Cooking Light

ANNUAL
RECIPES 2012

Oxmoor
House®

A Year at
Cooking Light®

2011 was quite a year in the healthy-eating world.
Much fuss on the government side of things: Food
labels began evolving, new dietary guidelines were
introduced, and the hopelessly confusing last version
of the iconic food pyramid vanished, replaced by
a simple-to-understand plate. But the real news
in healthy eating continues to be the confluence
between "delicious" and "good for you." Lines and
divisions blur: So-called health foods seem quaint;
highly processed diet foods lack appeal. Whole
foods, local when possible, globally flavored,
cooked with joy, are in. And the rules are
simpler: more plants, less meat, healthy
fats, and regular exercise—all things
we strive to communicate to our readers.

This year, as with every year at *Cooking Light*, we led the charge on defining what delicious healthy eating is, and published some of our best-ever recipes along the way:

- In January we introduced our new sustainable fish icon, which points out recipes that call for fish or shellfish with healthy populations that are caught (or raised) by environmentally friendly means. We continued this theme in May with a guide to cooking delicious, healthy dishes from five sustainable species of seafood (page 112).

- Each month in "Oops!" we featured a common cooking mistake and how to avoid it. We know all cooks make mistakes every now and then, but we want to help keep those mishaps from becoming habits.

- The magazine's popular "Cooking Class" series focused on classic dishes, from simmering stews and braising meats (pages 36 and 285) to baking brownies and soufflés (pages 262 and 148). Our Test Kitchen staff delighted in preserving the delicious essence of traditional comfort-food recipes while converting them into modern, lighter dishes.

- Our annual "Summer Cookbook" (page 137) was a glorious celebration of seasonable bounty. Our fresh twists on classic recipes created perfect summer fare.

- The "Pork Tenderloin, 25 Ways" (page 248) feature in September showcased a lean, quick-cooking cut that, when prepared using 5 easy techniques, led to 25 easy, healthy dinners.

- And as always, we began the holidays with our traditional, reader-favorite "Holiday Cookbook" (page 299) in November. Here, we included a variety of appetizers and drinks, entrées, sides, and desserts to ensure that you had all you needed to make your holiday celebrations just right—from Thanksgiving to New Year's.

At *Cooking Light,* we hear every month from enlightened cooks who have responded to our recipes and want to share great ideas that inform our future issues. To all of you, thanks. We hope this compilation inspires all our readers in your pursuit of light, great eating.

Scott Mowbray
Editor

◀ **Piña Colada Sorbet**
(page 146)
Feel like you're on a beach with this cool, creamy, pineapple-coconut dessert. For an adult version, top with a drizzle of rum.

▼ **Tequila-Glazed Grilled Chicken Thighs** *(page 141)*
Lime, pineapple juice, and tequila make these tangy-sweet chicken thighs tender and juicy. They'll be one of your go-to dishes for alfresco summer meals.

Our Favorite Recipes

Not all recipes are created equal.

At *Cooking Light,* only those that have passed muster with our Test Kitchen staff and food editors—not an easy crowd to please—make it onto the pages of our magazine. We rigorously test each recipe, often two or three times, to ensure that it's healthy, reliable, and tastes as good as it possibly can. So which of our recipes are our favorites? They're the dishes that are the most memorable. They're the ones readers keep calling and writing about, the ones our staff whip up for their own families and friends.

◄ **Brown Sugar Soufflés with Crème Anglaise** *(page 148)*
Have a sweet tooth? The brown sugar and brown butter in this melt-in-your-mouth soufflé deliver an exceptional caramel flavor that's sure to satisfy your sugar craving.

▼ **Barbecue Pulled Chicken Sliders** *(page 79)*
Cider vinegar, dry mustard, ketchup, and a host of other spices create that tangy-sweet barbecue sauce that tastes wonderful on a pulled chicken sandwich.

Paella with Poblanos, Corn, and Clams *(page 122)* The festive and colorful appearance of this dish reflects its sweet spiciness. And the layer of crisp browned rice on the bottom of the pan— known as the socarrat—is an unexpected must-try.

Skillet Pork Chop Sauté with Peaches *(page 161)*
Peaches, butter, and honey combine to make a sweet, rich sauce that pairs perfectly with pork chops. This quick dish is ready in 20 minutes.

▲ Guinness Lamb Stew *(page 37)*
In this stew, lamb and dark beer simmers to perfection.
Hearty and warm, this dish is the ultimate winter meal.

▲ Frozen Orange Tortes with Cranberry Compote *(page 330)*
Jeweled cranberry topping cascades down a fluffy, creamy, citrusy ice
cream filling.

▲ Crispy Chickpea Salad with Grilled Prawns *(page 40)*
Combine fried chickpeas, crisp arugula, spinach , and smoky
prawns to create a fresh, guilt-free salad.

▲ Onion Tart *(page 106)*
Woodsy thyme, sweet onions, and tangy feta cheese mingle in this vegetarian tart. Use a refrigerated pie dough to cut down on cooking time.

Pan-Fried Trout with Tomato-Basil Sauté
(page 268)
This special occasion–worthy dish has a secret: It's super quick and easy to make. Tomato sauce keeps the trout moist, while smoky pancetta intensifies this dish's complex flavors.

Shaved Summer Squash Salad with Prosciutto Crisps *(page 144)*
Raw yellow squash and zucchini juxtapose beautifully with sautéed prosciutto. Choose either creamy feta or ricotta salata to round out this summer salad.

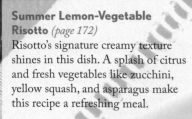

Summer Lemon-Vegetable Risotto *(page 172)*
Risotto's signature creamy texture shines in this dish. A splash of citrus and fresh vegetables like zucchini, yellow squash, and asparagus make this recipe a refreshing meal.

▲ **Browned Butter Asparagus** *(page 119)*
A hint of tarragon adds bold fresh flavor to this side.

▲ **Grilled Zucchini Caprese Sandwiches** *(page 207)*
Grilled zucchini elevates the classic caprese, while crusty ciabatta provides the perfect crunch.

▲ **Brazilian Feijoada** *(page 57)*
Dried beans get creamy soft in this hearty Brazilian treat.

▲ **Grilled Stuffed Jalapeños** *(page 174)*
Cheddar cheese, cream cheese, and bacon tame hot jalapeño peppers in this spicy, fun appetizer.

Chicken Fried Rice with Leeks and Dried Cranberries *(page 39)*
With seared chicken, leeks softened in olive oil, slightly plump dried cranberries, and a hint of sage, this dish is about as far from restaurant fried rice as you can go.

Argentinean Pork *(page 249)*
The pungent marinade emphasizes the flavor of the pork. Serve it with mashed potatoes for a full meal.

▲ **Crispy Topped Brussels Sprouts and Cauliflower Gratin** *(page 53)*
This creamy gratin finishes under the broiler to make the top beautifully browned and crunchy.

▲ **Truffle Roasted Potatoes** *(page 118)*
Potatoes get fancy with a splash of truffle oil. This recipe is easy enough make on a weeknight, yet impressive enough to serve to guests.

▲ **Pear Chutney Bruschetta with Pecans and Blue Cheese** *(page 278)*
Served on toasted baguette slices, the sweet-tangy chutney with buttery soft fruit pairs beautifully with blue cheese and toasty pecans.

▲ **Caramel-Pecan Dacquoise** *(page 330)*
A creamy caramel mousse is nestled between discs of airy, crispy meringues.

Classic Meat Loaf *(page 281)*
Everyone knows not to mess with a classic, home-cooked dish like meat loaf. That's why there's nothing showy here, just a timeless and delicious dish.

◄ Melon Gazpacho with Frizzled Prosciutto *(page 196)*
A cold soup may sound like an oxymoron to some, but you'll be wondering why you didn't try it sooner after tasting this gazpacho. Sweet cantaloupe and peaches blend with cool mint and smoky prosciutto.

Peanut Butter Caramel Corn *(page 274)*
There's no resisting this sweet and salty snack. Nutty, crunchy, caramelized popcorn is perfect for a Halloween treat—or an any-time snack.

Lemony Chicken Saltimbocca *(page 43)*
Lemon adds citrusy refreshment to this hearty meal of chicken and prosciutto. An aura of delicacy shines through with the addition of sage leaves and extra-virgin olive oil.

◄ Roasted Sweet Potato Salad with Cranberry-Chipotle Dressing *(page 285)*
When a mix of cranberries and chipotle peppers dress roasted sweet potatoes, tart, sweet, and spicy flavors unite to form a delectable fit-for-fall salad.

Blueberry Thrill *(page 138)*
Blueberry-infused gin makes for a summer sipper that's refreshing without being overly sweet. It can be served straight up or on the rocks with club soda.

Butternut Squash, Caramelized Onion, and Spinach Lasagna *(page 331)*
Cheesy and warm, this lasagna defines vegetarian comfort food. Butternut squash, caramelized onions, and spinach take it to cosmopolitan heights.

◄ Blackened Tilapia Tacos *(page 63)*
Fish tacos are fast becoming mainstay Mexican fare and are a healthier option, too. These get their spicy kick from jalapeño peppers and their crunch from onion relish.

Herb-Crusted Rack of Lamb *(page 103)*
Dijon mustard and aromatic herbs lend a fresh flavor to this prime, lean cut of lamb. Crispy breadcrumbs complement the tender meat.

Creamy, Light Macaroni and Cheese *(page 260)*
Butternut squash in mac and cheese? It sounds like a strange idea, but you'll be surprised by the creaminess it imparts. A trio of cheeses—pecorino Romano, Parmigiano-Reggiano, and Gruyère—makes this a rich and a luscious dish.

► Creamy Chicken Salad *(page 123)*
Our take on chicken salad is light on mayonnaise, but not on flavor. Juicy poached chicken gets a tangy twist from Greek yogurt, Dijon mustard, dried cranberries, and smoked almonds.

Beet, Blood Orange, Kumquat, and Quinoa Salad *(page 33)*
Blood oranges and kumquats make this grain-based salad vibrant and exciting. The fresh coriander, cumin, and citrus dressing burst with flavor.

◄ Cumin-Spiced Chickpeas and Carrots on Couscous *(page 202)*
Looking for a flavorful and filling vegetarian entrée? This stir-fry, which includes garlic, red pepper, and cumin, delivers a fiery flare that's subdued by the couscous.

Smoky Baked Beans with Chorizo *(page 144)*
These smoky beans have a distinct, complex flavor that can only be achieved through slow cooking. Spanish chorizo adds even more spice and heartiness to this dish.

Real Bagels *(page 336)*
It doesn't take a trip to New York City to find a good bagel. These traditional boiled bagels are chewy and delicious.

◄ Roasted Banana Pudding *(page 202)*
This rich and creamy dessert gets a fat-free but intense flavor boost from roasting the bananas. Banana pudding traditionalists say this tastes better the next day, but who can resist digging in after it has chilled?

Triple-Chocolate Cake *(page 329)*
With a rich chocolate filling between chocolate cake layers and topped with chocolate-espresso glaze, this dessert is the cure for even the most diehard chocoholic.

Vanilla Cupcakes with Vanilla Bean Frosting *(page 363)*
These sweet treats please the palate across all ages. A rich, vanilla bean frosting elevates them to a heavenly dessert.

► Sparkling Pear Cocktail *(page 313)*
This sophisticated sipper is surprisingly simple to make. The mix of pears and Champagne creates a cocktail that is fragrant and full-bodied.

CONTENTS

A Year at *Cooking Light*®   2

Our Favorite Recipes   4

January/February   19

March   50

April   82

May   112

June featuring   137
The *Cooking Light*® Summer Cookbook

July   167

August   190

September   248

October   274

November featuring   299
The *Cooking Light*® Holiday Cookbook

December   351

Contributors   383
Seasonal Produce Guide   384
Time-Saving Tools & Gadgets   385
Nutritional Analysis   386
Metric Equivalents   387
Menu Index   388
Recipe Title Index   391
Month-by-Month Index   396
General Recipe Index   402

©2011 by Time Home Entertainment Inc.
135 West 50th Street, New York, NY 10020

ISBN-13: 978-0-8487-3474-9
ISBN-10: 0-8487-3474-2
ISSN: 1091-3645

Printed in the United States of America
First Printing 2011

Be sure to check with your health-care provider before making any changes in your diet.

Oxmoor House
VP, Publishing Director: Jim Childs
Editorial Director: Susan Payne Dobbs
Creative Director: Felicity Keane
Brand Manager: Michelle Turner Aycock
Senior Editor: Heather Averett
Managing Editor: Laurie S. Herr

Cooking Light Annual Recipes 2012
Editors: Holly D. Smith, Rachel Quinlivan West, RD
Senior Production Manager: Greg A. Amason

Contributors
Designer: Carol Damsky
Copy Editors: Jacqueline Giovanelli, Dolores Hydock
Proofreaders: Julie Bosche, Adrienne Davis
Indexer: Mary Ann Laurens
Interns: Erin Bishop, Jessica Cox, R.D., Sarah H. Doss,
Laura Hoxworth, Alison Loughman, Caitlin Watzke

Time Home Entertainment Inc.
Publisher: Richard Fraiman
VP, Strategy & Business Development: Steven Sandonato
Executive Director, Marketing Services: Carol Pittard
Executive Director, Retail & Special Sales: Tom Mifsud
Executive Director, New Product Development: Peter Harper
Director, Bookazine Development & Marketing: Laura Adam
Publishing Director: Joy Butts
Finance Director: Glenn Buonocore
Assistant General Counsel: Helen Wan

Cooking Light
Editor: Scott Mowbray
Creative Director: Carla Frank
Deputy Editor: Phillip Rhodes
Executive Editor, Food: Ann Taylor Pittman
Special Publications Editor: Mary Simpson Creel, MS, RD
Senior Food Editor: Julianna Grimes
Senior Editor: Cindy Hatcher
Associate Food Editor: Timothy Q. Cebula
Assistant Editor, Nutrition: Sidney Fry, MS, RD
Assistant Editors: Kimberly Holland, Phoebe Wu
Test Kitchen Director: Vanessa T. Pruett
Assistant Test Kitchen Director: Tiffany Vickers Davis
Recipe Testers and Developers: Robin Bashinsky, Adam Hickman, Deb Wise
Art Directors: Fernande Bondarenko, Shawna Kalish
Associate Art Director: Rachel Lasserre
Designer: Chase Turbeville
Junior Designer: Hagen Stegall
Photo Director: Kristen Schaefer
Assistant Photo Editor: Amy Delaune
Senior Photographer: Randy Mayor
Senior Photo Stylist: Cindy Barr
Photo Stylist: Leigh Ann Ross
Chief Food Stylist: Charlotte Autry
Senior Food Stylist: Kellie Gerber Kelley
Food Styling Assistant: Blakeslee Wright
Copy Chief: Maria Parker Hopkins
Assistant Copy Chief: Susan Roberts
Research Editor: Michelle Gibson Daniels
Editorial Production Editor: Liz Rhoades
Production Editor: Hazel R. Eddins
Assistant Production Editor: Josh Rutledge
Administrative Coordinator: Carol D. Johnson
CookingLight.com Editor: Allison Long Lowery
CookingLight.com Nutrition Editor: Holley Johnson Grainger, MS, RD
CookingLight.com Production Assistant: Mallory Daughtery

To order additional publications, call 1-800-765-6400 or 1-800-491-0551.

For more books to enrich your life, visit **oxmoorhouse.com**

To search, savor, and share thousands of recipes, visit **myrecipes.com**

Cover: *Provençal Beef Daube (page 57)*
Back Cover (left to right): *Herbed Shrimp and White Bean Salad (page 242); Tandoori-Spiced Chicken (page 19); Sponge Cake with Orange Curd and Strawberries (page 94)*
Front Flap: *Pasta Puttanesca (page 130)*
Page 1: *Salted Caramel Brownies, Peanut Butter Cup Blondies, Cherry Cheesecake Brownies, Classic Fudge-Walnut Brownies (pages 262-263)*

CHICKEN BREASTS 25 WAYS

No more boring bird! Five simple techniques, with variations, give healthy weeknight cooking a makeover.

MARINATING

Chicken breasts are naturally tender, so marinating simply adds flavor. It's best to choose bold ingredients and avoid soaking the delicate meat in acidic liquids for too long—it may become stringy and tough.

Tandoori-Spiced Chicken

(pictured on page 209)

Hands-on time: 31 min. Total time: 2 hr. 21 min.

1½ cups plain 2% reduced-fat Greek yogurt
2 tablespoons grated onion
1 tablespoon grated peeled fresh ginger
1 tablespoon canola oil
1 teaspoon ground cumin
½ teaspoon ground red pepper
¼ teaspoon ground turmeric
3 garlic cloves, minced
4 (6-ounce) skinless, boneless chicken breast halves
½ teaspoon salt
Cooking spray

1. Combine first 8 ingredients in a heavy-duty zip-top plastic bag. Add chicken to bag; seal. Marinate in refrigerator 2 hours, turning occasionally.
2. Place a small roasting pan in oven. Preheat broiler to high. Remove chicken from bag; discard marinade.

Sprinkle both sides of chicken evenly with salt. Place chicken on preheated pan coated with cooking spray. Broil in lower third of oven 15 minutes or until done, turning after 7 minutes. Yield: 4 servings (serving size: 1 breast half).

CALORIES 152; FAT 2.2g (sat 0.6g, mono 0.6g, poly 0.5g); PROTEIN 30.4g; CARB 0.7g; FIBER 0.1g; CHOL 74mg; IRON 1mg; SODIUM 381mg; CALC 24mg

If you like **Chile Paste** try:

Thai Coconut Chicken

Combine 1 cup light coconut milk, ¼ cup lower-sodium soy sauce, 2 tablespoons fresh lime juice, 1 tablespoon grated peeled fresh ginger, 2 teaspoons Thai chile paste, ½ teaspoon sugar, and 2 thinly sliced shallots. Reserve ½ cup coconut mixture; pour remaining coconut mixture into a zip-top plastic bag. Add 4 (6-ounce) skinless, boneless chicken breast halves; seal. Marinate in refrigerator 2 hours. Heat a grill pan over medium-high heat. Coat pan with cooking spray. Remove chicken from bag; discard marinade in bag. Sprinkle chicken with ½ teaspoon salt. Add chicken to pan; cook 7 minutes on each side or until done. Serve with reserved coconut sauce. Yield: 4 servings.

CALORIES 205; FAT 5.2g (sat); SODIUM 510mg

If you like **Hot Sauce** try:

Quick & Easy
Buffalo Chicken

Combine ¾ cup hot sauce, ¼ cup melted butter, 2 teaspoons Worcestershire sauce, and ½ teaspoon onion powder into a bowl. Reserve ¼ cup hot sauce mixture; pour remaining hot sauce mixture in a zip-top plastic bag. Add 4 (6-ounce) skinless, boneless chicken breast halves to bag; seal. Marinate at room temperature 20 minutes. Heat a large skillet over medium-high heat. Coat pan with cooking spray. Remove chicken from bag; discard marinade in bag. Sprinkle chicken with ¼ teaspoon salt. Add chicken to pan; sauté 6 minutes on each side or until done. Brush reserved marinade over chicken. Serve with light ranch dressing, if desired. Yield: 4 servings.

CALORIES 221; FAT 8.1g (sat 3.7g); SODIUM 655mg

If you like **Herbs** try:

Quick & Easy
Herbed Chicken

Combine 3 tablespoons extra-virgin olive oil, 2 tablespoons minced shallots, 1 tablespoon chopped fresh rosemary, 2 teaspoons chopped fresh thyme, and 2 minced garlic cloves in a zip-top plastic bag. Add 4 (6-ounce) skinless, boneless chicken breast halves. Marinate in refrigerator 2 hours. Remove chicken from bag; sprinkle with ½ teaspoon salt and ¼ teaspoon black pepper. Brush herb mixture evenly over chicken. Heat a grill pan over medium-high heat. Coat pan with cooking spray. Add chicken to pan; cook 6 minutes on each side or until done. Yield: 4 servings.

CALORIES 279; FAT 14.1g (sat 2.5g); SODIUM 378mg

Chicken Fajitas

Hands-on time: 32 min. Total time: 1 hr. 32 min.

3/4 cup dark Mexican beer
2 tablespoons lower-sodium soy sauce
2 tablespoons fresh lime juice
1 tablespoon canola oil
1 tablespoon Worcestershire sauce
3 garlic cloves, crushed
1 pound skinless, boneless chicken breast halves, cut across grain into 1/2-inch-thick strips
1 cup sliced onion
1 orange bell pepper, seeded and sliced
1 yellow bell pepper, seeded and sliced
Cooking spray
1/4 teaspoon salt
1/4 teaspoon freshly ground black pepper
8 (6-inch) flour tortillas
1 jalapeño pepper, thinly sliced
Salsa (optional)
Reduced-fat sour cream (optional)
Fresh cilantro leaves (optional)

1. Combine first 6 ingredients, stirring well. Place chicken in a zip-top plastic bag. Add 3/4 cup beer mixture to bag; seal. Reserve remaining beer mixture. Marinate in refrigerator 1 hour, turning occasionally. Combine onion, bell peppers, and remaining beer mixture in a zip-top plastic bag, and seal. Marinate 1 hour at room temperature.
2. Heat a grill pan over medium-high heat. Coat pan with cooking spray. Remove chicken from bag; discard marinade. Sprinkle chicken with salt and black pepper. Add chicken to pan; cook 2 minutes on each side or until done. Remove chicken from pan; keep warm. Remove onion and bell peppers from bag; discard marinade. Add onion mixture to pan; cook 6 minutes or until tender, turning after 3 minutes. Toast tortillas in pan, if desired. Place 2 tortillas on each of 4 plates; divide chicken mixture and onion mixture among tortillas. Garnish with jalapeño slices. Serve with salsa, sour cream, and cilantro, if desired. Yield: 4 servings.

CALORIES 377; **FAT** 9.4g (sat 1.5g, mono 4.7g, poly 2.3g); **PROTEIN** 31.6g; **CARB** 39.8g; **FIBER** 4.3g; **CHOL** 66mg; **IRON** 1.9mg; **SODIUM** 668mg; **CALC** 67mg

BEER NOTE: With Chicken Fajitas, a dark Mexican beer serves as both a marinade ingredient and the ideal thirst-quenching companion. This style of beer arrived in Mexico from Germany. Classic examples like Negra Modelo ($8/six-pack) offer clean, malty flavors that balance spicy jalapeños, while caramel and chocolate nuances work with the smoky grilled flavors.

Hawaiian Chicken

Hands-on time: 15 min. Total time: 4 hr. 23 min.

1/4 cup pineapple juice
2 tablespoons ketchup
2 tablespoons lower-sodium soy sauce
1 1/2 teaspoons minced peeled fresh ginger
2 garlic cloves, minced
4 (6-ounce) skinless, boneless chicken breast halves
Cooking spray
3/4 teaspoon salt, divided
1/4 teaspoon black pepper
2 cups hot cooked long-grain white rice
1/4 cup chopped fresh cilantro

1. Combine first 5 ingredients. Reserve 1/4 cup marinade; place remaining marinade in a zip-top plastic bag. Add chicken to bag; seal. Chill 4 hours.
2. Heat a grill pan over medium-high heat. Coat pan with cooking spray. Remove chicken from bag; discard marinade in bag. Sprinkle chicken with 1/2 teaspoon salt and pepper. Add chicken to pan; baste with 2 tablespoons reserved marinade. Cook 6 minutes. Turn chicken over; baste with 2 tablespoons reserved marinade. Cook 6 minutes.
3. Combine rice, remaining 1/4 teaspoon salt, and cilantro. Yield: 4 servings (serving size: 1 breast half and 1/2 cup rice).

CALORIES 247; **FAT** 1.8g (sat 0.5g, mono 0.4g, poly 0.4g); **PROTEIN** 29.9g; **CARB** 25.2g; **FIBER** 0.5g; **CHOL** 68mg; **IRON** 1.9mg; **SODIUM** 674mg; **CALC** 26mg

POUNDING

Thin cutlets cook in a flash and remain supremely tender and juicy. After cooking the chicken, use the tasty browned bits left behind in the pan as the base for a speedy sauce.

Sautéed Chicken with Sage Browned Butter

Hands-on time: 25 min. Total time: 25 min.

4 (6-ounce) skinless, boneless chicken breast halves
1/4 teaspoon salt
1/4 teaspoon black pepper
Cooking spray
1/2 cup all-purpose flour
3 tablespoons butter
2 sage sprigs
1 tablespoon minced shallots
1 teaspoon chopped fresh thyme
2 tablespoons lemon juice
Fresh sage leaves (optional)

1. Place each breast half between 2 sheets of plastic wrap; pound to 1/4-inch thickness. Sprinkle with salt and pepper. Heat a large skillet over medium-high heat; coat with cooking spray. Place flour in a shallow dish; dredge chicken in flour. Add chicken to pan; sauté 4 minutes on each side or until done. Remove chicken from pan.
2. Add butter and sage sprigs to pan; cook over medium heat until butter browns. Discard sage. Add shallots and thyme; cook 30 seconds. Add lemon juice; cook 30 seconds. Serve with chicken. Garnish with sage leaves, if desired. Yield: 4 servings (serving size: 1 breast half and 1 tablespoon sauce).

CALORIES 326; **FAT** 11.1g (sat 6.1g, mono 2.8g, poly 0.9g); **PROTEIN** 41.1g; **CARB** 13.1g; **FIBER** 0.5g; **CHOL** 122mg; **IRON** 2mg; **SODIUM** 320mg; **CALC** 26mg

If you like **Dijon Mustard** try:

Quick & Easy

Chicken Cutlets with Creamy Dijon Sauce

Place 4 (6-ounce) skinless, boneless chicken breast halves between 2 sheets of plastic wrap; pound to ½-inch thickness. Sprinkle chicken with ½ teaspoon salt and ¼ teaspoon black pepper. Heat a large skillet over medium-high heat. Add 1 tablespoon olive oil to pan. Add chicken; sauté 3 minutes on each side or until done. Transfer to a serving platter. Add 3 tablespoons chopped shallots to pan; sauté 2 minutes. Stir in ½ cup fat-free, lower-sodium chicken broth and 1 rosemary sprig; bring to a boil. Cook 2 minutes. Stir in 3 tablespoons whipping cream; cook 2 minutes. Remove from heat, and discard rosemary. Stir in 2 teaspoons Dijon mustard. Spoon over chicken. Yield: 4 servings.

CALORIES 266; **FAT** 9.7g (sat 3.6g); **SODIUM** 519mg

If you like **Soy Sauce** try:

Quick & Easy

Sweet and Sour Chicken

Place 4 (6-ounce) skinless, boneless chicken breast halves between 2 sheets of plastic wrap; pound to ½-inch thickness. Sprinkle chicken with ½ teaspoon salt and ¼ teaspoon black pepper. Heat a large skillet over medium-high heat. Add 1 tablespoon olive oil to pan. Add chicken; sauté 3 minutes on each side or until done. Transfer chicken to a serving platter. Add ¼ cup fat-free, lower-sodium chicken broth, 3 tablespoons apricot preserves, and 1½ tablespoons lower-sodium soy sauce to pan; bring to a boil. Stir. Cook 1 minute. Remove from heat; stir in 2 tablespoons fresh lime juice and 2 teaspoons Thai chile paste. Spoon over chicken; garnish with fresh cilantro leaves. Yield: 4 servings.

CALORIES 264; **FAT** 5.5g (sat 1g); **SODIUM** 576mg

If you like **Cherry Tomatoes** try:

Quick & Easy • Kid Friendly

Chicken with Cherry Tomato Sauce

Place 4 (6-ounce) skinless, boneless chicken breast halves between 2 sheets of plastic wrap; pound to ½-inch thickness. Sprinkle chicken with ½ teaspoon salt and ¼ teaspoon black pepper. Heat a large skillet over medium-high heat. Add 2 tablespoons olive oil to pan. Add chicken; sauté 3 minutes on each side or until done. Transfer to a serving platter. Add 5 coarsely chopped garlic cloves to pan; sauté 1 minute, stirring constantly. Stir in 1 pint cherry tomatoes and ⅓ cup fat-free, lower-sodium chicken broth, and bring to a boil. Cook 5 minutes, stirring occasionally. Spoon over chicken. Garnish with ¼ cup small basil leaves. Yield: 4 servings.

CALORIES 268; **FAT** 9.1g (sat 1.5g); **SODIUM** 442mg

SECRETS OF THE EVER-EXPANDING CHICKEN BREAST

A lean, skinless chicken breast half contains 182 calories and 4 grams fat (only 1.1 grams sat fat). It's a great source of protein in a convenient package. But boy, that package has grown—from 4 to 6 to almost 8 ounces. Most U.S. chickens are bred for big breasts, which are then plumped by injecting with saline solution during processing.

Plumping renders lean meat more foolproof; the added liquid makes it more difficult to get tough, dry results, even when you overcook. But it also means you're paying for water, and flavor isn't always the best. Look for organic and less-processed chicken breasts—now very common. We've found them to be smaller and less likely to be pumped full of saltwater or broth.

Quick & Easy

Chicken with Mushroom Sauce

Hands-on time: 35 min. Total time: 35 min.

- 4 (6-ounce) skinless, boneless chicken breast halves
- 2 teaspoons canola oil
- ½ teaspoon salt, divided
- ¼ teaspoon freshly ground black pepper
- ¼ cup chopped shallots
- 1 (8-ounce) package presliced mushrooms
- 2 minced garlic cloves
- ½ cup dry white wine
- 1½ teaspoons all-purpose flour
- ¾ cup fat-free, lower-sodium chicken broth
- 2 tablespoons butter
- 1 teaspoon minced fresh thyme

1. Place each chicken breast half between 2 sheets of heavy-duty plastic wrap, and pound to ½-inch thickness using a meat mallet or small heavy skillet.

2. Heat a large nonstick skillet over medium-high heat. Add canola oil to pan; swirl to coat. Sprinkle chicken with ¼ teaspoon salt and pepper. Add chicken to pan; cook 3 minutes on each side or until done. Transfer chicken to a serving platter; keep warm.

3. Add shallots and mushrooms to pan; sauté 4 minutes or until browned, stirring occasionally. Add garlic; sauté 1 minute, stirring constantly. Stir in wine, scraping pan to loosen browned bits; bring to a boil. Cook until liquid almost evaporates. Sprinkle mushroom mixture with remaining ¼ teaspoon salt and flour; cook 30 seconds, stirring frequently. Add broth to pan; bring to a boil. Cook 2 minutes or until slightly thick. Remove pan from heat; add butter and thyme, stirring until butter melts. Serve with chicken. Yield: 4 servings (serving size: 1 breast half and ⅓ cup sauce).

CALORIES 290; **FAT** 10.5g (sat 4.4g, mono 3.5g, poly 1.5g); **PROTEIN** 42.1g; **CARB** 5.5g; **FIBER** 0.8g; **CHOL** 114mg; **IRON** 1.9mg; **SODIUM** 526mg; **CALC** 34mg

STUFFING

The impressive-looking results of stuffed chicken breasts belie the ease of preparation. You can stuff them up to a day ahead, keep refrigerated, and then simply cook and serve.

Pimiento Cheese Chicken

Hands-on time: 15 min. Total time: 34 min.

1 applewood-smoked bacon slice
¾ cup (3 ounces) shredded cheddar cheese
2 tablespoons minced green onions
1½ tablespoons diced pimientos
1 tablespoon canola mayonnaise
2 teaspoons fresh lemon juice
½ teaspoon hot sauce
½ teaspoon salt, divided
4 (6-ounce) skinless, boneless chicken breast
   halves
½ teaspoon black pepper
1 tablespoon canola oil

1. Preheat oven to 350°.
2. Cook bacon in a large ovenproof skillet until crisp. Remove bacon, reserving drippings in pan; crumble bacon. Combine bacon, next 6 ingredients, and ¼ teaspoon salt. Cut a 1-inch-wide slit into the thick end of each breast half; carefully cut down to center of chicken to form a deep pocket. Divide cheese mixture evenly among pockets. Secure with wooden picks. Sprinkle chicken with remaining ¼ teaspoon salt and pepper.
3. Heat pan over medium-high heat. Add oil to drippings. Add chicken to pan; sauté 4 minutes. Turn chicken over. Bake at 350° for 12 minutes; let stand 5 minutes. Yield: 4 servings (serving size: 1 stuffed breast half).

CALORIES 299; FAT 16g (sat 5.8g, mono 6.1g, poly 2.3g); PROTEIN 36.8g; CARB 1.3g; FIBER 0.2g; CHOL 100mg; IRON 1.2mg; SODIUM 606mg; CALC 171mg

If you like Blue Cheese try:

Spinach and Blue Cheese Chicken

Preheat oven to 350°. Heat a large ovenproof skillet over medium-high heat. Add 2 teaspoons oil. Add 3 cups baby spinach and 1 minced garlic clove, and sauté 2 minutes. Combine spinach, ¼ cup blue cheese, 1 tablespoon flour, and 1 ounce chopped prosciutto. Cut a 1-inch-wide slit into the thick end of 4 (6-ounce) skinless, boneless chicken breast halves, and carefully cut down to center of chicken to form a pocket. Divide spinach mixture evenly among pockets. Secure with wooden picks. Sprinkle chicken with ¼ teaspoon salt and ¼ teaspoon pepper. Heat pan over medium-high heat; coat pan with cooking spray. Add chicken; sauté 4 minutes. Turn chicken over. Bake at 350° for 12 minutes; let stand 5 minutes. Yield: 4 servings.

CALORIES 263; FAT 9.4g (sat 3.3g); SODIUM 566mg

If you like Bacon try:

Bacon and Goat Cheese Chicken

Preheat oven to 350°. Combine 2 tablespoons sliced green onions; ⅓ cup (3 ounces) goat cheese; and 1 slice cooked, crumbled bacon. Cut a 1-inch-wide slit into the thick end of 4 (6-ounce) skinless, boneless chicken breast halves, and carefully cut down to center of chicken to form a pocket. Divide cheese mixture evenly among pockets. Secure with wooden picks. Sprinkle chicken with ½ teaspoon salt and ¼ teaspoon pepper. Heat a large ovenproof skillet over medium-high heat. Add 1 tablespoon canola oil. Add chicken to pan; sauté 4 minutes. Turn chicken over. Bake at 350° for 12 minutes; let stand 5 minutes. Yield: 4 servings.

CALORIES 283; FAT 12.8g (sat 4.8g); SODIUM 503mg

If you like Olives try:

Mediterranean Chicken

Preheat oven to 350°. Combine ¼ cup prepared hummus, ¼ cup feta cheese, 3 tablespoons diced tomato, and 2 tablespoons chopped kalamata olives. Cut a 1-inch-wide slit into the thick end of 4 (6-ounce) skinless, boneless chicken breast halves, and carefully cut down to center of chicken to form a pocket. Divide cheese mixture evenly among pockets. Secure with wooden picks. Sprinkle chicken with ¼ teaspoon salt and ¼ teaspoon pepper. Heat a large ovenproof skillet over medium-high heat. Add 1 tablespoon olive oil to pan. Add chicken to pan; sauté 4 minutes. Turn chicken over. Bake at 350° for 12 minutes; let stand 5 minutes. Yield: 4 servings.

CALORIES 290; FAT 13.3g (sat 3.3g); SODIUM 567mg

Couscous-Stuffed Chicken

Hands-on time: 45 min. Total time: 45 min.

⅓ cup fat-free, lower-sodium chicken broth
¼ cup uncooked couscous
½ teaspoon salt, divided
½ teaspoon black pepper, divided
3 tablespoons chopped plum tomato
2 tablespoons kalamata olives, chopped
2 tablespoons crumbled feta cheese
2 tablespoons extra-virgin olive oil
2 teaspoons chopped fresh oregano
2 teaspoons chopped fresh parsley
1 teaspoon grated lemon rind
1 minced garlic clove
4 (6-ounce) skinless, boneless chicken breast
   halves
Cooking spray

1. Bring broth to a boil in a small saucepan; remove from heat. Stir in couscous. Cover and let stand 4 minutes. Place couscous in a small bowl; fluff with a fork. Cool 10 minutes. Add ¼ teaspoon salt, ¼ teaspoon pepper, and next 8 ingredients; toss.

2. Place chicken between 2 sheets of plastic wrap; pound to ¼-inch thickness. Divide couscous mixture evenly among breast halves; roll up jelly-roll fashion. Secure with wooden picks. Sprinkle chicken with remaining ¼ teaspoon salt and ¼ teaspoon pepper.
3. Preheat oven to 400°.
4. Heat a large ovenproof skillet over medium-high heat. Coat pan with cooking spray. Add chicken to pan, and cook 6 minutes or until browned; turn chicken over. Bake at 400° for 5 minutes or until chicken is done. Yield: 4 servings (serving size: 1 stuffed breast half).

CALORIES 271; **FAT** 10.7g (sat 2.2g, mono 6.5g, poly 1.3g); **PROTEIN** 31.9g; **CARB** 10g; **FIBER** 0.8g; **CHOL** 78mg; **IRON** 1.2mg; **SODIUM** 546mg; **CALC** 49mg

PAN-FRYING

Dip chicken in buttermilk to add a tangy flavor, and coat it with flour and nuts or other tasty breading ingredients. Then pan-fry it in a sensible amount of heart-healthy oil to create a crisp exterior.

Kid Friendly
Coconut Chicken Fingers

Hands-on time: 28 min. Total time: 28 min.

4 (6-ounce) skinless, boneless chicken breast halves, cut into ½-inch-thick strips
½ teaspoon salt
¼ teaspoon ground red pepper
1 cup rice flour
1 cup whole buttermilk
1 large egg
1½ cups flaked unsweetened coconut
3 tablespoons canola oil
Sweet chile sauce (optional)

1. Sprinkle chicken with salt and pepper. Place flour in a shallow dish. Combine buttermilk and egg in a shallow dish, stirring well. Place coconut in a shallow dish. Dredge chicken in flour; shake off excess. Dip chicken in egg mixture; dredge in coconut.

2. Heat a large skillet over medium-high heat. Add oil to pan; swirl to coat. Add chicken to pan; cook 6 minutes or until done, turning to brown. Serve with chile sauce, if desired. Yield: 6 servings (serving size: about 4.5 ounces).

CALORIES 298; **FAT** 12.7g (sat 4.1g, mono 5.4g, poly 2.6g); **PROTEIN** 28.7g; **CARB** 15.9g; **FIBER** 1.7g; **CHOL** 102mg; **IRON** 1.4mg; **SODIUM** 318mg; **CALC** 20mg

If you like **Pecans** try:
Pecan Chicken

Preheat oven to 425°. Place 4 (6-ounce) skinless, boneless chicken breast halves in a zip-top plastic bag. Combine 1 cup whole buttermilk and 1 large egg. Add egg mixture to bag; seal. Marinate in refrigerator 4 hours. Remove chicken from bag; discard marinade. Sprinkle chicken with ½ teaspoon salt and ½ teaspoon black pepper. Combine ⅔ cup all-purpose flour and ½ cup finely ground pecans. Dredge chicken in flour mixture; shake off excess. Heat a large ovenproof skillet over medium-high heat. Add 2 tablespoons canola oil to pan; swirl to coat. Add chicken to pan; sauté 4 minutes or until browned. Turn chicken over. Place pan in oven; bake at 425° for 10 minutes or until done. Yield: 4 servings.

CALORIES 443; **FAT** 22.6g (sat 3.3g); **SODIUM** 422mg

If you like **Oatmeal** try:
Oatmeal-Crusted Chicken

Preheat oven to 425°. Place 4 (6-ounce) skinless, boneless chicken breast halves in a zip-top plastic bag. Combine 1 cup buttermilk and 1 large egg. Add egg mixture to bag, and seal. Marinate in refrigerator 4 hours. Remove chicken from bag; discard marinade. Sprinkle chicken with ½ teaspoon salt and ½ teaspoon pepper. Combine ⅔ cup flour and ½ cup ground oats. Dredge chicken in flour mixture. Heat 2 tablespoons oil in a large ovenproof skillet over

medium-high heat. Add chicken; sauté 4 minutes. Turn chicken over. Bake at 425° for 10 minutes or until done. Yield: 4 servings.

CALORIES 387; **FAT** 13.6g (sat 2.6g); **SODIUM** 422mg

Kid Friendly
Crispy Buttermilk Chicken

Hands-on time: 20 min. Total time: 4 hr. 20 min.

4 (6-ounce) skinless, boneless chicken breast halves
1¾ cups whole buttermilk
1 large egg
¾ teaspoon onion powder, divided
¾ teaspoon ground red pepper, divided
½ teaspoon kosher salt
1 cup all-purpose flour
2 teaspoons black pepper
1 teaspoon celery salt
2 tablespoons canola oil

1. Place chicken in a zip-top plastic bag. Combine buttermilk, egg, ¼ teaspoon onion powder, and ¼ teaspoon red pepper; add to bag. Seal. Marinate in refrigerator 4 hours.
2. Preheat oven to 425°.
3. Remove chicken from bag; discard marinade. Sprinkle kosher salt over chicken. Combine remaining ½ teaspoon onion powder, remaining ½ teaspoon red pepper, flour, black pepper, and celery salt in a shallow dish. Dredge chicken in flour mixture. Place chicken on a wire rack.
4. Heat a large ovenproof skillet over medium-high heat. Add oil to pan; swirl to coat. Add chicken; sauté 4 minutes. Turn chicken over. Bake chicken at 425° for 10 minutes. Yield: 4 servings. (serving size: 1 chicken breast half).

CALORIES 425; **FAT** 12.5g (sat 2.7g, mono 5.5g, poly 2.7g); **PROTEIN** 46.3g; **CARB** 28.4g; **FIBER** 1.2g; **CHOL** 152mg; **IRON** 3mg; **SODIUM** 629mg; **CALC** 36mg

GRINDING

Combine skinless, boneless chicken breast halves in the food processor with pungent ingredients like garlic, spicy peppers, or curry paste. Puree them together so the flavor permeates the meat.

Quick & Easy
Chicken Larb

Hands-on time: 27 min. Total time: 27 min.

2 tablespoons red curry paste
1 pound skinless, boneless chicken breast halves
½ teaspoon salt
1 tablespoon canola oil
⅓ cup chopped English cucumber
¼ cup finely chopped shallots
3 tablespoons chopped fresh cilantro
2 tablespoons fresh lime juice
8 cabbage leaves
Thai chile paste (optional)

1. Place curry paste, chicken, and salt in a food processor; process until smooth. Heat a large skillet over medium-high heat. Add oil to pan; swirl to coat. Add chicken mixture to pan; sauté 6 minutes or until done, stirring to crumble. Remove pan from heat; stir in cucumber and next 3 ingredients. Place 2 cabbage leaves on each of 4 plates; divide chicken mixture evenly among leaves. Serve with chile paste, if desired. Yield: 4 servings (serving size: 2 filled cabbage leaves).

CALORIES 174; **FAT** 4.9g (sat 0.6g, mono 2.6g, poly 1.3g); **PROTEIN** 26.7g; **CARB** 4.1g; **FIBER** 0.3g; **CHOL** 66mg; **IRON** 1mg; **SODIUM** 507mg; **CALC** 29mg

---

If you like **Jalapeño Peppers** try:
Chicken Tacos

Combine 1 cup chopped onion, 5 garlic cloves, and 2 trimmed jalapeño peppers in a food processor; process until ground. Add 1 pound skinless, boneless chicken breast halves; process until finely ground. Heat a large skillet over medium-high heat. Add 1 tablespoon canola oil. Add chicken mixture; sprinkle with ½ teaspoon salt and ¼ teaspoon black pepper. Sauté 10 minutes, stirring to crumble. Heat 8 (6-inch) corn tortillas according to package directions. Place 2 tortillas on each of 4 plates; divide chicken mixture evenly among tortillas. Combine 1 cup sliced radishes, 1 cup chopped avocado, and 2 tablespoons fresh lime juice; divide mixture evenly among tacos. Garnish with cilantro leaves. Yield: 4 servings.

CALORIES 386; **FAT** 12.5g (sat 1.5g); **SODIUM** 455mg

If you like **Ketchup** try:

Quick & Easy • Kid Friendly
Chicken Meat Loaf

Preheat oven to 350°. Combine ½ cup sliced green onions, 4 ounces button mushrooms, and 5 garlic cloves in a food processor; process until ground. Add 1 pound skinless, boneless chicken breast halves; process until finely ground. Add ¾ cup panko (Japanese breadcrumbs), 1 tablespoon lower-sodium soy sauce, ½ teaspoon pepper, ¼ teaspoon salt, and 1 large egg; pulse. Shape mixture into a 9 x 5–inch loaf on a broiler pan coated with cooking spray. Combine ⅓ cup ketchup, 1 tablespoon yellow mustard, and 1 teaspoon sugar; brush mixture over meat loaf. Bake at 350° for 45 minutes. Let stand 10 minutes. Slice. Yield: 4 servings.

CALORIES 229; **FAT** 4.6g (sat 1.2g); **SODIUM** 620mg

Quick & Easy
Greek-Style Chicken

Hands-on time: 15 min. Total time: 25 min.

3 tablespoons chopped fresh oregano
¼ teaspoon crushed red pepper
6 garlic cloves, coarsely chopped
4 (6-ounce) skinless, boneless chicken breast halves, cut into 1-inch pieces
½ teaspoon kosher salt, divided
1 tablespoon canola oil
½ cup plain 2% reduced-fat Greek yogurt
¼ cup diced onion
¼ cup chopped English cucumber
1 tablespoon chopped fresh dill
1 tablespoon fresh lemon juice
4 green leaf lettuce leaves
2 plum tomatoes, cut into 12 slices
¼ teaspoon black pepper
3 ounces feta cheese, sliced
2 whole-wheat pitas, cut into wedges

1. Place first 4 ingredients and ¼ teaspoon salt in a food processor; process until ground. Divide mixture into 8 equal portions; shape each into a ½-inch-thick patty. Heat a large skillet over medium-high heat. Add oil to pan. Add patties to pan; cook 4 minutes on each side.
2. Combine yogurt and next 4 ingredients; stir in remaining ¼ teaspoon salt. Place 1 lettuce leaf on each of 4 plates. Top evenly with tomato slices; sprinkle with black pepper. Divide cheese evenly among servings. Arrange 2 patties on top of tomato mixture; top each serving with about 2 tablespoons yogurt mixture. Serve with pita wedges. Yield: 4 servings.

CALORIES 359; **FAT** 11.4g (sat 4.5g, mono 3.7g, poly 1.9g); **PROTEIN** 39.6g; **CARB** 25g; **FIBER** 3.4g; **CHOL** 95mg; **IRON** 2.5mg; **SODIUM** 751mg; **CALC** 192mg

Chicken Burgers

Hands-on time: 18 min. Total time: 26 min.

1 tablespoon capers, drained
2 shallots, trimmed and peeled
1 pound skinless, boneless chicken breast
  halves
¼ teaspoon salt
¼ teaspoon black pepper
Cooking spray
4 whole-wheat hamburger buns
¼ cup canola mayonnaise
4 green leaf lettuce leaves
8 plum tomato slices
2 tablespoons Dijon mustard

1. Place first 5 ingredients in a food processor; process until finely ground. Divide chicken mixture into 4 equal portions; shape each into a ½-inch-thick patty. Heat a large grill pan over medium high heat. Coat pan with cooking spray. Add patties to pan; cook 5 minutes on each side.
2. Place bottom half of each bun on a plate, and spread 1 tablespoon mayonnaise over each. Top each burger with 1 lettuce leaf, 1 patty, and 2 tomato slices. Spread 1½ teaspoons mustard over each bun top, then place bun tops on burgers. Yield: 4 servings.

CALORIES 335; **FAT** 9.2g (sat 1.1g, mono 3.9g, poly 3g); **PROTEIN** 29.2g; **CARB** 34.9g; **FIBER** 3.8g; **CHOL** 63mg; **IRON** 2.8mg; **SODIUM** 764mg; **CALC** 69mg

3 LITTLE SECRETS FOR BIG FLAVORS

Concentrate the flavors of shrimp, chicken, or mushrooms to instantly jazz up sauces, sautés, sides, and more.

In France, tricks of the culinary trade are called *trucs* or *astuces*—little tips and techniques with ingredients, passed down from generations of cooks. They add special depth to a dish.

Here are three little preparations that fill the bill: chicken glace, duxelles, and shrimp butter. Each magically adds flavor, texture, aroma, and complexity. Flavor boosters like these are part of "classic" cooking, but they're not difficult, and they elevate dishes from the everyday to the special.

Make Ahead • Freezable • Vegetarian
Duxelles

Hands-on time: 51 min. Total time: 51 min.
Keep a batch handy to liven up a simple fish (such as Arctic Char with Duxelles and Leeks, page 26). Stir into stews, or layer them into a gratin (such as Potato Gratin with Duxelles, page 26). Use white button mushrooms. Refrigerate for up to three days, or freeze in ¼-cup portions (try using muffin tins) for up to three months. Thaw frozen duxelles before adding them to a recipe. Duxelles give earthy, aromatic notes to meat and fish stuffings, soups, stews, pastas, and casseroles.

10¾ cups sliced mushrooms (about
  3 pounds)
1 tablespoon olive oil
¾ cup minced onion
½ cup minced leek (about 1 small)
2 garlic cloves, minced
½ cup minced fresh parsley
3 tablespoons minced fresh chives
¾ teaspoon salt
¼ teaspoon freshly ground black pepper

1. Place about 2 cups mushrooms in a food processor, and pulse 12 times or until finely chopped, scraping sides of bowl occasionally. Place chopped mushrooms in a large bowl. Repeat procedure in batches with remaining mushrooms.
2. Heat a large nonstick skillet over medium-high heat. Add oil to pan; swirl to coat. Add onion, leek, and garlic to pan; sauté 3 minutes or until tender. Stir in mushrooms; sauté 30 minutes or until liquid evaporates, stirring occasionally. Remove from heat; stir in parsley, chives, salt, and pepper. Cool completely. Yield: 4 cups (serving size: ¼ cup).

CALORIES 32; **FAT** 1g (sat 0.1g, mono 0.6g, poly 0.1g); **PROTEIN** 1.7g; **CARB** 4.3g; **FIBER** 0.3g; **CHOL** 0mg; **IRON** 0.5mg; **SODIUM** 118mg; **CALC** 11mg

A VERSATILE INGREDIENT LIKE DUXELLES DELIVERS DEEP, RICH, EARTHY DELIGHT WITH EVERY BITE.

THREE SECRET INGREDIENTS

1 SHRIMP BUTTER
Shells that you might otherwise discard capture the soul of the sea. Recipe page 27.

Chefs make this special ingredient, sometimes called shellfish butter, with lobster, crab, or crawfish shells. At home, shrimp is the easiest and cheapest alternative.

We've simplified the traditional way of making shrimp butter, which involved pounding shells by hand and mixing with butter, and then straining the shells out. Even using a food processor to grind shells involves laborious shell extraction later. So we simply cook raw shrimp shells in butter to draw off flavor. The resulting butter can be used as a last-minute aromatic addition to sauces, soups, and sautés. Stir it into a seafood pasta toss, use it to enliven fish chowder, or mix it into side dishes for a briny touch of the sea. The late Edna Lewis—an icon of Southern cooking—developed an American twist on shrimp butter with finely chopped shrimp meat, a touch of sherry, lemon juice, and cayenne.

2 CHICKEN GLACE
Beyond chicken stock lies this amazingly concentrated flavor of the bird. Recipe page 27.

Glace is made by reducing homemade stock to a fraction of its original volume, yielding rich flavor and a syrupy consistency. Julia Child extolled its power in *Mastering the Art of French Cooking:* "Half a teaspoon stirred into a sauce or a soup will often give it just that particular boost of flavor which it lacks." Glace imparts its velvety richness with almost no added fat.

Glace can also be made from beef or fish stock. But chicken glace is hearty enough to use in a pan sauce for beef, yet light enough to glaze vegetables. You can stir in a tablespoon to fortify and enrich starchy sides like polenta and risotto. Commercially prepared glace sold at specialty food shops is an option, but making your own lets you control sodium and avoid additives.

While it takes some time to prepare, most of the cooking is hands-off. Don't overapply it, though! Our recipe's yield is only about 6 tablespoons, but a little goes a long way—that's enough for at least three dishes.

3 DUXELLES
Onions, herbs, and mushrooms evoke the essence of forest and garden. Recipe page 25.

The original recipe for this chunky paste of mushrooms, onions, and herbs dates to the 17th century. And, yes, you find duxelles deployed in rather dated, regal dishes like veal Prince Orloff and beef Wellington. But this is really a very down-to-earth, timeless concoction, a perfect flavor booster for casual dishes like meat loaf and omelets. You can even spread the paste on toasted bread and broil with a bit of cheese—shaved Parmigiano-Reggiano or little dollops of goat cheese—for a quick cocktail snack. Some recipes for duxelles suggest squeezing excess liquid from the finely chopped mushrooms before cooking, but this carries away much of the mushroom flavor. The technique we use in our recipe allows liquid from the finely chopped mushrooms to evaporate as they cook, retaining maximum mushroom taste.

Potato Gratin with Duxelles

Hands-on time (assuming Duxelles are prepared): 35 min. Total time: 1 hr. 30 min.

4½ cups (⅛-inch-thick) slices peeled baking potato (about 2 pounds)
2½ cups whole milk
1 teaspoon salt
1 teaspoon minced garlic
¾ teaspoon chopped fresh thyme
¼ teaspoon black pepper
Cooking spray
¾ cup Duxelles (page 25)
½ cup (2 ounces) grated fresh Parmesan cheese, divided

1. Preheat oven to 375°.
2. Combine first 6 ingredients in a medium saucepan over medium heat; bring to a boil. Reduce heat, and simmer 10 minutes, stirring frequently. Drain potatoes through a sieve over a bowl; reserve potatoes and liquid.
3. Arrange half of potatoes in an 11 x 7–inch glass or ceramic baking dish coated with cooking spray. Spread Duxelles evenly over potatoes; sprinkle with ¼ cup cheese. Top with remaining potatoes. Pour reserved cooking liquid over potatoes; sprinkle with remaining ¼ cup cheese. Bake at 375° for 50 minutes or until cheese begins to brown. Let stand 5 minutes. Yield: 10 servings.

CALORIES 136; **FAT** 4g (sat 2g, mono 0.7g, poly 0.2g); **PROTEIN** 6.3g; **CARB** 19.2g; **FIBER** 1.2g; **CHOL** 10mg; **IRON** 0.4mg; **SODIUM** 399mg; **CALC** 157mg

Arctic Char with Duxelles and Leeks

Hands-on time (assuming Duxelles are prepared): 22 min. Total time: 34 min.

Cooking spray
1½ cups thinly sliced leek (about 1½ large)
½ cup dry white wine, divided
½ cup Duxelles (page 25)
4 (6-ounce) Arctic char fillets, skinned
½ teaspoon salt

1. Preheat oven to 400°.
2. Heat a medium nonstick skillet over medium heat. Coat pan with cooking spray. Add leek to pan; cook 5 minutes or until tender. Add 2 tablespoons wine; cook 1 minute. Arrange leek mixture in bottom of an 11 x 7–inch glass or ceramic baking dish coated with cooking spray.
3. Spread Duxelles evenly over leek mixture. Place fish on top of Duxelles; sprinkle with salt. Drizzle with remaining 6 tablespoons wine. Bake at 400° for 12 minutes or until desired degree of doneness. Serve fish with leeks and cooking liquid. Yield: 4 servings (serving size: 1 fillet and about 2 tablespoons sauce).

Sustainable Choice | *Arctic char is a smart option when wild salmon isn't available.*

CALORIES 310; **FAT** 13.7g (sat 3.2g, mono 6g, poly 3.3g); **PROTEIN** 37.6g; **CARB** 7.3g; **FIBER** 0.8g; **CHOL** 87mg; **IRON** 1.6mg; **SODIUM** 443mg; **CALC** 48mg

Chicken Glace

Hands-on time: 25 min. Total time: 13 hr. 45 min.
Yes, this is a weekend project, but it has a big flavor payoff. (Or buy some at a gourmet store, or order from bonewerksculinarte.com). To store, spoon 1-tablespoon portions of cooled Glace into an ice-cube tray. Cover with plastic wrap; freeze. Place cubes in a container; freeze up to three months.

3 pounds bone-in chicken thighs, skinned
Cooking spray
3 quarts cold water, divided
4 cups coarsely chopped yellow onion
2 cups coarsely chopped celery
1 cup coarsely chopped carrot
12 black peppercorns
10 parsley sprigs
3 thyme sprigs
2 bay leaves

1. Preheat oven to 425°.
2. Place chicken in a broiler pan or shallow roasting pan coated with cooking spray. Bake at 425° for 1 hour, turning thighs after 30 minutes.
3. Place chicken in a large stockpot. Carefully add 2 cups cold water to broiler pan, scraping to loosen browned bits; pour liquid into stockpot. Add onion and next 6 ingredients. Add remaining 10 cups cold water; bring to a boil. Reduce heat, and simmer 2 hours; skim surface occasionally, discarding foam.
4. Strain stock through a fine sieve lined with cheesecloth or a thin cotton dish towel into a large bowl; discard solids. Cool stock to room temperature. Cover and chill stock 8 hours or overnight.
5. Skim solidified fat from surface of stock, and discard. Place stock in a medium saucepan; bring to a boil. Reduce heat, and simmer until syrupy and reduced to 6 tablespoons (about 1 hour and 15 minutes), skimming foam as needed. Yield: 6 tablespoons (serving size: 1 tablespoon).

CALORIES 27; FAT 1.3g (sat 0.4g, mono 0.5g, poly 0.3g); PROTEIN 3.2g; CARB 0.4g; FIBER 0.1g; CHOL 11mg; IRON 0.2mg; SODIUM 14mg; CALC 4mg

Beef Tenderloin with Mushroom–Red Wine Sauce

Hands-on time (assuming Glace is prepared): 17 min. Total time: 19 min.

Cooking spray
2 (4-ounce) beef tenderloin steaks, trimmed
½ teaspoon salt, divided
¼ teaspoon freshly ground black pepper, divided
1¼ cups sliced mushrooms
¼ cup minced shallots
½ cup dry red wine
2 tablespoons Chicken Glace (at left)

1. Heat a large nonstick skillet over medium-high heat. Coat pan with cooking spray. Sprinkle steaks with ¼ teaspoon salt and ⅛ teaspoon pepper. Add steaks to pan; cook 3 minutes on each side or until desired degree of doneness. Remove steaks from pan; keep warm.
2. Add mushrooms and shallots to pan; sauté 3 minutes. Add wine, scraping pan to loosen browned bits; bring to a boil. Reduce heat, and simmer 4 minutes. Stir in Chicken Glace and remaining ¼ teaspoon salt and ⅛ teaspoon pepper; cook 1 minute or until Glace is blended into sauce. Yield: 2 servings (serving size: 1 steak and about ⅓ cup sauce).

CALORIES 222; FAT 8.1g (sat 2.9g, mono 3.2g, poly 0.6g); PROTEIN 29.1g; CARB 6.7g; FIBER 0.4g; CHOL 79mg; IRON 2.4mg; SODIUM 665mg; CALC 34mg

Herb-Glazed Carrots

Hands-on time (assuming Glace is prepared): 18 min. Total time: 28 min.
This is a delicious, versatile side dish for roast chicken, pork tenderloin, or steak.

18 ounces baby carrots, peeled and halved lengthwise
2 teaspoons olive oil
2 tablespoons Chicken Glace (at left)
¼ teaspoon salt
¼ teaspoon black pepper
2 tablespoons minced fresh flat-leaf parsley
2 teaspoons minced fresh chives
1 teaspoon minced fresh tarragon

1. Cook carrots in boiling water 8 minutes or until tender. Drain well.
2. Heat a large nonstick skillet over medium heat. Add oil to pan; swirl to coat. Add carrots; cook 1 minute. Add Chicken Glace, salt, and pepper; cook 3 minutes. Stir in parsley, chives, and tarragon. Yield: 4 servings (serving size: about 1 cup).

CALORIES 94; FAT 3.3g (sat 0.6g, mono 1.9g, poly 0.6g); PROTEIN 3g; CARB 14.3g; FIBER 4.2g; CHOL 6mg; IRON 0.7mg; SODIUM 255mg; CALC 54mg

Shrimp Butter

Hands-on time: 47 min. Total time: 47 min.
Cooking the shrimp shells until they're uniformly pink and give off a toasty aroma ensures that they've infused the butter. Spoon 1-tablespoon portions of cooled Shrimp Butter into an ice-cube tray. Cover with plastic wrap; freeze until solid. Keep butter cubes frozen in an airtight container for up to three months. Thaw before using.

1 cup butter
4 cups raw shrimp shells (about 6 ounces)

1. Melt butter in a medium saucepan over medium heat. Add shrimp shells to pan, and cook 15 minutes, stirring frequently.
2. Strain butter mixture through a fine sieve over a bowl, reserving butter. Discard solids. Yield: 8 tablespoons (serving size: 1 tablespoon).

CALORIES 113; FAT 12.7g (sat 7.9g, mono 3.7g, poly 0.5g); PROTEIN 0.2g; CARB 0g; FIBER 0g; CHOL 34mg; IRON 0mg; SODIUM 1mg; CALC 1mg

Shrimp Sautéed with Broccolini
(pictured on page 210)

Hands-on time (assuming Shrimp Butter is prepared): 18 min. Total time: 67 min. Shrimp Butter stirred into this quick sauté brings out its briny ocean essence. This ginger-spiced dish is a tasty way to enjoy a serving of vegetables.

1 pound Broccolini, trimmed
2 teaspoons olive oil
1/4 cup sliced green onions
1 tablespoon thinly sliced peeled fresh ginger
3/4 pound medium shrimp, peeled and deveined
1/2 teaspoon salt
2 tablespoons Shrimp Butter (page 27)
3 cups hot cooked long-grain brown rice

1. Cook Broccolini in boiling water 2 minutes or until nearly tender; drain.
2. Heat a large nonstick skillet over medium-high heat. Add oil to pan; swirl to coat. Add onions and ginger; sauté 1 minute. Add shrimp, salt, and Broccolini; sauté 4 minutes or until shrimp are done. Stir in Shrimp Butter; cook 30 seconds or until butter melts. Serve over rice. Yield: 4 servings (serving size: about 1 cup shrimp mixture and 3/4 cup rice).

CALORIES 364; FAT 11.8g (sat 4.9g, mono 4.2g, poly 1.7g); PROTEIN 24.7g; CARB 41g; FIBER 6.1g; CHOL 146mg; IRON 3.8mg; SODIUM 461mg; CALC 118mg

WINE NOTE: For the Shrimp Sautéed with Broccolini, an off-dry white wine such as riesling marries the varied flavors of sweet shrimp, savory Broccolini, earthy green onions, and spicy ginger. The 2009 Pacific Rim Riesling (Columbia Valley, $11) is bright and crisp with an underlying sweetness that complements this colorful dish.

Rice and Green Peas with Shrimp Butter

Hands-on time (assuming Shrimp Butter is prepared): 11 min. Total time: 43 min. Serve with roasted fish, or use as a bed for broiled shrimp skewers.

Cooking spray
1/4 cup minced shallots
1/4 cup diced carrot
3/4 cup uncooked long-grain rice
1 1/2 cups hot water
1 teaspoon chopped fresh thyme
1/2 teaspoon salt
1 cup frozen green peas, thawed
2 tablespoons Shrimp Butter (page 27), cut into small pieces

1. Heat a medium saucepan over medium-high heat. Coat pan with cooking spray. Add shallots to pan; sauté 1 minute or until tender. Add carrot; sauté 1 minute. Stir in rice; sauté 2 minutes. Add 1 1/2 cups hot water, thyme, and salt; bring to a boil. Cover, reduce heat, and simmer 23 minutes or until rice is tender and liquid is absorbed. Remove from heat; stir in peas and Shrimp Butter. Let stand 5 minutes or until peas are thoroughly heated and Shrimp Butter melts. Yield: 6 servings (serving size: about 2/3 cup).

CALORIES 150; FAT 4.5g (sat 2.7g, mono 1.3g, poly 0.2g); PROTEIN 3.2g; CARB 24.5g; FIBER 1.5g; CHOL 11mg; IRON 1.3mg; SODIUM 238mg; CALC 17mg

STARCHY SIDES ARE TRANSFORMED WITH A DAB OF SHRIMP BUTTER.

5 OTHER WAYS TO BOOST FLAVOR

The same flavor-elevating principle applies to pastes, oils, and sauces.

CHUTNEY: There are more and more varieties of this sweet-tart condiment in stores. It can brighten a variety of dishes. Stir a few tablespoons into lentil soup just before serving, or toss sautéed shrimp or chicken strips with chutney and serve over rice for a quick, flavorful entrée.

CURRY PASTE: Another Indian short-cut pantry item, this blend of chiles, herbs, and spices ranges from mild to fiery. Add a teaspoon to the pot when steaming mussels, make a pan sauce for chicken with white wine or broth, or add some to eggplant puree for a zingy dip.

PESTO: The herby Italian staple can do far more than coat pasta. Spread it over a fish fillet before baking, toss it with steamed green beans, or stir a bit into salad dressing for a great leap in flavor. Find good prepared versions in the refrigerated section of the supermarket.

TRUFFLE OIL: Costly, small bottles go a long way. Mere drizzles of the black (more earthy-mushroomy) or white (quite heady and pungent) can lift a dish. Just before serving, stir into mashed potatoes, drizzle over soup, or toss with pasta and sautéed mushrooms.

HOT PEPPER SAUCE: This blend of chiles, vinegar, and salt gives dimension and kick to so many savory foods. Add a bit to tartar sauce for zip, blend some into ground beef for meatballs, add to a tomato-based soup, or enliven a vegetable stir-fry.

WHAT TO EAT RIGHT NOW
EGGS

Pretty much everyone now knows that the bad rap that eggs got during the Great Cholesterol Scare of the '80s was unfair—cholesterol in food isn't the culprit. Recently the egg has been elevated to the status of Gourmet Object, to be fussed over and coddled. On restaurant menus of a certain pretension, eggs are now called "hen eggs," a term that must make for some snickering back in the chicken coop. Our position is this: Amid the general tendency to lighten up in January, don't put the eggs away. Start your morning with a soft-cooked egg, featuring a nicely set white and a rich, molten yolk. Make dinner more interesting by perching poached, fried, or scrambled eggs atop salad greens or pizza crust. It's a simply delicious way to eat light.

EGGS, UPGRADED?

Egg cartons are dotted with claims these days.

- **Omega-3:** Hens that eat flaxseeds lay eggs that can be higher in these heart-healthy fatty acids.

- **Vegetarian-fed:** No nutritional difference, but perhaps more appealing to egg-eating vegetarians.

- **Hormone-free:** Nice to know, but there are no hormone products approved for egg production.

- **Cage-free:** Implies more humane treatment than battery crowding, but the claim is lightly regulated.

Vegetarian
Walnut-Breadcrumb Pasta with a Soft Egg

Hands-on time: 20 min. Total time: 44 min.

A soft-cooked egg coats the pasta and adds rich flavor to this rustic dish. The key to success with the eggs is to plunge them quickly into ice water to stop the cooking.

4 large eggs
1 (2-ounce) piece French bread baguette, torn into small pieces
¼ cup walnuts
3 tablespoons olive oil
4 garlic cloves, minced
½ teaspoon kosher salt
½ teaspoon freshly ground black pepper
8 ounces uncooked fresh linguine
⅓ cup chopped fresh flat-leaf parsley
2 tablespoons finely chopped fresh chives
⅓ cup (1½ ounces) crumbled goat cheese

1. Bring 3 inches of water to a boil in a medium saucepan. Add eggs to pan; boil 5½ minutes. Drain. Plunge eggs into ice water, and let stand 5 minutes. Drain and peel.
2. Place bread in a food processor; process until finely ground. Add nuts to bread; pulse until finely ground. Heat a large skillet over medium-high heat. Add olive oil to pan, and swirl to coat. Add garlic, and sauté 30 seconds, stirring constantly. Add breadcrumb mixture, salt, and pepper to pan; sauté 5 minutes or until toasted, stirring frequently.
3. Cook pasta according to package directions, omitting salt and fat; drain. Add pasta to breadcrumb mixture; toss to combine. Sprinkle with parsley and chives; toss to combine. Divide pasta mixture evenly among 4 shallow bowls, and top each serving with 1 egg and 1½ tablespoons cheese. Serve immediately. Yield: 4 servings.

CALORIES 492; **FAT** 23.2g (sat 5.3g, mono 10.5g, poly 5.4g); **PROTEIN** 19.2g; **CARB** 53.3g; **FIBER** 3g; **CHOL** 216mg; **IRON** 4.1mg; **SODIUM** 448mg; **CALC** 80mg

MASTERING THE SOFT BOIL

Soft-cooked eggs—perfect peeled ovoids holding pockets of creamy yolk inside—are impressive on the plate, more so, even, than poached. Served on a bed of pasta, they add an extra dimension and sauce up the dish. Part of the trick is immersing the eggs in ice water: For the whole technique, see the recipe for Walnut-Breadcrumb Pasta with a Soft Egg at left.

Quick & Easy
Smoked Salmon and Egg Sandwich

4 cups water
1 tablespoon white vinegar
4 large eggs
¼ cup (2 ounces) ⅓-less-fat cream cheese
2 tablespoons minced red onion
1 tablespoon chopped dill
⅜ teaspoon kosher salt
4 (1-ounce) slices whole-grain bread, toasted
1 cup fresh arugula
4 ounces smoked wild salmon
¼ teaspoon black pepper

1. Bring 4 cups water and vinegar to a simmer in a 12-inch skillet over medium heat. Add eggs, 1 at a time; simmer 3 minutes or until desired degree of doneness.
2. Combine cheese, onion, dill, and ⅛ teaspoon salt; spread 1 tablespoon cheese mixture over each bread slice. Top each serving with ¼ cup arugula and 1 ounce salmon. Remove eggs from pan with a slotted spoon; place 1 egg on top of each serving. Top each sandwich with remaining ¼ teaspoon salt and pepper. Yield: 4 servings.

Sustainable Choice

Look for salmon that's labeled "wild Alaskan salmon," and you can be sure you're getting sustainable seafood.

CALORIES 219; **FAT** 10.7g (sat 3.9g, mono 0g, poly 0g); **PROTEIN** 0g; **CARB** 0g; **FIBER** 0g; **CHOL** 0mg; **IRON** 0mg; **SODIUM** 640mg; **CALC** 0mg

THE COMFORT OF CURRIES

Get bold when it gets cold. Store-bought curry pastes are easy and delicious. A home blend of spices adds fragrant complexity.

Vegetarian

Green Curry with Bok Choy

Hands-on time: 20 min. Total time: 35 min.

½ cup chopped fresh cilantro
2 tablespoons chopped peeled fresh ginger
2 teaspoons ground coriander
2 teaspoons ground cumin
8 garlic cloves, peeled
3 small serrano chiles, seeded
2 large shallots, coarsely chopped
4 cups coarsely chopped broccoli florets (about 1 head)
2 cups (½-inch-thick) slices baby bok choy
2 teaspoons dark sesame oil
4 teaspoons sugar
1 tablespoon lower-sodium soy sauce
¾ teaspoon kosher salt
3 Kaffir lime leaves
1 (13.5-ounce) can light coconut milk
1 (14-ounce) package water-packed organic firm tofu, drained and cut into ¾-inch cubes
¼ cup fresh lime juice
2 cups hot cooked long-grain white rice
¼ cup chopped fresh basil
2 tablespoons chopped fresh mint

1. Place first 7 ingredients in a food processor; process until smooth. Set aside.
2. Cook broccoli florets in boiling water in a large Dutch oven 3 minutes or until crisp-tender. Remove broccoli from water with a slotted spoon; drain and rinse with cold water. Drain; set aside. Return water to a boil. Add baby bok choy to pan; cook 1 minute. Drain and rinse with cold water. Drain; set aside.
3. Heat Dutch oven over medium-high heat. Add oil to pan; swirl to coat. Add cilantro mixture to pan, and sauté 1 minute, stirring constantly. Add sugar and next 4 ingredients to pan; bring to a boil. Add tofu; cover, reduce heat, and simmer 6 minutes or until slightly thick. Add broccoli, bok choy, and juice, and cook 1 minute or until heated, tossing to combine. Discard lime leaves. Place ½ cup rice in each of 4 bowls, and spoon 1½ cups tofu mixture over each serving. Sprinkle 1 tablespoon basil and 1½ teaspoons mint over each serving. Yield: 4 servings.

CALORIES 338; FAT 12.8g (sat 5.3g, mono 2.2g, poly 4.1g); PROTEIN 16.6g; CARB 44.2g; FIBER 4.1g; CHOL 0mg; IRON 5mg; SODIUM 566mg; CALC 333mg

Vegetarian

Curried Chickpea Stew with Brown Rice Pilaf

Hands-on time: 20 min. Total time: 60 min. This curry hails from the Indian region of Punjab. The cardamom pods puff up to almost twice their size and float to the top, so they're easy to find and discard before serving. In just one serving, you get close to 10 grams of fiber, thanks to brown rice, chickpeas, tomatoes, and plenty of onion.

Pilaf:
1 tablespoon canola oil
1 cup finely chopped onion
1 cup uncooked brown rice
½ teaspoon ground turmeric
3 cardamom pods, crushed
1 (3-inch) cinnamon stick
1 garlic clove, minced
1⅔ cups water
1 bay leaf

Stew:
1 tablespoon canola oil
2 cups chopped onion
1 tablespoon grated peeled fresh ginger
1 teaspoon ground cumin
1 teaspoon ground coriander
¾ teaspoon ground turmeric
¼ teaspoon ground red pepper
4 garlic cloves, minced
3 cardamom pods, crushed
1 (3-inch) cinnamon stick
2½ cups water
1 cup diced carrot
¼ teaspoon kosher salt
1 (15-ounce) can chickpeas (garbanzo beans), rinsed and drained
1 (14.5-ounce) can fire-roasted crushed tomatoes, undrained (such as Muir Glen)
½ cup plain fat-free yogurt
¼ cup chopped fresh cilantro

1. To prepare pilaf, heat a large non-stick skillet over medium heat. Add 1 tablespoon oil; swirl to coat. Add 1 cup onion; cook 6 minutes or until golden, stirring frequently. Add rice and next 4 ingredients; cook 1 minute, stirring constantly. Add 1⅔ cups water and bay leaf; bring to a boil. Cover, reduce heat, and simmer 45 minutes. Let stand 5 minutes. Discard cardamom, cinnamon, and bay leaf. Keep warm.
2. To prepare stew, heat a large Dutch oven over medium-high heat. Add 1 tablespoon oil, and swirl to coat. Add 2 cups onion; sauté 6 minutes or until golden. Add ginger and next 7 ingredients; cook 1 minute, stirring constantly. Add 2½ cups water, carrot, ¼ teaspoon salt, chickpeas, and tomatoes; bring to a boil. Cover, reduce heat, and simmer 20 minutes or until carrots are tender and sauce is slightly thick. Discard cardamom and cinnamon stick.
3. Place 1 cup rice mixture into each of 4 bowls; spoon 1¼ cups chickpea mixture over rice. Top each serving with 2 tablespoons yogurt and 1 tablespoon cilantro. Yield: 4 servings.

CALORIES 431; FAT 9.6g (sat 1g, mono 5.1g, poly 2.9g); PROTEIN 11.9g; CARB 77.9g; FIBER 9.6g; CHOL 1mg; IRON 3.1mg; SODIUM 626mg; CALC 121mg

Vegetarian
Curry-Spiced Noodles

Hands-on time: 20 min. Total time: 35 min.

8 ounces dry udon noodles (thick, round fresh
    Japanese wheat noodles) or spaghetti
4 teaspoons peanut oil, divided
2 cups julienne-cut carrot
2 cups julienne-cut red bell pepper
1 cup julienne-cut green bell pepper
4 cups thinly sliced shiitake mushroom caps
3 tablespoons chopped peeled fresh
    lemongrass
1 tablespoon grated peeled fresh ginger
1 tablespoon red curry paste
2 teaspoons ground cumin
1 teaspoon ground turmeric
8 garlic cloves, minced
1 cup organic vegetable broth
½ cup water
2 teaspoons lower-sodium soy sauce
¼ teaspoon kosher salt
3 green onions, thinly sliced
⅓ cup cilantro leaves
¼ cup chopped dry-roasted, unsalted cashews

1. Cook noodles according to package
directions, omitting salt and fat. Set
noodles aside; keep warm.
2. Heat a large nonstick skillet over
medium-high heat. Add 2 teaspoons
peanut oil to pan; swirl to coat. Add
carrot to pan; sauté 2 minutes. Add bell
peppers; sauté 2 minutes. Remove carrot mixture from pan.
3. Heat remaining 2 teaspoons oil in
pan over medium-high heat; swirl
to coat. Add mushrooms; sauté 2
minutes. Add lemongrass and next 5
ingredients; cook 1 minute, stirring
constantly. Add broth, ½ cup water, soy
sauce, and salt. Bring to a boil; cover,
reduce heat, and simmer 2 minutes
or until slightly thick. Add noodles,
carrot mixture, and onions; cook 2
minutes, tossing to combine. Divide
noodle mixture among 4 bowls; top
with cilantro and cashews. Yield: 4
servings (serving size: 1½ cups noodle
mixture, about 4 teaspoons cilantro,
and 1 tablespoon cashews).

CALORIES 402; **FAT** 10.8g (sat 1.7g, mono 4.5g, poly 2.3g);
PROTEIN 12.7g; **CARB** 66g; **FIBER** 8.5g; **CHOL** 0mg;
IRON 4.4mg; **SODIUM** 555mg; **CALC** 77mg

HOW TO PREPARE
LEMONGRASS FOR CURRY

Lemongrass adds citrusy punch and floral fragrance to some curries, but this tough plant
needs proper prep to release its essence.

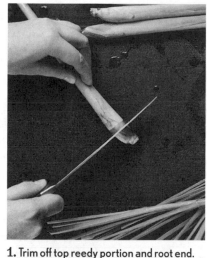

1. Trim off top reedy portion and root end.

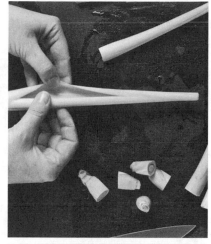

2. Peel and discard tough, dry outer layers.

3. Place knife blade flat against trimmed
stalk; pound to release aromatic oils.

4. Mince finely for the recipe.

USE ONLY THE LOWER BULB OF
THE LEMONGRASS STALK, AND
REMOVE THE TOUGH OUTER LEAVES
BEFORE CHOPPING.

Vegetarian Country Captain

Hands-on time: 20 min. Total time: 30 min. Traditionally, Country Captain is a mild chicken stew seasoned with curry powder. Myth has it that a British sea captain working in the spice trade introduced this comforting dish to the southern U.S. in the 19th century. Here, we've replaced chicken with edamame and cauliflower for a version loaded with vegetables.

1 tablespoon canola oil
1½ cups finely chopped onion
1½ cups diced peeled Granny Smith apple
1 tablespoon all-purpose flour
1 tablespoon curry powder
3 garlic cloves, minced
2 cups organic vegetable broth
2 tablespoons mango chutney
2 tablespoons whipping cream
½ teaspoon kosher salt
3 cups cauliflower florets
2 cups frozen shelled edamame (green
  soybeans)
3 cups hot cooked long-grain white rice
¼ cup dried currants
¼ cup sliced almonds, toasted
Chopped fresh cilantro (optional)
Sliced green onions (optional)

1. Heat a large, heavy nonstick skillet over medium heat. Add oil to pan, and swirl to coat. Add chopped onion, and cook 7 minutes or until tender, stirring frequently. Add apple; cook 5 minutes, stirring frequently. Add flour, curry powder, and garlic; cook 1 minute, stirring constantly. Add broth, and bring to a boil. Reduce heat, and simmer 2 minutes or until slightly thick. Stir in chutney, cream, and salt. Add cauliflower and edamame; cook 8 minutes or until cauliflower is tender, stirring occasionally. Serve over rice, and top with currants and almonds. Garnish with cilantro and green onions, if desired. Yield: 4 servings (serving size: 1¼ cups cauliflower mixture, ¾ cup rice, 1 tablespoon currants, and 1 tablespoon almonds).

CALORIES 473; FAT 14.9g (sat 3.4g, mono 6g, poly 4.4g); PROTEIN 16.7g; CARB 70.6g; FIBER 5.8g; CHOL 10mg; IRON 4.4mg; SODIUM 641mg; CALC 122mg

THE WINTER WARMTH OF CITRUS

Juicy, tangy, sweet, vibrant, and supremely fresh— the season's finest fruits add life and lightness to any dish.

For those lucky enough to live among citrus trees, the cheerful yellows and oranges, the glistening deep reds and shiny lime greens add such bright notes to your day. And that's before you even eat the fruit.

Citrus offers an easy cure for the common cold-weather blahs, no matter where you live. Winter foods shouldn't be stodgy, of course, but they often can get a refreshing lift from citrus. Citrus power comes not only from the juice and flesh but also, critically, from the rind, which is filled with aromatic oils that allow the flavor to carry through time and temperature. Just one lemon—juice, rind, and a little flesh—gives an acidic punch to Poached Halibut with Lemon-Herb Sauce (page 34), a dish that is delicious hot or cold.

Citrus is a natural for winter salads. In our quinoa recipe, blood orange sections cut through the earthiness of quinoa, and beets add vivid color. In the spinach and endive salad, tart tangelo stands up to flavorful walnut oil and toasted walnuts.

Finally, citrus gives so much to the sweet side of the menu. Tangerine infuses a light citrus pudding here, and there is also a more substantial Clementine-Date Cake (page 33) that includes two entire clementines, fragrant skin and all. Dense and moist, it keeps for days and is a winter standby.

For an utterly light dessert, meanwhile, there's Grapefruit-Buttermilk Sherbet (page 33), a clean little ice that will be quite festive if you serve it in a Champagne flute, then cover it with Champagne. Raise your glass in a toast to winter and to the warming gift that is citrus.

Spinach, Endive, and Tangelo Salad

Hands-on time: 15 min. Total time: 15 min.

2 tablespoons torn fresh mint leaves
1½ teaspoons grated tangelo rind
1 tablespoon fresh tangelo juice
2 teaspoons thinly sliced green onions
½ teaspoon Champagne vinegar
¼ teaspoon salt
2 tablespoons walnut oil
4 cups baby spinach leaves
¾ cup sliced peeled tangelo
2 heads Belgian endive, halved and thinly
  sliced
⅓ cup walnuts, toasted
¼ teaspoon freshly ground black pepper

1. Combine first 6 ingredients in a medium bowl. Gradually add walnut oil, stirring constantly with a whisk.
2. Combine spinach, tangelo slices, and endive in a large bowl. Drizzle dressing over salad, tossing to coat. Arrange 1 cup salad on each of 6 plates, and sprinkle evenly with walnuts and black pepper. Serve immediately. Yield: 6 servings.

CALORIES 119; FAT 9.1g (sat 0.8g, mono 1.6g, poly 6g); PROTEIN 2.3g; CARB 10.6g; FIBER 3.3g; CHOL 0mg; IRON 0.9mg; SODIUM 115mg; CALC 54mg

Vegetarian

Beet, Blood Orange, Kumquat, and Quinoa Salad

(pictured on page 211)

Hands-on time: 22 min. Total time: 32 min.

1/4 cup finely chopped green onions
2 teaspoons grated blood orange rind
1 teaspoon grated lemon rind
2 tablespoons blood orange juice
1 tablespoon fresh lemon juice
2 teaspoons finely chopped cilantro
1/4 teaspoon salt
1/4 teaspoon ground coriander
1/4 teaspoon ground cumin
1/4 teaspoon paprika
3 tablespoons extra-virgin olive oil
1 cup uncooked quinoa
1 3/4 cups water
1/2 teaspoon salt, divided
1 cup blood orange sections, chopped (about 4 medium)
1 cup diced peeled avocado
6 whole kumquats, seeded and sliced
2 medium beets, cooked and cut into wedges

1. Combine first 10 ingredients in a medium bowl, stirring with a whisk. Gradually add oil, stirring constantly with a whisk. Set aside.
2. Place quinoa in a fine sieve, and place sieve in a large bowl. Cover quinoa with water. Using your hands, rub grains together for 30 seconds; rinse and drain. Repeat procedure twice. Drain well.
3. Combine 1 3/4 cups water, quinoa, and 1/4 teaspoon salt in a medium saucepan; bring to a boil. Cover, reduce heat, and simmer 10 minutes or until liquid is absorbed. Remove from heat; fluff with a fork. Combine quinoa, remaining 1/4 teaspoon salt, blood orange sections, avocado, and kumquats in a large bowl, tossing gently to combine. Add dressing; toss gently to coat salad. Spoon 1 cup salad onto each of 4 plates; top each serving with about 1/2 cup beets. Yield: 4 servings.

CALORIES 442; **FAT** 20.7g (sat 2.7g, mono 12.3g, poly 2.1g); **PROTEIN** 9.1g; **CARB** 58g; **FIBER** 10.7g; **CHOL** 0mg; **IRON** 3.9mg; **SODIUM** 486mg; **CALC** 117mg

---

Make Ahead • Kid Friendly

Clementine-Date Cake

Hands-on time: 30 min. Total time: 1 hr. 15 min.

Cooking spray
2 teaspoons all-purpose flour
1/2 cup walnut halves, divided
6 pitted dates
2 unpeeled clementines, quartered
1/2 cup packed brown sugar
3 tablespoons unsalted butter, softened
2 tablespoons toasted walnut oil
3/4 teaspoon vanilla extract
1 large egg
9 ounces all-purpose flour (about 2 cups)
3/4 teaspoon baking soda
3/8 teaspoon salt
1/2 cup nonfat buttermilk
1/3 cup chopped pitted dates
1 cup powdered sugar
5 teaspoons fresh tangerine juice

1. Preheat oven to 350°.
2. Coat a 9-inch round cake pan with cooking spray. Line bottom of pan with parchment paper; coat with cooking spray. Dust with 2 teaspoons flour.
3. Reserve 5 walnut halves. Place remaining walnuts, 6 dates, and clementines in a food processor; process until ground.
4. Combine brown sugar, butter, and oil in a bowl; beat with a mixer at medium speed until well blended. Beat in vanilla and egg.
5. Weigh or lightly spoon 9 ounces flour into dry measuring cups; level with a knife. Combine flour, baking soda, and salt. Add flour mixture and buttermilk alternately to sugar mixture, beginning and ending with flour mixture; mix after each addition. Add nut mixture and chopped dates; beat with a mixer at medium speed 3 minutes. Pour batter into prepared pan. Bake at 350° for 45 minutes or until a wooden pick inserted in center comes out clean. Cool in pan 10 minutes on a wire rack; remove from pan.
6. Combine powdered sugar and juice, stirring with a whisk until smooth. Drizzle glaze over warm cake; spread to coat top. Top with reserved 5 walnut halves. Cool cake on wire rack 30 minutes. Yield: 12 servings.

CALORIES 266; **FAT** 8.5g (sat 2.5g, mono 1.8g, poly 3.7g); **PROTEIN** 4.1g; **CARB** 44.8g; **FIBER** 1.7g; **CHOL** 25mg; **IRON** 1.4mg; **SODIUM** 172mg; **CALC** 39mg

---

Make Ahead • Freezable

Grapefruit-Buttermilk Sherbet

(pictured on page 211)

Hands-on time: 26 min. Total time: 2 hr.

1 cup water
2 tablespoons finely chopped red grapefruit rind
1 cup sugar
1 cup fresh red grapefruit juice
2 cups whole buttermilk
2 tablespoons vodka

1. Bring 1 cup water to a boil in a small saucepan. Add rind to pan; reduce heat, and simmer 2 minutes. Drain, reserving rind. Combine rind, sugar, and juice in pan; bring to a boil, stirring constantly until sugar dissolves. Reduce heat, and simmer 20 minutes. Remove from heat; pour into a bowl. Chill 1 hour. Strain juice mixture, and discard solids. Combine juice mixture, buttermilk, and vodka in the freezer can of an ice-cream freezer; freeze according to manufacturer's instructions. Yield: 8 servings (serving size: about 2/3 cup).

CALORIES 157; **FAT** 2g (sat 1.3g, mono 0.6g, poly 0.1g); **PROTEIN** 2.2g; **CARB** 31.4g; **FIBER** 0.2g; **CHOL** 9mg; **IRON** 0.1mg; **SODIUM** 73mg; **CALC** 5mg

IF A DISH SEEMS A LITTLE UNINSPIRED, ADD A SQUEEZE OF JUICE OR A GRATING OF AROMATIC RIND. IT WILL LIKELY ADD THE SPARK YOU'RE LOOKING FOR.

NINE CITRUS TYPES

1 KUMQUAT: Tiny fruit with curiously sweet, pungent peel that adds interest to salads or baking.

2 LIME: Hugely aromatic peel; complex tang adds tropical spritz to tacos, soups, cocktails, and more.

3 LEMON: More neutral than lime, an all-purpose acidic brightener.

4 BLOOD ORANGE: Sweet and tangy with hints of raspberry; dazzling flesh.

5 TANGELO: Easy to peel like a tangerine, but the best have a tart, grapefruity zing.

6 RED GRAPEFRUIT: Tart and sweet, with a delightful bitter edge and lovely perfume.

7 NAVEL ORANGE: Mildly sweet, juicy fruit—the basic workhorse orange.

8 CLEMENTINE: Small, usually seedless fruit that's sweet-tangy and easy to peel.

9 TANGERINE: Look for firm fruit, which promises that nice balance of sweet and sour; great for eating out of hand or for salads.

Make Ahead • Kid Friendly

Citrus Pudding with Whipped Cream

Hands-on time: 14 min. Total time: 2 hr. 30 min.

3 tablespoons sugar
1/2 teaspoon grated tangerine rind
1/2 teaspoon grated orange rind
1 cup fresh tangerine juice
1 cup fresh orange juice
3 tablespoons cornstarch
1/4 teaspoon salt
1 tablespoon fresh lemon juice
1 teaspoon unsalted butter
1/4 cup heavy whipping cream

1. Combine first 3 ingredients in a small saucepan; crush with a wooden spoon. Stir in tangerine juice, orange juice, cornstarch, and salt, stirring well. Bring to a boil, stirring constantly. Boil 2 minutes or until thickened, stirring constantly. Remove from heat; stir in lemon juice and butter. Pour pudding into a bowl; cover surface of pudding with plastic wrap. Chill.
2. Place cream in a bowl; beat with a mixer at high speed until stiff peaks form. Fold half of cream into pudding. Spoon 1/2 cup pudding into each of 4 dessert bowls or glasses; top each serving with 1 tablespoon whipped cream. Yield: 4 servings (serving size: 1/2 cup).

CALORIES 177; FAT 6.8g (sat 4.1g, mono 1.9g, poly 0.3g); PROTEIN 1.2g; CARB 28.7g; FIBER 0.4g; CHOL 23mg; IRON 0.3mg; SODIUM 162mg; CALC 25mg

---

Quick & Easy

Poached Halibut with Lemon-Herb Sauce

Hands-on time: 10 min. Total time: 22 min.

3 tablespoons olive oil
1 1/2 tablespoons chopped seeded jalapeño pepper
1 tablespoon grated lemon rind
1 1/2 tablespoons fresh lemon juice
4 teaspoons chopped fresh cilantro
4 teaspoons chopped fresh parsley
1/2 teaspoon salt
3 lemon sections, finely chopped
6 cups water
1 teaspoon salt
1/2 teaspoon black peppercorns
2 green onions, coarsely chopped
1 parsley sprig
1 cilantro sprig
4 (6-ounce) halibut fillets

1. Combine first 8 ingredients.
2. Combine 6 cups water and next 5 ingredients in a large skillet; bring to a low simmer (180° to 190°). Add fish; cook 10 minutes or until desired degree of doneness. Remove fish from pan with a slotted spoon; drain on paper towels. Serve with sauce. Yield: 4 servings (serving size: 1 fillet and 1 tablespoon sauce).

Sustainable Choice

Halibut is a readily available, sustainable option with mild flavor and firm flesh.

CALORIES 217; FAT 11.2g (sat 1.6g, mono 7.5g, poly 1.4g); PROTEIN 27g; CARB 1.3g; FIBER 0.4g; CHOL 65mg; IRON 0.8mg; SODIUM 447mg; CALC 22mg

---

READER RECIPES
FROM YOUR KITCHEN TO OURS

Marie Rizzio wanted a quicker route to breakfast for overnight guests, and she found it in a convenience product. Low-fat baking mix shortcuts the process because the flour, salt, and baking soda are already added in the proper ratios—allowing Rizzio to be the baking rock star, in less time, with less fuss.

Personal Chef Karen Tedesco loves to experiment with spicy Asian flavors, and her basil chicken meatballs are a perfect example of her success. Tedesco wanted to come up with a recipe that was versatile enough to serve as an appetizer but could also be served over rice or noodles as a light meal. "The sweet and sour Asian condiments in the meatballs add tangy, spicy, fresh flavors without high-fat ingredients."

Fresh ingredients—from Jersey tomatoes to homemade breadcrumbs—are something about which Kathy Pickens will never compromise. "Cooking with fresh ingredients is more fun. The food just smells and tastes better," she says. Breadcrumbs are made from a day-old baguette and help this delightfully simple recipe shine, adding a buttery, garlicky, toasty crunch to the baked shrimp. The shrimp stay moist and plump from a brief turn in the oven.

Chocolate Chip Scones

Hands-on time: 10 min. Total time: 35 min.
"I love chocolate, so I added semisweet minichips to complement the currants. The scones are great with my morning cup of tea."
—Marie Rizzio, Interlochen, Michigan

½ cup currants, chopped
2 tablespoons water
3 cups low-fat baking mix (such as reduced-fat Bisquick)
5 tablespoons granulated sugar, divided
½ teaspoon ground cinnamon
2 tablespoons butter, chilled and cut into small pieces
⅔ cup fat-free half-and-half
2 tablespoons semisweet chocolate minichips
1 large egg, separated
1 tablespoon fat-free half-and-half
½ cup powdered sugar
1½ teaspoons water

1. Preheat oven to 400°.
2. Combine ½ cup currants and 2 tablespoons water in a microwave-safe bowl. Microwave at HIGH 45 seconds, stirring every 15 seconds. Cool 10 minutes (do not drain).
3. Combine baking mix, ¼ cup granulated sugar, and cinnamon in a large bowl. Cut in butter with 2 knives until mixture resembles coarse meal. Add currants, ⅔ cup half-and-half, chips, and egg white; stir just until moist. Drop dough by ¼ cupfuls onto a foil-lined baking sheet; place pan in freezer 5 minutes. Combine egg yolk and 1 tablespoon half-and-half; brush over tops and sprinkle with remaining 1 tablespoon granulated sugar. Bake at 400° for 12 minutes or until golden. Cool on a wire rack.
4. Combine powdered sugar and 1½ teaspoons water; drizzle over scones. Yield: 1 dozen (serving size: 1 scone).

CALORIES 205; FAT 4.8g (sat 1.7g, mono 2g, poly 0.5g); PROTEIN 3.2g; CARB 37.9g; FIBER 1g; CHOL 23mg; IRON 1.4mg; SODIUM 360mg; CALC 133mg

Basil Chicken Meatballs with Ponzu Sauce

Hands-on time: 15 min. Total time: 19 min.
"My kids like to wrap a meatball in a lettuce leaf and pick it up to eat."
—Karen Tedesco, Webster Groves, Missouri

⅔ cup panko (Japanese breadcrumbs)
⅓ cup flaked sweetened coconut
¼ cup chopped green onions
¼ cup chopped fresh basil
2 tablespoons sweet chili sauce
2 teaspoons minced garlic
1½ teaspoons fish sauce
1½ pounds ground chicken
2 large egg whites, lightly beaten
Cooking spray
¼ cup lower-sodium soy sauce
2 tablespoons small basil leaves
1 tablespoon chopped green onions
2 tablespoons fresh orange juice
1 tablespoon fresh lemon juice
1½ teaspoons water
1½ teaspoons mirin (sweet rice wine)
Dash of crushed red pepper
Small basil leaves (optional)
Chopped green onions (optional)

1. Preheat oven to 425°.
2. Combine first 9 ingredients in a large bowl; shape into 16 (1½-inch) meatballs.
3. Heat a large nonstick skillet over medium-high heat. Coat pan with cooking spray. Add 8 meatballs to pan, and cook 6 minutes, browning on all sides. Remove meatballs from pan, and arrange on the rack of a broiler pan coated with cooking spray. Repeat procedure with remaining 8 meatballs.
4. Bake at 425° for 7 minutes or until done.
5. Combine soy sauce and next 7 ingredients in a small bowl. Serve sauce with meatballs. Garnish with basil leaves and additional chopped green onions, if desired. Yield: 8 servings (serving size: 2 meatballs and 1 tablespoon sauce).

CALORIES 194; FAT 10.2g (sat 3.9g, mono 3.9g, poly 1.9g); PROTEIN 16.8g; CARB 9.2g; FIBER 0.7g; CHOL 103mg; IRON 1.2mg; SODIUM 544mg; CALC 40mg

Baked Shrimp with Tomatoes

Hands-on time: 15 min. Total time: 30 min.
"Individual gratin dishes make a nice presentation, but you can also use a 13 x 9–inch glass baking dish."
—Kathy Pickens, Croton on Hudson, New York

1 (3-ounce) piece French bread baguette
½ cup finely chopped fresh parsley
2 garlic cloves, minced
2 tablespoons butter, divided
2 tablespoons olive oil, divided
1½ pounds large shrimp, peeled and deveined
¼ teaspoon salt, divided
¼ teaspoon black pepper, divided
2 medium tomatoes, cut into ¼-inch-thick slices (about 1 pound)
2 tablespoons balsamic vinegar

1. Preheat oven to 450°.
2. Place bread in a food processor; pulse until fine crumbs measure 1½ cups. Combine breadcrumbs, parsley, and garlic. Heat 1 tablespoon butter and 1 tablespoon oil in a large skillet over medium-high heat. Add breadcrumb mixture; cook 3 minutes or until golden brown and garlic is fragrant, stirring frequently.
3. Coat 6 individual gratin dishes with remaining 1 tablespoon oil. Arrange shrimp in a single layer in dishes; sprinkle with ⅛ teaspoon salt and ⅛ teaspoon pepper. Sprinkle with ¾ cup breadcrumb mixture; top with tomato slices. Sprinkle with remaining ⅛ teaspoon salt and ⅛ teaspoon pepper. Top with remaining ¾ cup breadcrumb mixture; dot with remaining 1 tablespoon butter. Bake at 450° for 12 minutes or until shrimp are done. Drizzle with vinegar. Yield: 6 servings (serving size: about 5 shrimp, ¼ cup breadcrumb mixture, and 2 tomato slices).

CALORIES 364; FAT 16.5g (sat 5.4g, mono 7.1g, poly 2.7g); PROTEIN 37.1g; CARB 16g; FIBER 1.8g; CHOL 274mg; IRON 5.5mg; SODIUM 563mg; CALC 140mg

TODAY'S LESSON: STEWS

Stew-making is comfort-food alchemy: Bites of meat—usually taken from tough, sinewy muscles—cook low and slow with hearty veggies, bubbling away until flavors meld and the meat loosens and gains buttery texture.

The technique is straightforward, but the cook needs to avoid simple mistakes that often come from speeding the process—boiling rather than simmering, or skimping on the first steps that build deep flavor. Read on for foolproof, healthy results.

Make Ahead • Freezable
Kid Friendly
Italian Beef Stew

Hands-on time: 40 min. Total time: 2 hr. 40 min.

7 teaspoons olive oil, divided
1½ cups chopped onion
½ cup chopped carrot
1 tablespoon minced garlic
¼ cup all-purpose flour
2 pounds boneless chuck roast, trimmed and cut into cubes
¾ teaspoon salt, divided
½ teaspoon black pepper
1 cup dry red wine
3¾ cups chopped seeded peeled plum tomato (about 2 pounds)
1½ cups fat-free, lower-sodium beef broth
½ cup water
2 teaspoons chopped fresh oregano
2 teaspoons chopped fresh thyme
1 bay leaf
1 (8-ounce) package cremini mushrooms, quartered
¾ cup (¼-inch-thick) slices carrot
2 tablespoons chopped fresh basil
1 tablespoon chopped fresh parsley

1. Heat a Dutch oven over medium-high heat. Add 1 teaspoon oil to pan. Add onion and chopped carrot; sauté 8 minutes, stirring occasionally. Add garlic; sauté 45 seconds, stirring constantly. Remove from pan.
2. Add 1 tablespoon oil to pan. Place ¼ cup flour in a shallow dish. Sprinkle beef with ½ teaspoon salt and pepper; dredge in flour. Add half of beef to pan; sauté 6 minutes, browning on all sides. Remove from pan. Repeat procedure.
3. Add wine to pan, and bring to a boil, scraping pan to loosen browned bits. Cook until reduced to ⅓ cup (about 5 minutes). Return meat and onion mixture to pan. Add tomato and next 6 ingredients; bring to a boil. Cover, reduce heat, and simmer 45 minutes, stirring occasionally. Uncover, and stir in sliced carrot. Simmer, uncovered, 1 hour or until meat is very tender, stirring occasionally. Discard bay leaf. Stir in remaining ¼ teaspoon salt, basil, and parsley. Yield: 8 servings (serving size: 1 cup).

CALORIES 334; **FAT** 13g (sat 3.9g, mono 0.8g, poly 6.6g); **PROTEIN** 40.6g; **CARB** 12.2g; **FIBER** 2.4g; **CHOL** 86mg; **IRON** 4.1mg; **SODIUM** 387mg; **CALC** 51mg

3 STEPS TO SUCCULENT STEWS

Tough cuts of meat that lend themselves to stews tend to be fatty, so you need to trim them well for healthy results.

STEP 1: Build a flavor foundation by browning meat and aromatic ingredients. This step leaves tasty browned bits in the bottom of the pan that add complexity to the stew.

STEP 2: Add a flavorful (usually acidic) liquid like wine to the pan, scraping the bits off the bottom as you bring the mixture to a boil. Cook briefly to concentrate the flavor.

STEP 3: Stir in broth or water to cover; bring to a boil. Reduce heat, cover, and simmer gently. Then uncover and cook until the meat is fork-tender and the stew thickens.

Guinness Lamb Stew

*Hands-on time: 35 min. Total time: 3 hr. 20 min.
If you can't find Guinness, or if you don't like
it, substitute another dark beer. Cut meat
and veggies into roughly equal-sized pieces
so they'll cook evenly. Hearty ingredients like
onions hold up to long simmering. Add more
delicate items, like potatoes or herbs, midway
or near the end of cooking.*

8 teaspoons olive oil, divided
2 cups chopped onion
1 tablespoon chopped fresh thyme
1½ teaspoons chopped fresh rosemary
3 tablespoons all-purpose flour
2½ pounds boneless leg of lamb, trimmed
    and cut into 1-inch cubes
1 teaspoon salt, divided
¾ teaspoon freshly ground black pepper,
    divided
2 cups Guinness Stout
1 tablespoon tomato paste
3 cups fat-free, lower-sodium beef broth
1 bay leaf
2 cups cubed peeled Yukon gold potato
2 cups (1-inch-thick) diagonally cut carrot
8 ounces baby turnips, peeled and quartered
1 tablespoon whole-grain Dijon mustard
⅓ cup chopped fresh parsley

1. Heat a large Dutch oven over
medium-high heat. Add 2 teaspoons oil
to pan; swirl to coat. Add onion, thyme,
and rosemary; sauté 5 minutes, stirring
occasionally. Place onion mixture in a
large bowl. Place flour in a shallow dish.
Sprinkle lamb evenly with ½ teaspoon
salt and ½ teaspoon pepper. Dredge lamb
in flour, and shake off excess. Return pan
to medium-high heat. Add 1 tablespoon oil to pan; swirl to coat. Add
half of lamb mixture to pan; sauté 6
minutes, turning to brown on all sides.
Add browned lamb to onion mixture.
Repeat procedure with remaining lamb
and remaining 1 tablespoon oil.
2. Add beer to pan; bring to a boil,
scraping pan to loosen browned bits.
Cook until reduced to 1 cup (about
5 minutes). Return onion mixture and
lamb to pan. Stir in tomato paste; cook

30 seconds. Add broth and bay leaf;
bring to a boil. Cover, reduce heat, and
simmer 1 hour and 15 minutes, stirring
occasionally. Uncover and stir in potato,
carrot, and turnips. Simmer, uncovered,
1½ hours or until meat and vegetables
are tender. Stir in remaining ½ teaspoon
salt, remaining ¼ teaspoon pepper, and
1 tablespoon mustard. Ladle about 1
cup stew into each of 7 bowls; sprinkle
evenly with parsley. Yield: 7 servings.

CALORIES 430; FAT 22.9g (sat 8.3g, mono 11g, poly 2g);
PROTEIN 26.3g; CARB 24.2g; FIBER 3.4g; CHOL 83mg;
IRON 3.3mg; SODIUM 702mg; CALC 50mg

Chicken Verde Stew with Hominy

(pictured on page 213)

*Hands-on time: 35 min. Total time: 1 hr. 20 min.
Fresh tomatillos are encased in rough skins.
Remove the skins and rinse tomatillos before
roasting. Anaheim chiles are mild; try poblanos
or jalapeños if you want to turn up the heat on
this Latin-inspired stew.*

2 Anaheim chiles
Cooking spray
1½ pounds tomatillos
¼ cup finely chopped fresh cilantro
1½ teaspoons ground cumin
1 teaspoon dried oregano
2 cups fat-free, lower-sodium chicken broth,
    divided
2 tablespoons olive oil, divided
1½ cups finely chopped onion
½ cup chopped carrot
½ cup chopped celery
½ cup chopped red bell pepper
3 tablespoons all-purpose flour
4 teaspoons finely chopped garlic
1 pound skinless, boneless chicken thighs, cut
    into 1½-inch pieces
¾ teaspoon kosher salt, divided
½ teaspoon black pepper, divided
1 (29-ounce) can golden hominy, rinsed and
    drained
6 tablespoons reduced-fat sour cream
Cilantro leaves (optional)

1. Preheat broiler to high.
2. Halve, stem, and seed chiles. Place
chiles, skin sides up, on a foil-lined
baking sheet coated with cooking
spray; broil 5 minutes or until charred.
Place chiles in a paper bag; seal. Let
stand 15 minutes. Peel and discard
skins. Arrange tomatillos on prepared
baking sheet, and broil 14 minutes or
until blackened, turning once. Combine
chiles, tomatillos, ¼ cup cilantro, cumin,
and oregano in a blender. Add 1 cup
broth; process until smooth.
3. Heat a large Dutch oven over
medium-high heat. Add 2 teaspoons
olive oil; swirl to coat. Add onion, carrot,
celery, and bell pepper; sauté 2 minutes,
stirring occasionally. Stir in flour; sauté 2
minutes, stirring frequently. Add garlic;
sauté 30 seconds, stirring constantly.
Place onion mixture in a large bowl.
4. Sprinkle chicken with ½ teaspoon
salt and ¼ teaspoon black pepper. Add
2 teaspoons oil to pan, and swirl to
coat. Add half of chicken; sauté 3
minutes. Add browned chicken to
onion mixture. Repeat procedure with
remaining chicken and 2 teaspoons
oil. Combine remaining 1 cup broth,
tomatillo mixture, onion mixture, and
hominy in pan over medium-high heat;
bring to a boil. Cover, reduce heat, and
simmer 45 minutes, stirring occasionally. Stir in remaining ¼ teaspoon salt
and ¼ teaspoon black pepper. Ladle
1⅔ cups stew into each of 6 bowls, and
top each with 1 tablespoon sour cream.
Garnish with cilantro, if desired. Yield:
6 servings.

CALORIES 322; FAT 14.1g (sat 3.6g, mono 6.3g, poly 2.7g);
PROTEIN 18.7g; CARB 30.9g; FIBER 6.3g; CHOL 56mg;
IRON 2.9mg; SODIUM 651mg; CALC 69mg

FRIED BROWN RICE

By Mark Bittman

This grain-based meal offers easy opportunities to toss lots of vegetables—even fruit—into versions from Asian classics to fun American twists.

If you often have leftover brown rice in the fridge (and you should, if you don't), then you're often looking for something to do with it. Stir a spoonful into soup: check. Turn it into salad: check. Reheat it with milk for breakfast: check. Use it for fried rice? Not so much, since a pile of grains, drenched in fat and flecked with some dried-out scrambled eggs, isn't exactly your idea of dinner.

Nor is that exactly my idea of fried rice. When you take the more-vegetables-less-meat approach to this Chinese restaurant classic, you get a crisp, fresh-tasting skillet meal—essentially a stir-fry with rice, an impromptu dish that can just as readily take advantage of leftovers as it can showcase seasonal ingredients. And your flavorings don't necessarily have to be Asian.

The first recipe here is a spin on tradition, loaded up with everyday vegetables. The pork and egg are still there for flavor and texture (what would fried rice be without those little chewy bits?), but you almost have to look for them. And since the rice is brown—with far more nutritional benefit than its white counterpart—it's so hearty you need less of it.

I hope the second example inspires you to think outside the takeout box. With seared chicken, leeks softened in olive oil, slightly plump dried cranberries, and a hint of sage, this dish is about as far from restaurant fried rice as you can go. (It even skips the egg.)

And that's precisely the point. Take a look in the fridge: Common storage vegetables, like celery, carrots, winter squash, onions, garlic, and cabbage, take on new life when chopped or grated and stir-fried with rice, especially if you turn to interesting seasonings like chili or curry powder, or warm spices like cinnamon or five-spice powder.

Even unexpected vegetables like chard, green beans, shiitake mushrooms, kohlrabi, and Brussels sprouts are fair game. Same goes for the meat: Use what you've got. If it's already cooked, all the better. You can either crisp it in the hot oil in step 1 or add it at the very end just to warm. Grilled seafood or chicken, small bits of smoked sausage or ham, or shredded roast beef are all possibilities.

When there is no leftover brown rice (a box from your neighborhood restaurant is all you need, of course), turn to other cooked whole grains. Quinoa, wheat berries, bulgur or even steel-cut oats are all fine stand-ins. Simply crumble them into the hot fat, just like you would rice.

You can also cook a fresh batch of rice or grains, but it's best if it's cold. What makes leftover rice so ideal is the same thing that makes eating a forkful of chalky kernels right out of the fridge rarely enjoyable: You need the kernels to dry out and the starch to firm up. And as with all good stir-fries, work in batches and avoid overcrowding the pan. Otherwise you're steaming, not frying.

STRETCH THE FRIED RICE TEMPLATE WITH UNEXPECTED ADDITIONS LIKE GREEN BEANS, BRUSSELS SPROUTS, OR CHARD.

Quick & Easy • Make Ahead
Kid Friendly

Almost Classic Pork Fried Rice

Hands-on time: 24 min. Total time: 24 min. (or 4 hr. 24 min. if you don't have leftover chilled rice)

2 tablespoons peanut oil or olive oil, divided
½ teaspoon kosher salt, divided
½ pound boneless loin pork chop, cut into ½-inch pieces
½ cup chopped carrot
½ cup chopped celery
½ cup chopped green onion bottoms (white part)
2 tablespoons minced garlic
2 tablespoons minced peeled fresh ginger
3 cups cooked, chilled long-grain brown rice
1 large egg
3 tablespoons mirin (sweet rice wine)
3 tablespoons lower-sodium soy sauce
1 teaspoon dark sesame oil
¼ teaspoon freshly ground black pepper
2 cups fresh bean sprouts
¼ cup canned diced water chestnuts, rinsed and drained
1 cup chopped green onion tops

1. Heat a large skillet over medium-high heat. Add 1 tablespoon peanut oil to pan, swirling to coat. Sprinkle ⅛ teaspoon salt over pork. Add pork to pan, and sauté 2 minutes or until browned on all sides. Remove pork from pan. Add carrot and celery to pan, and sauté 2 minutes or until lightly browned, stirring frequently. Add carrot mixture to pork.
2. Add remaining 1 tablespoon peanut oil to pan, swirling to coat. Stir in green onion bottoms, garlic, and ginger; cook 15 seconds, stirring constantly. Add rice, stirring well to coat rice with oil; cook, without stirring, 2 minutes or until edges begin to brown. Stir rice mixture, and cook, without stirring, 2 minutes or until edges begin to brown. Make a well in center of rice mixture. Add egg; stir-fry 30 seconds or until soft-scrambled, stirring constantly.
3. Return pork mixture to pan. Stir in mirin, and cook 1 minute or until mirin is absorbed. Stir in remaining

⅜ teaspoon salt, soy sauce, sesame oil, and pepper. Remove from heat, and stir in bean sprouts and water chestnuts. Sprinkle with green onion tops. Yield: 4 servings (serving size: about 2 cups).

CALORIES 408; **FAT** 12.4g (sat 2.6g, mono 5.4g, poly 3.6g); **PROTEIN** 21g; **CARB** 49.3g; **FIBER** 6.5g; **CHOL** 82mg; **IRON** 2.4mg; **SODIUM** 627mg; **CALC** 79mg

Staff Favorite • Quick & Easy
Make Ahead • Kid Friendly

Chicken Fried Rice with Leeks and Dried Cranberries

Hands-on time: 26 min. Total time: 26 min. (or 4 hr. 26 min. if you don't have leftover chilled rice)

2 tablespoons olive oil, divided
¾ teaspoon kosher salt, divided
½ pound skinless, boneless chicken thighs, cut into ½-inch pieces
3 cups thinly sliced leek (about 1½ pounds)
¼ teaspoon freshly ground black pepper
3½ cups cooked, chilled long-grain brown rice
1 cup dried cranberries
1 tablespoon chopped fresh sage
¼ cup dry white wine

1. Heat a large skillet over medium-high heat. Add 1 tablespoon olive oil to pan, swirling to coat. Sprinkle ⅛ teaspoon salt over chicken. Add chicken to pan; sauté 3 minutes or until browned, stirring occasionally. Remove chicken from pan. Add leek, black pepper, and remaining ⅝ teaspoon salt to pan; sauté 4 minutes or until leek is tender and golden. Add leek mixture to chicken.
2. Add remaining 1 tablespoon oil to pan, swirling to coat. Add rice, stirring well to coat rice with oil; cook, without stirring, 2 minutes or until edges begin to brown. Stir rice mixture; cook, without stirring, 2 minutes or until edges begin to brown. Stir in chicken mixture, cranberries, and sage. Add wine; cook 2 minutes or until mixture is dry, stirring constantly. Yield: 4 servings (serving size: about 1⅓ cups).

CALORIES 452; **FAT** 11.1g (sat 1.9g, mono 6.2g, poly 2.1g); **PROTEIN** 16.6g; **CARB** 74g; **FIBER** 6g; **CHOL** 47mg; **IRON** 3mg; **SODIUM** 433mg; **CALC** 70mg

BREAKFAST, LUNCH & DINNER IN VANCOUVER

Vancouver's dining scene looks a lot different from the one predicted before the 2010 Winter Olympics began. Flashy pre-game restaurant openings such as Jean-Georges Vongerichten's Market and Daniel Boulud's DB Bistro Moderne (Gordon Ramsay was also spied scouting locations) were expected to usher in a new era of celebrity-chef, high-end dining.

But these high-profile rooms have struggled to capture the city's fancy. Instead, Vancouver's dining scene clung to its easygoing roots: West Coast casual with Canadian manners—even the French waiters are polite to a fault here. This slavish devotion to all things local persists (Vancouver was, after all, the birthplace of The 100-Mile Diet). The corporate-catering-giant Sysco truck is a four-wheeled pariah, and if you ask for bottled water from Italy, expect a raised eyebrow as your server mentally calculates your carbon footprint.

Thanks to the Vancouver Aquarium's pioneering Ocean Wise program (learn more at oceanwise.ca), the Ark of the Covenant is easier to find than a menu containing the severely overfished Chilean sea bass.

Strict government regulations mean many trends that sweep other cities can't germinate here. Food carts serving anything other than hot dogs? None, until just last August—hyperattentive health inspectors need to guarantee safety, of course. Even beachside stands are largely absent, with one glorious exception: Go Fish (604-730-5040), a great take-out shack near Granville Island that attracts long lines even during the rain-soaked months.

Owner and former punk singer Gord Martin offers unfussy fare like wild salmon tacones—the fish travels no more than a few hundred feet from the nearby fisherman's dock—drizzled with a light chipotle crema. It comes with a crunchy, mayo-free Pacific Rim slaw, with ingredients—mostly ginger, red and green cabbage, and rice wine vinegar—sourced from the Granville Island public market, mere blocks away.

While it's rare to find a Vancouver restaurant that doesn't have local salmon on the menu, when it comes to true seafood restaurants here, diners prefer their fish raw: The city has an estimated 300-plus sushi restaurants, and locals allegedly eat more per capita than the Japanese.

Ironically, until recently, one of the few places that didn't have any standout Asian fare was the city's expansive Chinatown. The area serves as a mecca for tourists who make do with marginal cart-service dim sum because the city's huge Chinese population (20% in the last census) has largely settled in the neighboring suburb of Richmond to live and eat. They've transformed a former bastion of proper English living into a collection of foodie-heaven strip malls, heavy with Cantonese script and unrecognizable brands that appear to have been transported from Guangzhou lock, stock, and barrel. For the adventurous, the food courts here (try Yaohan Centre for superauthentic, Aberdeen Centre for more refinement) offer the closest thing to southern Chinese street food in North America. It's a culinary day ticket to the overwhelming excitement of mainland China for less than $10, all a short SkyTrain ride away.

Vegetarian
Breakfast

Libanais Breakfast

Hands-on time: 15 min. Total time: 20 min.
It wasn't that long ago that breakfast in Vancouver was a choice between a cheap greasy spoon or an elaborate overpriced hotel buffet. Now we have Medina (medinacafe.com), a Belgian breakfast spot—a seemingly odd choice given that when Chef Nico Schuermans moved to town, he likely doubled the existing Belgian population. Medina started out its life selling just Belgian waffles with a variety of sauces, but popular demand has led them to expand into the most creative breakfast menu in the city. This Middle Eastern–inspired breakfast is a popular selection at Medina, where the dish includes a boiled egg and three salads—tabbouleh, cucumber salad, and baba ghanoush—complemented with crisp pita toasts. Our simplified version features just one salad: tabbouleh.

3 (6-inch) pitas, each cut into 8 wedges
¼ cup extra-virgin olive oil, divided
1 cup water
¼ cup uncooked bulgur
1 cup chopped seeded plum tomato
¾ cup chopped fresh parsley
3 tablespoons finely chopped red onion
2 tablespoons chopped fresh mint
3 tablespoons fresh lemon juice
¾ teaspoon salt, divided
½ teaspoon freshly ground black pepper, divided
⅛ teaspoon ground red pepper
6 large eggs

1. Preheat oven to 350°.
2. Arrange pita wedges in a single layer on a baking sheet. Lightly brush pita wedges with 2 tablespoons oil; bake at 350° for 20 minutes or until golden.
3. Combine 1 cup water and bulgur in a large bowl. Let stand 30 minutes or until bulgur is tender. Drain bulgur through a fine sieve; discard liquid. Place bulgur in a medium bowl. Add remaining 2 tablespoons oil, tomato, parsley, onion, mint, juice, ½ teaspoon salt, ¼ teaspoon black pepper, and red pepper; toss well. Refrigerate 30 minutes.
4. Bring a medium saucepan of water to a boil. With a slotted spoon, carefully lower eggs into pan; cook 6 minutes.

Drain and rinse eggs with cold running water until cool (about 1 minute). Peel eggs. Place ⅓ cup tabbouleh and 4 pita wedges on each of 6 plates; top each serving with 1 egg. Sprinkle eggs with remaining ¼ teaspoon salt and ¼ teaspoon black pepper. Yield: 6 servings.

CALORIES 262; FAT 14.2g (sat 2.8g, mono 8.5g, poly 1.7g); PROTEIN 11g; CARB 23.9g; FIBER 2.3g; CHOL 212mg; IRON 3mg; SODIUM 452mg; CALC 65mg

Lunch

Crispy Chickpea Salad with Grilled Prawns

Hands-on time: 30 min. Total time: 1 hr. 30 min.
Even as Chef Robert Belcham was being honored as Vancouver Magazine's Chef of the Year in 2009, he knew the type of food he was cooking at his high-end eatery, Fuel, had little or no future in Vancouver. "True fine dining is dead," was his oft-repeated quote. So he rebranded the restaurant refuel (refuelrestaurant.com), brought the menu back to locally sourced basics, and hasn't looked back. Ingredients like watercress and English peas share space with seared hanger steak and the city's best buttermilk fried chicken. Too cold to grill? Broil the shrimp skewers, or cook them on the stovetop in a grill pan.

¼ cup extra-virgin olive oil, divided
4 teaspoons grated lemon rind, divided
¼ cup fresh lemon juice, divided
1 tablespoon chopped fresh flat-leaf parsley
2½ teaspoons crushed red pepper, divided
¾ teaspoon salt, divided
½ teaspoon freshly ground black pepper
1 garlic clove, minced
18 large shrimp, peeled and deveined (about ¾ pound)
6 cups canola oil
3 cups rinsed and drained canned chickpeas (garbanzo beans)
Cooking spray
4 cups fresh baby arugula
2 cups fresh baby spinach
½ cup fresh mint, torn
⅓ cup fresh flat-leaf parsley leaves
⅓ cup (¼-inch) diagonally cut green onions

1. Combine 1 tablespoon olive oil, 1½ teaspoons lemon rind, 1 tablespoon juice, parsley, 1 teaspoon red pepper, ½ teaspoon salt, black pepper, and garlic in a medium bowl. Add shrimp; toss well. Marinate in refrigerator 1 hour, stirring occasionally.
2. Clip a candy/fry thermometer onto the side of a Dutch oven. Add canola oil to pan; heat oil to 385°.
3. Dry chickpeas thoroughly in a single layer on paper towels. Place 1½ cups chickpeas in hot oil; fry 4 minutes or until crisp, stirring occasionally. Make sure oil temperature remains at 375°. Remove peas from pan using a slotted spoon; drain on paper towels. Keep warm. Return oil to 385°. Repeat procedure with remaining chickpeas.
4. Remove shrimp from marinade; discard marinade. Thread 3 shrimp onto each of 6 (5-inch) skewers.
5. Preheat grill to medium-high heat.
6. Place shrimp on grill rack coated with cooking spray. Grill shrimp 2½ minutes on each side or until done.
7. Combine remaining 3 tablespoons olive oil, 2½ teaspoons rind, 3 tablespoons juice, 1½ teaspoons red pepper, and ¼ teaspoon salt in a large bowl; stir with a whisk. Add chickpeas, arugula, spinach, and next 3 ingredients, and toss gently to combine. Place 1¼ cup chickpea mixture in each of 6 shallow bowls. Top each serving with 3 grilled shrimp. Yield: 6 servings.

CALORIES 262; FAT 15.8g (sat 1.7g, mono 9.6g, poly 2.5g); PROTEIN 10.2g; CARB 21.6g; FIBER 5.7g; CHOL 32mg; IRON 2.6mg; SODIUM 628mg; CALC 80mg

THE ARK OF THE COVENANT IS EASIER TO FIND THAN A VANCOUVER MENU OFFERING UNSUSTAINABLE FISH.

Dinner
Yogurt-Marinated Chicken with Beet Salad

*Hands-on time: 55 min. Total time: 4 hr. 40 min.
If there's one iconic moment in Vancouver dining, it's the nightly lineup at the no-reservations temple of modern Indian cuisine that is Vij's (vijs. ca). It doesn't matter who you are, proprietor Vikram Vij is graciously inflexible about his no-reservations rule. So everyone waits. The reward for such patience? Vij's pairing of his classical Indian training with nontraditional ingredients to create Indian food like none you've tried before. Tamarind lends the marinade a pleasant sweet-sour note. You can substitute 2 tablespoons lemon juice if tamarind paste isn't available.*

¾ cup plain low-fat yogurt
1 tablespoon garam masala
3 tablespoons finely chopped garlic
2 tablespoons canola oil
1 tablespoon tamarind paste
1¼ teaspoons ground red pepper
1 teaspoon ground cumin
1 teaspoon minced peeled fresh ginger
12 skinless, boneless chicken thighs (about 2½ pounds)
1½ cups diced seeded tomato
1 cup thinly sliced peeled beet
¾ cup thinly sliced peeled daikon radish (about 4 ounces)
½ cup vertically sliced red onion
½ cup finely chopped fresh cilantro
3 tablespoons fresh lemon juice
1 tablespoon extra-virgin olive oil
1 teaspoon salt, divided
Cooking spray

1. Combine first 8 ingredients in a large bowl. Add chicken thighs; toss to coat. Cover and chill at least 4 hours.
2. Combine tomato and next 4 ingredients in a bowl. Combine juice, olive oil, and ½ teaspoon salt. Pour juice mixture over beet mixture; toss to coat. Cover and chill at least 2 hours.
3. Heat a grill pan over high heat. Coat pan with cooking spray. Remove chicken from marinade, and discard marinade. Sprinkle chicken evenly with remaining ½ teaspoon salt. Add half of chicken to pan; cook chicken 4 minutes on each side or until done. Repeat procedure with remaining chicken. Serve with salad. Yield: 6 servings (serving size: 2 chicken thighs and ½ cup salad).

CALORIES 385; FAT 20.9g (sat 5g, mono 9.4g, poly 4.7g); PROTEIN 37.6g; CARB 11.2g; FIBER 2.6g; CHOL 125mg; IRON 2.6mg; SODIUM 550mg; CALC 69mg

5-INGREDIENT COOKING

Simple Lobster Risotto

Hands-on time: 39 min. Total time: 1 hr. 3 min.

Simmering the shells infuses the broth with lobster flavor.

Directions: Bring broth and 1½ cups water to a boil in a saucepan. Add lobster; cover and cook 4 minutes. Remove lobster from pan; cool 5 minutes. Remove meat from cooked lobster tails, reserving shells. Chop meat. Place shells in a large zip-top plastic bag. Coarsely crush shells using a meat mallet or heavy skillet. Return crushed shells to broth mixture. Reduce heat to medium-low. Cover and cook 20 minutes. Strain shell mixture through a sieve over a bowl, reserving broth; discard solids. Return broth mixture to pan; keep warm over low heat. Heat 1 tablespoon butter in a medium saucepan over medium-high heat. Add rice to pan; cook 2 minutes, stirring constantly. Stir in 1 cup broth mixture; cook 5 minutes or until liquid is nearly absorbed, stirring constantly. Reserve 2 tablespoons broth mixture. Add remaining broth mixture, ½ cup at a time, stirring constantly until each portion is absorbed before adding the next (about 22 minutes total). Remove from heat; stir in lobster, reserved 2 tablespoons broth mixture, remaining 2 tablespoons butter, and green peas. Yield: 4 servings (serving size: 1 cup).

Sustainable Choice

The American lobster population is well managed in Canada and the U.S.

CALORIES 374; FAT 10.7g (sat 5.8g, mono 2.6g, poly 0.9g); PROTEIN 24.7g; CARB 44.4g; FIBER 4.1g; CHOL 80mg; IRON 2mg; SODIUM 620mg; CALC 63mg

THE FIVE INGREDIENTS

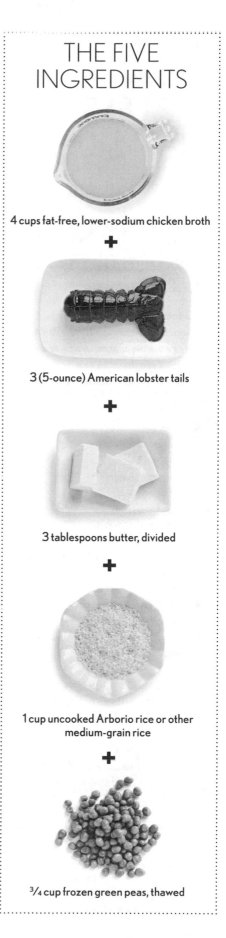

4 cups fat-free, lower-sodium chicken broth

+

3 (5-ounce) American lobster tails

+

3 tablespoons butter, divided

+

1 cup uncooked Arborio rice or other medium-grain rice

+

¾ cup frozen green peas, thawed

FEED 4 FOR LESS THAN $10

These simple, hearty, filling meals are lean on cost.

Make Ahead

Garbanzo Beans and Greens

$7.00 total, $1.75 per serving
Hands-on time: 10 min. Total time: 45 min.
Substitute escarole or another hearty green like collards if you don't like kale. Serve with torn baguette bread to soak up all the tasty juices.

2 center-cut bacon slices
1 cup chopped carrot
1/2 cup chopped onion
2 garlic cloves, minced
1 teaspoon paprika
1/4 teaspoon kosher salt
1/2 teaspoon ground cumin
1/2 teaspoon crushed red pepper
2 1/2 cups fat-free, lower-sodium chicken broth
1 cup water
2 (15-ounce) cans organic chickpeas (garbanzo beans), rinsed and drained
4 cups chopped fresh kale
1/2 cup plain 2% reduced-fat Greek yogurt
4 lemon wedges (optional)

1. Cook bacon in a Dutch oven over medium heat until crisp. Remove bacon from pan using a slotted spoon, and crumble. Add 1 cup carrot and chopped onion to drippings in pan, and cook 4 minutes, stirring occasionally. Add garlic, and cook 1 minute, stirring constantly. Add paprika, 1/4 teaspoon salt, cumin, and red pepper; cook 30 seconds, stirring constantly. Stir in chicken broth, 1 cup water, and beans; bring to a boil. Reduce heat, and simmer 20 minutes, stirring occasionally.
2. Add 4 cups kale to bean mixture. Cover and simmer 10 minutes or until kale is tender, stirring occasionally. Ladle about 1 1/4 cups bean mixture into each of 4 bowls; top each serving with 2 tablespoons yogurt. Sprinkle with bacon, and serve with lemon wedges, if desired. Yield: 4 servings.

CALORIES 216; **FAT** 4.2g (sat 0.9g, mono 0.2g, poly 0.1g); **PROTEIN** 15.1g; **CARB** 33.7g; **FIBER** 6g; **CHOL** 4mg; **IRON** 4mg; **SODIUM** 595mg; **CALC** 197mg

Smoky Potato Pancakes

$7.40 total, $1.85 per serving
Hands-on time: 20 min. Total time: 45 min. Spinach salad with red onion and tangy vinaigrette is a lovely companion to these potato cakes.

2 center-cut hickory-smoked bacon slices
2 cups chopped onion
1 cup thinly sliced leek
3 garlic cloves, chopped
1 1/2 pounds shredded peeled baking potato (about 2 large)
1/3 cup (1 1/2 ounces) shredded sharp cheddar cheese
3/4 teaspoon salt
1/2 teaspoon freshly ground black pepper
2 large eggs
Cooking spray
1/4 cup reduced-fat sour cream

1. Preheat oven to 425°.
2. Cook bacon in a large skillet over medium heat until crisp. Remove bacon from pan using a slotted spoon, and crumble. Add onion to drippings in pan, and cook 5 minutes, stirring occasionally. Add leek and garlic; cook 2 minutes, stirring frequently. Combine onion mixture, shredded potato, cheddar cheese, 3/4 teaspoon salt, black pepper, and 2 large eggs in a medium bowl, stirring well.
3. Divide potato mixture into 8 equal portions, and shape each portion into a 1/2-inch-thick patty. Place patties on a baking sheet coated with cooking spray. Bake at 425° for 25 minutes or until golden and set. Top with crumbled bacon and sour cream. Yield: 4 servings (serving size: 2 potato patties, 1 tablespoon sour cream, and 1/2 bacon slice).

CALORIES 335; **FAT** 12g (sat 6.3g, mono 2.2g, poly 0.7g); **PROTEIN** 11.5g; **CARB** 46.6g; **FIBER** 4.9g; **CHOL** 133mg; **IRON** 1.7mg; **SODIUM** 631mg; **CALC** 151mg

Make Ahead • Freezable

Green Chile Chili

$9.96 total, $2.49 per serving
Hands-on time: 35 min. Total time: 65 min. Serve this chili with corn bread or corn muffins.

1 tablespoon canola oil
12 ounces ground sirloin
1 1/2 cups chopped onion
1 tablespoon chili powder
1 teaspoon hot paprika
5 garlic cloves, minced
1 (12-ounce) bottle dark beer
1/2 cup salsa verde
1 (4-ounce) can diced green chiles, undrained
1 (15-ounce) can no-salt-added tomatoes, undrained and crushed
1 (15-ounce) can organic kidney beans, rinsed and drained
1/4 cup (1 ounce) shredded sharp cheddar cheese
1 green onion, sliced

1. Heat a large Dutch oven over medium-high heat. Add oil to pan; swirl to coat. Add beef; sauté 5 minutes or until no longer pink, stirring to crumble. Add chopped onion, chili powder, and paprika; sauté 4 minutes, stirring occasionally. Add garlic; sauté 1 minute, stirring constantly.
2. Stir in beer, and bring to a boil. Cook 15 minutes or until liquid almost evaporates. Add salsa and next 3 ingredients; bring to a boil. Reduce heat, and simmer 30 minutes, stirring occasionally. Ladle 1 1/4 cups chili into each of 4 bowls, and top each serving with 1 tablespoon cheese. Sprinkle with green onions. Yield: 4 servings.

CALORIES 310; **FAT** 10.6g (sat 3.3g, mono 1.5g, poly 4.4g); **PROTEIN** 24.1g; **CARB** 25.1g; **FIBER** 4.3g; **CHOL** 52mg; **IRON** 4.8mg; **SODIUM** 575mg; **CALC** 95mg

SUPERFAST

Prosciutto, balsamic vinegar, goat cheese, hazelnuts: Simple ingredients create memorable 20-minute Italian weeknight dishes.

Quick & Easy

Lemony Chicken Saltimbocca

(pictured on page 212)

Serve over a bed of angel hair pasta or polenta to catch all the sauce.

4 (4-ounce) chicken cutlets
1/8 teaspoon salt
12 fresh sage leaves
2 ounces very thinly sliced prosciutto, cut into 8 thin strips
4 teaspoons extra-virgin olive oil, divided
1/3 cup fat-free, lower-sodium chicken broth
1/4 cup fresh lemon juice
1/2 teaspoon cornstarch
Lemon wedges (optional)

1. Sprinkle chicken evenly with salt. Place 3 sage leaves on each cutlet; wrap 2 prosciutto strips around each cutlet, securing sage leaves in place.
2. Heat a large skillet over medium heat. Add 1 tablespoon oil to pan, and swirl to coat. Add chicken to pan; cook 2 minutes on each side or until done. Remove chicken from pan; keep warm.
3. Combine broth, lemon juice, and cornstarch in a small bowl; stir with a whisk until smooth. Add cornstarch mixture and remaining 1 teaspoon olive oil to pan; bring to a boil, stirring constantly. Cook 1 minute or until slightly thickened, stirring constantly with a whisk. Spoon sauce over chicken. Serve with lemon wedges, if desired. Yield: 4 servings (serving size: 1 cutlet and 2 tablespoons sauce).

CALORIES 202; FAT 7.5g (sat 1.5g, mono 4.3g, poly 0.9g); PROTEIN 30.5g; CARB 2.3g; FIBER 0.2g; CHOL 77mg; IRON 1.1mg; SODIUM 560mg; CALC 18mg

Broccoli Rabe with Onions and Pine Nuts: Trim 1½ pounds broccoli rabe (rapini); cut into 3-inch-long pieces. Cook in boiling water 1½ minutes; drain and rinse. Drain well. Heat 1 tablespoon olive oil and 1½ teaspoons butter in a skillet over medium-high heat. Add 1 cup sliced onion; sauté 2 minutes or until lightly browned. Add broccoli rabe; sprinkle with ¼ teaspoon salt, and toss to combine. Cook 1 minute. Sprinkle with 2 tablespoons toasted pine nuts. Yield: 4 servings.

CALORIES 132; FAT 7.7g (sat 1.6g); SODIUM 209mg

Quick & Easy

Chicken Dish of the Month

Herb-Crusted Chicken and Parsley Orzo

3/4 cup uncooked orzo
2 tablespoons chopped fresh parsley
2 tablespoons butter, divided
1/2 teaspoon salt, divided
1/4 teaspoon black pepper, divided
4 (6-ounce) skinless, boneless chicken breast halves
4 teaspoons dried fines herbes
1 tablespoon olive oil

1. Cook orzo according to package directions, omitting salt and fat. Drain. Stir in parsley, 2 teaspoons butter, ¼ teaspoon salt, and ⅛ teaspoon pepper. Keep warm.
2. While pasta cooks, sprinkle chicken with remaining ¼ teaspoon salt and remaining ⅛ teaspoon pepper; sprinkle fines herbes over both sides of chicken, pressing gently to adhere.
3. Melt remaining 4 teaspoons butter in a large nonstick skillet over medium heat. Add oil to pan, and swirl to coat. Add chicken to pan; cook 5 minutes or until browned. Turn chicken over; cook 7 minutes or until done. Remove chicken from pan; let stand 3 minutes. Serve chicken over orzo mixture. Yield: 4 servings (serving size: 1 breast half and ½ cup orzo mixture).

CALORIES 342; FAT 11.4g (sat 5g, mono 4.3g, poly 0.9g); PROTEIN 33.9g; CARB 24.4g; FIBER 2.6g; CHOL 89mg; IRON 2.6mg; SODIUM 428mg; CALC 96mg

Quick & Easy • Vegetarian
Pasta of the Month

Fettuccine with Mushrooms and Hazelnuts

Look for blanched hazelnuts, which should have most or all of their skins removed.

1 (9-ounce) package refrigerated fresh fettuccine
1 tablespoon butter
1/4 cup chopped blanched hazelnuts
1 tablespoon olive oil
4 garlic cloves, thinly sliced
3 (4-ounce) packages presliced exotic mushroom blend
1/2 teaspoon salt, divided
1/4 teaspoon freshly ground black pepper
2 teaspoons chopped fresh sage
2 ounces Parmigiano-Reggiano cheese, shaved
2 tablespoons finely chopped chives

1. Cook pasta according to package directions, omitting salt and fat. Drain in a colander over a bowl, reserving ¾ cup cooking liquid.
2. While water for pasta comes to a boil, melt butter in a large nonstick skillet over medium-high heat. Add hazelnuts to pan; sauté 3 minutes or until toasted and fragrant. Remove from pan with a slotted spoon. Add oil to pan, and swirl to coat. Add garlic and mushrooms to pan; sprinkle with ¼ teaspoon salt and black pepper. Sauté mushroom mixture 5 minutes; stir in sage. Add pasta, reserved cooking liquid, and remaining ¼ teaspoon salt to pan; toss well to combine. Remove from heat; top with cheese, toasted hazelnuts, and chives. Yield: 4 servings (serving size: about 1½ cups pasta mixture, about 2 tablespoons cheese, and 1 tablespoon hazelnuts).

CALORIES 364; FAT 16.5g (sat 5.7g, mono 7.6g, poly 1.2g); PROTEIN 16.8g; CARB 40.2g; FIBER 3.2g; CHOL 56mg; IRON 2.4mg; SODIUM 563mg; CALC 204mg

Endive Spears with Spicy Goat Cheese

You can make the cheese mixture up to a day ahead. It also makes a great sandwich or bagel spread or a thick dip for crudités.

½ cup (4 ounces) goat cheese
⅓ cup plain fat-free Greek yogurt
¼ teaspoon kosher salt
⅛ teaspoon ground red pepper
1 garlic clove, pressed
1¼ teaspoons Hungarian sweet paprika, divided
36 Belgian endive leaves (about 3 heads)

1. Combine first 5 ingredients and 1 teaspoon paprika in a medium bowl; mash with a fork until smooth. Top each endive leaf with about 1 teaspoon cheese mixture. Sprinkle remaining ¼ teaspoon paprika evenly over cheese mixture. Yield: 6 servings (serving size: 6 filled leaves).

CALORIES 105; **FAT** 4.8g (sat 3.1g, mono 0.9g, poly 0.3g); **PROTEIN** 8g; **CARB** 9.5g; **FIBER** 2.1g; **CHOL** 9mg; **IRON** 2.6mg; **SODIUM** 210mg; **CALC** 175mg

Spinach with Garlic Vinaigrette

1½ tablespoons extra-virgin olive oil
1 tablespoon white wine vinegar
½ teaspoon Dijon mustard
¼ teaspoon freshly ground black pepper
⅛ teaspoon salt
2 garlic cloves, minced
6 cups fresh baby spinach leaves (about 6 ounces)
¼ cup vertically sliced red onion

1. Combine first 6 ingredients in a large bowl, stirring well with a whisk. Add 6 cups spinach and red onion; toss to coat. Yield: 4 servings (serving size: 1¾ cups).

CALORIES 66; **FAT** 5.1g (sat 0.7g, mono 3.7g, poly 0.5g); **PROTEIN** 1.1g; **CARB** 5.2g; **FIBER** 19g; **CHOL** 0mg; **IRON** 1.3mg; **SODIUM** 147mg; **CALC** 31mg

Cook ½ cup mini farfalle according to package directions. Drain. Rinse with cold water; drain. Add garlic vinaigrette, 3 cups baby spinach, and ¼ cup chopped red onion. Yield: 4 servings.

CALORIES 106; **FAT** 5.4g (sat 0.8g); **SODIUM** 108mg

Increase garlic to 3 thinly sliced cloves. Heat vinaigrette in a large skillet over medium-high heat. Add onion and garlic; sauté 2 minutes. Gradually add 1 (9-ounce) package fresh spinach; toss until wilted. Yield: 4 servings.

CALORIES 78; **FAT** 5.1g (sat 0.7g); **SODIUM** 191mg

Microwave 4 (6-ounce) Yukon gold potatoes at HIGH 13 minutes or until tender. Prepare wilted spinach; divide spinach among potatoes. Top each with 1½ tablespoons crumbled feta cheese. Yield: 4 servings.

CALORIES 255; **FAT** 8.1g (sat 2.8g); **SODIUM** 358mg

Pork Tenderloin with Red and Yellow Bell Peppers

Anchovies add a savory, salty quality. If you don't like anchovies, substitute 3 tablespoons minced olives. Serve with mashed potatoes.

1 (1-pound) pork tenderloin, trimmed and cut crosswise into 1-inch-thick medallions
½ teaspoon kosher salt
½ teaspoon freshly ground black pepper
1 tablespoon extra-virgin olive oil
1½ teaspoons chopped fresh rosemary, divided
4 canned anchovy fillets, drained and mashed
3 garlic cloves, thinly sliced
1 red bell pepper, cut into 1½-inch strips
1 yellow bell pepper, cut into 1½-inch strips
2 teaspoons balsamic vinegar

1. Heat a large skillet over medium-high heat. Sprinkle pork with salt and pepper. Add oil to pan; swirl to coat. Add pork to pan; cook 5 minutes. Reduce heat to medium; turn pork over. Add 1 teaspoon rosemary, anchovies, garlic, and bell peppers; cook 7 minutes or until peppers are tender and pork is done. Drizzle with vinegar. Top with remaining ½ teaspoon rosemary. Yield: 4 servings (serving size: 3 ounces pork and about ½ cup bell pepper mixture).

CALORIES 215; **FAT** 10.1g (sat 2.7g, mono 5.4g, poly 1.2g); **PROTEIN** 25.2g; **CARB** 5g; **FIBER** 1.4g; **CHOL** 78mg; **IRON** 2mg; **SODIUM** 441mg; **CALC** 26mg

Snapper in Tomato Broth

½ teaspoon kosher salt
4 (6-ounce) snapper fillets
2 tablespoons all-purpose flour
5 teaspoons olive oil, divided
1 cup diced plum tomato (about 2)
¾ cup clam juice
½ cup frozen green peas
¼ cup chopped fresh mint, divided
1 tablespoon fresh lemon juice
½ teaspoon dried oregano

1. Sprinkle salt over fillets. Dredge fillets in flour, shaking off excess.
2. Heat 4 teaspoons olive oil in a large nonstick skillet over medium-high heat. Add fillets, and cook 3 minutes on each side or until done.
3. Combine remaining 1 teaspoon olive oil, tomato, clam juice, peas, 2 tablespoons mint, juice, and oregano in pan; bring to a boil. Reduce heat, and simmer 2 minutes. Spoon about ¼ cup broth mixture into each of 4 bowls, and top each serving with 1 fillet. Sprinkle with remaining 2 tablespoons mint. Yield: 4 servings.

 Sustainable Choice | *At the seafood counter, look for Hawaiian gray snapper or Northwest Hawaiian ruby snapper.*

CALORIES 263; **FAT** 8.1g (sat 1.3g, mono 4.6g, poly 1.5g); **PROTEIN** 37g; **CARB** 8.6g; **FIBER** 2g; **CHOL** 64mg; **IRON** 1.3mg; **SODIUM** 444mg; **CALC** 78mg

DINNER TONIGHT

Here is a batch of fast weeknight menus from the *Cooking Light* Test Kitchens.

READY IN
40
MINUTES

The SHOPPING LIST

Beef Tagine with Butternut Squash

4 shallots
1 medium butternut squash
cilantro
garlic
paprika
ground cinnamon
ground ginger
crushed red pepper
olive oil
fat-free, lower-sodium chicken broth
14.5-ounce can no-salt-added diced
    tomatoes
1-pound beef shoulder roast

Scallion Couscous

green onions
fat-free, lower-sodium chicken broth
couscous

The GAME PLAN

While beef and shallots cook:
 ▪ Chop garlic.
While broth mixture cooks:
 ▪ Prep squash.
While tagine simmers:
 ▪ Prepare couscous.

Quick & Easy • Make Ahead

Beef Tagine with Butternut Squash
with Scallion Couscous
(pictured on page 213)

Simple Sub: You can use 1 medium onion, cut into thin wedges, in place of shallots.
Time-Saver: Save prep work by purchasing precut fresh butternut squash.
Flavor Hit: A good dose of cinnamon adds complex sweet-spicy notes to the tagine.

2 teaspoons paprika
1 teaspoon ground cinnamon
3/4 teaspoon salt
1/2 teaspoon ground ginger
1/2 teaspoon crushed red pepper
1/4 teaspoon freshly ground black pepper
1 (1-pound) beef shoulder roast or petite
    tender roast, trimmed and cut into 1-inch
    cubes
1 tablespoon olive oil
4 shallots, quartered
4 garlic cloves, chopped
1/2 cup fat-free, lower-sodium chicken broth
1 (14.5-ounce) can no-salt-added diced
    tomatoes, undrained
3 cups (1-inch) cubed peeled butternut
    squash (about 1 pound)
1/4 cup chopped fresh cilantro

1. Combine first 6 ingredients in a medium bowl. Add beef; toss well to coat.
2. Heat oil in a Dutch oven over medium-high heat. Add beef and shallots; cook 4 minutes or until browned, stirring occasionally. Add garlic; cook 1 minute, stirring frequently. Stir in broth and tomatoes; bring to a boil. Cook 5 minutes. Add squash; cover, reduce heat, and simmer 15 minutes or until squash is tender. Sprinkle with cilantro. Yield: 4 servings (serving size: 1½ cups).

CALORIES 283; **FAT** 9.5g (sat 2g, mono 4.8g, poly 0.5g); **PROTEIN** 25.6g; **CARB** 25.7g; **FIBER** 4.8g; **CHOL** 67mg; **IRON** 4.6mg; **SODIUM** 617mg; **CALC** 103mg

---

Quick & Easy • Vegetarian
For the Scallion Couscous:
Bring ¾ cup fat-free, lower-sodium chicken broth and ½ cup water to a boil in a medium saucepan. • Gradually stir in 1 cup uncooked couscous. • Remove from heat; cover and let stand 5 minutes. • Fluff couscous with a fork. • Stir in ⅓ cup chopped green onions. Yield: 4 servings.

CALORIES 169; **FAT** 0.3g (sat 0.1g); **SODIUM** 80mg

READY IN
30
MINUTES

The SHOPPING LIST

**Sautéed Halibut with Romesco
    Sauce**

2 medium-sized red bell peppers
garlic
1 dried ancho pepper
sliced whole-wheat bread
1 lemon
slivered almonds
hazelnut or olive oil
red wine vinegar
sugar
ground red pepper
4 (6-ounce) halibut fillets

Nutty Rice

green onions
basmati rice
slivered almonds

The GAME PLAN

While broiler preheats:
 ▪ Prep bell peppers.
 ▪ Cook rice.
While bell peppers steam in bag:
 ▪ Toast almonds for sauce and rice.
While fish cooks:
 ▪ Blend sauce.

continued

Sautéed Halibut with Romesco Sauce

with Nutty Rice

Simple Sub: Try hazelnuts in place of almonds in the sauce and/or rice.
Flavor Hit: Basmati rice has a nutty essence that's enhanced by the almonds.
Make-Ahead Tip: Prepare sauce up to two days in advance.

2 medium-sized red bell peppers
1 dried ancho pepper, stemmed and seeded
1/2 teaspoon salt, divided
1 1/2 tablespoons slivered almonds, toasted
1 tablespoon hazelnut oil or olive oil
1 tablespoon red wine vinegar
1/4 teaspoon sugar
1/4 teaspoon freshly ground black pepper
1/8 teaspoon ground red pepper
2 garlic cloves, chopped
1 (1-ounce) slice whole-wheat bread
4 (6-ounce) halibut fillets
Cooking spray
4 lemon wedges

1. Preheat broiler.
2. Cut bell peppers in half; discard seeds and membranes. Place bell peppers, skin sides up, on a baking sheet; flatten. Broil 10 minutes or until blackened. Add ancho; broil 2 minutes. Place bell peppers in a paper bag; close tightly. Let stand 5 minutes; peel. Place bell peppers, ancho, 1/4 teaspoon salt, and next 8 ingredients in a food processor; process until smooth.
3. Heat a large skillet over medium-high heat. Sprinkle remaining 1/4 teaspoon salt over fish. Coat pan with cooking spray. Add fish to pan; cook 6 minutes on each side or until desired degree of doneness. Top with sauce; serve with lemon wedges. Yield: 4 servings (serving size: 1 fillet and 1/4 cup sauce).

CALORIES 267; **FAT** 8.9g (sat 0.9g, mono 4.7g, poly 2g); **PROTEIN** 26.3g; **CARB** 9.5g; **FIBER** 2.1g; **CHOL** 52mg; **IRON** 2.1mg; **SODIUM** 427mg; **CALC** 93mg

For the Nutty Rice:
Cook 1 cup basmati rice according to package directions. • Stir in 1/4 cup thinly sliced green onions, 2 tablespoons toasted slivered almonds, 1/4 teaspoon salt, and 1/4 teaspoon black pepper. Yield: 4 servings.

CALORIES 191; **FAT** 2g (sat 0.2g); **SODIUM** 152mg

READY IN 40 MINUTES

The SHOPPING LIST

Smoky Pan-Grilled Pork Chops
cumin seeds
brown sugar
hot smoked paprika
4 (4-ounce) boneless center-cut loin pork chops

Caramelized Onion Mashed Potatoes
prechopped onion
1 1/2 pounds baking potatoes
olive oil
nonfat buttermilk
butter

Lemon Broccolini
2 (6-ounce) bunches Broccolini
1 lemon
olive oil

The GAME PLAN

While onion caramelizes:
- Prep and boil potatoes.
- Coat pork with spice mixture.
While pork cooks:
- Prepare Broccolini.
- Mash potatoes.

Smoky Pan-Grilled Pork Chops

with Caramelized Onion Mashed Potatoes and Lemon Broccolini

Prep Pointer: Toasting cumin seeds deepens their smoky flavor.
Vegetarian Swap: The spice rub would be equally good on tofu or tempeh.

1 tablespoon cumin seeds
1 tablespoon brown sugar
1/2 teaspoon hot smoked paprika
1/4 teaspoon salt
1/4 teaspoon freshly ground black pepper
4 (4-ounce) boneless center-cut loin pork chops
Cooking spray

1. Cook cumin seeds in a small skillet over medium heat 1 minute or until fragrant, stirring frequently. Place in a clean coffee grinder or blender; process until ground. Combine ground cumin, sugar, paprika, salt, and pepper; rub evenly over pork.
2. Heat a grill pan over medium-high heat. Coat pan with cooking spray. Add pork to pan; cook 5 minutes on each side or until done. Yield: 4 servings (serving size: 1 chop).

CALORIES 224; **FAT** 11.5g (sat 4.1g, mono 5.2g, poly 0.9g); **PROTEIN** 24.8g; **CARB** 4.3g; **FIBER** 0.3g; **CHOL** 70mg; **IRON** 1.9mg; **SODIUM** 201mg; **CALC** 47mg

For the Caramelized Onion Mashed Potatoes:
Heat 2 teaspoons olive oil in a large skillet over medium-high heat. • Add 1 1/2 cups prechopped onion; sauté 15 minutes or until golden. • Place 1 1/2 pounds chopped peeled baking potatoes in a saucepan; cover with water, and bring to a boil. • Cover, reduce heat, and simmer 15 minutes or until tender; drain. • Stir in 1/2 cup nonfat buttermilk, 2 tablespoons butter, 1/4 teaspoon salt, and 1/4 teaspoon black pepper; mash with a potato masher. • Stir in onion. Yield: 4 servings.

CALORIES 235; **FAT** 8.1g (sat 4g); **SODIUM** 229mg

For the Lemon Broccolini:

Heat 2 teaspoons olive oil in a large skillet. • Add 2 (6-ounce) bunches Broccolini, ¼ teaspoon salt, and ¼ teaspoon freshly ground black pepper; sauté 5 minutes or until crisp-tender. • Remove from heat; stir in 1 teaspoon grated lemon rind. Yield: 4 servings.

CALORIES 55; FAT 2.3g (sat 0.3g); SODIUM 173mg

READY IN
40
MINUTES

The SHOPPING LIST

Cheesy Meat Loaf Minis
small onion
garlic
parsley
sliced white bread
ketchup
prepared horseradish
Dijon mustard
dried oregano
3 ounces white cheddar cheese
Parmesan cheese
eggs
1½ pounds ground sirloin

Salad with Balsamic Vinaigrette
1 small shallot
5-ounce package herb salad mix
carrots
1 small red onion
balsamic vinegar
Dijon mustard
olive oil
sugar

The GAME PLAN

While oven preheats:
■ Toast breadcrumbs.
■ Chop onion and garlic.
While onion and garlic sauté:
■ Dice cheese.
■ Chop parsley.
While meat loaves cook:
■ Prepare salad.

Cheesy Meat Loaf Minis

with Salad with Balsamic Vinaigrette

Flavor Hit: Toasting fresh breadcrumbs makes them sturdy, hearty, and nutty-tasting.
Kid Tweak: Omit horseradish for a sweeter meat loaf.
Prep Pointer: Diced cheese melts into yummy-gooey pockets as the meat loaves cook.

½ cup fresh breadcrumbs (about 1 ounce)
Cooking spray
1 cup chopped onion
2 garlic cloves, chopped
½ cup ketchup, divided
¾ cup (3 ounces) white cheddar cheese, diced
¼ cup chopped fresh parsley
2 tablespoons grated Parmesan cheese
1 tablespoon prepared horseradish
1 tablespoon Dijon mustard
¾ teaspoon dried oregano
¼ teaspoon salt
¼ teaspoon freshly ground black pepper
1½ pounds ground sirloin
1 large egg, lightly beaten

1. Preheat oven to 425°.
2. Heat a skillet over medium-high heat. Add breadcrumbs; cook 3 minutes or until toasted, stirring frequently.
3. While breadcrumbs cook, heat a large skillet over medium-high heat. Coat pan with cooking spray. Add onion and garlic; sauté 3 minutes. Combine onion mixture, breadcrumbs, ¼ cup ketchup, and next 10 ingredients. Shape into 6 (4 x 2–inch) loaves on a broiler pan coated with cooking spray; spread 2 teaspoons ketchup over each. Bake at 425° for 25 minutes or until done. Yield: 6 servings (serving size: 1 meat loaf).

CALORIES 256; FAT 11.6g (sat 5.7g, mono 3.9g, poly 0.9g); PROTEIN 28.5g; CARB 11.2g; FIBER 0.9g; CHOL 112mg; IRON 2.6mg; SODIUM 620mg; CALC 159mg

---

For the Salad with Balsamic Vinaigrette:

Combine 2 tablespoons balsamic vinegar, 2 tablespoons olive oil, 1 tablespoon minced shallots, and ½ teaspoon Dijon mustard in a large bowl. • Stir in ¼ teaspoon sugar and ⅛ teaspoon salt. • Add 1 (5-ounce) package herb salad mix, 1 cup carrot ribbons, and ½ cup thinly sliced red onion; toss. Yield: 6 servings.

CALORIES 63; FAT 4.6g (sat 0.6g); SODIUM 94mg

RECIPE MAKEOVER
MEXICAN CASSEROLE, TWO-THIRDS LIGHTER!

Yup, the same cheesy, gooey goodness in an American comfort favorite—without the heft.

The classic one-dish combination of ground beef, refried beans, fried tortillas, and lots of melty cheese is a crowd-pleaser, no question. But a single serving of most versions of Mexican Casserole can add up to nearly an entire day's worth of both saturated fat and sodium.

The best way to lighten this monster was to create a base of familiar flavors, starting with a homemade salsa and traditional corn tortillas. We then swapped in lean chicken breast and nutrient-rich veggies for the ground beef and frijoles. The finishing touch is an unconventional but interesting blend of creamy Monterey Jack and sharp feta cheese; the latter adds a welcome tang. This casserole has less than one-third of the original's calories, saturated fat, and sodium. And you'll be able to get off the couch afterward unassisted.

continued

Kid Friendly

Mexican Chicken Casserole with Charred Tomato Salsa

Hands-on time: 25 min. Total time: 1 hr. 10 min.

Salsa:
8 plum tomatoes, halved and seeded
3 garlic cloves, peeled and crushed
1 small onion, peeled and chopped
1 seeded jalapeño pepper, quartered
Cooking spray
⅓ cup chopped fresh cilantro
3 tablespoons fresh lime juice
⅛ teaspoon black pepper

Casserole:
1 cup chopped onion
1 cup fresh or frozen corn kernels, thawed
1 cup diced zucchini
1 cup chopped red bell pepper
3 cups shredded cooked chicken breast
1 tablespoon minced garlic
2 teaspoons chili powder
1 teaspoon ground cumin
1 (10-ounce) can green chile enchilada sauce
1 (4-ounce) can chopped green chiles
12 (6-inch) corn tortillas
1 cup (4 ounces) shredded Monterey Jack cheese
1 cup (4 ounces) crumbled feta cheese

1. Preheat broiler.
2. To prepare salsa, combine first 4 ingredients on a baking sheet coated with cooking spray. Broil 20 minutes or until charred, stirring once. Remove from oven; cool slightly. Place tomato mixture in a food processor; add cilantro, lime juice, and black pepper. Process until smooth. Set aside.
3. Preheat oven to 350°.
4. To prepare casserole, heat a large nonstick skillet over medium-high heat. Lightly coat pan with cooking spray. Add 1 cup onion, corn, zucchini, and bell pepper; sauté 6 minutes or until tender. Add chicken and next 5 ingredients; sauté 2 minutes or until thoroughly heated. Remove from heat.
5. Spread ½ cup salsa over the bottom of a 13 x 9–inch glass or ceramic baking dish coated with cooking spray. Arrange half of tortillas over salsa. Spoon 2 cups chicken mixture evenly over tortillas. Top with ¾ cup salsa. Sprinkle with ½ cup of each cheese. Repeat layers, starting with remaining tortillas and ending with remaining cheeses. Bake at 350° for 25 minutes until bubbly. Yield: 8 servings.

CALORIES 331; FAT 12.3g (sat 6.1g, mono 2.8g, poly 1.2g); PROTEIN 26.1g; CARB 30.8g; FIBER 4.2g; CHOL 74mg; IRON 1.6mg; SODIUM 535mg; CALC 242mg

CHARRED TOMATO SALSA

Broiling allows smoky flavors to build and natural sugars to caramelize, leaving vegetables crispy and brown on the outside.

The heat of the jalapeño is concentrated in the seeds and veins. For maximum heat, skip the seeding process.

Broiling condenses flavor by evaporating the juices slowly. Stir the vegetables once for an even char.

The longer the salsa is allowed to sit, the more the flavors will meld. Make extra and use to enhance other dishes.

OLD WAY	OUR WAY
1,084 calories per serving	331 calories per serving
28 grams saturated fat	6.1 grams saturated fat
2,075 milligrams sodium	535 milligrams sodium
Greasy, processed ground beef	Skinless, boneless chicken breast
Beans: fried and fried again	Veggies: lightly seasoned and sautéed
A pound of cheese	A hearty sprinkle of Jack cheese and feta

OOPS!
YOU BURN
THE BROWN
BUTTER

Don't cross the thin line between nutty and bitter.
By Tim Cebula

Browning butter is a sure way to suffuse a dish with a great deal of nutty, buttery flavor without using a lot of fat. Example: Sautéed Chicken with Sage Browned Butter, page 20. But the process is a little tricky because once the butter begins to brown, it can race right into burnt. Then nutty becomes bitter.

Success depends on visual cues, so use a stainless steel pan—you can see the butter change color better. Use no more than medium heat so that the browning proceeds gradually. First the butter will foam in the pan: The milk solids are separating from the butterfat, and the water is evaporating. Then the foam subsides and the milk solids begin to brown. Now the butter gives off its characteristic nutty aroma (the French call brown butter *beurre noisette,* or hazelnut butter). Some recipes call for adding lemon juice at this point; the tartness complements the sweet butter, while the juice cools it and slows the browning. Either way, when the butter turns amber-brown, take the pan off the heat. If you're not using it immediately (say, drizzling it over steamed vegetables), get it out of the hot pan and into a bowl so the residual heat doesn't continue to push the butter from brown to burnt.

(butter gone bad)

(perfect)

YOUR SECRET ELEMENT

The underused oven broiler delivers sizzling flavor with little added fat. Here are tips and recipes so you can broil your best.

You have a grill in your house in winter months: It's upside down, hanging from the top of your oven. Fired up, your broiler can cook at 550° or hotter and quickly brown casseroles and gratins; sear and cook steaks, chops, and fish fillets in a flash; and toast foods like garlic bread. It delivers crusty exteriors while preserving succulence within.

The broiler is a go-to tool for confident cooks. Yet it's underused because, badly deployed, it can both scorch and undercook food at once.

You can use the broiler at home with brilliant success if you master a few tricks and principles laid out in these pages. The successful broiling formula, as with all cooking, balances time and heat. Proximity to the heat source is absolutely key (think about the grilling analogy again). You want food near enough to the element for good browning action but not so close that the surface burns before the interior is done. Our recipes call for putting the food about 5 inches from the broiler, which puts it on the second rack position from the top in most ovens (you will want to measure). It's also critical to keep a sharp eye on progress. You might stock up on a few broiler accessories shown in this story, including, if you're a bit of a kitchen nerd, a nifty infrared instant-read thermometer that can tell you the surface temperature of any point in your oven. Read on to become a master broiler in no time.

Quick & Easy
Broiled Tenderloin Steaks with Ginger-Hoisin Glaze

Hands-on time: 5 min. Total time: 12 min.

1½ tablespoons hoisin sauce
1½ teaspoons grated peeled fresh ginger
1½ teaspoons honey
1½ teaspoons lower-sodium soy sauce
¼ teaspoon chili garlic sauce or crushed red pepper
4 (4-ounce) beef tenderloin steaks, trimmed (1 inch thick)
Cooking spray
⅛ teaspoon salt

1. Preheat broiler to high.
2. Combine first 5 ingredients in a small bowl; stir with a whisk.
3. Place steaks on a foil-lined broiler pan coated with cooking spray; sprinkle with salt. Broil steaks 5 inches from heat 2 minutes, and turn steaks over. Broil 2 minutes; turn steaks over. Brush steaks with half of hoisin mixture; broil 1 minute. Turn steaks over, and brush with remaining hoisin mixture; broil 2 minutes or until desired degree of doneness. Yield: 4 servings (serving size: 1 steak).

CALORIES 194; FAT 7.8g (sat 2.7g, mono 2.7g, poly 0.3g); PROTEIN 24.5g; CARB 4.9g; FIBER 0g; CHOL 67mg; IRON 1.6mg; SODIUM 278mg; CALC 16mg

Quick & Easy
Broiled Oysters with Garlic-Buttered Breadcrumbs

Hands-on time: 17 min. Total time: 20 min.

1 tablespoon butter
2 teaspoons extra-virgin olive oil
2 garlic cloves, minced
1 teaspoon fresh lemon juice
1 (2-ounce) slice French bread baguette
⅛ teaspoon salt
⅛ teaspoon freshly ground black pepper
24 shucked oysters
Cooking spray
1 tablespoon chopped fresh flat-leaf parsley

1. Preheat broiler to high.
2. Melt butter in a skillet over medium heat. Add oil and garlic; cook 1 minute, stirring occasionally. Remove from heat, and stir in lemon juice.
3. Place bread in a food processor; pulse 10 times or until coarse crumbs measure 1 cup. Combine breadcrumbs, butter mixture, salt, and pepper, and mix well.
4. Arrange oysters on a broiler pan coated with cooking spray; top oysters with breadcrumb mixture. Broil 5 inches from heat 3 minutes or until breadcrumbs are golden. Sprinkle with parsley. Yield: 6 servings (serving size: 4 oysters).

CALORIES 90; FAT 5.1g (sat 1.9g, mono 1.8g, poly 0.9g); PROTEIN 4.6g; CARB 6.4g; FIBER 0.2g; CHOL 35mg; IRON 4mg; SODIUM 232mg; CALC 39mg

BABY, IT'S HOT IN HERE

These things determine whether food browns or burns.

KNOW YOUR TEMPERATURES

On high broil, food cooks at a sizzling 550° on the top rack. The temperature drops about 50° to 75° on each rack level, down to a balmy 325° at the bottom position in our Test Kitchens ovens. Your oven may be different, hence the appeal of an instant-read thermometer (see page 54).

WHEN TO SET HIGH, WHEN TO SET LOW

Most ovens offer two broiler settings: high (550°) and low (450° or less). Some deluxe models (like the $8,400 Wolf dual-fuel range at left) come with convection broil, which swirls hot air around and cuts cook times. *High broil* works best with delicate or quick-cooking foods, like shrimp or steak cooked to medium-rare. *Low broil* allows for longer cooking times, useful for thicker meats, but you won't see as much searing and browning action.

PICK YOUR POSITION

Use the top two rack positions (3 to 5 inches from the heating element) to brown gratins and cook thin cuts of meat. If you choose to use the top rack, keep an eagle eye on the food—it can go from browned to scorched in seconds. Middle rack positions are for items like bone-in chicken or thick steaks, to ensure they don't burn before they finish cooking.

DOOR: OPEN OR CLOSED?

Consult your oven's user's manual on this one. Some manufacturers call for leaving the oven door open a few inches while broiling (set at the "broiler stop") so the heating element remains on and the stove can vent smoke. Others won't even operate with the door open: They have catalyst filters that vent the oven.

NOT COOKING WITH GAS?

Gas broilers run a little hotter than electric, cranking up to about 600° (that temperature is the industry standard for gas). But don't fret: The slightly cooler electric broiler distributes its heat more evenly, which really helps with tasks like browning gratins.

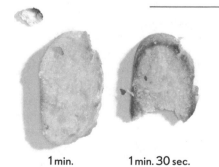

TIMING IS CRITICAL

When you set food under the broiler's intense direct heat, timing is critical. A point illustrated here with garlic bread toasted 5 inches from the heating element. (See Broiler Garlic Bread, page 52.)

1 min.   1 min. 30 sec.

2 min.   2 min. 30 sec.

FOOD SHOULD BE ABOUT 5 INCHES FROM THE BROILER

Your Broiler Here

0"

(Actual Distance)

5"

Your Food Here

Broiler Garlic Bread

Preheat broiler. Melt 2 tablespoons butter in a small saucepan over low heat. Add 2 crushed garlic cloves to pan; cook 15 minutes, stirring occasionally. Arrange 8 (½-ounce) slices French bread baguette in a single layer on a baking sheet. Broil bread 5 inches from heat 1 minute or until lightly browned. Turn slices over; brush with melted butter. Discard garlic. Top each bread slice with 1½ teaspoons grated Parmigiano-Reggiano cheese. Broil 2 minutes or until cheese is melted and golden brown. Yield: 4 servings.

CALORIES 118; FAT 4.1g (sat 2.4g); SODIUM 243mg

Kid Friendly

Broiled Herb-Marinated Shrimp Skewers

Hands-on time: 15 min. Total time: 45 min.

These skewers are a simple, quick, and fresh-tasting entrée. Shrimp cook fast, making them great for the broiler—but watch the time and keep an eye on them so they don't overcook and dry out.

3/4 cup fresh cilantro leaves
3/4 cup fresh parsley leaves
1/2 cup fresh basil leaves
3 tablespoons extra-virgin olive oil
3 tablespoons fresh orange juice
1 tablespoon fresh lime juice
1/2 teaspoon ground cumin
1/2 teaspoon salt
1/4 teaspoon freshly ground black pepper
2 garlic cloves
24 jumbo shrimp (about 1½ pounds), peeled and deveined
Cooking spray

1. Combine first 10 ingredients in a food processor; process until smooth. Place in a bowl; add shrimp, tossing to coat. Marinate in refrigerator 30 minutes, stirring occasionally.
2. Preheat broiler to high.
3. Remove shrimp from marinade; thread 6 shrimp onto each of 4 (8-inch)

wooden skewers. Place skewers on a broiler pan coated with cooking spray; top with any remaining marinade. Broil 5 inches from heat 2 minutes on each side or until shrimp are done. Yield: 4 servings (serving size: 6 shrimp).

CALORIES 285; FAT 13.3g (sat 2g, mono 7.9g, poly 2.3g); PROTEIN 35.3g; CARB 4.6g; FIBER 0.7g; CHOL 259mg; IRON 5.2mg; SODIUM 555mg; CALC 121mg

SHRIMP COOK FAST, MAKING THEM GREAT FOR THE BROILER—BUT WATCH THE TIME AND KEEP AN EYE ON THEM SO THEY DON'T OVERCOOK AND DRY OUT.

Quick & Easy

Broiled Pineapple with Bourbon Caramel over Vanilla Ice Cream

Hands-on time: 15 min. Total time: 30 min. Sugar-coated fruit caramelizes beautifully under the broiler, which deepens and intensifies its flavor.

1/2 cup granulated sugar
3 tablespoons plus 2 teaspoons bourbon, divided
3 tablespoons water
1 teaspoon fresh lemon juice
1/4 cup heavy whipping cream
1 teaspoon vanilla extract
1 pineapple, peeled and cored
Cooking spray
3 tablespoons brown sugar
2 cups vanilla fat-free ice cream
1/4 cup flaked sweetened coconut, toasted

1. Combine granulated sugar, 3 tablespoons bourbon, 3 tablespoons water, and juice in a medium saucepan over medium-high heat; cook 2 minutes or until sugar dissolves, stirring constantly. Bring to a boil; reduce heat to medium and cook, without stirring, 10 minutes or until golden. Remove from heat. Carefully add cream, stirring constantly (mixture will bubble vigorously). Cool slightly. Stir in remaining 2 teaspoons bourbon and vanilla.

2. Preheat broiler to high.

3. Cut pineapple lengthwise into 12 slices; cut each slice in half crosswise. Arrange pineapple on a foil-lined broiler pan coated with cooking spray; sprinkle evenly with brown sugar. Broil 5 inches from heat 12 minutes or until golden brown.

4. Scoop ⅓ cup ice cream into each of 6 bowls. Arrange 4 pineapple slices in each bowl; top each serving with 2½ tablespoons caramel sauce. Sprinkle each serving with 2 teaspoons coconut; serve immediately. Yield: 6 servings.

CALORIES 309; FAT 5.3g (sat 3.5g, mono 1.2g, poly 0.2g); PROTEIN 3.1g; CARB 61g; FIBER 2.3g; CHOL 14mg; IRON 0.6mg; SODIUM 48mg; CALC 86mg

Staff Favorite
Crispy Topped Brussels Sprouts and Cauliflower Gratin

Hands-on time: 33 min. Total time: 63 min.

You can also try this dish with broccoli.

4 cups cauliflower florets (about 1 pound)
4 cups trimmed quartered Brussels sprouts (about 1¾ pounds)
1.1 ounces all-purpose flour (about ¼ cup)
1½ cups 1% low-fat milk
⅔ cup half-and-half
¾ teaspoon salt
¼ teaspoon freshly ground black pepper
⅛ teaspoon freshly ground nutmeg
4 center-cut bacon slices, chopped
2 cups chopped Vidalia or other sweet onion
3 garlic cloves, minced
Cooking spray
½ cup (2 ounces) grated Parmigiano-Reggiano cheese
¼ cup panko (Japanese breadcrumbs)

1. Preheat oven to 375°.

2. Cook cauliflower and Brussels sprouts in boiling water 2 minutes; drain.

3. Weigh or lightly spoon flour into a dry measuring cup; level with a knife. Combine flour, milk, and next 4 ingredients in a bowl; stir well with a whisk.

4. Heat a large skillet over medium heat. Add bacon to pan; cook 3 minutes or until bacon begins to brown, stirring occasionally. Add onion and garlic; cook 5 minutes, stirring occasionally. Stir in milk mixture; bring to a simmer. Cook 5 minutes or until thick, stirring constantly. Remove from heat; stir in cauliflower and Brussels sprouts. Spoon vegetable mixture into an 11 x 7–inch broiler-safe ceramic baking dish coated with cooking spray. Cover dish with foil coated with cooking spray. Bake at 375° for 20 minutes or until bubbly. Remove from oven.

5. Preheat broiler to high.

6. Remove foil from dish. Combine cheese and panko; sprinkle evenly over vegetables. Broil 5 inches from heat 4 minutes or until browned. Let stand 5 minutes before serving. Yield: 8 servings (serving size: about 1 cup).

CALORIES 148; FAT 5.2g (sat 2.9g, mono 0.6g, poly 0.2g); PROTEIN 8.7g; CARB 18.3g; FIBER 3.8g; CHOL 17mg; IRON 1.2mg; SODIUM 399mg; CALC 173mg

THIS CREAMY GRATIN BAKES FOR 20 MINUTES, THEN FINISHES UNDER THE BROILER TO MAKE THE TOP BEAUTIFULLY BROWNED AND CRUNCHY.

Quick & Easy
Lump Crab–Stuffed Trout

Hands-on time: 25 min. Total time: 35 min.

Sweet crabmeat fills these whole trout and helps keep the fillets moist under high broiler heat.

3 center-cut bacon slices, chopped
⅓ cup finely chopped onion
3 tablespoons finely chopped red bell pepper
3 tablespoons finely chopped carrot
2 teaspoons chopped fresh thyme
2 garlic cloves, minced
1 cup finely chopped mushrooms (about 4 ounces)
4 ounces lump crabmeat, drained and shell pieces removed
2 tablespoons chopped fresh parsley
2 tablespoons fresh lemon juice
4 (8-ounce) dressed whole rainbow trout
¼ teaspoon salt
⅛ teaspoon freshly ground black pepper
Cooking spray
Lemon wedges (optional)

1. Preheat broiler to high.

2. Heat a large nonstick skillet over medium-high heat. Add bacon to pan; sauté 4 minutes. Add onion and next 4 ingredients; sauté 4 minutes. Stir in mushrooms; sauté 4 minutes. Place in a medium bowl; cool slightly. Stir in crabmeat, parsley, and juice.

3. Open trout flat as you would a book. Sprinkle trout evenly with salt and black pepper. Spoon about ¼ cup crabmeat mixture onto 1 side of each fish, and fold other side over to cover. Arrange fish on a foil-lined broiler pan coated with cooking spray. Broil 5 inches from heat 5 minutes on each side or until desired degree of doneness. Serve with lemon wedges, if desired. Yield: 4 servings (serving size: 1 stuffed trout).

CALORIES 324; FAT 9.5g (sat 2g, mono 2.6g, poly 2.9g); PROTEIN 53g; CARB 4.2g; FIBER 0.9g; CHOL 163mg; IRON 2.2mg; SODIUM 442mg; CALC 176mg

WHAT THE MASTER BROILER OWNS

Equipment that works perfectly well at 350° may not cut it at 550° or 600°. Avoid shattered casserole dishes, burned hands, and scorched suppers: Buy a few broiler-handy items.

PROTECT YOUR HANDS AND ARMS
With food just 5 inches from a red-hot element, and timing critical, it's easy to get burned. Don't use a damp towel; don't use a thin or too-short mitt. The Oxo Good Grips Silicone Oven Mitt boasts silicone on the outside and breathable fabric inside, with protection up to 600°. At 13 inches long, it guards your wrists and forearms.
Price: $15
Buy: amazon.com

MARK THE TIME
Your first defense against burning is a watchful eye. Your backup is a precise timer. There are many options, but digital is better than mechanical when seconds count.
Price: $20, Oxo
Buy: Bed Bath & Beyond (bedbathandbeyond.com)

CHECK THE TEMP
Most oven thermometers measure the ambient temperature. What matters with broiling is the surface temperature. Get rid of guesswork with an instant-read thermometer, which takes the surface temperature anywhere—even the bubbling top of a gratin. We loved the MicroTemp MT-PRO Digital Infrared Thermometer. (It's also fun to check the temperature of pretty much anything in the house!)
Price: $30–$70
Buy: microtempusa.com

PREVENT CRACKING
Some glass or ceramic baking dishes crack at broiler temps, but the durable clay Emile Henry 13 x 10-inch Lasagna Baker is good for casseroles, steaks, fish fillets, or chicken breasts.
Price: $66
Buy: emilehenryusa.com

REDUCE THE SMOKE
Broiler pans catch liquid that drips from the slotted top into the pan below, which also helps prevent smoke and flares. The nonstick Range Kleen Porcelain Broiler Pan with Porcelain Grill makes cleanup easy.
Price: $20
Buy: Kmart (kmart.com)

COOK WITH IRON
Cast iron can handle high heat forever. Here, a Lodge 12-inch preseasoned model.
Price: $34
Buy: lodgemfg.com

THE DELICIOUS PLEASURES OF SLOW COOKING

The slow cooker promises ultra-easy food preparation, but coaxing delicious, picture-perfect results from it can be a little tricky. We have a three-step process that will help you turn out mouthwatering results every time.

Slow cookers have been back in fashion for so long that in some kitchens they're probably out of favor again, collecting dust in the cupboard. Such is the life cycle of a slow cooker when imperfectly understood: It beckons with the promise of fork-tender meat, perfectly cooked veggies, and a succulent sauce that integrates the sum of its parts. It disappoints, sometimes, with chewy bits of beef or pork; thin, murky liquids; and unbalanced flavors. If you heed three simple principles, though, you can keep the slow cooker in your fast lane.

First, don't skip the browning step. It's true that sautéing meat and veggies produces sticky splatters and makes an extra pan you'll have to scrub (cooking inserts, which can go directly from stovetop to slow cooker, save some labor). But if you don't brown, the slow cooker won't do it for you: Foods do not caramelize sealed in a bubbling bath. And both flavor and appearance will suffer.

Second, remember to use a cautious hand with added liquid, especially alcohol. Wine or other acidic ingredients add harmonious layers of flavor to dishes that are slowly simmered in a stovetop stew pot whose lid can be removed to let liquids evaporate. But the slow cooker holds in all liquid, and then creates more as it is released from the food, so nothing reduces. For this sealed environment, you must reduce total added liquid by about half compared to what you would use in a classic braise or stew. When you do that, the liquid may look paltry, and you may be tempted to add just a bit more. Resist! That will make the dish soupy, not saucy. (If that happens, all is not lost: You can remove a small amount of the cooking liquid an hour or so before the dish is done and make a slurry with a bit of flour. Stir until smooth; add it back to the cooker and let the dish cook at least 30 minutes or until it reaches a desirable thickness; in fact, one of our recipes calls for this step.)

Third and finally, let the slow cooker do its work slowly. Many of the recipes here have total cooking times of 7, 8, even 9 hours. While it's tempting to simply reduce the cooking time by cranking up the heat, that may not produce the best results. This means beginning a dinner dish midmorning, lest you be tempted to rush at the end or find yourself eating later than planned. Don't lift the lid to peek too often, or you'll slow the process even more.

One other consideration in some cases: Add ingredients in stages. Hunks of sinewy meat and dried beans need to cook much longer than most veggies. And fresh herbs and other delicate ingredients retain their vibrant appearance and fresh flavor if added after the dish is completely cooked.

Make Ahead • Freezable
Chickpea Chili
(pictured on page 215)

Hands-on time: 30 min. Total time: 9 hr. 30 min.

1 cup dried chickpeas
2 quarts boiling water
2 tablespoons olive oil, divided
1½ cups chopped onion
5 garlic cloves, minced
1 tablespoon tomato paste
1½ teaspoons ground cumin
1 teaspoon kosher salt
½ teaspoon ground red pepper
½ teaspoon ground cinnamon
¼ teaspoon ground turmeric
2½ cups fat-free, lower-sodium chicken broth
⅔ cup sliced pimiento-stuffed olives
½ cup water
½ cup golden raisins
1 (28-ounce) can whole tomatoes, undrained and crushed
4 cups chopped peeled butternut squash
1 cup frozen green peas, thawed
¼ cup chopped fresh cilantro
6 cups hot cooked couscous
8 lime wedges

1. Place chickpeas in a saucepan; add 2 quarts boiling water. Cover and let stand 1 hour; drain. Place beans in a 6-quart electric slow cooker.
2. Heat a large skillet over medium-high heat. Add 1 tablespoon oil to pan; swirl to coat. Add onion; sauté 4 minutes, stirring occasionally. Add garlic; sauté 1 minute, stirring constantly. Stir in tomato paste and next 5 ingredients; sauté 30 seconds, stirring constantly. Add onion mixture, broth, and next 4 ingredients to slow cooker; cover and cook on HIGH 8 hours.
3. Heat a large skillet over medium-high heat. Add remaining 1 tablespoon oil; swirl to coat. Add squash; sauté 5 minutes. Add squash to slow cooker. Cover and cook on HIGH 1 hour; stir in peas. Sprinkle with cilantro. Serve over couscous with lime wedges. Yield: 8 servings (serving size: 1 cup chili and ¾ cup couscous).

CALORIES 382; **FAT** 7.6g (sat 0.9g, mono 4.1g, poly 0.8g); **PROTEIN** 12.9g; **CARB** 69.4g; **FIBER** 8.6g; **CHOL** 0mg; **IRON** 4mg; **SODIUM** 790mg; **CALC** 133mg

Beef Pot Roast with Turnip Greens

Hands-on time: 25 min. Total time: 8 hr. 38 min.

Cipollini onions are small, flat Italian onions. If you can't find them, substitute pearl onions. Other large full-flavored greens like mustard greens or kale will work, as well.

³/₄ cup all-purpose flour
1 (3-pound) boneless chuck roast, trimmed
1 teaspoon kosher salt
¹/₂ teaspoon freshly ground black pepper
1 tablespoon olive oil
1 pound fresh turnip greens, trimmed and coarsely chopped
3 cups (2-inch) diagonally cut parsnip (about 1 pound)
3 cups cubed peeled Yukon gold potato (about 1 pound)
2 cups cipollini onions, peeled and quartered
2 tablespoons tomato paste
1 cup dry red wine
1 (14-ounce) can fat-free, lower-sodium beef broth
1 tablespoon black peppercorns
4 thyme sprigs
3 garlic cloves, crushed
2 bay leaves
1 bunch fresh flat-leaf parsley
Thyme sprigs (optional)

1. Place flour in a shallow dish. Sprinkle beef evenly with salt and pepper; dredge in flour. Heat a large skillet over medium-high heat. Add oil to pan; swirl to coat. Add beef; sauté 10 minutes, turning to brown on all sides. Place turnip greens in a 6-quart electric slow cooker; top with parsnips, potatoes, and onions. Transfer beef to slow cooker. Add tomato paste to pan; cook 30 seconds, stirring constantly. Stir in wine and broth; bring to a boil, scraping pan to loosen browned bits. Cook 1 minute, stirring constantly. Pour broth mixture into slow cooker.
2. Place peppercorns and next 4 ingredients on a double layer of cheesecloth. Gather edges of cheesecloth together; secure with kitchen twine. Add cheesecloth bundle to slow cooker. Cover and cook on LOW 8 hours or until beef and vegetables are tender. Discard cheesecloth bundle. Remove roast from slow cooker; slice. Serve with vegetable mixture and cooking liquid. Garnish with thyme sprigs, if desired. Yield: 12 servings (serving size: 3 ounces beef, ¾ cup vegetable mixture, and ⅓ cup sauce).

CALORIES 424; **FAT** 21.3g (sat 8.1g, mono 9.4g, poly 0.9g); **PROTEIN** 33g; **CARB** 23.5g; **FIBER** 2.9g; **CHOL** 99mg; **IRON** 3.8mg; **SODIUM** 348mg; **CALC** 90mg

Slow-Simmered Meat Sauce

Hands-on time: 25 min. Total time: 8 hr. 30 min.

Mafaldine is a flat noodle with ruffled edges. You can substitute spaghetti.

1 tablespoon olive oil
2 cups chopped onion
1 cup chopped carrot
6 garlic cloves, minced
2 (4-ounce) links hot Italian sausage, casings removed
1 pound ground sirloin
¹/₂ cup kalamata olives, pitted and sliced
¹/₄ cup no-salt-added tomato paste
1¹/₂ teaspoons sugar
1 teaspoon kosher salt
¹/₂ teaspoon crushed red pepper
1 (28-ounce) can no-salt-added crushed tomatoes, undrained
1 cup no-salt-added tomato sauce
1 tablespoon chopped fresh oregano
16 ounces uncooked mafaldine pasta
¹/₂ cup torn fresh basil
3 ounces shaved fresh Parmigiano-Reggiano cheese

1. Heat a large skillet over medium-high heat. Add oil to pan; swirl to coat. Add onion and carrot to pan; sauté 4 minutes, stirring occasionally. Add garlic; sauté 1 minute, stirring constantly. Place vegetable mixture in a 6-quart electric slow cooker. Add sausage and beef to pan; sauté 6 minutes or until browned, stirring to crumble. Remove beef mixture from pan using a slotted spoon. Place beef mixture on a double layer of paper towels; drain. Add beef mixture to slow cooker. Stir olives and next 6 ingredients into slow cooker. Cover and cook on LOW 8 hours. Stir in oregano.
2. Prepare pasta according to package directions, omitting salt and fat. Serve sauce with hot cooked pasta; top with basil and cheese. Yield: 8 servings (serving size: 1 cup pasta, 1 cup sauce, 1 tablespoon basil, and 2 tablespoons cheese).

CALORIES 503; **FAT** 16.7g (sat 5.7g, mono 8g, poly 2g); **PROTEIN** 26.3g; **CARB** 59.7g; **FIBER** 5.6g; **CHOL** 48mg; **IRON** 4.8mg; **SODIUM** 766mg; **CALC** 198mg

IT MAY BE TEMPTING TO ADD LIQUID TO THE SLOW COOKER, BUT RESIST! THIS ENVIRONMENT IS SEALED AND NO LIQUID ESCAPES AS THE DISH COOKS. IN FACT, MORE IS PRODUCED AS FOOD COOKS.

Provençal Beef Daube

Hands-on time: 29 min. Total time: 7 hr. 19 min.

If you can't find niçoise olives, use another meaty variety, such as kalamata or gaeta. For other ways to use dried porcini mushrooms, see below.

2 pounds boneless chuck roast, trimmed and cut into chunks
1 tablespoon extra-virgin olive oil
6 garlic cloves, minced
½ cup boiling water
½ ounce dried porcini mushrooms
¾ teaspoon salt, divided
Cooking spray
½ cup red wine
¼ cup fat-free, lower-sodium beef broth
⅓ cup pitted niçoise olives
½ teaspoon freshly ground black pepper
2 large carrots, peeled and thinly sliced
1 large onion, peeled and chopped
1 celery stalk, thinly sliced
1 (15-ounce) can whole tomatoes, drained and crushed
1 teaspoon whole black peppercorns
3 flat-leaf parsley sprigs
3 thyme sprigs
1 bay leaf
1 (1-inch) strip orange rind
1 tablespoon water
1 teaspoon cornstarch
1½ tablespoons chopped fresh flat-leaf parsley
1½ teaspoons chopped fresh thyme

1. Combine first 3 ingredients in a large zip-top plastic bag. Seal and marinate at room temperature 30 minutes, turning bag occasionally.
2. Combine ½ cup boiling water and mushrooms; cover and let stand 30 minutes. Drain through a sieve over a bowl, reserving mushrooms and ¼ cup soaking liquid. Chop mushrooms.
3. Heat a large skillet over medium-high heat. Sprinkle beef mixture with ¼ teaspoon salt. Coat pan with cooking spray. Add half of beef mixture to pan, and sauté 5 minutes, turning to brown on all sides. Place browned beef mixture in a 6-quart electric slow cooker. Repeat procedure with cooking spray and remaining beef mixture. Add wine and broth to pan; bring to a boil, scraping pan to loosen browned bits. Pour wine mixture into slow cooker. Add mushrooms, reserved ¼ cup soaking liquid, remaining ½ teaspoon salt, olives, and next 5 ingredients. Place peppercorns, parsley sprigs, thyme sprigs, bay leaf, and orange rind on a double layer of cheesecloth. Gather edges of cheesecloth together; secure with kitchen twine. Add cheesecloth bundle to slow cooker. Cover and cook on LOW 6 hours or until beef and vegetables are tender. Discard cheesecloth bundle.
4. Combine 1 tablespoon water and cornstarch in a small bowl, stirring until smooth. Add cornstarch mixture to slow cooker; cook 20 minutes or until slightly thick, stirring occasionally. Sprinkle with chopped parsley and chopped thyme. Yield: 8 servings (serving size: about ¾ cup).

CALORIES 360; FAT 22.5g (sat 8g, mono 10.6g, poly 1.1g); PROTEIN 30.2g; CARB 7.8g; FIBER 2.2g; CHOL 94mg; IRON 3.5mg; SODIUM 516mg; CALC 53mg

3 MORE WAYS WITH DRIED PORCINI MUSHROOMS

1. Rehydrate mushrooms with boiling water; use them and soaking liquid to flavor risotto.

2. Enrich soups and stews with soaking liquid and mushrooms.

3. Use soaking liquid and mushrooms as the base for pasta sauce.

Staff Favorite • Make Ahead
Freezable
Brazilian Feijoada

Hands-on time: 47 min. Total time: 9 hr. 47 min.

Feijoada (pronounced fay-ZWAH-da) is a delicious stew of pork and black beans that's traditionally served over rice with fresh orange slices. In Brazil, this dish is often served on special occasions, but preparing it in a slow cooker makes it possible to serve this rich dish on the busiest weeknights.

2 cups dried black beans
4 applewood-smoked bacon slices
1 pound boneless pork shoulder (Boston butt), trimmed and cut into ½-inch cubes
¾ teaspoon salt, divided
½ teaspoon freshly ground black pepper, divided
3 bone-in beef short ribs, trimmed (about 2 pounds)
3 cups finely chopped onion (about 2 medium)
1¼ cups fat-free, lower-sodium chicken broth
4 garlic cloves, minced
1 (9-ounce) smoked ham hock
1 tablespoon white vinegar
8 orange wedges

1. Place beans in a small saucepan; cover with cold water. Bring to a boil, and cook 2 minutes. Remove from heat; cover and let stand 1 hour. Drain.
2. Cook bacon in a large skillet over medium heat until crisp. Remove bacon from pan; crumble. Sprinkle pork evenly with ⅛ teaspoon salt and ¼ teaspoon pepper. Increase heat to medium-high. Add pork to drippings in pan; sauté 8 minutes, turning to brown on all sides. Transfer pork to a 6-quart electric slow cooker. Sprinkle ribs evenly with ⅛ teaspoon salt and remaining ¼ teaspoon pepper. Add ribs to pan; cook 3 minutes on each side or until browned. Place ribs in slow cooker. Add drained beans, remaining ½ teaspoon salt, onion, and next 3 ingredients to slow cooker, stirring to combine. Cover and cook on LOW 8 hours or until beans and meat are tender.

continued

3. Remove ribs from slow cooker, and let stand 15 minutes. Remove meat from bones; shred meat with 2 forks. Discard bones. Discard ham hock. Return beef to slow cooker. Stir in vinegar and crumbled bacon. Serve with orange wedges. Yield: 8 servings (serving size: about 1¼ cups bean mixture and 1 orange wedge).

CALORIES 458; FAT 17.4g (sat 6.8g, mono 6.7g, poly 1.1g); PROTEIN 39.5g; CARB 35.8g; FIBER 11.6g; CHOL 96mg; IRON 6.4mg; SODIUM 533mg; CALC 102mg

SLOW-COOKER SHOWDOWN

We tested our Provençal Beef Daube recipe in six slow cookers—all with at least a 6-quart capacity—ranging in price from $35 to a hefty $280. The results varied more in appearance and flavor than anticipated. In our favorite cookers, the meat was more broken down and succulent, and the cooking liquid was rich and harmonious. In other cookers, flavors were less deliciously integrated. Our conclusion: The more successful pots seemed to cook at a slightly higher temp—even on the LOW settings, the stews bubbled a bit as they simmered.

BEST OVERALL: Breville BSC560XL 7-Quart ($180)
Although this stainless cooker lacks a timer and operates with manual controls, it produced great results. We love the lightweight cooking insert, safe for the stovetop. This model also includes a meat rack and a long, detachable cord. One drawback: A metal lid makes it hard not to peek.

BEST VALUE: West Bend 84966 6-Quart ($60)
A close second, this model has a digital timer. The cooking pot is safe for stovetop use, and the warming element doubles as a griddle, so you can cook directly on it. There are three heat settings—high, low, and warm—a nice feature for entertaining or families who eat in shifts.

EVERYDAY VEGETARIAN

COMFORTING CASSEROLES

From pasta and strata to potpie and moussaka, these meatless mains deliver home-style flavor and hearty satisfaction.

Make Ahead • Vegetarian

Mushroom and Root Vegetable Potpie

Hands-on time: 50 min. Total time: 1 hr. 35 min.

2 cups (½-inch-thick) slices carrot
2 cups (½-inch-thick) slices rutabaga
2 cups (½-inch-thick) slices parsnip
3 cups organic vegetable broth
2 cups fat-free milk
1 bay leaf
1 tablespoon butter, divided
1 tablespoon chopped fresh thyme, divided
3 (4-ounce) packages presliced exotic mushroom blend
⅔ cup finely chopped shallots
2 garlic cloves, minced
1.5 ounces all-purpose flour (about ⅓ cup)
2 tablespoons heavy whipping cream
1 tablespoon dry sherry
Cooking spray
3.2 ounces whole-wheat flour (about ⅔ cup)
3 ounces all-purpose flour (about ⅔ cup)
1½ teaspoons baking powder
2 teaspoons minced fresh parsley
3 tablespoons chilled butter, cut into small pieces
⅔ cup plus 2 tablespoons nonfat buttermilk, divided

1. Place first 6 ingredients in a large saucepan, and bring to a boil. Reduce heat, and simmer 15 minutes or until vegetables are tender. Remove carrot mixture from pan with a slotted spoon; set aside. Reserve cooking liquid; set aside. Discard bay leaf.

2. Heat 1½ teaspoons butter in a large nonstick skillet over medium heat. Add 1½ teaspoons thyme and mushrooms; cook 12 minutes or until mushrooms are tender, stirring occasionally. Remove from heat.

3. Melt remaining 1½ teaspoons butter in a medium heavy saucepan over medium heat. Add ⅔ cup chopped shallots and garlic; cook 3 minutes or until tender, stirring frequently. Pour ½ cup reserved cooking liquid into a bowl. Weigh or lightly spoon 1.5 ounces (about ⅓ cup) all-purpose flour into a dry measuring cup; level with a knife. Add 1.5 ounces all-purpose flour to ½ cup reserved cooking liquid in bowl; stir with a whisk.

4. Add remaining reserved cooking liquid, remaining 1½ teaspoons thyme, cream, and sherry to pan with shallots; bring to a boil. Add flour mixture; stir with a whisk. Bring to a boil; reduce heat, and simmer until mixture thickens and is reduced to 3 cups (about 10 minutes), stirring frequently.

5. Place reserved carrot mixture, mushrooms, and shallot mixture in a large bowl, and stir to combine. Spoon 1⅓ cups mixture into each of 6 (10-ounce) ramekins coated with cooking spray.

6. Preheat oven to 400°.

7. Weigh or lightly spoon whole-wheat flour and 3 ounces all-purpose flour into dry measuring cups, and level with a knife. Combine whole-wheat flour, 3 ounces all-purpose flour (about ⅔ cup), baking powder, and parsley in a medium bowl, stirring with a whisk. Cut in 3 tablespoons chilled butter with a pastry blender or 2 knives until mixture resembles coarse meal. Add ⅔ cup buttermilk to whole-wheat flour mixture, stirring just until moist. Drop dough by tablespoonfuls onto vegetable mixture, dividing evenly among ramekins. Brush remaining 2 tablespoons buttermilk over topping. Bake at 400° for 45 minutes or until crust is golden brown. Yield: 6 servings.

CALORIES 351; FAT 10.5g (sat 6.2g, mono 2.6g, poly 0.8g); PROTEIN 12.2g; CARB 53.7g; FIBER 6.9g; CHOL 29mg; IRON 2.7mg; SODIUM 561mg; CALC 253mg

CRUNCHY-TOPPED AND CREAMY, IT'S LIKE MAC AND CHEESE FOR GROWN-UPS.

Kid Friendly • Vegetarian

Baked Pasta with Spinach, Lemon, and Cheese

Hands-on time: 12 min. Total time: 1 hr. 33 min.

Casarecce pasta is a short noodle with a curled edge that provides a large groove to hold the creamy sauce. If you can't find it, use fusilli, campanelle, or radiatore. Use a large, deep pot for the pasta so the spinach will fit inside, as well.

10 ounces casarecce pasta or fusilli (short twisted spaghetti)
1 (5-ounce) package fresh baby spinach
1 tablespoon olive oil
4 cups chopped onion
1.1 ounces all-purpose flour (about ¼ cup)
4 garlic cloves, minced
2½ cups 1% low-fat milk
½ cup dry white wine
1 cup (4 ounces) grated Parmigiano-Reggiano cheese, divided
¾ teaspoon salt
¼ teaspoon grated lemon rind
½ teaspoon black pepper
Cooking spray
¾ cup panko (Japanese breadcrumbs), divided

1. Preheat oven to 350°.
2. Cook pasta in boiling water 8 minutes or until almost al dente, omitting salt and fat. Remove from heat; stir in spinach. Let stand 2 minutes or until spinach wilts. Drain pasta mixture well.
3. Heat a large nonstick skillet over medium heat. Add olive oil to pan; swirl to coat. Add onion; cook 15 minutes or until golden brown, stirring frequently. Weigh or lightly spoon flour into a dry measuring cup; level with a knife. Add flour and garlic to pan; cook 1 minute, stirring constantly with a whisk. Gradually add milk and wine; cook 8 minutes or until sauce boils and thickens, stirring constantly. Stir in ¾ cup cheese, salt, and rind. Remove from heat; stir in pepper.

Add pasta mixture to onion mixture, and toss gently to coat.

4. Spoon pasta mixture into a 13 x 9–inch glass or ceramic baking dish coated with cooking spray. Sprinkle half of panko over pasta, and top evenly with remaining ¼ cup cheese. Sprinkle remaining half of panko over cheese. Bake at 350° for 50 minutes or until browned and bubbly. Yield: 6 servings.

CALORIES 396; FAT 8.2g (sat 3.5g, mono 3.1g, poly 0.5g); PROTEIN 18.4g; CARB 63.3g; FIBER 4.9g; CHOL 17mg; IRON 3mg; SODIUM 611mg; CALC 325mg

Vegetarian

Vegetarian Moussaka

Hands-on time: 60 min. Total time: 1 hr. 50 min.

In this meatless version of the classic Greek dish, bulgur wheat stands in for ground meat in a spiced-tomato filling surrounded by eggplant layers and topped with a béchamel sauce. The eggplant and bulgur pack this dish with fiber.

3 peeled eggplants, cut into ½-inch-thick slices (about 2½ pounds)
2 tablespoons extra-virgin olive oil, divided
Cooking spray
2 cups chopped onion
4 garlic cloves, minced
½ cup uncooked bulgur
¼ teaspoon ground allspice
¼ teaspoon ground cinnamon
⅛ teaspoon ground cloves
2 cups organic vegetable broth
2 teaspoons chopped fresh oregano
1 (14.5-ounce) can no-salt-added diced tomatoes, undrained
1 tablespoon butter
2 tablespoons all-purpose flour
1 cup 1% low-fat milk
2 tablespoons finely grated fresh Romano cheese
¼ teaspoon salt
1 large egg, lightly beaten

1. Preheat broiler to high.
2. Brush eggplant slices with 1 tablespoon oil. Place half of eggplant on a foil-lined baking sheet coated with cooking spray; broil 5 inches from heat 5 minutes on each side or until browned. Repeat procedure with remaining eggplant. Set eggplant aside.
3. Heat a large skillet over medium-high heat. Add remaining 1 tablespoon oil to pan; swirl to coat. Add chopped onion to pan; sauté 8 minutes. Add garlic; sauté 1 minute. Add bulgur; cook 3 minutes or until bulgur is lightly toasted, stirring frequently. Add allspice, cinnamon, and cloves; cook 1 minute, stirring constantly. Stir in vegetable broth, oregano, and tomatoes. Bring to a boil; reduce heat, and simmer 20 minutes or until thick, stirring occasionally.
4. Melt butter in a saucepan over medium heat. Add flour; cook 1 minute, stirring constantly with a whisk until well blended. Gradually add milk, stirring constantly with a whisk. Bring to a boil; reduce heat to medium-low, and simmer 5 minutes or until thick, stirring frequently. Stir in cheese and salt. Remove from heat, and cool slightly. Add egg, stirring well with a whisk.
5. Preheat oven to 350°.
6. Arrange half of eggplant in an 11 x 7–inch glass or ceramic baking dish coated with cooking spray. Spread bulgur mixture evenly over eggplant; arrange remaining eggplant over bulgur mixture. Top with milk mixture. Bake at 350° for 40 minutes, and remove from oven. Increase oven temperature to 475°. Return dish to oven 4 minutes or until top is browned. Let stand 10 minutes before serving. Yield: 4 servings.

CALORIES 343; FAT 13.1g (sat 4.2g, mono 6.4g, poly 1.3g); PROTEIN 11.4g; CARB 47.8g; FIBER 13.4g; CHOL 57mg; IRON 2.3mg; SODIUM 583mg; CALC 203mg

Artichoke and Goat Cheese Strata

Hands-on time: 29 min. Total time: 1 hr. 39 min.

To make ahead, prepare through step 2, cover, and chill. Before baking, let bread mixture stand at room temperature 10 minutes while the oven preheats. Then assemble and bake. The cook time will increase by about 10 minutes. Garnish with parsley, if desired.

1 teaspoon olive oil
½ cup finely chopped shallots (about 1 large)
1 (10-ounce) package frozen artichoke hearts, thawed
2 garlic cloves, minced
½ teaspoon dried herbes de Provence
1¾ cups 1% low-fat milk
½ teaspoon freshly ground black pepper
¼ teaspoon salt
4 large eggs
⅓ cup (about 1½ ounces) grated Parmigiano-Reggiano cheese
½ (1-pound) loaf country-style white bread, cut into 1-inch cubes (about 5 cups)
Cooking spray
¾ cup (3 ounces) crumbled goat cheese, divided

1. Heat a large nonstick skillet over medium heat. Add olive oil to pan; swirl to coat. Add shallots, and cook 2 minutes, stirring frequently. Stir in artichoke hearts and garlic; cook 8 minutes or until artichoke hearts begin to brown, stirring occasionally. Remove from heat, and stir in herbes de Provence. Cool 10 minutes.
2. Combine milk, black pepper, salt, and eggs in a large bowl, stirring with a whisk. Add Parmigiano-Reggiano cheese and bread; toss gently to combine. Stir in artichoke mixture, and let stand 20 minutes.
3. Preheat oven to 375°.
4. Spoon half of bread mixture into an 8-inch square glass or ceramic baking dish coated with cooking spray. Sprinkle with half of goat cheese, and top with remaining bread mixture. Sprinkle remaining half of goat cheese over top. Bake at 375° for 50 minutes or until browned and bubbly. Yield: 6 servings.

CALORIES 286; **FAT** 10.7g (sat 5.1g, mono 3.4g, poly 0.9g); **PROTEIN** 16.8g; **CARB** 31.1g; **FIBER** 2.7g; **CHOL** 139mg; **IRON** 2.5mg; **SODIUM** 561mg; **CALC** 272mg

READER RECIPES
FROM YOUR KITCHEN TO OURS

Leanne Guido teaches cooking classes for kids and adults at her local community center, and her Turkey Tenders pass muster with all ages. Panko-crumb crunch and Parmesan notes will please adult palates, but "kids love them too, and they are healthier than fast-food nuggets." For an easy, sweet-tangy-creamy dipping sauce, combine equal parts ketchup and mayonnaise with a dash of honey.

When it comes to cooking, Jan Valdez has an eye for presentation. Arctic char fillets topped with fresh, colorful vegetables are steamed in individual parchment pouches in this recipe, unwrapped by each diner at the table. "Parchment packets allow the fish and vegetables to cook in their own juices and thus maintain the flavor of each ingredient," she says.

Although she spends long hours on the job as a chef, Nicolette Manescalchi enjoys cooking at home. "It's my chance to experiment and create new dishes that are outside the boundaries and restrictions of the cuisine at work," she says. Here, Manescalchi riffs on tradition by incorporating a Honeycrisp apple, native to her former home in Minneapolis, into classic French onion soup. The fruit adds an unusual combination of tart and sweet to the soup's savory broth. Key to success: allowing enough time for the onions to caramelize over moderate heat until they reach a silky, buttery texture.

Turkey Tenders

Hands-on time: 20 min. Total time: 30 min.

"I try to cook fresh, real food that's easy for students to duplicate at home."
—Leanne Guido, Herndon, Virginia

1 (1-pound) turkey tenderloin
¼ cup all-purpose flour
⅓ cup egg substitute
¾ cup panko (Japanese breadcrumbs)
2 tablespoons grated Parmesan cheese
¼ teaspoon garlic salt
¼ teaspoon black pepper
1 tablespoon canola oil

1. Preheat oven to 425°.
2. Cut tenderloin in half lengthwise; cut into 20 (2-inch) pieces.
3. Place flour in a shallow dish. Place egg substitute in another shallow dish. Combine panko, cheese, garlic salt, and pepper in a third shallow dish. Dredge turkey in flour; dip in egg substitute, and dredge in panko mixture. Heat oil in a large nonstick skillet over medium-high heat, swirling to coat. Add turkey pieces to pan; cook 2 minutes on each side. Place turkey pieces on a broiler pan. Bake at 425° for 5 minutes. Turn turkey pieces over, and bake an additional 5 minutes or until golden. Yield: 4 servings (serving size: 5 pieces).

CALORIES 227; **FAT** 6.1g (sat 1.2g, mono 2.7g, poly 1.3g); **PROTEIN** 32.9g; **CARB** 11g; **FIBER** 0.5g; **CHOL** 47mg; **IRON** 2mg; **SODIUM** 237mg; **CALC** 36mg

6 STEPS FOR FISH COOKED IN PARCHMENT

Cooking fish *en papillote*—in parchment paper—yields moist, tender results with little fuss. The key is a folded seal on the paper packet.

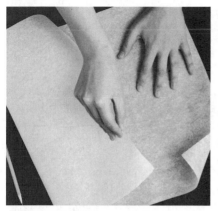

1. Fold parchment paper in half.

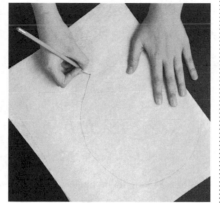

2. Draw half of a heart shape.

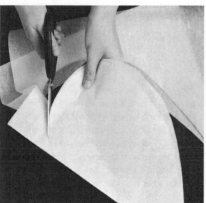

3. Cut out shape as shown.

4. Arrange fish and veggies on one side of paper.

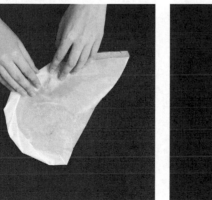

5. Make small, tight, overlapping folds down the outside edge to close packet.

6. Twist tail end to seal.

Arctic Char and Vegetables in Parchment Hearts

Hands-on time: 15 min. Total time: 30 min.

"This dish offers a really great way to introduce a variety of colorful and flavor-packed veggies into your family's diet."
—Jan Valdez, Chicago, Illinois

1½ tablespoons unsalted butter, softened
1 teaspoon grated lemon rind
1 tablespoon fresh lemon juice
1 teaspoon chopped fresh dill
2 (6-ounce) arctic char fillets (about 1 inch thick)
¼ teaspoon kosher salt
⅛ teaspoon black pepper
¼ cup julienne-cut leek
¼ cup julienne-cut red bell pepper
¼ cup julienne-cut carrot
¼ cup julienne-cut snow peas

1. Preheat oven to 450°.
2. Combine first 4 ingredients in a small bowl; stir until blended.
3. Cut 2 (15 x 24–inch) pieces of parchment paper. Fold in half crosswise. Draw a large heart half on each piece, with the fold of the paper along the center of the heart. Cut out the heart, and open. Sprinkle both sides of fillets with salt and pepper. Place 1 fillet near fold of each parchment heart. Top each fillet with half of vegetables and half of butter mixture. Start at top of heart and fold edges of parchment, sealing edges with narrow folds. Twist end tip to secure tightly. Place packets on a baking sheet. Bake at 450° for 15 minutes. Place on plates; cut open. Serve immediately. Yield: 2 servings (serving size: 1 fillet, ½ cup vegetables, and about 1 tablespoon sauce).

Sustainable Choice | *If arctic char is not available from your fishmonger, substitute frozen wild Alaskan salmon.*

CALORIES 301; **FAT** 14.6g (sat 6.4g, mono 3.8g, poly 2.7g); **PROTEIN** 34.8g; **CARB** 6g; **FIBER** 1.4g; **CHOL** 111mg; **IRON** 1.8mg; **SODIUM** 369mg; **CALC** 45mg

French Onion and Apple Soup

Hands-on time: 25 min. Total time: 2 hr. 10 min.

"I thought, why not try combining the flavors of my favorite apple with the sweet richness of French onion soup? And my recipe was born."
—Nicolette Manescalchi,
San Francisco, California

3 tablespoons unsalted butter
15 cups sliced yellow onion (about 4 pounds)
¾ teaspoon black pepper
1 Honeycrisp or Pink Lady apple, peeled, quartered, and cut into julienne strips
3 thyme sprigs
2 bay leaves
½ cup Madeira wine or dry sherry
6 cups lower-sodium beef broth
½ cup apple cider
1 tablespoon sherry vinegar
10 (½-ounce) slices sourdough bread, cut into 1-inch cubes
2 cups (8 ounces) grated Gruyère or Swiss cheese
Thyme leaves (optional)

1. Melt butter in a Dutch oven over medium heat. Add onion to pan; cook 5 minutes, stirring frequently. Continue cooking 50 minutes or until deep golden brown, stirring occasionally. Add pepper, apple, thyme sprigs, and bay leaves; cook 3 minutes or until apples soften. Add wine; cook 2 minutes, scraping pan. Add broth and cider; bring to a boil. Reduce heat; simmer 45 minutes. Discard bay leaves; stir in vinegar.
2. Preheat broiler.
3. Arrange bread cubes in a single layer on a jelly-roll pan; broil 2 minutes or until toasted, turning after 1 minute.
4. Preheat oven to 500°.
5. Ladle 1 cup soup into each of 10 ovenproof bowls. Divide croutons evenly among bowls, and top each serving with about 3 tablespoons cheese. Place bowls on jelly-roll pan. Bake at 500° for 8 minutes or until cheese melts. Garnish with thyme leaves, if desired. Yield: 10 servings.

CALORIES 254; **FAT** 11g (sat 6.4g, mono 3.1g, poly 0.7g); **PROTEIN** 11.1g; **CARB** 29.2g; **FIBER** 4.1g; **CHOL** 33mg; **IRON** 1.1mg; **SODIUM** 426mg; **CALC** 278mg

TAKEOUT MAKEOVERS

Yum! Your favorite restaurant dishes made lighter in 30 minutes or less!

Quick & Easy • Make Ahead
Kid Friendly

Chicken Fried Rice

Hands-on time: 25 min. Total time: 25 min.

2 (3½-ounce) bags boil-in-bag long-grain white rice
7 teaspoons lower-sodium soy sauce, divided
1 teaspoon cornstarch
12 ounces skinless, boneless chicken breast halves, cut into ½-inch pieces
2 tablespoons hoisin sauce
2 tablespoons rice wine vinegar
2 tablespoons fresh lime juice
1 teaspoon chili paste with garlic
2 tablespoons canola oil, divided
2 large eggs, lightly beaten
1 cup chopped white onion
1 teaspoon grated peeled fresh ginger
3 garlic cloves, minced
1 cup frozen green peas, thawed
½ cup chopped green onions

1. Cook rice according to package directions, omitting salt and fat.
2. Combine 1 tablespoon soy sauce, cornstarch, and chicken in a bowl; toss well. Combine remaining 4 teaspoons soy sauce, hoisin sauce, and next 3 ingredients in a small bowl.
3. Heat 1 tablespoon oil in a wok or large nonstick skillet over medium-high heat. Add chicken mixture; stir-fry 4 minutes or until lightly browned. Push chicken to 1 side of pan; add eggs to open side of pan. Cook 45 seconds, stirring constantly; stir eggs and chicken mixture together. Remove chicken mixture from pan; keep warm. Return pan to medium-high heat. Add remaining 1 tablespoon oil to pan. Add white onion, ginger, and garlic; cook 2 minutes or until fragrant.

Add rice; cook 1 minute. Add peas; cook 1 minute. Add chicken mixture and soy sauce mixture; cook 2 minutes or until thoroughly heated. Remove pan from heat; stir in green onions. Yield: 4 servings (serving size: about 1½ cups).

CALORIES 477; **FAT** 11.7g (sat 1.7g, mono 5.7g, poly 2.7g); **PROTEIN** 30.2g; **CARB** 58.3g; **FIBER** 3.5g; **CHOL** 139mg; **IRON** 3.5mg; **SODIUM** 488mg; **CALC** 58mg

---

CHICKEN FRIED RICE

Along with iridescent sweet- and-sour pork, fried rice is a comforting Chinese-American hybrid that populates every Chinese takeout menu in the country. Almost everyone who loves fried rice is drawn to its salty, greasy goodness. The problem is the salty, greasy part, because underneath is a reasonable rice and lean-protein dish, flecked with vegetables. Our riff uses a bit of lower-sodium soy sauce, and then boosts the savor with sweet-salty hoisin sauce and fiery chili paste. Sodium savings: about 60%. Comfort factor: still high.

NUTRITION INFORMATION

CALORIES
Takeout: 455
Ours: 477

FAT
Takeout: 13.5g
Ours: 11.7g

SATURATED FAT
Takeout: 3g
Ours: 1.7g

SODIUM
Takeout: 1,122mg
Ours: 488mg

Ready in 25 min.

FISH TACOS

The food truck trend offers everything from Korean-fusion tacos at Yumbii in Atlanta (yumbii.com) to traditional fish tacos at the Mariscos German trucks in San Diego. We decided to lighten the Baja fish taco because it's both mighty good and mighty fatty. The batter on the traditional fried fish soaks up fat, and then salt gets poured on afterward. We forgo the fryer, coat the fish with a bold spice rub, and then sauté it in a bit of oil.

NUTRITION INFORMATION

CALORIES
Takeout: 500
Ours: 362

FAT
Takeout: 26g
Ours: 13.6g

SATURATED FAT
Takeout: 4g
Ours: 3.1g

SODIUM
Takeout: 840mg
Ours: 388mg

Ready in 20 min.

Quick & Easy
Blackened Tilapia Tacos

Hands-on time: 20 min. Total time: 20 min.

¼ cup reduced-fat sour cream
2 tablespoons chopped fresh cilantro
2 tablespoons fresh lime juice
1 jalapeño pepper, seeded and chopped
1 cup thinly sliced white onion
1½ teaspoons paprika
1½ teaspoons brown sugar
1 teaspoon dried oregano
¾ teaspoon garlic powder
½ teaspoon salt
½ teaspoon ground cumin
¼ teaspoon ground red pepper
4 (6-ounce) tilapia fillets
1 tablespoon canola oil
8 (6-inch) corn tortillas
½ ripe peeled avocado, thinly sliced
4 lime wedges

1. Combine first 4 ingredients in a food processor; process until smooth. Combine jalapeño sauce and onion in a small bowl.
2. Combine paprika and next 6 ingredients; sprinkle evenly over fish. Heat oil in a large cast-iron skillet over medium-high heat. Add fish to pan; cook 3 minutes on each side or until desired degree of doneness.
3. Warm tortillas according to package directions. Divide fish, onion mixture, and avocado evenly among tortillas. Serve with lime wedges. Yield: 4 servings (serving size: 2 tacos).

CALORIES 362; **FAT** 13.6g (sat 3.1g, mono 6.4g, poly 2.8g); **PROTEIN** 37g; **CARB** 27.1g; **FIBER** 4.9g; **CHOL** 79mg; **IRON** 1.5mg; **SODIUM** 388mg; **CALC** 74mg

---

PIZZA SUPREME

Authentic wood-fired pizza is all the rage, but a great deal of the pies eaten in America are still pepperoni, meat-lover's, and supreme versions from national chains. But why eat heavy when you can have the same pleasure in a lighter pizza package? We attacked the supreme formula, leaning on veggies and walking back the meat (just one sausage link for the whole pizza). It's enough for flavor but doesn't leave you with pools of grease to blot. Lean turkey sausage stands in for pork, and lower-sodium marinara anchors the toppings. But, knowing when a low-fat swap is not worth it, we use full-fat mozzarella (and a generous amount of it)—which makes our pizza irresistible.

NUTRITION INFORMATION

CALORIES
Takeout: 507
Ours: 344

FAT
Takeout: 24g
Ours: 11.3g

SATURATED FAT
Takeout: 10.7g
Ours: 4.1g

SODIUM
Takeout: 1,333mg
Ours: 640mg

Ready in 30 min.

Quick & Easy • Kid Friendly
Pizza Supreme

Hands-on time: 15 min. Total time: 30 min.

Purchase fresh pizza dough from your supermarket's bakery section. Or you may be able to swing by your favorite pizza parlor and pick some up.

1 (16-ounce) refrigerated pizza crust dough
Cooking spray
2 teaspoons olive oil
1 (4-ounce) link turkey Italian sausage
1 cup sliced mushrooms
1 cup thinly sliced red bell pepper
1 cup thinly sliced orange bell pepper
1 cup thinly sliced onion
¼ teaspoon crushed red pepper
3 garlic cloves, thinly sliced
¾ cup lower-sodium marinara sauce
5 ounces fresh mozzarella cheese, thinly sliced

1. Preheat oven to 500°.
2. Roll dough into a 14-inch circle on a lightly floured surface. Place dough on a 14-inch pizza pan or baking sheet coated with cooking spray.
3. Heat oil in a large nonstick skillet over medium-high heat. Remove casing from sausage. Add sausage to pan; cook 2 minutes, stirring to crumble. Add mushrooms, bell peppers, onion, crushed red pepper, and garlic; sauté 4 minutes, stirring occasionally.
4. Spread sauce over dough, leaving a 1-inch border. Arrange cheese evenly over sauce. Arrange turkey mixture evenly over cheese. Bake at 500° for 15 minutes or until crust and cheese are browned. Cut into 12 wedges. Yield: 6 servings (serving size: 2 wedges).

CALORIES 344; **FAT** 11.3g (sat 4.1g, mono 3.9g, poly 1.8g); **PROTEIN** 14.4g; **CARB** 53.4g; **FIBER** 2.4g; **CHOL** 31mg; **IRON** 2.8mg; **SODIUM** 640mg; **CALC** 132mg

CHEESEBURGER

The burger craze is red-hot, ranging from the wagyu-brisket fads of big-city chefs to the megaburgers at the chains. Those giants can serve up most of a day's calories, more than a day's fat, and a shakerful of salt. We decided to start with something more reasonable yet still iconic: the legendary In-N-Out cheeseburger. Ours is a tasty handful, with a similar addictive sauce, but about 40% less fat and saturated fat, thanks to lean ground sirloin and lower-sodium, lighter cheese.

NUTRITION INFORMATION

CALORIES
Takeout: 480
Ours: 389

FAT
Takeout: 27g
Ours: 16.5g

SATURATED FAT
Takeout: 10g
Ours: 5.8g

SODIUM
Takeout: 1,000mg
Ours: 806mg

Ready in 22 min.

Quick & Easy • Kid Friendly
Out-N-In California Burger

Hands-on time: 22 min. Total time: 22 min.

3 tablespoons ketchup
2 tablespoons canola mayonnaise
2 teaspoons sweet pickle relish
1 teaspoon Dijon mustard
1 pound ground sirloin
⅛ teaspoon salt
⅛ teaspoon freshly ground black pepper
Cooking spray
4 (1-ounce) slices reduced-fat, lower-sodium Swiss cheese
4 green leaf lettuce leaves
4 (1½-ounce) hamburger buns
4 (¼-inch-thick) slices red onion
8 (¼-inch-thick) slices tomato
½ ripe peeled avocado, cut into ⅛-inch-thick slices
8 bread-and-butter pickle chips

1. Combine first 4 ingredients in a bowl.
2. Divide beef into 4 equal portions, gently shaping each into a ½-inch-thick patty. Press a nickel-sized indentation in the center of each patty; sprinkle patties evenly with salt and pepper. Heat a large skillet or grill pan over medium-high heat. Coat pan with cooking spray. Add patties to pan; cook 3 minutes on each side. Top each patty with 1 cheese slice; cook 2 minutes or until cheese melts and patties are desired degree of doneness.
3. Place 1 lettuce leaf on bottom half of each hamburger bun; top with 1 patty, 1 onion slice, 2 tomato slices, about 2 avocado slices, 2 pickle chips, about 1½ tablespoons sauce, and top half of bun. Yield: 4 servings (serving size: 1 burger).

CALORIES 389; FAT 16.5g (sat 5.8g, mono 6.1g, poly 2.4g); PROTEIN 38g; CARB 34.7g; FIBER 2.4g; CHOL 72mg; IRON 3.3mg; SODIUM 806mg; CALC 271mg

---

SHRIMP PAD THAI

Pad Thai is the "safe" choice of Thai takeout. But it's also a delicious version of a real Thai dish. Its flavors are complex—salty, slightly fishy-fermenty, a tad sweet. The main nutrition killer here is sodium (well over a full-day's worth in a single serving), found mostly in the fish sauce that's key to the flavor. But a small amount of this fragrant staple provides the right notes without overpowering the American palate. We keep the palate intrigued with an interesting interplay of textures: silky noodles, crisp bean sprouts, and crunchy nuts.

NUTRITION INFORMATION

CALORIES
Takeout: 668
Ours: 462

FAT
Takeout: 14.5g
Ours: 16.1g

SATURATED FAT
Takeout: 2.5g
Ours: 1.6g

SODIUM
Takeout: 2,771mg
Ours: 779mg

Ready in 25 min.

Quick & Easy
Shrimp Pad Thai

Hands-on time: 25 min. Total time: 25 min.

8 ounces uncooked flat rice noodles (pad Thai noodles)
2 tablespoons dark brown sugar
2 tablespoons lower-sodium soy sauce
1½ tablespoons fish sauce
1½ tablespoons fresh lime juice
1 tablespoon Sriracha or chili garlic sauce
3 tablespoons canola oil
1 cup (2-inch) green onion pieces
8 ounces peeled and deveined large shrimp
5 garlic cloves, minced
1 cup fresh bean sprouts
¼ cup chopped unsalted, dry-roasted peanuts
3 tablespoons thinly sliced fresh basil

1. Cook noodles according to package directions; drain.
2. While water for noodles comes to a boil, combine sugar and next 4 ingredients in a small bowl.
3. Heat a large skillet or wok over medium-high heat. Add oil to pan; swirl to coat. Add onion pieces, shrimp, and garlic; stir-fry 2 minutes or until shrimp are almost done. Add cooked noodles; toss to combine. Stir in sauce; cook 1 minute, stirring constantly to combine. Arrange about 1 cup noodle mixture on each of 4 plates; top each serving with ¼ cup bean sprouts, 1 tablespoon peanuts, and about 2 teaspoons basil. Yield: 4 servings.

CALORIES 462; FAT 16.1g (sat 1.6g, mono 9.1g, poly 4.8g); PROTEIN 15.8g; CARB 64.3g; FIBER 2.6g; CHOL 86mg; IRON 3.7mg; SODIUM 779mg; CALC 90mg

CHICKEN SOUVLAKI

The lure of Greek takeout begins at the altar of the gyro—hot slivers carved from cones of lamb or other meat that turn and sizzle in the windows of small restaurants across the land, calling out to passersby. But garlicky grilled souvlaki can be even better. Our version stars lean chicken breast, served in pitas with a tangy sesame-yogurt-cucumber sauce. The sauce flavors the sandwich but does not drown it, keeping calories in check. The astronomical sodium in the takeout probably comes from simple added salt, easily adjusted at home. We use just ¼ teaspoon, cutting sodium by 75%. Garlicky-herby-savory deliciousness: unchanged.

NUTRITION INFORMATION

CALORIES
Takeout: 492
Ours: 390

FAT
Takeout: 16g
Ours: 8g

SATURATED FAT
Takeout: 3.6g
Ours: 1.3g

SODIUM
Takeout: 1,553mg
Ours: 398mg

Ready in 25 min.

A SMART PORTION SIZE OF THE TANGY SESAME-YOGURT-CUCUMBER SAUCE HELPS KEEP CALORIES IN CHECK.

Quick & Easy
Chicken Souvlaki Pitas with Tahini Sauce

Hands-on time: 25 min. Total time: 25 min.

6 tablespoons plain fat-free Greek yogurt
2 tablespoons shredded cucumber
1½ tablespoons tahini (roasted sesame seed paste)
5 teaspoons fresh lemon juice, divided
5 garlic cloves, minced
1 tablespoon extra-virgin olive oil
1 teaspoon dried oregano
¼ teaspoon salt
¼ teaspoon freshly ground black pepper
1 pound skinless, boneless chicken breast halves, cut into 1-inch pieces
Cooking spray
4 (6-inch) pitas, cut in half
1 cup shredded iceberg lettuce
½ cup thinly sliced red onion
16 (¼-inch-thick) slices cucumber
16 (¼-inch-thick) slices plum tomato

1. Combine yogurt, shredded cucumber, tahini, 1 tablespoon lemon juice, and garlic in a small bowl; set aside.
2. Combine remaining 2 teaspoons lemon juice, olive oil, and next 4 ingredients in a small bowl. Heat a grill pan over medium-high heat. Thread chicken pieces evenly onto 4 (8-inch) skewers. Coat grill pan with cooking spray. Add chicken to pan; cook 10 minutes or until done, turning every 2 minutes. Remove chicken from skewers.
3. Divide chicken evenly among pita halves. Fill each pita half with 2 tablespoons lettuce, 1 tablespoon onion, 2 cucumber slices, 2 tomato slices, and 1 tablespoon sauce. Yield: 4 servings (serving size: 2 stuffed pita halves).

CALORIES 390; FAT 8g (sat 1.3g, mono 4g, poly 2.1g); PROTEIN 37.3g; CARB 419g; FIBER 2.9g; CHOL 66mg; IRON 4.3mg; SODIUM 398mg; CALC 103mg

---

RECIPE MAKEOVER
THE COMPLETELY DREAMY COCONUT CREAM PIE

We fluff up the flavor, deploy an Italian meringue, and re-create a blue-ribbon dessert that won't march your diet into madness.

When it comes to creamy, dreamy coconut pie, never settle for anything less than mile-high. But even when the traditional version comes across so light and fluffy, it's supplying as much as a quarter of your 2,000-calorie daily requirement and 75% of your saturated fat limit. That's a pie *too* high.

To rein things in, our Test Kitchens used a smart technique of steeping a combo of milk and half-and-half with real coconut and vanilla bean, drawing out richer flavor than you'd get from bottled extracts. The coconut is then strained out, along with most of its calories and saturated fat. A creamy, fluffy Italian meringue and a shower of toasted coconut seal this delectable deal with a top Test Kitchens rating, half the calories, 65% less saturated fat, and flavor even better than the original.

continued

Coconut Cream Pie

Hands-on time: 34 min. Total time: 4 hr. 10 min.

½ (14.1-ounce) package refrigerated pie dough
Cooking spray
2 cups 1% low-fat milk
1 cup half-and-half
1½ cups flaked sweetened coconut
1 vanilla bean, split lengthwise
⅔ cup sugar
⅓ cup cornstarch
¼ teaspoon salt
4 large eggs yolks
2 tablespoons butter
3 large egg whites, at room temperature
½ teaspoon cream of tartar
½ cup sugar
¼ cup water
¼ cup flaked sweetened coconut, toasted

1. Preheat oven to 425°.
2. Fit dough into a 9-inch pie plate coated with cooking spray. Fold edges under; flute. Line dough with foil; arrange pie weights or dried beans on foil. Bake at 425° for 10 minutes; remove weights and foil, and bake an additional 10 minutes or until golden. Cool completely on a wire rack.
3. Combine milk and half-and-half in a medium saucepan over medium heat.

Add 1½ cups coconut. Scrape seeds from vanilla bean; stir seeds and pod into milk mixture. Bring milk mixture to a simmer; immediately remove from heat. Cover and let stand 15 minutes. Strain through a cheesecloth-lined sieve into a bowl. Gather edges of cheesecloth; squeeze over bowl to release moisture. Discard solids.
4. Combine ⅔ cup sugar, cornstarch, salt, and egg yolks in a large bowl, stirring with a whisk. Gradually add milk mixture to egg yolk mixture, stirring constantly. Return milk mixture to pan; bring to a boil, whisking constantly. Remove from heat. Add butter; whisk until smooth. Place pan in a large ice-filled bowl for 6 minutes, stirring to

cool. Pour into prepared crust. Cover and chill at least 1 hour.
5. Place 3 egg whites and cream of tartar in a large bowl; beat with a mixer at high speed until soft peaks form. Combine ½ cup sugar and ¼ cup water in a saucepan; bring to a boil. Cook, without stirring, until candy thermometer registers 250°. Pour hot sugar syrup in a thin stream over egg whites, beating at high speed until thick. Spread meringue over pie. Cover and refrigerate at least 2 hours. Top with toasted coconut before serving. Yield: 12 servings (serving size: 1 wedge).

CALORIES 266; **FAT** 11.5g (sat 5.7g, mono 1.3g, poly 0.3g); **PROTEIN** 4.2g; **CARB** 36.4g; **FIBER** 0.3g; **CHOL** 79mg; **IRON** 0.4mg; **SODIUM** 189mg; **CALC** 79mg

OLD WAY	OUR WAY
478 calories per serving	266 calories per serving
32 grams total fat	11.5 grams total fat
16 grams saturated fat	5.7 grams saturated fat
Three cups half-and-half	Two parts low-fat milk; one part half-and-half
Flavor from a bottled coconut extract	Flavor from real coconut flakes and vanilla bean
Heavy whipped cream topping	Light, fluffy Italian meringue topping

PERFECTING THE ITALIAN MERINGUE

An Italian meringue is a fluffy, stable mixture made by adding boiling sugar syrup—instead of granulated sugar—to whipped egg whites. This heats the egg to a safe temperature. The mixture stands in as a yummy, lighter replacement for a topping made with whipped cream.

1. Before beating, make sure both the bowl and egg whites are at room temperature, as chilled egg whites take longer to reach full volume.

2. The sugar syrup is ready when the candy thermometer reaches 250°.

3. With the mixer running, carefully and slowly pour the syrup in a thin, steady stream into the egg whites, whipping constantly.

4. Continue whipping until the meringue is smooth, satiny, and completely cool, and stiff peaks have formed. Spread immediately on pie.

A LITTLE ODE TO THE OTHER LEMON

The Meyer lemon, that is—a fragrant, cold-weather fruit worth searching for.

Of the citrus fruits, the lemon may seem the most unchanging—until you meet the Meyer. This tangy-sweet citrus is thought to be a cross between a regular lemon and a mandarin orange (though exact origins of citrus are often obscure because the fruits crossbreed like mad). The best, freshest examples have beautifully unblemished, taut skin that ranges (as do its flesh and juice) from sunny yellow to a deeper, egg-yolk yellow-orange. The Meyer is plump and full of juice and has thin skin. And, most important, it doesn't taste like an ordinary lemon. Its flavor ranges from a teensy bit to a lot sweeter and has a floral essence that's unlike that of any other citrus. Imagine a cocktail of fresh lemon juice mixed with sweet orange juice and a whiff of jasmine blossom. The juice is lovely in beverages, salads, entrées, and desserts, adding depth that regular lemons don't have. The grated rind releases a perfume that adds complexity to desserts, even vegetables. That said, the Meyer lacks the acid punch that regular lemons give to sauces and desserts—it's more delicate, more nuanced.

Quick & Easy

Meyer Lemon Chicken Piccata

Hands-on time: 36 min. Total time: 36 min.

2 (8-ounce) skinless, boneless chicken breast halves
1/2 teaspoon kosher salt
1/4 teaspoon freshly ground black pepper
1/4 cup all-purpose flour
2 tablespoons unsalted butter, divided
1/3 cup sauvignon blanc or other crisp, tart white wine
1/2 cup fat-free, lower-sodium chicken broth
1/3 cup fresh Meyer lemon juice (about 3 lemons)
2 tablespoons capers, rinsed and drained
1/4 cup chopped fresh flat-leaf parsley

1. Split chicken breast halves in half horizontally to form 4 cutlets. Place each cutlet between 2 sheets of heavy-duty plastic wrap; pound each cutlet to 1/4-inch thickness using a meat mallet or small heavy skillet. Sprinkle cutlets evenly with salt and pepper. Place flour in a shallow dish; dredge cutlets in flour.
2. Melt 1 tablespoon butter in a large skillet over medium-high heat. Add 2 cutlets to pan, and sauté 2 minutes. Turn cutlets over; sauté 1 minute. Remove cutlets from pan. Repeat procedure with remaining 1 tablespoon butter and 2 cutlets.
3. Add wine to pan, and bring to a boil, scraping pan to loosen browned bits. Cook 1 minute or until liquid almost evaporates. Stir in chicken broth; bring to a boil. Cook until broth mixture is reduced to 2 tablespoons (about 4 minutes). Stir in juice and capers. Serve over chicken. Sprinkle with parsley. Yield: 4 servings (serving size: 1 cutlet, 2 tablespoons sauce, and 1 tablespoon parsley).

CALORIES 214; **FAT** 7.3g (sat 4.1g, mono 1.9g, poly 0.6g); **PROTEIN** 27.5g; **CARB** 8.5g; **FIBER** 0.6g; **CHOL** 81mg; **IRON** 1.6mg; **SODIUM** 502mg; **CALC** 26mg

---

Sparkling Meyer Lemon Cocktail

Hands-on time: 10 min. Total time: 46 min.

1 cup water
1/3 cup sugar
1 rosemary sprig
1 cup fresh Meyer lemon juice, chilled (about 8 lemons)
1/3 cup chilled vodka
2 cups chilled prosecco or other sparkling wine, chilled

1. Combine first 3 ingredients in a microwave-safe liquid measuring cup. Microwave at HIGH 2½ minutes; stir until sugar dissolves. Let stand 10 minutes; discard rosemary. Chill.
2. Combine sugar mixture, juice, vodka, and prosecco, stirring gently. Serve immediately. Yield: 6 servings (serving size: about 2/3 cup).

CALORIES 147; **FAT** 0g; **PROTEIN** 0.2g; **CARB** 16g; **FIBER** 0.2g; **CHOL** 0mg; **IRON** 0.1mg; **SODIUM** 1mg; **CALC** 4mg

---

SELECTING MEYERS

Meyer lemons are relatively rare and not always in the best condition when you do come upon them. Often, you'll find lemons that are too soft, or dry and shriveled. Avoid these. What you want are plump, shiny-skinned fruits that are firm but not hard and seemingly heavy for their size—a good sign, as with any citrus, that they're full of juice. You can store Meyer lemons in a plastic bag in the refrigerator for up to two weeks; when they start feeling squishy, though, they've passed their prime.

Seared Scallops with Meyer Lemon Beurre Blanc

Hands-on time: 32 min. Total time: 40 min.

Ask for "dry" scallops—this means they haven't soaked in a salty brine. And they'll release less moisture in the pan as they cook, making it easier to get a gorgeous golden crust.

⅔ cup fresh Meyer lemon juice (about 6 lemons)
⅓ cup dry white wine
3 tablespoons minced shallots
2 thyme sprigs
3 tablespoons chilled butter, cut into pieces
¾ teaspoon sugar
½ teaspoon salt, divided
¼ teaspoon freshly ground black pepper, divided
Cooking spray
1½ pounds dry sea scallops
1½ teaspoons chopped fresh thyme (optional)

1. Combine first 4 ingredients in a small heavy saucepan over medium-high heat; bring to a boil. Cook until reduced to about ¼ cup (about 8 minutes). Remove from heat; discard thyme sprigs. Add butter, 1 piece at a time, stirring constantly with a whisk until butter is thoroughly incorporated. Strain mixture through a fine sieve over a bowl, pressing to release all of the sauce; discard solids. Stir in sugar, ¼ teaspoon salt, and ⅛ teaspoon pepper.
2. Heat a large cast-iron skillet over high heat. Coat pan with cooking spray. Sprinkle both sides of scallops evenly with remaining ¼ teaspoon salt and remaining ⅛ teaspoon pepper. Add scallops to pan; cook 2 minutes. Turn scallops over; cook 1 minute or until desired degree of doneness. Serve scallops with sauce; sprinkle with chopped thyme, if desired. Yield: 4 servings (serving size: 4½ ounces scallops, and 2 tablespoons sauce).

CALORIES 247; **FAT** 10g (sat 5.6g, mono 2.3g, poly 0.8g); **PROTEIN** 29g; **CARB** 10g; **FIBER** 0.2g; **CHOL** 79mg; **IRON** 0.7mg; **SODIUM** 633mg; **CALC** 52mg

Meyer Lemon Curd Tart

Hands-on time: 46 min. Total time: 4 hr. 52 min.

Crust:
⅓ cup macadamia nuts
¼ cup flaked sweetened coconut
2 tablespoons brown sugar
⅛ teaspoon salt
36 vanilla wafers
3 tablespoons butter, melted
Filling:
½ cup granulated sugar
2½ teaspoons cornstarch
Dash of salt
½ cup fresh Meyer lemon juice (about 5 lemons)
3 large egg yolks
2 tablespoons butter
½ teaspoon grated Meyer lemon rind
Meringue:
3 large egg whites
⅛ teaspoon salt
¼ cup granulated sugar
¼ cup water

1. Preheat oven to 400°.
2. To prepare crust, place first 5 ingredients in a food processor; process until finely ground. With processor on, drizzle 3 tablespoons melted butter through food chute, and process until blended. Press crumb mixture into bottom and up sides of a 9-inch metal tart pan. Bake at 400° for 10 minutes or until toasted. Cool on a wire rack.
3. To prepare filling, combine ½ cup granulated sugar, cornstarch, and dash of salt in a medium heavy saucepan, stirring with a whisk. Stir in lemon juice and egg yolks; bring to a boil over medium heat, stirring constantly with a whisk. Reduce heat, and simmer 1 minute or until slightly thick, stirring constantly. Remove from heat; add 2 tablespoons butter and rind, stirring gently until butter melts. Spoon mixture into a medium bowl; cool slightly. Place plastic wrap directly over surface of lemon curd, and chill at least 4 hours or overnight (mixture will thicken as it cools).

4. Preheat broiler.
5. Spoon curd evenly into prepared crust. To prepare meringue, place 3 egg whites and ⅛ teaspoon salt in a large bowl, and beat with a mixer at high speed until soft peaks form. Combine ¼ cup granulated sugar and ¼ cup water in a saucepan; bring to a boil. Cook, without stirring, until a thermometer registers 238°. Pour hot syrup in a thin stream over egg whites, beating until stiff peaks form. Spread meringue over tart. Broil 30 seconds or until lightly browned. Yield: 10 servings (serving size: 1 wedge).

CALORIES 246; **FAT** 13.2g (sat 5.6g, mono 5.3g, poly 0.5g); **PROTEIN** 2.8g; **CARB** 31.6g; **FIBER** 1.1g; **CHOL** 80mg; **IRON** 0.8mg; **SODIUM** 183mg; **CALC** 24mg

Fennel Salad with Lemon

Hands-on time: 25 min. Total time: 1 hr. 25 min.

¼ cup coarsely chopped fresh parsley
2 fennel bulbs, trimmed, halved, and cut into thin vertical slices
1 shallot, halved and cut into thin vertical slices
2 tablespoons extra-virgin olive oil
1 teaspoon sugar
½ teaspoon kosher salt
¼ teaspoon freshly ground black pepper
⅔ cup Meyer lemon sections (about 3 lemons)
2 ounces goat cheese, cut into 6 slices

1. Combine first 3 ingredients in a bowl. Drizzle mixture with oil; sprinkle with sugar, salt, and pepper. Toss. Add lemon sections; toss gently to combine. Cover and chill 1 hour. Top with cheese. Yield: 6 servings (serving size: 1 cup salad and 1 cheese slice).

CALORIES 107; **FAT** 6.9g (sat 2.1g, mono 3.8g, poly 0.8g); **PROTEIN** 3.3g; **CARB** 10.5g; **FIBER** 3.3g; **CHOL** 4mg; **IRON** 1.2mg; **SODIUM** 238mg; **CALC** 65mg

Quick & Easy • Vegetarian
Roasted Asparagus with Browned Butter

Hands-on time: 14 min. Total time: 25 min.

1 pound asparagus spears, trimmed
1 tablespoon olive oil
½ teaspoon kosher salt
¼ teaspoon black pepper
2 tablespoons butter
2 tablespoons fresh Meyer lemon juice
1½ teaspoons chopped fresh thyme
1 teaspoon grated Meyer lemon rind

1. Preheat oven to 450°.
2. Place asparagus in a roasting pan; drizzle with oil. Sprinkle evenly with salt and pepper. Bake at 450° for 8 minutes or until crisp-tender.
3. Melt butter in a small skillet over medium heat; cook 3 minutes or until lightly browned, shaking pan occasionally. Remove from heat; stir in juice. Drizzle butter mixture over asparagus; toss well to coat. Sprinkle thyme and rind over asparagus. Yield: 4 servings (serving size: about 3 ounces).

CALORIES 107; FAT 9.2g (sat 4.1g, mono 4g, poly 0.7g); PROTEIN 2.6g; CARB 5.8g; FIBER 2.6g; CHOL 15mg; IRON 0.5mg; SODIUM 220mg; CALC 29mg

SUBSTITUTIONS

If you can't find Meyer lemons, you can use other citrus fruits. The flavor won't be as complex but will still be tasty. For every ¼ cup Meyer lemon juice, try 3 tablespoons lemon juice plus 1 tablespoon orange juice plus ½ teaspoon sugar. For fruit sections (as in our salad), try tangerines. For rind, just substitute regular lemon rind in the same quantity.

COOKING CLASS
TODAY'S LESSON: ROAST CHICKEN

Many classic roast chicken recipes call for steady heat throughout, or start high and then reduce the heat. We discovered something different, and it yielded our juiciest bird ever. We baked at 350° for about 45 minutes, and then cranked the heat up to 450° for the last few minutes. The chicken browned beautifully, and the high-temp finish speeded the cooking. Have a meat thermometer handy so you can remove the chicken from the oven the moment it's done.

Kid Friendly
Classic Roast Chicken

Hands-on time: 30 min. Total time: 1 hr. 40 min.

Be prepared to turn on your vent: The high-heat finishing may generate some smoke. Allow the chicken to stand at least 10 minutes before you slice it so the juices redistribute throughout the meat.

1 (4-pound) whole roasting chicken
2 teaspoons unsalted butter, softened
1½ teaspoons minced fresh thyme
1 teaspoon paprika
1 teaspoon ground coriander
2 teaspoons extra-virgin olive oil
¾ teaspoon salt
¼ teaspoon freshly ground black pepper
2 garlic cloves, minced
3 shallots, peeled and halved
3 thyme sprigs
1 lemon, quartered

1. Preheat oven to 350°.
2. Discard giblets and neck from chicken. Starting at neck cavity, loosen skin from breasts and drumsticks by inserting fingers, gently pushing between skin and meat.
3. Combine butter and next 7 ingredients in a small bowl. Rub mixture under loosened skin over flesh; rub over top of skin. Tie ends of legs together with twine. Lift wing tips up and over back; tuck under chicken. Place chicken, breast side up, on a broiler pan; place in roasting pan. Place shallots, thyme sprigs, and lemon in cavity of chicken.

4. Bake at 350° for 45 minutes. Increase oven temperature to 450° (do not remove chicken); bake at 450° for 15 minutes or until a thermometer inserted into meaty part of leg registers 165°. Remove chicken from pan; let stand 10 minutes. Discard skin. Carve chicken. Yield: 4 servings (serving size: 1 breast half or 1 leg quarter).

CALORIES 278; FAT 13.6g (sat 4.1g, mono 5.7g, poly 2.5g); PROTEIN 35.7g; CARB 0.9g; FIBER 0.3g; CHOL 111mg; IRON 1.9mg; SODIUM 563mg; CALC 23mg

Kid Friendly
Italian-Seasoned Roast Chicken Breasts

Hands-on time: 18 min. Total time: 53 min.

Rosemary, fennel seeds, lemon, olive oil, and garlic give chicken Mediterranean flavor. Lean breast meat needs to be shielded as it cooks, so leave the skin on (and enjoy it—see Nutrition Note, page 70).

1 tablespoon chopped fresh rosemary
1 teaspoon grated lemon rind
2 tablespoons fresh lemon juice
4 teaspoons extra-virgin olive oil
½ teaspoon fennel seeds, crushed
½ teaspoon salt
¼ teaspoon freshly ground black pepper
3 garlic cloves, minced
4 bone-in chicken breast halves (about 3 pounds)
Cooking spray

continued

1. Preheat oven to 425°.

2. Combine first 8 ingredients in a bowl, stirring well. Loosen skin from chicken by inserting fingers, gently pushing between skin and meat. Rub rosemary mixture under loosened skin over flesh; rub over top of skin. Place chicken, bone side down, on a broiler pan coated with cooking spray. Coat skin lightly with cooking spray. Bake at 425° for 35 minutes or until a thermometer inserted into thickest portion of the breast registers 155°. Remove chicken from pan; let stand 10 minutes. Yield: 4 servings (serving size: 1 breast half).

CALORIES 240; FAT 12.2g (sat 2.8g, mono 6.3g, poly 2.1g); PROTEIN 29.5g; CARB 1.8g; FIBER 0.3g; CHOL 82mg; IRON 1.2mg; SODIUM 366mg; CALC 24mg

NUTRITION NOTE

Since chicken breast meat is low in calories and saturated fat, you can eat the skin and still keep saturated fat within allowable limits. If you like dark meat, which is higher in saturated fat, remove and discard the skin.

Asian-Glazed Chicken Thighs

Hands-on time: 22 min. Total time: 1 hr. 52 min.

Thigh meat is forgiving, even if overcooked. In fact, it becomes more tender when cooked to at least 160°. Soy sauce, garlic, and honey combine for a tangy, salty, sweet counterbalance to the heat of chile paste. The tasty glaze gives these chicken thighs a mahogany sheen. Rich thigh meat is higher in fat than lean white meat, so the thighs stay moist even when they're roasted without skin. Garnish with fresh cilantro and sliced green onions, if desired.

⅓ cup rice vinegar

¼ cup lower-sodium soy sauce

3 tablespoons honey

2 tablespoons dark sesame oil

1½ tablespoons chile paste (such as sambal oelek)

10 garlic cloves, minced

12 bone-in chicken thighs, skinned

Cooking spray

½ teaspoon salt

1. Combine vinegar, soy sauce, honey, sesame oil, chile paste, and garlic, stirring until honey dissolves. Pour vinegar mixture into a zip-top plastic bag. Add chicken to bag; seal. Marinate in refrigerator 1 hour, turning occasionally. Remove chicken from bag, reserving marinade.

2. Preheat oven to 425°.

3. Place reserved marinade in a small saucepan over medium-high heat; bring to a boil. Cook 2 minutes or until syrupy, stirring occasionally. Place chicken on a broiler pan coated with cooking spray, and place in a roasting pan. Baste chicken with reserved marinade; sprinkle evenly with salt. Bake at 425° for 10 minutes; baste. Bake an additional 10 minutes; baste. Discard remaining marinade. Bake an additional 10 minutes or until done. Let stand 5 minutes before serving. Yield: 6 servings (serving size: 2 thighs).

CALORIES 306; FAT 15.9g (sat 3.8g, mono 6.1g, poly 4.5g); PROTEIN 27.9g; CARB 12g; FIBER 0.2g; CHOL 99mg; IRON 1.7mg; SODIUM 646mg; CALC 24mg

HOW TO ROAST A WHOLE CHICKEN

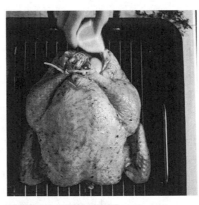

TRUSS
Simply cross the legs and tie them together with kitchen twine. Next, lift the wing tips up and tuck them under the bird. Once cooked, discard the twine, and the chicken will hold this tidy shape.

SEASON AND ROAST
Season the flesh, leaving the skin intact. (Season the skin too for a nice presentation.) Then place the chicken on a broiler pan in a roasting pan. Elevating the bird allows air to circulate and promotes even browning.

TEMPERATURE CHECK
Cooking to the proper temperature is the most critical step. Insert a thermometer into a meaty part of the leg (avoiding the bone). When the temperature reaches 165°, pull the bird from the oven. Let rest 10 minutes.

HAMBURGER HAS A NEW HELPER

By Mark Bittman

The less-meat approach turns a single burger's worth of ground beef into the flavorful center of dishes that are loaded with vegetable goodness.

The convenience of ground beef is enormously appealing, especially for full-on meat-eaters: Press a handful into a burger and away you go. Try adding vegetables, grains, or beans to the patty, however, and things can quickly fall apart. Literally. You can do it, of course (and I have), but forget about simplicity or speed with the high-vegetable-content burger.

Let's move past the burger proposition but stick with the ground beef. I take the amount of ground beef you might find in a single typical backyard burger—8 ounces—and then reach for my skillet. I build in a load of colorful vegetables, sauté away, and finish the dish under the broiler or in a hot oven for extra flavor. The convenience, the meat, the lack of mess—it's all still there. Only now you've got a bunch of other good stuff in the mix.

The first dish is a gorgeous, violet-tinted hash. To make the texture more interesting, the beets and cabbage are shredded (to speed up the prep time, by all means use a food processor). This helps them cook quickly so that some parts stay sort of crisp while other parts get downright silky. Although this hash stays moist, you can try to crisp it a bit if you want—walk away from the pan and let it do its thing on the stove. No stirring! After a few minutes, break the hash up a bit, flip the pieces over, and pop the skillet under the broiler for a final frizzle.

For the second recipe, I turn to another retro classic: tamale pie.

Instead of cornmeal, though, I use masa harina for the topping. Because this is the same flour used for tamales, it has that distinctive tortilla-like, limey flavor. (Masa harina is available in almost all supermarkets now.) The water-based batter couldn't be easier and "proofs" while the filling (a mixture of ground beef, chiles, tomatillos, and lima beans) comes together in the pan. Once you dollop and smear on the topping, into the oven it goes while you make a salad.

In fact, a salad is all you need to turn either of these dishes into a full meal. But if you plan a little ahead, a baked potato is a natural companion for the hash. Since the tamale is more substantial, a splash of salsa is probably the only side you need. When you cook hamburger like this, the only thing left to do is help yourself.

A HASH AND A TAMALE PIE: RETRO CLASSICS THAT ARE SKILLET-COOKED, LIGHTENED UP, EASY, AND GOOD.

Quick & Easy

Red Flannel Hash

Hands-on time: 30 min. Total time: 30 min.

2 tablespoons olive oil
8 ounces ground sirloin
1 cup chopped red onion
1 teaspoon kosher salt, divided
½ teaspoon freshly ground black pepper
3 garlic cloves, minced
2 cups shredded red cabbage (about ½ small head)
2 cups grated beet (about 3 medium beets)
½ cup water
2 tablespoons cider vinegar
¼ cup plain 2% reduced-fat Greek yogurt
2 tablespoons chopped fresh dill

1. Heat a large skillet over medium-high heat. Add oil to pan; swirl to coat. Add beef to pan; cook 4 minutes, stirring to crumble. Add onion, ½ teaspoon salt, pepper, and garlic; sauté 5 minutes or until translucent. Add cabbage, beet, ½ cup water, vinegar, and remaining ½ teaspoon salt; cook about 10 minutes or until cabbage begins to wilt and liquid almost evaporates. Spoon 1¼ cups hash into each of 4 bowls; top each serving with 1 tablespoon yogurt and 1½ teaspoons dill. Yield: 4 servings.

CALORIES 187; FAT 9.8g (sat 2.2g, mono 6g, poly 1g); PROTEIN 14.3g; CARB 12.7g; FIBER 2.9g; CHOL 31mg; IRON 1.9mg; SODIUM 577mg; CALC 50mg

Green Chile Tamale Pie

Hands-on time: 20 min. Total time: 1 hr. 10 min.

1 cup masa harina
1 teaspoon kosher salt, divided
¼ teaspoon ground red pepper
1 cup boiling water
1 tablespoon olive oil
8 ounces ground sirloin
1½ cups chopped onion
3 garlic cloves, minced
1 poblano chile, seeded and chopped
½ teaspoon freshly ground black pepper
8 ounces tomatillos (about 8 small), chopped
1 cup frozen baby lima beans
2 tablespoons butter, melted
½ teaspoon baking powder
¼ cup (1 ounce) crumbled queso fresco
2 tablespoons chopped fresh cilantro
4 lime wedges

1. Preheat oven to 400°.
2. Combine masa harina, ¼ teaspoon salt, and ground red pepper, stirring well with a whisk. Add 1 cup boiling water to masa mixture, and stir until a soft dough forms. Cover until ready to use.
3. Heat a 9-inch cast-iron skillet over medium-high heat. Add olive oil to pan; swirl to coat. Add beef to pan; cook 5 minutes or until browned, stirring to crumble. Add onion, garlic, poblano chile, remaining ¾ teaspoon

continued

salt, and black pepper to pan; sauté 5 minutes or until onion is tender, stirring frequently. Add tomatillos and lima beans to pan, and cook 2 minutes. Remove from heat.

4. Add butter and baking powder to masa mixture, stirring until smooth. Dollop batter over filling, and spread into an even layer. Cover pan with foil; bake at 400° for 30 minutes. Uncover and bake an additional 10 minutes or until crust is lightly browned around edges. Remove from oven; let stand 3 minutes. Sprinkle with crumbled queso fresco and cilantro; serve with lime wedges. Yield: 4 servings (serving size: 1½ cups pie, 1 tablespoon queso fresco, and 1 lime wedge).

CALORIES 378; FAT 15.2g (sat 6.2g, mono 5.7g, poly 1.9g); PROTEIN 20.5g; CARB 43.4g; FIBER 8.6g; CHOL 50mg; IRON 5mg; SODIUM 643mg; CALC 154mg

WHAT TO EAT RIGHT NOW

TROPICAL FRUIT

The fantastic armored pineapple, with its Sideshow Bob hairdo, is almost as common in supermarkets as the basic navel orange, yet retains a happy essence of the exotic. So, too, is the rosy, orange-fleshed papaya, with its odd slimy seeds and sweet whiff of tropical funk (which is beautifully cut by a spritz of lime juice).

Yes, eating fresh and local is good, but in a month when fresh and local amounts to turnips in some parts of the country, God bless these breezy out-of-towners.

Make sure you buy ripe fruit, though. Papayas yellow as they ripen: Look for full, yellowish skin with slightly soft flesh for the best musky melon flavor. If the base of a pineapple is a red-orange color (even if the rest of the fruit is green), it was picked at the proper time, signaling a juicy texture. Hold the pineapple to your nose and check for a sweet aroma, too.

Make Ahead

Spicy Crab-Papaya Salad

Hands-on time: 20 min. Total time: 50 min.

Combine 1½ cups diced peeled papaya, ⅓ cup thinly sliced green onions, ¼ cup finely chopped celery, 1 finely chopped jalapeño pepper, and 1 pound lump crabmeat (shell pieces removed). Combine 3 tablespoons canola oil, 2 tablespoons cider vinegar, 2 teaspoons sugar, 1 teaspoon Dijon mustard, ¼ teaspoon freshly ground black pepper, and ⅛ teaspoon salt, stirring with a whisk. Drizzle vinegar mixture over crab mixture; toss. Chill. Yield: 4 servings (serving size: 1 cup).

CALORIES 246; FAT 12.6g (sat 1.1g, mono 7g, poly 3.8g); PROTEIN 23.3g; CARB 8.7g; FIBER 1.5g; CHOL 113mg; IRON 1.3mg; SODIUM 430mg; CALC 141mg

Quick & Easy

Tamarind Pork with Pineapple-Ginger Chutney

Hands-on time: 30 min. Total time: 40 min.

Tamarind is a pod containing sticky, tart pulp and large seeds. Tamarind paste is more convenient, as it's seedless. Buy it at Asian, Latin, or Indian markets. Or substitute 2 tablespoons lime juice for less-complex flavor.

Chutney:
1½ teaspoons butter
1 cup chopped onion
1 tablespoon grated peeled fresh ginger
1 serrano chile, seeded and minced
3 cups chopped pineapple
¼ cup packed light brown sugar
2 tablespoons gold rum
¼ teaspoon salt
¼ cup chopped fresh cilantro
⅛ teaspoon ground red pepper

Pork:
1 tablespoon sweet chili sauce
1 tablespoon lower-sodium soy sauce
1 teaspoon rice vinegar
2 teaspoons tamarind paste
2 (1-pound) pork tenderloins
¾ teaspoon salt
¾ teaspoon freshly ground black pepper
1 tablespoon canola oil

1. To prepare chutney, melt butter in a small saucepan over medium heat. Add onion, ginger, and chile to pan; cover and cook 6 minutes or until onion is tender. Uncover. Stir in pineapple and next 3 ingredients; bring to a boil. Reduce heat, and simmer, uncovered, 20 minutes or until pineapple is tender, stirring occasionally. Cool 20 minutes; stir in cilantro and red pepper.

2. Preheat oven to 400°.

3. To prepare pork, combine chili sauce and next 3 ingredients, stirring to combine. Reserve half of soy mixture. Heat a cast-iron grill pan over medium-high heat. Sprinkle pork with ¾ teaspoon salt and black pepper; coat pork with oil. Add pork to pan; sauté 4 minutes on 1 side or until browned. Brush pork with half of soy mixture; turn pork over. Place pan in oven; bake at 400° for 16 minutes or until a thermometer inserted into thickest portion of pork registers 155° (slightly pink). Remove pork from pan; let stand 10 minutes. Brush pork evenly with reserved soy mixture. Slice pork crosswise into ½-inch-thick medallions. Serve with chutney. Yield: 8 servings (serving size: 3 ounces pork and about ¼ cup chutney).

CALORIES 227; FAT 5.6g (sat 1.6g, mono 2.4g, poly 1g); PROTEIN 23.1g; CARB 19.1g; FIBER 1.4g; CHOL 64mg; IRON 1.4mg; SODIUM 460mg; CALC 26mg

Tropical Sherbet

Hands-on time: 25 min. Total time: 2 hr. 55 min.

You don't hear much about sherbet these days, but this recipe will cause you to reconsider the milky, fruity 1970s staple. Full-fat coconut milk adds creaminess and tames the bright tang of pineapple, papaya, and fresh lime. If you want a modern twist on grown-up party punch, drizzle a couple of tablespoons of golden rum over the top of each serving.

²/₃ cup sugar
²/₃ cup water
3 cups cubed pineapple
1 cup cubed papaya
³/₄ cup coconut milk
1 tablespoon fresh lime juice
1 tablespoon light-colored corn syrup
⅛ teaspoon salt

1. Combine sugar and ⅔ cup water in a microwave-safe dish; microwave at HIGH 4 minutes. Stir until sugar dissolves; cool completely. Combine syrup, pineapple, and remaining ingredients in a blender; process until smooth. Strain mixture though a fine sieve over a bowl; discard solids. Pour into the freezer can of an ice-cream freezer; freeze according to manufacturer's instructions. Spoon into a freezer-safe container; cover and freeze 2 hours or until firm. Yield: 6 servings (serving size: about ½ cup).

CALORIES 204; FAT 6.2g (sat 5.4g, mono 0.3g, poly 0.1g); PROTEIN 1.2g; CARB 39.4g; FIBER 1.6g; CHOL 0mg; IRON 1.2mg; SODIUM 57mg; CALC 22mg

BUDGET COOKING
FEED 4 FOR LESS THAN $10

Fragrant, heady spices infuse comforting soups, stews, and casseroles with a bit of extra warmth.

Pork Posole

$2.46 per serving, $9.84 total
Hands-on time: 25 min. Total time: 1 hr. 35 min.

1 tablespoon olive oil
12 ounces boneless pork shoulder, trimmed and cut into ½-inch pieces
1 cup chopped onion
4 garlic cloves, minced
1½ teaspoons ground cumin
½ teaspoon ground red pepper
½ cup beer
2 cups fat-free, lower-sodium chicken broth
½ cup salsa verde
1 (28-ounce) can hominy, drained
¼ cup cilantro leaves
4 radishes, sliced
4 lime wedges

1. Heat a Dutch oven over medium-high heat. Add oil; swirl to coat. Add pork; sauté 5 minutes, turning to brown on all sides. Remove pork from pan. Add onion; sauté 4 minutes, stirring occasionally. Add garlic; sauté 1 minute, stirring constantly. Return pork to pan; stir in cumin and pepper. Add beer; bring to a boil. Cook until liquid almost evaporates (about 9 minutes).
2. Add broth, salsa, and hominy; bring to a boil. Cover, reduce heat, and simmer 1 hour and 10 minutes or until pork is very tender, stirring occasionally. Ladle 1½ cups soup into each of 4 bowls. Top each serving with 1 tablespoon cilantro and 1 sliced radish. Serve with lime wedges. Yield: 4 servings.

CALORIES 315; FAT 11.5g (sat 2.8g, mono 5.6g, poly 1.6g); PROTEIN 21.2g; CARB 30.4g; FIBER 6.1g; CHOL 57mg; IRON 3.6mg; SODIUM 736mg; CALC 77mg

Spaghetti Bolognese

$1.53 per serving, $6.12 total
Hands-on time: 30 min. Total time: 40 min.

1 (³/₄-ounce) slice French bread
¼ cup 1% low-fat milk
2 teaspoons olive oil
1 cup finely chopped onion
½ cup finely chopped carrot
3 garlic cloves, minced
1 tablespoon tomato paste
2 tablespoons red wine vinegar
2 teaspoons dried oregano
½ teaspoon salt
¼ teaspoon black pepper
⅛ teaspoon ground red pepper
12 ounces ground sirloin
1 (14.5-ounce) can diced tomatoes with basil, garlic, and oregano, undrained
4 cups hot cooked spaghetti (about 8 ounces uncooked)
¼ cup (1 ounce) shaved fresh Parmigiano-Reggiano cheese

1. Pulse bread in a food processor until coarse crumbs measure ½ cup. Combine crumbs and milk in a bowl.
2. Heat olive oil in a large skillet over medium-high heat. Add onion and carrot; sauté 8 minutes. Add garlic and tomato paste; sauté 1 minute, stirring constantly. Add vinegar; cook 30 seconds. Add oregano, salt, peppers, and beef; cook 7 minutes, stirring to crumble. Stir in breadcrumb mixture and tomatoes; bring to a boil. Reduce heat, and simmer 6 minutes, stirring occasionally. Serve over spaghetti; top with cheese. Yield: 4 servings (serving size: 1 cup spaghetti, about ¾ cup sauce, and 1 tablespoon cheese).

CALORIES 440; FAT 9.6g (sat 3.4g, mono 4g, poly 1.2g); PROTEIN 29.8g; CARB 59.1g; FIBER 6g; CHOL 51mg; IRON 5.1mg; SODIUM 682mg; CALC 164mg

Moroccan Shepherd's Pie

$2.11 per serving, $8.44 total
Hands-on time: 29 min. Total time: 1 hr. 24 min.

You can also bake the entire mixture in an 8-inch square glass or ceramic baking dish. Assemble up to a day ahead, cover, refrigerate, and bake just before serving.

1 tablespoon olive oil
1 pound bone-in lamb shoulder, trimmed and cut into 1/2-inch pieces
1 teaspoon ground cumin, divided
1/2 teaspoon kosher salt, divided
1 1/2 cups chopped onion
4 garlic cloves, minced
1 tablespoon tomato paste
1 1/2 cups fat-free, lower-sodium chicken broth
1/2 cup water
1/3 cup sliced pimiento-stuffed green olives
1/3 cup raisins
2 tablespoons honey
1/2 teaspoon ground red pepper
1/4 teaspoon ground turmeric
1/2 teaspoon ground cinnamon, divided
1 cup frozen green peas
4 cups chopped peeled sweet potato
1 large egg, lightly beaten
Cooking spray

1. Preheat oven to 350°.
2. Heat a large skillet over medium-high heat. Add olive oil to pan, and swirl to coat. Sprinkle lamb evenly with 1/2 teaspoon cumin and 1/4 teaspoon salt. Add lamb to pan, and sauté 4 minutes, turning to brown on all sides. Remove lamb from pan. Add onion to pan; sauté 3 minutes, stirring occasionally. Add garlic; sauté 30 seconds, stirring constantly. Stir in tomato paste, and sauté 30 seconds, stirring frequently.
3. Add chicken broth and 1/2 cup water to pan, and bring to a boil, scraping pan to loosen browned bits. Return lamb to pan. Stir in remaining 1/2 teaspoon cumin, olives, raisins, honey, ground red pepper, and turmeric. Stir in 1/8 teaspoon cinnamon. Reduce heat, and simmer 30 minutes, stirring occasionally. Remove from heat; stir in peas.
4. Cook potato in a large saucepan of boiling water 10 minutes or until tender; drain. Cool 5 minutes. Place potato in a bowl. Sprinkle potato with remaining 1/4 teaspoon salt and remaining 3/8 teaspoon cinnamon. Beat potato with a mixer at high speed until smooth. Add egg, and beat until combined. Spoon lamb mixture into 4 (10-ounce) ramekins coated with cooking spray; spread potato mixture evenly over lamb mixture. Place ramekins on a baking sheet; bake at 350° for 25 minutes or until bubbly. Yield: 4 servings.

CALORIES 515; FAT 22g (sat 7.9g, mono 10.6g, poly 2.1g); PROTEIN 22.1g; CARB 58.3g; FIBER 79g; CHOL 105mg; IRON 4mg; SODIUM 885mg; CALC 112mg

SWEET POTATOES PROVIDE A NICE FOIL FOR THE FULL-FLAVORED LAMB, TANGY OLIVES, AND EARTHY SPICES.

Make Ahead

Vegetable Korma

$1.84 per serving, $7.36 total
Hands-on time: 15 min. Total time: 50 min.

1 1/2 tablespoons butter
1 cup chopped onion
1 tablespoon minced peeled fresh ginger
3 garlic cloves, minced
1 tablespoon tomato paste
1 1/2 teaspoons ground cumin
1/2 teaspoon ground red pepper
1/4 teaspoon ground turmeric
1/8 teaspoon ground cinnamon
1 cup frozen shelled edamame
1 (12-ounce) baking potato, peeled and diced
1 cup fat-free, lower-sodium chicken broth
1 teaspoon all-purpose flour
1 (13.5-ounce) can light coconut milk
3 cups cauliflower florets
2 cups hot cooked long-grain white rice

1. Melt butter in a saucepan over medium-high heat. Add onion, and sauté 2 minutes. Add 1 tablespoon ginger and garlic; sauté 30 seconds, stirring constantly. Stir in tomato paste and next 4 ingredients; sauté 1 minute, stirring frequently. Stir in edamame and potato. Combine chicken broth, flour, and milk, stirring until smooth. Add broth mixture to pan, and bring to a boil. Reduce heat, and simmer 8 minutes, stirring occasionally. Stir in 3 cups cauliflower, and simmer 9 minutes or until vegetables are tender. Serve over white rice. Yield: 4 servings (serving size: 1 1/4 cups vegetable mixture and 1/2 cup rice).

CALORIES 370; FAT 11.1g (sat 7.1g, mono 2.1g, poly 0.6g); PROTEIN 12.9g; CARB 57.9g; FIBER 7.6g; CHOL 11mg; IRON 4.1mg; SODIUM 238mg; CALC 95mg

Kid Friendly

Chicken Enchilada Casserole

$2.47 per serving, $9.88 total
Hands-on time: 50 min. Total time: 65 min.

Cooking spray
4 bone-in chicken thighs, skinned
1/3 cup chopped fresh cilantro, divided
1 cup frozen whole-kernel corn, thawed
1/3 cup (3 ounces) 1/3-less-fat cream cheese, softened
1/2 teaspoon ground red pepper
1/2 teaspoon ground cumin
1/4 teaspoon kosher salt
1/4 teaspoon black pepper
2 cups chopped onion, divided
6 garlic cloves, minced and divided
1 cup fat-free, lower-sodium chicken broth
2/3 cup salsa verde
1/4 cup water
2 tablespoons chopped pickled jalapeño pepper
9 (6-inch) corn tortillas
1/4 cup (1 ounce) shredded sharp cheddar cheese

1. Preheat oven to 425°.
2. Heat a large ovenproof skillet over medium-high heat. Coat pan with cooking spray. Add chicken to pan; sauté 4 minutes on each side. Place pan

in oven; bake at 425° for 10 minutes or until done. Remove chicken from pan; let stand 15 minutes. Remove meat from bones; shred. Discard bones. Place chicken in a medium bowl. Add 1½ tablespoons cilantro, corn, and next 5 ingredients to chicken; toss to combine.

3. Return pan to medium-high heat. Add ½ cup onion; sauté 5 minutes, stirring occasionally. Add 3 garlic cloves; sauté 30 seconds, stirring constantly. Add onion mixture to chicken mixture; stir to combine.

4. Combine remaining 1½ cups onion, remaining 3 garlic cloves, broth, salsa, ¼ cup water, and jalapeño in a medium saucepan over medium-high heat; bring to a boil. Reduce heat, and simmer 15 minutes, stirring occasionally. Remove from heat; let stand 10 minutes. Carefully pour mixture into a blender; add 2 tablespoons cilantro. Process until smooth.

5. Heat a large skillet over medium-high heat. Add 2 tortillas; cook 1½ minutes on each side. Remove tortillas from pan; repeat procedure with remaining tortillas. Cut tortillas into quarters.

6. Spread ½ cup salsa mixture in bottom of an 8-inch square glass or ceramic baking dish coated with cooking spray. Arrange 12 tortilla quarters over salsa mixture. Spoon half of chicken mixture over tortillas. Repeat layers, ending with tortillas. Pour remaining salsa mixture over tortillas; sprinkle evenly with cheddar cheese. Bake at 425° for 15 minutes or until bubbly and lightly browned. Top with remaining cilantro. Yield: 4 servings (serving size: about 1¾ cups).

CALORIES 371; **FAT** 12.4g (sat 5g, mono 2.9g, poly 1.8g); **PROTEIN** 23.1g; **CARB** 45.3g; **FIBER** 5.4g; **CHOL** 80mg; **IRON** 1.5mg; **SODIUM** 759mg; **CALC** 141mg

5-INGREDIENT COOKING

Easy Braised Brisket

Hands-on time: 25 min. Total time: 4 hr.

Directions: Sprinkle brisket evenly with ¾ teaspoon salt and ¼ teaspoon freshly ground black pepper. Heat a large Dutch oven over medium-high heat. Coat pan with cooking spray. Add brisket to pan; cook 10 minutes, browning on all sides. Remove brisket from pan. Add onion and oregano to pan; sauté 3 minutes. Return brisket to pan; add ½ cup water. Cover; reduce heat, and simmer 2 hours. Add olives and tomatoes; cover and cook 1 hour. Remove brisket from pan. Let stand 5 minutes. Cut brisket across grain into thin slices; return brisket slices to pan. Cover and cook over medium-low heat 30 minutes. Yield: 8 servings (serving size: about 3½ ounces brisket and about ⅓ cup sauce).

CALORIES 224; **FAT** 7.3g (sat 2.3g, mono 3.7g, poly 0.5g); **PROTEIN** 31.4g; **CARB** 6g; **FIBER** 1g; **CHOL** 58mg; **IRON** 3.2mg; **SODIUM** 557mg; **CALC** 42mg

THIS DISH REHEATS BEAUTIFULLY– AND MAY BE EVEN BETTER THE SECOND DAY.

THE FIVE INGREDIENTS

1 (2½-pound) beef brisket, trimmed

+

1½ cups chopped onion

+

1 teaspoon dried oregano

+

⅓ cup chopped pitted kalamata olives

+

1 (14.5-ounce) can diced tomatoes, undrained

DINNER TONIGHT

Here is a batch of fast weeknight menus from the *Cooking Light* Test Kitchens.

READY IN
30
MINUTES

········· *The* ·········
SHOPPING LIST

Chicken with Italian Sweet-Sour Fennel
small fennel bulb
dried rosemary
extra-virgin olive oil
fat-free, lower-sodium chicken broth
raisins
red wine vinegar
pine nuts
4 (4-ounce) chicken cutlets
dry white wine

Creamy Polenta
instant dry polenta
2 cups 2% milk
⅓-less-fat cream cheese

Herbed Green Beans
1 pound green beans
fresh thyme
fresh chives
olive oil

········· *The* ·········
GAME PLAN

While milk mixture comes to a boil for polenta:
■ Trim and cut fennel.
■ Cook chicken.
■ Trim green beans, and set up steamer.
While fennel sauce cooks:
■ Cook polenta.
■ Steam green beans.

Quick & Easy
Chicken with Italian Sweet-Sour Fennel
with Creamy Polenta and Herbed Green Beans

Time-Saver: Chicken cutlets are thin and cook in a flash.
Simple Sub: If you don't have white wine, use 2 teaspoons lemon juice plus enough broth to equal ¼ cup.
Flavor Hit: Toasted nuts have at least twice as much impact as untoasted.

1 small fennel bulb with stalks
2 teaspoons extra-virgin olive oil
4 (4-ounce) chicken cutlets
½ teaspoon kosher salt, divided
½ teaspoon dried rosemary, crushed
¼ teaspoon freshly ground black pepper
¼ cup dry white wine
¾ cup fat-free, lower-sodium chicken broth
¼ cup raisins
2 teaspoons red wine vinegar
1 tablespoon pine nuts, toasted

1. Mince 1 tablespoon fennel fronds. Thinly slice bulb to measure 2 cups (discard core).
2. Heat oil in a large skillet over medium-high heat. Sprinkle chicken with ¼ teaspoon salt, rosemary, and pepper. Add chicken to pan; cook 3 minutes on each side or until done. Remove from pan. Add fennel bulb to pan; sauté 1 minute. Stir in wine. Add remaining ¼ teaspoon salt, broth, raisins, and vinegar; cover and cook 4 minutes or until fennel is tender. Return chicken to pan. Sprinkle with nuts and fennel fronds. Yield: 4 servings (serving size: 1 cutlet and ⅓ cup fennel mixture).

CALORIES 209; FAT 5.3g (sat 0.8g, mono 2.4g, poly 1.3g); PROTEIN 28g; CARB 12.3g; FIBER 2.5g; CHOL 66mg; IRON 1.8mg; SODIUM 419mg; CALC 53mg

For the Creamy Polenta:
Bring 2 cups 2% milk and 1 cup water to a simmer in a saucepan. • Whisk in ¾ cup instant dry polenta. • Cook 5 minutes or until thick, stirring frequently. • Stir in ¼ cup ⅓-less-fat cream cheese and ¼ teaspoon salt. Yield: 4 servings.

CALORIES 197; FAT 5.6g (sat 3.4g); SODIUM 245mg

For the Herbed Green Beans:
Steam 1 pound green beans 5 minutes. • Drizzle with 1 tablespoon olive oil; sprinkle with 1 teaspoon chopped fresh thyme, 1 teaspoon chopped fresh chives, and ⅛ teaspoon salt. Yield: 4 servings.

CALORIES 57; FAT 3.4g (sat 0.5g); SODIUM 74mg

READY IN
40
MINUTES

········· *The* ·········
SHOPPING LIST

Caramel Pork
Vidalia onion
garlic
bottled ground fresh ginger
1 lime
sushi rice or short-grain rice
rice vinegar
lower-sodium soy sauce
fat-free, lower-sodium chicken broth
dark brown sugar
crushed red pepper
anchovies
frozen green peas
1 pound pork tenderloin

Radish-Squash Slaw
carrots
daikon radish
1 yellow squash
cilantro
dark sesame oil
rice vinegar
lower-sodium soy sauce
honey

········· *The* ·········
GAME PLAN

While rice cooks:
■ Cut pork into cubes.
■ Prepare slaw; cover and chill.
While rice stands:
■ Cook pork mixture.

Caramel Pork
with Radish-Squash Slaw

Prep Pointer: Use a mandoline or julienne slicer to help the slaw come together faster.
Flavor Hit: Anchovies are readily available and add a savory quality similar to that of Asian fish sauce.
Kid Tweak: Kids will love the sweet-salty pork, especially if you omit the crushed red pepper.

1 cup water
¾ cup uncooked sushi rice or short-grain rice
½ teaspoon kosher salt, divided
½ cup frozen green peas, thawed
1 tablespoon rice vinegar
Cooking spray
1 pound pork tenderloin, cut into 1-inch pieces
½ cup chopped Vidalia or other sweet onion
3 garlic cloves, minced
½ cup fat-free, lower-sodium chicken broth
3 tablespoons dark brown sugar
1 tablespoon lower-sodium soy sauce
1 teaspoon bottled ground fresh ginger
½ teaspoon crushed red pepper
2 canned anchovy fillets, rinsed and minced
8 lime wedges

1. Combine 1 cup water, rice, and ¼ teaspoon salt in a small saucepan; bring to a boil. Cover, reduce heat, and simmer 15 minutes; remove from heat. Let stand 10 minutes; gently stir in peas and vinegar.
2. Heat a medium skillet over high heat. Coat pan with cooking spray. Add pork; sauté 5 minutes. Sprinkle with remaining ¼ teaspoon salt. Add onion and garlic; stir-fry 2 minutes. Stir in broth and next 5 ingredients; bring to a boil. Reduce heat; simmer 5 minutes or until slightly thick. Spoon ½ cup rice onto each of 4 plates; top each serving with ½ cup pork mixture. Serve with lime wedges. Yield: 4 servings.

CALORIES 295; **FAT** 2.9g (sat 0.9g, mono 1g, poly 0.5g); **PROTEIN** 27.8g; **CARB** 37.3g; **FIBER** 2.1g; **CHOL** 75mg; **IRON** 2.7mg; **SODIUM** 577mg; **CALC** 31mg

For the Radish-Squash Slaw:
Combine 2 tablespoons dark sesame oil, 2 tablespoons rice vinegar, 1 tablespoon lower-sodium soy sauce, 2 teaspoons honey, and ¼ teaspoon salt in a medium bowl. • Add ¾ cup each of julienne-cut carrot, daikon radish, and yellow squash; toss. • Top with 3 tablespoons cilantro leaves. Yield: 4 servings.

CALORIES 101; **FAT** 7.5g (sat 1g); **SODIUM** 234mg

READY IN
40
MINUTES

The SHOPPING LIST

Seared Scallops with Cauliflower Puree
cauliflower
1 Yukon gold potato
fat-free, lower-sodium chicken broth
canola oil
crushed red pepper
unsalted butter
1½ pounds sea scallops

Tarragon Carrots and Peas
fresh tarragon
sugar snap peas
matchstick-cut carrots
Dijon mustard
cider vinegar
butter

The GAME PLAN

While cauliflower mixture cooks:
■ Pat scallops dry.
■ Prep sugar snap peas.
While cauliflower mixture stands:
■ Sear scallops.
■ Cook carrots and peas.
■ Chop herbs.
■ Puree cauliflower mixture, and serve.

Seared Scallops with Cauliflower Puree
with Tarragon Carrots and Peas

Simple Sub: These flavors would go equally well with halibut in place of the scallops.
Prep Pointer: Patting scallops dry before cooking helps ensure a great seared crust.
Time-Saver: Precut carrots save you prep work; the small pieces cook quickly, too.

2 cups chopped cauliflower florets
1 cup cubed peeled Yukon gold potato
1 cup water
½ cup fat-free, lower-sodium chicken broth
1 tablespoon canola oil
1½ pounds sea scallops
¾ teaspoon kosher salt, divided
½ teaspoon coarsely ground black pepper
1½ tablespoons unsalted butter
⅛ teaspoon crushed red pepper

1. Bring first 4 ingredients to a boil in a saucepan; cover, reduce heat, and simmer 6 minutes or until potato is tender. Remove from heat. Let stand, uncovered, 10 minutes.
2. Heat a large skillet over high heat. Add oil; swirl to coat. Pat scallops dry with paper towels; sprinkle with ¼ teaspoon salt and black pepper. Add scallops to pan; cook 3 minutes on each side or until desired degree of doneness. Remove scallops from pan.
3. Pour cauliflower mixture into a blender. Add remaining ½ teaspoon salt, butter, and red pepper. Remove center piece of blender lid (to allow steam to escape); secure lid on blender. Place a clean towel over opening in lid (to avoid splatters). Blend until smooth. Serve puree with scallops. Yield: 4 servings (serving size: ½ cup puree and about 4 scallops).

CALORIES 232; **FAT** 8.9g (sat 3.1g, mono 3.4g, poly 1.5g); **PROTEIN** 23.8g; **CARB** 13g; **FIBER** 2g; **CHOL** 54mg; **IRON** 1.1mg; **SODIUM** 632mg; **CALC** 46mg

continued

For the Tarragon Carrots and Peas:
Place 1 cup sugar snap peas and ⅓ cup water in a saucepan. • Bring to a boil; cover and cook 2 minutes. • Add 1 cup matchstick-cut carrot and 1½ teaspoons butter; cover and cook 2 minutes. • Stir in 1 teaspoon chopped tarragon, 1½ teaspoons Dijon mustard, 1 teaspoon cider vinegar, and ⅛ teaspoon salt. Yield: 4 servings.

CALORIES 41; FAT 1.5g (sat 0.9g); SODIUM 150mg

READY IN
40
MINUTES

The
SHOPPING LIST

Arctic Char with Orange-Caper Relish

3 large oranges
small red onion
fresh flat-leaf parsley
capers
extra-virgin olive oil
rice vinegar
ground red pepper
4 (6-ounce) arctic char fillets

Frisée and Arugula Salad

fresh dill
frisée
baby arugula
small fennel bulb
cucumber
radishes
canola mayonnaise
sherry vinegar
Dijon mustard
pine nuts

The
GAME PLAN

■ Prepare relish; cover and chill.
While fish cooks:
■ Prepare salad.

Quick & Easy
Arctic Char with Orange-Caper Relish
with Frisée and Arugula Salad

Flavor Hit: Capers add briny, salty essence—a nice foil to sweet oranges.
Simple Sub: You can try radicchio or endive in place of frisée.
Make-Ahead Tip: Prepare the relish up to a day in advance.

1 cup orange sections
2 tablespoons slivered red onion
1 tablespoon chopped fresh flat-leaf parsley
1 tablespoon capers, minced
1 teaspoon grated orange rind
1 tablespoon fresh orange juice
1 tablespoon extra-virgin olive oil
1 teaspoon rice vinegar
⅛ teaspoon ground red pepper
4 (6-ounce) arctic char fillets
½ teaspoon kosher salt
½ teaspoon freshly ground black pepper
Cooking spray

1. Combine first 9 ingredients in a small bowl; toss gently to combine. Cover and chill until ready to serve.
2. Heat a large heavy skillet over medium-high heat. Sprinkle fish with salt and pepper. Coat pan with cooking spray. Add fish to pan; cook 4 minutes on each side or until desired degree of doneness. Place 1 fillet on each of 4 plates; top each serving with about ¼ cup relish. Yield: 4 servings.

CALORIES 295; FAT 18.5g (sat 2.9g, mono 7.7g, poly 2.4g); PROTEIN 26.5g; CARB 6.7g; FIBER 1.4g; CHOL 78mg; IRON 1.3mg; SODIUM 366mg; CALC 77mg

For the Frisée and Arugula Salad:
Combine ¼ cup canola mayonnaise, 1 tablespoon chopped fresh dill, 2 tablespoons water, 1 tablespoon sherry vinegar, 1½ teaspoons Dijon mustard, ½ teaspoon black pepper, and ¼ teaspoon salt in a large bowl; stir with a whisk. • Add 2 cups frisée, 2 cups baby arugula, ½ cup thinly sliced fennel bulb, ½ cup thinly sliced cucumber, and ½ cup thinly sliced radish. • Toss gently to combine. • Sprinkle with 2 tablespoons toasted pine nuts. Yield: 4 servings.

CALORIES 147; FAT 14.1g (sat 0.7g); SODIUM 303mg

SUPERFAST

Try a meaty stir-fry, sloppy-saucy barbecue sliders, spicy tortilla soup, cheesy pesto pizza, and other speedy options for easy weeknight suppers.

Quick & Easy
Beef-Broccoli Stir-Fry

2 (3½-ounce) bags boil-in-bag long-grain white rice
2 tablespoons dry sherry, divided
2 tablespoons lower-sodium soy sauce, divided
1 teaspoon sugar
1 pound boneless sirloin steak, cut diagonally across grain into thin slices
½ cup lower-sodium beef broth
1 tablespoon cornstarch
1 tablespoon hoisin sauce
1 teaspoon Sriracha (hot chile sauce) or ½ teaspoon crushed red pepper
2 tablespoons canola oil, divided
1 tablespoon bottled ground fresh ginger
2 teaspoons minced garlic
4 cups prechopped broccoli florets
¼ cup water
⅓ cup sliced green onions

1. Cook rice according to directions.
2. While rice cooks, combine 1 tablespoon sherry, 1 tablespoon soy sauce, sugar, and beef. Stir together remaining 1 tablespoon sherry, remaining 1 tablespoon soy sauce, broth, cornstarch, hoisin sauce, and Sriracha.
3. Heat 1 tablespoon oil in a large skillet over medium-high heat. Add beef mixture; sauté 3 minutes or until browned. Remove beef from pan. Add remaining 1 tablespoon oil to pan. Add ginger and garlic; cook 30 seconds, stirring constantly. Add broccoli and ¼ cup water; cook 1 minute. Add onions; cook 1 minute, stirring constantly. Add broth mixture and beef mixture; cook 2 minutes or until beef is thoroughly heated and sauce is slightly thick. Serve beef mixture over rice. Yield: 4 servings (serving size: about 1⅓ cups beef mixture and ½ cup rice).

CALORIES 476; FAT 12.9g (sat 2.4g, mono 6.3g, poly 2.3g); PROTEIN 32.1g; CARB 52g; FIBER 2.5g; CHOL 48mg; IRON 4.2mg; SODIUM 523mg; CALC 71mg

Spicy Tortilla Soup with Shrimp and Avocado

Chipotle chile and fire-roasted tomatoes lend smokiness to the soup.

1 tablespoon olive oil
1 cup prechopped onion
1/3 cup prechopped celery
1/3 cup chopped carrot
1 tablespoon minced chipotle chile, canned in adobo sauce
1 teaspoon ground cumin
1 teaspoon chili powder
2 teaspoons minced garlic
4 cups fat-free, lower-sodium chicken broth
1 (15-ounce) can white hominy, rinsed and drained
1 (15-ounce) can no-salt-added fire-roasted diced tomatoes, undrained
12 ounces peeled and deveined medium shrimp
1 tablespoon fresh lime juice
1/8 teaspoon salt
1/2 cup lightly crushed baked tortilla chips (about 1 ounce)
1 cup diced avocado (about 1/2 pound)
2 tablespoons fresh cilantro leaves (optional)

1. Heat a Dutch oven over medium-high heat. Add oil to pan; swirl to coat. Add onion and next 6 ingredients; cook 6 minutes or until carrot is crisp-tender, stirring occasionally. Add broth, hominy, and tomatoes; bring to a boil. Cover and cook 6 minutes, stirring occasionally. Add shrimp; cook 2 minutes or until shrimp are done.
2. Remove from heat; stir in juice and salt. Divide shrimp mixture evenly among 4 bowls; top evenly with chips and avocado. Garnish with cilantro, if desired. Yield: 4 servings (serving size: about 1¾ cups soup, 2 tablespoons chips, and ¼ cup avocado).

CALORIES 357; **FAT** 13.9g (sat 2.3g, mono 7.6g, poly 2.5g); **PROTEIN** 25.9g; **CARB** 32.7g; **FIBER** 7g; **CHOL** 130mg; **IRON** 3.7mg; **SODIUM** 570mg; **CALC** 97mg

Mini Farfalle with Roasted Peppers, Onions, Feta, and Mint

8 ounces mini farfalle pasta
1/4 cup pine nuts
1 tablespoon extra-virgin olive oil
1 cup prechopped onion
1/4 cup golden raisins
1 tablespoon minced garlic
1 cup sliced bottled roasted red bell peppers, rinsed and drained
1 cup (4 ounces) crumbled feta cheese
2 tablespoons chopped fresh mint
2 tablespoons chopped fresh basil
1/4 teaspoon black pepper

1. Cook pasta according to package directions, omitting salt and fat. Drain pasta over a bowl; reserve ½ cup cooking liquid.
2. While pasta cooks, heat a small nonstick skillet over medium heat. Add nuts; cook 4 minutes or until golden brown, stirring frequently.
3. Heat a large skillet over medium heat. Add oil; swirl to coat. Add onion, raisins, and garlic; cook 8 minutes or until onion begins to brown, stirring frequently. Add bell peppers; cook 4 minutes or until heated, stirring occasionally. Add pasta and ½ cup reserved cooking liquid; cook 1 minute, stirring to combine. Remove from heat; stir in feta, mint, basil, and black pepper. Sprinkle with nuts. Yield: 4 servings (serving size: about 1½ cups pasta mixture and 1 tablespoon nuts).

CALORIES 453; **FAT** 17.4g (sat 5.1g, mono 4.1g, poly 3.3g); **PROTEIN** 16.6g; **CARB** 59.7g; **FIBER** 4.2g; **CHOL** 25mg; **IRON** 3.5mg; **SODIUM** 558mg; **CALC** 131mg

Barbecue Pulled Chicken Sliders

For a less sweet option, use sliced dill pickles.

1/2 cup no-salt-added ketchup
1 tablespoon dark brown sugar
1 tablespoon cider vinegar
1 teaspoon chili powder
1/2 teaspoon garlic powder
1/2 teaspoon onion powder
1/2 teaspoon dry mustard
1/2 teaspoon smoked paprika
1/2 teaspoon ground cumin
1/8 teaspoon ground allspice
2 cups shredded skinless, boneless rotisserie chicken breast
8 (1.3-ounce) sliders mini buns
8 bread-and-butter pickle chips

1. Combine first 10 ingredients in a small saucepan over medium heat. Bring to a simmer; cook 3 minutes or until slightly thick, stirring occasionally. Add chicken to ketchup mixture; stir to combine. Cook 2 minutes or until chicken is thoroughly heated.
2. Spoon 3 tablespoons chicken mixture onto bottom half of each bun, and top each with 1 pickle chip and top half of bun. Yield: 4 servings (serving size: 2 sandwiches).

CALORIES 400; **FAT** 7.5g (sat 2.3g, mono 0.9g, poly 0.5g); **PROTEIN** 30g; **CARB** 52.7g; **FIBER** 1.9g; **CHOL** 60mg; **IRON** 2.7mg; **SODIUM** 481mg; **CALC** 83mg

Snack of the Month

Black Bean Hummus

You can also serve with assorted crudités.

½ cup chopped fresh cilantro, divided
2 tablespoons tahini (roasted sesame seed paste)
2 tablespoons water
2 tablespoons fresh lime juice
1 tablespoon extra-virgin olive oil
¾ teaspoon ground cumin
¼ teaspoon salt
1 (15-ounce) can no-salt-added black beans, rinsed and drained
1 garlic clove, peeled
½ small jalapeño pepper, seeded
3 (6-inch) pitas

1. Preheat oven to 425°.
2. Place ¼ cup cilantro, tahini, and next 8 ingredients in a food processor; process until smooth. Spoon into a bowl; sprinkle with remaining ¼ cup cilantro.
3. Cut each pita into 8 wedges. Arrange on a baking sheet. Bake at 425° for 6 minutes, turning once. Yield: 8 servings (serving size: about 3½ tablespoons hummus and 3 pita wedges).

CALORIES 127; **FAT** 4g (sat 0.5g, mono 2g, poly 1.1g); **PROTEIN** 5.1g; **CARB** 18.5g; **FIBER** 2.4g; **CHOL** 0mg; **IRON** 1.7mg; **SODIUM** 138mg; **CALC** 41mg

Pizza of the Month

White Pizza with Tomato and Basil

(pictured on page 214)

Heating a baking sheet in the oven before you put the pizza on it gives you a crisper crust.

1 (10-ounce) Italian cheese-flavored thin pizza crust
1 teaspoon cornmeal
Cooking spray
3 tablespoons refrigerated pesto with basil
½ cup (2 ounces) shredded fresh mozzarella cheese
½ cup part-skim ricotta cheese
½ cup sliced small tomatoes (such as Campari tomatoes)
¼ teaspoon black pepper
¼ cup small basil leaves
Crushed red pepper (optional)

1. Preheat broiler to high.
2. Place a baking sheet in oven; heat 10 minutes.
3. While baking sheet heats, place crust on another baking sheet sprinkled with cornmeal. Lightly coat crust with cooking spray. Spread pesto evenly over crust, leaving a 1-inch border; sprinkle mozzarella evenly over pesto. Dollop ricotta, by teaspoonfuls, evenly over mozzarella. Slide crust onto preheated baking sheet, using a spatula as a guide. Broil 5 inches from heat 5 minutes or until cheese begins to melt. Remove from oven; top evenly with tomato, black pepper, and basil. Sprinkle with red pepper, if desired. Cut into 8 slices. Yield: 4 servings (serving size: 2 slices).

CALORIES 352; **FAT** 13.8g (sat 4.8g, mono 3.2g, poly 3.2g); **PROTEIN** 15.8g; **CARB** 40.2g; **FIBER** 2g; **CHOL** 24mg; **IRON** 2.6mg; **SODIUM** 643mg; **CALC** 297mg

Soup of the Month

Escarole, Bean, and Sausage Soup with Parmesan Cheese

Escarole has a milder flavor than endive but still offers a slight bitterness that is balanced by the creamy beans and sweet sausage.

2 teaspoons extra-virgin olive oil
1 cup prechopped onion
½ cup thinly sliced fennel bulb
1 tablespoon minced garlic
3 (3.2-ounce) links sweet turkey Italian sausage, casings removed
2 cups fat-free, lower-sodium chicken broth
1 cup water
1 (15-ounce) can no-salt-added cannellini beans or other white beans, rinsed and drained
4 cups chopped escarole
2 tablespoons grated Parmesan cheese

1. Heat a large saucepan over medium-high heat. Add olive oil to pan; swirl to coat. Add onion, fennel, garlic, and sausage; cook 7 minutes or until sausage is browned, stirring frequently to crumble. Add broth, 1 cup water, and beans. Cover; bring to a boil, and cook 5 minutes, stirring occasionally. Stir in escarole; cook 4 minutes or until escarole wilts. Divide soup evenly among 4 bowls; sprinkle with Parmesan cheese. Yield: 4 servings (serving size: about 1¼ cups soup and 1½ teaspoons cheese).

CALORIES 230; **FAT** 4.6g (sat 2.6g, mono 1.7g, poly 0.3g); **PROTEIN** 17.9g; **CARB** 15.5g; **FIBER** 4.7g; **CHOL** 49mg; **IRON** 1.3mg; **SODIUM** 624mg; **CALC** 87mg

Quick & Easy

Sautéed Brussels Sprouts with Bacon

3 center-cut bacon slices, finely chopped
¼ teaspoon dried thyme
1½ cups presliced onion
⅓ cup fat-free, lower-sodium chicken broth
1 pound Brussels sprouts, trimmed and halved

1. Heat a large skillet over medium-high heat. Add bacon; cook 7 minutes or until crisp. Remove bacon from pan with a slotted spoon; drain.
2. Add thyme and onion to pan; sauté 3 minutes. Add broth and Brussels sprouts; bring to a boil. Cover and simmer 6 minutes or until crisp-tender. Sprinkle with bacon. Yield: 4 servings (serving size: about 1 cup).

CALORIES 81; FAT 1.5g (sat 0.5g, mono 0.1g, poly 0.2g); PROTEIN 6.1g; CARB 13.7g; FIBER 4.9g; CHOL 4mg; IRON 1.8mg; SODIUM 101mg; CALC 58mg

Quick & Easy
Lemon and Pecan Variation: Omit bacon; use 1 teaspoon olive oil in place of bacon drippings. Substitute 1 cup prechopped onion for sliced onion. To finish, stir in ¼ cup chopped pecans, 2 teaspoons grated lemon rind, 1 tablespoon fresh lemon juice, and ¼ teaspoon black pepper. Yield: 4 servings.

CALORIES 132; FAT 6.7g (sat 0./g); SODIUM 36mg

Quick & Easy
Sesame, Garlic, and Ginger Variation: Omit bacon and thyme; use 1 tablespoon dark sesame oil in place of drippings. Substitute 1 cup prechopped onion for sliced onion; add 2 teaspoons minced ginger and 1 minced garlic clove. To finish, add ¼ cup sliced green onions and 1 tablespoon lower-sodium soy sauce. Yield: 4 servings.

CALORIES 107; FAT 4g (sat 0.5g); SODIUM 181mg

Quick & Easy
Garlic and Pecorino Variation: Omit bacon; use 1 teaspoon olive oil in place of drippings. Substitute 1 cup prechopped onion for sliced onion; add 6 sliced garlic cloves. To finish, add ¼ teaspoon black pepper and ⅛ teaspoon salt. Sprinkle with 2 tablespoons shaved pecorino Romano cheese. Yield: 4 servings.

CALORIES 115; FAT 4.7g (sat 1.1g); SODIUM 156mg

OOPS! YOUR BACON IS BURNED AND CRINKLY

There's a surefire way to avoid those tangled ribbons: Bake your bacon.
By Tim Cebula

Pan-frying is the standard way to cook bacon, but it has drawbacks. Only a few strips fit flat in most skillets—any more than that will slope up the sides, cooking unevenly. And bacon strips can shrink more than they need to in a hot pan. (Starting them in a cold pan helps, but you'll still need to flip often.)

Take a cue from chefs—bake your bacon. Heat hits from all sides, cooking more evenly. The result: consistently flat strips.

Line a jelly-roll pan with foil or parchment paper to make cleanup easier. Set a wire rack on the pan so the bacon doesn't sit in fat. Place bacon slices in a single layer on the rack, and bake at 400° for about 20 minutes (depending on bacon thickness and how crisp you like it). Unless your oven has major hot spots, you don't have to flip the bacon or turn the pans. You can even put the bacon in while the oven preheats—the gradual temperature increase will render the fat more slowly and won't shrink the meat as much.

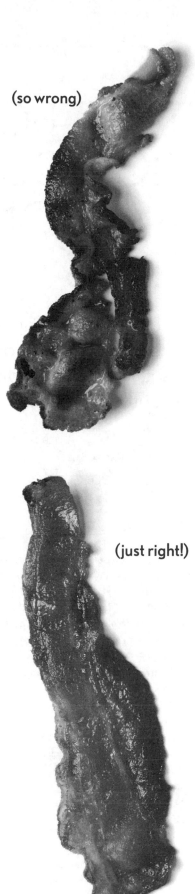

(so wrong)

(just right!)

STORE-BOUGHT SHORTCUTS FOR EASY, HOME-COOKED MEALS

Speed up the cooking with versatile, healthy supermarket convenience foods that help you turn out vibrant, healthy main dishes. Prep time is cut to about 20 minutes.

Kid Friendly • Vegetarian

Roasted Vegetable and Ricotta Pizza

Hands-on time: 20 min. Total time: 1 hr.

Store-bought dough yields pizzeria quality. Ask for it in the bakery of your supermarket, or check specialty retailers. In a pinch, buy dough in tubes from the refrigerated section of the grocery store (it's higher in sodium than fresh dough).

1 pound refrigerated fresh pizza dough
2 cups sliced cremini mushrooms
1 cup (¼-inch-thick) slices zucchini
¼ teaspoon black pepper
1 medium yellow bell pepper, sliced
1 medium red onion, cut into thick slices
5½ teaspoons olive oil, divided
1 tablespoon yellow cornmeal
⅓ cup tomato sauce
1 cup (4 ounces) shredded part-skim
  mozzarella cheese, divided
½ teaspoon crushed red pepper
⅓ cup part-skim ricotta cheese
2 tablespoons small fresh basil leaves

1. Position an oven rack in the lowest setting; place a pizza stone on rack. Preheat oven to 500°.
2. Remove dough from refrigerator. Let stand, covered, 30 minutes.
3. Combine mushrooms and next 4 ingredients in a large bowl; drizzle with 1½ tablespoons oil. Toss. Arrange vegetables on a jelly-roll pan. Bake at 500° for 15 minutes.
4. Punch dough down. Sprinkle a lightly floured baking sheet with cornmeal; roll dough out to a 15-inch circle on prepared baking sheet. Brush dough with remaining 1 teaspoon oil. Spread sauce over dough, leaving a ½-inch border. Sprinkle ½ cup mozzarella over sauce; top with vegetables. Sprinkle remaining ½ cup mozzarella and red pepper over zucchini mixture. Dollop with ricotta. Slide pizza onto preheated pizza stone. Bake at 500° for 11 minutes or until crust is golden. Sprinkle with basil. Yield: 6 servings (serving size: 2 slices).

CALORIES 347; **FAT** 11.1g (sat 3.7g, mono 4.4g, poly 2g); **PROTEIN** 14.8g; **CARB** 48.5g; **FIBER** 2.7g; **CHOL** 15mg; **IRON** 3mg; **SODIUM** 655mg; **CALC** 193mg

5 MORE WAYS WITH **PIZZA DOUGH**

1. Brush with olive oil and top with cheese and herbs to make flavorful **flatbreads.**

2. Cut into small portions, roll small circles, bake, and top with salad or meats for **piadines.**

3. Make great **calzones** with dough, pasta sauce, cheese, wilted spinach, and cooked, crumbled sausage.

4. Roll into a rectangle, brush with butter, and sprinkle with cinnamon sugar for **roll-ups.** Cut crosswise and bake.

5. Cut into strips and make garlicky **cheese sticks.**

HEALTHY DISHES HAVE A MADE-WITH-CARE FRESHNESS. ONLY YOU KNOW THE TIME SAVED.

5 MORE WAYS WITH **PIE DOUGH**

1. Roll dough into an 11-inch circle; fill with sautéed veggies. Fold dough toward center. Bake a savory **galette**.

2. Use dough to top individual or casserole-style **potpies**.

3. Divide dough; roll into small circles. Fill with cooked meat, beans, cheese. Fold, crimp, and bake for **empanadas**.

4. Bake in mini muffin cups, and fill with crab or shrimp salad for **appetizers**.

5. Wrap seasoned chicken or fish, and bake for an **en croûte entrée**.

FOR DINNER ON THE RUN, FILL FLAKY PASTRY WITH A CHUNKY VEGGIE AND SAUSAGE MIXTURE AND TOP WITH CHEESE.

Quick & Easy • Kid Friendly

Savory Sausage, Spinach & Onion Turnovers

Hands-on time: 21 min. Total time: 39 min.

The nutritional difference between refrigerated dough and one made from scratch is actually quite small, so on a weeknight, this is a shortcut that's worth the trade-off.

Cooking spray
²⁄₃ cup diced peeled red potatoes
¹⁄₃ cup diced red bell pepper
¹⁄₃ cup diced yellow onion
2 (3.5-ounce) links hot chicken Italian sausage, casings removed
3 cups bagged washed baby spinach
2 tablespoons finely chopped fresh basil
¼ teaspoon salt
¼ teaspoon crushed red pepper
½ (14.1-ounce) package refrigerated pie dough
2 tablespoons water
1 large egg white, lightly beaten
3 tablespoons grated fresh Parmigiano-Reggiano cheese

1. Preheat oven to 400°.
2. Heat a medium nonstick skillet over medium-high heat. Coat pan with cooking spray. Add potatoes, bell pepper, and onion to pan; sauté 4 minutes or until onion begins to brown, stirring frequently. Add sausage; cook 4 minutes or until browned, stirring to crumble. Stir in spinach; cook 2 minutes or until spinach wilts. Stir in basil, salt, and crushed red pepper. Remove from heat.
3. Cut dough into 4 equal portions. Roll each portion into a 5-inch circle. Spoon about ½ cup potato mixture on half of each circle, leaving a ½-inch border. Fold dough over potato mixture until edges almost meet. Bring bottom edge of dough over top edge; crimp edges of dough to form a rim.
4. Place turnovers on a baking sheet coated with cooking spray. Combine 2 tablespoons water and egg white in a small bowl, stirring with a whisk; brush evenly over dough. Sprinkle about 2 teaspoons cheese over each turnover. Bake at 400° for 18 minutes or until golden brown. Let stand at least 5 minutes before serving. Yield: 4 servings (serving size: 1 turnover).

CALORIES 344; FAT 17.9g (sat 6.3g, mono 6g, poly 4.1g); PROTEIN 12.1g; CARB 33g; FIBER 1.9g; CHOL 44mg; IRON 4mg; SODIUM 691mg; CALC 91mg

---

5 MORE WAYS WITH **ROTISSERIE CHICKEN**

1. Combine with salsa and cheddar cheese for **enchilada filling**.

2. Toss shredded chicken with a favorite barbecue sauce. Add greens for a **hearty salad**.

3. Make a classic béchamel sauce; stir in chicken and cheese, and fill **crepes**.

4. Make a **noodle bowl** with coconut milk, broth, chicken, peanuts, chile paste, and lime wedges.

5. Stir shredded or cubed white and dark meat into **chili**.

Thai Chicken Salad with Peanut Dressing

(pictured on page 218)

Hands-on time: 10 min. Total time: 17 min.

When you purchase a rotisserie chicken, look for a just-done bird. Most stores follow a schedule, and packages are marked with the time the chickens came off the spit. Stick with the original, unflavored version, as it's the most versatile.

6 cups torn romaine lettuce
2 cups shredded skinless, boneless rotisserie
   chicken breast
2 cups fresh bean sprouts
1 cup shredded carrots
¾ cup sliced celery
⅔ cup light coconut milk
1 tablespoon brown sugar
2 tablespoons creamy peanut butter
2 tablespoons lower-sodium soy sauce
1 tablespoon fresh lime juice
⅛ teaspoon ground red pepper
2 tablespoons coarsely chopped unsalted,
   dry-roasted peanuts
4 lime wedges (optional)

1. Combine first 5 ingredients in a large bowl. Combine coconut milk and next 5 ingredients in a small saucepan; bring to a boil. Reduce heat, and simmer 5 minutes or until mixture thickens slightly, stirring occasionally. Remove from heat, and cool 2 minutes. Pour warm coconut milk mixture over lettuce mixture. Sprinkle with peanuts; serve with lime wedges, if desired. Serve immediately. Yield: 4 servings (serving size: 3 cups salad and 1½ teaspoons peanuts).

CALORIES 262; **FAT** 11.2g (sat 3.7g, mono 4.5g, poly 2.5g);
PROTEIN 27.5g; **CARB** 17.1g; **FIBER** 4.4g; **CHOL** 63mg;
IRON 2.3mg; **SODIUM** 599mg; **CALC** 67mg

5 MORE WAYS WITH CANNED CHICKPEAS

1. Sauté onions and garlic; add Indian simmer sauce and chickpeas for a **quick curry.**

2. Use in your favorite **baked beans** recipe for a firmer texture—try all chickpeas or just half.

3. Toss rinsed and drained beans with canola oil and spices. Then toast them in the oven for a **healthy snack.**

4. Puree with canola mayonnaise or Greek yogurt and lemon juice for a **sandwich spread.**

5. Add to **soups and stews** for an al dente bite of earthy flavor.

Mediterranean Barley with Chickpeas & Arugula

Hands-on time: 11 min. Total time: 31 min.

Use organic or no-salt-added beans to keep sodium levels in check.

1 cup uncooked pearl barley
1 cup packed arugula leaves
1 cup finely chopped red bell pepper
3 tablespoons finely chopped sun-dried
   tomatoes, packed without oil
1 (15½-ounce) can no-salt-added chickpeas,
   rinsed and drained
2 tablespoons fresh lemon juice
2 tablespoons extra-virgin olive oil
1 teaspoon salt
½ teaspoon crushed red pepper
2 tablespoons chopped pistachios

1. Cook barley according to package directions, omitting salt. Combine barley, arugula, bell pepper, tomatoes, and chickpeas in a large bowl.
2. Combine lemon juice, oil, salt, and crushed red pepper, stirring with a whisk. Drizzle over barley mixture, and toss. Sprinkle with pistachios. Yield: 4 servings (serving size: 1¼ cups barley mixture and 1½ teaspoons pistachios).

CALORIES 360; **FAT** 10.1g (sat 1.4g, mono 6.1g, poly 2g);
PROTEIN 10.1g; **CARB** 59.9g; **FIBER** 12.4g; **CHOL** 0mg;
IRON 2.9mg; **SODIUM** 682mg; **CALC** 55mg

5 MORE WAYS WITH BAGGED SPINACH

1. Stir into **scrambled eggs** or omelets during the last minute of cooking.

2. Up your veggie intake by adding chopped or whole leaves to **rice or pasta.**

3. Toss with olive oil, thinly sliced shallots, and crumbled bacon. Put on a **pizza** after it's baked.

4. Stir into **soups** just before serving for a boost of garden flavor.

5. Sauté spinach and garlic until wilted, and use it to fill **savory tarts.**

Stir-Fried Rice Noodles with Beef and Spinach

Hands-on time: 7 min. Total time: 24 min.

Rinsing, drying, stemming, and chopping supermarket spinach is a messy time-eater. Ready-to-use baby spinach from the bag cuts out that process. Inspect in the store to make sure it's in prime condition.

6 ounces uncooked wide rice sticks (rice-flour noodles)
1 tablespoon canola oil
1 cup thinly sliced green onions
²/₃ pound top sirloin steak, cut into thin strips
2 cups sliced shiitake mushroom caps
2 garlic cloves, finely minced
1 (6-ounce) bag washed baby spinach
3 tablespoons lower-sodium soy sauce
2 tablespoons rice vinegar
1 tablespoon fresh lime juice
2 teaspoons grated peeled fresh ginger
2 teaspoons Sriracha (hot chile sauce)
1 tablespoon dark sesame oil
¼ teaspoon salt
2 teaspoons sesame seeds, toasted

1. Cook noodles according to package directions, omitting salt and fat. Drain and rinse under cold water; drain.
2. Heat a large skillet or wok over high heat. Add canola oil to pan; swirl to coat. Add onions and steak; stir-fry 1 minute. Add mushrooms and garlic; stir-fry 1 minute. Add spinach; stir-fry 1 minute or until greens wilt.
3. Combine soy sauce and next 4 ingredients in a small bowl, stirring with a whisk. Add vinegar mixture to steak mixture; cook 30 seconds, stirring constantly. Stir in noodles, sesame oil, and salt; cook 1 minute or until noodles are thoroughly heated, tossing to combine. Sprinkle with sesame seeds. Yield: 4 servings (serving size: 1½ cups).

CALORIES 408; **FAT** 13.2g (sat 2.9g, mono 5.9g, poly 3.1g); **PROTEIN** 16.7g; **CARB** 56.1g; **FIBER** 5g; **CHOL** 37mg; **IRON** 5.1mq; **SODIUM** 616mg; **CALC** 8.3mg

---

3 MORE WAYS WITH RICE NOODLES

1. Make **pad thai** with shrimp, chicken, or tofu.

2. Prepare a **noodle salad** with dark sesame oil, toasted sesame seeds, rice vinegar, and sliced green onions.

3. Add hydrated noodles to pho, a flavorful, brothy **beef soup**.

EVERYDAY VEGETARIAN

VEGGIE SKILLET SUPPERS

Kid Friendly • Vegetarian

Paella with Soy Chorizo and Edamame

Hands-on time: 23 min. Total time: 55 min.

Paella is a rice dish that hails from the Valencia region on the east coast of Spain. If Valencia rice is not available, use Arborio rice, but be sure not to stir the dish too much because paella is not meant to be creamy like a risotto.

6 ounces meatless soy chorizo
2 tablespoons extra-virgin olive oil
2¼ cups chopped yellow onion (about 1 large)
¼ teaspoon saffron threads, crushed
4 garlic cloves, minced
1 cup Valencia or other medium-grain rice
1 cup (½-inch) pieces red bell pepper
½ cup dry white wine
2 cups organic vegetable broth
¼ teaspoon salt
1½ cups frozen shelled edamame (green soybeans), thawed
¼ cup coarsely chopped fresh flat-leaf parsley
¼ cup chopped green onions

1. Heat a large nonstick skillet over medium heat. Add soy chorizo to pan, and cook 12 minutes or until browned, crumbling and stirring occasionally. Place in a small bowl, and set aside.
2. Return pan to medium heat. Add olive oil, swirling to coat. Add yellow onion; cover and cook 10 minutes or until tender, stirring occasionally. Add saffron and garlic; cook 1 minute, stirring constantly. Add 1 cup rice and bell pepper; cook 2 minutes, stirring frequently. Stir in white wine, and cook 2 minutes or until liquid is nearly absorbed, stirring frequently. Add vegetable broth and salt; bring to a simmer. Cover, reduce heat, and simmer 20 minutes or until rice is tender and liquid is absorbed.
3. Return soy chorizo to pan, and stir in edamame. Cook 5 minutes or until edamame is thoroughly heated, stirring occasionally. Sprinkle with chopped parsley and ¼ cup green onions. Yield: 6 servings (serving size: about 1 cup rice mixture, 2 teaspoons parsley, and 2 teaspoons green onions).

CALORIES 313; **FAT** 11.2g (sat 1g, mono 6.5g, poly 2.7g); **PROTEIN** 12g; **CARB** 41.7g; **FIBER** 6.1g; **CHOL** 0mg; **IRON** 4.3mg; **SODIUM** 525mg; **CALC** 79mg

---

3 MORE WAYS TO USE SOY CHORIZO

1. Stir into a black bean **chili**.

2. Add smoky appeal to **queso dip**.

3. Cook with **scrambled eggs**, and serve over corn tortillas.

Quick White Bean, Asparagus, and Mushroom Cassoulet

Hands-on time: 26 min. Total time: 38 min.

Cassoulet—a rich, slow-cooked bean stew with meat—is reinvented here as a quick-cooking vegetarian dish, starting with canned beans and using mushrooms to lend a meaty mouthfeel and earthy flavor.

5 cups water
3 cups (2-inch) sliced asparagus (about
  1 pound)
2 tablespoons extra-virgin olive oil, divided
3 cups sliced chanterelle or oyster
  mushrooms (about 10 ounces)
1/3 cup finely chopped shallots
6 garlic cloves, minced
1/4 cup dry white wine
1 1/2 cups organic vegetable broth
1/2 teaspoon dried marjoram or dried oregano
2 (15-ounce) cans no-salt-added cannellini
  beans, rinsed and drained
1/4 teaspoon freshly ground black pepper
2 ounces French bread, cut into 1-inch cubes
1 tablespoon butter, cut into small pieces
1/2 cup (2 ounces) grated fresh Parmigiano-
  Reggiano cheese

1. Bring 5 cups water to a boil in a large stainless-steel skillet, and add asparagus to pan. Cover and cook 2 minutes; drain. Rinse asparagus with cold water, and drain well. Set aside.
2. Return pan to medium-high heat. Add 1 tablespoon oil, swirling to coat. Add mushrooms, shallots, and garlic; sauté 8 minutes or until mushrooms are tender. Add wine; cook 3 minutes or until liquid evaporates. Stir in broth, marjoram, and beans; bring to a simmer. Reduce heat to medium, and cook 12 minutes or until thick and beans are very tender. Stir in black pepper.
3. Preheat broiler.
4. Place French bread and butter in a food processor, and pulse until coarse crumbs form. Add remaining 1 tablespoon oil and cheese to coarse breadcrumbs; pulse until combined. Stir

asparagus into bean mixture; sprinkle coarse breadcrumb mixture evenly over bean mixture. Broil 3 minutes or until crumbs are golden brown. Yield: 4 servings (serving size: about 1 3/4 cups).

CALORIES 328; FAT 14.2g (sat 4.6g, mono 6.5, poly 1g); PROTEIN 15.7g; CARB 36.3g; FIBER 8.8g; CHOL 16mg; IRON 5.7mg; SODIUM 530mg; CALC 198mg

CREAMY BEANS AND VEGGIES WITH A CRISPY, CHEESY BREAD-CRUMB TOPPING MAKE FOR A HEARTY MEATLESS ONE-DISH MEAL.

Tempeh and Green Bean Stir-Fry with Peanut Sauce

Hands-on time: 25 min. Total time: 30 min.

Peanut Sauce:
1/4 cup water
1 tablespoon brown sugar
3 tablespoons natural-style, chunky peanut
  butter
1 teaspoon Sriracha (hot chile sauce)
1 teaspoon lower-sodium soy sauce
Stir-Fry:
2 teaspoons brown sugar
5 teaspoons lower-sodium soy sauce
1 teaspoon Sriracha
4 garlic cloves, chopped
1 tablespoon plus 2 teaspoons sesame oil,
  divided
1 (8-ounce) package organic tempeh, cut into
  1/3-inch strips
2 cups thinly sliced carrot
1 cup (2-inch) strips red bell pepper
1 pound green beans, trimmed
1/2 cup water
3/4 cup thinly sliced green onions, divided
6 ounces mung bean sprouts

1. To prepare peanut sauce, combine 1/4 cup water, 1 tablespoon brown sugar, 3 tablespoons peanut butter, 1 teaspoon Sriracha, and 1 teaspoon soy sauce in a medium bowl, stirring well with a whisk. Set aside.
2. To prepare stir-fry, combine 2 teaspoons sugar, 5 teaspoons soy sauce, 1 teaspoon Sriracha, and garlic in a small bowl, stirring with a whisk.
3. Heat a large heavy skillet over medium-high heat. Add 1 tablespoon sesame oil to pan, swirling to coat. Add tempeh and half of soy sauce mixture; stir-fry 5 minutes or until tempeh is golden brown. Remove tempeh mixture from pan, and keep warm. Add remaining 2 teaspoons oil to pan, swirling to coat. Add carrot, bell pepper, and green beans to pan; stir-fry 3 minutes. Add 1/2 cup water; reduce heat to medium. Cover and simmer 5 minutes or until beans are crisp-tender. Stir in remaining half of soy sauce mixture, tempeh mixture, half of onions, and bean sprouts; cook 2 minutes or until sprouts are tender. Serve with peanut sauce and remaining half of onions. Yield: 4 servings (serving size: 2 cups tempeh mixture, 2 tablespoons peanut sauce, and 1 1/2 tablespoons green onions).

CALORIES 357; FAT 18.3g (sat 2.9g, mono 7.1g, poly 6.7g); PROTEIN 18.4g; CARB 35.2g; FIBER 8.2g; CHOL 0mg; IRON 4mg; SODIUM 353mg; CALC 158mg

WINE NOTE: Hogue Late Harvest Riesling ($10) has a seductive touch of sweetness from dense peach and apricot notes to balance the spicy Sriracha. At the same time, its tangy acidity cuts through the rich flavors of peanut butter and sesame oil.

TEMPEH IS A HIGH-PROTEIN SOY PRODUCT; SUBSTITUTE EXTRA-FIRM TOFU, IF DESIRED.

Fingerling Potato–Leek Hash with Swiss Chard and Eggs

Hands-on time: 25 min. Total time: 63 min.

To trim Swiss chard, pull or cut the stems out of the leaves.

2 tablespoons extra-virgin olive oil
2 cups sliced leek (about 2 large)
12 ounces fingerling potatoes, cut in half
  lengthwise (about 4 cups)
2 garlic cloves, minced
1¼ teaspoons Spanish smoked paprika, divided
½ teaspoon salt, divided
½ teaspoon coarsely ground black pepper,
  divided
4 cups thinly sliced trimmed Swiss chard
  (about 1 bunch)
4 large eggs
¼ cup (1 ounce) shredded Gruyère cheese

1. Heat a large skillet over medium heat. Add oil to pan. Add leek; cook 8 minutes, stirring frequently. Add potatoes and garlic; cook 15 minutes or until potatoes are tender, stirring occasionally. Stir in 1 teaspoon paprika, ¼ teaspoon salt, and ¼ teaspoon pepper. Add chard; cook 4 minutes, stirring constantly. Using a spoon, push potato mixture aside to make 4 egg-sized spaces. Crack 1 egg into each space, and sprinkle remaining ¼ teaspoon salt, remaining ¼ teaspoon pepper, and remaining ¼ teaspoon paprika over eggs. Cover and cook 3 minutes; sprinkle cheese over potato mixture. Cover and cook 2 minutes or until egg yolks are lightly set. Yield: 4 servings (serving size: about 1½ cups potato mixture and 1 egg).

CALORIES 261; **FAT** 13.5g (sat 3.5g, mono 7.6g, poly 1.8g); **PROTEIN** 11.6g; **CARB** 23.6g; **FIBER** 3.2g; **CHOL** 188mg; **IRON** 3.4g; **SODIUM** 480mg; **CALC** 156mg

4 STEPS FOR PREPPING LEEKS

With their mild onion flavor, leeks have a reserved, subtle, almost creamy presence in dishes. Prep is important: Leeks grow partly underground, and the overlapping layers can trap dirt. Follow these steps.

1. Trim off and discard dark, tough tops and root.

2. Cut in half lengthwise.

3. Slice thinly.

4. Swish in a bowl of water to release all grit (which should sink); scoop out clean leeks and drain.

GRASS VERSUS GRAIN

We bought half a cow: Grass-fed, locally raised. We talked to farmers and butchers, and then got cooking.

A large herd's worth of beef cattle has passed through the *Cooking Light* Test Kitchen over the past 24 years, almost all of it standard-issue, grain-fed supermarket meat. But with beef, as with everything in the American diet, change is afoot. Shoppers are seeing more and more grass-fed beef in regular grocery stores, along with meat from breeds marketed as special (like Angus), and meat from organically raised animals. The local/sustainable movement has been singing the praises of the grass-fed cow, while the grain-fed industry has been under attack by food activists. The grass-fed cow, which eats from a pasture and is not "finished" on a diet of grains and supplements for rapid weight gain, is said by its promoters to be better for the planet (less energy goes into growing grass than grain); better for the beef eater (less overall fat, and more omega-3s and other "good" fats); and better for the cow (critics decry feedlot practices as inhumane). In this article, though, we're looking not at meat politics but at three things that most cooks are acutely interested in: price, nutrition, and taste.

Price may be the first thing you notice about grass-fed beef: In supermarkets, small-production, grass-fed meat can be more expensive than the average grain-fed beef, just as artisanal cheese costs more than industrial cheddar. But the cook will notice that the meat often looks different, too—sometimes a lot darker, often with less of the coveted fat-marbling you see in the highest-grade grain-fed meat.

To dive into the subject, we bought half a cow. Specifically, we bought half of a 648-pound Brangus cow (an Angus-Brahman hybrid), pasture-raised by Alabama farmer Melissa Boutwell, who is pretty local: She works about 175 miles from our main editorial offices. Boutwell Farms (boutwellfarms.com) supplies regional restaurants, which have included James Beard Award–winning Chef Frank Stitt's restaurants in Birmingham.

We talked to Boutwell about her husbandry. We saw our meat through the butchering process, took delivery of 243 pounds of meat (plus bones) cut to our specifications, and conducted blind tastings in our Test Kitchens. We learned that we could dodge supermarket prices by buying in bulk: Our cost per pound of Boutwell's beef was $5.32, including everything from ground beef to liver to filet mignon, which made it only marginally higher than similar quantities of regular grain-fed beef prices in local supermarkets, and a lot less than we would have paid for premium grass-fed or grain-fed meat.

As for nutrition, we put fat-content claims to the test by sending some of our finest grass-fed steaks for nutritional analysis, along with supermarket and specialty grain-fed cuts. And on the matter of taste, we confirmed that grass-fed beef can be delicious and versatile but, if it comes from a lean cow like the one we bought, requires careful cooking lest the extra effort of buying it go to waste on the plate. Buying beef directly from farmers not only is a logical next step in the "buy local" movement but also hearkens back to the way many of our parents or grandparents bought meat. All you need is to do some digging for local suppliers and buy a good-sized freezer for the supply (see Cow-Pooling Made Easy, page 90).

Pan-Seared Strip Steak

Hands-on time: 10 min. Total time: 51 min.

A little butter adds richness and keeps leaner-than-usual beef moist without adding much total fat. WARNING: Smoky! Keep exhaust fan on high, or cook in skillet on a hot outdoor grill.

2 (12-ounce) lean, grass-fed New York strip steaks
1 teaspoon kosher salt
¾ teaspoon black pepper
1 tablespoon olive oil
2 tablespoons butter
2 thyme sprigs
2 garlic cloves, crushed

1. Let steaks stand 30 minutes at room temperature.
2. Sprinkle salt and pepper evenly over steaks. Heat a large cast-iron skillet over high heat. Add oil to pan; swirl to coat. Add steaks to pan; cook 3 minutes on each side or until browned. Reduce heat to medium-low; add butter, thyme, and garlic to pan. Carefully grasp pan handle using an oven mitt or folded dish towel. Tilt pan toward you so butter pools; cook 1½ minutes, basting steaks with butter constantly. Remove steaks from pan; cover loosely with foil. Let stand 10 minutes. Reserve butter mixture.
3. Cut steak diagonally across grain into thin slices. Discard thyme and garlic; spoon reserved butter mixture over steak. Yield: 6 servings (3 ounces beef and ¾ teaspoon butter mixture).

CALORIES 197; FAT 10.2g (sat 4.4g, mono 2.2g, poly 0.7g); PROTEIN 26.3g; CARB 0.3g; FIBER 0g; CHOL 73mg; IRON 2.1mg; SODIUM 410mg; CALC 13mg

THE SKINNY ON GRASS-FED BEEF

All cows graze on pasture for the first six months to a year of their lives, but most finish at a feedlot on a concentrated mix of corn, soy, grains, and other supplements, plus hormones and antibiotics. This growth-spurt formula is the backbone of a hugely productive U.S. beef industry. A feedlot cow can grow to slaughter weight up to a year faster than a cow fed only forage, grass, and hay. "That's one year that you don't have to feed the cows in the feedlot," notes Eatwild.com founder Jo Robinson, who spent the past decade examining scientific research comparing grass-fed and grain-fed animals. "Conventional factory meat is so cheap because they've done everything to speed growth and lower the cost of feed."

The feedlot process not only speeds the animal to slaughter weight but also enhances fat marbling, which is one factor that determines a cut of beef's USDA rating—the more fat within the red meat, the richer the taste, the higher the grade. Most supermarket beef is Choice, which is one step below Prime, the top grade typically found in steak houses.

Boosting fat levels changes the nutritional composition of the meat, of course, and, from a health point of view, not for the better. A study by researchers at California State University in Chico examined three decades of research and found that beef from pasture-raised cows fits more closely into goals for a diet lower in saturated fat and higher in "good fats" and other beneficial nutrients. Grass-fed beef is lower in calories, contains more healthy omega-3 fats, more vitamins A and E, higher levels of antioxidants, and up to seven times the beta-carotene.

Skeptics such as Chris Raines, a professor of meat science at Penn State, say the benefits of the different fat profiles are overblown: "Some people get very excited about the fatty-acid profile of grass-fed beef. Then, in the same breath, they'll talk about how wonderfully lean it is. We're talking up the good fats that aren't really there."

The National Cattlemen's Beef Association, which says it supports all forms of beef production, echoes this much-ado-about-not-much theme. Shalene McNeill, who has a PhD in human nutrition and is Executive Director for Human Nutrition Research at the association, acknowledges that "if you feed (cows) grass, you can slightly increase the omega-3 content, but if you look at it in terms of a whole diet, it's not a significant advantage to human health." Ditto, McNeill says, for some other "good" nutrients.

Yet a 6-ounce grass-fed beef tenderloin may have 92 fewer calories than the same cut from a grain-fed cow. "If you eat a typical amount of beef per year," Robinson points out in *Pasture Perfect*, a book about the benefits of pasture-raised animals, "which in the United States is

about 67 pounds, switching to grass-fed beef will save you 16,642 calories a year." It would also, if you paid supermarket prices and dined on tenderloin, cost you about $300 more.

Meeting the Meat

Another lesson about grass-fed beef: It's not only about the grass, but also the breed, and the cow.

We were looking for a lower-fat cow, so we chose the Brangus. Though lean, it was still blanketed with a jacket of fat that would play a flavor role in the evolution of the meat. The fat would mostly get trimmed away during the butchering, but before then it would protect the meat during the dry-aging period, usually 10 to 14 days, in which the carcass hangs in a cold locker while natural enzymes break down tough muscle fiber and tenderize the meat. It's worth noting that although the best steakhouse steaks are dry-aged, most supermarket beef is wet-aged in a plastic vacuum-sealed bag that prevents shrinkage but also precludes the concentration of beefy flavor that occurs with water loss. The amount of fat cover also determines how much is available to go into the ground beef—which we ordered in 85/15 and 90/10 meat-to-fat ratios.

The fat on our grass-fed cow looked different from the fat we have been accustomed to cooking. Compared to the bright, white fat of conventional beef, grass-fed fat is often yellower, stemming from the higher levels of beta-carotene. And as we would learn, the quantity and the quality of our cow's fat would play a key role in cooking.

Taste and Tenderness

Our Test Kitchens experimented with various cuts of grass-fed beef, both from our Brangus cow and from local supermarkets. The meat had good, clean beefy flavor but tended to be a lot chewier than we were used to, and sometimes drier. There can be such a thing as too lean in beef cuts that are conventionally fairly high in fat, like strip steaks and other luxury cuts. Adjustments had to be made for these steaks, which were producing less fat in the pan than we were used to and could turn tough.

"Fat is an insulator," says Deborah Krasner, author of *Good Meat*, the first major cookbook dedicated to sustainable meats. "So if you cook something that's very fatty, and you cook it badly, it's still going to taste pretty good because fat insulates the meat. When you have leaner meat, you don't have that safety net, so you have to cook it carefully." Cook with care, or chew like crazy, basically.

"Carefully" means that tougher cuts like short ribs or brisket require the very-low-and-slow approach—long cooking at low temperatures. But it also means cooking a tender steak

more aggressively than you might be used to for such a pricey cut. We decided to really turn up the heat on a thick, 12-ounce grass-fed New York strip purchased at Whole Foods, preheating a cast-iron pan on high, turning on the fan, and nearly smoking out the kitchen when the meat hit the metal. Testers were coughing and shaking their heads as the vent fans roared. After a billowing 3-minute sear on each side, there was very little fat in the pan. Previous tests suggested that the meat, though good, would lack the buttery deliciousness many of us like in this rare treat. Recipe tester Robin Bashinsky turned down the heat and began basting the steak with two pats of butter (see recipe, page 88, for this method). When done, the meat got a short rest under foil and then was sliced; it was perfectly medium-rare within.

Could a grass-fed cut, with its lower-fat content, rival a grain-fed cut? Yes: It was succulent, buttery, and robust, with a perfectly caramelized crust. The juices formed a simple, rich sauce.

But is this a paradoxical way to cook a steak bought in part for its lean fat profile—adding butter to "beef" up the flavor? (After all, grass-fed fans suggest it just takes time to come to love what Deborah Krasner calls "meatier, purer, more mineral" flavors.) Not necessarily. First, most of the butter does not cling to the beef, so we estimate the process adds less than half a gram of saturated fat to the final meat. (If you use the pan juices as a sauce, more is added, but total saturated fat for a serving is still only 4.4 grams.) Second, a cook may have bought grass-fed meat for many reasons—ecological, ethical, or to support local businesses—but still desires a hit of full-on steak-house flavor now and then.

As we tasted more beef, however, we found that there aren't clear-cut, consistent taste differences between grass-fed and grain-fed meat. This emerged after a blind tasting of eight New York strips, cooked identically. Samples included regular supermarket beef; steak from our grass-fed cow; and meat from a variety of grass-fed and grain-fed animals of different breeds raised in different states. The latter came from a "Discover Beef" tasting pack from The Artisan Beef Institute in Santa Rosa, California, whose founder, Carrie Oliver, applies the wine-tasting model to meats.

Our testers liked several samples but discovered no universal preference for grass-fed or grain-fed, finding various degrees of beefiness and juiciness across the samples. Beef really is like cheese or tomatoes or any other food: The proof is in the pudding, not in claims about the pudding. The cook needs to explore and sample with an open mind.

MORE ABOUT COWS

COW-POOLING MADE EASY

At *Cooking Light*, we dove into the subject of grass-fed versus grain-fed cows by starting our own cow-pool. Of course, most cooks won't want to buy a whole grass-fed cow or even a half-cow. One option is to "cow-pool" with curious friends. Another is to turn to a CSA, or community-supported agriculture group. CSAs have been popping up like mushrooms in many cities, and many deliver quantities of meat on a weekly or monthly basis. Here's a 10-point guide from what we learned:

1. FIND YOUR COW. Locate a pasture-based farm near you by searching the state-by-state directory on Eatwild.com, which also has a library of scientific research on the topic. If you don't want to buy in bulk, Google "meat CSA" and the name of the nearest city. Sometimes the best place to start is a farmers' market—find one near you on LocalHarvest.org.

2. ASK QUESTIONS. Legit grass-fed producers welcome them. Do they practice rotational grazing? What breeds are best? (The "right" answer varies by region, but generally small-framed breeds—Angus, Hereford, Red Hereford, British White, Shorthorn, Murray Gray, and others—gain weight on grass best. If you can't visit the farm, at least taste a sample before you buy.

3. BUY IN SEASON. Like produce, meat has peak seasons. For beef, it's typically mid-spring to September, after the lushest, greenest pastures. Many farmers need advance notice, so order 2 to 6 weeks ahead.

4. DO THE MATH. A half-cow will feed a family of four for almost a year and costs around $1200 to $1500. The per-pound price—which ranges from $3.50 to $5.00 a pound nationally—is the hanging weight (the hot carcass weight after slaughter). After butchering, expect to take home about 55% to 65% of that.

5. FILL OUT A CUT SHEET. Most farmers provide a planning sheet that walks you through the key decisions. Think about how you cook: Do you want more ground beef or stew meat? Ground chuck and sirloin can comprise 30%-45% of your take-home meat (we got 80 pounds). If you enjoy braising or slow-cooking, you might want more roasts. If you're a Superfast cook, quick-defrosting ground beef is your friend.

6. MAKE ROOM. A half-cow, including organs and meat, takes up about 10 cubic feet of freezer space. To save space and money, roast the bones to make stock, and then freeze the liquid in gallon zippered bags laid flat—they'll fit in the nooks and crannies of your freezer.

7. CHOOSE PAPER OR PLASTIC. Some people claim the meat tastes better when tightly wrapped in butcher paper, but plastic tends to last longer. "If you're looking for the best quality product in your freezer, cryovac is the way to go," says Chris Raines, Professor of Meat Science at Penn State University. Vacuum-packed meat can wet age in the refrigerator for several days to a week, tenderizing the meat without spoiling.

8. PROLONG SHELF LIFE. Minimize handling, which can puncture the seal, exposing meat to air and freezer-burn. "You could keep well-packaged paper-wrapped meats for six months, and cryovac meats for a year," Raines says. "But I've had meat that's two years old and it's been fine."

9. DEFROST PROPERLY. Never nuke it! Defrosting in a microwave will produce a dry, rubbery mess. Defrost overnight in a nonreactive dish in the refrigerator. If you've purchased paper-wrapped meat, it may bleed out, but don't worry—just turn the meat so it will reabsorb the juices. For quick defrosting, run cryovac-packed beef under cold water for 20 minutes.

10. COOK IT RIGHT. As a rule, cook hot and fast or low and slow. For tougher cuts, explore techniques beyond braising, says Krasner. "Meat destined for roasting or grilling can be marinated overnight in red wine and spices, or yogurt and garlic, before cooking, or it can be roasted for a long time at an extremely low temperature, or pounded before cooking, or sliced thinly against the grain to make a more tender mouthfeel."

HOW OUR COW STACKED UP

Nutrition and pricing: our grass-fed beef against basic grain-fed supermarket beef

OUR GRASS-FED COW
What Do the Terms Mean?
The USDA has a less rigorous definition, but among pasture purists, grass-fed means a cow lives its life eating only grass and forage after weaning. Never treated with hormones or antibiotics. Our cow fit those standards.

Nutrition: How Did the Total Fat Compare?*
Our cow was really lean. Lab tests on a 4-ounce serving sample of our sirloin strip steak showed 4.1g total fat, 1.7g sat fat.

What About the "Good" Fats?
Our grass-fed cow did not have a significantly higher ratio of monounsaturated fats, or of omega-3 fatty acids. It was just a low-fat cow.

What Our Cow Cost Versus Supermarket Prices
We paid, on average, $5.32 per pound for our half-cow of grass-fed Brangus (243 pounds of meat, including organs).

GRAIN-FED BEEF
What Do the Terms Mean?
Pastured on grass and forage at first, then confined to fatten up on a concentrated feed of grains and supplements. Treated with hormones and antibiotics to promote growth and prevent illness.

Nutrition: How Did the Total Fat Compare?*
Lab tests of supermarket grain-fed sirloin strip steak showed almost three times the fat: 11.5g total fat, 4.7g sat fat. A Prime-grade steak had four times as much total fat and sat fat.

What About the "Good" Fats?
Grain-fed steaks were higher in saturated and trans fats, but also in monounsaturated and polyunsaturated fats.

What Our Cow Cost Versus Supermarket Prices
We would have paid $5.03 per pound, on average, for the same quantities and cuts of regular grain-fed beef in a local supermarket.

*We tested the fat content of fully trimmed steaks using an accredited lab. Fat content varies significantly depending on the degree of trimming. A lean grass-fed steak with a good ribbon of external fat can have more fat than a well-trimmed, well-marbled Choice grain-fed cut, as another test showed.

HOW OUR HALF-COW BROKE DOWN

We got 42% of our meat in cuts suitable for roasting or for braising, 21% was good for sautéing or grilling, and 37% was ground. We also got bones and offal.

A CELEBRATION OF TRADITIONS

When you grow up eating both Easter and Passover meals, you have lots of delicious flavors to draw on for one of the first feasts of spring. *Cooking Light* contributing editor Allison Fishman shares her experience.

I was born with lifelong passports to the joys of both Easter and Passover tables: holiday dual citizenship. My mother was raised Protestant and converted to Judaism after college. I was raised Jewish, attended Hebrew school three days a week, had a bat mitzvah, and continue to practice Jewish traditions today. My extended family was Protestant, however, and we celebrated holidays together, so I was blessed to enjoy the culinary traditions of Christmas and Easter.

For Easter, my mom bought baskets at the drugstore and filled them with chocolate bunnies, jelly beans, and squishy Peeps. We dyed Easter eggs and played hide and seek. The Jewish kids had an edge when it came to Easter-egg hunting: We'd already hunted down the *afikomen* at Passover earlier that week. By Easter, our seeking skills were honed.

This open-mindedness abounded as my family grew, and it continues today. My Christmas-celebrating Protestant cousin recently married a Polish Catholic man who has a lot of Greek relatives in his extended family. This year, I'll be celebrating Greek Easter with his family; they will be roasting a whole lamb on a spit.

On these pages is a feast I developed, deriving from both traditions—a mashup. There were some challenges (I wanted a grand dessert but could use no leavening), but the first work was easy: I said buh-bye to pork and separated milk from meat (combining the two is a violation of kosher rules). Although there is dairy in the beet salad that comes at the beginning of the meal (before any meat is served), the entrée, sides, and desserts are completely dairy-free.

Both holiday meal traditions tend to feature foods of spring, and so does this menu: eggs (in the orange curd); spring produce (artichokes, strawberries); and lots of herbs (dill, parsley, thyme, and cilantro). With winter still in the rearview mirror, I also included citrus and beets. The carrots are a nod to the Easter bunny, seasoned with Israeli flavors (the carrots, not the bunny). The Lemon Chicken Soup with Dumplings is a twist on a Passover classic, matzo ball soup. The sweet crowning glory at feast's end is the sponge cake, leavened only with eggs, topped with tangy curd and first-of-the-season berries.

When we eat with friends and family, we share our faith in fundamental human connection. Blending food traditions is a pleasure and an honor. Spring is the most hopeful time of year, a time to share our heritage, and our foods, with guests new and familiar.

CELEBRATION OF SPRING MENU

serves 8

Beets with Walnuts, Goat Cheese, and Baby Greens

Lemon Chicken Soup with Dumplings

Quinoa Salad with Artichokes and Parsley

Brown Sugar–Glazed Capon with Bourbon Gravy

Israeli Carrots

Green Beans with Shallots and Hazelnuts

Sponge Cake with Orange Curd and Strawberries

Date and Almond Truffles

Vegetarian

Beets with Walnuts, Goat Cheese, and Baby Greens

Hands-on time: 20 min. Total time: 2 hr.

If you're keeping kosher, you can have dairy before meat is served, so have this salad first, before the chicken soup or capon. You can roast the beets up to two days in advance.

6 medium beets (red and golden), about 1½ pounds
1 cup water
8 cups mixed baby salad greens
1 cup loosely packed fresh flat-leaf parsley leaves
1 tablespoon white balsamic vinegar
¼ teaspoon kosher salt
¼ teaspoon black pepper
2 tablespoons extra-virgin olive oil
½ cup (2 ounces) crumbled goat cheese
¼ cup coarsely chopped walnuts, toasted

continued

1. Preheat oven to 375°.

2. Leave root and 1-inch stem on beets; scrub with a brush. Place beets and 1 cup water in a 13 x 9–inch glass or ceramic baking dish; cover tightly with foil. Bake at 375° for 1 hour and 30 minutes or until tender. Cool beets slightly. Trim off roots; rub off skins. Cut beets into wedges; cool completely.

3. Place greens and parsley in a large bowl; toss. Combine vinegar, salt, and pepper, stirring with a whisk. Gradually drizzle in oil, stirring constantly with a whisk. Drizzle dressing over greens mixture; toss gently. Arrange 1 cup salad on each of 8 plates; top evenly with beets. Top each serving with 1 tablespoon cheese and 1½ teaspoons nuts. Yield: 8 servings.

CALORIES 125; FAT 8.2g (sat 2.4g, mono 3.3g, poly 1.9g); PROTEIN 4.1g; CARB 10.1g; FIBER 3.1g; CHOL 7mg; IRON 1.5mg; SODIUM 178mg; CALC 63mg

Make Ahead

Lemon Chicken Soup with Dumplings

Hands-on time: 1 hr. Total time: 4 hr.

Roasting the bones adds richer, deeper flavor to the stock. Take your time when tempering the egg (used to add body to the soup) with the hot broth; the payoff is a smooth, silky texture.

2 pounds chicken bones (such as necks and backs)
2 large carrots, cut into 3-inch pieces
2 celery stalks, cut into 3-inch pieces
1 large onion, halved
12 cups water
1 bay leaf
1 teaspoon ground turmeric
3/4 teaspoon kosher salt, divided
2/3 cup matzo meal
1 tablespoon chopped fresh flat-leaf parsley
2 tablespoons canola oil
2 tablespoons sparkling water
2 teaspoons grated lemon rind
1/4 teaspoon freshly ground black pepper
3 large eggs, lightly beaten and divided
1/2 pound skinless, boneless chicken breast halves
2 tablespoons fresh lemon juice
1½ tablespoons chopped fresh dill

1. Preheat oven to 425°.

2. Arrange first 4 ingredients on a jelly-roll pan. Bake at 425° for 45 minutes or until browned.

3. Combine chicken mixture, 12 cups water, and bay leaf in a stockpot over high heat. Bring to a boil. Reduce heat to low, and simmer gently 2 hours, skimming fat and foam from surface occasionally. Strain stock through a fine sieve into a large bowl; discard solids. Skim fat from surface of stock; discard fat. Return stock to pan; stir in turmeric and ½ teaspoon salt.

4. Combine remaining ¼ teaspoon salt, matzo meal, and next 5 ingredients. Add 2 eggs; stir until combined. Cover and refrigerate 30 minutes. With moist hands, shape mixture into 24 (1-inch) balls. Bring stock to a simmer (do not boil). Add dumplings to stock, and cook 15 minutes. Add chicken, and continue cooking 15 minutes or until chicken is done. Remove pan from heat. Remove chicken from stock, and let stand 5 minutes. Cut chicken into thin slices; return to pan. Remove 1 cup hot broth mixture. Place remaining 1 egg in a medium bowl. Gradually add 1 cup hot broth mixture to egg, stirring constantly with a whisk. Slowly pour beaten egg mixture into pan, stirring constantly with a whisk. Stir in lemon juice, and sprinkle with dill. Yield: 8 servings (serving size: about 1¼ cups).

CALORIES 138; FAT 5.7g (sat 0.9g, mono 3.1g, poly 1.4g); PROTEIN 10.9g; CARB 10.6g; FIBER 0.6g; CHOL 88mg; IRON 0.9mg; SODIUM 232mg; CALC 18mg

Quick & Easy • Make Ahead

Quinoa Salad with Artichokes and Parsley

Hands-on time: 20 min. Total time: 32 min.

Parsley has its own spot on the seder plate; it represents spring. Although quinoa is considered a whole grain, it is, in fact, a seed—making it a welcome addition to a Passover meal.

1 tablespoon olive oil
1 cup chopped spring or sweet onion
½ teaspoon chopped fresh thyme
1 (9-ounce) package frozen artichoke hearts, thawed
1 cup fat-free, lower-sodium chicken broth
½ cup uncooked quinoa
1 cup chopped fresh parsley
5 teaspoons grated lemon rind
1½ tablespoons fresh lemon juice
¼ teaspoon kosher salt

1. Heat oil in a medium saucepan over medium-high heat. Add onion and thyme; sauté 5 minutes or until onion is tender. Add artichokes; sauté 2 minutes or until thoroughly heated. Add broth and quinoa; bring to a simmer. Cover and cook 18 minutes or until liquid is completely absorbed.

2. Remove pan from heat. Stir in parsley, rind, juice, and salt. Serve warm or at room temperature. Yield: 8 servings (serving size: about ⅓ cup).

CALORIES 83; FAT 2.8g (sat 0.3g, mono 1.4g, poly 0.6g); PROTEIN 3g; CARB 12.4g; FIBER 3.5g; CHOL 0mg; IRON 1.2mg; SODIUM 135mg; CALC 39mg

LEMON CHICKEN SOUP WITH DUMPLINGS MAKE-AHEAD TIP: COOK AND CHILL THE STOCK A DAY AHEAD; SKIM SOLIDIFIED FAT FROM COLD STOCK BEFORE HEATING AND PROCEEDING WITH RECIPE.

Brown Sugar–Glazed Capon with Bourbon Gravy

Hands-on time: 21 min. Total time: 1 hr. 41 min.

Capons are great for a special occasion, but a 6-pound roasting chicken works equally well (cook times stay the same). Potato starch thickens the gravy and fits within Passover dietary restrictions.

1 (6-pound) whole capon or roasting chicken
¼ cup packed brown sugar
3½ teaspoons Dijon mustard, divided
¾ teaspoon kosher salt, divided
Cooking spray
1 cup water
1 (14-ounce) can fat-free, lower-sodium chicken broth, divided
⅓ cup minced shallots
3 tablespoons bourbon
2 tablespoons potato starch
1 tablespoon water
¼ cup chopped fresh flat-leaf parsley
½ teaspoon freshly ground black pepper

1. Preheat oven to 425°.
2. Remove and discard giblets and neck from capon. Trim excess fat. Starting at neck cavity, loosen skin from breast and drumsticks by inserting fingers, gently pushing between skin and meat. Combine sugar, 2 teaspoons mustard, and ½ teaspoon salt; rub sugar mixture under loosened skin and over breast and drumsticks. Tie ends of legs together with twine. Lift wing tips up and over back; tuck under capon. Place capon, breast side up, on the rack of a broiler pan coated with cooking spray. Pour 1 cup water into bottom of pan; place rack in pan. Bake at 425° for 30 minutes.

3. Baste capon with 1 cup broth; loosely cover capon with foil. Reduce oven temperature to 350° (do not remove capon from oven). Bake at 350° for 30 minutes. Uncover and baste with remaining broth. Bake an additional 20 minutes or until a thermometer inserted in meaty part of thigh registers 165°. Remove from oven; let stand 20 minutes. Discard skin before serving.
4. Place a zip-top plastic bag inside a 2-cup glass measure. Pour drippings from pan into bag. Let stand 2 minutes (fat will rise to top). Seal bag, and carefully snip off 1 bottom corner of bag. Drain drippings into measuring cup, stopping before fat layer reaches opening; discard fat. Pour drippings into a small sauccpan; stir in shallots. Bring to a boil; reduce heat, and simmer 2 minutes. Add remaining 1½ teaspoons mustard and bourbon, stirring with a whisk; simmer 1 minute. Combine potato starch and 1 tablespoon water in a small bowl, stirring with a whisk; stir starch mixture into bourbon mixture. Simmer 1 minute or until thick. Remove from heat; stir in remaining ¼ teaspoon salt, parsley, and pepper. Serve gravy with capon. Yield: 8 servings (serving size: about 4 ounces capon meat and ¼ cup gravy).

NOTE: Bourbon is generally not permissible on Passover; however, the issue gets rather complicated, and there do seem to be cases where the spirit may be allowed. If you'd like to make this dish for Passover without bourbon, simply omit it and add 3 tablespoons more chicken broth. For a full discussion, go to CookingLight.com/passover.

CALORIES 244; FAT 4.8g (sat 1.2g, mono 1.5g, poly 1.2g); PROTEIN 36g; CARB 10.7g; FIBER 0.3g; CHOL 113mg; IRON 2.2mg; SODIUM 445mg; CALC 32mg

---

Quick & Easy • Vegetarian
Israeli Carrots

Hands-on time: 20 min. Total time: 20 min.

This became an instant classic at my Passover table when I first served it years ago. The vivid garlic-and-herb vinaigrette contrasts with the sweet carrots, which are a natural Easter vegetable, what with all those hungry Easter bunnies looking for something to munch. If you can find carrots in a variety of colors, such as orange, yellow, and purple, by all means use them! If you can't find baby carrots, simply cut a regular carrot in half crosswise, halve the skinny bottom lengthwise, and quarter the thicker top section. What we're looking for here are long pieces, a visual contrast to most of the other dishes.

2 quarts water
1 pound baby carrots, trimmed and halved lengthwise
1 garlic clove, chopped
½ cup chopped fresh cilantro
2 tablespoons chopped fresh dill
1 tablespoon olive oil
1 tablespoon fresh orange juice
½ teaspoon ground cumin
¼ teaspoon kosher salt

1. Bring 2 quarts water to a boil in a saucepan. Add carrots; cook 3 minutes or until crisp-tender. Drain.
2. Place garlic in a food processor; pulse 3 times or until finely chopped. Add cilantro; pulse 3 times or until combined. Add dill and next 4 ingredients; pulse 3 times or until well combined. Spoon dill mixture over carrots; toss gently to coat. Serve warm or at room temperature. Yield: 8 servings (serving size: about ⅓ cup).

CALORIES 38; FAT 1.9g (sat 0.3g, mono 1.2g, poly 0.2g); PROTEIN 0.5g; CARB 5.2g; FIBER 1.5g; CHOL 0mg; IRON 0.2mg; SODIUM 95mg; CALC 19mg

Vegetarian

Green Beans with Shallots and Hazelnuts

Hands-on time: 15 min. Total time: 30 min.

2 quarts water
1 tablespoon kosher salt
1½ pounds green beans, trimmed and cut into
   3-inch pieces
2 tablespoons olive oil
4 shallots, thinly sliced
¼ teaspoon kosher salt
¼ teaspoon freshly ground black pepper
¼ cup chopped hazelnuts, toasted

1. Combine 2 quarts water and 1 tablespoon salt in a large Dutch oven; bring to a boil. Add green beans; cook 3 minutes or until crisp-tender. Drain and plunge beans into ice water; drain.
2. Heat olive oil in a large nonstick skillet over medium-high heat, swirling to coat. Add shallots, and sauté 3 minutes or until golden brown. Add beans, ¼ teaspoon salt, and pepper; toss to coat. Cook 2 minutes or until beans are thoroughly heated. Sprinkle with hazelnuts. Yield: 8 servings (serving size: ¾ cup).

CALORIES 88; FAT 5.7g (sat 0.7g, mono 4.1g, poly 0.7g);
PROTEIN 2.6g; CARB 9.1g; FIBER 3.3g; CHOL 0mg;
IRON 1.3mg; SODIUM 137mg; CALC 36mg

MATZO AND ALMOND FLOUR SPONGE CAKE IS DELIGHTFUL— FLORAL AND SWEET, WITH LEMON, ORANGE, AND TANGY BERRIES.

Sponge Cake with Orange Curd and Strawberries

(pictured on page 219)

Hands-on time: 40 min. Total time: 1 hr. 55 min.

Dairy- and flour-free, this cake is a winner year-round. Matzo cake meal—finely ground matzo—stands in for wheat flour.

Cake:
1 cup sugar
1 tablespoon grated lemon rind
8 large egg yolks
8 large egg whites
½ cup almond flour
¼ cup matzo cake meal
¼ cup potato starch
Cooking spray
Orange Curd:
1 teaspoon grated orange rind
¾ cup fresh orange juice
½ cup sugar
1 tablespoon potato starch
3 large eggs
1 pound strawberries, halved

1. Preheat oven to 325°.
2. To prepare cake, place first 3 ingredients in a large bowl; beat with a mixer at high speed 5 minutes or until thick and pale. Place 8 egg whites in a separate large bowl; beat with a mixer at high speed 3 minutes or until stiff peaks form, using clean, dry beaters. Gently fold egg whites into egg yolk mixture.
3. Sift together almond flour, cake meal, and ¼ cup potato starch; gently fold into egg mixture.
4. Coat 2 (8 x 2–inch) round metal cake pans with cooking spray; line bottoms of pans with wax paper. Coat wax paper with cooking spray. Spoon batter into prepared pans. Bake at 325° for 30 minutes or until cake springs back when lightly touched. Invert pans on a wire rack; cool cake completely in inverted pans.
5. To prepare curd, place orange rind, orange juice, ½ cup sugar, 1 tablespoon potato starch, and 3 eggs in a small saucepan; stir with a whisk until smooth. Place pan over medium-low heat; cook 6 minutes or until thick, stirring constantly. Spoon curd into a bowl, and place plastic wrap on surface of curd. Chill.
6. Loosen cakes from sides of pans using a narrow metal spatula. Place 1 cake layer, upside down, on a plate. Remove and discard wax paper. Spread half of curd over cake, and arrange half of strawberries over curd. Top with remaining cake layer, upside down. Spread remaining curd over cake. Arrange remaining strawberry halves over curd. Yield: 12 servings (serving size: 1 wedge).

CALORIES 230; FAT 5.9g (sat 1.2g, mono 3g, poly 1.2g);
PROTEIN 7.2g; CARB 37.5g; FIBER 1.4g; CHOL 165mg;
IRON 1.2mg; SODIUM 65mg; CALC 43mg

Date and Almond Truffles

Hands-on time: 35 min. Total time: 35 min.

This dessert is for those at the table who want just a little something sweet. Store truffles in an airtight container for up to five days.

2½ cups whole pitted dates
2 cups slivered blanched almonds, toasted
1 tablespoon honey
½ teaspoon ground cinnamon
⅛ teaspoon kosher salt
1 cup flaked unsweetened coconut, toasted

1. Place first 5 ingredients in a food processor. Process 45 seconds, scraping down sides as needed, or until mixture forms a thick paste.
2. Place coconut in a shallow bowl. Shape almond mixture into 36 (1-inch) balls. Roll balls in toasted coconut. Yield: 18 servings (serving size: 2 truffles).

CALORIES 158; FAT 9.1g (sat 3g, mono 4g, poly 1.6g);
PROTEIN 3.3g; CARB 19g; FIBER 3.6g; CHOL 0mg;
IRON 0.8mg; SODIUM 15mg; CALC 47mg

THE GLORIOUS NOODLES OF SPRING

April warmth brings the first farm-fresh vegetables, and some of the year's best at that. Pair vegetables with pasta for simple and delicious dinners that celebrate this lovely season.

Pasta makes an ideal partner for the lightest, most delicately flavored veggies of the year. These dishes showcase fresh, vibrant items like snappy green peas, earthy asparagus, peppery radishes, sweet spring onions, and nutty fava beans. The job of the noodles is to make them a substantial, but never heavy, meal. It's also fitting to celebrate the season's produce bounty with pasta that's just as varied: tidy farfalle bow ties and fluted garganelli tubes; long, hollow bucatini noodles and broad, elegant pappardelle ribbons. We chose dried pastas, rather than fresh—they're pantry-friendly and offer a more satisfying chew when cooked al dente.

Most of these recipes are vegetarian but are easily transformed for seafood or meat eaters by adding sautéed shrimp or even a little crumbled bacon. And a few of them use a secret weapon from the savvy Italian cook's arsenal: pasta cooking liquid. Starchy and lightly salted, it becomes a quick, simple sauce that won't mask the taste of the veggies, moistening the pasta and marrying flavors in the dish.

Quick & Easy • Kid Friendly
Garganelli with Asparagus and Pecorino Cheese

Hands-on time: 20 min. Total time: 29 min.

Substitute penne if garganelli is unavailable.

8 ounces uncooked garganelli pasta
1 tablespoon kosher salt
2 tablespoons olive oil
2 1/2 cups (1-inch) sliced asparagus (about 1 pound)
1 cup fat-free, lower-sodium chicken broth
1 tablespoon grated lemon rind
1 garlic clove, minced
1/4 cup (1 ounce) grated fresh pecorino Romano cheese
1/2 teaspoon kosher salt
1/2 teaspoon freshly ground black pepper
2 tablespoons shaved fresh pecorino Romano cheese

1. Cook pasta in boiling water with 1 tablespoon kosher salt according to package directions, omitting additional fat. Drain.
2. Heat a large skillet over medium-high heat. Add oil to pan, swirling to coat. Add asparagus to pan; cook 3 minutes or until crisp-tender, stirring occasionally. Remove from pan; keep warm. Add broth, lemon rind, and garlic to pan; cook until liquid is reduced to 1/2 cup (about 6 minutes). Return asparagus to pan. Add pasta, grated cheese, 1/2 teaspoon salt, and pepper; toss well. Place about 1 1/4 cups pasta mixture in each of 4 shallow bowls; top each serving with 1 1/2 teaspoons shaved cheese. Yield: 4 servings.

CALORIES 340; FAT 11.9g (sat 3g, mono 6.4g, poly 1.9g); PROTEIN 14.1g; CARB 46g; FIBER 4.7g; CHOL 54mg; IRON 4.9mg; SODIUM 610mg; CALC 138mg

Fusilli with Caramelized Spring Onions and White Wine

Hands-on time: 36 min. Total time: 48 min.

Spring onions are those that have been harvested early—they look like scallions with large white bulbs. If they're unavailable, use Vidalia onions.

1/2 cup panko (Japanese breadcrumbs)
3 tablespoons olive oil, divided
2 teaspoons minced garlic, divided
1/2 teaspoon kosher salt, divided
2 cups thinly sliced spring onions (about 1 pound)
1/2 cup dry white wine
1/4 cup fat-free, lower-sodium chicken broth
8 ounces uncooked fusilli (short twisted spaghetti)
1 tablespoon kosher salt
1/4 teaspoon freshly ground black pepper

1. Preheat oven to 375°.
2. Combine panko, 1 tablespoon oil, 1 teaspoon garlic, and a dash of salt in a small bowl. Spread panko mixture in a single layer on a baking sheet. Bake at 375° for 6 minutes or until golden brown, stirring after 3 minutes. Cool.
3. Heat a large skillet over medium-low heat. Add remaining 2 tablespoons oil to pan, swirling to coat. Add onions to pan; cook 20 minutes or until golden brown, stirring occasionally. Add remaining 1 teaspoon garlic and wine. Increase heat to medium-high; cook 1 minute. Add broth; cook until liquid is reduced to 1/2 cup (about 4 minutes).
4. Cook pasta in boiling water with 1 tablespoon kosher salt according to package directions, omitting additional fat. Drain. Add pasta, remaining salt, and pepper to onion mixture; toss gently. Place about 1 cup pasta in each of 4 shallow bowls; sprinkle each serving with 2 tablespoons panko mixture. Yield: 4 servings.

CALORIES 364; FAT 11.7g (sat 1.7g, mono 7.6g, poly 1.8g); PROTEIN 9.5g; CARB 55.6g; FIBER 3.5g; CHOL 0mg; IRON 2.2mg; SODIUM 438mg; CALC 35mg

Orzo Salad with Radish and Fennel

Hands-on time: 20 min. Total time: 58 min.

Lemony dressing and fresh mint add vibrant flavor to this pasta salad. Serve chilled or at room temperature, and garnish with pretty mint leaves, if desired.

8 ounces uncooked orzo (rice-shaped pasta)
1 tablespoon kosher salt
1/4 cup fresh lemon juice
3 tablespoons olive oil
1 teaspoon Dijon mustard
1/2 teaspoon freshly ground black pepper
1 1/2 cups diced fennel (about 1 bulb)
1/2 cup chopped radish
3 tablespoons chopped fresh mint
3 tablespoons minced green onions
1/2 teaspoon kosher salt
1/3 cup pine nuts, toasted

1. Cook orzo pasta with 1 tablespoon kosher salt according to package directions, omitting additional fat. Drain and rinse with cold water. Drain well.
2. Combine lemon juice and next 3 ingredients in a large bowl; stir well with a whisk. Add orzo, fennel, and next 4 ingredients; toss well to coat. Cover and chill. Top with nuts before serving. Yield: 4 servings (serving size: 1¼ cups pasta and 4 teaspoons nuts).

CALORIES 393; **FAT** 19.1g (sat 2.3g, mono 9.6g, poly 5.4g); **PROTEIN** 10g; **CARB** 48.8g; **FIBER** 4.1g; **CHOL** 0mg; **IRON** 3.3mg; **SODIUM** 517mg; **CALC** 46mg

Pappardelle with Baby Spinach, Herbs, and Ricotta

(pictured on page 216)

Hands-on time: 17 min. Total time: 27 min.

Fettuccine will also work if you can't find pappardelle. Have all the ingredients prepped and ready to go before beginning to cook—the pasta needs to be hot when mixed with the other ingredients to create a creamy consistency.

8 ounces uncooked pappardelle (wide ribbon pasta)
1 tablespoon kosher salt
1/3 cup whole-milk ricotta cheese
3 cups baby spinach leaves
1/4 cup chopped fresh chives
1/4 cup chopped fresh flat-leaf parsley
1/4 cup chopped fresh dill
3 tablespoons grated fresh pecorino Romano cheese
2 tablespoons olive oil
1/2 teaspoon freshly ground black pepper
1/4 teaspoon kosher salt

1. Cook pasta with 1 tablespoon kosher salt according to package directions, omitting additional fat. Drain in a colander over a bowl, and reserve 1 cup cooking liquid.
2. Place ½ cup reserved hot cooking liquid and ricotta cheese in a food processor or blender, and process until well blended.
3. Combine hot pasta, cheese mixture, spinach, and next 7 ingredients in a large bowl; toss gently to coat. Add additional cooking liquid to moisten, if needed. Yield: 4 servings (serving size: 1¾ cups).

CALORIES 329; **FAT** 11.6g (sat 3.6g, mono 6.1g, poly 1.1g); **PROTEIN** 12.2g; **CARB** 45.5g; **FIBER** 2.9g; **CHOL** 14mg; **IRON** 2.9mg; **SODIUM** 373mg; **CALC** 118mg

Bucatini with Green Peas and Pancetta

Hands-on time: 30 min. Total time: 45 min.

Use frozen, thawed green peas if fresh are unavailable. Substitute linguine for bucatini, which is a thick, spaghetti-like pasta with a hollow center.

1 tablespoon olive oil
1/2 cup chopped pancetta (about 2 ounces)
1/4 cup finely chopped shallots
1 1/4 cups fresh shelled green peas (about 1 1/2 pounds unshelled)
1 garlic clove, minced
1/4 cup dry white wine
2 teaspoons chopped fresh thyme
1/2 pound uncooked bucatini pasta
1 tablespoon kosher salt
2 tablespoons extra-virgin olive oil
1/2 teaspoon kosher salt
1/4 teaspoon freshly ground black pepper
1/2 cup (2 ounces) grated fresh Parmigiano-Reggiano cheese

1. Heat a large skillet over medium heat. Add 1 tablespoon oil to pan, swirling to coat. Add pancetta; cook 10 minutes or until browned and crisp, stirring occasionally. Remove pancetta from pan, reserving 1 tablespoon drippings in pan; set pancetta aside. Add shallots; cook 4 minutes or until tender, stirring occasionally. Add peas and garlic; cook 1 minute, stirring occasionally. Add wine and thyme. Increase heat to medium-high. Bring to a boil; cook until liquid reduces to 2 tablespoons (about 3 minutes). Remove from heat.
2. Cook pasta in boiling water with 1 tablespoon salt according to package directions, omitting additional fat. Drain pasta in a colander over a bowl, and reserve ½ cup cooking liquid. Add pasta, 2 tablespoons extra-virgin olive oil, ½ teaspoon salt, and black pepper to pea mixture; toss well. Stir in reserved cooking liquid. Place about 1¼ cups pasta mixture in each of 4 shallow bowls; top each serving evenly with grated cheese and pancetta. Yield: 4 servings.

CALORIES 403; **FAT** 16.8g (sat 4.3g, mono 7.5g, poly 1.6g); **PROTEIN** 13.5g; **CARB** 51.1g; **FIBER** 4.2g; **CHOL** 12mg; **IRON** 2.8mg; **SODIUM** 639mg; **CALC** 64mg

Vegetarian

Farfalle with Fava Beans, Morel Mushrooms, and Mascarpone

Hands-on time: 35 min. Total time: 1 hr. 22 min.

You can also use shiitake mushrooms and edamame, good year-round alternatives to morels and fava beans.

½ ounce dried morel mushrooms
1 cup boiling water
1½ cups shelled fava beans (about 1½ pounds unshelled)
1 tablespoon olive oil
½ cup finely chopped onion
1 cup fresh morel mushrooms, halved lengthwise
1 garlic clove, minced
1 tablespoon chopped fresh marjoram or oregano
8 ounces uncooked farfalle (bow tie pasta)
1 tablespoon kosher salt
⅓ cup (about 3 ounces) mascarpone cheese
½ teaspoon kosher salt
¼ teaspoon freshly ground black pepper

1. Combine dried mushrooms and boiling water in a bowl; cover and let stand 30 minutes or until tender. Drain mushrooms in a sieve lined with a paper towel over a bowl; reserve liquid. Rinse mushrooms; drain well. Chop.
2. Place fava beans in a large pot of boiling water; cook 40 seconds. Drain; rinse with cold water. Drain well. Remove tough outer skins from beans.
3. Heat a large skillet over medium-high heat. Add oil to pan, swirling to coat. Add onion to pan; sauté 3 minutes or until tender. Add fresh mushrooms and garlic; sauté 2 minutes. Add chopped rehydrated mushrooms, reserved liquid, fava beans, and marjoram. Cook until liquid is reduced to ½ cup (about 5 minutes).
4. Cook pasta in boiling water with 1 tablespoon salt according to package directions, omitting additional fat. Drain. Add pasta, mascarpone, and remaining ingredients to fava bean mixture; toss gently to coat. Yield: 4 servings (serving size: about 1½ cups).

CALORIES 386; **FAT** 14.5g (sat 6.1g, mono 5.9g, poly 1.3g); **PROTEIN** 13.5g; **CARB** 51.9g; **FIBER** 4.2g; **CHOL** 27mg; **IRON** 3.5mg; **SODIUM** 421mg; **CALC** 59mg

WINE NOTE: The wait for weather warm enough to crack open a bottle of rosé has always been a difficult one. By the time the birds start chirping, we're up to our eyeballs in pink.

Rosés come in styles that range from light and dry to full and fruity. And when they are from Spain, all the better. This morel and fava bean pasta dish begs for a full, tropical fruit–laden rosé from Bodegas Muga, Rioja Rosé, 2009 ($13). Its elegant, fresh citrus flavors cut the creamy mascarpone, while its laid-back herbal notes pair remarkably with the meaty morels.

> SEEK OUT THE FRESHEST PRODUCE YOU CAN FIND. THE SUCCESS OF SIMPLE DISHES DEPENDS ON THE QUALITY OF THEIR INGREDIENTS.

FIRST BITES

THE PERFECT DISH TO PAIR WITH CHIANTI

Try this with a Da Vinci 2008 Chianti ($12), with bright plum notes and hints of smoke.

Kid Friendly • Vegetarian

Slow-Roasted Tomato Pasta

Hands-on time: 10 min. Total time: 4 hr. 32 min.

3 pounds plum tomatoes, cored and halved lengthwise
¼ cup extra-virgin olive oil, divided
2¼ teaspoons kosher salt, divided
¼ teaspoon black pepper
6 whole peeled garlic cloves
¼ teaspoon crushed red pepper
12 ounces uncooked fettuccine
¾ cup (3 ounces) shaved fresh Parmigiano-Reggiano cheese
3 tablespoons torn fresh basil

1. Preheat oven to 225°.
2. Place tomatoes on a jelly-roll pan; sprinkle with 2 tablespoons oil, ¾ teaspoon salt, and black pepper. Bake at 225° for 4 hours.
3. Heat a large skillet over low heat. Add remaining 2 tablespoons oil and garlic; cook 10 minutes, stirring occasionally. Remove garlic, and chop. Combine garlic, tomatoes, and red pepper in pan.
4. Cook pasta in boiling water with remaining 1½ teaspoons salt 8 minutes or until almost al dente. Drain, reserving ¾ cup cooking liquid. Increase heat to medium-high under tomato mixture; stir in reserved cooking liquid. Bring to a boil. Cook 3 minutes. Add cooked pasta; cook 1 minute, tossing to combine. Remove from heat; sprinkle with cheese and basil. Yield: 6 servings (serving size: 1 cup).

CALORIES 389; **FAT** 14.3g (sat 4g, mono 7.8g, poly 1.3g); **PROTEIN** 15.2g; **CARB** 52g; **FIBER** 4.4g; **CHOL** 13mg; **IRON** 2.7mg; **SODIUM** 631mg; **CALC** 196mg

CARROT CAKE, 1,000 CALORIES LIGHTER!

We radically slim down one of the most egregiously over-the-top cakes in the universe.

Some time back, carrot cake became the poster child for a healthy-sounding food that is actually a fat and calorie disaster. But we'd forgotten how much of a disaster it could be until we looked at an online recipe from a celebrity chef who shall go unnamed. There it was, in all its splendor, weighing in at 1,460 calories and 28 grams of saturated fat in one gargantuan three-layer slice.

Few are the recipes that have been made over quite this dramatically. We shaved about 1,000 calories and 89 grams of total fat. Yet, it's delicious: Creamy butter and smooth buttermilk create a perfectly moist, tender texture. Earthy brown sugar brings out the warm cinnamon spices. Real-deal cream cheese and butter maximize frosting flavor. Low-fat fromage blanc and a light sprinkle of toasted pecans make it a special, vastly lighter treat.

Make Ahead • Kid Friendly
Carrot Cake

Hands-on time : 35 min. Total time: 1 hr. 53 min.

Warm spices and brown sugar add rich, caramelized flavors to this carrot cake. If you can't find fromage blanc, use more cream cheese.

Cake:
10.1 ounces all-purpose flour (about 2¼ cups)
2 teaspoons baking powder
1½ teaspoons ground cinnamon
¼ teaspoon salt
2 cups grated carrot
1 cup granulated sugar
½ cup packed brown sugar
6 tablespoons butter, softened
3 large eggs
1 teaspoon vanilla extract
½ cup low-fat buttermilk
Cooking spray
Frosting:
6 ounces cream cheese, softened
1 ounce fromage blanc
2 tablespoons butter, softened
½ teaspoon vanilla extract
⅛ teaspoon salt
3 cups powdered sugar
¼ cup chopped pecans, toasted

1. Preheat oven to 350°.
2. To prepare cake, weigh or lightly spoon flour into dry measuring cups; level with a knife. Combine flour, 2 teaspoons baking powder, ground cinnamon, and ¼ teaspoon salt in a medium bowl, stirring with a whisk. Add 2 cups grated carrot, tossing to combine.
3. Place granulated sugar, brown sugar, and 6 tablespoons butter in a large bowl. Beat with a mixer at medium speed until combined. Add eggs, 1 at a time, beating well after each addition. Stir in 1 teaspoon vanilla. Add flour mixture and buttermilk alternately to sugar mixture, beginning and ending with flour mixture. Spread batter into a 13 x 9–inch metal baking pan coated with cooking spray. Bake at 350° for 28 minutes or until a wooden pick inserted in center comes out clean. Cool cake completely on a wire rack.
4. To prepare frosting, place softened cream cheese and next 4 ingredients in a medium bowl. Beat with a mixer at medium speed until fluffy. Gradually add powdered sugar, beating at medium speed until combined (don't overbeat). Spread frosting evenly over top of cake. Sprinkle evenly with toasted pecans. Yield: 20 servings (serving size: 1 piece).

CALORIES 284; FAT 9.7g (sat 4.9g, mono 2.8g, poly 0.8g); PROTEIN 3.6g; CARB 46.6g; FIBER 0.9g; CHOL 49mg; IRON 1mg; SODIUM 172mg; CALC 68mg

OLD WAY	OUR WAY
1,460 calories per slice	284 calories per slice
99 grams total fat	9.7 grams total fat
28 grams saturated fat	4.9 grams saturated fat
24 tablespoons oil for moisture	6 tablespoons butter and a rich splash of buttermilk
Frosted with one stick of butter and a pound of cream cheese	Frosted with a hint of butter, cream cheese, and fromage blanc
Pecan extravaganza	A perfectly toasted sprinkle

BUILDING A BETTER CAKE

A successful cake finds perfect balance among these four essential ingredients:

1 FLOUR
Flour contributes body, structure, and texture to the framework of a cake. Weigh the flour and measure it carefully; this is essential to lower-fat baking.

2 SUGAR
Sugar adds volume, tenderness, and texture to the batter. Granulated and brown sugars team up to provide a level of sweetness that rounds out the warm spices.

3 BUTTER
Real butter lends a softer texture, firm crumb, and melt-in-your-mouth goodness. Soften butter to a range of 65° to 70° for maximum leavening.

4 EGGS
Eggs bind ingredients, provide structure, and aerate the cake. To incorporate more air, beat the eggs after each addition, resulting in a great rise.

LESS MEAT, MORE FLAVOR
QUESADILLAS, DONE BETTER
By Mark Bittman

Crisped tortillas encase bold ingredients—peppery greens, robust cheeses, a hint of meat—with just enough cheese to seal the deal.

Quesadillas are, by definition, cheesy; the word translates as "cheese in tortilla." But that doesn't mean they can't be a little more interesting—and a lot less gooey—than the standard oozy and pretty tasteless ones.

I start by demoting cheese to the job of glue. Obviously cheese has good flavor, but a big mouthful is no more flavorful than a small one, especially when it's hot and melting. If you drastically reduce the amount of cheese, there's room for more vegetables, along with delicious bits of meat, seafood, or poultry—ingredients that enhance taste, texture, and nutrition.

I usually go with whole-wheat flour tortillas, since they have a little more fiber than those made with white flour, and I like the deeper flavor. Both bake up crisp and a little flaky. Choose corn tortillas if you want a little chew along with the crunch, and expect a pronounced corn taste that intensifies in the oven. (Corn tortillas are often smaller, so you may need to use an extra one or two for the amount of filling in the recipes here.) Whatever tortilla you pick, scan the label for unnecessary additives and hidden trans fat. For my money, lard is better.

For fillings, draw on combinations of ingredients that work well together without a tortilla. They don't have to be Mexican: Use what you like and what you have handy. The tortillas are going to partially enclose the filling—and the cheese will hold everything together—so you have more options than you do with sandwiches, where you have to worry about losing food out the sides.

I gravitate toward hearty greens: They're compact, chewy, flavorful, and versatile. Escarole and mustard greens are the two examples in these recipes, but you can also try chard, kale (especially Lacinato or so-called black kale), or even cabbage. Some other vegetables that work well are mushrooms (I like a mixture of fresh and reconstituted dried porcini for more intensity with less bulk) and grated root vegetables such as carrots, parsnips, or beets. You want to avoid anything that's too wet. And you definitely want to precook the fillings until they shrink and dry a bit since that will make them easier to handle. Most raw ingredients won't have time to cook in the oven and will just turn the tortillas into a soggy mess as they release their liquid.

For meat I follow the same guidelines and choose things that deliver a lot of flavor in small quantities, like the chicken thighs and sausage I use here. Shrimp, crab, lobster, cured or smoked pork or fish, or chopped hard-cooked eggs are other good choices. For vegetarian quesadillas, you could use stir-fried tofu or lightly mashed beans. Again, you want to precook the meat, poultry, or fish. Stir-frying them with the vegetables is simple and quick. Even easier is to use leftovers—grilled or roasted foods are especially nice. Just chop everything up a bit first.

And then there's the cheese. Any cheese that melts will do the job, including hard grating cheeses like Parmesan, Manchego, or pecorino. Creamy cheeses like Brie, Gorgonzola, or goat cheese are other good choices. You can use mozzarella, but since there isn't going to be much in your slimmed-down quesadilla, I veer toward cheeses that have more flavor.

You can make quesadillas on the stove one or two at a time; the oven offers the advantage of making more than a couple at once. The technique I use is a simple fold and a flip. The results are crisp on the outside and interesting on the inside, without a drop of goo in sight.

Chicken, Mustard Greens, and Gruyère Quesadillas

Hands-on time: 26 min. Total time: 26 min.

2 tablespoons olive oil, divided
½ teaspoon black pepper, divided
⅛ teaspoon kosher salt
2 skinless, boneless chicken thighs (about 5 ounces), chopped
4 cups chopped stemmed mustard greens
1 tablespoon minced fresh garlic
Dash of kosher salt
¼ teaspoon grated lemon rind
4 (6-inch) whole-wheat tortillas
¼ cup (1 ounce) grated Gruyère cheese

1. Preheat oven to 400°.
2. Heat a large skillet over medium-high heat. Add 1 tablespoon olive oil to pan; swirl to coat. Sprinkle ¼ teaspoon pepper and ⅛ teaspoon salt over chicken; toss to coat. Add chicken to pan; cook 2 minutes or until browned, stirring occasionally. Add greens, garlic, and dash of salt; cook 3 minutes or until greens wilt, stirring frequently. Stir in remaining ¼ teaspoon pepper and rind.
3. Brush remaining 1 tablespoon oil over a jelly-roll pan; arrange tortillas in a single layer on pan. Sprinkle 1 tablespoon cheese evenly over each tortilla; top each tortilla with about ⅔ cup chicken mixture. Bake at 400° for 5 minutes or until cheese begins to melt. Remove pan from oven; carefully fold each tortilla in half, pressing gently to close. Bake quesadillas an additional 10 minutes or until browned and crisp, turning carefully after 5 minutes. Yield: 2 servings (serving size: 2 quesadillas).

CALORIES 476; FAT 22.9g (sat 5.2g, mono 12.2g, poly 2.4g); PROTEIN 25.3g; CARB 41.3g; FIBER 8g; CHOL 74mg; IRON 5mg; SODIUM 736mg; CALC 400mg

Escarole, Sausage, and Fontina Quesadillas

Hands-on time: 26 min. Total time: 26 min.

2 tablespoons olive oil, divided
5 ounces hot pork Italian sausage, casings removed
4 cups chopped escarole
1 tablespoon minced fresh garlic
¼ teaspoon freshly ground black pepper
4 (6-inch) whole-wheat tortillas
¼ cup (1 ounce) grated fontina cheese

1. Preheat oven to 400°.
2. Heat a large skillet over medium-high heat. Add 1 tablespoon oil to pan; swirl to coat. Add Italian sausage, and cook 5 minutes or until browned, stirring to crumble. Drain sausage, and return to pan. Add escarole, garlic, and black pepper; cook 2 minutes or until escarole wilts, stirring frequently.
3. Brush remaining 1 tablespoon olive oil over a jelly-roll pan; arrange tortillas in a single layer on pan. Sprinkle 1 tablespoon cheese evenly over each tortilla; top each with about ⅔ cup sausage mixture. Bake at 400° for 3 minutes or until cheese begins to melt. Remove from oven, and carefully fold each tortilla in half, pressing to close. Bake an additional 10 minutes, turning after 5 minutes. Yield: 2 servings (serving size: 2 quesadillas).

CALORIES 441; FAT 23.2g (sat 5.4g, mono 11.7g, poly 1.8g); PROTEIN 18g; CARB 40.5g; FIBER 7.3g; CHOL 23mg; IRON 4mg; SODIUM 826mg; CALC 305mg

CONVENIENCE COOKING

START WITH A CAN OF WHITE BEANS

...such as cannellini, navy, or Great Northern. Look for organic versions, which are low in sodium.

Artichoke, Spinach, and White Bean Dip

Hands-on time: 15 min. Total time: 35 min.

If you can't find baby artichoke hearts, use quartered artichoke hearts and chop them.

¼ cup (1 ounce) grated fresh pecorino Romano cheese
¼ cup canola mayonnaise
1 teaspoon fresh lemon juice
¼ teaspoon salt
¼ teaspoon freshly ground black pepper
⅛ teaspoon ground red pepper
2 garlic cloves, minced
1 (15-ounce) can organic white beans, rinsed and drained
1 (14-ounce) can baby artichoke hearts, drained and quartered
1 (9-ounce) package frozen chopped spinach, thawed, drained, and squeezed dry
Cooking spray
½ cup (2 ounces) shredded part-skim mozzarella cheese

1. Preheat oven to 350°.
2. Place pecorino Romano cheese, ¼ cup mayonnaise, 1 teaspoon lemon juice, salt, black pepper, red pepper, minced garlic, and white beans in a food processor, and process until smooth. Spoon into a medium bowl. Stir in artichokes and spinach. Spoon mixture into a 1-quart glass or ceramic baking dish coated with cooking spray. Sprinkle with ½ cup mozzarella. Bake

at 350° for 20 minutes or until bubbly and brown. Yield: 12 servings (serving size: ¼ cup).

CALORIES 87; FAT 5.4g (sat 1.4g, mono 2.3g, poly 1g); PROTEIN 3.7g; CARB 4.9g; FIBER 1g; CHOL 6mg; IRON 0.7mg; SODIUM 232mg; CALC 91mg

---

Quick & Easy

Tuna and White Bean Salad

Hands-on time: 30 min. Total time: 30 min.

20 asparagus spears
1 tablespoon capers, drained
1 tablespoon chopped fresh flat-leaf parsley
2 tablespoons white wine vinegar
2 tablespoons fresh lemon juice
2 tablespoons extra-virgin olive oil
1 tablespoon butter, melted
¼ teaspoon salt
¼ teaspoon black pepper
1 cup cherry tomatoes, quartered
1 (15-ounce) can organic white beans, rinsed and drained
4 cups torn butter lettuce (about 1 head)
2 (5-ounce) cans solid white tuna packed in olive oil, drained and broken into chunks

1. Snap off tough ends of asparagus spears. Steam asparagus, covered, 3 minutes. Drain and rinse with cold water; drain.
2. Combine capers and next 7 ingredients in a small bowl, stirring well with a whisk.
3. Place ¼ cup juice mixture, cherry tomatoes, and beans in a small bowl; toss gently to combine.
4. Place 1 cup lettuce on each of 4 plates, and top each serving with 5 asparagus spears. Spoon about ½ cup white bean mixture over each serving, and divide tuna evenly among servings. Drizzle each salad with about 1 tablespoon remaining juice mixture. Yield: 4 servings.

Sustainable Choice

Buy solid white (albacore) tuna. Look on the label for sustainable pole-caught fish.

CALORIES 270; FAT 14.6g (sat 3.5g, mono 7.4g, poly 2.5g); PROTEIN 20.2g; CARB 16g; FIBER 5.6g; CHOL 24mg; IRON 2.4mg; SODIUM 467mg; CALC 65mg

---

Quick & Easy • Kid Friendly

Chicken and White Bean Soup

Hands-on time: 30 min. Total time: 40 min.

Cannellini beans, native to Tuscany, work beautifully in this rustic soup because they hold their shape after simmering in the flavorful broth. Serve with a crusty Italian bread, such as ciabatta, and a salad of bitter greens.

2 smoked bacon slices, chopped
12 ounces skinless, boneless chicken thighs, trimmed and cut into 2-inch pieces
½ cup chopped onion
1 garlic clove, minced
1 cup chopped plum tomato
2 tablespoons chopped fresh oregano
¼ teaspoon black pepper
2 cups water
2 cups fat-free, lower-sodium chicken broth
⅔ cup uncooked orzo (rice-shaped pasta)
1 (15-ounce) can organic white beans, rinsed and drained
2 tablespoons chopped fresh flat-leaf parsley
1 tablespoon white wine vinegar
¼ teaspoon salt

1. Cook bacon in a large saucepan over medium heat 7 minutes or until crisp. Remove bacon from pan, reserving drippings in pan; set bacon aside.
2. Add chicken to drippings in pan; sauté 6 minutes. Remove chicken from pan. Add onion and garlic to pan; cook 4 minutes or until tender. Add tomato, oregano, and pepper; cook 1 minute, stirring constantly. Return bacon and chicken to pan. Stir in 2 cups water and broth, scraping pan to loosen browned bits. Bring to a boil. Add orzo, and cook 9 minutes or until al dente. Add beans; cook 2 minutes or until heated. Remove from heat; stir in parsley, vinegar, and salt. Yield: 4 servings (serving size: 1¼ cups).

CALORIES 335; FAT 9.9g (sat 2.8g, mono 2.5g, poly 1.5g); PROTEIN 26g; CARB 35.4g; FIBER 5.1g; CHOL 61mg; IRON 3.2mg; SODIUM 530mg; CALC 64mg

---

Quick & Easy • Vegetarian

Southwestern White Bean Pita Pockets

Hands-on time: 25 min. Total time: 25 min.

1½ tablespoons lime juice, divided
4 teaspoons extra-virgin olive oil, divided
½ teaspoon ground cumin
¼ teaspoon salt, divided
¼ teaspoon ground red pepper
2 (15-ounce) cans organic white beans, rinsed, drained, and divided
½ cup diced plum tomato
¼ cup diced red bell pepper
¼ cup diced seeded peeled cucumber
3 tablespoons diced red onion
1 tablespoon chopped fresh cilantro
1 small jalapeño pepper, seeded and minced
2 (6-inch) pitas, cut in half
4 Boston lettuce leaves
½ cup crumbled queso fresco
4 lime wedges

1. Place 1 tablespoon lime juice, 2 teaspoons oil, cumin, ⅛ teaspoon salt, red pepper, and 1 cup beans in a food processor; process until smooth, scraping sides of bowl as needed.
2. Place remaining 1½ teaspoons lime juice, remaining 2 teaspoons olive oil, remaining ⅛ teaspoon salt, remaining beans, tomato, bell pepper, cucumber, red onion, cilantro, and jalapeño in a bowl; toss well to combine.
3. Spread about 3½ tablespoons processed bean mixture inside each pita half. Place 1 lettuce leaf, about ¾ cup tomato mixture, and 2 tablespoons cheese inside each pita half. Serve with lime wedges. Yield: 4 servings (serving size: 1 pita half and 1 lime wedge).

CALORIES 363; FAT 9g (sat 2.6g, mono 4.1g, poly 0.9g); PROTEIN 16g; CARB 54.9g; FIBER 7.6g; CHOL 10mg; IRON 4mg; SODIUM 546mg; CALC 196mg

TODAY'S LESSON: ROAST LAMB

Roast lamb is a seasonal classic, but time, temperature, and roasting technique differ according to the cut. We'll walk you through the basics for four cuts of this delicious spring meat.

HOW TO ROAST A LAMB LEG

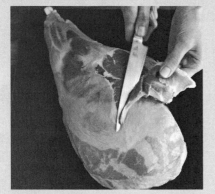

1. TRIM The exterior of this cut is covered with a layer of tough connective tissue and fat. Be sure to trim away all visible fat and silver skin (that thin, pearly-looking membrane). Use a thin utility or carving knife for this job.

2. INFUSE FLAVOR With a large muscle like this, you need to go beneath the surface to ensure the flavor permeates the meat. Make small slits in the meat and insert slivers of garlic directly into them for maximum impact.

3. SEASON Make a flavorful rub. We used a mixture of lemon, fresh herbs, and olive oil. Other citrus, shallots, and spices are also good options. Then sprinkle salt and freshly ground black pepper directly onto the trimmed roast.

4. LET STAND AND CARVE Once the lamb is cooked, let it stand at least 15 minutes before slicing. This allows the meat to relax and the juices to redistribute, ensuring you won't lose the flavor and moisture on your cutting board.

Garlicky Leg of Lamb with Yogurt Sauce

Hands-on time: 35 min. Total time: 7 hr.

1 tablespoon grated lemon rind
3 tablespoons fresh lemon juice
2 tablespoons extra-virgin olive oil
1 tablespoon chopped fresh rosemary
1 tablespoon chopped fresh oregano
1 (6-pound) bone-in leg of lamb, trimmed
10 garlic cloves, halved
1 teaspoon salt
½ teaspoon freshly ground black pepper
Cooking spray
1 cup plain 2% reduced-fat Greek yogurt
¼ cup diced English cucumber
¼ cup diced plum tomato
¼ cup diced red onion
2 tablespoons chopped fresh chives
1 tablespoon red wine vinegar
⅛ teaspoon salt
1 garlic clove, minced

1. Combine first 5 ingredients in a small bowl. Cut 20 (¾-inch-deep) slits in lamb. Press 1 garlic half into each slit. Rub lamb with lemon mixture. Cover and marinate in refrigerator at least 5 hours.
2. Preheat oven to 450°.
3. Sprinkle lamb with 1 teaspoon salt and pepper. Place lamb on a wire rack coated with cooking spray; place rack in a roasting pan. Let stand at room temperature 20 minutes. Bake lamb at 450° for 20 minutes.
4. Reduce oven temperature to 375° (do not remove lamb from oven).
5. Bake an additional 55 minutes or until a thermometer inserted in thickest part of lamb registers 130°. Let stand 15 minutes; cut across grain into slices.
6. Combine yogurt and next 7 ingredients in a medium bowl. Serve with lamb. Yield: 16 servings (serving size: 3 ounces lamb and about 1 tablespoon sauce).

CALORIES 276; FAT 11.9g (sat 4g, mono 5.6g, poly 0.8g); PROTEIN 37.8g; CARB 2.2g; FIBER 0.2g; CHOL 114mg; IRON 2.8mg; SODIUM 259mg; CALC 33mg

LOIN CHOPS

These affordable, versatile chops are quick-cooking, so they're great for weeknight meals. Marinate overnight so flavor permeates, or simply season and cook. For best flavor and visual appeal, sear them and roast at high heat.

Marinated Lamb Chops

Hands-on time: 20 min. Total time: 8 hr. 20 min.

Chermoula, *a North African herb and spice paste, imparts bold flavors with minimal effort.*

1/4 cup finely chopped fresh cilantro
2 tablespoons finely chopped fresh flat-leaf parsley
2 tablespoons minced onion
2 tablespoons fresh lemon juice
1 tablespoon extra-virgin olive oil
3/4 teaspoon smoked paprika
1/2 teaspoon ground coriander
2 garlic cloves, minced
8 (4-ounce) lamb loin chops, trimmed
Cooking spray
1/4 teaspoon salt
1/4 teaspoon freshly ground black pepper

1. Combine first 8 ingredients in a large zip-top plastic bag. Add lamb; seal and marinate in refrigerator 8 hours or overnight.
2. Preheat oven to 450°.
3. Heat a large nonstick skillet over medium-high heat. Coat pan with cooking spray. Remove lamb from bag, and discard marinade. Sprinkle both sides of lamb evenly with salt and black pepper. Add half of lamb to pan, and sauté 2 minutes or until browned. Transfer lamb, browned side up, to a broiler pan coated with cooking spray. Repeat procedure with remaining lamb. Bake lamb at 450° for 6 minutes or until desired degree of doneness. Yield: 4 servings (serving size: 2 lamb chops).

CALORIES 246; FAT 12.9g (sat 3.8g, mono 6.5g, poly 1g); PROTEIN 28.9g; CARB 2g; FIBER 0.4g; CHOL 90mg; IRON 2.1mg; SODIUM 230mg; CALC 27mg

RACK OF LAMB

Rack of lamb is a prime cut for special occasions. Sear in a hot pan, coat with breadcrumbs or other flavorful ingredients, and roast the lamb at high heat. Its lean meat becomes tough if overcooked, so we recommend removing it from the oven when it reaches an internal temperature of 130°. Then allow it to stand until it reaches 135° for medium-rare.

PLACE THE LEG OF LAMB ON A RACK IN A HEAVY ROASTING PAN SO AIR CIRCULATES AND IT BROWNS AND COOKS EVENLY.

Quick & Easy
Herb-Crusted Rack of Lamb

Hands-on time: 24 min. Total time: 50 min.

Coat the lamb with Dijon mustard to add flavor and help the breadcrumbs stick.

1/3 cup dry breadcrumbs
3 tablespoons finely chopped fresh mint
2 tablespoons finely chopped fresh flat-leaf parsley
1 garlic clove, minced
2 (1 1/2-pound) French-cut racks of lamb (8 ribs each), trimmed
1/2 teaspoon salt
1/4 teaspoon freshly ground black pepper
Cooking spray
2 tablespoons Dijon mustard

1. Preheat oven to 450°.
2. Combine first 4 ingredients in a small bowl.
3. Sprinkle lamb evenly with salt and pepper. Heat a large nonstick skillet over medium-high heat. Coat pan with cooking spray. Add 1 lamb rack to pan; cook 2 minutes on each side or until browned. Remove lamb from pan. Repeat with remaining lamb rack. Brush Dijon mustard over lamb, and press breadcrumb mixture over lamb. Place lamb on a pan coated with cooking spray; place pan in a roasting pan. Bake at 450° for 18 minutes or until a thermometer inserted in thickest part of lamb registers 130°. Let stand 10 minutes. Cut into chops. Yield: 8 servings (serving size: 2 chops).

CALORIES 293; FAT 15.3g (sat 6.6g, mono 5.8g, poly 0.6g); PROTEIN 32.2g; CARB 4.4g; FIBER 0.3g; CHOL 102mg; IRON 2.4mg; SODIUM 376mg; CALC 23mg

IF THE RIB BONES ARE NOT ALREADY SCRAPED CLEAN, ASK YOUR BUTCHER TO "FRENCH" THE RACK FOR YOU.

SHANKS

Lamb shanks are a tough cut with loads of connective tissue that breaks down over time when cooked at a low temperature. Slow roasting renders the meat tender and succulent.

Slow-Roasted Lamb Shanks

Hands-on time: 26 min. Total time: 3 hr. 38 min.

1 tablespoon chopped fresh rosemary
1 tablespoon chopped fresh thyme
6 garlic cloves
1 medium shallot, peeled
3 tablespoons extra-virgin olive oil, divided
4 (12-ounce) lamb shanks
³⁄₄ teaspoon kosher salt
¹⁄₂ teaspoon black pepper
¹⁄₃ cup fruity, earthy red wine
1¹⁄₂ teaspoons all-purpose flour
1¹⁄₂ tablespoons Dijon mustard
¹⁄₂ cup dried porcini mushrooms
¹⁄₂ cup panko (Japanese breadcrumbs)
Cooking spray

1. Preheat oven to 450°.
2. Combine first 4 ingredients in a mini food processor. Add 1¹⁄₂ teaspoons oil; process until finely ground. Sprinkle lamb evenly with salt and pepper; coat with herb mixture. Place lamb in a single layer in a large ovenproof skillet; roast at 450° for 30 minutes, turning after 20 minutes.
3. Reduce oven temperature to 225° (do not remove lamb from oven).

4. Cover lamb with foil. Bake an additional 2¹⁄₂ hours or until lamb is tender. Remove lamb from pan; keep warm. Place a zip-top plastic bag inside a 2-cup glass measure or bowl. Pour drippings into bag; let stand 10 minutes (fat will rise to the top). Seal bag, and carefully snip off 1 bottom corner of bag. Drain ¹⁄₂ cup drippings into a bowl, stopping before fat layer reaches opening; discard fat. Return drippings and wine to pan over medium heat; bring to a boil, scraping pan to loosen browned bits. Cook until reduced to ¹⁄₂ cup (about 8 minutes). Remove 2 tablespoons wine mixture from pan; stir in flour. Return flour mixture to pan; cook 2 minutes or until slightly thick. Remove from heat; keep warm.
5. Preheat broiler.
6. Combine mustard and 1¹⁄₂ teaspoons oil in a small bowl; brush evenly over lamb. Place mushrooms in a food processor; process until finely ground. Combine ground mushrooms and panko in a shallow dish. Toss panko mixture with remaining 2 tablespoons oil. Press panko mixture evenly over lamb. Place lamb on a broiler pan coated with cooking spray. Broil 4 minutes or until golden brown, turning after 2 minutes. Serve with sauce. Yield: 4 servings (serving size: 1 shank).

CALORIES 388; FAT 19.2g (sat 4.5g, mono 11.1g, poly 1.7g); PROTEIN 38.6g; CARB 12.5g; FIBER 1.5g; CHOL 111mg; IRON 3.8mg; SODIUM 604mg; CALC 29mg

WHAT TO EAT RIGHT NOW

TASTES OF SPRING

Meet the elusive ramp: a beautifully wispy distant cousin to the onion. Ramps appear briefly—for only about six weeks—in farmers' markets before vanishing for another year. Don't be deceived by their delicate, lily-like leaves: These alliums pack a pungent, garlicky bite balanced by a faint whiff of musk. Edible from end to end, a few go a long way. They're worth hunting down and then pairing with other peak ingredients like grassy asparagus, nutty morel mushrooms, and tiny new potatoes for the first feasts of the season.

Another one of spring's finest offerings is the morel mushroom, with its nutty, meaty flavor and wonderfully whimsical appearance. The nooks and crannies hide lots of grit, so be sure to submerge the mushrooms in cold water, swish vigorously, and gently pat dry before you cook and eat them. Sauté in a bit of butter or oil, and pair with scrambled eggs, pasta tosses, or pizza.

Make Ahead

Pickled Ramps and Asparagus

Hands-on time: 8 min. Total time: 48 hr. 26 min.

2 cups white wine vinegar
2 cups dry white wine
1¹⁄₂ tablespoons sugar
1¹⁄₂ tablespoons salt
1 tablespoon mustard seeds
1 tablespoon crushed red pepper
5 thyme sprigs
5 bay leaves
2 pounds ramps
2 pounds asparagus, trimmed and cut into 3-inch pieces

1. Combine first 8 ingredients in a large saucepan over medium-high heat; bring to a boil. Remove and discard roots and outer leaves from ramps; rinse and drain ramps. Pat ramps dry; cut white bulb ends into 3-inch pieces. Reserve greens for another use. Add ramps to vinegar mixture; cook 2 minutes. Place asparagus in a large bowl. Pour hot vinegar mixture over asparagus; cool completely. Cover and chill 2 days. Yield: 12 servings (serving size: about 5 ramp pieces and 5 asparagus pieces).

CALORIES 44; FAT 0.3g (sat 0.1g, mono 0g, poly 0.1g); PROTEIN 3.1g; CARB 8.8g; FIBER 3.6g; CHOL 0mg; IRON 2.8mg; SODIUM 102mg; CALC 73mg

Smoky Asparagus and Mushroom Sauté

Hands-on time: 16 min. Total time: 16 min.

Cook 2 slices applewood-smoked bacon in a large skillet over medium heat until crisp. Remove bacon from pan; crumble. Add 1 tablespoon butter to drippings in pan; swirl to coat. Add 6 ounces quartered fresh morel mushrooms; sauté 4 minutes, stirring occasionally. Stir in 1 pound (1-inch) asparagus pieces, ¼ teaspoon salt, and ¼ teaspoon freshly ground black pepper; sauté 5 minutes or until asparagus is crisp-tender, stirring occasionally. Remove from heat; sprinkle with bacon and 3 tablespoons chopped ramp greens or fresh chives. Yield: 4 servings (serving size: about ⅔ cup).

CALORIES 89; FAT 5.3g (sat 2.8g); SODIUM 283mg

Warm Potato Salad with Ramps and Bacon

Hands-on time: 10 min. Total time: 70 min.

1½ pounds new potatoes
3 tablespoons water
3 tablespoons extra-virgin olive oil
2 tablespoons white wine vinegar
1½ tablespoons Dijon mustard
2 bacon slices, cut into ½-inch pieces
10 ramps
1 cup thinly sliced radishes (about 8 radishes)
¼ teaspoon salt
¼ teaspoon freshly ground black pepper

1. Preheat oven to 375°.
2. Place potatoes in a 13 x 9–inch glass or ceramic baking dish, and drizzle with 3 tablespoons water. Cover with foil and bake at 375° for 45 minutes or until tender. Remove foil, and cool 15 minutes. Halve potatoes.
3. Combine olive oil, vinegar, and mustard in a small bowl, stirring with a whisk. Cook bacon in a large nonstick skillet over medium heat until crisp, stirring occasionally. Remove bacon

from pan using a slotted spoon, reserving drippings in pan. Increase heat to medium-high. Place potatoes, cut sides down, in pan; cook 5 minutes or until golden brown. Place potatoes in a medium bowl.
4. Remove and discard roots and outer leaves from ramps; rinse and drain ramps. Pat ramps dry. Thinly slice bulb ends and leaves crosswise to measure ½ cup. Add ramps, bacon, and radishes to potatoes. Drizzle dressing over potato mixture, and sprinkle with salt and pepper. Toss. Yield: 6 servings (serving size: ⅔ cup).

CALORIES 170; FAT 8.7g (sat 1.6g, mono 5g, poly 1.1g); PROTEIN 3.8g; CARB 21.2g; FIBER 2.8g; CHOL 3mg; IRON 1.3mg; SODIUM 223mg; CALC 33mg

READER RECIPE

FROM YOUR KITCHEN TO OURS

Creative, healthy cooking is nothing new to Lauren Zembron. She considers culinary invention to be one of life's greatest joys (she shares her ideas on her blog healthyfoodforliving.com). This burger recipe combines her husband's two favorite dishes—chicken Parmesan and hamburgers—into one great-tasting, hearty, healthy meal.

Chicken Parmesan Burgers

Chicken Parmesan Burgers

Hands-on time: 22 min. Total time: 30 min.

"Nutritious food can taste downright delicious and even decadent if made at home with wholesome, unprocessed ingredients."
—Lauren Zembron, Boston, Massachusetts

2 (3-ounce) square ciabatta rolls
1 garlic clove, halved
½ pound ground chicken
⅓ cup plus 2 tablespoons lower-sodium marinara sauce, divided
½ teaspoon chopped fresh rosemary
½ teaspoon chopped fresh thyme
¼ teaspoon crushed red pepper
⅛ teaspoon kosher salt
⅛ teaspoon black pepper
Cooking spray
¼ cup (1 ounce) shredded part-skim mozzarella cheese
8 basil leaves

1. Preheat broiler.
2. Cut rolls in half. Place bread, cut sides up, on a baking sheet. Broil 3 minutes or until lightly browned. Remove bread from pan. Rub each slice with cut side of garlic. Set aside.
3. Reduce oven temperature to 375°.
4. Combine chicken, ⅓ cup marinara, rosemary, thyme, red pepper, salt, and black pepper. Divide into 2 portions, shaping each into a ¼-inch-thick patty. Heat an ovenproof skillet over medium-high heat. Coat pan with cooking spray. Add patties to pan; cook 3 minutes. Turn patties, and place pan in oven. Bake at 375° for 8 minutes. Top each patty with 2 tablespoons cheese; bake 1 minute.
5. Layer bottom half of each roll with 2 basil leaves, 1 patty, 1 tablespoon marinara, 2 basil leaves, and roll top. Yield: 2 servings (serving size: 1 burger).

CALORIES 427; FAT 14.4g (sat 4.5g, mono 5.3g, poly 2.3g); PROTEIN 28.9g; CARB 55.4g; FIBER 1.2g; CHOL 83mg; IRON 2.9mg; SODIUM 742mg; CALC 112mg

FEED 4 FOR LESS THAN $10

The heady aroma of roasting onions, a perfectly simple bowl of noodles, and a gorgeous spring risotto

Staff Favorite • Vegetarian
Onion Tart

$9.81 total, $2.45 per serving
Hands-on time: 20 min. Total time: 70 min.

The earthy flavor of this tart, with touches of feta tang, pairs beautifully with a peppery, nutty salad—and we've suggested just that.

1 tablespoon olive oil
2½ pounds onion, sliced
2 tablespoons chopped fresh thyme
¾ teaspoon kosher salt
¼ teaspoon black pepper
½ (14.1-ounce) package refrigerated pie dough
¼ cup (1 ounce) crumbled reduced-fat feta cheese
¼ cup (1 ounce) shredded reduced-fat Swiss cheese
1 large egg, lightly beaten
2 tablespoons water

1. Preheat oven to 425°.
2. Heat oil in a large skillet over medium-high heat. Add onion, thyme, salt, and pepper; cook 20 minutes, stirring occasionally.
3. Roll dough out on a parchment paper–lined baking sheet. Sprinkle feta cheese in center, leaving a 1½-inch border; top with onion mixture. Sprinkle with Swiss cheese. Fold piecrust border up and over onion mixture, pleating as you go, leaving a 6-inch-wide opening. Combine egg and water; brush over dough. Bake at 425° for 25 minutes or until golden. Cool 10 minutes. Yield: 4 servings (serving size: 1 wedge).

CALORIES 402; **FAT** 18.9g (sat 6.7g, mono 6.8g, poly 3.7g); **PROTEIN** 7.6g; **CARB** 51.4g; **FIBER** 5g; **CHOL** 13mg; **IRON** 0.8mg; **SODIUM** 676mg; **CALC** 146mg

Arugula and Walnut Salad:
Combine 6 tablespoons toasted walnuts and 4 ounces arugula. Combine 2 tablespoons olive oil, 1 tablespoon red wine vinegar, and 1 teaspoon Dijon mustard. Drizzle over salad; sprinkle with ¼ cup crumbled feta cheese. Toss. Yield: 4 servings.

CALORIES 159; **FAT** 15.6g (sat 2.7g); **SODIUM** 191mg

Quick & Easy • Vegetarian
Fettuccine with Olive Oil, Garlic, and Red Pepper

$5.59 total, $1.40 per serving
Hands-on time: 28 min. Total time: 28 min.

Serve this simple pasta with zucchini sautéed in 1 tablespoon olive oil.

¼ cup olive oil, divided
3 garlic cloves, minced
½ teaspoon crushed red pepper
6 quarts water
3¼ teaspoons kosher salt, divided
8 ounces uncooked fettuccine
½ cup (2 ounces) grated fresh Parmesan cheese
⅓ cup coarsely chopped fresh flat-leaf parsley

1. Heat a large skillet over medium heat. Add 2 tablespoons oil; swirl to coat. Add garlic; cook 30 seconds, stirring constantly. Stir in pepper. Remove from heat.
2. Bring 6 quarts water and 1 tablespoon salt to a boil in a large pot. Add pasta; cook 8 minutes or until almost al dente. Drain pasta in a colander over a bowl, reserving ½ cup cooking liquid. Add hot pasta, reserved cooking liquid, remaining ¼ teaspoon salt, and cheese to garlic mixture. Increase heat to medium-high; cook 2 minutes or until pasta is al dente, tossing to combine. Remove from heat. Add parsley; toss. Place 1½ cups pasta on each of 4 plates; drizzle each serving with 1½ teaspoons olive oil. Yield: 4 servings.

CALORIES 397; **FAT** 19g (sat 4.6g, mono 11.3g, poly 2.5g); **PROTEIN** 13.2g; **CARB** 44g; **FIBER** 2.1g; **CHOL** 12mg; **IRON** 2.4mg; **SODIUM** 559mg; **CALC** 180mg

Quick & Easy • Kid Friendly
Spring Risotto

$9.60 total, $2.40 per serving
Hands-on time: 30 min. Total time: 30 min.

Fresh asparagus is most economical in the spring when it's in season.

6 cups water, divided
1 pound asparagus, trimmed and cut into ¾-inch pieces
1¾ cups fat-free, lower-sodium chicken broth
2 tablespoons olive oil
1½ cups chopped onion
2 garlic cloves, minced
1 cup uncooked Arborio rice
1 cup frozen shelled edamame
¾ teaspoon kosher salt
¼ cup ⅓-less-fat cream cheese
½ teaspoon freshly ground black pepper
¼ cup (1 ounce) shaved fresh Parmesan cheese
2 tablespoons chopped fresh thyme

1. Bring 4 cups water to a boil in a saucepan. Add asparagus, and cook 2 minutes. Drain. Bring remaining 2 cups water and chicken broth to a simmer in a saucepan.
2. Heat a large saucepan over medium heat. Add olive oil, and swirl to coat. Add onion; cook 4 minutes. Add garlic, and cook 2 minutes, stirring constantly. Stir in rice, edamame, and salt; cook 1 minute. Stir in 1 cup broth mixture; cook 4 minutes or until liquid is nearly absorbed, stirring constantly. Add remaining broth mixture, ½ cup at a time, stirring constantly until liquid is absorbed before adding more (about 20 minutes total).
3. Stir in asparagus, cream cheese, and pepper; cook 1 minute. Spoon 1 cup risotto into each of 4 bowls. Top each serving with 1 tablespoon Parmesan cheese; sprinkle evenly with thyme. Yield: 4 servings.

CALORIES 398; **FAT** 14.2g (sat 4.3g, mono 5.6g, poly 0.8g); **PROTEIN** 17g; **CARB** 53.2g; **FIBER** 7.6g; **CHOL** 15mg; **IRON** 4.4mg; **SODIUM** 748mg; **CALC** 169mg

DINNER TONIGHT

Here is a batch of fast weeknight menus from the *Cooking Light* Test Kitchens.

READY IN 40 MINUTES

········ *The* ········
SHOPPING LIST

Chipotle Pork Tacos
3 large shallots
1 lime
fresh oregano
bottled minced garlic
chipotle chiles in adobo sauce
olive oil
brown sugar
(6-inch) corn tortillas
1 (1-pound) pork tenderloin
reduced-fat sour cream

Radish and Fennel Salad
radishes
fennel bulb
celery
niçoise olives
2 lemons
extra-virgin olive oil

········ *The* ········
GAME PLAN

- Prepare salad.
- Pound and slice pork.

While pork marinates:
- Sauté shallots.
- Cook pork.
- Warm tortillas, and assemble tacos.

Quick & Easy • Kid Friendly
Chipotle Pork Tacos
with Radish and Fennel Salad

*Flavor Hit: Cook tortillas over an open gas flame or in a grill pan for chargrilled flavor.
Keep It Fresh: Store fresh herbs with a damp paper towel in a zip-top plastic bag.
Simple Sub: Use agave nectar or honey in place of brown sugar.*

1 (1-pound) pork tenderloin, trimmed
1½ teaspoons finely grated lime rind
1 tablespoon fresh lime juice
2 teaspoons minced fresh oregano
1 teaspoon brown sugar
2 teaspoons chopped chipotle chile in adobo sauce
2 teaspoons bottled minced garlic
¼ teaspoon salt
Cooking spray
1 cup thinly sliced shallots
2 teaspoons olive oil
8 (6-inch) corn tortillas
¼ cup reduced-fat sour cream
Chopped fresh cilantro (optional)

1. Place pork tenderloin between 2 sheets of heavy-duty plastic wrap; pound to ¼-inch thickness using a meat mallet or small heavy skillet. Remove plastic wrap. Cut pork into thin strips. Combine pork, lime rind, and next 6 ingredients.
2. Heat a large nonstick skillet over medium-high heat. Coat pan with cooking spray. Add shallots to pan; sauté 4 minutes or until tender. Place shallots in a large bowl. Add oil to pan. Add pork; sauté 3 minutes or until no longer pink. Add pork to shallots.
3. Warm tortillas according to package directions. Spoon ⅓ cup pork mixture onto each tortilla, and top each tortilla with 1½ teaspoons sour cream and cilantro, if desired. Fold in half. Yield: 4 servings (serving size: 2 tacos).

CALORIES 299; FAT 9.3g (sat 2.8g, mono 3.9g, poly 1.2g); PROTEIN 27.3g; CARB 27.4g; FIBER 2.6g; CHOL 80mg; IRON 2mg; SODIUM 253mg; CALC 61mg

---

For the Radish and Fennel Salad:
Combine 1 cup thinly sliced radishes, 1 cup thinly sliced fennel, ½ cup thinly sliced celery, and 1 tablespoon finely chopped niçoise olives in a large bowl. • Combine 5 tablespoons fresh lemon juice, 2 teaspoons extra-virgin olive oil, ¼ teaspoon salt, and ¼ teaspoon black pepper. • Drizzle juice mixture over radish mixture. Yield: 4 servings.

CALORIES 48; FAT 2.7g (sat 0.4g); SODIUM 199mg

READY IN 30 MINUTES

········ *The* ········
SHOPPING LIST

Grilled Lamb Chops and Mint Chimichurri
fresh flat-leaf parsley
fresh mint
shallots
garlic
crushed red pepper
extra-virgin olive oil
white vinegar
fat-free, lower-sodium chicken broth
8 (4-ounce) lamb loin chops

Buttermilk Mashed Potatoes
1 pound Yukon gold potatoes
low-fat buttermilk
butter
extra-virgin olive oil

········ *The* ········
GAME PLAN

While water for potatoes comes to a boil:
- Prepare chimichurri.

While potatoes simmer:
- Cook lamb.

While lamb rests:
- Mash and finish potatoes.

continued

Grilled Lamb Chops and Mint Chimichurri
with Buttermilk Mashed Potatoes

Simple Sub: If you don't like lamb, substitute 4-ounce beef tenderloin steaks.
Shopping Tip: Fruity, peppery olive oil will make the most intensely flavored sauce.

1½ cups fresh mint
½ cup fresh flat-leaf parsley
2½ tablespoons extra-virgin olive oil
2 tablespoons fat-free, lower-sodium chicken broth
1½ tablespoons white vinegar
2 teaspoons minced shallots
⅛ teaspoon crushed red pepper
2 garlic cloves, minced
¾ teaspoon kosher salt, divided
½ teaspoon freshly ground black pepper, divided
8 (4-ounce) lamb loin chops, trimmed
Cooking spray

1. Place first 8 ingredients, ¼ teaspoon salt, and ¼ teaspoon black pepper in a food processor; process until blended.
2. Sprinkle lamb loin chops on both sides with remaining ½ teaspoon salt and remaining ¼ teaspoon black pepper. Heat a grill pan over medium-high heat. Coat pan with cooking spray. Add lamb; cook 5 minutes on each side or until desired degree of doneness. Let stand 5 minutes. Serve with chimichurri. Yield: 4 servings (serving size: 2 lamb chops and 2 tablespoons chimichurri).

CALORIES 303; FAT 18.4g (sat 4.7g, mono 10.3g, poly 2g); PROTEIN 30.1g; CARB 4.4g; FIBER 2.7g; CHOL 90mg; IRON 6.6mg; SODIUM 472mg; CALC 101mg

For the Buttermilk Mashed Potatoes:
Cut 1 pound peeled Yukon gold potato into 1-inch pieces. Place in a medium saucepan; cover with water. • Bring to a boil. Reduce heat; simmer 15 minutes or until potato is tender. • Drain well; mash potato with a potato masher. • Stir in ½ cup room temperature low-fat buttermilk, 4 teaspoons butter, and ½ teaspoon kosher salt. • Drizzle with 4 teaspoons extra-virgin olive oil. Yield: 4 servings.

CALORIES 182; FAT 8.8g (sat 3.3g); SODIUM 306mg

READY IN 40 MINUTES

The SHOPPING LIST

Herb and Goat Cheese–Stuffed Chicken Breasts
1 (10-ounce) package fresh spinach
fresh flat-leaf parsley
fresh mint
panko (Japanese breadcrumbs)
olive oil
crushed red pepper
4 (6-ounce) skinless, boneless chicken breast halves
1 (4-ounce) package goat cheese

Red Pepper Couscous
onion
red bell pepper
olive oil
couscous

The GAME PLAN

■ Combine couscous and boiling water.
While couscous stands:
  ■ Stuff chicken breasts.
  ■ Brown stuffed breasts in pan.
While chicken broils:
  ■ Fluff couscous.
  ■ Cook red pepper mixture, and combine with couscous.
  ■ Cook spinach mixture.

Herb and Goat Cheese–Stuffed Chicken Breasts
with Red Pepper Couscous
(pictured on page 217)

Simple Sub: Use regular dried breadcrumbs in place of panko.
Flavor Hit: Mint adds a bright, fresh, lightly sweet note to the stuffing.
Shopping Tip: Look for soft, tangy goat cheese.

¼ cup panko (Japanese breadcrumbs)
2 tablespoons chopped fresh mint
2 tablespoons chopped fresh flat-leaf parsley
1 (4-ounce) package goat cheese
4 (6-ounce) skinless, boneless chicken breast halves
½ teaspoon kosher salt, divided
4 teaspoons olive oil, divided
¼ teaspoon crushed red pepper
1 (10-ounce) package fresh spinach
Lemon wedges (optional)

1. Preheat broiler.
2. Combine first 4 ingredients in a small bowl. Cut a horizontal slit through thickest portion of each breast half to form a pocket. Stuff 2 tablespoons cheese mixture into each pocket; close opening with a wooden pick. Sprinkle chicken with ¼ teaspoon salt.
3. Heat a large nonstick skillet over medium-high heat; add 1 tablespoon olive oil to pan. Add chicken; cook 2 minutes on 1 side or until browned. Arrange chicken on a baking sheet (browned side up); broil 8 minutes or until done.
4. Heat pan over medium-high heat. Add remaining 1 teaspoon oil, red pepper, and spinach; cook 2 minutes or until spinach wilts. Stir in remaining ¼ teaspoon salt. Serve with lemon wedges, if desired. Yield: 4 servings (serving size: 1 chicken breast half and about ½ cup spinach).

CALORIES 348; FAT 12.9g (sat 5.4g, mono 5.2g, poly 1.3g); PROTEIN 46.8g; CARB 10.7g; FIBER 3.7g; CHOL 112mg; IRON 4.2mg; SODIUM 579mg; CALC 114mg

For the Red Pepper Couscous:
Cook 1 cup couscous according to package directions. • Heat 2 teaspoons olive oil in a skillet over medium-high heat. • Add ½ cup chopped onion, ½ cup chopped red bell pepper, and ¼ teaspoon salt; sauté 7 minutes. • Toss with couscous. Yield: 4 servings.

CALORIES 197; FAT 2.6g (sat 0.4g), SODIUM 153mg

READY IN
30
MINUTES

The
SHOPPING LIST

Linguine with Clams and Fresh Herbs
fresh flat-leaf parsley
fresh oregano
1 lemon
2 red onions
garlic
olive oil
crushed red pepper
8 ounces linguine
1½ pounds littleneck clams
white wine
butter

Baby Romaine Salad
baby romaine lettuce leaves
olive oil
balsamic vinegar
honey
Dijon mustard

The
GAME PLAN

While water for the pasta comes to a boil:
■ Chop herbs and grate lemon rind.
While pasta cooks:
■ Prepare clam mixture.
■ Combine pasta, clam mixture, butter, and herb mixture.
■ Toss salad.

Quick & Easy
Linguine with Clams and Fresh Herbs
with Baby Romaine Salad

Prep Pointer: Scrub the littleneck shells before cooking to remove any sand or grit.
Flavor Hit: Cooking the crushed red pepper with the onions distributes its heat evenly.
Time-Saver: Fresh refrigerated linguine will cook in about 3 minutes.

8 ounces uncooked linguine
⅓ cup flat-leaf parsley leaves
1 tablespoon chopped fresh oregano
2 teaspoons grated lemon rind
2 tablespoons olive oil
2 cups vertically sliced red onion
¼ teaspoon crushed red pepper
4 garlic cloves, sliced
½ cup white wine
1½ pounds littleneck clams
2 tablespoons butter
¾ teaspoon salt
½ teaspoon freshly ground black pepper

1. Cook pasta according to package directions, omitting salt and fat; drain well.
2. Finely chop parsley; add oregano and rind.
3. Heat a large skillet over medium-high heat. Add olive oil to pan; swirl to coat. Add onion, red pepper, and garlic; sauté 4 minutes. Add wine and clams; cover and simmer 5 minutes or until shells open. Discard any unopened shells.
4. Combine clam mixture, pasta, butter, salt, and black pepper in a large bowl; toss until butter melts. Sprinkle with parsley mixture; toss well. Yield: 4 servings (serving size: 1½ cups pasta mixture and 6 clams).

Sustainable Choice

Fresh clams are not only sustainable but also require no feed, and they filter the water in which they live.

CALORIES 373; FAT 14.2g (sat 5g, mono 6.6g, poly 1.4g); PROTEIN 15g; CARB 47.5g; FIBER 2.5g; CHOL 32mg; IRON 9.5mg; SODIUM 521mg; CALC 61mg

For the Baby Romaine Salad:
Combine 2 tablespoons balsamic vinegar, 1 tablespoon olive oil, 2 teaspoons honey, 1 teaspoon Dijon mustard, ¼ teaspoon salt, and ⅛ teaspoon black pepper in a bowl. Drizzle mixture over 6 cups baby romaine lettuce leaves; toss well to coat. Yield: 4 servings.

CALORIES 63, FAT 3.7g (sat 0.5g), SODIUM 185mg

OOPS! YOUR GREEN VEGGIES TURN BROWN

Baby them a bit, and your bright spring vegetables will stay vibrant.
By Tim Cebula

When vegetables take a sad turn from bright green to khaki drab, it conjures memories of grade-school cafeteria food and the ruined texture of canned asparagus. The most common culprits: overcooking and acidic dressings. A cook has to know how to care for the delicate source of the green: chlorophyll.

Vegetables such as green beans, broccoli, and asparagus lose their bright color—and crisp texture, for that matter—after six or seven minutes of cooking. If you know you'll be eating them immediately, just remove, drain, and serve. But if you'll be busy assembling other dishes, consider blanching and shocking. Cook for two minutes in salted boiling water, and then remove vegetables immediately and plunge into ice water. The ice bath halts the cooking process and helps set the color. Later, the chilled vegetables can be quickly reheated—by sautéing in olive oil, for instance—without losing their green.

Blanching won't keep veggies vibrant if you dress them too soon with an acid such as vinegar or lemon juice. Wait until just before serving (as we do with our Superfast asparagus sides, page 111).

SUPERFAST

Spring brings fresh flavors and more delicate offerings: leafy salad with steak, lighter seafood mains, asparagus aplenty, and more.

Quick & Easy

Salmon Sandwiches

4 (6-ounce) skinless wild Alaskan salmon fillets (about 1 inch thick)
Cooking spray
1 teaspoon olive oil
¼ teaspoon salt, divided
⅛ teaspoon black pepper
½ cup chopped peeled cucumber
½ cup plain fat-free Greek yogurt
1 tablespoon minced fresh mint
2 teaspoons fresh lemon juice
⅛ teaspoon ground red pepper
8 (1-ounce) slices 100% whole-wheat bread, toasted
½ cup trimmed watercress

1. Preheat oven to 450°.
2. Place fillets in a 13 x 9–inch baking dish coated with cooking spray. Drizzle with olive oil; sprinkle with ⅛ teaspoon salt and black pepper. Bake at 450° for 8 minutes or until desired degree of doneness.
3. Combine remaining ⅛ teaspoon salt, cucumber, and next 4 ingredients. Place 1 fillet on each of 4 bread slices; top with ¼ cup sauce, 2 tablespoons watercress, and 1 bread slice. Yield: 4 servings (serving size: 1 sandwich).

Sustainable Choice | *Wild Alaskan salmon is available for a few months. If unavailable, buy frozen Alaskan salmon.*

CALORIES 455; **FAT** 17.6g (sat 2.7g, mono 7.8g, poly 4.5g); **PROTEIN** 44.7g; **CARB** 28.5g; **FIBER** 3.7g; **CHOL** 105mg; **IRON** 2.6mg; **SODIUM** 448mg; **CALC** 212mg

Quick & Easy

Steak with Cucumber-Radish Salad

If you can't find mâche, use butter lettuce.

3 tablespoons red wine vinegar, divided
2 teaspoons extra-virgin olive oil, divided
1 teaspoon black pepper, divided
⅝ teaspoon salt, divided
1 (1-pound) flank steak, trimmed
Cooking spray
1½ cups thinly sliced radishes
1 English cucumber, halved lengthwise, peeled, and cut into ¼-inch-thick slices
1 (5-ounce) package prewashed mâche (about 8 cups)
¼ cup (1 ounce) crumbled blue cheese

1. Heat a grill pan over medium-high heat. Combine 1 tablespoon vinegar, 1 teaspoon oil, ½ teaspoon pepper, and ⅜ teaspoon salt; rub evenly over surface of steak. Coat grill pan with cooking spray. Add steak to pan, and cook 5 minutes on each side or until desired degree of doneness. Remove steak from pan, and let stand 5 minutes. Cut steak diagonally across grain into thin slices.
2. While steak cooks, combine remaining 2 tablespoons red wine vinegar, remaining 1 teaspoon oil, remaining ½ teaspoon pepper, remaining ¼ teaspoon salt, radishes, and cucumber in a large bowl, and toss well to coat. Add mâche; toss gently to combine. Serve steak with salad. Sprinkle evenly with cheese. Yield: 4 servings (serving size: about 3 ounces steak, about 2 cups salad, and 1 tablespoon cheese).

CALORIES 229; **FAT** 10.7g (sat 4g, mono 3.9g, poly 0.5g); **PROTEIN** 27.2g; **CARB** 3.9g; **FIBER** 0.9g; **CHOL** 44mg; **IRON** 2.1mg; **SODIUM** 560mg; **CALC** 113mg

Quick & Easy

Scallops with Spinach and Paprika Syrup

(pictured on page 218)

¼ cup sugar
¼ cup fresh lemon juice
¼ teaspoon paprika
⅛ teaspoon ground red pepper
2 teaspoons olive oil, divided
1½ pounds jumbo sea scallops
¼ teaspoon salt, divided
¼ teaspoon black pepper
1 teaspoon minced fresh garlic
10 ounces fresh baby spinach
¼ cup pine nuts, toasted

1. Bring first 4 ingredients to a boil in a saucepan; cook 4 minutes or until mixture thickens. Cool slightly.
2. While paprika mixture cooks, heat a large skillet over medium-high heat. Add 1 teaspoon olive oil to pan; swirl to coat. Pat scallops dry with paper towels; sprinkle with ⅛ teaspoon salt and black pepper. Add scallops to pan; cook 2 minutes on each side or until done. Remove from pan; keep warm.
3. Add remaining 1 teaspoon oil and garlic to pan; cook 30 seconds, stirring constantly. Add half of spinach; cook 1 minute, stirring constantly. Add remaining spinach; cook 2 minutes or until wilted. Stir in remaining ⅛ teaspoon salt.
4. Divide spinach mixture evenly among 4 plates, and divide scallops evenly among servings. Drizzle paprika mixture evenly over scallops; sprinkle 1 tablespoon pine nuts over each serving. Yield: 4 servings.

CALORIES 313; **FAT** 9.5g (sat 0.9g, mono 3.3g, poly 3.6g); **PROTEIN** 31.5g; **CARB** 27g; **FIBER** 3.8g; **CHOL** 56mg; **IRON** 3.3mg; **SODIUM** 535mg; **CALC** 94mg

Soup of the Month

Cucumber Gazpacho with Shrimp Relish

2 teaspoons extra-virgin olive oil
¾ pound peeled and deveined medium
    shrimp, chopped
½ teaspoon salt, divided
½ teaspoon black pepper, divided
¼ teaspoon ground cumin
¼ teaspoon paprika
2 cups quartered grape tomatoes
⅓ cup fresh cilantro leaves
2½ cups chopped English cucumber
1 cup fat-free, lower-sodium chicken broth
1 cup plain whole-milk Greek yogurt
¼ cup chopped onion
2 tablespoons fresh lime juice
Dash of ground red pepper
1 large garlic clove, peeled

1. Heat oil in a large skillet over
medium-high heat. Sprinkle shrimp
with ¼ teaspoon salt, ¼ teaspoon black
pepper, cumin, and paprika. Add shrimp
to pan; sauté 2 minutes or until done.
Stir in tomatoes; remove from heat.
Add cilantro.
2. Place remaining ¼ teaspoon salt,
remaining ¼ teaspoon black pepper,
cucumber, and next 6 ingredients in a
blender; process until smooth. Ladle
1 cup soup into each of 4 bowls; top
each serving with ¾ cup relish. Yield: 4
servings.

Look for shrimp that are certified
sustainable. U.S.-farmed shrimp
or wild Northern shrimp from
Canada are the best options. Avoid imported
wild and farmed species.

Sustainable
Choice

CALORIES 225; **FAT** 9.6g (sat 5.1g, mono 1.9g, poly 0.9g);
PROTEIN 22.7g; **CARB** 11.5g; **FIBER** 2.2g; **CHOL** 139mg;
IRON 2.4mg; **SODIUM** 557mg; **CALC** 130mg

Side Dish of the Month

Asparagus with Balsamic Tomatoes

(pictured on page 217)

1 pound asparagus, trimmed
2 teaspoons extra-virgin olive oil
1½ cups halved grape tomatoes
½ teaspoon minced fresh garlic
2 tablespoons balsamic vinegar
¼ teaspoon salt
3 tablespoons crumbled goat cheese
½ teaspoon black pepper

1. Cook asparagus in boiling water 2
minutes or until crisp-tender. Drain.
2. Heat olive oil in a large skillet over
medium-high heat. Add tomatoes and
garlic; cook 5 minutes. Stir in vinegar;
cook 3 minutes. Stir in salt. Arrange
asparagus on a platter; top with tomato
mixture. Sprinkle with cheese and pepper. Yield: 4 servings.

CALORIES 69; **FAT** 3.9g (sat 1.4g, mono 2g, poly 0.3g);
PROTEIN 3g; **CARB** 6.5g; **FIBER** 2.1g; **CHOL** 4mg;
IRON 1.6mg; **SODIUM** 181mg; **CALC** 45mg

Raisin and Pine Nut Variation:
Omit tomatoes, garlic, vinegar, and goat
cheese. Cook ⅓ cup sliced red onion
and 2 tablespoons pine nuts in oil 4
minutes. Add 2½ tablespoons orange
juice, 3 tablespoons raisins, and 2 teaspoons honey; cook 2 minutes. Stir in
¼ teaspoon salt and ¼ teaspoon orange
rind. Spoon over asparagus; sprinkle
with pepper. Yield: 4 servings.

CALORIES 111; **FAT** 5.3g (sat 0.6g); **SODIUM** 151mg

Sesame-Ginger Glazed Variation:
Omit oil, tomatoes, vinegar, salt, cheese,
and pepper. Microwave 1 tablespoon
lower sodium soy sauce, 1 teaspoon
honey, 1 teaspoon lime juice, 1 teaspoon
minced peeled fresh ginger, and garlic
at HIGH 2 minutes. Drizzle over
asparagus; sprinkle with 2 teaspoons
toasted sesame seeds. Serve with lime
wedges. Yield: 4 servings.

CALORIES 43; **FAT** 0.8g (sat 0.1g); **SODIUM** 134mg

Lemon-Tarragon Variation:
Omit tomatoes, vinegar, and cheese;
decrease pepper to ¼ teaspoon.
Combine ⅛ teaspoon lemon rind, 1
tablespoon lemon juice, 2 teaspoons
chopped fresh tarragon, garlic, ½ teaspoon minced shallot, ½ teaspoon Dijon
mustard, salt, pepper, and oil. Drizzle
tarragon mixture over asparagus; toss
gently to coat. Yield: 4 servings.

CALORIES 49; **FAT** 2.3g (sat 0.3g); **SODIUM** 153mg

Snack of the Month

Black-Eyed Pea and Tomato Salsa

Adding the inner veins and seeds from the chile
will increase the heat in this salsa.

1 cup chopped tomatoes
¼ cup prechopped red onion
3 tablespoons chopped poblano chile
2 tablespoons chopped fresh cilantro
2½ tablespoons fresh lime juice
¼ teaspoon minced fresh garlic
⅛ teaspoon salt
⅛ teaspoon ground cumin
⅛ teaspoon freshly ground black pepper
1 (15.8-ounce) can black-eyed peas, rinsed
    and drained

1. Place all ingredients in a large bowl,
and toss to combine. Yield: 8 servings
(serving size: about ⅓ cup).

CALORIES 35; **FAT** 0.3g (sat 0.1g, mono 0g, poly 0.1g);
PROTEIN 1.9g; **CARB** 6.6g; **FIBER** 1.5g; **CHOL** 0mg;
IRON 0.4mg; **SODIUM** 139mg; **CALC** 11mg

ONE FISH, TWO FISH, GOOD FISH, GREEN FISH

Eat more (for your health), but choose wisely (for the ocean's sake): A guide to five species, with recipes

The next time you stare perplexed at your local seafood counter wondering what is good and sustainable, keep this in mind:

Sustainable seafood choices are often tricky and usually influenced by regional, seasonal, and even political conditions that take some homework to fully understand. Black-and-white choices are rare. But increasingly, there are better shades of gray. Barton Seaver, a Washington, D.C.–based chef, has been cooking through sustainability issues for his new book, *For Cod and Country,* and Paul Greenberg, a journalist who has reported on seafood for over a decade, discussed archetypal American seafood items. You'll find a distillation of what they concluded in "Sustainable Seafood Choices" on page 113.

It's true, by the way, that better-farmed and better-caught fish and shellfish cost a bit more. But in an era when we're starting to understand the ocean's limitations, no one should feel self-conscious about serving or accepting smaller portions. The more care we show enjoying the sea's resources, the more the sea will continue to reward us with its bounty.

Quick & Easy
Sautéed Shrimp with Sherry and Chiles

Hands-on time: 25 min. Total time: 25 min.

1½ tablespoons extra-virgin olive oil
1 cup chopped poblano chile (about 1 large)
½ teaspoon salt
4 garlic cloves, thinly sliced
1 large shallot, thinly sliced
1½ pounds large shrimp, peeled and deveined
2 teaspoons paprika
1 cup sherry
¼ cup fresh orange juice
2 tablespoons butter
1 tablespoon chopped fresh oregano
¼ teaspoon crushed red pepper

1. Heat a large nonstick skillet over medium-high heat. Add oil to pan; swirl to coat. Add poblano chile and next 3 ingredients; sauté 30 seconds, stirring frequently. Add shrimp and paprika; sauté 4 minutes or until shrimp are done, stirring frequently. Remove shrimp mixture from pan. Add sherry and orange juice to pan. Bring to a boil; reduce heat, and simmer 3 minutes or until slightly thick. Stir in butter, oregano, and red pepper. Return shrimp to pan; cook 2 minutes or until thoroughly heated. Yield: 4 servings (serving size: 1½ cups).

CALORIES 379; FAT 14g (sat 4.9g, mono 5.6g, poly 2g); PROTEIN 35.5g; CARB 6.8g; FIBER 0.6g; CHOL 274mg; IRON 4.6mg; SODIUM 589mg; CALC 104mg

Staff Favorite • Quick & Easy
Striped Bass with Cilantro-Onion Salad

Hands-on time: 10 min. Total time: 20 min.

Wild striped bass has a clean and assertive taste that is great with the strong flavors of southwestern cooking.

3 tablespoons fresh lime juice, divided
3 tablespoons plain 2% reduced-fat Greek yogurt
1 tablespoon water
¾ teaspoon salt, divided
1 avocado, peeled and pitted
3 tablespoons extra-virgin olive oil, divided
4 (6-ounce) wild or farmed striped bass fillets
½ teaspoon freshly ground black pepper
3 cups loosely packed fresh cilantro leaves (about 1 bunch)
2 cups thinly sliced onion
Chipotle Tabasco sauce (optional)

1. Preheat oven to 400°.
2. Combine 2 tablespoons lime juice, yogurt, 1 tablespoon water, ¼ teaspoon salt, and avocado in a small bowl; mash with a fork until smooth.
3. Heat a large ovenproof skillet over high heat. Add 1½ tablespoons oil to pan; swirl to coat. Sprinkle fish evenly with remaining ½ teaspoon salt and black pepper. Add fish to pan, skin side down, and sauté 2 minutes or until lightly browned. Place pan in oven; bake at 400° for 8 minutes or until desired degree of doneness.
4. Combine remaining 1 tablespoon lime juice and remaining 1½ tablespoons olive oil in a medium bowl, stirring with a whisk. Add cilantro and onion; toss gently to coat. Spoon about 3 tablespoons avocado mixture on each of 4 plates. Top each serving with 1 fillet and ½ cup cilantro-onion salad. Serve with Tabasco, if desired. Yield: 4 servings.

CALORIES 372; FAT 21.7g (sat 3.5g, mono 13.4g, poly 3.3g); PROTEIN 32.1g; CARB 13.4g; FIBER 4.9g; CHOL 132mg; IRON 1.9mg; SODIUM 567mg; CALC 63mg

SUSTAINABLE SEAFOOD CHOICES

Shrimp: No better example of seafood's troublesome gray area exists than shrimp. Catching wild shrimp often requires trawling gear that kills juvenile fish, sea turtles, and sea horses. Carelessly farmed shrimp can be tainted with antibiotics and destroy mangrove forests in sensitive tropical coastal zones. But good choices exist in each category. The Monterey Bay Aquarium and the Blue Ocean Institute have identified several American and Canadian wild shrimp fisheries as "best choices" either because of low-bycatch fishing gear—like the traps used to catch West Coast spot prawns—or because they are caught in a region where the ocean bottom is less susceptible to trawl impacts, as with the Northern Shrimp in Canada. Several shrimp-farming companies have emerged that grow shrimp in closed-containment facilities and spare the mangroves. One standard for sustainable shrimp is set by the Marine Stewardship Council—look for the Council's blue-and-white check mark on packaging. To date the Council has certified one U.S. fishery—wild Oregon pink shrimp—and three varieties of Canadian shrimp.

On the farmed-shrimp front, Whole Foods and Wegman's are particularly good at identifying farms with best practices. As a default choice, stick with U.S. or Canadian shrimp.

Striped bass, farmed or wild: Surprisingly, finding a basic piece of white fish turns out to be one of the harder things to do nowadays. Cod, haddock, red snapper—all have had their problems. Striped bass, another classic white-fleshed fish, suffered an enormous population collapse in the 1980s as a result of overfishing and habitat pollution. But wild striped bass have come roaring back thanks to good management. By 1995, the National Marine Fisheries Service had declared the fish "fully rebuilt." Size limits, as well as low-impact hook-and-line and gill nets practices, have kept them that way. That said, recent unlawful poaching has caused sport fishermen to wage a campaign to have the fish recategorized as a sport fish–only animal. And wild "stripers" carry a PCB risk. If all that turns you off, then farmed striped bass are a good alternative.

Wild American lobster: Whereas many fish and some wild shrimp are trawled in nets that pull in all kinds of things, lobsters are caught in traps or "pots" that don't disturb the seafloor and tend to catch only, well, lobsters. Mandated escape hatches mean that unwanted creatures can sneak out the back door, and a very carefully regulated management scheme has kept populations in decent shape.

Farmed Arctic char: Arctic char is a newcomer to aquaculture that's fairly closely related to salmon. Like salmon, char has a nice orange color and is high in omega-3s. But unlike farmed salmon, Arctic char are not farmed in the open sea, do not cause the spread of sea lice to the wild, and do not escape and dilute the genetics of wild populations.

Fresh or frozen U.S.-caught Pacific albacore tuna: Two questions govern any wild fish's sustainability: (1) How many are there? and (2) How many should we catch? With tuna it takes a lot of work to determine answers to these fundamental questions. Tuna are extremely migratory, sometimes traveling thousands of miles in their lifetimes. To know how many we can catch, we must gather fishing data from dozens of nations. Nevertheless, tuna is the most consumed finfish in America—with fish coming from all over the world. In looking through the different options, there seems to be consensus among ocean advocacy organizations that U.S.-caught Pacific Ocean albacore is a reasonable choice. Assessments indicate they are abundant. They are shorter-lived, quick to reproduce, and hence a little more resistant to fishing pressure than the larger bigeye and bluefin tunas. Ocean conservation organizations further stress selecting pole- or troll-caught albacore since the more industrial fishing methods like purse seining and long-lining can result in the bycatch of turtles, sharks, and billfish. But (and here's that darn seafood gray area again) as Gavin Gibbons at the National Fisheries Institute, a seafood industry advocacy organization, rightly points out, the purse seining and long-lining sectors have improved their bycatch numbers in recent years, and pole-catching tuna can lead to considerable bycatch of juvenile tuna. If you would like to sidestep the tuna question entirely, try U.S.-caught Spanish mackerel as a replacement.

Mixed Seafood Salad

Hands-on time: 50 min. Total time: 2 hr. 50 min.

Use any sustainable seafoods that look fresh. The key to squid is cooking it just until done. Any longer can cause it to turn rubbery.

1½ cups water
6 tablespoons fresh lemon juice (about 2 lemons), divided
1½ pounds mussels, scrubbed and debearded
½ pound peeled and deveined sustainable shrimp, such as pink
½ pound cleaned skinless squid
1 (1¼-pound) wild American lobster
⅛ teaspoon kosher salt
¼ teaspoon black pepper
2 tablespoons extra-virgin olive oil
2 cups fresh cilantro leaves
1 cup thinly sliced radicchio
1½ cups thinly sliced celery
1 cup thinly sliced red onion
¼ teaspoon crushed red pepper
1 head frisée, torn

1. Bring 1½ cups water and 3 tablespoons juice to a boil in a Dutch oven. Add mussels; cover and cook 2 minutes or until shells open. Remove mussels from pan with a slotted spoon; discard any unopened shells. Cool. Remove meat from mussels; discard shells. Place mussels in a large bowl.

2. Add shrimp to boiling liquid in pan; cook 2 minutes or until done. Remove shrimp from pan with a slotted spoon, and add to mussels. Cut squid crosswise into ¼-inch rings, and leave tentacles whole. Add squid to boiling liquid in pan; cook 1 minute. Remove squid from pan with a slotted spoon. Cool; add squid to mussels mixture. Add lobster to pan, and cover. Reduce heat, and simmer 8 minutes. Remove lobster from pan, reserving 1 tablespoon cooking liquid; cool lobster. Remove meat from lobster tail and claws; coarsely chop. Add lobster, salt, and black pepper to mussels mixture.

3. Combine remaining 3 tablespoons juice, reserved cooking liquid, and olive

continued

oil in a bowl, stirring with a whisk. Drizzle lemon mixture over seafood mixture; toss gently to coat. Cover and marinate in refrigerator 1½ hours. Add cilantro and remaining ingredients to seafood mixture, and toss gently. Yield: 4 servings (serving size: about 2 cups).

Sustainable Choice

What about Gulf shrimp? According to Monterey Bay Aquarium Seafood Watch, Gulf shrimp are considered a good alternative. Post-oil spill, the U. S. government says they've tested safe to eat.

CALORIES 339; FAT 11.2g (sat 1.8g, mono 5.6g, poly 2.1g); PROTEIN 44.4g; CARB 14.5g; FIBER 4.7g; CHOL 283mg; IRON 6.7mg; SODIUM 683mg; CALC 192mg

Sesame Albacore Tuna

Hands-on time: 40 min. Total time: 40 min.

Although it is one of the most popular species, tuna is tricky when it comes to sustainability. To be sure you're making a sustainable choice, buy U.S.-caught fresh or frozen Pacific albacore tuna. Fresh albacore is normally available only in the summer months.

1 tablespoon olive oil
4 cups thinly sliced shiitake mushroom caps (about 10 ounces)
¼ cup organic vegetable broth
¼ cup rice vinegar
2 medium baby bok choy, quartered lengthwise
1 tablespoon sesame oil
2 tablespoons lower-sodium soy sauce
2 teaspoons sesame seeds
2 tablespoons chopped fresh cilantro
1 tablespoon canola oil
4 (6-ounce) fresh or frozen U.S.-caught Pacific albacore tuna fillets, thawed
½ teaspoon salt
¼ teaspoon freshly ground black pepper
2 cups hot cooked long-grain white rice

1. Heat a medium skillet over medium-high heat. Add olive oil to pan, and swirl to coat. Add mushrooms, and sauté 5 minutes or until lightly browned, stirring occasionally. Add broth and vinegar; boil 1 minute or until liquid almost evaporates. Keep warm.

2. Steam bok choy 1 minute. Heat a medium skillet over medium-high heat. Add sesame oil to pan; swirl to coat. Add bok choy, cut sides down; cook 1 minute. Add soy sauce and sesame seeds; cook 1 minute or until thoroughly heated. Add 1 tablespoon bok choy cooking liquid and cilantro to mushroom mixture; stir to combine.

3. Heat a large cast-iron skillet over high heat. Add canola oil to pan; swirl to coat. Sprinkle fish evenly with salt and pepper. Add fish to pan; sauté 1 minute on each side or until desired degree of doneness. Let stand 1 minute. Cut into ¼-inch-thick slices. To serve, place ½ cup rice on each of 4 plates; top each serving with 2 bok choy quarters. Arrange 1 tuna fillet on each plate; top each serving with ¼ cup mushroom mixture. Yield: 4 servings.

CALORIES 445; FAT 17.6g (sat 2.9g, mono 8g, poly 5.5g); PROTEIN 35.4g; CARB 36.2g; FIBER 3.2g; CHOL 47mg; IRON 2.4mg; SODIUM 760mg; CALC 145mg

Quick & Easy • Kid Friendly

Arctic Char with Blistered Cherry Tomatoes

Hands-on time: 15 min. Total time: 15 min.

Farmed char is widely available and has a mild flavor and a great texture. It's similar to salmon but not quite as rich and fatty. Wild Arctic char from the northern seas is available only for a few weeks in late summer, when the ice has melted enough for the local fishermen to reach them. It is a sought-after delicacy, and one that will cost you. If you find fresh, it's well worth the splurge.

3 tablespoons extra-virgin olive oil, divided
4 (6-ounce) Arctic char fillets
³⁄₄ teaspoon coarse salt, divided
½ teaspoon black pepper, divided
4 garlic cloves, halved
3 pints multicolored cherry tomatoes
¼ cup thinly sliced fresh basil
2 shallots, thinly sliced

1. Preheat oven to 400°.

2. Heat a large ovenproof skillet over high heat. Add 1 tablespoon oil to pan; swirl to coat. Sprinkle fillets with ½ teaspoon salt and ¼ teaspoon pepper. Add fillets, flesh sides down, to pan, and sauté 2 minutes. Place pan in oven; bake at 400° for 3 minutes or until desired degree of doneness.

3. Heat a large cast-iron skillet over medium heat. Add remaining 2 tablespoons oil to pan; swirl to coat. Add garlic, and cook 2 minutes or until lightly browned, stirring occasionally. Increase heat to medium-high. Add tomatoes to pan; sauté 2 minutes or until skins blister, stirring frequently. Remove pan from heat. Sprinkle tomato mixture with remaining ¼ teaspoon salt, remaining ¼ teaspoon black pepper, basil, and shallots; toss to combine. Serve with fish. Yield: 4 servings (serving size: 1 fillet and about ¾ cup tomato mixture).

CALORIES 380; FAT 20.4g (sat 3.8g, mono 11.7g, poly 3.6g); PROTEIN 31.4g; CARB 20g; FIBER 2.9g; CHOL 65mg; IRON 2mg; SODIUM 514mg; CALC 49mg

TRY WITH...
Couscous and Pine Nuts

Bring ¾ cup fat-free, lower-sodium chicken broth and ⅓ cup water to a boil in a small saucepan. Stir in 1 cup couscous. Cover, remove from heat, and let stand 5 minutes. Uncover; fluff with a fork. Stir in ¼ cup toasted pine nuts, ¼ cup chopped fresh flat-leaf parsley, ¼ cup finely chopped roasted red bell pepper, 1 tablespoon extra-virgin olive oil, ¼ teaspoon salt, and ¼ teaspoon freshly ground black pepper.

CALORIES 254; FAT 9.5g (sat 1g); SODIUM 227mg

EASY BAKING
FIVE MUNCHABLE MUFFINS

These easy-to-prepare quick breads are perfect for breakfast, snacks, or dessert.

No. 1

Quick & Easy • Make Ahead
Freezable • Kid Friendly • Vegetarian

Tuscan Lemon Muffins

Hands-on time: 13 min. Total time: 29 min.

7.9 ounces all-purpose flour (about 1¾ cups)
¾ cup granulated sugar
2½ teaspoons baking powder
¼ teaspoon salt
¾ cup part-skim ricotta cheese
½ cup water
¼ cup olive oil
1 tablespoon grated lemon rind
2 tablespoons fresh lemon juice
1 large egg, lightly beaten
Cooking spray
2 tablespoons turbinado sugar

1. Preheat oven to 375°.
2. Weigh or lightly spoon flour into dry measuring cups; level with a knife. Combine flour and next 3 ingredients; make a well in center. Combine ricotta and next 5 ingredients. Add ricotta mixture to flour mixture, stirring just until moist.
3. Place 12 muffin-cup liners in muffin cups; coat with cooking spray. Divide batter evenly among prepared muffin cups. Sprinkle turbinado sugar over batter. Bake at 375° for 16 minutes or until a wooden pick inserted in center comes out clean. Cool 5 minutes in pan on a wire rack. Yield: 12 servings (serving size: 1 muffin).

CALORIES 186; FAT 6.2g (sat 1.5g, mono 3.4g, poly 0.6g); PROTEIN 4g; CARB 29.5g; FIBER 0.6g; CHOL 21mg; IRON 1mg; SODIUM 160mg; CALC 81mg

No. 2

Quick & Easy • Make Ahead
Freezable • Kid Friendly • Vegetarian

Chocolate–Chocolate Chip Muffins

Hands-on time: 12 min. Total time: 27 min.

Cocoa batter encases chocolate minichips, which also melt on top for chocolaty goodness. Did we mention chocolate?

7.9 ounces all-purpose flour (about 1¾ cups)
½ cup packed brown sugar
¼ cup unsweetened cocoa
1 teaspoon baking powder
1 teaspoon baking soda
¼ teaspoon salt
1 cup warm water
¼ cup canola oil
1 tablespoon red wine vinegar
1 teaspoon vanilla extract
1 large egg, lightly beaten
½ cup semisweet chocolate minichips, divided
Cooking spray

1. Preheat oven to 400°.
2. Weigh or lightly spoon flour into dry measuring cups; level with a knife. Combine flour and next 5 ingredients in a large bowl, stirring with a whisk. Make a well in center of mixture. Combine 1 cup warm water and next 4 ingredients in a bowl, stirring well with a whisk. Stir in ¼ cup minichips. Add oil mixture to flour mixture, stirring just until moist.
3. Place 12 muffin-cup liners in muffin cups, and coat liners with cooking spray. Divide batter evenly among prepared muffin cups. Sprinkle remaining ¼ cup minichips evenly over batter. Bake at 400° for 15 minutes or until a wooden pick inserted in center comes out clean. Cool 5 minutes in pan on a wire rack. Yield: 12 servings (serving size: 1 muffin).

CALORIES 191; FAT 7.6g (sat 1.9g, mono 3.9g, poly 1.5g); PROTEIN 3.1g; CARB 29g; FIBER 1.5g; CHOL 15mg; IRON 1.5mg; SODIUM 197mg; CALC 37mg

No. 3

Quick & Easy • Make Ahead
Freezable • Kid Friendly

Bacon-Cheddar Corn Muffins

Hands-on time: 15 min. Total time: 40 min.

Cheddar, jalapeño, and bacon make these muffins a great partner for chili or a savory grab-and-go breakfast.

4.5 ounces all-purpose flour (about 1 cup)
¾ cup yellow cornmeal
½ cup (2 ounces) shredded sharp cheddar cheese
2 tablespoons sugar
1 teaspoon baking powder
1 teaspoon baking soda
¾ teaspoon ground cumin
¼ teaspoon salt
4 center-cut bacon slices, cooked, drained, and crumbled
1 jalapeño pepper, seeded and minced
1¼ cups low-fat buttermilk
¼ cup canola oil
1 large egg, lightly beaten
Cooking spray

1. Preheat oven to 375°.
2. Weigh or lightly spoon flour into a dry measuring cup; level with a knife. Combine flour and next 7 ingredients in a large bowl, stirring with a whisk. Stir in bacon and jalapeño; make a well in center of mixture. Combine buttermilk, oil, and egg in a bowl, stirring well with a whisk. Add buttermilk mixture to flour mixture, stirring just until moist.
3. Place 12 muffin-cup liners in muffin cups; coat with cooking spray. Divide batter evenly among prepared muffin cups. Bake at 375° for 15 minutes or until a wooden pick inserted in center comes out clean. Cool 5 minutes in pan on a wire rack. Yield: 12 servings (serving size: 1 muffin).

CALORIES 160; FAT 7.9g (sat 2g, mono 3.3g, poly 1.6g); PROTEIN 4.8g; CARB 17.7g; FIBER 0.9g; CHOL 23mg; IRON 0.9mg; SODIUM 299mg; CALC 89mg

No. 4

Quick & Easy • Make Ahead
Freezable • Kid Friendly • Vegetarian

Pistachio-Chai Muffins

Hands-on time: 15 min. Total time: 30 min.

A simple sugar glaze anchors crunchy pistachios, while aromatic spices and black tea speckle the dough.

7.9 ounces all-purpose flour (about 1¾ cups)
½ cup packed brown sugar
1 teaspoon baking powder
1 teaspoon baking soda
¼ teaspoon salt
2 chai blend tea bags
1 cup low-fat buttermilk
¼ cup butter, melted
1½ teaspoons vanilla extract, divided
1 large egg, lightly beaten
Cooking spray
⅓ cup shelled dry-roasted pistachios, chopped
½ cup powdered sugar
1 tablespoon water

1. Preheat oven to 375°.
2. Weigh or lightly spoon flour into dry measuring cups; level with a knife. Combine flour and next 4 ingredients in a large bowl, stirring with a whisk. Cut open tea bags; add tea to flour mixture, stirring well. Make a well in center of mixture. Combine buttermilk, butter, 1 teaspoon vanilla, and egg in a bowl, stirring well with a whisk. Add buttermilk mixture to flour mixture, stirring just until moist.
3. Place 12 muffin-cup liners in muffin cups; coat liners with cooking spray. Divide batter evenly among prepared muffin cups. Sprinkle nuts evenly over batter. Bake at 375° for 15 minutes or until a wooden pick inserted in center comes out clean. Cool 5 minutes in pan on a wire rack.
4. Combine remaining ½ teaspoon vanilla, powdered sugar, and 1 tablespoon water, stirring until smooth. Drizzle evenly over muffins. Yield: 12 servings (serving size: 1 muffin).

CALORIES 192; FAT 6.2g (sat 2.8g, mono 2.1g, poly 0.8g); PROTEIN 3.9g; CARB 30.5g; FIBER 0.9g; CHOL 26mg; IRON 1.2mg; SODIUM 259mg; CALC 61mg

No. 5

Quick & Easy • Make Ahead
Freezable • Kid Friendly • Vegetarian

Cherry–Wheat Germ Muffins

Hands-on time: 12 min. Total time: 27 min.

Dried cherries enliven a hearty muffin featuring nutty wheat germ; vary the flavor with dried apricots or blueberries.

6.75 ounces all-purpose flour (about 1½ cups)
¾ cup dried cherries, coarsely chopped
½ cup toasted wheat germ
½ cup packed dark brown sugar
1 teaspoon baking powder
1 teaspoon baking soda
½ teaspoon salt
¼ teaspoon ground allspice
1 cup low-fat buttermilk
¼ cup canola oil
1 large egg, lightly beaten
Cooking spray

1. Preheat oven to 400°.
2. Weigh or lightly spoon flour into dry measuring cups; level with a knife. Combine flour and next 7 ingredients in a large bowl, stirring with a whisk. Make a well in center of mixture. Combine buttermilk, oil, and egg in a bowl, stirring well with a whisk. Add buttermilk mixture to flour mixture, stirring just until moist.
3. Place 12 muffin-cup liners in muffin cups, and coat liners with cooking spray. Divide batter evenly among prepared muffin cups. Bake at 400° for 15 minutes or until a wooden pick inserted in center comes out clean. Cool 5 minutes in pan on a wire rack. Yield: 12 servings (serving size: 1 muffin).

CALORIES 202; FAT 5.9g (sat 0.7g, mono 3.3g, poly 1.8g); PROTEIN 4.5g; CARB 32.4g; FIBER 2.2g; CHOL 16mg; IRON 1.5mg; SODIUM 268mg; CALC 68mg

FIVE TIPS FOR PERFECT MUFFINS

1. LEAVE A FEW LUMPS. Overstirring can toughen a muffin.

2. SPRAY THE LINERS with cooking spray before adding batter.

3. CHECK FOR DONENESS EARLY (about 5 minutes before specified time) since ovens can vary.

4. COOL IN THE PAN 5 minutes, and then eat warm or remove to a rack so muffins don't get soggy.

5. STORE CORRECTLY so muffins stay fresh. Keep in an airtight container for a day or two. Or wrap individually in plastic wrap, place all in a zip-top bag, and freeze up to one month. Thaw at room temperature or in microwave for 10 to 30 seconds.

THE AMAZING ONE-HOUR DINNER PARTY

We cooked up a tasty spring menu for eight happy people—and included the tips and game plan to pull it all together in 60 minutes.

Before you decide that preparing an elegant three-course dinner, plus signature cocktail, from start to finish in 60 minutes is too good to be true, consider this: Many home cooks make an entire meal in that amount of time most weeknights, deftly and intuitively moving from side dish to entrée and back again, from oven to stovetop to salad spinner. We simply decided to extend those skills to the challenge of the classic dinner for eight.

This isn't to say that a lot of fiddling and retesting didn't go into this menu. It did. We tested the whole game plan three times, tweaking recipes and choreographing to make sure it all came in at less than an hour. We rearranged the order of tasks; we gussied up a few smart convenience products (bagged salad greens, precut potatoes, frozen lemonade); and we introduced bold flavors from pickled Vidalia onions, white truffle oil, and fresh tarragon. The hour zips by, but it's more fun than frantic. The payoff will make your guests linger with delight.

Quick & Easy
Lemon-Gin Sparkling Cocktails

Hands-on time: 3 min. Total time: 3 min.

Loosely based on the French 75, a classic cocktail of gin, Champagne, lemon juice, and sugar, this welcoming beverage uses lemonade concentrate as a shortcut. Be sure to allow the concentrate to thaw ahead of time. You'll use almost a whole bottle of Champagne; the rest goes into the dessert. If time allows, you can use a quick simple syrup with lemon juice: Combine 3 tablespoons each of sugar, lemon juice, and water; microwave 1 minute, and cool.

1 cup gin, chilled
½ cup frozen lemonade concentrate, thawed
2⅔ cups Champagne or other sparkling wine, chilled
Tarragon sprigs (optional)

1. Combine gin and lemonade concentrate in a pitcher; chill until ready to serve.
2. Just before serving, add Champagne to gin mixture; stir gently. Garnish with tarragon sprigs, if desired. Yield: 8 servings (serving size: about ½ cup).

CALORIES 154; FAT 0g; PROTEIN 0.1g; CARB 9.9g; FIBER 0g; CHOL 0mg; IRON 0.1mg; SODIUM 1mg; CALC 1mg

THE ONE-HOUR GAME PLAN

To make the 60-minute menu, you'll want to study and follow this detailed time line. (Two do-ahead tasks: Thaw lemonade concentrate and chill Champagne and gin.)

1. Preheat oven to 450°.

2. Pickle onions (for salad).

3. Bring water to a boil (for blanching asparagus).

4. Prep berries for dessert—combine with macerating liquid.

5. Prep roast; sear and get in oven.

6. Prep potatoes; place potatoes in oven with beef.

7. Blanch asparagus; drain and rinse with cold water.

8. Combine gin and lemonade in pitcher; chill.

9. Make horseradish sauce for beef; chill.

10. Make vinaigrette for salad; pile greens on top (do not toss).

11. Whip cream for dessert; place in fridge.

12. Remove beef from oven; let rest.

13. Brown the butter; heat asparagus.

14. Add Champagne to cocktails.

15. Toss salad; top with cheese, onions, and berries.

16. Enjoy the meal, and soak in the praise from your guests.

serves 8

Lemon-Gin Sparkling Cocktails
(page 117)

Pickled Onion, Blue Cheese, and Berry Salad
(page 118)

Beef Tenderloin with Horseradish-Chive Sauce
(page 118)

Truffled Roasted Potatoes
(page 118)

Browned Butter Asparagus
(page 119)

Champagne-Soaked Berries with Whipped Cream
(page 119)

Quick & Easy • Vegetarian

Pickled Onion, Blue Cheese, and Berry Salad

Hands-on time: 9 min. Total time: 39 min.

¼ cup water
¼ cup sherry vinegar, divided
4 teaspoons agave nectar, divided
⅔ cup thinly vertically sliced Vidalia onion
1 teaspoon Dijon mustard
¼ teaspoon freshly ground black pepper
⅛ teaspoon salt
3 tablespoons extra-virgin olive oil
2 (4-ounce) packages baby mixed herb salad
½ cup (2 ounces) crumbled blue cheese
1 (6-ounce) package fresh raspberries

1. Combine ¼ cup water, 2 tablespoons vinegar, and 1 tablespoon agave nectar in a small bowl. Add onion; toss to coat. Marinate at room temperature 30 minutes; drain.
2. Combine remaining 2 tablespoons vinegar, remaining 1 teaspoon agave nectar, mustard, pepper, and salt in a large bowl, stirring with a whisk. Gradually add oil, stirring constantly with a whisk. Add salad greens; toss gently to coat. Arrange about 1 cup salad on each of 8 plates. Top each serving with about 1 tablespoon onion, 1 tablespoon cheese, and about 6 raspberries. Yield: 8 servings.

CALORIES 101; FAT 7.6g (sat 2.3g, mono 4.4g, poly 0.7g); PROTEIN 2.6g; CARB 6.7g; FIBER 2.3g; CHOL 6mg; IRON 0.5mg; SODIUM 180mg; CALC 53mg

Beef Tenderloin with Horseradish-Chive Sauce

(pictured on page 221)

Hands-on time: 13 min. Total time: 48 min.

1 (2-pound) beef tenderloin, trimmed
1 tablespoon olive oil
1½ teaspoons coarsely ground black pepper
¾ teaspoon kosher salt
⅔ cup light sour cream
2 tablespoons chopped fresh chives
3 tablespoons prepared horseradish
1 teaspoon fresh lemon juice
1 teaspoon Dijon mustard
⅛ teaspoon kosher salt

1. Preheat oven to 450°.
2. Heat a large skillet over medium-high heat. Rub beef with oil; coat on all sides with pepper and ¾ teaspoon salt. Add beef to pan; cook 3 minutes, browning on all sides.
3. Place beef on a broiler pan. Bake at 450° for 25 minutes or until a thermometer registers 125°. Remove from oven; let stand 10 minutes before slicing.
4. Combine sour cream and next 5 ingredients; serve with beef. Yield: 8 servings (serving size: 3 ounces beef and about 1½ tablespoons sauce).

CALORIES 210; FAT 10.1g (sat 4.1g, mono 3.9g, poly 0.5g); PROTEIN 25.7g; CARB 2.4g; FIBER 0.3g; CHOL 67mg; IRON 1.7mg; SODIUM 310mg; CALC 21mg

Quick & Easy • Vegetarian

Truffled Roasted Potatoes

Hands-on time: 5 min. Total time: 45 min.

White truffle oil delivers a powerful flavor punch, more so than black truffle oil. To save money, purchase a small bottle. Use leftover oil for finishing other dishes—drizzle on pizza, risotto, or potato hash.

2 (20-ounce) packages refrigerated red potato wedges
2 tablespoons olive oil
1 tablespoon minced garlic
½ teaspoon kosher salt
½ teaspoon freshly ground black pepper
1 tablespoon white truffle oil
2 teaspoons fresh thyme leaves

1. Preheat oven to 450°.
2. Place potatoes on a jelly-roll pan; drizzle with olive oil, and sprinkle with garlic, salt, and pepper. Toss well to combine. Bake at 450° for 35 minutes or until potatoes are browned and tender. Remove from oven. Drizzle potatoes with truffle oil, and sprinkle with thyme. Toss gently to combine. Yield: 8 servings (serving size: about ¾ cup).

CALORIES 134; FAT 5.1g (sat 0.7g, mono 3.7g, poly 0.5g); PROTEIN 3.6g; CARB 18g; FIBER 3.6g; CHOL 0mg; IRON 0.8mg; SODIUM 269mg; CALC 3mg

WINE SUGGESTIONS

LIGHT & WHITE: Try the zippy Kung-fu Girl Riesling by Charles Smith (2010 Washington State, $13).

PINKY! Keep it simple with a lip-smacker like the Bethel Heights Pinot Noir Rosé (2009 Willamette Valley, Oregon, $22).

RED DELICIOUS: Dark fruit and spice make the Sanford Pinot Noir (2007 Santa Rita Hills, California, $43) a delightful match.

TIME-SAVING CONVENIENCE PRODUCTS

AGAVE NECTAR: A versatile, ready-made liquid sweetener with a nice, neutral flavor you don't find in honey.
Time saved: 15 minutes.

BAGGED SALAD GREENS: No need to wash and spin or pat dry—just open the bag and toss with vinaigrette.
Time saved: about 6 minutes.

LEMONADE CONCENTRATE: Skip the whole job of making and chilling simple syrup, and then combining with fresh-squeezed lemon juice. Concentrate does the job for you.
Time saved: about 15 minutes.

PRECUT POTATO WEDGES: Just open a package and pour onto a baking sheet—no spud scrubbing or knife work necessary.
Time saved: 10 minutes.

Staff Favorite • Quick & Easy
Vegetarian
Browned Butter Asparagus

Hands-on time: 8 min. Total time: 18 min.

Tarragon adds unique, fresh flavor to the dish but use any herb you like.

2 bunches asparagus, trimmed (about 2 pounds)
3 tablespoons butter
³⁄₈ teaspoon kosher salt
¼ teaspoon freshly ground black pepper
1½ teaspoons chopped fresh tarragon

1. Bring a large saucepan of water to a boil. Add asparagus; cook 3 minutes or until crisp-tender. Drain and rinse under cold water; drain and set aside.
2. Melt butter in a large skillet over medium heat; cook 3 minutes or until browned and fragrant. Stir in salt and pepper. Add asparagus and tarragon; cook 1 minute or until heated, tossing to coat. Yield: 8 servings (serving size: about 4 ounces).

CALORIES 61; **FAT** 4.5g (sat 2.8g, mono 1.1g, poly 0.2g);
PROTEIN 2.6g; **CARB** 4.6g; **FIBER** 2.3g; **CHOL** 11mg;
IRON 2.5mg; **SODIUM** 123mg; **CALC** 29mg

Quick & Easy
Champagne-Soaked Berries with Whipped Cream

Hands-on time: 9 min. Total time: 39 min.

Agave nectar is great for dishes like this, where it dissolves instantly. A chilled bowl and beaters will help the cream whip faster.

½ cup Champagne or other sparkling wine
¼ cup agave nectar, divided
1 teaspoon grated orange rind
1 (16-ounce) package fresh strawberries, halved
2 (6-ounce) packages fresh blueberries
½ cup heavy whipping cream
8 amaretti cookies, coarsely crumbled

1. Combine Champagne, 3 tablespoons agave nectar, and rind in a large bowl. Add berries; toss gently to combine. Cover and chill 30 minutes.
2. Place cream in a medium bowl; beat with a mixer at high speed until stiff peaks form. Beat in remaining 1 tablespoon agave nectar. Place ¾ cup berry mixture in each of 8 bowls. Top each serving with 2 tablespoons whipped cream; divide crushed cookies evenly among servings. Yield: 8 servings.

CALORIES 155; **FAT** 6.1g (sat 3.5g, mono 1.7g, poly 0.4g);
PROTEIN 1.5g; **CARB** 23.4g; **FIBER** 2.4g; **CHOL** 21mg;
IRON 0.4mg; **SODIUM** 20mg; **CALC** 22mg

MORE MAKE-AHEAD OPTIONS

This menu comes together in an hour. But if you want to get a head start, do a few things a day or two ahead:

• Pickle onions.
• Blanch asparagus.
• Beat whipped cream.
• Combine gin and lemonade.
• Make horseradish sauce.
• Make vinaigrette.

MENU PLANNING
SIDES FOR MAY

Four vegetable dishes, and the entrées from this month to pair with them.

PERFECT MATCHES FOR MAY

Roasted Chile-Garlic Broccoli (page 120)

— pair with —

Beef Tenderloin with Horseradish-Chive Sauce (page 118)
Sesame Albacore Tuna (page 114)

New Potatoes with Parsley and Saffron (page 121)

— pair with —

Flank Steak with Spicy Lemon Sauce (page 134)
Arctic Char with Blistered Cherry Tomatoes (page 114)

Greens with Golden Raisins (page 121)

— pair with —

Maple-Mustard Chicken Thighs (page 130)
Spiced Lamb Kebabs (page 129)

Spanish Rice Salad (page 120)

— pair with —

Sautéed Shrimp with Sherry and Chiles (page 112)
Sausage and Egg Burrito (page 130)

Quick & Easy • Vegetarian

Roasted Chile-Garlic Broccoli

Hands-on time: 8 min. Total time: 18 min.

6 cups broccoli florets
2 tablespoons dark sesame oil
2 teaspoons sambal oelek (ground fresh chile paste)
³⁄₈ teaspoon salt
⅛ teaspoon sugar
6 large garlic cloves, coarsely chopped

1. Place a small roasting pan in oven. Preheat oven to 450°.
2. Place broccoli in a large bowl; drizzle with oil. Toss to coat. Add sambal, salt, and sugar to broccoli mixture; toss. Add broccoli mixture to hot roasting pan; toss. Bake at 450° for 5 minutes; remove from oven. Add garlic to pan; stir. Bake an additional 5 minutes or until broccoli is lightly browned. Yield: 4 servings (serving size: 1¼ cups).

CALORIES 99; **FAT** 7.2g (sat 1g, mono 2.7g, poly 3g); **PROTEIN** 3.5g; **CARB** 7.7g; **FIBER** 3.2g; **CHOL** 0mg; **IRON** 1mg; **SODIUM** 325mg; **CALC** 59mg

Make Ahead • Vegetarian

Spanish Rice Salad

Hands-on time: 26 min. Total time: 52 min.

1½ tablespoons extra-virgin olive oil
1 tablespoon fresh lemon juice
1 tablespoon red wine vinegar
1 teaspoon chopped fresh oregano
1 small garlic clove, minced
½ cup uncooked medium-grain rice
1 tablespoon fresh lemon juice
2 large globe artichokes
½ teaspoon salt
⅛ teaspoon black pepper
¾ cup canned chickpeas (garbanzo beans), rinsed and drained
¼ cup finely chopped red onion
¼ cup diced piquillo peppers or roasted red bell peppers
1½ tablespoons chopped fresh flat-leaf parsley

4 STEPS TO ARTICHOKE HEARTS

Fresh artichokes are abundant in spring, and trimming them down to their tender hearts is worth the effort—the flavor is fresh, nutty, slightly grassy, and far superior to the jarred or canned stuff. Follow these steps.

1. Cut off stem to within about an inch of the base.

2. Peel stem so that all parts will be tender.

3. Remove tough outer leaves; discard.

4. Halve artichoke lengthwise; scoop out and discard fuzzy, inedible thistle.

1. Combine first 5 ingredients in a small bowl, stirring well with a whisk. Set aside.
2. Cook rice according to package directions, omitting salt and fat.
3. Fill a medium bowl with cold water; stir in 1 tablespoon juice. Work with 1 artichoke at a time; cut off stem to within 1 inch of base. Peel stem. Remove bottom leaves and tough outer leaves, leaving tender heart and bottom. Cut artichoke in half lengthwise. Remove fuzzy thistle with a spoon. Slice artichoke heart into eighths; place in lemon water. Repeat with remaining artichoke. Drain.

4. Place artichokes in a saucepan; add water to cover by 1 inch. Bring to a boil over medium-high heat; cook 10 minutes or until tender. Drain well.
5. Transfer rice to a large bowl; stir in salt and black pepper. Add dressing, artichokes, chickpeas, and remaining ingredients to rice mixture; stir well. Serve warm or at room temperature. Yield: 8 servings (serving size: ½ cup).

CALORIES 117; **FAT** 2.9g (sat 0.4g, mono 1.9g, poly 0.4g); **PROTEIN** 3.4g; **CARB** 20.1g; **FIBER** 3.5g; **CHOL** 0mg; **IRON** 1.4mg; **SODIUM** 266mg; **CALC** 30mg

New Potatoes with Parsley and Saffron

Hands-on time: 6 min. Total time: 29 min.

The earthy sweetness of the saffron pairs well with steak or fish. This quick dish is also a welcome substitution for traditional roasted or boiled potatoes.

½ cup water
¼ cup chopped fresh parsley
1 tablespoon extra-virgin olive oil
½ teaspoon sea salt
½ teaspoon freshly ground black pepper
2 garlic cloves, minced
Dash of saffron threads
1 pound small red potatoes

1. Combine all ingredients in a medium saucepan over medium-high heat. Bring mixture to a boil. Cover and reduce heat to medium-low; cook 20 minutes or until potatoes are tender when pierced with a knife. Serve immediately. Yield: 4 servings (serving size: 4 potatoes).

CALORIES 114; **FAT** 3.6g (sat 0.5g, mono 2.5g, poly 0.4g); **PROTEIN** 2.4g; **CARB** 19g; **FIBER** 2.2g; **CHOL** 0mg; **IRON** 1.1mg; **SODIUM** 249mg; **CALC** 20mg

Greens with Golden Raisins

Hands-on time: 9 min. Total time: 20 min.

Escarole's bitter, assertive flavor will complement beef kebabs or roasted leg of lamb.

2 tablespoons canola oil
½ cup golden raisins
1 small white onion, halved and thinly sliced (about 2 cups)
6 ounces chopped escarole
1 pound fresh baby spinach
½ teaspoon kosher salt
½ teaspoon garam masala

1. Heat a large nonstick skillet over medium-high heat. Add oil to pan; swirl to coat. Add raisins and onion to pan; cook 3 minutes or until onions are lightly browned. Add half of escarole to pan; cook 2 minutes or until greens wilt. Repeat with remaining escarole. Add a third of spinach to pan; cook 2 minutes or until spinach wilts. Repeat in 2 more batches with remaining spinach. Stir in salt and garam masala. Yield: 6 servings (serving size: about ½ cup).

CALORIES 136; **FAT** 4.9g (sat 0.4g, mono 3g, poly 1.4g); **PROTEIN** 3.2g; **CARB** 23.7g; **FIBER** 5.9g; **CHOL** 0mg; **IRON** 3.1mg; **SODIUM** 290mg; **CALC** 89mg

LESS MEAT, MORE FLAVOR

HEATING THINGS UP WITH A FEW FRESH CHILES

By Mark Bittman

Both the variety and the prep method affect how much heat you get, and peppers add fantastic flavor to easy fajitas and a paella.

Cooking with chiles should be fun rather than daunting. Unless you're a chile-head, you can ignore the zillion different kinds; you only need to know how to use three or four. And you don't have to fret over roasting and peeling; in most cases, it's just fine to skip those steps.

It's helpful to look at the world of peppers on a spectrum with bell peppers at one end and habaneros and their insanely hot ilk at the other. The sweet ones tend to be the size of your hands, and the hot ones tend to be small like fingers. Poblanos—which look like a flattened, gnarled, darker version of a green bell pepper—fall right in the middle. They have a mild, slightly noticeable heat but retain a bit of sweetness. They're great for stuffing, grilling, and roasting, though their skin can peel off in an unpleasant way unless you remove it as part of the cooking process. My solution is to prepare them whole quite rarely. Instead, I use them sliced or chopped into relatively small bits so the skins are never a nuisance, even if they separate from the flesh. This way you can still enjoy the intensity they bring to dishes like the paella on page 122, where you might otherwise use milder bell peppers.

Next on the heat spectrum is the medium-hot jalapeño. Jalapeños are tapered and about the size of a man's thumb, thick-fleshed with not too many seeds. They're often sliced crosswise into thin rounds and served raw as a garnish for tacos or nachos, or finely chopped in fresh salsas or stir-fries. They taste even better pickled. But don't bother with the stuff that comes in jars. Instead, pickle them quickly in fresh lime juice as explained in the vegetable-loaded fajitas here.

Building in heat are the smaller, similarly shaped serranos. Thai or Thai bird chiles are small and narrow—and spicier than serranos—but all can be used the same ways. Finally, you get to the brightly colored habaneros. They look like cute little bell peppers, but don't be fooled: These are among the hottest chiles you can buy. They have an irresistible citrus flavor that many cooks find addictive, so I'm not saying avoid them; just use them carefully.

Chile seeds and interior white membranes pack a wallop. For maximum heat, use the whole fruit. But if you'd rather temper the fire, remove the insides and use only the flesh. You can don rubber gloves to protect your skin and anything you might touch after the chiles. But I often just grab the fruit by the stem, slit it lengthwise, and cut the seeds and white parts free. Then I mince or slice the flesh—all without ever coming into much contact. Washing my hands with warm, soapy water is the only additional precaution. When I'm paranoid, I wash twice.

The single most important thing to learn about cooking with chiles: nick and taste. No two chiles have the same level of heat, even if they're the same type. So cut a teeny fleck from one side, let it sit on your tongue, and take

continued

a temperature reading. When in doubt, add a little to a dish at a time. Unless, of course, you're one of those chile-heads. Fortunately, these two recipes are perfect for wherever you fall on the heat spectrum.

Staff Favorite

Paella with Poblanos, Corn, and Clams

Hands-on time: 35 min. Total time: 1 hr. 30 min.

The part of paella I couldn't dare change is the socarrat—the crisp browned rice on the bottom of the pan. The crust won't form until all of the liquid from the clams and the tomatoes has boiled off, so be patient with that last step: I promise you, it's worth it.

2 tablespoons olive oil
2 cups chopped yellow onion
3 garlic cloves, minced
2 poblano chiles, seeded and chopped
1¼ teaspoons kosher salt, divided
½ teaspoon black pepper, divided
¾ cup uncooked short-grain brown rice
¼ teaspoon saffron threads, crushed
2 cups water
⅛ teaspoon ground red pepper
1½ cups fresh corn kernels (about 2 ears)
1 cup halved cherry tomatoes
2 pounds littleneck clams
2 tablespoons chopped fresh flat-leaf parsley
8 lemon wedges

1. Preheat oven to 450°.
2. Heat oil in a 12-inch ovenproof skillet over medium-high heat. Add onion, garlic, poblanos, ½ teaspoon salt, and ¼ teaspoon black pepper; sauté 3 minutes. Add rice and saffron. Cook 2 minutes; stir constantly. Add 2 cups water, remaining ¾ teaspoon salt, remaining ¼ teaspoon black pepper, and red pepper; bring to a boil.
3. Bake at 450° for 50 minutes or until rice is done. Stir in corn and tomatoes. Nestle clams into rice mixture. Bake at 450° for 12 minutes or until shells open, and discard unopened shells.
4. Return pan to medium-high heat, and cook without stirring 10 minutes or until liquid evaporates and rice browns. (It

should smell toasty but not burned.) Top with parsley; serve with lemon wedges. Yield: 4 servings (serving size: 1¼ cups rice mixture and about 7 clams).

CALORIES 340; FAT 9.1g (sat 1.1g, mono 5.2g, poly 1.3g); PROTEIN 14.8g; CARB 52.7g; FIBER 5.6g; CHOL 21mg; IRON 10mg; SODIUM 651mg; CALC 68mg

Quick & Easy

Vegetable and Steak Fajitas with "Killed" Jalapeños

Hands-on time: 45 min. Total time: 45 min.

Fajitas can be a little boring, don't you think? Not when they're topped with these lime-softened jalapeños. If you like a big burst of lime, drain but don't rinse the chiles before garnishing. Placing the steak briefly in the freezer firms it up, making it easier to slice thinly.

12 ounces flank steak
2 tablespoons hot water
2 tablespoons lime juice
½ teaspoon sugar
2 jalapeño peppers, seeded and cut lengthwise into strips
2 tablespoons olive oil, divided
¾ teaspoon kosher salt, divided
¾ teaspoon black pepper, divided
4 cups sliced mushrooms
2 cups sliced zucchini
2 cups sliced onion
1½ cups red bell pepper strips
3 garlic cloves, minced
1 teaspoon chili powder
12 (6-inch) corn tortillas
½ cup chopped fresh cilantro

1. Place beef in freezer.
2. Combine 2 tablespoons hot water, juice, and sugar in a bowl. Add jalape-ños; toss well.
3. Heat a large, heavy skillet over high heat. Cut beef across grain into thin slices. Add 1 tablespoon oil and beef to pan; sprinkle with ¼ teaspoon salt and ¼ teaspoon black pepper. Sauté 3 minutes or until done; remove from pan. Add sliced mushrooms, zucchini, ¼ teaspoon salt, and ¼ teaspoon black pepper to pan; sauté 4 minutes. Remove

from pan. Add remaining 1 tablespoon oil to pan. Add onion, red bell pepper, garlic, chili powder, remaining ¼ teaspoon salt, and remaining ¼ teaspoon black pepper; sauté 5 minutes or until crisp-tender. Add beef and mushroom mixture; cook 2 minutes or until heated.
4. Heat corn tortillas according to directions. Place 3 tortillas on each of 4 plates, and top each with ⅓ cup beef mixture. Top evenly with jalapeños and cilantro. Yield: 4 servings (serving size: 3 fajitas).

CALORIES 361; FAT 13.5g (sat 2.8g, mono 6.6g, poly 1.8g); PROTEIN 25.6g; CARB 39.1g; FIBER 6.1g; CHOL 28mg; IRON 2.3mg; SODIUM 455mg; CALC 77mg

RECIPE MAKEOVER
SMARTER CHICKEN SALAD

Creamy, crunchy, and fresh, our version of this classic has less than half the calories and salt of the traditional version.

Often seen lurking on the "lighter fare" side of restaurant menus, your standard chicken salad consists of lean chicken breast bathed with a fatty, salty, mayo-based dressing. You might as well go for the everything-fried platter: With a typical wallop of mayo, this "salad" can contain nearly 750 calories and 1,160mg sodium per cup.

Our Test Kitchens began the makeover by perfecting an easy poaching method for chicken breasts to lock in moisture (see end of this article). Creamy, fat-free Greek yogurt and light mayo combine for a tangy, slimmer dressing—and we dress, not drown, the meat. You can actually taste the chicken. Crispy celery and dried cranberries add texture and tartness. A surprising hit of bold smoked almonds is the crowning, crunchy touch.

Make Ahead

Creamy Chicken Salad

Hands-on time: 24 min. Total time: 2 hr. 19 min.

Poaching the chicken keeps it moist and succulent, so you'll need less dressing to bind the salad.

2 pounds skinless, boneless chicken breast halves
½ cup light mayonnaise
½ cup plain fat-free Greek yogurt
1 tablespoon fresh lemon juice
1 tablespoon white wine vinegar
1 tablespoon Dijon mustard
1 teaspoon honey
½ teaspoon kosher salt
½ teaspoon freshly ground black pepper
⅓ cup chopped celery
⅓ cup sweetened dried cranberries
7 tablespoons (about 2 ounces) coarsely chopped smoked almonds
6 cups mixed salad greens

OLD WAY	OUR WAY
748 calories per cup	339 calories per cup
8.1 grams saturated fat	1.9 grams saturated fat
1,161 milligrams sodium	525 milligrams sodium
Dry, leftover chicken	Perfectly poached chicken
Dressed in heavy mayonnaise madness	Dressed in light mayo and fat-free Greek yogurt
Salty, nutty overload	Smoked–almond satisfaction

1. Fill a Dutch oven two-thirds full of water; bring to a boil.
2. Wrap each chicken breast half completely and tightly in heavy-duty plastic wrap. Add chicken to boiling water. Cover and simmer 20 minutes or until a thermometer registers 165°. Remove from pan; let stand 5 minutes. Unwrap chicken; shred. Refrigerate 30 minutes or until cold.

3. Combine mayonnaise and next 7 ingredients in a large bowl, stirring with a whisk until combined. Add chicken, ⅓ cup celery, cranberries, and almonds; toss well to coat. Cover and refrigerate 1 hour. Serve over salad greens. Yield: 6 servings (serving size: about 1 cup chicken salad and 1 cup salad greens).

CALORIES 339; FAT 13.6g (sat 1.9g, mono 5.1g, poly 5.1g); PROTEIN 39.5g; CARB 14.6g; FIBER 2.8g; CHOL 95mg; IRON 2mg; SODIUM 525mg; CALC 54mg

PERFECTLY POACHED CHICKEN

No fat or seasonings are necessary in this cooking process, which retains the natural flavor of the chicken, making it ideal for salads, soups, tacos, and sandwiches. The result is a lower-fat, lower-sodium chicken that is more moist than any heat-lamp-exhausted rotisserie bird.

1. Tightly rolling each breast half in plastic wrap creates a mini steam bath. Twist the ends in opposite directions to ensure a secure cylinder for poaching.

2. Simmer chicken about 20 minutes or until a meat thermometer registers 165°. Turn the chicken at least once for even cooking throughout.

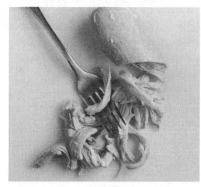

3. Allow chicken to sit, wrapped, for at least five minutes before shredding to avoid drying out. Cool in the refrigerator before dressing for proper food safety practice.

TODAY'S LESSON: CREAM PIES

Fluffy topping, silky filling, and crisp crust: Cream pies are dreamy. Lightened versions are tricky to pull off, though, since you don't have loads of fat and sugar to hide flaws. A good custard is the key. We offer a formula that yields a smooth, rich filling that's sturdy enough to slice whether you like your pie chocolate, lemon, or exotic chai.

KITCHEN NOTE

The nutritional difference between store-bought and homemade dough is negligible, so we opt for convenience.

Make Ahead • Kid Friendly
Lemon Cream Pie
(pictured on page 222)

Hands-on time: 25 min. Total time: 4 hr.

This lightened classic is sweet-tart perfection and a delicious ending to any meal. You'll love the make-ahead convenience. Brush edges of crust with egg wash for nice browning.

½ (14.1-ounce) package refrigerated pie dough
Cooking spray
½ cup sugar
1 tablespoon grated lemon rind, divided
¼ cup fresh lemon juice
3 tablespoons cornstarch
¼ teaspoon salt
2 large eggs
1½ cups fat-free milk
¼ cup (2 ounces) ⅓-less-fat cream cheese, softened
2 tablespoons butter, softened
1½ cups frozen fat-free whipped topping, thawed

1. Roll dough into a 12-inch circle; fit into a 9-inch pie plate coated with cooking spray. Fold edges under, and flute. Bake piecrust according to package directions. Cool completely on a wire rack.
2. Combine sugar, 2½ teaspoons rind, and next 4 ingredients in a large bowl, stirring well. Combine milk and cheese in a medium, heavy saucepan over medium-high heat; cook until mixture reaches 180° or until tiny bubbles form around edge (do not boil). Gradually add hot milk mixture to sugar mixture, stirring constantly with a whisk. Return milk mixture to pan, and cook over medium heat 10 minutes or until thick and bubbly, stirring constantly. Remove from heat; stir in butter.
3. Place pan in a large ice-filled bowl 10 minutes or until mixture cools to room temperature, stirring occasionally. Spoon filling into prepared crust, and cover surface of filling with plastic wrap. Chill 3 hours or until set, and remove plastic wrap. Spread whipped topping evenly over chilled pie, and sprinkle with remaining ½ teaspoon lemon rind. Yield: 8 servings (serving size: 1 slice).

CALORIES 264; FAT 11.9g (sat 5.9g, mono 3.4g, poly 1.9g); PROTEIN 4.6g; CARB 34.8g; FIBER 0.1g; CHOL 61mg; IRON 0.3mg; SODIUM 296mg; CALC 72mg

KITCHEN NOTE

Avoid scrambling the eggs: Slowly add hot milk, whisking constantly. Then cook custard over moderate heat.

Make Ahead
Mexican Chocolate Cream Pie

Hands-on time: 35 min. Total time: 4 hr.

Ground red pepper adds a subtle but distinct kick to the pie, while instant espresso powder intensifies the flavor. Omit either or both if you prefer a standard chocolate cream pie.

Crust:
1½ cups graham cracker crumbs (about 10 cookie sheets), divided
2 tablespoons sugar
1 teaspoon ground cinnamon
⅛ teaspoon salt
2 tablespoons egg white
2 tablespoons butter, melted
Cooking spray
Filling:
½ cup sugar
2 tablespoons cornstarch
1 tablespoon unsweetened cocoa
¼ teaspoon instant espresso powder
⅛ teaspoon salt
⅛ teaspoon ground red pepper
1 large egg
1 large egg yolk
1¾ cups 2% reduced-fat milk
2 ounces dark chocolate, chopped
1½ cups frozen reduced-calorie whipped topping, thawed

1. Preheat oven to 375°.
2. To prepare crust, reserve 1 tablespoon crumbs for topping. Combine remaining crumbs, 2 tablespoons sugar, cinnamon, and ⅛ teaspoon salt in a bowl, stirring well. Stir in egg white and butter. Press crumb mixture into bottom and up sides of a 9-inch pie plate coated with cooking spray. Bake at 375° for 9 minutes or until lightly toasted; cool completely on a wire rack.
3. To prepare filling, combine ½ cup sugar and next 7 ingredients in a bowl,

stirring well with a whisk. Place milk in a medium, heavy saucepan over medium-high heat; cook until milk reaches 180° or until tiny bubbles form around edge (do not boil). Gradually add hot milk to egg mixture, stirring constantly with a whisk. Return milk mixture to pan; cook over medium heat 10 minutes or until thick and bubbly, stirring constantly. Remove from heat. Add chocolate; stir until smooth.

4. Place pan in a large ice-filled bowl 10 minutes or until mixture cools, stirring occasionally. Spoon filling into crust, and cover surface of filling with plastic wrap. Chill 3 hours or until set; remove plastic wrap. Spread whipped topping over filling; sprinkle with reserved cracker crumbs. Yield: 8 servings (serving size: 1 slice).

CALORIES 278; **FAT** 10.3g (sat 5.8g, mono 2.8g, poly 1g); **PROTEIN** 5g; **CARB** 42.1g; **FIBER** 1.3g; **CHOL** 57mg; **IRON** 1.5mg; **SODIUM** 231mg; **CALC** 81mg

BY THE NUMBERS

Store-bought chocolate cream pie can contain as much as 85% (17 grams) of the recommended daily allowance of saturated fat per serving. You save 9.2 grams of sat fat per serving with this luscious pie!

Make Ahead • Kid Friendly
Chai Cream Pie

Hands-on time: 45 min. Total time: 4 hr.

½ (14.1-ounce) package refrigerated pie dough
Cooking spray
2 cups 2% reduced-fat milk
8 cardamom pods, crushed
8 whole cloves
1 (3-inch) cinnamon stick, broken
1 (½-inch) piece peeled fresh ginger, crushed
1 black tea bag
½ cup sugar
3 tablespoons cornstarch
⅛ teaspoon salt
2 large eggs
1½ tablespoons butter, softened
1½ cups frozen fat-free whipped topping, thawed
⅛ teaspoon ground cinnamon

1. Roll dough into a 12-inch circle; fit into a 9-inch pie plate coated with cooking spray. Fold edges under, and flute. Bake piecrust according to package directions. Cool completely on a wire rack.

2. Combine milk and next 4 ingredients in a medium, heavy saucepan over medium-high heat; cook until mixture reaches 180° or until tiny bubbles form around edge. Remove from heat. Add tea bag; cover and let stand 15 minutes. Strain mixture through a sieve over a bowl, and discard solids. Return milk mixture to pan, and cook over medium-high heat until milk reaches 180° or until tiny bubbles form around edge.

3. Combine sugar, cornstarch, salt, and eggs in a large bowl, stirring well. Gradually add hot milk mixture to sugar mixture, stirring constantly with a whisk. Return milk mixture to pan, and cook over medium heat 10 minutes or until thick and bubbly, stirring constantly. Remove from heat; stir in butter.

4. Place pan in a large ice-filled bowl 10 minutes or until filling cools, stirring occasionally. Spoon mixture into crust; cover surface with plastic wrap. Chill 3 hours or until set; remove plastic wrap. Top pie with whipped topping; sprinkle with ground cinnamon. Yield: 8 servings (serving size: 1 slice).

CALORIES 253; **FAT** 10.9g (sat 5.2g, mono 3.5g, poly 1.9g); **PROTEIN** 4.6g; **CARB** 34.3g; **FIBER** 0.1g; **CHOL** 58mg; **IRON** 0.4mg; **SODIUM** 232mg; **CALC** 79mg

KITCHEN TIP

Spoon filling into the crust, and place plastic wrap directly onto custard to prevent a film from forming on top.

CREAM PIE BASICS

PREBAKE THE CRUST
Toast a crumb crust to seal it; completely bake and cool a pastry crust before spooning in the filling. This ensures the crust will stand up to the moisture in the custard without becoming soggy.

COOL AND CHILL FILLING
The filling will continue to thicken as it cools, so it's important to chill it well before slicing and serving. Place the saucepan directly in an ice bath, stirring occasionally to speed along the cooling process.

VEGGIE PASTA SALADS

Noodles are the base of these one-dish meals, but the real stars are vegetables. Make ahead for lunch, dinner, or even a picnic.

Quick & Easy • Make Ahead
Vegetarian

Roasted Asparagus and Tomato Penne Salad with Goat Cheese

Hands-on time: 15 min. Total time: 35 min.

Serve immediately or cover and chill for two hours for a cold pasta salad.

2 cups uncooked penne or mostaccioli (tube-shaped pasta)
12 asparagus spears
12 cherry tomatoes
4 tablespoons extra-virgin olive oil, divided
½ teaspoon black pepper, divided
⅜ teaspoon kosher salt, divided
1 tablespoon minced shallots
2 tablespoons fresh lemon juice
1 tablespoon Dijon mustard
1 teaspoon dried herbes de Provence
1½ teaspoons honey
½ cup pitted kalamata olives, halved
2 cups baby arugula
½ cup (2 ounces) crumbled goat cheese

1. Preheat oven to 400°.
2. Cook pasta according to package directions, omitting salt and fat; drain and set aside.
3. Place asparagus and tomatoes on a jelly-roll pan. Drizzle with 1 tablespoon olive oil; sprinkle with ¼ teaspoon pepper and ¼ teaspoon salt. Toss gently to coat; arrange asparagus and tomato mixture in a single layer. Bake at 400° for 6 minutes or until asparagus is crisp-tender. Remove asparagus from pan. Place pan back in oven, and bake tomatoes an additional 4 minutes. Remove tomatoes from pan; let asparagus and tomatoes stand 10 minutes. Cut asparagus into 1-inch lengths; halve tomatoes.
4. Combine shallots and next 4 ingredients in a small bowl, stirring with a whisk. Gradually add remaining 3 tablespoons oil, stirring constantly with a whisk. Stir in remaining ¼ teaspoon pepper and remaining ⅛ teaspoon salt.
5. Place pasta, asparagus, tomato, olives, and arugula in a large bowl; toss. Drizzle juice mixture over pasta mixture; toss. Sprinkle with cheese. Yield: 4 servings (serving size: about 1¼ cups pasta mixture and 2 tablespoons cheese).

CALORIES 408; FAT 22.3g (sat 5.5g, mono 13.7g, poly 2.1g); PROTEIN 11.3g; CARB 42.9g; FIBER 3.5g; CHOL 11mg; IRON 3.6mg; SODIUM 584mg; CALC 101mg

Make Ahead • Vegetarian

Udon Noodle Salad with Broccolini and Spicy Tofu

Hands-on time: 25 min. Total time: 60 min.

Broccolini is blanched in salted water to get the vegetable crisp-tender while also keeping it bright green and full-flavored. If you make the salad ahead, wait to dress it until just before serving to preserve the Broccolini's color.

8 ounces water-packed extra-firm tofu
5 tablespoons peanut oil, divided
2 tablespoons lower-sodium tamari or soy sauce
1½ teaspoons Sriracha (hot chile sauce), divided
Cooking spray
6 ounces uncooked dried udon noodles (thick Japanese wheat noodles)
6 cups water
1½ teaspoons kosher salt
8 ounces Broccolini
3 tablespoons rice wine vinegar
1 tablespoon grated peeled fresh ginger
1 teaspoon dark sesame oil
½ cup thinly sliced radishes (about 3 medium)
2 tablespoons chopped dry-roasted cashews, toasted

1. Cut tofu into ¾-inch-thick slices. Place tofu slices in a single layer on several layers of paper towels; cover with additional paper towels. Let tofu stand 30 minutes to drain, pressing down occasionally. Remove tofu from paper towels, and cut into ¾-inch cubes.
2. Preheat oven to 350°.
3. Combine 2 tablespoons peanut oil, tamari, and 1 teaspoon Sriracha in a large bowl, stirring well with a whisk. Add tofu cubes to tamari mixture, and toss gently to coat. Let stand 15 minutes. Remove tofu from bowl with a slotted spoon; reserve tamari mixture in bowl. Arrange tofu in a single layer on a foil-lined baking sheet coated with cooking spray, and bake tofu at 350° for 10 minutes or until lightly golden.
4. Cook udon noodles according to package directions, omitting salt and fat. Drain and rinse with cold water; drain well.
5. Combine 6 cups water and salt in a large saucepan over high heat, and bring to a boil. Add Broccolini to pan; cook 3 minutes or until crisp-tender. Drain and plunge Broccolini into ice water; drain well. Chop Broccolini.
6. Add remaining 3 tablespoons peanut oil, remaining ½ teaspoon Sriracha, rice wine vinegar, ginger, and sesame oil to reserved tamari mixture in bowl; stir mixture well with a whisk. Add baked tofu, udon noodles, Broccolini, and ½ cup thinly sliced radishes to bowl; toss gently to coat. Sprinkle salad with cashews. Yield: 4 servings (serving size: 1¼ cups noodle mixture and 1½ teaspoons cashews).

CALORIES 438; FAT 24.7g (sat 4.1g, mono 10.1g, poly 8.2g); PROTEIN 14.3g; CARB 38.4g; FIBER 3.4g; CHOL 0mg; IRON 3mg; SODIUM 572mg; CALC 97mg

Quick & Easy • Make Ahead
Vegetarian

Gemelli Salad with Green Beans, Pistachios, and Lemon-Thyme Vinaigrette

Hands-on time: 20 min. Total time: 30 min.

Haricots verts are thin, tender green beans. If you can't find them, use trimmed regular green beans, but add them to the pasta after 8 minutes of cooking since they'll take longer to cook. You can make the salad ahead, but dress it just before serving so the beans don't turn drab.

8 ounces uncooked gemelli (short twisted tube pasta)
1 cup (1½-inch) cut haricots verts (about 4 ounces)
½ cup chopped shelled pistachios
2 tablespoons fresh thyme leaves, divided
2 tablespoons grated lemon rind, divided
1 tablespoon minced shallots
2 tablespoons Champagne or white wine vinegar
3 garlic cloves, crushed
5 tablespoons extra-virgin olive oil
½ teaspoon kosher salt
½ teaspoon freshly ground black pepper
⅓ cup (1 ounce) shaved fresh Parmesan cheese

1. Cook pasta according to package directions, omitting salt and fat. Add haricots verts during final 2 minutes of cooking. Drain and rinse pasta mixture under cold water; drain well.
2. Place pasta mixture, pistachios, 1 tablespoon thyme, and 1 tablespoon lemon rind in a large bowl; toss gently to combine.
3. Combine remaining 1 tablespoon thyme, remaining 1 tablespoon lemon rind, shallots, Champagne or white wine vinegar, and garlic in a small bowl, stirring well with a whisk. Gradually add olive oil, stirring constantly with a whisk. Add salt and black pepper; stir with a whisk. Drizzle over pasta mixture, and toss gently to coat. Top each serving with Parmesan cheese. Yield: 4 servings (serving size: about 1¼ cups pasta mixture and about 1 tablespoon cheese).

CALORIES 491; FAT 26.9g (sat 4.7g, mono 16.6g, poly 4g); PROTEIN 14.6g; CARB 50.8g; FIBER 4.9g; CHOL 6mg; IRON 3.2mg; SODIUM 416mg; CALC 131mg

Quick & Easy • Make Ahead
Vegetarian

Orzo Salad with Spicy Buttermilk Dressing

Hands-on time: 30 min. Total time: 30 min.

1 cup uncooked orzo
1 cup frozen whole-kernel corn, thawed and drained
12 cherry tomatoes, quartered
3 green onions, sliced
1 (15-ounce) can black beans, rinsed and drained
¼ cup low-fat buttermilk
3 tablespoons chopped fresh cilantro, divided
3 tablespoons fresh lime juice
2 tablespoons light sour cream
2 tablespoons canola mayonnaise
1 teaspoon chili powder
½ teaspoon kosher salt
¼ teaspoon black pepper
¼ teaspoon ground red pepper
2 garlic cloves, crushed
1 peeled avocado, cut into 8 wedges
1 tablespoon chopped fresh parsley

1. Cook orzo according to package directions, omitting salt and fat. Drain and rinse; drain well. Place orzo, corn, and next 3 ingredients in a large bowl, and toss.
2. Combine buttermilk, 2 tablespoons cilantro, and next 8 ingredients in a small bowl, stirring well with a whisk. Drizzle over orzo mixture; toss. Top with avocado; garnish with remaining 1 tablespoon cilantro and parsley. Yield: 4 servings (serving size: 1¾ cups orzo mixture, 2 avocado wedges, ¾ teaspoon cilantro, and ¾ teaspoon parsley).

CALORIES 424; FAT 15.3g (sat 2.3g, mono 8.4g, poly 2.7g); PROTEIN 12.7g; CARB 63.8g; FIBER 10.1g; CHOL 6mg; IRON 1.8mg; SODIUM 607mg; CALC 80mg

MATCH A DISH WITH CHARDONNAY

In America, oak-barrel notes are a hallmark of chardonnay. But winemakers around the globe are returning to France's Chablis style, making wine sans wood. The result: crisp wines with lean fruit. Without oak, you taste apple, pear, melon, and citrus.

This chowder includes flavors that complement chardonnay grapes, and the creaminess is balanced by the jolt of acidity from the wines. Our top pairing is Kim Crawford Marlborough Unoaked Chardonnay 2009, New Zealand, $17, with white peach and citrus notes.

A RANGE OF CHOICES FROM AFFORDABLE TO SPLURGE

WEEKNIGHT WINE
Clos LaChance Glittering-Throated Emerald Chardonnay 2009, California; $12. Apple, pear, and floral aromas.

ORGANIC OPTION
Emiliana Natura Unoaked Chardonnay 2010, Chile; $11. Peach, pineapple, and mango with a crisp, refreshing finish.

DINNER PARTY
Domaine Christian Moreau Père & Fils Chablis 2009, France; $23. Green apple and tart citrus with a mineral quality.

SPLURGE
William Fèvre "Champs Royaux" Chablis 2009, France; $25. Fresh as sea air, with nectarine and slate flavors.

Clam Chowder

Hands-on time: 37 min. Total time: 1 hr. 7 min.

1½ cups chopped onion, divided
½ cup unoaked chardonnay
3½ pounds littleneck clams
1 (8-ounce) bottle clam juice
1 bay leaf
1 tablespoon butter
1 bacon slice, chopped
3 cups diced red potato
½ cup chopped celery
⅛ teaspoon ground red pepper
3 tablespoons all-purpose flour
⅓ cup water
¾ cup half-and-half
¾ cup 2% reduced-fat milk
2 tablespoons chopped fresh chives
1 teaspoon chopped fresh thyme

1. Combine ½ cup onion, wine, and next 3 ingredients in a Dutch oven over medium-high heat; bring to a boil. Cover and cook 2 minutes or until clams open; discard any unopened shells. Strain through a cheesecloth-lined sieve over a bowl, reserving cooking liquid and clams. Remove meat from clams; chop. Discard shells.
2. Wipe pan clean. Melt butter in pan. Add bacon; sauté 3 minutes. Stir in remaining 1 cup onion, potato, celery, and red pepper; sauté 4 minutes. Stir in flour; cook 1 minute. Stir in cooking liquid and ⅓ cup water; bring to a boil. Cover and reduce heat; simmer 30 minutes, stirring occasionally. Stir in clams, half-and-half, and milk; cook 1 minute or until heated. Stir in herbs. Yield: 4 servings (serving size: 1¼ cups).

CALORIES 337; **FAT** 11.1g (sat 6.1g, mono 1.4g, poly 2.1g); **PROTEIN** 24.3g; **CARB** 34.9g; **FIBER** 3.1g; **CHOL** 78mg; **IRON** 20.6mg; **SODIUM** 310mg; **CALC** 204mg

WHAT TO EAT RIGHT NOW
PEAS

Green peas are one of spring's finest fleeting pleasures, remarkably sweet and so crisp they snap when you bite. They lend an unmistakable starchy, grassy sweetness to any dish—a far cry from the frozen, shriveled pellets we turn to for winter stews. You may have tried the stunning delicate green shoots (likely cut from immature snow peas) in Chinese restaurants. With a faint pea flavor, pea shoots are lovely additions to salads, stir-fries, pizzas, and soups. Look for them at farm stands or Asian markets, and get them while you can—the flavor turns bitter at the end of the growing season.

Vegetarian

Pea Shoot Salad with Radishes and Pickled Onion

Combine 1 cup cider vinegar, ½ cup water, and ½ teaspoon sugar, stirring until sugar dissolves. Add ¾ cup thinly vertically sliced red onion; let stand 30 minutes. Drain. Cook 1 cup shelled fresh English peas in boiling water with 1 teaspoon salt 2 minutes. Drain, and rinse peas with cold water. Combine onion, peas, 6 cups pea shoots, and 10 thinly sliced radishes in a large bowl. Combine 2 tablespoons extra-virgin olive oil, 1½ tablespoons white wine vinegar, ¼ teaspoon salt, and ¼ teaspoon freshly ground black pepper. Drizzle oil mixture over pea mixture; toss gently. Yield: 6 servings (serving size: 1 cup).

CALORIES 79; **FAT** 4.6g (sat 0.7g); **SODIUM** 163mg

Quick & Easy

Seared Scallops with Lemony Sweet Pea Relish

Hands-on time: 27 min. Total time: 27 min.

Pat your scallops dry with paper towels, and sear them in a superhot cast-iron skillet.

1 cup shelled fresh English peas
1½ teaspoons salt, divided
¼ cup extra-virgin olive oil, divided
1½ teaspoons grated lemon rind
2 tablespoons fresh lemon juice
1 tablespoon chopped fresh flat-leaf parsley
¼ cup minced shallots
½ teaspoon freshly ground black pepper, divided
2¼ pounds large sea scallops
1½ cups pea shoots
6 lemon wedges

1. Cook English peas in boiling water with 1 teaspoon salt 2 minutes. Drain and rinse with cold water; drain. Combine peas, 3 tablespoons oil, rind, juice, parsley, and shallots. Stir in ¼ teaspoon salt and ¼ teaspoon pepper; toss gently.
2. Heat a large cast-iron skillet over medium-high heat. Add 1½ teaspoons oil to pan; swirl to coat. Sprinkle remaining ¼ teaspoon salt and remaining ¼ teaspoon black pepper over scallops. Add half of scallops to pan; cook 2 minutes on each side or until desired degree of doneness. Repeat procedure with remaining 1½ teaspoons oil and scallops. Divide scallops evenly among 6 plates; top each serving with 2½ tablespoons pea mixture and ¼ cup pea shoots. Serve with lemon wedges. Yield: 6 servings.

CALORIES 260; **FAT** 10.4g (sat 1.4g, mono 6.6g, poly 1.4g); **PROTEIN** 30.2g; **CARB** 10.6g; **FIBER** 1.5g; **CHOL** 56mg; **IRON** 1.1mg; **SODIUM** 513mg; **CALC** 53mg

DRIZZLE, DRESS & DIP

Pea oil, a healthy alternative to saturated fat–laden butter, tastes sweet and green like spring. Drizzle it over sautéed, roasted, or grilled veggies. Use it to dress salads, or sprinkle coarse salt and freshly ground black pepper over the top and dunk a hunk of bread in it. If you make a batch of oil and strain it, you can keep it chilled for up to a week. Combine 3 cups pea shoots and 1 cup canola oil in a food processor; process until smooth. Strain through a fine sieve.

Quick & Easy • Vegetarian

Fresh Pea and Garlic Gazpacho

Cook 2½ cups shelled fresh English peas in boiling water 4 minutes. Drain and rinse with cold water until cool. Set aside ½ cup peas. Combine remaining peas, 2¼ cups ice water, 1½ cups chopped peeled English cucumber, 1 cup (½-inch) French bread cubes, 2 tablespoons extra-virgin olive oil, 1½ tablespoons sherry vinegar, and 2 garlic cloves in a blender; process until smooth. Stir in ½ teaspoon kosher salt and ½ teaspoon freshly ground black pepper. Ladle 1 cup soup into each of 6 bowls. Garnish with reserved peas, fresh pea shoots, 1 tablespoon small fresh mint leaves, and 1½ teaspoons extra-virgin olive oil. Yield: 6 servings.

CALORIES 128; **FAT** 6.1g (sat 0.9g); **SODIUM** 222mg

5-INGREDIENT COOKING

Spiced Lamb Kebabs

Hands-on time: 20 min. Total time: 1 hr. 20 min.

Combine yogurt, cumin, paprika, and garlic in a bowl. Cut lamb into 24 (1-inch) cubes; sprinkle with ½ teaspoon kosher salt and ¼ teaspoon black pepper. Combine lamb and ½ cup yogurt mixture in a zip-top plastic bag (refrigerate remaining yogurt mixture); seal. Marinate in refrigerator at least 1 hour. Remove lamb; discard marinade. Thread 3 lamb pieces onto each of 8 (10-inch) skewers. Heat a grill pan over medium-high heat; coat with cooking spray. Arrange 4 skewers on pan; cook 7 minutes or until desired degree of doneness, turning frequently. Remove from pan. Repeat with remaining skewers. Serve with remaining yogurt mixture. Yield: 4 servings (serving size: 2 skewers and 3 tablespoons sauce).

CALORIES 187; **FAT** 5.2g (sat 1.8g, mono 2.1g, poly 0.5g); **PROTEIN** 29.6g; **CARB** 3.4g; **FIBER** 0.2g; **CHOL** 73mg; **IRON** 2.3mg; **SODIUM** 338mg; **CALC** 60mg

THE FIVE INGREDIENTS

1¼ cups plain fat-free Greek yogurt

+

1 teaspoon ground cumin

+

½ teaspoon hot paprika

+

1 garlic clove, minced

+

1 pound boneless leg of lamb, trimmed

READER RECIPE

FROM YOUR KITCHEN TO OURS

Walla Walla onions are mild in flavor, so a generous amount enhances, not overwhelms, a casserole.

Vegetarian

Sweet Onion Casserole

Hands-on time: 20 min. Total time: 65 min.

"This recipe is a great complement to a pork roast with roasted potatoes and carrots."
—Irene Lilja, Corvallis, Oregon

1 tablespoon canola oil
4 cups chopped sweet onion (about 1¾ pounds)
½ cup uncooked long-grain rice
⅔ cup 2% reduced-fat milk
½ cup (2 ounces) shredded Gruyère cheese
¼ teaspoon salt
¼ teaspoon freshly ground black pepper
⅛ teaspoon ground allspice
Cooking spray
⅓ cup (1⅓ ounces) grated fresh Parmesan cheese
2 tablespoons chopped fresh parsley (optional)

1. Preheat oven to 325°.
2. Heat a large skillet over medium-high heat. Add oil; swirl to coat. Add onion; sauté 5 minutes or until tender. Place onion in a large bowl.
3. Cook rice in a large pot of boiling water 5 minutes. Drain.
4. Stir rice and next 5 ingredients into onions. Spoon onion mixture into an 8-inch square glass or ceramic baking dish coated with cooking spray. Sprinkle evenly with Parmesan cheese. Cover and bake at 325° for 40 minutes. Uncover and bake an additional 5 minutes. Top with parsley, if desired. Yield: 6 servings (serving size: about ⅔ cup).

CALORIES 192; **FAT** 7.4g (sat 3.1g, mono 3g, poly 0.9g); **PROTEIN** 7.6g; **CARB** 23.9g; **FIBER** 2.1g; **CHOL** 16mg; **IRON** 1mg; **SODIUM** 213mg; **CALC** 203mg

FEED 4 FOR LESS THAN $10

Smart flavor boosters—tangy mustard, tomatoes, lemon, capers, and vinegar—brighten up easy weekday meals.

Kid Friendly
Maple-Mustard Chicken Thighs

$7.63 total, $1.91 per serving
Hands-on time: 31 min. Total time: 2 hr. 43 min.

Speed up prep by marinating only 30 minutes. Serve with cabbage-carrot slaw.

⅓ cup spicy brown mustard
2 tablespoons brown sugar
3 tablespoons maple syrup
2 tablespoons yellow mustard
1 tablespoon grated onion
1 tablespoon cider vinegar
2 teaspoons lower-sodium soy sauce
½ teaspoon black pepper
1 garlic clove, minced
8 bone-in chicken thighs, skinned
¼ teaspoon kosher salt
Cooking spray

1. Combine first 9 ingredients. Place half of mixture in a zip-top plastic bag; reserve remaining mixture. Add chicken to bag; seal. Chill 2 hours.
2. Preheat grill to medium-high heat.
3. Remove chicken from bag. Sprinkle chicken with salt. Place chicken on grill rack coated with cooking spray; grill 8 minutes on each side or until done. Serve with reserved mustard mixture. Yield: 4 servings (serving size: 2 thighs and 2 tablespoons sauce).

CALORIES 314; **FAT** 11.7g (sat 3.2g, mono 4.5g, poly 2.7g); **PROTEIN** 27.6g; **CARB** 18.2g; **FIBER** 0.4g; **CHOL** 99mg; **IRON** 1.8mg; **SODIUM** 565mg; **CALC** 36mg

Quick & Easy
Pasta Puttanesca

$8.86 total, $2.22 per serving
Hands-on time: 23 min. Total time: 35 min.

Serve with a salad of green leaf lettuce, red onion, and fresh parsley, dressed with 1 tablespoon olive oil and fresh lemon juice.

3 tablespoons olive oil, divided
2 garlic cloves, minced
3 anchovy fillets
1½ cups canned crushed tomatoes
¾ cup pitted kalamata olives, coarsely chopped
1 tablespoon minced fresh parsley
1 tablespoon drained capers
¼ teaspoon crushed red pepper
6 quarts water
8 ounces uncooked fettuccine
¼ cup (1 ounce) grated fresh Parmesan cheese

1. Heat a large nonstick skillet over medium heat. Add 2 tablespoons oil to pan; swirl to coat. Add garlic; cook 30 seconds, stirring constantly. Add anchovies; mash in pan to form a paste. Stir in tomatoes and next 4 ingredients; cook 5 minutes, stirring occasionally.
2. Bring 6 quarts water to a boil. Add pasta; cook 8 minutes or until almost al dente. Drain in a colander over a bowl, reserving ½ cup pasta water. Add pasta and reserved pasta water to tomato mixture; increase heat to medium-high. Cook 5 minutes or until pasta is al dente, tossing to combine. Spoon 1½ cups pasta into each of 4 bowls. Drizzle each serving with ¾ teaspoon oil; sprinkle with cheese. Yield: 4 servings.

CALORIES 404; **FAT** 17.5g (sat 3.5g, mono 11.1g, poly 2.2g); **PROTEIN** 13.1g; **CARB** 51.5g; **FIBER** 3.9g; **CHOL** 7mg; **IRON** 3.5mg; **SODIUM** 648mg; **CALC** 144mg

Quick & Easy
Sausage and Egg Burrito

$8.42 total, $2.11 per serving,
Hands-on time: 20 min. Total time: 20 min.

Serve with a salad of fresh spinach, sliced red onion, and cubed cantaloupe.

⅓ cup thinly sliced radish
¼ cup thinly vertically sliced red onion
1 tablespoon fresh lemon juice
½ medium-sized ripe avocado, chopped
¼ teaspoon kosher salt, divided
¼ teaspoon freshly ground black pepper, divided
2 teaspoons butter
4 garlic cloves, coarsely chopped
2 ounces reduced-fat pork sausage
6 large eggs, lightly beaten
4 (8-inch) whole-wheat flour tortillas
1 (15-ounce) can organic pinto beans, rinsed, drained, and mashed
1 serrano chile, thinly sliced
¼ cup thinly sliced green onions

1. Combine first 4 ingredients in a bowl; sprinkle with ⅛ teaspoon salt and ⅛ teaspoon black pepper. Toss gently to coat.
2. Melt butter in a medium nonstick skillet over medium heat. Add garlic and sausage to pan; cook 3 minutes or until sausage is browned, stirring to crumble. Stir in eggs; sprinkle with remaining ⅛ teaspoon salt and remaining ⅛ teaspoon pepper. Cook to desired consistency, stirring to scramble. Remove from heat.
3. Heat tortillas according to package directions. Place 1 tortilla on each of 4 plates. Divide beans evenly among tortillas, spreading to a thin layer, leaving a ¼-inch border. Divide egg mixture evenly among tortillas; top with radish mixture and chile slices. Roll up each burrito jelly-roll fashion. Sprinkle 1 tablespoon green onions over each serving. Yield: 4 servings (serving size: 1 burrito).

CALORIES 370; **FAT** 14.4g (sat 4.2g, mono 6.5g, poly 1.8g); **PROTEIN** 20.1g; **CARB** 39.7g; **FIBER** 5.8g; **CHOL** 285mg; **IRON** 2.8mg; **SODIUM** 645mg; **CALC** 80mg

Pork Salad Provençal

$9.96 total, $2.49 per serving
Hands-on time: 25 min. Total time: 35 min.

Serve this elegant salad with baguette slices toasted with feta cheese.

2 garlic cloves, divided
1 (1-pound) pork tenderloin
Cooking spray
¾ teaspoon black pepper, divided
½ teaspoon salt, divided
½ teaspoon grated lemon rind
3 tablespoons fresh lemon juice
2 tablespoons olive oil
½ teaspoon dried thyme
5 cups chopped romaine lettuce
½ cup chopped fresh flat-leaf parsley
2 celery stalks, thinly sliced
1 plum tomato, diced

1. Preheat grill to medium-high heat.
2. Thinly slice 1 garlic clove. With a sharp knife, make 8 small slits in pork; insert garlic slices into slits. Coat pork with cooking spray; sprinkle with ½ teaspoon pepper and ¼ teaspoon salt. Place pork on grill rack coated with cooking spray; grill 20 minutes or until a thermometer registers 155°, turning once. Let stand 5 minutes; slice.
3. Mince remaining garlic clove. Combine minced garlic, remaining ¼ teaspoon pepper, remaining ¼ teaspoon salt, lemon rind, lemon juice, olive oil, and thyme in a large bowl, stirring well. Add lettuce and next 3 ingredients; toss. Arrange 1½ cups salad on each of 4 plates; top evenly with pork. Yield: 4 servings.

CALORIES 212; FAT 9.7g (sat 1.8g, mono 5.9g, poly 1.3g); PROTEIN 25.2g; CARB 5.8g; FIBER 2.3g; CHOL 74mg; IRON 2.7mg; SODIUM 382mg; CALC 57mg

DINNER TONIGHT

Here is a batch of fast weeknight menus from the *Cooking Light* Test Kitchens.

READY IN
30
MINUTES

The
SHOPPING LIST

Peach and Gorgonzola Chicken Pizza
1 peach
extra-virgin olive oil
balsamic vinegar
1 (10-ounce) prebaked thin pizza crust
cooked chicken breast
Gorgonzola cheese
part-skim mozzarella cheese

Arugula Salad
lemon
shallot
arugula
red onion
honey
extra-virgin olive oil

The
GAME PLAN

While oven heats:
■ Shred chicken.
■ Crumble cheese.
■ Slice peach.
While pizza bakes:
■ Prepare balsamic reduction.
■ Toss salad.

Peach and Gorgonzola Chicken Pizza
with Arugula Salad

Kid-Pleaser: Use crumbled goat cheese instead of Gorgonzola for milder flavor.
Buy the Best: Find fragrant peaches that yield slightly to the touch.
Flavor Hit: Tangy balsamic reduction balances the sweetness of the peach.

1 (10-ounce) prebaked thin pizza crust
Cooking spray
1 teaspoon extra-virgin olive oil
½ cup (2 ounces) shredded part-skim mozzarella cheese, divided
1 cup shredded cooked chicken breast
⅓ cup (about 1½ ounces) crumbled Gorgonzola cheese
1 medium unpeeled peach, thinly sliced
⅓ cup balsamic vinegar

1. Preheat oven to 400°.
2. Place pizza crust on a baking sheet coated with cooking spray. Brush 1 teaspoon extra-virgin olive oil evenly over crust. Top evenly with ¼ cup shredded mozzarella cheese, chicken, Gorgonzola cheese, and peach slices. Top with remaining ¼ cup mozzarella. Bake at 400° for 11 minutes or until crust browns.
3. Place vinegar in a small saucepan over medium-high heat; cook until reduced to 2 tablespoons (about 5 minutes). Drizzle balsamic reduction evenly over pizza. Cut pizza into 8 wedges. Yield: 4 servings (serving size: 2 pizza wedges).

CALORIES 384; FAT 12.5g (sat 4.9g, mono 2.1g, poly 0.5g); PROTEIN 24.3g; CARB 42.5g; FIBER 2.1g; CHOL 46mg; IRON 2.9mg; SODIUM 643mg; CALC 264mg

For the Arugula Salad:
Combine 1 teaspoon minced shallots, 2 teaspoons lemon juice, and ½ teaspoon honey in a large bowl; gradually whisk in 1 tablespoon extra-virgin olive oil. Add 4 cups loosely packed arugula and ⅓ cup vertically sliced red onion to bowl; toss gently to coat. Yield: 4 servings.

CALORIES 44; FAT 3.6g (sat 0.5g); SODIUM 6mg

The SHOPPING LIST

Roasted Shrimp and Broccoli
broccoli florets
lemon
extra-virgin olive oil
crushed red pepper
1½ pounds peeled and deveined large
   shrimp

Garlic-Basil Corn
4 ears corn
fresh basil
garlic
butter

The GAME PLAN

While oven heats and water comes to a boil:
- Prepare garlic-basil butter.
- Toss shrimp with seasonings.
- Blanch broccoli.

While broccoli and shrimp roast:
- Cook corn.

Dress corn and broccoli.

Quick & Easy

Roasted Shrimp and Broccoli
with Garlic-Basil Corn

Time-Saver: Purchase fresh, trimmed corn on the cob that has been cleaned of silks.
Simple Sub: Scallops or chunks of chicken breast can stand in for the shrimp.
Flavor Hit: Lemon rind adds zing to broccoli without acid that would dull its color.

5 cups broccoli florets
1 tablespoon grated lemon rind, divided
1 tablespoon fresh lemon juice
½ teaspoon salt, divided
½ teaspoon freshly ground black pepper,
   divided
1½ pounds peeled and deveined large shrimp
Cooking spray
2 tablespoons extra-virgin olive oil
¼ teaspoon crushed red pepper

1. Preheat oven to 425°.
2. Cook broccoli in boiling water 1 minute. Drain and plunge into ice water; drain.
3. Combine 1½ teaspoons rind, juice, ¼ teaspoon salt, and ¼ teaspoon black pepper in a medium bowl. Add shrimp; toss to combine. Arrange broccoli and shrimp in a single layer on a jelly-roll pan coated with cooking spray. Bake at 425° for 8 minutes or until shrimp are done.
4. Combine oil, remaining 1½ teaspoons rind, remaining ¼ teaspoon salt, remaining ¼ teaspoon black pepper, and crushed red pepper in a large bowl. Add broccoli; toss to combine. Yield: 4 servings (serving size: 1 cup broccoli and about 9 shrimp).

Sustainable Choice
For more information on sustainable shrimp, see page 113.

CALORIES 268; **FAT** 10g (sat 1.5g, mono 5.4g, poly 2g); **PROTEIN** 37.3g; **CARB** 7g; **FIBER** 2.9g; **CHOL** 259mg; **IRON** 5mg; **SODIUM** 571mg; **CALC** 135mg

---

For the Garlic-Basil Corn:
Combine 2 tablespoons softened butter, 1 tablespoon chopped fresh basil, and 1 minced garlic clove in a small bowl. Place 4 ears shucked corn in a large saucepan of boiling water; cook 4 minutes. Drain. Spoon 1 teaspoon butter mixture over each ear of corn. Yield: 4 servings.

CALORIES 130; **FAT** 6.8g (sat 3.8g); **SODIUM** 55mg

The SHOPPING LIST

Greek Lamb Chops and Mint Yogurt Sauce
lemon
fresh oregano
fresh mint
garlic
canola oil
plain fat-free yogurt
8 (4-ounce) lamb loin chops

Tomato-Parsley Salad
lemon
fresh flat-leaf parsley
yellow bell pepper
red onion
1 pint grape tomatoes
extra-virgin olive oil
Dijon mustard
honey

The GAME PLAN

- Cook lamb.

While lamb rests:
- Prepare yogurt sauce.
- Make salad.

Quick & Easy

Greek Lamb Chops and Mint Yogurt Sauce

with Tomato-Parsley Salad

Prep Pointer: Let the lamb stand at room temp for 30 minutes so it cooks evenly and quickly.
Simple Sub: Use mixed greens in place of parsley in the salad.
Make-Ahead Tip: Prepare and chill the yogurt sauce up to a day ahead.

If you have trouble finding the right size lamb loin chops, ask the butcher to cut them to the size you need. For a thicker sauce, use Greek-style yogurt.

2 tablespoons fresh lemon juice
2 teaspoons chopped fresh oregano
2 garlic cloves, minced
8 (4-ounce) lamb loin chops, trimmed
¼ teaspoon kosher salt
¼ teaspoon freshly ground black pepper
2 teaspoons canola oil
½ cup plain fat-free yogurt
1 tablespoon chopped fresh mint
½ teaspoon fresh lemon juice
⅛ teaspoon kosher salt
1 garlic clove, minced

1. Combine first 3 ingredients in a small bowl. Sprinkle lamb with ¼ teaspoon salt and pepper; rub with oregano mixture. Heat a large skillet over high heat. Add oil to pan, swirling to coat. Add lamb, and cook 3 minutes on each side or until desired degree of doneness. Let stand 5 minutes.
2. Combine yogurt and next 4 ingredients in a small bowl. Serve sauce with lamb. Yield: 4 servings (serving size: 2 lamb chops and 2 tablespoons sauce).

CALORIES 347; FAT 14.1g (sat 4.9g, mono 6.2g, poly 1.3g); PROTEIN 48.2g; CARB 3.9g, FIBER 0.1g; CHOL 147mg; IRON 4.5mg; SODIUM 347mg; CALC 86mg

For the Tomato-Parsley Salad:

Combine 2 tablespoons fresh lemon juice, 1½ teaspoons Dijon mustard, and ½ teaspoon honey in a large bowl; gradually whisk in 1 tablespoon extra-virgin olive oil. Add 2 cups fresh flat-leaf parsley leaves, 1 cup diced yellow bell pepper, ½ cup diced red onion, and 1 pint halved grape tomatoes; toss gently to coat. Yield: 4 servings.

CALORIES 82; FAT 3.9g (sat 0.6g); SODIUM 68mg

READY IN 40 MINUTES

The
SHOPPING LIST

Parmesan Polenta and Spicy Sausage Sauce

onion
garlic
fresh oregano
fresh basil
olive oil
crushed red pepper
fat-free, lower-sodium chicken broth
quick-cooking polenta
2 (14.5-ounce) cans no-salt-added diced tomatoes
sun-dried tomato chicken sausage
Parmesan cheese

Sautéed Spinach and Pine Nuts
shallot
1 (9-ounce) bag fresh spinach
canola oil
pine nuts

The
GAME PLAN

While sauce simmers:
■ Cook polenta.
■ Cook spinach.

Quick & Easy • Kid Friendly

Parmesan Polenta and Spicy Sausage Sauce

with Sautéed Spinach and Pine Nuts

Time-Saver: Use prechopped onion.
Simple Sub: Try sweet Italian chicken sausage if you're not a sun-dried tomato fan.
Prep Pointer: Green shoots inside a garlic clove mean the head is older and the garlic may be bitter; discard it.

1 tablespoon olive oil
3 ounces (2 links) sun-dried tomato chicken sausage, sliced
1 cup chopped onion
3 garlic cloves, minced
1 tablespoon chopped fresh oregano
½ teaspoon crushed red pepper
2 (14.5-ounce) cans no-salt-added diced tomatoes, undrained
½ cup chopped fresh basil, divided
2 cups fat-free, lower-sodium chicken broth
1 cup water
¾ cup quick-cooking polenta
½ cup grated fresh Parmesan cheese, divided

1. Heat a medium saucepan over medium-high heat. Add oil to pan, swirling to coat. Add sausage; sauté 3 minutes or until browned. Add onion; sauté 5 minutes or until tender. Add garlic; sauté 30 seconds. Add oregano, pepper, and tomatoes; bring to a boil. Reduce heat, and simmer 15 minutes, stirring occasionally. Add ¼ cup basil to pan; cook 5 minutes or until sauce thickens.
2. Combine broth and 1 cup water in a large saucepan; bring to a boil. Add polenta; reduce heat, and simmer 5 minutes or until thick, stirring frequently with a whisk. Stir in ¼ cup cheese. Place ⅔ cup polenta in each of 4 bowls; top with about ¾ cup sauce. Top each serving with 1 tablespoon basil and 1 tablespoon cheese. Yield: 4 servings.

CALORIES 279; FAT 8.3g (sat 2.7g, mono 4.1g, poly 1g); PROTEIN 12.6g; CARB 31g; FIBER 5.3g; CHOL 25mg; IRON 1.7mg; SODIUM 524mg; CALC 170mg

continued

For the Sautéed Spinach and Pine Nuts:
Heat 2 teaspoons canola oil in a large skillet over medium-high heat. Add 1 tablespoon minced shallots; sauté 2 minutes. Add 1 (9-ounce) bag fresh baby spinach; sauté 2 minutes or until spinach wilts. Stir in 1 tablespoon toasted pine nuts and ⅛ teaspoon salt. Yield: 4 servings.

CALORIES 64; FAT 3.8g (sat 0.3g); SODIUM 175mg

SUPERFAST

Lots of crunch from fresh ingredients—romaine salad, cabbage slaw, cucumbers, and watercress—boosts speedy weeknight dishes.

Quick & Easy

Shrimp Cobb Salad

(pictured on page 220)

Typical Cobb salads include chicken and hard-cooked eggs; this riff uses shrimp and corn.

4 center-cut bacon slices
1 pound large shrimp, peeled and deveined
½ teaspoon paprika
¼ teaspoon black pepper
Cooking spray
¼ teaspoon salt, divided
2½ tablespoons fresh lemon juice
1½ tablespoons extra-virgin olive oil
½ teaspoon whole-grain Dijon mustard
1 (10-ounce) package romaine salad
2 cups cherry tomatoes, quartered
1 cup shredded carrots (about 2 carrots)
1 cup frozen whole-kernel corn, thawed
1 ripe peeled avocado, cut into 8 wedges

1. Cook bacon in a large nonstick skillet over medium heat until crisp. Remove bacon from pan; cut in half crosswise. Wipe pan clean with paper towels. Increase heat to medium-high. Sprinkle shrimp with paprika and pepper. Coat pan with cooking spray. Add shrimp to pan; cook 2 minutes on each side or until done. Sprinkle with ⅛ teaspoon salt; toss to coat.
2. While shrimp cooks, combine remaining ⅛ teaspoon salt, juice, oil, and mustard in a large bowl, stirring with a whisk. Add lettuce; toss to coat.
3. Arrange about 1½ cups lettuce mixture on each of 4 plates. Top each serving with about 6 shrimp, ½ cup tomatoes, ¼ cup carrot, ¼ cup corn, 2 avocado wedges, and 2 bacon pieces. Yield: 4 servings.

CALORIES 332; FAT 15.2g (sat 2.9g, mono 8g, poly 2.6g); PROTEIN 30g; CARB 21.8g; FIBER 7.5g; CHOL 181mg; IRON 4.3mg; SODIUM 551mg; CALC 110mg

Quick & Easy • Kid Friendly

Ancho Chicken Tacos with Cilantro Slaw and Avocado Cream

1 pound skinless, boneless chicken breasts, cut into ¼-inch strips
¾ teaspoon ancho chile powder
½ teaspoon garlic salt
¼ teaspoon ground cumin
Cooking spray
⅛ teaspoon grated lime rind
2 tablespoons fresh lime juice, divided
¼ cup light sour cream
2 tablespoons 1% low-fat milk
½ ripe peeled avocado, diced
2 cups packaged angel hair slaw
½ cup thinly sliced green onions
¼ cup chopped fresh cilantro
1 tablespoon canola oil
¼ teaspoon salt
8 (6-inch) corn tortillas

1. Heat a large skillet over high heat. Sprinkle chicken evenly with chile powder, garlic salt, and cumin. Coat pan with cooking spray. Add chicken to pan; cook 4 minutes, stirring frequently. Remove chicken from pan.
2. Place rind, 1 tablespoon juice, and next 3 ingredients in a blender or food processor; process until smooth.
3. Combine remaining 1 tablespoon juice, slaw, onions, cilantro, oil, and salt, tossing to coat.
4. Heat tortillas according to package directions. Divide chicken mixture evenly among tortillas. Top each tortilla with about 1 tablespoon avocado mixture and ¼ cup slaw mixture. Yield: 4 servings (serving size: 2 tacos).

CALORIES 319; FAT 11.6g (sat 2.3g, mono 5.5g, poly 2.4g); PROTEIN 30g; CARB 25.3g; FIBER 5.1g; CHOL 72mg; IRON 1.3mg; SODIUM 385mg; CALC 80mg

Quick & Easy

Flank Steak with Spicy Lemon Sauce

1 (1-pound) flank steak, trimmed
½ teaspoon salt
½ teaspoon black pepper
Cooking spray
¼ cup reduced-fat sour cream
3 tablespoons prepared horseradish
1 tablespoon canola mayonnaise
1 teaspoon Dijon mustard
½ teaspoon grated lemon rind
1 tablespoon fresh lemon juice
2 tablespoons chopped fresh chives
1 tablespoon chopped fresh parsley

1. Heat a large skillet over medium-high heat. Sprinkle both sides of steak with salt and pepper. Coat pan with cooking spray. Add steak to pan; cook 5 minutes on each side or until desired degree of doneness. Place steak on a cutting board; let stand 5 minutes. Cut steak diagonally across grain into thin slices.
2. While steak cooks, combine sour cream and next 5 ingredients in a small bowl, stirring with a whisk. Stir in chives and parsley. Serve sour cream mixture with steak. Yield: 4 servings (serving size: 3 ounces steak and about 3 tablespoons sour cream mixture).

CALORIES 224; FAT 11.4g (sat 4g, mono 4.4g, poly 1.1g); PROTEIN 25.8g; CARB 3.3g; FIBER 0.6g; CHOL 44mg; IRON 1.9mg; SODIUM 459mg; CALC 60mg

Side Dish of the Month

Sesame-Miso Cucumber Salad

Miso is a thick soybean paste with a salty, slightly sweet flavor. Look for it in the refrigerated part of the produce section or with the dairy products, or substitute soy sauce.

1½ tablespoons sesame seeds, toasted
2 tablespoons white miso (soybean paste) or lower-sodium soy sauce
1 tablespoon rice vinegar
1 tablespoon honey
1 tablespoon hot water
1 teaspoon crushed red pepper
2 teaspoons dark sesame oil
4 cups thinly sliced seeded cucumber

1. Combine first 7 ingredients in a large bowl, stirring with a whisk. Add cucumber; toss to coat. Yield: 6 servings (serving size: ¾ cup).

CALORIES 60; FAT 2.7g (sat 0.2g, mono 0.6g, poly 0.7g); PROTEIN 1.9g; CARB 7.2g; FIBER 1.6g; CHOL 0mg; IRON 3.8mg; SODIUM 182mg; CALC 12mg

Sautéed Miso Variation:

Omit seeds, honey, and red pepper; decrease miso to 1½ tablespoons. Combine miso, vinegar, 1 tablespoon hot water, 1 tablespoon sliced green onions, ¼ teaspoon black pepper, and ⅛ teaspoon salt. Heat 1 tablespoon sesame oil in a large skillet over medium heat. Add cucumber to pan; sauté 4 minutes. Toss cucumber with juice mixture. Yield: 6 servings.

CALORIES 38; FAT 2.4g (sat 0.3g); SODIUM 186mg

Greek Variation:

Omit first 7 ingredients; decrease cucumber to 2 cups. Combine 1½ tablespoons minced red onion, 1 tablespoon chopped parsley, ¾ teaspoon chopped oregano, 1 tablespoon lemon juice, 1½ teaspoons olive oil, and ⅛ teaspoon salt. Toss with cucumber, 1 cup quartered cherry tomatoes, and ½ cup orange bell pepper strips. Yield: 4 servings.

CALORIES 40; FAT 1.9g (sat 0.3g); SODIUM 86mg

Spicy Pasta Variation:

Increase seeds to 3 tablespoons; add 1 cup thinly sliced green onions and ¼ teaspoon salt. Combine seeds and remaining ingredients in a large bowl. Cut 1 (9-ounce) package fresh linguine into thirds; cook according to directions. Drain; rinse with cold water. Toss pasta with cucumber mixture. Yield: 6 servings.

CALORIES 207; FAT 5.2g (sat 1.1g); SODIUM 294mg

Snack of the Month

Strawberry-Avocado Salsa with Cinnamon Tortilla Chips

Make the chips in advance, cool completely, and store in an airtight container until ready to serve.

2 teaspoons canola oil
6 (6-inch) whole-wheat flour tortillas
2 teaspoons sugar
½ teaspoon ground cinnamon
1½ cups finely chopped peeled ripe avocado (about 2)
1 cup finely chopped strawberries
2 tablespoons minced fresh cilantro
1 teaspoon minced seeded jalapeño pepper
2 teaspoons fresh lime juice
⅜ teaspoon salt

1. Preheat oven to 350°.
2. To prepare chips, brush oil evenly over 1 side of each tortilla. Combine sugar and cinnamon; sprinkle evenly over oil-coated sides of tortillas. Cut each tortilla into 12 wedges; arrange wedges in a single layer on 2 baking sheets. Bake at 350° for 10 minutes or until crisp.
3. Combine avocado and next 5 ingredients; stir gently to combine. Serve with chips. Yield: 12 servings (serving size: 6 chips and about 3 tablespoons avocado mixture).

CALORIES 138; FAT 6.7g (sat 1g, mono 3.8g, poly 0.9g); PROTEIN 2.8g; CARB 17.3g; FIBER 3.6g; CHOL 0mg; IRON 0.3mg; SODIUM 246mg; CALC 7mg

Sandwich of the Month

Roast Beef Sandwiches with Watercress Slaw

1 cup packaged angel hair slaw
1 cup chopped trimmed watercress
⅓ cup thinly sliced green onions
2 tablespoons minced fresh tarragon
3 tablespoons canola mayonnaise
¼ teaspoon black pepper
1 (8-ounce) French bread baguette
4 teaspoons butter, softened
8 ounces lower-sodium, thinly sliced deli roast beef
8 (¼-inch-thick) slices tomato

1. Combine first 6 ingredients.
2. Cut baguette crosswise into 4 pieces. Cut each piece in half horizontally using a serrated knife. Spread 1 teaspoon butter on each bottom half of baguette. Divide roast beef evenly over bottom halves of baguette. Arrange about 1 cup slaw mixture and 2 tomato slices over each sandwich; top with top halves of baguette. Yield: 4 servings (serving size: 1 sandwich).

CALORIES 358; FAT 14.8g (sat 4.2g, mono 6.5g, poly 2.4g); PROTEIN 21.3g; CARB 37.5g; FIBER 2.2g; CHOL 44mg; IRON 3.7mg; SODIUM 585mg; CALC 26mg

(soggy salad)

OOPS!
YOUR SALAD GOES LIMP

How and when you dress your greens can
make all the difference.
By Tim Cebula

A soggy pile of wilted greens makes
for a sorry salad indeed. Tender greens
like Boston lettuce, mâche, and arugula
are delicate little things that perish at
the mere rumor of mistreatment (tear-
ing or roughly handling lettuce bruises
it), but even crisp, hearty lettuces like
romaine need to be treated with care.
To keep them at their best, you need
to consider three factors: time, volume,
and temperature.

Only dress your greens just before
serving, particularly when using vinaigrette: Oil quickly permeates the waxy
surface of leafy greens, turning them
dark green and droopy. If you've washed
your greens, use a salad spinner or blot
them delicately with paper towels to
dry them. Water clinging to leaves
will repel oil-based vinaigrettes and
thin out creamy dressings, leading to
bland salad.

Put dry greens in a salad bowl. Add
less dressing than you think you'll need
(to avoid overdressing), and pour it
down the sides of the bowl, not onto
the greens—you'll dress them more
evenly this way. Gently toss, adding
dressing as needed, until the greens are
lightly coated. If you do overdress them,
a quick whirl in the salad spinner will
shake off any excess.

Finally, follow the lead of professional
chefs and serve your salad on chilled
plates to help keep the greens crisp as
you enjoy them.

(gorgeous greens)

THE 25 DISHES OF SUMMER

Delicious classics given fresh twists—recipes you'll just have to try this summer!

STARTERS & DRINKS

A watermelon cooler, a lettuce wedge with green goddess dressing—these are the sorts of classic recipes that, with just a little twist to keep them light and lively, make summer eating the most fun eating of the year. Porch and patio eating. Late-Sunday-brunch eating. Picnic and family-reunion eating. The dishes in this chapter and throughout our annual Summer Cookbook will sweeten your days in the shade and spice up your cool-breeze nights under a waxing moon.

RECIPES

Chilled Avocado Soup with Seared Chipotle Shrimp
(page 137)

Four-Herb Green Goddess Dressing
(page 138)

Minted Lemon-Lime Watermelon Agua Fresca
(page 138)

Blueberry Thrill
(page 138)

Quick & Easy • Make Ahead

Chilled Avocado Soup with Seared Chipotle Shrimp

Hands-on time: 19 min. Total time: 30 min.

A delicious combination of tastes and textures, this first-course soup combines smoky chile heat, crisp sweet corn, and silky-rich avocado.

Soup:
3 cups fat-free, lower-sodium chicken broth
1½ cups diced peeled avocado (about 2)
2 tablespoons chopped fresh cilantro
2 tablespoons fresh lime juice
¼ teaspoon kosher salt
¼ teaspoon freshly ground black pepper
Lime cream:
¾ cup reduced-fat sour cream
1 tablespoon chopped fresh cilantro
1 teaspoon grated lime rind
½ teaspoon freshly ground black pepper
Shrimp:
¾ pound medium shrimp, peeled and deveined
½ teaspoon ground cumin
½ teaspoon freshly ground black pepper
¼ teaspoon kosher salt
1 (7-ounce) can chipotle chiles in adobo sauce
Cooking spray
1 cup fresh corn kernels (about 2 ears)
¼ cup finely chopped red onion
1 garlic clove, minced
1 tablespoon fresh lime juice

1. To prepare soup, place chicken broth and next 5 ingredients in a blender or food processor, and process until smooth. Cover and chill.

2. To prepare lime cream, combine sour cream and next 3 ingredients in a bowl; stir well. Cover and chill.

3. To prepare shrimp, sprinkle shrimp with cumin, ½ teaspoon black pepper, and ¼ teaspoon salt; set aside. Remove 1 chipotle chile and 1 tablespoon adobo sauce from can, and finely chop chile. Reserve remaining chiles and adobo sauce for another use.

4. Heat a large nonstick skillet over medium-high heat. Coat pan with cooking spray. Add shrimp, and cook 2 minutes. Turn shrimp over. Add corn, onion, and garlic; sauté 2 minutes. Add chopped chipotle chile, 1 table-spoon adobo sauce, and 1 tablespoon lime juice; sauté 2 minutes or until shrimp are done and vegetables are crisp-tender.

5. To serve, ladle about ½ cup soup into each of 8 bowls. Top with 1½ tablespoons lime cream, one-eighth of shrimp, and about 2 tablespoons corn mixture. Yield: 8 servings.

CALORIES 184; FAT 10.5g (sat 2.9g, mono 5.3g, poly 1.3g); PROTEIN 12g; CARB 13g; FIBER 4.6g; CHOL 63mg; IRON 1.7mg; SODIUM 286mg; CALC 28mg

COOLING AVOCADO AND SOUR CREAM TEMPER THE HEAT OF CHIPOTLE CHILES IN THIS STARTER SOUP.

NOTHING MAKES A SUMMER EVENING MORE ENJOYABLE THAN THE COMPANY AND CONVERSATION OF GOOD FRIENDS...AND A COLD DRINK OVER WHICH TO LINGER.

Quick & Easy • Make Ahead

Four-Herb Green Goddess Dressing

Hands-on time: 17 min. Total time: 17 min.

Drape over greens, or serve as a dip for your favorite summery crudités.

1 cup plain fat-free Greek yogurt
½ cup reduced-fat mayonnaise
2 teaspoons Worcestershire sauce
2 teaspoons fresh lemon juice
½ teaspoon hot pepper sauce
3 canned anchovy fillets
1 garlic clove, minced
⅔ cup fresh parsley leaves
¼ cup fresh tarragon leaves
¼ cup chopped fresh chives
¼ cup fresh chervil leaves (optional)

1. Place first 7 ingredients in a blender or food processor; process until smooth. Add parsley, tarragon, chives, and, if desired, chervil; process until herbs are minced. Yield: 1½ cups (serving size: about 2½ tablespoons).

CALORIES 36; **FAT** 1.8g (sat 0g, mono 0.1g, poly 0.8g); **PROTEIN** 2.6g; **CARB** 3.6g; **FIBER** 0.1g; **CHOL** 1mg; **IRON** 0.4mg; **SODIUM** 171mg; **CALC** 30mg

Quick & Easy • Kid Friendly

Minted Lemon-Lime Watermelon Agua Fresca

Hands-on time: 20 min. Total time: 40 min.

This beverage is one the whole family can enjoy.

1¼ cups water
½ cup sugar
⅓ cup coarsely chopped fresh mint
1 tablespoon grated lime rind
1 tablespoon grated lemon rind
12 cups cubed seeded watermelon
¼ cup fresh lime juice
3 tablespoons fresh lemon juice

1. Combine 1¼ cups water and sugar in a small saucepan; bring to a boil over medium-high heat. Cook 30 seconds or until sugar dissolves, stirring frequently.
2. Remove from heat; stir in mint, lime rind, and lemon rind. Let stand 20 minutes. Strain mixture through a sieve over a bowl; discard solids.
3. Place one-third each of sugar syrup and watermelon in a blender; process until smooth. Pour puree into a large pitcher. Repeat procedure twice with remaining sugar syrup and watermelon. Stir in lime juice and lemon juice. Serve over ice, or refrigerate until ready to serve. Stir before serving. Yield: 9 servings (serving size: 1 cup).

CALORIES 108; **FAT** 0.3g (sat 0g, mono 0.1g, poly 0.1g); **PROTEIN** 1.3g; **CARB** 27.7g; **FIBER** 1g; **CHOL** 0mg; **IRON** 0.6mg; **SODIUM** 3mg; **CALC** 19mg

Blueberry Thrill
(pictured on page 223)

Hands-on time: 11 min. Total time: 1 hr. 11 min.

Sweet blueberries infuse spicy gin for summer's most refreshing sipper. For a fizzy cocktail, pour gin, cardamom syrup, and lemon juice over crushed ice in a glass; top with chilled club soda.

2 cups blueberries
1½ cups dry gin
¾ cup water
½ cup sugar
3 cardamom pods
Crushed ice
½ cup fresh lemon juice
Additional blueberries (optional)

1. Place 2 cups blueberries in a large, heavy stainless-steel saucepan; mash with a fork or potato masher. Place over medium-high heat, and cook 3 minutes or until berries begin to release juice. Remove from heat; add gin. Cover and let stand at least 1 hour or overnight. Strain mixture through a sieve into a bowl, pressing berries with the back of a spoon to remove as much juice as possible; discard solids.
2. Combine ¾ cup water, sugar, and cardamom pods in a small saucepan; bring to a boil. Cook 2 minutes or until sugar dissolves. Cool completely; discard cardamom pods.
3. To serve, add crushed ice to a cocktail shaker to come halfway up sides of container. Add ¼ cup blueberry-gin, 1½ tablespoons cardamom syrup, and 1 tablespoon lemon juice; shake until chilled. Strain cocktail into a chilled martini glass. Garnish with additional blueberries, if desired. Serve immediately. Repeat procedure with remaining ingredients. Yield: 8 servings.

CALORIES 159; **FAT** 0g; **PROTEIN** 0.1g; **CARB** 14.5g; **FIBER** 0.2g; **CHOL** 0mg; **IRON** 0mg; **SODIUM** 1mg; **CALC** 1mg

HOT & COLD MAINS

RECIPES

Grill-Braised Clams and Chorizo in Tomato-Saffron Broth
(page 139)

Grilled Char with Yukon Golds and Tomato—Red Onion Relish
(page 140)

Burgers with Blue Cheese Mayo and Sherry Vidalia Onions
(page 140)

Tequila-Glazed Grilled Chicken Thighs
(page 141)

Orecchiette with Peas, Shrimp, and Buttermilk-Herb Dressing
(page 140)

Grilled Pizza with Prosciutto, Arugula, and Lemon
(page 142)

Yakitori
(page 142)

Curry Chicken Wraps with Nectarine Chutney
(page 142)

Grill-Braised Clams and Chorizo in Tomato-Saffron Broth

Hands-on time: 25 min. Total time: 50 min.

3 cups hickory wood chips, divided
1½ cups fat-free, lower-sodium chicken broth
1 tablespoon chopped fresh thyme
½ teaspoon saffron threads
¼ teaspoon crushed red pepper
¼ teaspoon freshly ground black pepper
7 garlic cloves, thinly sliced
1 (14.5-ounce) can diced tomatoes, undrained
1 poblano chile
1 ear shucked corn
Cooking spray
4 green onions
1 (6-ounce) link dry-cured Spanish chorizo, cut in half lengthwise
24 littleneck clams (about 2½ pounds)
2 tablespoons chopped fresh flat-leaf parsley
1 tablespoon fresh lemon juice
4 (¾-inch-thick) slices Italian or French bread

1. Preheat grill to medium-high heat.
2. Pierce the bottom of a disposable foil pan several times with the tip of a knife. Line pan with newspaper or paper towels; place 2 cups wood chips on top of paper in pan.
3. Combine broth and next 6 ingredients in a medium-sized ovenproof saucepan. Place disposable pan on 1 side of grill rack; ignite newspaper with a long match. Place saucepan on other side of grill rack. Cover grill. Bring sauce to a simmer, and grill 15 minutes. Remove saucepan from grill, and keep warm.
4. Place poblano and corn on grill rack coated with cooking spray. Cover and grill 10 minutes, turning occasionally. Add green onions and chorizo, cut sides down, to grill rack; cover and grill 4 minutes or until poblano is blackened and charred and corn is lightly charred, turning occasionally. Place poblano in a paper bag; fold to close tightly. Let stand 5 minutes. Peel and discard skins; cut poblano in half lengthwise. Discard stem, seeds, and membranes. Chop poblano, cut kernels from corn cob, slice green onions, and dice chorizo; add to broth mixture.
5. Add remaining 1 cup wood chips to disposable pan. Return saucepan to grill rack. Cover grill, and simmer. Place clams on grill rack. Cover and grill 2 minutes or until clams just begin to open. Discard unopened shells. Add clams to broth mixture; cover and grill 4 minutes or until shells open completely. Remove saucepan from grill; stir in parsley and juice. Cover and keep warm.
6. Place bread on grill rack, and grill 1 to 2 minutes on each side or until toasted. Ladle clam mixture into bowls. Serve with grilled bread. Yield: 4 servings (serving size: about 6 clams, about 1 cup broth, and 1 bread slice).

CALORIES 319; **FAT** 12.7g (sat 4.3g, mono 5.6g, poly 2.2g); **PROTEIN** 25.5g; **CARB** 27.6g; **FIBER** 2g; **CHOL** 28mg; **IRON** 13.5mg; **SODIUM** 500mg; **CALC** 142mg

SPANISH FLAVORS INSPIRE THIS SIMPLE BUT INTENSE SUMMERY BRAISE. SAFFRON GIVES THE TOMATO BROTH A NUTTY COMPLEXITY, WHILE THE SPICE AND HEAT OF CHORIZO LIVEN UP THE CLAMS.

Grilled Char with Yukon Golds and Tomato–Red Onion Relish

Hands-on time: 20 min. Total time: 1 hr. 30 min.

Soaking the onions in cool water removes some of their harsh bite.

1 small red onion, vertically sliced
4 (6-ounce) center-cut Arctic char or salmon fillets
1 pound small Yukon gold or red potatoes
1 tablespoon chopped fresh thyme
2 tablespoons extra-virgin olive oil, divided
1 teaspoon kosher salt, divided
½ teaspoon freshly ground black pepper, divided
1 pint heirloom cherry or grape tomatoes, quartered
2 tablespoons finely chopped fresh mint
1 tablespoon capers, chopped
2 teaspoons sherry vinegar
2 teaspoons Dijon mustard
Cooking spray

1. Place onion in a small bowl; add water to cover. Let stand for 30 minutes. Drain. Set aside.
2. Arrange fish in a single layer on a large plate lined with paper towels. Let stand, uncovered, in refrigerator 1 hour (to allow surface to dry).
3. Preheat grill to medium-high heat.
4. Place potatoes in a large saucepan. Cover with water to 2 inches above potatoes; bring to a boil. Reduce heat; simmer 15 minutes or until tender. Drain; cool slightly. Cut potatoes in half. Combine potatoes, thyme, 1 tablespoon olive oil, ½ teaspoon salt, and ⅛ teaspoon pepper in a bowl, tossing to coat. Thread potatoes onto 4 (6-inch) skewers with cut sides facing out.
5. Combine onion, remaining 1 tablespoon oil, ⅛ teaspoon salt, ⅛ teaspoon pepper, tomatoes, mint, capers, vinegar, and mustard in a bowl; toss gently. Set aside.
6. Sprinkle remaining ⅜ teaspoon salt and remaining ¼ teaspoon pepper evenly over fish. Place fish and potatoes, cut sides down, on grill rack coated with cooking spray. Cover and grill potatoes 6 minutes without turning. Grill fish 3 to 4 minutes on each side or until desired degree of doneness. Serve fish with potatoes; top with tomato-onion relish. Yield: 4 servings (serving size: 1 fillet, about 5 potato halves, and ½ cup relish).

Sustainable Choice | *Arctic char is a sound choice; you can use wild Alaskan salmon in its place.*

CALORIES 357; **FAT** 13.4g (sat 2.8g, mono 6.5g, poly 2.3g); **PROTEIN** 32.1g; **CARB** 25.6g; **FIBER** 2.8g; **CHOL** 141mg; **IRON** 1.9mg; **SODIUM** 704mg; **CALC** 47mg

---

SWEET HEIRLOOM TOMATOES ARE THE CROWNING GLORY ON THIS GRILLED MEAL.

Kid Friendly

Burgers with Blue Cheese Mayo and Sherry Vidalia Onions
(pictured on page 224)

Hands-on time: 45 min. Total time: 45 min.

½ cup (2 ounces) crumbled blue cheese
¼ cup canola mayonnaise
2 teaspoons chopped fresh thyme, divided
¼ teaspoon hot pepper sauce
1 pound lean ground sirloin
1 teaspoon black pepper, divided
⅛ teaspoon kosher salt
½ teaspoon extra-virgin olive oil
4 (¼-inch-thick) slices Vidalia or other sweet onion
Cooking spray
2 teaspoons sherry vinegar
4 (1½-ounce) whole-wheat hamburger buns, toasted
2 cups loosely packed arugula

1. Preheat grill to medium-high heat.
2. Combine ½ cup blue cheese, mayonnaise, 1 teaspoon thyme, and hot pepper sauce in a small bowl; stir well.
3. Divide beef into 4 equal portions, shaping each portion into a ½-inch-thick patty. Sprinkle beef evenly with ½ teaspoon black pepper and salt.
4. Brush oil evenly over both sides of onion slices; sprinkle with remaining ½ teaspoon pepper. Place patties and onions on grill rack coated with cooking spray; cover and grill 3 minutes on each side. Set patties aside; keep warm. Place onion slices in a zip-top plastic bag; seal. Let stand 5 minutes; toss with remaining 1 teaspoon thyme and vinegar.
5. Spread cut sides of buns evenly with mayonnaise mixture. Arrange ½ cup arugula on bottom half of each bun; top with 1 patty, 1 onion slice, and bun top. Yield: 4 servings (serving size: 1 burger).

CALORIES 420; **FAT** 21.8g (sat 5.1g, mono 10.6g, poly 5.2g); **PROTEIN** 31.5g; **CARB** 26.7g; **FIBER** 4.2g; **CHOL** 76mg; **IRON** 3.2mg; **SODIUM** 623mg; **CALC** 149mg

---

LEAN SIRLOIN HAS ABOUT THE SAME SAT FAT AS GROUND TURKEY. WITH BLUE CHEESE MAYO AND TANGY-SWEET ONIONS, IT MAKES A MIGHTY JUICY BURGER.

Tequila-Glazed Grilled Chicken Thighs

Hands-on time: 40 min. Total time: 1 hr.

Rich chicken thighs hold their own against a sweet-spicy-savory glaze. If you would rather not use tequila, you can substitute 1/3 cup pineapple juice. Start the grilling over direct heat to get good grill marks and charred bits, and then move to indirect heat to gently finish the cooking.

1 1/2 teaspoons ground cumin
1 teaspoon chili powder
3/4 teaspoon kosher salt
1/4 teaspoon chipotle chile powder
6 bone-in chicken thighs (about 2 pounds), skinned
3/4 cup pineapple juice
1/3 cup tequila
1/4 cup honey
2 teaspoons cornstarch
2 teaspoons water
2 teaspoons grated lime rind
3 tablespoons fresh lime juice
1/4 teaspoon crushed red pepper
Cooking spray

1. Preheat grill to medium-high heat using both burners. After preheating, turn the left burner off (leave the right burner on).
2. Combine first 4 ingredients in a small bowl; rub evenly over chicken.
3. Bring pineapple juice, tequila, and honey to a boil in a small saucepan; cook until reduced to 3/4 cup (about 10 minutes). Combine cornstarch and 2 teaspoons water in a small bowl, and stir well. Add cornstarch mixture to juice mixture, stirring constantly with a whisk. Bring to a boil, and cook 1 minute, stirring constantly. Remove from heat, and stir in lime rind, 3 tablespoons lime juice, and red pepper.
4. Place chicken on grill rack coated with cooking spray over right burner (direct heat). Cover and grill 5 minutes on each side, basting occasionally with juice mixture. Move chicken to grill rack over left burner (indirect heat).

Cover and grill an additional 5 minutes on each side or until done, basting occasionally. Yield: 6 servings (serving size: 1 thigh).

CALORIES 241; FAT 7.6g (sat 2.1g, mono 2.8g, poly 1.7g); PROTEIN 18g; CARB 17.2g; FIBER 0.4g; CHOL 64mg; IRON 1.2mg; SODIUM 374mg; CALC 19mg

STICKY-DELICIOUS AND JUST PLAIN IRRESISTIBLE, THIS CHICKEN WILL BE THE STANDOUT HIT OF YOUR NEXT BARBECUE.

Quick & Easy • Kid Friendly

Orecchiette with Peas, Shrimp, and Buttermilk-Herb Dressing

Hands-on time: 30 min. Total time: 30 min.

Medium shell-shaped pasta will also work in place of orecchiette.

8 ounces uncooked orecchiette pasta
1 cup shelled green peas (about 1 pound unshelled green peas) or frozen green peas
1/2 pound medium shrimp, peeled and deveined
1 cup thinly sliced radishes
1/3 cup reduced-fat mayonnaise
1/4 cup nonfat buttermilk
3 tablespoon minced fresh chives
1 tablespoon chopped fresh dill
1/2 teaspoon salt
1/2 teaspoon grated lemon rind
1 tablespoon fresh lemon juice
1/4 teaspoon freshly ground black pepper
1/8 teaspoon ground red pepper
2 garlic cloves, minced

1. Cook pasta according to package directions, omitting salt and fat. Add peas and shrimp during last 2 minutes of cooking. Drain and rinse with cold water; drain.
2. Combine pasta mixture and radishes in a large bowl. Combine mayonnaise and next 9 ingredients in a small bowl; stir well with a whisk. Pour over pasta mixture, tossing to coat. Cover and let stand 20 minutes. Serve at room temperature, or cover and chill until ready to serve. Yield: 4 servings (serving size: 1 1/2 cups).

CALORIES 340; FAT 3.4g (sat 0.4g, mono 0.3g, poly 1.5g); PROTEIN 22.2g; CARB 54.7g; FIBER 4.7g; CHOL 86mg; IRON 4.1mg; SODIUM 585mg; CALC 84mg

WINE NOTE: Sweet shrimp, peppery summer radishes, and the refreshing dill and buttermilk dressing all point to a wine with tangy acidity, fresh berry fruit, and a zip of citrus. The Fleur, Pinot Noir, Rosé (2009, Carneros, Calif.; $15)—with its shocking bright-red hue—is a hands-down crowd-pleaser and an excellent value.

THIS HERBY PASTA SALAD IS PERFECT FOR A PICNIC OR POTLUCK GATHERING; DOUBLE THE RECIPE TO SERVE A CROWD.

Grilled Pizza with Prosciutto, Arugula, and Lemon

Hands-on time: 35 min. Total time: 25 hr. 35 min.

10 ounces bread flour (about 2 cups plus 2 tablespoons)
1 cup warm water (100° to 110°), divided
1 teaspoon chopped fresh thyme
1 teaspoon chopped fresh oregano
1 garlic clove, crushed
1 package dry yeast (about 2¼ teaspoons)
⅛ teaspoon kosher salt
Cooking spray
2 teaspoons cornmeal
1¼ cups (5 ounces) shredded fontina cheese
4 ounces thinly sliced prosciutto
1 teaspoon cracked black pepper
1 tablespoon extra-virgin olive oil
1 teaspoon lemon juice
3 cups packed baby arugula
4 lemon wedges

1. Weigh or lightly spoon flour into dry measuring cups and spoons; level with a knife. Combine flour, ¾ cup warm water, thyme, oregano, and garlic in bowl of a stand mixer with dough hook attached; mix until combined. Cover and let stand 20 minutes.
2. Dissolve yeast in remaining ¼ cup warm water in a small bowl; let stand 5 minutes or until bubbly. Add yeast mixture and salt to flour mixture; beat at low speed 5 minutes or until a soft dough forms. Place dough in a large bowl coated with cooking spray; cover dough with plastic wrap coated with cooking spray. Refrigerate 24 hours.
3. Remove dough from refrigerator. Let stand, covered, 1 hour or until dough reaches room temperature. Punch dough down. Divide dough into 4 equal portions. Press each portion into a 7-inch circle on a baking sheet sprinkled with cornmeal. Cover loosely with plastic wrap.
4. Preheat grill to medium-high heat.
5. Place pizza dough rounds, cornmeal side up, on grill rack coated with cooking spray, and grill 3 minutes or until blistered. Turn dough over; grill 3 minutes. Remove from grill.

6. Sprinkle about 5 tablespoons fontina cheese over each pizza. Top evenly with prosciutto and pepper. Combine oil and lemon juice in a bowl; add arugula, and toss gently. Divide arugula mixture evenly among pizzas. Serve immediately with lemon wedges. Yield: 4 servings (serving size: 1 pizza).

CALORIES 497; FAT 18.6g (sat 8.4g, mono 7g, poly 2.1g); PROTEIN 25.7g; CARB 56.3g; FIBER 2.8g; CHOL 58mg; IRON 4.4mg; SODIUM 778mg; CALC 261mg

Yakitori

Hands-on time: 25 min. Total time: 1 hr. 30 min.

1 cup sake
¼ cup sugar
3½ tablespoons lower-sodium soy sauce
1 (1-inch) piece peeled fresh ginger, sliced
½ teaspoon crushed red pepper
4 (6-ounce) skinless, boneless chicken breast halves, cut into 36 (¾-inch) cubes
5 garlic cloves, crushed
5 cilantro sprigs
3 tablespoons rice vinegar
1 tablespoon dark sesame oil
9 green onions (white and light green parts only), cut into 36 (2-inch) pieces
Cooking spray

1. Combine first 4 ingredients in a small saucepan; bring to a boil. Remove from heat; let stand 15 minutes. Remove ginger with a slotted spoon, and place in a medium bowl. Add 2 tablespoons soy sauce mixture, pepper, chicken, garlic, and cilantro to ginger in bowl; toss well. Cover and chill 1 hour, stirring occasionally.
2. Preheat grill to medium-high heat.
3. Bring remaining soy sauce mixture to a boil; cook 10 minutes or until reduced to ¼ cup. Remove from heat; slowly add vinegar and oil, stirring with a whisk. Divide soy sauce mixture into 2 equal portions (about ¼ cup each); set aside.
4. Remove chicken from marinade; discard marinade. Thread 3 chicken pieces and 3 green onion pieces alternately onto each of 12 (8-inch) skewers. Place skewers on grill rack coated with cooking spray. Cover and grill 8 minutes

or until done, turning after 4 minutes and basting occasionally with ¼ cup reserved soy sauce mixture.
5. Place skewers on a serving platter; serve with remaining ¼ cup soy sauce mixture. Yield: 4 servings (serving size: 3 skewers).

CALORIES 365; FAT 7.6g (sat 1.7g, mono 2.8g, poly 2.3g); PROTEIN 36.2g; CARB 20.6g; FIBER 1.1g; CHOL 94mg; IRON 2mg; SODIUM 556mg; CALC 51mg

Curry Chicken Wraps with Nectarine Chutney

Hands-on time: 30 min. Total time: 2 hr. 20 min.

Indian spices pair well with tangy nectarines. You can also use peaches.

1 cup plain fat-free yogurt
3 tablespoons curry powder
3 tablespoons lime juice, divided
4 (6-ounce) skinless, boneless chicken breast halves
10 cilantro sprigs
6 garlic cloves, crushed
2 cups chopped nectarines
¾ cup finely sliced green onions
⅓ cup mango chutney
2 tablespoons chopped fresh cilantro
2 tablespoons chopped fresh mint
1 tablespoon grated peeled fresh ginger
¼ teaspoon ground red pepper
½ teaspoon salt
Cooking spray
6 (1.9-ounce) light whole-wheat flatbreads
24 (⅛-inch-thick) slices cucumber
1½ cups loosely packed baby arugula
1 cup vertically sliced red onion

1. Combine yogurt, curry powder, and 1 tablespoon lime juice in a large heavy-duty zip-top plastic bag; squeeze bag to mix. Cut 3 shallow slits in each chicken breast half. Add chicken, cilantro sprigs, and garlic to bag, squeezing to coat chicken. Seal and marinate in refrigerator 2 hours, turning occasionally.
2. Combine remaining 2 tablespoons lime juice, nectarines, and next 6 ingredients in a bowl; toss gently. Cover and set aside.

3. Preheat grill to medium-high heat.
4. Remove chicken from bag; discard marinade. Sprinkle chicken with salt; place chicken on grill rack coated with cooking spray. Cover and grill 4 minutes on each side or until chicken is done. Let stand 5 minutes. Cut chicken across grain into thin slices.
5. Place ⅓ cup nectarine chutney in center of each flatbread. Divide chicken evenly among flatbreads. Top each with 4 cucumber slices, ¼ cup arugula, and about 2½ tablespoons red onion; roll up. Cut each wrap in half diagonally. Yield: 6 servings (serving size: 1 wrap).

CALORIES 283; FAT 3.9g (sat 0.3g, mono 0.4g, poly 0.4g); PROTEIN 30.8g; CARB 38.4g; FIBER 11g; CHOL 49mg; IRON 2.8mg; SODIUM 732mg; CALC 89mg

SALADS & SIDES

RECIPES

Fig, Tomato, and Sweet Onion Salad
(page 143)

Summer Tomato, Feta, and Basil Galette
(page 143)

Shaved Summer Squash Salad with Prosciutto Crisps
(page 144)

Smoky Baked Beans with Chorizo
(page 144)

Curried Potato Salad
(page 144)

Grilled Corn on the Cob with Roasted Jalapeño Butter
(page 145)

Golden Beet Salad with Wheat Berries and Pumpkinseed Vinaigrette
(page 145)

Stuffed Zucchini with Cheesy Breadcrumbs
(page 145)

Quick & Easy • Vegetarian
Fig, Tomato, and Sweet Onion Salad

Hands-on time: 20 min. Total time: 20 min.

For this recipe, use any fig variety you like or a combination of varieties.

2 tablespoons red wine vinegar
2 teaspoons extra-virgin olive oil
¼ teaspoon freshly ground black pepper
2 cups quartered fresh figs (about ½ pound)
2 cups torn romaine lettuce
1 cup cherry tomatoes, halved
¾ cup vertically sliced Vidalia or other sweet onion
3 tablespoons chopped fresh mint
¼ cup (1 ounce) crumbled feta cheese

1. Combine first 3 ingredients in a large bowl; stir well with a whisk. Add figs, lettuce, tomatoes, onion, and mint; toss gently to coat. Sprinkle with cheese. Yield: 4 servings (serving size: 1½ cups).

CALORIES 128; FAT 4.8g (sat 1.8g, mono 2.2g, poly 0.6g); PROTEIN 3.4g; CARB 20.1g; FIBER 4.2g; CHOL 8mg; IRON 1.5mg; SODIUM 114mg; CALC 105mg

Kid Friendly • Vegetarian
Summer Tomato, Feta, and Basil Galette

Hands-on time: 20 min. Total time: 2 hr.

Pair this summery side with grilled flank steak, chicken, or salmon.

3.4 ounces all-purpose flour (about ¾ cup)
¼ cup yellow cornmeal
3½ tablespoons chilled unsalted butter, cut into small pieces
¾ teaspoon salt, divided
3 tablespoons ice water
1 pint jewel box tomatoes or multicolored pear tomatoes, halved lengthwise
¼ teaspoon freshly ground black pepper
½ cup (2 ounces) crumbled reduced-fat feta cheese
¼ cup small basil leaves

1. Weigh or lightly spoon flour into dry measuring cups, and level with a knife. Combine flour, cornmeal, butter, and ½ teaspoon salt in a food processor; process until mixture resembles coarse meal. With processor on, slowly add 3 tablespoons ice water through food chute, and process just until combined (do not form a ball). Gently press mixture into a 4-inch circle on heavy-duty plastic wrap. Cover and chill 30 minutes.
2. Preheat oven to 425°.
3. Unwrap dough, and roll dough into a 13-inch circle on a lightly floured surface. Place dough on a baking sheet lined with parchment paper. Arrange tomatoes, cut sides up, on top of dough, leaving a 1½-inch border. Sprinkle with remaining ¼ teaspoon salt and pepper. Fold edges of dough over tomatoes to partially cover. Bake at 425° for 25 minutes or until golden brown. Sprinkle evenly with cheese. Bake an additional 5 minutes. Cool 5 minutes, and sprinkle with basil. Cut into 8 wedges. Yield: 8 servings (serving size: 1 wedge).

CALORIES 127; FAT 6.2g (sat 3.8g, mono 1.3g, poly 0.3g); PROTEIN 3.5g; CARB 14.7g; FIBER 1.1g; CHOL 15mg; IRON 1mg; SODIUM 322mg; CALC 26mg

TANGY FETA, FRESH TOMATOES, FRAGRANT BASIL: A PERFECT TART

A VEGETABLE PEELER TURNS SQUASH INTO DELICATE RIBBONS—A FOIL FOR THE SALTY HAM.

Quick & Easy • Kid Friendly

Shaved Summer Squash Salad with Prosciutto Crisps

Hands-on time: 20 min. Total time: 20 min.

Summer squash is delicious raw when it's shaved and marinated with a bit of salt.

1 medium zucchini
2 medium yellow squash
¼ teaspoon salt
2 tablespoons thinly sliced fresh mint
1 tablespoon extra-virgin olive oil
½ teaspoon grated lemon rind
1 teaspoon fresh lemon juice
¼ teaspoon freshly ground black pepper
3 thin slices prosciutto (1 ounce), chopped
¼ cup (1 ounce) crumbled ricotta salata or feta cheese

1. Shave zucchini and squash into thin strips using a vegetable peeler. Discard seeds. Place zucchini and squash in a medium bowl, and toss with salt.
2. Combine mint and next 4 ingredients in a small bowl; stir with a whisk. Pour over zucchini and squash; toss.
3. Heat a small nonstick skillet over medium heat. Add prosciutto; sauté 2 minutes or until crisp.
4. Place ¾ cup salad on each of 4 plates. Top each serving with 1 tablespoon cheese; sprinkle evenly with prosciutto. Yield: 4 servings.

CALORIES 68; FAT 4.9g (sat 1.1g, mono 3g, poly 0.7g); PROTEIN 3.5g; CARB 3.6g; FIBER 1.1g; CHOL 6mg; IRON 0.5mg; SODIUM 269mg; CALC 36mg

Make Ahead • Kid Friendly

Smoky Baked Beans with Chorizo

Hands-on time: 20 min. Total time: 10 hr. 30 min.

Be sure to use firm, dry-cured Spanish chorizo and not soft, raw Mexican chorizo for this recipe.

1 pound dried Great Northern beans (2½ cups)
1 cup diced dry-cured Spanish chorizo
4 cups chopped onion
8 garlic cloves, thinly sliced
4 cups water
2 tablespoons chopped fresh oregano
2 tablespoons chopped fresh thyme
1½ teaspoons salt
1 teaspoon ground cumin
½ teaspoon smoked paprika
½ teaspoon paprika
2 bay leaves
2 tablespoons brown sugar
3 tablespoons no-salt-added tomato paste
3 tablespoons molasses
¼ teaspoon crushed red pepper
2½ tablespoons red wine vinegar
¼ teaspoon black pepper
⅛ teaspoon ground red pepper
½ cup chopped green onions
2 tablespoons chopped fresh flat-leaf parsley

1. Sort and wash beans; place in a Dutch oven. Cover with water to 2 inches above beans. Cover; let stand 8 hours. Drain.
2. Heat a large Dutch oven over medium heat. Add chorizo; cook 4 minutes or until fat begins to render. Add onion and garlic; sauté 10 minutes or until tender. Add beans, water, and next 7 ingredients; bring to a boil. Cover, reduce heat, and simmer 45 minutes or until beans are just tender.
3. Preheat oven to 350°.
4. Stir brown sugar and next 3 ingredients into bean mixture; bring to a simmer. Cover; bake at 350° for 1½ hours or until beans are very tender and sauce is thick. Remove from oven; stir in vinegar, black pepper, and ground red pepper. Discard bay leaves; sprinkle with green onions and parsley. Yield: 12 servings (serving size: ⅔ cup).

CALORIES 184; FAT 2.9g (sat 1g, mono 1.2g, poly 0.5g); PROTEIN 10.6g; CARB 30.3g; FIBER 7.5g; CHOL 0mg; IRON 2.8mg; SODIUM 306mg; CALC 98mg

Make Ahead • Vegetarian

Curried Potato Salad

Hands-on time: 20 min. Total time: 1 hr. 30 min.

Madras curry powder adds an extra degree of heat to this fun take on the classic side.

2 pounds Red Bliss potatoes, peeled and cut into 1-inch pieces
¾ cup plain 2% reduced-fat Greek yogurt
2 teaspoons Madras or regular curry powder
1½ teaspoons hot pepper sauce
¾ teaspoon salt
¾ cup shredded carrot
½ cup thinly sliced green onions, divided
⅓ cup thinly sliced celery
2 tablespoons chopped unsalted cashews

1. Place potatoes in a medium saucepan; cover with cold water. Bring to a boil. Reduce heat, and simmer 10 minutes or until tender. Drain and cool.
2. Combine yogurt and next 3 ingredients, stirring with a whisk.
3. Place cooled potatoes in a large bowl. Add carrot, 5 tablespoons green onions, celery, and yogurt mixture; toss gently to combine. Sprinkle with remaining 3 tablespoons green onions and cashews. Serve chilled. Yield: 8 servings (serving size: about 1 cup).

CALORIES 117; FAT 1.8g (sat 0.6g, mono 0.6g, poly 0.3g); PROTEIN 4.9g; CARB 21.7g; FIBER 2.7g; CHOL 1mg; IRON 1.3mg; SODIUM 275mg; CALC 48mg

CHARRING THE PEPPER EASES THE HEAT, YIELDING A VERSATILE, NOT-TOO-SPICY BUTTER.

Quick & Easy • Vegetarian

Grilled Corn on the Cob with Roasted Jalapeño Butter

Hands-on time: 25 min. Total time: 25 min.

1 jalapeño pepper
Cooking spray
7 teaspoons unsalted butter, softened
1 teaspoon grated lime rind
2 teaspoons honey
¼ teaspoon salt
6 ears shucked corn

1. Preheat grill to medium-high heat.
2. Place jalapeño on grill rack coated with cooking spray; cover and grill 10 minutes or until blackened and charred, turning occasionally.
3. Place jalapeño in a small paper bag, and fold tightly to seal. Let stand 5 minutes. Peel and discard skins; cut jalapeño in half lengthwise. Discard stem, seeds, and membranes. Finely chop jalapeño. Combine jalapeño, butter, lime rind, honey, and salt in a small bowl; stir well.
4. Place corn on grill rack. Cover and grill 10 minutes or until lightly charred, turning occasionally. Place corn on serving plate; brush with jalapeño butter. Yield: 6 servings (serving size: 1 ear corn).

CALORIES 124; **FAT** 5.5g (sat 3g, mono 1.5g, poly 0.7g); **PROTEIN** 3g; **CARB** 19.2g; **FIBER** 2.5g; **CHOL** 12mg; **IRON** 0.5mg; **SODIUM** 113mg; **CALC** 4mg

Make Ahead • Vegetarian

Golden Beet Salad with Wheat Berries and Pumpkinseed Vinaigrette

Hands-on time: 20 min. Total time: 1 hr. 40 min.

4 medium golden beets
3 tablespoons extra-virgin olive oil, divided
1 cup uncooked wheat berries
2 cups water
½ cup unsalted pumpkinseed kernels, toasted and divided
1 tablespoon honey
1 tablespoon Dijon mustard
1 tablespoon sherry vinegar
¼ teaspoon kosher salt
¼ teaspoon black pepper
⅓ cup diced celery
¼ cup thinly sliced shallots
2 tablespoons chopped fresh chives
¼ cup celery leaves

1. Preheat oven to 400°.
2. Leave root and 1 inch of stem on beets; scrub with a brush. Place beets in center of a 16 x 12–inch sheet of foil; drizzle with 1 tablespoon oil. Fold foil over beets; tightly seal edges. Bake at 400° for 1 hour and 20 minutes or until tender. Unwrap beets; cool. Trim off beet roots; rub off skins. Cut beets into wedges.
3. While beets cook, combine wheat berries and 2 cups water in a medium saucepan; bring to a boil. Cover, reduce heat, and simmer 1 hour or until tender, stirring occasionally. Drain; cool slightly.
4. Place ¼ cup pumpkinseed kernels in a large bowl, and coarsely crush with the back of a spoon. Add honey and next 4 ingredients; stir well with a whisk. Gradually add remaining 2 tablespoons olive oil, stirring constantly with a whisk. Add beets, wheat berries, celery, shallots, and chives; toss gently. Sprinkle with remaining ¼ cup pumpkinseed kernels and celery leaves. Yield: 8 servings (serving size: about ⅔ cup).

CALORIES 203; **FAT** 9g (sat 1.5g, mono 3.8g, poly 1g); **PROTEIN** 6.2g; **CARB** 27.2g; **FIBER** 5g; **CHOL** 0mg; **IRON** 0.9mg; **SODIUM** 174mg; **CALC** 16mg

Kid Friendly • Vegetarian

Stuffed Zucchini with Cheesy Breadcrumbs

Hands-on time: 30 min. Total time: 1 hr. 30 min.

3 (1.3-ounce) slices day-old whole-wheat bread
3 medium zucchini
½ teaspoon freshly ground black pepper, divided
⅜ teaspoon salt, divided
2 tablespoons extra-virgin olive oil
1 tablespoon unsalted butter
1 cup finely chopped onion
⅓ cup canned artichoke hearts, drained and chopped
1 tablespoon chopped fresh thyme
3 garlic cloves, minced
3 tablespoons dry white wine
5 tablespoons grated Parmesan cheese
¼ cup chopped fresh flat-leaf parsley
3 tablespoons pine nuts, toasted
2 tablespoons chopped fresh basil
2 teaspoons finely grated lemon rind

1. Preheat oven to 350°.
2. Place bread in a food processor; pulse until fine crumbs form. Set aside.
3. Cut zucchini in half lengthwise; scoop out pulp, leaving a ¼-inch-thick shell. Chop pulp. Place zucchini halves, cut sides up, on a baking sheet lined with parchment paper; sprinkle with ¼ teaspoon pepper and ⅛ teaspoon salt.
4. Heat oil and butter in a large skillet over medium heat. Add zucchini pulp and onion; sauté 5 minutes. Add remaining ¼ teaspoon pepper, remaining ¼ teaspoon salt, artichoke hearts, thyme, and garlic; cook 45 seconds. Add wine; cook 1 minute or until most of liquid evaporates. Combine breadcrumbs and onion mixture in a large bowl; stir in cheese and next 4 ingredients. Spoon ½ cup breadcrumb mixture into each zucchini shell. Bake at 350° for 45 minutes or just until tender. Yield: 6 servings (serving size: 1 zucchini half).

CALORIES 177; **FAT** 12g (sat 2.8g, mono 5g, poly 2.3g); **PROTEIN** 6.9g; **CARB** 13.6g; **FIBER** 3.8g; **CHOL** 9mg; **IRON** 1.6mg; **SODIUM** 343mg; **CALC** 107mg

SWEETS & TREATS

RECIPES

Rich Chocolate Pudding Pie
(page 146)

Piña Colada Sorbet
(page 146)

Watermelon-Jalapeño Ice Pops
(page 146)

Cherry-Almond Crisp
(page 147)

Margarita Ice-Cream Sandwiches
(page 147)

Make Ahead • Kid Friendly

Rich Chocolate Pudding Pie

Hands-on time: 20 min. Total time: 4 hr. 45 min.

Melted chocolate binds cookie crumbs for the crust—and makes it extra delicious. Substitute 1 teaspoon vanilla extract for the rum.

Crust:
30 chocolate wafers
3 ounces bittersweet chocolate, melted
1 tablespoon canola oil
Filling:
3/4 cup sugar
1/4 cup cornstarch
1/4 cup unsweetened cocoa
1/4 teaspoon salt
1 3/4 cups 1% low-fat milk, divided
2 large egg yolks
4 ounces bittersweet chocolate, finely
  chopped
1 tablespoon white rum
1/2 cup fresh raspberries
10 tablespoons frozen fat-free whipped
  topping, thawed

1. To prepare crust, place wafers in a food processor; process until finely ground. Add 3 ounces melted chocolate and oil; process until blended. Press into bottom and up sides of a 9-inch pie plate. Freeze 15 minutes or until set. **2.** To prepare filling, combine sugar, cornstarch, cocoa, and salt in a large saucepan; stir with a whisk. Add half of milk and 2 yolks; stir with a whisk until smooth. Stir in remaining milk. Cook over medium heat 5 minutes or until thick and bubbly, stirring constantly. Remove from heat. Add 4 ounces chocolate, and stir until smooth. Stir in rum. Pour filling into prepared crust. Cover with plastic wrap; chill 4 hours or until set. Serve with raspberries and whipped topping. Yield: 10 servings (serving size: 1 pie slice, about 1 tablespoon berries, and 1 tablespoon whipped topping).

CALORIES 311; FAT 14.2g (sat 5.9g, mono 5.3g, poly 1.8g); PROTEIN 5.3g; CARB 47g; FIBER 3.2g; CHOL 44mg; IRON 1.7mg; SODIUM 193mg; CALC 76mg

THIS CRUST IS MADE FROM CHOCOLATE WAFERS AND...MORE CHOCOLATE.

Make Ahead • Freezable • Kid Friendly

Piña Colada Sorbet

Hands-on time: 10 min. Total time: 5 hr.

Three kinds of coconut products—coconut water, coconut milk, and cream of coconut—offer the best flavor and texture. Look for coconut water near the fruit juices. For an adult treat, drizzle rum over your serving.

3 cups cubed fresh pineapple
1 cup coconut water
1/2 cup sugar
1 cup light coconut milk
2/3 cup cream of coconut

1. Place first 3 ingredients in a blender, and process until smooth and sugar dissolves. Combine pureed pineapple mixture, coconut milk, and cream of coconut in a bowl; stir with a whisk. Cover and refrigerate until thoroughly chilled. **2.** Pour mixture into freezer can of an ice-cream freezer, and freeze according to manufacturer's instructions. Spoon sorbet into a freezer-safe container; cover and freeze 2 hours or until firm. Yield: 10 servings (serving size: 1/2 cup).

CALORIES 136; FAT 4g (sat 3.3g, mono 0g, poly 0g); PROTEIN 0.7g; CARB 26.4g; FIBER 0.3g; CHOL 0mg; IRON 0.3mg; SODIUM 40mg; CALC 12mg

Make Ahead • Freezable

Watermelon-Jalapeño Ice Pops

Hands-on time: 10 min. Total time: 6 hr. 10 min.

A bit of pectin helps keep all the ingredients incorporated evenly; without it, they tend to separate.

3 cups fresh red or yellow watermelon cubes,
  chilled
1/2 cup sugar
1/4 cup fresh lime juice
1 tablespoon light-colored corn syrup
1 tablespoon liquid pectin
1 large jalapeño pepper, halved and seeded
2 teaspoons grated lime rind

1. Combine first 6 ingredients in a blender, and process until pureed. Stir in lime rind. Pour into 8 (3-ounce) ice pop molds. Freeze 6 hours or until firm. Yield: 8 servings (serving size: 1 ice pop).

CALORIES 76; FAT 0.1g (sat 0g, mono 0g, poly 0.1g); PROTEIN 0.4g; CARB 19.7g; FIBER 0.4g; CHOL 0mg; IRON 0.2mg; SODIUM 3mg; CALC 6mg

POPS ARE A GREAT PARTY PLEASER.

A COMBO OF DRIED TART CHERRIES AND FRESH SWEET CHERRIES OFFERS THE BEST BALANCE AND FLAVOR.

Kid Friendly

Cherry-Almond Crisp

Hands-on time: 30 min. Total time: 1 hr. 35 min.

Fresh tart cherries can be hard to find, which is why we add some dried ones to boost the flavor of this crisp. If you have access to fresh tart cherries, use 3 pounds and omit the dried fruit. Serve with vanilla low-fat ice cream, if desired; a small (¼-cup) scoop will add 55 calories and 0.5 grams of saturated fat to each serving.

1 cup dried tart cherries
1 cup boiling water
2 pounds sweet cherries, pitted
²/₃ cup granulated sugar
3 tablespoons all-purpose flour
1 teaspoon vanilla extract
¼ teaspoon ground cinnamon
Cooking spray
3.4 ounces all-purpose flour (about ³/₄ cup)
³/₄ cup old-fashioned rolled oats
½ cup packed brown sugar
¼ cup sliced almonds
½ teaspoon salt
5 tablespoons unsalted butter, melted
¼ teaspoon almond extract

1. Combine dried cherries and 1 cup boiling water in a small bowl; cover and let stand 30 minutes.
2. Preheat oven to 375°.
3. Combine dried cherries with soaking liquid, 2 pounds sweet cherries, and next 4 ingredients in a large bowl; stir well. Let stand 15 minutes.
4. Pour cherry mixture into a 13 x 9–inch glass or ceramic baking dish coated with cooking spray. Bake at 375° for 40 minutes or until thick and bubbly.
5. While cherry mixture bakes, weigh or lightly spoon 3.4 ounces flour into dry measuring cups, and level with a knife. Combine flour, oats, brown sugar, almonds, and salt in a medium bowl, and stir well. Combine butter and almond extract in a small bowl, and drizzle over oat mixture, stirring until moist clumps form.
6. Remove cherry mixture from oven, and sprinkle evenly with streusel topping. Bake an additional 20 minutes or until streusel is golden brown. Let stand 5 minutes; serve warm. Yield: 12 servings (serving size: about ⅔ cup).

CALORIES 277; **FAT** 7g (sat 3.3g, mono 2.2g, poly 0.8g); **PROTEIN** 3.3g; **CARB** 52.2g; **FIBER** 5.5g; **CHOL** 13mg; **IRON** 1.5mg; **SODIUM** 103mg; **CALC** 36mg

Make Ahead • Freezable • Kid Friendly

Margarita Ice-Cream Sandwiches

Hands-on time: 27 min. Total time: 8 hr.

Fresh lime zest and coarse sea salt mimic the flavors of a margarita in this treat that kids and adults will love.

1 cup granulated sugar
½ cup unsalted butter, softened
1 large egg
5 teaspoons grated lime rind, divided
2 tablespoons fresh lime juice
11.25 ounces all-purpose flour (about 2½ cups)
1½ teaspoons baking powder
⅛ teaspoon table salt
1 teaspoon turbinado sugar
½ teaspoon coarse sea salt
2 cups vanilla reduced-fat ice cream, softened
2 cups lime sherbet, softened

1. Place granulated sugar and butter in a large bowl; beat with a mixer at medium speed 5 minutes or until light and fluffy. Add egg, 1 tablespoon lime rind, and lime juice; beat 2 minutes or until well combined.
2. Weigh or lightly spoon flour into dry measuring cups; level with a knife. Combine flour, baking powder, and ⅛ teaspoon table salt; stir with a whisk. Add flour mixture to butter mixture, and beat just until combined.
3. Divide dough into 2 equal portions. Shape each portion into a 6-inch log. Wrap logs individually in plastic wrap; chill 3 hours or until firm.
4. Preheat oven to 350°.
5. Cut each log into 16 (about ⅓-inch-thick) slices, and place 1 inch apart on baking sheets lined with parchment paper. Sprinkle cookies evenly with remaining 2 teaspoons lime rind, turbinado sugar, and sea salt. Bake at 350° for 10 minutes or until edges are lightly browned. Cool 2 minutes on pans on a wire rack. Remove from baking sheets, and cool completely on wire rack.
6. Place vanilla ice cream and sherbet in a medium bowl; lightly fold and swirl together. Scoop ¼ cup ice cream mixture onto bottom of 1 cookie, and top with 1 cookie. Cover each sandwich with plastic wrap; freeze 4 hours or until firm. Yield: 16 servings (serving size: 1 sandwich).

CALORIES 231; **FAT** 7.1g (sat 4.2g, mono 1.7g, poly 0.4g); **PROTEIN** 3.4g; **CARB** 38.6g; **FIBER** 1.1g; **CHOL** 28mg; **IRON** 1.1mg; **SODIUM** 138mg; **CALC** 74mg

SEA SALT AND COARSE SUGAR YIELD A SALTY-SWEET CRUNCH.

3 STEPS TO SOARING SOUFFLÉS

COAT THE DISHES
Lightly coat dishes with cooking spray. Then add a coarse ingredient to provide traction. Granulated sugar works for sweet soufflés, and breadcrumbs are good for savory.

WHIP THE EGG WHITES
Soufflés are leavened only by egg whites; separate the eggs carefully so they'll whip nicely. Beat whites just to medium peaks: Test to see if they stand at a 45° angle to be sure.

GENTLY FOLD
Incorporate the egg whites into the heavier base by pushing lightly down and pulling the heavier custard mixture up and over the whites, using a sweeping S motion as you work.

TODAY'S LESSON: SOUFFLÉS

Every cook likes to show off sometimes, and few dishes are as dazzling as the old-fashioned but remarkably light soufflé, sweet or savory. The secret to these ethereal puffs has everything to do with egg whites. Whip in a blast of air, and carefully incorporate the billowy froth into a creamy base. Then serve right away—these delicate creations defy gravity for a few fleeting moments.

Kid Friendly

Brown Sugar Soufflés with Crème Anglaise

Hands-on time: 48 min. Total time: 1 hr. 18 min.

The combination of brown sugar and browned butter gives this rich dessert an intense caramel flavor.

½ cup fat-free milk
1 (2-inch) piece vanilla bean, split lengthwise
2 tablespoons granulated sugar
1 large egg, lightly beaten
Cooking spray
2½ tablespoons granulated sugar
½ cup packed brown sugar
3 tablespoons all-purpose flour
⅛ teaspoon salt
4½ tablespoons butter
1¼ cups fat-free milk
1 teaspoon vanilla extract
1 large egg yolk
6 large egg whites
½ teaspoon cream of tartar

1. Pour ½ cup milk into a medium saucepan over medium heat. Scrape seeds from vanilla bean; add seeds and bean to milk. Cook 6 minutes (do not boil); discard bean. Combine 2 tablespoons granulated sugar and egg in a bowl. Gradually add hot milk mixture to bowl, stirring constantly with a whisk. Return mixture to pan. Cook over medium heat 4 minutes or until mixture coats the back of a spoon, stirring constantly. Immediately pour into a bowl. Cover and chill.
2. Place a baking sheet in oven. Preheat oven to 425°.
3. Lightly coat 6 (8-ounce) ramekins with cooking spray. Sprinkle evenly with 2½ tablespoons granulated sugar, tilting and turning dishes to coat sides.
4. Combine brown sugar, flour, and salt. Place butter in a medium, heavy saucepan over medium heat; cook 3 minutes or until butter browns slightly. Stir in flour mixture and 1¼ cups milk; bring to a boil. Cook 2 minutes or until slightly thick, stirring constantly, and remove from heat. Let stand 5 minutes. Stir in vanilla and egg yolk.
5. Combine egg whites and cream of tartar in a large bowl; let stand at room temperature 15 minutes. Beat with a mixer at high speed until medium peaks form. Gently stir one-fourth of egg whites into milk mixture; gently fold in remaining egg whites. Gently spoon mixture into prepared dishes. Sharply tap dishes 2 or 3 times on

counter to level. Place dishes on preheated baking sheet, and return baking sheet to 425° oven. Immediately reduce oven temperature to 350°; bake soufflés at 350° for 30 minutes or until puffy and golden. Serve immediately with sauce. Yield: 6 servings (serving size: 1 soufflé and 2 tablespoons sauce).

CALORIES 274; **FAT** 11.1g (sat 6.2g, mono 3.2g, poly 0.7g); **PROTEIN** 9.1g; **CARB** 34.9g; **FIBER** 0.1g; **CHOL** 125mg; **IRON** 0.8mg; **SODIUM** 225mg; **CALC** 123mg

Kid Friendly

Lemon-Almond Soufflés

Hands-on time: 16 min. Total time: 36 min.

A dusting of powdered sugar or cocoa powder is a traditional garnish for this classic dessert. We sprinkle the tops with sliced almonds before baking to add contrasting flavor and texture.

Cooking spray
1/2 cup plus 2 tablespoons sugar, divided
2 large egg yolks
3/4 cup low-fat buttermilk
1 tablespoon grated lemon rind
1/3 cup fresh lemon juice
2 tablespoons butter, melted
1.13 ounces all-purpose flour (about 1/4 cup)
6 large egg whites
1/2 teaspoon cream of tartar
1/4 cup sliced almonds, lightly toasted

1. Place a baking sheet in oven. Preheat oven to 425°.
2. Lightly coat 6 (8-ounce) ramekins with cooking spray; sprinkle evenly with 2 tablespoons sugar, tilting dishes to coat sides completely.
3. Combine 1/4 cup sugar and egg yolks in a large bowl; beat with a mixer at high speed until thick and pale (about 2 minutes). Add 3/4 cup buttermilk and

next 4 ingredients; beat at medium speed just until blended.
4. Combine egg whites and cream of tartar in a large bowl; let stand at room temperature 15 minutes. Using clean dry beaters, beat with a mixer at high speed until soft peaks form. Gradually add remaining 1/4 cup sugar, 1 tablespoon at a time, beating until medium peaks form.
5. Gently stir one-fourth of egg whites into lemon mixture; gently fold in remaining egg whites. Gently spoon mixture into prepared ramekins. Sharply tap dishes 2 or 3 times on counter to level. Sprinkle evenly with almonds. Place dishes on preheated baking sheet; return baking sheet to 425° oven. Immediately reduce oven temperature to 350°; bake soufflés at 350° for 20 minutes or until puffy and lightly browned. Serve immediately. Yield: 6 servings (serving size: 1 soufflé).

CALORIES 207; **FAT** 7.6g (sat 3.3g, mono 2.9g, poly 0.9g); **PROTEIN** 7g; **CARB** 29.2g; **FIBER** 0.8g; **CHOL** 81mg; **IRON** 0.6mg; **SODIUM** 117mg; **CALC** 60mg

Vegetarian

Spinach and Parmesan Soufflés

Hands-on time: 24 min. Total time: 57 min.

Italian Parmigiano-Reggiano cheese has a superior nutty flavor you won't find in the domestic alternatives. It's worth seeking out— be sure to buy a wedge and grate it yourself.

Cooking spray
1 1/2 tablespoons dry breadcrumbs
1 (6-ounce) package fresh baby spinach
2/3 cup fat-free milk
2 tablespoons all-purpose flour
1/8 teaspoon salt
1/8 teaspoon ground nutmeg
1/8 teaspoon freshly ground black pepper
1/2 cup (2 ounces) grated fresh Parmigiano-Reggiano cheese
2 large egg yolks
4 large egg whites
1/4 teaspoon cream of tartar

1. Place a baking sheet in oven. Preheat oven to 425°.
2. Coat 4 (6-ounce) ramekins with cooking spray; sprinkle evenly with breadcrumbs, tilting and turning dishes to coat sides completely.
3. Heat a large nonstick skillet over medium-high heat. Lightly coat pan with cooking spray. Add spinach; cook 2 minutes or until spinach wilts, stirring constantly. Place spinach in a colander; let stand 5 minutes. Squeeze excess liquid from spinach. Coarsely chop spinach.
4. Combine 2/3 cup milk and next 4 ingredients in a small saucepan over medium-high heat, stirring with a whisk until smooth. Cook 2 minutes or until mixture is thick and bubbly, stirring constantly. Spoon mixture into a large bowl, and let stand 10 minutes. Stir in spinach, cheese, and egg yolks.
5. Combine egg whites and cream of tartar in a large bowl, and let stand at room temperature 15 minutes. Beat with a mixer at high speed until medium peaks form (do not overbeat). Gently stir one-fourth of egg whites into spinach mixture, and gently fold in remaining egg whites. Gently spoon mixture into prepared dishes. Sharply tap dishes 2 or 3 times on counter to level. Place dishes on preheated baking sheet; return baking sheet to 425° oven. Immediately reduce oven temperature to 350°; bake soufflés at 350° for 21 minutes or until puffy and golden brown. Serve immediately. Yield: 4 servings (serving size: 1 soufflé).

CALORIES 163; **FAT** 6g (sat 2.8g, mono 1.9g, poly 0.6g); **PROTEIN** 13.2g; **CARB** 14.6g; **FIBER** 1.4g; **CHOL** 115mg; **IRON** 1.7mg; **SODIUM** 405mg; **CALC** 218mg

BEAN SALADS WITH BITE

By Mark Bittman

Crunchy add-ins, bold dressings, and a few surprises for lovely summer entrées

I've called a truce in my battle against canned beans. Making a big pot of plain-cooked chickpeas, kidneys, or cannellini once a week—and using them in all sorts of dishes—will change your life. But since the canned stuff is absolutely acceptable in a pinch, why ask people to give it up?

In exchange, I recommend a bit more effort when assembling your next bean salad. The dump-from-the-can, dress-and-toss method can only take you so far. To develop a rich variety of flavors and textures, you might need to heat the beans, ratchet up the seasonings, or consider unexpected ingredients. In the recipes here, I do all three.

At their worst, beans—especially canned beans—are soft and bland depending on the variety and brand, so they perform best when paired with crunchy foods that have some bite. I often go for an element of surprise, too, like macerating fresh fruit, using arugula as an herb and cheese as a seasoning, or turning small pieces of steak into crunchy bits that function like croutons.

Because beans are heartier than salad greens, they require bold dressings that either contrast or complement their heft. The bright citrus dressing and floral spices in the chickpea salad and the piquant, rich mayo vinaigrette on the edamame are examples of each approach. To help the dressing flavor and coat the beans, I often heat them and toss them warm, or bathe them in spices first to grab the liquid and help it adhere. Another trick: Dress the beans ahead, and then toss in the more fragile ingredients right before serving.

If you're with me so far, then you might be receptive to my pot-of-beans pitch. Home-cooked dried beans have a deeper flavor than canned and allow control over texture and salt. Cook a big, simply flavored batch once a week, and they're always on hand for salads, stir-fries, soups, pasta, or spontaneous side dishes. Or freeze them in their liquid, and then thaw and use them as you would canned.

Don't avoid making beans because you forgot to soak them. Just put the beans in a large pot, and cover with two or three inches of cold water. Throw in a couple of bay leaves, if you like, a big pinch of salt, and lots of black pepper. Bring to a boil, and then reduce the heat so that the liquid bubbles gently. Cover the pot and cook, without checking, for 30 minutes (or 20 minutes for lentils). After that, take a peek every 15 minutes or so, and stir; if they look too dry, add a splash of water. Cook until they're the texture you like (just tender inside with the skins still intact is ideal for salads). Then drain and dry them well, especially if you're toasting the beans, as in the chickpea salad here. The whole process can take from 30 minutes to two hours depending on what beans you use—and all are fair game for salads. But you do virtually nothing. You don't even need to open a can.

Quick & Easy • Kid Friendly

Edamame Salad with Crisp Steak Bits

Hands-on time: 22 min. Total time: 22 min.

3 cups frozen shelled edamame
2 tablespoons lower-sodium soy sauce
1 tablespoon minced peeled fresh ginger
1 tablespoon mayonnaise
1 tablespoon Dijon mustard
2 teaspoons rice wine vinegar
1 teaspoon dark sesame oil
1 pint cherry tomatoes, halved
1½ cups chopped seeded English cucumber (about 1)
4 green onions, chopped
1 tablespoon olive oil
8 ounces flank steak, cut into small pieces
¼ teaspoon kosher salt
¼ teaspoon freshly ground black pepper

1. Cook edamame according to package directions. Drain. Rinse with cold water; drain.
2. Combine soy sauce and next 5 ingredients in a large bowl, stirring with a whisk. Add edamame, tomatoes, cucumber, and onions; toss to coat.
3. Heat a medium cast-iron skillet over high heat. Add olive oil to pan; swirl to coat. Combine steak, salt, and pepper, tossing to coat steak. Add steak mixture to pan; cook 5 minutes or until well browned and crisp, stirring frequently. Spoon 1½ cups edamame mixture onto each of 4 plates; top evenly with steak. Yield: 4 servings.

CALORIES 277; FAT 14.8g (sat 2.7g, mono 6.7g, poly 2.8g); PROTEIN 23.1g; CARB 14.6g; FIBER 6.1g; CHOL 20mg; IRON 3.5mg; SODIUM 540mg; CALC 97mg

Quick & Easy • Vegetarian

Toasted Chickpea and Apricot Salad

Hands-on time: 30 min. Total time: 30 min.

3 cups cooked or canned chickpeas, rinsed, drained, and patted dry
2 teaspoons ground cumin
1 teaspoon ground coriander
¼ cup olive oil, divided
1 teaspoon grated orange rind
1½ tablespoons white wine vinegar
1½ tablespoons fresh orange juice
¼ teaspoon kosher salt
¼ teaspoon freshly ground black pepper
½ cup thinly vertically sliced red onion
4 large apricots, pitted and sliced
4 cups baby arugula leaves
½ cup (2 ounces) crumbled feta cheese

1. Preheat oven to 450°.
2. Combine first 3 ingredients in a roasting pan; drizzle with 2 tablespoons oil, shaking pan to coat beans. Roast at 450° for 20 minutes, stirring once.
3. Combine remaining 2 tablespoons oil, rind, vinegar, juice, salt, and pepper in a large bowl, stirring with a whisk. Stir in onion and apricots, tossing gently to coat. Add warm beans and arugula, tossing to combine. Sprinkle

with cheese. Yield: 4 servings (serving size: about 1⅔ cups salad and 2 tablespoons cheese).

CALORIES 340; FAT 19.3g (sat 4g, mono 10.7g, poly 1.6g); PROTEIN 10.9g; CARB 32.8g; FIBER 7.4g; CHOL 13mg; IRON 3mg; SODIUM 567mg; CALC 150mg

VEGGIE SANDWICHES

These comforting entrées don't need meat to deliver bold flavor and hearty satisfaction.

Quick & Easy • Vegetarian

Tempeh Greek Salad Wraps

Hands-on time: 20 min. Total time: 25 min.

2 tablespoons olive oil, divided
1 (8-ounce) package organic tempeh, cut into 24 pieces
1 cup water
3 tablespoons lemon juice, divided
2 tablespoons plain low-fat yogurt
1½ teaspoons dried Italian seasoning, divided
1 teaspoon grated lemon rind
½ teaspoon paprika
¼ teaspoon salt
1 garlic clove, minced
2 cups bagged baby spinach
1 cup shredded romaine lettuce
⅔ cup sliced cherry tomato
⅔ cup sliced English cucumber
¼ cup (1 ounce) crumbled feta cheese
¼ teaspoon freshly ground black pepper
4 (8-inch) whole-wheat tortillas

1. Heat a 10-inch skillet over medium-high heat. Add 1 tablespoon oil; swirl to coat. Add tempeh; sauté 4 minutes or until lightly browned, turning once. Add 1 cup water and 2 tablespoons juice to pan; reduce heat to medium, and simmer 10 minutes, turning once.
2. Combine 2 tablespoons yogurt, ½ teaspoon Italian seasoning, and next 4 ingredients in a bowl.

3. Combine remaining 1 tablespoon olive oil, remaining 1 tablespoon lemon juice, remaining 1 teaspoon Italian seasoning, spinach, and next 5 ingredients in a bowl.
4. Warm tortillas according to the package directions. Spread 2 teaspoons yogurt mixture over each tortilla. Top each tortilla with ¾ cup spinach mixture and 6 pieces tempeh; roll up. Cut each rolled tortilla in half crosswise. Yield: 4 servings (serving size: 2 wrap halves).

CALORIES 319; FAT 16.2g (sat 3.7g, mono 7.1g, poly 3g); PROTEIN 16.4g; CARB 29.8g; FIBER 2.4g; CHOL 9mg; IRON 2.9mg; SODIUM 468mg; CALC 194mg

Vegetarian

Lemongrass Tofu Banh Mi

(pictured on page 223)

Hands-on time: 26 min. Total time: 50 min.

The bread and Vietnamese filling (carrot and radish, cilantro, mayonnaise, and cucumber) are traditional in this vegetarian take on the classic. Prepare the mayonnaise mixture and toast the bread while the tofu and vegetable mixture marinate.

1 (14-ounce) package water-packed extra-firm tofu, drained
2 tablespoons finely chopped peeled fresh lemongrass
2 tablespoons water
1 tablespoon lower-sodium soy sauce
2 teaspoons sesame oil, divided
¼ cup rice vinegar
¼ cup water
1 tablespoon sugar
¼ teaspoon salt
1¼ cups matchstick-cut carrot
1¼ cups matchstick-cut peeled daikon radish
1½ tablespoons chopped fresh cilantro
3 tablespoons canola mayonnaise
1½ teaspoons Sriracha (hot chile sauce)
1 (12-ounce) French bread baguette, halved lengthwise and toasted
Cooking spray
1 cup thinly sliced English cucumber

1. Cut tofu crosswise into 6 (⅔-inch-thick) slices. Arrange tofu on several

layers of paper towels. Cover with additional paper towels; top with a cast-iron skillet or heavy pan. Let stand 15 minutes. Remove tofu from paper towels.
2. Combine 2 tablespoons lemongrass, 2 tablespoons water, soy sauce, and 1 teaspoon sesame oil in a 13 x 9–inch glass or ceramic baking dish. Arrange tofu slices in a single layer in soy mixture, turning to coat. Let stand 15 minutes.
3. Combine vinegar and next 3 ingredients in a medium bowl, stirring until sugar and salt dissolve. Add carrot and radish; toss well. Let stand 30 minutes, stirring occasionally. Drain; stir in cilantro.
4. Combine remaining 1 teaspoon sesame oil, mayonnaise, and Sriracha in a small bowl, stirring with a whisk. Spread mayonnaise mixture evenly on cut sides of bread.
5. Heat a large nonstick skillet over medium-high heat. Coat pan with cooking spray. Remove tofu from marinade, and discard marinade. Pat tofu slices dry with paper towels. Add tofu slices to pan, and cook 4 minutes on each side or until crisp and golden. Arrange tofu slices on bottom half of bread; top tofu slices with carrot mixture and cucumber slices. Cut loaf crosswise into 6 equal pieces. Yield: 6 servings (serving size: 1 sandwich).

CALORIES 297; FAT 12g (sat 1.1g, mono 4.3g, poly 4g); PROTEIN 12g; CARB 34.9g; FIBER 3.1g; CHOL 3mg; IRON 2.8mg; SODIUM 499mg; CALC 91mg

PRESSING TOFU FIRMS IT UP AND ALLOWS IT TO ABSORB FLAVORS. PAT IT COMPLETELY DRY AFTER MARINATING SO IT CRISPS AND BROWNS AS IT COOKS.

White Bean and Sage Pita Burgers

Hands-on time: 27 min. Total time: 27 min.

The bean mixture is sticky, so it helps to wet the measuring cup before scooping to form patties.

1 tablespoon extra-virgin olive oil, divided
½ cup chopped onion
2 garlic cloves, minced
⅓ cup old-fashioned rolled oats
⅓ cup sliced almonds, toasted
2 tablespoons cornstarch
1½ teaspoons chopped fresh sage
2 teaspoons Dijon mustard
½ teaspoon salt
¼ teaspoon freshly ground black pepper
2 (15-ounce) cans cannellini beans, rinsed
    and drained
1 large egg, lightly beaten
½ cup reduced-fat sour cream
2 tablespoons grated fresh onion
2 tablespoons crumbled feta cheese
3 (6-inch) pitas, cut in half
6 green leaf lettuce leaves
6 (¼-inch-thick) slices tomato

1. Heat a large nonstick skillet over medium heat. Add 1 teaspoon oil to pan, and swirl to coat. Add ½ cup chopped onion and garlic; cook 2 minutes, stirring frequently. Place mixture in food processor. Add oats and next 8 ingredients; process until smooth.
2. Wipe pan with a paper towel. Return pan to medium heat. Add remaining 2 teaspoons olive oil to pan, and swirl to coat. Working with 1 portion at a time, spoon bean mixture into a ½-cup dry measuring cup, and carefully remove bean mixture with a rubber spatula onto pan. (Bean mixture is very soft and sticky.) Using spatula, shape mixture into a ¾-inch-thick round patty. Repeat procedure 5 times to form 6 patties. Cook 8 minutes or until golden, turning after 4 minutes.
3. Combine sour cream, 2 tablespoons grated onion, and cheese in a small bowl. Spread about 2 tablespoons sour cream mixture into each pita half; top each with 1 lettuce leaf, 1 tomato slice, and 1 bean patty. Yield: 6 servings (serving size: 1 burger).

CALORIES 315; FAT 10g (sat 3.1g, mono 4.7g, poly 1.5g); PROTEIN 13.2g; CARB 43.8g; FIBER 6g; CHOL 40mg; IRON 3.8mg; SODIUM 471mg; CALC 158mg

Grilled Farmers' Market Sandwiches

Hands-on time: 33 min. Total time: 33 min.

The stacked vegetables are quite a mouthful but still tasty to eat.

2 tablespoons olive oil, divided
8 (½-inch-thick) slices eggplant
2 (½-inch-thick) slices red onion
1 large zucchini, cut lengthwise into 4 pieces
2 teaspoons chopped fresh rosemary
¼ teaspoon black pepper
⅛ teaspoon salt
1 tablespoon white balsamic vinegar
4 (2½-ounce) ciabatta bread portions, cut in
    half horizontally
Cooking spray
4 (1-ounce) slices provolone cheese, halved
8 (¼-inch-thick) slices tomato
8 fresh basil leaves

1. Preheat grill to medium-high heat.
2. Brush 1 tablespoon olive oil evenly over both sides of eggplant, onion, and zucchini. Sprinkle with rosemary, pepper, and salt.
3. Combine remaining 1 tablespoon oil and vinegar in a bowl. Brush vinegar mixture over cut sides of bread.
4. Place onion on grill rack coated with cooking spray, and grill 6 minutes on each side or until tender. Remove from grill, and separate into rings. Grill eggplant and zucchini 4 minutes on each side or until tender. Cut zucchini pieces in half crosswise.
5. Place bread, cut sides down, on grill rack; grill 2 minutes. Remove from grill. Place 1 piece of cheese on bottom half of bread portion; top each serving with 1 eggplant slice, 1 tomato slice, 1 basil leaf, 2 pieces zucchini, one-fourth of onion rings, 1 eggplant slice, 1 tomato slice, 1 basil leaf, 1 piece of cheese, and top half of bread. Place sandwiches on grill rack; grill 2 minutes, covered, or until cheese melts. Yield: 4 servings (serving size: 1 sandwich).

CALORIES 386; FAT 16.2g (sat 5.9g, mono 7.1g, poly 1.1g); PROTEIN 15.8g; CARB 45.5g; FIBER 6.4g; CHOL 20mg; IRON 3.2mg; SODIUM 670mg; CALC 249mg

MATCH A DISH WITH PINOT NOIR

Few white wines can stand up to salmon's robust flavor and buttery texture, and many reds are too tannic. Medium-bodied with an ethereal quality and bright acidity, pinot noir makes a great match. To mimic the oak often found in pinot noir, we've cooked our fish on a wood plank. Our top pairing is Pali Wine Co. Alphabets, Pinot Noir 2009, Willamette Valley, Oregon; $20. Wild berries and earthy notes.

A RANGE OF CHOICES FROM AFFORDABLE TO SPLURGE

WEEKNIGHT WINE
Veramonte Pinot Noir Reserva 2009, Chile; $14. Medium-bodied with cherry and cola flavors.

WIDELY AVAILABLE
Castle Rock Pinot Noir Central Coast 2008, California; $13. Plump and juicy black and red fruits.

DINNER PARTY
Cuvaison Carneros, Pinot Noir Napa Valley 2008, California; $30. Strawberry and plum with clove and anise.

FRENCH FAVORITE
Domaine Faiveley, Cuvée Joseph Faiveley Bourgogne Rouge 2008, France; $20. Toasty dry cherry.

Plank-Grilled Salmon with Grape Relish

Hands-on time: 22 min. Total time: 1 hr. 22 min.

This unusual combo does a beautiful job of showing off this complex wine: Briny olives, sweet grapes, and rich salmon match well with pinot noir's balance of earthiness and acidity. Substitute picholine or other green olives, if necessary.

1 (15 x 6½ x ⅜–inch) alder wood grilling plank
4 (6-ounce) wild Alaskan salmon fillets
½ teaspoon black pepper
¼ teaspoon kosher salt
1 tablespoon butter
⅓ cup chopped leek
3 tablespoons chopped shallots
1 cup seedless red grapes, quartered
12 Castelvetrano olives, pitted and chopped
4 teaspoons red wine vinegar

1. Immerse and soak plank in water 1 hour; drain.
2. Preheat grill to medium-high heat.
3. Place plank on grill rack; grill 3 minutes or until lightly charred. Sprinkle fillets with pepper and salt. Carefully turn plank over using sturdy long-handled tongs. Place fillets, skin sides down, on charred side of plank. Grill 12 minutes or until desired degree of doneness.
4. Melt butter in a small skillet over medium-high heat. Add leek and shallots; sauté 2 minutes. Stir in grapes and olives; remove from heat. Stir in vinegar. Serve with fillets. Yield: 4 servings (serving size: 1 fillet and about ⅓ cup relish).

CALORIES 370; **FAT** 18.3g (sat 4.1g, mono 7.1g, poly 5.4g); **PROTEIN** 39.3g; **CARB** 10.4g; **FIBER** 0.6g; **CHOL** 115mg; **IRON** 2.1mg; **SODIUM** 412mg; **CALC** 40mg

CONVENIENCE COOKING

START WITH A CAN OF LIGHT COCONUT MILK

Turn to this global pantry staple to lend subtly sweet, rich goodness to breakfast, dinner, or dessert.

Creamy coconut milk is traditionally used in saucy Asian curries, marinades, and soups. We take it a bit further, pairing it with tropical fruit for French toast and sherbet. You'll find coconut milk on the Asian-foods aisle of your supermarket, but be sure to reach for the light version, which has about 75% less saturated fat than the regular.

Quick & Easy • Kid Friendly
Vegetarian

Coconut French Toast with Grilled Pineapple

Hands-on time: 19 min. Total time: 22 min.

1 cup light coconut milk
¼ cup sugar
¼ cup fat-free milk
3 large eggs
1 (12-ounce) loaf French bread, cut into 15 slices
Cooking spray
10 (¼-inch-thick) slices peeled pineapple
½ cup flaked sweetened coconut

1. Place a baking sheet in oven. Preheat oven to 200°.
2. Combine coconut milk, sugar, fat-free milk, and eggs in a shallow dish, stirring with a whisk. Working in batches, dip bread in milk mixture, and let stand 1 minute on each side.
3. Heat a large nonstick skillet over medium-high heat; coat pan with cooking spray. Add 5 coated bread slices to pan, and cook 2 minutes on each side or until browned. Place on warm pan in oven to keep warm. Repeat procedure in batches with cooking spray, remaining bread slices, and milk mixture.
4. Heat a grill pan over medium-high heat. Add pineapple, and grill 2 minutes on each side or until well marked. Chop pineapple. Place 3 slices French toast on each of 5 plates, and divide pineapple among servings. Top with coconut. Yield: 5 servings.

CALORIES 394; **FAT** 9.1g (sat 5.2g, mono 1.3g, poly 0.5g); **PROTEIN** 11.4g; **CARB** 67.8g; **FIBER** 3.6g; **CHOL** 108mg; **IRON** 3.2mg; **SODIUM** 523mg; **CALC** 88mg

Make Ahead • Freezable
Kid Friendly

Mango-Coconut Sherbet

Hands-on time: 5 min. Total time: 2 hr. 30 min.

To toast flaked unsweetened coconut, spread it in an even, single layer on a rimmed baking sheet. Then, bake in a 350° preheated oven for 5 minutes or until golden, stirring once.

2 cups cubed peeled ripe mango
¾ cup sugar
1 tablespoon fresh lime juice
1 (13.5-ounce) can light coconut milk
¼ cup flaked unsweetened coconut, toasted

1. Combine cubed mango, sugar, 1 tablespoon lime juice, and coconut milk in a blender; process until mixture is smooth, scraping sides as necessary. Pour mixture into the freezer can of an ice-cream freezer, and freeze according to manufacturer's instructions to soft-serve consistency. Spoon sherbet into a freezer-safe container; cover and freeze 2 hours or until firm. Sprinkle each serving with toasted coconut. Yield: 6 servings (serving size: about ⅔ cup sherbet and 2 teaspoons coconut).

CALORIES 171; **FAT** 4.1g (sat 3.8g, mono 0.1g, poly 0g); **PROTEIN** 1.1g; **CARB** 35.4g; **FIBER** 1g; **CHOL** 0mg; **IRON** 0.4mg; **SODIUM** 26mg; **CALC** 4mg

Quick & Easy

Curried Coconut Mussels

Hands-on time: 20 min. Total time: 25 min.

1 tablespoon olive oil
2 cups chopped onion
1 tablespoon finely chopped peeled fresh
　ginger
2 garlic cloves, minced
1 jalapeño pepper, chopped
2 teaspoons red curry paste
1 cup light coconut milk
½ cup dry white wine
1 teaspoon dark brown sugar
¼ teaspoon kosher salt
2 pounds small mussels, scrubbed and
　debearded (about 60)
¾ cup small fresh basil leaves, divided
3 tablespoons fresh lime juice
4 lime wedges

1. Heat a large Dutch oven over medium-high heat. Add oil to pan; swirl to coat. Add onion, ginger, garlic, and jalapeño; sauté 3 minutes, stirring frequently. Stir in curry paste; cook 30 seconds, stirring constantly. Add coconut milk, wine, sugar, and salt; bring to a boil. Cook 2 minutes. Stir in mussels; cover and cook 5 minutes or until mussels open. Discard any unopened shells. Stir in ½ cup basil and juice. Divide mussels mixture evenly among 4 bowls, and spoon coconut mixture evenly over mussels. Sprinkle each serving with remaining 1 tablespoon basil; serve with lime wedges. Yield: 4 servings (serving size: about 15 mussels, about ½ cup coconut mixture, 1 tablespoon basil, and 1 lime wedge).

CALORIES 241; **FAT** 9.9g (sat 4g, mono 3.2g, poly 1.3g); **PROTEIN** 20g; **CARB** 19.1g; **FIBER** 1.7g; **CHOL** 42mg; **IRON** 6.8mg; **SODIUM** 594mg; **CALC** 80mg

WINE NOTE: Columbia Winery Cellarmaster's Riesling, Columbia Valley ($10), has a dense texture and honey-sweet flavor that's balanced with spice and mineral notes. Tart lime cuts through the rich coconutty broth of the mussels.

RECIPE MAKEOVER

FRESHER, LIGHTER FISH STICKS

It was time to reclaim the pleasures of this frozen finger-food delight.

This month's makeover question: Could we capture the real crunch appeal of those super-convenient frozen-aisle fish sticks but get them out of the nutrition doghouse? After all, your basic fried fish stick, dunked in tangy tartar sauce, can add up to about half a day's sodium allowance and half a day's saturated fat.

The answer is yes, and in our version you get delicious fresh-fish flavor that grown-ups will love. Our makeover starts with strips of meaty halibut, seasoned and breaded in a panko-pumpkinseed coating—the seeds add extra crunch and heart-healthy fats. The fish is then oven-baked on a lightly oiled, preheated pan to crispy perfection. Splashed with lime and served with a zesty rémoulade sauce, our fish sticks have 40% fewer calories, half the sodium, and double the crunch and flavor.

Quick & Easy • Kid Friendly

Fancy Fish Sticks

Hands-on time: 25 min. Total time: 40 min.

¼ cup reduced-fat mayonnaise
¼ cup fat-free sour cream
1 tablespoon Creole mustard
2 teaspoons fresh lime juice
½ teaspoon Cajun seasoning
Cooking spray
1 tablespoon canola oil
½ cup all-purpose flour
¼ teaspoon freshly ground black pepper
½ cup lager-style beer
1½ tablespoons creamy mustard blend
1 tablespoon fresh lime juice
2 large egg whites
1 large egg
⅔ cup panko (Japanese breadcrumbs)
⅓ cup unsalted pumpkinseed kernels,
　toasted
1 teaspoon ground cumin
½ teaspoon ground chipotle chile pepper
1 pound halibut or other lean white fish fillets
　(such as cod or pollack), cut into 4 x 1-inch
　pieces (about 12 pieces)
¼ teaspoon kosher salt
4 lime wedges

1. Combine first 5 ingredients in a small bowl, stirring with a whisk. Cover and chill.

2. Preheat oven to 425°.

3. Coat a baking sheet with cooking spray, and spread evenly with oil; heat in oven 12 minutes.

4. Combine flour and black pepper in a shallow dish. Combine ½ cup beer, mustard blend, lime juice, egg whites, and egg in a shallow dish; stir with a whisk until foamy. Place panko, pumpkinseeds, cumin, and chipotle pepper in a food processor; pulse 20 times or until coarse crumbs form. Place panko mixture in a shallow dish.

5. Sprinkle fish evenly with salt. Working with 1 piece at a time, dredge fish in flour mixture. Dip in egg mixture, and dredge in panko mixture until completely covered.

6. Remove preheated baking sheet from oven; place fish on pan, and return to oven. Bake at 425° for 15 minutes or until desired degree of doneness, turning once. Serve immediately with sauce and lime wedges. Yield: 4 servings (serving size: about 3 fish sticks, 2 tablespoons sauce, and 1 lime wedge).

Sustainable Choice

If Pacific halibut is not available, you can use Alaskan pollack and U.S. Pacific cod as alternatives.

CALORIES 425; **FAT** 17g (sat 2.5g, mono 6g, poly 6.2g); **PROTEIN** 36.9g; **CARB** 29.5g; **FIBER** 1.8g; **CHOL** 91mg; **IRON** 5mg; **SODIUM** 597mg; **CALC** 98mg

TIPS FOR BREADING

A lightly oiled, preheated pan ensures fried-like crunch. Turn the fish once for even crisping.

Season fish directly with salt. For less mess, assign one hand for the dry mixture and one for the wet mixture.

A light flour dusting helps the egg mixture adhere to the fish. Shake off excess before dipping in egg.

The frothy beer keeps the egg mixture light and fluffy so the breading doesn't get gummy.

We use hearty panko and nutty pumpkin-seeds for ultimate crunch.

OLD WAY	OUR WAY
750 calories per serving	425 calories per serving
1,212 milligrams sodium	597 milligrams sodium
9 grams saturated fat	2.5 grams saturated fat
Minced, processed fish	Fresh, sustainable fillets
Prebreaded, soggy, and frozen	Crispy, crunchy, and fresh
From deep fryer to freezer	From oven to table

WHAT TO EAT RIGHT NOW
APRICOTS

Now is the time to seek out these delicate sweet-tart fruits. Beneath the velvety skin of the perfect apricot is flesh that somehow manages to be dense and fragile at the same time. Baking or simmering melts the fruit, intensifying the flavor. Grilling produces a lovely, caramelized result, while the skin holds the fruit's shape.

The gold standard apricot is the small, puckery-sweet, perfumed Blenheim. Or try the Candy Cot, which is almost sugary by comparison. Stewed, this fruit is gorgeous over ice cream or a light cake. Fresh slices can be served alongside beef, poultry, pork, or shellfish. And pureed peeled apricots make for one delicious Bellini.

Make Ahead • Vegetarian
Apricot-Fig Chutney

Hands-on time: 15 min. Total time: 30 min.

3 cups apricots, peeled, quartered, and pitted
1/2 cup dried figs, quartered
1/2 cup white wine
1/3 cup sugar
1/4 cup golden raisins
1 1/2 teaspoons chopped fresh thyme
1 tablespoon honey
1 tablespoon fresh lemon juice
1 teaspoon mustard seeds
1/2 teaspoon ground cumin
1/2 teaspoon ground ginger
1/4 teaspoon kosher salt
Dash of ground red pepper
1/2 jalapeño pepper, finely chopped
1/2 shallot, sliced
2 tablespoons chopped cilantro

1. Combine all ingredients except cilantro in a large Dutch oven over medium heat, and simmer. Cook 15 minutes. Stir in cilantro. Yield: 2½ cups (serving size: ¼ cup).

CALORIES 99; FAT 0.4g (sat 0g, mono 0.2g, poly 0.1g); PROTEIN 1.4g; CARB 23.5g; FIBER 2g; CHOL 0mg; IRON 0.6mg; SODIUM 61mg; CALC 24mg

Grilled Apricot Halves

Hands-on time: 10 min. Total time: 35 min.

Perch on salad or even pizzas, or serve as a side dish.

1 tablespoon olive oil
1 teaspoon honey
6 apricots, halved and pitted (about
    ³/₄ pound)
Cooking spray
⅛ teaspoon kosher salt
⅛ teaspoon black pepper
1 teaspoon fresh thyme leaves

1. Preheat grill to medium-high heat.
2. Combine olive oil and honey; brush over cut sides of apricots. Arrange apricots, cut sides down, on grill rack coated with cooking spray. Remove from grill; sprinkle with salt, black pepper, and thyme. Yield: 6 servings (serving size: 2 apricot halves).

CALORIES 40; **FAT** 2.4g (sat 0.3g, mono 1.7g, poly 0.3g); **PROTEIN** 0.5g; **CARB** 4.9g; **FIBER** 0.7g; **CHOL** 0mg; **IRON** 0.2mg; **SODIUM** 40mg; **CALC** 5mg

Make Ahead • Freezable

Sparkling Apricot Sorbet

Combine 1 cup sugar; 2 cups sparkling wine; 2 (2-inch) strips lemon peel; 1½ pounds peeled, halved, and pitted apricots; and a dash of salt in a medium saucepan over medium-high heat. Bring to a boil. Reduce heat, and simmer 10 minutes. Remove from heat, and cool. Discard lemon peel. Transfer mixture to a blender; process until smooth. Pour mixture through a sieve over a bowl; discard solids. Cover and chill. Transfer mixture to the freezer can of an ice cream freezer; freeze according to manufacturer's instructions. Scrape sorbet into a freezer-safe container; freeze 2 hours or until firm. Yield: about 4 cups (serving size: ½ cup).

CALORIES 178; **FAT** 0.3g (sat 0g); **SODIUM** 19mg

5-INGREDIENT COOKING

Quick & Easy • Kid Friendly

Grilled Flank Steak with Onions, Avocado, and Tomatoes

Hands-on time: 20 min. Total time: 30 min.

Use colorful in-season heirloom tomatoes for a pretty presentation.

Directions: Preheat grill to high heat. Lightly coat onions with cooking spray. Place onions on grill rack; grill 10 minutes on each side or until tender. Place onions in a medium bowl; cover tightly with foil. Keep warm. Lightly coat steak with cooking spray; sprinkle steak with ¾ teaspoon kosher salt and ¾ teaspoon black pepper. Place steak on grill rack; grill 6 minutes on each side or until desired degree of doneness. Let stand 3 minutes. Cut steak diagonally across grain into thin slices. Add tomatoes, balsamic vinegar, ¼ teaspoon kosher salt, and ¼ teaspoon black pepper to onions; toss gently to combine. Divide steak evenly among 6 plates; top with ½ cup tomato mixture. Cut avocado wedges in thirds crosswise. Top each serving with 4 avocado pieces. Yield: 6 servings.

CALORIES 262; **FAT** 13.6g (sat 4g, mono 7.7g, poly 1g); **PROTEIN** 24.3g; **CARB** 10.3g; **FIBER** 3.6g; **CHOL** 50mg; **IRON** 2.9mg; **SODIUM** 393mg; **CALC** 31mg

THE FIVE INGREDIENTS

2 medium red onions, cut into
½-inch-thick slices

+

1½ pounds flank steak, trimmed

+

2 cups cherry tomatoes, halved

+

¼ cup balsamic vinegar

+

1 ripe peeled avocado, cut into 8 wedges

FEED 4 FOR LESS THAN $10

Saucy chicken wraps, a fresh take on tuna melts, shrimp pasta, and updated chicken and rice make for laid-back, family-friendly meals.

$9.67 total, $2.42 per serving

Quick & Easy • Kid Friendly

Grilled Chicken Wraps

Hands-on time: 35 min. Total time: 35 min.

½ cup canola mayonnaise
3 tablespoons white wine vinegar, divided
2½ teaspoons black pepper, divided
¼ teaspoon kosher salt, divided
1 teaspoon fresh lemon juice
1 cup shredded cabbage
2 teaspoons bread-and-butter pickle juice
2 (6-ounce) skinless, boneless chicken breast halves
Cooking spray
4 light flatbread sandwich wraps
4 sandwich-cut bread-and-butter pickles

1. Preheat grill to medium-high heat.
2. Combine mayonnaise, 2 tablespoons vinegar, 2 teaspoons black pepper, ⅛ teaspoon salt, and lemon juice in a small bowl, stirring well. Combine remaining 1 tablespoon vinegar, cabbage, and pickle juice in a medium bowl; toss.
3. Sprinkle chicken with remaining ½ teaspoon black pepper and remaining ⅛ teaspoon salt. Place chicken on a grill rack coated with cooking spray, and grill 6 minutes on each side or until done. Cool; shred chicken. Combine chicken and mayonnaise mixture in a medium bowl; toss to coat. Place 1 flatbread on each of 4 plates; divide chicken mixture evenly among flatbreads. Top each serving with about ¼

cup cabbage mixture and 1 pickle; roll up. Cut each wrap in half diagonally. Yield: 4 servings (serving size: 1 wrap).

CALORIES 288; FAT 12.6g (sat 0.2g, mono 7.2g, poly 3.2g); PROTEIN 24.3g; CARB 24.4g; FIBER 10.1g; CHOL 37mg; IRON 0.7mg; SODIUM 802mg; CALC 37mg

---

$9.64 total, $2.41 per serving

Quick & Easy • Kid Friendly

Tuna Melts with Avocado

Hands-on time: 11 min. Total time: 14 min.

You can serve these with carrot and celery sticks and a bit of light ranch dressing on the side for dipping.

2½ tablespoons olive oil
2 tablespoons thinly sliced shallots
1 tablespoon Dijon mustard
¼ teaspoon black pepper
⅛ teaspoon salt
1 (6-ounce) can solid white tuna in water, drained and flaked
1½ tablespoons fresh lemon juice
1 avocado
1 cup cherry tomatoes, quartered
⅓ cup shredded Swiss cheese
2 (6-ounce) pieces French bread, halved lengthwise and toasted

1. Preheat broiler to high.
2. Combine first 6 ingredients in a medium bowl, stirring well to coat. Place juice in a small bowl. Peel, seed, and chop avocado. Add avocado to juice; toss. Add avocado mixture and tomatoes to tuna mixture; toss well to combine. Sprinkle cheese evenly over cut sides of bread, and broil 3 minutes or until cheese is bubbly. Place 1 bread slice, cheese side up, on each of 4 plates, and divide tuna mixture evenly among bread slices. Yield: 4 servings.

Sustainable Choice | *Solid white tuna is albacore, the most sustainable choice among the varieties of tuna.*

CALORIES 455; FAT 19.7g (sat 3.9g, mono 10.6g, poly 1.7g); PROTEIN 20.1g; CARB 49.7g; FIBER 5.3g; CHOL 26mg; IRON 3mg; SODIUM 860mg; CALC 140mg

---

$7.45 total, $1.86 per serving

Black Beans and Yellow Rice

Hands-on time: 23 min. Total time: 10 hr. 53 min.

4 ounces dried black beans
Cooking spray
4 ounces Spanish chorizo, thinly sliced
6 cups water, divided
½ teaspoon salt, divided
½ teaspoon black pepper, divided
¼ teaspoon ground cumin
1½ cups chopped onion
1 orange bell pepper, chopped
1 jalapeño pepper, minced
2 garlic cloves, minced
1 cup uncooked long-grain rice
¼ teaspoon ground turmeric
3 cups chopped fresh tomato
2 tablespoons chopped fresh cilantro

1. Sort and wash beans; place in a bowl. Cover with water to 2 inches above beans; let stand 8 hours. Drain.
2. Heat a large saucepan over medium-high heat. Coat pan with cooking spray. Add chorizo; sauté 3 minutes. Add beans and 4 cups water; bring to a boil. Reduce heat, and simmer 2½ hours or until beans are tender. Stir in ¼ teaspoon salt, ¼ teaspoon black pepper, and cumin.
3. Heat a medium skillet over medium heat. Coat pan with cooking spray. Add 1½ cups onion, bell pepper, jalapeño, and garlic; cook 8 minutes, stirring occasionally. Stir remaining ¼ teaspoon black pepper and onion mixture into bean mixture.
4. Bring remaining 2 cups water to a boil in a small saucepan over medium-high heat. Stir in remaining ¼ teaspoon salt, rice, and turmeric. Cover, reduce heat, and simmer 20 minutes or until liquid evaporates and rice is tender. Spoon ¾ cup rice into each of 4 bowls, and top each serving with about ⅔ cup bean mixture, ¾ cup tomato, and 1½ teaspoons cilantro. Yield: 4 servings.

CALORIES 438; FAT 11.6g (sat 4.2g, mono 5.4g, poly 1.2g); PROTEIN 17.5g; CARB 64.6g; FIBER 5.7g; CHOL 25mg; IRON 4.6mg; SODIUM 657mg; CALC 40mg

$9.69 total, $2.42 per serving

Quick & Easy • Kid Friendly

Creamy Linguine with Shrimp and Veggies

Hands-on time: 30 min. Total time: 30 min.

6 quarts water
1 teaspoon salt, divided
8 ounces uncooked linguine
3 cups small broccoli florets
1½ tablespoons butter
1 cup chopped onion
8 ounces sliced mushrooms
2 garlic cloves, minced
12 ounces peeled and deveined medium shrimp
1 julienne-cut carrot
¾ cup ⅓-less-fat cream cheese
¼ teaspoon ground black pepper

1. Bring 6 quarts water to a boil in a saucepan. Add ½ teaspoon salt and pasta; cook 5 minutes. Add broccoli; cook 3 minutes or until pasta is al dente. Drain through a sieve over a bowl, reserving ½ cup pasta water.
2. Melt butter in a Dutch oven over medium-high heat. Add onion and mushrooms to pan; sauté 5 minutes, stirring occasionally. Add garlic, and sauté 1 minute, stirring constantly. Add remaining ½ teaspoon salt, shrimp, and carrot; sauté 3 minutes, stirring occasionally. Add pasta mixture, reserved ½ cup pasta water, cream cheese, and pepper to pan; cook 3 minutes or until cheese melts and shrimp are done, stirring occasionally. Yield: 4 servings (serving size: 2 cups).

Sustainable Choice

Look for the Marine Stewardship Council stamp to ensure you're making an eco-friendly choice.

CALORIES 501; FAT 16.3g (sat 9.4g, mono 3.9g, poly 1.2g); PROTEIN 32.2g; CARB 57g; FIBER 5.6g; CHOL 171mg; IRON 4.8mg; SODIUM 691mg; CALC 136mg

---

$9.97 total, $2.49 per serving

Cold Chicken and Rice Salad

Hands-on time: 25 min. Total time: 1 hr. 10 min.

Serve with cantaloupe and a crisp white wine.

2 (6-ounce) skinless, boneless chicken breast halves
¾ teaspoon salt, divided
¾ teaspoon black pepper, divided
Cooking spray
¾ cup uncooked long-grain rice
3 tablespoons fresh lemon juice
2 tablespoons olive oil
⅓ cup dried cranberries
¼ cup diced celery
¼ cup thinly sliced green onions
¼ cup diced red bell pepper
¼ cup chopped pimiento-stuffed olives
12 green leaf lettuce leaves, torn
¼ cup thinly sliced green onion tops
4 lemon wedges

1. Preheat oven to 400°.
2. Sprinkle chicken with ¼ teaspoon salt and ½ teaspoon black pepper. Heat a medium ovenproof skillet over medium-high heat. Coat pan with cooking spray. Add chicken to pan; cook 3 minutes. Turn chicken over. Place pan in oven; bake at 400° for 8 minutes or until done. Remove chicken from pan, and let stand 5 minutes. Shred chicken, and chill 30 minutes.
3. Cook rice according to package directions, omitting salt and fat. Coat a jelly-roll pan with cooking spray. Spread rice in an even layer in pan; chill 30 minutes.
4. Combine remaining ½ teaspoon salt, remaining ¼ teaspoon black pepper, juice, and oil in a large bowl, stirring with a whisk. Add chicken, rice, cranberries, and next 5 ingredients to juice mixture in bowl; toss gently. Divide rice mixture evenly among 4 plates; sprinkle with green onion tops. Serve with lemon wedges. Yield: 4 servings (serving size: about 2 cups salad, 1 tablespoon green onion tops, and 1 lemon wedge).

CALORIES 325; FAT 9.2g (sat 1.2g, mono 5.7g, poly 1.6g); PROTEIN 18.7g; CARB 41.9g; FIBER 2.7g; CHOL 37mg; IRON 2.9mg; SODIUM 634mg; CALC 59mg

---

DINNER TONIGHT

Here is a batch of fast weeknight menus from the *Cooking Light* Test Kitchens.

READY IN 30 MINUTES

········· *The* ·········
SHOPPING LIST

Open-Faced Blackened Catfish Sandwiches
1 package cabbage-and-carrot coleslaw
fresh cilantro
lime
paprika
dried oregano
ground red pepper
olive oil
honey
4 (6-ounce) catfish fillets
plain fat-free Greek yogurt
sourdough bread

Stewed Okra and Fresh Tomato
onion
1 pound fresh okra pods
tomato
1 ear fresh corn
vegetable broth
olive oil

········· *The* ·········
GAME PLAN

- Cook stewed okra.
  While okra cooks:
- Cook fish.
- Prepare slaw.

Open-Faced Blackened Catfish Sandwiches

with Stewed Okra and Fresh Tomato

Prep Pointer: You can chop the tender tops of cilantro stems along with the leaves.
Keep It Fresh: Wrap extra sourdough bread in foil, and freeze for up to two months.
Time-Saver: Frozen cut okra will cook in just a few minutes.

1¾ teaspoons paprika
1 teaspoon dried oregano
¾ teaspoon ground red pepper
¼ teaspoon salt
¼ teaspoon freshly ground black pepper
4 (6-ounce) catfish fillets
2 teaspoons olive oil
⅓ cup plain fat-free Greek yogurt
3 tablespoons fresh lime juice
1 tablespoon honey
2 cups packaged cabbage-and-carrot coleslaw
1 cup chopped fresh cilantro
4 (1-ounce) slices sourdough bread, toasted

1. Combine first 5 ingredients in a small bowl. Sprinkle both sides of fish with paprika mixture. Heat a large cast-iron skillet over high heat. Add oil to pan; swirl to coat. Add fish; cook 4 minutes on each side or until desired degree of doneness.
2. Combine yogurt, juice, and honey in a medium bowl. Add coleslaw and cilantro; toss well to coat. Top each bread slice with about ½ cup slaw and 1 fillet. Top each fillet with remaining slaw. Yield: 4 servings (serving size: 1 open-faced sandwich).

Sustainable Choice Choose farmed catfish, which is an eco-friendly option.

CALORIES 362; FAT 16g (sat 3.4g, mono 7.8g, poly 3.2g); PROTEIN 31.3g; CARB 22.6g; FIBER 2.2g; CHOL 80mg; IRON 2.4mg; SODIUM 414mg; CALC 63mg

Quick & Easy • Vegetarian
For the Stewed Okra and Fresh Tomato:
Heat a Dutch oven over medium-high heat. Add 2 teaspoons olive oil to pan, swirling to coat. Add ¾ cup chopped onion; sauté 2 minutes. Add 1 pound fresh okra pods, 1 cup chopped tomato, 1 cup vegetable broth, ¾ cup fresh corn kernels, and ¼ teaspoon salt; bring to a boil. Cover, reduce heat, and simmer 20 minutes or until vegetables are tender, stirring occasionally. Yield: 4 servings (serving size: about 1¼ cups).

CALORIES 102; FAT 2.8g (sat 0.3g); SODIUM 303mg

READY IN 30 MINUTES

The SHOPPING LIST

Chipotle-Rubbed Flank Steak
shallot
garlic
fresh flat-leaf parsley
ground chipotle chile pepper
paprika
1 (1-pound) flank steak
olive oil
all-purpose flour
1% low-fat milk
butter
1 ounce crumbled Gorgonzola cheese

Couscous
vegetable broth
couscous

Spinach with Toasted Almonds
1 (6-ounce) package fresh baby spinach
sliced almonds

The GAME PLAN

▪ Cook couscous.
▪ Broil steak.
While steak cooks:
▪ Prepare spinach.
While steak rests:
▪ Make sauce.

Chipotle-Rubbed Flank Steak

with Couscous and Spinach with Toasted Almonds

Flavor Hit: Chipotle chile pepper brings spicy, smoky taste to the dish.
Prep Pointer: Slice the steak thinly to keep it tender.
Keep It Fresh: Store extra Gorgonzola wrapped tightly in foil.

1 teaspoon ground chipotle chile pepper
1 teaspoon paprika
¼ teaspoon salt
1 (1-pound) flank steak, trimmed
1 teaspoon olive oil
2 tablespoons finely chopped shallots
1 garlic clove, finely chopped
1 teaspoon all-purpose flour
⅔ cup 1% low-fat milk
¼ cup (1 ounce) crumbled Gorgonzola cheese
1 teaspoon butter
2 teaspoons chopped fresh flat-leaf parsley

1. Preheat broiler to high.
2. Combine first 3 ingredients. Sprinkle steak with chipotle mixture. Place on a broiler pan; broil 5 minutes on each side. Let stand 5 minutes. Cut thinly across grain.
3. Heat oil in a saucepan over medium heat. Add shallots and garlic; cook 1 minute. Add flour; cook 30 seconds, stirring. Add milk; bring to a boil. Cook until reduced by half. Remove from heat; stir in cheese and next 2 ingredients. Yield: 4 servings (serving size: 3 ounces steak and 3 tablespoons sauce).

CALORIES 240; FAT 11.8g (sat 5.5g, mono 4g, poly 0.5g); PROTEIN 27.9g; CARB 4.2g; FIBER 0.5g; CHOL 58mg; IRON 2.1mg; SODIUM 353mg; CALC 123mg

Quick & Easy • Kid Friendly • Vegetarian
For the Couscous:
Bring 1¾ cups vegetable broth to a boil in a saucepan. Add ¾ cup uncooked couscous. Cover, remove from heat, and let stand 5 minutes. Fluff with a fork. Yield: 4 servings (serving size: about ½ cup).

CALORIES 138; FAT 1.3g (sat 0.2g); SODIUM 253mg

For the Spinach with Toasted Almonds:
Heat a large nonstick skillet over medium-high heat. Coat pan with cooking spray. Add 1 (6-ounce) package fresh baby spinach; sauté 2 minutes or until spinach wilts. Add ⅛ teaspoon salt. Sprinkle with 3 tablespoons toasted sliced almonds. Yield: 4 servings (serving size: about ⅓ cup).

CALORIES 42; **FAT** 2.1g (sat 0.2g); **SODIUM** 141mg

The
SHOPPING LIST

Shrimp Korma and Basmati Rice
red bell pepper
onion
fresh ginger
garlic
tomato
Madras curry powder
garam masala
coconut milk
basmati rice
1 pound peeled and deveined large shrimp
frozen green peas
plain fat-free yogurt
butter
organic vegetable broth
all-purpose flour

Roasted Summer Squash with Parsley
zucchini
yellow squash
fresh parsley

The
GAME PLAN

■ Roast squash.
While squash cooks:
■ Prepare shrimp mixture.
■ Chop parsley for squash.

Quick & Easy

Shrimp Korma and Basmati Rice
with Roasted Summer Squash with Parsley

Veg Swap: Substitute 1 pound extra-firm diced tofu for the shrimp.
Shopping Tip: Thick, tangy Greek-style yogurt will give you a creamy sauce.
Time-Saver: Use prechopped bell pepper.

2 teaspoons butter
1 cup chopped red bell pepper
½ cup chopped onion
1½ tablespoons all-purpose flour
1 teaspoon grated peeled fresh ginger
3 garlic cloves, finely chopped
2 teaspoons Madras curry powder
2 teaspoons garam masala
½ teaspoon salt, divided
2 cups organic vegetable broth
⅓ cup water
⅓ cup coconut milk
¼ cup diced tomato
¼ cup frozen green peas
1 pound peeled and deveined large shrimp
4 cups hot cooked basmati rice
¼ cup plain fat-free yogurt

1. Melt butter in a Dutch oven over medium-high heat. Add bell pepper and onion to pan; sauté 2 minutes. Add flour, ginger, and garlic; cook 1 minute, stirring constantly. Add curry powder, garam masala, and ¼ teaspoon salt; cook 30 seconds, stirring. Stir in broth and ⅓ cup water; bring to a boil. Stir in milk and tomato; reduce heat, and simmer 5 minutes. Add peas, shrimp, and remaining ¼ teaspoon salt; cook 5 minutes or until shrimp are done. Spoon about ⅔ cup rice into each of 6 bowls. Top each serving with about 1 cup shrimp mixture and 2 teaspoons yogurt. Yield: 6 servings.

CALORIES 295; **FAT** 5.9g (sat 3.5g, mono 0.7g, poly 0.7g); **PROTEIN** 20.1g; **CARB** 39.1g; **FIBER** 2g; **CHOL** 119mg; **IRON** 4.3mg; **SODIUM** 524mg; **CALC** 71mg

---

For the Roasted Summer Squash with Parsley:
Preheat oven to 425°. Arrange 2 cups chopped zucchini and 2 cups chopped yellow squash on a jelly-roll pan; sprinkle with ¼ teaspoon salt. Bake at 425° for 17 minutes or until crisp-tender. Toss with ¼ cup chopped fresh parsley. Yield: 6 servings (serving size: about ⅓ cup).

CALORIES 16; **FAT** 0.2g (sat 0g); **SODIUM** 104mg

The
SHOPPING LIST

Grilled Chicken Sliders and Apricot Chutney Spread
3 medium apricots
garlic
ground red pepper
Dijon mustard
cider vinegar
1½ pounds skinless, boneless chicken thighs
8 (1.3-ounce) mini sandwich buns

Guacamole
onion
fresh cilantro
avocado

The
GAME PLAN

■ Make guacamole.
■ Cook chicken.
While chicken cools slightly:
■ Cook apricots.
■ Shred chicken.
■ Process chutney.
■ Assemble sliders.

Grilled Chicken Sliders and Apricot Chutney Spread
wth Guacamole

Flavor Hit: Dijon mustard gives the chutney peppery tang.
Simple Sub: Use white wine vinegar in place of cider vinegar.
Shopping Tip: Buy the smallest container of red pepper available to help it stay fresh.

3/8 teaspoon ground red pepper
1/2 teaspoon freshly ground black pepper
1/8 teaspoon salt
1 1/2 pounds skinless, boneless chicken thighs
Cooking spray
3 apricots, halved and pitted
1 tablespoon water
1 tablespoon cider vinegar
1 tablespoon Dijon mustard
2 garlic cloves, chopped
8 (1.3-ounce) mini sandwich buns

1. Combine first 3 ingredients in a small bowl. Sprinkle chicken with pepper mixture. Place a large grill pan over medium-high heat; coat pan with cooking spray. Add chicken to pan; cook 5 minutes on each side or until done. Cool slightly; shred meat.
2. Recoat pan with cooking spray. Place apricots, cut sides down, on pan; cook over medium-high heat 6 minutes or until tender and lightly browned, turning after 4 minutes. Place apricots, 1 tablespoon water, and next 3 ingredients in a food processor; process until smooth.
3. Spread 1/2 teaspoon apricot chutney over cut side of each sandwich bun half. Place about 1/3 cup chicken on bottom bun; cover with top half of bun. Yield: 4 servings (serving size: 2 sliders).

CALORIES 430; **FAT** 11g (sat 3.7g, mono 4.1g, poly 1.7g); **PROTEIN** 42.3g; **CARB** 41.9g; **FIBER** 2.7g; **CHOL** 141mg; **IRON** 2mg; **SODIUM** 644mg; **CALC** 24mg

Quick & Easy • Kid Friendly • Vegetarian
For the Guacamole:
Combine 2 tablespoons chopped onion, 2 tablespoons chopped fresh cilantro, 1/8 teaspoon salt, and 1 medium chopped avocado in a food processor; pulse 8 times or until combined. Yield: 4 servings (serving size: about 3 tablespoons guacamole).

CALORIES 65; **FAT** 5.6g (sat 0.6g); **SODIUM** 74mg

SUPERFAST

Quick weeknight dishes featuring bright, bold flavors: herby shrimp salad, sweet-spicy chicken skewers, mushroom-packed sloppy joes, and more

Quick & Easy • Kid Friendly

Skillet Pork Chop Sauté with Peaches

Serve over quick-cooking couscous.

2 teaspoons olive oil
4 (4-ounce) center-cut boneless loin pork chops, trimmed
1/2 teaspoon salt
1/2 teaspoon freshly ground black pepper
2 tablespoons thinly sliced shallots
2 teaspoons chopped fresh thyme
2 peaches, each cut into 8 wedges
1/2 cup dry white wine
1/2 cup fat-free, lower-sodium chicken broth
2 teaspoons honey
2 teaspoons butter

1. Heat a large skillet over medium-high heat. Add oil to pan; swirl to coat. Sprinkle chops with salt and pepper. Add chops to pan; cook 3 minutes on each side or until done. Remove chops from pan; keep warm. Add shallots, thyme, and peaches to pan; cook 2 minutes. Stir in wine, scraping pan to loosen browned bits; bring to a boil. Cook until reduced to 1/3 cup (about 2 minutes). Stir in broth and honey; bring to a boil. Cook until reduced to 1/3 cup (about 2 minutes). Remove from heat; stir in butter. Spoon sauce over chops. Yield: 4 servings (serving size: 1 chop, 4 peach wedges, and about 1 1/2 tablespoons broth mixture).

CALORIES 235; **FAT** 8.6g (sat 2.8g, mono 3.7g, poly 0.8g); **PROTEIN** 26.2g; **CARB** 13.6g; **FIBER** 1.1g, **CHOL** 83mg; **IRON** 1.3mg; **SODIUM** 433mg; **CALC** 26mg

Quick & Easy • Kid Friendly

Beef and Mushroom Sloppy Joes

Cremini offer deeper, richer flavor, but you can also use regular button mushrooms.

1 tablespoon olive oil
12 ounces ground sirloin
2 (8-ounce) packages presliced cremini mushrooms
1 cup prechopped onion
3 garlic cloves, minced
1/2 cup no-salt-added tomato paste
1 tablespoon minced fresh oregano
2 tablespoons red wine vinegar
2 tablespoons Worcestershire sauce
1 tablespoon molasses
1/4 teaspoon salt
3/4 teaspoon freshly ground black pepper
1/2 teaspoon hot sauce
4 (2-ounce) Kaiser rolls or hamburger buns, toasted

1. Heat a large nonstick skillet over medium-high heat. Add oil; swirl to coat. Add beef; cook 4 minutes or until browned, stirring to crumble.
2. While beef cooks, place mushrooms in a food processor; pulse 10 times or until finely chopped. Add mushrooms, onion, and garlic to pan; cook 3 minutes or until onion is tender. Add tomato paste and next 5 ingredients to pan; cook 5 minutes or until mushrooms are tender and liquid evaporates. Stir in pepper and hot sauce. Spoon about 1 cup beef mixture on bottom half of each bun; top with top halves of buns. Yield: 4 servings (serving size: 1 sandwich).

CALORIES 439; **FAT** 14.7g (sat 4.6g, mono 6.8g, poly 1.9g); **PROTEIN** 27.3g; **CARB** 49.2g; **FIBER** 4g; **CHOL** 55mg; **IRON** 6.1mg; **SODIUM** 618mg; **CALC** 160mg

Quick Shrimp Chowder

Quick & Easy • Kid Friendly

2 cups organic vegetable broth
2 teaspoons minced fresh thyme
½ teaspoon freshly ground black pepper
1 tablespoon olive oil
½ cup prechopped carrot
½ cup prechopped onion
¼ cup prechopped celery
2 tablespoons all-purpose flour
1 pound peeled and deveined medium shrimp
⅓ cup heavy whipping cream

1. Pour broth into a 2-cup glass measure. Microwave at MEDIUM-HIGH 1 minute.
2. Combine broth, thyme, and black pepper in a large saucepan over medium-high heat, and simmer.
3. Heat a medium skillet over medium-high heat. Add oil to pan; swirl to coat. Add carrot, onion, and celery; sauté 3 minutes or until tender. Add flour, stirring with a whisk. Stir carrot mixture and shrimp into broth mixture. Cover; simmer 5 minutes. Stir in cream; cover and simmer 4 minutes. Yield: 4 servings (serving size: 1¼ cups).

Be sure to buy U.S. wild-caught or farmed shrimp for the best sustainable option.

Sustainable Choice

CALORIES 258; **FAT** 12.9g (sat 5.5g, mono 4.9g, poly 1.4g); **PROTEIN** 24.3g; **CARB** 9.9g; **FIBER** 1.1g; **CHOL** 200mg; **IRON** 3.1mg; **SODIUM** 478mg; **CALC** 88mg

Quick & Easy

Chicken Puttanesca

Serve with angel hair pasta.

1½ tablespoons olive oil, divided
4 (4-ounce) skinless, boneless chicken breast cutlets
¼ cup minced fresh onion
3 garlic cloves, minced
2 cups chopped tomato
¼ cup sliced green olives
1 tablespoon chopped fresh oregano
1½ teaspoons capers, chopped
½ teaspoon crushed red pepper
¼ teaspoon salt
1 canned anchovy fillet, chopped

1. Heat a large nonstick skillet over medium-high heat. Add 1 tablespoon oil to pan; swirl to coat. Add chicken to pan; cook 5 minutes or until done, turning once. Remove chicken from pan; keep warm. Add remaining 1½ teaspoons oil, onion, and garlic; sauté 1 minute. Add tomato and next 6 ingredients. Bring to a simmer, and cook 9 minutes or until sauce is slightly thickened, stirring occasionally. Serve chicken with tomato mixture. Yield: 4 servings (serving size: 1 chicken cutlet and about ⅓ cup tomato mixture).

CALORIES 241; **FAT** 9.9g (sat 1.1g, mono 5.8g, poly 1.5g); **PROTEIN** 30.9g; **CARB** 6.6g; **FIBER** 1.4g; **CHOL** 87mg; **IRON** 1.2mg; **SODIUM** 602mg; **CALC** 33mg

Quick & Easy

Pineapple Chicken Satay

¼ cup lower-sodium soy sauce
¼ cup sweet chili sauce
¼ cup natural-style, crunchy peanut butter
2 teaspoons peanut oil
½ teaspoon curry powder
1 pound chicken breast tenders, cut lengthwise into 8 pieces
Cooking spray
1½ cups diced pineapple
⅓ cup vertically sliced red onion
2 tablespoons chopped fresh cilantro
2 tablespoons fresh lime juice
⅛ teaspoon ground red pepper

1. Combine first 3 ingredients in a bowl, stirring with a whisk.
2. Place peanut oil, curry powder, and chicken in a bowl, and toss to coat. Thread chicken onto 8 (6-inch) skewers.
3. Heat a grill pan over medium-high heat. Coat pan with cooking spray. Add chicken to pan; cook 4 minutes on each side or until chicken is done.
4. While chicken cooks, combine 1½ cups pineapple, ⅓ cup red onion, 2 tablespoons cilantro, 2 tablespoons lime juice, and ⅛ teaspoon ground red pepper. Serve chicken with soy sauce mixture and pineapple mixture. Yield: 4 servings (serving size: 2 skewers, about ⅓ cup pineapple mixture, and about 3 tablespoons soy sauce mixture).

CALORIES 330; **FAT** 11.9g (sat 1.8g, mono 5.4g, poly 3.4g); **PROTEIN** 31.2g; **CARB** 22.7g; **FIBER** 2.2g; **CHOL** 66mg; **IRON** 1.4mg; **SODIUM** 528mg; **CALC** 28mg

Quick & Easy • Kid Friendly
Vegetarian

Microwave Smashed Potatoes

4 (6-ounce) baking potatoes, peeled and cut into 1-inch pieces
½ cup reduced-fat sour cream
½ cup 1% low-fat milk
2 tablespoons minced fresh chives
½ teaspoon salt
½ teaspoon freshly ground black pepper

1. Place potato pieces in a large microwave-safe bowl. Cover bowl with plastic wrap; cut a 1-inch slit in center of plastic wrap. Microwave at HIGH 10 minutes. Let stand 2 minutes. Add sour cream and remaining ingredients to bowl; mash with a potato masher. Yield: 4 servings (serving size: about 1 cup).

CALORIES 225; **FAT** 4.1g (sat 2.5g, mono 1.1g, poly 0.2g); **PROTEIN** 5.6g; **CARB** 42.6g; **FIBER** 2.8g; **CHOL** 13mg; **IRON** 0.8mg; **SODIUM** 333mg; **CALC** 78mg

Southwest Variation:

Omit sour cream and chives; decrease milk to 2 tablespoons and salt to ¼ teaspoon. Add ¾ cup plain low-fat yogurt; 1 tablespoon chopped chipotle chile, canned in adobo sauce; and ¼ teaspoon ground cumin. Yield: 4 servings (serving size: about 1 cup).

CALORIES 206; **FAT** 1g (sat 0.6g); **SODIUM** 236mg

Roasted Garlic Variation:

You can find roasted garlic cloves at the salad bar in many grocery stores. Omit sour cream and chives; increase milk to ¾ cup. Add ¼ cup coarsely chopped roasted garlic cloves and 1 tablespoon chopped fresh sage. Yield: 4 servings (serving size: about 1 cup).

CALORIES 223; **FAT** 2.9g (sat 0.7g); **SODIUM** 329mg

Bacon and Cheddar Variation:
Decrease salt to ¼ teaspoon. Add ¼ cup (1 ounce) reduced-fat shredded extrasharp cheddar cheese and 1 slice center-cut bacon, cooked and crumbled; mash with a potato masher to desired consistency. Yield: 4 servings (serving size: about 1 cup).

CALORIES 254; **FAT** 6.1g (sat 3.7g); **SODIUM** 280mg

Quick & Easy
Shrimp and Arugula Salad

The white balsamic won't discolor the shrimp or bright veggies. For something a little sharper, substitute white wine vinegar.

4 cups loosely packed baby arugula
1 cup (¼ x 3-inch) julienne-cut red bell pepper
½ cup matchstick-cut carrot
3 tablespoons extra-virgin olive oil, divided
2 teaspoons minced fresh rosemary
½ teaspoon crushed red pepper
2 garlic cloves, thinly sliced
16 large shrimp, peeled and deveined (about ¾ pound)
3 tablespoons white balsamic vinegar

1. Combine first 3 ingredients in a large bowl.
2. Heat a large skillet over medium heat. Add 2 tablespoons oil to pan; swirl to coat. Add rosemary, red pepper, and garlic to pan; cook 2 minutes or until garlic is tender, stirring constantly. Increase heat to medium-high. Add shrimp to pan; sauté 6 minutes or until shrimp are done. Remove shrimp mixture from pan. Add remaining 1 tablespoon oil and vinegar to pan; cook 15 seconds. Drizzle warm vinegar mixture over arugula mixture; toss gently to coat. Divide arugula mixture among 4 plates; top with shrimp. Serve immediately. Yield: 4 servings (serving size: 1 cup arugula mixture and 4 shrimp).

CALORIES 208; **FAT** 12g (sat 1.7g, mono 7.6g, poly 1.8g); **PROTEIN** 18.5g; **CARB** 6.9g; **FIBER** 1.5g; **CHOL** 129mg; **IRON** 2.7mg; **SODIUM** 149mg; **CALC** 101mg

¡TACO! ¡TACO!

A simple plan for some grown-up fun: 2 tacos, 2 toppings, and a fab margarita = one great party

MIX & MATCH TACO MENU

serves 6
Blackberry Margaritas
+
Baked Black Beans with Chorizo
+
Flank Steak Tacos
+
Chimichurri Halibut Tacos
+
Cabbage Slaw
+
Grilled Pineapple-Avocado Salsa

Quick & Easy • Make Ahead
Blackberry Margaritas

Hands-on time: 30 min. Total time: 30 min.

Combine 1½ tablespoons granulated sugar and ½ teaspoon kosher salt in a dish. Cut 1 lime into 9 wedges; rub rims of 8 glasses with 1 lime wedge. Dip rims of glasses in salt mixture. Combine 1 cup water and ½ cup sugar in a microwave-safe glass measuring cup. Microwave at HIGH 2½ minutes, stirring to dissolve sugar; cool. Combine syrup, 1 cup 100% agave blanco tequila, ¾ cup Grand Marnier, ⅔ cup fresh lime juice, and 12 ounces fresh blackberries in a blender; process until smooth. Strain mixture through a cheesecloth-lined sieve over a pitcher; discard solids. Serve over ice. Garnish with remaining lime wedges. Yield: 8 servings (serving size: about ½ cup).

CALORIES 204; **FAT** 0.2g (sat 0g); **SODIUM** 121mg

Kid Friendly
Flank Steak Tacos

Hands-on time: 30 min. Total time: 2 hr. 30 min.

2 tablespoons olive oil
2¼ teaspoons hot paprika
2¼ teaspoons ground cumin
1½ teaspoons dark brown sugar
½ teaspoon Spanish smoked paprika
½ teaspoon ground red pepper
¼ teaspoon celery seeds
3 garlic cloves, minced
1 (1½-pound) flank steak, trimmed
1 teaspoon kosher salt
½ teaspoon black pepper
Cooking spray
12 (6-inch) corn tortillas

1. Combine first 8 ingredients. Rub steak evenly with spice mixture. Cover and refrigerate at least 2 hours.
2. Preheat grill to high heat.
3. Sprinkle steak evenly with 1 teaspoon salt and black pepper. Place steak on grill rack coated with cooking spray, and grill 6 minutes on each side or until desired degree of doneness. Remove steak from grill, and let stand 10 minutes. Cut steak across grain into thin slices. Heat tortillas according to package directions. Divide steak evenly among tortillas. Yield: 6 servings (serving size: 2 tacos).

CALORIES 256; **FAT** 10.7g (sat 2.4g, mono 5g, poly 1.2g); **PROTEIN** 20.9g; **CARB** 20.7g; **FIBER** 2.8g; **CHOL** 28mg; **IRON** 2mg; **SODIUM** 380mg; **CALC** 54mg

WELL AHEAD:
Shop for nonperishable items, and order specialty products.

2 DAYS BEFORE:
Prepare and assemble black beans, omitting green onions.
Make Pineapple-Avocado Salsa, omitting avocado.

1 DAY BEFORE:
Prepare margaritas.
Cut lime wedges for margaritas.
Chop green onions for beans.
Marinate flank steak.
Prepare chimichurri (do not add fish).
Slice cabbage, radish, and green onions.

2 HOURS BEFORE:
Coat the rims of margarita glasses.
Marinate fish.
Add juice and oil to slaw; toss.

JUST BEFORE GUESTS ARRIVE:
Bake black beans.
Grill beef; let stand at room temperature (unsliced) until ready to serve.

WHEN YOU'RE READY TO SERVE:
Grill fish; break into chunks.
Garnish beans.
Warm tortillas.
Slice steak.
Stir mint, salt, and pepper into slaw.
Chop avocado; stir into salsa.

Quick & Easy • Make Ahead
Vegetarian

Cabbage Slaw

Hands-on time: 15 min. Total time: 15 min.

4 cups shredded cabbage
1½ cups thinly sliced radishes
½ cup diagonally cut green onions
3 tablespoons olive oil
2 tablespoons fresh lemon juice
⅓ cup chopped fresh mint
½ teaspoon salt
¼ teaspoon ground red pepper

1. Combine first 5 ingredients; toss. Sprinkle with mint, salt, and pepper. Yield: 6 servings (serving size: ½ cup).

CALORIES 81; **FAT** 6.9g (sat 1g, mono 4.9g, poly 0.8g);
PROTEIN 1g; **CARB** 5g; **FIBER** 2g; **CHOL** 0mg;
IRON 0.6mg; **SODIUM** 218mg; **CALC** 36mg

Make Ahead

Baked Black Beans with Chorizo

Hands-on time: 35 min. Total time: 1 hr. 5 min.

Serve this versatile dish warm or at room temperature as a tasty side to accompany the tacos or as a dip with chips.

1 tablespoon olive oil
½ cup diced Spanish chorizo
Cooking spray
1½ cups chopped onion
1 jalapeño pepper, sliced
½ teaspoon salt
½ teaspoon ground cumin
¼ teaspoon ground red pepper
5 garlic cloves, minced
¾ cup fat-free, lower-sodium chicken broth
2 (15-ounce) cans no-salt-added black beans, rinsed and drained
1 cup chopped seeded tomato
½ cup (2 ounces) shredded Monterey Jack cheese
¼ cup thinly sliced green onions

1. Preheat oven to 425°.
2. Heat a large nonstick skillet over medium-high heat. Add oil to pan; swirl to coat. Add chorizo; sauté 2 minutes. Remove chorizo from pan. Coat pan with cooking spray. Add onion and jalapeño; sauté 4 minutes, stirring occasionally. Add salt, cumin, red pepper, and garlic; sauté 1 minute, stirring constantly. Stir in broth and beans; bring to a boil. Cook 5 minutes. Mash to desired consistency. Spoon bean mixture into an 8-inch square baking dish coated with cooking spray.
3. Top with chorizo, tomato, and cheese. Bake at 425° for 30 minutes or until lightly browned. Top with green onions. Yield: 6 servings (serving size: about ½ cup).

CALORIES 189; **FAT** 8.4g (sat 3g, mono 3.6g, poly 0.7g);
PROTEIN 10.2g; **CARB** 19.4g; **FIBER** 6.2g; **CHOL** 8mg;
IRON 1.7mg; **SODIUM** 307mg; **CALC** 142mg

Vegetarian

Grilled Pineapple-Avocado Salsa

Hands-on time: 25 min. Total time: 25 min.

1 tablespoon olive oil
1 tablespoon honey
1 pineapple, peeled, cored, and cut into ½-inch-thick slices
Cooking spray
⅓ cup finely chopped red onion
¼ cup minced fresh cilantro
1 tablespoon fresh lime juice
½ teaspoon salt
½ teaspoon ground red pepper
¼ teaspoon ground cumin
1 serrano chile, minced
1 avocado

1. Preheat grill to high heat.
2. Combine oil and honey, stirring well. Brush oil mixture over pineapple. Place pineapple on grill rack coated with cooking spray; grill 2 minutes on each side or until golden. Remove from grill; cool 5 minutes. Chop. Combine pineapple, onion, and next 6 ingredients; toss gently.
3. Peel, seed, and dice avocado. Add avocado to pineapple mixture, and toss gently. Yield: 6 servings (serving size: ½ cup).

CALORIES 166; **FAT** 7.5g (sat 1.1g, mono 5g, poly 0.9g);
PROTEIN 1.7g; **CARB** 26.8g; **FIBER** 4.6g; **CHOL** 0mg;
IRON 0.7mg; **SODIUM** 201mg; **CALC** 27mg

SET OUT THE FIXINGS AND LET THE GUESTS MAKE THEIR OWN CREATIVE COMBOS.

Chimichurri Halibut Tacos

Hands-on time: 25 min. Total time: 2 hr. 25 min.

2 cups fresh flat-leaf parsley leaves
2 tablespoons fresh oregano
3/4 teaspoon ground cumin
1/4 teaspoon ground red pepper
5 garlic cloves, crushed
1/3 cup extra-virgin olive oil
5 (6-ounce) halibut fillets
1 teaspoon kosher salt
1/2 teaspoon black pepper
Cooking spray
12 (6-inch) corn tortillas

1. Place first 5 ingredients in a food processor; process until finely chopped. Slowly pour oil through food chute; process until smooth. Place fish in a shallow dish; rub mixture over fish. Cover and chill 2 hours.
2. Preheat grill to high heat.
3. Sprinkle fish with salt and black pepper. Place fish on grill rack coated with cooking spray, and grill for 4 minutes on each side or until desired degree of doneness. Remove from grill. Break fish into chunks. Heat tortillas according to package directions. Divide fish evenly among tortillas. Yield: 6 servings (serving size: 2 tacos).

Sustainable Choice | *Wild-caught Alaskan halibut is the best option. If it's not available, opt for other U.S. or Canadian wild-caught Pacific halibut, or substitute striped bass or U.S. line-caught cod.*

CALORIES 266; **FAT** 10.4g (sat 1.3g, mono 5.8g, poly 2g); **PROTEIN** 24.6g; **CARB** 19.8g; **FIBER** 2.6g; **CHOL** 34mg; **IRON** 1.6mg; **SODIUM** 394mg; **CALC** 93mg

OOPS! INCINERATING CHICKEN ON THE GRILL

How to avoid a backyard poultry flame-out.
By Tim Cebula

Grilling bone-in, skin-on chicken breasts feels like it should be simple enough. Even experienced grillers often try to cook them entirely over direct heat, figuring it's just a matter of timing. At which point dripping fat causes flare-ups that engulf the breasts, charring the skin while the meat remains rare deep within. Yet perfectly grilled chicken—with crisp, browned skin and juicy, succulent meat—is relatively simple if you learn to manipulate the heat.

First, establish two temperature zones: Set one side of a gas grill to medium-high and the other to low, or build a fire on one side of a charcoal grill. (Make sure your grate is clean and oiled to prevent sticking.) Start the chicken skin side up on the low- or no-heat side, and cover the grill. After a few minutes, when the chicken fat starts to render, flip the meat skin side down. Point the breasts' thicker ends toward the hot side to help them cook evenly. Cover and grill for about 25 minutes. When the meat is done (165° at the thickest part of the breast), crisp the skin on the hot side for a minute or two, moving it as needed to avoid flare-ups. Wait until the last few minutes to brush on barbecue sauce: The sugars in the sauce will char quickly.

(indirect heat)

(flamethrower?)

FROM YOUR KITCHEN TO OURS

When Daniel Croddy moved from California to Maine, he found the local Mexican food lacking the zip and zing he was used to back home. "New Englanders are not fond of hot spice," he says, wistfully. To get his fiery fix, Croddy turned to developing his favorite Mexican recipes at home. One of his favorites is a lighter, quicker chile rellenos recipe with a pan-seared (instead of deep-fried) chile—a party pleaser with plenty of heat.

Vegetarian

Chiles Rellenos Made Easy

Hands-on time: 43 min. Total time: 1 hr. 6 min.

"Using the green salsa bypasses toasting and peeling fresh tomatillos, which can take up time."
— Daniel Croddy, Portland, Maine

Cooking spray
1¼ cups coarsely chopped onion
2 cups chopped tomatoes
½ cup low-sodium salsa verde
¼ teaspoon salt
¼ cup fresh cilantro
4 poblano chiles
1 cup (4 ounces) shredded reduced-fat
   Monterey Jack cheese, divided
2 tablespoons goat cheese, divided
3 large egg yolks
3 large egg whites
1.1 ounces all-purpose flour (about ¼ cup)
¼ teaspoon freshly ground black pepper
3 tablespoons cornmeal
¼ cup canola oil

1. Preheat broiler to high.
2. Heat a large skillet over medium-high heat. Coat pan with cooking spray. Add onion; sauté 4 minutes or until tender. Stir in chopped tomatoes,

4 STEPS TO CHILES RELLENOS

Roasted fresh chiles stuffed with cheese are gooey-char-wonderful. Follow these steps to keep cooked, softened chiles whole and their stems intact.

1. Broil poblanos until charred, and then steam in a bag and slip off skins.

2. Cut a slit into each chile. Take your time carefully removing seeds; leave stems intact.

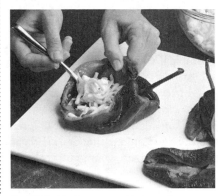
3. Stuff with cheese; coat in breading.

4. Turn gently to keep crunchy coating from falling off.

salsa verde, and ¼ teaspoon salt; cook 15 minutes or until thick, stirring frequently. Place tomato mixture in a food processor; add cilantro. Process mixture until smooth. Set aside.
3. Place poblanos on a foil-lined baking sheet; broil 3 inches from heat 8 minutes or until blackened and charred, turning after 6 minutes. Place in a paper bag; fold to close tightly. Let stand 15 minutes. Peel and discard skins. Cut a lengthwise slit in each chile; discard seeds, leaving stems intact. Spoon ¼ cup Jack cheese and 1½ teaspoons goat cheese into cavity of each chile.
4. Preheat oven to 350°.
5. Lightly beat egg yolks in a small bowl. Place egg whites in a medium bowl; beat with a mixer at high speed until stiff peaks form. Fold egg yolks

into egg whites. Combine flour and black pepper in a shallow dish. Place cornmeal in another shallow dish. Dredge poblanos in flour mixture, and dip into egg mixture. Dredge in cornmeal.
6. Heat oil in a large stainless-steel skillet over medium-high heat until hot; reduce heat to medium. Add coated poblanos to oil; cook 6 minutes or until crisp, turning to cook on all sides. Place chiles on a baking sheet, and bake at 350° for 8 minutes or until cheese melts. Serve with tomato sauce. Yield: 4 servings (serving size: 1 chile and about ⅓ cup sauce).

CALORIES 297; **FAT** 14.8g (sat 5.8g, mono 4.1g, poly 1.8g); **PROTEIN** 16.1g; **CARB** 25.6g; **FIBER** 2.7g; **CHOL** 159mg; **IRON** 1.9mg; **SODIUM** 562mg; **CALC** 254mg

PLUM WONDERFUL

Turn one of summer's more humble fruits into dazzling salads, sauces, drinks, and sweet-tart desserts.

Stone fruits of all sorts jumble the farm stands each summer, none more diverse than the puckery-sweet but curiously neglected plum. The plum ranges from inky purple to burnished gold in color. Its flesh may be anything from astringent to syrupy sweet—sometimes in the same single fruit—and its diversity makes it as versatile as, say, the apple. Yet we Americans mostly like our plums fresh and don't cook them as often as we should.

Others know better. In China, crisp-skinned roast duck is often served with thick, spiced sweet-and-sour plum sauce. Salted, dried plums are an almost shockingly sour Chinese snack. Eastern Europeans will use almost anything to make a dumpling, and no exception is made for the plum, which is coddled in a pillow of potato dough, boiled to create a hot, syrupy fruit filling, and then rolled in sugary breadcrumbs and even sautéed in butter for good measure. Plums are also distilled into *slivovitz*, a singe-your-hair firewater. There's a more delicate French plum *eau-de-vie*, too.

Probably the most famous American plum dish is Marian Burros' plum torte, published in 1983 in *The New York Times* and one of the paper's most requested recipes. Tart prune plums sink into a thick batter that becomes almost cookie-crunchy in the oven. Our own Plum Kuchen echoes the pleasures of that dish.

Make Ahead • Kid Friendly
Plum Kuchen

Hands-on time: 35 min. Total time: 1 hr. 10 min.

Almost any slightly firm plum will work in this lovely cake. In fact, we prefer a mix of black, red, and yellow fruit for contrasting flavor and color.

6.75 ounces all-purpose flour (about 1½ cups)
⅔ cup plus 2 tablespoons granulated sugar, divided
2 tablespoons brown sugar
1 teaspoon baking powder
⅜ teaspoon salt, divided
⅛ teaspoon ground cardamom
7 tablespoons butter, divided
½ cup fat-free milk
½ teaspoon vanilla extract
1 large egg
Cooking spray
1½ pounds plums, quartered and pitted
1 teaspoon grated lemon rind
¼ teaspoon ground allspice

1. Preheat oven to 425°.
2. Weigh or lightly spoon flour into dry measuring cups; level with a knife. Combine flour, 2 tablespoons granulated sugar, brown sugar, baking powder, ¼ teaspoon salt, and cardamom in a medium bowl, stirring well with a whisk. Cut in 4 tablespoons butter with a pastry blender or 2 knives until mixture resembles coarse meal.
3. Combine milk, vanilla, and egg in a bowl, stirring with a whisk. Add milk mixture to flour mixture, and stir until just combined.
4. Spoon batter into a 9-inch round metal cake pan coated with cooking spray. Arrange plums in a circular pattern over batter.
5. Combine remaining ⅔ cup granulated sugar, remaining ⅛ teaspoon salt, lemon rind, and allspice in a small bowl, stirring well. Place remaining 3 tablespoons butter in a microwave-safe bowl. Microwave at HIGH 30 seconds or until butter melts. Stir into sugar mixture. Sprinkle plums evenly with sugar mixture. Bake at 425° for 35 minutes or until browned and bubbling. Cool in pan 1 hour on a wire rack. Cut into wedges. Yield: 10 servings (serving size: 1 wedge).

CALORIES 256; FAT 8.7g (sat 5.3g, mono 2.3g, poly 0.5g); PROTEIN 3.6g; CARB 42.5g; FIBER 1.5g; CHOL 40mg; IRON 1.2mg; SODIUM 144mg; CALC 48mg

---

PLUM THE PARTY!

We asked ourselves: With everything from mangoes to blackberries finding their way into summer cocktails, doesn't the plum deserve a moment in the sun? Result: a fresh plum Bellini and a gingery drink based on plum sake.

FIZZY PLUM BELLINI
Combine ½ cup water, 3 tablespoons sugar, and 2 pitted, quartered ripe red-skinned plums in a medium saucepan over medium-high heat; bring to a boil. Cook 5 minutes, stirring occasionally. Remove from heat; cool completely. Strain syrup through a sieve over a bowl; reserve plums. Stir 1 tablespoon eau-de-vie or brandy into syrup; chill. Discard plum skins; puree flesh until smooth. Chill puree. Spoon 2 teaspoons puree into each of 6 flutes; discard remaining puree. Divide syrup evenly among glasses. Top each serving with ⅓ cup prosecco; stir. Yield: 6 servings.

CALORIES 94; FAT 0.1g (sat 0g); SODIUM 0mg

SWEET & SOUR PLUM QUENCHER
Thinly slice 1 lime; place in a cocktail shaker. Add 2 ounces cachaça, 6 thin ginger slices, and 6 fresh mint leaves; muddle. Add 6 ounces Japanese plum sake and ice to shaker. Cover and shake 30 seconds. Strain and divide mixture evenly between 2 glasses. Float 1 ounce sparkling rosé wine atop each serving. Garnish with a thin plum slice. Yield: 2 servings.

CALORIES 214; FAT 0g; SODIUM 2mg

RETURN OF THE PLUMS

America's romance with heirloom produce means more plum varieties each year. Flavorful light-skinned plums—like Greengage—had been mostly replaced by larger, darker fruits, which hide bruises. And because they're often harvested before ripe, they sometimes lack flavor. Happily, more interesting varieties are making a comeback.

BLACKAMBER: A popular American commercial variety with black skin and light-yellow flesh. If you can find tree-ripened ones, they will be sweet and tasty.

DAMSON: One of the more tart varieties, these purple-skinned plums are popular in cooked applications, such as jam or stewed fruit.

ELEPHANT HEART: With mottled brownish-gold skin, this ruby red–fleshed fruit is so juicy when ripe that it's almost drinkable. The flavor is tropical with a hint of vanilla.

FRENCH PRUNE: Compact purple European-style plums—about the size of a large walnut—that are deliciously sweet when soft, deliciously tart when firm. Also often called sugar plums.

FRIAR: Another popular variety in American supermarkets. Inky black skin and light flesh; taste best when picked fully ripe.

GREENGAGE: This superior European variety is rare. The fruit is small with greenish-yellow speckled skin and fantastic honey-sweet flesh.

MIRABELLE: Small yellow-crimson blushed plums used to make French plum eau-de-vie. Intensely sweet, these plums are good raw or cooked.

MYROBALAN (CHERRY PLUMS): Sweet plums the size of cherry tomatoes. Their skin can be red, yellow, or purple.

SANTA ROSA: Another deliciously sweet-tart plum that can be hard to find. Crimson skin with blondish-amber flesh.

SATSUMA: Not to be confused with the mandarin orange of the same name, these are meaty-fleshed, sweet plums with deep red flesh. Often called blood plum.

Vegetarian
Yellow Plum Salad
(pictured on page 227)

Hands-on time: 29 min. Total time: 2 hr. 2 min.

Serve it with grilled chicken, pork, steaks, or seafood.

2 yellow bell peppers
4 golden beets (about 12 ounces)
2½ tablespoons extra-virgin olive oil
1 tablespoon white wine vinegar
1 tablespoon chopped fresh chives
1 teaspoon chopped fresh thyme
1 teaspoon Dijon mustard
¼ teaspoon salt
⅛ teaspoon freshly ground black pepper
8 yellow-fleshed plums, halved and pitted (about 1 pound)
½ pint yellow pear tomatoes, halved lengthwise
½ cup (2 ounces) crumbled goat cheese

1. Preheat broiler to high.
2. Cut bell peppers in half lengthwise; discard seeds and membranes. Place pepper halves, skin sides up, on a foil-lined baking sheet; flatten with hand. Broil 13 minutes or until blackened. Place in a paper bag, and fold tightly to seal. Let stand 20 minutes. Peel and cut bell peppers into ½-inch-thick strips.
3. Preheat oven to 450°.
4. Leave root and 1-inch stem on beets; scrub with a brush. Place beets in an 11 x 7–inch glass or ceramic baking dish. Add 1 inch of water to dish; cover tightly with foil. Bake at 450° for 1 hour or until tender. Cool; peel and cut into ½-inch-thick slices.
5. Combine olive oil and next 6 ingredients in a small bowl, stirring well with a whisk. Place sliced beets in a medium bowl. Drizzle beets with 3 tablespoons vinaigrette; toss gently. Let stand at least 15 minutes. Divide beets evenly among 6 salad plates, and top each serving evenly with peppers, plums, and tomatoes. Drizzle with remaining vinaigrette. Sprinkle evenly with cheese. Yield: 6 servings.

CALORIES 158; FAT 8g (sat 2.2g, mono 4.6g, poly 0.7g); PROTEIN 4.2g; CARB 20.2g; FIBER 3.5g; CHOL 4mg; IRON 1.4mg; SODIUM 194mg; CALC 35mg

---

Roast Pork Tenderloin with Plum Barbecue Sauce

Hands-on time: 15 min. Total time: 1 hr. 5 min.

Asian spices give this barbecue sauce a complex flavor, which enhances the sweet-tart flavor of the plums. Once it's cooked, set aside 2½ cups sauce to serve with the pork, and use the remaining sauce to baste the pork as it cooks.

Sauce:
2 tablespoons canola oil
1 cup chopped onion
2 garlic cloves, finely chopped
¼ cup packed brown sugar
¼ cup rice wine vinegar
¼ cup ketchup
2 tablespoons lower-sodium soy sauce
2 teaspoons dry mustard
1 teaspoon ground ginger
½ teaspoon black pepper
⅛ teaspoon crushed red pepper
2 whole cloves
1½ pounds black plums, quartered and pitted
1 star anise
Pork:
2 tablespoons canola oil
2 (1-pound) pork tenderloins, trimmed
½ teaspoon salt
½ teaspoon freshly ground black pepper

1. Heat a large saucepan over medium-high heat. Add 2 tablespoons canola oil to pan, and swirl to coat. Add onion and garlic; sauté 5 minutes, stirring constantly. Add sugar and next 10 ingredients; bring to a boil. Reduce heat, and simmer, partially covered, 30 minutes or until plums break down and sauce thickens, stirring occasionally. Discard cloves and anise.
2. Preheat oven to 450°.
3. Heat a large skillet over medium-high heat. Add 2 tablespoons oil to pan; swirl to coat. Sprinkle pork evenly with ½ teaspoon salt and ½ teaspoon black pepper. Add pork to pan; sauté 7 minutes, turning to brown on all sides.
4. Transfer pork to a foil-lined jelly-roll pan; coat with ½ cup plum sauce. Roast pork at 450° for 15 minutes. Remove pork from oven. Turn pork over; coat

with an additional ½ cup plum sauce. Roast 10 minutes or until a thermometer inserted in thickest portion of pork registers 155°. Remove from pan; let stand 10 minutes. Slice crosswise. Serve with remaining plum sauce. Yield: 8 servings (serving size: 3 ounces pork and about ⅓ cup sauce).

CALORIES 378; FAT 10.3g (sat 1.6g, mono 5.6g, poly 2.4g); PROTEIN 25.2g; CARB 50.7g; FIBER 4.7g; CHOL 62mg; IRON 2mg; SODIUM 417mg; CALC 22mg

Make Ahead • Kid Friendly

Stone Fruit Cobbler

Hands-on time: 45 min. Total time: 4 hr. 55 min.

Tender and buttery, this cobbler's crust is a nice foil for the intense filling. You can bake in any 2-quart baking dish, from round to rectangular. For a special treat (and an extra 55 calories and half a gram of saturated fat), top with a small scoop of vanilla low-fat ice cream.

Crust:
9 ounces all-purpose flour (about 2 cups)
1 tablespoon sugar
½ teaspoon salt
6 tablespoons butter
2 teaspoons fresh lemon juice
4 to 5 tablespoons ice water
Filling:
1¼ cups sugar
6 tablespoons all-purpose flour
½ teaspoon salt
½ teaspoon ground nutmeg
¼ teaspoon ground allspice
2½ pounds red plums, pitted and cut into
    ½-inch-thick slices
2 peaches (about 1 pound), pitted and cut into
    ½-inch-thick slices
1 tablespoon butter, melted
½ teaspoon vanilla extract
Remaining ingredients:
Cooking spray
2 teaspoons fat-free milk
1 tablespoon sugar

1. Weigh or lightly spoon 9 ounces flour into dry measuring cups, and level with a knife. Combine flour, 1 tablespoon sugar, and ½ teaspoon salt in a bowl; cut in 6 tablespoons butter with a pastry blender or 2 knives until mixture resembles

coarse meal. Sprinkle surface with juice and ice water, 1 tablespoon at a time; toss with a fork until moist and crumbly (do not form a ball). Gently press two-thirds of dough into a 4-inch circle on plastic wrap, and cover. Press remaining dough into a 4-inch circle on plastic wrap, and cover. Chill 3 hours or overnight.
2. Preheat oven to 425°. Place a foil-lined baking sheet on middle rack.
3. To prepare filling, combine 1¼ cups sugar and next 4 ingredients in a small bowl, stirring with a whisk. Combine plums and peaches in a large bowl; sprinkle flour mixture over plum mixture. Drizzle with melted butter and vanilla; toss gently.
4. Working with large portion, roll dough out on a lightly floured surface into a 13 x 9–inch rectangle. Fit into a 2-quart glass or ceramic baking dish coated with cooking spray. Spoon plum mixture into crust. Roll remaining portion of dough into an 11 x 7–inch rectangle. Cut dough lengthwise into ½-inch-thick strips; arrange strips in a lattice design over plum mixture. Seal dough strips around edges of crust. Lightly brush strips with milk; sprinkle evenly with 1 tablespoon sugar. Place baking dish on preheated pan; bake at 425° for 20 minutes.
5. Reduce oven temperature to 375° (do not remove cobbler from oven). Bake 50 minutes or until crust is golden and filling is bubbly. Cool at least 1 hour. Yield: 12 servings (serving size: about ¾ cup).

CALORIES 301; FAT 7.1g (sat 4.3g, mono 1.8g, poly 0.4g); PROTEIN 3.7g; CARB 58g; FIBER 2.5g; CHOL 18mg; IRON 1.5mg; SODIUM 199mg; CALC 10mg

SAVORY SIDE: PLUMS WITH BEETS AND TOMATOES, OR COOKED TO A THICK SAUCE FOR PORK

Make Ahead • Freezable

Basil Plum Granita

Hands-on time: 20 min. Total time: 5 hr. 20 min.

Although complex black plums, with their winey flavor, taste and look spectacular in this refreshing granita, you can use most any variety.

1 cup water
⅔ cup sugar
¼ teaspoon vanilla extract
⅛ teaspoon salt
5 whole allspice
1½ pounds black plums, quartered and pitted
¾ cup fresh basil leaves
2 tablespoons fresh lime juice

1. Place first 6 ingredients in a large saucepan over medium-high heat; bring to a boil. Reduce heat; simmer 15 minutes or until plums begin to fall apart, stirring occasionally. Place pan in a large ice-filled bowl; cool completely, stirring occasionally. Discard allspice.
2. Place plum mixture, basil, and lime juice in a blender; process until well blended. Press plum mixture through a fine sieve over a bowl, and discard solids. Pour mixture into an 8-inch square glass or ceramic baking dish. Cover and freeze until partially frozen (about 2 hours). Scrape with a fork, crushing any lumps. Freeze, scraping with a fork every hour, 3 hours or until completely frozen. Yield: 4 servings (serving size: about 1 cup).

CALORIES 215; FAT 0.1g (sat 0g, mono 0g, poly 0.1g); PROTEIN 1.4g; CARB 56.3g; FIBER 2.7g; CHOL 0mg; IRON 0.7mg; SODIUM 74mg; CALC 19mg

FEAST OF THE PERFECT TOMATOES

By Mark Bittman

Use these juicy fruits as much as you can when they're at their peak. Often, you don't even have to peel or seed.

You can recognize a super-ripe tomato a mile away. Approach happily, and give it a squeeze: Your fingertips meet virtually no resistance. With a little more pressure, the fruit might turn to pulp in your hands. You can almost hear juice slosh around inside.

When tomatoes are this good, the more the merrier. Dishes at the peak of summer should spin around these meaty beasts, whether they're everyday beefsteak, plump cherries, or some gorgeous heirloom variety. And that's what we've got here: two main courses loaded with the red—or yellow, orange, or green—stuff.

Since I want to capture all that juice (and since I'm lazy), I don't bother to seed or peel perfect tomatoes. And I often leave them raw, or warm them ever so gently, coddling them so they retain their shape and texture. That's the trick in these two recipes.

The prep, then, is easy: Just core the tomatoes (cut a circle all the way around the top with a paring knife, creating a cone that pops right out), and then roughly chop and salt them. You want to make sure the pieces are big enough to chew a bit without becoming an unwieldy mouthful. The salt seasons the tomatoes and pulls out some of their watery juices. There's

flavor in that water, though, and it comes in handy as you can reduce the amount of olive oil in the dressing.

A little something starchy—in the form of whole grains—is the obvious choice to soak up this liquid. I like to use just enough starch to do the job, and then balance the carbohydrates with a full spectrum of flavors and lots of crisp textures. In these two dishes, still-warm pasta and toasted bread cubes absorb the liquid beautifully and lightly warm the tomatoes as you toss everything together, which intensifies their rich, fruity taste. Together the starch and the tomatoes meld to provide a backdrop for all sorts of other ingredients.

Tomatoes pair well with foods that play off their natural sweetness and acidity—sweet seafood like clams and shrimp (or other light, protein-rich food), sweet-tart balsamic vinegar, or tangy lemon juice. In Pasta with Fresh Tomato Sauce and Clams, the tomatoes are seasoned to become a vibrant raw sauce, developing in their own juices for a few minutes while you get the pasta ready. Drain the tomato liquid into the pan and use it to cook the clams, turning it into a rich sauce. A similar concept works to create the dressing for the herb-fueled Tomato Panzanella with Shrimp and Basil (a spin on the classic bread salad). What you're essentially doing is making two highly flavored warm tomato vinaigrettes.

Once you nail the concept, it's easy to change things up. Maybe the pasta becomes Asian noodles, like soba or rice sticks. And you use soy sauce for seasoning instead of salt, and swap sesame oil for olive oil. For the panzanella, try corn bread and cilantro to get something totally different but equally delicious—and satisfying. Funny how meaty tomatoes work their magic like that.

Quick & Easy

Pasta with Fresh Tomato Sauce and Clams

Hands-on time: 24 min. Total time: 32 min.

5 cups chopped tomato (about 4 large)
6½ tablespoons chopped fresh chives, divided
2½ tablespoons minced garlic, divided
1 tablespoon balsamic vinegar
¾ teaspoon kosher salt
½ teaspoon ground black pepper
2 quarts water
1 tablespoon kosher salt
8 ounces uncooked whole-wheat spaghetti or linguine
1 tablespoon butter
1 tablespoon olive oil
16 littleneck clams

1. Combine tomatoes, ⅓ cup chives, 1 tablespoon garlic, vinegar, ¾ teaspoon salt, and pepper in a large bowl; let stand 15 minutes. Drain mixture in a colander over a bowl, reserving liquid.
2. While tomatoes stand, bring 2 quarts water to a boil in a large saucepan. Add 1 tablespoon salt and pasta. Cook pasta 10 minutes or until al dente, and drain.
3. Heat butter, olive oil, and remaining 1½ tablespoons garlic in a large skillet over low heat; cook 4 minutes or until fragrant. Increase heat to medium-high. Add reserved tomato liquid, and bring to a boil; cook until reduced to ½ cup (about 6 minutes). Add clams; cover and cook 4 minutes or until shells open. Remove clams from pan, and discard any unopened shells. Add reserved tomato mixture and pasta to pan; cook 2 minutes or until thoroughly heated. Top with remaining chives. Yield: 4 servings (serving size: about 2 cups pasta mixture and 4 clams).

Sustainable Choice

Because they help filter the water in which they live, clams and other bivalves are sustainable superstars.

CALORIES 332; FAT 7.9g (sat 2.6g, mono 3.4g, poly 1.1g); PROTEIN 15.4g; CARB 55g; FIBER 10.2g; CHOL 20mg; IRON 8mg; SODIUM 563mg; CALC 79mg

Quick & Easy • Kid Friendly

Tomato Panzanella with Shrimp and Basil

Hands-on time: 23 min. Total time: 42 min.

Use multicolored tomatoes for a prettier plate.

4 cups (¾-inch) cubed whole-wheat French
 bread baguette (about 6 ounces)
5 cups ripe tomato wedges (about 4 large)
½ teaspoon kosher salt, divided
½ pound medium shrimp, peeled and
 deveined
¼ teaspoon freshly ground black pepper
2 tablespoons olive oil
¼ teaspoon crushed red pepper
6 garlic cloves, thinly sliced
1 tablespoon fresh lemon juice
1½ cups small fresh basil leaves

1. Preheat oven to 375°.
2. Place bread cubes on a jelly-roll pan.
Bake at 375° for 20 minutes or until
crisp and golden brown, turning cubes
once.
3. Combine tomatoes and ¼ teaspoon
salt in a large bowl. Sprinkle shrimp
with remaining ¼ teaspoon salt and
black pepper. Heat olive oil, red pepper,
and garlic in a large nonstick skillet
over low heat; cook 5 minutes or until
warm and fragrant. Increase heat to
medium-high. Add shrimp to pan; sauté 2 minutes or until shrimp are done,
stirring frequently. Stir in lemon juice.
Add bread, shrimp mixture, and basil
to tomatoes; toss gently to coat. Let
stand 5 minutes before serving. Yield:
4 servings (serving size: 2½ cups).

CALORIES 272; FAT 8.7g (sat 1.2g, mono 5.2g, poly 1.4g);
PROTEIN 17.9g; CARB 30.9g; FIBER 3.8g; CHOL 86mg;
IRON 3.7mg; SODIUM 557mg; CALC 89mg

EVERYDAY VEGETARIAN

PEAK OF THE CROP

With tomatoes and corn sweet as candy
in farmers' markets, meatless dishes are at
their absolute best. Dig into these treats.

Vegetarian

Market Salad with Goat Cheese and Champagne-Shallot Vinaigrette

Hands-on time: 27 min. Total time: 1 hr. 17 min.

*Fresh herbs make all the difference in this
versatile dressing. Try it on any combination of
greens and vegetables from your local farmers'
market.*

2 medium beets (about ¾ pound)
8 ounces green beans, trimmed and cut into
 2-inch pieces
1 (15-ounce) can no-salt-added chickpeas,
 rinsed and drained
3 tablespoons finely chopped shallots
2 tablespoons chopped fresh mint
1 tablespoon chopped fresh tarragon
3 tablespoons walnut or olive oil
2 tablespoons Champagne vinegar
1 tablespoon fresh lemon juice
1½ teaspoons Dijon mustard
¼ teaspoon salt
⅛ teaspoon freshly ground black pepper
2 medium heirloom tomatoes, each cut into
 8 wedges
½ cup (2 ounces) crumbled goat cheese

1. Preheat oven to 350°.
2. Leave root and 1-inch stem on
beets; scrub with a brush. Wrap beets
in heavy-duty foil. Bake at 350° for
1 hour and 15 minutes or until tender.
Remove from oven; cool. Trim off beet
roots and stems; rub off skins. Cut each
beet into 8 wedges.

3. Cook beans in boiling water 4 minutes or until crisp-tender. Drain and
plunge beans into ice water; drain well.
Combine beans and chickpeas in a
medium bowl.
4. Combine shallots and next 8 ingredients in a small bowl, stirring with a
whisk. Add 2 tablespoons dressing to
beets; toss well. Combine 2 tablespoons
dressing and tomatoes in a bowl; toss
gently to coat. Add remaining ¼ cup
dressing to bean mixture, tossing well
to combine. Place ¾ cup bean mixture
on each of 4 plates. Arrange 4 pieces
each of beets and tomatoes around bean
mixture. Sprinkle each serving with 2
tablespoons cheese. Yield: 4 servings.

CALORIES 345; FAT 15.8g (sat 3.9g, mono 3.4g, poly 6.8g);
PROTEIN 13g; CARB 40.1g; FIBER 10.5g; CHOL 11mg;
IRON 3.2mg; SODIUM 370mg; CALC 161mg

JUICY HEIRLOOM
TOMATOES ARE
THE HEART OF THIS
SALAD. CHOOSE
TOMATOES THAT
FEEL HEAVY FOR
THEIR SIZE, AND
STORE THEM
AT ROOM
TEMPERATURE
UNTIL READY
TO EAT.

Kid Friendly • Vegetarian

Local Farmers' Market Pizza

Hands-on time: 32 min. Total time: 1 hr.

1 tablespoon extra-virgin olive oil
2 cups thinly sliced onion
1 teaspoon chopped fresh thyme
2 cups thinly sliced red bell pepper
5 garlic cloves, thinly sliced
1 cup fresh corn kernels (about 2 ears)
¼ teaspoon salt
¼ teaspoon black pepper
1 (16-ounce) refrigerated fresh pizza crust dough
Cooking spray
5 ounces thinly sliced fresh mozzarella cheese
⅓ cup (1½ ounces) grated Parmigiano-Reggiano cheese
1 cup cherry tomatoes, halved
⅓ cup fresh basil leaves

1. Preheat oven to 425°. Position an oven rack in the next to lowest setting. Place a 16-inch pizza pan on rack.
2. Heat a large nonstick skillet over medium-high heat. Add olive oil to pan, and swirl to coat. Add 2 cups onion and thyme to pan; cook 3 minutes or until onion is tender, stirring occasionally. Add bell pepper and garlic to pan; cook 2 minutes, stirring occasionally. Add corn, salt, and black pepper to pan; cook 1 minute or until thoroughly heated.
3. Roll dough into a 16-inch circle on a lightly floured surface. Remove pan from oven. Coat pan with cooking spray. Place dough on pan. Arrange mozzarella slices evenly over dough. Spread corn mixture evenly over cheese, and top with Parmigiano-Reggiano cheese. Bake at 425° for 23 minutes. Arrange tomatoes evenly over pizza; bake an additional 5 minutes or until crust is browned. Remove from oven; sprinkle with basil. Cut into 6 slices. Yield: 6 servings (serving size: 1 slice).

CALORIES 355; **FAT** 11.6g (sat 4.6g, mono 1.8g, poly 1.8g); **PROTEIN** 14.2g; **CARB** 51.4g; **FIBER** 3.5g; **CHOL** 23mg; **IRON** 2.9mg; **SODIUM** 611mg; **CALC** 87mg

ALLOWING THE DOUGH TO COME TO ROOM TEMPERATURE WILL EASE THE ROLLING-OUT PROCESS.

Kid Friendly • Vegetarian

Summer Lemon-Vegetable Risotto

Hands-on time: 59 min. Total time: 59 min.

Reserving some of the cooking liquid for the very end helps to keep the risotto creamy.

8 ounces asparagus, trimmed and cut into 1-inch pieces
8 ounces sugar snap peas, trimmed and cut in half
5 teaspoons extra-virgin olive oil, divided
1 (8-ounce) zucchini, halved lengthwise and cut into ½-inch-thick slices
1 (8-ounce) yellow squash, halved lengthwise and cut into ½-inch-thick slices
4¾ cups organic vegetable broth
½ cup finely chopped shallots
1 cup uncooked Arborio rice
¼ cup dry white wine
½ cup (2 ounces) grated fresh pecorino Romano cheese
¼ cup chopped fresh chives
1 teaspoon grated lemon rind
2 tablespoons fresh lemon juice
1 tablespoon unsalted butter
¼ teaspoon salt

1. Bring a large saucepan of water to a boil. Add asparagus and peas; cook 3 minutes or until crisp-tender. Drain and rinse under cold water.
2. Heat a large nonstick skillet over medium-high heat. Add 2 teaspoons olive oil to pan; swirl to coat. Add zucchini and squash to pan; cook 7 minutes or until lightly browned, stirring occasionally. Set aside.
3. Bring vegetable broth to a simmer in a medium saucepan (do not boil). Keep warm over low heat.
4. Heat remaining 1 tablespoon olive oil in a Dutch oven over medium heat. Add shallots, and cook 3 minutes or until tender. Stir in rice, and cook 1 minute, stirring constantly. Stir in wine; cook until liquid is absorbed (about 30 seconds), stirring constantly. Stir in 1 cup broth; cook 5 minutes or until liquid is nearly absorbed, stirring constantly. Reserve ¼ cup broth. Add remaining broth, ½ cup at a time, stirring constantly until each portion of broth is absorbed before adding the next (about 22 minutes total). Stir in vegetables; cook 1 minute or until thoroughly heated. Remove from heat; stir in reserved ¼ cup broth and remaining ingredients. Yield: 4 servings (serving size: 1½ cups).

CALORIES 395; **FAT** 12.3g (sat 4.7g, mono 4.9g, poly 0.8g); **PROTEIN** 10.6g; **CARB** 56.2g; **FIBER** 7.1g; **CHOL** 18mg; **IRON** 3.1mg; **SODIUM** 512mg; **CALC** 191mg

IN SOME RISOTTOS, RICE RULES; EVERYTHING ELSE PLAYS A MINOR ROLE. NOT SO HERE: THIS ONE BURSTS WITH GARDEN BOUNTY.

TODAY'S LESSON: GRILLED VEGETABLES

Throwing a few vegetables onto the barbie to complement a burger or a chop gives short shrift to the true power of char and flame. The natural sugars in vegetables are caramelized by the high heat and suffused by the smoke. Yes, they're good right off the fire. But go even further: Make a gazpacho, or grill stuffed jalapeños, or make a grilled Caesar salad. Fear not the fire: Techniques are revealed here.

Quick & Easy • Vegetarian

Grilled Romaine with Creamy Herb Dressing

Hands-on time: 16 min. Total time: 36 min.

A brief turn over hot coals wilts hearty romaine lettuce ever so slightly and infuses it with a delicious smoky flavor, yielding a special salad that's simple to prepare. Serve with any type of grilled meat, fish, or burgers.

1 large head romaine lettuce, trimmed and halved lengthwise
2 teaspoons olive oil
Cooking spray
½ teaspoon freshly ground black pepper, divided
³/₈ teaspoon salt, divided
¼ cup canola mayonnaise
1 tablespoon chopped fresh flat-leaf parsley
1½ teaspoons chopped fresh dill
2 tablespoons fresh lemon juice
1 tablespoon water
2 garlic cloves, minced

1. Preheat grill to medium-high heat.
2. Brush cut sides of lettuce evenly with oil. Place lettuce, cut sides down, on grill rack coated with cooking spray, and grill 2 minutes. Remove from heat; cut each lettuce half lengthwise in half again to form 4 quarters. Sprinkle cut sides of lettuce with ¼ teaspoon black pepper and ⅛ teaspoon salt.
3. Combine remaining ¼ teaspoon pepper, remaining ¼ teaspoon salt, mayonnaise, and next 5 ingredients in a small bowl, stirring well. Place 1 lettuce quarter on each of 4 salad plates; drizzle each serving with about 4 teaspoons dressing. Serve immediately. Yield: 4 servings.

CALORIES 132; **FAT** 13.4g (sat 1.3g, mono 7.7g, poly 3.3g); **PROTEIN** 0.7g; **CARB** 2.7g; **FIBER** 1g; **CHOL** 5mg; **IRON** 0.5mg; **SODIUM** 325mg; **CALC** 19mg

> GRILL TIP: The greens that can best take the heat are tougher—like romaine, radicchio, and endive.

GAS IS FAST, BUT CHARCOAL IS CHARMING

LIGHT THE PAPER.
A chimney starter is indispensable for charcoal grilling. Stuff newspaper in the bottom. Place charcoal in the top, and light the paper. Now wait until the coals catch fire. If you don't see smoke pouring out of the top and, eventually, flames, you need to relight.

WAIT. WAIT A BIT MORE.
Yes, it can take its own sweet time. But don't rush: Allow the flames to die down and the coals to take on a bright-red glow with a gray, ashy look. These cues signal that it's time to put down your beverage and dump the coals into the bottom of your grill.

SPREAD THE BED OF COALS.
Arrange coals in a pattern suited to what you're cooking. For veggies that take longer than 20 minutes to cook (like dense potatoes), pile coals to one side of the grill for indirect heat. For quicker-cooking ingredients, pile coals in the center of the grill.

Make Ahead • Vegetarian

Grilled Vegetable Gazpacho

Hands-on time: 50 min. Total time: 1 hr. 5 min.

Make this soup up to two days ahead, cover, and chill until you're ready to serve. If you prepare it ahead, you may need to stir in a bit of water before serving, as it may thicken slightly as it sits. For more heat, leave the seeds in the jalapeño, or remove them to tame the flames.

3 ripe beefsteak tomatoes, cored and cut in half crosswise (about 3 pounds)
1 onion, sliced crosswise into ¼-inch-thick slices
¼ cup extra-virgin olive oil, divided
1 (1-ounce) piece French bread baguette, cut into 2 slices
Cooking spray
1 red bell pepper
1 jalapeño pepper
½ cup water
2½ tablespoons fresh lemon juice, divided
¾ teaspoon kosher salt, divided
¼ teaspoon freshly ground black pepper
2 garlic cloves, crushed
2 cups thinly sliced, quartered English cucumber
¼ cup minced green onions
3 tablespoons fresh cilantro leaves

1. Preheat grill to medium-high heat.
2. Brush cut sides of tomatoes and onion slices with 1 tablespoon oil. Lightly coat bread with cooking spray. Place bread on grill rack, and grill 1½ minutes on each side or until toasted. Remove from grill. Place peppers on grill rack coated with cooking spray. Grill 8 minutes or until blistered, turning peppers after 4 minutes. Remove peppers from grill. Place peppers in a small paper bag; fold tightly to seal. Let stand 20 minutes. Arrange onion on grill rack; grill 10 minutes. Turn onion over. Arrange tomatoes, cut sides down, on grill rack; grill onion and tomatoes 10 minutes. Peel and seed peppers.

3. Combine 2 tablespoons oil, bread, grilled vegetables, ½ cup water, 2 tablespoons juice, ½ teaspoon salt, black pepper, and garlic in a blender; process until smooth. Combine remaining 1 tablespoon olive oil, remaining 1½ teaspoons lemon juice, remaining ¼ teaspoon salt, cucumber, and next 2 ingredients; toss. Ladle about ⅔ cup soup into each of 6 bowls, and top each serving with about ⅓ cup cucumber mixture. Yield: 6 servings.

CALORIES 134; FAT 9.4g (sat 1.3g, mono 6.6g, poly 1.1g); PROTEIN 2.2g; CARB 11.5g; FIBER 2.5g; CHOL 0mg; IRON 0.8mg; SODIUM 280mg; CALC 29mg

GRILL TIP: A simple brush with oil prevents the annoyance of grill-stick and promotes even charring.

Quick & Easy

Grilled Stuffed Jalapeños

Hands-on time: 30 min. Total time: 40 min.

The rich and creamy combination of bacon, cream cheese, and cheddar is a nice foil for the muted spice of grilled jalapeño peppers. This recipe is a healthy, fresh alternative to the popular breaded and fried version. If making these poppers for a party, you can stuff the peppers, cover, and chill. Then grill just before your guests arrive.

2 center-cut bacon slices
½ cup (4 ounces) cream cheese, softened
½ cup (4 ounces) fat-free cream cheese, softened
¼ cup (1 ounce) shredded extra-sharp cheddar cheese
¼ cup minced green onions
1 teaspoon fresh lime juice
¼ teaspoon kosher salt
1 small garlic clove, minced
14 jalapeño peppers, halved lengthwise and seeded
Cooking spray
2 tablespoons chopped fresh cilantro
2 tablespoons chopped seeded tomato

1. Preheat grill to medium-high heat.
2. Cook bacon in a skillet over medium heat until crisp. Remove bacon from pan, and drain on paper towels. Crumble bacon. Combine crumbled bacon, cheeses, and next 4 ingredients in a bowl, stirring to combine. Divide cheese evenly and fill pepper halves. Place peppers, cheese sides up, on grill rack or grill grate coated with cooking spray. Cover and grill peppers 8 minutes or until bottoms of peppers are charred and cheese mixture is lightly browned. Place peppers on a serving platter. Sprinkle with cilantro and tomato. Yield: 14 servings (serving size: 2 pepper halves).

CALORIES 56; FAT 4.1g (sat 2.2g, mono 1.1g, poly 0.2g); PROTEIN 2.9g; CARB 2.1g; FIBER 0.5g; CHOL 13mg; IRON 0.2mg; SODIUM 157mg; CALC 55mg

GRILL TIP: Avoid the aggravation of veggies plunging into the coals—try a dedicated grill pan.

THE STEAK LOVER'S GUIDE TO LEAN MEAT & HIGH HEAT

Hot & fast are watchwords for healthy, lean cuts on the grill. But that can mean dry-as-desert meat unless you follow our guide to keeping the juice in.

When we bought a side of 100% grass-fed beef, we learned plenty about grilling superlean meat, whether grass- or grain-fed. Because it doesn't have extra fat to insulate it, lean beef offers less room for error on the part of the cook. It cooks faster and can go from perfectly cooked to dry and overdone in about a minute. Lean steaks are very suitable for high-heat cooking methods like grilling but need a cook with a quick hand.

With chipotle-spiced flank steak, for instance, we grill the meat over high heat for a scant four minutes a side. (We call for medium-high heat in recipes that include grilled vegetables so the veggies won't char.) Depending on your grill, you may need to cook it longer, but remember—it's better to err on the side of undercooking. You can always re-fire the meat, but once it's overcooked, there's no fixing it. Because lean beef turns bone-dry when well done, cooking it to rare or medium-rare is the ticket. After it rests, use your sharpest knife to cut thinly across the grain to keep the meat tender.

Tuscan-Style New York Strip with Arugula-Artichoke Salad

Hands-on time: 33 min. Total time: 4 hr. 53 min.

Based on the classic bistecca Fiorentina—grilled porterhouse—this dish uses sirloin strip steaks, which are leaner (and, because they're boneless, a little easier to grill) than porterhouse. Lemon juice is a traditional accent in the dish, meant to cut the richness of the meat. Use a mandoline to slice the artichokes thinly and evenly.

4 tablespoons extra-virgin olive oil, divided
10 garlic cloves, crushed
10 thyme sprigs
6 (2-inch) strips lemon rind
2 (12-ounce) New York strip steaks, trimmed
1 teaspoon kosher salt, divided
1 teaspoon freshly ground black pepper, divided
6 medium red potatoes
1 bay leaf
2 cups water
½ cup fresh lemon juice, divided
3 medium artichokes (about 1¾ pounds)
5 cups baby arugula (about 5 ounces)
1 cup thinly vertically sliced red onion
3 lemons, quartered
Cooking spray
2 teaspoons fresh thyme leaves
½ cup (2 ounces) shaved Parmigiano-Reggiano cheese

1. Combine 1 tablespoon oil, garlic, thyme sprigs, and lemon rind in a large zip-top plastic bag. Add steaks to bag; seal and marinate in refrigerator 3½ hours, turning occasionally. Remove bag from refrigerator, and let stand 30 minutes. Remove steaks from marinade, and discard marinade. Sprinkle with ½ teaspoon salt and ½ teaspoon black pepper.
2. Place potatoes and bay leaf in a saucepan; cover with water. Bring to a boil; reduce heat, and simmer 15 minutes or until crisp-tender. Drain; discard bay leaf. Cool potatoes completely; cut into 24 (⅓-inch-thick) slices.
3. Preheat grill to medium-high heat.
4. Combine 2 cups water and ¼ cup juice in a large bowl. Trim about 2 inches from top of each artichoke. Cut each in half vertically. Remove fuzzy thistle from bottom with a spoon. Trim any remaining leaves and dark green layer from base. Place artichoke halves in lemon water. Combine 2 tablespoons oil, 2 tablespoons juice, ¼ teaspoon salt, and ¼ teaspoon pepper in a large bowl; stir with a whisk. Thinly vertically slice artichokes. Add sliced artichokes, arugula, and thinly vertically sliced onion to bowl; toss gently to combine.
5. Place steak, potato slices, and lemons on grill rack coated with cooking spray. Grill steak 4 minutes on each side or until desired degree of doneness. Grill potatoes 3 minutes on each side or until tender. Grill lemons 2 minutes on each cut side. Let steak stand 5 minutes. Cut steak diagonally across grain into thin slices.
6. Place 4 potato slices on each of 6 plates. Sprinkle evenly with remaining ¼ teaspoon salt, remaining ¼ teaspoon black pepper, and thyme leaves. Place 1 cup arugula mixture on each plate, and top each serving with 4 teaspoons cheese. Arrange 3 ounces steak on each serving, and drizzle evenly with remaining 1 tablespoon olive oil and remaining 2 tablespoons lemon juice. Serve with grilled lemon. Yield: 6 servings.

CALORIES 390; FAT 13.3g (sat 3.9g, mono 7g, poly 1.2g); PROTEIN 36.8g; CARB 35.8g; FIBER 10.6g; CHOL 71mg; IRON 5.1mg; SODIUM 664mg; CALC 238mg

WHY BOTHER WITH LEAN? HERE'S THE SKINNY.

A cooked 3.5-ounce portion of these lean, grill-friendly steaks has less total fat than a same-size serving of skinless chicken thighs.

CUT	FAT	COOKING TIPS
Top sirloin steak	Total: 4.9g Saturated: 1.9g	The USDA defines top sirloin as "extra lean" because it has fewer than 5g fat and 2g saturated fat per serving. Not as tender as a strip steak, but it's still good for grilled kebabs.
New York strip steak	Total: 6g Saturated: 2.3g	Relatively tender with a satisfying chew and deep flavor, this sirloin cut is a steak-house star that needs little more than salt and pepper to shine.
Flank steak	Total: 6.4g Saturated: 2.6g	A great all-purpose cut, flank needs to be sliced very thinly across the grain to keep it from seeming tough.
Tri-tip steak	Total: 6.9g Saturated: 2.5g	A triangular cut that comes from the end tip of the sirloin section. More tender than flank, its beefiness stands up to bold flavorings.
Tenderloin steak	Total: 6.5g Saturated: 2.5g	The most tender of the lean cuts, tenderloin steaks benefit from spice rubs or flavorful sauces.

Spice-Rubbed Flank Steak with Fresh Salsa

Hands-on time: 27 min. Total time: 32 min.

Chipotle powder gives the rub a smoky hit.

Salsa:
2 cups chopped seeded tomato
½ cup finely chopped red onion
¼ cup chopped fresh cilantro
3 tablespoons fresh lime juice
1 tablespoon extra-virgin olive oil
½ teaspoon kosher salt
¼ teaspoon ground red pepper

Steak:
2 teaspoons ground cumin
2 teaspoons paprika
1 teaspoon garlic powder
1 teaspoon chipotle chile powder
¾ teaspoon freshly ground black pepper
½ teaspoon kosher salt
½ teaspoon ground cinnamon
1 (1½-pound) flank steak, trimmed
1 tablespoon extra-virgin olive oil
Cooking spray

1. Preheat grill to high heat.
2. To prepare salsa, combine first 7 ingredients in a bowl.

3. To prepare steak, combine cumin and next 6 ingredients. Brush both sides of steak with olive oil, and sprinkle with spice mixture. Place steak on grill rack coated with cooking spray, and grill 4 minutes on each side or until desired degree of doneness. Let stand 5 minutes. Cut steak diagonally across grain into thin slices. Serve with salsa. Yield: 6 servings (serving size: about 3 ounces steak and ⅓ cup salsa).

CALORIES 253; **FAT** 14.4g (sat 4.2g, mono 8.1g, poly 1g); **PROTEIN** 25g; **CARB** 5.6g; **FIBER** 1.7g; **CHOL** 65mg; **IRON** 3.2mg; **SODIUM** 415mg; **CALC** 30mg

Sirloin Skewers with Grilled Vegetable Couscous and Fiery Pepper Sauce

Hands-on time: 15 min. Total time: 1 hr. 11 min.

A spicy North African–style pepper sauce amps up the flavor in these beef kebabs. Prepare the sauce up to one day ahead.

Pepper sauce:
4 red bell peppers
1/2 cup fresh cilantro leaves
1/4 cup extra-virgin olive oil
3 tablespoons fresh lemon juice
1 1/2 teaspoons ground coriander
1 1/2 teaspoons ground cumin
1/2 teaspoon kosher salt
1/2 teaspoon caraway seeds
1/2 teaspoon crushed red pepper
Couscous:
1 cup water
1 cup fat-free, lower-sodium chicken broth
1 bay leaf
2 cups uncooked couscous
8 ounces eggplant, cut lengthwise into
   1/2-inch-thick slices
8 ounces squash, cut lengthwise into
   1/2-inch-thick slices
8 ounces zucchini, cut lengthwise into
   1/2-inch-thick slices
4 green onions, trimmed
Cooking spray
Skewers:
1 1/2 pounds top sirloin steak, cut into 1-inch
   cubes
3/4 teaspoon freshly ground black pepper
1/2 teaspoon kosher salt

1. Preheat broiler.
2. To prepare pepper sauce, cut bell peppers in half lengthwise; discard seeds and membranes. Place bell pepper halves, skin sides up, on a foil-lined baking sheet; flatten with hand. Broil 12 minutes or until blackened. Place in a paper bag, and fold to close tightly. Let stand 20 minutes. Peel. Place peppers and next 8 ingredients in a blender, and process until smooth.
3. Preheat grill to medium-high heat.
4. To prepare couscous, combine 1 cup water, broth, and bay leaf in a medium saucepan; bring to a boil. Stir in couscous; cover. Remove from heat; let stand 10 minutes. Fluff with a fork; discard bay leaf.
5. Arrange eggplant and next 3 ingredients on grill rack coated with cooking spray; grill 3 minutes on each side or until vegetables are tender and well marked. Remove from heat; coarsely chop vegetables. Combine 1/2 cup pepper sauce, couscous, and chopped vegetables in a large bowl; toss gently. Keep warm.
6. To prepare skewers, thread beef onto 12 (7-inch) skewers. Lightly coat beef with cooking spray, and sprinkle with black pepper and 1/2 teaspoon salt. Place skewers on grill rack coated with cooking spray; grill 8 minutes or until desired degree of doneness, turning once. Serve with couscous mixture and remaining sauce. Yield: 6 servings (serving size: 2 skewers, about 1 1/3 cups couscous mixture, and about 1/4 cup sauce).

CALORIES 526; **FAT** 15.4g (sat 3.3g, mono 9.3g, poly 1.4g); **PROTEIN** 36.7g; **CARB** 58.5g; **FIBER** 8.2g; **CHOL** 49mg; **IRON** 3.7mg; **SODIUM** 461mg; **CALC** 75mg

WINE NOTE: Brazin Lodi Old Vine Zinfandel ($16), a big, juicy wine loaded with vanilla, dark fruit, spice, and acidity to balance the lemony tang of the Tuscan-Style New York Strip.

NOW GET SAUCY!

ZINGY CHIMICHURRI
Hands-on time: 15 min. Total time: 45 min.

This Argentinian herb sauce is a classic topping for grilled beef.

Combine 1 1/2 cups finely chopped red onion, 1/2 cup red wine vinegar, 1/4 cup chopped fresh oregano, 2 tablespoons extra-virgin olive oil, 1 teaspoon crushed red pepper, 1/2 teaspoon kosher salt, and 2 minced garlic cloves in a small bowl; let stand 30 minutes. Stir in 3 tablespoons chopped fresh cilantro. Yield: 12 servings (serving size: 5 teaspoons).

CALORIES 32; **FAT** 2.3g (sat 0.3g); **SODIUM** 82mg

TANGY COFFEE BARBECUE SAUCE
Hands-on time: 5 min. Total time: 15 min.

This zesty condiment is great with grilled steaks, pork, or chicken. Refrigerate extra up to a week.

Combine 1 cup no-salt-added ketchup, 1 cup brewed coffee, 2 tablespoons dark brown sugar, 1 teaspoon onion powder, 1 teaspoon garlic powder, and 1 teaspoon chili powder in a small saucepan; bring to a boil. Reduce heat, and simmer 10 minutes or until slightly thick, stirring occasionally. Remove from heat; stir in 1 1/2 teaspoons black pepper, 1 1/2 tablespoons balsamic vinegar, and 1 1/2 teaspoons lower-sodium soy sauce. Yield: 12 servings (serving size: about 2 1/2 tablespoons).

CALORIES 47; **FAT** 0g; **SODIUM** 24mg

LEAN MEAT CAN STILL DRY OUT AFTER COOKING! LET IT REST FOR AT LEAST FIVE MINUTES. JUICES WILL REDISTRIBUTE AND WON'T FLOOD OUT WHEN YOU SLICE.

THE PORTABLE 4TH OF JULY

Crunchy slaw, baked beans, potato salad: You'll love the classics even more spiked with a few jazzy new ingredients. Perfect for packing off to a picnic or patio, for a hero's welcome.

Favorite foods on national holidays must strum the heartstrings, but we're all for a twist or two to keep the tune fresh. Potato salad, for example, needs to hit creamy, starchy, comforting notes, but why not update it by ditching the mayo and swathing the spuds in a combo of nutty crème fraîche, tangy buttermilk, and a handful of fresh herbs? Baked beans are a favorite gooey treat—made more interesting with a trio of legumes for fun colors and textures; a hit of smoked paprika deepens the bacon-y flavor throughout every bite. Standard coleslaw is a crunchy must-have, and something spectacular happens when you opt for a fresh lime dressing and load in lots of jalapeño peppers and cilantro. For something sweet, we have shortbread-crusted cheesecake bars made zippy with fresh cherries. The following recipes are all designed to be made ahead and are perfectly portable—ideal for toting or setting out at your own patriotic bash.

PORTABLE 4TH OF JULY MENU

Marinated Shrimp Salad

Tabbouleh Salad

Creamy Buttermilk-Herb Potato Salad

Lemony Cucumber Salad

Jalapeño-Lime Slaw

Smoky Three-Bean Bake

Fresh Cherry Cheesecake Bars

Make Ahead
Marinated Shrimp Salad

Hands-on time: 40 min. Total time: 8 hr. 43 min.

Offer this salad as a main-dish option, or set it out for a starter snack. You can reserve some of the feathery fennel fronds for a pretty garnish.

3 pounds large shrimp, unpeeled
3 quarts water
1 cup (3-inch) julienne-cut yellow bell pepper
1 cup thinly sliced fennel bulb
2/3 cup thinly sliced shallots
3 garlic cloves, thinly sliced
1 teaspoon grated lemon rind
1/2 cup fresh lemon juice
1 teaspoon kosher salt
1 teaspoon mustard seeds
1 teaspoon fennel seeds
1/2 teaspoon sugar
1/2 teaspoon crushed red pepper
1/3 cup extra-virgin olive oil
4 bay leaves

1. Peel and devein shrimp, leaving tails intact; discard shells.
2. Bring 3 quarts water to a boil in a Dutch oven. Add shrimp; cook 3 minutes or just until shrimp turn pink. Drain and rinse with cold water; drain. Place shrimp in a large bowl. Add bell pepper, fennel, shallots, and garlic; toss to combine.
3. Combine rind and next 6 ingredients in a medium bowl, stirring with a whisk. Gradually add oil, stirring constantly with a whisk. Stir in bay leaves. Combine oil mixture and shrimp mixture in a large zip-top plastic bag; toss well to coat. Seal and marinate in refrigerator at least 8 hours or up to 24 hours, turning bag occasionally. Discard bay leaves. Yield: 8 servings (serving size: about 1½ cups salad).

CALORIES 289; FAT 12.2g (sat 1.8g, mono 7.1g, poly 2.1g); PROTEIN 35.5g; CARB 8.2g; FIBER 1.1g; CHOL 259mg; IRON 4.6mg; SODIUM 501mg; CALC 109mg

Make Ahead • Vegetarian
Tabbouleh Salad

Hands-on time: 15 min. Total time: 3 hr. 10 min.

This classic Middle Eastern salad, chock-full of herbs and spiked with lemon, is a perfect make-ahead and portable option.

2½ cups boiling water
1½ cups uncooked bulgur wheat (about 8 ounces)
2 cups chopped fresh flat-leaf parsley
1 cup diced seeded tomato
3/4 cup diagonally sliced green onions
1/4 cup chopped fresh mint
6 tablespoons fresh lemon juice
3 tablespoons extra-virgin olive oil
1 teaspoon kosher salt
1 teaspoon freshly ground black pepper
1/2 teaspoon ground cumin

1. Combine 2½ cups boiling water and bulgur in a large bowl; cover and let stand 1 hour. Add parsley and remaining ingredients to bulgur; toss well. Cover and chill at least 2 hours. Yield: 8 servings (serving size: about 2/3 cup).

CALORIES 161; FAT 5.7g (sat 0.8g, mono 3.8g, poly 0.8g); PROTEIN 4.6g; CARB 25.6g; FIBER 6.6g; CHOL 0mg; IRON 2.6mg; SODIUM 259mg; CALC 54mg

Make Ahead • Kid Friendly
Vegetarian

Creamy Buttermilk-Herb Potato Salad

Hands-on time: 12 min. Total time: 57 min.

Crème fraîche is a thickened cream product with a mildly tangy, nutty flavor; you'll often find it in tubs near the gourmet cheeses. If you can't find it, you can substitute full-fat sour cream.

3 pounds small red potatoes, quartered
1/2 cup crème fraîche or sour cream
1/3 cup fat-free buttermilk
1/4 cup chopped fresh parsley
2 tablespoons chopped fresh chives
1 tablespoon chopped fresh dill
1 1/4 teaspoons kosher salt
1/2 teaspoon freshly ground black pepper
1 large garlic clove, minced

1. Place potatoes in a Dutch oven, and cover with water. Bring to a boil. Reduce heat, and simmer 15 minutes or until just tender; drain. Cool 30 minutes.
2. Combine crème fraîche and next 7 ingredients in a large bowl; stir with a whisk. Add warm potatoes; toss gently to coat. Serve at room temperature or chilled. Yield: 8 servings (serving size: about 1 cup).

CALORIES 176; **FAT** 5.5g (sat 3.3g, mono 1.5g, poly 0.3g); **PROTEIN** 4.1g; **CARB** 28g; **FIBER** 3g; **CHOL** 14mg; **IRON** 1.4mg; **SODIUM** 326mg; **CALC** 34mg

THESE CRUNCHY SIDES MAKE FUN, HEALTHY BURGER TOPPINGS, TOO.

Quick & Easy • Make Ahead
Kid Friendly • Vegetarian

Lemony Cucumber Salad

Hands-on time: 22 min. Total time: 22 min.

Don't forget that something fresh, vibrant, and crunchy is often missing from potluck gatherings; this easy salad will get gobbled up quickly because it satisfies on those levels.

1 cup thinly sliced radishes
1/2 cup finely chopped orange bell pepper
1/4 cup chopped fresh flat-leaf parsley
2 English cucumbers, thinly sliced (about 6 cups)
1 teaspoon finely grated lemon rind
2 tablespoons fresh lemon juice
1 tablespoon extra-virgin olive oil
1 1/2 teaspoons white wine vinegar
1/2 teaspoon salt
1/4 teaspoon freshly ground black pepper

1. Combine first 4 ingredients in a large bowl.
2. Combine lemon rind and next 5 ingredients in a small bowl, stirring with a whisk. Pour over cucumber mixture; toss well to coat. Serve at room temperature or chilled. Yield: 8 servings (serving size: 2/3 cup).

CALORIES 33; **FAT** 1.8g (sat 0.3g, mono 1.2g, poly 0.2g); **PROTEIN** 0.8g; **CARB** 4.3g; **FIBER** 0.9g; **CHOL** 0mg; **IRON** 0.4mg; **SODIUM** 156mg; **CALC** 20mg

Make Ahead • Vegetarian

Jalapeño-Lime Slaw

(pictured on page 227)

Hands-on time: 7 min. Total time: 1 hr. 7 min.

Leave the seeds in more peppers for added fire, or seed all of them for a milder dish.

1/3 cup fresh lime juice
1 teaspoon sugar
3/4 teaspoon kosher salt
1/4 teaspoon freshly ground black pepper
3 tablespoons olive oil
1/2 cup thinly vertically sliced red onion
1/2 cup coarsely chopped fresh cilantro
1 (16-ounce) package cabbage-and-carrot coleslaw
4 jalapeño peppers, halved crosswise

1. Combine first 4 ingredients in a large bowl, stirring with a whisk. Gradually add olive oil, stirring constantly with a whisk. Add onion, cilantro, and coleslaw. Thinly slice 1 jalapeño half crosswise (keeping seeds), and remove seeds from remaining jalapeño halves. Cut remaining halves into thin crosswise slices. Add jalapeños to onion mixture, and toss well to coat. Cover and chill at least 1 hour. Yield: 8 servings (serving size: about 3/4 cup).

CALORIES 71; **FAT** 5.2g (sat 0.7g, mono 3.7g, poly 0.6g); **PROTEIN** 0.9g; **CARB** 6.3g; **FIBER** 1.8g; **CHOL** 0mg; **IRON** 0.4mg; **SODIUM** 198mg; **CALC** 26mg

THIS CITRUSY TAKE ON COLESLAW IS FRESH AND PLEASANTLY SPICY.

Smoky Three-Bean Bake

Hands-on time: 29 min. Total time: 1 hr. 29 min.

4 applewood-smoked bacon slices, chopped
2 cups finely chopped onion
1 cup finely chopped green bell pepper
6 garlic cloves, minced
¾ cup no-salt-added tomato sauce
⅓ cup packed brown sugar
1 tablespoon cider vinegar
1 tablespoon honey
1 tablespoon Dijon mustard
1 teaspoon smoked paprika
¾ teaspoon kosher salt
½ teaspoon freshly ground black pepper
¼ teaspoon ground red pepper
1 (15-ounce) can organic black beans, rinsed and drained
1 (15-ounce) can organic chickpeas (garbanzo beans), rinsed and drained
1 (15-ounce) can organic Great Northern beans, rinsed and drained
Cooking spray

1. Preheat oven to 325°.
2. Heat a large nonstick skillet over medium-high heat. Add bacon to pan, and sauté 5 minutes or until crisp. Remove bacon from pan with a slotted spoon, reserving 1½ tablespoons drippings in pan. Set bacon aside. Add 2 cups onion, bell pepper, and minced garlic to drippings in pan, and sauté 6 minutes or until tender, stirring occasionally. Remove from heat, and cool slightly.
3. Combine tomato sauce and next 8 ingredients in a large bowl, stirring with a whisk. Stir in onion mixture and beans. Spoon bean mixture into an 11 x 7–inch glass or ceramic baking dish coated with cooking spray, and sprinkle with reserved bacon. Cover and bake at 325° for 30 minutes. Uncover; bake an additional 30 minutes. Yield: 8 servings (serving size: about ¾ cup).

CALORIES 204; **FAT** 4.7g (sat 1.4g, mono 1.8g, poly 0.5g); **PROTEIN** 7.3g; **CARB** 33.2g; **FIBER** 6g; **CHOL** 7mg; **IRON** 1.7mg; **SODIUM** 382mg; **CALC** 71mg

Fresh Cherry Cheesecake Bars

Hands-on time: 20 min. Total time: 4 hr. 5 min.

With their combo of shortbread-like crust, creamy cheesecake, and fresh summer cherry goodness, these bars will make you the hit of the picnic.

4.5 ounces all-purpose flour (about 1 cup)
3 tablespoons powdered sugar
⅛ teaspoon salt
5 tablespoons chilled butter, cut into small pieces
3½ teaspoons ice water
1¼ cups chopped pitted fresh cherries
1 tablespoon granulated sugar
1 tablespoon water
2 teaspoons fresh lemon juice
½ teaspoon cornstarch
¾ cup (6 ounces) ⅓-less-fat cream cheese
⅓ cup plain fat-free Greek yogurt
⅓ cup granulated sugar
½ teaspoon vanilla extract
1 large egg

1. Preheat oven to 350°.
2. Line an 8-inch square glass or ceramic baking dish with parchment paper. Weigh or lightly spoon flour into a dry measuring cup; level with a knife. Place flour, powdered sugar, and salt in a food processor; pulse 2 times to combine. Add chilled butter, and drizzle with ice water. Pulse 10 times or until mixture resembles coarse meal. Pour mixture into prepared baking dish (mixture will be crumbly). Press mixture into bottom of prepared dish. Bake at 350° for 23 minutes or until lightly browned. Cool completely. Reduce oven temperature to 325°.
3. Place cherries, 1 tablespoon granulated sugar, and 1 tablespoon water in a small saucepan. Bring to a boil. Reduce heat, and simmer 5 minutes or until cherries are tender. Combine lemon juice and cornstarch in a small bowl, stirring with a whisk. Stir cornstarch mixture into cherry mixture; cook 1 minute or until thick. Cool mixture slightly. Spoon cherry mixture into food processor, and process until smooth.

Spoon pureed mixture into a bowl, and set aside.
4. Wipe food processor clean. Place cream cheese and next 4 ingredients in food processor; process until smooth. Spoon cream cheese mixture over cooled crust; spread evenly. Dollop cherry mixture over cream cheese mixture, and swirl together with a knife. Bake at 325° for 36 minutes or until set. Cool on a wire rack. Cover and chill at least 3 hours. Yield: 15 servings (serving size: 1 bar).

CALORIES 136; **FAT** 6.9g (sat 4g, mono 1.8g, poly 0.3g); **PROTEIN** 2.9g; **CARB** 16g; **FIBER** 0.5g; **CHOL** 33mg; **IRON** 0.5mg; **SODIUM** 92mg; **CALC** 23mg

PACK WELL, KEEP COOL (OR HOT), EAT SAFE

If you're taking one of these dishes to a picnic or party, follow a few rules for safety. Prep less than 1 day from picnic so food tastes fresh.

TRANSPORT ON ICE. Except for the baked beans, all the recipes should be chilled and packed in a cooler with ice or ice packs to keep them cold while they travel.

HEAT JUST BEFORE TAKING. Baked beans can be cooked the day before. Reheat just before heading out; wrap the hot container in a towel, and tote carefully to the picnic.

SERVE—THEN STOW. Once folks have gone through the line and served themselves, put chilled dishes back in the cooler to keep them cold. Anyone who wants seconds can dig back into the cooler.

USE THE TWO-HOUR/ONE-HOUR RULE. Don't let food sit out for more than 2 hours (or 1 hour if it's a hot day over 90 degrees).

TOSS THE LEFTOVERS. The food will have been handled a lot and possibly will have been sitting out for a while.

FEED 4 FOR LESS THAN $10

Chicken, pork, and beef: Family favorites for healthy meals, all for much less than a fast-food night out.

$2.39 per serving, $9.54 total

Quick & Easy • Kid Friendly

Pork Chops with Cherry Couscous

(pictured on page 229)

Hands-on time: 19 min. Total time: 39 min.

3 tablespoons olive oil, divided
4 (6-ounce) bone-in center-cut pork chops
1 teaspoon salt, divided
¼ teaspoon freshly ground black pepper
Cooking spray
1 cup uncooked couscous
¾ cup boiling water
1 cup coarsely chopped pitted cherries
½ cup sliced green onions
⅓ cup dry-roasted almonds, chopped
2 teaspoons grated lemon rind
2 tablespoons fresh lemon juice

1. Preheat grill to medium-high heat.
2. Brush 1 tablespoon olive oil evenly over both sides of pork, and sprinkle evenly with ½ teaspoon salt and black pepper. Place pork on grill rack coated with cooking spray, and grill 4 minutes on each side or until desired degree of doneness. Let pork stand 5 minutes.
3. Place couscous in a large bowl. Add ¾ cup boiling water; cover and let stand 5 minutes. Uncover and fluff with a fork. Stir in remaining 2 tablespoons oil, remaining ½ teaspoon salt, cherries, and next 4 ingredients. Serve with pork. Yield: 4 servings (serving size: 1 pork chop and about ¾ cup couscous).

CALORIES 495; FAT 22.3g (sat 3.6g, mono 13.4g, poly 3.3g); PROTEIN 29.7g; CARB 43.8g; FIBER 5g; CHOL 66mg; IRON 2mg; SODIUM 683mg; CALC 76mg

$1.96 per serving, $7.82 total

Quick & Easy • Kid Friendly

Grilled Steak with Onions and Scallions

Hands-on time: 31 min. Total time: 51 min.

Grilling onions caramelizes their natural sugars and makes them sweeter as well as smoky. Cook the potatoes while you wait for the grill to heat. Serve with sautéed fresh green beans.

1 (1-pound) boneless sirloin steak
¾ teaspoon salt, divided
½ teaspoon pepper, divided
4 (½-inch-thick) slices red onion
4 green onions
Cooking spray
1 pound baking potato, peeled and chopped
⅓ cup reduced-fat sour cream
⅓ cup fat-free milk
2 teaspoons butter

1. Preheat grill to medium-high heat.
2. Sprinkle steak evenly with ⅜ teaspoon salt and ¼ teaspoon pepper. Sprinkle red onion with ⅛ teaspoon salt. Coat green onions with cooking spray. Place steak on grill rack coated with cooking spray; grill 3 minutes on each side or until desired degree of doneness. Let stand 10 minutes. Cut steak diagonally across grain into thin slices. Grill red onion 5 minutes on each side or until tender. Grill green onions 1½ minutes on each side; cut into 3-inch pieces.
3. Place potato in a saucepan; cover with cold water. Bring to a boil; cook 10 minutes or until tender. Drain. Return potato to pan; add remaining ¼ teaspoon salt, sour cream, milk, and butter. Mash to desired consistency. Garnish with ¼ teaspoon pepper. Yield: 4 servings (serving size: 3 ounces steak, 1 onion slice, 1 green onion, and ½ cup potatoes).

CALORIES 333; FAT 12.6g (sat 5.8g, mono 3.5g, poly 0.6g); PROTEIN 25g; CARB 29.4g; FIBER 2.9g; CHOL 71mg; IRON 4.1mg; SODIUM 547mg; CALC 99mg

$2.45 per serving, $9.80 total

Chicken Satay

Hands-on time: 27 min. Total time: 1 hr. 27 min.

Serve skewers with rice noodles tossed with cilantro, sesame seeds, and dark sesame oil; top with thinly sliced cucumber. If using a gas grill, preheat it during the last 20 minutes of marinating time. By the time the chicken is threaded onto skewers, the grill should be heated.

⅓ cup unsalted, dry-roasted peanuts
1 tablespoon toasted cumin seeds
2 tablespoons fresh lime juice
1 tablespoon dark sesame oil
1 teaspoon toasted coriander seeds
2 garlic cloves
1 shallot, peeled
⅓ cup light coconut milk
3 tablespoons brown sugar
1 tablespoon grated peeled fresh ginger
¼ teaspoon ground turmeric
1 serrano chile, stem removed
6 skinless, boneless chicken thighs, cut into 36 pieces
½ teaspoon salt

1. Combine first 7 ingredients in a food processor, and process until smooth. Add coconut milk and next 4 ingredients; process until smooth. Spoon peanut mixture into a large zip-top plastic bag. Add chicken to bag, and seal. Marinate in refrigerator 1 hour, turning after 30 minutes.
2. Preheat grill to medium-high heat.
3. Remove chicken from bag, and discard marinade. Thread chicken evenly onto 12 (6-inch) skewers; sprinkle evenly with salt. Grill 6 minutes on each side or until chicken is done. Yield: 4 servings (serving size: 3 skewers).

CALORIES 300; FAT 15.2g (sat 2.7g, mono 6.1g, poly 4.7g); PROTEIN 24.6g; CARB 17.5g; FIBER 2.1g; CHOL 86mg; IRON 2.2mg; SODIUM 508mg; CALC 51mg

WINE NOTE: The slightly floral-scented Pie de Palo, Viognier (Mendoza, Argentina, $10) is layered with unctuous ripe peach and provides a fierce backbone of bright orange acidity on which this fiery-sweet dish can hang its intricate flavors.

DINNER TONIGHT

Here is a batch of fast weeknight menus from the *Cooking Light* Test Kitchens.

READY IN
40
MINUTES

The
SHOPPING LIST

Baked Ziti and Summer Veggies
yellow squash
zucchini
onion
tomato
garlic
fresh basil
fresh oregano
crushed red pepper
olive oil
ziti
4 ounces part-skim mozzarella cheese
2 ounces part-skim ricotta cheese
1 large egg

Mixed Greens Salad
lemon
mixed salad greens
pine nuts

The
GAME PLAN

While pasta cooks:
■ Sauté veggies.
While pasta bakes:
■ Prepare salad.

Quick & Easy • Vegetarian
Baked Ziti and Summer Veggies
With Mixed Greens Salad

Simple Sub: Use eggplant instead of yellow squash.
Shopping Tip: Hit a farmers' market for the freshest local produce.
Flavor Hit: Kick up the heat in the dish by using ¼ teaspoon crushed red pepper.

4 ounces uncooked ziti
1 tablespoon olive oil
2 cups chopped yellow squash
1 cup chopped zucchini
½ cup chopped onion
2 cups chopped tomato
2 garlic cloves, minced
1 cup (4 ounces) shredded part-skim mozzarella cheese, divided
2 tablespoons chopped fresh basil
2 teaspoons chopped fresh oregano
¾ teaspoon salt, divided
⅛ teaspoon crushed red pepper
¼ cup (2 ounces) part-skim ricotta cheese
1 large egg, lightly beaten
Cooking spray

1. Cook pasta according to package directions, omitting salt and fat; drain.
2. Preheat oven to 400°.
3. Heat a large skillet over medium-high heat. Add oil to pan. Add squash, zucchini, and onion; sauté 5 minutes. Add tomato and garlic; sauté 3 minutes. Remove from heat; stir in pasta, ½ cup mozzarella, herbs, ½ teaspoon salt, and pepper.
4. Combine ricotta, remaining ¼ teaspoon salt, and egg. Stir into pasta mixture. Spoon into an 8-inch square glass or ceramic baking dish coated with cooking spray; sprinkle with remaining ½ cup mozzarella. Bake at 400° for 15 minutes or until bubbly and browned. Yield: 4 servings (serving size: about 1½ cups).

CALORIES 301; FAT 12.1g (sat 5.3g, mono 5g, poly 0.9g); PROTEIN 16.5g; CARB 32.8g; FIBER 4.1g; CHOL 65mg; IRON 1.9mg; SODIUM 640mg; CALC 291mg

---

For the Mixed Greens Salad:
Combine 3 tablespoons fresh lemon juice and 2 tablespoons olive oil in a large bowl. Add 4 cups mixed salad greens; toss. Sprinkle with 1 tablespoon toasted pine nuts. Yield: 4 servings (serving size: about 1 cup).

CALORIES 85; FAT 8.2g (sat 1g); SODIUM 7mg

READY IN
40
MINUTES

The
SHOPPING LIST

Pan-Fried Shrimp with Creole Mayonnaise
salt-free Creole seasoning
dry breadcrumbs
olive oil
all-purpose flour
canola mayonnaise
Worcestershire sauce
hot sauce
1½ pounds peeled and deveined large shrimp
fat-free milk

Tomato, Cucumber, and Fennel Salad
lemon
English cucumber
cherry tomatoes
fennel bulb
olive oil

The
GAME PLAN

■ Prepare salad.
■ Dredge shrimp.
While shrimp cooks:
■ Prepare Creole mayonnaise.

Pan-Fried Shrimp with Creole Mayonnaise

With Tomato, Cucumber, and Fennel Salad

Flavor Hit: Creole seasoning is a zesty spice blend with heat from ground red pepper.
Simple Sub: Use panko in place of regular dry breadcrumbs for extra crunch.
Prep Pointer: Get the oil hot before adding the shrimp so they don't absorb too much of it.

2.25 ounces all-purpose flour (about ½ cup)
1¼ teaspoons salt-free Creole seasoning, divided
⅛ teaspoon salt
¼ cup fat-free milk
¾ cup dry breadcrumbs
1½ pounds peeled and deveined large shrimp
3 tablespoons olive oil, divided
2 tablespoons canola mayonnaise
1 teaspoon Worcestershire sauce
¼ teaspoon hot sauce

1. Combine flour, 1 teaspoon Creole seasoning, and salt in a shallow dish. Pour milk into a shallow dish. Place breadcrumbs in a shallow dish. Dredge shrimp in flour mixture; dip in milk. Dredge shrimp in breadcrumbs; shake off excess breading.
2. Heat a large nonstick skillet over medium-high heat. Add 1½ tablespoons oil to pan; swirl to coat. Add half of shrimp; cook 2 minutes on each side or until done. Repeat procedure with remaining oil and shrimp.
3. Combine mayonnaise, remaining ¼ teaspoon Creole seasoning, Worcestershire, and hot sauce in a small bowl; stir with a whisk. Serve Creole mayonnaise with shrimp. Yield: 4 servings (serving size: about 5 ounces shrimp and 2 teaspoons Creole mayonnaise).

Sustainable Choice | Buy U.S. or Canadian wild-caught or farmed shrimp for the best sustainable option.

CALORIES 427; FAT 19.5g (sat 2.5g, mono 11.3g, poly 4g); PROTEIN 38.4g; CARB 22g; FIBER 0.9g; CHOL 261mg; IRON 4.7mg; SODIUM 511mg; CALC 111mg

For the Tomato, Cucumber, and Fennel Salad:
Combine 1½ tablespoons lemon juice, 1 tablespoon olive oil, ⅛ teaspoon salt, and ⅛ teaspoon pepper in a small bowl. Combine 2 cups sliced cucumber, ½ cup cherry tomato wedges, and ¼ cup sliced fennel bulb in a bowl. Pour dressing over vegetables; toss. Yield: 4 servings (serving size: about ⅔ cup).

CALORIES 45; FAT 3.5g (sat 0.5g); SODIUM 79mg

READY IN 40 MINUTES

The SHOPPING LIST

Chicken Kebabs and Nectarine Salsa
3 nectarines
red bell pepper
2 red onions
lime
1 jalapeño pepper
fresh cilantro
bottled minced garlic
avocado
olive oil
brown sugar
chili powder
ground cumin
1½ pounds skinless, boneless chicken breast halves

Herbed Couscous
fat-free, lower-sodium chicken broth
1 cup uncooked couscous
fresh parsley
fresh chives

The GAME PLAN

■ Prepare spice rub for chicken.
While chicken marinates:
■ Prepare salsa.
While chicken broils:
■ Make couscous.

Chicken Kebabs and Nectarine Salsa

With Herbed Couscous

Simple Sub: Use peaches or plums instead of nectarines.
Prep Pointer: Stir in avocado just before serving so it doesn't get mushy or brown.
Make-Ahead Tip: Prepare spice rub up to 1 day ahead, and store in the fridge.

1 tablespoon brown sugar
1 tablespoon olive oil
1 tablespoon fresh lime juice
2 teaspoons chili powder
1 teaspoon bottled minced garlic
½ teaspoon kosher salt
½ teaspoon ground cumin
¼ teaspoon freshly ground black pepper
1½ pounds skinless, boneless chicken breast halves, cut into 24 (2-inch) pieces
1 large red onion, cut into 32 (2-inch) pieces
Cooking spray
2 cups diced nectarine (about 3)
½ cup diced red bell pepper
¼ cup thinly sliced red onion
2 tablespoons fresh cilantro leaves
1½ tablespoons fresh lime juice
2 teaspoons minced seeded jalapeño pepper
¼ teaspoon kosher salt
½ cup diced peeled avocado

1. Preheat broiler. Combine first 9 ingredients in a shallow dish; let stand 15 minutes.
2. Thread 4 onion pieces and 3 chicken pieces alternately onto each of 8 (12-inch) skewers. Place skewers on broiler pan coated with cooking spray. Broil 12 minutes or until chicken is done, turning occasionally.
3. Combine nectarines and next 6 ingredients in a bowl. Gently stir in avocado. Yield: 4 servings (serving size: 2 skewers and ¾ cup salsa).

CALORIES 324; FAT 8.9g (sat 1.5g, mono 4.9g, poly 1.3g); PROTEIN 41.2g; CARB 18.5g; FIBER 3.8g; CHOL 99mg; IRON 1.9mg; SODIUM 547mg; CALC 44mg

continued

For the Herbed Couscous:
Combine ¾ cup fat-free, lower-sodium chicken broth and ½ cup water in a saucepan; boil. Stir in 1 cup uncooked couscous. Remove from heat; cover and let stand 5 minutes. Fluff with a fork. Stir in 2 tablespoons chopped fresh parsley, 2 tablespoons chopped fresh chives, and ¼ teaspoon salt.

CALORIES 167; **FAT** 0.4g (sat 0.1g); **SODIUM** 226mg

READY IN
40
MINUTES

The
....
SHOPPING LIST

Pork Tenderloin Medallions and Balsamic Reduction

shallots
1 fresh garlic clove
fresh rosemary
olive oil
Dijon mustard
balsamic vinegar
white granulated sugar
1 (1-pound) pork tenderloin

Grilled Peaches

2 peaches

Wild Rice Salad

green onions
dried sweet cherries
pecans
fast-cooking white and wild rice

The
....
GAME PLAN

- Prepare rice salad.
  While rice cooks:
- Cook peaches.
- Start reduction.
  While vinegar reduces:
- Cook pork.

Quick & Easy
Pork Tenderloin Medallions and Balsamic Reduction
With Grilled Peaches and Wild Rice Salad

Flavor Hit: Fresh rosemary infuses the sauce with pinelike fragrance and taste.
Prep Pointer: Keep your stove's exhaust fan on as the vinegar cooks to draw off pungent fumes.
Budget Buy: Inexpensive balsamic vinegar will work just fine in the reduction.

1 tablespoon olive oil
1 tablespoon minced shallots
1 garlic clove, minced
1 cup balsamic vinegar
1½ teaspoons sugar
1 teaspoon chopped fresh rosemary
1 teaspoon Dijon mustard
Cooking spray
1 (1-pound) pork tenderloin, cut into 12 slices
½ teaspoon salt
½ teaspoon freshly ground black pepper

1. Heat oil in a small saucepan over medium-high heat. Add shallots and garlic; sauté 2 minutes. Add vinegar and next 3 ingredients; cook until reduced to ½ cup.
2. Heat a large skillet over medium-high heat. Coat pan with cooking spray. Sprinkle pork with salt and pepper. Place pork in pan; cook 2 minutes on each side. Add balsamic reduction; cook 1 minute, turning pork to coat. Yield: 4 servings (serving size: 3 pork medallions and 2 tablespoons reduction).

CALORIES 222; **FAT** 6g (sat 1.3g, mono 3.4g, poly 0.8g); **PROTEIN** 24.2g; **CARB** 13.6g; **FIBER** 0.1g; **CHOL** 74mg; **IRON** 1.7mg; **SODIUM** 400mg; **CALC** 27mg

For the Grilled Peaches:
Heat a grill pan over medium-high heat. Coat pan with cooking spray. Add 4 peach halves to pan; cook 2 minutes on each side. Cut each half into 3 wedges. Yield: 4 servings (serving size: 3 wedges).

CALORIES 34; **FAT** 0.2g (sat 0g); **SODIUM** 0mg

For the Wild Rice Salad:
Cook 1 cup fast-cooking white and wild rice per package directions, omitting seasoning. Stir in ¼ cup chopped green onions, 2 tablespoons chopped dried cherries, and 2 tablespoons chopped pecans. Yield: 4 servings (serving size: ½ cup).

CALORIES 199; **FAT** 2.8g (sat 0.3g); **SODIUM** 153mg

SUPERFAST

Very fresh is ideal for Superfast: Summer's perfect produce captured in a flash.

Quick & Easy
Open-Faced Prosciutto and Plum Sandwiches

Sweet fig preserves balance the tartness of the plums. Choose red or purple plums with bright, unblemished skin that are firm and plump to the touch.

¼ cup fig preserves
1 tablespoon fresh lemon juice
¼ teaspoon grated peeled fresh ginger
⅓ cup (3 ounces) soft goat cheese
4 (2-ounce) slices country wheat bread, toasted
1 cup loosely packed arugula
2 ripe plums, cut into thin wedges
3 ounces very thin slices prosciutto

1. Combine first 3 ingredients, stirring with a whisk; set aside.
2. Spread ¾ ounce cheese evenly over each bread slice; divide arugula, plum wedges, and prosciutto evenly over sandwiches. Drizzle each sandwich with about 1 tablespoon fig preserves mixture. Yield: 4 servings (serving size: 1 sandwich).

CALORIES 318; **FAT** 9.1g (sat 5.1g, mono 3.1g, poly 0.6g); **PROTEIN** 13.1g; **CARB** 45.5g; **FIBER** 1.9g; **CHOL** 26mg; **IRON** 4.4mg; **SODIUM** 689mg; **CALC** 161mg

Linguine with Two-Cheese Sauce

8 ounces uncooked linguine
1 cup 1% low-fat milk
2 tablespoons chopped fresh basil, divided
1/2 teaspoon salt
1/8 teaspoon freshly ground black pepper
1 tablespoon extra-virgin olive oil
1 tablespoon all-purpose flour
1/2 cup (2 ounces) shaved fresh Parmigiano-
  Reggiano cheese, divided
1 1/2 tablespoons mascarpone cheese

1. Cook pasta according to package directions, omitting salt and fat. Drain; keep warm.
2. While pasta cooks, combine milk, 2 teaspoons basil, salt, and pepper in a bowl; stir milk mixture with a whisk.
3. Heat a small saucepan over medium heat. Add oil to pan; swirl to coat. Add flour to pan, and cook 2 minutes, stirring constantly. Add milk mixture; cook 3 minutes or until slightly thick, stirring frequently. Remove from heat, and add 1 1/2 ounces Parmigiano-Reggiano and mascarpone cheese to milk mixture. Add cheese mixture to pasta; toss to combine. Sprinkle with remaining 4 teaspoons basil and remaining 1/2 ounce Parmigiano-Reggiano. Yield: 4 servings (serving size: 1 cup pasta mixture and 1 teaspoon basil).

CALORIES 376; **FAT** 13.7g (sat 6.2g, mono 3.8g, poly 0.6g); **PROTEIN** 16.2g; **CARB** 47.4g; **FIBER** 1.9g; **CHOL** 29mg; **IRON** 2.1mg; **SODIUM** 547mg; **CALC** 258mg

Green Beans with Toasted Garlic

1 pound green beans, trimmed
2 teaspoons butter
1 teaspoon olive oil
4 garlic cloves, thinly sliced
1/4 teaspoon salt
1/4 teaspoon black pepper

1. Bring a large saucepan of water to a boil. Add beans; cook 5 minutes. Plunge beans into ice water; drain.
2. Heat a large skillet over medium-high heat. Add butter and oil; swirl until butter melts. Add garlic; sauté 30 seconds. Remove garlic; set aside. Add beans; sprinkle with salt and pepper. Cook 2 minutes, tossing frequently. Top with garlic. Yield: 4 servings (serving size: about 1 cup).

CALORIES 67; **FAT** 3.2g (sat 1.4g, mono 1.3g, poly 0.3g); **PROTEIN** 2.3g; **CARB** 9.2g; **FIBER** 4g; **CHOL** 5mg; **IRON** 1.3mg; **SODIUM** 169mg; **CALC** 49mg

Sesame-Soy Variation:
Prepare beans through step 1. Heat 1 tablespoon dark sesame oil in a skillet over medium-high heat. Add 2 minced garlic cloves and 1/4 teaspoon crushed red pepper; sauté 30 seconds. Add beans, 1 tablespoon lower-sodium soy sauce, and 1/8 teaspoon salt; cook 2 minutes, tossing frequently. Sprinkle with 1/2 teaspoon toasted sesame seeds. Yield: 4 servings.

CALORIES 72; **FAT** 3.8g (sat 0.5g); **SODIUM** 214mg

Citrus-Nut Variation:
Prepare green beans through step 1. Combine beans, 1 tablespoon extra-virgin olive oil, 1/4 teaspoon salt, and 1/4 teaspoon freshly ground black pepper; toss. Combine 2 tablespoons finely chopped blanched hazelnuts, 2 tablespoons chopped fresh parsley, 1/2 teaspoon grated orange rind, and 1 minced garlic clove; sprinkle over beans. Yield: 4 servings.

CALORIES 90; **FAT** 5.7g (sat 0.7g); **SODIUM** 156mg

Peppery Bacon Variation:
Prepare green beans through step 1. Cook 2 chopped bacon slices in a skillet over medium-high heat until crisp. Remove bacon, reserving 2 teaspoons drippings in pan. Add 2 tablespoons chopped shallots; sauté 2 minutes. Add beans; sprinkle with 1/2 teaspoon pepper and 1/4 teaspoon salt. Cook 2 minutes. Top with bacon. Yield: 4 servings.

CALORIES 76; **FAT** 3.6g (sat 1.3g); **SODIUM** 231mg

Greek Yogurt with Warm Black and Blueberry Sauce
(pictured on page 225)

Substitute fresh berries for frozen when making this year-round treat in the summer. This sauce also pairs well with biscuits or as a stand-in for syrup on pancakes.

2/3 cup frozen blueberries
2/3 cup frozen blackberries
1/2 cup water
1/4 cup sugar
2 tablespoons fresh lemon juice
1 tablespoon butter
2 cups plain 2% reduced-fat Greek yogurt

1. Combine first 5 ingredients in a small saucepan. Bring mixture to a boil. Reduce heat to medium-low; gently boil 10 minutes or until sauce thickens. Stir in butter.
2. Spoon 1/2 cup yogurt into each of 4 bowls; top each serving with about 1/4 cup sauce. Serve immediately. Yield: 4 servings.

CALORIES 192; **FAT** 5.8g (sat 3.8g, mono 0.8g, poly 0.2g); **PROTEIN** 11.8g; **CARB** 25.7g; **FIBER** 2g; **CHOL** 14mg; **IRON** 0.3mg; **SODIUM** 64mg; **CALC** 131mg

Bombay Shrimp Curry with Coconut Rice

5 teaspoons canola oil, divided
1 pound peeled and deveined shrimp
¾ teaspoon salt, divided
¼ teaspoon black pepper
1½ cups prechopped onion
1½ tablespoons curry powder
1 tablespoon mustard seeds
¼ teaspoon ground cinnamon
⅛ teaspoon ground red pepper
1⅓ cups hot water
1 cup frozen peas and carrots
1 cup light coconut milk
1 cup uncooked instant rice
1 tablespoon chopped fresh cilantro

1. Heat a Dutch oven over medium-high heat. Add 2 teaspoons oil; swirl to coat. Sprinkle shrimp with ⅛ teaspoon salt and black pepper. Add shrimp to pan; cook 2 minutes on each side or until done. Remove from pan.
2. Reduce heat to medium; add remaining 3 teaspoons oil; swirl to coat. Add onion; cook 2 minutes, stirring constantly. Add ½ teaspoon salt, curry powder, and next 3 ingredients; cook 1 minute, stirring constantly. Add hot water and peas and carrots; bring to a boil. Cover and reduce heat to medium-low; simmer 4 minutes. Return shrimp to pan; cook 1 minute.
3. While curry cooks, bring milk to a boil in a saucepan. Stir in remaining ⅛ teaspoon salt and rice. Cover and remove from heat. Let stand 5 minutes or until liquid is absorbed.
4. Place about ⅓ cup rice on each of 4 plates; top each serving with about 1 cup shrimp mixture. Sprinkle each serving with ¾ teaspoon cilantro. Yield: 4 servings.

Sustainable Choice | Buy U.S. or Canadian wild-caught or farmed shrimp for the best sustainable option.

CALORIES 366; FAT 12.5g (sat 3.8g, mono 4.7g, poly 2.7g); PROTEIN 28.4g; CARB 36.1g; FIBER 4g; CHOL 172mg; IRON 5.9mg; SODIUM 660mg; CALC 115mg

WHAT TO EAT RIGHT NOW
PACIFIC SALMON

Rich, buttery salmon is a rock star when it comes to nutrition because it's one of the best sources of heart-healthy omega-3 fats. Even better, the unctuous flavor and meaty-fatty texture make it seem luxurious and indulgent, a real treat to eat. Its high fat content keeps it moist even when slightly overcooked—so it's a perfect option for the intense heat of the grill. Now is the best time of year to find wild Pacific king salmon—the premier, largest, and most full-flavored species. Many fish return to fresh water to spawn beginning in May and continuing through July. Sockeye and coho salmon are also abundant during summer months and offer a milder flavor. If you're concerned about sustainability, stick with wild Pacific salmon, especially Alaskan.

FISHING FOR FLAVORS

Versatile salmon pairs with bold and subtle tastes.

SALTY: lower-sodium soy sauce, capers, miso, olives

SWEET: honey, brown sugar, maple syrup, orange juice or rind

SOUR: fresh lemon, fresh lime, vinegar

PUNGENT: onion, shallot, garlic, ginger, horseradish, sesame

CREAMY: cream cheese, yogurt, crème fraîche, butter

SMOKY: chipotle chiles, smoked paprika, cumin

GREEN: fresh herbs (especially dill, chives, and mint), cucumber, asparagus

Grilled King Salmon with Tomato-Peach Salsa
(pictured on page 226)

Hands-on time: 15 min. Total time: 25 min.

Use a peach that's just ripe so it's juicy but still holds its shape. King (also called chinook) salmon is the best quality and works well in this dish, though sockeye works, too.

1 cup chopped peeled peach
¾ cup quartered cherry tomatoes
¼ cup thinly vertically sliced red onion
3 tablespoons small fresh mint leaves
3 tablespoons small fresh basil leaves
2 tablespoons fresh lemon juice
1 tablespoon extra-virgin olive oil
1 tablespoon honey
1 jalapeño pepper, thinly sliced (optional)
1 teaspoon kosher salt, divided
4 (6-ounce) wild Alaskan king salmon fillets
¼ teaspoon freshly ground black pepper
Cooking spray

1. Preheat grill to high heat.
2. Combine first 8 ingredients in a bowl; add jalapeño, if desired. Sprinkle mixture with ¼ teaspoon salt; toss gently. Sprinkle fillets evenly with remaining ¾ teaspoon salt and black pepper. Place fillets on grill rack coated with cooking spray, and grill 10 minutes or until desired degree of doneness, turning after 5 minutes. Serve with salsa. Yield: 4 servings (serving size: 1 fillet and about ½ cup salsa).

CALORIES 325; FAT 21.9g (sat 3.3g, mono 10.2g, poly 2.8g); PROTEIN 26.7g; CARB 6.4g; FIBER 1.2g; CHOL 78mg; IRON 1.4mg; SODIUM 544mg; CALC 68mg

DID YOU KNOW? SALMON STOP EATING WHEN THEY ENTER FRESH WATER TO SPAWN.

OOPS! YOUR HARD-COOKED EGGS ARE ICKY

For a perfect egg every time, heat slowly and cool quickly.
By Hannah Klinger

We've all puzzled, after following someone's can't-fail advice, over less-than-perfect hard-cooked eggs—the eggs with rubbery whites, chalky yolks, and that tell-tale green-gray film between yolk and white. The cause? Temperature differential: The white of an egg dropped into boiling water cooks much faster than the yolk at the center, and that's trouble. By the time the yolk sets, the white is tough. And if the egg stays over high heat too long, or isn't cooled quickly after cooking, sulfur in the white will react with iron in the yolk, creating that nasty off-colored ring.

Here's the fix: To keep the temperature of the egg white and yolk close, heat the eggs gradually. Place them in a saucepan, cover them with an inch or two of cold water, and set the pan over high heat. When the water reaches a full boil, remove from heat, cover the pan, and let the eggs stand for 10 minutes. This cooks them gently and keeps the whites from toughening. Peel the eggs immediately under cold running water; or, if you're not using them right away, set them in an ice-water bath. This lowers the eggs' temperature and minimizes the pressure that causes sulfur rings to form.

(bad news)

(good egg)

THE PERFECT DISH FOR ROSÉ

And 5 American bottles to uncork on the Fourth of July.

The crisp, berry-floral essence of American rosé wines pairs beautifully with creamy, lemony lobster rolls. Rosés start with any red grape variety (or sometimes a blend), but the juice stays in contact with the skins for a brief soak, resulting in less color and softer flavor than red wine. Color ranges from a pale salmon to brilliant magenta. Our top pairing is Heitz Cellar 2010 Grignolino Rosé ($18), with tart cranberry notes that slice through the buttery lobster.

Kid Friendly
Picnic-Perfect Lobster Rolls

Hands-on time: 12 min. Total time: 1 hr. 12 min.

This classic New England sandwich comes together in a snap if you purchase lobster tails and have them steamed at the fish counter.

1/3 cup chopped celery
2 tablespoons chopped green onions
1 tablespoon finely chopped fresh tarragon
3 tablespoons canola mayonnaise
1/2 teaspoon grated lemon rind
1 1/2 tablespoons fresh lemon juice
1/2 teaspoon Dijon mustard
1/4 teaspoon kosher salt
1/4 teaspoon black pepper
1/8 teaspoon ground red pepper
3/4 pound lobster meat, steamed and chopped
4 (1 1/2-ounce) New England–style hot dog buns, toasted

1. Combine first 11 ingredients in a large bowl, stirring well; cover and chill at least 1 hour. Divide lobster mixture evenly among buns. Yield: 4 servings (serving size: 1 sandwich).

CALORIES 284; FAT 10.3g (sat 0.8g, mono 4.9g, poly 2.7g); PROTEIN 21.7g; CARB 22.4g; FIBER 0.3g; CHOL 65mg; IRON 1.5mg; SODIUM 731mg; CALC 61mg

A RANGE OF CHOICES, FROM AFFORDABLE TO SPLURGE

BARGAIN PICK
Toad Hollow 2010 Dry Rosé, Sonoma County; $11. Hints of cherry, violets, and pepper. Bone dry.

BASTILLE DAY
Copain Rosé Wine Anderson Valley, Calif.; $20. French-style: flint, strawberries, and watermelon rind.

SPECIAL OCCASION
Schramsberg Mirabelle Brut Rosé, Calistoga, Calif.; $21. Berries, vanilla, and licorice.

DINNER PARTY
Kuleto Estate Rosato 2009, Napa Valley; $24. Rose petals, as well as fresh strawberries.

READER RECIPE
FROM YOUR KITCHEN TO OURS

Summer's garden bounty allows Katie Koonce to feed her family food that is as local and organic as can be. "I try to incorporate a lot of the veggies from our garden into the dishes I make because we know where they're coming from," she says. But with so much squash and zucchini on hand, there's the usual challenge: How do you get kids to eat these bland-at-first-bite vegetables? Koonce thought to make quiche: With a creamy filling and flaky crust, it's a family-pleasing favorite her 4-year-old likes to call "pie." Try pairing this quiche with a green salad for a hearty brunch or light dinner.

Make Ahead • Kid Friendly
Summer Squash, Bacon, and Mozzarella Quiche

Hands-on time: 25 min. Total time: 2 hr. 40 min.

"To save time, I often make a big batch of dough for piecrusts, shape it into discs, and then freeze them in a zip-top bag."
—Katie Koonce, Santa Barbara, California

Crust:
6.75 ounces all-purpose flour (about 1 1/2 cups)
1/2 teaspoon salt
3 tablespoons chilled unsalted butter, cut into small pieces
2 tablespoons vegetable shortening, cut into small pieces
1/4 cup ice water
Cooking spray
Filling:
1 tablespoon extra-virgin olive oil
2 cups (1/8-inch-thick) slices yellow squash
2 cups (1/8-inch-thick) slices zucchini
1/4 cup chopped shallots
1 tablespoon chopped fresh thyme
1 cup 2% reduced-fat milk
3/4 teaspoon salt
1/4 teaspoon freshly ground black pepper
4 center-cut bacon slices, cooked and crumbled
3 large eggs
3 large egg whites
3/4 cup (3 ounces) shredded part-skim mozzarella cheese

1. To prepare crust, weigh or lightly spoon flour into dry measuring cups; level with a knife. Combine flour and 1/2 teaspoon salt in a food processor, and pulse 2 times or until combined. Add butter and shortening; pulse 4 times or until mixture resembles coarse meal. With processor on, add ice water through food chute, processing just until mixture is combined (do not form a ball). Press mixture into a 4-inch circle on plastic wrap, and cover. Refrigerate 1 hour.

2. Preheat oven to 400°.

3. Slightly overlap 2 sheets of plastic wrap on a slightly damp flat surface. Unwrap and place chilled dough on plastic wrap. Cover dough with 2 additional sheets of overlapping plastic wrap. Roll dough, still covered, into a 12-inch circle. Place dough in freezer 5 minutes or until plastic wrap can easily be removed. Remove top sheets of plastic wrap, and fit dough, plastic wrap side up, into a 9½-inch deep-dish pie plate coated with cooking spray. Remove remaining plastic wrap from dough. Fold edges under, and flute. Pierce bottom and sides of dough with a fork. Bake at 400° for 15 minutes. Cool on a wire rack.

4. Reduce oven temperature to 350°.

5. To prepare filling, heat a large nonstick skillet over medium-high heat. Add oil to pan; swirl to coat. Add squash, zucchini, shallots, and thyme; sauté 5 minutes or until squash and zucchini are tender, stirring frequently. Cool squash mixture slightly.

6. Combine 1 cup reduced-fat milk and next 5 ingredients in a large bowl, stirring with a whisk. Arrange squash mixture evenly over crust, and sprinkle with ¾ cup mozzarella cheese. Pour egg mixture over cheese. Bake at 350° for 45 minutes or until filling is set. Cool 15 minutes on wire rack. Yield: 8 servings (serving size: 1 wedge).

CALORIES 265; **FAT** 14.1g (sat 6.3g, mono 4.3g, poly 1.5g); **PROTEIN** 11.2g; **CARB** 22.4g; **FIBER** 1.2g; **CHOL** 90mg; **IRON** 1.7mg; **SODIUM** 556mg; **CALC** 134mg

PRETTY AS PIE (BUT IT'S QUICHE)

Nothing equals the satisfaction of a homemade piecrust, and fluting the pastry adds a lovely grace note.

1. Press chilled dough into pie plate, allowing it to conform to the shape of the dish; remove plastic wrap.

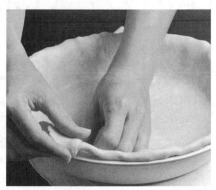

2. Fold under overhanging edges of dough.

3. Use the thumb of one hand to push the rim of dough between the thumb and index finger of the other hand; repeat around entire edge of pie plate.

4. Pierce bottom and sides of dough with a fork to help the crust hold its shape as it bakes.

THE CLAMBAKE COMES HOME

Beach is nice, but backyard is easy for this classic American summer seafood feast.

A New England purist might get all huffy to see that our simple clambake requires no surf-pounded beach, no seaweed-lined hole, not even a backyard dig—just a grill and a stove. We (including the New Englanders on staff) believe that a clambake is too much fun to deny landlocked Americans its pleasures, and this menu bursts with the essence of clambake fun: briny clams that taste of the ocean; smoky, lightly charred corn; good old potato nourishment spiced up with Portuguese sausage; and the luxury of succulent lobster. You can opt to end the meal with a simple slice of watermelon, but we wrap up with a delightful blueberry crisp.

Some of these dishes need a little advance prep—soaking wood chips, corn, and clams, for example—but the food is simple and straightforward. Our Game Plan makes planning a snap. If you're unfamiliar with the finer points of buying or cooking lobster or steamers, there's a Landlubber's Guide on page 192. Beach? Pshaw!

Quick & Easy • Vegetarian
Butter Sauce

Hands-on time: 5 min. Total time: 5 min.

This simple sauce is an emulsion—the end product should have a thick, creamy consistency and the light color of cold butter. It's an indulgent sauce but perfect for pairing with low-fat lobsters and steamed clams.

1 tablespoon fresh lemon juice
6 tablespoons chilled butter, cut into small
   pieces
Dash of ground red pepper

1. Heat lemon juice in a small saucepan over low heat. Gradually add pieces of butter, stirring constantly with a whisk until butter is melted and well blended. Stir in red pepper. Yield: 8 servings (serving size: about 1 tablespoon).

CALORIES 77; FAT 8.6g (sat 5.5g, mono 2.2g, poly 0.3g);
PROTEIN 0.1g; CARB 0.2g; FIBER 0g; CHOL 23mg;
IRON 0mg; SODIUM 61mg; CALC 3mg

Beer-Steamed Soft-Shell Clams

Hands-on time: 25 min. Total time: 2 hr. 10 min.

For a charcoal grill, simply toss the wood on the coals just as you begin to cook—no need for a foil pan. Make sure the pan you choose for the clams will fit inside your grill. If soft-shell clams aren't available, scrubbed littleneck clams will also work in the recipe, and they don't require soaking in cornmeal—check for doneness after 10 minutes. Serve with strained steaming liquid or heated clam broth to dunk the clams in for one last rinse, and then dip in Butter Sauce (left).

2 cups wood chips
2 pounds soft-shell clams
⅓ cup yellow cornmeal
1 tablespoon kosher salt
12 ounces room temperature medium-bodied
   beer, such as pale ale
1 cup warm water (100° to 110°)
2 tablespoons minced garlic
1 lemon, thinly sliced

LOBSTERS & STEAMERS: Lobsters trapped off waters near the Northeast U.S. and Canada are smart sustainable options, as are wild-caught or farmed soft-shell clams.

1. Soak wood chips in water 1 hour, and drain.
2. Place clams in sink, and cover with cool water. Rinse clams well, rubbing together to dislodge grit, and drain. Repeat until water is clear. Drain clams. Place in a large bowl, and cover clams with cold water. Stir in cornmeal and salt. Refrigerate and soak 30 minutes.
3. Preheat grill to medium-high heat.
4. Remove grill rack; set aside. Pierce bottom of a disposable aluminum foil pan several times with the tip of a knife. Place pan directly on heat element on bottom of grill; add wood chips to pan. Place grill rack on grill. Arrange clams in a grill-safe roasting pan, large shallow baking pan, or sturdy disposable foil pan. Pour beer and 1 cup warm water over clams; arrange garlic and lemon over clams. Place pan on grill; cover grill, and cook 15 minutes. Stir clams. Cover grill, and cook 5 minutes or until clams open. Discard any unopened shells. Yield: 8 servings (serving size: about 6 clams).

CALORIES 36; FAT 0.3g (sat 0g, mono 0g, poly 0.1g);
PROTEIN 4.6g; CARB 3.3g; FIBER 0.1g; CHOL 11mg;
IRON 4.8mg; SODIUM 95mg; CALC 23mg

CLAMS, CORN & POTATOES WITH A SPICY KICK. PLUS ALL THE LUXURY OF LOBSTER.

Vegetarian
Grilled Corn on the Cob

Hands-on time: 13 min. Total time: 1 hr. 13 min.

Grilled in its husk, the corn takes on a wonderful, lightly charred flavor while its sugars caramelize and intensify. Soaking in salted water lightly seasons the corn and helps keep it moist as it grills. Then, since the silks have been removed, just peel and enjoy.

8 ears corn with husks
1 tablespoon kosher salt
2 tablespoons butter, melted

1. Preheat grill to medium-high heat.
2. Pull husks back from corn, keeping husks intact; scrub off silks, and pull husks back over corn to cover. Place corn and salt in a large stockpot; cover with water. Let stand 45 minutes; drain.
3. Place corn on grill rack, and grill for 8 minutes on each side or until husks are blackened. Serve grilled corn with butter. Yield: 8 servings (serving size: 1 ear of corn and ¾ teaspoon butter).

CALORIES 148; **FAT** 4.6g (sat 2.1g, mono 1.2g, poly 0.9g); **PROTEIN** 4.6g; **CARB** 27.2g; **FIBER** 3.9g; **CHOL** 8mg; **IRON** 0.7mg; **SODIUM** 114mg; **CALC** 4mg

New Potatoes with Onions and Spicy Sausage

Hands-on time: 33 min. Total time: 1 hr. 19 min.

Linguica is a Portuguese sausage—you can substitute Spanish-style chorizo or kielbasa. Leave the root end intact on the onions so they don't fall apart as they cook.

3 cups water
2 tablespoons Dijon mustard
1 teaspoon sweet paprika
2 teaspoons white vinegar
½ teaspoon ground red pepper
1 (14-ounce) can fat-free, lower-sodium chicken broth
2 bay leaves
16 small red and yellow potatoes, halved lengthwise (about 18 ounces)
8 small boiling onions, peeled (root end left intact)
Cooking spray
4 ounces linguica sausage, diced
1 tablespoon chopped fresh flat-leaf parsley
½ teaspoon kosher salt

1. Remove grill rack, and set aside. Prepare grill for indirect grilling, heating one side to medium-high and leaving one side with no heat. Place grill rack on grill.
2. Combine 3 cups water, Dijon mustard, and next 5 ingredients in a large saucepan. Bring to a boil, and cook 2 minutes. Add potatoes and onions; bring to a boil. Reduce heat to low, and simmer 12 minutes. Remove from heat, and let stand 10 minutes in cooking liquid; drain. Cut onions in half.
3. Pierce bottom of a disposable aluminum foil pan several times with the tip of a knife. Place potatoes and onions in pan, and coat with cooking spray. Place pan on grill rack over unheated side of grill; cover grill, and cook 25 minutes or until lightly browned.
4. Heat a large nonstick skillet over medium-high heat. Coat pan with cooking spray. Add sausage, and sauté 4 minutes or until lightly browned. Combine sausage, potato mixture, parsley, and salt in a large bowl; toss gently. Yield: 8 servings (serving size: about ½ cup).

CALORIES 133; **FAT** 5.7g (sat 2.1g, mono 2.6g, poly 0.5g); **PROTEIN** 5.3g; **CARB** 15.8g; **FIBER** 2.1g; **CHOL** 12mg; **IRON** 0.8mg; **SODIUM** 311mg; **CALC** 21mg

Grilled Maine Lobsters

Hands-on time: 17 min. Total time: 1 hr. 32 min.

If you don't have the grill capacity to cook all the lobsters at once, the relatively brief cooking time makes it easy to do them in batches. The lobsters will be bright red with a few blackened spots when done cooking. To check doneness, break a lobster open where the tail and body meet—the meat should be opaque and white. Serve with Butter Sauce (page 190).

8 (1⅛-pound) whole live lobsters
8 lemon wedges

1. Preheat grill to medium-high heat.
2. Plunge a heavy chef's knife through each lobster head just above the eyes, making sure the knife goes all the way through the head. Pull the knife in a downward motion between the eyes.
3. Place lobsters on grill rack; grill 6 minutes on each side or until done. Serve with lemon wedges. Yield: 8 servings (serving size: 1 lobster).

CALORIES 122; **FAT** 0.7g (sat 0.1g, mono 0.2g, poly 0.1g); **PROTEIN** 25.2g; **CARB** 2.2g; **FIBER** 0.2g; **CHOL** 88mg; **IRON** 0.5mg; **SODIUM** 466mg; **CALC** 77mg

A LANDLUBBER'S GUIDE TO LOBSTERS & SOFT-SHELL CLAMS

Both lobsters and soft-shell clams (commonly called steamers) need to be alive until as close to cooking time as possible—preferably right up to the minute. With lobsters this can be off-putting, but our instructions make it as easy as possible. With clams, the concern is grit.

BUYING AND DISPATCHING LOBSTERS
When buying, ask how long they've been there: A lobster that has languished in a tank for a couple of weeks will be sluggish and have mushy, withered meat. Pick the liveliest beasts—they should wave their claws and flap their tails rapidly when pulled from the water.

Before grilling, you'll need to pierce them in the middle of their heads to kill them first. The exact method is detailed in the recipe for Grilled Maine Lobsters on page 191. Of course, you can have your fishmonger take care of this piece of business—but you'll be in a race to cook them as soon as possible for maximum freshness.

SELECTING AND CLEANING SOFT-SHELL CLAMS
Most steamers are about 2 to 2½ inches long. The sheathed "necks" or siphons stick out from the side of the shell. Touch the siphon: It'll draw into the shell slightly. If it doesn't move, the clam may be dead. The clams should smell fresh and sweet, not fishy. Have your fishmonger put them in an open or perforated bag—clams breathe.

Steamers often carry a lot of sand and grit, which is why you soak them in salt water with a little cornmeal before cooking them—the clams are thought to feed on the cornmeal and expel grit.

When cooked, the clamshells open. Discard any that don't. Pull out the meat, remove the sheath, dunk the meat in hot clam broth for a last rinse, and then dip in melted butter to boost its briny deliciousness.

Make Ahead • Kid Friendly
Blueberry Crisp

Hands-on time: 20 min. Total time: 55 min.

Ripe, fresh blueberries are perfect for this dish, though frozen berries will also work. But keep them frozen, and bake the crisp 10 or 15 minutes longer as needed. Thawed berries are too fragile to toss and give off lots of liquid. Serve warm or at room temperature with low-fat vanilla ice cream—a ¼-cup scoop adds only about 55 calories per serving.

Cooking spray
4 teaspoons cornstarch, divided
2 tablespoons brown sugar
½ teaspoon vanilla extract
1 pound fresh or frozen blueberries
2.25 ounces all-purpose flour (about ½ cup)
½ cup packed brown sugar
¼ cup old-fashioned rolled oats
3 tablespoons chopped walnuts
2 tablespoons cornmeal
½ teaspoon salt
¼ teaspoon ground cinnamon
¼ cup chilled butter, cut into small pieces

1. Preheat oven to 375°.
2. Coat an 8-inch square glass or ceramic baking dish with cooking spray. Sprinkle 2 teaspoons cornstarch evenly in dish.
3. Combine remaining 2 teaspoons cornstarch, 2 tablespoons brown sugar, vanilla, and blueberries in a large bowl; toss. Place in prepared baking dish.
4. Weigh or lightly spoon flour into a dry measuring cup; level with a knife. Combine flour and next 6 ingredients in bowl of a food processor; pulse twice to combine. Add butter; pulse 5 times or until mixture resembles coarse meal. Spoon topping evenly over blueberries, packing down lightly. Bake at 375° for 30 minutes or until filling is bubbly and topping is golden. Yield: 8 servings (serving size: about ½ cup).

CALORIES 217; FAT 8.1g (sat 3.9g, mono 1.8g, poly 1.7g); PROTEIN 2.2g; CARB 35.9g; FIBER 2.4g; CHOL 15mg; IRON 0.9mg; SODIUM 195mg; CALC 25mg

---

Make Ahead • Kid Friendly
Fresh Raspberry Lemonade

Hands-on time: 26 min. Total time: 26 min.

¾ cup sugar
2 cups water, divided
2 cups fresh raspberries
½ cup fresh orange juice (about 1 orange)
1¾ cups fresh lemon juice (about 13 medium lemons)
16 ounces sparkling water, chilled

1. Combine sugar and ¾ cup water in a small saucepan; bring to a boil. Cook 2 minutes, stirring until sugar dissolves. Cool to room temperature.
2. Combine remaining 1¼ cups water and raspberries in a blender; pulse 10 times or until well blended. Strain mixture through a fine sieve into a large pitcher; discard solids. Add orange juice, lemon juice, sparkling water, and cooled syrup to pitcher; stir to combine. Serve immediately over ice. Yield: 8 servings (serving size: about 1 cup).

CALORIES 115; FAT 0.3g (sat 0g, mono 0g, poly 0.2g); PROTEIN 0.8g; CARB 30g; FIBER 0.5g; CHOL 0mg; IRON 0.4mg; SODIUM 15mg; CALC 21mg

---

CLAMBAKE WINES

Reach for chilled chardonnays with a touch of toasty oak to complement the smoky flavors in this open-fire feast. The 2009 J.J. Vincent "JJ" Bourgogne Blanc (France, $15) has a minerality that enhances the brininess of shellfish, while its lively acidity and crisp citrus flavors balance creamy butter sauce. For a slightly richer option, look for 2009 Concha y Toro Marques de Concha Chardonnay (Chile, $18). With its lush texture and a fresh butter note, it's a perfect match for sweet grilled corn, potatoes, and lobster.

5-INGREDIENT COOKING
SO-O-O-O SIMPLE!

These easy five-ingredient* entrées mean you can spend more time chilling, and less time shopping and chopping. (*salt, pepper, water, and cooking spray are freebies)

THE FIVE INGREDIENTS

Jalapeño pepper

+

Onion

+

Bell peppers

+

Tilapia

+

Tortillas

Quick & Easy
Sautéed Tilapia Tacos with Grilled Peppers and Onion
(pictured on page 231)

Hands-on time: 20 min. Total time: 30 min.

Slice the onion just before placing it on the grill. If given time to set, the onion rings will begin to separate and will not have good grill marks.

2 (½-inch-thick) slices white onion
1 (8-ounce) package mini sweet bell peppers
Cooking spray
³/₄ teaspoon salt, divided
½ teaspoon freshly ground black pepper, divided
4 (5-ounce) tilapia fillets
8 (6-inch) corn tortillas
1 small jalapeño pepper, thinly sliced
8 lime wedges (optional)

1. Preheat grill to high heat.
2. Arrange onion slices and bell peppers on grill rack coated with cooking spray. Grill onions 12 minutes, turning after 6 minutes. Grill bell peppers 12 minutes, turning occasionally. Remove onions and bell peppers from grill, and let stand 5 minutes. Slice onion rings in half. Thinly slice bell peppers; discard stems and seeds. Combine onion, bell peppers, ¼ teaspoon salt, and ⅛ teaspoon black pepper in a small bowl.
3. Sprinkle fish evenly with remaining ½ teaspoon salt and remaining ⅜ teaspoon black pepper. Heat a large nonstick skillet over medium-high heat. Coat pan with cooking spray. Add fish to pan, and cook 3 minutes on each side or until fish flakes easily when tested with a fork or until desired degree of doneness.
4. Warm tortillas according to package directions. Divide fish, onion mixture, and jalapeño slices evenly among tortillas. Serve with lime wedges, if desired. Yield: 4 servings (serving size: 2 tacos).

CALORIES 292; **FAT** 4.4g (sat 1.2g, mono 1.2g, poly 1.3g); **PROTEIN** 32.6g; **CARB** 32g; **FIBER** 4.8g; **CHOL** 71mg; **IRON** 1.9mg; **SODIUM** 526mg; **CALC** 120mg

THE FIVE INGREDIENTS

Watermelon

+

Farro

+

Parsley

+

Green peas

+

Pecorino Romano cheese

Quick & Easy • Vegetarian
Summer Pea, Watermelon, and Farro Salad

Hands-on time: 9 min. Total time: 32 min.

This unusual yet delicious combination of flavors makes a good substitute for traditional pasta salad at your next cookout.

1 cup uncooked farro or wheat berries
1 cup shelled green peas (about ³/₄ pound unshelled)
½ teaspoon salt
¼ teaspoon freshly ground black pepper
1 cup cubed seeded watermelon
1 cup coarsely chopped fresh flat-leaf parsley
¹/₃ cup (1½ ounces) shaved fresh pecorino Romano cheese

1. Place farro in a large saucepan, and cover with water to 2 inches above farro. Bring to a boil. Cover, reduce heat, and simmer 23 minutes or until desired degree of doneness.
2. Add green peas to pan with farro, and cook 2 minutes or until crisp-tender. Drain and rinse farro mixture with cold water; drain.
3. Combine farro mixture, ½ teaspoon salt, and ¼ teaspoon black pepper in a large bowl. Add watermelon cubes and 1 cup chopped parsley, and toss gently to combine. Top salad with Romano cheese. Yield: 4 servings (serving size: 1 cup).

CALORIES 188; **FAT** 4.2g (sat 1.9g, mono 0.9g, poly 0.2g); **PROTEIN** 10g; **CARB** 35.5g; **FIBER** 6g; **CHOL** 11.1mg; **IRON** 1.7mg; **SODIUM** 433mg; **CALC** 146mg

THE FIVE INGREDIENTS

Bread-and-butter pickles

+

Dijon mustard

+

Pork tenderloin

+

Cilantro

+

Swiss cheese

Quick & Easy • Kid Friendly

Stuffed Cuban Pork Tenderloin

Hands-on time: 15 min. Total time: 37 min.

While the pork is cooking, add fresh vegetables to the grill for a complete meal.

1 (1-pound) pork tenderloin, trimmed
2 tablespoons whole-grain Dijon mustard
1/3 cup chopped fresh cilantro
3 thin slices Swiss cheese, halved
1/3 cup chopped bread-and-butter pickles
1/4 teaspoon salt
1/4 teaspoon freshly ground black pepper
Cooking spray

1. Preheat grill to medium-high heat.
2. Cut a lengthwise slit down center of tenderloin two-thirds of way through the meat. Open halves, laying tenderloin flat. Place tenderloin between 2 sheets of plastic wrap; pound to ½-inch thickness using a meat mallet or heavy skillet. Spread mustard evenly over pork. Sprinkle with cilantro. Arrange cheese and pickles over pork in a single layer. Roll up, starting with long side; secure pork at 1-inch intervals with twine. Sprinkle evenly with salt and pepper.
3. Place pork on grill rack coated with cooking spray. Grill 22 minutes or until a thermometer registers 155°, turning after 11 minutes. Remove from grill. Let stand, covered, 5 minutes. Cut into 12 slices. Yield: 4 servings (serving size: 3 slices).

CALORIES 215; FAT 8.5g (sat 4.5g, mono 2.4g, poly 0.6g); PROTEIN 30.6g; CARB 4.6g; FIBER 0g; CHOL 93mg; IRON 1.2mg; SODIUM 507mg; CALC 172mg

WINE NOTE: A dry, medium-weight rosé, like Crios de Susana Balbo Rose of Malbec, Argentina ($12), has enough crisp acidity to match the stuffed pork's sweet-tart pickles and tangy Dijon mustard yet just a smidgen of tannins to tango with the melted Swiss cheese.

THE FIVE INGREDIENTS

Peaches

+

Lemon juice

+

Bourbon

+

Brown sugar

+

Chicken breast halves

Make Ahead

Grilled Chicken with Bourbon Peach Butter

Hands-on time: 15 min. Total time: 3 hr. 12 min.

1½ pounds coarsely chopped peeled peaches (about 5 medium)
¼ cup fresh lemon juice
3 tablespoons water
½ cup bourbon
1/3 cup packed dark brown sugar
3/4 teaspoon salt, divided
½ teaspoon freshly ground black pepper
6 (6-ounce) skinless, boneless chicken breast halves
Cooking spray

1. Preheat oven to 250°.
2. Combine first 3 ingredients in a saucepan. Bring to a boil; cover, reduce heat, and simmer 30 minutes. Combine peach mixture, bourbon, brown sugar, and ¼ teaspoon salt in a food processor or blender, and process 1 minute or until smooth. Transfer peach mixture to a 13 x 9–inch glass or ceramic baking dish. Bake at 250° for 2 hours and 15 minutes or until thickened.
3. Preheat grill to medium-high heat.
4. Sprinkle remaining ½ teaspoon salt and pepper evenly over chicken. Place chicken on grill rack coated with cooking spray; grill 6 minutes on each side or until done. Serve with sauce. Yield: 6 servings (serving size: 1 breast half and ¼ cup sauce).

CALORIES 304; FAT 2.5g (sat 0.6g, mono 0.6g, poly 0.6g); PROTEIN 40.4g; CARB 23.8g; FIBER 1.7g; CHOL 99mg; IRON 1.6mg; SODIUM 409mg; CALC 37mg

Bonus
Mixed Greens and Avocado Salad

Combine 1½ tablespoons extra-virgin olive oil, 1 tablespoon fresh lemon juice, ½ teaspoon Dijon mustard, ¼ teaspoon black pepper, and 1/8 teaspoon salt in a large bowl, stirring well with a whisk. Add 6 cups mixed salad greens; toss to coat. Top with 1 chopped peeled avocado. Yield: 4 servings (serving size: about 1¾ cups).

CALORIES 142; FAT 12.4g (sat 1.8g); SODIUM 122mg

OUR HANDS-FREE OVEN METHOD HELPS PREVENT THE SUGARY FRUIT BUTTER FROM SCORCHING.

Quick & Easy • Kid Friendly

Shredded Chicken Tacos with Tomatoes and Grilled Corn

(pictured on page 231)

Hands-on time: 20 min. Total time: 35 min.

2 ears shucked corn
1 (12-ounce) package baby heirloom tomatoes
½ teaspoon freshly ground black pepper
¼ teaspoon salt
8 (6-inch) corn tortillas
2 cups shredded skinless, boneless rotisserie chicken breast
1 peeled avocado, cut into 16 slices
8 lime wedges (optional)

1. Preheat broiler.
2. Place corn on a jelly-roll pan; broil 18 minutes or until charred on all sides, rotating every 6 minutes. Cut kernels from corn; place kernels in a medium bowl. Cut tomatoes into quarters. Add tomatoes to corn, and sprinkle corn mixture with black pepper and salt.
3. Heat tortillas according to package directions. Divide chicken evenly among tortillas; top each taco with ¼ cup corn mixture and 2 avocado slices. Serve with lime wedges, if desired. Yield: 4 servings (serving size: 2 tacos).

CALORIES 420; **FAT** 13.5g (sat 2.3g, mono 7.1g, poly 2.4g); **PROTEIN** 39.2g; **CARB** 40.6g; **FIBER** 8.4g; **CHOL** 101mg; **IRON** 2mg; **SODIUM** 554mg; **CALC** 123mg

QUICK MENUS
OUR FIRST APP GETS COOKING

Our Quick & Healthy Menu Maker combines two reader favorites: fast recipes and healthy menu suggestions.

What is the calorie, sat-fat, and sodium count in a dinner serving of chicken tacos with salsa, chorizo-studded beans, and a fruity ginger parfait? Or a bowl of pasta with mushroom Bolognese, an arugula-pear salad, and a dessert of figs with orange and ginger? Our first iPad® and iPhone® app gives you running nutrition calculations as you pick the dishes you want to make for dinner. After picking a main, side, or dessert, build a 3- or 4-course dinner around that dish, or have the app suggest an entire menu—and the nutrition numbers change as the dishes are swapped in and out.

You can save your dishes and menus. And if you want to share, recipes can be e-mailed along with their photos. Vegetarian dishes and menus are also available.

Quick & Easy • Kid Friendly

Mango-Ginger Parfaits

Hands-on time: 12 min. Total time: 12 min.

2 cups plain 2% Greek yogurt
2 tablespoons mascarpone cheese
2 tablespoons brown sugar
2 tablespoons fresh lime juice
2 ripe mangoes, peeled and chopped
¼ cup gingersnap crumbs (4 cookies)
2 tablespoons flaked sweetened coconut, toasted

1. Combine yogurt and mascarpone.
2. Combine sugar, lime juice, and mango in a small bowl; toss to coat.
3. Combine gingersnaps and coconut.
4. Place ¼ cup yogurt mixture into each of 4 parfait glasses; top with ¼ cup mango mixture and 1½ teaspoons gingersnap mixture. Repeat layers once. Yield: 4 servings.

CALORIES 270; **FAT** 10.5g (sat 5.9g, mono 2.6g, poly 0.3g); **PROTEIN** 11.5g; **CARB** 35.9g; **FIBER** 2.2g; **CHOL** 25mg; **IRON** 0.7mg; **SODIUM** 95mg; **CALC** 118mg

LESS MEAT, MORE FLAVOR
COLD SUMMER SOUPS
By Mark Bittman

Chilled, creamy purees, crunchy vegetable stir-ins, and warm bits of meat make for satisfying light mains on a hot evening.

Puree fruit in a blender, pour it in a glass, and drink it with a straw: You've just made a smoothie. Puree fruit in a blender, pour it in a bowl, and eat it with a spoon: Now you've made a cold soup.

It's true that sometimes there is little or nothing to differentiate one from the other, but the best cold soups (like the ones here, I must say) escape the smooth, sweet comfort zone of the glass and straw. They have a simple anatomy: something creamy and something crunchy, something sweet and something tart, a kick of salt here, or a hint of spice there.

This time of year the markets are brimming with perfect produce, but it's just too hot to cook it. Exit pot; enter blender. Start by pureeing fresh fruit and/or vegetables (you can leave the mixture a bit chunky if you like). Melons, berries, stone fruits, corn, tomatoes, peppers, and cucumbers are all prime possibilities. You'll need some liquid to get the machine going: Juice or water will do the trick, keeping everything light and fresh.

Taste the "broth"; it always needs something. With Avocado-Corn Chowder with Grilled Chicken on page 196, the combination of avocado and

continued

orange juice lacks a hit of sweetness to mellow the acidity of the citrus: Honey is perfect. The cantaloupe and peaches in Melon Gazpacho with Frizzled Prosciutto (right) require the opposite, something with a sharp edge to gently rise up underneath their natural sugars: shallots, vinegar, and lemon juice. Add these ingredients to taste, and then stash the mixture in the freezer to chill quickly (not so much that it numbs your taste buds).

You could eat the smooth puree as is, and it would be delicious, but not as dynamic as it could be. The contrasts and counterpoints are what really bring these soups to life. To add crunch, I typically turn to raw vegetables. Corn, red bell pepper, and green onions turn the silky avocado-orange broth into a full-on chowder, hearty but light. Onions and radishes are other obvious choices; jicama, cabbage, and summer squash may be a bit more surprising.

Meat can also be part of the supporting cast. Crispy strips of prosciutto lace the melon gazpacho with crunch and a burst of salt, and charred cubes of chicken breast add an irresistibly smoky chew (and a touch of spice, if you choose) to the chowder. Here, the meat brings new textures and flavors to the bowl, but it also works wonders with temperature. That first bite of hot, just-cooked meat swimming in cool, bright broth truly tickles the tongue.

If you haven't already noticed, I'm playing with some pretty classic flavor combinations here: prosciutto and melon; avocado, green onions, cilantro, and lime. That's really as good a place as any to start: Take the flavors you know and love, and turn them into summer soup. Maybe you puree avocado and cucumber with a touch of soy sauce, and sprinkle with edamame or toasted peanuts; add a splash of coconut milk and a dash of curry powder to the peaches and melon, and top with grilled shrimp; or simply puree tomatoes and top with chopped mozzarella and basil. The possibilities are nearly endless, so long as you're willing to leave your glass and straw behind.

Avocado-Corn Chowder with Grilled Chicken

Hands-on time: 28 min. Total time: 28 min.

2 ripe avocados, divided
1½ cups water
½ cup fresh orange juice
1 teaspoon honey
1 teaspoon kosher salt, divided
½ teaspoon freshly ground black pepper, divided
¼ teaspoon ground red pepper (optional)
12 ounces skinless, boneless chicken breast
1 teaspoon olive oil
1 small garlic clove, cut in half
1½ cups fresh corn kernels (about 3 ears)
1 cup chopped red bell pepper
⅓ cup chopped green onions
¼ cup chopped fresh cilantro
4 lime wedges

1. Peel and coarsely chop 1 avocado; place in a blender. Add water, orange juice, honey, ¾ teaspoon salt, ¼ teaspoon black pepper, and red pepper, if desired; blend until smooth. Place in freezer to chill while chicken cooks.
2. Heat a grill pan over medium-high heat. Brush chicken with oil; sprinkle with remaining ¼ teaspoon salt and ¼ teaspoon black pepper. Place chicken in pan; cook 4 minutes on each side or until done. Remove chicken from pan; rub chicken with cut sides of garlic halves. Let chicken stand 10 minutes; cut or shred into bite-sized pieces.
3. Peel and dice remaining avocado. Stir diced avocado, corn, bell pepper, and onions into chilled avocado puree. Spoon chowder into bowls; top with chicken and cilantro. Serve with lime wedges. Yield: 4 servings (serving size: 1¼ cups chowder, about 2 ounces chicken, 1 tablespoon cilantro, and 1 lime wedge).

CALORIES 359; FAT 17.9g (sat 2.7g, mono 11.2g, poly 2.6g); PROTEIN 24.5g; CARB 30g; FIBER 9.7g; CHOL 49mg; IRON 2mg; SODIUM 558mg; CALC 39mg

Melon Gazpacho with Frizzled Prosciutto

Hands-on time: 27 min. Total time: 27 min.

Pair with prosecco or other sparkling wine for a lovely, light summer dinner. Serve half-sized portions for a starter course.

5 cups cubed peeled cantaloupe (about 3½ pounds)
4 cups chopped ripe peaches (about 4 large)
½ cup water
2 tablespoons minced shallots
2 tablespoons fresh lemon juice
1 tablespoon sherry vinegar
⅜ teaspoon kosher salt
2 teaspoons olive oil
4 ounces thinly sliced prosciutto, cut into ribbons
4 teaspoons chopped fresh mint
¼ teaspoon freshly ground black pepper

1. Place first 7 ingredients in a blender; process until smooth (process in batches, if necessary). Place in freezer to chill while prosciutto cooks.
2. Heat a large skillet over medium heat. Add oil to pan; swirl to coat. Add prosciutto; cook 10 minutes or until crisp, stirring occasionally. Drain on paper towels.
3. Spoon soup into bowls; top with prosciutto, mint, and pepper. Yield: 4 servings (serving size: about 1¾ cups soup, about 1 ounce prosciutto, 1 teaspoon mint, and dash of pepper).

CALORIES 206; FAT 5.6g (sat 1.3g, mono 3g, poly 0.9g); PROTEIN 9.7g; CARB 32.7g; FIBER 4g; CHOL 16.7mg; IRON 1.3mg; SODIUM 638mg; CALC 34mg

USE CLASSIC FLAVOR COMBOS—AVOCADO WITH CORN AND LIME, MELON WITH PROSCIUTTO—OR GET CREATIVE WITH NEW PAIRINGS.

CHICKEN OF THE YEAR!

And other incredibly delicious, easy dishes from the guru of backyard smoking, Steven Raichlen.

With all the fuss made about smoking food these days, you'd think you had to be one of those hard-core hobbyists who'll spend $3,000 on a pellet smoker and devote their free time to getting a master's degree in the ancient art. Or one of those high-end chefs who smoke everything in sight (smoked yogurt, anyone?). In the almost religious vogue for smoke lies a suggestion that this is not a job for the average home cook. Not so: You can smoke pork shoulder, poultry, brisket, even oysters and potato salad at home on your charcoal or gas grill to dazzling effect, as the recipes on these pages show. Assuming you're not looking to become a Carolina-style pitmaster, we've got what you need to know right here.

First, you don't need a special smoker; you can use your grill—gas or charcoal. Second, although this is not a quick-cooking technique, the pleasure of mostly-hands-off food prep (while delicious smells waft about) will be familiar to anyone who uses a slow cooker in winter. It takes about two hours to smoke-roast Steven Raichlen's Fantastic Bourbon Smoked Chicken (page 200), and it's pretty much the tastiest bird we've ever had: You'd best believe this is two hours well spent. Yes, large meat cuts take several hours to reach meltingly tender, juicy, smoke-saturated perfection, but you don't have to do much more than tend the fire and sip cold beer, wine, or tea, working up an appetite.

Raichlen offers a quick primer on smoking versus grilling: "The difference has to do with the fuel, heat, and configuration of the food and fire. In grilling, food cooks close to and directly over the fire. You work over high heat—500° to 700°—and the brief cooking time is measured in minutes.

"In smoking, the food is positioned away from the fire, and you work at moderate to low temperatures, 225° to 350°, for an extended time, typically measured in hours or half-days.

"Smoking always involves wood smoke, generated by smoldering chunks, chips, or pellets of hardwood [see Wood Chip Wisdom, page 200]. The heat can come from charcoal, gas, or wood, but the soul of the dish is the smoke."

Can you get good results from gas? Raichlen strongly prefers charcoal. But we tested these recipes on both and found that, though there was an unbeatable smoky deliciousness to charcoal, gas-grill smoking is absolutely worth doing. With gas grills, you put the soaked wood chips in a perforated aluminum pan. With charcoal, you put the chips directly on the hot coals. Then the smoking begins.

Quick & Easy • Make Ahead

All-Purpose Spice Rub

Hands-on time: 2 min. Total time: 2 min.

Use 1 tablespoon per pound of pork, chicken, or beef. Store extra in a sealed container at room temp.

1½ tablespoons garlic powder
1½ tablespoons black pepper
1 tablespoon salt
1 tablespoon sugar
1 tablespoon dry mustard
1 tablespoon paprika
1½ teaspoons no-salt lemon pepper
1½ teaspoons ground cumin
1½ teaspoons ground red pepper

1. Combine all ingredients in a small bowl. Yield: ½ cup.

CALORIES 6; FAT 0.2g; PROTEIN 0.2g; CARB 1.1g; FIBER 0.3g; CHOL 0mg; IRON 0.1mg; SODIUM 222mg; CALC 3mg

---

OLD-SCHOOL HEAT CONTROL

With larger cuts like pork shoulder or brisket that need to smoke for hours, maintaining an even temperature is critical to prevent overcooking or drying out your meat. On a gas grill, you can regulate temperature easily via the burners and monitor it from the built-in thermometer in the lid. But charcoal grills require a little more finesse.

WORK THE VENTS
Charcoal grills have vents at the top and bottom. To raise the heat, open the vents wide. To decrease the heat, partially close the vents. Remember: More oxygen means a hotter fire; less oxygen, a cooler fire.

ADJUST THE CHARCOAL
When smoke-roasting (at temps of 300° to 350°) in a charcoal grill, use the normal amount (one chimney-full) of charcoal. When low-heat smoking (225° to 275°), use a half-chimney's worth. Replenish as needed.

KEEP IT MOIST
We call for keeping a small pan of water in the grill for the longer-cooking dishes, which humidifies the air and helps prevent meat from drying out. This is good practice in gas grills, too.

Smoked Oysters with Olive Relish

Hands-on time: 45 min. Total time: 1 hr. 45 min.

This dish is near to Steve's heart. He makes it often with the briny oysters raised in Katama Bay, close to his home on Martha's Vineyard. If your experience with smoked oysters is limited to the oily, strong-flavored bivalves sold canned, you're in for a revelation. The brininess of the olive- and caper-laced relish echoes the fresh, oceany notes of the oysters. Keep as much of the oysters' juices as possible in the shells while shucking and grilling.

1½ cups hickory wood chips
½ cup chopped pitted kalamata olives
½ cup chopped seeded peeled plum tomato
2 tablespoons chopped fresh basil
2 tablespoons extra-virgin olive oil
1 tablespoon capers
1 tablespoon fresh lemon juice
½ teaspoon freshly ground black pepper
24 large shucked oysters (on the half shell)
12 lemon wedges

1. Soak wood chips in water 1 hour; drain.
2. Combine olives and the next 6 ingredients in a small bowl.
3. Remove grill rack, and set aside. Prepare grill for indirect grilling, heating one side to medium-high and leaving one side with no heat. Maintain temperature at 300°. Pierce bottom of a disposable aluminum foil pan several times with the tip of a knife. Place pan on heat element on heated side of grill; add wood chips to pan. Place another disposable aluminum foil pan (do not pierce pan) on unheated side of grill. Pour 2 cups water in pan. Place grill rack on grill. Place the oysters on grill rack over foil pan on unheated side, and close lid. Grill 9 minutes; remove oysters from grill. Top each oyster with

1½ teaspoons olive mixture; serve immediately with lemon wedges. Yield: 6 servings (serving size: 4 topped oysters and 2 tablespoons relish).

Sustainable Choice

Farmed or wild oysters are smart seafood options.

CALORIES 120; FAT 9.3g (sat 1.5g, mono 6.1g, poly 1.4g); PROTEIN 4.3g; CARB 5.1g; FIBER 0.7g; CHOL 30mg; IRON 3.9mg; SODIUM 373mg; CALC 37mg

Make Ahead • Kid Friendly

Pulled Pork Sandwiches with Mustard Sauce

(pictured on page 230)

Hands-on time: 1 hr. Total time: 7 hr. 15 min.

7 to 8 cups hickory wood chips
2 tablespoons brown sugar
1 tablespoon dry mustard
1 tablespoon smoked paprika
1 tablespoon black pepper
1½ teaspoons kosher salt
1 (5-pound) boneless Boston Butt pork roast
2 tablespoons olive oil
¾ cup finely chopped onion
⅓ cup packed brown sugar
⅔ cup Dijon mustard
⅔ cup cider vinegar
⅓ cup molasses
1 teaspoon hot sauce
½ teaspoon kosher salt
16 (1½-ounce) whole-wheat hamburger buns

1. Soak the wood chips in water at least 1 hour; drain.
2. Combine sugar and next 4 ingredients in a bowl. Pat pork dry, and rub with sugar mixture.
3. Remove grill rack, and set aside. Prepare grill for indirect grilling, heating one side to high and leaving one side with no heat. Pierce bottom of a disposable aluminum foil pan several times with the tip of a knife. Place pan on heat element on heated side of grill; add 1½ cups wood chips to pan. Place another disposable aluminum foil pan (do not pierce pan) on unheated side of grill. Pour 2 cups water in pan. Let chips stand for 15 minutes or until smoking; reduce heat to medium.

Maintain temperature at 300°. Place grill rack on grill. Place pork on grill rack over unheated side. Close lid, and grill 6 hours at 300° or until a meat thermometer registers 195°, covering pork loosely with foil after 5 hours. Drain and add 1 cup additional wood chips every 45 minutes. Refill water pan and add charcoal to fire as needed. Remove pork from grill; let stand 20 minutes. Unwrap pork; trim and discard fat. Shred pork.
4. Heat oil in a medium saucepan over medium heat; swirl to coat. Add onion; cook 2 minutes, stirring frequently. Add ⅓ cup sugar and next 5 ingredients; bring to a simmer. Cook 15 minutes or until thickened. Arrange about 3 ounces pork and 2 tablespoons sauce on each bun. Yield: 16 servings (serving size: 1 sandwich).

CALORIES 438; FAT 19.2g (sat 6.2g, mono 8.5g, poly 2.5g); PROTEIN 29.8g; CARB 36.1g; FIBER 3.6g; CHOL 2.5mg; IRON 3.3mg; SODIUM 792mg; CALC 99mg

Coffee-Rubbed Texas-Style Brisket

Hands-on time: 1 hr. Total time: 7 hr. 15 min.

6 cups oak or hickory wood chips
1 tablespoon ground coffee
1 tablespoon kosher salt
1 tablespoon dark brown sugar
2 teaspoons smoked paprika
2 teaspoons ancho chile powder
1 teaspoon garlic powder
1 teaspoon onion powder
1 teaspoon ground cumin
1 teaspoon freshly ground black pepper
1 (4½-pound) flat-cut brisket (about 3 inches thick)

1. Soak wood chips in water at least 1 hour; drain.
2. Combine coffee and the next 8 ingredients in a bowl. Pat brisket dry; rub with coffee mixture.
3. Remove grill rack, and set aside. Prepare grill for indirect grilling, heating one side to high and leaving one side with no heat. Pierce bottom of a disposable aluminum foil pan several times with the tip of a knife. Place pan on heat element on heated side of grill;

SET UP YOUR GRILL FOR SMOKING SUCCESS

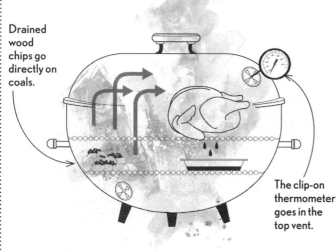

Drained wood chips go directly on coals.

The clip-on thermometer goes in the top vent.

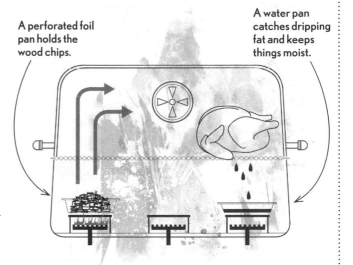

A perforated foil pan holds the wood chips.

A water pan catches dripping fat and keeps things moist.

CHARCOAL GRILL
Set up for indirect grilling: One pile of charcoal on one end, or two smaller piles on each end, leaving the middle unheated (Steve's method).

GAS GRILL
Indirect heat here means lighting one burner and leaving the others off. Begin with the burner on high so the wood smokes, and then reduce the heat.

---

add 1½ cups wood chips to pan. Place another disposable aluminum foil pan (do not pierce pan) on unheated side of grill. Pour 2 cups water in pan. Let chips stand 15 minutes or until smoking; reduce heat to medium-low. Maintain temperature at 225°. Place grill rack on grill. Place brisket in a small roasting pan, and place pan on grill rack on unheated side. Close lid; grill 6 hours or until a meat thermometer registers 195°. Add 1½ cups wood chips every hour for first 4 hours; cover roasting pan with foil for remaining 2 hours. Remove from grill. Let stand, covered, 30 minutes.
4. Unwrap brisket, reserving juices; trim and discard fat. Place a large zip-top plastic bag inside a 4-cup glass measure. Pour juices through a sieve into bag; discard solids. Let drippings stand 10 minutes (fat will rise to the top). Seal bag; carefully snip off 1 bottom corner of bag. Drain drippings into a bowl, stopping before fat reaches opening; discard fat. Cut brisket across grain into thin slices; serve with juices. Yield: 18 servings (serving size: 3 ounces).

CALORIES 156; **FAT** 4.4g (sat 1.6g, mono 1.8g, poly 0.2g); **PROTEIN** 24.9g; **CARB** 2.3g; **FIBER** 0.2g; **CHOL** 47mg; **IRON** 2.4mg; **SODIUM** 414mg; **CALC** 25mg

Vegetarian
Smoked Potato Salad

Hands-on time: 15 min. Total time: 1 hr. 30 min.

2 cups mesquite wood chips
¼ cup olive oil, divided
½ teaspoon black pepper
¼ teaspoon kosher salt
1½ pounds small potatoes
⅓ cup sliced pitted kalamata olives
2 thinly sliced green onions
2 tablespoons chopped fresh flat-leaf parsley
1 tablespoon red wine vinegar
2 teaspoons celery seed
1 teaspoon Dijon mustard

1. Soak wood chips in water 1 hour; drain.
2. Remove the grill rack, and set aside. Prepare grill for indirect grilling, heating one side to medium-high and leaving one side with no heat. Maintain temperature at 400°. Pierce bottom of a disposable aluminum foil pan several times with the tip of a knife. Place pan on heat element on heated side of grill; add 1 cup wood chips to pan. Place grill rack on grill. Combine 1 tablespoon oil, pepper, salt, and potatoes in a medium bowl; toss to coat. Arrange potatoes in a single layer in a disposable foil pan. Place pan over unheated side; close lid. Grill 30 minutes at 400° or until tender, and add remaining 1 cup wood chips after 15 minutes. Remove potatoes from grill. Combine potatoes, olives, and onions in a medium bowl.
3. Combine remaining 1 tablespoon oil, parsley, and remaining ingredients in a small bowl; stir with a whisk. Drizzle oil mixture over potato mixture; toss well. Yield: 8 servings (serving size: about ¾ cup).

CALORIES 162; **FAT** 8.8g (sat 1.2g, mono 6.4g, poly 1g); **PROTEIN** 2.4g; **CARB** 19.4g; **FIBER** 2.2g; **CHOL** 0mg; **IRON** 1.4mg; **SODIUM** 194mg; **CALC** 29mg

WOOD CHIP WISDOM

Steven Raichlen thinks of wood as "the spice of barbecue." As a rule, use hardwoods (from deciduous trees) for smoking, not soft woods (like pine, spruce, and other evergreens)—the latter produce a sooty, unpleasantly resinous smoke. Never use scraps of pressure-treated lumber, which may contain arsenic and other toxins.

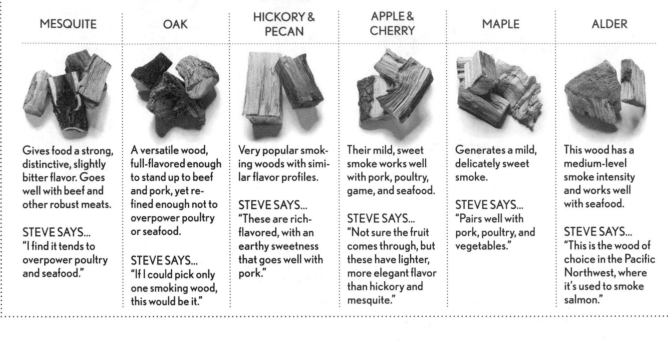

MESQUITE	OAK	HICKORY & PECAN	APPLE & CHERRY	MAPLE	ALDER
Gives food a strong, distinctive, slightly bitter flavor. Goes well with beef and other robust meats. STEVE SAYS... "I find it tends to overpower poultry and seafood."	A versatile wood, full-flavored enough to stand up to beef and pork, yet refined enough not to overpower poultry or seafood. STEVE SAYS... "If I could pick only one smoking wood, this would be it."	Very popular smoking woods with similar flavor profiles. STEVE SAYS... "These are rich-flavored, with an earthy sweetness that goes well with pork."	Their mild, sweet smoke works well with pork, poultry, game, and seafood. STEVE SAYS... "Not sure the fruit comes through, but these have lighter, more elegant flavor than hickory and mesquite."	Generates a mild, delicately sweet smoke. STEVE SAYS... "Pairs well with pork, poultry, and vegetables."	This wood has a medium-level smoke intensity and works well with seafood. STEVE SAYS... "This is the wood of choice in the Pacific Northwest, where it's used to smoke salmon."

Fantastic Bourbon Smoked Chicken

Hands-on time: 20 min. Total time: 20 hr. 35 min.

To reinforce the whiskey flavor in the brine and basting butter, use whiskey barrel chips for smoking. This bird is so wonderfully moist and flavorful, it doesn't need added embellishment.

2 quarts water
9 tablespoons bourbon, divided
¼ cup packed dark brown sugar
3 tablespoons kosher salt
2 quarts ice water
1 tablespoon black peppercorns
1 tablespoon coriander seeds
3 bay leaves
3 garlic cloves, peeled
1 small onion, quartered
1 small Fuji apple, cored and quartered
1 lemon, quartered
1 (4-pound) whole chicken
2 cups applewood chips
½ teaspoon freshly ground black pepper
Cooking spray
1 tablespoon butter, melted

1. Combine 2 quarts water, ½ cup bourbon, sugar, and kosher salt in a large Dutch oven, and bring to a boil, stirring until salt and sugar dissolve. Add ice water and next 7 ingredients, and cool to room temperature. Add chicken to brine; cover and refrigerate 18 hours, turning chicken occasionally.
2. Soak wood chips in water for 1 hour, and drain.
3. Remove the chicken from brine; pat chicken dry with paper towels. Strain brine through a sieve; discard brine and reserve 2 apple quarters, 2 lemon quarters, 2 onion quarters, and garlic. Discard remaining solids. Sprinkle chicken cavity with pepper; add reserved solids to chicken cavity. Lift wing tips up and over back; tuck under chicken. Tie legs.
4. Remove grill rack, and set aside. Prepare grill for indirect grilling, heating one side to high and leaving one side with no heat. Pierce bottom of a disposable aluminum foil pan several times with the tip of a knife. Place pan on heat element on heated side of grill; add 1 cup wood chips to pan. Place another disposable aluminum foil pan (do not pierce pan) on unheated side of grill. Pour 2 cups water in pan. Let chips stand 15 minutes or until smoking; reduce heat to medium-low. Maintain temperature at 275°.
5. Coat grill rack with cooking spray; place on grill. Place chicken, breast side up, on grill rack over foil pan on unheated side. Combine remaining 1 tablespoon bourbon and butter; baste chicken with the bourbon mixture. Close lid, and grill 2 hours at 275° or until thermometer inserted into meaty part of thigh registers 165°. Add remaining 1 cup wood chips halfway through cooking time. Place chicken on a platter; cover with foil. Let stand for 15 minutes. Discard skin before serving. Yield: 4 servings (serving size: 5 ounces chicken).

CALORIES 299; FAT 12.6g (sat 4.4g, mono 4.3g, poly 2.3g); PROTEIN 35.8g; CARB 6.2g; FIBER 1g; CHOL 114mg; IRON 1.8mg; SODIUM 560mg; CALC 30mg

MUST-HAVE TOOLS OF A BACKYARD SMOKER

DISPOSABLE ALUMINUM PAN
If you're cooking with gas, use it to hold wood chips atop the heat element (less than $1 each at the supermarket).

CLIP-ON THERMOMETER
A grill thermometer helps you keep the heat low and slow.

CHARCOAL CHIMNEY
Start a fire fast or feed it on the fly with a chimney starter.

Cajun-Spiced Smoked Shrimp with Rémoulade

Hands-on time: 23 min. Total time: 2 hr. 5 min.

No grilling skillet, no problem: Thread the shrimp on skewers instead.

1½ cups hickory wood chips
Shrimp:
1½ teaspoons sweet paprika
½ teaspoon kosher salt
½ teaspoon ground white pepper
½ teaspoon ground sage
½ teaspoon freshly ground black pepper
¼ teaspoon onion powder
¼ teaspoon garlic powder
¼ teaspoon dried thyme
¼ teaspoon dried oregano
¼ teaspoon ground red pepper
2 tablespoons extra-virgin olive oil
1½ pounds large shrimp, peeled and deveined
Rémoulade:
½ cup reduced-fat mayonnaise
3 tablespoons finely chopped green onions
2 tablespoons finely chopped celery
2 tablespoons ketchup
1 tablespoon finely chopped fresh parsley
1 tablespoon capers, chopped
1 tablespoon fresh lemon juice
1 tablespoon Creole-style mustard
1 teaspoon prepared horseradish
1 teaspoon Worcestershire sauce
1 garlic clove, minced
2 hard-cooked large eggs
Cooking spray

1. Soak wood chips in water 1 hour, and drain.
2. To prepare shrimp, combine paprika and next 9 ingredients. Combine olive oil and shrimp in a bowl, and toss to coat. Sprinkle shrimp with rub, and toss to coat. Cover and refrigerate 30 minutes.
3. To prepare rémoulade, combine mayonnaise and next 10 ingredients in a medium bowl. Remove yolks from eggs; discard yolks or reserve for another use. Finely chop egg whites, and stir into mayonnaise mixture. Cover; chill.
4. Remove grill rack, and set aside. Prepare grill for indirect grilling, heating one side to high and leaving one side with no heat. Pierce bottom of a disposable aluminum foil pan several times with the tip of a knife. Place pan on heat element on heated side of grill; add wood chips to pan. Let wood chips stand 15 minutes or until smoking; reduce heat to medium. Coat grill rack with cooking spray; place on grill. Place shrimp in a grilling skillet; place skillet on grill rack over unheated side. Cover and grill 15 minutes or until shrimp are done, stirring after 7 minutes. Serve with rémoulade. Yield: 8 servings (serving size: 4 shrimp and 3 tablespoons rémoulade).

CALORIES 159; FAT 7g (sat 1.3g, mono 2.7g, poly 1g); PROTEIN 18.4g; CARB 5.1g; FIBER 0.3g; CHOL 129mg; IRON 2.3mg; SODIUM 493mg; CALC 54mg

RECIPE MAKEOVER
BANANA PUDDING: BEST DESSERT EVER?

Some Southerners say so. And this classic dish became magically richer and more decadent as we lightened it up.

Southern cooks love their banana pudding the way New Yorkers love their cheesecake. It's a traditional dessert that starts off innocently enough (with fruit, after all), until the bananas are nestled inside several layers of heavy custard, cookies, and whipped cream. A sampling of this sweet, unctuous treat can add up to 800 calories and 19 grams of saturated fat—all in one modest-sized bowl.

We start by giving the bananas a little boost, roasting the fruit in its peel to concentrate the flavor. Half then gets mashed into the custard to make it richer and creamier, and the other half is sliced for texture. Our homemade custard stays light by using 2% milk instead of half-and-half, while fluffy whipped topping steps in for heavy whipped cream. Vanilla wafers remain, for old-fashioned goodness; they soften into cakelike disks as they sit. Our new dessert has about 90% less saturated fat, 60% fewer calories—and all the southern charm of the original.

BANANAS, ROASTED
Cooking the fruit in the peel sweetens and intensifies the flavor.

LIGHT 2% MILK FOR CUSTARD BASE
Replaces half-and-half and saves 180 calories per serving.

NONFAT WHIPPED TOPPING
Sub for heavy whipping cream and knock out 7g saturated fat per serving.

Roasted Banana Pudding

Hands-on time: 36 min. Total time: 2 hr. 26 min.

Many folks say banana pudding is best the next day, after the flavors have blended overnight and the cookies have softened.

5 ripe unpeeled medium bananas (about
   2 pounds)
2 cups 2% reduced-fat milk
²/₃ cup sugar, divided
2 tablespoons cornstarch
¼ teaspoon salt
2 large eggs
1 tablespoon butter
2 teaspoons vanilla extract
1 (12-ounce) container frozen fat-free
   whipped topping, thawed and divided
45 vanilla wafers, divided

1. Preheat oven to 350°.
2. Place bananas on a jelly-roll pan covered with parchment paper. Bake at 350° for 20 minutes. Remove 3 bananas; cool completely. Peel and cut into ½-inch-thick slices. Bake remaining 2 bananas at 350° for an additional 20 minutes. Carefully peel and place 2 bananas in a small bowl, and mash with a fork until smooth.
3. Combine milk and ⅓ cup sugar in a saucepan over medium-high heat. Bring to a simmer (do not boil).
4. Combine remaining ⅓ cup sugar, cornstarch, salt, and eggs in a medium bowl; stir well with a whisk. Gradually add hot milk mixture to sugar mixture, stirring constantly with a whisk. Return milk mixture to pan. Cook over medium

heat until thick and bubbly (about 3 minutes), stirring constantly. Remove from heat. Add mashed bananas, butter, and vanilla, stirring until butter melts. Place pan in a large ice-filled bowl 15 minutes or until mixture comes to room temperature, stirring occasionally. Fold half of whipped topping into pudding.
5. Spread 1 cup custard evenly over bottom of an 11 x 7–inch baking dish. Top with 20 vanilla wafers and half of banana slices. Spoon half of remaining custard over banana. Repeat procedure with 20 wafers, banana slices, and custard. Spread remaining half of whipped topping evenly over top. Crush remaining 5 wafers; sprinkle over top. Refrigerate 1 hour or until chilled. Yield: 10 servings (serving size: about ⅔ cup).

CALORIES 295; FAT 5.6g (sat 2.1g, mono 1.7g, poly 0.2g); PROTEIN 3.9g; CARB 56.6g; FIBER 2g; CHOL 46mg; IRON 1mg; SODIUM 165mg; CALC 73mg

OLD WAY	OUR WAY
819 calories per serving	295 calories per serving
49 grams total fat	5.6 grams total fat
19 grams saturated	2.1 grams saturated

CREATING A BLACK BANANA

Roasting an ordinary banana adds richness to the pudding without extra fat or sugar.

1. Leave the peel on the bananas when roasting. Be aware that they'll turn black. The skin keeps the flesh intact while the fruit cooks and helps lock in the flavor.

2. Remove three of the bananas halfway through roasting. The flavors have developed, but the bananas remain firm, adding texture to the pudding.

3. Allow the remaining two bananas to roast longer. This breaks down the pulp, adding a rich creaminess to the custard. Mash bananas with a fork until smooth.

EVERYDAY VEGETARIAN

VEGGIE STIR-FRIES

Fresh, globally inspired dishes bring a skillet full of tasty vegetables and grains to your dinner table in 35 minutes or less.

Quick & Easy • Make Ahead
Vegetarian

Cumin-Spiced Chickpeas and Carrots on Couscous

Hands-on time: 30 min. Total time: 30 min.

½ cup organic vegetable broth
1 tablespoon grated lemon rind
3 tablespoons fresh lemon juice
1 tablespoon tomato paste
2 (15½-ounce) cans chickpeas (garbanzo
   beans), rinsed and drained
3 tablespoons canola oil, divided
1 cup chopped red bell pepper
1 cup julienne-cut carrots
1 jalapeño pepper, finely chopped
1 teaspoon cumin seeds
¼ teaspoon salt
¼ teaspoon black pepper
¼ teaspoon ground allspice
⅛ teaspoon ground red pepper
6 garlic cloves, minced
4 cups warm cooked couscous (about
   2 cups dry)
½ cup fresh cilantro leaves
Lemon wedges (optional)

1. Combine first 4 ingredients, stirring with a whisk.
2. Dry chickpeas thoroughly in a single layer on paper towels. Heat 2 tablespoons oil in a large skillet over high heat, and swirl to coat. Add chickpeas to pan, and stir-fry 3 minutes or until lightly browned. Remove chickpeas from pan with a slotted spoon; wipe pan clean with a paper towel. Add remaining 1 tablespoon oil to pan, and swirl to coat. Add bell pepper, carrots, and jalapeño to pan,

and stir-fry for 2 minutes or until vegetables are slightly tender. Add cumin seeds and next 5 ingredients to pan, and stir-fry for 30 seconds. Add reserved broth mixture and chickpeas. Bring to a boil, and remove from heat. Serve over couscous, and top with cilantro. Serve with lemon wedges, if desired. Yield: 4 servings (serving size: 1 cup couscous, about ¾ cup chickpea mixture, and 2 tablespoons cilantro).

CALORIES 420; FAT 12.8g (sat 0.9g, mono 6.7g, poly 3.2g); PROTEIN 12.7g; CARB 64.5g; FIBER 8.8g; CHOL 0mg; IRON 2.6mg; SODIUM 586mg; CALC 66mg

WINE NOTE: The light and lively Pine Ridge Chenin Blanc-Viognier 2010 ($14) pairs perfectly with this dish's bold spices. Floral aromas and a hint of sweetness temper the fiery jalapeño and red pepper.

Quick & Easy • Vegetarian
Rice Noodle Salad

Hands-on time: 35 min. Total time: 35 min.

Wide rice noodles are great for stir-fries and cook better when broken into shorter lengths. Soften in hot water, and stir-fry as directed. If unavailable, substitute linguine or fettuccine.

8 ounces uncooked wide rice sticks (banh pho)
2 tablespoons plus 1 teaspoon sesame oil, divided
½ cup organic vegetable broth
6 tablespoons ketchup
2 tablespoons lime juice
2 tablespoons lower-sodium soy sauce
1 teaspoon Sriracha (hot chile sauce)
8 ounces tempeh, cut into ½-inch cubes
6 garlic cloves, minced
2 shallots, thinly sliced
2 large eggs, lightly beaten
2 cups fresh bean sprouts
1½ cups thinly sliced English cucumber
5 thinly sliced green onions
1½ cups matchstick-cut carrots
½ cup fresh basil leaves
½ cup fresh mint leaves
½ cup chopped fresh cilantro
2 tablespoons finely chopped unsalted, dry-roasted peanuts
12 lime wedges

1. Cook noodles according to package directions. Drain and toss with 1 teaspoon sesame oil.
2. Combine broth and next 4 ingredients, stirring with a whisk.
3. Heat remaining 2 tablespoons oil in a large nonstick skillet over medium-high heat; swirl to coat. Add tempeh, and stir-fry 3 minutes or until lightly browned. Add garlic and shallots; stir-fry 1 minute or until shallots begin to soften. Add eggs; stir-fry 30 seconds or until soft-scrambled, stirring constantly. Add soy sauce mixture, and bring to a boil. Add noodles and bean sprouts; toss gently to coat. Cook 1 minute or until sauce is thickened.
4. Remove from heat, and top with cucumber and next 5 ingredients. Sprinkle each serving with 1 teaspoon dry-roasted peanuts and juice from 2 lime wedges. Yield: 6 servings (serving size: 1⅓ cups).

CALORIES 370; FAT 12.6g (sat 2.3g, mono 4.7g, poly 4.5g); PROTEIN 13g; CARB 55.3g; FIBER 3.9g; CHOL 60mg; IRON 3.4mg; SODIUM 420mg; CALC 112mg

MAKING MATCHSTICKS

Slender matchstick-cut (or julienned) carrots are pretty and quick-cooking. Uniform size is important.

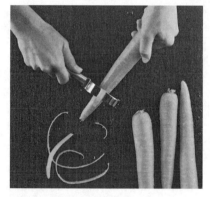

1. Peel carrots to remove bitterness.

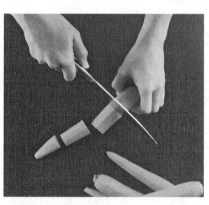

2. Cut into 2- to 3-inch pieces.

3. Slice into thin planks.

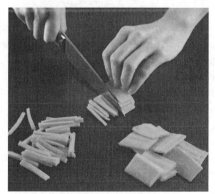

4. Stack planks, and cut into strips.

Quick & Easy • Vegetarian

Ginger-Scented Corn and Asparagus Stir-Fry

Hands-on time: 30 min. Total time: 30 min.

4 tablespoons canola oil, divided
10 ounces extra-firm tofu, drained and cut
    into ¾-inch cubes
⅔ cup fresh corn kernels
1 tablespoon grated peeled fresh ginger
4 garlic cloves, minced
1 small onion, vertically sliced (about ¾ cup)
1 julienne-cut red bell pepper (about 1 cup)
6 ounces asparagus, steamed and cut into
    1-inch pieces (about 2 cups)
¼ cup organic vegetable broth
2 tablespoons lower-sodium soy sauce
3 tablespoons rice wine vinegar
¼ teaspoon crushed red pepper
2 cups hot cooked short-grain rice
2 thinly sliced green onions (about ¼ cup)

1. Heat 2 tablespoons oil in a large cast-iron skillet over medium-high heat; swirl to coat. Add tofu; sauté 10 minutes or until golden brown, stirring frequently. Remove tofu from pan with a slotted spoon; wipe pan dry with a paper towel. Heat remaining 2 tablespoons oil in pan; swirl to coat. Add corn and next 4 ingredients; stir-fry 5 minutes. Add reserved tofu, asparagus, and next 4 ingredients. Stir-fry 1 minute or until asparagus and tofu are heated. Divide the rice evenly among 4 plates. Spoon about 1 cup corn mixture over rice, and top evenly with 1 tablespoon green onions. Yield: 4 servings (serving size: about 1½ cups).

CALORIES 380; **FAT** 18.8g (sat 1.6g, mono 12.1g, poly 4.6g); **PROTEIN** 12.2g; **CARB** 43.8g; **FIBER** 4g; **CHOL** 0mg; **IRON** 4.2mg; **SODIUM** 421mg; **CALC** 153mg

---

Quick & Easy • Vegetarian

Fried Rice with Sweet Soy Sauce

Hands-on time: 20 min. Total time: 35 min.

3 tablespoons peanut oil, divided
4 large eggs, lightly beaten
3 finely chopped shallots
2 garlic cloves, minced
1 chopped serrano chile
4 cups cooked long-grain brown rice
2 tablespoons Sweet Soy Sauce or Indonesian
    sweet soy sauce (kecap manis)
¼ teaspoon salt
¼ teaspoon black pepper
1½ cups thinly sliced daikon radish
⅓ cup fresh basil leaves
⅓ cup fresh mint leaves
⅓ cup chopped fresh cilantro
4 lime wedges

1. Heat 1 tablespoon oil in a large skillet over medium-high heat; swirl to coat. Pour eggs into pan; cook for 2 minutes or until set, stirring once. Remove eggs from pan.
2. Increase heat to high, and add remaining 2 tablespoons oil to pan. Add shallots, garlic, and chile; stir-fry 1 minute. Add rice; stir-fry 3 minutes or until lightly browned. Add cooked eggs, soy sauce, salt, and pepper; toss to combine.
3. Top with radish and herbs, and serve with lime. Yield: 4 servings (serving size: 1¼ cups rice and 1 lime wedge).

CALORIES 430; **FAT** 16.1g (sat 3.3g, mono 7.2g, poly 4.7g); **PROTEIN** 12.8g; **CARB** 58.2g; **FIBER** 5.2g; **CHOL** 180mg; **IRON** 2.6mg; **SODIUM** 377mg; **CALC** 83mg

Sweet Soy Sauce:
Bring ¼ cup lower-sodium soy sauce and ¼ cup packed dark brown sugar to a boil in a small saucepan over medium heat. Simmer 2 minutes or until reduced to ¼ cup. Yield: 4 servings (serving size: 1 tablespoon).

CALORIES 61; **FAT** 0g; **PROTEIN** 0.9g; **CARB** 14.9g; **FIBER** 0.1g; **CHOL** 0mg; **IRON** 0.4mg; **SODIUM** 537mg; **CALC** 14mg

---

OOPS! YOUR TURKEY BURGERS ARE PARCHED PUCKS

A simple stir-in makes for juicy, delicious patties.
By Hannah Klinger

A well-made turkey burger is a delicious, lower-fat backyard grill treat, but if you don't compensate for the leanness of the meat, you could be eating turkey-flavored particleboard. Mostly it's a matter of getting the patty off the grill before it dries out (or sticks and falls apart)—a job made trickier by the need to cook poultry to 165°. So, to avoid sawdust syndrome, add a little fat to the meat. Yes, add fat. This might seem counterproductive, but it's not if you use a fat that's heart-healthy.

The fat in question? Olive oil. Stirring in two tablespoons olive oil per pound of ground turkey keeps the burgers moist and juicy and also helps them form a nicely browned crust on the outside that won't stick to the grill.

Even better: Sauté 1 cup diced onion in 2 tablespoons olive oil until nice and tender, let cool slightly, and then mix the onion and oil from the pan into a pound of ground turkey to form four patties. The oil-coated onions do a marvelous job of adding both moisture and flavor to lean poultry burgers, and you get a hit of that nice, oniony sweetness, too.

SLICE, FILL, EAT, SMILE

Different breads create entirely different sandwich effects, even when the filling is the same. Here, great summer satisfiers, plus variations.

▼ Peanut-Sauced Chicken in pita bread
Rich dark meat stands up to the robust pea-nutty sauce. To pack, combine chicken mixture, sprouts, carrot, and cilantro; put in a sealed container; stuff into pita just when you're ready to eat. Look for satay sauce and chile paste on the Asian-food aisle of your supermarket.
Mix and Match: Wrap the filling inside a whole-grain flatbread or piece of naan.

Quick & Easy • Make Ahead
Peanut-Sauced Chicken Pitas

Hands-on time: 24 min. Total time: 24 min.

1 cup shredded skinless, boneless rotisserie chicken thigh or drumstick meat
⅓ cup thinly sliced green onions
2 tablespoons thin red bell pepper strips
2 tablespoons peanut satay sauce
⅛ teaspoon kosher salt
1 teaspoon chile paste with garlic (optional)
1 (6-inch) whole-wheat pita, cut in half
½ cup fresh mung bean sprouts, rinsed, drained, and patted dry
2 tablespoons diagonally-cut carrot
2 tablespoons chopped fresh cilantro

1. Combine first 5 ingredients, tossing well to coat. Stir in chile paste, if desired. Fill each pita half with about ½ cup chicken mixture, ¼ cup bean sprouts, 1 tablespoon carrot, and 1 tablespoon cilantro. Yield: 2 servings (serving size: 1 stuffed pita half).

CALORIES 275; FAT 9.6g (sat 2.4g, mono 3.6g, poly 2.5g); PROTEIN 21.4g; CARB 25.7g; FIBER 3.9g; CHOL 52.5mg; IRON 2.5mg; SODIUM 620mg; CALC 32mg

---

▼ Caesar Salad on a bagel
Maybe we're going too far, thinking of the toasty bagel here as a kind of oversized crouton for the light Caesar salad filling. Maybe not.
  To brown-bag, pack sandwich components separately—the leaves and the cheese; a mixture of the dressing and pepper; and the toasted bagel. For the vegetarians in your crew, choose salad dressing that doesn't contain anchovies.
Mix and Match: Toss lettuce, cheese, pepper, and dressing together; tuck into a pita or a whole-wheat flatbread.

Quick & Easy
Caesar Salad Bagels

Hands-on time: 6 min. Total time: 6 min.

3 tablespoons organic creamy Caesar salad dressing
2 (4-ounce) whole-grain, onion, or "everything" bagels, split and toasted
½ teaspoon black pepper
2 thin red onion slices
1 cup torn or shredded romaine lettuce
½ cup (2 ounces) shaved Parmigiano-Reggiano cheese

1. Spread dressing evenly on cut sides of bagels. Sprinkle with pepper.
2. Arrange half of red onion, romaine lettuce, and cheese on bottom halves of bagels, and repeat layers. Top with the top halves of bagels. Yield: 2 servings (serving size: 1 sandwich).

CALORIES 394; FAT 16g (sat 4.2g, mono 5.4g, poly 2.7g); PROTEIN 16.6g; CARB 51.9g; FIBER 8.6g; CHOL 17.9mg; IRON 1.9mg; SODIUM 757mg; CALC 396mg

---

▼ Steak and pesto on baguette
Grill the steak and toast the baguette over the same flame for a delicious charred effect. This sandwich holds up well, so you can pack it for lunch, fully assembled.
Mix and Match: Try also on a toasted Kaiser roll. Or pile high onto a toasted boule slice for an open-faced, knife-and-fork version.

Quick & Easy • Make Ahead
Kid Friendly
Steak Baguettes with Pesto Mayo

Hands-on time: 20 min. Total time: 20 min.

1 (12-ounce) boneless beef sirloin steak (about 1 inch thick), trimmed
¼ teaspoon kosher salt
⅛ teaspoon freshly ground black pepper
2 tablespoons canola mayonnaise
2 tablespoons refrigerated pesto sauce
1 (12-ounce) piece white or whole-grain baguette, split in half horizontally
1 cup packed baby arugula (about 1 ounce)
3 (⅛-inch-thick) slices red onion
2 plum tomatoes, thinly sliced lengthwise

1. Heat a grill pan over medium-high heat. Sprinkle steak with salt and pepper. Add steak to pan, and cook 2½ minutes on each side or until desired degree of doneness. Remove steak from pan, and let stand 5 minutes. Cut steak across grain into thin slices.
2. Combine mayonnaise and pesto, stirring until well blended. Spread mayonnaise mixture evenly over cut sides of bread. Layer bottom half of bread with arugula, red onion, steak, and tomato; top with top half of bread. Cut sandwich diagonally into 4 equal pieces. Yield: 4 servings (serving size: 1 sandwich piece).

CALORIES 346; FAT 9.1g (sat 1.6g, mono 4.6g, poly 1.4g); PROTEIN 21g; CARB 41.4g; FIBER 2.3g; CHOL 26mg; IRON 3.3mg; SODIUM 701mg; CALC 41mg

▼ **Herbed Chicken Salad on rye bread**
Pick up a rotisserie chicken from the market, and this sandwich is a snap. That said, if you make the chicken salad a day or so ahead, the flavors will marry nicely as the filling chills.
Mix and Match: Try on a wedge of focaccia, and toast in a grill pan for a chicken salad panini. Or for a sweet touch, try on toasted cinnamon-raisin sandwich bread.

Quick & Easy • Make Ahead
Kid Friendly

Herbed Chicken Salad Sandwiches

Hands-on time: 14 min. Total time: 14 min.

1 tablespoon finely chopped fresh tarragon
3 tablespoons canola mayonnaise
3 tablespoons 2% plain Greek yogurt
1 tablespoon fresh lemon juice
⅛ teaspoon kosher salt
2 cups chopped skinless, boneless rotisserie chicken breast
¼ cup minced sweet onion
8 (1½-ounce) slices rye sandwich bread
4 red leaf lettuce leaves
1 cup microgreens or arugula

1. Combine first 5 ingredients in a large bowl. Stir in chicken and onion. Top each of 4 bread slices with 1 lettuce leaf, about ½ packed cup chicken salad, ¼ cup microgreens, and 1 bread slice. Yield: 4 servings (serving size: 1 sandwich).

CALORIES 382; FAT 9g (sat 1.4g, mono 3.9g, poly 2.4g); PROTEIN 30.2g; CARB 42.9g; FIBER 5.1g; CHOL 60mg; IRON 3.2mg; SODIUM 745mg; CALC 89mg

8 GOOD BREADS

Good bread is the essential foundation here. If you're working with a saucy mix, you want sturdy bread that resists turning soggy. If fillings are subtle, avoid one with too much flavor (such as rye).

1. Baguette: Oh, that all the limp, fake baguettes were banished and only the sturdy, crusty loaves survived. The crunch factor counterpoints nicely with creamy or soft fillings, cheeses, or grilled vegetables.

2. Sandwich loaves: The difference between a flabby superwhite supermarket loaf and a substantial Pullman loaf is...staggering. Try 100% whole grains and multigrains when you want grainy flavors. Dense bread, toasted and served hot with tuna salad, is delicious.

3. Hamburger buns: These and other soft rolls are great for barbecue-chicken, pulled-pork, or classic deli meats. Toasting helps the bread hold up if the filling is moist.

4. Ciabatta: Italian bread with a crispy-chewy exterior and moist, spongy, dense interior. Works nicely with salad-type fillings that turn weaker breads soggy.

5. Bagels: A real bagel is chewy, substantial, and flavorful. Look for modest ones, not monsters. Plain is best for many sandwiches, but seedy varieties can add a nice note. Don't fill too high—contents squeeze out.

6. Flatbreads: Beyond pita, blistered Indian naans and pliable tortilla-like wraps make for a nice change. One large flatbread may equal two or three regular bread servings.

7. Boule: The rounded loaf shape yields large, flat slices—ideal for open-faced sandwiches where you want more surface area.

8. Focaccia: Often comes as large, flat rounds that you can cut into wedges for interesting shapes, and then slice open for filling. Herbs, olive oil, and toasty flavors match with Italian/Mediterranean ingredients.

Quick & Easy • Make Ahead
Kid Friendly • Vegetarian

Grilled Zucchini Caprese Sandwiches

Hands-on time: 15 min. Total time: 15 min.

1 medium zucchini, trimmed and cut lengthwise into 6 slices
4 teaspoons extra-virgin olive oil, divided
1 garlic clove, minced
1½ teaspoons balsamic vinegar
⅛ teaspoon kosher salt
⅛ teaspoon black pepper
4 (2-ounce) ciabatta rolls, split and toasted
8 large fresh basil leaves
1 medium tomato, thinly sliced
6 ounces fresh mozzarella cheese, thinly sliced

1. Heat a large grill pan over medium-high heat. Place zucchini in a shallow dish. Add 2 teaspoons oil and garlic; toss to coat. Arrange zucchini in grill pan; cook 2 minutes on each side or until grill marks appear. Cut each zucchini piece in half crosswise. Return zucchini to shallow dish. Drizzle with vinegar. Sprinkle with salt and black pepper.
2. Brush bottom halves of rolls with remaining 2 teaspoons oil. Top evenly with zucchini, basil, tomatoes, and mozzarella.
3. Brush cut side of roll tops with remaining liquid from shallow dish, and place on sandwiches. Heat sandwiches in pan until warm. Yield: 4 servings (serving size: 1 sandwich).

CALORIES 343; **FAT** 16.8g (sat 6.6g, mono 8g, poly 1.3g); **PROTEIN** 15.4g; **CARB** 35.3g; **FIBER** 2g; **CHOL** 33.6mg; **IRON** 2.3mg; **SODIUM** 722mg; **CALC** 229mg

COOKING CLASS

TODAY'S LESSON: ICE POPS

There is a delicious moment in the making of ice pops that simply doesn't happen with the supermarket variety, as you feel the pop slip the bonds of its frozen mold and come sliding out, still frosty but showing the first signs of melting. Your mouth waters, ready for a cold summer shock and a burst of intense, homemade flavors.

Make Ahead • Freezable

Limoncello Pops

Hands-on time: 15 min. Total time: 4 hr. 15 min.

1¼ cups water
⅔ cup sugar
1 tablespoon grated lemon rind
1 cup fresh lemon juice
½ cup limoncello (lemon-flavored liqueur)

1. Combine 1¼ cups water and sugar in a microwave-safe bowl; microwave at HIGH 3 minutes or until boiling. Stir until sugar dissolves. Stir in rind. Cool completely.
2. Strain mixture through a sieve into a bowl; discard rind. Stir in juice and liqueur. Divide mixture among 6 (4-ounce) ice-pop molds. Top with lid; insert craft sticks. Freeze 4 hours or until thoroughly frozen. Yield: 6 servings (serving size: 1 pop).

CALORIES 133; **FAT** 0g; **PROTEIN** 0.2g; **CARB** 29.2g; **FIBER** 0.3g; **CHOL** 0mg; **IRON** 0mg; **SODIUM** 1mg; **CALC** 5mg

POP PARTY

Kick off a summer party with our limoncello or Champagne-based pops in place of the usual cocktail.

Make Ahead • Freezable

Sparkling Strawberry Pops

Hands-on time: 20 min. Total time: 4 hr. 20 min.

For a kid version, use nonalcoholic sparkling grape juice.

¾ cup sugar
¼ cup water
6 cups sliced fresh strawberries (2 pounds)
2 tablespoons fresh lemon juice
2 teaspoons light-colored corn syrup
1¼ cups chilled Champagne

1. Combine sugar and ¼ cup water in a microwave-safe bowl; microwave at HIGH 3 minutes or until boiling. Stir until sugar dissolves; cool. Combine berries, juice, and corn syrup in a food processor; process until smooth. Strain through a sieve over a bowl, pressing to extract juices; discard solids. Combine sugar syrup, strawberry mixture, and Champagne. Divide mixture among 8 (4-ounce) ice-pop molds. Top with lid; insert craft sticks. Freeze 4 hours or until thoroughly frozen. Yield: 8 servings (serving size: 1 pop).

CALORIES 146; **FAT** 0.4g (sat 0g, mono 0.1g, poly 0.2g); **PROTEIN** 0.9g; **CARB** 30.8g; **FIBER** 2.5g; **CHOL** 0mg; **IRON** 0.5mg; **SODIUM** 2mg; **CALC** 21mg

Chocolate Pudding Pops

Hands-on time: 15 min. Total time: 4 hr. 15 min.

2½ cups 2% reduced-fat milk
½ cup sugar
½ cup unsweetened cocoa
1 tablespoon cornstarch
Dash of salt
1 large egg yolk
1 teaspoon vanilla extract
2 ounces bittersweet chocolate, finely chopped

1. Combine first 6 ingredients in a medium saucepan over medium-high heat, stirring well with a whisk. Cook 8 minutes or until thick and bubbly, stirring constantly.
2. Remove pan from heat. Add 1 teaspoon vanilla and chocolate, stirring until smooth. Transfer mixture to a bowl; place bowl in an ice-filled bowl. Cover surface of pudding directly with plastic wrap; cool completely. Spoon chocolate mixture evenly into 6 (4-ounce) ice-pop molds. Top with lid; insert craft sticks. Freeze 4 hours or until thoroughly frozen. Yield: 6 servings (serving size: 1 pop).

CALORIES 196; **FAT** 7.8g (sat 4.2g, mono 1.2g, poly 0.2g); **PROTEIN** 5.9g; **CARB** 31.8g; **FIBER** 3.1g; **CHOL** 43.1mg; **IRON** 1.4mg; **SODIUM** 69mg; **CALC** 132mg

KITCHEN TIP: Sugar and alcohol lower the freezing point of the liquid, resulting in pops that have a softer, slushier texture.

Blueberry-Peach Ice Pops

Hands-on time: 30 min. Total time: 5 hr. 30 min.

An icy-fruity blueberry layer sandwiches creamy summer peach mousse for a stunning and delicious treat that children and adults will love.

⅔ cup sugar, divided
3 tablespoons fresh lemon juice, divided
3 cups fresh blueberries
1 cup peeled, pitted, and sliced peach (about 1 large peach)
⅓ cup heavy whipping cream

1. Combine 3 tablespoons sugar, 2 tablespoons fresh lemon juice, and berries in a food processor, and process until smooth. Strain mixture through a fine-mesh sieve over a bowl, pressing to extract juices, and discard solids.
2. Place remaining 1 tablespoon juice and peach in a food processor; process until smooth. Place cream in a large bowl; beat with a mixer at high speed until soft peaks form. Gradually add remaining sugar, beating until stiff peaks form. Stir one-quarter of whipped cream into peach mixture. Gently fold remaining cream into peach mixture; chill. Divide half of blueberry mixture evenly among 10 (4-ounce) ice-pop molds. Top with lid. Freeze 25 minutes or until set. Uncover and top each serving with peach mixture; top with lid. Insert craft sticks into center of each mold; freeze 25 minutes or until set. Uncover and top each serving with remaining blueberry mixture. Freeze 4 hours or until thoroughly frozen. Yield: 10 servings (serving size: 1 pop).

CALORIES 140; **FAT** 3.9g (sat 2.3g, mono 1.1g, poly 0.2g); **PROTEIN** 0.8g; **CARB** 27.5g; **FIBER** 1.6g; **CHOL** 13.6mg; **IRON** 0.2mg; **SODIUM** 4mg; **CALC** 11mg

KITCHEN TIP: No molds? Use paper cups and insert sticks into the center after freezing the mixture about 30 minutes.

STEP-BY-STEPS

WHY IT'S GOOD TO STRAIN FRUIT
When working with fresh fruit purees, you'll get the smoothest texture if you strain the mixture through a fine-mesh sieve. Chunks of whole fruit may freeze rock-hard, while seeds may create an unpleasant grittiness.

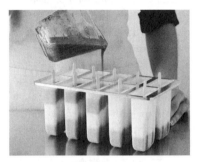

HOW TO GET NICE LAYERS
Start with chilled mixtures so they'll freeze quicker. For separate and defined stripes, it's important to freeze each layer until set. That way, when you pour on the next layer, it won't bleed into the mixture beneath it.

UNMOLDING: ALL OR SOME
Submerge the mold about halfway in warm water for 20 to 30 seconds or until the pops begin to release. Or to remove just one or two pops, wrap a towel dampened in warm water around individual molds for the same amount of time.

Tandoori-Spiced Chicken,
page 19

Shrimp Sautéed with Broccolini,
page 28

Grapefruit-Buttermilk
Sherbet, page 33

Beet, Blood Orange, Kumquat,
and Quinoa Salad, page 33

Lemony Chicken Saltimbocca,
page 43

Chicken Verde Stew with Hominy,
page 37

Beef Tagine with
Butternut Squash,
page 45

White Pizza with Tomato and Basil, page 80

Chickpea Chili, page 55

Pappardelle with Baby Spinach, Herbs, and Ricotta, page 96

Asparagus with Balsamic Tomatoes, page 111

Herb and Goat Cheese-Stuffed Chicken Breasts, page 108

Thai Chicken Salad with
Peanut Dressing, page 84

Scallops with Spinach and
Paprika Syrup, page 110

Sponge Cake with Orange Curd
and Strawberries, page 94

Shrimp Cobb Salad,
page 134

Beef Tenderloin with Horseradish-Chive Sauce, page 118

Lemon Cream Pie, page 124

Blueberry Thrill, page 138

Lemongrass Tofu Banh Mi,
page 151

Burgers with Blue Cheese Mayo
and Sherry Vidalia Onions,
page 140

Greek Yogurt with Warm Black and Blueberry Sauce, page 185

Grilled King Salmon with
Tomato-Peach Salsa, page 186

Jalapeño-Lime Slaw, page 179

Yellow Plum Salad, page 168

Lemon-Parmesan
Broccoli, page 295

Creamy, Light Mac
and Cheese, page 260

228

Pork Chops with Cherry
Couscous, page 181

Pulled Pork Sandwiches with
Mustard Sauce, page 198

230

Sautéed Tilapia Tacos with Grilled Peppers and Onion (left), page 193, and Shredded Chicken Tacos with Tomatoes and Grilled Corn (right), page 195

Mozzarella Omelet with Sage
and Red Chile Flakes, page 258

Cherry Cheesecake
Brownies, page 262

Tortilla Meatball Soup, page 280

Pepperoni, Onion, and
Olive Pizza, page 298

Soy and Cola–Braised
Pork Shoulder, page 287

Orange and Avocado Salsa and Spicy
Tortilla Strips, page 325

236

Pan-Seared Chicken with Tomato-Olive Relish, page 344

Triple-Chocolate Cake, page 329

Rich Chocolate Babka,
page 335

Indian-Spiced Roasted Squash
Soup, page 318

Roasted Rosemary
Fingerling Potatoes
(page 310), Mashed
Potato Casserole,
Parmesan-Coated Potato
Wedges (page 309)

Spiced Cinnamon Rolls
with Maple Glaze,
page 317

Quinoa-Stuffed Squash,
page 315

WHAT TO EAT RIGHT NOW
PEACHES

A peach is a peach until July and August roll around, and then, as the fruit hangs on the trees soaking up sunshine during summer's hottest days, all the magic happens. Crisp flesh softens, and sugar levels rise to balance the tart acidity. One juicy bite and you understand again why peach fanciers are so obsessed with this luscious, fuzzy fruit. No question: Peak peach time is worth the wait.

Quick & Easy
Bourbon-Glazed Peaches with Yogurt

Hands-on time: 10 min. Total time: 30 min.

1 (2-inch) piece vanilla bean, split lengthwise
1 cup plain 2% reduced-fat Greek yogurt
5½ tablespoons dark brown sugar, divided
⅛ teaspoon fine sea salt, divided
3 tablespoons bourbon
½ teaspoon vanilla extract
4 firm, ripe peaches, halved and pitted

1. Scrape seeds from vanilla bean into a medium bowl. Combine seeds, bean, yogurt, 1½ tablespoons sugar, and a dash of salt. Let stand 1 hour, and discard bean.
2. Preheat oven to 350°.
3. Combine remaining ¼ cup sugar, remaining dash of salt, bourbon, and vanilla extract in a large bowl, stirring with a whisk. Add peaches; toss gently. Arrange peaches, cut sides down, on a parchment-lined baking sheet. Reserve sugar mixture. Bake peaches at 350° for 10 minutes. Turn peach halves over; drizzle cavities with reserved sugar mixture. Bake an additional 10 minutes or until just tender. Serve with yogurt and juices. Yield: 4 servings (serving size: 2 peach halves and about ¼ cup yogurt).

CALORIES 201; **FAT** 1.8g (sat 1g, mono 0g, poly 0g); **PROTEIN** 6.7g; **CARB** 36.4g; **FIBER** 2g; **CHOL** 3mg; **IRON** 0.5mg; **SODIUM** 87mg; **CALC** 76mg

Quick & Easy • Make Ahead
Sparkling Peach Sangria

Combine 1 cup water and ⅓ cup packed brown sugar in a microwave-safe dish; microwave at HIGH 3½ minutes. Stir to dissolve sugar. Cool. Peel and pit 3 large ripe peaches. Combine sugar syrup and peeled peaches in a food processor; process until smooth. Pour peach mixture into a pitcher; stir in 2½ cups tart white wine (such as albariño) and ⅓ cup Grand Marnier. Chill at least 4 hours; strain mixture through a cheesecloth-lined sieve. Squeeze cloth to extract juices. Discard solids. Stir in 1 (750-milliliter) bottle chilled cava or other sparkling wine. Garnish with blueberries, mint leaves, and peach slices, if desired. Yield: 10 servings (serving size: ¾ cup).

CALORIES 179; **FAT** 0.2g (sat 0g); **SODIUM** 2.3mg

DID YOU KNOW?

In China—where peaches originated—the fruit symbolizes immortality.

READER RECIPE
FROM YOUR KITCHEN TO OURS

Although Linda Stoneking enjoys the challenge of creating new dishes with unusual produce (Hakurei turnips, anyone?), she still finds inspiration in the good old zucchini. "I already make zucchini patties," she says, "but I wanted to add something to make them a more satisfying lunch." For a heartier texture, Stoneking improvised by throwing in leftover pasta, which creates a crisp, toasty crust. Instead of individual patties, a single pancake also streamlines the process for an easy, fuss-free dish. Here, Stoneking serves the pancake with marinara, but for a variation, try a fresh tomato salsa or pine nut pesto.

Quick & Easy • Kid Friendly
Vegetarian
Zucchini Angel Hair Pancake

Hands-on time: 35 min. Total time: 35 min.

3 cups shredded zucchini
1 teaspoon salt, divided
1 (8-ounce) package angel hair pasta, broken into 3-inch pieces
½ cup lower-sodium marinara sauce
1.5 ounces all-purpose flour (about ⅓ cup)
⅓ cup reduced-fat sour cream
¼ cup (1 ounce) grated fresh Parmesan cheese
2 tablespoons minced shallots
1 tablespoon chopped fresh basil
1 teaspoon chopped fresh oregano
½ teaspoon baking powder
½ teaspoon black pepper
2 large eggs, lightly beaten
1 garlic clove, minced
1 tablespoon butter

1. Place zucchini in a colander, and sprinkle with ½ teaspoon salt. Toss well. Drain 20 minutes, tossing occasionally. Press zucchini between paper towels until barely moist.
2. Cook pasta according to package directions, omitting salt and fat.
3. Bring marinara to a simmer in a small saucepan; keep warm.
4. Weigh or lightly spoon flour into a dry measuring cup, and level with a knife. Combine remaining ½ teaspoon salt, flour, and next 9 ingredients in a large bowl. Add zucchini and pasta to bowl; toss well.
5. Melt butter in a large nonstick skillet over medium-high heat. Add zucchini mixture to pan, pressing down. Cook 5 minutes or until bottom is lightly browned. Carefully turn pancake over; cook 5 minutes or until bottom is lightly browned. Cut into 8 wedges. Serve with marinara. Yield: 4 servings (serving size: 2 wedges and 2 tablespoons marinara).

CALORIES 401; **FAT** 11.2g (sat 5.5g, mono 3.2g, poly 1.6g); **PROTEIN** 16.7g; **CARB** 65.9g; **FIBER** 3.2g; **CHOL** 109mg; **IRON** 3.1mg; **SODIUM** 598mg; **CALC** 159mg

DINNER TONIGHT

Here is a batch of fast weeknight menus from the *Cooking Light* Test Kitchens.

READY IN
30
MINUTES

The
SHOPPING LIST

Herbed Shrimp and White Bean Salad

1 medium-sized red bell pepper
arugula
1 red onion
fresh chives
fresh basil
fresh flat-leaf parsley
1 lemon
garlic
pine nuts
1 (15-ounce) can cannellini beans
extra-virgin olive oil
1 pound peeled and deveined large shrimp

Tomato Toast
tomato
1 French bread baguette
butter

The
GAME PLAN

While pepper broils:
- Chop herbs.
- Prepare juice mixture.
While toast broils:
- Cook tomato.
- Cook shrimp.
- Toss salad.

Quick & Easy
Herbed Shrimp and White Bean Salad
With Tomato Toast

Time-Saver: Bottled roasted red pepper can sub for fresh in a pinch.
Prep Pointer: Delicate arugula wilts quickly—serve immediately once dressed.
Simple Sub: Chopped roasted pistachios would work well in place of pine nuts.

1 medium-sized red bell pepper
4 cups arugula, loosely packed
½ cup thinly vertically sliced red onion
2 tablespoons chopped fresh chives
2 tablespoons chopped fresh basil
1 tablespoon chopped fresh flat-leaf parsley
1 (15-ounce) can cannellini beans or other white beans, rinsed and drained
½ teaspoon grated lemon rind
2 tablespoons fresh lemon juice
1 garlic clove, minced
3 tablespoons extra-virgin olive oil
¼ teaspoon salt, divided
¼ teaspoon black pepper, divided
Cooking spray
1 pound peeled and deveined large shrimp
2 tablespoons pine nuts, toasted

1. Preheat broiler to high.
2. Halve bell pepper lengthwise; discard seeds and membranes. Place halves, skin sides up, on a baking sheet. Broil 12 minutes or until blackened. Seal in a paper bag. Let stand 5 minutes. Peel; chop. Combine bell pepper and next 6 ingredients. Combine rind, juice, garlic, oil, ⅛ teaspoon salt, and ⅛ teaspoon pepper.
3. Heat a large skillet over medium-high heat. Coat pan with cooking spray. Sprinkle shrimp with remaining salt and pepper. Cook 2 minutes on each side or until done. Add shrimp, lemon mixture, and nuts to arugula mixture; toss. Yield: 4 servings (serving size: 2 cups).

CALORIES 326; **FAT** 15.7g (sat 2.1g, mono 9.2g, poly 3.3g); **PROTEIN** 28.9g; **CARB** 17.4g; **FIBER** 4.8g; **CHOL** 172mg; **IRON** 4.5mg; **SODIUM** 494mg; **CALC** 136mg

---

For the Tomato Toast:
Broil 8 (½-inch-thick) slices baguette 3 minutes. Melt 1½ teaspoons butter in a small skillet over medium-high heat. Add 1 cup chopped tomato; sauté 2 minutes. Stir in 1 tablespoon chopped parsley. Serve over toast. Yield: 4 servings (serving size: 2 toasts).

CALORIES 97; **FAT** 1.5g (sat 0.9g); **SODIUM** 197mg

READY IN
40
MINUTES

The
SHOPPING LIST

Peppered Flank Steak and Salsa
1 large red tomato
1 large yellow tomato
green onions
fresh oregano
extra-virgin olive oil
red wine vinegar
ground white pepper
ground coriander
ground cumin
ground red pepper
1 (1-pound) flank steak

Two-Bean Toss
green beans
wax beans
1 lime
extra-virgin olive oil
fresh flat-leaf parsley

The
GAME PLAN

While grill heats:
- Combine spice mix, and season steak.
While steak cooks:
- Prepare salsa.
While steak rests:
- Cook beans.

Peppered Flank Steak and Salsa
With Two-Bean Toss

Make-Ahead Tip: Prepare salsa up to two hours ahead; cover and store at room temperature. Keep It Fresh: To preserve your tomatoes' texture and flavor, never refrigerate them. Simple Sub: Use basil in place of oregano in the salsa.

Serve with bread to bulk up this light meal.

½ teaspoon salt
½ teaspoon ground cumin
½ teaspoon freshly ground black pepper
¼ teaspoon ground white pepper
¼ teaspoon ground coriander
⅛ teaspoon ground red pepper
1 (1-pound) flank steak, trimmed
Cooking spray
1½ cups diced red and yellow tomato
2 tablespoons sliced green onions
4 teaspoons chopped fresh oregano
1 tablespoon extra-virgin olive oil
2 teaspoons red wine vinegar
⅛ teaspoon salt
⅛ teaspoon freshly ground black pepper

1. Preheat grill to medium-high heat.
2. Combine first 6 ingredients in a small bowl. Rub spice mixture evenly over both sides of steak. Place steak on grill rack coated with cooking spray; grill 6 minutes on each side or until desired degree of doneness. Let stand 5 minutes. Cut steak diagonally across grain into thin slices.
3. Combine 1½ cups tomato and remaining ingredients. Serve salsa over steak. Yield: 4 servings (serving size: 3 ounces steak and ⅓ cup salsa).

CALORIES 210; **FAT** 10g (sat 2.8g, mono 4.9g, poly 0.6g); **PROTEIN** 25.2g; **CARB** 3.6g; **FIBER** 1.2g; **CHOL** 37mg; **IRON** 2.2mg; **SODIUM** 437mg; **CALC** 47mg

Quick & Easy • Kid Friendly
Vegetarian

For the Two-Bean Toss:

Cook 2 cups trimmed green beans and 1 cup trimmed wax beans in boiling water 4 minutes or until crisp-tender; drain and rinse with cold water. Combine 1 teaspoon grated lime rind, 1 tablespoon fresh lime juice, 1 tablespoon extra-virgin olive oil, 1 tablespoon chopped fresh flat-leaf parsley, ¼ teaspoon salt, and ¼ teaspoon black pepper in a medium bowl. Add beans; toss to coat. Yield: 4 servings (serving size: ¾ cup).

CALORIES 52; **FAT** 3.4g (sat 0.5g); **SODIUM** 148mg

READY IN 30 MINUTES

The SHOPPING LIST

Grilled Scallop Salad

1 English cucumber
1 (10-ounce) package prewashed romaine salad
cubed seedless watermelon
fresh mint leaves
1 avocado
1 lime
extra-virgin olive oil
12 large sea scallops (dry-packed)

Radish-Yogurt Dip and Pita Wedges

1 small bunch radishes
2 fresh garlic cloves
plain 2% reduced-fat Greek yogurt
red wine vinegar
2 (6-inch) pitas

The GAME PLAN

While grill heats:
■ Make dip.
■ Prep salad ingredients.
While scallops cook:
■ Combine and plate lettuce-watermelon mixture.

Grilled Scallop Salad
With Radish-Yogurt Dip and Pita Wedges

Prep Pointer: Remove the small, tough muscle that may still be attached to the scallop. Time-Saver: Look for cubed watermelon in the refrigerated produce section. Keep It Fresh: Rub lemon juice on the cut side of leftover avocado to help keep it from browning.

½ teaspoon freshly ground black pepper, divided
⅜ teaspoon salt, divided
12 large sea scallops (about 1½ pounds)
1 English cucumber, halved lengthwise
Cooking spray
2 tablespoons fresh lime juice
2 teaspoons extra-virgin olive oil
4 cups torn romaine lettuce
3 cups (1-inch) cubed seedless watermelon
¼ cup fresh mint leaves, torn
½ peeled avocado, cut into 8 slices

1. Preheat grill to medium-high heat.
2. Sprinkle ¼ teaspoon pepper and ¼ teaspoon salt over scallops and cucumber. Arrange in a single layer on grill rack coated with cooking spray. Grill 3 minutes on each side or until scallops are done and cucumber is well marked. Remove from heat; cut cucumber into ¼-inch slices.
3. Combine remaining ⅛ teaspoon salt, juice, and oil in a large bowl; stir with a whisk. Add cucumber, lettuce, watermelon, and mint; toss gently to coat. Divide watermelon mixture evenly among 4 plates. Top each serving with 3 scallops and 2 avocado slices. Sprinkle evenly with remaining ¼ teaspoon freshly ground black pepper. Yield: 4 servings.

Sustainable Choice

All scallops, whether farmed, diver-caught, or wild-caught, are great options.

CALORIES 263; **FAT** 7.5g (sat 1g, mono 4.2g, poly 1.3g); **PROTEIN** 31.4g; **CARB** 18.6g; **FIBER** 3.7g; **CHOL** 56mg; **IRON** 2mg; **SODIUM** 501mg; **CALC** 92mg

continued

Quick & Easy • Vegetarian

For the Radish-Yogurt Dip and Pita Wedges:

Cut 2 (6-inch) pitas into 6 wedges each. Combine ½ cup plain 2% reduced-fat Greek yogurt, 2 teaspoons minced garlic, 1 teaspoon red wine vinegar, and ¼ teaspoon black pepper in a small bowl. Stir in ¼ cup grated radish. Serve with pita wedges. Yield: 4 servings.

CALORIES 106; **FAT** 0.7g (sat 0.5g); **SODIUM** 94mg

READY IN
40
MINUTES

The
SHOPPING LIST

Lamb Chops and Cilantro Relish
1 fresh medium lemon
1 large yellow onion
1 jalapeño pepper
1 bunch fresh cilantro
extra-virgin olive oil
ground cumin
1 (1½-pound) French-cut rack of lamb (8 ribs)

Fresh Lima Beans
2 cups fresh shelled lima beans
1 pint grape tomatoes
fresh flat-leaf parsley
10 pitted kalamata olives
red wine vinegar
olive oil

The
GAME PLAN

- Preheat oven.
- Cook lima beans.
While beans cook:
- Prepare bean dressing and tomato mixture.
- Brown lamb.
While lamb roasts:
- Combine bean mixture.
- Prepare relish.

Quick & Easy

Lamb Chops and Cilantro Relish
With Fresh Lima Beans

Flavor Hit: Leave seeds in the jalapeño for a spicier relish.
Budget Buy: Use less expensive lamb loin chops in place of rack of lamb.
Time-Saver: Prechopped onion speeds prep for the relish.

1 teaspoon extra-virgin olive oil
½ teaspoon grated lemon rind
¼ teaspoon ground cumin
Cooking spray
1 (1½-pound) French-cut rack of lamb (8 ribs), trimmed
¼ teaspoon kosher salt
¼ teaspoon freshly ground black pepper
1 cup finely chopped onion
1 jalapeño pepper, seeded and finely chopped
¾ cup chopped fresh cilantro
1 tablespoon fresh lemon juice
2 teaspoons extra-virgin olive oil
¼ teaspoon kosher salt

1. Preheat oven to 400°.
2. Combine first 3 ingredients.
3. Heat a large ovenproof skillet over medium-high heat. Coat pan with cooking spray. Sprinkle lamb with ¼ teaspoon salt and black pepper. Add lamb to pan; cook 2 minutes on each side. Spread oil mixture over lamb; place pan in oven. Bake at 400° for 15 minutes or until a thermometer registers 138°. Remove lamb from pan; let stand 8 minutes. Cut into chops.
4. Heat a skillet over medium-high heat. Coat pan with cooking spray. Add onion and jalapeño; sauté 5 minutes. Combine onion mixture, cilantro, and remaining ingredients. Serve relish with chops. Yield: 4 servings (serving size: 2 chops and 3 tablespoons relish).

CALORIES 319; **FAT** 18.4g (sat 7g, mono 8.3g, poly 0.9g); **PROTEIN** 32g; **CARB** 4.5g; **FIBER** 1g; **CHOL** 102mg; **IRON** 2.5mg; **SODIUM** 347mg; **CALC** 3mg

---

Quick & Easy • Kid Friendly
Vegetarian

For the Fresh Lima Beans:

Cook 2 cups fresh lima beans in simmering water 20 minutes or until tender. Rinse with cold water; drain. Combine 1 tablespoon olive oil, 2 teaspoons red wine vinegar, and ⅛ teaspoon salt in a bowl. Add beans, ½ cup quartered grape tomato, ¼ cup sliced kalamata olives, and 2 tablespoons chopped parsley; toss well. Yield: 4 servings (serving size: ½ cup).

CALORIES 140; **FAT** 4.6g (sat 0.7g); **SODIUM** 176mg

BUDGET COOKING
FEED 4 FOR LESS THAN $10

This month: Creamy, lemony ricotta that takes less than 15 minutes, plus a kids' treat that the whole family will happily munch.

$2.49 per serving, $9.96 total

Kid Friendly • Vegetarian

Summer Veggie Pizza

Hands-on time: 33 min. Total time: 45 min.

If you have dough left over, freeze it; thaw overnight in the refrigerator before use.

8 ounces store-bought pizza dough
Cooking spray
2 tablespoons olive oil, divided
2 garlic cloves, crushed
1 cup sliced onion
1 red bell pepper, cut into thin strips
8 ounces asparagus, trimmed and cut into 1-inch pieces
2 ears corn
1 tablespoon cornmeal
¾ cup (3 ounces) shredded part-skim mozzarella cheese
½ teaspoon kosher salt
½ teaspoon crushed red pepper
⅓ cup small fresh basil leaves

1. Preheat oven to 500°.
2. Place dough in a bowl coated with cooking spray; cover and let stand 30 minutes. Heat a small skillet over medium heat. Add 4 teaspoons olive oil and garlic to pan; cook 2 minutes or until fragrant (do not brown). Remove garlic from oil, and discard garlic. Remove garlic oil from pan; set aside. Increase heat to medium-high. Add remaining 2 teaspoons oil to pan; swirl to coat. Add onion and bell pepper; sauté 5 minutes. Place onion mixture in a bowl, and add asparagus. Cut corn from cob; add corn to vegetable mixture.
3. Scatter cornmeal over a lightly floured surface; roll dough into a 13-inch circle on prepared surface. Transfer dough to a baking sheet; brush with garlic oil. Top with vegetable mixture, leaving a ½-inch border; sprinkle cheese, salt, and pepper over top. Bake at 500° for 15 minutes or until golden. Top with basil. Cut into 8 slices. Yield: 4 servings (serving size: 2 slices).

CALORIES 356; FAT 12.8g (sat 3.4g, mono 5.1g, poly 2g); PROTEIN 14.8g; CARB 49.3g; FIBER 4.8g; CHOL 11mg; IRON 3.7mg; SODIUM 728mg; CALC 185mg

$2.20 per serving, $8.79 total

Quick & Easy

Linguine with Quick Lemon Ricotta

Hands-on time: 30 min. Total time: 50 min.

Our fresh ricotta is easy to prepare; it cooks in the microwave and takes less than 15 minutes.

2 cups 2% reduced-fat milk
½ cup plain Greek yogurt
2 teaspoons cider vinegar
1½ teaspoons grated lemon rind
1 teaspoon kosher salt, divided
8 ounces uncooked linguine
1 tablespoon olive oil
2 small yellow squash, chopped
1 small zucchini, chopped
1 pint grape tomatoes, halved
4 garlic cloves, coarsely chopped
⅓ cup fat-free, lower-sodium chicken broth
½ teaspoon black pepper
¼ cup small fresh mint leaves

1. Combine first 3 ingredients in a microwave-safe 1-quart liquid measuring cup; microwave at HIGH 4 minutes. Stir to form small curds. Strain through a sieve lined with a double layer of cheesecloth; let stand 5 minutes. Discard liquid. Scrape cheese mixture into a small bowl; stir in rind and ¼ teaspoon salt.
2. Cook pasta according to package directions, omitting salt and fat, and drain. Heat a large skillet over medium-high heat. Add olive oil to pan; swirl to coat. Add squash and zucchini to pan; sauté 1 minute. Add ¼ teaspoon salt, tomatoes, and garlic; sauté 4 minutes. Add broth and pasta to pan, and cook 2 minutes or until thoroughly heated, tossing to combine. Place 2 cups pasta mixture in each of 4 shallow bowls; sprinkle each serving evenly with remaining ½ teaspoon salt and pepper. Top each serving with 2 tablespoons cheese mixture and 1 tablespoon mint. Serve immediately. Yield: 4 servings.

CALORIES 372; FAT 9.8g (sat 4.6g, mono 3.2g, poly 0.6g); PROTEIN 15.9g; CARB 56.5g; FIBER 4.1g; CHOL 15mg; IRON 2.6mg; SODIUM 587mg; CALC 212mg

$1.27 per serving, $5.09 total

Quick & Easy • Kid Friendly

Kid-tastic Pizzadillas

Hands-on time: 5 min. Total time: 25 min.

1 tablespoon canola oil
4 (8-inch) fat-free flour tortillas
1½ cups (6 ounces) shredded part-skim mozzarella cheese
1 ounce turkey pepperoni
1 cup marinara sauce

1. Preheat oven to 400°.
2. Brush canola oil over a jelly-roll pan, and top with tortillas. Sprinkle 3 tablespoons cheese over each tortilla, and divide pepperoni among tortillas. Top each with 3 tablespoons cheese. Bake at 400° for 5 minutes. Remove from oven, and carefully fold each tortilla in half. Bake an additional 10 minutes or until browned and crisp, turning after 5 minutes. Serve with

marinara. Yield: 4 servings (serving size: 1 pizzadilla and ¼ cup sauce).

CALORIES 308; FAT 15.5g (sat 6.7g, mono 5.2g, poly 1.2g); PROTEIN 17.6g; CARB 37.4g; FIBER 11g; CHOL 37.3mg; IRON 1mg; SODIUM 849mg; CALC 413mg

$2.50 per serving, $9.99 total

Kid Friendly

Maple-Brined Pork

Hands-on time: 26 min. Total time: 9 hr.

3 cups water
½ cup fat-free, lower-sodium chicken broth
1 tablespoon black peppercorns
1½ teaspoons whole allspice
4 garlic cloves, crushed
1 bay leaf, crushed
2 tablespoons plus ½ teaspoon kosher salt, divided
2½ tablespoons maple syrup, divided
4 (4-ounce) boneless pork chops
½ teaspoon freshly ground black pepper, divided
Cooking spray
2 tablespoons butter, melted
2 ripe plums, halved and pitted
2 ripe peaches, halved and pitted
2 green onions, sliced (optional)

1. Place first 6 ingredients, 2 tablespoons salt, and 2 tablespoons syrup in a pan. Bring to a boil; dissolve salt. Cool. Place pork and brine in a zip-top plastic bag; seal. Chill 8 hours; drain.
2. Preheat grill to medium-high heat.
3. Sprinkle pork with ¼ teaspoon salt and ¼ teaspoon ground pepper. Grill pork on rack coated with cooking spray 3 minutes on each side or until done. Combine remaining ½ tablespoon syrup and butter; brush onto fruit. Sprinkle with remaining ¼ teaspoon salt and ¼ teaspoon ground pepper. Grill fruit, cut sides down, on rack coated with cooking spray 3 minutes. Cut each peach and plum half in half again; serve with pork. Top with onions, if desired. Yield: 4 servings (serving size: 1 chop and 4 fruit pieces).

CALORIES 243; FAT 11.7g (sat 5.4g, mono 3.6g, poly 0.9g); PROTEIN 22.2g; CARB 12.7g; FIBER 1.5g; CHOL 82mg; IRON 1mg; SODIUM 620mg; CALC 33mg

Tomato Soup with Roasted Chickpeas

Hands-on time: 20 min. Total time: 1 hr. 8 min.

1 red bell pepper, halved lengthwise
3 tablespoons olive oil, divided
8 garlic cloves, divided
¼ cup heavy whipping cream
1 (28-ounce) can no-salt-added whole peeled tomatoes, crushed
½ teaspoon smoked paprika
³⁄₈ teaspoon salt, divided
¼ teaspoon ground red pepper
2 ounces country ham, finely chopped
1 (15.5-ounce) can organic chickpeas, rinsed and drained
¼ teaspoon ground cumin
¼ cup fresh flat-leaf parsley
2 tablespoons sliced almonds, toasted and chopped

1. Preheat broiler.
2. Discard seeds and membranes from bell pepper; place, skin sides up, on a foil-lined baking sheet. Broil 8 minutes or until blackened. Seal in a bag; let stand 10 minutes. Peel.
3. Reduce oven to 450°.
4. Heat 1 tablespoon oil in a saucepan over medium heat. Add 3 garlic cloves; cook 1 minute. Add cream and tomatoes; bring to a simmer. Add paprika, ¼ teaspoon salt, and ground red pepper; simmer 20 minutes, stirring occasionally. Cool 10 minutes. Combine tomato mixture and bell pepper in a blender, and puree.
5. Combine 5 garlic cloves, ham, and chickpeas in a roasting pan; drizzle with 2 tablespoons oil, cumin, and ⅛ teaspoon salt. Toss. Roast at 450° for 12 minutes, stirring once. Ladle ¾ cup soup into each of 4 bowls; top evenly with chickpea mixture, parsley, and almonds. Yield: 4 servings.

CALORIES 288; FAT 12.6g (sat 0.2g, mono 7.2g, poly 3.2g); PROTEIN 24.3g; CARB 24.4g; FIBER 10.1g; CHOL 37mg; IRON 0.7mg; SODIUM 802mg; CALC 37mg

SUPERFAST

Get ready for the end of summer with two back-to-school kid-pleasers, fresh tomatoes, grilled chicken, and more.

Quick & Easy • Kid Friendly
Vegetarian

Baked Mozzarella Bites

Serve this quick after-school snack to your kids as an alternative to traditional fried cheesesticks.

⅓ cup panko (Japanese breadcrumbs)
3 (1-ounce) sticks part-skim mozzarella string cheese
3 tablespoons egg substitute
Cooking spray
¼ cup lower-sodium marinara sauce

1. Preheat oven to 425°.
2. Heat a medium skillet over medium heat. Add ⅓ cup panko to pan, and cook 2 minutes or until toasted, stirring frequently. Remove from heat, and place panko in a shallow dish.
3. Cut mozzarella sticks into 1-inch pieces. Working with one piece at a time, dip cheese in egg substitute; dredge in panko. Place cheese on a baking sheet coated with cooking spray. Bake at 425° for 3 minutes or until cheese is softened and thoroughly heated.
4. Pour marinara sauce into a microwave-safe bowl. Microwave at HIGH 1 minute or until thoroughly heated, stirring after 30 seconds. Serve with mozzarella pieces. Yield: 4 servings (serving size: 3 mozzarella bites and 1 tablespoon sauce).

CALORIES 91; FAT 5.1g (sat 2.8g, mono 1.3g, poly 0.3g); PROTEIN 7.2g; CARB 6.7g; FIBER 0.1g; CHOL 12mg; IRON 0.3mg; SODIUM 162mg; CALC 162mg

Quick & Easy • Kid Friendly

Bacon-Corn Chowder with Shrimp

This soup can also serve 6 as a first course instead of an entrée·

6 center-cut bacon slices, chopped
1 cup prechopped onion
½ cup prechopped celery
1 teaspoon chopped fresh thyme
1 garlic clove, minced
4 cups fresh or frozen corn kernels, thawed
2 cups fat-free, lower-sodium chicken broth
¾ pound peeled and deveined medium shrimp
⅓ cup half-and-half
¼ teaspoon freshly ground black pepper
⅛ teaspoon salt

1. Heat a large Dutch oven over medium-high heat. Add bacon to pan; sauté 4 minutes or until bacon begins to brown. Remove 2 slices bacon. Drain on paper towels. Add onion and next 3 ingredients to pan, and sauté 2 minutes. Add corn, and cook 2 minutes, stirring occasionally. Add broth; bring to a boil, and cook 4 minutes.
2. Place 2 cups of corn mixture in a blender. Remove center piece of blender lid (to allow steam to escape), and secure lid on blender. Place a clean towel over opening in blender lid (to avoid splatters). Blend until smooth. Return pureed corn mixture to pan. Stir in shrimp; cook 2 minutes or until shrimp are done. Stir in half-and-half, pepper, and salt. Crumble reserved bacon over soup. Yield: 4 servings (serving size: about 1⅔ cups).

CALORIES 294; FAT 7g (sat 2.7g, mono 1.3g, poly 1.2g); PROTEIN 26.8g; CARB 34.8g; FIBER 4.3g; CHOL 144mg; IRON 3.1mg; SODIUM 547mg; CALC 94mg

BBQ Chicken and Blue Cheese Pizza

For a kid-friendly pie, substitute fresh mozzarella for the blue cheese.

1 (8-ounce) prebaked thin pizza crust
1/3 cup barbecue sauce
1 1/2 cups shredded skinless, boneless
    rotisserie chicken breast
1/2 cup vertically sliced red onion
1/2 cup coarsely chopped yellow bell pepper
1/2 cup (2 ounces) crumbled blue cheese
2 plum tomatoes, thinly sliced (about
    1/4 pound)

1. Preheat oven to 500°.
2. Place pizza crust on a baking sheet. Spread sauce over crust, leaving a 1/2-inch border. Top with chicken and remaining ingredients. Bake at 500° for 10 minutes or until cheese melts and crust is crisp. Cut into 12 wedges. Yield: 6 servings (serving size: 2 wedges).

CALORIES 252; FAT 8.5g (sat 3.1g, mono 2.2g, poly 2.7g); PROTEIN 16.7g; CARB 27.4g; FIBER 1.8g; CHOL 38mg; IRON 1.6mg; SODIUM 494mg; CALC 92mg

Grilled Chicken Thighs with Pineapple, Corn, and Bell Pepper Relish

Cooking spray
1 teaspoon garlic powder
1 teaspoon ground cumin
3/4 teaspoon salt, divided
1/4 teaspoon freshly ground black pepper
8 skinless, boneless chicken thighs (about
    1 1/4 pounds)
2 cups cubed fresh pineapple (about
    1/2 pineapple)
1/2 cup fresh corn kernels (about 1 ear)
1/3 cup finely chopped red bell pepper
1/4 cup thinly sliced fresh basil
3 tablespoons finely chopped red onion
1 tablespoon cider vinegar
1 teaspoon sugar

1. Heat a grill pan over medium-high heat; lightly coat with cooking spray. Combine garlic powder, cumin, 1/2 teaspoon salt, and pepper in a small bowl; sprinkle over chicken. Add chicken to pan; cook 10 minutes on each side or until done.
2. Meanwhile, combine remaining 1/4 teaspoon salt, pineapple, and remaining ingredients in a medium bowl. Serve relish over chicken. Yield: 4 servings (serving size: 2 thighs and 3/4 cup relish).

CALORIES 242; FAT 6.1g (sat 1.5g, mono 1.8g, poly 1.5g); PROTEIN 29.6g; CARB 17.4g; FIBER 1.3g; CHOL 118mg; IRON 2.2mg; SODIUM 571mg; CALC 38mg

Ham and Swiss Egg Sandwiches

Cooking spray
4 ounces thinly sliced lower-sodium deli ham
4 large eggs
4 English muffins, split and toasted
4 (1-ounce) slices Emmentaler or Swiss
    cheese

1. Preheat broiler to high.
2. Heat a nonstick skillet over medium-high heat. Coat pan with cooking spray. Add ham to pan; sauté 2 minutes or until lightly browned. Remove from pan. Recoat pan with cooking spray. Crack eggs into pan. Cover and cook 4 minutes or until desired degree of doneness. Remove from heat.
3. Place 4 muffin halves, cut sides up, on a baking sheet. Top each half with 1 cheese slice. Broil 2 minutes or until cheese melts. Divide ham among cheese-topped muffin halves; top each with 1 egg and 1 muffin half. Yield: 4 servings (serving size: 1 sandwich).

CALORIES 344; FAT 14.7g (sat 6.7g, mono 4.1g, poly 1.5g); PROTEIN 23.5g; CARB 29.1g; FIBER 0g; CHOL 250mg; IRON 2mg; SODIUM 553mg; CALC 351mg

Summer Tomato, Mozzarella, and Basil Panini with Balsamic Syrup

Serve with sweet potato chips or a simple green salad.

1/2 cup balsamic vinegar
1 (8-ounce) piece Cuban bread, cut in half
    horizontally
1 tablespoon extra-virgin olive oil
12 large fresh basil leaves
5 ounces fresh mozzarella cheese, thinly
    sliced
2 medium tomatoes, thinly sliced
1/4 teaspoon salt
1/8 teaspoon freshly ground black pepper
Cooking spray

1. Bring balsamic vinegar to a boil in a small saucepan over medium-high heat; cook until reduced to 3 tablespoons (about 8 minutes).
2. While vinegar reduces, brush cut side of top half of bread with oil. Top evenly with basil, cheese, and tomatoes. Sprinkle evenly with salt and pepper. Brush cut side of bottom half of bread with reduced vinegar; place on top of sandwich. Invert sandwich.
3. Heat a large grill pan over medium-high heat. Coat pan with cooking spray. Add sandwich to pan. Place a cast-iron or heavy skillet on top of sandwich, and gently press to flatten. Leave skillet on; cook 3 minutes on each side or until cheese melts and bread is toasted. Cut sandwich into 4 equal pieces. Yield: 4 servings.

CALORIES 325; FAT 13.4g (sat 5.5g, mono 5.5g, poly 1.1g); PROTEIN 13.6g; CARB 37.4g; FIBER 2.5g; CHOL 28mg; IRON 2.1mg; SODIUM 726mg; CALC 225mg

PORK TENDERLOIN, 25 WAYS

This lean, quick-cooking cut is the chicken breast of the pork world. It stands up to bold flavors and is so versatile it can move from down-home casual to elegant to global. We've dived into 5 easy techniques that let you marinate, roast, grill, stuff, or slice-and-dice your way to 25 easy, healthy dinners.

ROAST

Roasting tender pork at high heat browns the exterior, adding deep, savory flavor, but leaves the interior juicy and rosy pink (see guidelines at top right).

Spicy North African Pork Tenderloin

Hands-on time: 15 min. Total time: 1 hr.

1/4 cup bottled roasted red bell pepper
3 tablespoons olive oil, divided
3 tablespoons lemon juice, divided
1 tablespoon sambal oelek (ground fresh chile paste)
3/4 teaspoon kosher salt, divided
1 1/2 teaspoons ground cumin, divided
1/4 teaspoon ground coriander
2 garlic cloves
1 cup plain 2% reduced-fat Greek yogurt
1/4 cup chopped fresh mint
1 (1-pound) pork tenderloin, trimmed

1. Place bell pepper, 2 tablespoons olive oil, 2 tablespoons juice, sambal oelek, 1/4 teaspoon salt, 1/2 teaspoon cumin, coriander, and garlic in a food processor; process until smooth. Place harissa in a large bowl.

2. Preheat oven to 425°.
3. Combine yogurt, mint, remaining 1 tablespoon juice, and remaining 1 teaspoon cumin.
4. Heat a large skillet over medium-high heat. Add 1 tablespoon olive oil; swirl to coat. Sprinkle pork with remaining 1/2 teaspoon salt. Add pork to pan, and cook 6 minutes, browning on all sides. Add pork to harissa, turning to coat. Place pork on a roasting rack in a pan; brush with remaining harissa. Roast at 425° for 11 minutes or until a thermometer registers 145°. Remove from oven; let stand 5 minutes; cut crosswise into 12 slices. Serve with yogurt sauce. Yield: 4 servings (serving size: 3 pork slices and 3 tablespoons sauce).

CALORIES 283; FAT 14.3g (sat 3.2g, mono 8.3g, poly 1.5g); PROTEIN 30.2g; CARB 8.2g; FIBER 1.4g; CHOL 77mg; IRON 1.7mg; SODIUM 446mg; CALC 84mg

SERVE WITH BLISTERED CHERRY TOMATOES OR OTHER ROASTED VEGGIES.

If you like **Maple Syrup** try:

Quick & Easy • Kid Friendly

Roasted Pork Tenderloin and Maple-Glazed Apples

Preheat oven to 425°. Combine 1/2 teaspoon salt, 1/4 teaspoon black pepper, and 1/4 teaspoon ground cinnamon; rub over 2 (12-ounce) trimmed pork tenderloins. Heat a large ovenproof skillet over medium-high heat. Add 1 tablespoon olive oil. Add pork; cook 4 minutes on each side. Remove pork, and reduce heat. Melt 2 tablespoons butter in pan. Add 2 pounds 1/2-inch-thick sliced peeled Granny Smith apples and 1 thinly sliced shallot to pan; sauté 1 minute. Stir in 3 tablespoons maple syrup, 1 1/2 tablespoons lemon juice, 1/4 teaspoon salt, and 1/4 teaspoon ground cinnamon; cook 4 minutes. Stir. Return pork to pan. Roast at 425° for 12 minutes or until a thermometer registers 145°. Remove pork from pan; let stand 5 minutes. Slice pork; serve with apples. Yield: 6 servings (serving size: 3 ounces pork and 1/3 cup apple mixture).

CALORIES 281; FAT 8.8g (sat 3.6g); SODIUM 302mg

If you like **Goat Cheese** try:

Pork Tenderloin with Tangy Grape Salad

Preheat oven to 400°. Sprinkle 2 (1-pound) pork tenderloins with ½ teaspoon salt. Heat 1 tablespoon olive oil in a large ovenproof skillet over medium-high heat. Add pork; sauté 4 minutes on each side. Roast at 400° for 12 minutes or until a thermometer registers 145°. Remove pork; let stand. Heat a medium skillet over medium-high heat. Add 2 teaspoons olive oil. Add 1 cup sliced shallots and 1 tablespoon chopped thyme; sauté 4 minutes. Add ¾ cup fat-free, lower-sodium chicken broth and ½ cup riesling wine; bring to a boil. Cook 3 minutes. Stir in 1½ cups halved seedless grapes and 2 tablespoons Dijon mustard. Stir in ½ cup chopped toasted pecans. Slice pork; serve with salad. Sprinkle with ¾ cup crumbled goat cheese. Yield: 8 servings (serving size: 3 ounces pork, ½ cup grape mixture, and 1½ tablespoons cheese).

CALORIES 269; **FAT** 12.4g (sat 3.2g); **SODIUM** 342mg

If you like **Butternut Squash** try:

Roast Pork with Potatoes and Butternut Squash

Preheat oven to 425°. Combine 2½ cups halved small red potatoes and 2 cups cubed peeled butternut squash in an 11 x 7–inch baking dish. Combine 1 tablespoon olive oil, 1½ teaspoons chopped thyme, 1½ teaspoons chopped sage, ½ teaspoon salt, and ¼ teaspoon pepper; toss with vegetables. Roast at 425° for 15 minutes. Heat a large skillet over medium-high heat. Add 1 tablespoon olive oil. Sprinkle 1 (1-pound) pork tenderloin with ½ teaspoon salt. Add pork to pan; cook 4 minutes. Stir vegetables; add pork and ¼ cup dry sherry. Roast for 12 minutes or until a thermometer registers 145°. Remove pork; let stand 5 minutes. Yield: 4 servings (serving size: 3 ounces pork and 1 cup vegetables).

CALORIES 319; **FAT** 9.5g (sat 1.8g); **SODIUM** 664mg

MARINATE/ RUB

Because tenderloin is already tender, the point of marinating is to impart great flavors into what can be a bland cut. Marinating can take anywhere from 30 minutes to 24 hours.

Argentinean Pork

Hands-on time: 20 min. Total time: 1 hr. 30 min.

6 tablespoons olive oil, divided
1 cup fresh parsley leaves, divided
⅔ cup fresh cilantro leaves, divided
½ teaspoon ground cumin
¼ teaspoon crushed red pepper
1 (1-pound) pork tenderloin, trimmed
¾ teaspoon kosher salt, divided
½ teaspoon black pepper
Cooking spray
1 tablespoon fresh oregano leaves
1 tablespoon fresh lemon juice
1 tablespoon sherry vinegar
2 garlic cloves, chopped
1 shallot, chopped

1. Combine 2 tablespoons oil, ¼ cup parsley, ⅓ cup cilantro, cumin, and red pepper in a shallow dish. Add pork. Cover with plastic wrap, and refrigerate 1 hour, turning once.
2. Preheat grill to medium-high.
3. Sprinkle pork with ½ teaspoon salt and black pepper. Place pork on grill rack coated with cooking spray, and grill 8 minutes. Turn pork over; grill 7 minutes or until a thermometer registers 145°. Remove pork from grill. Let stand 5 minutes. Slice pork crosswise.
4. Combine ¾ cup parsley, ⅓ cup cilantro, ¼ teaspoon salt, oregano, and remaining ingredients in a food processor; pulse 10 times. Drizzle ¼ cup olive oil through food chute with food processor on. Serve with pork. Yield: 4 servings (serving size: 3 ounces pork and 2 tablespoons sauce).

CALORIES 319; **FAT** 23g (sat 3.6g, mono 15.7g, poly 2.6g); **PROTEIN** 24.5g; **CARB** 2.9g; **FIBER** 0.7g; **CHOL** 74mg; **IRON** 2.4mg; **SODIUM** 430mg; **CALC** 39mg

Spanish Pork with Apple-Citrus Salsa

Hands-on time: 25 min. Total time: 59 min.

Pimenton is a Spanish paprika made from peppers that have been smoked and dried over oak fires. If pimenton is not available, use Spanish smoked paprika. Garnish this smoky pork with lime wedges and fresh cilantro leaves, if desired.

1½ teaspoons chili powder
½ teaspoon dried oregano
½ teaspoon ground cumin
⅛ teaspoon pimenton
¾ teaspoon kosher salt, divided
½ teaspoon freshly ground black pepper, divided
2 tablespoons olive oil, divided
1 (1-pound) pork tenderloin, trimmed
2 cups diced Granny Smith apple
2 tablespoons chopped fresh cilantro
2 tablespoons apple juice
½ teaspoon grated lime rind
1½ teaspoons fresh lime juice
2 green onions, thinly sliced
½ jalapeño pepper, thinly sliced
Cooking spray

1. Combine first 4 ingredients. Stir in ½ teaspoon salt and ¼ teaspoon black pepper. Brush 1 tablespoon olive oil over pork, and sprinkle evenly with chili powder mixture. Let stand 30 minutes at room temperature.
2. Preheat grill to medium-high heat.
3. Combine remaining 1 tablespoon olive oil, remaining ¼ teaspoon salt, remaining ¼ teaspoon black pepper, apple, and next 6 ingredients in a medium bowl; toss.
4. Place pork on grill rack coated with cooking spray; grill 6 minutes on each side or until a thermometer registers 145°. Remove pork from grill; let stand 5 minutes. Slice pork crosswise; serve with salsa. Yield: 4 servings (serving size: 3 ounces pork and ½ cup salsa).

CALORIES 227; **FAT** 9.6g (sat 1.8g, mono 5.8g, poly 1.2g); **PROTEIN** 24.2g; **CARB** 10.7g; **FIBER** 2.0g; **CHOL** 74mg; **IRON** 1.5mg; **SODIUM** 453mg; **CALC** 21mg

Indian-Spiced Pork with Raita

Combine 1 teaspoon each coriander seeds, cumin seeds, and fennel seeds; ¼ teaspoon salt; and ¼ teaspoon black pepper in a spice grinder, and process until finely ground. Brush 1 tablespoon canola oil over 1 (1-pound) trimmed pork tenderloin. Rub with spice mixture. Place pork on a roasting rack in pan; let stand at room temperature 30 minutes. Preheat oven to 425°. Roast pork at 425° for 15 minutes or until a thermometer registers 145°. Remove from oven. Let stand 5 minutes; slice. Squeeze moisture from 1 cup grated English cucumber. Combine cucumber, ⅔ cup plain 2% Greek yogurt, 1½ teaspoons grated lemon rind, ¼ teaspoon salt, a dash of ground red pepper, and 1 minced garlic clove. Serve with pork. Yield: 4 servings (serving size: 3 ounces pork and about ¼ cup raita).

CALORIES 178; **FAT** 4.9g (sat 1.6g); **SODIUM** 317mg

If you like Avocado try:

Tequila Pork with Tomatillo Guacamole

Combine ¼ cup tequila, ¼ cup lemon juice, 1 teaspoon ground cumin, ¼ teaspoon crushed red pepper, and 1 chopped jalapeño in a zip-top plastic bag. Add 1 (1-pound) trimmed pork tenderloin to bag; seal. Marinate in refrigerator 2 hours. Boil 4 tomatillos 2 minutes; drain. Place tomatillos, 1 tablespoon lime juice, ¼ teaspoon salt, 6 cilantro sprigs, 2 peeled avocados, and 2 garlic cloves in a food processor; process until smooth. Preheat grill to medium-high. Remove pork from bag; discard marinade. Sprinkle pork with ¼ teaspoon salt. Place pork on grill rack coated with cooking spray; grill 8 minutes. Turn; grill 7 minutes or until a thermometer registers 145°. Remove; let stand 5 minutes; slice. Serve with guacamole. Yield: 4 servings (serving size: 3 ounces pork and ½ cup guacamole).

CALORIES 316; **FAT** 18.8 (sat 3.1g); **SODIUM** 407mg

If you like Dark Sesame Oil try:

Soy-Ginger Sesame Pork

Combine ½ cup lower-sodium soy sauce, 2 tablespoons dark sesame oil, 1 tablespoon grated peeled fresh ginger, and 2 crushed garlic cloves in a large zip-top plastic bag. Add 1 (1-pound) trimmed pork tenderloin to bag; seal. Marinate in refrigerator 1½ hours, turning occasionally. Preheat grill to medium-high heat. Remove pork from marinade; discard marinade. Sprinkle both sides of pork evenly with ½ teaspoon kosher salt. Place pork on grill rack coated with cooking spray; grill 8 minutes. Turn pork over; grill 7 minutes or until a thermometer inserted into thickest portion of pork registers 145°. Remove from grill; let stand 5 minutes. Cut crosswise into 12 slices. Yield: 4 servings (serving size: 3 slices).

CALORIES 132; **FAT** 3.1g (sat 0.9g); **SODIUM** 378mg

SLICE/DICE

Slices, strips, and cubes are the perfect building blocks for the cook in a hurry.

Quick & Easy

Baja Pork Stir-Fry

Hands-on time: 26 min. Total time: 26 min.

Serve this dish over cooked rice or rice noodles.

¼ cup fat-free, lower-sodium chicken broth
1½ teaspoons cornstarch
½ teaspoon ground cumin
2 garlic cloves, minced
1 (1-pound) pork tenderloin, cut into 1-inch pieces
¾ teaspoon salt, divided
½ teaspoon black pepper, divided
2 tablespoons canola oil, divided
½ red onion, cut into wedges
½ cup julienne-cut yellow bell pepper
½ cup julienne-cut green bell pepper
½ cup julienne-cut red bell pepper
½ jalapeño pepper, minced
10 cherry tomatoes, halved
¼ cup fresh cilantro leaves

1. Combine first 4 ingredients.
2. Sprinkle pork with ¼ teaspoon salt and ¼ teaspoon black pepper; toss. Heat a large skillet over medium-high heat. Add 1 tablespoon canola oil; swirl. Add pork, and cook 3 minutes, browning on all sides. Remove pork from pan; keep warm.
3. Heat pan over high heat, and add remaining 1 tablespoon canola oil, and swirl to coat. Add onion, and stir-fry for 1 minute. Add bell peppers and jalapeño; stir-fry 1 minute. Return pork to pan, and stir-fry 1 minute. Stir in broth mixture, remaining ½ teaspoon salt, and remaining ¼ teaspoon black pepper, and bring to a boil. Remove from heat, and stir in tomatoes. Sprinkle with cilantro. Yield: 4 servings (serving size: 1¼ cups).

CALORIES 221; **FAT** 9.8g (sat 1.3g, mono 5.3g, poly 2.5g); **PROTEIN** 25g; **CARB** 7.4g; **FIBER** 1.9g; **CHOL** 74mg; **IRON** 1.6mg; **SODIUM** 536mg; **CALC** 22mg

Quick & Easy

Vietnamese Salad

Hands-on time: 10 min. Total time: 48 min.

1 (1-pound) pork tenderloin, trimmed
1 teaspoon canola oil
Cooking spray
3 tablespoons fresh lime juice
1½ tablespoons fish sauce
1½ tablespoons lower-sodium soy sauce
1½ teaspoons sugar
1½ teaspoons grated peeled fresh ginger
⅛ teaspoon ground red pepper
1 serrano chile, thinly sliced
¾ cup small fresh mint leaves
½ cup thinly sliced red onion
3 thinly diagonally sliced green onions
1 halved, seeded, and thinly sliced cucumber
8 cups sliced romaine lettuce
½ cup fresh cilantro leaves

1. Preheat grill to medium-high heat.
2. Brush pork with oil. Place pork on grill rack coated with cooking spray, and grill 6 minutes on each side or until a thermometer inserted into thickest portion of pork registers 145°. Remove from grill; let pork stand 5 minutes. Slice pork crosswise in half; slice each

half, lengthwise, into thin strips. Cool. Combine juice and next 6 ingredients in a large bowl. Add pork to juice mixture; toss to coat. Add mint and next 3 ingredients to bowl; toss. Arrange 2 cups lettuce on each of 4 plates; top each serving with about ⅔ cup pork mixture. Sprinkle with cilantro. Yield: 4 servings (serving size: 1 salad).

CALORIES 200; FAT 4.3g (sat 1g, mono 1.7g, poly 1g); PROTEIN 27.7g; CARB 13.9g; FIBER 5g; CHOL 74mg; IRON 3.4mg; SODIUM 653mg; CALC 95mg

Make Ahead
Hungarian Goulash

Hands-on time: 28 min. Total time: 1 hr. 28 min.

1 garlic clove, crushed
1 teaspoon kosher salt, divided
¼ teaspoon caraway seeds, crushed
¼ teaspoon black pepper, divided
Cooking spray
1 (1-pound) pork tenderloin, cut into 1-inch pieces
2 cups coarsely chopped onion
1 bacon slice, finely chopped
1¾ cups water, divided
1 cup chopped seeded tomato
1 tablespoon paprika
¾ cup beer
⅛ teaspoon crushed red pepper
3 Hungarian wax chiles, seeded and cut into 1-inch pieces
1½ tablespoons all-purpose flour
8 ounces uncooked egg noodles
1 tablespoon butter
3 tablespoons sour cream
Chopped fresh parsley (optional)

1. Place garlic in a small bowl; mash with the back of a spoon to form a paste. Add ¼ teaspoon salt, caraway seeds, and ⅛ teaspoon black pepper.
2. Heat a large Dutch oven over high heat. Coat pan with cooking spray. Combine ¼ teaspoon salt, remaining ⅛ teaspoon black pepper, and pork in a medium bowl; toss. Add pork to pan; sauté 6 minutes, browning on all sides. Remove pork from pan.
3. Reduce heat to medium-high; return pan to heat. Add onion and bacon; sauté 7 minutes or until bacon is

done, stirring frequently. Stir in garlic mixture; cook 1 minute, stirring constantly. Add 1½ cups water, tomato, paprika, and beer; bring to a boil. Reduce heat, and simmer 30 minutes, stirring occasionally. Stir in red pepper and chiles; simmer 15 minutes. Add pork to pan; simmer 15 minutes, stirring occasionally. Combine remaining ¼ cup water and flour in a small bowl; stir with a whisk. Stir flour mixture and remaining ½ teaspoon salt into pork mixture. Bring to a boil; cook 1 minute, stirring constantly.
4. Cook noodles according to package directions, omitting salt and fat. Combine noodles and butter in a medium bowl, stirring until butter melts. Place 1 cup noodles in each of 4 shallow bowls; top with 1 cup pork mixture. Top each serving with about 2 teaspoons sour cream. Garnish with parsley, if desired. Yield: 4 servings.

CALORIES 476; FAT 11.3g (sat 5g, mono 2.2g, poly 0.9g); PROTEIN 35g; CARB 56.1g; FIBER 5.4g; CHOL 154mg; IRON 3.9mg; SODIUM 626mg; CALC 69mg

If you like **Saffron** try:
Make Ahead
Tagine-Style Pork with Squash and Pearl Onions

Sprinkle 1 pound cubed pork tenderloin with ½ teaspoon salt and ½ teaspoon black pepper. Heat 1 tablespoon canola oil in a Dutch oven over medium-high heat. Add pork, and sauté 2 minutes. Add ⅔ cup chopped onion, ¾ teaspoon Hungarian sweet paprika, ½ teaspoon ground cumin, ¼ teaspoon ground red pepper, ⅛ teaspoon saffron threads, and 3 minced garlic cloves; sauté 1 minute. Stir in 1½ cups water; 1 cup fat-free, lower-sodium chicken broth; and 1 (3-inch) cinnamon stick. Bring to a boil. Cover, reduce heat, and simmer 15 minutes. Stir in 3 cups cubed butternut squash and 12 peeled pearl onions. Cook, covered, 15 minutes or until vegetables are tender. Remove from heat, and stir in ½ cup chopped fresh

parsley, 2 tablespoons lemon juice, and ¼ teaspoon salt. Yield: 4 servings (serving size: 1 cup).

CALORIES 248; FAT 6.3g (sat 1.1g); SODIUM 669mg

If you like **Pecans** try:
Pecan-Crusted Pork Noisettes

Preheat oven to 350°. Combine ⅓ cup coarsely ground pecans and ⅓ cup panko; spread on a jelly-roll pan. Bake at 350° for 10 minutes. Place crumbs in a shallow dish. Place ⅓ cup all-purpose flour in a shallow dish. Combine 1 tablespoon water and 1 large egg in a shallow dish. Slice 1 (1-pound) trimmed pork tenderloin crosswise into 8 slices. Place each pork slice between 2 sheets of heavy-duty plastic wrap; pound to ¼-inch thickness using a meat mallet. Sprinkle pork with ¼ teaspoon salt and ¼ teaspoon pepper. Dredge in flour. Dip pork in egg mixture; dredge in crumbs. Melt 1½ teaspoons butter in a large skillet over medium heat. Add half of pork to pan; cook 2 minutes on each side. Place pork on a jelly-roll pan. Repeat procedure with remaining pork and butter. Bake at 350° for 5 minutes. Serve with lemon wedges. Yield: 4 servings (serving size: 3 ounces pork).

CALORIES 396; FAT 24.7g (sat 4.6g); SODIUM 260mg

Make Ahead

Choucroute

Sprinkle 1 pound cubed pork tenderloin with ¼ teaspoon pepper and ⅛ teaspoon salt. Melt 1 tablespoon butter in a Dutch oven over medium-high heat. Add pork; sauté 5 minutes, browning on all sides. Remove pork. Reduce heat. Add 2 teaspoons canola oil, 2 cups chopped onion, 1 teaspoon crushed juniper berries, ½ teaspoon crushed caraway seeds, and 2 chopped bacon slices to pan; cook 10 minutes, stirring occasionally. Stir in 4 cups thinly sliced cabbage; 1 cup dry riesling wine; 1 cup fat-free, lower-sodium chicken broth; and 1 (16-ounce) jar prepared sauerkraut. Bring to a boil. Cover and simmer 1 hour and 15 minutes, stirring occasionally. Add pork; cook 15 minutes, stirring occasionally. Yield: 4 servings (serving size: 1¾ cups).

CALORIES 308; FAT 9g (sat 3.4g); SODIUM 679mg

STUFF

Stuffing a butterflied pork tenderloin makes for an easy prep-ahead meal, yet the results look impressive enough for special occasions.

Cheese and Pear Pork

Hands-on time: 47 min. Total time: 1 hr. 6 min.

Serve with a spinach, pear, and parsley salad.

2 tablespoons olive oil, divided
4 shallots, thinly sliced
1 cup chopped firm Anjou pear
½ cup riesling or other white wine
1 tablespoon chopped fresh thyme
Dash of ground red pepper
½ cup chopped walnuts, toasted
½ cup crumbled blue cheese
⅓ cup fresh breadcrumbs
2 tablespoons chopped fresh parsley
2 (12-ounce) pork tenderloins
½ teaspoon kosher salt
1¼ cups fat-free, lower-sodium chicken broth

1. Preheat oven to 425°.
2. Heat 1 tablespoon oil in a pan over medium heat. Add shallots; cook 6 minutes. Add pear, wine, thyme, and pepper; cook 2 minutes. Cool. Stir in nuts, cheese, crumbs, and parsley.
3. Slice pork lengthwise, cutting to, but not through, other side. Open halves. Place pork between sheets of plastic wrap; pound to ¼ inch. Top pork with pear mixture; leave ½-inch border. Roll, starting with long side; secure pork with picks. Sprinkle with salt.
4. Heat remaining 1 tablespoon oil in a large ovenproof pan over medium-high heat. Add pork; sauté 5 minutes, browning all sides. Bake at 425° for 12 minutes or until a thermometer registers 145°. Remove pork from pan, and let stand 5 minutes. Slice. Bring broth to a boil in pan over medium-high heat; scrape pan to loosen browned bits. Cook 4 minutes. Serve with pork. Yield: 6 servings (serving size: 3 ounces pork and 1 tablespoon sauce).

CALORIES 321; FAT 16.1g (sat 3.8g, mono 5.8g, poly 5.6g); PROTEIN 28.7g; CARB 13g; FIBER 1.8g; CHOL 81mg; IRON 2mg; SODIUM 478mg; CALC 72mg

Pork with Figs and Farro

Hands-on time: 35 min. Total time: 1 hr. 15 min.

2 cups water
⅔ cup uncooked farro
1 (3-inch) cinnamon stick
1½ tablespoons olive oil, divided
¾ cup minced onion
1 garlic clove, minced
½ cup chopped dried figs
¼ cup chopped fresh flat-leaf parsley
1¼ teaspoons kosher salt, divided
¾ teaspoon freshly ground black pepper, divided
1 teaspoon sherry vinegar
⅛ teaspoon ground allspice
⅛ teaspoon ground cloves
1 large egg, lightly beaten
2 (1-pound) pork tenderloins, trimmed

1. Combine first 3 ingredients in a saucepan; bring to a boil. Cover and simmer 20 minutes or until tender. Drain; discard cinnamon stick.
2. Heat 1½ teaspoons olive oil in a medium skillet over medium heat. Add onion; sauté 6 minutes or until tender. Add garlic; sauté 1 minute, stirring constantly.
3. Combine farro, onion mixture, figs, parsley, ½ teaspoon salt, ¼ teaspoon pepper, and next 4 ingredients in a medium bowl.
4. Preheat oven to 425°.
5. Slice pork lengthwise, cutting to, but not through, other side. Open halves. Place pork between sheets of plastic wrap; pound to ¼ inch. Top pork with farro mixture, and leave ½-inch border. Roll, starting with long side; secure pork with picks.
6. Sprinkle pork evenly with remaining ¾ teaspoon salt and remaining ½ teaspoon pepper. Heat remaining 1 tablespoon olive oil in a large ovenproof skillet. Add pork; cook 6 minutes, browning all sides. Place pan in oven; bake pork at 425° for 15 minutes or until a thermometer registers 145°. Remove pork from pan; let stand 5 minutes. Slice. Yield: 8 servings (serving size: 4 ounces pork).

CALORIES 202; FAT 5.8g (sat 1.3g, mono 3g, poly 0.8g); PROTEIN 25.7g; CARB 12.2g; FIBER 2.2g; CHOL 96mg; IRON 3.3mg; SODIUM 371mg; CALC 31mg

FARRO IS AN ANCIENT WHEAT GRAIN. IF YOU CAN'T FIND IT, SUBSTITUTE WHEAT BERRIES.

Pork Tenderloin with Orange Compote

Hands-on time: 1 hr. 4 min. Total time: 2 hr. 21 min.

Serve with couscous and fresh green beans.

1 (1-pound) pork tenderloin, trimmed
4 teaspoons extra-virgin olive oil, divided
¾ teaspoon kosher salt, divided
½ teaspoon freshly ground black pepper, divided
¼ teaspoon ground cumin
¼ teaspoon ground red pepper
1½ cups thinly sliced onion
½ teaspoon grated orange rind
½ cup fresh orange juice
2 tablespoons dried currants
2 tablespoons sherry vinegar
1 teaspoon sugar
1 cup fat-free, lower-sodium chicken broth
¼ cup dry white wine

1. Slice pork lengthwise, cutting to, but not through, other side. Open halves. Place pork between sheets of plastic wrap; pound to ¼ inch.
2. Combine 1 teaspoon olive oil, ¼ teaspoon salt, ¼ teaspoon black pepper, cumin, and red pepper in a small bowl. Brush pork with mixture. Cover and refrigerate 1 hour.
3. Heat remaining 1 tablespoon oil in a large skillet over medium-low heat. Add onion; cook 20 minutes or until golden brown, stirring occasionally. Add remaining ½ teaspoon salt, remaining ¼ teaspoon black pepper, rind, and next 4 ingredients; bring to a boil. Cook 14 minutes or until liquid almost evaporates, stirring occasionally. Cool slightly.
4. Spread onion mixture over pork; leave ½-inch border. Roll, starting with long side. Secure pork with wooden picks.
5. Combine broth and wine in a large Dutch oven; bring to a boil. Add tenderloin; cover, reduce heat, and simmer 15 minutes or until a thermometer registers 145°. Remove pork from pan; keep warm. Bring cooking liquid to a boil; cook 8 minutes or until reduced to ½ cup. Strain cooking liquid through a sieve into a bowl; discard solids. Remove and discard wooden picks from pork; slice crosswise. Yield: 4 servings (serving size: 3 pork slices and 2 tablespoons sauce).

CALORIES 229; **FAT** 7.1g (sat 1.4g, mono 4.2g, poly 0.9g); **PROTEIN** 24.9g; **CARB** 12.4g; **FIBER** 1.2g; **CHOL** 74mg; **IRON** 1.5mg; **SODIUM** 536mg; **CALC** 28mg

If you like **Fresh Herbs** try:
Pork Roulade

Preheat oven to 425°. Slice 1 (1-pound) pork tenderloin lengthwise, cutting to, but not through, other side. Open halves. Place between sheets of plastic wrap; pound to ½ inch. Combine 1 tablespoon olive oil, ⅓ cup chopped fresh parsley, 2 tablespoons chopped fresh chives, and ½ teaspoon chopped fresh rosemary; spread on pork. Roll, starting with long side. Secure pork with picks. Sprinkle with ¼ teaspoon salt and ¼ teaspoon pepper. Heat a large ovenproof skillet over medium-high heat. Add 1 tablespoon olive oil and pork; cook 6 minutes, browning all sides. Bake at 425° for 12 minutes or until a thermometer registers 145°. Remove pork; let stand 5 minutes. Slice. Yield: 4 servings (servings size: 3 ounces pork).

CALORIES 187; **FAT** 9.3g (sat 1.7g); **SODIUM** 211mg

If you like **Balsamic Vinegar** try:
Pepper Pork

Combine 1 cup chopped roasted red bell pepper and 1 tablespoon balsamic vinegar. Slice 1 (1-pound) pork tenderloin lengthwise, cutting to, but not through, other side. Open halves. Place between sheets of plastic wrap; pound to ½ inch. Top pork with peppers; leave ½-inch border. Roll, starting with long side. Secure pork with wooden picks. Sprinkle with ¼ teaspoon salt. Heat a Dutch oven over medium-high heat. Add 1 tablespoon olive oil and pork; cook 6 minutes, browning all sides. Add 2 cups fat-free, lower-sodium chicken broth; bring to a boil. Cover; reduce heat, and simmer 12 minutes or until a thermometer registers 145°. Remove pork from pan; let stand 5 minutes. Combine 1 teaspoon flour and 1 tablespoon balsamic vinegar. Add flour mixture and ⅓ cup kalamata olives to pan; cook 16 minutes. Slice pork. Yield: 4 servings (serving size: 3 pork slices and 2 tablespoons sauce).

CALORIES 213; **FAT** 9.7g (sat 1.7g); **SODIUM** 667mg

TRY 2011'S "IN" DRINK: THE MICHELADA

This beer-based Mexican refresher is a good way to kick off your taco night. The tangy, spicy flavors are a perfect match for the smoky, spicy pork and sweet-tart pineapple salsa in Tacos Al Pastor with Grilled Pineapple Salsa (page 254). Prepare the base ahead, chill, and stir in the beer just before serving.

—Julianna Grimes

Combine 6 tablespoons spicy Bloody Mary mix (such as Tabasco), ¼ cup fresh lime juice, 1 tablespoon lower-sodium soy sauce, 1 teaspoon hot pepper sauce, and 2 (12-ounce) bottles light beer. Serve over ice. Yield: 4 servings (serving size: about 7 ounces).

CALORIES 64; **FAT** 0g; **SODIUM** 199mg

GRILL

Cooks from the American South to Southeast Asia know that when pork hits the grill—often with a sweet or spicy sauce—something magical happens.

Kid Friendly

Apricot-Glazed Pork Kebabs

Hands-on time: 27 min. Total time: 57 min.

Serve these glazed grilled pork skewers with a summer salad of nectarines, tomatoes, and mint. Brown rice pilaf completes the meal.

1 (10-ounce) jar apricot preserves
2 tablespoons lower-sodium soy sauce
1 tablespoon fresh lemon juice
2 garlic cloves, minced
2 (1-pound) pork tenderloins, trimmed and cut into 1-inch pieces
3/4 teaspoon salt
3/4 teaspoon freshly ground black pepper
Cooking spray

1. Preheat grill to medium-high heat.
2. Place preserves in a 2-cup glass measure. Microwave at HIGH 1 minute, stirring after 30 seconds. Stir in soy sauce, juice, and garlic. Place 3/4 cup apricot mixture in a large zip-top plastic bag; reserve remaining apricot mixture. Add pork to bag, and seal. Marinate at room temperature 30 minutes. Remove pork from bag, and discard marinade. Thread pork evenly onto 16 (8-inch) skewers. Sprinkle pork evenly with salt and black pepper. Set aside 1/4 cup apricot mixture. Place pork on grill rack coated with cooking spray; baste with half of remaining apricot mixture. Grill 3½ minutes. Turn pork over; baste with other half of remaining apricot mixture. Grill 3½ minutes or until desired degree of doneness. Remove pork from grill. Brush with reserved 1/4 cup apricot mixture. Yield: 8 servings (serving size 2 kebabs).

CALORIES 233; FAT 2.9g (sat 0.9g, mono 1g, poly 0.5g); PROTEIN 27g; CARB 23.9g; FIBER 0.1g; CHOL 83mg; IRON 1.4mg; SODIUM 422mg; CALC 9mg

---

Kid Friendly

Tacos Al Pastor with Grilled Pineapple Salsa

Hands-on time: 34 min. Total time: 1 hr. 8 min.

If you want to tame the spice, seed the jalapeño and chop it, or simply omit it.

Pork:
1 chipotle chile, canned in adobo sauce
1 tablespoon olive oil
1 (1-pound) pork tenderloin, trimmed
1 tablespoon chopped fresh oregano
2 teaspoons ancho chile powder
1/2 teaspoon ground cumin
1/2 teaspoon kosher salt
1/4 teaspoon freshly ground black pepper
Cooking spray
Salsa:
4 (1/2-inch-thick) slices fresh pineapple
1/4 cup fresh cilantro leaves
3 tablespoons thinly sliced red onion
3 tablespoons fresh lime juice
1/4 teaspoon kosher salt
1/2 jalapeño, thinly sliced
Remaining ingredients:
8 (6-inch) corn tortillas
8 lime wedges

1. To prepare pork, preheat grill to high heat.
2. Mince chipotle chile. Combine chipotle and oil in a small bowl; rub evenly over pork. Combine oregano and next 4 ingredients. Sprinkle spice mixture evenly over pork, and let stand 30 minutes. Place pork on grill rack coated with cooking spray, and grill 6 minutes on each side or until a thermometer registers 145°. Remove pork from grill; let stand 5 minutes. Coarsely chop pork; keep warm.
3. To prepare salsa, place pineapple on grill rack coated with cooking spray; grill 5 minutes on each side. Coarsely chop pineapple, and place in a medium bowl. Add cilantro and next 4 ingredients; toss to combine.
4. Warm tortillas according to package directions. Place 2 tortillas on each of 4 plates, and divide pork evenly among tortillas. Top each taco with about 3 tablespoons salsa. Serve with lime wedges. Yield: 4 servings (serving size: 2 tacos).

CALORIES 305; FAT 7.1g (sat 1.3g, mono 3.4g, poly 1.3g); PROTEIN 26.6g; CARB 36.9g; FIBER 4.7g; CHOL 74mg; IRON 1.7mg; SODIUM 513mg; CALC 51mg

---

Grilled Pork Salad

Hands-on time: 40 min. Total time: 45 min.

Escarole, a variety of chicory, tastes less bitter than its cousins, frisée and endive. Apples are also abundant this time of year, so substitute your favorite red-skinned variety if you prefer a sweet-tart note.

1/2 cup pecans
2 teaspoons canola oil
1 teaspoon salt, divided
Dash of sugar
2½ tablespoons extra-virgin olive oil, divided
1½ tablespoons white wine vinegar
1/2 teaspoon freshly ground black pepper, divided
1 (1-pound) pork tenderloin, trimmed
Cooking spray
5 cups chopped escarole
1⅓ cups thinly diagonally sliced celery
2 cups thinly sliced red Bartlett or Comice pear (about 2)

1. Preheat oven to 350°.
2. Combine pecans and canola oil in a small bowl; toss well. Place pecans on a baking sheet. Sprinkle with 1/4 teaspoon salt and sugar. Bake at 350° for 5 minutes.
3. Preheat grill to medium-high heat.
4. Combine 1/4 teaspoon salt, 2 tablespoons olive oil, vinegar, and 1/4 teaspoon pepper in a large bowl, stirring with a whisk.
5. Brush pork with remaining 1½ teaspoons olive oil; sprinkle with remaining 1/2 teaspoon salt and remaining 1/4 teaspoon pepper. Place pork on a grill rack coated with cooking spray; grill 6 minutes on each side or until a thermometer registers 145°. Remove from grill. Let stand 10 minutes. Cut, crosswise, into 1/4-inch-thick slices.
6. Add escarole and celery to vinegar mixture; toss gently to coat. Place 1 cup

escarole mixture on each of 6 plates; top each serving with ⅓ cup pears and 3 ounces pork. Sprinkle evenly with pecans. Yield: 6 servings (serving size: 1 salad).

CALORIES 250; FAT 15g (sat 2g, mono 9.1g, poly 3.2g); PROTEIN 17.5g; CARB 12.5g; FIBER 4.2g; CHOL 49mg; IRON 1.5mg; SODIUM 459mg; CALC 45mg

If you like **Peanuts** try:

Quick & Easy

Pork Satay with Peanut Sauce

Slice 1 (1-pound) pork tenderloin crosswise into 16 slices. Place each pork slice between 2 sheets of plastic wrap; pound to ¼-inch thickness using a meat mallet. Combine ¼ cup coconut milk and 1 tablespoon red curry paste in a medium bowl. Add pork to bowl; toss. Cover and marinate in refrigerator 1 hour. Combine ⅔ cup coarsely ground peanuts, ¼ cup coconut milk, 1 tablespoon brown sugar, 2 tablespoons lower-sodium soy sauce, 1 tablespoon lime juice, and 1 tablespoon red curry paste. Preheat grill to medium-high heat. Remove pork from bag; discard marinade. Thread pork evenly onto 8 skewers; sprinkle evenly with ½ teaspoon kosher salt. Place skewers on grill rack coated with cooking spray. Grill 3 minutes on each side. Serve with peanut sauce. Yield: 4 servings (serving size: 2 skewers and ¼ cup sauce).

CALORIES 321; FAT 16.4g (sat 5.6g); SODIUM 650mg

If you like **Barbecue Sauce** try:

Quick & Easy • Kid Friendly

Barbecued Pork Tenderloin

Preheat grill to medium-high heat. Melt 2 tablespoons butter in a saucepan over medium-high heat. Add 1 cup chopped onion and 3 minced garlic cloves; sauté 4 minutes, stirring constantly. Stir in ⅓ cup brown sugar, ⅓ cup cider vinegar, 3 tablespoons ketchup,

and 1 tablespoon lower-sodium soy sauce; bring to a boil. Cook 6 minutes. Process mixture until smooth. Reserve 6 tablespoons sauce. Sprinkle 2 (12-ounce) pork tenderloins with ¾ teaspoon salt; brush with remaining sauce. Place pork on grill rack coated with cooking spray. Grill 6 minutes on each side or until thermometer registers 145°. Remove pork; let stand for 5 minutes. Slice. Yield: 6 servings (serving size: 3 ounces pork and 1 tablespoon reserved sauce).

CALORIES 227; FAT 6.5g (sat 3.2g); SODIUM 483mg

CHICKEN 3 WAYS
GRILL AND GLAZE

Turn up the flavor on skinless, boneless chicken breasts with smoky char and a slathering of sauce.

Kid Friendly

Grilled Chicken with Cola Sauce

Hands-on time: 21 min. Total time: 54 min.

1 tablespoon canola oil
2½ tablespoons finely chopped onion
1 garlic clove, minced
¾ cup cola
⅓ cup ketchup
1 tablespoon cider vinegar
2 teaspoons Worcestershire sauce
1½ teaspoons chili powder
1½ tablespoons dark brown sugar
1 tablespoon sweet paprika
½ teaspoon salt
½ teaspoon ground cumin
6 (6-ounce) skinless, boneless chicken breast halves
Cooking spray

1. Preheat grill to medium-high heat.
2. Heat a medium saucepan over medium-high heat. Add oil to pan; swirl to coat. Add onion to pan; sauté

2 minutes, stirring occasionally. Add garlic; sauté 1 minute, stirring constantly. Stir in cola and next 4 ingredients; bring to a boil. Reduce heat, and simmer 15 minutes or until sauce reduces to ¾ cup, stirring occasionally. Reserve 6 tablespoons sauce.
3. Combine sugar and next 3 ingredients, stirring well. Rub spice mixture evenly over both sides of chicken. Arrange chicken on grill rack coated with cooking spray; baste with 3 tablespoons remaining sauce. Grill 5 minutes. Turn chicken over; baste with 3 tablespoons sauce. Grill 5 minutes or until done. Serve with reserved 6 tablespoons sauce. Yield: 6 servings (serving size: 1 breast half and 1 tablespoon sauce).

CALORIES 254; FAT 4.7g (sat 0.7g, mono 2g, poly 1.5g); PROTEIN 39.8g; CARB 11.2g; FIBER 0.5g; CHOL 99mg; IRON 1.7mg; SODIUM 498mg; CALC 32mg

Quick & Easy

Bourbon-Glazed Chicken

Preheat grill to medium-high heat. Melt 2 tablespoons butter in a medium saucepan over medium heat. Add 2 tablespoons finely chopped shallots and 2 minced garlic cloves; cook 2 minutes, stirring constantly. Stir in 3 tablespoons bourbon, 2 tablespoons Dijon mustard, and 2 tablespoons maple syrup; bring to a boil. Cook 1 minute, stirring occasionally. Remove from heat. Sprinkle 4 (6-ounce) skinless, boneless chicken breast halves evenly with ½ teaspoon kosher salt and ½ teaspoon freshly ground black pepper. Arrange chicken on grill rack coated with cooking spray; baste with half of bourbon mixture. Grill 5 minutes. Turn chicken over; baste with remaining bourbon mixture. Grill 5 minutes or until chicken is done. Yield: 4 servings (serving size: 1 breast half).

CALORIES 297; FAT 9.7g (sat 4.8g); SODIUM 545mg

Spicy-Sweet Glazed Chicken

Combine ¼ cup lower-sodium soy sauce, 3 tablespoons rice vinegar, 2 tablespoons sesame oil, 2 tablespoons honey, 1½ tablespoons chile paste, and 6 minced garlic cloves. Place 6 (6-ounce) skinless, boneless chicken breast halves in a large zip-top plastic bag. Add soy mixture; seal. Marinate in refrigerator 1 hour. Preheat grill to medium-high heat. Remove chicken from bag. Place marinade in a saucepan; bring to a boil. Cook 4 minutes. Sprinkle chicken with ¼ teaspoon salt; place on grill rack coated with cooking spray. Baste with half of sauce. Grill 5 minutes. Turn chicken over; baste with remaining sauce. Grill 5 minutes or until done. Yield: 6 servings (serving size: 1 breast half).

CALORIES 258; FAT 8.5g (sat 1.8g); SODIUM 503mg

READER RECIPES

GRANOLA GETS FANCY

Christin Holcomb had a mission: She scoured grocery store shelves looking for granola that wasn't laden with oil and sweeteners. She never found one that lived up to her standards, so she tried her hand at granola making. Her creation is perfect as a cereal or oatmeal add-in for hearty crunch. But Holcomb doesn't limit her granola to just breakfast: She combines the nutty oats and pecans with sweet, honey-roasted figs and tangy yogurt for a simple late-summer dessert. "The figs give it richness," she says. "The recipe is light but still creamy, sweet, and satisfying." You can easily double the granola and place individual portions into containers for time-pressed mornings and snacks on the run.

Make Ahead • Kid Friendly

Granola with Honey-Scented Yogurt and Baked Figs

Hands-on time: 18 min. Total time: 53 min.

"Help extra granola stay fresh for up to two weeks by placing it in a sealed, airtight container."

—Christin Holcomb, Rancho Santa Margarita, Calif.

1 cup old-fashioned rolled oats
⅓ cup chopped pecans
1 large egg white
1⅛ teaspoons vanilla extract, divided
2 tablespoons packed brown sugar
⅜ teaspoon ground cinnamon, divided
¼ teaspoon salt, divided
⅛ teaspoon ground nutmeg
2 tablespoons maple syrup
Cooking spray
2 tablespoons plus 2 teaspoons honey, divided
9 firm, fresh dark-skinned figs, stemmed and quartered
3 cups plain fat-free Greek yogurt

1. Preheat oven to 300°.
2. Combine oats and pecans in a small bowl. Combine egg white and ⅛ teaspoon vanilla in a medium bowl; beat egg mixture with a mixer at medium speed until foamy. Fold oat mixture into egg white mixture. Combine brown sugar, ¼ teaspoon cinnamon, ⅛ teaspoon salt, and nutmeg; fold sugar mixture into oat mixture. Fold in maple syrup.
3. Spread granola evenly on a foil-lined baking sheet coated with cooking spray. Bake at 300° for 25 minutes, stirring once. Remove granola from oven; stir to loosen granola from foil. Cool on a wire rack.
4. Increase oven temperature to 350°.
5. Combine 2 teaspoons honey and remaining 1 teaspoon vanilla in a large bowl; add figs, stirring gently to coat fruit. Arrange figs, cut sides up, in a single layer on a foil-lined baking sheet. Sprinkle figs evenly with the remaining ⅛ teaspoon ground cinnamon and remaining ⅛ teaspoon salt.

---

6. Bake at 350° for 10 minutes or until fig juices begin to bubble. Remove from oven, and cool completely. Combine remaining 2 tablespoons honey and yogurt in a small bowl. Spoon ½ cup yogurt mixture into each of 6 bowls; top each serving with about 2½ tablespoons granola and 6 fig quarters. Yield: 6 servings.

CALORIES 277; FAT 5.6g (sat 0.6g, mono 2.9g, poly 1.8g); PROTEIN 13.3g; CARB 45.7g; FIBER 4.2g; CHOL 0mg; IRON 1.2mg; SODIUM 152mg; CALC 117mg

---

LESS MEAT, MORE FLAVOR

WHOLE-GRAIN SALADS

By Mark Bittman

Fruits, veggies, herbs, and nuts make full-flavored partners for chewy steel-cut oats and bulgur.

Green salads are mostly greens. But grain salads—for me, at least—are mostly fruits, vegetables, and herbs. I want the whole grains to be the backbone of the dish, to give the salad structure and texture, but not necessarily form the bulk. Whole grains can lend substance and subtle earthiness to pretty much any salad you can devise.

These salads taste very different, but the idea is the same: Complement the grains with a range of tastes and textures, and take advantage of their satisfying chew. Use a classic salad (or any dish, really) for inspiration, or just start with whatever produce is in season.

Although these dishes are more produce than grain, you have to cook the grains properly or the salads will fall flat. Here "properly" means you want dry and fluffy grains (as opposed to wet and starchy). Only add more water if the grains really start sticking to the pot, and don't stir too much (vigorous stirring helps release the starch). Don't worry if the oats clump a bit; they'll disperse as you toss them through the salad. Of course, any whole grains (quinoa, barley, farro, and wheat berries) or varieties of rice—preferably brown—are fair game; cooking times and methods will vary from one to the next.

Now, you have a smallish batch of dry, just-tender, pleasantly chewy grains: What next? I usually turn to classic combinations for inspiration. When I hear "bulgur," I immediately think of tabbouleh. It's an ancient Syrian dish; a bit of bulgur, a ton of fresh herbs, juicy tomatoes, and scallions (I add a touch of minced garlic, too). Stirring in some sautéed chicken thighs—rich and meaty—turns what's normally served as a side into a satisfying entrée. You could do the same with pork, lamb, beef, or shrimp. Traditionally, tabbouleh is dressed with olive oil and lemon juice, but I like to add some richness: tahini, Greek yogurt, and lemon juice whisked together and thinned with a little water. Drizzle it over the top instead of tossing it, so the salad doesn't get gloppy.

Steel-cut oats are a bit more unusual in salads than bulgur. Thinking that almost any salad can benefit from the addition of a few whole grains, I look to one of the all-time greats: the Waldorf salad. That combination of walnuts, apples, and grapes is stellar, but for all its juicy crunch, the Waldorf lacks that perfect chewiness. Steel-cut oats fit in seamlessly. I also add a bit of torn radicchio for some bitterness, and I caramelize the walnuts in honey and cayenne to balance out the dish. Instead of the classic mayonnaise dressing, I toss the salad with olive oil and sherry vinegar, and top it with a few crumbles of blue cheese, a tribute to the fatty richness of the original.

You'll want to try your own combinations. Fresh fruits and vegetables will add juiciness and crunch; some lend sweetness, others tartness. A hint of heat can be great: cayenne, garlic, chiles, or even milder ground spices. If you like, round out the dish with a touch of richness: cheese, yogurt, sour cream, peanut butter, or sometimes just olive oil. When these good grains stay in the background, the salad comes to life.

Quick & Easy • Make Ahead
Vegetarian

Waldorf Salad with Steel-Cut Oats

Hands-on time: 26 min. Total time: 26 min.

Oats are a delicious base for a meal that plays up the beloved flavors of Waldorf salad. Rinsing the oats removes excess starch on the outside of the grains, preventing them from becoming too sticky.

1 cup steel-cut oats, rinsed and drained
1 cup water
1 teaspoon kosher salt, divided
2/3 cup coarsely chopped walnuts
1 1/2 teaspoons honey
1/8 teaspoon ground red pepper
3 tablespoons extra-virgin olive oil
2 tablespoons sherry vinegar
1/2 teaspoon freshly ground black pepper
1 1/2 cups diced Granny Smith apple (about 1 large)
1 1/2 cups torn radicchio
1 1/2 cups seedless red grapes, halved
1/2 cup (2 ounces) crumbled blue cheese

1. Combine oats, 1 cup water, and 1/2 teaspoon kosher salt in a medium saucepan; bring to a boil. Reduce heat; simmer 7 minutes (do not stir) or until liquid almost evaporates. Remove from heat; fluff with a fork. Place oats in a medium bowl; let stand 10 minutes.
2. Combine walnuts, honey, and red pepper in a small nonstick skillet over medium heat; cook 4 minutes or until nuts are fragrant and honey is slightly caramelized, stirring occasionally.
3. Combine remaining 1/2 teaspoon salt, olive oil, vinegar, and black pepper in a small bowl, stirring with a whisk. Add dressing, apple, radicchio, and grapes to oats; toss well. Place 1 1/2 cups oat mixture on each of 4 plates, and top each serving with about 3 tablespoons walnut mixture and 2 tablespoons blue cheese. Yield: 4 servings (serving size: 1 salad).

CALORIES 410; FAT 26.5g (sat 5.4g, mono 10.5g, poly 9.6g); PROTEIN 9g; CARB 37.9g; FIBER 5.1g; CHOL 11mg; IRON 2mg; SODIUM 683mg; CALC 106mg

Quick & Easy • Make Ahead

Chicken Tabbouleh with Tahini Drizzle

Hands-on time: 26 min. Total time: 37 min.

One sure sign that the bulgur is done is that little holes will form on top.

1 1/4 cups water
1 cup uncooked bulgur, rinsed and drained
2 tablespoons olive oil, divided
1 teaspoon kosher salt, divided
1/2 pound skinless, boneless chicken thighs
1/2 teaspoon freshly ground black pepper
3 cups chopped tomato
1 cup chopped fresh parsley
1 cup chopped fresh mint
1 cup chopped green onions
1 teaspoon minced garlic
1/4 cup tahini (roasted sesame seed paste)
1/4 cup plain 2% reduced-fat Greek yogurt
3 tablespoons fresh lemon juice
1 tablespoon water

1. Combine 1 1/4 cups water, 1 cup bulgur, 1 tablespoon olive oil, and 1/2 teaspoon salt in a medium saucepan; bring to a boil. Reduce heat; simmer 10 minutes (do not stir) or until the liquid almost evaporates. Remove from heat; fluff with a fork. Place bulgur in a medium bowl; let stand 10 minutes.
2. Heat remaining 1 tablespoon oil in a large nonstick skillet over medium-high heat. Add chicken to pan; sprinkle with 1/4 teaspoon salt and black pepper. Sauté 4 minutes on each side or until done; shred chicken. Combine bulgur, chicken, tomato, and next 4 ingredients in a large bowl; toss gently.
3. Combine remaining 1/4 teaspoon salt, tahini, and remaining ingredients in a small bowl, stirring with a whisk. Drizzle over salad. Yield: 4 servings (serving size: about 1 1/2 cups).

CALORIES 395; FAT 18.2g (sat 3g, mono 8.8g, poly 5.1g); PROTEIN 21.5g; CARB 41g; FIBER 10.9g; CHOL 48mg; IRON 4.2mg; SODIUM 573mg; CALC 127mg

LADIES AND GENTLEMEN, BREAKFAST IS NOW SERVED, FOR DINNER

Moving rise-and-shine favorites to the evening time slot feels both fun and indulgent. We've dressed up those favorites.

Cooking first-of-the-day dishes for dinner seems oddly indulgent, somehow, and liberating, maybe a bit frisky, like lounging around in pajamas with a martini. It's also a little like eating dessert first: You're an adult, and you're going to eat what you want, when you want it! That said, a breakfast dish time-shifted to the dinner hour needs some dressing up. A few ingredient twists or technique tweaks are required. Upgrade French toast, for instance, with chewy, crusty Italian ciabatta bread stuffed with savory Gruyère cheese, and top it with a fresh, tart apple syrup. Or, make over your basic egg sandwich by pairing fried eggs with sweet caramelized onions, peppery arugula, and smoky bacon—still striking breakfast notes, but the tune seems downright decadent.

This isn't complication for complication's sake, though: Part of the appeal of breakfast at dinner is that it's a marvelously simple change-up solution for busy weeknights. These recipes clock in at under an hour, most around 30 minutes, and that means they deliver the convenience of breakfast dishes with the amped-up flavor of evening entrées. Get out the PJs, pour a nice bottle of red, and dig in.

Quick & Easy
Bacon and Egg Sandwiches with Caramelized Onions and Arugula

Hands-on time: 32 min. Total time: 32 min.

This upscale twist on the traditional breakfast sandwich features sweet, tender caramelized onion and peppery arugula. A fresh fruit salad would be a good accompaniment.

4 center-cut bacon slices
2 cups thinly sliced onion
1 tablespoon water
½ teaspoon Mexican hot sauce
1 tablespoon butter
Dash of sugar
Cooking spray
4 (½-ounce) slices whole-wheat bread
2 large eggs
⅛ teaspoon salt
¼ teaspoon freshly ground black pepper
1 cup arugula

1. Cook bacon in a nonstick skillet over medium heat until crisp (about 8 minutes). Remove bacon from pan, reserving drippings; drain on paper towels. Add onion, water, and hot sauce to drippings in pan; cover and cook 3 minutes. Stir in butter and sugar; cover and cook 3 minutes. Uncover and cook 5 minutes or until golden brown, stirring frequently. Set aside; keep warm.
2. Heat a large nonstick skillet over medium-high heat. Coat pan with cooking spray. Place bread in pan, and cook 3 minutes on each side or until lightly browned. Set aside; keep warm.
3. Recoat pan with cooking spray. Crack eggs into pan, and cook 2 minutes. Gently turn eggs, one at a time; cook 1 minute or until desired degree of doneness. Sprinkle evenly with salt and black pepper.
4. Place one bread slice on each of 2 plates; arrange onion mixture evenly over bread. Place 1 egg, 2 bacon slices, and ½ cup arugula over each serving; top with remaining bread slices. Serve immediately. Yield: 2 servings (serving size: 1 sandwich).

CALORIES 277; FAT 13.9g (sat 5.9g, mono 3.7g, poly 1.4g); PROTEIN 14.7g; CARB 24.3g; FIBER 3.8g; CHOL 205mg; IRON 2.1mg; SODIUM 622mg; CALC 71mg

MOZZARELLA AND SAGE TAKE THE BASIC OMELET INTO GOOEY, EARTHY NEW TERRITORY.

Quick & Easy • Vegetarian
Mozzarella Omelet with Sage and Red Chile Flakes
(pictured on page 232)

Hands-on time: 27 min. Total time: 27 min.

An omelet makes for a quick and easy dinner, but it doesn't have to be boring. Gooey mozzarella, vibrant sage, and a generous hit of red pepper make this a standout dish.

¼ cup water
1 tablespoon chopped fresh sage
½ teaspoon crushed red pepper
¼ teaspoon salt
4 large eggs
1 large egg white
1 tablespoon olive oil, divided
¼ cup (1 ounce) shredded part-skim mozzarella cheese, at room temperature
Fresh sage leaves (optional)

1. Combine first 6 ingredients in a bowl, stirring gently with a whisk.

2. Heat an 8-inch nonstick skillet over medium-high heat. Add 1½ teaspoons oil to pan; swirl to coat. Add half of egg mixture to pan, and spread evenly in pan. Cook egg mixture until edges begin to set (about 1 minute). Slide front edge of spatula between edge of omelet and pan. Gently lift edge of omelet, tilting pan to allow some uncooked egg mixture to come in contact with pan. Repeat procedure on opposite edge of omelet. Continue cooking until center is just set (about 2 minutes). Sprinkle half of cheese evenly over half of omelet. Loosen omelet with a spatula, and fold in half. Carefully slide omelet onto a plate. Repeat procedure with remaining oil, egg mixture, and cheese. Garnish with sage leaves, if desired. Serve immediately. Yield: 2 servings (serving size: 1 omelet).

CALORIES 256; FAT 19.7g (sat 5.8g, mono 9.6g, poly 2.2g); PROTEIN 18.2g; CARB 1.8g; FIBER 0.1g; CHOL 431mg; IRON 2mg; SODIUM 538mg; CALC 165mg

Quick & Easy • Kid Friendly
Vegetarian

Ciabatta French Toast with Warm Apple Maple Syrup

Hands-on time: 35 min. Total time: 35 min.

¼ cup apple cider
1 teaspoon cornstarch
2 teaspoons butter
2 tablespoons finely chopped shallots
2 cups sliced McIntosh apples
¼ cup maple syrup
6 (2-ounce) slices ciabatta bread
3 ounces Gruyère cheese, cut into thin slices
½ cup fat-free milk
⅓ cup low-fat buttermilk
¼ teaspoon salt
⅛ teaspoon ground nutmeg
⅛ teaspoon freshly ground black pepper
1 large egg
1 large egg white
4 teaspoons butter, divided
3 tablespoons chopped pecans, toasted

1. Combine cider and cornstarch in a small bowl, stirring with a whisk. Melt 2 teaspoons butter in a large nonstick skillet over medium heat. Add shallots to pan; cook 1 minute, stirring frequently. Add cider mixture, apples, and syrup to pan. Bring to a boil, stirring frequently. Reduce heat to low; cook 3 minutes or until apples begin to soften, stirring occasionally. Set aside, and keep warm.

2. Cut a horizontal slit through bottom crust of each bread slice to form a pocket; stuff ½ ounce cheese evenly into each pocket. Combine fat-free milk, buttermilk, and next 5 ingredients in a shallow dish, stirring well with a whisk. Working with 1 stuffed bread slice at a time, place bread slice into milk mixture, turning gently to coat both sides.

3. Heat a large nonstick skillet over medium-high heat. Melt 2 teaspoons butter in pan. Add 3 coated bread slices to pan, and cook 2 minutes on each side or until lightly browned. Repeat procedure with remaining 2 teaspoons butter and remaining 3 coated bread slices.

4. Place 1 French toast slice onto each of 6 plates; top each serving with about 3 tablespoons sauce and 1½ teaspoons pecans. Yield: 6 servings.

CALORIES 373; FAT 14.3g (sat 5.9g, mono 6.1g, poly 1.5g); PROTEIN 12.8g; CARB 51.3g; FIBER 2.4g; CHOL 57mg; IRON 2.4mg; SODIUM 607mg; CALC 205mg

GRUYÈRE-STUFFED CIABATTA—NOW THAT TAKES FRENCH TOAST TO THE NEXT LEVEL!

NEXT: DINNER FOR BREAKFAST?

Lots of cultures favor a day begun with savory dishes that feel more in line with the American approach to dinner.

THE DISH: Ful
WHERE IT'S EATEN: Egypt and Lebanon
WHAT IT IS: Fava beans cooked with garlic and lemon juice, served with tomato or hard-cooked egg. Paired with lots of flatbread—an economical way to fill up before work.

THE DISH: Menudo
WHERE IT'S EATEN: Mexico
WHAT IT IS: A spicy tripe stew made with red chiles, onions, cilantro, and posole—it's also prized as a hangover cure.

THE DISH: Congee
WHERE IT'S EATEN: Cambodia, China, Thailand
WHAT IT IS: A rice porridge that has chunks of meat, mushrooms, or green onions stirred in. It's often eaten with salted eggs, dried or grilled fish, and pickled veggies.

THE DISH: Hoppers
WHERE IT'S EATEN: Sri Lanka
WHAT IT IS: Wafer-thin, cup-shaped pancakes made from rice flour, coconut milk, and palm toddy (fermented liquor from the palm tree). These make perfect nests for the fiery curries they're typically paired with.

THE DISH: Pho
WHERE IT'S EATEN: Vietnam
WHAT IT IS: A protein-rich broth seasoned with warm spices like cinnamon and star anise, featuring delicate rice noodles, thin slices of meat, and a variety of fresh garnishes, such as bean sprouts, onion, lime, fresh chile, and cilantro and basil leaves.

Savory Bread Puddings with Ham and Cheddar

Hands-on time: 22 min. Total time: 42 min.

Bread pudding becomes a main dish inspired by the flavors of a loaded baked potato. Here, a strata-like bread pudding is infused with cheddar and ham and topped with sour cream—serve it as a main course. Preparing the puddings in individual ramekins gives them a dressier feel and shortens the cook time.

8 ounces multigrain bread with seeds, cut into 3/4-inch cubes
Cooking spray
3/4 cup (3 ounces) shredded sharp cheddar cheese, divided
1/4 cup chopped green onions, divided
3/4 cup fat-free milk
1/4 cup fat-free, lower-sodium chicken broth
1/8 teaspoon freshly ground black pepper
3 ounces lower-sodium ham, minced
2 large egg yolks, lightly beaten
3 large egg whites
4 teaspoons reduced-fat sour cream

1. Preheat oven to 375°.
2. Place bread cubes on a jelly-roll pan; coat with cooking spray. Bake at 375° for 10 minutes or until lightly toasted, turning once. Remove from oven; cool.
3. Combine bread, ½ cup cheese, 3 tablespoons onions, and next 5 ingredients in a large bowl. Place egg whites in a small bowl, and beat with a mixer at high speed until foamy (about 30 seconds). Gently fold egg whites into bread mixture.
4. Spoon about 1 cup bread mixture into each of 4 (7-ounce) ramekins coated with cooking spray. Sprinkle the remaining ¼ cup cheese and remaining 1 tablespoon onions evenly over ramekins. Bake at 375° for 20 minutes or until lightly browned. Top each serving with 1 teaspoon sour cream. Yield: 4 servings (serving size: 1 bread pudding).

CALORIES 272; **FAT** 11.2g (sat 5g, mono 3.3g, poly 0.6g); **PROTEIN** 18.5g; **CARB** 28.4g; **FIBER** 8.6g; **CHOL** 140mg; **IRON** 2mg; **SODIUM** 536mg; **CALC** 400mg

CREAMY, LIGHT MAC AND CHEESE

We squashed out half the calories and three-fourths of the sat fat by using a new trick in the sauce.

Nothing defines comfort food better than mac and cheese, and nothing gives "comfort" a bad nutritional name quite so deliciously. A typical bowl can contain a half-day's worth of calories and two days' saturated fat.

This isn't the first time we've tackled this dish, of course, but this time we wanted to retain as much cheese as possible for both flavor and that non-negotiable gooey texture, so the real work happened with the béchamel. Instead of the traditional buttery, heavy sauce, we turned to an unlikely hero for a boost: butternut squash. Combined with fat-free milk and Greek yogurt, the squash adds a rich, nutty flavor; sneaks in some vegetable; and brilliantly mimics the color and creaminess of cheddar sauce. A trio of bold cheeses packs more flavor than a one-cheese approach, while grooved pasta ensures full sauce coverage for a saucy favorite with all kinds of comforting goodness.

OLD WAY	OUR WAY
908 calories per serving	390 calories per serving
36 grams saturated fat	6.1 grams saturated fat
963 milligrams sodium	589 milligrams sodium

Creamy, Light Macaroni and Cheese
(pictured on page 228)

Hands-on time: 1 hr. Total time: 1 hr. 25 min.

3 cups cubed peeled butternut squash (about 1 [1-pound] squash)
1¼ cups fat-free, lower-sodium chicken broth
1½ cups fat-free milk
2 garlic cloves
1 teaspoon kosher salt
½ teaspoon freshly ground black pepper
2 tablespoons fat-free Greek yogurt
1¼ cups (5 ounces) shredded Gruyère cheese
1 cup (4 ounces) grated pecorino Romano cheese
¼ cup (1 ounce) finely grated fresh Parmigiano-Reggiano cheese, divided
1 pound uncooked cavatappi
Cooking spray
1 teaspoon olive oil
½ cup panko (Japanese breadcrumbs)
2 tablespoons chopped fresh parsley

1. Preheat oven to 375°.
2. Combine squash, broth, milk, and garlic in a medium saucepan; bring to a boil over medium-high heat. Reduce heat to medium, and simmer until squash is tender when pierced with a fork, about 25 minutes. Remove from heat.

3. Place hot squash mixture in a blender. Add salt, pepper, and Greek yogurt. Remove the center piece of blender lid (to allow steam to escape); secure blender lid on blender. Place a clean towel over opening in blender lid (to avoid splatters). Blend until smooth. Place blended squash mixture in a large bowl; stir in Gruyère, pecorino Romano, and 2 tablespoons Parmigiano-Reggiano. Stir until combined.

4. Cook pasta according to package directions, omitting salt and fat; drain well. Add pasta to squash mixture, and stir until combined. Spread mixture evenly into a 13 x 9–inch glass or ceramic baking dish coated with cooking spray.

5. Heat oil in a medium skillet over medium heat. Add panko, and cook 2 minutes or until golden brown. Remove from heat; stir in remaining 2 tablespoons Parmigiano-Reggiano cheese. Sprinkle panko mixture evenly over hot pasta mixture. Lightly coat topping with cooking spray.

6. Bake at 375° for 25 minutes or until bubbly. Sprinkle with parsley, and serve immediately. Yield: 8 servings (serving size: 1⅓ cups).

CALORIES 390; FAT 10.9g (sat 6.1g, mono 2.1g, poly 0.4g); PROTEIN 19.1g; CARB 53.9g; FIBER 3.2g; CHOL 31mg; IRON 2.4mg; SODIUM 589mg; CALC 403mg

CHEESE TRIO
Parmigiano-Reggiano, pecorino Romano, and Gruyère save 336 calories worth of cheese per serving.

CUBED BUTTERNUT SQUASH
Subs in for butter in our creamy sauce, saving 7g sat fat per serving.

FAT-FREE MILK
Replaces half-and-half and whole milk in the sauce to cut a total of 5g sat fat per serving.

BUTTERNUT SQUASH "BÉCHAMEL"

1. Boil the squash with milk, broth, and garlic to help marry the sweet and savory flavors for an intensely rich base. No roux, no clumps, no mess.

2. Puree the butternut squash mixture until smooth. Fat-free Greek yogurt adds tang, richness, and thickening power to the sweet butternut.

3. Stir the three cheeses into the pureed butternut sauce while it's still hot to ensure they all melt evenly.

4. Use a pasta shape that holds on to the sauce. We like cavatappi because of its corkscrew shape and grooved ridges; penne rigate would also work well.

TODAY'S LESSON: BROWNIES

The best brownies are fudgy, chewy, and dense, with the thinnest sugar crust on top. Achieving all this in a light recipe can be tricky: If you use too little fat or too much flour, or leave the brownies just a minute too long in the oven, results will range from springy cakes to dry pucks. These recipes, though, yield decadent success, from full-throttle chocolate with meaty walnuts to salty-sweet caramel-drenched bars and even a bonus blondie.

in a large bowl. Combine ½ cup chocolate and milk in a microwave-safe bowl; microwave at HIGH 1 minute, stirring after 30 seconds. Stir in butter, vanilla, and eggs. Add milk mixture, remaining ½ cup chocolate, and ¼ cup nuts to flour mixture; stir to combine.

3. Pour batter into a 9-inch square metal baking pan coated with cooking spray; sprinkle with remaining ¼ cup nuts. Bake at 350° for 19 minutes or until a wooden pick inserted in center comes out with moist crumbs clinging. Cool in pan on a wire rack. Cut into squares. Yield: 20 servings (serving size: 1 brownie).

CALORIES 186; **FAT** 9.1g (sat 4.2g, mono 2.2g, poly 1.7g); **PROTEIN** 2.8g; **CARB** 25.4g; **FIBER** 1.4g; **CHOL** 30mg; **IRON** 0.9mg; **SODIUM** 74mg; **CALC** 23mg

> KITCHEN TIP: For taller brownies, bake them in an 8-inch square pan and add about 5 minutes to the cook time.

STEP-BY-STEPS

MEASURE DRY INGREDIENTS CAREFULLY
Proper measuring of flour is probably the most crucial factor when baking light brownies. Weigh or measure carefully for the correct amount. Then place all the dry ingredients in a bowl, and whisk to combine.

COMBINE WET INGREDIENTS
Place melted butter and chocolate in a bowl with eggs, milk, vanilla, and any other wet ingredients; stir just until mixture is smooth. Fats like butter and chocolate, even in small amounts, add flavor and moisten the brownies.

TEST FOR DONENESS EARLY
It's critical to bake the brownies just until set and remove them from the oven before they dry out. The best test of doneness is to insert a wooden pick into the center of the pan. When moist crumbs cling to the pick, the brownies are perfectly baked.

Make Ahead • Kid Friendly

Classic Fudge-Walnut Brownies

Hands-on time: 15 min. Total time: 45 min.

To ensure a nice fudgy texture, take care not to overbake. Large chocolate chunks create big, luxurious pockets of melty chocolate in the brownies, but you can always substitute chocolate chips.

3.38 ounces all-purpose flour (about ¾ cup)
1 cup granulated sugar
¾ cup unsweetened cocoa
½ cup packed brown sugar
½ teaspoon baking powder
¼ teaspoon salt
1 cup bittersweet chocolate chunks, divided
⅓ cup fat-free milk
6 tablespoons butter, melted
1 teaspoon vanilla extract
2 large eggs, lightly beaten
½ cup chopped walnuts, divided
Cooking spray

1. Preheat oven to 350°.
2. Weigh or lightly spoon flour into dry measuring cups; level with a knife. Combine flour and next 5 ingredients

Make Ahead • Kid Friendly

Cherry Cheesecake Brownies
(pictured on page 233)

Hands-on time: 34 min. Total time: 1 hr. 24 min.

Cheesecake:
½ cup chopped dried tart cherries
1 tablespoon cherry liqueur
¼ cup sugar
6 ounces ⅓-less-fat cream cheese
1 tablespoon matzo cake meal
¼ teaspoon vanilla extract
1 large egg, lightly beaten
Brownies:
Cooking spray
1½ teaspoons unsweetened cocoa
3 ounces bittersweet chocolate, finely chopped
1 ounce unsweetened chocolate, finely chopped
6 tablespoons butter, cut into small pieces
½ teaspoon vanilla extract
2 large egg whites
1 large egg
3.38 ounces all-purpose flour (about ¾ cup)
¾ cup sugar
½ teaspoon baking powder
⅛ teaspoon salt

1. Preheat oven to 325°.
2. To prepare cheesecake, place cherries and liqueur in a microwave-safe bowl. Microwave at HIGH 45 seconds or until boiling; let stand 20 minutes. Place ¼ cup sugar and cream cheese in a large bowl; beat with a mixer at medium speed 1 minute or until smooth. Add matzo meal, ¼ teaspoon vanilla, and 1 egg; beat just until blended. Stir in cherry mixture.
3. To prepare brownies, coat a 9-inch square metal baking pan with cooking spray; dust with cocoa. Combine chocolates and butter in a microwave-safe dish; microwave at HIGH 1 minute, stirring every 20 seconds. Let stand 5 minutes. Stir in ½ teaspoon vanilla, egg whites, and 1 egg. Weigh or lightly spoon flour into dry measuring cups; level with a knife. Combine flour, ¾ cup sugar, baking powder, and salt in a large bowl. Stir chocolate mixture into flour mixture.
4. Scrape half the brownie batter into prepared pan. Dot half of cheesecake batter on top. Top with remaining brownie batter. Dot with remaining cheesecake batter. Swirl batters using tip of a knife. Bake at 325° for 50 minutes or until a wooden pick inserted in center comes out with moist crumbs clinging. Cool completely in pan on a wire rack. Cut into squares. Yield: 20 servings (serving size: 1 brownie).

CALORIES 164; FAT 8.3g (sat 4.9g, mono 1.3g, poly 0.3g); PROTEIN 2.8g; CARB 20.8g; FIBER 1.1g; CHOL 33mg; IRON 0.8mg; SODIUM 96mg; CALC 16mg

KITCHEN TIP: Matzo cake meal thickens the cheesecake batter but allows the texture to remain creamy when baked. You can always substitute all-purpose flour for the cake meal. (The recipe also works with all matzo cake meal—no flour.) Cherry liqueur reinforces the fruity flavor, but sub plain brandy, if necessary.

Make Ahead • Kid Friendly

Salted Caramel Brownies

Hands-on time: 30 min. Total time: 1 hr. 30 min.

Brownies:
3.38 ounces all-purpose flour (about ¾ cup)
1 cup granulated sugar
¾ cup unsweetened cocoa
½ cup packed brown sugar
½ teaspoon baking powder
6 tablespoons butter, melted
2 large eggs
1 teaspoon vanilla extract
Cooking spray
Topping:
¼ cup butter
¼ cup packed brown sugar
3½ tablespoons evaporated fat-free milk, divided
¼ teaspoon vanilla extract
½ cup powdered sugar
1 ounce bittersweet chocolate, coarsely chopped
⅛ teaspoon coarse sea salt

1. Preheat oven to 350°.
2. To prepare brownies, weigh or lightly spoon flour into dry measuring cups; level with a knife. Combine flour and next 4 ingredients in a large bowl, stirring well with a whisk. Combine 6 tablespoons butter, eggs, and 1 teaspoon vanilla. Add butter mixture to flour mixture; stir to combine. Scrape batter into a 9-inch square metal baking pan lightly coated with cooking spray. Bake at 350° for 19 minutes or until a wooden pick inserted in center comes out with moist crumbs clinging. Cool in pan on a wire rack.
3. To prepare topping, melt ¼ cup butter in a saucepan over medium heat. Add ¼ cup brown sugar and 1½ tablespoons milk; cook 2 minutes. Remove from heat. Add vanilla and powdered sugar; stir with a whisk until smooth. Spread mixture evenly over cooled brownies. Let stand 20 minutes or until set.
4. Combine remaining 2 tablespoons milk and chocolate in a microwave-safe bowl; microwave at HIGH 45 seconds or until melted, stirring after 20 seconds.

Stir just until smooth; drizzle over caramel. Sprinkle with sea salt; let stand until set. Cut into squares. Yield: 20 servings (serving size: 1 brownie).

CALORIES 180; FAT 7.2g (sat 4.1g, mono 1.7g, poly 0.3g); PROTEIN 2.1g; CARB 27.8g; FIBER 0.8g; CHOL 37mg; IRON 0.9mg; SODIUM 76mg; CALC 26mg

KITCHEN TIP: For sparkle and a salty kick, substitute large flake salt for the coarse sea salt.

Make Ahead • Kid Friendly

Peanut Butter Cup Blondies

Hands-on time: 20 min. Total time: 2 hr.

5.6 ounces all-purpose flour (about 1¼ cups)
1 cup granulated sugar
½ teaspoon baking powder
¼ teaspoon salt
⅓ cup creamy peanut butter
¼ cup butter, melted and cooled slightly
2 tablespoons 2% reduced-fat milk
1 teaspoon vanilla extract
2 large eggs, lightly beaten
¼ cup semisweet chocolate chips
Cooking spray
4 (0.75-ounce) peanut butter cups, coarsely chopped

1. Preheat oven to 350°.
2. Weigh or lightly spoon flour into dry measuring cups; level with a knife. Combine flour and next 3 ingredients, stirring well with a whisk. Combine peanut butter and next 4 ingredients, stirring well. Add peanut butter mixture to flour mixture; stir until combined. Stir in chocolate chips.
3. Scrape batter into a 9-inch square metal baking pan lightly coated with cooking spray, and arrange the peanut butter cups over batter. Bake at 350° for 19 minutes or until a wooden pick inserted in center comes out with moist crumbs clinging. Cool in pan on a wire rack. Yield: 20 servings (serving size: 1 brownie).

CALORIES 153; FAT 7g (sat 2.9g, mono 2g, poly 0.8g); PROTEIN 3.2g; CARB 20.8g; FIBER 0.7g; CHOL 28mg; IRON 0.7mg; SODIUM 98mg; CALC 17mg

CHILE HEAT INDEX

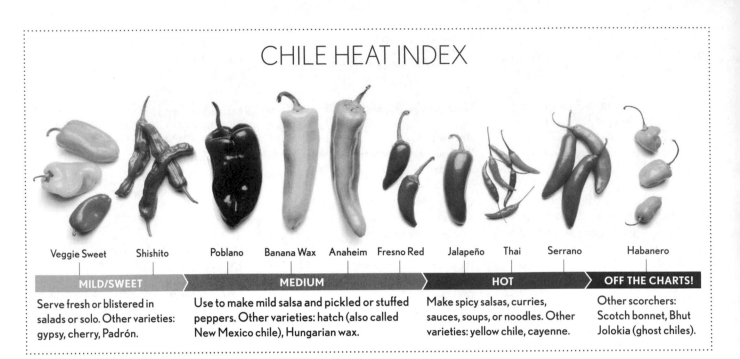

Veggie Sweet	Shishito	Poblano	Banana Wax	Anaheim	Fresno Red	Jalapeño	Thai	Serrano	Habanero

MILD/SWEET	MEDIUM	HOT	OFF THE CHARTS!

Serve fresh or blistered in salads or solo. Other varieties: gypsy, cherry, Padrón.

Use to make mild salsa and pickled or stuffed peppers. Other varieties: hatch (also called New Mexico chile), Hungarian wax.

Make spicy salsas, curries, sauces, soups, or noodles. Other varieties: yellow chile, cayenne.

Other scorchers: Scotch bonnet, Bhut Jolokia (ghost chiles).

WHAT TO EAT RIGHT NOW
CHILE PEPPERS

Quick & Easy • Make Ahead

Salsa Verde

Instead of buying bottled salsa, make it fresh with two kinds of chiles.

Preheat broiler to high. Broil 2 poblano peppers 5 minutes per side or until blackened. Place in a small paper bag; seal. Let stand 10 minutes; peel and chop. Bring ½ cup fat-free, lower-sodium chicken broth and 1 pound peeled tomatillos to a boil in a saucepan over medium heat. Cover and simmer 8 minutes. Remove from heat; let stand 20 minutes. Pour into a blender. Add 2 tablespoons fresh lime juice and 2 garlic cloves; process until smooth. Pour into a bowl; stir in poblanos, ⅔ cup chopped white onion, ⅓ cup chopped cilantro, ½ teaspoon kosher salt, and 1 finely chopped fresh serrano chile. Chill. Yield: 8 servings (serving size: ¼ cup).

CALORIES 34; **FAT** 0.7g (sat 0.1g); **SODIUM** 146mg

Make Ahead • Vegetarian

Marinated Peppers and Mozzarella

Preheat broiler to high. Arrange 4 cups baby sweet peppers in a single layer on a foil-lined jelly-roll pan; broil peppers 4 minutes on each side or until blackened and tender. Cool. Combine peppers, ½ cup extra-virgin olive oil, 3 crushed garlic cloves, 1 teaspoon grated lemon rind, ½ teaspoon crushed red pepper, ½ teaspoon salt, and 3 ounces fresh baby mozzarella balls; toss. Cover and refrigerate overnight, tossing occasionally. Let stand at room temperature 30 minutes. Stir in ¼ cup fresh small basil leaves and 1 teaspoon fresh lemon juice before serving. Serve with a slotted spoon. Yield: 6 servings (serving size: about ¼ cup).

CALORIES 83; **FAT** 7.7g (sat 1.8g); **SODIUM** 86mg

> **KITCHEN NOTES:** Serve this stunning dish solo as a predinner nosh, or spoon over mixed lettuces for a fresh spin on salad. Reserve excess oil, and toss it with steamed brown rice or noodles.

EVERYDAY VEGETARIAN
20-MINUTE VEGGIE MAINS

We set out to make some fast fall entrées that use eggs, beans, polenta, and multigrain bread for a hearty result.

Quick & Easy • Vegetarian

Rotini with White Beans and Escarole

Hands-on time: 20 min. Total time: 20 min.

8 ounces uncooked rotini
2 tablespoons extra-virgin olive oil
8 garlic cloves, thinly sliced
½ teaspoon crushed red pepper
1 (12-ounce) bag chopped escarole
¾ cup organic vegetable broth
1 (15-ounce) can no-salt-added cannellini beans, rinsed and drained
½ teaspoon salt
¼ cup (1 ounce) shaved Parmigiano-Reggiano cheese

1. Cook pasta according to package directions, omitting salt and fat; drain.
2. Heat a large nonstick skillet over medium-high heat. Add oil to pan, and swirl to coat. Add garlic and red pepper; cook 45 seconds or until garlic begins to brown, stirring constantly. Add escarole; cook 1 minute or until escarole begins to wilt. Add broth; bring to a boil. Reduce heat to medium; cook 5 minutes or until escarole is tender and liquid nearly evaporates. Stir in pasta, beans, and salt. Top with cheese. Yield: 4 servings (serving size: 1¾ cups pasta mixture and 1 tablespoon cheese).

CALORIES 356; FAT 9.7g (sat 2.2g, mono 4.9g, poly 0.8g); PROTEIN 13.8g; CARB 55.1g; FIBER 7g; CHOL 4mg; IRON 3.5mg; SODIUM 391mg; CALC 158mg

WINE NOTE: With earthy beans, bitter greens, and sharp Parmesan cheese, this dish needs a dose of fruit to bring it to life. Try a pinot grigio with lively melon and citrus flavors, such as Lungarotti Torre di Giano 2010 ($15).

Make Ahead • Kid Friendly
Vegetarian

Arugula Pizza with Poached Eggs

Hands-on time: 20 min. Total time: 20 min.

You can also try using fresh dough. Look to your local pizzeria for homemade dough, as many will sell theirs for only a few dollars. Try with other crisp greens such as spinach or watercress.

1 (11-ounce) package refrigerated pizza crust dough
Cooking spray
½ cup part-skim ricotta cheese
½ cup (2 ounces) shaved fresh Romano cheese, divided
1 tablespoon white vinegar
6 large eggs
1 (5-ounce) package baby arugula
4 teaspoons extra-virgin olive oil
½ teaspoon grated fresh lemon rind
1 tablespoon fresh lemon juice
⅛ teaspoon salt
¼ teaspoon freshly ground black pepper

1. Preheat oven to 450°.
2. Unroll pizza dough on a baking sheet lightly coated with cooking spray; place in preheating oven. Bake as oven heats for 7 minutes.
3. Combine ricotta and ¼ cup Romano. Remove pan from oven. Quickly spread cheese mixture over dough, leaving a ½-inch border around edges. Return pan to oven, and bake at 450° for 5 minutes.
4. While pizza bakes, add water to a large skillet, filling two-thirds full; bring to a boil. Reduce heat; simmer. Add vinegar. Break each egg into a custard cup, and pour gently into pan. Cook 3 minutes or until desired degree of doneness. Carefully remove eggs from pan using a slotted spoon.
5. Combine arugula, remaining ¼ cup Romano cheese, and next 4 ingredients in a large bowl; toss well. Top pizza with arugula mixture and eggs, and sprinkle with pepper. Cut into 6 pieces. Yield: 6 servings (serving size: 1 piece).

CALORIES 323; FAT 15.4g (sat 5.2g, mono 6.7g, poly 2g); PROTEIN 15.8g; CARB 27.9g; FIBER 1.3g; CHOL 192mg; IRON 2.6mg; SODIUM 605mg; CALC 237mg

Quick & Easy • Vegetarian

Grilled Gruyère and Olive Tapenade Sandwiches

Hands-on time: 20 min. Total time: 20 min.

You can easily shave thin slices of cheese in a snap using an inexpensive kitchen tool: a vegetable peeler. This is a perfect technique for many hard cheeses like Gruyère.

1 (8.5-ounce) jar oil-packed sun-dried tomatoes
12 pitted kalamata olives
2 garlic cloves
8 (1-ounce) slices multigrain bread
¼ cup (1 ounce) grated Parmigiano-Reggiano cheese
8 (¼-inch-thick) slices large tomato
2 ounces Gruyère cheese, shaved

1. Remove 4 sun-dried tomatoes and 2 tablespoons oil from jar. Reserve remaining tomatoes and oil for another use. Set 1 tablespoon oil aside. Combine tomatoes, 1 tablespoon oil, olives, and garlic in a mini food processor; process until mostly smooth, scraping sides of bowl once.
2. Brush one side of each bread slice with remaining 1 tablespoon olive oil. Spread 1½ tablespoons olive mixture on each of 4 bread slices, oil side down. Top each bread slice with 1 tablespoon cheese, 2 tomato slices, and ½ ounce Gruyère. Top each with remaining 4 bread slices, oil side up.
3. Heat a skillet over medium-high heat. Add sandwiches to pan. Place a cast-iron or other heavy skillet on top of sandwiches; press gently to flatten sandwiches (leave cast-iron skillet on sandwiches while they cook). Cook 2 minutes on each side or until cheese melts and bread is toasted. Yield: 4 servings (serving size: 1 sandwich).

CALORIES 346; FAT 20.2g (sat 5.1g, mono 8.9g, poly 1.4g); PROTEIN 14.7g; CARB 28.9g; FIBER 5.8g; CHOL 21mg; IRON 1.6mg; SODIUM 618mg; CALC 290mg

BOOST FLAVOR WITH SUN-DRIED TOMATO-INFUSED OIL.

Quick & Easy • Vegetarian

Blue Cheese Polenta with Vegetables

Hands-on time: 15 min. Total time: 15 min.

2 tablespoons extra-virgin olive oil, divided
2 (4-ounce) packages presliced exotic
  mushroom blend
1 teaspoon chopped fresh thyme
1½ cups thinly sliced sweet onion
1 red bell pepper, thinly sliced
1 teaspoon minced garlic
½ teaspoon kosher salt, divided
¼ teaspoon black pepper, divided
3 cups 1% low-fat milk
½ cup water
⅔ cup quick-cooking polenta
¾ cup (3 ounces) crumbled Gorgonzola
  cheese
¼ cup chopped fresh parsley

1. Heat a large nonstick skillet over
medium-high heat. Add 1 tablespoon
olive oil to pan, and swirl to coat. Add
mushrooms and thyme; sauté for 4
minutes or until mushrooms are tender.
Add remaining 1 tablespoon olive oil,
onion, bell pepper, garlic, ¼ teaspoon
salt, and ⅛ teaspoon black pepper;
sauté 8 minutes or until vegetables
are tender.
2. Combine milk, ½ cup water, remaining ¼ teaspoon salt, and remaining ⅛
teaspoon black pepper in a medium
saucepan; bring to a boil. Stir in polenta; cook 5 minutes, stirring frequently.
Remove from heat, and stir in cheese.
Serve with vegetables. Sprinkle with
parsley. Yield: 4 servings (serving size:
1 cup polenta, ¾ cup vegetables, and 1
tablespoon parsley).

CALORIES 340; FAT 15g (sat 6.1g, mono 5.5g, poly 0.9g);
PROTEIN 15.3g; CARB 32.1g; FIBER 4.9g; CHOL 29mg;
IRON 0.8mg; SODIUM 594mg; CALC 337mg

BUDGET COOKING

FEED 4 FOR LESS THAN $10

Back-to-school season means less time in
the kitchen: These family-friendly recipes
help you get dinner on the table in a hurry.

$1.31 per serving, $5.24 total

Quick & Easy • Vegetarian

Stir-Fried Chinese Egg Noodles

Hands-on time: 27 min. Total time: 27 min.

*Though the chewy texture of Chinese egg
noodles is fantastic, you can substitute rice
sticks or linguine. Omit or decrease the amount
of chile paste if serving to kids.*

8 ounces fresh or frozen Chinese egg
  noodles, thawed
1 tablespoon canola oil
1 cup sliced cremini mushrooms
5 garlic cloves, minced
3 green onions, diagonally sliced
¼ cup lower-sodium soy sauce
1 tablespoon brown sugar
1½ tablespoons fresh lime juice
1 tablespoon dark sesame oil
1 tablespoon ketchup
1 tablespoon chile paste (such as sambal
  oelek)
2 large eggs
2 cups fresh spinach, trimmed

1. Cook egg noodles according to package directions, omitting salt and fat.
Drain. Set aside.
2. Heat a large skillet over medium-
high heat. Add canola oil to pan, and
swirl to coat. Add mushrooms; sauté
4 minutes, stirring occasionally. Add
garlic and green onions; sauté 1 minute,
stirring constantly. Combine soy sauce
and next 5 ingredients, stirring well.
Stir soy sauce mixture into mushroom
mixture; bring to a boil.

3. Add noodles to pan; toss to coat.
Add eggs; cook 2 minutes or until eggs
are set, tossing well. Remove from heat;
stir in spinach. Yield: 4 servings (serving size: 1 cup).

CALORIES 304; FAT 10.3g (sat 1.8g, mono 4.5g, poly 2.8g);
PROTEIN 14.4g; CARB 39.6g; FIBER 2.3g; CHOL 106mg;
IRON 1.8mg; SODIUM 662mg; CALC 54mg

IF YOU WANT TO PUMP UP THE PROTEIN, ADD CUBED TOFU.

$1.64 per serving, $6.56 total

Quick & Easy • Kid Friendly
Vegetarian

French Toast Peanut Butter and Jelly

Hands-on time: 15 min. Total time: 15 min.

*What kid (or grown-up, for that matter)
wouldn't love this ooey-gooey sandwich? Serve
the souped-up PB&Js with fresh fruit.*

⅔ cup 2% reduced-fat milk
1 large egg, lightly beaten
½ teaspoon baking powder
½ teaspoon vanilla extract
⅛ teaspoon salt
8 white whole-wheat sandwich bread slices
½ cup strawberry preserves
6 tablespoons creamy peanut butter
1 tablespoon canola oil, divided
1 tablespoon powdered sugar

1. Combine first 5 ingredients in a
medium shallow dish, stirring well with
a whisk. Place bread slices on a flat
surface. Spread 2 tablespoons preserves
over each of 4 bread slices, and spread
1½ tablespoons peanut butter over each
of remaining 4 bread slices. Assemble
sandwiches. Carefully dip 2 sandwiches
in milk mixture, turning to coat.
2. Heat a large skillet over medium-
high heat. Add 1½ teaspoons canola
oil to pan; swirl to coat. Place coated

sandwiches in pan; cook 2 minutes on each side or until toasted. Remove sandwiches from pan. Repeat procedure with remaining oil, 2 sandwiches, and milk mixture. Sprinkle powdered sugar evenly over sandwiches; cut each sandwich in half diagonally. Yield: 4 servings (serving size: 1 sandwich).

CALORIES 394; FAT 19.4g (sat 4.6g, mono 8.7g, poly 5.1g); PROTEIN 14.9g; CARB 43.2g; FIBER 5.4g; CHOL 48mg; IRON 1.6mg; SODIUM 519mg; CALC 124mg

---

$2.43 per serving, $9.70 total

Quick & Easy • Kid Friendly

Cheese Ravioli with Pesto

Hands-on time: 12 min. Total time: 12 min.

Fresh herbs are premium ingredients that can easily break a budget. Stretch the pesto by adding a little fresh baby spinach.

1 (9-ounce) package fresh 3-cheese ravioli
1⅓ cups fresh baby spinach
⅔ cup fresh basil leaves
½ teaspoon salt
¼ teaspoon crushed red pepper
2 garlic cloves
2 tablespoons fat-free, lower-sodium chicken broth
2 tablespoons olive oil
1 tablespoon fresh lemon juice
1 plum tomato, diced
½ cup (2 ounces) shaved fresh Parmesan cheese
⅓ cup pine nuts, toasted
Fresh basil leaves (optional)

1. Cook ravioli according to package directions; omit salt and fat. Drain.
2. Combine spinach, basil, salt, red pepper, and garlic in a food processor. With processor running, add broth, olive oil, and lemon juice through chute until mixture is smooth.
3. Combine ravioli, pesto, and tomato in medium saucepan over medium-high heat; cook 1 minute or until warm. Spoon ¾ cup into each of 4 bowls; sprinkle each serving with 2 tablespoons cheese and about 4 teaspoons nuts.

Garnish with basil leaves, if desired. Yield: 4 servings.

CALORIES 389; FAT 23.4g (sat 6.9g, mono 7.9g, poly 4.7g); PROTEIN 14.5g; CARB 31.7g; FIBER 3g; CHOL 45mg; IRON 2.3mg; SODIUM 811mg; CALC 223mg

WINE NOTE: This rich dish needs a crisp white to refresh the palate. Costamolino Vermentino di Sardegna 2010 ($10) is zesty and refreshing with tropical fruit and an herbal edge to match the basil.

$2.22 per serving, $8.89 total

Quick & Easy

Buffalo Chicken Thighs

Hands-on time: 16 min. Total time: 45 min.

Play up the buffalo theme with a side of celery sticks and light ranch dressing.

6 tablespoons all-purpose flour
½ teaspoon salt
¼ teaspoon garlic powder
¼ teaspoon ground red pepper
8 bone-in chicken thighs, skinned
1 tablespoon olive oil, divided
3 tablespoons hot sauce
1 tablespoon butter

1. Preheat oven to 375°.
2. Combine first 4 ingredients in a heavy-duty zip-top plastic bag; seal. Shake to blend. Add half of chicken to bag; seal. Shake to coat. Remove chicken from bag, shaking to remove excess flour mixture. Heat a large nonstick skillet over medium-high heat. Add 1½ teaspoons oil to pan; swirl to coat. Add flour-coated chicken to pan; sauté 4 minutes on each side or until browned. Transfer browned chicken to a jelly-roll pan. Repeat procedure with remaining uncooked chicken, flour mixture, and oil. Discard remaining flour mixture. Bake chicken at 375° for 8 minutes or until done.
3. Combine hot sauce and butter in a microwave-safe dish; microwave at HIGH 30 seconds or until butter melts, stirring to blend. Place chicken in a

shallow dish; drizzle with butter sauce. Toss to coat. Yield: 4 servings (serving size: 2 thighs).

CALORIES 318; FAT 17.8g (sat 5.5g, mono 7.5g, poly 3.1g); PROTEIN 28.4g; CARB 9.2g; FIBER 0.4g; CHOL 106mg; IRON 2.1mg; SODIUM 474mg; CALC 17mg

Buttermilk–Blue Cheese Smashed Potatoes:
Place 1 pound small red potatoes in a saucepan; cover with cold water to 2 inches above potatoes. Bring mixture to a boil over medium-high heat. Reduce heat to medium, and simmer 15 minutes or until tender; drain. Return potatoes to pan. Add ⅓ cup buttermilk, ¼ cup crumbled blue cheese, ¼ teaspoon salt, and ¼ teaspoon freshly ground black pepper to pan; mash with potato masher to desired consistency. Yield: 4 servings.

CALORIES 117; FAT 2.9g (sat 1.8g); SODIUM 277mg

WHAT IS BUDGET COOKING?

Prices derived from midsized-city supermarkets. For specialty or highly perishable ingredients, like some Asian sauces or fresh herbs, we account for the entire cost of the ingredient. For staples and other ingredients, we include the cost for only the amount used. Salt, pepper, and cooking spray are freebies.

SUPERFAST

As summer wanes, snap up the best ingredients for these fast recipes. And it's time for some back-to-school inspiration: Try our bagel pizzas and chocolate-covered apple snacks.

Quick & Easy

Pan-Fried Trout with Tomato Basil Sauté

A tomato sauce moistens the fish, making this company-worthy recipe foolproof.

2 ounces chopped pancetta
2 cups cherry tomatoes, halved
1 teaspoon minced garlic
1 teaspoon freshly ground black pepper, divided
½ teaspoon salt, divided
¼ cup fresh small basil leaves
1 tablespoon canola oil, divided
4 (6-ounce) trout fillets, divided
4 lemon wedges

1. Heat pancetta in a medium skillet over low heat. Cook 4 minutes or just until pancetta begins to brown. Add cherry tomatoes, garlic, ½ teaspoon pepper, and ⅛ teaspoon salt; cook 3 minutes or until tomatoes begin to soften. Remove from heat, and stir in basil leaves.
2. Heat a large nonstick skillet over medium-high heat. Add 1½ teaspoons oil to pan; swirl to coat. Sprinkle fish evenly with remaining ½ teaspoon pepper and remaining ⅜ teaspoon salt. Add 2 fillets to pan; cook 2 minutes on each side or until fish flakes easily when tested with a fork. Remove fish from pan; keep warm. Repeat procedure with remaining 1½ teaspoons oil and remaining 2 fillets. Top fish with tomato mixture. Serve fish with lemon wedges. Yield: 4 servings (serving size: 1 fillet and about ⅓ cup sauce).

 Sustainable Choice | *When shopping, look for U.S.-farmed rainbow trout. Avoid wild-caught lake trout.*

CALORIES 388; **FAT** 20.5g (sat 5.9g, mono 7.9g, poly 5.5g); **PROTEIN** 44.3g; **CARB** 4.3g; **FIBER** 1.3g; **CHOL** 126mg; **IRON** 1.1mg; **SODIUM** 604mg; **CALC** 169mg

Quick & Easy

Spicy Asian Chicken and Noodle Soup

This broth packs a lot of flavor in just a little time. If you don't have the Sriracha on hand, thin slices of jalapeño pepper make a good substitute.

3 cups fat-free, lower-sodium chicken broth
1½ cups water
1½ cups shredded rotisserie chicken breast
½ cup grated carrot (about 1 medium)
½ cup thinly sliced snow peas
2 teaspoons Sriracha (hot chile sauce)
2 teaspoons lower-sodium soy sauce
1½ teaspoons Thai red curry paste
1 (2-inch) piece peeled fresh ginger
6 cups water
3 ounces uncooked wide rice sticks (rice-flour noodles)
1 tablespoon fresh lime juice
¼ cup chopped fresh mint
¼ cup chopped fresh cilantro
¼ cup thinly sliced green onions

1. Bring first 9 ingredients to a simmer in a medium saucepan; keep warm.
2. Bring 6 cups water to a boil in a large saucepan. Add rice noodles; cook 3 minutes. Drain. Place about ¼ cup rice noodles in each of 4 bowls.
3. Discard ginger in broth mixture. Add juice to broth mixture; stir. Ladle 1⅓ cups broth mixture over each serving; top with 1 tablespoon each mint, cilantro, and green onions. Yield: 4 servings.

CALORIES 197; **FAT** 2.1g (sat 0.5g, mono 0.8g, poly 0.3g); **PROTEIN** 19.9g; **CARB** 23.5g; **FIBER** 2.7g; **CHOL** 47mg; **IRON** 2.1mg; **SODIUM** 635mg; **CALC** 53mg

Quick & Easy

Salmon and Bok Choy

3 tablespoons lower-sodium soy sauce
2 tablespoons honey
2 teaspoons grated peeled fresh ginger
2 teaspoons dark sesame oil
½ teaspoon garlic powder
1 pound baby bok choy or bok choy
4 (6-ounce) salmon fillets
¼ cup diagonally cut green onions

1. Preheat broiler.
2. Combine first 5 ingredients in a small bowl, stirring with a whisk.
3. Coarsely chop bok choy leaves, and arrange on one end of a jelly-roll pan. Coarsely chop bok choy stems and arrange in a single layer on opposite end of jelly-roll pan. Place salmon, skin sides down, in a single layer on top of leafy greens. Pour half of soy sauce mixture evenly over salmon; pour remaining half evenly over bok choy stems. Broil 5 minutes; stir stems. Broil an additional 4 minutes or until desired degree of doneness. Arrange ⅓ cup bok choy on each of 4 plates. Top each serving with 1 fillet and 1 tablespoon green onions. Yield: 4 servings.

CALORIES 320; **FAT** 13.4g (sat 2g, mono 4.6g, poly 5.4g); **PROTEIN** 36.3g; **CARB** 12.8g; **FIBER** 1.5g; **CHOL** 94mg; **IRON** 2.5mg; **SODIUM** 444mg; **CALC** 147mg

Quick & Easy • Vegetarian

Grilled Zucchini with Sea Salt

For more tender zucchini, leave slices in the pan an extra 1 minute on each side. When the flesh starts to look translucent, the zucchini is done.

2 teaspoons extra-virgin olive oil
¼ teaspoon coarse sea salt
¼ teaspoon freshly ground black pepper
2 medium zucchini, cut diagonally into ½-inch-thick slices

1. Preheat grill pan over medium-high heat. Combine all ingredients in a bowl; toss well to coat. Arrange zucchini in a single layer in pan; grill 4 minutes, turning after 2 minutes. Yield: 4 servings (serving size: about 4 slices).

CALORIES 36; **FAT** 2.4g (sat 0.4g, mono 1.7g, poly 0.3g); **PROTEIN** 1.2g; **CARB** 3.4g; **FIBER** 1.1g; **CHOL** 0mg; **IRON** 0.4mg; **SODIUM** 130mg; **CALC** 15mg

PARMIGIANO-CRUMBED

Prepare base recipe. Chop 1½ ounces ciabatta bread. Place bread and ½ teaspoon fresh thyme in a food processor; pulse 10 times. Heat a skillet over medium-high heat. Add 2 teaspoons olive oil. Add bread mixture; cook

5 minutes, stirring frequently. Combine zucchini, bread mixture, and 2 tablespoons grated fresh Parmigiano-Reggiano. Yield: 4 servings.

CALORIES 94; FAT 5.9g (sat 1.2g); SODIUM 241mg

CAPRESE "SALSA"

Prepare base recipe. Combine ⅓ cup diced tomato, 2 ounces sliced fresh mozzarella cheese, 3 tablespoons chopped fresh basil, and 1 minced garlic clove in a bowl. Add 1 tablespoon extra-virgin olive oil and 1 teaspoon red wine vinegar to tomato mixture; stir gently. Divide zucchini evenly among 4 plates. Top zucchini evenly with tomato mixture. Yield: 4 servings.

CALORIES 106; FAT 8.1g (sat 2.3g); SODIUM 246mg

MINT GREMOLATA

Prepare base recipe. Combine ¼ cup finely chopped fresh flat-leaf parsley, ¼ cup finely chopped fresh mint, 1½ tablespoons grated lemon rind, 1 tablespoon olive oil, and 2 minced garlic cloves. Divide zucchini evenly among 4 plates; top evenly with gremolata. Yield: 4 servings.

CALORIES 72; FAT 5.9g (sat 0.8g); SODIUM 133mg

Quick & Easy • Kid Friendly
Cheesy Chicken Bagel Pizzas

2 (4½-inch, 2¼-ounce) plain bagels, sliced in half
½ cup lower-sodium marinara sauce
1 cup shredded rotisserie chicken breast
1 cup preshredded part-skim mozzarella cheese

1. Preheat broiler.
2. Place bagel halves, cut sides up, on a baking sheet. Broil 2 minutes or until lightly toasted.
3. Spread 2 tablespoons marinara on cut side of each bagel half. Top each half with ¼ cup chicken, and sprinkle with ¼ cup cheese. Broil bagel halves an additional 2 minutes or until cheese melts. Yield: 4 servings (serving size: 1 bagel pizza).

CALORIES 268; FAT 8g (sat 4.2g, mono 2.4g, poly 0.6g); PROTEIN 22.1g; CARB 32.7g; FIBER 1g; CHOL 47mg; IRON 2.9mg; SODIUM 516mg; CALC 251mg

BAGEL HALVES ARE A QUICK, KID-FRIENDLY STAND-IN FOR TRADITIONAL PIZZA CRUST.

Quick & Easy • Make Ahead
Kid Friendly
Chocolate-Granola Apple Wedges

If you can't find Braeburn apples, Gala or Fuji varieties also stand up to dipping and add a touch more sweetness.

2 ounces semisweet chocolate, finely chopped
⅓ cup low-fat granola without raisins
1 large Braeburn apple, cut into 16 wedges

1. Place chocolate in a medium microwave-safe bowl. Microwave at HIGH 1 minute, stirring every 15 seconds, or until chocolate melts.
2. Place granola in a shallow dish. Dip apple wedges, skin side up, in chocolate; allow excess chocolate to drip back into bowl. Dredge wedges in granola. Place wedges, chocolate side up, on a large plate. Refrigerate 5 minutes or until set. Yield: 4 servings (serving size: 4 apple wedges).

CALORIES 132; FAT 4.8g (sat 2.6g, mono 1.4g, poly 0.1g); PROTEIN 1.5g; CARB 23.9g; FIBER 2.6g; CHOL 0mg; IRON 0.8mg; SODIUM 22mg; CALC 13mg

OOPS! YOUR RICE GETS GUMMY

For light, fluffy grains, try a technique so simple you'll kick yourself for not thinking of it.
By Hannah Klinger

Rice is the great staple grain of much of the world, but it can strike fear in the hearts of some American cooks who have learned that the famous 2:1 water-to-rice ratio is not reliable in many cases or for many varieties. And stovetop prep can be tricky (rice cookers are reliable, so if you love rice, consider buying one). Slightly under-cooked rice can sometimes be fixed with more water and time, but the dreaded gummy rice is a dead loss.

When rice is cooked in the traditional way—simmering in a lidded pot—the close-packed grains rub together and release starch, often leading to stickiness. The solution is blessedly ratio-free, though it may seem counterintuitive: Use more water. Lots more, so you cook the rice like pasta until it reaches the proper consistency, and then drain. The pasta method keeps rice from rubbing together too much as it cooks; draining ensures it won't suck up more water than it needs.

Check brown rice for doneness at around 25 minutes. You can also sauté brown rice in olive oil after it's drained, to evaporate excess moisture. For white rice, which absorbs water more readily, try sautéing the grains before boiling, for about two minutes in a tablespoon of oil. Then add roughly four times as much cold water as rice to the pan, and boil. Check for doneness at around 15 minutes (timing starts when water boils). The oil forms a protective layer around the white grains during boiling—and sautéing lends the rice deliciously toasty flavor.

DINNER TONIGHT

Here is a batch of fast weeknight menus from the *Cooking Light* Test Kitchens.

READY IN 30 MINUTES

The SHOPPING LIST

Chicken Lettuce Cups
red onion
tomato
fresh oregano
fresh flat-leaf parsley
lemon
1 head Bibb lettuce
1/2 cup canned artichoke hearts
pitted green olives (preferably Castelvetrano)
1 pound ground chicken
3 ounces fresh mozzarella cheese

Orzo with Spinach
3 cups fresh spinach
orzo (rice-shaped pasta)
white balsamic vinegar
olive oil

The GAME PLAN

- Cook orzo.
  While pasta cooks:
- Prepare chicken mixture.
- Finish orzo dish.
- Fill lettuce cups.

Quick & Easy

Chicken Lettuce Cups
With Orzo with Spinach

Simple Sub: Use ground turkey breast in place of ground chicken.
Keep It Fresh: Store extra fresh mozzarella in lightly salted water.
Shopping Tip: Castelvetrano olives are meaty and add mildly fruity taste and gorgeous color.

Cooking spray
1 pound ground chicken
1/4 teaspoon freshly ground black pepper
1/8 teaspoon salt
1 cup vertically sliced red onion
1/2 cup canned artichoke hearts, drained and coarsely chopped
1/4 cup diced tomato
1 tablespoon chopped fresh oregano
1 tablespoon chopped fresh flat-leaf parsley
10 pitted green olives, chopped
1/2 cup (about 3 ounces) diced fresh mozzarella cheese
1 tablespoon fresh lemon juice
8 Bibb lettuce leaves

1. Heat a large nonstick skillet over medium-high heat. Coat pan with cooking spray. Add chicken, pepper, and salt to pan; cook 3 minutes, stirring to crumble. Stir in onion and next 5 ingredients; cook 3 minutes or until chicken is done. Stir in cheese and juice. Spoon 1/4 cup chicken mixture into each lettuce leaf. Yield: 4 servings (serving size: 2 lettuce cups).

CALORIES 284; **FAT** 18g (sat 6.4g, mono 8g, poly 2.4g); **PROTEIN** 24.2g; **CARB** 6.9g; **FIBER** 0.9g; **CHOL** 113mg; **IRON** 1.6mg; **SODIUM** 543mg; **CALC** 24mg

For the Orzo with Spinach:

Cook 1 1/4 cups orzo (rice-shaped pasta) in boiling water according to package directions, omitting salt and fat. Drain pasta in a colander over a bowl, reserving 1/4 cup cooking liquid. Heat a large skillet over medium-high heat. Add 2 teaspoons olive oil to pan; swirl to coat. Add orzo, 1/4 teaspoon salt, and 1/4 teaspoon black pepper; cook 1 minute, stirring constantly. Stir in reserved 1/4 cup cooking liquid, 3 tablespoons

---

white balsamic vinegar, and 3 cups chopped fresh spinach; cook 2 minutes or until spinach wilts. Yield: 4 servings (serving size: 1 cup).

CALORIES 234; **FAT** 3.3g (sat 0.3g); **SODIUM** 168mg

READY IN 40 MINUTES

The SHOPPING LIST

Chicken Tostadas and Avocado Dressing
avocado
lemon
garlic
1 jalapeño pepper
iceberg lettuce
tomato
6-inch flour tortillas
ground red pepper
canola oil
fat-free, lower-sodium chicken broth
rotisserie chicken
queso fresco
reduced-fat sour cream

Mexican Rice
green bell pepper
tomato
ground cumin
long-grain rice
fat-free, lower-sodium chicken broth

The GAME PLAN

- Cook rice.
  While rice simmers:
- Prepare dressing.
- Cook tortillas.
- Sauté filling mixture.

Chicken Tostadas and Avocado Dressing
With Mexican Rice

Prep Pointer: Remove the ribs and seeds from the jalapeño before mincing to tame the heat.
Simple Sub: Use shredded Monterey Jack cheese if you can't find queso fresco.
Keep It Fresh: Sprinkle lemon juice on surface of leftover avocado before tightly wrapping.

2 tablespoons reduced-fat sour cream
2 tablespoons fat-free, lower-sodium chicken broth
2 tablespoons fresh lemon juice
2 teaspoons canola oil
¼ teaspoon ground red pepper
⅛ teaspoon salt
½ ripe peeled avocado
1½ tablespoons canola oil, divided
4 (6-inch) flour tortillas
2 garlic cloves, minced
1 jalapeño pepper, minced
2 cups shredded skinless, boneless rotisserie chicken breast
1 cup shredded iceberg lettuce
½ cup chopped tomato
¼ cup (1 ounce) crumbled queso fresco

1. Combine the first 7 ingredients in a food processor, and process until smooth.
2. Heat a large nonstick skillet over medium-high heat. Add ¾ teaspoon oil to pan. Cook 1 tortilla 2 minutes on each side or until golden brown. Repeat procedure with 2¼ teaspoons oil and remaining tortillas.
3. Add remaining ½ tablespoon oil to pan. Add garlic and jalapeño; sauté 1½ minutes. Add chicken; cook 2 minutes. Place 1 tortilla on each of 4 plates; top each tortilla with ½ cup chicken mixture, ¼ cup lettuce, 2 tablespoons tomato, and 1 tablespoon cheese. Top each serving with 3 tablespoons dressing. Yield: 4 servings (serving size: 1 tostada).

CALORIES 428; **FAT** 20g (sat 4.1g, mono 10.8g, poly 3.6g); **PROTEIN** 39.2g; **CARB** 24.2g; **FIBER** 20g; **CHOL** 109mg; **IRON** 2mg; **SODIUM** 658mg; **CALC** 96mg

For the Mexican Rice:
Combine ¾ cup uncooked long-grain rice; 1½ cups fat-free, lower-sodium chicken broth; ½ cup minced green bell pepper; ½ cup diced tomato; and ½ teaspoon ground cumin in a medium saucepan; bring to a boil. Cover, reduce heat, and simmer 20 minutes. Yield: 4 servings (serving size: ½ cup).

CALORIES 138; **FAT** 0.4g (sat 0.1g); **SODIUM** 173mg

READY IN
40
MINUTES

The
SHOPPING LIST

Shrimp Fettuccine Alfredo
2 green onions
garlic
fresh parsley
olive oil
9-ounce package refrigerated fettuccine
1 pound peeled and deveined medium shrimp
2 ounces Parmigiano-Reggiano cheese
half-and-half
⅓-less-fat cream cheese

Roasted Asparagus
1 pound asparagus
lemon
ground red pepper
olive oil

The
GAME PLAN

While oven preheats:
■ Cook pasta.
■ Sauté shrimp mixture.
■ Roast asparagus.
While asparagus cooks:
■ Prepare sauce.
■ Toss pasta.

Shrimp Fettuccine Alfredo
With Roasted Asparagus

Refrigerated pasta is a time-pressed cook's secret weapon, cooking up in a flash. Reserved pasta water will give your sauce the right consistency.

Vegetarian Swap: Substitute 10 ounces sliced mushrooms for shrimp.
Flavor Hit: Parmigiano-Reggiano adds a sharp, nutty contrast to the creamy pasta sauce.
Time-Saver: Buy fresh or frozen shrimp that have already been peeled and deveined.

1 (9-ounce) package refrigerated fettuccine
1 pound peeled and deveined medium shrimp
2 green onions, chopped
2 garlic cloves, minced
2 teaspoons olive oil
½ cup (2 ounces) grated Parmigiano-Reggiano cheese
⅓ cup half-and-half
3 tablespoons (1½ ounces) ⅓-less-fat cream cheese
¼ teaspoon freshly ground black pepper
2 tablespoons chopped fresh parsley

1. Cook pasta according to package directions, omitting salt and fat. Drain pasta in a colander over a bowl, reserving ¼ cup cooking liquid. Combine shrimp, onions, and garlic in a small bowl. Heat a large skillet over medium-high heat. Add olive oil; swirl to coat. Add shrimp mixture, and sauté 4 minutes or until shrimp are done. Remove from pan; keep warm.
2. Reduce heat to medium. Add reserved cooking liquid, Parmigiano-Reggiano, half-and-half, cream cheese, and pepper to pan. Cook 2 minutes or until cheeses melt. Combine pasta, cheese mixture, and shrimp mixture. Sprinkle with parsley. Yield: 4 servings (serving size: about 1 cup).

CALORIES 442; **FAT** 14.3g (sat 6.1g, mono 3.1g, poly 1.2g); **PROTEIN** 37.4g; **CARB** 40g; **FIBER** 2.1g; **CHOL** 200mg; **IRON** 3.2mg; **SODIUM** 565mg; **CALC** 256mg

continued

For the Roasted Asparagus:
Combine 2 teaspoons olive oil, ¼ teaspoon salt, ⅛ teaspoon ground red pepper, and 1 pound trimmed asparagus on a jelly-roll pan. Bake at 450° for 6 minutes or until crisp-tender. Serve with lemon wedges. Yield: 4 servings.

CALORIES 43; **FAT** 2.4g (sat 0.4g); **SODIUM** 150mg

READY IN
40
MINUTES

The
SHOPPING LIST

Crab Cakes and Mustard Sauce
prechopped red bell pepper
2 green onions
fresh parsley
canola mayonnaise
Dijon mustard
white wine vinegar
olive oil
panko
1 pound lump crabmeat
reduced-fat sour cream
eggs
ground red pepper

Tomato and Arugula Salad
grape tomatoes
arugula
white wine vinegar

The
GAME PLAN

- Form and dredge cakes.
- Brown cakes.
While cakes cook:
- Prepare sauce.
- Toss salad.

Quick & Easy
Crab Cakes and Spicy Mustard Sauce
With Tomato and Arugula Salad

Make Ahead: Make mustard sauce up to a day ahead; store in an airtight container.
Shopping Tip: Panko has a crisper, airier texture than regular breadcrumbs.
Prep Pointer: Toss salad just before serving so arugula doesn't wilt.

⅓ cup prechopped red bell pepper
2 tablespoons canola mayonnaise
¼ teaspoon kosher salt
¼ teaspoon freshly ground black pepper
2 green onions, chopped
1 large egg, lightly beaten
1 large egg yolk, lightly beaten
1⅓ cups panko (Japanese breadcrumbs), divided
1 pound lump crabmeat, drained and shell pieces removed
2 tablespoons olive oil, divided
2 tablespoons canola mayonnaise
2 tablespoons reduced-fat sour cream
2 teaspoons chopped fresh parsley
2 teaspoons Dijon mustard
1 teaspoon white wine vinegar
⅛ teaspoon ground red pepper

1. Combine first 7 ingredients. Add ⅓ cup panko and crab; toss gently. Divide crab mixture into 8 equal portions; shape each into a ¾-inch-thick patty. Place remaining panko in a shallow dish. Gently dredge patties in panko.
2. Heat a large skillet over medium-high heat. Add 1 tablespoon oil to pan. Add 4 crab cakes to pan; cook 4 minutes on each side. Remove from pan; keep warm. Repeat procedure with remaining oil and crab cakes.
3. Combine 2 tablespoons mayonnaise and remaining ingredients. Serve with crab cakes. Yield: 4 servings (serving size: 2 crab cakes and 1½ tablespoons sauce).

CALORIES 404; **FAT** 23.7g (sat 3.1g, mono 13.5g, poly 5.4g); **PROTEIN** 2g; **CARB** 16.3g; **FIBER** 1.2g; **CHOL** 219mg; **IRON** 1.6mg; **SODIUM** 670mg; **CALC** 149mg

For the Tomato and Arugula Salad:
Combine 2 tablespoons white wine vinegar, 1 tablespoon olive oil, ⅛ teaspoon salt, and 1 pint halved grape tomatoes in a medium bowl. Add 4 cups arugula, and toss. Yield: 4 servings (serving size: ¾ cup).

CALORIES 46; **FAT** 3.5g (sat 0.5g); **SODIUM** 80mg

5-INGREDIENT COOKING

Quick & Easy • Make Ahead
Tuna-Fennel Pasta Salad

Hands-on time: 24 min. Total time: 24 min.

Sure, premium oil-packed tuna is a splurge, but the texture and rich flavor are worth it.

Cook 8 ounces penne (tube–shaped pasta) according to package directions, omitting salt and fat. Drain pasta in a large colander over a bowl, reserving ½ cup cooking liquid. Rinse pasta under cold water; drain. Drain 1 (7.8-ounce) jar solid white tuna packed in oil, reserving 2 tablespoons oil. Grate 2 teaspoons rind from lemon; squeeze 3 tablespoons juice. Combine reserved oil, rind, and juice in a large bowl; stir with a whisk. Add pasta to oil mixture, tossing to coat. Fold in tuna and apple. Remove fronds from 1 small fennel bulb; finely chop fronds to measure 3 tablespoons. Remove and discard stalks. Thinly slice fennel bulb. Stir fronds and sliced fennel into pasta mixture. Add reserved pasta liquid and ½ teaspoon salt, tossing to coat pasta salad evenly. Yield: 4 servings (serving size: 2 cups).

Sustainable Choice

Industry label regulations require solid white tuna to be from the albacore variety.

CALORIES 411; **FAT** 12.1g (sat 1.9g, mono 6.7g, poly 2.4g); **PROTEIN** 23.3g; **CARB** 53.3g; **FIBER** 5.1g; **CHOL** 17mg; **IRON** 2.8mg; **SODIUM** 549mg; **CALC** 52mg

THE FIVE INGREDIENTS

8 ounces uncooked penne
(tube-shaped pasta)

+

1 (7.8-ounce) jar solid white tuna
packed in oil

+

1 lemon

+

1 Fuji apple, sliced (about 1½ cups)

+

1 small fennel bulb with stalks

PREPARING FENNEL

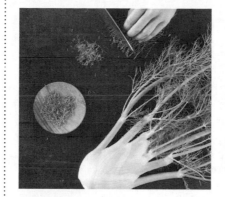

1. Remove fronds; chop.

2. Trim and discard stalks.

3. Cut away fibrous core.

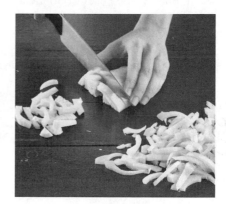

4. Slice trimmed fennel bulb.

USE CRUNCHY FENNEL BULB
EITHER RAW OR COOKED,
AND SAVE SOME OF THE FEATHERY
FRONDS (WHICH LOOK LIKE DILL
BUT TASTE LIKE ANISE) FOR A
DELICATE GARNISH.

TRICKS WITH TREATS

Scary-good sweets with grown-up twists.

Halloween treats are too much fun for kids to have all the fun: sorry, kids. These treats have a nice grown-up kick that will spice things up at your next Halloween party—and they're lighter, too.

Sharp shards of crisp Thai Cashew Brittle combine salty cashews and hot chile paste. The glossy coating on our Cinnamon-Cider Candied Apples contains a splash of brandy. The Peanut Butter Caramel Corn would tempt any dieter. And which of these marshmallows is more devilishly tempting: cocoa-flavored—with a nice bite from dark chocolate drizzle—or orange-and-honey?

All treats can be made ahead, leaving plenty of time to decorate the house, pull together a costume, and spike a vat of witch's brew.

Make Ahead • Kid Friendly
Peanut Butter Caramel Corn

Hands-on time: 30 min. Total time: 1 hr. 30 min.

Cooking spray
2 tablespoons canola oil
1/2 cup unpopped popcorn kernels
1/2 cup sliced almonds
2/3 cup packed brown sugar
2/3 cup light-colored corn syrup
2 1/2 tablespoons butter
1/2 teaspoon salt
1/2 cup creamy peanut butter
1 teaspoon vanilla extract

1. Preheat oven to 250°.
2. Line a jelly-roll pan with parchment paper; coat paper with cooking spray.
3. Heat oil in a large Dutch oven over medium-high heat. Add popcorn; cover and cook 4 minutes, shaking pan frequently. When popping slows, remove pan from heat. Let stand until popping stops. Uncover; add almonds.
4. Combine sugar, syrup, butter, and salt in a medium saucepan; bring to a boil. Cook 3 minutes, stirring occasionally. Remove from heat. Add peanut butter and vanilla; stir until smooth. Drizzle over popcorn; toss well. Spread mixture

out onto prepared pan. Bake at 250° for 1 hour, stirring every 15 minutes. Cool completely. Yield: 20 servings (serving size: about 3/4 cup).

CALORIES 155; FAT 7.4g (sat 1.8g, mono 3.5g, poly 1.6g); PROTEIN 2.6g; CARB 21.3g; FIBER 1.4g; CHOL 4mg; IRON 0.4mg; SODIUM 108mg; CALC 17mg

Make Ahead
Thai Cashew Brittle

Hands-on time: 35 min. Total time: 2 hr. 35 min.

Cooking spray
2 cups sugar
1 cup light-colored corn syrup
1/2 cup water
1 cup coarsely chopped dry-roasted cashews, salted
1 tablespoon butter
1 tablespoon chile paste (sambal oelek)
1 teaspoon baking soda
1 teaspoon grated fresh lemongrass
1 teaspoon grated peeled fresh ginger

1. Line a baking sheet with parchment paper; lightly coat with cooking spray.
2. Combine sugar, corn syrup, and 1/2 cup water in a medium heavy saucepan over medium-high heat, stirring just until combined; bring to a boil.

Cook, without stirring, until a candy thermometer reaches 335°. Remove from heat; stir in cashews and remaining ingredients (mixture will bubble). Quickly pour mixture onto prepared pan, spreading evenly. Cool completely (about 2 hours); break into pieces. Yield: 24 servings.

CALORIES 144; FAT 3.2g (sat 0.8g, mono 1.7g, poly 0.5g); PROTEIN 0.9g; CARB 30.2g; FIBER 0.2g; CHOL 1mg; IRON 0.3mg; SODIUM 118mg; CALC 5mg

Make Ahead
Cinnamon-Cider Candied Apples

Hands-on time: 40 min. Total time: 1 hr. 10 min.

Wash apples well to remove any waxy coating, and dry thoroughly before dipping them. Work quickly, but if the syrup begins to set, you can reheat it over low heat to liquefy.

Cooking spray
1 3/4 cups apple cider
1/2 cup brandy
2/3 cup cinnamon-flavored candies
1 3/4 cups sugar
1/8 teaspoon kosher salt
12 wooden craft sticks
12 small Granny Smith apples, washed and dried

1. Line a baking sheet with parchment paper; coat paper with cooking spray. Combine cider and brandy in a small saucepan; bring to a boil. Cook until reduced to 3/4 cup (about 14 minutes). Add candies to pan, stirring constantly until melted. Add sugar and salt, stirring just until sugar dissolves. Cook, without stirring, until a candy thermometer registers 310° (about 8 minutes). Remove from heat; let cool to 210° (about 15 minutes).
2. Stick craft sticks in apples; dip apples in hot syrup. Place apples on prepared baking sheet; cool until set. Yield: 12 servings (serving size: 1 apple).

CALORIES 272; FAT 0.2g (sat 0.1g, mono 0g, poly 0.1g); PROTEIN 0.5g; CARB 64.1g; FIBER 1.7g; CHOL 0mg; IRON 0.1mg; SODIUM 23mg; CALC 7mg

Bittersweet Chocolate Cookies

Hands-on time: 39 min. Total time: 1 hr. 51 min.

Gingerbread cutters work if you're making skeletons. You can also use 2½-inch cat or bat cutters. Look for meringue powder at craft stores or in the craft section of some big-box retailers.

Cookies:
1 cup granulated sugar
½ cup butter, softened
½ cup canola oil
1 teaspoon vanilla extract
1 large egg
5.6 ounces all-purpose flour (about 1¼ cups)
4.75 ounces whole-wheat flour (about 1 cup)
¾ cup unsweetened dark cocoa
½ teaspoon salt

Icing:
1 tablespoon water
1 teaspoon meringue powder
1 tablespoon 2% reduced-fat milk
¼ teaspoon vanilla extract
2 cups powdered sugar

1. To prepare cookies, place first 3 ingredients in a large bowl; beat with a mixer at medium speed until well blended. Add 1 teaspoon vanilla and egg; beat until well blended.
2. Weigh or lightly spoon flours into dry measuring cups, and level with a knife. Combine flours, cocoa, and salt, stirring with a whisk. Add flour mixture to sugar mixture; beat at low speed just until flour is incorporated.
3. Place half of dough between 2 sheets of plastic wrap; roll to a ¼-inch thickness. Repeat procedure with remaining dough. Place dough (still wrapped in plastic wrap) on a baking sheet. Chill 45 minutes or until firm.
4. Preheat oven to 375°.
5. Cut dough with a 2½- to 3-inch cutter to form 40 cookies (reroll scraps as necessary). Arrange 20 cookies on a baking sheet lined with parchment paper (keep remaining cookies chilled). Bake at 375° for 9 minutes or until set.

Cool on pan on a wire rack 5 minutes; remove cookies from pan. Cool completely on wire rack. Repeat procedure with remaining dough.
6. To prepare icing, combine 1 tablespoon water and meringue powder in a medium bowl, stirring with a whisk until smooth. Add milk and ¼ teaspoon vanilla. Add powdered sugar, stirring until smooth. Spoon icing into a small zip-top plastic bag. Snip a tiny hole in 1 bottom corner of bag; pipe designs on cookies. Yield: 40 servings (serving size: 1 cookie).

CALORIES 118; FAT 6.1g (sat 1.7g, mono 2.4g, poly 0.9g); PROTEIN 1.2g; CARB 16.7g; FIBER 0.6g; CHOL 11mg; IRON 0.6mg; SODIUM 48mg; CALC 4mg

Chocolate Spider Cupcakes

Hands-on time: 42 min. Total time: 1 hr. 50 min.

To make spiderweb designs on cupcakes, pipe concentric circles and drag a wooden pick through wet frosting. For kid-friendly cupcakes, use water instead of bourbon in the frosting.

Cupcakes:
4 ounces cake flour (about 1 cup)
⅓ cup unsweetened cocoa
½ teaspoon baking soda
⅛ teaspoon salt
¾ cup granulated sugar
¼ cup butter, softened
2 large eggs
1 teaspoon vanilla extract
½ cup low-fat buttermilk
1 ounce bittersweet chocolate, finely chopped and melted

Icing:
½ cup packed brown sugar
2 tablespoons bourbon
3 large egg whites
½ teaspoon cream of tartar
⅛ teaspoon salt
¼ cup butter, softened
1 teaspoon meringue powder
1 tablespoon water
1 cup powdered sugar
Black food coloring

1. Preheat oven to 350°.
2. To prepare cupcakes, weigh or lightly spoon flour into a dry measuring cup; level with a knife. Combine flour, cocoa, baking soda, and ⅛ teaspoon salt, stirring with a whisk.
3. Place ¾ cup sugar and ¼ cup butter in a large bowl; beat with a mixer at medium speed until well combined (about 3 minutes). Add eggs and vanilla, beating well. Add flour mixture and buttermilk alternately to egg mixture, beginning and ending with flour mixture. Fold in chocolate. Spoon batter into 12 muffin cups lined with muffin cup liners. Bake at 350° for 18 minutes or until a wooden pick inserted in center comes out with moist crumbs clinging. Remove from pan; cool completely on a wire rack.
4. To prepare icing, combine ½ cup brown sugar and bourbon in a saucepan; bring to a boil. Cook, without stirring, 3 minutes or until a candy thermometer registers 250°. Combine egg whites, cream of tartar, and ⅛ teaspoon salt in a large bowl; using clean, dry beaters, beat with a mixer at high speed until foamy. Pour hot sugar syrup in a thin stream over egg whites, beating at high speed until stiff peaks form, about 3 minutes. Reduce mixer speed to low, and continue beating until egg white mixture cools (about 3 minutes).
5. Place ¼ cup butter in a large bowl; beat until light and fluffy. Fold in 1 cup egg white mixture. Fold butter mixture into remaining egg white mixture. Spread about 3 tablespoons icing over each cooled cupcake. Combine meringue powder and 1 tablespoon water in a bowl, stirring with a whisk until smooth. Add powdered sugar, beating with a mixer at medium speed until thick and smooth. Stir in black food coloring to desired shade. Scrape powdered sugar mixture into a zip-top plastic bag, and snip a tiny hole in 1 corner of bag. Pipe black spiders or webs over frosted cupcakes. Yield: 12 servings (serving size: 1 cupcake).

CALORIES 280; FAT 10g (sat 5.7g, mono 2.3g, poly 0.5g); PROTEIN 4g; CARB 43.9g; FIBER 0.8g; CHOL 56mg; IRON 1.5mg; SODIUM 196mg; CALC 30mg

Honey-Orange Marshmallows

Hands-on time: 50 min. Total time: 2 hr. 50 min.

1 cup water, divided
3 (¼-ounce) packages unflavored gelatin
1½ cups granulated sugar
¾ cup light-colored corn syrup
¼ cup orange blossom honey
Dash of salt
1 teaspoon vanilla extract
5 drops orange oil
20 drops orange food coloring
Cooking spray
⅓ cup powdered sugar
⅓ cup cornstarch

1. Pour ½ cup water into a small microwave-safe bowl, and sprinkle with gelatin.
2. Combine remaining ½ cup water, granulated sugar, corn syrup, honey, and salt in a medium heavy saucepan over medium-high heat; bring to a boil, stirring occasionally. Cook, without stirring, until a candy thermometer registers 250°. Pour sugar mixture into the bowl of a stand mixer, and let stand until a candy thermometer registers 210°.
3. Microwave gelatin mixture at HIGH 20 seconds or until gelatin melts, stirring after 10 seconds. With mixer on low speed, beat sugar mixture using a whip attachment; gradually pour gelatin mixture in a thin stream into sugar mixture. Add vanilla, orange oil, and food coloring. Increase speed to high; whip mixture at high speed until light and fluffy (about 5 minutes). Using a spatula coated with cooking spray, scrape mixture into an 11 x 7–inch baking pan coated with cooking spray; smooth top. Let stand 2 hours.
4. Sift together powdered sugar and cornstarch into a jelly-roll pan. Using an offset spatula coated with cooking spray, remove marshmallow from pan and place into powdered sugar mixture. Using scissors well dusted with powdered sugar mixture, cut marshmallows into 78 (1-inch) squares. Dust with powdered sugar mixture; shake marshmallows lightly to remove excess sugar mixture. Yield: 26 servings (serving size: 3 marshmallows).

CALORIES 99; FAT 0g; PROTEIN 0.7g; CARB 25.1g; FIBER 0g; CHOL 0mg; IRON 0mg; SODIUM 14mg; CALC 2mg

Chocolate Marshmallows

Hands-on time: 50 min. Total time: 2 hr. 50 min.

1 cup water, divided
3 (¼-ounce) packages unflavored gelatin
1½ cups granulated sugar
1 cup light-colored corn syrup
Dash of salt
1 teaspoon vanilla extract
¼ cup sifted unsweetened cocoa
Cooking spray
⅓ cup powdered sugar
⅓ cup cornstarch
2 teaspoons unsweetened cocoa
2 ounces bittersweet chocolate, chopped

1. Pour ½ cup water into a small microwave-safe bowl, and sprinkle with gelatin.
2. Combine remaining ½ cup water, sugar, corn syrup, and salt in a medium heavy saucepan over medium-high heat; bring to a boil, stirring occasionally. Cook, without stirring, until a candy thermometer registers 250°. Pour sugar mixture into the bowl of a stand mixer; let stand until a candy thermometer registers 210°.
3. Microwave gelatin mixture at HIGH 20 seconds or until gelatin melts, stirring after 10 seconds. With mixer on low speed, beat sugar mixture using a whip attachment; gradually pour gelatin mixture in a thin stream into sugar mixture. Add 1 teaspoon vanilla. Increase speed to high; whip mixture at high speed until light and fluffy (about 5 minutes). Reduce mixer to medium speed, and gradually add ¼ cup cocoa; beat until combined. Using a spatula coated with cooking spray, scrape mixture into an 11 x 7–inch baking pan coated with cooking spray; smooth top. Let stand 2 hours.
4. Sift together powdered sugar, cornstarch, and 2 teaspoons cocoa into a jelly-roll pan. Using an offset spatula coated with cooking spray, remove marshmallow from pan; place in sugar mixture. Using scissors well coated with powdered sugar mixture, cut marshmallows into 78 (1-inch) squares. Dust with powdered sugar mixture; shake to remove excess sugar mixture.
5. Arrange marshmallows on a cooling rack placed on a rimmed baking sheet. Place bittersweet chocolate in a small microwave-safe bowl; microwave at HIGH 1 minute or until melted, stirring every 20 seconds until smooth. Drizzle melted chocolate over marshmallows; let stand until chocolate is set. Yield: 26 servings (serving size: 3 marshmallows).

CALORIES 112; FAT 1.1g (sat 0.6g, mono 0.1g, poly 0g); PROTEIN 1.1g; CARB 26.7g; FIBER 0.5g; CHOL 0mg; IRON 0.2mg; SODIUM 16mg; CALC 4mg

FOR MORE PRONOUNCED CHOCOLATE FLAVOR, INCREASE THE COCOA POWDER IN THE MARSHMALLOWS.

FOR THE LOVE OF A PERFECT PEAR

What's not to adore about fall's most luscious fruit? Thin skins give way to creamy, juicy flesh that's a pleasure, raw or cooked, in desserts, salads, and more.

Pears are a truly seasonal crop, and all the more wonderful for it. Most of the year, if you do happen upon a pear in the supermarket, it's usually an Anjou, often rock-hard, and probably not worth the bother. Then, around September, the Bartlett, Bosc, and Comice begin to pop up. By October it's a pear profusion, with lovely colors echoing fall-leaf tones: russet, crimson, gold, and chartreuse. And that flavor! That texture! A ripe pear is plump and juicy, gorgeously sweet, with a pleasing give to the bite and a faint grittiness. The taste is hauntingly subtle, yet also strong and unlike any other. Explore the varieties. Get to know the Comice, Seckel, and Starkrimson, and be inspired to include them in your cooking. These recipes show off pears' affinity for nuts, cheese, and warm spices—other great flavors of fall.

Make Ahead • Kid Friendly
Vegetarian

Pear and Gruyère Strata

Hands-on time: 20 min. Total time: 9 hr. 25 min.

Think of this as stuffed French toast in a casserole. Here, sweet cinnamon bread meets juicy pears and the savory bite of Gruyère cheese. You want a pear variety that will hold its shape and won't exude too much moisture as the strata bakes—we liked Anjou and Concorde.

4 cups sliced peeled Anjou or Concorde pear
2 teaspoons butter, melted
6 tablespoons granulated sugar, divided
12 (1-ounce) slices cinnamon swirl bread (such as Pepperidge Farm), cut in half diagonally
Cooking spray
1 cup (4 ounces) shredded Gruyère cheese
1½ cups 1% low-fat milk
1 cup egg substitute
½ teaspoon ground cinnamon
1 tablespoon turbinado sugar
½ cup maple syrup

1. Combine pear, butter, and 1 tablespoon sugar in a large bowl, and toss gently.
2. Arrange half of bread in an 11 x 7–inch glass or ceramic baking dish coated with cooking spray. Spoon pear mixture evenly over bread; top evenly with cheese. Arrange remaining bread over cheese.
3. Combine remaining 5 tablespoons granulated sugar, milk, egg substitute, and cinnamon, stirring with a whisk. Pour milk mixture over bread, pressing down to submerge. Cover and chill 8 hours or overnight.
4. Preheat oven to 350°.
5. Uncover dish. Sprinkle turbinado sugar evenly over bread. Bake at 350° for 55 minutes or until a knife inserted in center comes out clean. Let stand 10 minutes. Cut into 8 equal pieces; drizzle with syrup. Yield: 8 servings (serving size: 1 strata piece and 1 tablespoon syrup).

CALORIES 355; **FAT** 10g (sat 4.3g, mono 3.7g, poly 0.6g); **PROTEIN** 13.1g; **CARB** 55.1g; **FIBER** 5.3g; **CHOL** 20mg; **IRON** 1.6mg; **SODIUM** 295mg; **CALC** 216mg

Vegetarian

Whole Roasted Endives with Pear, Arugula, and Walnut Salad

Hands-on time: 35 min. Total time: 50 min.

1 cup apple cider
1 teaspoon sugar
2 whole cloves
1 (2-inch) cinnamon stick
1 small bay leaf
1 teaspoon olive oil
4 heads Belgian endive, halved lengthwise
³⁄₈ teaspoon salt, divided
½ teaspoon freshly ground black pepper, divided
1 tablespoon fresh lemon juice
1 tablespoon toasted walnut oil or olive oil
4 cups arugula
¼ cup chopped walnuts, toasted
1 large ripe Bosc pear, cored and thinly sliced

1. Preheat oven to 450°.
2. Combine first 5 ingredients in a small saucepan; bring to a boil. Cook until reduced to ⅓ cup (about 20 minutes). Strain cider mixture through a sieve into a bowl; discard solids.
3. Brush olive oil on a baking sheet; arrange endive halves, cut sides down, on prepared pan. Brush 2 tablespoons cider mixture over endive; sprinkle with ⅛ teaspoon salt and ¼ teaspoon pepper. Bake at 450° for 10 minutes. Remove from oven; turn endive halves over. Brush cut sides with 2 tablespoons cider mixture.
4. Preheat broiler.
5. Broil endive 4 minutes or until edges begin to brown.
6. Combine remaining ¼ teaspoon salt, remaining ¼ teaspoon pepper, remaining cider mixture, lemon juice, and walnut oil in a large bowl, stirring with a whisk. Add arugula, walnuts, and pear, tossing to coat. Arrange 2 endive halves on each of 4 salad plates, and top each serving with 1½ cups arugula mixture. Yield: 4 servings (serving size: 1 salad).

CALORIES 180; **FAT** 9.7g (sat 1g, mono 2.3g, poly 5.9g); **PROTEIN** 3.1g; **CARB** 23.5g; **FIBER** 5.8g; **CHOL** 0mg; **IRON** 0.9mg; **SODIUM** 230mg; **CALC** 66mg

A PANOPLY OF PEARS

These are the varieties you are most likely to see.

ANJOU Available in red and green, this is the most abundant variety and usually the one you'll find year-round. Juicy, slightly dense flesh makes this pear great for raw and cooked uses—salads, snacks, chutneys, and pies.

BARTLETT Deep, quintessential pear flavor and intense pear-floral aroma make this variety a favorite. You'll find both green and red Bartletts. They perform well in raw and cooked dishes.

BOSC Firm texture (even when ripe) and gorgeously russeted brown skin differentiate this variety. Because it holds its shape well, the Bosc is the go-to for poaching and preserve-making.

COMICE Arguably the most delicious variety for eating fresh, these are buttery-creamy, juicy, and highly sweet. Because they drip with juice, they're best to eat raw and may not cook well.

CONCORDE This pale-green pear has a firm texture and resists browning when cut, making it perfect for a fruit tray or cheese plate. It is also a good choice for pies, crisps, chutneys, and other cooked dishes.

FORELLE Stunning petite variety that boasts green skin spotted with red freckles. The fruit is slightly crisp with a tart-sweet flavor.

SECKEL The smallest commercially grown variety, Seckels are often used as garnishes. They're very sweet, though, and should be enjoyed for snacking, too.

STARKRIMSON Crimson skin contrasts milky-white flesh in this beautiful variety. Its juicy texture, floral aroma, and striking color are best enjoyed in raw applications like salads.

Make Ahead • Vegetarian

Pear Chutney Bruschetta with Pecans and Blue Cheese

Hands-on time: 10 min. Total time: 35 min.

Sweet-tangy chutney pairs beautifully with pungent blue cheese and toasty pecans.

2 teaspoons olive oil
1/4 cup finely chopped shallots
1 1/2 cups finely chopped peeled Anjou, Bartlett, or Bosc pear
1/2 cup pear nectar
1/4 cup finely chopped dried apricots
2 tablespoons sugar
1 1/2 tablespoons cider vinegar
1/8 teaspoon salt
1 (3-inch) cinnamon stick
4 ounces French bread baguette, cut diagonally into 16 thin slices and toasted
8 teaspoons chopped pecans, toasted
8 teaspoons crumbled blue cheese
1 tablespoon chopped fresh chives
1 teaspoon chopped fresh thyme

1. Heat a small saucepan over medium-high heat. Add olive oil to pan; swirl to coat. Add shallots, and sauté 2 minutes or until soft. Add pear and next 6 ingredients; bring to a boil. Reduce heat to medium; cook 20 minutes or until pear is tender and mixture is thick. Cool to room temperature. Discard cinnamon stick.
2. Spoon about 1 1/2 tablespoons chutney over each baguette slice; top each with 1/2 teaspoon pecans and 1/2 teaspoon cheese. Sprinkle evenly with chopped chives and thyme. Yield: 8 servings (serving size: 2 topped bruschetta).

CALORIES 124; **FAT** 3.6g (sat 0.8g, mono 2g, poly 0.7g); **PROTEIN** 2.4g; **CARB** 21.9g; **FIBER** 1.7g; **CHOL** 2.1mg; **IRON** 0.8mg; **SODIUM** 170mg; **CALC** 24mg

---

FALL'S FINEST

Pears cook down to a buttery softness in this bruschetta; the juicy snap of raw pear slices enlivens the roasted endive salad (page 277).

Make Ahead • Kid Friendly

Frangipane Pear Tarts

Hands-on time: 40 min. Total time: 1 hr. 5 min.

Sheets of crisp, paper-thin phyllo dough encase a filling of toasted ground almonds, with red-skinned pears as the crowning touch. We call for Anjou, but you can also use Bartlett, Bosc, or Concorde pears.

2/3 cup blanched whole almonds, toasted
1/2 cup sugar
2 tablespoons butter, divided
3/4 teaspoon vanilla extract
1/8 teaspoon salt
1 large egg
12 (14 x 9-inch) sheets frozen phyllo dough, thawed
Cooking spray
2 red Anjou pears, cored and thinly sliced
2 tablespoons apple jelly

1. Preheat oven to 375°.
2. Place almonds and sugar in a food processor; process until very finely ground. Add 1 1/2 teaspoons butter, vanilla, salt, and egg; process to form a sticky paste.
3. Place remaining 1 1/2 tablespoons butter in a small microwave-safe bowl; microwave at HIGH 20 seconds or until butter melts. Arrange 1 phyllo sheet on a cutting board or other work surface (cover remaining phyllo to keep from drying); brush lightly with butter. Top with another phyllo sheet; brush lightly with butter. Fold phyllo stack in half lengthwise to form a 9 x 7-inch stack. Loosely fold edges of phyllo up toward the center to create a 4 1/2-inch rimmed tart shell. Place on a baking sheet lined with parchment paper; coat phyllo shell with cooking spray. Repeat procedure with remaining phyllo sheets, butter, and cooking spray to form 6 shells.
4. Spread about 2 tablespoons almond mixture over each tart shell; top each with about 6 slightly overlapping pear slices. Bake at 375° for 23 minutes or until phyllo is browned and crisp.
5. Place jelly in a small microwave-safe bowl; microwave at HIGH 20 seconds or until jelly melts. Brush jelly evenly

over tarts. Yield: 6 servings (serving size: 1 tart).

CALORIES 314; FAT 14g (sat 3.6g, mono 7.1g, poly 2.4g); PROTEIN 6.2g; CARB 43.6g; FIBER 3.9g; CHOL 45.4mg; IRON 1.5mg; SODIUM 185mg; CALC 48mg

Honey-Wheat Pizza with Pear-Prosciutto Salad

Hands-on time: 24 min. Total time: 2 hr. 8 min.

A showy, crimson-skinned pear is beautiful here, but any pear variety you like will work.

1 cup warm water (100° to 110°)
1 tablespoon honey
2 tablespoons extra-virgin olive oil, divided
1½ teaspoons dry yeast
9 ounces all-purpose flour (about 2 cups)
2.38 ounces whole-wheat flour (about ½ cup)
¾ teaspoon kosher salt
Cooking spray
1½ cups (6 ounces) crumbled goat cheese
1 tablespoon cornmeal
4 cups fresh mâche or baby spinach
2 teaspoons chopped fresh thyme
2 teaspoons fresh lemon juice
½ teaspoon freshly ground black pepper
3 ounces very thinly sliced prosciutto, chopped
2 ripe Starkrimson or red Bartlett pears, cored and thinly sliced

1. Combine 1 cup warm water, honey, and 1 teaspoon oil in a small bowl, stirring with a whisk. Stir in yeast; let stand 10 minutes. Weigh or lightly spoon flours into dry measuring cups; level with a knife. Combine flours and salt in a food processor, and pulse 2 times or until blended. Add yeast mixture, pulsing to combine (dough will feel sticky). Turn dough out onto a floured surface; knead lightly 3 to 4 times.
2. Place dough in a large bowl coated with cooking spray, turning to coat top. Cover and let rise in a warm place (85°), free from drafts, 1 hour or until doubled in size. (Gently press two fingers into dough. If indentation

remains, dough has risen enough.) Punch dough down; cover and let rest 10 minutes.
3. Preheat oven to 450°.
4. Place a baking sheet in oven. Roll dough into a 14-inch circle on a floured surface. Brush dough evenly with 1 tablespoon oil, and sprinkle evenly with cheese. Place dough on a baking sheet sprinkled with 1 tablespoon cornmeal. Transfer dough carefully to preheated pan; bake at 450° for 12 minutes or until crust is crisp and golden. Combine remaining 2 teaspoons oil, mâche, and remaining ingredients; toss to combine. Arrange salad over crust. Yield: 6 servings (serving size: 1 slice).

CALORIES 393; FAT 12.7g (sat 5.2g, mono 5.3g, poly 0.9g); PROTEIN 18.1g; CARB 56.8g; FIBER 5.3g; CHOL 21mg; IRON 3.7mg; SODIUM 559mg; CALC 95mg

WHAT TO EAT RIGHT NOW
APPLES

The return of the righteous ripe apple is upon us, as dozens of obscure and heirloom varieties tumble into farmers' markets from coast to coast. Thank goodness for the tough old trees that lingered on out-of-the-way land, waiting for their fruits to be rediscovered. The flavors, textures, and colors—even the inside colors, as with lovely, pink-fleshed Hidden Rose—are there to be discovered. October is peak apple time. Get crunching.

TOP HEIRLOOM PICKS

HIDDEN ROSE Notes of fresh, tart cranberry and wine with a pleasant perfumy, floral scent.

ASHMEAD'S KERNEL Tart and crisp. Tastes of citrus and Champagne.

WINESAP Best for juicing and baking. Sweet-tart flavor with hints of wine and spice.

TOMPKINS KING A juicy jumbo-sized apple with the perfect balance of sweet and tart.

Quick & Easy
Serrano, Manchego, and Apple Sandwiches

Hands-on time: 20 min. Total time: 20 min.

Ashmead's Kernel, a very old English apple, is smallish and lumpy with a russet exterior that blankets the green skin. We like its crisp flavor here, though any apple would work.

1½ tablespoons canola mayonnaise
2 teaspoons Dijon mustard, divided
4 (1-ounce) slices sourdough bread, toasted
¼ cup sliced shallot
4 ounces paper-thin sliced serrano ham or prosciutto
⅓ cup (1½ ounces) shredded Manchego cheese
½ teaspoon black pepper, divided
1 tablespoon olive oil
1 teaspoon sherry vinegar
2 cups arugula
1 tart apple, peeled, cored, and thinly sliced

1. Preheat broiler.
2. Combine mayonnaise and 1 teaspoon mustard; spread mayonnaise mixture over each bread slice. Top each slice with 1 tablespoon shallot, 1 ounce ham, and 4 teaspoons cheese, and sprinkle evenly with ¼ teaspoon pepper. Broil 3 minutes. Combine remaining 1 teaspoon mustard, oil, and vinegar. Combine arugula and apple slices in a bowl; drizzle with vinaigrette. Toss gently. Divide apple mixture evenly among sandwiches, and sprinkle with remaining ¼ teaspoon pepper. Yield: 4 servings (serving size: 1 sandwich).

CALORIES 298; FAT 15.2g (sat 4.3g, mono 6g, poly 2.2g); PROTEIN 14.7g; CARB 27.3g; FIBER 2.4g; CHOL 29mg; IRON 2.5mg; SODIUM 790mg; CALC 213mg

DID YOU KNOW?

The preference for big, durable, unblemished fruit ensured that a tiny number of apple varieties would dominate supermarket sales. Heirlooms can be odd-shaped and even ugly, belying their delicious flavor.

START WITH A POUND OF GROUND BEEF...

... and turn out one of our six delicious dishes, including an Italian ragù over polenta, comforting all-American meat loaf, and chipotle-spiked meatballs in a new take on tortilla soup.

Ground beef is America's favorite go-to meat for good reason. It's cheap and versatile—you can shape it into meatballs or loaves, crumble it into chilis or casseroles. But if it's an American standard, it also requires a canny customer. The two main issues: What's the cut, and how much fat is there? We prefer leaner ground sirloin and even think it's worth experimenting with grass-fed meat to see if you like the flavor. Use our handy guide on page 281 to ensure you get a beautifully beefy serving with much less fat.

Quick & Easy • Make Ahead
Kid Friendly

Quick Pastitsio

Hands-on time: 17 min. Total time: 40 min.

Use any short pasta—ziti or rotini also work.

8 ounces uncooked penne (tube-shaped pasta)
Cooking spray
1 pound ground sirloin
1 tablespoon olive oil
1½ cups chopped onion
5 garlic cloves, minced
¾ teaspoon kosher salt
1 tablespoon all-purpose flour
2 cups fat-free milk
1 (14.5-ounce) can diced tomatoes, drained
½ cup (4 ounces) ⅓-less-fat cream cheese
1 (3-ounce) package fat-free cream cheese
¾ cup (3 ounces) shredded part-skim mozzarella cheese
2 tablespoons chopped fresh flat-leaf parsley

1. Preheat broiler.
2. Cook pasta according to package directions, omitting salt and fat. Drain.
3. Heat a large skillet over medium-high heat. Coat pan with cooking spray. Add beef to pan; sauté 5 minutes or until browned, stirring to crumble. Remove beef from pan; drain. Wipe pan clean with paper towels. Add oil to pan; swirl to coat. Add onion; sauté 4 minutes, stirring occasionally. Add garlic; sauté 1 minute, stirring constantly. Add beef; sprinkle with salt. Add flour; cook 1 minute, stirring frequently. Stir in milk, tomatoes, and cream cheeses, stirring until smooth; bring to a simmer. Cook 2 minutes or until thoroughly heated. Stir in pasta.
4. Spoon pasta mixture into a 13 x 9–inch broiler-safe baking dish coated with cooking spray. Sprinkle mozzarella evenly over top. Broil 4 minutes or until golden. Sprinkle with parsley. Yield: 6 servings (serving size: 1⅓ cups).

CALORIES 431; FAT 15.9g (sat 6.9g, mono 6.1g, poly 0.7g); PROTEIN 27.8g; CARB 41.9g; FIBER 1.9g; CHOL 61mg; IRON 2.43mg; SODIUM 679mg; CALC 289mg

Make Ahead

Tortilla Meatball Soup
(pictured on page 234)

Hands-on time: 43 min. Total time: 1 hr. 30 min.

If you can't find fresh corn on the cob, substitute 2 cups frozen corn kernels, and broil them with peppers. Use extra chipotle chiles to spice up a pot of beans, rice, stews, or canola mayonnaise.

2 jalapeño peppers
1 red bell pepper
2 ears corn on the cob
4 (6-inch) corn tortillas, cut into ½-inch-thick strips
Cooking spray
¾ teaspoon kosher salt, divided
6 garlic cloves, minced and divided
⅓ cup panko (Japanese breadcrumbs)
1 pound ground sirloin
1 large egg, lightly beaten
1 chipotle chile, canned in adobo sauce, minced
1 tablespoon olive oil
2 cups chopped onion
2 cups (¾-inch) cubed red potatoes
1 cup (½-inch-thick) slices carrot
3 cups fat-free, lower-sodium chicken broth
2 cups water
½ cup (2 ounces) shredded Monterey Jack cheese
¼ cup (1 ounce) shredded extra-sharp cheddar cheese
½ cup chopped fresh cilantro

1. Preheat broiler.
2. Cut jalapeños and bell pepper in half lengthwise; discard seeds and membranes. Place pepper halves, skin sides up, on a foil-lined baking sheet. Arrange corn on baking sheet with peppers. Broil 4 to 6 minutes or until blackened, turning corn once. Place peppers in a paper bag; fold to seal. Let stand 15 minutes; peel. Mince jalapeños, and coarsely chop bell pepper. Cut corn kernels from cobs. Set aside.
3. Place tortilla strips in a single layer on a baking sheet; lightly coat with cooking spray. Broil 3 minutes or until golden brown, turning after 2 minutes. Set aside.
4. Combine ¼ teaspoon salt, 1 garlic clove, panko, and next 3 ingredients in

a large bowl, and gently mix until just combined. With moist hands, shape meat mixture into 24 meatballs (about 2 tablespoons each).

5. Place a Dutch oven over medium-high heat. Add oil to pan; swirl to coat. Add meatballs to pan; sauté for 8 minutes, turning to brown on all sides. Remove from pan. Add onion, potatoes, and carrot to pan; sauté 5 minutes, stirring occasionally. Add remaining 5 garlic cloves; cook 1 minute, stirring constantly. Add peppers, broth, and 2 cups water; bring to a boil. Reduce heat; simmer 20 minutes or until vegetables are almost tender, stirring occasionally. Return meatballs to pan. Add remaining ½ teaspoon salt and corn; return to a simmer. Cook 10 minutes or until meatballs are done. Ladle 1½ cups soup into each of 6 bowls; top each serving with 4 teaspoons Monterey Jack cheese, 2 teaspoons cheddar cheese, and 4 teaspoons cilantro. Top evenly with tortilla strips. Yield: 6 servings.

CALORIES 380; **FAT** 16.3g (sat 6.5g, mono 6.1g, poly 1g); **PROTEIN** 25g; **CARB** 33.1g; **FIBER** 4.7g; **CHOL** 98mg; **IRON** 3mg; **SODIUM** 631mg; **CALC** 159mg

---

Make Ahead • Kid Friendly
Classic Meat Loaf

Hands-on time: 12 min. Total time: 57 min.

This is the iconic, traditional meat loaf like your mom used to make (or that you wished your mom would make). Mix the ingredients gently, just until combined, and don't compact the meat when shaping the loaf for best results. For extra pizzazz, garnish with parsley.

Cooking spray
½ cup chopped onion
6 tablespoons ketchup, divided
½ cup panko (Japanese breadcrumbs)
¼ cup chopped fresh flat-leaf parsley
1 teaspoon Worcestershire sauce
¾ teaspoon dried oregano
¼ teaspoon salt
¼ teaspoon freshly ground black pepper
1 pound ground sirloin
1 large egg white

1. Preheat oven to 350°.
2. Heat a small skillet over medium heat. Coat pan with cooking spray. Add onion to pan; cook 6 minutes or until tender, stirring occasionally. Remove from heat; cool slightly. Combine onion, 3 tablespoons ketchup, and remaining ingredients in a bowl, and gently stir just until combined.
3. Place meat mixture on a baking sheet coated with cooking spray; shape into an 8 x 4–inch loaf. Brush top of loaf with remaining 3 tablespoons ketchup. Bake at 350° for 35 minutes or until a thermometer registers 160°. Let stand 10 minutes; cut into 8 slices. Yield: 4 servings (serving size: 2 slices).

CALORIES 264; **FAT** 11.8g (sat 4.6g, mono 5g, poly 0.4g); **PROTEIN** 25.3g; **CARB** 13.3g; **FIBER** 0.9g; **CHOL** 74mg; **IRON** 3.1mg; **SODIUM** 525mg; **CALC** 33mg

---

GROUND BEEF KNOW-HOW

When shopping, you'll find lots of choices but inconsistent labeling. Some packages tout the cut of beef (like ground chuck). Others list percentages or ratios that may be confusing, like 90/10. Beef with 10% fat by weight gets 51% of its calories from fat because fat is more caloric than meat. Know these terms:

GROUND HAMBURGER Ground from the trimmings of any cut of beef. Fat can be added, but the total fat content allowable is capped at a whopping 30% by weight (81% calories from fat, raw).

GROUND BEEF Like hamburger but no added fat.

GROUND CHUCK Beef ground from the chuck (shoulder section) that contains about 15% to 20% fat (63% to 71% calories from fat, raw).

GROUND ROUND From the round (rump to hind leg), about 10% to 15% fat (51% to 63% calories from fat, raw)

GROUND SIRLOIN We like beef ground from the lean sirloin, which contains about 8% to 10% fat (up to 51% calories from fat, raw). In a recent blind tasting of several types of ground sirloin (grain-fed, organic, grass-fed, and Angus), the beefy tasting grass-fed was the unanimous winner.

Quick & Easy
Thai Beef Cabbage Cups

Hands-on time: 27 min. Total time: 27 min.

In Thailand, the spicy ground beef mixture is called larb. Serve with lime wedges.

2½ teaspoons dark sesame oil, divided
2 teaspoons minced peeled fresh ginger
3 garlic cloves, minced
1 pound ground sirloin
1 tablespoon sugar
2 tablespoons fresh lime juice
1½ tablespoons fish sauce
1 tablespoon water
¼ teaspoon crushed red pepper
½ cup vertically sliced red onion
½ cup chopped fresh cilantro
8 large green cabbage leaves
2 tablespoons finely chopped unsalted, dry-roasted peanuts

1. Heat a large nonstick skillet over medium-high heat. Add 2 teaspoons oil to pan; swirl to coat. Add ginger and garlic; cook 1 minute, stirring constantly. Add beef; cook 5 minutes or until browned, stirring to crumble.
2. Combine remaining ½ teaspoon oil, sugar, and next 4 ingredients in a large bowl. Add beef mixture, onion, and cilantro; toss well. Place 2 cabbage leaves on each of 4 plates; divide beef mixture evenly among leaves. Top each serving with 1½ teaspoons peanuts. Yield: 4 servings (serving size: 2 filled cabbage leaves).

CALORIES 292; **FAT** 16.7g (sat 5.4g, mono 7.3g, poly 2.4g); **PROTEIN** 25.4g; **CARB** 10.9g; **FIBER** 2.4g; **CHOL** 74mg; **IRON** 3.1mg; **SODIUM** 516mg; **CALC** 51mg

Italian-Style Beef with Polenta

Hands-on time: 40 min. Total time: 40 min.

This hearty meat sauce with cheesy polenta is a nice change from spaghetti.

1 cup dry coarse-ground polenta
1 teaspoon dried oregano
Dash of kosher salt
2 cups water
1 cup 2% reduced-fat milk
¾ cup (3 ounces) grated Parmigiano-Reggiano cheese, divided
Cooking spray
1 pound ground sirloin
1 cup chopped onion
1 teaspoon crushed red pepper
⅛ teaspoon kosher salt
3 garlic cloves, minced
2 cups lower-sodium marinara sauce
½ cup torn fresh basil

1. Place first 3 ingredients in a large saucepan. Gradually add 2 cups water and milk, stirring constantly with a whisk. Bring to a boil; reduce heat to medium, and cook 20 minutes, stirring frequently. Stir in ⅓ cup cheese.
2. Heat a nonstick skillet over medium-high heat; coat with cooking spray. Add beef; sauté 5 minutes. Stir to crumble. Remove beef; drain. Wipe pan; coat with cooking spray. Add onion, pepper, ⅛ teaspoon salt, and garlic; sauté 4 minutes, stirring frequently. Add beef and sauce; simmer 8 minutes.
3. Divide polenta evenly among 4 shallow bowls. Top each serving with 1 cup beef mixture; sprinkle with 2 teaspoons cheese and 2 tablespoons basil. Yield: 4 servings.

CALORIES 487; FAT 15.5g (sat 7.2g, mono 5.3g, poly 0.6g); PROTEIN 29.3g; CARB 80.9g; FIBER 5g; CHOL 73mg; IRON 3.2mg; SODIUM 695mg; CALC 266mg

Chili-Corn Chip Pie

Hands-on time: 40 min. Total time: 40 min.

This recipe is a healthy version of Chili Pie. Often served from concession stands at fairs, festivals, and sporting events, this crowd-pleaser usually involves splitting the bag of chips open, ladling chili into the bag, and then topping with cheese, onions, and other garnishes.

Cooking spray
1 pound ground sirloin
1¼ cups chopped onion
6 garlic cloves, minced
½ teaspoon ground cumin
½ teaspoon ground red pepper
⅛ teaspoon kosher salt
1 tablespoon no-salt-added tomato paste
1 cup fat-free, lower-sodium beef broth
⅓ cup water
1 (10-ounce) can diced tomatoes and green chiles, undrained
4 ounces lightly salted corn chips
⅓ cup (1½ ounces) shredded sharp cheddar cheese
¼ cup fat-free sour cream
½ cup diagonally sliced green onion tops

1. Heat a large skillet over medium-high heat. Coat pan with cooking spray. Add beef to pan; sauté 5 minutes, stirring to crumble. Remove beef; drain. Wipe pan clean with paper towels. Add onion to pan; sauté 4 minutes, stirring occasionally. Add garlic; sauté 1 minute, stirring constantly. Stir in beef, cumin, pepper, and salt.
2. Stir in tomato paste; cook 1 minute, stirring occasionally. Add broth, ⅓ cup water, and tomatoes; bring to a boil. Reduce heat to medium, and simmer 15 minutes or until slightly thick, stirring occasionally. Remove from heat.
3. Place 1 ounce chips in each of 4 bowls, and top each serving with about ⅔ cup beef mixture, 2 tablespoons cheese, and 1 tablespoon sour cream. Sprinkle each serving with 2 tablespoons green onions. Yield: 4 servings.

CALORIES 414; FAT 21.9g (sat 7g, mono 7.6g, poly 5.5g); PROTEIN 24.5g; CARB 29.2g; FIBER 3.2g; CHOL 68mg; IRON 2.6mg; SODIUM 682mg; CALC 160mg

CHICKEN 3 WAYS
3 SPEEDY SOUPS

Chicken Gumbo

Hands-on time: 35 min. Total time: 35 min.

1 (3½-ounce) bag boil-in-bag long-grain rice
1 bay leaf
Cooking spray
2 bone-in chicken breast halves, skinned
¼ teaspoon kosher salt
¼ teaspoon black pepper
2 cups fat-free, lower-sodium chicken broth
2 cups water
3 tablespoons all-purpose flour
2½ tablespoons canola oil
¾ cup chopped onion
½ cup chopped green bell pepper
½ cup chopped celery
1 garlic clove, minced
1 cup frozen sliced okra, thawed
½ teaspoon Cajun seasoning
¼ teaspoon hot pepper sauce
⅓ cup chopped green onions

1. Cook rice and bay leaf according to rice package directions, omitting salt and fat; drain. Discard bay leaf.
2. Heat a saucepan over medium-high heat, and coat pan with cooking spray. Sprinkle chicken with salt and black pepper. Sauté chicken in pan 5 minutes. Add broth and 2 cups water; bring to a boil. Reduce heat; simmer 20 minutes. Remove chicken; shred. Reserve cooking liquid.
3. Cook flour and oil in a cast-iron skillet 15 minutes over medium heat, stirring constantly. Add onion, bell pepper, ½ cup celery, and garlic; cook 4 minutes. Add cooking liquid, chicken, okra, Cajun seasoning, and hot sauce. Cook 3 minutes. Serve over rice; sprinkle with green onions. Yield: 4 servings (serving size: 1¼ cups gumbo and ½ cup rice).

CALORIES 297; FAT 9.8g (sat 0.9g, mono 5.8g, poly 2.7g); PROTEIN 18.6g; CARB 32.1g; FIBER 2.8g; CHOL 34mg; IRON 2.2mg; SODIUM 469mg; CALC 57mg

If you like **Wild Rice** try:

Quick & Easy • Make Ahead

Chicken and Wild Rice Soup

Combine ½ cup brown and wild rice blend and 1 bay leaf in a large saucepan; cook according to rice package directions, omitting salt and fat. Discard bay leaf. Heat pan over medium-high heat; coat with cooking spray. Add 1 cup chopped onion, ½ cup thinly sliced celery, and ½ cup thinly sliced carrot; sauté 3 minutes. Add 2 minced garlic cloves; sauté 30 seconds, stirring constantly. Stir in 2 cups shredded cooked dark meat chicken, and cook 3 minutes, stirring occasionally. Add ¼ cup dry white wine; cook 1 minute. Add 2½ cups fat-free, lower-sodium chicken broth and 1 cup water; bring to a boil. Reduce heat, and simmer 5 minutes. Stir in rice. Remove from heat, and stir in ½ cup half-and-half, 1½ teaspoons chopped fresh sage, ¼ teaspoon salt, and ¼ teaspoon black pepper. Yield: 4 servings (serving size: 1½ cups).

CALORIES 313; FAT 11.5g (sat 4.3g); SODIUM 492mg

If you like **Bacon** try:

Quick & Easy • Make Ahead

Chicken Club Soup

Preheat oven to 375°. Combine 2½ ounces cubed sourdough wheat bread and 1 minced garlic clove; drizzle with 1½ teaspoons olive oil. Toss. Spread bread in a single layer on a baking sheet. Bake at 375° for 8 minutes or until toasted, stirring once. Heat a saucepan over medium heat. Add 1 tablespoon olive oil. Add 1 cup sliced red onion and 1 minced garlic clove; sauté 2 minutes. Stir in 2½ cups fat-free, lower-sodium chicken broth; 2 cups chopped cooked chicken breast; 1½ cups water; 1⅓ cups chopped plum tomato; 2 tablespoons fresh lemon juice; 2 teaspoons chopped thyme; and ½ teaspoon black pepper. Bring to a simmer. Cook 5 minutes. Ladle about

1½ cups soup into each of 4 bowls. Sprinkle with croutons; ⅓ cup sliced green onions; 2 slices cooked, crumbled bacon; and 1 ripe pitted, peeled, and chopped avocado. Yield: 4 servings.

CALORIES 353; FAT 17.2g (sat 3.2g); SODIUM 512mg

READER RECIPE

BEANS, GREENS, AND ACCOLADES

The women in Erin McCall's family are a talented group of cooks, and to impress them has been Erin's fun challenge. When her mother, aunt, and sister visited, Erin wanted to create a recipe that would stand out. "I wanted a dish that was something they'd never tried before," she says. Her blend of beans, spinach, and fennel with Parmesan cheese received winning marks from a tough crowd.

Quick & Easy • Vegetarian

Warm White Beans with Roasted Fennel

Hands-on time: 14 min. Total time: 34 min.

4 cups thinly sliced fennel bulb
3 tablespoons olive oil, divided
¾ teaspoon freshly ground black pepper, divided
½ teaspoon salt, divided
¼ teaspoon ground red pepper
2 garlic cloves, minced
Cooking spray
3 tablespoons grated Parmigiano-Reggiano cheese
2 (15.8-ounce) cans Great Northern beans, rinsed and drained
4 cups fresh baby spinach

1. Preheat oven to 450°.
2. Combine fennel, 1 tablespoon oil, ½ teaspoon black pepper, ¼ teaspoon salt, red pepper, and garlic in a large bowl;

toss to coat fennel. Arrange fennel mixture in a single layer on a baking sheet coated with cooking spray. Bake at 450° for 15 minutes or until fennel begins to brown. Stir; sprinkle cheese evenly over fennel mixture. Bake an additional 5 minutes or until golden brown.
3. Heat a large nonstick skillet over medium heat; add remaining 2 tablespoons oil. Add beans; cook 2 minutes or until heated. Add fennel mixture, spinach, remaining ¼ teaspoon black pepper, and remaining ¼ teaspoon salt. Cook 2 minutes; serve immediately. Yield: 8 servings (serving size: about ⅔ cup).

CALORIES 140; FAT 6.1g (sat 1.1g, mono 3.9g, poly 0.7g); PROTEIN 5.8g; CARB 17.4g; FIBER 5.2g; CHOL 2mg; IRON 1.8mg; SODIUM 231mg; CALC 90mg

> "I LIKE THE WARMTH OF THIS SIDE DISH, THE SPICE AS WELL AS THE TEMPERATURE, AND THE DIFFERING CREAMY, CRUNCHY TEXTURES."
>
> —ERIN McCALL, ATLANTA, GEORGIA

FALL VEGETABLE SALADS

By Mark Bittman

Hearty sweet potatoes and fennel turn into interesting side salads when paired with robust flavors like chipotle or olives.

The most delicate summer greens need only the gentlest kiss to bring them to life: a quick drizzle of olive oil, a couple drops of vinegar or lemon, a few grains of salt. Well, it's not summer anymore, and fall greens and vegetables are stronger, sturdier, and more resilient than their summer brethren: Turning them into salads requires a dressing to match, something with deep flavor and heft. We think of fall vegetables as perfect candidates for roasting, in part because after a long, hot summer, we get a strange thrill from turning on the oven and not melting. In fact, those classic roasting vegetables like squash, celery root, beets, Brussels sprouts, and fennel are also fantastic to eat uncooked. I'm splitting the difference here: one raw salad, and one roasted.

On the raw side, you can always rely on the classic (and sort of perfect) combination of raw shaved fennel, orange, and olives. Here I use green olives instead of the more traditional black for a little extra freshness, and add pistachios for that perfect salty crunch. The dressing is substantial and boldly flavored but comes together in just a few minutes: Chopped orange segments and zest go into a bowl with the chopped olives, olive oil, salt, and pepper. The salt extracts enough of the orange juice to moisten the shaved (or thinly sliced) fennel without making it too wet. If you're at all skeptical about all that raw, licorice-y fennel, replace half of it with green apple (also a classic).

When you're ready to fire up the oven, there's not a lot better than roasted sweet potatoes: golden and crisp on the outside, just tender in the middle, sweet and earthy at the same time. I start with exactly that in my Roasted Sweet Potato Salad with Cranberry-Chipotle Dressing; chunks of sweet potato are roasted with olive oil, salt, and pepper. The dressing is a mixture of cranberries (a quintessential fall ingredient) and canned chipotles in adobo (smoky, spicy peppers that are pretty much made for sweet potatoes). They're simmered until the cranberries are soft, mixed with a little honey to round out the tartness and heat, and mashed with a splash of water to get the perfect texture and consistency. For crunch and brightness, I add toasted pumpkinseeds, chopped green onions, and cilantro. Toss it all together, and you've got a roasted sweet potato salad with some serious oomph—a complex, rich, surprising dish.

These salads are easy to customize. In the fennel dish, citrus like grapefruit, tangerines, or clementines could sub for the orange, and something salty or briny (like capers or even anchovies) could take the place of the olives. For the sweet potato salad, some other fresh, frozen, or dried fruits could do the job of the cranberries (I'm thinking dried cherries, or even fresh raspberries). The idea here is to build the dressing around ingredients that have some serious flavor and texture, because splashing the lightest possible vinaigrette over some raw fennel could make you feel like you're eating a pile of vegetables that would have been better off somewhere other than a salad bowl.

Quick & Easy • Make Ahead
Vegetarian

Shaved Fennel Salad with Orange, Green Olives, and Pistachios

Hands-on time: 20 min. Total time: 20 min.

A mandoline is great for shaving the fibrous fennel bulbs into delicate, thin slices.

1 tablespoon grated orange rind
¾ cup orange sections (about 2 large oranges)
¾ cup coarsely chopped pitted green olives (about 3 ounces)
2 tablespoons extra-virgin olive oil
1 tablespoon fresh lemon juice
¼ teaspoon freshly ground black pepper
⅛ teaspoon kosher salt
2 medium fennel bulbs with stalks (about 2 pounds)
1 cup shelled unsalted dry-roasted pistachios

1. Combine first 7 ingredients in a large bowl; toss gently to combine.
2. Trim tough outer leaves from fennel, and mince feathery fronds to measure 2 tablespoons. Remove and discard stalks. Cut fennel bulbs in half lengthwise, and discard core. Thinly slice fennel bulbs. Add fennel slices to juice mixture, and toss gently to combine. Sprinkle with fennel fronds and nuts. Yield: 8 servings (serving size: ¾ cup).

CALORIES 168; FAT 12.7g (sat 1.3g, mono 7.8g, poly 2.7g); PROTEIN 4.1g; CARB 11.9g; FIBER 3t.8g; CHOL 0mg; IRON 1.1mg; SODIUM 280mg; CALC 52mg

ONE RAW SALAD, ONE ROASTED: CRUNCHY FENNEL MINGLES WITH JUICY ORANGES, WHILE TENDER SWEET POTATOES MEET A TANGY-SPICY-SMOKY FOIL.

Vegetarian

Roasted Sweet Potato Salad with Cranberry-Chipotle Dressing

Hands-on time: 25 min. Total time: 1 hr.

Let the cranberries cook long enough that they start to pop; the juice helps to thicken the dressing.

2½ pounds sweet potatoes, peeled and cut into 2-inch pieces
3 tablespoons olive oil, divided
¾ teaspoon kosher salt
½ teaspoon freshly ground black pepper
¾ cup fresh or frozen cranberries
¼ cup water
2 teaspoons honey
1 (7-ounce) can chipotle chiles in adobo sauce
½ cup pepitas (pumpkinseeds)
¾ cup chopped green onions
¼ cup fresh cilantro leaves

1. Preheat oven to 450°.
2. Place sweet potatoes on a large jelly-roll pan. Drizzle with 2 tablespoons oil, and sprinkle with salt and pepper; toss to coat. Bake at 450° for 30 minutes or until tender, turning after 15 minutes.
3. Place remaining 1 tablespoon oil, cranberries, water, and honey in a saucepan. Remove 1 or 2 chiles from can; finely chop to equal 1 tablespoon. Add chopped chipotle and 1 teaspoon adobo sauce to pan (reserve remaining chiles and sauce for another use). Place pan over medium-low heat; bring to a boil. Cover, reduce heat, and cook 10 minutes or until cranberries pop, stirring occasionally. Remove from heat. Mash with a potato masher or fork until chunky.
4. Place pepitas in a medium skillet; cook over medium heat 4 minutes or until lightly browned, shaking pan frequently.
5. Combine potatoes, pepitas, onions, and cilantro in a bowl. Add cranberry mixture to bowl; toss gently to coat. Yield: 8 servings (serving size: ¾ cup).

CALORIES 189; **FAT** 8.4g (sat 1.3g, mono 5.5g, poly 0.9g); **PROTEIN** 3.7g; **CARB** 25.5g; **FIBER** 4.5g; **CHOL** 0mg; **IRON** 1.3mg; **SODIUM** 335mg; **CALC** 40mg

COOKING CLASS

TODAY'S LESSON: BRAISED MEATS

A braising pot is a heavy slow cooker without a plug: In go tough, inexpensive cuts of meat, such as beefy short ribs or bone-in chicken thighs, and out come melt-in-your-mouth treats—after a long simmer. Few other cooking methods achieve this type of total transformation. But for best braising magic, it's critical to follow a few steps, outlined on page 286.

Make Ahead

Chicken with Dates, Olives, and Cinnamon

Hands-on time: 34 min. Total time: 1 hr.

Serve over couscous.

12 bone-in chicken thighs, skinned
¼ teaspoon freshly ground black pepper
⅛ teaspoon kosher salt
2 tablespoons butter, divided
2 tablespoons olive oil, divided
4 cups sliced onion
1 teaspoon minced peeled fresh ginger
18 pitted manzanilla (or green) olives, chopped
2 tablespoons all-purpose flour
¾ teaspoon ground cumin
½ teaspoon ground coriander
⅛ teaspoon ground red pepper
1 (3-inch) cinnamon stick
2 cups fat-free, lower-sodium chicken broth
½ cup whole pitted dates, chopped
3 tablespoons fresh lemon juice
¼ cup fresh basil leaves

1. Sprinkle chicken with pepper and salt. Melt 1 tablespoon butter in a 10-quart Dutch oven over medium-high heat. Add 1 tablespoon oil to pan; swirl to coat. Add 6 chicken thighs to pan; cook 4 minutes on each side or until browned. Remove chicken from pan. Repeat with remaining 1 tablespoon butter, remaining 1 tablespoon oil, and remaining 6 chicken thighs.
2. Add onion and ginger to pan; sauté 8 minutes, stirring frequently. Add olives; sauté for 1 minute. Add flour and next 4 ingredients; cook 1 minute, stirring constantly. Add broth; bring to a boil, scraping pan to loosen browned bits. Cook 1 minute. Return chicken to pan. Cover, reduce heat to low, and cook 12 minutes. Stir in dates; simmer 10 minutes or until chicken is done. Stir in juice, and garnish with basil. Discard cinnamon stick before serving. Yield: 6 servings (serving size: 2 thighs and ½ cup sauce).

CALORIES 350; **FAT** 16g (sat 4.5g, mono 7g, poly 3g); **PROTEIN** 29.1g; **CARB** 21.9g; **FIBER** 2.7g; **CHOL** 125mg; **IRON** 2mg; **SODIUM** 580mg; **CALC** 47mg

KITCHEN TIP: Stovetop braising is ideal for small, quicker-cooking meats, like chicken thighs; oven braising is suited to larger cuts.

STEP-BY-STEP

BROWN THE MEAT
Heat the pan, add a bit of fat, swirl it around, and then brown the meat. This step helps the appearance of the meat, but more important, it's how you begin to build the flavor foundation for these rich braises. Remove the meat, and set aside.

SAUTÉ AROMATICS
Add ingredients like onion, carrot, celery, garlic, or ginger, and sauté to continue to add complexity to the dish. Don't worry if browned bits start to collect on the bottom of the pan as you work. This adds depth.

SIMMER IN A FLAVORFUL LIQUID
Usually a broth balanced with an acid—such as wine or vinegar—works best. Return meat to the pan, and nestle it in until partially covered. Meat should not be totally submerged. Cover and simmer gently until the meat is fork-tender.

Cabernet Short Ribs with Parmesan Polenta

Hands-on time: 30 min. Total time: 2 hr. 21 min.

Serve with a chunk of bread to soak up all the sauce.

Ribs:
16 (3-ounce) bone-in beef short ribs, trimmed
⅝ teaspoon kosher salt
½ teaspoon black pepper
2 teaspoons olive oil, divided
1 cup chopped onion
¾ cup chopped shallots
½ cup chopped carrot
½ cup chopped celery
6 garlic cloves, sliced
1 rosemary sprig
2½ cups cabernet sauvignon or other dry red wine
1¼ cups lower-sodium beef broth
1 teaspoon all-purpose flour
2 teaspoons water
1 tablespoon balsamic vinegar
Gremolata:
⅓ cup chopped fresh flat-leaf parsley
½ teaspoon grated lemon rind
1 garlic clove, minced
Polenta:
3 cups fat-free milk
1 cup water
⅝ teaspoon kosher salt
⅛ teaspoon freshly ground black pepper
1 cup quick-cooking polenta
¼ cup (1 ounce) grated fresh Parmigiano-Reggiano cheese

1. To prepare ribs, sprinkle ribs with salt and pepper. Heat a large ovenproof Dutch oven over medium-high heat. Add 1 teaspoon olive oil to pan. Add 8 ribs, and sauté 6 minutes, turning to brown on all sides. Remove ribs. Repeat procedure with remaining 1 teaspoon oil and 8 ribs. Add onion and next 5 ingredients to pan; sauté 3 minutes, stirring constantly. Add wine to pan, and bring to a boil, scraping pan to loosen browned bits. Cook 13 minutes or until reduced to 2 cups.
2. Preheat oven to 350°.
3. Add broth to pan, and bring to a boil. Return ribs to pan. Cover and bake at 350° for 1½ hours, turning ribs after 45 minutes. Remove ribs from pan, and strain cooking liquid through a fine-mesh sieve over a bowl. Discard solids. Skim fat; discard. Return cooking liquid to pan. Combine flour and 2 teaspoons water in a small bowl, stirring well. Add to pan, and bring to a boil. Cook 11 minutes or until reduced to about 1 cup. Stir in vinegar.
4. To prepare gremolata, combine ⅓ cup parsley, ½ teaspoon lemon rind, and minced garlic.
5. To prepare polenta, bring 3 cups milk, 1 cup water, ⅝ teaspoon salt, and ⅛ teaspoon black pepper to a boil over medium heat. Slowly stir in 1 cup polenta. Cook 5 minutes or until thick, stirring frequently. Stir in cheese. Place ½ cup polenta in each of 8 shallow bowls, and top each serving with 2 ribs, 2 tablespoons sauce, and about 2 teaspoons gremolata. Yield: 8 servings.

CALORIES 483; FAT 19.1g (sat 7.7g, mono 7.9g, poly 0.7g); PROTEIN 34.3g; CARB 29g; FIBER 2.2g; CHOL 85mg; IRON 5.2mg; SODIUM 694mg; CALC 210mg

> **KITCHEN TIP:** For longer braises, add quicker-cooking ingredients like vegetables in stages so they don't turn to mush over time.

Make Ahead
Beer-Braised Brisket

Hands-on time: 30 min. Total time: 5 hr. 45 min.

2 teaspoons ground cumin
2 teaspoons sweet Hungarian paprika
½ teaspoon dried thyme
1¼ teaspoons kosher salt, divided
2½ pounds flat-cut beef brisket, trimmed
1 tablespoon olive oil
1½ cups pale ale
4 cups lower-sodium beef broth
5 garlic cloves, sliced
6 carrots, cut diagonally into 1½-inch pieces
6 celery stalks, cut diagonally into 1½-inch pieces
2 medium onions, each cut into 12 wedges
2 tablespoons all-purpose flour
½ cup water

1. Preheat oven to 325°.
2. Combine first 3 ingredients in a small bowl; stir in 1 teaspoon salt. Rub spice mixture evenly over both sides of brisket. Heat an ovenproof Dutch oven over medium-high heat. Add oil to pan; swirl to coat. Add brisket; sauté 3 minutes on each side or until browned. Remove brisket from pan. Add beer; bring to a boil, scraping pan to loosen browned bits. Add broth and garlic; return to a boil. Return brisket to pan. Cover and cook at 325° for 2 hours. Turn brisket over; cook an additional 2 hours. Turn brisket over. Add carrot, celery, and onion; cook an additional 1 hour or until brisket is very tender.
3. Remove brisket and vegetables from pan using a slotted spoon. Skim fat from cooking liquid; discard fat. Bring cooking liquid to a boil over medium-high heat. Place flour in a small bowl; stir in ½ cup water. Add flour mixture to pan, stirring until smooth; bring to a boil, stirring constantly. Cook 2 minutes or until slightly thickened. Stir in remaining ¼ teaspoon salt. Serve sauce with beef and vegetables. Yield: 8 servings (serving size: 3 ounces beef, ⅔ cup vegetables, and ⅓ cup sauce).

CALORIES 253; **FAT** 7g (sat 2.1g, mono 3.3g, poly 0.5g); **PROTEIN** 30.2g; **CARB** 12.6g; **FIBER** 2.7g; **CHOL** 52mg; **IRON** 3.2mg; **SODIUM** 674mg; **CALC** 64mg

---

DUTCH OVENS
A Dutch oven made of cast iron—or enameled cast iron—with a tight-fitting lid is the best pot for the job. Cast iron is heavy and a good, even conductor of heat. Thin aluminum or other metal or clay pots can have hot spots and burn food more easily, which will leave a bitter, scorched flavor that will permeate the dish.

Kid Friendly
Soy and Cola–Braised Pork Shoulder
(pictured on page 235)

Hands-on time: 35 min. Total time: 2 hr. 25 min.

Serve this East-meets-West pulled pork on hamburger buns or Kaiser rolls with shaved cucumber and carrot ribbons tossed with rice vinegar. Or stuff it into tortillas for Asian-style tacos with matchstick-cut cucumber and carrot.

1 tablespoon dark sesame oil
1 (3½-pound) bone-in pork shoulder (Boston butt), trimmed
½ teaspoon kosher salt
1 tablespoon minced peeled fresh ginger
4 garlic cloves, minced
2 cups cola
½ cup hoisin sauce
¼ cup rice vinegar
¼ cup lower-sodium soy sauce
1 cup diagonally sliced green onions

1. Preheat oven to 300°.
2. Heat an ovenproof Dutch oven over medium-high heat. Add oil to pan. Sprinkle pork evenly with salt. Add pork to pan; sauté 8 minutes, turning to brown all sides. Remove pork. Add ginger and garlic; sauté 1 minute, stirring constantly. Stir in cola and next 3 ingredients; bring to a boil. Return pork to pan; cover. Bake at 300° for 1 hour and 50 minutes or until tender, turning occasionally. Remove pork from pan, and let stand 10 minutes. Shred pork with 2 forks. Skim fat from cooking liquid.
3. Place pan over medium-high heat; bring cooking liquid to a boil. Cook 15 minutes or until reduced to about 2 cups, stirring occasionally. Combine pork and ¾ cup sauce in a bowl; toss to coat. Top with green onions. Serve pork with remaining 1¼ cups sauce. Yield: 10 servings (serving size: about 3 ounces pork and 2 tablespoons sauce).

CALORIES 316; **FAT** 18.3g (sat 6.4g, mono 8.2g, poly 2.8g); **PROTEIN** 24.3g; **CARB** 12.8g; **FIBER** 0.7g; **CHOL** 91mg; **IRON** 2.1mg; **SODIUM** 574mg; **CALC** 39mg

---

RECIPE MAKEOVER
MONKEY BREAD LIGHTENS UP

This pull-apart brunch favorite undergoes a slimming transformation yet miraculously keeps all its irresistible sticky-buttery essence.

Monkey around with the likes of canned biscuit dough, a stick of butter, and gobs of cinnamon-sugar, and you've got a mountain of fatty calories. We knew that the nutrition analysis of the traditional monkey bread recipe would show that—but 960mg of sodium per serving surprised us.

To build a better base, we give the premade biscuits a pass—they're high in sodium and contain trans fats. Instead (and here's where convenience takes a backseat to quality), we start with fresh, homemade dough, made with nutty whole-wheat flour and delicately sweetened with orange juice and honey. In place of the stick of butter, each bite is dipped in a combo of milk and butter, and then rolled in cinnamon and sugar. A finishing drizzle of cream cheese icing sends this treat over the top in taste—with about 80% less sodium and saturated fat than the original.

CANNED BISCUITS
A nifty kitchen convenience, but you pay a price in fat, and they can contain a surprising amount of sodium.

HOMEMADE WHOLE-WHEAT DOUGH
You'll save 3g saturated fat and 677mg sodium per serving by making your own light, fluffy whole-wheat dough.

---

continued

PERFECTING THE PULL-APART

Easy to make, and fun to eat: Investing a little extra time in this easy dough is worth the tender, melt-in-your-mouth results.

1. Use kitchen shears or scissors to cut each rope into 8 equal portions, shaping each cut portion into a 1-inch ball.

2. A quick skinny dip in a milk-and-butter bath evenly coats the dough, so there's no need for a heavy butter basting.

3. The milk bath allows maximum cinnamon-sugar coverage on the dough for full flavor in every bite.

4. Layer the bites in the pan for the final rise. The sugar coating caramelizes in the oven.

Kid Friendly • Vegetarian
Monkey Bread

Hands-on time: 45 min. Total time: 3 hr. 18 min.

13.5 ounces all-purpose flour (about 3 cups)
4.75 ounces whole-wheat flour (about 1 cup)
1 teaspoon salt
1 package quick-rise yeast (about 2¼ teaspoons)
1 cup very warm fat-free milk (120° to 130°)
¼ cup very warm orange juice (120° to 130°)
¼ cup honey
2 tablespoons butter, melted
Cooking spray
½ cup granulated sugar
½ cup packed brown sugar
2 teaspoons ground cinnamon
4½ tablespoons fat-free milk, divided
2 tablespoons butter, melted
½ cup powdered sugar
1 tablespoon ⅓-less-fat cream cheese
1 teaspoon vanilla extract

1. Weigh or lightly spoon flours into dry measuring cups; level with a knife. Combine flours, salt, and yeast in the bowl of a stand mixer with dough hook attached; mix until combined. With mixer on, slowly add 1 cup milk, juice, honey, and 2 tablespoons butter; mix dough at medium speed 7 minutes or until smooth and elastic. Place dough in a large bowl coated with cooking spray, turning to coat top. Cover and let rise in a warm place (85°), free from drafts, 1 hour or until doubled in size. (Gently press two fingers into dough. If indentation remains, dough has risen enough.)
2. Combine granulated sugar, brown sugar, and cinnamon in a shallow dish. Combine 3 tablespoons milk and 2 tablespoons butter in a shallow dish, stirring with a whisk.
3. Punch dough down; divide into 8 equal portions. Working with one portion at a time (cover remaining dough to prevent drying), roll into an 8-inch rope. Cut each dough rope into 8 equal pieces, shaping each piece into a 1-inch ball. Dip each ball in milk mixture, turning to coat, and roll in sugar mixture. Layer balls in a 12-cup Bundt pan coated with cooking spray. Repeat procedure with remaining 7 dough ropes. Sprinkle any remaining sugar mixture over dough. Cover and let rise in a warm place (85°), free from drafts, 1 hour or until almost doubled in size.
4. Preheat oven to 350°.
5. Bake at 350° for 25 minutes or until golden. Cool 5 minutes in pan on a wire rack. Place a plate upside down on top of bread; invert onto plate. Combine powdered sugar, remaining milk, and remaining ingredients in a small bowl, stirring with a whisk. Microwave at HIGH 20 seconds or until warm. Drizzle over bread. Yield: 16 servings (serving size: 4 pieces and 1 teaspoon sauce).

CALORIES 234; **FAT** 3.4g (sat 2g, mono 0.8g, poly 0.3g); **PROTEIN** 4.5g; **CARB** 47.2g; **FIBER** 1.9g; **CHOL** 9mg; **IRON** 1.5mg; **SODIUM** 184mg; **CALC** 43mg

OLD WAY	OUR WAY
556 calories per serving	234 calories per serving
960 milligrams sodium	184 milligrams sodium
13 grams saturated fat	2 grams saturated fat

MEATLESS MEXICAN MAINS

No chance of needing chicken or beef when chiles, limes, and other bright-flavored ingredients spice up these hearty dishes.

Vegetarian

Migas con Salsa Verde

Hands-on time: 28 min. Total time: 55 min.

Enjoy this one-skillet dish for breakfast, lunch, or dinner.

1 medium-sized red bell pepper
6 large eggs
4 large egg whites
2 tablespoons chopped fresh cilantro
¼ teaspoon salt
4 teaspoons olive oil
4 (6-inch) corn tortillas, cut into ½-inch strips
1½ cups chopped onion
2 garlic cloves, minced
1 jalapeño pepper, seeded and chopped
6 tablespoons salsa verde
¼ cup crumbled queso fresco

1. Preheat broiler.
2. Cut bell pepper in half lengthwise; discard seeds and membranes. Place pepper halves, skin sides up, on a foil-lined baking sheet; flatten with hand. Broil 10 minutes or until blackened. Place in a paper bag; fold to close tightly. Let stand 10 minutes. Peel and chop.
3. Combine eggs, egg whites, cilantro, and salt in a bowl, stirring with a whisk. Heat a large nonstick skillet over medium-high heat. Add olive oil to pan; swirl to coat. Add tortilla strips; sauté 2 minutes, stirring frequently.

Reduce heat to medium. Add onion, garlic, and jalapeño; sauté 5 minutes or until tender, stirring occasionally. Add roasted bell pepper and egg mixture; cook 2½ minutes or until eggs are set, stirring occasionally. Divide egg mixture evenly among 4 plates; top each serving with 1½ tablespoons salsa and 1 tablespoon cheese. Yield: 4 servings.

CALORIES 273; **FAT** 14.5g (sat 3.8g, mono 6.6g, poly 2g); **PROTEIN** 17g; **CARB** 20.3g; **FIBER** 2.7g; **CHOL** 278mg; **IRON** 1.8mg; **SODIUM** 509mg; **CALC** 115mg

Make Ahead • Freezable • Vegetarian

Black Bean and Cheese Enchiladas with Ranchero Sauce

Hands-on time: 55 min. Total time: 1 hr. 10 min.

2 dried ancho chiles, stemmed and seeded
2 cups water
2 teaspoons olive oil
1 cup chopped yellow onion
5 garlic cloves, sliced
¼ teaspoon kosher salt
2 cups organic vegetable broth
2 tablespoons chopped fresh oregano
2 tablespoons no-salt-added tomato paste
½ teaspoon ground cumin
1 tablespoon fresh lime juice
⅛ teaspoon ground red pepper
1 (15-ounce) can black beans, rinsed and drained
2 cups (8 ounces) preshredded reduced-fat 4-cheese Mexican-blend cheese, divided
3 thinly sliced green onions, divided
Cooking spray
12 (6-inch) corn tortillas
6 tablespoons light sour cream

1. Preheat oven to 400°.
2. Combine chiles and 2 cups water in a saucepan; bring to a boil, reduce heat, and simmer 5 minutes. Remove from heat; let stand 5 minutes. Drain chiles in a colander over a bowl, reserving 1 cup cooking liquid.
3. Heat oil in a medium saucepan over high heat. Add onion; sauté 1 minute. Reduce heat to medium; add garlic and salt. Cook 5 minutes or until golden,

stirring occasionally. Add broth and next 3 ingredients; cook 8 minutes or until thickened, stirring occasionally.
4. Pour onion mixture into a blender; add chiles and reserved liquid. Remove center piece of blender lid (to allow steam to escape); secure lid on blender. Place a clean towel over opening in lid. Blend until smooth; stir in lime juice and red pepper.
5. Combine beans, 1 cup cheese, and half the green onions in a bowl. Spread ½ cup sauce in bottom of a 13 x 9–inch glass or ceramic baking dish coated with cooking spray. Warm tortillas according to package directions. Spoon 3 tablespoons bean mixture down center of each tortilla; roll up. Place, seam sides down, in prepared dish. Pour remaining sauce over filled tortillas. Top with remaining cheese. Bake at 400° for 15 minutes or until lightly browned. Sprinkle with remaining green onions; serve with sour cream. Yield: 6 servings (serving size: 2 enchiladas and 1 tablespoon sour cream).

CALORIES 302; **FAT** 12.9g (sat 5.3g, mono 3.9g, poly 1.3g); **PROTEIN** 17.3g; **CARB** 36.1g; **FIBER** 6.4g; **CHOL** 32mg; **IRON** 1.7mg; **SODIUM** 574mg; **CALC** 426mg

GET AHEAD: MAKE RANCHERO SAUCE A DAY OR TWO IN ADVANCE.

Vegetarian

Mexican Stuffed Poblanos

Hands-on time: 45 min. Total time: 1 hr. 5 min.

4 poblano chiles
½ cup organic vegetable broth
½ cup uncooked bulgur
1 tablespoon olive oil
1 cup chopped onion
3 garlic cloves, minced
1 (15-ounce) can no-salt-added pinto beans, drained
1 (4-ounce) can chopped green chiles, undrained
2 teaspoons cumin
Cooking spray
¾ cup shredded Monterey Jack cheese
2 cups chopped seeded tomato (about 2)
½ cup finely chopped red onion
¼ cup chopped fresh cilantro
2 tablespoons fresh lime juice
¼ teaspoon kosher salt
⅛ teaspoon ground red pepper
1 jalapeño pepper, seeded and finely chopped

1. Preheat broiler.
2. Place poblanos on a foil-lined baking sheet. Broil 5 minutes on each side or until blackened and charred. Place poblanos in a paper bag; fold to close tightly. Let stand 15 minutes; peel. Cut a slit lengthwise in each poblano; discard seeds, keeping chiles intact. Set aside.
3. Reduce oven temperature to 400°.
4. Bring vegetable broth to a boil in a medium saucepan; gradually stir in bulgur. Remove from heat; cover and let stand 30 minutes.
5. Heat a large nonstick skillet over medium-high heat. Add oil to pan; swirl to coat. Add onion and garlic to pan; sauté 5 minutes or until the onion is lightly browned. Add beans, green chiles, and cumin. Bring to a boil, reduce heat, and simmer 10 minutes or until thickened, stirring occasionally. Remove from heat; let stand 10 minutes. Stir in cooked bulgur.
6. Divide bean mixture evenly among poblanos. Press poblanos gently to close. Place poblanos, seam-sides up, on a foil-lined baking sheet coated with cooking spray. Top each poblano with

3 tablespoons cheese. Bake poblanos at 400° for 15 minutes or until lightly browned.
7. Combine tomato and remaining ingredients in a medium bowl. Serve with poblanos. Yield: 4 servings (serving size: 1 poblano and ⅓ cup salsa).

CALORIES 307; **FAT** 10.7g (sat 4.6g, mono 4.4g, poly 0.8g); **PROTEIN** 14g; **CARB** 41.5g; **FIBER** 10.7g; **CHOL** 19mg; **IRON** 3.4mg; **SODIUM** 442mg; **CALC** 256mg

Vegetarian

Grilled Portobello and Poblano Tacos with Pico de Gallo

Hands-on time: 47 min. Total time: 1 hr.

1½ cups chopped seeded plum tomato (about 3)
½ cup julienne-cut jicama
2 tablespoons chopped fresh cilantro
2 tablespoons fresh lime juice
⅛ teaspoon crushed red pepper
1 minced serrano chile
½ teaspoon salt, divided
4 portobello mushroom caps (about 1 pound)
4 (¼-inch-thick) slices onion
1 whole poblano chile
Cooking spray
4 teaspoons olive oil
3 garlic cloves, thinly sliced
½ teaspoon ground cumin
8 (6-inch) corn tortillas
1 cup sliced peeled avocado
1 cup (4 ounces) shredded reduced-fat colby-Jack cheese

1. Preheat grill to medium-high heat.
2. Combine the first 6 ingredients and ⅛ teaspoon salt in a small bowl.
3. Remove gills from undersides of mushrooms using a spoon; discard gills. Place mushrooms, onion, and poblano on grill rack coated with cooking spray, and grill mushrooms and poblano 5 minutes on each side or until tender. Grill onion 6 minutes on each side or until tender. Remove from heat. Seed poblano and remove stem, and cut mushrooms and poblano into thin strips. Chop onion, and combine vegetables in a bowl.

4. Heat olive oil in a large nonstick skillet over medium-high heat. Add garlic; sauté 1 minute or until lightly browned. Add mushroom mixture, remaining ⅜ teaspoon salt, and cumin; cook 2 minutes or until thoroughly heated.
5. Heat tortillas according to package directions. Divide mushroom mixture, pico de gallo, and avocado evenly among tortillas. Top each with 2 tablespoons cheese. Yield: 4 servings (serving size: 2 tacos).

CALORIES 327; **FAT** 16.7g (sat 5g, mono 7.2g, poly 1.8g); **PROTEIN** 14g; **CARB** 35.9g; **FIBER** 8.4g; **CHOL** 15mg; **IRON** 1.5mg; **SODIUM** 554mg; **CALC** 460mg

PREPPING PORTOBELLOS

1. Wipe off dirt with a damp paper towel.

2. Twist and pull off stems.

3. Scoop out dark brown gills with a spoon (they'll discolor food). Slice as recipe requires.

FEED 4 FOR LESS THAN $10

Creamy spinach casseroles, cheese-stuffed pork, and saucy spiced lentils are guest-worthy. Potato chip chicken will make you a hero with your kids.

$2.42 per serving, $9.69 total
Make Ahead

Garlicky Spinach-Sausage Gratin

Hands-on time: 25 min. Total time: 37 min.

Go fancier by baking in individual dishes.

2 tablespoons olive oil, divided
1 cup chopped onion
8 garlic cloves, coarsely chopped
6 ounces pork sausage
¼ teaspoon kosher salt
¼ teaspoon ground red pepper
2 tablespoons all-purpose flour
2 cups 2% reduced-fat milk
2 large eggs, lightly beaten
12 ounces fresh spinach, trimmed
Cooking spray
2 ounces French bread baguette, torn into 1-inch pieces
⅓ cup grated Parmesan cheese

1. Preheat oven to 450°.
2. Heat a Dutch oven over medium-high heat. Add 1½ teaspoons oil, and swirl. Add onion; sauté 4 minutes. Add garlic; sauté 1 minute, stirring constantly. Add sausage, salt, and pepper; sauté 5 minutes, stirring to crumble. Remove mixture from pan; drain. Wipe pan.
3. Return sausage mixture to pan. Stir in flour, and sauté 30 seconds, stirring constantly. Combine milk and eggs, stirring well. Reduce heat to medium. Stir milk mixture into sausage mixture, and bring to a boil. Cook 2 minutes, stirring constantly. Remove from heat, and stir in spinach. Spoon spinach mixture into an 11 x 7–inch glass or ceramic baking dish coated with cooking spray.
4. Place bread in a food processor, and pulse until 1 cup coarse crumbs form. Heat a large skillet over medium-high heat. Add remaining 1½ tablespoons olive oil to pan, and swirl to coat. Stir in crumbs, and sauté 3 minutes or until toasted, stirring frequently. Sprinkle crumbs over spinach mixture, and top with cheese. Bake at 450° for 12 minutes or until bubbly. Yield: 4 servings (serving size: 1 cup).

CALORIES 396; FAT 23.6g (sat 8g, mono 11.2g, poly 2.6g); PROTEIN 21g; CARB 26.6g; FIBER 3.1g; CHOL 148mg; IRON 4.1mg; SODIUM 732mg; CALC 382mg

$2.41 per serving, $9.62 total

Blue Cheese–Stuffed Pork Chops with Pears

Hands-on time: 24 min. Total time: 24 min.

4 (4-ounce) boneless center-cut loin pork chops, trimmed
½ cup (2 ounces) crumbled blue cheese
½ teaspoon kosher salt, divided
½ teaspoon freshly ground black pepper, divided
1½ teaspoons olive oil
1½ teaspoons butter
1 ripe pear, cored and cut into 16 wedges

1. Cut a horizontal slit through thickest portion of each pork chop to form a pocket. Stuff 2 tablespoons crumbled blue cheese into each pocket. Sprinkle ¼ teaspoon salt and ¼ teaspoon pepper evenly over both sides of pork. Heat a large nonstick skillet over medium-high heat. Add olive oil to pan; swirl to coat. Add pork to pan; sauté 3 minutes on each side or until desired degree of doneness. Remove pork from pan, and let stand 5 minutes.
2. Melt butter in pan; swirl to coat. Add pear; sprinkle with remaining ¼ teaspoon salt and remaining ¼ teaspoon pepper. Sauté 4 minutes or until lightly browned, stirring occasionally. Serve with pork. Yield: 4 servings (serving size: 1 stuffed pork chop and 4 pear wedges).

CALORIES 246; FAT 13g (sat 5.5g, mono 1g, poly 4.8g); PROTEIN 24.4g; CARB 7.3g; FIBER 1.4g; CHOL 81mg; IRON 0.8mg; SODIUM 493mg; CALC 98mg

$2.33 per serving, $9.30 total
Make Ahead • Freezable

Indian-Spiced Lentils and Lamb

Hands-on time: 30 min. Total time: 1 hr. 10 min.

2 teaspoons olive oil
6 ounces lean ground lamb
1 teaspoon red curry powder
1 teaspoon ground cumin
½ teaspoon kosher salt
¼ teaspoon ground red pepper
1½ cups chopped onion
¾ cup chopped carrot
1 jalapeño pepper, chopped
5 garlic cloves, minced
1 tablespoon tomato paste
¾ cup brown lentils
2 cups fat-free, lower-sodium chicken broth
1 cup water
¾ cup light coconut milk
1 (15-ounce) can whole peeled tomatoes, drained and coarsely chopped
¼ cup plain 2% reduced-fat Greek yogurt
¼ cup fresh cilantro leaves

1. Heat a saucepan over medium-high heat. Add oil to pan; swirl. Add lamb and next 4 ingredients; sauté 4 minutes, stirring to crumble. Add onion, carrot, and jalapeño; sauté 4 minutes or until lamb is browned. Add garlic; sauté 1 minute, stirring constantly. Stir in tomato paste; sauté 30 seconds.
2. Add lentils; sauté 30 seconds. Stir in broth and next 3 ingredients; bring to a boil. Reduce heat, and simmer 40 minutes or until lentils are tender. Ladle about 1 cup lentil mixture into each of 4 bowls; top each serving with 1 tablespoon yogurt and 1 tablespoon cilantro. Yield: 4 servings.

CALORIES 371; FAT 16g (sat 7.1g, mono 5.8g, poly 1.1g); PROTEIN 19.8g; CARB 40.5g; FIBER 9g; CHOL 32mg; IRON 4.3mg; SODIUM 619mg; CALC 107mg

Quick & Easy • Kid Friendly

Potato-Crusted Chicken Fingers

Hands-on time: 40 min. Total time: 40 min.

Serve with broccoli and buttered penne.

6 ounces baked potato chips
¾ cup all-purpose flour
½ cup 2% reduced-fat milk
1 large egg, lightly beaten
4 (6-ounce) skinless, boneless chicken
   breast halves, cut into strips
½ teaspoon salt
3 tablespoons canola oil, divided

1. Grind chips in a food processor, and place in a shallow dish. Place ¾ cup flour in a shallow dish. Combine milk and egg in a shallow dish. Sprinkle chicken with salt; dredge in flour. Dip chicken in milk mixture; dredge in ground chips.
2. Heat 1½ tablespoons oil in a large skillet over medium-high heat. Add half of chicken; cook 2 minutes on each side or until done. Repeat with remaining oil and chicken. Yield: 4 servings.

CALORIES 444; **FAT** 19.7g (sat 3g, mono 10.7g, poly 5g); **PROTEIN** 38.7g; **CARB** 25.2g; **FIBER** 1.3g; **CHOL** 140mg; **IRON** 2.1mg; **SODIUM** 596mg; **CALC** 69mg

WHAT IS BUDGET COOKING?

Prices derived from midsized-city supermarkets. For specialty or highly perishable ingredients, like some Asian sauces or fresh herbs, we account for the entire cost of the ingredient. For staples and other ingredients, we include the cost for only the amount used. Salt, pepper, and cooking spray are freebies.

5-INGREDIENT COOKING

Beef Tenderloin with Cherry–Black Pepper Sauce

Hands-on time: 20 min. Total time: 45 min.

Preheat oven to 425°. Sprinkle beef with ¾ teaspoon salt and ½ teaspoon black pepper. Melt 1 tablespoon butter in a large skillet over medium-high heat. Add beef; cook 2 minutes on each side or until browned. Transfer beef to a jelly-roll pan coated with cooking spray. Bake at 425° for 25 minutes or until a thermometer registers 135° or desired degree of doneness. Remove beef from oven; let stand 10 minutes. Return skillet to medium heat. Add shallots; cook 3 minutes or until shallots are translucent, stirring occasionally. Add 1 teaspoon black pepper, ¼ teaspoon salt, vinegar, and preserves. Bring to a boil, scraping pan to loosen browned bits. Reduce heat to low, and simmer 6 minutes or until sauce slightly thickens. Stir in remaining 2 tablespoons butter. Serve sauce with beef. Yield: 8 servings (serving size: 3 ounces beef and 1½ tablespoons sauce).

CALORIES 288; **FAT** 12.5g (sat 5.7g, mono 4.3g, poly 0.5g); **PROTEIN** 25.4g; **CARB** 16.8g; **FIBER** 0.1g; **CHOL** 93mg; **IRON** 2.1mg; **SODIUM** 310mg; **CALC** 41mg

ENTERTAINING? POP THE BEEF IN THE OVEN AS GUESTS ARRIVE, AND MAKE THE SAUCE JUST BEFORE THEY'RE SEATED.

THE FIVE INGREDIENTS

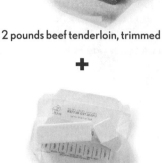

2 pounds beef tenderloin, trimmed

+

3 tablespoons unsalted butter, divided

+

¼ cup sliced shallots

+

½ cup balsamic vinegar

+

½ cup cherry preserves

Butternut Squash Risotto

Hands-on time: 45 min. Total time: 45 min.

Combine 2 cups squash and 2½ cups water in a saucepan; bring to a boil. Reduce heat; simmer 5 minutes. Remove pan from heat; let stand 5 minutes. Place mixture in a food processor. Process until smooth. Return mixture to pan. Stir in broth; bring to a simmer. Reserve ¼ cup squash mixture. Keep pan warm over low heat. Heat a large Dutch oven over medium-high heat. Coat pan with cooking spray. Add rice; cook 2 minutes, stirring constantly. Stir in remaining 1 cup squash, 2½ cups squash mixture, and ⅛ teaspoon salt. Cook 2 minutes or until liquid is nearly absorbed, stirring constantly. Add remaining squash mixture, 1 cup at a time, stirring until each cup is absorbed before adding the next (about 20 minutes). Remove from heat; stir in reserved ¼ cup squash mixture. Top with parsley and bacon. Yield: 4 servings (serving size: 1¼ cups).

CALORIES 447; FAT 4.9g (sat 1.4g, mono 1.6g, poly 0.6g); PROTEIN 13.9g; CARB 89.8g; FIBER 7.1g; CHOL 8mg; IRON 1.7mg; SODIUM 583mg; CALC 67mg

STIRRING IS ESPECIALLY IMPORTANT TO PREVENT BOTH THE RICE AND SQUASH FROM STICKING TO THE PAN.

THE FIVE INGREDIENTS

3 cups (½-inch) cubed peeled butternut squash, divided

+

3½ cups fat-free, lower-sodium chicken broth

+

2 cups uncooked Arborio rice

+

2 tablespoons chopped fresh flat-leaf parsley

+

5 ounces applewood-smoked bacon, cooked and crumbled

SUPERFAST

Discover bright flavors for chilly fall days with Caribbean-spiced pork chops, lemony chickpea soup, roasted red pepper salmon, and more.

Quick & Easy

Salmon with Red Pepper Pesto

If you don't like the bite of raw garlic, drop the clove in boiling water for 1 minute to blanch, and then proceed with the pesto.

4 (6-ounce) fresh or frozen salmon fillets (such as wild Alaskan)
¾ teaspoon kosher salt, divided
Cooking spray
⅓ cup chopped bottled roasted red bell peppers, rinsed and drained
1 tablespoon tomato paste
1 teaspoon extra-virgin olive oil
7 whole blanched almonds
1 garlic clove

1. Heat a grill pan over medium-high heat. Sprinkle fish evenly with ½ teaspoon salt. Coat pan with cooking spray. Arrange fish in pan; cook 4 minutes on each side or until fish flakes easily when tested with a fork or until desired degree of doneness.
2. While fish cooks, combine remaining ¼ teaspoon salt, bell peppers, and remaining ingredients in a blender or food processor, and process until smooth. Serve pesto over fish. Yield: 4 servings (serving size: 1 fillet and 3 tablespoons pesto).

Sustainable Choice | *Look for salmon that's labeled "wild Alaskan," and you can be sure that you're getting a sustainable option.*

CALORIES 309; FAT 14.8g (sat 2.2g, mono 5.6g, poly 5.4g); PROTEIN 39.3g; CARB 2.4g; FIBER 0.6g; CHOL 107mg; IRON 1.8mg; SODIUM 506mg; CALC 31mg

Pork Chops with Caribbean Rub and Mango Salsa

The smoky-spicy rub would also work well with grilled chicken breasts.

1½ teaspoons ground coriander
1½ teaspoons ground cumin
¾ teaspoon sugar
¾ teaspoon ground ginger
½ teaspoon salt
¼ teaspoon ground allspice
⅛ teaspoon ground red pepper
4 (6-ounce) bone-in center-cut pork chops (about ½-inch-thick)
Cooking spray
½ cup diced peeled mango
½ cup diced plum tomato
½ cup chopped fresh cilantro
1 tablespoon red wine vinegar
2 teaspoons extra-virgin olive oil

1. Combine first 7 ingredients in a small bowl. Rub pork chops with spice mixture.
2. Heat a grill pan over medium-high heat. Coat pan with cooking spray. Add pork to pan; grill 3 minutes on each side or until a thermometer registers 145° (slightly pink). Remove from pan. Let stand 5 minutes.
3. Combine mango and remaining ingredients in a small bowl, and toss gently. Serve salsa with pork. Yield: 4 servings (serving size: 1 chop and ¼ cup salsa).

CALORIES 192; **FAT** 7g (sat 1.6g, mono 3.2g, poly 0.7g); **PROTEIN** 24.9g; **CARB** 6.3g; **FIBER** 1.4g; **CHOL** 76mg; **IRON** 1.2mg; **SODIUM** 363mg; **CALC** 38mg

WINE NOTE #1: A lively, fruity red.
A light red with an extra dose of acidity can handle both the grilled chops and tangy salsa.
With its fresh tomatoes and mangoes and tart vinegar, this zesty salsa steamrolls the fruit in most reds, leaving them flat and lifeless. But Burgundy's Beaujolais-Villages, a naturally low-tannin wine made from the gamay grape, is power-packed with enough red berry flavor to stand up to the dish.

Its secret weapon is its white wine–like crispness, which squarely takes on the salsa's acidity and allows the fruit to shine through.
1. Louis Jadot, Beaujolais-Villages, France 2009 ($13)
2. Georges Duboeuf, Beaujolais-Villages, France 2009 ($10)
3. Joseph Drouhin, Beaujolais-Villages, France 2009 ($12)

WINE NOTE #2: A crisp, off-dry white.
A refreshing, slightly sweet white softens the edges of the salsa and keeps the bold rub from dominating.
Try a riesling from Washington, where the climate produces wines that are well-suited for the global table. The hint of sweetness in these low-octane whites mellows the assertive spices and peppery heat in this jerk-inspired Caribbean dish. Citrus and stone fruit flavors complement the mango.
1. Charles Smith Wines, Kung Fu Girl, Riesling, Washington 2010 ($12)
2. Milbrandt, Traditions Riesling, Washington 2009 ($13)
3. Chateau Ste. Michelle, Riesling, Washington 2010 ($9)

Mashed Chickpea Pitas

Pair this sandwich with a mixed green salad or cup of soup for a light dinner.

2 garlic cloves, minced
6 tablespoons plain fat-free Greek yogurt, divided
2 tablespoons reduced-fat mayonnaise
1 tablespoon fresh lemon juice
½ teaspoon salt
1 (15-ounce) can no-salt-added chickpeas (garbanzo beans), rinsed and drained
½ cup diced peeled English cucumber
1 tablespoon chopped fresh dill
1 carrot, shredded
2 (6-inch) pitas, cut in half
4 curly leaf lettuce leaves

1. Combine garlic, 5 tablespoons yogurt, and next 4 ingredients in a bowl. Mash with a potato masher or fork until almost smooth or to desired consistency. Stir in cucumber and dill.
2. Combine remaining 1 tablespoon yogurt and carrot in a small bowl; stir well to coat.
3. Line each pita half with 1 lettuce leaf; fill with ½ cup chickpea mixture and 2 tablespoons carrot mixture. Yield: 4 servings (serving size: 1 sandwich).

CALORIES 185; **FAT** 1.6g (sat 0.3g, mono 0.3g, poly 0.5g); **PROTEIN** 9.5g; **CARB** 33.4g; **FIBER** 3.8g; **CHOL** 0mg; **IRON** 2.2mg; **SODIUM** 477mg; **CALC** 74mg

Spinach, Pasta, and Pea Soup

For a vegetarian version of this lemony soup, use organic or lower-sodium vegetable broth in place of chicken broth.

1 tablespoon extra-virgin olive oil
3 garlic cloves, thinly sliced
2 thinly sliced green onions
4 cups fat-free, lower-sodium chicken broth
2 cups water
¾ cup uncooked orzo
1 tablespoon grated lemon rind
1 (15-ounce) can no-salt-added chickpeas (garbanzo beans), drained
1 tablespoon chopped fresh oregano
1 tablespoon lemon juice
½ teaspoon freshly ground black pepper
⅛ teaspoon salt
1 (6-ounce) package fresh baby spinach
⅓ cup grated Parmesan cheese

1. Heat a large saucepan over high heat. Add olive oil to pan; swirl to coat. Add garlic and onions; sauté 30 seconds, stirring constantly. Add chicken broth and 2 cups water; bring to a boil. Add orzo, lemon rind, and chickpeas. Cover and cook 10 minutes or until orzo is done. Stir in oregano and next 4 ingredients. Ladle 1¾ cups soup into each of 4 bowls; top each serving with about 4 teaspoons cheese. Yield: 4 servings.

CALORIES 290; **FAT** 6.7g (sat 1.7g, mono 3.1g, poly 0.5g); **PROTEIN** 14g; **CARB** 43.8g; **FIBER** 7.2g; **CHOL** 6mg; **IRON** 2.8mg; **SODIUM** 648mg; **CALC** 163mg

Lemon-Parmesan Broccoli

(pictured on page 228)

12 ounces broccoli florets (5 cups raw)
2 tablespoons extra-virgin olive oil
2 garlic cloves, minced
½ teaspoon grated lemon rind
1 teaspoon fresh lemon juice
¼ teaspoon kosher salt
3 tablespoons shaved fresh Parmesan

1. Arrange broccoli in a steamer. Steam, covered, 4 minutes or until crisp-tender. Place broccoli in a large bowl.
2. Heat a small skillet over medium-high heat. Add oil and garlic; cook 2 minutes or until garlic is fragrant. Add oil mixture, rind, juice, and salt to broccoli; toss to coat. Sprinkle broccoli mixture with cheese. Yield: 6 servings (serving size: ⅔ cup).

CALORIES 71; **FAT** 5.7g (sat 1.2g, mono 3.3g, poly 0.6g); **PROTEIN** 2.9g; **CARB** 3.5g; **FIBER** 1.7g; **CHOL** 3mg; **IRON** 0.5mg; **SODIUM** 146mg, **CALC** 67mg

Spicy Chile and Garlic

Prepare base recipe through step 1. Heat a skillet over medium-high. Add 2 tablespoons olive oil, 1½ teaspoons crushed red pepper, and 4 sliced garlic cloves; cook 2 minutes. Add 1 tablespoon lemon juice. Pour over broccoli. Sprinkle with 1 teaspoon grated lemon rind and ¼ teaspoon kosher salt. Yield: 6 servings.

CALORIES 61; **FAT** 4.8g (sat 0.7g); **SODIUM** 96mg

Dijon, Thyme, and Pine Nut

Prepare base recipe through step 1. Combine 1 tablespoon minced shallots, 2 tablespoons olive oil, 1 tablespoon fresh lemon juice, 1 tablespoon Dijon mustard, and 2 teaspoons chopped fresh thyme in a large bowl; stir with a whisk. Add broccoli and 2 tablespoons toasted pine nuts to oil mixture; toss. Yield: 6 servings.

CALORIES 79; **FAT** 6.6g (sat 0.8g); **SODIUM** 76mg

Cheddar-Beer Sauce

Whisk ¼ cup beer and 1½ tablespoons flour in a bowl. Combine ¾ cup fat-free milk and ¼ cup beer in a pan; bring to a simmer. Stir in flour mixture; bring to a boil. Reduce heat; simmer 2 minutes. Add ¾ cup reduced-fat cheddar, 1 tablespoon chives, ½ teaspoon grated lemon rind, and ¼ teaspoon kosher salt. Yield: 6 servings.

CALORIES 79; **FAT** 3.3g (sat 1.8g); **SODIUM** 227mg

Linguine with Easy Meat Sauce

For picky eaters, try serving this meat sauce over whimsically shaped pasta, like bow ties, rotini, or wagon wheels.

1 (9-ounce) package fresh linguine
½ pound extra-lean ground beef
½ cup prechopped onion
1 tablespoon minced fresh garlic
1 teaspoon dried oregano
¼ teaspoon salt
3 tablespoons tomato paste
1 (14.5-ounce) can diced tomatoes, undrained
¼ cup (1 ounce) shaved Parmigiano-Reggiano cheese
1 tablespoon fresh flat-leaf parsley leaves

1. Cook pasta according to package directions, omitting salt and fat. Drain.
2. While pasta cooks, heat a large skillet over medium-high heat. Add beef, onion, garlic, oregano, and salt; cook 5 minutes or until beef is browned, stirring to crumble. Stir in tomato paste; cook 1 minute, stirring frequently. Add tomatoes. Bring to a boil; cook 1 minute. Reduce heat to medium-low; cook 3 minutes or until thickened. Serve over pasta; top with cheese and parsley. Yield: 4 servings.

CALORIES 296; **FAT** 4.9g (sat 2g, mono 1g, poly 0.3g); **PROTEIN** 20.7g; **CARB** 43.6g; **FIBER** 3.3g; **CHOL** 68mg; **IRON** 3.4mg; **SODIUM** 530mg; **CALC** 66mg

Apple, Goat Cheese, and Pecan Pizza

Crumbled feta can be substituted for the goat cheese in this recipe.

1 (1-pound) six-grain pizza crust
Cooking spray
3 cups thinly sliced Fuji apple (about 8 ounces)
1 cup (4 ounces) crumbled goat cheese
2 teaspoons chopped fresh thyme
1 tablespoon extra-virgin olive oil
2 teaspoons Dijon mustard
1 teaspoon fresh lemon juice
1½ teaspoons honey
2 cups baby arugula
3 tablespoons chopped pecans, toasted

1. Preheat oven to 450°.
2. Place pizza crust on a baking sheet coated with cooking spray. Arrange apple slices evenly over pizza crust; top with cheese. Sprinkle thyme evenly over cheese. Bake at 450° for 8 minutes or until cheese melts and begins to brown.
3. Combine oil and next 3 ingredients in a medium bowl, stirring with a whisk. Add arugula; toss gently to coat. Sprinkle pecans evenly over pizza; top with arugula mixture. Cut pizza into 6 wedges. Yield: 6 servings (serving size: 1 wedge).

CALORIES 316; **FAT** 11.2g (sat 4.4g, mono 4.3g, poly 1.1g); **PROTEIN** 11.3g; **CARB** 43.2g; **FIBER** 3g; **CHOL** 15mg; **IRON** 0.7mg; **SODIUM** 419mg; **CALC** 77mg

DINNER TONIGHT

Here is a batch of fast weeknight menus from the *Cooking Light* Test Kitchens.

READY IN
40
MINUTES

The
SHOPPING LIST

Bacon, Tomato, and Arugula Pizza
1 pint grape tomatoes
1 cup baby arugula
lower-sodium marinara sauce
5 applewood-smoked bacon slices
1 pound refrigerated fresh pizza dough
3 ounces part-skim mozzarella cheese
yellow cornmeal
crushed red pepper
white wine vinegar
extra-virgin olive oil

Poached Pears
3 large firm pears
sweet white wine
granulated sugar
star anise
cinnamon stick
plain 2% reduced-fat Greek yogurt

The
GAME PLAN

While oven preheats and dough stands:
- Poach pears.
- Cook bacon and tomato mixture.
- Roll out and top dough.
- Bake pizza.

Quick & Easy • Kid Friendly
Bacon, Tomato, and Arugula Pizza
With Poached Pears

1 pound refrigerated fresh pizza dough
Cooking spray
5 applewood-smoked bacon slices
2 cups grape tomatoes, halved lengthwise
½ teaspoon crushed red pepper
1 tablespoon yellow cornmeal
½ cup lower-sodium marinara sauce
¾ cup (3 ounces) shredded part-skim
   mozzarella cheese
1 cup baby arugula
1 teaspoon extra-virgin olive oil
½ teaspoon white wine vinegar

1. Preheat oven to 450°.
2. Place dough in a bowl coated with cooking spray; let dough stand, covered, for 15 minutes.
3. Cook bacon in a skillet over medium heat until crisp. Remove bacon; crumble. Add tomatoes and pepper to drippings in pan; cook 2 minutes, stirring occasionally.
4. Sprinkle a baking sheet with cornmeal; roll dough into a 12-inch circle on prepared baking sheet. Spread sauce evenly over dough, leaving a ½-inch border. Top with tomatoes and crumbled bacon. Sprinkle cheese over top. Bake at 450° on bottom oven rack for 17 minutes or until crust is golden. Combine arugula and remaining ingredients; top pizza with arugula mixture. Yield: 6 servings (serving size: 1 slice).

CALORIES 314; **FAT** 9.1g (sat 4.5g, mono 2.1g, poly 2.1g); **PROTEIN** 13.5g; **CARB** 50.2g; **FIBER** 2.1g; **CHOL** 17mg; **IRON** 2.5mg; **SODIUM** 770mg; **CALC** 124mg

For the Poached Pears:
Combine 2 cups sweet white wine, 1 cup water, ¼ cup sugar, ⅛ teaspoon salt, 1 star anise, and 1 (3-inch) cinnamon stick in a medium saucepan; bring to a simmer. Add 3 large firm pears, peeled,

---

cored, and halved lengthwise; cover and simmer 25 minutes or until tender. Serve 1 pear half with ¼ cup cooking liquid and 2 teaspoons plain 2% reduced-fat Greek yogurt. Yield: 6 servings.

CALORIES 123; **FAT** 0.3g (sat 0.2g); **SODIUM** 54mg

READY IN
40
MINUTES

The
SHOPPING LIST

Chicken and Herb White Pizza
red onion
fresh oregano
fresh chives
fresh parsley
garlic
all-purpose flour
yellow cornmeal
12 ounces rotisserie chicken breast (about 1
   rotisserie chicken)
1 pound refrigerated fresh pizza dough
2 ounces fresh pecorino Romano cheese
¾ cup 2% reduced-fat milk
butter

Apple Iced Tea
2 cups strong brewed tea
unfiltered apple cider
granulated sugar
2 cups bottled lemon sparkling water

The
GAME PLAN

While oven preheats and dough stands:
- Cook white sauce.
- Roll out and top dough.
While pizza bakes:
- Mix iced tea.

Chicken and Herb White Pizza
With Apple Iced Tea

Prep Pointer: Shape the dough by hand rather than using a rolling pin for an airy crust.
Simple Sub: Use dark meat for deeper chicken flavor.
Kid Friendly: Lose the oregano to give the dish more kid appeal.

1 pound refrigerated fresh pizza dough
Cooking spray
1 tablespoon butter
2 garlic cloves, minced
2 tablespoons all-purpose flour
½ teaspoon freshly ground black pepper
¾ cup 2% reduced-fat milk
½ cup (2 ounces) grated fresh pecorino
    Romano cheese
1 tablespoon yellow cornmeal
1½ cups shredded rotisserie chicken breast
¼ cup diced red onion
1 tablespoon chopped fresh oregano
1 tablespoon chopped fresh chives
1 tablespoon chopped fresh parsley

1. Preheat oven to 450°.
2. Place dough in a bowl coated with cooking spray; let dough stand, covered, 15 minutes.
3. Melt butter in a medium saucepan over medium heat. Add garlic; cook 30 seconds, stirring constantly. Add flour and pepper; cook 1 minute, stirring constantly with a whisk. Gradually add milk, stirring constantly with a whisk. Cook 3 minutes or until thick and bubbly, stirring constantly with a whisk. Remove from heat; add cheese, stirring until cheese melts.
4. Sprinkle a baking sheet with cornmeal; roll dough into a 12-inch circle on prepared baking sheet. Spread white sauce over dough, leaving a ½-inch border. Top with chicken and onion. Bake at 450° on bottom oven rack for 17 minutes or until crust is golden. Sprinkle with herbs. Yield: 6 servings (serving size: 1 slice).

CALORIES 363; **FAT** 8.6g (sat 3.4g, mono 1.5g, poly 1.7g); **PROTEIN** 26.1g; **CARB** 45.8g; **FIBER** 1.7g; **CHOL** 65mg; **IRON** 2.9mg; **SODIUM** 805mg; **CALC** 117mg

---

For the Apple Iced Tea:
Combine 2 cups chilled strong brewed tea, 2 cups apple cider, and ¼ cup sugar, stirring until sugar dissolves. Add 2 cups lemon sparkling water. Serve over ice. Yield: 6 servings (serving size: 1 cup).

CALORIES 69; **FAT** 0g; **SODIUM** 8mg

READY IN 40 MINUTES

The SHOPPING LIST

Spicy Sausage and Mushroom Pizza
1 large yellow or white onion
1 (8-ounce) package presliced mushrooms
1 red or green bell pepper
1 pound refrigerated fresh pizza dough
yellow cornmeal
lower-sodium marinara sauce
4 ounces hot turkey Italian sausage
    (about 1 link)
2 ounces part-skim mozzarella cheese
1 ounce Parmigiano-Reggiano cheese

Lemony Arugula Salad
1 lemon
8 cups arugula
1 red onion
extra-virgin olive oil

The GAME PLAN

While oven preheats and dough stands:
■ Cook sausage mixture.
■ Roll out and top dough.
While pizza bakes:
■ Prepare salad.

Spicy Sausage and Mushroom Pizza
With Lemony Arugula Salad

Flavor Hit: Hot sausage gives the pizza a welcome spicy kick.
Time-Saver: Store-bought precooked crust offers choices: thin, regular, or whole-wheat.
Budget Buy: Pecorino Romano is a cheaper alternative to Parmigiano-Reggiano.

1 pound refrigerated fresh pizza dough
Cooking spray
4 ounces hot turkey Italian sausage
1 cup thinly sliced onion
1 (8-ounce) package presliced mushrooms
1 cup diced red or green bell pepper
1 tablespoon yellow cornmeal
½ cup lower-sodium marinara sauce
½ cup (2 ounces) shredded part-skim
    mozzarella cheese
¼ cup (1 ounce) grated Parmigiano-Reggiano
    cheese

1. Preheat oven to 450°.
2. Place dough in a bowl coated with cooking spray; let dough stand, covered, 15 minutes.
3. Heat a large nonstick skillet over medium-high heat; coat pan with cooking spray. Remove casings from sausage. Add sausage to pan; cook 3 minutes, stirring to crumble. Add onion and mushrooms; sauté 4 minutes. Add bell pepper; sauté 2 minutes.
4. Sprinkle a baking sheet with cornmeal; roll dough into a 12-inch circle on prepared baking sheet. Spread sauce over dough, leaving a ½-inch border. Top with sausage mixture. Sprinkle cheeses over sausage mixture. Bake at 450° on bottom oven rack for 17 minutes or until crust is golden. Yield: 6 servings (serving size: 1 slice).

CALORIES 311; **FAT** 7.3g (sat 1.9g, mono 2.8g, poly 1.5g); **PROTEIN** 15.6g; **CARB** 51.8g; **FIBER** 2.4g; **CHOL** 21mg; **IRON** 3.1mg; **SODIUM** 751mg; **CALC** 134mg

continued

For the Lemony Arugula Salad:
Combine 2 tablespoons extra-virgin olive oil, ½ teaspoon grated lemon rind, 1 tablespoon fresh lemon juice, and ¼ teaspoon salt in a large bowl. Add 8 cups arugula and ⅓ cup thinly sliced red onion; toss well. Yield: 6 servings (serving size: about 1 cup).

CALORIES 50; **FAT** 4.7g (sat 0.7g); **SODIUM** 111mg

READY IN
40
MINUTES

The
SHOPPING LIST

Pepperoni, Onion, and Olive Pizza
1 sweet onion (such as Vidalia)
10 niçoise olives
1 pound refrigerated fresh pizza dough
lower-sodium marinara sauce
2 ounces pepperoni slices
yellow cornmeal
3 ounces preshredded reduced-fat
   Italian-blend cheese

Greens and Sherry Vinaigrette
mixed gourmet salad greens
sherry vinegar
extra-virgin olive oil
Dijon mustard

The
GAME PLAN

While oven preheats and dough stands:
■ Prep toppings.
■ Roll out and top dough.
While pizza bakes:
■ Prepare salad.

Quick & Easy • Kid Friendly
Pepperoni, Onion, and Olive Pizza
With Greens and Sherry Vinaigrette
(pictured on page 235)

Flavor Hit: Sweet onion like Vidalia helps balance the bold, briny olives in this pizza.
Simple Sub: Turkey pepperoni is a lower-fat (but higher-sodium) alternative.
Kid-Friendly: Omit olives from the recipe to make it more appealing to younger palates.

1 pound refrigerated fresh pizza dough
Cooking spray
1 tablespoon yellow cornmeal
½ cup lower-sodium marinara sauce
½ cup thinly sliced sweet onion
2 ounces pepperoni slices
10 niçoise olives, pitted and halved lengthwise
¾ cup (3 ounces) preshredded reduced-fat
   Italian-blend cheese

1. Preheat oven to 450°.
2. Place dough in a bowl coated with cooking spray; let dough stand, covered, 15 minutes.
3. Sprinkle a baking sheet with cornmeal; roll dough into a 12-inch circle on prepared baking sheet. Spread sauce evenly over dough, leaving a ½-inch border. Top with onion, pepperoni, and olives; sprinkle with cheese. Bake at 450° on bottom oven rack for 17 minutes or until crust is golden. Yield: 6 servings (serving size: 1 slice).

CALORIES 307; **FAT** 8.7g (sat 3.3g, mono 3.1g, poly 1.7g); **PROTEIN** 13.5g; **CARB** 48.4g; **FIBER** 1.7g; **CHOL** 15mg; **IRON** 2.8mg; **SODIUM** 799mg; **CALC** 109mg

For the Greens and Sherry Vinaigrette:
Combine 2 tablespoons sherry vinegar, 2 tablespoons extra-virgin olive oil, ½ teaspoon Dijon mustard, ¼ teaspoon salt, and ¼ teaspoon freshly ground black pepper in a large bowl; stir well with a whisk. Add 8 cups mixed salad greens; toss gently to coat. Yield: 6 servings (serving size: about 1½ cups).

CALORIES 55; **FAT** 4.5g (sat 0.6g); **SODIUM** 135mg

OOPS! YOUR CARAMEL MEETS A BURNT, BITTER END

A little water—and patience—goes a long way.
By Hannah Klinger

Caramel is a one-ingredient recipe for experts, two for more cautious cooks who add water to the sugar—but either way it can quickly go wrong. The problem is a rapid acceleration of browning, which can quickly move your sugar sauce into bitter, burnt territory.

Sugar behaves differently from other foods when it's cooked. While most ingredients absorb heat from the pan, sugar actually generates its own heat as it breaks down, causing the temperature to rise about 1 degree per second. When you remove the pan from the heat as the caramel reaches the perfect light-amber hue, it can still burn (residual heat from the pan keeps the action going).

The key is watchful, hands-off cooking, as slow and even as possible. Adding ¼ cup of water per cup of sugar dissolves the sugar uniformly and slows boiling, providing more control as you look for that honey-gold color. Use a light-colored stainless steel or enamel saucepan and a candy thermometer.

To make the caramel, cook the sugar and water, without stirring (or minimal stirring, if you must), over medium-low heat until golden and fragrant, about 335°. With experience, you'll learn to trust color more than temperature.

The hands-off approach works best because stirring can cause hot caramel to crystallize when it hits the cool sides of the pan, and that can set off a chain reaction that ruins the sauce.

Set the pan in an ice bath for 2 to 3 seconds to stop the cooking (any longer and the caramel will seize), and then use immediately.

THE CROWD-PLEASER'S HOLIDAY COOKBOOK

Wow your table with variations on the 5 best-loved dishes of the Thanksgiving table: turkey, stuffing, veggies, potatoes, and pie.

THE TURKEY

It may be the star, but turkey is often wildly overcooked—we've all seen white meat served as dried slabs and shreds after so much time in the oven. In fact, it's a good bet some folks have never tasted a properly cooked turkey. Two words: meat thermometer. But there is more than one path to a juicy, flavorful bird. If guests expect the ritual carving at the head of the table, opt for a classic whole presentation, like Maple-Cider Brined Turkey with Bourbon-Cider Gravy (page 302), or the enticingly simple roasted bird with gorgeous, golden butter-basted skin (Butter-Basted Turkey, page 302). Note the tips on page 301 for maximizing moistness.

Still, if you're cooking for real turkey aficionados, take the cheffy route to perfection: Cut the bird into parts and slow roast them, basting with a touch of cream, which gives you fantastically moist, rich meat, white and dark alike. For smaller crowds—and those even less tradition-bound—try the creative elegance of braised turkey roulade stuffed with meaty porcini mushrooms and peppery Italian bacon (Braised Turkey Roulade with Pancetta, Shallots, and Porcini Gravy, page 300). Another smaller option: a smoked turkey breast with sweet-tart pomegranate glaze (recipe at right).

Kid Friendly
Smoke-Roasted Turkey Breast with Pomegranate-Thyme Glaze

Hands-on time: 30 min. Total time: 2 hr. 10 min.

Late November may not be prime time for grilling, but adding smoke and fire to the holiday bird is worth the momentary chill. Because this is a turkey breast (and not a whole bird), it cooks relatively quickly over an indirect fire, but it's still plenty big to feed a crowd.

2 cups cherry or apple wood chips
1 (6-pound) whole bone-in turkey breast
1 tablespoon chopped fresh thyme, divided
2 teaspoons kosher salt, divided
1 teaspoon freshly ground black pepper
3 garlic cloves, thinly sliced
1 teaspoon olive oil
1 large shallot, finely chopped
1½ cups pomegranate juice
¼ cup sugar
Cooking spray

1. Soak wood chips in water 1 hour; drain well.
2. Trim excess fat from turkey. Loosen skin from breast by inserting fingers, gently pushing between skin and meat. Combine 2 teaspoons thyme, 1½ teaspoons salt, pepper, and garlic, stirring well. Rub thyme mixture under loosened skin.

3. Heat oil in small saucepan over medium-high heat; swirl to coat. Add remaining 1 teaspoon thyme, remaining ½ teaspoon salt, and shallot; sauté 2 minutes. Add juice and sugar. Bring to a boil; reduce heat, and simmer 15 minutes or until syrupy and reduced to about ½ cup. Remove from heat.
4. To prepare turkey for indirect grilling, remove grill rack. Preheat grill to medium-high using both burners. After preheating, turn the left burner off (leave the right burner on). Place 1 cup wood chips on heat element on right side. Place a disposable aluminum foil pan on heat element on left (unheated) side. Pour 2 cups water in pan. Coat grill rack with cooking spray, and place on grill. Place turkey on grill rack covering left burner. Cover and grill 1 hour and 20 minutes or until a thermometer registers 165°, turning halfway during cooking time. Add remaining 1 cup wood chips halfway during cooking time, and brush turkey with half of pomegranate mixture during last 5 minutes of cooking. Place turkey on a platter. Let stand 30 minutes. Discard skin. Serve with remaining pomegranate mixture. Yield: 8 servings (serving size: 6 ounces turkey and about 1½ teaspoons sauce).

CALORIES 349; FAT 2.2g (sat 0.6g, mono 0.7g, poly 0.5g); PROTEIN 64.3g; CARB 14.3g; FIBER 0.1g; CHOL 176mg; IRON 3.5mg; SODIUM 597mg; CALC 39mg

Braised Turkey Roulade with Pancetta, Shallots, and Porcini Gravy

Kid Friendly

Hands-on time: 1 hr. 10 min. Total time: 1 hr. 50 min.

The combination of shallots and porcini soaking liquid creates a savory, earthy gravy.

2 cups boiling water
¾ cup dried porcini mushrooms (about ¾ ounce)
1 tablespoon extra-virgin olive oil, divided
3½ ounces thinly sliced pancetta (about 9 slices), divided
2 cups chopped shallots (about 10 ounces), divided
1½ tablespoons chopped fresh rosemary, divided
1 teaspoon salt, divided
¾ teaspoon freshly ground black pepper, divided
2 (1¼-pound) skinless, boneless turkey breast halves
½ cup coarsely chopped carrot
½ cup coarsely chopped celery
½ cup dry white wine
¼ cup water
3 tablespoons all-purpose flour

1. Combine 2 cups boiling water and porcini mushrooms in a bowl; cover and let stand 15 minutes or until mushrooms are soft. Drain through a sieve over a bowl, reserving soaking liquid. Chop porcini mushrooms.
2. Heat a large nonstick skillet over medium heat. Add 1½ teaspoons olive oil to pan, and swirl to coat. Coarsely chop 1 pancetta slice. Add chopped pancetta to pan; cook 3 minutes, stirring occasionally. Add 1¾ cups shallots, 2 teaspoons rosemary, ¼ teaspoon salt, and ¼ teaspoon pepper; cook 7 minutes or until shallots are tender, stirring occasionally. Stir in reserved mushrooms. Cool slightly.
3. Slice 1 turkey breast half lengthwise, cutting to, but not through, other side. Open halves, laying turkey breast flat. Place plastic wrap over turkey breast;

pound to ½-inch thickness using a meat mallet or small heavy skillet. Spread half of shallot mixture over turkey breast; roll up jelly-roll fashion, starting with long sides. Sprinkle with ⅜ teaspoon salt and ¼ teaspoon pepper. Arrange 4 pancetta slices evenly on top of turkey roll. Secure at 2-inch intervals with twine. Repeat procedure with remaining turkey breast half, shallot mixture, ⅜ teaspoon salt, ¼ teaspoon pepper, and 4 pancetta slices.
4. Preheat oven to 325°.
5. Heat a large Dutch oven over medium-high heat. Add remaining 1½ teaspoons oil to pan; swirl to coat. Add turkey rolls to pan; cook 6 minutes or until browned, turning after 3 minutes. Add remaining ¼ cup shallots, carrot, celery, and wine to pan. Bring to a boil; cook until liquid is reduced by half (about 2 minutes). Stir in reserved porcini liquid and remaining 2½ teaspoons rosemary. Cover and bake at 325° for 40 minutes or until a thermometer inserted in thickest portion registers 165°. Remove turkey rolls from pan; let stand 15 minutes. Cut each roll crosswise into 12 slices.
6. Strain cooking liquid through a fine mesh sieve over a bowl; discard solids. Combine ¼ cup water and flour, stirring with a whisk until smooth. Return remaining cooking liquid to pan; add flour mixture, stirring with a whisk. Bring to a boil; cook 1 minute or until thickened, stirring constantly. Serve gravy with turkey. Yield: 8 servings (serving size: 3 turkey slices and ¼ cup gravy).

CALORIES 277; FAT 6.8g (sat 2.3g, mono 3.3g, poly 0.6g); PROTEIN 38.9g; CARB 11.6g; FIBER 0.9g; CHOL 97mg; IRON 2.9mg; SODIUM 585mg; CALC 38mg

THIS IS A PERFECT DISH FOR AN ELEGANT HOLIDAY DINNER AND SIMPLER TO CARVE THAN A WHOLE TURKEY.

Slow-Roasted Turkey with Cream Gravy

Kid Friendly

Hands-on time: 30 min. Total time: 10 hr.

Cut the bird into pieces (to help ensure even cooking), salt overnight, and cook slowly for juicy, tender meat. If breaking down the turkey seems too advanced, have your butcher do it.

1 (12-pound) fresh or frozen whole turkey, thawed
1 tablespoon kosher salt
10 cups cold water
4 celery stalks, quartered and divided
2 medium onions, peeled, quartered, and divided
2 carrots, quartered and divided
½ cup heavy whipping cream, divided
1½ teaspoons freshly ground black pepper
2 tablespoons cornstarch

1. Remove giblets and neck from turkey; set aside. Discard liver. Place turkey, breast side up, on a cutting board. Pull legs away from body; using a boning knife, cut through skin at leg joint. Using both hands, turn leg quarter away from body until joint pops out of socket. When flesh and joint are exposed, place knife firmly against joint to make cut. Cut through joint to remove leg quarters, and set aside. Remove wings along the joint, and reserve wings. Using kitchen shears, cut along backbone on both sides from tail to neck to remove backbone; reserve backbone. Place breast, meat side down, on a cutting board. Using a large, heavy knife, cut breast in half lengthwise.
2. Place breast halves and leg quarters in a large bowl; sprinkle with salt. Cover and chill 8 hours or overnight.
3. Combine reserved giblets, wings, and backbone in a large Dutch oven. Add 10 cups water, 8 celery pieces, 4 onion quarters, and 4 carrot pieces. Bring to a boil over medium-high heat. Reduce heat and simmer 5 hours or until mixture measures 8 cups. Cool to room temperature. Cover and chill stock 8 hours or overnight.
4. Skim solidified fat from surface of stock; discard fat. Return stock to high

heat; bring to a boil. Boil 30 minutes or until stock measures 3 cups. Strain mixture through a sieve, reserving stock. Discard the solids.

5. Remove turkey from refrigerator, and let stand at room temperature 30 minutes.

6. Preheat oven to 325°.

7. Arrange turkey pieces, skin side up, in a roasting pan, and arrange remaining 8 celery pieces, 4 onion quarters, and 4 carrot pieces in pan. Brush turkey skin with 2 tablespoons cream; sprinkle with black pepper. Bake at 325° for 1½ hours or until a thermometer inserted in the thickest part of breast registers 165°, basting every 30 minutes with 2½ tablespoons stock. Remove from oven. Place breast halves and leg quarters on a jelly-roll pan or cutting board. Let stand, covered, 30 minutes. Discard skin.

8. Add 1 cup stock to bottom of roasting pan; carefully scrape browned bits from bottom of pan. Place a zip-top plastic bag inside a 2-cup glass measure. Pour drippings into bag; let stand 10 minutes (fat will rise to top). Seal bag, and carefully snip off 1 bottom corner of bag. Strain drippings through a sieve into a medium saucepan, stopping before fat layer reaches opening; discard fat and solids. Add remaining 1½ cups stock to pan; bring to a boil over medium-high heat. Combine remaining 6 tablespoons cream and cornstarch, stirring with a whisk until smooth. Stir cream mixture into stock mixture, stirring with a whisk. Boil 1 minute or until slightly thick, stirring constantly. Serve gravy with turkey. Yield: 12 servings (serving size: about 5 ounces turkey and 3 tablespoons gravy).

CALORIES 254; **FAT** 7.4g (sat 3.5g, mono 1.9g, poly 1.2g); **PROTEIN** 42.2g; **CARB** 2g; **FIBER** 0.2g; **CHOL** 153mg; **IRON** 2.8mg; **SODIUM** 581mg; **CALC** 37mg

---

Kid Friendly

Roasted Turkey with Rosemary-Garlic Butter Rub and Pan Gravy

Hands-on time: 35 min. Total time: 2 hr. 15 min.

1 (12-pound) fresh or frozen turkey, thawed
¼ cup butter, softened
1 tablespoon chopped fresh rosemary, divided
1¼ teaspoons salt, divided
½ teaspoon freshly ground black pepper, divided
½ teaspoon ground coriander
4 garlic cloves, minced
2 carrots, coarsely chopped (1¼ cups)
2 celery stalks, coarsely chopped (about 1 cup)
1 medium onion, coarsely chopped (about 2½ cups)
Cooking spray
3 cups fat-free, lower-sodium chicken broth, divided
3 tablespoons all-purpose flour
3 tablespoons water

1. Preheat oven to 425°.

2. Remove giblets and neck from turkey; discard liver. Reserve neck and giblets. Pat turkey dry. Trim excess fat. Starting at neck cavity, loosen skin from breast and drumsticks by inserting fingers, gently pushing between skin and meat. Lift wing tips up and over back; tuck under turkey.

3. Combine butter, 2 teaspoons rosemary, 1 teaspoon salt, ¼ teaspoon pepper, coriander, and garlic in a small bowl. Rub butter mixture under loosened skin and over breasts and drumsticks. Tie legs together with kitchen string. Place remaining 1 teaspoon rosemary, reserved giblets, neck, carrots, celery, and onion in the bottom of a large roasting pan coated with cooking spray. Add ½ cup broth. Place roasting rack in pan. Arrange turkey, breast side up, on roasting rack. Bake turkey at 425° for 30 minutes.

4. Reduce oven temperature to 325° (do not remove turkey from oven). Add ½ cup broth to pan. Bake an additional 30 minutes. Rotate pan in oven; bake an additional 30 minutes or until a thermometer inserted into meaty part of thigh registers 165°. Remove from oven; let stand on a cutting board 30 minutes. Discard skin.

5. Place a large zip-top plastic bag inside a 4-cup glass measure. Strain pan drippings into bag; let stand 10 minutes. Discard solids. Seal bag; snip off 1 bottom corner of bag. Drain pan drippings into a medium saucepan, stopping before fat layer reaches opening. Add remaining 2 cups broth to pan; bring to a boil. Combine 3 tablespoons flour and 3 tablespoons water in a small bowl, stirring with a whisk until smooth. Stir flour mixture into broth mixture, and boil 1 minute or until thickened, stirring constantly. Stir in remaining ¼ teaspoon salt and remaining ¼ teaspoon pepper. Serve gravy with turkey. Yield: 12 servings (serving size: about 6 ounces turkey and ¼ cup gravy).

CALORIES 304; **FAT** 8.4g (sat 3.9g, mono 2g, poly 1.5g); **PROTEIN** 51.3g; **CARB** 2.6g; **FIBER** 0.5g; **CHOL** 177mg; **IRON** 3.6mg; **SODIUM** 486mg; **CALC** 43mg

---

MOIST TURKEY, GUARANTEED

The biggest challenge is keeping the white meat moist while the dark meat cooks through. High heat or low? Does basting help? What about the recent vogue for brining? To take the last one first, brining does boost moistness since it adds seasoned liquid to the meat, but it isn't a miracle. As for basting—it browns the skin but does little for the meat. A meat thermometer (preferably digital, with an alarm), however, is a must so you can get the bird out when the deepest thigh meat hits 165°. This may happen a lot faster than you expect. Don't worry. Just remove to a cutting board (no need to cover with foil). Then, patience. Let the turkey stand at least 30 minutes so the juices redistribute and don't spill out when you slice. (A big uncarved bird will stay warm for a long time.) There isn't one perfect cooking temp, by the way, though brined birds better handle high heat (375° to 425°). For unbrined turkey, we prefer 325° to 350°.

Maple-Cider Brined Turkey with Bourbon-Cider Gravy

Hands-on time: 40 min. Total time: 20 hr. 40 min.

Use your largest stockpot for brining the bird, or a brining bag.

Brine:
2 quarts apple cider
½ cup kosher salt
½ cup maple syrup
1 teaspoon whole allspice berries
¾ teaspoon whole black peppercorns
½ teaspoon whole cloves
6 (2-inch) strips orange rind
2 rosemary sprigs
2 bay leaves
1 gallon cold water

Turkey:
1 (12-pound) fresh or frozen turkey, thawed
3 tablespoons butter, softened
2 teaspoons chopped fresh rosemary
2 teaspoons chopped fresh sage
½ teaspoon freshly ground black pepper
1 apple, cut into wedges
6 garlic cloves
1 rosemary sprig
1 sage sprig
½ orange, cut into wedges
½ onion, cut into wedges
Cooking spray

Gravy:
1 tablespoon butter
1 tablespoon chopped fresh thyme
1 shallot, finely chopped
½ cup apple cider
¼ cup bourbon
1¼ cups fat-free, lower-sodium chicken broth, divided
3 tablespoons all-purpose flour
1 tablespoon chopped fresh flat-leaf parsley
1 tablespoon cider vinegar

1. To prepare brine, combine first 9 ingredients in a large stockpot over high heat; cook 6 minutes or until salt dissolves, stirring occasionally. Remove from heat; add 1 gallon cold water. Cool to room temperature.
2. To prepare turkey, remove giblets and neck from turkey; reserve neck. Trim excess fat; add turkey to brine. Refrigerate 18 to 24 hours, turning occasionally.
3. Preheat oven to 375°.
4. Remove turkey from brine; discard brine. Pat turkey dry. Starting at neck cavity, loosen skin from breast and drumsticks by inserting fingers, gently pushing between skin and meat. Combine 3 tablespoons butter and next 3 ingredients in a small bowl; rub butter mixture under loosened skin and over breast and drumsticks. Lift wing tips up and over back; tuck under turkey. Place apple and next 5 ingredients in body cavity. Secure legs with kitchen twine. Place turkey on rack of a roasting pan coated with cooking spray. Place neck in bottom of roasting pan; place rack with turkey in pan. Bake at 375° for 1 hour and 15 minutes. Cover turkey loosely with foil; bake an additional 45 minutes or until a thermometer inserted into thickest part of thigh registers 165°. Remove from oven; place turkey on a cutting board. Let stand, covered, 20 minutes; discard neck and skin.
5. To prepare gravy, place a zip-top plastic bag inside a 2-cup glass measure. Pour pan drippings into bag; let stand 10 minutes (fat will rise to the top). Seal bag; carefully snip off one bottom corner of bag. Drain drippings into a small bowl, stopping before fat layer reaches opening; discard fat.
6. Melt 1 tablespoon butter in a medium saucepan over medium-high heat. Add thyme and shallot; sauté 2 minutes. Add ½ cup cider and bourbon; boil 3 minutes or until liquid is reduced by half. Combine ¼ cup broth and flour, stirring with a whisk. Add flour mixture, remaining 1 cup broth, and drippings to pan; bring to a boil. Reduce heat, and simmer 4 minutes or until thickened. Stir in parsley and vinegar. Yield: 12 servings (serving size: 6 ounces turkey and 2½ tablespoons gravy).

CALORIES 326; **FAT** 8.4g (sat 3.9g, mono 2g, poly 1.5g); **PROTEIN** 51g; **CARB** 7g; **FIBER** 0.2g; **CHOL** 177mg; **IRON** 3.6mg; **SODIUM** 566mg; **CALC** 42mg

Kid Friendly
Butter-Basted Turkey

Hands-on time: 20 min. Total time: 2 hr. 5 min.

This wonderfully simple bird uses clarified butter (with milk solids removed) to achieve a gorgeous golden brown color on the skin. Visit CookingLight.com for how to prepare clarified butter.

Preheat oven to 325°. Remove giblets and neck from turkey; reserve for another use. Pat turkey dry. Trim excess fat. Lift wing tips up and over back; tuck under turkey. Tie legs together with kitchen string. Brush turkey with ⅓ cup clarified butter; sprinkle evenly with 1 tablespoon kosher salt. Place roasting rack in large roasting pan. Arrange turkey, breast side up, on roasting rack. Bake turkey at 325° for 1 hour and 10 minutes, basting with remaining clarified butter after 1 hour. Increase oven temperature to 450° (do not remove turkey from oven); bake an additional 25 minutes or until a thermometer inserted into meaty part of thigh registers 165°. Remove turkey from oven; let turkey stand 30 minutes before carving. Discard skin. Yield: 12 servings (serving size: about 6 ounces turkey).

CALORIES 261; **FAT** 5.1g (sat 1.9g); **SODIUM** 594mg

THE LACTOSE-FREE MENU

Roasted Rosemary Fingerling Potatoes
(page 310)

Old-Fashioned Cranberry Sauce
(page 303)

Fennel, Sausage, and Caramelized Apple Stuffing (page 305)

Smoke-Roasted Turkey Breast with Pomegranate-Thyme Glaze (page 299)

Brussels Sprouts with Bacon, Garlic, and Shallots (page 306)

French Apple Tart (page 310)
(Hold the crème fraîche.)

Quick & Easy • Make Ahead
Vegetarian

Old-Fashioned Cranberry Sauce

Hands-on time: 15 min. Total time: 15 min.

1 tablespoon canola oil
½ cup chopped onion
1¼ cups sugar
½ cup water
¼ cup port wine
¼ teaspoon ground ginger
1 (12-ounce) package fresh cranberries
2 teaspoons grated orange rind

1. Heat oil in a medium saucepan over medium-high heat. Add onion, and sauté 4 minutes. Add sugar and next 4 ingredients; bring to a boil. Reduce heat, and simmer 8 minutes or until cranberries pop. Remove from heat, and stir in orange rind. Serve chilled or at room temperature. Yield: 12 servings (serving size: ¼ cup).

CALORIES 112; FAT 1.2g (sat 0.1g, mono 0.7g, poly 0.4g); PROTEIN 0.2g; CARB 25.5g; FIBER 1.5g; CHOL 0mg; IRON 0.1mg; SODIUM 1mg; CALC 5mg

South-of-the-Border Cranberry Sauce: Add 3 tablespoons chopped fresh cilantro; 1 teaspoon grated lime rind; and 1 minced chipotle chile, canned in adobo sauce, to Old-Fashioned Cranberry Sauce. Yield: 12 servings (serving size: ¼ cup).

CALORIES 112; FAT 1.2g (sat 0.1g); SODIUM 6mg

Apple-Cranberry Sauce: Add 2 cups diced apple to Old-Fashioned Cranberry Sauce. Yield: 16 servings (serving size: ¼ cup).

CALORIES 90; FAT 0.9g (sat 0.1g); SODIUM 1mg

Dried Cherry-Cranberry Sauce: Combine 1 cup dried cherries and 1 cup cherry juice in a small saucepan over medium-high heat; bring to a boil. Remove from heat; let stand 10 minutes. Drain. Add drained cherries to Old-Fashioned Cranberry Sauce. Yield: 14 servings (serving size: ¼ cup).

CALORIES 137; FAT 1g (sat 0.1g); SODIUM 3mg

Raspberry-Walnut Cranberry Sauce: Add 1 cup fresh raspberries and ½ cup coarsely chopped toasted walnuts to Old-Fashioned Cranberry Sauce. Yield: 16 servings (serving size: ¼ cup).

CALORIES 112; FAT 3.3g (sat 0.3g); SODIUM 1mg

"FRESH SAUCE IS SO MUCH BETTER."

Good, fresh cranberry sauce is incredibly easy and rewarding to make. The berries quickly pop under heat and release lots of pectin for beautiful texture and a bit of crunch. The basic recipe at left, spiked with lush port wine and brightened by citrus, takes all of 15 minutes to prepare. Think of it as what chefs call a "mother sauce"—a sauce to which other ingredients can be added to suit your taste. We've provided four simple stir-in suggestions, from chipotle-spiced sauce to fruit- and nut-studded versions with dried cherries, crisp apple, or fresh raspberries.

CARVE THAT BIRD LIKE A PRO

REMOVE LEG QUARTER
Cut through the skin between the leg quarter and breast, and then pull the leg quarters away from the turkey. Cut through the joint between the thigh and backbone to separate the leg quarter, or just twist it off.

SEPARATE LEG AND THIGH
Find the joint between the thigh and drumstick, and then cut through it.

REMOVE WHOLE BREAST
Cut parallel to the breastbone, from wing to tail end. Stay close to the bone and work downward. Make a long cut at the bottom of the breastbone, almost parallel to the work surface. Take off the entire breast.

CARVE BREAST
Slice the breast crosswise, against the grain.

THE STUFFING

The bread vs. corn bread divide is so deeply established in many families that switching up the foundation ingredient is next to heresy. But that doesn't mean you can't experiment with your bread stuffing or your corn bread dressing (that's what it's called in the South)—check out the recipes here. Sourdough bread, sausage, and apple is a classic combo, but our bread stuffing also has licorice notes from fresh fennel. On the corn bread side, our version veers away from Dixie toward the Southwest, with chorizo sausage and a little kick from a jalapeño pepper.

If your family is less resolute on this issue, stray further afield into whole-grain territory. Farro has earthy flavor and a satisfying chew—a bold choice for nontraditional stuffing, blended with shiitakes. Wild rice stuffing flecked with pecans and dried cherries offers another whole-grain medium, while ciabatta stuffing with chestnuts and raisins gives bread-lovers another option.

Kid Friendly
Ciabatta Stuffing with Chestnuts and Raisins

Hands-on time: 35 min. Total time: 1 hr. 25 min.

10 cups (1-inch) cubed ciabatta bread (about 14 ounces)
2 tablespoons extra-virgin olive oil
1½ cups chopped celery
1 cup chopped onion
½ cup coarsely chopped fresh flat-leaf parsley
1 tablespoon chopped fresh rosemary
1 tablespoon chopped fresh sage
½ teaspoon freshly ground black pepper
¼ teaspoon salt
2 cups peeled bottled chestnuts, finely chopped
½ cup golden raisins
3 cups fat-free, lower-sodium chicken broth
1 large egg, lightly beaten
Cooking spray

1. Preheat oven to 350°.
2. Arrange bread in a single layer on a baking sheet. Bake at 350° for 25 minutes or until golden. Place bread in a large bowl.
3. Heat a large skillet over medium heat. Add oil to pan; swirl to coat. Add celery and next 6 ingredients to pan; cook 15 minutes or until vegetables are tender, stirring occasionally. Add celery mixture, chestnuts, and raisins to bread; toss well. Combine chicken broth and egg, stirring with a whisk. Add broth mixture to bread mixture, tossing gently to combine. Spoon bread mixture into a 13 x 9–inch glass or ceramic baking dish coated with cooking spray. Bake at 350° for 50 minutes or until top is lightly browned. Yield: 12 servings.

CALORIES 205; FAT 4.5g (sat 0.9g, mono 2.3g, poly 1g); PROTEIN 5.3g; CARB 36.1g; FIBER 3.1g; CHOL 18mg; IRON 1.7mg; SODIUM 358mg; CALC 55mg

Fennel, Sausage, and Caramelized Apple Stuffing

Hands-on time: 48 min. Total time: 1 hr. 28 min.

12 ounces sourdough bread, cut into ½-inch cubes
Cooking spray
9 ounces Italian sausage
5 teaspoons extra-virgin olive oil, divided
4 cups chopped onion
1¼ cups sliced fennel bulb
1¼ cups chopped carrot
2 tablespoons chopped fresh sage
½ teaspoon fennel seeds, crushed
5 garlic cloves, minced
½ teaspoon freshly ground black pepper, divided
3 cups chopped Golden Delicious apple
2 teaspoons sugar
1½ cups fat-free, lower-sodium chicken broth
2 large eggs

1. Preheat oven to 400°.
2. Arrange bread cubes in a single layer on a baking sheet coated with cooking spray. Bake at 400° for 16 minutes or until golden, stirring after 8 minutes. Place in a large bowl.
3. Heat a large skillet over medium-high heat. Remove casings from sausage. Coat pan with cooking spray. Add sausage to pan; cook 8 minutes or until browned, stirring to crumble. Add sausage to bread.
4. Return pan to medium-high heat. Add 3 teaspoons oil to pan; swirl to coat. Add onion and next 5 ingredients. Add ¼ teaspoon pepper; sauté 8 minutes or until vegetables are tender, stirring occasionally. Add vegetables to sausage mixture.
5. Return pan to medium-high heat. Add remaining 2 teaspoons oil to pan; swirl to coat. Add apple and sugar; sauté 5 minutes or until apple caramelizes, stirring occasionally. Add to sausage mixture.
6. Combine broth and eggs in a small bowl, stirring with a whisk. Add broth mixture and remaining ¼ teaspoon pepper to sausage mixture; toss well to combine.
7. Spoon sausage mixture into a 13 x 9–inch glass or ceramic baking dish coated with cooking spray. Cover with foil. Bake at 400° for 20 minutes. Uncover dish; bake at 400° for 20 minutes or until browned and crisp. Yield: 12 servings (serving size: about ⅔ cup).

CALORIES 180; FAT 5.4g (sat 1.3g, mono 2.5g, poly 0.7g); PROTEIN 8.4g; CARB 26.3g; FIBER 3g; CHOL 42mg; IRON 1.9mg; SODIUM 359mg; CALC 66mg

Corn Bread, Chorizo, and Jalapeño Dressing

Hands-on time: 40 min. Total time: 2 hr.

Corn bread:
4.5 ounces all-purpose flour (about 1 cup)
1¼ cups low-fat buttermilk
1 cup yellow cornmeal
2 tablespoons sugar
2 tablespoons unsalted butter, melted
1 tablespoon baking powder
2 large eggs, lightly beaten
¾ cup shredded reduced-fat sharp cheddar cheese
Cooking spray
Dressing:
1 jalapeño pepper, halved
1 teaspoon olive oil
3 ounces Mexican chorizo, casing removed and crumbled
1¼ cups diced red bell pepper (1 large)
1 cup thinly sliced green onions
2 cups (½-inch) cubed French bread baguette (crusts removed)
¼ cup chopped fresh cilantro
2 large egg whites, lightly beaten
1 (14.5-ounce) can fat-free, lower-sodium chicken broth
1 lime, cut into wedges

1. Preheat oven to 350°. Place a 10-inch cast-iron skillet in oven as it preheats.
2. To prepare corn bread, weigh or lightly spoon flour into a dry measuring cup; level with a knife. Combine flour and next 6 ingredients in a large bowl; fold in cheese.
3. Remove skillet from oven. Coat pan with cooking spray. Pour batter into hot skillet. Bake at 350° for 35 minutes or until edges are lightly browned and a wooden pick inserted in center comes out clean. Cool corn bread completely on a wire rack. Crumble corn bread into a large bowl.
4. To prepare dressing, remove seeds and membrane from half of jalapeño. Coarsely chop both jalapeño halves. Heat a large skillet over medium-high heat. Add oil to pan; swirl to coat. Add chorizo; sauté 2 minutes. Add jalapeño, bell pepper, and onions; sauté 3 minutes. Remove from heat. Add chorizo mixture to corn bread; stir in baguette, cilantro, egg whites, and broth, stirring until bread is moist.
5. Spoon corn bread mixture into a 13 x 9–inch glass or ceramic baking dish coated with cooking spray. Bake at 350° for 45 minutes or until lightly browned. Serve with lime wedges. Yield: 12 servings (serving size: ¾ cup).

CALORIES 218; FAT 8.1g (sat 3.6g, mono 3g, poly 0.7g); PROTEIN 8.9g; CARB 27.7g; FIBER 1.9g; CHOL 53mg; IRON 1.9mg; SODIUM 374mg; CALC 232mg

A GLUTEN-FREE MENU

Slow-Roasted Turkey with Cream Gravy
(page 300)
(Our gravy is thickened with cornstarch, which is gluten-free.)

Old-Fashioned Cranberry Sauce
(page 303)

Wild Rice Stuffing with Dried Cherries and Toasted Pecans (page 306)
(Use a gluten-free chicken broth or water.)

Brussels Sprouts with Bacon, Garlic, and Shallots (page 306)
(Use a gluten-free chicken broth.)

Truffled Pommes Anna (page 308)

Ginger Pumpkin Pie with Toasted Coconut (page 312)
(Forget the crust; just make the filling. Divide it and bake in individual ramekins.)

Farro, Caramelized Onion, and Wild Mushroom Stuffing

Hands-on time: 45 min. Total time: 1 hr. 30 min.

3 cups boiling water
½ cup dried porcini mushrooms (about
   ½ ounce)
2 tablespoons olive oil, divided
2½ cups finely chopped onion
1½ cups uncooked farro
1 teaspoon kosher salt, divided
6 cups sliced shiitake mushroom caps
   (about 12 ounces mushrooms)
1 cup finely chopped celery
1 tablespoon chopped fresh thyme
1 tablespoon chopped fresh sage
½ teaspoon freshly ground black pepper
½ cup dry white wine
Cooking spray
¼ cup celery leaves

1. Combine 3 cups boiling water and dried porcini mushrooms in a bowl; cover and let stand 30 minutes. Drain through a sieve over a bowl, reserving soaking liquid. Finely chop mushrooms.
2. Preheat oven to 350°.
3. Heat 1 tablespoon oil in a large saucepan over medium-high heat; swirl to coat. Add onion; sauté 2 minutes, stirring frequently. Reduce heat to low; cook 30 minutes or until onion is tender and lightly browned, stirring occasionally. Add reserved porcini liquid, chopped porcini, farro, and ½ teaspoon salt; cover. Bring to a boil; reduce heat, and simmer 30 minutes or until farro is al dente and liquid is reduced to about ⅓ cup. Remove from heat.
4. Heat remaining 1 tablespoon oil in a large skillet over medium-high heat; swirl to coat. Add shiitake mushrooms, celery, thyme, and sage; sprinkle with remaining ½ teaspoon salt and pepper. Sauté 6 minutes or until mushrooms are lightly browned, stirring occasionally. Add wine to skillet; cook 3 minutes or until liquid evaporates. Add shiitake mixture to farro mixture; stir to combine. Spoon stuffing into an

11 x 7–inch glass or ceramic baking dish coated with cooking spray; cover dish with foil. Bake at 350° for 30 minutes. Let stand 5 minutes, uncover, and top with celery leaves. Yield: 8 servings (serving size: about ½ cup).

CALORIES 228; FAT 4.7g (sat 0.6g, mono 2.6g, poly 0.6g); PROTEIN 10.1g; CARB 37.6g; FIBER 6.8g; CHOL 0mg; IRON 4mg; SODIUM 258mg; CALC 40mg

Wild Rice Stuffing with Dried Cherries and Toasted Pecans

Hands-on time: 30 min. Total time: 1 hr. and 30 min.

¼ cup butter, divided
2 cups thinly sliced leek (about 1 large)
1 tablespoon chopped fresh thyme
1 teaspoon kosher salt, divided
3 cups water
2 cups fat-free, lower-sodium chicken broth
1 cup uncooked wild rice
2 cups uncooked long-grain brown rice
½ cup finely chopped peeled turnip
⅓ cup finely chopped celery
⅓ cup finely chopped carrot
⅔ cup chopped pecans, toasted
½ cup chopped dried sweet cherries
2 green onions, thinly sliced

1. Heat 2 tablespoons butter in a large saucepan over medium heat; swirl to coat. Add leek, thyme, and ½ teaspoon salt; sauté 8 minutes, stirring occasionally. Add 3 cups water, broth, and wild rice; cover. Increase heat to high; bring to a boil. Reduce heat, and simmer 30 minutes. Stir in brown rice; cover and simmer 30 minutes. Remove from heat.
2. Preheat oven to 400°.
3. Heat remaining 2 tablespoons butter over high heat in a large skillet; swirl to coat. Add turnip, celery, carrot, and remaining ½ teaspoon salt; sauté 1 minute. Reduce heat to medium; cook 4 minutes, stirring occasionally. Remove from heat.
4. Combine rice mixture, turnip mixture, pecans, cherries, and onions in a large bowl. Spoon stuffing into a

13 x 9–inch glass or ceramic baking dish. Cover with foil; bake at 400° for 20 minutes or until liquid is absorbed. Let stand 5 minutes before serving. Yield: 12 servings (serving size: about 1 cup).

CALORIES 277; FAT 9.4g (sat 3g, mono 3.8g, poly 1.9g); PROTEIN 5.9g; CARB 43.1g; FIBER 3.9g; CHOL 10mg; IRON 1.5mg; SODIUM 268mg; CALC 40mg

THE VEGETABLES

You almost can't have too many vegetable side dishes, starting with those little green cruciferous Brussels sprouts. When did the lowly sprout become a side dish superstar? It's a flavor-packed veggie that is both meaty and pleasingly bitter when sautéed or roasted, perfect for pairing with smoky bacon. Traditionalists will enjoy a lightened-up green bean casserole that still hits the required GBC flavor notes, with a retro topping of canned fried onion rings. With the basics covered, veer this way or that and add another green: Maybe go all garlicky and feisty, with broccoli rabe seasoned with spicy red pepper. If your audience favors a creamier approach, serve Swiss chard enriched with crème fraîche—a dish that's ready in about 15 minutes.

Brussels Sprouts with Bacon, Garlic, and Shallots

Hands-on time: 16 min. Total time: 16 min.

6 center-cut bacon slices, chopped
½ cup sliced shallot (about 1 large)
1½ pounds Brussels sprouts, trimmed and
   halved
6 garlic cloves, thinly sliced
¾ cup fat-free, lower-sodium chicken broth
⅛ teaspoon salt
⅛ teaspoon freshly ground black pepper

1. Heat a large nonstick skillet over medium-high heat. Add bacon, and sauté 5 minutes or until bacon begins to brown. Remove pan from heat. Remove bacon from pan with a slotted spoon, reserving 1 tablespoon drippings in pan (discard remaining drippings).
2. Return pan to medium-high heat, and stir in bacon, shallot, and Brussels sprouts; sauté 4 minutes. Add garlic, and sauté 4 minutes or until garlic begins to brown, stirring frequently. Add broth, and bring to a boil. Cook 2 minutes or until broth mostly evaporates and sprouts are crisp-tender, stirring occasionally. Remove from heat; stir in salt and pepper. Yield: 6 servings (serving size: about ⅔ cup).

CALORIES 90; FAT 2.4g (sat 1.1g, mono 0.6g, poly 0.3g); PROTEIN 6.7g; CARB 13.5g; FIBER 4.5g; CHOL 8mg; IRON 2mg; SODIUM 263mg; CALC 60mg

Kid Friendly
Green Bean Casserole with Madeira Mushrooms

Hands-on time: 40 min. Total time: 1 hr.

Here's a deliciously updated version of the classic, with fresh green beans and wine-infused mushrooms. We just had to keep the fried onion topping, which is arguably the best part.

1½ pounds green beans, trimmed and halved crosswise
2 tablespoons olive oil
3 cups chopped sweet onion
1 teaspoon chopped fresh thyme
8 ounces shiitake mushrooms, stemmed and sliced
1 (8-ounce) package presliced button mushrooms
⅓ cup Madeira wine or dry sherry
¼ teaspoon salt
¼ teaspoon freshly ground black pepper
3 tablespoons all-purpose flour
1 cup fat-free, lower-sodium chicken broth
1 cup (about 2 ounces) canned fried onions
½ cup (2 ounces) grated fresh Parmigiano-Reggiano cheese

1. Preheat oven to 425°.
2. Place beans into a large saucepan of boiling water; cook 4 minutes. Drain and rinse with cold water; drain well. Place beans in a large bowl; set aside.
3. Heat a large skillet over medium-high heat. Add oil to pan; swirl to coat. Add onion and thyme to pan; sauté 4 minutes or until onion is tender, stirring occasionally. Add mushrooms; sauté 10 minutes or until liquid almost evaporates, stirring frequently. Stir in wine, salt, and pepper; cook 2 minutes or until liquid almost evaporates. Stir in flour; cook 1 minute, stirring constantly. Gradually stir in chicken broth; bring to a boil. Cook 1 minute or until thick, stirring constantly. Add mushroom mixture to green beans; toss well. Place green bean mixture in a 2-quart glass or ceramic baking dish. Combine fried onions and grated cheese in a small bowl. Top green bean mixture evenly with fried onion mixture. Bake at 425° for 17 minutes or until top is lightly browned. Yield: 8 servings (serving size: ¾ cup).

CALORIES 1/3; FAT 8.5g (sat 2.3g, mono 4.9g, poly 0.6g); PROTEIN 6.6g; CARB 18.7g; FIBER 5g; CHOL 4mg; IRON 1.2mg; SODIUM 249mg; CALC 119mg

"I CAN'T BELIEVE GREEN BEAN CASSEROLE IS LIGHT."

It is, and has none of the mush sometimes found in this classic American dish. The fresh flavors of green beans are an essential part of the Thanksgiving plate. Do cook more than one...

Quick & Easy • Make Ahead
Vegetarian
Spicy Sautéed Broccoli Rabe with Garlic

Hands-on time: 25 min. Total time: 25 min.

Bring some bold Italian flavor to your holiday table with this speedy stovetop side. The recipe doubles easily if you're serving a larger crowd.

1¼ pounds broccoli rabe (rapini), trimmed and cut into 2-inch pieces (about 10 cups)
2 tablespoons extra-virgin olive oil
1 cup thinly sliced red onion
¼ teaspoon crushed red pepper
5 garlic cloves, thinly sliced
½ teaspoon salt

1. Cook broccoli rabe in boiling water 2 minutes; drain and rinse with cold water.
2. Heat olive oil in a large skillet over medium-high heat. Add onion, red pepper, and garlic to pan; sauté 3 minutes, stirring occasionally. Add broccoli rabe and ½ teaspoon salt to pan, and cook 2 minutes or until heated, stirring frequently. Yield: 6 servings (serving size: ½ cup).

CALORIES 79; FAT 4.5g (sat 0.6g, mono 3.3g, poly 0.5g); PROTEIN 3.7g; CARB 7.1g; FIBER 0.4g; CHOL 0mg; IRON 0.9mg; SODIUM 226mg; CALC 54mg

THE VEGAN MENU

Roasted Rosemary Fingerling Potatoes (page 310)

Apple-Cranberry Sauce (page 303)

Spicy Sautéed Broccoli Rabe with Garlic (above)

Farro, Caramelized Onion, and Wild Mushroom Stuffing (page 306)

French Apple Tart (page 310)
(Use a vegan pastry dough—one made with vegetable shortening—and leave off the crème fraîche.)

Balsamic-Glazed Green Beans and Pearl Onions

Hands-on time: 30 min. Total time: 40 min.

1¼ pounds green beans, trimmed
1 tablespoon butter, divided
6 ounces red pearl onions, halved lengthwise
   and peeled
¼ cup fat-free, lower-sodium chicken broth
3 tablespoons balsamic vinegar
1 tablespoon sugar
½ teaspoon kosher salt
½ teaspoon freshly ground black pepper

1. Place beans into a large saucepan of boiling water; cook 3 minutes. Drain and rinse with cold water; drain well. Place beans in a large bowl; set aside.
2. Heat 1½ teaspoons butter in a large nonstick skillet over medium-high heat. Add onions; sauté 3 minutes or until lightly browned, stirring frequently. Add broth, vinegar, and sugar; bring to a boil. Simmer 3 minutes or until syrupy. Add beans, remaining 1½ teaspoons butter, salt, and pepper; toss to coat. Cook 2 minutes or until thoroughly heated. Yield: 8 servings (serving size: about ⅔ cup).

CALORIES 56; FAT 1.6g (sat 0.9g, mono 0.4g, poly 0.1g); PROTEIN 1.7g; CARB 9.8g; FIBER 2.8g; CHOL 4mg; IRON 0.9mg; SODIUM 149mg; CALC 34mg

Swiss Chard with Crème Fraîche

Hands-on time: 5 min. Total time: 16 min.

1½ pounds Swiss chard, trimmed
1 tablespoon olive oil
⅓ cup crème fraîche
¼ teaspoon salt
¼ teaspoon freshly ground black pepper

1. Remove stems and center ribs from chard. Cut stems and ribs into ½-inch pieces; set aside. Coarsely chop leaves; set aside.
2. Bring a large pot of water to a boil. Add stems and ribs; cook 5 minutes. Stir in leaves; cook 2 minutes or until leaves wilt. Drain well, pressing chard with back of a spoon to remove as much water as possible.
3. Return pan to medium heat. Add oil to pan; swirl to coat. Add chard, crème fraîche, salt, and pepper. Cook 4 minutes or until chard is tender. Yield: 8 servings (serving size: ½ cup).

CALORIES 64; FAT 5.3g (sat 2.4g, mono 2.3g, poly 0.3g); PROTEIN 1.7g; CARB 3g; FIBER 1.3g; CHOL 9mg; IRON 1.4mg; SODIUM 244mg; CALC 40mg

THE POTATOES

When addressing the two sides of the potato debate (sweet potatoes versus white mashed), you could just double down on the love and please everyone. Twice-baked sweet potatoes mix with a spicy-smoky chipotle butter to balance the sugar, while a cheese-laced mashed potato casserole delivers old-school comfort. To limit the number of dishes, mix both varieties in the same serving: Sweet and Idaho roasted potato wedges play well together when coated in savory Italian cheese and golden bread-crumbs. Fingerlings roasted with fresh rosemary are as simple a potato side as you can get, while cooks doing something more elegant can put out white truffle–scented pommes Anna.

POTATO TIPS

WHITE
If you're making a mashed dish, stick to russets (baking potatoes) and Yukon golds—waxy potatoes (like red-skinned varieties) can get gluey.

SWEET
Not to be confused with yams (which have white flesh and thick skins), these super-versatile spuds can be roasted, mashed, boiled, and even baked into pies.

FINGERLING
They'd be a pain to peel, but there's no need: Leave the tender skins on these tiny taters as they roast and halve them lengthwise to make the most of their elegant shape.

Truffled Pommes Anna

Hands-on time: 25 min. Total time: 1 hr. 5 min.

A small amount of truffle oil infuses the whole dish with loads of earthy essence. If you don't have truffle oil, you can use olive oil for a more subtle flavor. Use a mandoline for quick, easy, uniform potato slices.

2½ teaspoons chopped fresh thyme, divided
1 teaspoon kosher salt
1½ tablespoons unsalted butter, melted
Cooking spray
2½ pounds baking potatoes, peeled and cut
   into ⅛-inch-thick slices
2½ teaspoons white truffle oil, divided

1. Preheat oven to 450°.
2. Combine 2 teaspoons thyme and kosher salt in a small bowl.
3. Drizzle butter into a 10-inch cast-iron skillet coated with cooking spray. Arrange a layer of slightly overlapping potato slices in a circular pattern in pan; sprinkle with about ½ teaspoon salt mixture and drizzle with ½ teaspoon truffle oil. Repeat layers 4 times, ending with truffle oil. Press potato mixture firmly to pack. Cook over medium-high heat 6 minutes without stirring.
4. Cover with foil, and bake at 450° for 20 minutes on bottom rack in oven.
5. Uncover and bake an additional 20 minutes or until potatoes are tender when pierced with a knife. Loosen edges of potatoes with a spatula or knife. Place a plate upside down on top of pan; invert potatoes onto plate. Sprinkle with remaining ½ teaspoon thyme. Yield: 6 servings (serving size: 1 wedge).

CALORIES 215; FAT 8.9g (sat 2.7g, mono 5.3g, poly 0.6g); PROTEIN 2.9g; CARB 31.4g; FIBER 2.2g; CHOL 8mg; IRON 0.6mg; SODIUM 328mg; CALC 9mg

Mashed Potato Casserole

(pictured on page 239)

Hands-on time: 25 min. Total time: 49 min.

Buttery Yukon gold and fluffy baking potatoes contrast both in flavor and texture. If you don't have a food mill, cream the potatoes and cooking liquid with a potato masher.

1½ pounds Yukon gold potatoes, peeled and cut into ½-inch-thick slices
1½ pounds baking potatoes, peeled and cut into ½-inch-thick slices
5 garlic cloves, thinly sliced
1¼ teaspoons kosher salt, divided
¾ cup (6 ounces) ⅓-less-fat cream cheese, softened
Cooking spray
½ cup (2 ounces) grated fresh Parmigiano-Reggiano cheese
½ cup panko (Japanese breadcrumbs)
4 green onions, thinly sliced

1. Preheat oven to 350°.
2. Place potatoes, garlic, and ½ teaspoon salt in a large saucepan, and cover with water. Bring to a boil. Reduce heat, and simmer 15 minutes or until tender. Drain in a colander over a bowl, reserving ½ cup cooking liquid.
3. Place a food mill over a large bowl, and place potato mixture in food mill. Press mixture through food mill into bowl. Stir in reserved ½ cup cooking liquid, remaining ¾ teaspoon salt, and cream cheese.
4. Spoon potato mixture into an 11 x 7–inch glass or ceramic baking dish coated with cooking spray. Bake at 350° for 20 minutes or until thoroughly heated.
5. Preheat broiler.
6. Combine Parmigiano-Reggiano and panko; sprinkle over top of potatoes. Broil 4 minutes or until golden brown. Sprinkle with onions. Yield: 8 servings (serving size: about ⅔ cup).

CALORIES 243; **FAT** 6.5g (sat 3.6g, mono 1.7g, poly 0.3g); **PROTEIN** 8.3g; **CARB** 37.9g; **FIBER** 2.6g; **CHOL** 20mg; **IRON** 1.2mg; **SODIUM** 361mg; **CALC** 93mg

Twice-Roasted Sweet Potatoes with Chipotle

Hands-on time: 20 min. Total time: 1 hr. 45 min.

Look for similar-sized sweet potatoes so they'll cook at an even rate. To make ahead, stuff the potato halves, cover, and refrigerate up to one day. Set out at room temperature as the oven preheats to take the chill off.

6 medium sweet potatoes, unpeeled (about 3½ pounds)
¼ cup butter, softened
1 tablespoon finely chopped chipotle chiles, canned in adobo sauce
1 teaspoon adobo sauce
½ teaspoon salt
3 green onions

1. Preheat oven to 400°.
2. Pierce potatoes with a fork; place on a baking sheet. Bake at 400° for 1 hour and 15 minutes or until done. Cool slightly. Cut each potato in half lengthwise; scoop out pulp, leaving a ¼-inch-thick shell. Combine potato pulp, butter, chiles, adobo sauce, and salt in a food processor. Finely chop white bottom part of onions; add to pulp mixture. (Reserve green onion tops.) Pulse mixture 5 times to combine.
3. Arrange potato shells on baking sheet. Spoon potato mixture into shells. Bake at 400° for 10 minutes or until hot. Thinly slice green top part of onions, and sprinkle over potatoes. Yield: 12 servings (serving size: 1 potato half).

CALORIES 116; **FAT** 4.1g (sat 2.5g, mono 1.1g, poly 0.2g); **PROTEIN** 1.5g; **CARB** 18.8g; **FIBER** 2.8g; **CHOL** 10mg; **IRON** 0.8mg; **SODIUM** 253mg; **CALC** 32mg

Parmesan-Coated Potato Wedges

(pictured on page 239)

Hands-on time: 20 min. Total time: 50 min.

Crunchy on the outside and creamy within, these wedges are like amped-up oven fries with the added appeal of Parmesan cheese.

1.5 ounces all-purpose flour (about ⅓ cup)
¾ teaspoon kosher salt
3 large egg whites
1 tablespoon water
¾ cup (3 ounces) grated fresh Parmigiano-Reggiano cheese
½ cup panko (Japanese breadcrumbs), finely crushed
2 (8-ounce) baking potatoes, each cut lengthwise into 8 wedges
2 (8-ounce) sweet potatoes, each cut lengthwise into 8 wedges

1. Preheat oven to 425°.
2. Combine flour and salt in a shallow dish. Combine egg whites and water in a shallow dish, stirring with a whisk. Combine cheese and panko in another shallow dish.
3. Dredge potato wedges in flour mixture. Dip in egg white mixture; dredge in cheese mixture. Divide potato wedges between 2 baking sheets lined with parchment paper. Bake at 425° for 30 minutes or until golden, rotating pans after 20 minutes. Yield: 8 servings (serving size: 4 wedges).

CALORIES 165; **FAT** 2.4g (sat 1.3g, mono 0.6g, poly 0.1g); **PROTEIN** 7.4g; **CARB** 28.5g; **FIBER** 2.7g; **CHOL** 7mg; **IRON** 1.2mg; **SODIUM** 360mg; **CALC** 109mg

ESSENTIAL EQUIPMENT

FOOD MILL AND MANDOLINE

To elevate potato dishes from tasty to sublime, two pieces of gear are indispensable. First, a sturdy food mill makes mashed potatoes ethereally fluffy and smooth. Potato mashers can leave big chunks of potato in the mix. The food mill ensures the potatoes are evenly mashed and, just as important, not overworked, so they won't get gluey. The mill also works great for pureeing roasted or stewed tomatoes or making applesauce.

For dishes like Truffled Pommes Anna (page 308) that call for thin potato slices, a mandoline makes it a snap. The sharp blade cuts uniformly thin slices (so they'll cook evenly) in a fraction of the time it would take with a knife.

Roasted Rosemary Fingerling Potatoes

(pictured on page 239)

Hands-on time: 15 min. Total time: 42 min.

These potatoes are perfect for a holiday meal: quick and convenient, but still plenty dressy. They cook in about the same time it takes for a large roast to rest before carving. Bake the potatoes in their jackets so the outsides get nice and browned while the buttery interiors gently cook through.

1 tablespoon chopped fresh rosemary
2 tablespoons olive oil
¾ teaspoon kosher salt
½ teaspoon black pepper
3 shallots, thinly sliced
2 pounds fingerling potatoes, halved
   lengthwise (about 6 cups)
Cooking spray
2 teaspoons minced fresh chives

1. Preheat oven to 425°.
2. Combine first 6 ingredients in a large bowl, tossing to coat. Arrange potato mixture on a foil-lined jelly-roll pan coated with cooking spray. Bake at 425° for 27 minutes or until potatoes are tender, turning after 15 minutes. Sprinkle evenly with chives. Yield: 10 servings (serving size: ⅔ cup).

CALORIES 94; FAT 2.8g (sat 0.4g, mono 2g, poly 0.3g); PROTEIN 2g; CARB 16g; FIBER 1.6g; CHOL 0mg; IRON 0.8mg; SODIUM 150mg; CALC 10mg

THE PIES

Everyone saves room for pie, and it's usually the same pie every year. So we took the classics and jazzed them up without reimagining them in any way that would alarm traditionalists at the table: We added a spicy hit of ginger to the pumpkin pie and poured a hint of maple into the pecan. All good.

Now, in the spirit of bounty, why not add one more dessert? The free-form French apple tart is mighty easy because it works from a store-bought

crust—yet it's just spectacular, and so evocative of the season. The apple-cranberry pie combines two iconic ingredients of the table. Or, for that elegant dinner, consider a pine nut–studded quince tart—an exotic Old World sweet to give thanks for.

A PERFECT PIECRUST

Homemade piecrust has few ingredients and a quick method, so you needn't be daunted: Keep it cool (temperature-wise), and don't overwork it. Cut very cold butter into flour with a pastry blender, mixing just until pebbly, with pea-sized clumps. These melt and steam in the oven, creating a flaky crust. Stir in ice water, 1 tablespoon at a time, just until dough is tacky. Wrap, chill, and roll out, touching the dough as little as possible so that warm hands don't melt the fat or knead unnecessarily. If blind baking, prick with a fork and use pie weights to prevent the sides from shrinking.

Make Ahead • Kid Friendly
French Apple Tart

Hands-on time: 20 min. Total time: 55 min.

½ (14.1-ounce) package refrigerated pie
   dough
3 tablespoons apple jelly, melted and divided
1 vanilla bean, split lengthwise
3 tablespoons packed brown sugar
⅛ teaspoon freshly ground nutmeg
1½ pounds Granny Smith apples, peeled and
   thinly sliced
8 teaspoons crème fraîche

1. Preheat oven to 425°.
2. Roll dough to a 12-inch circle; place on a 12-inch pizza pan. Brush dough with 1 tablespoon jelly. Place pan in freezer 5 minutes.
3. Scrape seeds from vanilla bean. Combine seeds, brown sugar, and nutmeg in a small bowl, stirring with a whisk. Sprinkle 1 tablespoon sugar mixture over dough. Arrange apple slices in concentric circles on prepared crust. Sprinkle apples with remaining sugar mixture. Bake at 425° for 35

minutes or until apples are tender and crust is golden brown.
4. Brush remaining 2 tablespoons jelly over hot tart. Cut into 8 wedges; top each wedge with 1 teaspoon crème fraîche. Yield: 8 servings (serving size: 1 wedge).

CALORIES 205; FAT 8.7g (sat 4.1g, mono 3g, poly 0g); PROTEIN 1.4g; CARB 32.6g; FIBER 1.1g; CHOL 8mg; IRON 0.1mg; SODIUM 141mg; CALC 9mg

Make Ahead
Maple-Bourbon Pecan Pie

Hands-on time: 12 min. Total time: 1 hr. 23 min.

Maple syrup and bourbon infuse the pie with distinctive sweetness. For a decadent treat, top warm pie with low-fat vanilla ice cream.

½ (14.1-ounce) package refrigerated pie
   dough
Cooking spray
¾ cup pecan halves
¼ cup finely chopped pecans
½ cup maple syrup
½ cup dark corn syrup
3 tablespoons brown sugar
2 tablespoons butter, melted
2 tablespoons bourbon
1 teaspoon vanilla extract
¼ teaspoon kosher salt
2 large eggs, lightly beaten
2 large egg whites, lightly beaten

1. Preheat oven to 350°.
2. Roll dough into a 12-inch circle. Fit dough into a 9-inch pie plate coated with cooking spray, draping excess dough over edges. Fold edges under, and flute. Chill in freezer 15 minutes.
3. Combine pecans and remaining ingredients in a bowl, stirring well to combine. Pour filling into prepared crust. Bake at 350° for 38 minutes or until center of pie is almost set (shield edges of piecrust with foil if crust gets too brown). Cool on wire rack. Yield: 10 servings (serving size: 1 wedge).

CALORIES 308; FAT 16.2g (sat 4.4g, mono 7g, poly 3.8g); PROTEIN 3.3g; CARB 37.6g; FIBER 1g; CHOL 51mg; IRON 0.7mg; SODIUM 203mg; CALC 29mg

Quince Tart with Pine Nut Caramel Glaze

Hands-on time: 15 min. Total time: 2 hr. 21 min.

Quince is a hard fall fruit with sweet-tangy flavor. You'll find quince paste in specialty stores and most supermarkets.

4.5 ounces all-purpose flour (about 1 cup)
1 teaspoon sugar
1/2 teaspoon salt
3 tablespoons chilled butter, cut into pieces
3 tablespoons chilled vegetable shortening, cut into pieces
3 tablespoons ice water
1 (10-ounce) container quince paste
4 teaspoons fresh lemon juice, divided
1/4 cup sugar
3 tablespoons honey
1/8 teaspoon salt
2 tablespoons butter
1/2 cup pine nuts, toasted

1. To prepare crust, weigh or lightly spoon flour into a dry measuring cup; level with a knife. Combine flour, 1 teaspoon sugar, and 1/2 teaspoon salt in a medium bowl; cut in 3 tablespoons butter and shortening with a pastry blender or 2 knives until mixture resembles coarse meal. Sprinkle surface with ice water, 1 tablespoon at a time; toss with a fork until moist and crumbly (do not form a ball). Press mixture gently into a 5-inch circle on plastic wrap; cover. Chill 1 hour.
2. Preheat oven to 375°.
3. Unwrap dough. Roll into an 11-inch circle on a lightly floured surface. Fit dough into a 9-inch tart pan with a removable bottom. Press dough against bottom and sides of pan. Chill in freezer 10 minutes.
4. Line bottom of dough with a piece of foil; arrange pie weights or dried beans on foil. Bake at 375° for 15 minutes or until edge is lightly browned. Carefully remove pie weights and foil; bake an additional 7 minutes or until center is lightly browned. Cool 1 minute on a wire rack.
5. To prepare filling, combine quince paste and 1 tablespoon juice in a food processor; process until smooth. Spread quince mixture evenly over warm tart shell. Bake at 375° for 15 minutes or until filling is bubbly. Reduce oven temperature to 350°.
6. Combine remaining 1 teaspoon juice, 1/4 cup sugar, honey, and 1/8 teaspoon salt in a small saucepan over medium heat. Bring to a boil, stirring until sugar dissolves. Boil 2 minutes. Remove from heat; carefully add 2 tablespoons butter, stirring until butter melts. Stir in nuts. Pour nut mixture over quince paste. Carefully spread evenly. Bake at 350° for 10 minutes or until topping bubbles. Cool 1 hour on wire rack. Yield: 12 servings (serving size: 1 wedge).

CALORIES 239; FAT 11.8g (sat 4.1g, mono 3.3g, poly 2.9g); PROTEIN 1.9g; CARB 33g; FIBER 0.5g; CHOL 13mg; IRON 0.8mg; SODIUM 157mg; CALC 4mg

Cranberry-Apple Pie

Hands-on time: 50 min. Total time: 3 hr.

Grade B maple syrup is less refined and has a stronger maple taste, though grade A will work fine in this recipe.

9 ounces all-purpose flour (about 2 cups)
2 teaspoons sugar
1 1/4 teaspoons salt, divided
6 tablespoons chilled butter, cut into small pieces
6 tablespoons chilled vegetable shortening, cut into small pieces
6 tablespoons ice water
1 1/2 cups fresh cranberries
1/3 cup packed dark brown sugar
5 tablespoons all-purpose flour
1/4 teaspoon ground cinnamon
2 1/2 pounds Gala apples (about 6), peeled and cut into 1/2-inch pieces
2/3 cup grade B maple syrup
Cooking spray

1. Weigh or lightly spoon 9 ounces (2 cups) flour into dry measuring cups; level with a knife. Combine 9 ounces flour, 2 teaspoons sugar, and 1 teaspoon salt in a large bowl, stirring well with a whisk; cut in butter and shortening with a pastry blender or 2 knives until mixture resembles coarse meal. Gradually add ice water; toss with a fork until flour mixture is moist. Divide dough into 2 equal portions. Gently press each portion into a 5-inch circle on heavy-duty plastic wrap; cover and chill 1 hour.
2. Combine remaining 1/4 teaspoon salt, cranberries, and next 4 ingredients in a large bowl, tossing gently to coat. Add syrup, tossing to coat.
3. Slightly overlap 2 sheets of plastic wrap on a damp surface. Unwrap dough; place 1 portion of chilled dough on plastic wrap. Cover dough with 2 additional sheets of overlapping plastic wrap. Roll dough, still covered, into a 12-inch circle. Chill dough in freezer 5 minutes or until plastic wrap can be easily removed. Remove top sheets of plastic wrap; fit dough, plastic wrap side up, into a 9-inch pie plate coated with cooking spray. Remove remaining plastic wrap. Spoon apple mixture into prepared crust.
4. Slightly overlap 2 sheets of plastic wrap on a slightly damp surface. Unwrap; place remaining portion of chilled dough on plastic wrap. Cover dough with 2 additional sheets of overlapping plastic wrap. Roll dough, still covered, into an 11-inch circle. Chill dough in freezer 5 minutes or until plastic wrap can be easily removed. Remove top sheets of plastic wrap; fit dough, plastic wrap side up, over apple mixture. Remove remaining plastic wrap. Press edges of dough together. Fold edges under; flute. Cut several slits in top of dough to allow steam to escape. Chill pie in refrigerator 10 minutes.
5. Preheat oven to 425°.
6. Place pie plate on a foil-lined baking sheet. Place baking sheet on bottom oven rack; bake at 425° for 25 minutes. Reduce oven temperature to 375° (do not remove pie from oven); bake an additional 45 minutes or until browned. Cool on a wire rack. Yield: 12 servings (serving size: 1 wedge).

CALORIES 312; FAT 12.2g (sat 5.2g, mono 3.5g, poly 1.9g); PROTEIN 2.9g; CARB 49.2g; FIBER 2.3g; CHOL 15mg; IRON 1.5mg; SODIUM 291mg; CALC 28mg

Make Ahead • Kid Friendly
Ginger Pumpkin Pie with Toasted Coconut

Hands-on time: 18 min. Total time: 3 hr. 58 min.

Ginger and coconut add warm, flavorful accents to this Thanksgiving classic. If you'd like a dollop of something creamy, top with fat-free whipped topping.

¼ cup packed brown sugar
1½ tablespoons grated peeled fresh ginger
½ teaspoon ground cinnamon
¼ teaspoon salt
⅛ teaspoon ground allspice
2 large eggs
1 (15-ounce) can pumpkin
1 (14-ounce) can fat-free sweetened condensed milk
½ (14.1-ounce) package refrigerated pie dough
½ cup flaked or shaved sweetened coconut, toasted

1. Preheat oven to 375°.
2. Combine first 8 ingredients in a large bowl, stirring with a whisk until smooth.
3. Roll dough into an 11-inch circle; fit into a 9-inch pie plate. Fold edges under, and flute.
4. Pour pumpkin mixture into prepared crust. Place pie plate on a baking sheet. Place baking sheet on lowest oven rack. Bake at 375° for 40 minutes or until a knife inserted into center comes out clean. Remove from baking sheet; cool 1 hour on a wire rack. Refrigerate 2 hours or until chilled. Sprinkle coconut over pie. Yield: 12 servings (serving size: 1 wedge).

CALORIES 224; **FAT** 6.5g (sat 3.2g, mono 2.4g, poly 0.1g); **PROTEIN** 4.8g; **CARB** 37.7g; **FIBER** 1.5g; **CHOL** 41mg; **IRON** 0.8mg; **SODIUM** 200mg; **CALC** 104mg

THE COCKTAILS

Serving up a signature cocktail is a special way to lift the mood. We built these five around bubbly, but don't sweat the cost: If you're thumbing your nose at the recession, try real Champagne with dry French pear brandy (Poire William). But if the recession has been thumbing its nose at you, dip into Spanish cava or Italian prosecco for the bubbles: Some cost less than $10 per bottle and are delicious in the citrusy Clementine Sparkler at right (basically a sophisticated twist on a standard mimosa) or the lime-tangy Pomegranate Fizz (page 313). Another classic combo—sparkling wine, cognac, sugar, and a dash of bitters—makes for an elegant drink worthy of a special celebration. And a little rosé pairs wonderfully with bitter Campari.

Quick & Easy
Campari and Orange Sparkling Cocktail

Hands-on time: 6 min. Total time: 6 min.

Campari, an Italian aperitif, gives the drink a bitter edge and beautiful rosy color.

1⅓ cups sparkling rosé wine, chilled
6 tablespoons fresh orange juice, chilled
6 tablespoons Campari, chilled
Orange rind curls (optional)

1. Combine first 3 ingredients. Garnish with rind, if desired. Yield: 4 servings (serving size: ½ cup).

CALORIES 127; **FAT** 0g; **PROTEIN** 0.2g; **CARB** 10g; **FIBER** 0.1g; **CHOL** 0mg; **IRON** 0.1mg; **SODIUM** 0mg; **CALC** 3mg

Quick & Easy
Clementine Sparkler

Hands-on time: 8 min. Total time: 8 min.

Like a modern mimosa, this fruity drink is ideal for a holiday brunch.

1⅓ cups cava or other sparkling wine, chilled
¾ cup fresh clementine juice, chilled
Clementine slices (optional)

1. Combine cava and juice. Garnish with clementine slices, if desired. Yield: 4 servings (serving size: about ½ cup).

CALORIES 77; **FAT** 0.1g (sat 0g, mono 0.1g, poly 0g); **PROTEIN** 0.3g; **CARB** 6.2g; **FIBER** 0.1g; **CHOL** 0mg; **IRON** 0.1mg; **SODIUM** 0mg; **CALC** 5mg

Quick & Easy
Cognac Sparkling Wine Cocktail

Hands-on time: 5 min. Total time: 5 min.

The original Champagne cocktail, this one packs a wallop.

4 drops Angostura bitters
4 sugar cubes
1½ cups demi-sec sparkling wine, chilled
½ cup cognac, chilled

1. Place 1 drop of bitters onto each sugar cube; place 1 sugar cube into bottom of each of 4 Champagne flutes. Combine wine and cognac. Pour ½ cup wine mixture into each flute. Yield: 4 servings (serving size: ½ cup).

CALORIES 149; **FAT** 0g; **PROTEIN** 0g; **CARB** 4.8g; **FIBER** 0g; **CHOL** 0mg; **IRON** 0mg; **SODIUM** 0mg; **CALC** 0mg

"LET'S ALL GIVE THANKS."

Raise a glass to the importance of family and friends near the end of a very bumpy year—with a nod to the cook who made the best Thanksgiving dinner ever.

Pomegranate Fizz

Hands-on time: 4 min. Total time: 4 min.

1¼ cups demi-sec sparkling wine, chilled
⅔ cup pomegranate juice, chilled
1 tablespoon fresh lime juice
Lime wedges (optional)

1. Combine first 3 ingredients. Garnish with lime wedges, if desired. Yield: 4 servings (serving size: ½ cup).

CALORIES 77; **FAT** 0g; **PROTEIN** 0.2g; **CARB** 7.4g; **FIBER** 0g; **CHOL** 0mg; **IRON** 0.1mg; **SODIUM** 5mg; **CALC** 7mg

Quick & Easy
Sparkling Pear Cocktail

Hands-on time: 3 min. Total time: 3 min.

This beautifully aromatic sipper is surprisingly stout.

1⅓ cups brut sparkling wine, chilled
⅔ cup pear liqueur (such as Poire William), chilled
Seckel pear slices (optional)

1. Combine wine and liqueur. Garnish with pear slices, if desired. Yield: 4 servings (serving size: ½ cup).

CALORIES 142; **FAT** 0g; **PROTEIN** 0g; **CARB** 1.3g; **FIBER** 0g; **CHOL** 0mg; **IRON** 0mg; **SODIUM** 0mg; **CALC** 0mg

"HERE'S TO THE COOK!"

It's a lot harder for the family grump—if there is one—to be crabby with a bright sparkling cocktail in hand. These drinks range from almost soda-pop light to a cognac-tinged glass of pure golden elegance.

PLAYING WITH FLAVORS
FUN USES FOR FRESH CRANBERRIES

Three ways to make the tart red fruit go beyond the one-time Thanksgiving nod.

Quick & Easy
Tangy Cranberry Tea

Combine 1 cup fresh cranberries, 3 tablespoons sugar, 2 teaspoons orange pekoe tea, and 2 (3 x 1–inch) strips orange rind in a heavy nonreactive saucepan. Cover with 4¼ cups water; bring to a simmer. Simmer 10 minutes. Remove from heat; cover and let stand 10 minutes. Strain mixture through a sieve over a liquid measuring cup; discard solids. Yield: 4 servings (serving size: about 1 cup).

CALORIES 39; **FAT** 0g; **SODIUM** 7mg

Make Ahead • Kid Friendly
Vegetarian
Cranberry Ketchup

Slather on a burger, or serve with sweet potato fries or pork.

Combine 1⅔ cups fresh cranberries, ½ cup packed brown sugar, ½ cup chopped shallots, ¼ cup cider vinegar, ¼ cup water, ½ teaspoon salt, and ½ teaspoon crushed red pepper in a medium, heavy saucepan over medium-high heat; bring to a boil. Cook 10 minutes or until thick, stirring occasionally. Remove from heat; let stand 10 minutes. Pour into a blender; process until smooth. Transfer to a bowl; cover and chill. Yield: 8 servings (serving size: about 1½ tablespoons).

CALORIES 72; **FAT** 0g; **SODIUM** 154mg

Make Ahead • Vegetarian
Pickled Cranberries

Serve this tangy-sweet combo with ham, pork tenderloin, or roast chicken.

Combine 1¼ cups sugar, 1¼ cups water, 1 cup white balsamic vinegar, and 1½ tablespoons pickling spice in a nonreactive saucepan over medium-high heat; bring to a boil. Reduce heat, and cook until reduced by half. Strain vinegar mixture through a sieve over another medium nonreactive saucepan; discard solids. Add 3 cups fresh cranberries to strained mixture, and place pan over medium heat. Bring mixture to a simmer, and cook just until cranberries begin to pop (about 5 minutes), stirring occasionally. Remove from heat; cool. Chill at least 24 hours. Yield: 12 servings (serving size: about ¼ cup).

CALORIES 116; **FAT** 0.3g (sat 0g); **SODIUM** 5mg

LESS MEAT, MORE FLAVOR
LEFTOVERS: CURRY YOUR TURKEY!
By Mark Bittman

Because a little warming spice is mighty nice.

It's the day after Thanksgiving. Your fridge is stuffed with leftovers, and you are oh-so tempted to make yourself the same plate of delicious food that put you to sleep at 6 p.m. the night before. Me too. The leftover Thanksgiving sandwich is very close to my heart (and probably closer still to my arteries). But I often find myself craving a totally different kind of turkey: something lighter and brighter. Turkey transformed.

Cue curry, the intensely flavorful spice blend that can redeploy roast turkey from New England to Asia. Curry dishes are eaten all over Asia, from India and Pakistan, to Thailand and Malaysia,

continued

to China and Japan. They can be made with spice blends (most often including turmeric, coriander, and cumin, at the very least) or pastes, and eaten as thin soups, thick stews, and everything in between. They can be remarkably simple to make, or a bit more complex; here, we have one of each.

The quick fix here is actually a take on a dish that has become an American classic: curried chicken salad. I use turkey, of course, instead of chicken—and not too much of it, because baby spinach (a leafy green thing that I certainly didn't eat the night before) takes over for most of the meat. The turkey and spinach get many of the familiar accompaniments that make curried salads so perfect: sweet, chewy, golden raisins; salty, crunchy cashews; and spicy red onions. The dressing is thick Greek yogurt whisked with a drizzle of honey to balance the acidity, black pepper, a splash of water, and curry powder, which gives you a ton of exotic flavor in absolutely no time and should always be in your spice drawer.

The Thai-style stew is more involved since it starts with making your own curry mixture, which sounds daunting but isn't. You start by rehydrating a few dried chiles in warm water, and blend them with garlic, ginger, cilantro, light coconut milk, and ground, toasted cumin and coriander seeds, which, since I said this was the "involved" recipe, you toast and grind yourself (if you don't have a spice or coffee grinder, just use preground.) Add this mixture to a pot with sautéing chopped onions and grated carrots; it caramelizes and turns golden brown (color equals flavor) and fragrant as it sticks to the bottom of the pot. Then, you add broth and scrape that beautiful curry off the bottom of the pot with a wooden spoon. Chunks of zucchini provide the bulk: They break down as they simmer and thicken the liquid, turning it from a thin soup into a hearty stew. As for the turkey, all you need to do is chop it and stir it in at the end to warm. Garnish with the classic Thai trio of peanuts, cilantro, and lime, and eat the stew on its own or over rice.

Thai Curry Stew with Turkey and Zucchini

Hands-on time: 35 min. Total time: 1 hr. 25 min.

For a looser stew, skip the mashing step.

1 to 2 dried Thai or other hot red dried chiles, stems discarded
¼ cup boiling water
½ teaspoon coriander seeds
½ teaspoon cumin seeds
1 teaspoon grated lime rind
15 cilantro sprigs, coarsely chopped
2 garlic cloves, crushed
1 (½-inch) piece peeled fresh ginger, coarsely chopped
1 cup light coconut milk
2 tablespoons olive oil
1½ cups grated peeled carrot
1 cup chopped yellow onion
½ teaspoon kosher salt
¼ teaspoon freshly ground black pepper
4 cups fat-free, lower-sodium chicken broth
3½ cups coarsely chopped zucchini (about 2 medium), divided
3 cups chopped cooked skinless turkey (light and dark meat)
3 cups hot cooked brown basmati rice
¼ cup chopped unsalted, dry-roasted peanuts
2 tablespoons chopped fresh cilantro leaves
6 lime wedges

1. Combine chiles and ¼ cup boiling water in a bowl; let stand 15 minutes or until chiles are soft. Remove chiles; discard water.
2. Combine coriander and cumin in a small skillet over medium heat. Cook 3 minutes or until toasted, shaking pan frequently. Place spice mixture in a spice or coffee grinder, and process until finely ground. Combine ground spices, chiles, rind, cilantro sprigs, garlic, and ginger in a food processor; process until finely chopped. Add coconut milk, and process until smooth.
3. Heat a Dutch oven over medium heat. Add oil to pan; swirl to coat. Add carrot and onion; cook 5 minutes or until onion is tender, stirring occasionally. Add coconut milk mixture, salt, and pepper. Increase heat to high, and

cook 4 minutes or until mixture reduces and begins to brown, stirring frequently. Reduce heat to medium-high; add broth, scraping pan to loosen browned bits. Bring to a boil; stir in 2 cups zucchini. Simmer 45 minutes or until zucchini is very tender.
4. Remove pan from heat. Mash zucchini mixture with a potato masher, or blend with an immersion blender. Return pan to medium-high heat. Stir in remaining 1½ cups zucchini and turkey; cook 2 minutes or until thoroughly heated.
5. Spoon ½ cup rice into each of 6 shallow bowls; top each serving with about 1 cup stew, 2 teaspoons nuts, and 1 teaspoon cilantro. Serve with lime wedges. Yield: 6 servings.

CALORIES 328; **FAT** 11.3g (sat 2.2g, mono 5.3g, poly 2.1g); **PROTEIN** 27.5g; **CARB** 31.1g; **FIBER** 4.8g; **CHOL** 69mg; **IRON** 3mg; **SODIUM** 497mg; **CALC** 61mg

Curried Turkey, Spinach, and Cashew Salad

Hands-on time: 30 min. Total time: 30 min.

¼ cup plain fat-free Greek yogurt
1 tablespoon water
1 tablespoon olive oil
1 teaspoon curry powder
1 teaspoon honey
¼ teaspoon kosher salt
¼ teaspoon freshly ground black pepper
5 cups loosely packed baby spinach
2 cups chopped cooked skinless turkey (light and dark meat)
½ cup coarsely chopped roasted, salted cashews
½ cup golden raisins
½ cup thinly sliced red onion

1. Combine first 7 ingredients in a large bowl; stir with a whisk. Add spinach and remaining ingredients; toss well to combine. Yield: 4 servings (serving size: 2 cups).

CALORIES 321; **FAT** 13.3g (sat 2.7g, mono 7.6g, poly 2.3g); **PROTEIN** 26.1g; **CARB** 27g; **FIBER** 3.1g; **CHOL** 69mg; **IRON** 3.9mg; **SODIUM** 333mg; **CALC** 69mg

WINTER SQUASH

Impressive on the table. Sweet and rich on the palate. Behold the squash. Then cook it.

It's true that the winter squash has a sort of Quasimodo quality: often knobby, misshapen, mottled, and leather-skinned. Its charm is the beauty of dignified, old-looking things. Nor does the flesh inside seem too promising in its raw state. But therein lies the miracle of cooking: As it roasts, the meat of the squash caramelizes beautifully around the edges and turns buttery and sweet in the center, while holding its gorgeous autumn hue. It's delicious served chunky, sprinkled with coarse salt, or whipped with a touch of butter or cream for a rich, smooth side. Dessert, even, can be helped by squash: The flesh, pureed, adds natural sweetness to baked goods like our cinnamon rolls. And know that these dependable vegetables deliver a good dose of potassium, beta-carotene, and other phytonutrients and antioxidants—the stuff healthy cells dream of.

Make Ahead
Quinoa-Stuffed Squash
(pictured on page 240)

Hands-on time: 37 min. Total time: 1 hr. 47 min.

Golden nugget squash looks and tastes like a pumpkin and combines with a whole grain for a comforting fall entrée. As the hard squash softens, caramelizes, and sweetens, it becomes succulent. You can cook the squash, prepare the filling, and refrigerate up to 2 days ahead. Then assemble and bake just before serving.

4 (1-pound) golden nugget squashes
Cooking spray
2 (4-ounce) links hot turkey Italian sausage, casings removed
½ cup finely chopped carrot
½ cup finely chopped onion
2 garlic cloves, minced
½ cup water
2 cups cooked quinoa
2 tablespoons chopped fresh parsley
½ teaspoon chopped fresh thyme
¼ teaspoon kosher salt
¼ teaspoon black pepper
¾ cup (3 ounces) shredded 2% reduced-fat Monterey Jack cheese, divided

1. Cut top quarter off each squash, and reserve tops. Discard seeds. Arrange squashes, cut sides down, in 2 (11 x 7–inch) baking dishes. Fill each dish with 1-inch of water; microwave 1 dish at HIGH 15 minutes. Remove dish; repeat with remaining dish. Cool.
2. Preheat oven to 350°.
3. Heat a large skillet over medium-high heat. Coat pan with cooking spray. Add sausage; sauté 5 minutes or until browned, stirring to crumble. Remove sausage with a slotted spoon. Add carrot, onion, and garlic to drippings in pan; sauté 2 minutes, stirring frequently. Stir in ½ cup water; bring to a boil. Reduce heat to medium; cover and cook 8 minutes or until carrot is tender.
4. Combine sausage, carrot mixture, quinoa, parsley, thyme, salt, and pepper; stir in ½ cup cheese. Stuff about 1 cup quinoa mixture into each squash, and top each serving with 1 tablespoon cheese. Arrange stuffed squashes in a broiler-safe baking dish, and place tops in dish. Bake at 350° for 20 minutes or until thoroughly heated. Remove from oven.
5. Preheat broiler to high.
6. Broil squashes 4 minutes or until cheese is golden. Yield: 4 servings (serving size: 1 stuffed squash).

CALORIES 362; **FAT** 14.6g (sat 4.4g, mono 5.4g, poly 1.8g); **PROTEIN** 21.5g; **CARB** 39.4g; **FIBER** 4.7g; **CHOL** 53mg; **IRON** 4.6mg; **SODIUM** 620mg; **CALC** 238mg

Vegetarian

Cheese and Squash Soufflés

Hands-on time: 48 min. Total time: 1 hr. 48 min.

The skin of the sweet dumpling squash is edible when cooked, so you don't have to peel these gems: Simply chop, roast, puree, and proceed with the recipe. If you can't find it, substitute peeled butternut. If you prefer, serve this soufflé as a side to accompany roast chicken, pork, or beef. Simply serve eight smaller portions.

1 tablespoon butter
3 cups (1-inch) cubed sweet dumpling squash (about 2 medium squashes)
1 tablespoon extra-virgin olive oil
2 teaspoons chopped fresh thyme
1 shallot, peeled and cut into 6 wedges
½ teaspoon salt, divided
¼ teaspoon freshly ground black pepper
1 (1-ounce) slice French bread
Cooking spray
1.5 ounces all-purpose flour (about ⅓ cup)
1 cup fat-free milk
¾ cup (3 ounces) shredded Gruyère cheese
3 tablespoons grated fresh Parmigiano-Reggiano cheese
3 large egg yolks
6 large egg whites

1. Place a small roasting pan in oven. Preheat oven to 450°.
2. Remove hot pan from oven; melt butter in pan. Add squash and next 3 ingredients to pan. Sprinkle squash mixture with ¼ teaspoon salt and pepper; toss. Bake at 450° for 20 minutes or until tender, turning once. Cool squash mixture. Place squash mixture in a food processor; process until smooth. Scrape squash mixture into a bowl.
3. Reduce oven temperature to 425°, and place a rimmed baking sheet in oven.
4. Place the French bread in a food processor, and pulse 10 times or until fine breadcrumbs measure about ½ cup. Lightly coat 5 (8-ounce) soufflé ramekins with cooking spray; sprinkle crumbs evenly over dishes.
5. Weigh or lightly spoon flour into a dry measuring cup; level with a knife. Combine flour and remaining ¼ teaspoon salt in a medium, heavy saucepan over medium heat. Gradually add milk, stirring constantly with a whisk; bring to a boil. Cook 1 minute or until thick and bubbly. Remove from heat; let stand 5 minutes. Add cheeses; stir until smooth. Stir in squash mixture and egg yolks.
6. Place egg whites in a large mixing bowl; beat with a mixer at high speed until medium peaks form (do not overbeat). Gently stir one quarter of egg whites into squash mixture; gently fold in remaining egg whites. Divide mixture evenly among prepared dishes. Sharply tap dishes on counter 2 to 3 times to level. Place dishes on preheated baking sheet; place in 425° oven. Immediately reduce oven temperature to 350°. Bake soufflés at 350° for 45 minutes or until golden, puffed, and set. Serve immediately. Yield: 5 servings (serving size: 1 soufflé).

CALORIES 268; FAT 13.4g (sat 6g, mono 5.5g, poly 1.2g); PROTEIN 16.2g; CARB 22.3g; FIBER 2.6g; CHOL 151mg; IRON 1.6mg; SODIUM 478mg; CALC 309mg

Make Ahead • Freezable

Beef and Butternut Chili

Hands-on time: 36 min. Total time: 2 hr. 40 min.

Cooking spray
1 tablespoon canola oil, divided
1½ pounds boneless chuck roast, trimmed and cut into ½-inch cubes
¾ teaspoon salt
1½ cups chopped onion
½ cup chopped green bell pepper
2 tablespoons tomato paste
1 tablespoon minced fresh garlic
2 teaspoons diced jalapeño pepper
⅔ cup dry red wine
1½ teaspoons ground ancho chile pepper
1 teaspoon dried oregano
½ teaspoon ground red pepper
¼ teaspoon ground cumin
¼ teaspoon ground coriander
⅛ teaspoon ground cinnamon
1 (28-ounce) can whole tomatoes, undrained and chopped
1 (15-ounce) can no-salt-added kidney beans, rinsed and drained
2 cups (½-inch) cubed peeled butternut squash
1 cup coarsely chopped carrot
6 tablespoons reduced-fat sour cream
2 tablespoons fresh cilantro leaves

1. Heat a large Dutch oven over medium-high heat. Coat pan with cooking spray. Add 1 teaspoon oil; swirl. Sprinkle beef with salt. Add beef to pan; sauté 8 minutes, turning to brown on all sides. Remove beef.
2. Add 2 teaspoons oil to pan. Add onion and bell pepper; sauté 3 minutes. Add tomato paste, garlic, and jalapeño; sauté 2 minutes, stirring constantly. Add wine; bring to a boil, scraping pan. Cook 2 minutes. Return beef to pan.

3. Stir in ancho chile pepper and next 7 ingredients, and bring to a boil. Cover, reduce heat to medium, and simmer gently 1 hour. Add butternut squash and 1 cup carrot, and simmer 1 hour or until beef is tender. Ladle 1⅓ cups chili into each of 6 bowls, and top each with 1 tablespoon sour cream and 1 teaspoon cilantro. Yield: 6 servings.

CALORIES 308; FAT 9.9g (sat 3.3g, mono 3.6g, poly 1g); PROTEIN 28.4g; CARB 25.5g; FIBER 5.8g; CHOL 55mg; IRON 4.7mg; SODIUM 606mg; CALC 138mg

NUTTY, CARAMEL-FLAVORED SQUASH IS WHIRRED WITH BUTTER AND BROWN SUGAR FOR A SURPRISINGLY SIMPLE SIDE.

Make Ahead • Kid Friendly

Kabocha Squash Puree

Hands-on time: 12 min. Total time: 1 hr. 27 min.

If you can't find kabocha, use two medium delicata or acorn squashes. Serve this rich, delicious puree alongside roast pork tenderloin or chicken.

1 (3-pound) kabocha squash
½ cup water
½ cup packed brown sugar
3 tablespoons butter, melted
¾ teaspoon salt
¼ teaspoon freshly ground black pepper

1. Preheat oven to 450°.
2. Cut squash in half, and discard seeds. Place squash halves, cut sides down, in a 13 x 9–inch glass or ceramic baking dish, and add ½ cup water to dish. Cover and bake at 450° for 40 minutes or until squash is tender. Remove squash from pan, and let stand 10 minutes. Remove pulp from skin, and discard skin. Combine squash pulp, ½ cup brown sugar, and remaining ingredients in a food processor, and process until smooth. Yield: 6 servings (serving size: ½ cup).

CALORIES 201; FAT 5.8g (sat 3.7g, mono 1.5g, poly 0.2g); PROTEIN 2.8g; CARB 36.8g; FIBER 2.7g; CHOL 15mg; IRON 1.1mg; SODIUM 341mg; CALC 71mg

Make Ahead • Kid Friendly

Spiced Cinnamon Rolls with Maple Glaze
(pictured on page 240)

Hands-on time: 23 min. Total time: 2 hr. 25 min.

Delicata squash adds a golden-orange hue and soft sweetness. It is a great choice for dessert recipes. Roasting it intensifies the sweet flavor.

Rolls:
1 cup warm water (100° to 110°)
1 tablespoon granulated sugar
1 package dry yeast (about 2¼ teaspoons)
11.9 ounces bread flour (about 2½ cups)
6.47 ounces all-purpose flour, divided (about 1¼ cups plus 3 tablespoons)
1 teaspoon salt
1½ teaspoons ground cinnamon, divided
¼ teaspoon ground nutmeg
Dash of ground cloves
1 cup mashed cooked delicata squash (about 1 [1-pound] squash)
1 tablespoon canola oil
Cooking spray
½ cup packed brown sugar
2 tablespoons butter, melted
2 teaspoons water
3 tablespoons finely chopped walnuts, toasted
Glaze:
⅓ cup water
½ cup maple sugar or light brown sugar
1 tablespoon butter
1 tablespoon half-and-half
½ teaspoon vanilla extract

1. To prepare rolls, combine first 3 ingredients in a small bowl, and let stand 10 minutes.

2. Weigh or lightly spoon bread flour and 5.63 ounces (about 1¼ cups) all-purpose flour into dry measuring cups; level with a knife. Combine bread flour, 5.63 ounces all-purpose flour, salt, ½ teaspoon cinnamon, nutmeg, and cloves in a large bowl, stirring with a whisk. Add yeast mixture, squash, and oil, and stir just until moist. Turn dough out onto a lightly floured surface, and knead until smooth and elastic (about 6 minutes), adding enough of remaining all-purpose flour, 1 tablespoon at a time, to prevent dough from sticking to hands (dough will feel tacky).
3. Place dough in a large bowl coated with cooking spray, turning to coat top. Cover and let rise in a warm place (85°), free from drafts, 45 minutes or until doubled in size. (Gently press 2 fingers into dough. If indentation remains, dough has risen enough.) Punch dough down; cover and let rest 5 minutes. Turn dough out onto a lightly floured surface, and roll dough into a 20 x 12–inch rectangle. Combine remaining 1 teaspoon cinnamon, brown sugar, 2 tablespoons melted butter, and 2 teaspoons water in a small bowl; spread mixture evenly over dough, leaving a ¼-inch border. Sprinkle evenly with nuts. Roll dough, jelly-roll fashion, starting with long side. Cut roll crosswise into 16 equal slices. Arrange rolls, cut sides up, in a 13 x 9–inch glass or ceramic baking dish coated with cooking spray. Cover and let rise 30 minutes or until doubled in size.
4. Preheat oven to 375°.
5. Bake at 375° for 33 minutes or until brown. Cool 5 minutes on a wire rack.
6. To prepare glaze, combine ⅓ cup water and maple sugar in a small saucepan over medium-high heat; bring to a boil. Reduce heat to medium; simmer 5 minutes, stirring occasionally. Remove from heat; stir in 1 tablespoon butter, half-and-half, and vanilla. Cool 5 minutes; drizzle over rolls. Yield: 16 servings (serving size: 1 roll).

CALORIES 205; FAT 4.5g (sat 1.7g, mono 1.3g, poly 1.2g); PROTEIN 4.2g; CARB 36.9g; FIBER 1.2g; CHOL 6mg; IRON 1.8mg; SODIUM 167mg; CALC 22mg

Indian-Spiced Roasted Squash Soup

(pictured on page 238)

Hands-on time: 15 min. Total time: 1 hr. 3 min.

Garnish this curry-spiced soup with toasted squash seeds for crunchy contrast.

1 cup chopped yellow onion
8 ounces carrot, chopped
4 garlic cloves, peeled
1 (1-pound) butternut squash, peeled and cut into (½-inch) cubes
1 (8-ounce) acorn squash, quartered
1 tablespoon olive oil
½ teaspoon black pepper
2 cups water
1 teaspoon Madras curry powder
½ teaspoon garam masala
¼ teaspoon ground red pepper
2 (14-ounce) cans fat-free, lower-sodium chicken broth
¼ teaspoon kosher salt
6 tablespoons Greek yogurt
6 teaspoons honey

1. Preheat oven to 500°.
2. Arrange first 5 ingredients on a jelly-roll pan. Drizzle with oil; sprinkle with pepper. Toss. Roast at 500° for 30 minutes or until vegetables are tender, turning once. Cool 10 minutes. Peel acorn squash; discard skin.
3. Combine vegetable mixture, 2 cups water, curry powder, garam masala, and red pepper in a food processor; pulse to desired consistency. Scrape mixture into a large saucepan over medium heat. Stir in broth; bring to a boil. Cook 10 minutes, stirring occasionally; stir in salt. Combine yogurt and honey, stirring well. Serve with soup. Yield: 6 servings (serving size: 1 cup soup and 4 teaspoons yogurt mixture).

CALORIES 143; **FAT** 3.1g (sat 0.7g, mono 1.8g, poly 0.4g); **PROTEIN** 4.8g; **CARB** 27g; **FIBER** 4.4g; **CHOL** 1mg; **IRON** 1.5mg; **SODIUM** 343mg; **CALC** 98mg

CHICKEN 3 WAYS
LEGS & THIGHS

Three recipes that highlight the rich, moist meat of the muscular part of the bird.

Make Ahead
Braised Chicken with Kale

Hands-on time: 20 min. Total time: 1 hr. 40 min.

2 tablespoons canola oil, divided
4 chicken leg quarters, skinned
½ teaspoon freshly ground black pepper
¼ teaspoon salt
1.1 ounces all-purpose flour (about ¼ cup)
5 garlic cloves, chopped
1 (16-ounce) package cut prewashed kale
1 (14.5-ounce) can no-salt-added fire-roasted diced tomatoes, undrained
1 (14.5-ounce) can fat-free, lower-sodium chicken broth
1 tablespoon red wine vinegar

1. Preheat oven to 325°.
2. Heat a Dutch oven over medium-high heat. Add 2 teaspoons canola oil. Sprinkle chicken with pepper and ¼ teaspoon salt. Place flour in a dish, and dredge chicken. Place 2 leg quarters in pan, and cook 1½ minutes on each side. Remove from pan. Repeat procedure with 2 teaspoons oil and remaining 2 leg quarters. Remove from pan.
3. Add remaining 2 teaspoons oil to pan. Add garlic; cook 20 seconds. Add half of kale; cook 2 minutes. Add remaining half of kale; cook 3 minutes. Stir in tomatoes and broth; bring to a boil. Return chicken to pan. Cover and bake at 325° for 1 hour and 15 minutes. Remove chicken from pan; stir in vinegar. Serve chicken over kale mixture. Yield: 4 servings (serving size: 1¼ cups kale mixture and 1 leg quarter).

CALORIES 412; **FAT** 15.7g (sat 2.6g, mono 6.9g, poly 4.4g); **PROTEIN** 45.9g; **CARB** 22.8g; **FIBER** 3.7g; **CHOL** 161mg; **IRON** 5.4mg; **SODIUM** 604mg; **CALC** 215mg

If you like **Kalamata Olives** try:
Greek Chicken Thighs

Preheat oven to 375°. Combine ⅓ cup lemon juice, 3 tablespoons chopped fresh oregano, 2 tablespoons olive oil, and 3 chopped garlic cloves in a large zip-top plastic bag. Add 8 skinned bone-in chicken thighs (about 4 pounds), and seal. Marinate in refrigerator 30 minutes, turning bag occasionally. Place chicken on a jelly-roll pan coated with cooking spray; sprinkle with ½ teaspoon salt and ½ teaspoon pepper. Bake at 375° for 30 minutes or until done, turning after 15 minutes. Sprinkle with 2 tablespoons chopped fresh flat-leaf parsley and 2 tablespoons chopped pitted kalamata olives. Yield: 4 servings (serving size: 2 thighs).

CALORIES 258; **FAT** 14.3g (sat 2.5g); **SODIUM** 531mg

If you like **Chipotle Chiles** try:
Chipotle-Orange Thighs

Combine ½ cup orange marmalade, 1 tablespoon cider vinegar, 1 teaspoon minced chipotle chile in adobo sauce, and 1 teaspoon adobo sauce in a saucepan; bring to a boil. Reduce heat, and simmer 10 minutes or until syrupy. Place a grill pan over medium-high heat; coat pan with cooking spray. Sprinkle 8 (3-ounce) skinless, boneless chicken thighs evenly with ½ teaspoon salt and ¼ teaspoon pepper. Add chicken to pan; cook 5 minutes on each side or until done. Brush cooked chicken with chipotle sauce. Sprinkle with 2 tablespoons diagonally cut green onions. Yield: 4 servings (serving size: 2 thighs and 1½ tablespoons sauce).

CALORIES 306; **FAT** 6.8g (sat 1.7g); **SODIUM** 492mg

BREAKFAST, LUNCH & DINNER IN HONOLULU

Honolulu has emerged as an eating destination in its own right, thanks to a newfound love affair with amazing fresh ingredients.

For most of the previous century, Honolulu was a town whose take on fine dining was shaped by decades of catering to military brass and regiments of tourists. A big night out meant fried frozen shrimp, mainland steaks, and flambéed desserts. Locals dug into heavy, traditional plate lunches: a multicultural comfort-food affair of Japanese-style fried chicken or Filipino pork adobo surrounded by heaping scoops of sticky rice and macaroni salad.

Hawaii's pride in being the state with the highest per capita consumption of Spam lingers even today—locals still enjoy it in Spam musubi, a brick of rice topped by a slice of the canned meat and a drizzle of teriyaki (see our surprisingly tasty, lightened version on page 322).

That said, the islands were not immune to mainland trends. By the 1970s, island-bred chefs were venturing forth and bringing back what they learned, while food wizards from far-flung places were alighting on Oahu to share their skills—and discover the fantastic supply of local fish and produce. As the food revolution has heated up, Honolulu has emerged as a genuinely interesting destination in its own right. A newfound desire to highlight those amazing ingredients is gaining popularity, altering how Hawaiians eat—and it's increasingly evident in the fresher, lighter food served in the very places where your only previous option was the thudding heft of a classic plate lunch.

The evolution of the dining scene here can be credited to the chefs who pioneered the Hawaii Regional Cuisine movement 20 years ago. The idea, characteristic of any local movement: Start with fresh ingredients instead of frozen, flown-in foods. Many of these chefs are now internationally known food celebrities. George Mavrothalassitis (owner of Chef Mavro), Roy Yamaguchi (Roy's), and Alan Wong (Alan Wong's) are all James Beard Award winners and are all still upping the eating ante in the islands today.

The menus at Chef Mavro (chefmavro.com) are on par with those at elite restaurants in any major city and might include Hawaii-raised shrimp dusted with garam masala and served with a hearts of palm and green apple rémoulade or poached lobster with curried Pirie mango. At Alan Wong's (alanwongs.com), the emphasis is on Pacific fish. Onaga (long-tail red snapper) is crusted with ginger and served with a velvety miso-sesame vinaigrette, while for opakapaka (pink snapper), the Chinese treatment of ginger and pork hash is turned on its head with truffle nage and tapioca pearls. Chris Garnier, executive chef at Roy's (roysrestaurant.com), features a daily-changing menu of Hawaiian fusion cuisine, including a duck confit served with a passionfruit-and-mango sauce.

"Hawaii's rich cultural and ethnic composition lends itself to flavors and food preparations that are unlike anywhere else," says Joan Namkoong, coauthor with Roy Yamaguchi of *Hawaii Cooks* and author of the *Food Lover's Guide to Honolulu*. "While East-West fusion cuisines are common, Hawaii's is different. We, and Hawaii Regional Cuisine, started with ethnic dishes, and then added European techniques and flavors, compared to the usual—adding Asian flavors and techniques to a European base. Our flavors are bolder, exciting, and true to their origins, but with finesse."

Inspired by Hawaii's food pioneers, Chef Kevin Hanney of 12th Ave Grill (12thavegrill.com) offers a spin on contemporary American cooking that updates local comfort foods, such as pork chops with apple chutney and chicken glazed with ginger and honey from nearby Manoa Valley. Hanney also takes international cues: He smokes ahi to make a salty-sweet spread for bruschetta with pickled vegetable relish.

Recent arrival Quinten Frye, a Texan whose résumé includes the Shoreline Grill in Austin, is chef de cuisine at Hanney's new tapas-and-wine joint Salt Kitchen and Tasting Bar (808-744-7567). The sliver of a stylish space opened in June and has been packed with people hungry for a taste of Frye's squid stuffed with housemade chorizo.

Cheap and cheerful spots are jumping on the high-/low-brow bandwagon, too. Located across from the United Fishing Agency auction house, where the island's top chefs get their fresh catches, Nicolas Chaize gives the artery-blocking plate lunch a healthy upgrade at Nico's at Pier 38 (nicospier38.com). Order the pan-seared ahi with ginger-garlic-cilantro sauce and a simple green salad, which replaces the usual side of macaroni salad—all for about $9.

Wine bars are also part of the new guard. At Vino (vinohawaii.com), the food holds its own against stellar selections by master sommelier Chuck Furuya; Chef Keith Endo blends contemporary Italian cuisine with island

continued

ingredients, filling ravioli with Japanese kabocha pumpkin and Molokai sweet potato, and putting roasted mushrooms and Parmesan atop asparagus from the North Shore, an area generally better known for its world-class surf.

On the other side of the island, in a waterside shack in Kaneohe, Chef Mark Noguchi, an alum of famed Chef Mavro, uses indigenous ingredients, such as taro, from a local wetlands restoration project to spectacular effect at Heeia Pier General Store & Deli (heeiapier.com). Salty fishermen and island chowhounds alike sit on worn park benches and enjoy dishes such as a salad of pa'i 'ai (hand-pounded taro) and shoots of ho'io (a Hawaiian fern) brightened with a sesame dressing, along with a healthier hash made from corned brisket, breadfruit, onions, and palula, which are young sweet potato leaves.

You might guess that Honolulu's cultural mix would yield lots of international eating options, but up until five years ago, eating "foreign" largely meant Japanese. With a population that's about one-fifth Japanese, that archipelago's cuisine still figures large in local menus. At Matsugen (808-926-0255), buckwheat is ground at the restaurant to make nutty, light noodles that are delicious simply dressed with a light, cold broth, or made heartier in a warm soup dotted with tender pieces of duck. Fans wait on the sidewalk to get a seat at Sushi Izakaya Gaku (808-589-1329), where the fish is impeccable. Diners dip crisp squares of nori right into the spicy hamachi tartare, no rice needed.

Building on the international trend, a recent influx of cooks and entrepreneurs from around the world are adding new flavors. The revitalized Chinatown district—now the international nightlife nexus of Honolulu—is home to Soul de Cuba Cafe (souldecuba.com), Honolulu's first Cuban restaurant, which gives a Caribbean accent to native opakapaka, topping the light fish with a mix of cilantro, tomato, white wine, and garlic. At Himalayan Kitchen (himalayankitchen.net), Suman Basnet, who hails from Nepal, offers tasty Nepalese and Indian specialties, such as momo (steamed pork dumplings) and Himalayan curries.

Even with the multiculti infusion and an abundance of local produce (a tropical fruit bowl spritzed with lime can be pure heaven), vegetarian options are still admittedly few. Peace Café (peacecafehawaii.com) is one of the standouts. The cozy room features a country-rustic communal table and well-prepared vegan dishes such as hearty miso-tahini-flavored spinach and tofu cubes on ciabatta and fragrant Moroccan-inspired chickpea stew.

Kid Friendly • Vegetarian

Whole-Wheat Buttermilk Pancakes with Orange Sauce

Hands-on time: 42 min. Total time: 42 min.

Whipped egg whites and added leavening make these pancakes extra fluffy, which is Café Kaila's signature style.

Sauce:
¼ cup plus 1 teaspoon water, divided
¾ cup fresh orange juice
1 tablespoon sugar
1 teaspoon cornstarch
1 tablespoon butter
½ teaspoon grated orange rind
Pancakes:
3.6 ounces whole-wheat flour (about ¾ cup)
3.5 ounces all-purpose flour (about ¾ cup)
1 teaspoon baking powder
¼ teaspoon baking soda
⅛ teaspoon salt
½ cup nonfat buttermilk
2 teaspoons grated orange rind
1 teaspoon vanilla extract
1 large egg yolk
3 large egg whites
2 tablespoons sugar
½ cup sparkling water
1½ cups sliced banana

1. To prepare sauce, combine ¼ cup water, juice, and 1 tablespoon sugar in a small saucepan; bring to a boil. Cover, reduce heat, and cook until reduced to ⅔ cup (about 6 minutes). Combine cornstarch and remaining 1 teaspoon water in a small bowl, stirring with a whisk. Stir into juice mixture. Bring to a boil; cook 1 minute or until slightly thickened, stirring constantly. Remove from heat; stir in butter and ½ teaspoon orange rind. Keep warm.

2. To prepare pancakes, weigh or lightly spoon flours into dry measuring cups; level with a knife. Combine flours, baking powder, baking soda, and salt in a large bowl; stir with a whisk. Combine buttermilk and next 3 ingredients in a small bowl, stirring with a whisk. Add milk mixture to flour mixture, stirring with a whisk (batter will be thick). Place egg whites in a large bowl; beat with a mixer at high speed until soft peaks form. Add 2 tablespoons sugar, 1 tablespoon at a time, beating until stiff peaks form. Gently stir one-fourth of egg white mixture into batter. Gently fold in remaining egg white mixture. Gently stir in sparkling water.

3. Pour about ¼ cup batter per pancake onto a hot nonstick griddle or nonstick skillet, and spread gently with a spatula. Cook 2 minutes or until tops are covered with bubbles and edges look cooked. Carefully turn pancakes over; cook 2 minutes or until bottoms are lightly browned. Top with bananas. Serve with sauce. Yield: 4 servings (serving size: 2 pancakes, about ⅓ cup bananas, and 3 tablespoons sauce).

CALORIES 349; **FAT** 5g (sat 2.4g, mono 1.4g, poly 0.6g); **PROTEIN** 11.1g; **CARB** 67.5g; **FIBER** 5.4g; **CHOL** 60mg; **IRON** 2.5mg; **SODIUM** 340mg; **CALC** 157mg

BREAKFAST AT CAFÉ KAILA

The quintessential Hawaiian breakfast includes eggs, two scoops of rice, and fried slices of Portuguese sausage or Spam: Island diners like old-school comfort in the morning. But a new generation of cheery breakfast spots is serving freshened-up favorites. There is always a line outside sunny Café Kaila (808-732-3330), where fans can enjoy their signature salty-sweet buttermilk pancakes. Owner-chef Chrissie Kaila Castillo made countless batches of batter ("My mother had to eat so many pancakes," she says) before arriving at this winning recipe.

LUNCH AT TANGO CONTEMPORARY CAFÉ

Finnish chef Göran V. Streng makes clean, modern versions of traditional favorites such as Cobb salad and a grilled mahimahi sandwich served on a nori-flecked bun. But what makes Tango (tangocafehawaii.com) stand out in Honolulu are the references to Streng's Scandinavian background, such as the popular open-faced gravlax sandwich with Boursin, egg, and mustard-dill sauce, and the open, airy space punctuated with Marimekko wall hangings. Salmon, by the way, may be a key part of Scandinavian cuisine, but it's also featured locally. In the 1800s, western sailors introduced a salted-salmon-and-tomato salad that is now part of the Hawaiian-food menu and is known as lomi-lomi salmon.

Quick & Easy
Open-Faced Smoked Salmon Sandwiches

Hands-on time: 17 min. Total time: 17 min.

This sandwich is basically a riff on Hawaii's beloved lomi-lomi salmon, a salad of salted fish and tomatoes.

⅓ cup (3 ounces) ⅓-less-fat cream cheese, softened
1 teaspoon minced fresh chives
1 teaspoon chopped fresh flat-leaf parsley
1 teaspoon chopped fresh thyme
1 teaspoon plain low-fat yogurt
½ teaspoon lemon juice
1 garlic clove, minced
3 tablespoons Dijon mustard
1 tablespoon chopped fresh dill
1 tablespoon water
2 teaspoons honey
6 (1-ounce) slices rye bread
6 Bibb lettuce leaves, cut in half
12 ounces cold-smoked salmon, cut into thin strips
24 (¼-inch-thick) slices plum tomato
24 (⅛-inch-thick) slices cucumber
3 hard-cooked large egg whites, chopped
Dill sprigs (optional)

1. Combine first 7 ingredients in a bowl.
2. Combine mustard and next 3 ingredients; stir with a whisk.
3. Spread 2 tablespoons cheese mixture over each bread slice. Top each with 2 lettuce halves, 2 ounces salmon, 4 tomato slices, and 4 cucumber slices. Drizzle each sandwich with 2 teaspoons mustard mixture; sprinkle with 2 tablespoons egg whites. Garnish with dill sprigs, if desired. Yield: 6 servings (serving size: 1 open-faced sandwich).

CALORIES 231; FAT 6.9g (sat 2.6g, mono 1.2g, poly 0.7g); PROTEIN 17.2g; CARB 25.1g; FIBER 3g; CHOL 23mg; IRON 2.1mg; SODIUM 848mg; CALC 67mg

Quick & Easy
Pan-Roasted Fish with Mediterranean Tomato Sauce

Hands-on time: 32 min. Total time: 32 min.

Chef Ed Kenney uses Hawaiian fish such as mahimahi and onaga (long-tailed snapper), but any type of meaty, white fish like snapper will work.

1½ tablespoons olive oil
1½ teaspoons butter
2 cups chopped seeded plum tomato
1½ tablespoons capers
1 tablespoon Dijon mustard
3 garlic cloves, minced
1½ tablespoons chopped fresh flat-leaf parsley
1½ tablespoons minced fresh chives
1 tablespoon minced fresh tarragon
¾ teaspoon kosher salt, divided
¾ teaspoon freshly ground black pepper, divided
¼ teaspoon crushed red pepper
1 tablespoon canola oil
4 (6-ounce) yellowtail snapper fillets, skin on

1. Heat olive oil and butter in a medium skillet over medium-high heat. Add tomato to pan; cook 6 minutes, stirring frequently. Stir in capers, Dijon mustard, and minced garlic; bring to a boil. Reduce heat, and simmer 2 minutes or until slightly thickened, stirring occasionally. Remove from heat. Stir in parsley, chives, tarragon, ¼ teaspoon salt, ¼ teaspoon black pepper, and red pepper; keep warm.
2. Heat canola oil in a large nonstick skillet over medium-high heat. Sprinkle fish with remaining ½ teaspoon salt and remaining ½ teaspoon black pepper. Add fish to pan, skin side down; cook 3 minutes or until skin is browned. Turn fish over; cook 3 minutes or until desired degree of doneness. Serve fish with sauce. Yield: 4 servings (serving size: 1 fillet and ½ cup sauce).

Sustainable Choice | Use U.S. wild-caught yellowtail snapper; avoid red snapper.

CALORIES 282; FAT 12.4g (sat 2.6g, mono 7g, poly 1.8g); PROTEIN 36.1g; CARB 5.2g; FIBER 1.4g; CHOL 67mg; IRON 0.8mg; SODIUM 611mg; CALC 26mg

DINNER AT TOWN

At Town (townkaimuki.com), Chef-Owner Ed Kenney puts a Mediterranean spin on local produce—even the steaks are from island-raised beef. On the daily-changing menu you might find house-cured wild boar sausage, mussels in a Cinzano-spiked broth, or pan-roasted Hawaiian onaga topped with a vinegary sauce gribiche. This casual spot, with art by Oahu artists on the walls, was the de facto canteen for the *Lost* cast. It's a safe harbor for Honolulu's trendy arts crowd.

Pineapple Musubi Rolls

Hands-on time: 34 min. Total time: 59 min.

We just had to tackle Hawaii's Spam classic, adding pineapple and Sriracha to jazz things up.

¾ cup uncooked short-grain rice
¾ cup plus 1 tablespoon water
3 tablespoons rice wine vinegar
1 teaspoon mirin (sweet rice wine)
1 tablespoon plus 2 teaspoons sugar, divided
½ teaspoon kosher salt
1 tablespoon lower-sodium soy sauce
Cooking spray
4 ounces Spam Lite, cut into 2 (¾-inch-thick) pieces
2 nori (seaweed) sheets
4 (4-inch) julienne-cut pieces fresh pineapple
2 (8-inch) pieces green onions
½ teaspoon Sriracha (hot chile sauce)

1. Place rice in a fine sieve. Rinse under cold water, stirring rice until water runs clear (about 1 minute). Combine rice and ¾ cup plus 1 tablespoon water in a small saucepan, and cover. Bring to a boil; cook 1 minute. Reduce heat, and simmer 5 minutes. Increase heat to high, and cook 30 seconds. Remove from heat. Let stand, covered, 5 minutes.
2. Combine rice wine vinegar, mirin, 2 teaspoons sugar, and salt in a microwave-safe dish; microwave at HIGH 30 seconds, stirring until sugar dissolves. Cool.
3. Place rice and 2 tablespoons vinegar mixture in a bowl; toss. Cover with a paper towel soaked in remaining vinegar mixture.
4. Combine remaining sugar and soy sauce in a small bowl. Heat a large skillet over medium-high heat. Coat pan with cooking spray. Add Spam to pan; cook 4 minutes on each side or until lightly browned. Add to soy mixture; toss. Let stand 5 minutes. Remove Spam from soy mixture; cut in half lengthwise. Reserve remaining soy mixture.
5. Cut off top quarter of each nori sheet along short end. Place 1 nori sheet,

shiny side down, on a sushi mat covered with plastic wrap, with long end toward you. Pat about ¾ cup rice mixture evenly over nori with moist hands, leaving a 1-inch border on 1 long end of nori. Arrange 2 Spam slices, 2 pineapple pieces, and 1 green onion piece along top third of rice-covered nori. Top with ¼ teaspoon Sriracha and half of reserved soy mixture. Lift edge of nori closest to you; fold over filling. Lift bottom edge of sushi mat; roll toward top edge, pressing firmly on sushi roll. Continue rolling to top edge; press mat to seal sushi roll. Let rest, seam side down, 5 minutes. Slice roll crosswise into 10 pieces. Repeat procedure with remaining rice, nori, Spam, pineapple, onions, Sriracha, and soy mixture. Yield: 10 servings (serving size: 2 pieces).

CALORIES 90; **FAT** 1.7g (sat 0.5g, mono 0.8g, poly 0.2g); **PROTEIN** 3g; **CARB** 15.4g; **FIBER** 0.6g; **CHOL** 9mg; **IRON** 0.9mg; **SODIUM** 254mg; **CALC** 10mg

CONVENIENCE COOKING

START WITH... SWEETENED CONDENSED MILK

This old-fashioned, supersweet syrupy goo is actually an invaluable ally in lower-fat baking.

Condensed milk with added sugar seems like a processed food from a bygone prerefrigeration era, though it remains a star from Brazil to Vietnam and is used to make thick caramel, eye-opening coffee, and lots of other treats. It can also be a friend to the American cook because the viscous liquid inhibits gritty crystallization in fudge or ice cream, a textural flaw more commonly prevented by the generous application of cream and butter. The fat-free version of this milk is used here to smooth a peanutty fudge, a peppery brownie, a surprising pie, and a tangy-sweet ice cream with a cashew brittle.

FOR A RUSTIC, FLAVOR-PACKED GARNISH, SCRAPE A CINNAMON STICK ALONG A NUTMEG GRATER.

Make Ahead • Kid Friendly

Sweet Potato Pie with Spiced Cream Topping

Hands-on time: 20 min. Total time: 3 hr.

Tangy cream cheese and sweetened condensed milk combine for a creamy contrast to the sweet potato layer. You can prepare this pie up to 2 days ahead and refrigerate.

1½ pounds sweet potatoes
⅓ cup fat-free milk
1 (14-ounce) can fat-free sweetened condensed milk, divided
3 tablespoons brown sugar
2 tablespoons butter, melted
¾ teaspoon ground cinnamon, divided
½ teaspoon vanilla extract
¼ teaspoon salt
2 large eggs
½ (14.1-ounce) package refrigerated pie dough
Cooking spray
½ cup (4 ounces) ⅓-less-fat cream cheese, softened

1. Preheat oven to 350°.
2. Wrap potatoes in aluminum foil. Bake potatoes at 350° for 1½ hours or until tender, and discard foil. Let stand 10 minutes; peel. Place flesh in a large bowl; discard skins. Mash flesh with a fork. Stir in fat-free milk, ¼ cup sweetened condensed milk, sugar, butter, ½ teaspoon cinnamon, vanilla, and salt. Stir in eggs.
3. Fit dough into a 9½-inch pie plate coated with cooking spray. Press dough against bottom and sides of pan. Fold edges under, and flute. Spoon sweet potato mixture into prepared crust.

Bake at 350° for 45 minutes or until set.
4. Place remaining ¼ teaspoon cinnamon and cream cheese in a medium bowl. Beat with an electric mixer until combined. Add ½ cup plus 2 tablespoons sweetened condensed milk to cheese mixture; reserve remaining milk for another use. Beat at medium speed until well blended. Carefully pour cream mixture evenly over pie. Let stand 10 minutes. Cut into wedges. Yield: 12 servings (serving size: 1 wedge).

CALORIES 287; FAT 9.5g (sat 4.5g, mono 2.7g, poly 0.5g); PROTEIN 6g; CARB 43.6g; FIBER 1.8g; CHOL 49mg; IRON 0.6mg; SODIUM 254mg; CALC 126mg

DULCE DE LECHE STYLE: THE MILK, SLOWLY SIMMERED, TURNS INTO RICH, INTENSE CARAMEL.

Make Ahead
Spicy Caramel Brownies

Hands-on time: 15 min. Total time: 2 hr.

These brownies have a rich swirl of dulce de leche and a kick from ground red pepper. For a milder version, omit or reduce the pepper. Allow egg whites to stand at room temperature 15 minutes to take the chill off before using.

1 (14-ounce) can fat-free sweetened
  condensed milk
1 ounce bittersweet chocolate, chopped
½ cup sugar
6 tablespoons butter, softened
½ teaspoon vanilla extract
3 large egg whites
4.25 ounces all-purpose flour (almost 1 cup)
⅓ cup unsweetened cocoa
½ teaspoon baking powder
½ teaspoon ground red pepper
⅛ teaspoon salt
Cooking spray

1. Pour sweetened condensed milk into top of a double boiler; place over boiling water. Reduce heat to low; simmer 1½ hours or until mixture is thick and caramel-colored, stirring occasionally. Cool slightly.
2. Preheat oven to 350°.
3. Place chocolate in a microwave-safe dish, and microwave at HIGH 30 seconds or until almost melted, stirring after 15 seconds. Combine melted chocolate, ½ cup sugar, and butter in a medium bowl; beat with a mixer at high speed until well blended. Add vanilla and egg whites; beat until well blended. Weigh or lightly spoon flour into a dry measuring cup. Combine flour, ⅓ cup cocoa, baking powder, pepper, and salt. Add flour mixture to sugar mixture; beat just until blended. Stir half of sweetened condensed milk into batter. Spoon batter into a 9-inch square metal baking pan coated with cooking spray. Dollop remaining sweetened condensed milk by the spoonful over chocolate mixture; swirl together using a knife. Bake at 350° for 19 minutes or until a wooden pick inserted in center comes out clean. Cool in pan on a wire rack. Cut into 16 squares. Yield: 16 servings (serving size: 1 brownie).

CALORIES 179; FAT 5.3g (sat 3.1g, mono 1.1g, poly 0.2g); PROTEIN 3.9g; CARB 29.3 g; FIBER 0.7g; CHOL 14mg; IRON 0.7mg; SODIUM 96mg; CALC 77mg

Make Ahead • Freezable • Kid Friendly
Tangy Ice Cream with Cashew Brittle

Hands-on time: 7 min. Total time: 1 hr. 32 min.

1¼ cups 2% reduced-fat milk
1 cup half-and-half
¾ cup fat-free sweetened condensed milk
½ cup sour cream
¼ teaspoon salt
Cooking spray
¼ cup sugar
1 tablespoon water
2 teaspoons light-colored corn syrup
2 tablespoons dry-roasted salted cashews,
  coarsely chopped
1 tablespoon butter, softened

1. Combine first 5 ingredients, stirring well with a whisk. Place mixture in freezer can of a table-top ice-cream freezer, and freeze according to manufacturer's instructions. Spoon ice cream into a freezer-safe container; freeze 1 hour or until firm.
2. Coat a sheet of parchment paper with cooking spray. Combine sugar, 1 tablespoon water, and corn syrup in a small, heavy saucepan; bring to a boil. Cook 7 minutes or until golden, without stirring. Remove from heat. Stir in nuts and butter. Quickly spread sugar mixture in a thin, even layer over prepared parchment; cool completely. Chop brittle; serve over ice cream. Yield: 6 servings (serving size: ½ cup).

CALORIES 255; FAT 8.6g (sat 4.7g, mono 2.4g, poly 0.5g); PROTEIN 6.1g; CARB 38.9g; FIBER 0.1g; CHOL 26mg; IRON 0.2mg; SODIUM 145mg; CALC 204mg

CL KITCHEN SECRET: VANILLA IN VANILLA

THE CHALLENGE:
Whole vanilla beans impart generous flavor to custards and other sweets, but they don't come cheap. Storing in a dark pantry helps keep them soft, but they still often dry out, leaving you with an expensive pile of sticks.

THE SECRET:
Store them, snipped to fit, in your bottle of vanilla extract. Not only does the liquid keep the pods soft and pliable, but also the beans add further intensity to the extract.

Peanut Butter and Dark Chocolate Fudge

Hands-on time: 9 min. Total time: 2 hr. 11 min.

1 (14-ounce) can fat-free sweetened
   condensed milk, divided
3/4 cup semisweet chocolate chips
2 tablespoons unsweetened dark cocoa
   powder
1/4 teaspoon instant coffee granules
1 teaspoon vanilla extract, divided
3/4 cup peanut butter chips
1 tablespoon peanut butter
1/4 cup salted, dry-roasted peanuts, coarsely
   chopped

1. Line an 8-inch square baking dish
with wax paper. Place 9 tablespoons
milk in a microwave-safe bowl. Add
chocolate chips, cocoa, and coffee.
Microwave at HIGH 1 minute or
until melted. Stir in 1/2 teaspoon vanilla.
Spread into prepared pan.
2. Combine remaining milk, peanut
butter chips, and peanut butter in a
microwave-safe bowl. Microwave at
HIGH 1 minute or until melted. Stir
in remaining 1/2 teaspoon vanilla. Spread
evenly over chocolate layer, and sprinkle
with peanuts. Cover and chill 2 hours.
Cut into 25 squares. Yield: 25 servings
(serving size: 1 square).

CALORIES 123; FAT 4.7g (sat 3.1g, mono 0.7g, poly 0.1g);
PROTEIN 3.5g; CARB 17g; FIBER 0.6g; CHOL 2mg;
IRON 0.3mg; SODIUM 47mg; CALC 43mg

OH, FUDGE! DARK CHOCOLATE, PEANUT BUTTER, AND CRUNCHY NUTS MAKE FOR A DELICIOUS INDULGENCE.

DIPS: EASY, GOOEY, CHEWY TREATS

Never underestimate the power of a great dip to get a holiday party off to a cheery start.

Make Ahead
Baked Feta with Romesco and Olive Tapenade

Hands-on time: 45 min. Total time: 1 hr. 12 min.

Make the romesco sauce and tapenade up to three days ahead, and keep them chilled separately.

Romesco Sauce:
1 red bell pepper
Cooking spray
2 cups chopped peeled plum tomato
5 garlic cloves, minced
1/2 cup fat-free, lower-sodium chicken broth
2 tablespoons chopped hazelnuts, toasted
1 (1-ounce) slice white bread, chopped
1/4 teaspoon black pepper
Tapenade:
1/2 cup pitted kalamata olives
1/2 cup pitted picholine or other fruity olives
1/4 cup chopped fresh flat-leaf parsley
1 tablespoon olive oil
2 tablespoons sherry vinegar
1/4 teaspoon freshly ground black pepper
Remaining ingredients:
1 1/4 cups (5 ounces) crumbled feta cheese,
   divided
2 tablespoons fresh flat-leaf parsley

1. Preheat broiler to high.
2. To prepare romesco sauce, cut red
bell pepper in half lengthwise, and
discard seeds and membranes. Place
pepper halves, skin sides up, on a foil-
lined baking sheet; flatten with hand.

Broil 8 minutes or until blackened.
Place in a paper bag; fold to close
tightly. Let stand 10 minutes. Peel
and chop.
3. Reduce oven temperature to 425°.
4. Heat a large skillet over medium
heat. Coat pan with cooking spray. Add
tomato and garlic; cook 4 minutes or
until garlic lightly browns, stirring frequently. Add red bell pepper and broth;
cover and cook 10 minutes, stirring
occasionally. Stir in nuts and bread;
cook 1 minute. Transfer mixture to
a food processor or blender; add 1/4
teaspoon black pepper. Process until
smooth; transfer to a bowl.
5. To prepare tapenade, place olives, 1/4
cup parsley, and next 3 ingredients in
a food processor. Process until finely
chopped. Transfer to a bowl.
6. Coat a 1 1/2-quart broiler-safe glass
or ceramic baking dish with cooking
spray. Spoon half of romesco sauce
into prepared dish, and top with 3/4 cup
cheese. Dollop tapenade over cheese.
Spoon remaining romesco sauce over
tapenade, and top with remaining 1/2
cup crumbled feta cheese. Bake at 425°
for 20 minutes or until thoroughly
heated. Remove dish from oven.
7. Preheat broiler.
8. Broil 3 minutes or until top browns.
Sprinkle with 2 tablespoons parsley.
Yield: 12 servings (serving size: 1/4 cup).

CALORIES 88; FAT 6.1g (sat 2g, mono 2.4g, poly 0.6g);
PROTEIN 3.6g; CARB 4.9g; FIBER 0.7g; CHOL 8mg;
IRON 0.4mg; SODIUM 240mg; CALC 47mg

Toasted Parmesan Pita Crisps

Hands-on time: 9 min. Total time: 21 min.

6 (6-inch) whole-wheat pitas
Cooking spray
½ cup (2 ounces) grated fresh Parmigiano-
　Reggiano cheese
½ teaspoon freshly ground black pepper

1. Preheat oven to 350°.
2. Cut each pita in half horizontally; cut each pita half into 6 wedges to form 72 wedges. Divide wedges evenly among 2 baking sheets lined with parchment paper and coated with cooking spray. Lightly coat wedges with cooking spray. Sprinkle cheese and pepper evenly over wedges. Bake at 350° for 11 minutes or until crisp, rotating baking sheets after 5 minutes. Yield: 12 servings (serving size: 6 chips).

CALORIES 100; FAT 1.8g (sat 0.7g, mono 0.4g, poly 0.4g);
PROTEIN 4.4g; CARB 17g; FIBER 2.4g; CHOL 2.9mg;
IRON 1mg; SODIUM 221mg; CALC 42mg

Orange and Avocado Salsa

(pictured on page 236)

Hands-on time: 15 min. Total time: 15 min.

3 cups orange sections, chopped (about 4)
2½ cups pink grapefruit sections, chopped
　(about 2 large grapefruit)
¼ cup minced red onion
2 tablespoons chopped fresh cilantro
1 tablespoon minced jalapeño pepper
2 teaspoons fresh lime juice
½ teaspoon kosher salt
1 diced peeled avocado

1. Combine all ingredients in a bowl; toss gently. Serve immediately. Yield: 10 servings (serving size: ¼ cup).

CALORIES 86; FAT 3g (sat 0.4g, mono 2g, poly 0.4g);
PROTEIN 1.3g; CARB 14.7g; FIBER 3.5g; CHOL 0mg;
IRON 0.1mg; SODIUM 98mg; CALC 44mg

Spicy Tortilla Strips

(pictured on page 236)

Hands-on time: 20 min. Total time: 30 min.

Increase the ground red pepper to add a kick.

6 (8-inch) flour tortillas
Cooking spray
1½ tablespoons canola oil
⅜ teaspoon ground cumin
⅛ teaspoon ground red pepper

1. Preheat oven to 400°.
2. Cut tortillas in half, and cut each half into 5 strips to form 60 strips. Divide tortilla strips evenly among 2 baking sheets lined with parchment paper and coated with cooking spray. Brush strips evenly with canola oil. Combine cumin and red pepper in a small bowl, and sprinkle over strips. Bake at 400° for 10 minutes or until browned, rotating baking sheets after 5 minutes. Yield: 10 servings (serving size: 6 chips).

CALORIES 106; FAT 4.3g (sat 0.7g, mono 2.4g, poly 1g);
PROTEIN 2.3g; CARB 14.2g; FIBER 0.9g; CHOL 0mg;
IRON 1mg; SODIUM 176mg; CALC 36mg

Caramelized Onion, Gruyère, and Bacon Spread

Hands-on time: 35 min. Total time: 1 hr. 5 min.

Serve with crackers or bread slices. If you can't find Gruyère, substitute raclette, fontina, or Swiss cheese.

Cooking spray
3½ cups chopped onion
2 ounces Gruyère cheese, shredded and
　divided
2 tablespoons chopped fresh chives, divided
⅓ cup canola mayonnaise
⅓ cup fat-free sour cream
¼ teaspoon salt
¼ teaspoon black pepper
3 bacon slices, cooked and crumbled

1. Preheat oven to 425°.
2. Heat a large cast-iron skillet over medium-high heat. Coat pan lightly with cooking spray. Add onion to pan; sauté 5 minutes, stirring frequently. Reduce heat to low; cook 20 minutes or until golden brown, stirring occasionally. Cool slightly.
3. Reserve 2 tablespoons cheese. Combine remaining cheese, caramelized onion, 1 tablespoon chives, and remaining ingredients in a medium bowl. Transfer mixture to a 1-quart glass or ceramic baking dish coated lightly with cooking spray. Sprinkle with reserved 2 tablespoons cheese. Bake at 425° for 20 minutes or until browned and bubbly. Sprinkle with remaining 1 tablespoon chives. Yield: 8 servings (serving size: 3 tablespoons).

CALORIES 101; FAT 6.8g (sat 1.9g, mono 2.9g, poly 1.3g);
PROTEIN 4.2g; CARB 5.3g; FIBER 0.7g; CHOL 12mg;
IRON 0.2mg; SODIUM 236mg; CALC 97mg

Zesty Green Goddess Dip

Hands-on time: 12 min. Total time: 12 min.

2 cups trimmed watercress (about 2 bunches)
½ cup fresh basil leaves
⅓ cup canola mayonnaise
¼ cup fresh flat-leaf parsley leaves
¼ cup chopped green onions
¼ cup plain fat-free Greek yogurt
2 tablespoons extra-virgin olive oil
1 tablespoon white wine vinegar
1 teaspoon anchovy paste
½ teaspoon freshly ground black pepper
¼ teaspoon kosher salt
¼ teaspoon ground red pepper

1. Combine all ingredients in a food processor, and pulse 8 to 10 times or until just combined. Scrape mixture into a bowl or serving dish. Cover and chill 8 hours or overnight. Yield: 6 servings (serving size: 3 tablespoons).

CALORIES 92; FAT 8.7g (sat 0.7g, mono 5.5g, poly 1.8g);
PROTEIN 1.5g; CARB 1.2g; FIBER 0.4g; CHOL 3mg;
IRON 0.4mg; SODIUM 223mg; CALC 33mg

Cajun Hot Crab Dip

Hands-on time: 30 min. Total time: 1 hr. 5 min.

Spoon this dip into a baking dish up to a day ahead, but top with panko and chives just before baking. If it's chilled, leave the dish out at room temperature while the oven preheats.

Cooking spray
2 tablespoons minced shallots
1 teaspoon minced garlic
1 pound lump crabmeat, shell pieces removed, divided
¼ cup water
1 tablespoon hot pepper sauce
2 teaspoons salt-free Cajun seasoning
½ cup canola mayonnaise
⅓ cup ⅓-less-fat cream cheese, softened
¼ cup minced red bell pepper
2 tablespoons lemon juice
¼ teaspoon salt
¼ teaspoon black pepper
3 tablespoons panko
3 tablespoons minced fresh chives

1. Preheat oven to 450°.
2. Heat a small saucepan over medium heat. Coat pan with cooking spray. Add shallots and garlic to pan; cook 2 minutes, stirring frequently. Place 1 cup crab in a food processor. Add shallot mixture, ¼ cup water, pepper sauce, and Cajun seasoning to crab; process until smooth. Spoon mixture into a large bowl, and stir in remaining crab, mayonnaise, and next 5 ingredients.
3. Transfer mixture to a 1-quart glass or ceramic casserole dish coated lightly with cooking spray. Combine panko and chives in a small bowl; sprinkle over crab mixture. Coat panko mixture with cooking spray. Bake at 450° for 30 minutes or until browned and bubbly. Let stand 5 minutes. Yield: 12 servings (serving size: ¼ cup).

CALORIES 95; **FAT** 5.3g (sat 1.1g, mono 1.8g, poly 1.3g); **PROTEIN** 8.4g; **CARB** 2g; **FIBER** 0.1g; **CHOL** 43mg; **IRON** 0.4mg; **SODIUM** 253mg; **CALC** 46mg

READER RECIPE
PLUM GOOD CHOPS

Traditional Moroccan tagines are stewed for hours, but Anisa Abeytia's dish captures the flavors without the time crunch. Instead of cubes of lamb, Abeytia opts for chops. "You don't have to worry about a long cooking process," she says. Simmering the sauce separately also saves time and intensifies the flavor. Serve with couscous.

Spiced Lamb with Plum Sauce

Hands-on time: 22 min. Total time: 52 min.

"If you're short on time, the sauce can be made the night before."
—Anisa Abeytia, Dubai, U.A.E.

Lamb:
1 teaspoon ground cumin
1 teaspoon ground coriander
1 teaspoon ground cinnamon
1 teaspoon paprika
¼ teaspoon salt
¼ teaspoon freshly ground black pepper
2 (1½-pound) French-cut racks of lamb (8 ribs each)
1 tablespoon extra-virgin olive oil
1 onion, thinly sliced (about 3 cups)
Cooking spray
Sauce:
1¾ cups water
1½ cups pitted dried plums, chopped
½ teaspoon ground cumin
½ teaspoon ground coriander
½ teaspoon ground cinnamon
½ teaspoon paprika
¼ teaspoon salt
¼ teaspoon black pepper
1 tablespoon fresh lemon juice
2 tablespoons chopped fresh cilantro

1. Preheat oven to 375°.
2. To prepare lamb, combine first 6 ingredients. Coat lamb with oil. Rub spice mixture on lamb.
3. Arrange onion in a roasting pan coated with cooking spray; top with lamb. Bake at 375° for 30 minutes or until a thermometer inserted in thickest part of lamb registers 130°. Let stand 10 minutes. Cut lamb into chops. Discard onion.
4. To prepare sauce, combine 1¾ cups water and next 7 ingredients in a medium saucepan; bring to a boil. Reduce heat to medium; simmer 20 minutes or until sauce measures 2 cups. Stir in juice. Serve sauce with lamb. Sprinkle lamb with cilantro. Yield: 8 servings (serving size: 2 chops and ¼ cup sauce).

CALORIES 381; **FAT** 15.9g (sat 6.3g, mono 6.8g, poly 0.8g); **PROTEIN** 35.4g; **CARB** 22g; **FIBER** 2.4g; **CHOL** 112mg; **IRON** 3.7mg; **SODIUM** 291mg; **CALC** 33mg

5-INGREDIENT COOKING

Rice and Beans with Chicken and Chorizo

Hands-on time: 20 min. Total time: 25 min.

Cook 1 (5-ounce) package lower-sodium yellow rice according to package directions, omitting salt and fat. Heat a large skillet over medium-high heat; coat with cooking spray. Add 1 pound skinless, boneless chicken breast, cut into bite-sized pieces. Sauté 7 minutes or until browned. Stir in 1½ cups chopped seeded plum tomato, ⅓ cup water, ½ teaspoon kosher salt, ½ teaspoon black pepper, and 2 ounces Spanish chorizo sausage, diced; bring to a boil. Reduce heat, and simmer 6 minutes or until thickened. Stir in 1 (15-ounce) can lower-sodium black beans, rinsed and drained; cook 2 minutes or until thoroughly heated. Spoon ½ cup rice onto each of 4 plates; top each serving with 1 cup chicken mixture. Yield: 4 servings.

CALORIES 307; **FAT** 5.1g (sat 1.7g, mono 2g, poly 0.8g); **PROTEIN** 34.6g; **CARB** 31.9g; **FIBER** 4.2g; **CHOL** 66mg; **IRON** 2mg; **SODIUM** 472mg; **CALC** 41mg

OYSTERS

Quick & Easy • Make Ahead
Vegetarian
Rosemary–Green Peppercorn Mignonette

Combine 3 tablespoons minced
shallots, 1 tablespoon chopped fresh
rosemary, 1½ tablespoons crushed green
peppercorns, ½ cup red wine vinegar,
and ⅛ teaspoon salt; chill shallot
mixture 30 minutes. Serve with oysters.
Yield: 8 servings (serving size: 1½
tablespoons).

CALORIES 15; **FAT** 0.1g (sat 0.1g); **SODIUM** 154mg

Quick & Easy
Roasted Oysters with Pancetta and Breadcrumbs

Hands-on time: 19 min. Total time: 24 min.

2 tablespoons pine nuts, toasted
2 (1-ounce) slices white bread
Cooking spray
1 ounce finely chopped pancetta or cured
  bacon
2 tablespoons chopped fresh flat-leaf parsley
¼ teaspoon black pepper
18 shucked oysters on the half shell
6 lemon wedges

1. Preheat oven to 450°.
2. Combine nuts and bread in a mini
food processor; process until coarsely
ground. Heat a medium skillet over
medium-high heat, and lightly coat
pan with cooking spray. Add pancetta;
sauté 2 minutes or until crisp, stirring
frequently. Remove from heat. Stir in
pine nut mixture, parsley, and black
pepper. Carefully arrange oysters in a
single layer on a broiler pan, and spoon
1 tablespoon bread mixture onto each

oyster. Bake at 450° for 5 minutes or
until oysters are opaque. Serve immediately with lemon wedges. Yield: 6
servings (serving size: 3 oysters).

Sustainable Choice | *Oysters are filter feeders, so they help keep the waters they live in clean.*

CALORIES 92; **FAT** 4.9g (sat 1.1g, mono 0.7g, poly 1.4g);
PROTEIN 4.7g; **CARB** 7.7g; **FIBER** 0.7g; **CHOL** 26mg;
IRON 3.3mg; **SODIUM** 212mg; **CALC** 38mg

OYSTER BARS often offer dozens of varieties, making it hard to choose. Below are a
few of our favorites with tasting notes to
help you navigate with confidence next
time you belly up to the bar.

·············· **WEST COAST** ··············

FANNY BAY
Popular British Columbia oysters offer
consistently briny flavor with sweet
cucumber notes in the finish. (Available
September to June.)

GOOSE POINT
Tender, creamy, and low in brine, these
Washington state oysters come from
Willapa Bay, the cleanest estuary in
America. (Available year-round.)

PENN COVE SELECT
These big, fat, plump Puget Sound oysters
taste buttery, with a mild nutty flavor,
mellow mineral notes, and a clean finish.
(Available October to June.)

·············· **EAST COAST** ··············

WINTER POINT
Firm, chewy, and salty up front, these
Maine oysters follow with a beefy mineral
note and a sweet, clean finish. (Available
year-round.)

WELLFLEET
A popular oyster that hails from Wellfleet,
Mass., these superbriny bivalves finish on a
more rounded sweet note. (Available June
to November.)

CANADA CUP
Mild, creamy, grassy, and minerally oysters
from prized Prince Edward Island. This is
a crowd favorite. (Available May to
December.)

HOW TO SHUCK OYSTERS

1. Using an oyster knife and glove,
grasp oyster firmly in gloved hand, and
wedge the knife tip into the hinge.
Carefully push and twist simultaneously
to pop the oyster open. (Rösle knife
and mesh glove from Sur la Table.)

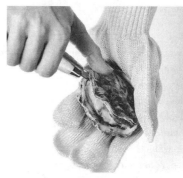

2. Swipe to free the oyster by sliding
the knife along the inside of the top
shell, using it as a guide. This will help
you avoid mangling the delicate meat.
Take care not to spill the delicious
oyster liquor.

3. Remove and discard top shell. Make
same swiping motion under the oyster,
carefully guiding the knife between
meat and the bottom shell to release
foot. Serve immediately, or place shells
on a bed of ice and chill up to 2 hours.

BEAUTIFUL HOLIDAY DESSERTS

These applause-worthy desserts will delight guests with a sweet, elegant full-stop ending to a great meal—and do so with a much lighter touch.

Make Ahead • Freezable • Kid Friendly
Apple-Cinnamon Bundt Cake

Hands-on time: 26 min. Total time: 2 hr. 16 min.

This homey comfort classic is made special with a dusting of sugar and a hidden filling of apples and nuts.

Filling:

1½ cups diced peeled Granny Smith or other tart apple

½ cup apple cider

1 tablespoon dark brown sugar

1 (3-inch) cinnamon stick

Streusel:

½ cup walnuts

2 tablespoons dark brown sugar

1 tablespoon all-purpose flour

½ teaspoon ground cinnamon

Cake:

Baking spray with flour

¾ cup granulated sugar

½ cup butter, softened

2 large eggs

1 large egg yolk

1 vanilla bean, split lengthwise

9 ounces all-purpose flour (about 2 cups)

2 teaspoons baking powder

1 teaspoon baking soda

¼ teaspoon salt

½ cup fat-free milk

¾ cup plain 2% reduced-fat Greek yogurt

1 teaspoon powdered sugar

1. Preheat oven to 350°.
2. To prepare filling, combine first 4 ingredients in a saucepan over medium-high heat; bring to a boil. Reduce heat to medium; simmer 20 minutes or until liquid almost evaporates and apple is tender, stirring occasionally. Cool to room temperature. Discard cinnamon stick.
3. To prepare streusel, combine walnuts and next 3 ingredients in a food processor. Pulse until mixture resembles coarse meal.
4. To prepare cake, coat a 12-cup bundt pan with baking spray. Place sugar and butter in a large bowl; beat with a mixer at medium speed until light and fluffy (about 3 minutes). Add eggs and egg yolk, 1 at a time, beating well after each addition. Scrape seeds from vanilla bean; add seeds to sugar mixture. Reserve bean for another use. Weigh or lightly spoon flour into dry measuring cups; level with a knife. Combine flour, baking powder, baking soda, and salt in a bowl, stirring well with a whisk. Combine milk and yogurt in a small bowl, stirring until smooth. Add flour mixture and milk mixture alternately to sugar mixture, beginning and ending with flour mixture; beat just until combined.
5. Spoon one-third of batter into prepared pan; sprinkle batter with half of apple mixture and half of walnut mixture. Repeat layers, ending with remaining third of batter; smooth with a spatula. Bake at 350° for 30 minutes or until a wooden pick inserted in center comes out with moist crumbs clinging. Cool on wire rack 15 minutes; remove cake from pan. Cool on a wire rack. Sprinkle with powdered sugar. Yield: 12 servings (serving size: 1 wedge).

CALORIES 279; **FAT** 11.7g (sat 5.5g, mono 2.9g, poly 2.5g); **PROTEIN** 5.9g; **CARB** 38.2g; **FIBER** 1.1g; **CHOL** 68mg; **IRON** 1.4mg; **SODIUM** 299mg; **CALC** 83mg

Make Ahead
Pumpkin-Almond Cheesecake

Hands-on time: 20 min. Total time: 12 hr.

If your springform pan is loose and prone to leaking, wrap the bottom of it completely with heavy-duty aluminum foil before scraping the batter into it and baking. You can also place the pan on a baking sheet in the oven so that nothing drips on the floor of your oven. Serve the cheesecake unadorned for informal dining, or garnish with the whipped topping and almond brittle to add a special touch to your holiday dessert buffet.

Almond cake:

6 tablespoons sugar

¼ cup butter, softened

⅛ teaspoon salt

4 ounces almond paste

2 large eggs

1 ounce cake flour (about ¼ cup)

1 tablespoon dark rum

Cooking spray

Cheesecake:

1 cup (8 ounces) ⅓-less-fat cream cheese, softened

⅓ cup (3 ounces) fat-free cream cheese, softened

½ cup sugar

Dash of salt

3 large eggs

1 vanilla bean, split lengthwise

1¼ cups canned unsweetened pumpkin

⅓ cup plain 2% reduced-fat Greek yogurt

⅛ teaspoon ground ginger

Brittle:

½ cup sugar

1½ tablespoons water

1½ teaspoons light-colored corn syrup

3 tablespoons sliced almonds, toasted

1 tablespoon butter

Remaining ingredient:

14 tablespoons frozen fat-free whipped topping, thawed

1. Preheat oven to 350°.
2. To prepare almond cake, combine 6 tablespoons sugar, ¼ cup butter, ⅛ teaspoon salt, and 4 ounces almond paste in a large bowl; beat with an electric mixer at medium speed until light and fluffy (about 3 minutes). Add 2

eggs, 1 at a time, beating well after each addition. Weigh or lightly spoon cake flour into a dry measuring cup; level with a knife. Stir flour and rum into sugar mixture. Spread batter evenly into a 9-inch springform pan coated with cooking spray. Bake at 350° for 20 minutes or until a wooden pick inserted in center comes out clean. Cool completely in pan on a wire rack (do not remove or loosen sides of springform pan).

3. Reduce oven temperature to 300°.

4. To prepare cheesecake, place softened cheeses, ½ cup sugar, and salt in a large bowl; beat with a mixer at medium speed just until blended. Add 3 eggs, 1 at a time, beating at low speed just until each addition is incorporated. Scrape seeds from vanilla bean, and reserve bean for another use. Add seeds, pumpkin, yogurt, and ginger to cream cheese mixture; beat at low speed just until blended. Pour cream cheese mixture evenly over top of cooled almond cake. Bake at 300° for 1 hour or until cheesecake center barely moves when pan is touched. Remove cheesecake from oven, and run a knife around outside edge. Cool to room temperature on a wire rack. Cover and chill 8 hours or overnight.

5. To prepare brittle, line a baking sheet with parchment paper; coat parchment paper with cooking spray. Combine ½ cup sugar, 1½ tablespoons water, and corn syrup in a small saucepan; bring to a boil, stirring just until sugar dissolves. Cook, without stirring, 7 minutes or until mixture is golden. Remove from heat. Stir in almonds and butter. Quickly spread sugar mixture in a thin, even layer over prepared parchment; cool completely. Break into 14 pieces. Slice cheesecake into 14 slices; top each serving with 1 tablespoon whipped topping and 1 piece brittle. Yield: 14 servings

CALORIES 263; **FAT** 12.2g (sat 5.7g, mono 3.6g, poly 1.1g); **PROTEIN** 6.3g; **CARB** 32.1g; **FIBER** 1.2g; **CHOL** 88mg; **IRON** 1mg; **SODIUM** 199mg; **CALC** 71mg

---

Make Ahead • Kid Friendly

Triple-Chocolate Cake

(pictured on page 237)

Hands-on time: 25 min. Total: 1 hr. 25 min.

Cake:
1 cup boiling water
½ cup plus 1 tablespoon unsweetened cocoa, divided
2 ounces bittersweet chocolate, finely chopped
Cooking spray
1¾ cups granulated sugar
6 tablespoons butter, softened
1 teaspoon vanilla extract
3 large egg whites
½ cup fat-free sour cream
8 ounces cake flour (about 2 cups)
1½ teaspoons baking powder
½ teaspoon baking soda
½ teaspoon salt
Filling:
⅓ cup fat-free milk
1 tablespoon granulated sugar
1 tablespoon cornstarch
Dash of salt
4 ounces milk chocolate, finely chopped
¾ cup frozen fat-free whipped topping, thawed
Glaze:
½ cup powdered sugar
¼ cup unsweetened cocoa
3 tablespoons fat-free milk
2 teaspoons butter
⅛ teaspoon instant espresso granules
Dash of salt
1 ounce bittersweet chocolate, finely chopped

1. Preheat oven to 350°.

2. To prepare cake, combine 1 cup boiling water and ½ cup cocoa. Add 2 ounces bittersweet chocolate; stir until smooth. Cool to room temperature. Coat 2 (8-inch) round metal cake pans with cooking spray; line bottoms of pans with wax paper. Coat wax paper with cooking spray; dust pans with remaining 1 tablespoon cocoa.

3. Place 1¾ cups granulated sugar, 6 tablespoons butter, and 1 teaspoon vanilla in a large bowl; beat with a mixer at medium speed 1 minute. Add

egg whites, 1 at a time, beating well after each addition. Add sour cream; beat at medium speed 2 minutes. Weigh or lightly spoon cake flour into dry measuring cups; level with a knife. Combine flour, baking powder, baking soda, and ½ teaspoon salt in a bowl, stirring with a whisk. Add flour mixture and cocoa mixture alternately to sugar mixture, beginning and ending with flour mixture; beat just until combined.

4. Divide batter evenly between prepared pans. Bake at 350° for 30 minutes or until a wooden pick inserted in center comes out with moist crumbs clinging. Cool 10 minutes in pans on wire racks. Remove from pans; cool on wire racks. Discard wax paper.

5. To prepare filling, combine ⅓ cup milk and next 3 ingredients in a saucepan over medium-low heat; bring to a boil, stirring constantly. Cook 1 minute or until thick, stirring constantly. Remove from heat. Add milk chocolate, stirring until smooth. Pour into a bowl. Cover and chill. Uncover; fold in whipped topping.

6. To prepare glaze, combine powdered sugar and remaining ingredients in a saucepan over low heat. Cook 2 minutes, stirring frequently. Place 1 cake layer on a plate. Spread filling over cake, leaving a ¼-inch border. Top with remaining layer. Drizzle glaze over top of cake, spreading it out over edges. Yield: 16 servings (serving size: 1 slice).

CALORIES 311; **FAT** 10.3g (sat 5.7g, mono 2.1g, poly 0.5g); **PROTEIN** 4.8g; **CARB** 50.6g; **FIBER** 1.8g; **CHOL** 49mg; **IRON** 2.2mg; **SODIUM** 224mg; **CALC** 66mg

Frozen Orange Tortes with Cranberry Compote

Hands-on time: 1 hr. Total time: 9 hr.

Crust:
2 tablespoons sugar
2 tablespoons Dutch process cocoa
16 chocolate wafer cookies
2 tablespoons butter, melted
Cooking spray
Filling:
2 large egg whites
1/8 teaspoon salt
1/3 cup sugar
3 tablespoons water
1 1/2 cups vanilla ice cream
1 tablespoon grated orange rind
1/4 cup fresh orange juice
Compote:
1 cup fresh cranberries
1/2 cup sugar
2 tablespoons water
1 tablespoon fresh lemon juice
1/4 cup orange-flavored liqueur

1. Preheat oven to 400°.
2. To prepare crust, combine first 3 ingredients in a food processor; process until finely ground. With motor running, pour butter through food chute; process until well blended. Divide crumb mixture evenly among 8 (6-ounce) straight-sided ramekins coated with cooking spray; press mixture into bottoms of ramekins. Place ramekins on a baking sheet; bake at 400° for 8 minutes or until toasted. Cool completely.
3. To prepare filling, place egg whites and salt in a bowl; beat with a mixer at high speed until foamy. Combine sugar and 3 tablespoons water in a small saucepan; bring to a boil. Cook, without stirring, until a candy thermometer registers 250°. Gradually pour hot sugar syrup in a thin stream into egg white mixture, beating at medium speed, then at high speed until stiff peaks form. Reduce mixer to medium speed; beat until mixture cools (about 8 minutes).
4. Allow ice cream to stand at room temperature 15 minutes or until very soft; stir rind and orange juice into ice cream. Fold one-third of egg white mixture into ice cream mixture. Gently fold remaining egg white mixture into ice cream mixture. Divide mixture evenly among ramekins; freeze 8 hours or overnight.
5. To prepare compote, combine 1 cup fresh cranberries, 1/2 cup sugar, 2 tablespoons water, and 1 tablespoon lemon juice in a small saucepan over medium heat; bring to a boil. Cook 10 minutes or until thick, stirring occasionally. Remove from heat, and stir in liqueur. Cover and chill 4 hours or overnight. Unmold tortes; serve with cranberry compote. Yield: 8 servings (serving size: 1 torte and 2 tablespoons compote).

CALORIES 270; **FAT** 7.4g (sat 4.2g, mono 2.2g, poly 0.4g); **PROTEIN** 3g; **CARB** 45.4g; **FIBER** 1.7g; **CHOL** 21mg; **IRON** 0.7mg; **SODIUM** 183mg; **CALC** 38mg

Maple-Gingerbread Pots de Crème

Hands-on time: 20 min. Total time: 4 hr. 20 min.

Dress up these custard cups by sprinkling each with 1/2 teaspoon sugar and broiling them until the sugar turns golden brown.

1/2 cup maple syrup
2 tablespoons dark brown sugar
2 large egg yolks
1 3/4 cups half-and-half
1/2 teaspoon ground ginger
Dash of salt
Dash of ground nutmeg
Dash of ground cloves (optional)
2 (3-inch) cinnamon sticks
1 vanilla bean, split lengthwise

1. Preheat oven to 300°.
2. Combine first 3 ingredients in a large bowl, stirring well with a whisk.
3. Combine half-and-half and remaining ingredients in a medium, heavy saucepan over medium-high heat; cook until mixture reaches 180° or until tiny bubbles form around edge (do not boil). Gradually add hot milk mixture to egg mixture, stirring constantly with a whisk. Return milk mixture to pan. Reduce temperature to medium, and cook until mixture thickens slightly (about 2 minutes), stirring constantly with a whisk. Remove from heat. Strain mixture through a sieve into a bowl; discard solids. Divide mixture evenly among 8 (4-ounce) ramekins or custard cups. Place ramekins in a 13 x 9–inch metal baking pan; add hot water to pan to a depth of 1 inch. Bake at 300° for 1 hour or until center barely moves when ramekins are touched. Remove ramekins from pan; cool completely on a wire rack. Cover and chill 4 hours. Yield: 8 servings (serving size: 1 cup).

CALORIES 192; **FAT** 10.6g (sat 5.4g, mono 3.8g, poly 1g); **PROTEIN** 4.3g; **CARB** 21.1g; **FIBER** 1g; **CHOL** 229mg; **IRON** 4.3mg; **SODIUM** 51mg; **CALC** 96mg

Caramel-Pecan Dacquoise

Hands-on time: 55 min. Total time: 3 hr. 55 min.

Meringues:
1 teaspoon fresh lemon juice
1/8 teaspoon salt
3 large egg whites
1/2 cup granulated sugar
1/2 cup finely chopped pecans, toasted
Mousse:
1/3 cup cold water
1 teaspoon unflavored gelatin
6 tablespoons brown sugar
1/3 cup heavy whipping cream, divided
1 tablespoon butter
1 tablespoon light-colored corn syrup
1/8 teaspoon salt
1/4 cup granulated sugar
1/4 cup water
2 large egg whites
Dash of salt
Remaining ingredient:
1 ounce bittersweet chocolate, chopped and melted

1. Preheat oven to 200°.
2. To prepare meringues, combine first 3 ingredients in a bowl; beat with a mixer at high speed until foamy. Add sugar, 1 tablespoon at a time, beating

until stiff peaks form. Fold in pecans. Carefully spoon meringue mixture into a zip-top plastic bag; seal. Trace 1 (10-inch) circle onto each of 2 sheets of parchment paper; tape 1 sheet onto each of 2 baking sheets. Cut ¼ inch off 1 corner of bag; squeeze meringue mixture onto prepared pans to form 2 (10-inch) circles. Bake meringues at 200° for 3 hours or until dry. Turn oven off; cool in closed oven. Carefully remove meringues.

3. To prepare mousse, combine water and gelatin; let stand 5 minutes. Place brown sugar, 4½ teaspoons whipping cream, butter, syrup, and salt in a saucepan over medium-high heat; bring to a boil, stirring until sugar dissolves. Cook 2 minutes without stirring; remove from heat. Stir in gelatin mixture; cook 30 seconds, stirring until gelatin dissolves. Remove from heat. Transfer mixture to a large bowl; cool completely.

4. Place remaining ¼ cup whipping cream in a medium bowl; beat with a mixer at high speed until stiff peaks form. Fold whipped cream into cooled gelatin mixture; chill 20 minutes or until almost set. Combine granulated sugar and ¼ cup water in a small saucepan over medium-high heat; bring to a boil, stirring just until sugar dissolves. Cook without stirring until a thermometer registers 250° (about 3 minutes). Place 2 egg whites and a dash of salt in a large bowl; using clean, dry beaters, beat with a mixer at high speed until foamy. Slowly pour hot sugar mixture in a thin stream into egg whites; continue beating until stiff peaks form. Reduce mixer to medium speed; beat until mixture cools (about 8 minutes).

5. Fold one-third of egg white mixture into caramel mixture; gently fold in remaining egg white mixture. Chill 1 hour. Place 1 baked meringue round on a platter; spread mousse evenly over meringue. Top with remaining meringue round. Drizzle melted chocolate over top. Cut into 6 wedges. Yield: 6 servings (serving size: 1 wedge).

CALORIES 320; **FAT** 14.8g (sat 5.5g, mono 4.6g, poly 2.1g); **PROTEIN** 5.6g; **CARB** 46.2g; **FIBER** 1.1g; **CHOL** 23mg; **IRON** 0.5mg; **SODIUM** 218mg; **CALC** 81mg

MEATLESS HOLIDAY MAINS

Join the President: Pardon a turkey, and still have a festive meal. Consider a cheesy pasta, spicy tamales, or even a fancy new take on beets.

Make Ahead • Freezable • Vegetarian
Butternut Squash, Caramelized Onion, and Spinach Lasagna

Hands-on time: 1 hr. 15 min. Total time: 2 hr.

6 cups (½-inch) cubed peeled butternut squash
2 tablespoons extra-virgin olive oil, divided
2 tablespoons chopped fresh sage
12 garlic cloves, unpeeled (about 1 head)
1 teaspoon kosher salt, divided
½ teaspoon black pepper
Cooking spray
1 large onion, vertically sliced
2 tablespoons water
2 (9-ounce) packages fresh spinach
5 cups 1% low-fat milk, divided
1 bay leaf
1 thyme sprig
5 tablespoons all-purpose flour
1½ cups (6 ounces) shredded fontina cheese, divided
⅜ teaspoon ground red pepper
¼ teaspoon grated whole nutmeg
9 no-boil lasagna noodles

1. Preheat oven to 425°.
2. Combine squash, 1 tablespoon oil, sage, garlic, ½ teaspoon salt, and black pepper in a large bowl; toss to coat. Arrange squash mixture on a baking sheet coated with cooking spray. Bake at 425° for 30 minutes or until squash is tender. Cool slightly; peel garlic. Place squash and garlic in a bowl; partially mash with a fork.

3. Heat remaining 1 tablespoon oil in a large Dutch oven over medium-high heat. Add onion, and sauté 4 minutes. Reduce heat to medium-low; continue cooking 20 minutes or until golden brown, stirring frequently. Place onion in a bowl.
4. Add 2 tablespoons water and spinach to Dutch oven; increase heat to high. Cover and cook 2 minutes or until spinach wilts. Drain in a colander; cool. Squeeze excess liquid from spinach. Add spinach to onion.
5. Heat 4½ cups milk, bay leaf, and thyme in a medium saucepan over medium-high heat. Bring to a boil; remove from heat. Let stand 10 minutes. Discard bay leaf and thyme. Return pan to medium heat. Combine remaining ½ cup milk and flour in a small bowl. Add to pan, stirring with a whisk until blended. Bring to a boil; reduce heat, and simmer 5 minutes or until thickened, stirring constantly. Remove from heat; stir in remaining ½ teaspoon salt, 1¼ cups cheese, red pepper, and nutmeg.
6. Spread ½ cup milk mixture in bottom of a 13 x 9–inch glass or ceramic baking dish coated with cooking spray. Arrange 3 noodles over milk mixture; top with half of squash mixture, half of spinach mixture, and ¾ cup milk mixture. Repeat layers, ending with noodles. Spread remaining milk mixture over noodles. Bake at 425° for 30 minutes, and remove from oven. Sprinkle with remaining ¼ cup cheese.
7. Preheat broiler.
8. Broil 2 minutes or until cheese is melted and lightly browned. Let stand 10 minutes before serving. Yield: 8 servings (serving size: 1 piece).

CALORIES 360; **FAT** 11.9g (sat 5.4g, mono 4.7g, poly 1g); **PROTEIN** 16.6g; **CARB** 50g; **FIBER** 6.5g; **CHOL** 31mg; **IRON** 4mg; **SODIUM** 576mg; **CALC** 406mg

> Serve with a fresh salad of grapefruit and fennel, and sip our Pomegranate Fizz, page 313.

Vegetarian
Black Bean and Sweet Potato Tamales with Tomatillo Sauce

Hands-on time: 1 hr. 45 min. Total time: 3 hr.

Complete this fiesta with Spicy Sautéed Broccoli Rabe with Garlic and a Clementine Sparkler (pages 307 and 312).

24 dried cornhusks
Filling:
1 (1-pound) sweet potato
2 teaspoons extra-virgin olive oil
1 cup chopped onion
1 teaspoon ground cumin
½ teaspoon ground cinnamon
1 (15-ounce) can black beans, rinsed and drained
1 (4-ounce) can chopped green chiles, drained
1¼ cups (5 ounces) preshredded reduced-fat Mexican cheese blend
¼ cup chopped fresh cilantro
Masa dough:
2 cups organic vegetable broth
1½ cups frozen corn kernels, thawed
3¾ cups masa harina
1½ teaspoons baking powder
¼ teaspoon salt
¼ cup butter, melted
Tomatillo sauce:
2 teaspoons extra-virgin olive oil
1 cup chopped onion
1 jalapeño pepper, seeded and chopped
3 garlic cloves, minced
1 pound fresh tomatillos, husked and rinsed (about 8)
⅓ cup organic vegetable broth
2 tablespoons chopped fresh oregano
1 teaspoon ground cumin
1 teaspoon chipotle chile powder
¼ teaspoon salt
½ cup fresh cilantro leaves

1. Place corn husks in a large bowl; cover with water. Weight husks down with a can; soak 30 minutes. Drain.
2. Preheat oven to 400°.
3. To prepare filling, pierce potato with a fork; wrap in foil. Bake at 400° for 1 hour or until tender. Peel potato; mash. Heat 2 teaspoons oil in a skillet over medium-high heat. Add 1 cup onion; sauté 4 minutes. Add 1 teaspoon cumin and cinnamon; sauté 30 seconds. Add beans and green chiles; sauté 2 minutes. Remove from heat. Combine potato, bean mixture, cheese, and chopped cilantro.
4. Increase oven temperature to 450°.
5. To prepare masa dough, combine 2 cups broth and corn in a blender; process until smooth.
6. Lightly spoon masa harina into dry measuring cups; level with a knife. Combine masa harina, baking powder, and salt in a large bowl. Add broth mixture and butter to masa mixture; stir until a soft dough forms. Cover.
7. To prepare sauce, heat 2 teaspoons oil in a medium saucepan over medium-high heat. Add 1 cup onion, jalapeño, and garlic; sauté 2 minutes. Add tomatillos and next 5 ingredients; bring to a boil. Cover, reduce heat, and simmer 10 minutes. Cool slightly.
8. Place tomatillo mixture and cilantro leaves in a blender. Remove center piece of blender lid (to allow steam to escape); secure blender lid on blender. Place a clean towel over opening in blender lid (to prevent splatters). Blend until smooth.
9. Working with 1 husk at a time, place 3 tablespoons masa dough in center of husk about ½ inch from top, and press dough into a 4 x 3–inch rectangle. Spoon 2 tablespoons bean mixture down 1 side of dough. Fold husk over tamale, being sure to cover filling with dough; fold over 1 more time. Fold bottom end of husk under. Place tamale, seam side down, on rack of a broiler pan lined with a damp towel. Repeat procedure with remaining husks, dough, and bean mixture. Cover filled tamales with another damp towel. Pour 2 cups hot water in bottom of a broiler pan; top with prepared rack.
10. Steam at 450° for 1 hour, adding water as necessary to maintain a depth of about ½ inch. Let stand 10 minutes. Serve with sauce. Yield: 12 servings (serving size: 2 tamales and ¼ cup sauce).

CALORIES 297; **FAT** 9.8g (sat 4g, mono 2.6g, poly 1.2g); **PROTEIN** 10g; **CARB** 47.1g; **FIBER** 6.6g; **CHOL** 19mg; **IRON** 3.4mg; **SODIUM** 473mg; **CALC** 225mg

TAMALE TIME!

Tamales are delicious, comforting, fun to make, and—after you find corn husks—require no special equipment.

1. Spread dough onto husk, and then spoon filling along one side.

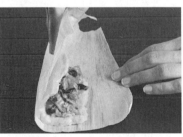

2. Fold husk over, making sure masa seals around filling.

3. Fold tapered end; turn tamale over.

4. Arrange on rack over a water-filled broiler pan lined with damp towels for steaming.

Vegetarian

Beet Wellingtons

Hands-on time: 1 hr. Total time: 2 hr. 5 min.

Pair these sophisticated but earthy delights with a fresh spinach salad and our scrumptious French Apple Tart (page 310).

1 large red beet (about 1 pound)
1 large golden beet (about 1 pound)
4 teaspoons extra-virgin olive oil, divided
¼ teaspoon salt, divided
½ teaspoon black pepper, divided
1 tablespoon unsalted butter
1 (8-ounce) package presliced exotic
   mushroom blend
1 tablespoon chopped fresh thyme
1 teaspoon chopped fresh rosemary
3 garlic cloves, minced
1 shallot, finely chopped
⅔ cup walnuts, toasted and chopped (about
   2¼ ounces)
2 tablespoons organic vegetable broth
2 tablespoons red wine
6 tablespoons crumbled goat cheese
8 (18 x 14-inch) sheets frozen phyllo dough,
   thawed and divided
Cooking spray
1 large egg, beaten

1. Preheat oven to 400°.
2. Pierce each beet with a fork; wrap in foil. Bake at 400° for 1 hour and 15 minutes or until tender; cool. Peel red beet; cut into 8 slices. Place in bowl with 2 teaspoons olive oil, ⅛ teaspoon salt, and ¼ teaspoon pepper. Toss gently. Repeat procedure with golden beet and remaining oil, salt, and pepper.
3. Reduce oven temperature to 375°.
4. Heat butter in a large skillet over medium-high heat. Add mushrooms and next 4 ingredients; sauté 4 minutes or until tender, stirring frequently. Add nuts, broth, and wine; cook 1 minute or until liquid evaporates. Transfer mushroom mixture to a medium bowl; cool. Stir in cheese.
5. Place 1 phyllo sheet on a large cutting board (cover remaining dough to prevent drying); coat phyllo sheet with cooking spray. Top with another phyllo sheet; coat with cooking spray. Gently press phyllo layers together. Arrange 2 slices red beet in center of 1 short edge of phyllo, leaving a 4-inch border. Top with ½ cup mushroom mixture, and arrange 2 slices golden beet over top of mushroom mixture. Fold over long edges to cover.
6. Starting at the short edge with 4-inch border, roll up jelly-roll fashion. Place packet seam side down on a baking sheet coated with cooking spray; brush with egg. Repeat with remaining phyllo, red beets, mushroom mixture, golden beets, and egg. Bake at 375° for 25 minutes or until golden. Yield: 4 servings (serving size: 1 packet).

CALORIES 403; FAT 25.7g (sat 6.1g, mono 7.5g, poly 10.3g); PROTEIN 10.9g; CARB 31.7g; FIBER 3.5g; CHOL 68mg; IRON 2.8mg; SODIUM 446mg; CALC 61mg

Wild Mushroom Pastitsio

Hands-on time: 33 min. Total time: 63 min.

4 teaspoons olive oil, divided
1 cup chopped onion
2 garlic cloves, minced
2 (8-ounce) packages presliced exotic
   mushroom blend, chopped
1 tablespoon chopped fresh oregano
½ teaspoon kosher salt, divided
¼ teaspoon black pepper
⅛ teaspoon ground nutmeg
1 (8-ounce) can tomato sauce
2 large eggs, lightly beaten
3 tablespoons chopped fresh parsley
1 teaspoon unsalted butter
1½ tablespoons all-purpose flour
2 cups 1% low-fat milk
1½ cups (6 ounces) shredded part-skim
   mozzarella cheese, divided
4 cups hot cooked fusilli pasta
Cooking spray

1. Preheat oven to 350°.
2. Heat 1 tablespoon oil in a Dutch oven over medium-high heat; swirl to coat. Add onion and garlic; sauté 3 minutes or until tender. Add mushrooms. Cook for 8 minutes or until liquid almost evaporates. Stir in oregano, ¼ teaspoon salt, black pepper, nutmeg, and tomato sauce. Cook 2 minutes, stirring frequently. Remove from heat; set aside.
3. Combine eggs and parsley in a large bowl. Heat remaining 1 teaspoon oil and butter in a medium saucepan over medium heat. Sprinkle flour evenly into pan; cook 2 minutes, stirring constantly. Gradually add milk to flour mixture, stirring with a whisk until smooth. Bring to a boil; cook 2 minutes or until thickened, stirring frequently. Remove from heat; let stand 4 minutes. Stir in remaining ¼ teaspoon salt and 1 cup cheese. Gradually add hot milk mixture to egg mixture, stirring constantly with a whisk. Add pasta to milk mixture; toss to combine.
4. Spread 2 cups pasta mixture in an 11 x 7–inch baking dish coated with cooking spray. Top with mushroom mixture. Top with remaining pasta mixture. Cover with foil coated with cooking spray. Bake at 350° for 30 minutes. Remove foil; sprinkle with remaining ½ cup cheese.
5. Preheat broiler.
6. Broil 5 minutes or until cheese melts. Let stand 15 minutes. Yield: 6 servings (serving size: 1 piece).

CALORIES 364; FAT 13.1g (sat 5.7g, mono 5g, poly 1.2g); PROTEIN 20.1g; CARB 42g; FIBER 3.5g; CHOL 92mg; IRON 2.6mg; SODIUM 574mg; CALC 341mg

....
Entertaining? Serve this alongside Swiss Chard with Crème Fraîche (page 308) and an earthy pinot noir.
....

TODAY'S LESSON: RUSTIC BREADS

Thanks to the artisanal boom, crusty, chewy loaves are pushing squishy breads out of the spotlight. But they're not in every store and not always well made. Nothing beats great home-baked bread in this robust, chewy style. For most recipes, a stand mixer makes it easy and takes the guesswork out of kneading.

Make Ahead • Freezable • Kid Friendly
Crusty French Boules

Hands-on time: 28 min. Total time: 52 hr. 20 min.

Spraying the dough with water produces a supercrisp crust. For best flavor, allow the pâte fermentée to rest for the full 48 hours. But you can chill it for as little as 8 hours.

Pâte fermentée:
5.63 ounces all-purpose flour, divided (about 1¼ cups)
½ teaspoon active dry yeast
½ teaspoon salt
½ cup warm water (100° to 110°)
Cooking spray
Dough:
¾ cup warm water (100° to 110°)
1 teaspoon active dry yeast
9 ounces all-purpose flour (about 2 cups)
4 ounces bread flour (about ⅔ cup)
1 teaspoon salt
1 tablespoon cornmeal

1. To prepare pâte fermentée, weigh or lightly spoon 4.5 ounces (about 1 cup) all-purpose flour into a dry measuring cup, and level with a knife. Combine 4.5 ounces all-purpose flour, ½ teaspoon yeast, and ½ teaspoon salt in bowl of a stand mixer fitted with paddle attachment. Add ½ cup warm water, and beat at low speed until mixture is thoroughly combined. Add enough of remaining 4 tablespoons flour, 1 tablespoon at a time, until dough just begins to pull away from sides of bowl. Increase mixer speed to medium, and beat 2 minutes. Place dough in a small bowl coated with cooking spray. Place a piece of plastic wrap coated with cooking spray directly on dough. Refrigerate 48 hours or up to 3 days.
2. Remove pâte fermentée from refrigerator; let stand at room temperature 30 minutes.
3. To prepare dough, place ¾ cup warm water in bowl of a stand mixer with dough hook attached, and sprinkle with 1 teaspoon yeast. Let mixture stand 5 minutes or until bubbles form. Add pâte fermentée to yeast mixture; let stand 10 minutes. Weigh or lightly spoon 9 ounces all-purpose flour (about 2 cups) and 4 ounces bread flour (about ⅔ cup) into dry measuring cups; level with a knife. Add flours and 1 teaspoon salt to bowl; beat at low speed until flour is incorporated. Increase mixer to medium speed, and beat 6 minutes. (Dough should form a ball.)
4. Place dough in a large bowl coated with cooking spray; lightly coat dough with cooking spray. Cover with plastic wrap, and let stand in a warm, dry place, free from drafts, 1½ hours or until doubled in size. (Gently press 2 fingers into dough. If indentation remains, dough has risen enough.) Punch dough down, and divide into 2 equal portions. Knead each portion 1 minute. Shape each dough portion into a 5-inch round by pulling the sides down, pinching and tucking them under the bottom center of dough, forming a smooth, taut surface on the top. Place dough rounds on a baking sheet sprinkled with cornmeal. Lightly coat surface of dough with cooking spray. Cover and let rise 1 hour and 15 minutes or until doubled in size.
5. Place a small ovenproof saucepan with 3 inches of water directly on the floor of oven. Preheat oven to 450°.
6. Uncover dough. Spray dough lightly with water. Make 4 (4-inch) cuts ¼ inch deep in dough to form a grid across top of each loaf using a sharp knife. Bake at 450° for 10 minutes. Remove water pan from oven. Bake an additional 15 minutes or until bread is golden brown and sounds hollow when bottom is tapped. Cool on a wire rack. Cut each boule, crosswise, into 12 slices. Yield: 24 servings (serving size: 1 slice).

CALORIES 82; FAT 0.3g (sat 0.1g, mono 0g, poly 0.1g); PROTEIN 2.5g; CARB 17g; FIBER 0.6g; CHOL 0mg; IRON 1.1mg; SODIUM 148mg; CALC 3mg

KEEP DOUGH ON HAND: WRAP IN PLASTIC AND FREEZE AFTER THE FIRST RISE. THAW IN REFRIGERATOR OVERNIGHT, AND PROCEED.

BOULE BASICS

DEVELOP FLAVOR
Start a day or two before you plan to bake by making a pâte fermentée. This step is well worth the time because it adds unparalleled flavor.

PROOF THE YEAST
Combine yeast and warm water; let stand about 5 minutes or until bubbles form. If the mixture fails to bubble, you'll need to start over.

SHAPE THE DOUGH
Work dough into a round and pull the sides down, pinching and tucking them under the bottom center, forming a smooth, taut surface.

Make Ahead • Kid Friendly
Rich Chocolate Babka
(pictured on page 238)

Hands-on time: 25 min. Total time: 3 hr. 40 min.

The dough is enriched with butter and eggs, making it a gorgeous, indulgent treat. Loosely rolling the dough will give it room to expand during the second rise.

Dough:
1 cup warm 2% reduced-fat milk (100° to 110°)
½ cup granulated sugar
1 package active dry yeast
¼ cup butter, melted
2 teaspoons vanilla extract
1 teaspoon salt
3 large eggs
23.6 ounces all-purpose flour, divided (about 5¼ cups)
Cooking spray

Filling:
⅓ cup granulated sugar
¼ cup unsweetened cocoa
1 large egg white
2 teaspoons 2% reduced-fat milk
¼ cup butter, divided
4 ounces bittersweet chocolate, chopped and divided

Additional ingredient:
1½ tablespoons turbinado sugar

1. To prepare dough, combine first 3 ingredients in a large bowl, and let stand 5 minutes or until bubbles form on surface. Add butter, vanilla, salt, and eggs; stir. Weigh or lightly spoon 22.5 ounces flour (about 5 cups) into dry measuring cups; level with a knife. Add flour to egg mixture; stir until combined. Turn dough out onto a lightly floured surface. Knead 4 minutes; add enough of remaining ¼ cup flour to prevent dough from sticking. Place dough in a large bowl coated with cooking spray, turning to coat top. Cover and let rise in a warm place, free from drafts, 1½ hours or until doubled in size.
2. To prepare filling, combine ⅓ cup sugar and cocoa in a small bowl, stirring well. Combine egg white and 2 teaspoons milk in a small bowl.
3. Divide dough into 2 equal portions. Working with 1 portion at a time (cover remaining dough to prevent drying), roll dough into a 12 x 9–inch rectangle. Melt ¼ cup butter; brush 1 tablespoon over dough. Sprinkle evenly with half of cocoa mixture, leaving a ¼-inch border. Sprinkle dough evenly with 2 ounces chopped chocolate. Drizzle with an additional 1 tablespoon butter. Brush far edge with milk mixture. Loosely roll up, starting with a long edge; pinch seam to seal, and tuck ends under. Place dough, seam side down, on a baking sheet lined with parchment paper. Repeat procedure with remaining dough, butter, cocoa mixture, chocolate, and egg white mixture. Reserve remaining milk mixture. Cover dough. Let rise in a warm place 1 hour or until doubled in size.
4. Preheat oven to 325°.
5. Brush dough with remaining milk mixture. Sprinkle each loaf with 2¼ teaspoons turbinado sugar. Bake at 325° for 40 minutes or until browned. Cool loaves completely on a wire rack. Cut each loaf into 12 slices. Yield: 24 servings (serving size: 1 slice).

CALORIES 213; FAT 7.1g (sat 3.8g, mono 1.3g, poly 0.4g); PROTEIN 5.1g; CARB 33g; FIBER 1.6g; CHOL 34mg; IRON 1.9mg; SODIUM 142mg; CALC 21mg

ROLL THE DOUGH TOO TIGHT AND THE DOUGH MAY SPLIT DURING BAKING.

Real Bagels

Hands-on time: 50 min. Total time: 2 hr. 40 min.

If you grew up on factory bagels, these are a chewy revelation. Omit barley malt syrup from the recipe if you can't find it.

2 cups warm water (100° to 110°)

1 teaspoon active dry yeast

28.5 ounces bread flour, divided (about 6½ cups)

1 tablespoon barley malt syrup

2 teaspoons kosher salt

Cooking spray

12 cups water

¾ cup sugar

1. Combine 2 cups warm water and yeast in bowl of a stand mixer fitted with dough hook; let stand 5 minutes or until bubbles form on the surface. Weigh or lightly spoon 28.13 ounces flour (about 6¼ cups) into dry measuring cups; level with a knife. Add flour, syrup, and salt to yeast mixture. Mix dough at low speed 6 minutes. Turn dough out onto a floured surface. Knead 2 minutes or until smooth and elastic; add enough of remaining ¼ cup flour, 1 tablespoon at a time, to prevent dough from sticking to hands. Place dough in a large bowl coated with cooking spray, turning to coat top. Cover and let rise in a warm place (85°), free from drafts, 30 minutes.

2. Turn dough out onto a lightly floured surface, and divide into 12 equal portions. Working with 1 portion at a time (cover remaining dough to prevent drying), shape each portion into a ball. Make a hole in center of each ball using your index finger. Using fingers of both hands, gently pull dough away from center to make a 1½-inch hole. Place bagels on a baking sheet coated with cooking spray. Lightly coat bagels with cooking spray; cover with plastic wrap. Let rise 10 minutes (bagels will rise only slightly).

3. Preheat oven to 450°.

4. Combine 12 cups water and ¾ cup sugar in a Dutch oven, and bring to a boil. Gently lower 3 bagels into pan.

Cook 30 seconds. Transfer bagels to a wire rack lightly coated with cooking spray. Repeat procedure with remaining bagels, working in batches of 3. Divide bagels between 2 baking sheets lined with parchment paper. Bake at 450° for 7 minutes. Rotate pans, and bake for 7 minutes or until golden. Cool on wire racks. Yield: 12 servings (serving size: 1 bagel).

CALORIES 255; FAT 1.1g (sat 0.2g, mono 0.1g, poly 0.5g); PROTEIN 8.3g; CARB 51.7g; FIBER 1.7g; CHOL 0mg; IRON 3mg; SODIUM 322mg; CALC 12mg

---

TOP WITH FUN!

For extra flavor, sprinkle about 1½ teaspoons sesame or poppy seeds, granulated garlic, or onion flakes on each bagel immediately after boiling.

Prosciutto Pizza with Tangy White Sauce

Hands-on time: 30 min. Total time: 27 hr. 50 min.

⅔ cup warm water (100° to 110°)

1 teaspoon active dry yeast

7.75 ounces bread flour, divided (about 1½ cups plus 2 tablespoons)

1½ tablespoons olive oil, divided

½ teaspoon kosher salt

Cooking spray

¾ cup 2% reduced-fat milk

2 teaspoons Dijon mustard

½ teaspoon freshly ground black pepper

1 large egg yolk

1½ tablespoons butter

1½ teaspoons minced fresh garlic

2 teaspoons all-purpose flour

¾ cup shredded Gruyère cheese

2 ounces thinly sliced prosciutto, torn

1 tablespoon chopped fresh chives

1. Combine ⅔ cup warm water and yeast in bowl of a stand mixer fitted with dough hook, and let stand 5 minutes or until bubbles form. Weigh or lightly spoon 6.75 ounces bread flour (about 1½ cups) into dry measuring cups; level with a knife. Sprinkle 6.75 ounces bread flour over yeast mixture. Add 1 tablespoon olive oil and salt.

Mix at low speed 2 minutes or until dough forms a ball. Increase speed to medium, and mix 8 minutes or until smooth and elastic. Place dough in a medium bowl coated with cooking spray, turning to coat top. Cover and let rise in a warm place, free from drafts, 1 hour or until doubled in size. (Gently press 2 fingers into dough. If indentation remains, dough has risen enough.) Punch dough down.

2. Cover surface of dough with plastic wrap lightly coated with cooking spray. Refrigerate 24 hours. Remove dough from refrigerator. Let stand, covered, 2 hours or until dough comes to room temperature. Punch dough down. Place a piece of parchment paper on a flat work surface, and sprinkle parchment with remaining 2 tablespoons bread flour. Roll dough out to a 13-inch circle. Slide parchment and dough onto a pizza peel or flat baking sheet. Brush dough evenly with remaining 1½ teaspoons olive oil. Cover dough lightly with plastic wrap.

3. Position an oven rack in the lowest setting, and place a pizza stone on rack. Preheat oven to 500°.

4. Combine milk and next 3 ingredients in a medium bowl, stirring with a whisk. Melt butter in a medium saucepan over low heat. Add garlic to pan; cook 3 minutes or just until butter and garlic begin to brown, stirring frequently. Add 2 teaspoons all-purpose flour to pan, and cook 30 seconds, stirring constantly with a whisk. Stir in milk mixture, and bring to a boil. Cook 1 minute or until thick, stirring constantly with a whisk. Spread sauce in an even layer over dough, leaving a ¼-inch border; sprinkle sauce evenly with cheese. Slide parchment and pizza onto preheated pizza stone. Bake at 500° for 18 minutes or until crust is golden. Arrange prosciutto on pizza, and sprinkle with chives. Cut pizza into 12 wedges. Yield: 6 servings (serving size: 2 wedges).

CALORIES 298; FAT 13.7g (sat 5.9g, mono 5.1g, poly 1.1g); PROTEIN 13g; CARB 30.2g; FIBER 1.1g; CHOL 67mg; IRON 2.1mg; SODIUM 534mg; CALC 186mg

ADVENTURES IN THE HOME KITCHENS OF THAILAND

In which an ordinary American cook learns to crush galangal and fry up hand-minced catfish from the wonderful women of Chiang Mai and Fang.

By Amy O'Connor

When I bragged to my foodie friends about my upcoming immersion cooking course in Thailand, they hinted the experience might be too much of a challenge for someone like me. Thai cooking, it seems, is so complex and laborious that a rookie home cook would be crouched in the corner relegated to rice-soaking duty while the experts butterflied tiger shrimp with a lemongrass twig. Plus, food in Thailand is taken very seriously, indeed reverentially: I should consider a crash course on fish sauce varieties before even getting on the plane.

So why were these same foodie friends clamoring for a dinner chez moi after I returned? Because hand-prepared, home-cooked Thai cuisine is seriously delicious—and distinct from anything you'll get at any Thai restaurant in the U.S. Over nine days I learned to make food that would haunt my dreams: spicy grilled pork, herbed steamed catfish patties, chicken poached in lemongrass-cilantro broth, tender meatballs spiked with garlic and ginger, gooey sticky rice pudding, and chopped salads bursting with texture and flavor. All without the benefit of a food processor or even a particularly sharp knife.

Thailand is a bona fide food-smacked place, with a France or Bay Area food focus and a comparable share of foodies, culinary preservationists, snobs, and upstarts. There was recently a brouhaha in Bangkok because the only two Michelin-starred Thai restaurants in the world are run by an Australian and a Dane. The editor of this magazine once went to a tasting—exactly like a wine tasting, but without the crackers—of super-pungent fish sauce, which many Southeast Asians take as seriously as wine.

Yet the Thais are not infected by the current urgent Western "discovery" of artisanal products and local ingredients. As an ancient and more demure culture, they ignore most loopy culinary innovation. Maybe that's because Thai ingredients have always been superb—the cuisine is a sort of symphonic expression of vivid, clear flavors. Their meals—often consumed in groups, on the floor, with just one's hands or a fork and spoon as utensils—are sublimely satisfying.

There, food is a source of fun, not pretension. People snack at all hours. They smile and share with strangers, and then laugh as you politely choke down a deep-fried silkworm. As I witnessed more than once, your typical foreign food snob will soon come a cropper in Thailand, trying, for example, to feign sophistication while chomping on sticky rice balls soaked in a cauterizing chili sauce.

Is real Thai food hard work? You bet. But if I can pull it off in a galley kitchen with budget ingredients from the local Korean-Asian market and get raves from my guests, anyone can. The trick is to learn the basic techniques and flavors, gain the confidence to adapt both to your taste, and then add the Thai special sauce: fun.

Kid Friendly • Vegetarian
Thai Sticky Rice

Hands-on time: 2 min. Total time: 8 hr. 30 min.

Thai sticky rice (which you'll find in Asian markets, labeled "sweet" or "glutinous" rice) is completely unlike other rice—its grains become semitranslucent when cooked, and the texture is pleasantly chewy. The moniker "sticky" is fitting, as the cooked rice can be pinched off in clumps that hold together firmly. To get the proper texture, it's prepared differently from most rice—soaked overnight, and then steamed over (not in) boiling water. If time is tight, quick-soak the rice in warm water for 2 hours, and then continue with recipe as written. If you have a rice cooker with a "sweet rice" or "sticky rice" setting, you can make it that way following manufacturer's instructions, though the texture is less sticky-chewy than you'll get with the traditional cooking method.

2 cups uncooked long-grain sweet or
  glutinous rice

1. Place rice in a large bowl. Cover rice with cool water to 2 inches above rice; cover and let stand 8 hours or overnight. Drain rice.
2. Line a bamboo steamer with a double layer of cheesecloth; pour rice over cheesecloth. Cover with steamer lid. Add water to a large skillet to a depth of 1 inch; bring to a boil. Place steamer in pan, making sure water doesn't touch rice; steam 25 minutes or until rice is shiny and cooked through. Yield: 8 servings (serving size: ½ cup).

CALORIES 171; FAT 0.3g (sat 0.1g, mono 0.1g, poly 0.1g); PROTEIN 3.2g; CARB 37.8g; FIBER 1.3g; CHOL 0mg; IRON 0.7mg; SODIUM 3mg; CALC 5mg

TRAVELING TO CHIANG MAI

My Thai cooking adventure, called Immersethrough, began in the legendary hippie-traveler destination Chiang Mai, about 400 miles north of Bangkok. A novice in Asia, I pictured a sleepy backwater with rickshaws and bamboo houses swaying on stilts. I landed in a fast-paced city buzzing with traffic, where several universities, wats, food markets, and canals jostle for square footage. This is a food mecca, still a hippie hangout, and a culinary melting pot where you can get everything from pizza to fish and chips to bouillabaisse, although we'd be getting none of that with Asian-food authority Naomi Duguid as our guide.

Duguid runs Immersethrough out of her Chiang Mai home base. It's less conventional cooking school than a chapter come to life from one of her famous books (which she wrote with her former partner, Jeffrey Alford). These coffee table volumes, including *Hot Sour Salty Sweet: A Culinary Journey through Southeast Asia* and *Beyond the Great Wall: Recipes and Travels in the Other China,* stew together gorgeous photography and recipes with scholarly essays and sharp profiles of obscure people and foodways. She is currently finishing up a solo book called *Rivers of Flavor: Recipes and Travel Stories from Burma,* due out next fall. In person, Duguid invites students to experience that near-baptismal connection to regional Thai culture in person and through food. Classes are taught not by trained chefs but by local home cooks, a singular privilege that I would truly come to appreciate later.

On our first night, we met at Duguid's apartment for Thai snacks and introductions. Duguid herself, at 5 foot 10 with a runner's physique, is an imposing presence. "That woman looks like she could tame a tiger," a friend who knows her says. This is not the politically correct earth mother you might expect from her respectful, lushly photographed books and her pensive blog entries. I encountered a high-octane intellect and a lapidary recall of facts and stories gathered over more than 30 years of traveling, photographing, learning indigenous languages, writing, and, later, raising two sons partially on the road. That she was also a successful attorney in her former life makes sense.

Munching peanuts tossed with chile peppers and fragrant Kaffir lime leaves, sipping a Thai "whiskey" made from sugar cane, Duguid started by toppling a few assumptions. First, those Thai dishes we think we love from neighborhood take-out restaurants? They are not what home cooks here make, and not what we'd be cooking.

Here, we'd be immersed in Northern Thai cuisine with Shan, Issaan, even Yunnan and Burmese influences, regions where the local soil can be dry and hard, the weather varies widely, and where there are no beaches. The cooks we would meet were the true food geniuses of Thailand, home cooks so skilled they can transform the humblest ingredients—roots, fibrous greens, bony river fish, yesterday's rice—into majestic meals. The results—cuisine that packs a forceful punch of spicy, salty, sweet, and sour in every bite, with pungent umami endnotes of fermented fish or dried meat—are like nothing most Americans have tasted.

Second, we were going to be learning to cook the traditional Thai way. No recipes. No fancy equipment. The markets would guide our daily shopping. No need for a Cuisinart, teacher insisted. "Village people without stovetops or food processors make this food every day. I say learn to do it right first, then you can simplify." Duguid would make sure we would gain as much appreciation for the people behind the wok as for what goes in.

All this began to make me a bit nervous. I love to cook, but my curriculum vitae includes a lot of ruined dishes (most recent blunder: whipping egg whites into packing peanuts). Duguid was talking about cooking freestyle, by hand, with fellow students who, it was turning out, were master home cooks or culinary professionals. Anne Winstanley, Anna Cleeves, and Colette Day, from Melbourne, Australia, have cooked on most continents and swapped tales about matters such as precision chocolate tempering and the paucity of spices in tribal Moroccan cuisine. Mizuho Hirokawa was a Tokyo-born student at The University of Gastronomic Sciences in Pollenzo, in the Piedmont region of Italy, which boasts a slow-foods curriculum. Brad Borchardt, an American chef who has run restaurants all over Asia, was in Chiang Mai on a sort of culinary bachelor party, two weeks into an executive position at P.F. Chang's in the United States.

Duguid passed around some small-batch fermented tofu, which was as sharp and creamy as Gorgonzola to some, and like a jar of stinky socks to the others. Then came three kinds of fried insects. The white silkworms were bland, but I passed on the larger mystery bug that looked like something that crawls out of bathtub drains. Cleeves took a bite and, with dry Aussie irony, reported it "fantastic." Fern Somrak, Duguid's Immersethrough partner, gave each of us a frozen lychee.

Duguid then led us to a night market where we ate more: fried rice cakes, sectioned pomelos sprinkled with sugar and chili powder (try that mix on grapefruit), raw jackfruit (like eating a flower), and bowl after bowl of Chiang Mai's famous street noodles. Finally, jet-lagged and staggering, we headed back to our hotel.

THE SOUND OF A MORTAR AND PESTLE IS A WAY FOR A MAN TO SCOUT OUT A GOOD SPOUSE.

Chiang Mai Pork Patties

Hands-on time: 15 min. Total time: 25 min.

Chiang Mai sausages are one of the glories of Northern Thai cuisine. The forcemeat used for the sausages makes a great patty full of vibrant flavor. Serve with Roasted Eggplant Salsa (page 340) and Thai Sticky Rice (page 337) for a delicious meal. Grill the patties for notes of smoke and char. You can find unfamiliar ingredients at Southeast Asian markets, or use the substitutes listed below.

1¼ pounds ground pork
¾ teaspoon salt
½ cup coarsely chopped shallots
¼ cup finely chopped fresh cilantro
2 tablespoons minced peeled fresh
    lemongrass
2 tablespoons thinly sliced Kaffir lime leaves
    or 1 tablespoon minced lime rind
1 tablespoon minced peeled fresh galangal or
    2 teaspoons minced peeled fresh ginger
3 garlic cloves, minced
3 fresh Thai red bird chiles, minced
15 Bibb or Boston lettuce leaves
⅔ cup fresh cilantro leaves
⅔ cup fresh mint leaves
10 lime wedges

1. Combine pork and salt in a medium bowl; toss to combine.
2. Place shallots in a food processor, and pulse until finely chopped. Add chopped cilantro and next 5 ingredients; process until mixture is finely chopped. Add pork mixture; pulse 5 times or until mixture is well combined.
3. Using wet hands, shape mixture into 15 (1-inch-thick) patties (about 2 tablespoons per patty). Heat a large grill pan over high heat. Add half of pork patties. Cook 5 minutes on each side or until done. Repeat procedure with remaining patties. Arrange 3 lettuce leaves and 3 pork patties on each of 5 plates, and serve each serving with about ¼ cup herbs and 2 lime wedges. Yield: 5 servings.

CALORIES 291; FAT 17.9g (sat 6.6g, mono 7.9g, poly 1.7g); PROTEIN 23.4g; CARB 8.8g; FIBER 1.4g; CHOL 80mg; IRON 2.2mg; SODIUM 424mg; CALC 50mg

COOKING IN CHIA MAI

The next morning, Duguid took us for a quick breakfast of hot, melt-on-your-tongue Thai doughnuts called pha thong ko. In Europe, they'd probably get protected status as a regional food. Here, you can find them at any local market, and the vendors get a kick out of twisting the dough into animal shapes so people like me can dunk their heads in Thai coffee and bite them off.

Afterward, Duguid took us shopping for ingredients. She made good on her promise to force "as much contact with non-English-speaking people as possible," pressing baht, the Thai currency, into our hands and sending us in different directions. "Anna, you buy shrimp paste," she urged. "Brad, we'll need pork—of course!—and grab some bags of beef blood."

Duguid's cooking studio has an open terrace lined with three clay braziers and a low table with mortars, tamarind cutting boards, and several medieval-looking cleavers. There is no oven and none of the machinery common to cooking-school kitchens. We would get "body memory" by watching and doing, not reading and making notes along the way. "I want you to take that leap off the trapeze and don't look at recipes," she said. "This way you can learn the technique and understand why flavors go together."

That's when we met Somrak's mother, whom everyone calls Khun Mae, a serene 70-year-old whose life experience preparing and cooking authentic Thai cuisine makes her the linchpin in Duguid's operation. Without a word—she doesn't speak English, and it doesn't matter—Khun Mae had us positioned like members of a scout group, each at our stations.

In one corner, the diminutive Hirokawa was whacking away at an even skinnier chicken in preparation for gai nung (chicken pieces rubbed with a spice paste and then steamed to yield a wonderful broth and tender meat). Day got engrossed in the art of catfish gutting; although the guts themselves would get tossed, nothing else, including the head and skin, would. When Hirokawa was done, she turned the cleavers over to Winstanley, who began mincing pork for ep moo (pork minced with lemongrass and other flavors, then shaped into small patties, wrapped in banana leaf, and grilled). Mincing is a technique Duguid urged us to adopt: "You can buy ground pork, but you don't know what it is or where it's been. This way you can control quality."

Just when we thought it was time to put the knives away and crack a beer, Khun Mae smudged some meat onto the cutting board, then shook her head; for these dishes, the pork—which is about 20% fat, compared to our much leaner American meat—had to be pummeled into a paste.

Duguid has a Zen quality. When she doesn't like a food, rather than avoiding it, she "opens a window on her palate" to let it in, over and over again, to try to understand why others do. She pretty much eats what she's offered, be it bugs, frogs, even raw pork and animal blood. Adopting Duguid's motto that "Not liking something holds you back" helped me enjoy fermented tofu, fatty pork, and the occasional searing chili sauce.

She also has a swashbuckling energy that makes you want to hitch a wagon to her life. She orders Thai whiskey by the bottle for the table at restaurants, sports her father's 1943 tuxedo jacket for special occasions, eats almost everything with her fingers, and is lean and fit at 61, despite constant snacking between epic meals. She can communicate in French, Spanish, Mandarin, Russian, Lao, Urdu, or Tibetan. Her advice to food-loving travelers who aren't fluent? "A kitchen vocabulary, an open face, and being unrushed are the essentials."

I stayed close to Duguid when she began demonstrating how not to screw up sticky rice, which Thais eat with every meal and which is a whole new rice experience if you're used to basic "converted" white rice. She showed how the grains of rice look distinct, holding one up to the light: The sticky variety is opaque, while the fluffy, drier rice most of the rest of the world prefers is kind of see-through. The reason: Sticky rice has more amylopectin, the starch that gives it that toothsome, roll-in-a-ball quality I have come to crave. While Duguid talked, Khun Mae and Somrak were at the table demonstrating several techniques at once: the most efficient way to prepare lime leaves (remove the stem with scissors or a knife, roll them up, and cut crosswise into fine slivers), and that you must remove the tough outer layers of lemongrass before slicing, but don't bother peeling young galangal, turmeric, ginger, or garlic. Oh, and if you take a minute to grill shallots before chopping them, their intensity will mellow into an almost hazelnut sweetness.

Confession: I have a mortar and pestle, but before I came to Thailand, I had used them just once to bruise mint for juleps. Thai cooks, it seems, keep them going all day, and for good reason: Pummeling creates surfaces, and the more surface area to an ingredient, the more flavor it will yield when cooked. An intense dish like laap pla lanna (catfish minced with cleavers, then fried with crushed aromatics, then mixed with separately fried heaps of crispy fried garlic and the skin, and topped with more crushed aromatics) asks that nine ingredients be pummeled into a

paste. One bite and the flavors explode, and linger and extend on your palate.

Khun Mae found my pestle method (tentative tap-tap-tapping followed by a swirl) exasperating. She grabbed my arms and showed how to let the heavy tool do the work. Through Somrak's translation, she told me the sound of a mortar and pestle was traditionally a way for a man to scout out a good spouse.

Despite all that, cooking the authentic Thai way is not all that difficult, although it can be an all-day affair. Duguid, who never stopped sharing her encyclopedic knowledge of ingredients, gave us helpful shortcuts for later use and tips for swapping ingredients and adapting recipes to Western kitchens. "Galangal is different from ginger—you can taste cedar and resin—but ginger is fine, too" … "we use catfish here, but you Aussies can swap in barramundi when you get home" … "try peanut oil, it has the best smoke point for wok-frying."

Meanwhile, Khun Mae walked among us, silent as a leopard, instructing us with the brush of her hand to hack that chicken closer to the joint, or with an exasperated smile, making it clear we were not done pulverizing those peanuts.

"IT WAS MY KARMA TO BUY THIS FARM," SOMRAK SAYS. "AND IT'S MY KARMA TO LET THEM LIVE ON IT."

Make Ahead

Roasted Eggplant Salsa

Hands-on time: 24 min. Total time: 44 min.

The perfect pairing to a bowl of sticky rice, this savory, garlicky paste gets toasty flavor from roasted eggplant and blackened garlic and peppers. In more traditional versions, you grill ingredients over charcoal for deeper flavor.

2 medium Asian eggplants (about 14 ounces)
8 garlic cloves, unpeeled
3 fresh banana peppers
3 medium shallots, unpeeled (about 4 ounces)
1½ tablespoons fresh lime juice
1 tablespoon fish sauce
3 tablespoons fresh cilantro leaves, divided

1. Preheat oven to 400°.
2. Pierce entire surface of eggplants with a fork, and place on a baking sheet. Bake at 400° for 22 minutes or until eggplants are very tender. Cool to room temperature.
3. Heat a medium cast-iron skillet over medium-high heat. Add garlic, peppers, and shallots; cook 15 minutes or until skins are blackened and shallots are tender, turning vegetables occasionally to blacken evenly. Cool 10 minutes.
4. Halve eggplants lengthwise; scoop out pulp with a spoon. Discard skins; place eggplant pulp in a food processor. Peel shallots and garlic; discard skins. Add garlic pulp and shallots to eggplants. Stem and seed peppers; add to eggplant mixture. Add juice and fish sauce; pulse 10 times or until finely chopped. Stir in 2 tablespoons cilantro; sprinkle remaining cilantro over dish. Yield: 6 servings (serving size: ¼ cup).

CALORIES 42; FAT 0.1g (sat 0g, mono 0g, poly 0.1g); PROTEIN 2.2g; CARB 10g; FIBER 2.4g; CHOL 0mg; IRON 0.4mg; SODIUM 235mg; CALC 12mg

After a few days cooking in Chiang Mai, we piled into a van and took a road trip north, through jungle-covered hills and rice fields. Our destination was the town of Fang, about 15 miles from the Myanmar border, where we would spend the night, with side trips to meet the people who produce by hand the fermented tofu and rice noodles we'd been sampling earlier in the week. We also spent a few hours shopping at a market, held every Wednesday, where groups of hill tribe people come down from the surrounding areas to buy and sell.

Like so much of what we experienced in Thailand, the market was a bracing mix of modern and traditional. Some of the vendors looked and dressed like the chic denizens of Chiang Mai, while others displayed distinctive jewelry and clothing; the Akha women, for example, wore headdresses with tassels, beads, and coins. While I sipped some of the best espresso I've tasted outside of Italy, Mizuho Hirokawa devoured a finch-sized fried grasshopper.

Back in the van we snaked our way through backcountry dirt roads to Somrak's 13-acre lychee farm, whose splendor left us speechless: lychee trees, lush flower and vegetable gardens, and giant parasols over open-air brick stoves. For the next few days, we would learn to prep and cook the Shan way.

The Shan, or Tai Ya, are an ethnic group who live primarily in Myanmar, Thailand, and Yunnan Province in China, though their ongoing war with the brutal Burmese army means many end up, undocumented and without rights, in border camps. That could have been the fate of our cooking instructors, Jam and Boon Ma, whose welcoming wais—palms pressed together and uplifted in the traditional Thai greeting—belied their history of repression and hardship. Somrak explained to us that Boon Ma fled the Burmese army, which had killed his brother; Jam almost died crossing the Thai border with their daughter after a visit to her mother-in-law. Both are

now residents of Thailand, thanks to Somrak's efforts, and the permanent caretakers of her property. "It was my karma to buy this farm," she says, "and it's my karma to let them live on it."

Repression, poverty, and the endlessly complicated political status of the Shan mean their culture remains marginalized and their food hard to find in Thailand. It is, however, transcendent, with soft, full flavors and a lightness that had us going back for second and third servings. We devoured a delicious salad with banana flower, cilantro root, and pork cracklings, and another that showcased fermented tea leaves, marveling that such an inventive cuisine could emerge from such scarcity. "When you come from poverty, you tend to be more careful and precise with ingredients because you paid in blood and sweat for them," Duguid explained.

I had wondered about the wisdom of having untrained cooks who don't speak English teach Duguid's classes. It proved to be ingenious. After cooking and eating, Duguid had us all gather in a circle sipping whiskey infused with lychee—a drink we dubbed Lycheetinis—for a debrief with Jam and Boon Ma. At first they were so shy they barely made eye contact. By the second day, our slapstick cooking efforts had bonded students to teachers. We pulverized tua nao (flavorful disks made from fermented soybeans), hung strips of spice-rubbed Shan-style beef out to dry (we'd eat them later), made lopsided Shan meatballs, and laughed a lot. The joy and effort of making these foods side by side with generous, patient teachers will stay with all of us. So will the memory of Boon Ma, sporting a dimpled grin and showing his 8-year-old daughter how to take a picture with someone's smartphone. And Jam, practicing her favorite, and possibly only, English word: "DEE-LIS-US." She said it several times, a mantra and a promise, as we pounded, ground, scissored, hacked, minced, and sliced the afternoon away. And when it was finally time to sit down together and eat, DEE-LIS-US it was.

Quick & Easy • Make Ahead

Simmered Cabbage, Shan Style

Hands-on time: 32 min. Total time: 32 min.

The name of this dish is galaam oop, which tells the cooking method (oop) used for cooking the cabbage (galaam). The "oop" method of cooking, found in Northern Thailand and among the Shan people in Myanmar, involves a slow simmer, under a tightly sealed lid, of ingredients that have been combined with very little water and little or no oil. There's depth of flavor from a little ground beef that gives extra succulence. For a vegetarian version, omit the beef and add 1 teaspoon brown miso paste partway through cooking the cabbage; reduce the salt a little.

2 tablespoons peanut oil
1 cup thinly vertically sliced shallots
1 teaspoon salt
1 teaspoon turmeric
½ teaspoon ground red pepper
¼ pound ground sirloin
4 cups finely shredded cabbage (about 1 small head)
1 cup thin plum tomato wedges (about 2 medium)
⅓ cup coarsely chopped unsalted, dry-roasted peanuts

1. Heat a wok or Dutch oven over medium heat. Add peanut oil to pan, and swirl to coat. Add shallots, salt, turmeric, and red pepper; cook 3 minutes or until shallots are tender, stirring frequently. Add beef; cook 2 minutes or until beef begins to brown. Add cabbage and tomato; toss well to combine. Reduce heat to medium-low, and cover. Cook 10 minutes or until cabbage wilts. Stir in peanuts; cover and cook 10 minutes or until cabbage is tender. Yield: 4 servings (serving size: 1 cup).

CALORIES 238; FAT 15.9g (sat 3.2g, mono 7.4g, poly 4.3g); PROTEIN 10.9g; CARB 15.7g; FIBER 3.4g; CHOL 18mg; IRON 2.1mg; SODIUM 629mg; CALC 59mg

FEED 4 FOR LESS THAN $10

Unexpected takes on familiar ingredients: savory stuffed apples, pizza turned into sandwiches, or olive-flecked cauliflower gratin.

$2.50 per serving, $9.98 total
Quick & Easy

Baked Italian-Style Cauliflower

Hands-on time: 28 min. Total time: 28 min.

1 tablespoon olive oil
1 cup chopped onion
4 garlic cloves, minced
6 ounces lean ground sirloin
$\frac{1}{4}$ teaspoon kosher salt
$\frac{1}{4}$ teaspoon crushed red pepper
$\frac{1}{4}$ teaspoon black pepper
$1\frac{1}{2}$ cups lower-sodium marinara sauce
2 ounces pitted kalamata olives, coarsely chopped
$1\frac{1}{2}$ pounds cauliflower, cut into florets
Cooking spray
1 ounce French bread baguette, torn into 1-inch pieces
$\frac{1}{4}$ cup (1 ounce) grated fresh pecorino Romano cheese

1. Heat a large skillet over medium-high heat. Add oil to pan; swirl. Add onion; sauté 4 minutes. Add garlic; sauté 30 seconds, stirring constantly. Stir in beef. Sprinkle with salt and peppers, and sauté 3 minutes or until browned, stirring to crumble. Stir in sauce and olives.
2. Preheat broiler.
3. Steam cauliflower 4 minutes or until crisp-tender. Place cauliflower in an 11 x 7–inch broiler-safe baking dish coated with cooking spray; top with sauce mixture.

4. Place bread in a mini chopper; pulse until coarse crumbs form. Combine crumbs and cheese; sprinkle over cauliflower mixture. Broil 4 minutes or until browned. Yield: 4 servings (serving size: about 2 cups).

CALORIES 306; FAT 14.9g (sat 4.3g, mono 7.8g, poly 1.2g); PROTEIN 16.3g; CARB 46.8g; FIBER 5.3g; CHOL 33.9mg; IRON 2.3mg; SODIUM 667mg; CALC 145mg

> **WINE MATCH**
> When in Rome, drink like the Romans: A light, easy-drinking Italian red with good acidity pairs well with the tomato-based sauce and beef in this Italian-style recipe. Try Castello Banfi's Col di Sasso 2008 ($8), a soft and fruity blend of cabernet sauvignon and sangiovese, which has a hint of earthiness that enhances the olives and cauliflower.

$2.27 per serving, $9.08 total
Make Ahead • Kid Friendly

Turkey Sausage, Mushroom, and Potato Gratin

Hands-on time: 27 min. Total time: 1 hr. 12 min.

Home fries meet casserole in this ultimate comfort food dish that's great for brunch or dinner. It's most economical to buy a block of cheese and shred it yourself.

2 (4-ounce) hot turkey Italian sausage links, casings removed
1 tablespoon butter
3 cups chopped onion
4 ounces sliced cremini mushrooms
$1\frac{1}{2}$ pounds red potatoes, coarsely chopped
$\frac{1}{2}$ teaspoon kosher salt
$\frac{1}{2}$ cup fat-free, lower-sodium chicken broth
Cooking spray
$\frac{3}{4}$ cup (3 ounces) shredded Swiss cheese
2 tablespoons chopped fresh thyme

1. Preheat oven to 400°.
2. Heat a large nonstick skillet over medium-high heat. Add sausage to pan, and sauté 5 minutes or until browned, stirring to crumble. Remove sausage from pan; drain. Wipe pan with paper towels. Melt butter in pan. Add onion; sauté 4 minutes, stirring occasionally. Add mushrooms; sauté 6 minutes, stirring occasionally. Add potatoes and salt; sauté 5 minutes or until browned, stirring occasionally.
3. Stir in sausage and broth. Remove from heat. Spoon potato mixture into an 11 x 7–inch glass or ceramic baking dish coated with cooking spray; top with cheese. Cover and bake at 400° for 30 minutes. Uncover and bake an additional 15 minutes or until golden. Sprinkle with thyme. Yield: 4 servings (serving size: about 1 cup).

CALORIES 358; FAT 13g (sat 6.9g, mono 3.9g, poly 1.6g); PROTEIN 19.5g; CARB 40.5g; FIBER 4g; CHOL 63mg; IRON 2.6mg; SODIUM 619mg; CALC 196mg

$1.87 per serving, $7.48 total
Kid Friendly

Savory Baked Apples

Hands-on time: 1 hr. Total time: 1 hr. 18 min.

Though pricier, Honeycrisp apples also hold their shape well when baked.

$\frac{2}{3}$ cup fat-free, lower-sodium chicken broth
$\frac{1}{3}$ cup uncooked brown rice
$\frac{1}{3}$ cup dried cranberries
$\frac{1}{3}$ cup apple cider
4 large Rome apples, cored
$1\frac{1}{2}$ tablespoons butter, melted and divided
1 (4-ounce) link sweet Italian sausage, casings removed
$\frac{3}{4}$ cup finely chopped yellow onion
$\frac{1}{3}$ cup finely chopped carrot
$\frac{1}{4}$ teaspoon ground cinnamon
$\frac{1}{8}$ teaspoon ground red pepper
3 garlic cloves, minced
$\frac{1}{4}$ cup chopped walnuts, toasted
3 tablespoons minced green onions
$\frac{3}{4}$ teaspoon kosher salt
$\frac{1}{2}$ teaspoon dried rubbed sage
$\frac{1}{2}$ cup shredded Swiss cheese

1. Preheat oven to 350°.
2. Bring broth to a boil in a saucepan. Stir in rice. Cover, reduce heat, and simmer 50 minutes. Remove from heat. Let stand 10 minutes.
3. Combine cranberries and cider in a microwave-safe bowl; microwave at HIGH 1 minute. Let stand 10 minutes. Add mixture to rice.

4. Using a small spoon, carefully scoop out centers of apples, leaving a ½-inch-thick shell, and chop apple flesh. Brush inside of apples with 1 tablespoon butter. Place apples on a baking sheet, and bake at 350° for 25 minutes or until just tender.

5. Preheat broiler to high.

6. Heat a large skillet over medium-high heat. Add sausage, and sauté 5 minutes, stirring to crumble. Remove from pan; drain. Wipe skillet, and melt remaining butter in pan. Add chopped apple, yellow onion, and next 3 ingredients; sauté 4 minutes. Add garlic; sauté 1 minute, stirring constantly. Add sausage, onion mixture, walnuts, and next 3 ingredients to rice; toss. Divide rice mixture evenly among apples; top with cheese. Broil 5 minutes or until golden. Yield: 4 servings (serving size: 1 stuffed apple).

CALORIES 363; FAT 16.1g (sat 6.7g, mono 4g, poly 4.2g); PROTEIN 12g; CARB 46.3g; FIBER 4.6g; CHOL 32mg; IRON 1.3mg; SODIUM 656mg; CALC 159mg

---

CL KITCHEN SECRET: GINGER MADE EASY

THE CHALLENGE: Grated fresh ginger lends a powerful, fragrant zing to noodles, stir-fries, holiday cookies, even teas. But grating the fresh, knobby root can result in a messy, fibrous pile.

THE SECRET: Freeze it, and then grate. Freezing keeps the root fresh. Then, when attacked with a sharp Microplane-style grater, the fibers are easily cut. The result is a pile of almost powdery ginger that quickly dissolves in curries, cranberry sauces—anything in which you want a bit of ginger heat. Don't add it directly to a hot pan, as it tends to stick and burn; in a curry, for example, add your onions and garlic first, and then add the ginger snow. Store the ginger in a freezer-safe zip-top bag. If you don't want to peel, just wash it; the peel virtually disappears when grated.

$2.39 per serving, $9.55 total
Kid Friendly

Ham and Pineapple Pizza Subs

Hands-on time: 20 min. Total time: 1 hr. 20 min.

Toss spinach and clementine segments with olive oil and juice from the fruit for a side.

1 (13.2-ounce) package refrigerated crusty French bread dough
½ cup lower-sodium marinara sauce
2 ounces Canadian bacon, sliced and coarsely chopped
½ cup (2 ounces) shredded part-skim mozzarella cheese
1 cup peeled cubed fresh pineapple
¼ cup sliced green onions (optional)

1. Preheat oven to 350°.
2. Roll dough out to a 24-inch rope; cut dough into 2 (12-inch) ropes. Place dough on a parchment-lined baking sheet. Bake at 350° for 25 minutes or until golden; cool completely on a wire rack. Cut bread into 4 (6-inch-long) pieces; split each piece crosswise.
3. Preheat broiler to high.
4. Open each bread portion flat. Spread 2 tablespoons sauce over each bread portion; divide Canadian bacon evenly among servings. Sprinkle bacon with cheese; top with pineapple. Broil 3 minutes or until golden. Garnish with green onions, if desired. Fold top half of bread over cheese mixture. Yield: 4 servings (serving size: 1 sandwich).

CALORIES 305; FAT 5.9g (sat 2.7g, mono 0.6g, poly 0.1g); PROTEIN 13.3g; CARB 58.5g; FIBER 1.9g; CHOL 17mg; IRON 2.8mg; SODIUM 803mg; CALC 116mg

---

SUPERFAST

Brothy clams, quick stir-fries, kid-friendly sliders, and other fast weeknight meals to ease you through the holiday rush.

Quick & Easy

Steamed Clams with White Wine and Tomatoes

Cook clams within 24 hours of purchasing in order to ensure freshness. Throw out any clams that don't close their shells when tapped.

4 (½-inch-thick) slices diagonally cut French bread baguette
1½ cups dry white wine
½ cup fat-free, lower-sodium chicken broth
¼ teaspoon freshly ground black pepper
1 (14.5-ounce) can diced tomatoes, undrained
1 teaspoon olive oil
½ cup prechopped onion
1 teaspoon chopped fresh oregano
1 teaspoon chopped fresh rosemary
1 teaspoon chopped fresh thyme
48 littleneck clams in shells, scrubbed (about 3 pounds)
1 tablespoon chopped fresh parsley

1. Preheat broiler.
2. Arrange baguette slices on a baking sheet. Broil 5 inches from heat 2 minutes or until toasted.
3. Combine white wine and next 3 ingredients in a microwave-safe bowl. Microwave at HIGH 1 minute. Heat a Dutch oven over medium-high heat. Add oil to pan; swirl to coat. Add onion and next 3 ingredients; sauté 2 minutes. Add wine mixture to pan; bring to a boil. Stir in clams; cover and cook 5 minutes or until clams open. Discard any unopened shells. Top with parsley, and serve with toasted baguette. Yield: 4 servings (serving size: about ⅓ cup broth, about 12 clams, and 1 toast slice).

Sustainable Choice | *Because they help filter the water in which they live, clams and other bivalves are a sustainable choice.*

CALORIES 237; FAT 2.8g (sat 0.4g, mono 1g, poly 0.6g); PROTEIN 17.8g; CARB 27.2g; FIBER 3.1g; CHOL 34mg; IRON 17.2mg; SODIUM 457mg; CALC 98mg

Grilled Chicken Caesar Salad

This salad dressing mimics the flavor of a typical Caesar but in a vinaigrette form.

2 ounces French bread, cut into ½-inch
    cubes (about 2 cups)
Cooking spray
2 (6-ounce) skinless, boneless chicken breast
    halves, halved lengthwise
½ teaspoon black pepper, divided
2 tablespoons white wine vinegar
2 tablespoons olive oil
1 teaspoon bottled minced garlic
1 teaspoon Dijon mustard
½ teaspoon anchovy paste
6 cups chopped romaine lettuce
2 cups chopped radicchio lettuce
¼ cup (1 ounce) grated fresh Parmesan

1. Preheat oven to 400°.
2. Spread bread cubes in a single layer on a baking sheet. Bake at 400° for 9 minutes or until lightly toasted.
3. Heat a grill pan over high heat. Coat pan with cooking spray. Sprinkle chicken with ¼ teaspoon pepper. Add chicken to pan, and cook 3½ minutes on each side or until done. Remove from pan; let stand 5 minutes. Cut chicken into slices.
4. Combine remaining ¼ teaspoon pepper, vinegar, and next 4 ingredients in a large bowl, stirring with a whisk. Add romaine and radicchio to bowl; toss well to coat. Divide lettuce and chicken evenly among each of 4 plates. Top each serving with ½ cup croutons and 1 tablespoon cheese. Yield: 4 servings.

CALORIES 272; **FAT** 10.4g (sat 2.3g, mono 5.7g, poly 1.3g);
PROTEIN 31.1g; **CARB** 12.6g; **FIBER** 2.1g; **CHOL** 72mg;
IRON 2.2mg; **SODIUM** 322mg; **CALC** 104mg

Cantonese-Style Shrimp and Napa Cabbage

Serve this dish with a side of brown rice or soba noodles.

⅓ cup fat-free, lower-sodium chicken broth
2 tablespoons medium dry sherry
1 teaspoon cornstarch
½ teaspoon salt
½ teaspoon sugar
½ teaspoon black pepper
2 teaspoons dark sesame oil
2 teaspoons peanut oil
1 pound peeled and deveined large shrimp
1 tablespoon bottled ground fresh ginger
1 teaspoon bottled minced garlic
4 cups shredded Napa cabbage
⅓ cup diagonally cut green onions

1. Combine first 6 ingredients in a small bowl; stir with a whisk.
2. Heat a wok or skillet over high heat. Add oils to pan; swirl to coat. Add shrimp; stir-fry 1 minute. Add ginger and garlic; stir-fry 30 seconds. Add broth mixture to pan; bring to a boil. Cook 2 minutes or until mixture thickens. Stir in cabbage; cook 1 minute. Top with onions. Yield: 4 servings (serving size: about ¾ cup).

CALORIES 186; **FAT** 6.7g (sat 1.1g, mono 2.4g, poly 2.5g);
PROTEIN 24.5g; **CARB** 5.4g; **FIBER** 1.6g; **CHOL** 172mg;
IRON 3.1mg; **SODIUM** 509mg; **CALC** 92mg

Sesame Beef Stir-Fry

1 tablespoon bottled minced ginger
1 tablespoon bottled minced garlic
2 tablespoons lower-sodium soy sauce
1½ teaspoons dark brown sugar
½ teaspoon crushed red pepper
1 tablespoon dark sesame oil
1 pound presliced stir-fry meat (such as flank
    or boneless sirloin steak)
8 green onions, cut into 1-inch pieces (white
    and light green parts only)
4 cups bagged baby spinach leaves
1 tablespoon sesame seeds

1. Combine first 5 ingredients in a small bowl.
2. Heat a wok or skillet over high heat. Add oil to pan; swirl to coat. Add half of beef to pan, and cook 3 minutes or until browned. Remove beef from pan. Repeat procedure with remaining beef. Add onions; cook 1 minute. Add soy sauce mixture; cook 1 minute. Return beef to pan; cook 1 minute. Stir in spinach, and cook 30 seconds. Top with sesame seeds. Yield: 4 servings (serving size: ¾ cup).

CALORIES 230; **FAT** 11g (sat 3g, mono 4.2g, poly 2.3g);
PROTEIN 26.5g; **CARB** 6.1g; **FIBER** 1.4g; **CHOL** 37mg;
IRON 3.3mg; **SODIUM** 356mg; **CALC** 94mg

Pan-Seared Chicken with Tomato-Olive Relish

(pictured on page 237)

Select olives from the supermarket olive bar to make the relish without leftovers.

2 teaspoons extra-virgin olive oil, divided
4 (6-ounce) skinless, boneless chicken breast
    halves
¼ teaspoon salt
¼ teaspoon black pepper
1 tablespoon finely chopped fresh basil
1 tablespoon sherry vinegar or balsamic
    vinegar
1 cup cherry tomatoes, quartered
⅓ cup chopped pitted olives

1. Heat a grill pan over medium-high heat. Add 1 teaspoon oil; swirl to coat. Sprinkle chicken with salt and pepper. Add chicken to pan; cook 6 minutes on each side or until done.
2. While chicken cooks, combine remaining 1 teaspoon olive oil, basil, and vinegar in a medium bowl, stirring with a whisk. Add cherry tomatoes and olives; toss to coat. Serve relish with chicken. Yield: 4 servings (serving size: 1 breast half and ¼ cup relish).

CALORIES 235; **FAT** 6g (sat 0.9g, mono 2.2g, poly 0.8g);
PROTEIN 39.6g; **CARB** 1.6g; **FIBER** 0.5g; **CHOL** 99mg;
IRON 1.4mg; **SODIUM** 511mg; **CALC** 24mg

Spanish-Style Cod in Tomato Broth

When stirring the shallot and broth mixtures, be careful not to break up the fish.

1 (3.5-ounce) bag boil-in-bag brown rice
1 tablespoon olive oil
½ teaspoon salt
½ teaspoon smoked paprika
½ teaspoon black pepper
1½ pounds wild Atlantic cod fillets, cut into 8 pieces
¼ cup sliced shallots
⅛ teaspoon crushed red pepper
3 large garlic cloves, thinly sliced
1½ cups chopped plum tomato
½ cup fat-free, lower-sodium chicken broth
⅓ cup dry white wine
1 thyme sprig
3 tablespoons chopped fresh flat-leaf parsley, divided
1 tablespoon fresh lemon juice
¼ cup sliced almonds

1. Cook rice according to package directions, omitting salt and fat. Drain.
2. While rice cooks, heat a skillet over high heat. Add oil to pan; swirl to coat. Combine salt, paprika, and black pepper; sprinkle evenly over fish. Add fish to pan, skin side down; cook 3 minutes or until lightly browned. Turn fish over; reduce heat to medium-high. Add shallots, red pepper, and garlic; cook 4 minutes or until shallots are translucent, stirring occasionally. Add tomatoes, broth, wine, and thyme; bring to a simmer, and cook 6 minutes. Add 1 tablespoon parsley and juice; stir gently to combine. Discard thyme sprig.
3. Combine cooked rice, remaining 2 tablespoons parsley, and almonds. Place about ⅓ cup rice mixture in each of 4 shallow bowls; top each serving with 2 pieces of fish and ½ cup tomato mixture. Yield: 4 servings.

Sustainable Choice | *Look for wild Atlantic cod from Iceland, Maine, or the Arctic to ensure a sustainable choice.*

CALORIES 348; **FAT** 9.3g (sat 1.2g, mono 4.7g, poly 1.9g); **PROTEIN** 39.7g; **CARB** 26.5g; **FIBER** 3g; **CHOL** 63mg; **IRON** 1.2mg; **SODIUM** 469mg; **CALC** 91mg

---

Mushroom, Corn, and Poblano Tacos

Keep your tortillas soft by wrapping them in foil and keeping them in a warm oven.

2 tablespoons olive oil, divided
1 (8-ounce) package presliced mushrooms
1 cup prechopped onion
1 teaspoon dried oregano
1 teaspoon bottled minced garlic
¾ teaspoon chili powder
¾ teaspoon ground cumin
1 poblano chile, chopped (about ½ cup)
1½ cups frozen whole-kernel corn
1 (14.5-ounce) can no-salt-added black beans, rinsed and drained
¼ cup salsa verde
1 tablespoon fresh lime juice
1 teaspoon hot sauce
½ teaspoon salt
8 (6-inch) corn tortillas
¾ cup (3 ounces) crumbled queso fresco
¼ cup chopped fresh cilantro
¼ cup light sour cream
8 lime wedges

1. Heat a large nonstick skillet over medium-high heat. Add 1 tablespoon oil to pan; swirl to coat. Add mushrooms to pan; cook 4 minutes, stirring occasionally. Add remaining 1 tablespoon oil to mushrooms. Stir in onion and next 5 ingredients; cook 4 minutes, stirring occasionally. Add corn and beans to pan; cook 4 minutes, stirring occasionally. Remove pan from heat; stir in salsa and next 3 ingredients.
2. Heat tortillas according to package directions. Divide vegetable mixture evenly among tortillas. Top each tortilla with 1½ tablespoons cheese, 1½ teaspoons cilantro, and 1½ teaspoons sour cream. Serve with lime wedges. Yield: 4 servings (serving size: 2 tacos and 2 lime wedges).

CALORIES 390; **FAT** 14.4g (sat 4.5g, mono 6.7g, poly 1.7g); **PROTEIN** 15.6g; **CARB** 56.6g; **FIBER** 9.8g; **CHOL** 20mg; **IRON** 2mg; **SODIUM** 553mg; **CALC** 225mg

---

Honey-Glazed Almonds

The smoky-spicy snack will store well in an airtight container for several days.

1½ cups raw, unblanched almonds
1 tablespoon sugar
1½ tablespoons honey
½ teaspoon ground chipotle chile powder
¼ teaspoon ground cumin
¼ teaspoon salt

1. Line a large baking sheet with parchment paper.
2. Place almonds in a medium nonstick skillet; cook over medium heat 6 minutes or until lightly toasted, shaking pan frequently. Combine remaining ingredients in a 2-cup glass measure. Microwave at HIGH 30 seconds. Add honey mixture to pan, and cook 2 minutes, stirring constantly. Arrange almond mixture on prepared baking sheet in a single layer; let stand 10 minutes. Break apart any clusters. Yield: 10 servings (serving size: about 16 almonds).

CALORIES 138; **FAT** 10.6g (sat 0.8g, mono 6.6g, poly 2.6g); **PROTEIN** 4.6g; **CARB** 8.5g; **FIBER** 2.6g; **CHOL** 0mg; **IRON** 0.8mg; **SODIUM** 63mg; **CALC** 57mg

SPICED NUTS ARE USUALLY BAKED; THIS STOVETOP VERSION SPEEDS UP THE PROCESS.

Sloppy Joe Sliders

1 large carrot
10 ounces lean ground beef
¾ cup prechopped onion
1 teaspoon garlic powder
1 teaspoon chili powder
¼ teaspoon freshly ground black pepper
¼ cup ketchup
1 tablespoon Dijon mustard
1 tablespoon Worcestershire sauce
1 tablespoon tomato paste
1 teaspoon red wine vinegar
1 (8-ounce) can no-salt-added tomato sauce
8 slider hamburger buns

1. Preheat broiler.
2. Heat a large nonstick skillet over medium-high heat. While pan is heating, grate carrot. Add carrot, beef, and onion to pan; cook 6 minutes or until beef is browned and vegetables are tender. Add garlic powder, chili powder, and pepper; cook 1 minute.
3. Combine ¼ cup ketchup and next 5 ingredients in a small bowl. Add ketchup mixture to pan, stirring to evenly coat beef mixture. Simmer 5 minutes or until thickened.
4. While sauce thickens, arrange buns, cut sides up, in a single layer on a baking sheet. Broil 2 minutes or until lightly toasted. Place about ¼ cup beef mixture on bottom half of each of 8 buns; top each slider with top half of bun. Yield: 4 servings (serving size: 2 sliders).

CALORIES 373; **FAT** 10g (sat 3.6g, mono 3.5g, poly 2.3g); **PROTEIN** 23.1g; **CARB** 52.2g; **FIBER** 4.2g; **CHOL** 38mg; **IRON** 4mg; **SODIUM** 736mg; **CALC** 111mg

Bananas Foster Parfaits

2 large ripe bananas
6 tablespoons dark brown sugar
2 tablespoons unsweetened apple juice
1 tablespoon unsalted butter
¼ teaspoon salt
2 cups plain 2% reduced-fat Greek yogurt
¼ cup chopped pecans, toasted

1. Peel bananas, and cut each banana in half lengthwise. Cut each half into 3 pieces.
2. Combine sugar and next 3 ingredients in a nonstick skillet. Cook over medium-low heat 3 minutes or until sugar mixture begins to bubble. Add bananas to pan; cook 2 minutes or until bananas begin to soften.
3. Spoon ½ cup yogurt into bottom of each of 4 parfait glasses. Divide banana mixture evenly among glasses. Top each serving with 1 tablespoon pecans. Yield: 4 servings (serving size: 1 parfait).

CALORIES 290; **FAT** 10.3g (sat 3.8g, mono 3.6g, poly 1.6g); **PROTEIN** 10.9g; **CARB** 42.2g; **FIBER** 2.4g; **CHOL** 15mg; **IRON** 0.5mg; **SODIUM** 192mg; **CALC** 102mg

WHEN MAKING THIS RECIPE FOR ADULTS, SUBSTITUTE AN EQUAL AMOUNT OF GOLD RUM FOR THE APPLE JUICE.

RECIPE MAKEOVER
GETTING GOOD WITH GUMBO

A fantastic American classic that can be salty and rather rife with calories. We cut both, but kept the soul.

Great gumbo requires two essentials: a dark, hearty roux for a rich flavor base, and a bayou full of seasonings to get the mouth tingling. But when sausage, duck, chicken, and assorted saltwater critters bathe in store-bought stock, followed by lashings of hot sauce, one delicious bowl can contain more than an entire day's worth of salt.

This is certainly not a soup to disrespect, though. To build all that great flavor with lower sodium, we began by making a quick homemade shrimp stock reduction, drawing lots of shrimp flavor from the shells. We slashed more sodium by ditching the sausage and instead using meaty chicken thighs for richness. The briny shrimp needed just a light dusting of smoked paprika to take the flavor to a whole new level—no extra salt required. Canola oil replaced saturated fat–heavy butter in the nicely darkened roux.

There is great brown rice from Louisiana (we gave a Tasties award to Cajun Grain brand in 2010), and a bowl of this lighter, but not light-weight, gumbo over chewy whole grains is something to celebrate.

HOMEMADE SHRIMP STOCK
Bursting with flavor and easy on salt, with 350mg less sodium per cup than the store-bought variety.

CANOLA OIL
Replaces butter or lard as the fat for our roux. Save 9g of saturated fat per serving by starting with this heart-healthy oil.

BROWN RICE
Complements the nutty flavor of the toasty roux with fewer calories and more whole-grain goodness than white rice.

Smoky Shrimp and Chicken Gumbo

Hands-on time: 58 min. Total time: 3 hr. 13 min.

Freeze leftover stock up to three months.

Stock:
1 pound unpeeled medium shrimp
8 cups water
1 teaspoon black peppercorns
4 garlic cloves, crushed
3 large celery stalks, chopped
3 bay leaves
3 medium carrots, coarsely chopped
1 large onion, coarsely chopped
Gumbo:
6 tablespoons canola oil, divided
2.25 ounces all-purpose flour (about ½ cup)
6 skinless, boneless chicken thighs, cut into
   bite-sized pieces
2 cups finely chopped white onion
1 tablespoon Creole seasoning
3 garlic cloves, minced
2 medium celery stalks, chopped
2 medium tomatoes, finely chopped
1 large green bell pepper, seeded and finely
   chopped
3 cups fat-free, lower-sodium chicken broth
2 bay leaves
1 cup frozen cut okra
2 teaspoons Worcestershire sauce
2 teaspoons hot pepper sauce
½ teaspoon black pepper
½ teaspoon smoked paprika
2 cups hot cooked brown rice

1. To prepare stock, peel and devein shrimp, reserving shells. Cut each shrimp in half lengthwise; cover shrimp, and refrigerate.
2. Combine reserved shrimp shells, 8 cups water, and next 6 ingredients in a large Dutch oven, and bring to a boil. Reduce heat, and simmer 1 hour. Strain mixture through a sieve into a bowl; discard solids. Set aside 3 cups stock; keep warm. Reserve remaining shrimp stock for another use.
3. To prepare gumbo, heat a large cast-iron skillet over low heat; add ¼ cup canola oil. Cook 2 minutes, swirling to coat pan. Weigh or lightly spoon flour into a dry measuring cup. Gradually add flour to oil, stirring constantly with a whisk until smooth. Increase heat to medium; cook 8 minutes or until flour mixture is caramel-colored, stirring frequently. Cook 2 minutes or until mixture is chestnut-colored, stirring constantly. Remove from heat; slowly add warm shrimp stock, stirring until smooth. Pour stock mixture into a large bowl.
4. Heat 1 tablespoon oil in a large Dutch oven over medium heat. Add chicken; cook 7 minutes, turning to brown on all sides. Add onion and next 5 ingredients; sauté 3 minutes. Return stock mixture to pan; add broth and bay leaves. Bring to a boil; reduce heat, and simmer 45 minutes.
5. Add okra and next 3 ingredients. Simmer 30 minutes.
6. Combine shrimp and paprika; toss to coat shrimp. Heat a large nonstick skillet over medium-high heat. Add remaining 1 tablespoon oil to pan; swirl to coat. Add shrimp; sauté 2 minutes or until shrimp are done. Stir shrimp into gumbo. Discard bay leaves. Serve over rice. Yield: 8 servings (serving size: 1 cup gumbo and ¼ cup rice).

CALORIES 334; FAT 14.3g (sat 1.6g, mono 7.6g, poly 4.1g);
PROTEIN 25.7g; CARB 24.5g; FIBER 3.1g; CHOL 130mg;
IRON 3.1mg; SODIUM 539mg; CALC 76mg

OLD WAY	OUR WAY
890 calories per serving	334 calories per serving
14.8 grams saturated fat	1.6 grams saturated fat
2,501 milligrams sodium	539 milligrams sodium

RULES OF A RIGHTEOUS ROUX

Both a flavor agent and thickener, a perfect roux imparts a nutty taste and a silken texture to gumbo. Be patient, and stir frequently.

1. Slowly whisk the flour into the hot oil to form a thick paste. The roux will thin out and grow smooth as it cooks.

2. Frequent stirring keeps the flour from clumping and burning. The color will first progress from white to blond.

3. Continue to stir as the color shifts from blond to brown. A deeper color yields a more flavorful, full-bodied roux.

4. Keep the shrimp stock warm, adding it slowly to the roux. This will keep the fat from coagulating and separating.

DINNER TONIGHT

Here is a batch of fast weeknight menus from the *Cooking Light* Test Kitchens.

READY IN 40 MINUTES

The SHOPPING LIST

Baked Mac and Cheese
fresh flat-leaf parsley
12 ounces uncooked penne pasta
panko (Japanese breadcrumbs)
1 (12-ounce) carton 2% low-fat cottage
   cheese
2 ounces Parmesan cheese
2 ounces sharp cheddar cheese

Spinach Salad
8 cups baby spinach
2 cups cherry tomatoes
1 small red onion
white wine vinegar
olive oil
fresh oregano

The GAME PLAN

While oven preheats:
- Cook pasta.
- Assemble and top mac and cheese.

While mac and cheese bakes:
- Prepare salad.

---

*Quick & Easy • Kid Friendly
Vegetarian*

Baked Mac and Cheese
With Spinach Salad

Great Technique: Blending the cottage cheese creates a smooth, silky sauce.
Make-Ahead Tip: Assemble, untopped, up to a day ahead.
Shopping Tip: Panko is available in supermarkets and makes for a lighter, crispier topping.

4½ cups (12 ounces) uncooked penne (tube-
   shaped pasta)
1 (12-ounce) carton 2% low-fat cottage
   cheese
½ cup (2 ounces) finely shredded sharp
   cheddar cheese
½ cup (2 ounces) grated fresh Parmesan
   cheese, divided
½ teaspoon salt
⅛ teaspoon freshly ground black pepper
Cooking spray
3 tablespoons panko (Japanese
   breadcrumbs)
1 tablespoon minced fresh flat-leaf parsley

1. Preheat oven to 375°.
2. Cook pasta according to package directions, omitting salt and fat. Drain; place in a large bowl.
3. Place cottage cheese in a food processor; process until smooth. Combine cottage cheese, cheddar cheese, ¼ cup Parmesan cheese, salt, and pepper. Add cheese mixture to pasta, and stir well. Spoon mixture into an 11 x 7–inch glass or ceramic baking dish coated with cooking spray.
4. Combine remaining ¼ cup Parmesan, panko, and parsley in a small bowl. Sprinkle evenly over pasta mixture. Bake at 375° for 10 minutes.
5. Preheat broiler (do not remove dish from oven).
6. Broil pasta 1 minute or until top browns. Yield: 6 servings (serving size: about 1⅓ cups).

CALORIES 329; **FAT** 7.4g (sat 4.4g, mono 0.8g, poly 0.1g); **PROTEIN** 19.1g; **CARB** 47g; **FIBER** 1.9g; **CHOL** 21mg; **IRON** 2mg; **SODIUM** 455mg; **CALC** 275mg

---

For the Spinach Salad:
Combine 8 cups baby spinach, 2 cups halved cherry tomatoes, and ¾ cup vertically sliced red onion in a large bowl. Combine ¼ cup white wine vinegar, 2 tablespoons olive oil, 1 tablespoon minced fresh oregano, ⅛ teaspoon salt, and ⅛ teaspoon freshly ground black pepper. Pour over spinach mixture; toss gently to combine. Yield: 6 servings (serving size: about 1 cup).

CALORIES 69; **FAT** 4.6g (sat 0.6g); **SODIUM** 104mg

READY IN 40 MINUTES

The SHOPPING LIST

Chicken and Sausage Jambalaya
onion
celery
green bell pepper
garlic
fresh thyme
canola oil
6 ounces reduced-fat smoked sausage
fat-free, lower-sodium chicken broth
1 (14.5-ounce) can no-salt-added diced
   tomatoes
long-grain white rice
rotisserie chicken breast
ground red pepper

Garlic Breadsticks
fresh parsley
garlic
1 (11-ounce) package refrigerated thin-crust
   pizza dough
butter

The GAME PLAN

While oven preheats:
- Cook sausage and veggies.
- Roll out and top dough.

While rice mixture simmers:
- Bake breadsticks.

Chicken and Sausage Jambalaya

With Garlic Breadsticks

Simple Sub: Use smoky chicken sausage if you can't find reduced-fat smoked links.
Flavor Hit: Simmering broth with thyme flavors the rice without overpowering it.
Leftover Tip: Make a mini pizza from the extra pizza dough.

2 teaspoons canola oil
6 ounces reduced-fat smoked sausage, halved lengthwise and cut into ¼-inch slices
½ cup chopped onion
½ cup chopped celery
½ cup chopped green bell pepper
2 garlic cloves, minced
1 cup uncooked long-grain white rice
1 cup water
¼ teaspoon ground red pepper
⅛ teaspoon salt
6 fresh thyme sprigs
1 (14.5-ounce) can fat-free, lower-sodium chicken broth
1 (14.5-ounce) can no-salt-added diced tomatoes, undrained
1 cup shredded skinless, boneless rotisserie chicken breast

1. Heat a Dutch oven over medium-high heat. Add oil to pan; swirl to coat. Add sausage; sauté 1 minute or until browned. Add onion, celery, bell pepper, and garlic; sauté 6 minutes or until tender. Add rice and next 5 ingredients; bring to a boil. Cover, reduce heat, and simmer 20 minutes or until rice is done. Remove thyme sprigs; discard. Stir in tomatoes and chicken. Cook 3 minutes or until thoroughly heated. Yield: 4 servings (serving size: about 1¼ cups).

CALORIES 341; **FAT** 5.8g (sat 1.3g, mono 2g, poly 0.9g); **PROTEIN** 19.3g; **CARB** 50.6g; **FIBER** 2.8g; **CHOL** 44mg; **IRON** 3.2mg; **SODIUM** 723mg; **CALC** 59mg

For the Garlic Breadsticks:

Preheat oven to 425°. Unroll 1 (11-ounce) package thin-crust pizza dough. Cut in half crosswise; reserve half of dough for another use. Combine 1 tablespoon melted butter and 2 minced garlic cloves; brush evenly over dough. Sprinkle with 2 teaspoons minced fresh parsley. Cut dough crosswise into 8 strips; twist each piece. Place twists on a baking sheet coated with cooking spray. Bake at 425° for 12 minutes or until golden brown. Yield: 4 servings (serving size: 2 breadsticks).

CALORIES 142; **FAT** 6.2g (sat 2.5g); **SODIUM** 247mg

READY IN 40 MINUTES

The SHOPPING LIST

Crispy Pork Medallions
fresh thyme
fresh parsley
Dijon mustard
panko (Japanese breadcrumbs)
1 (1-pound) pork tenderloin
extra-virgin olive oil

Roasted Root Vegetables
8 ounces small red potatoes
2 carrots
2 parsnips
garlic
olive oil

The GAME PLAN

While oven preheats:
■ Slice root vegetables.
While vegetables roast:
■ Coat pork medallions.
■ Sauté pork.
■ Roast pork.

Crispy Pork Medallions

With Roasted Root Vegetables

Flavor Hit: Mustard adds tanginess to the pork and helps the crust adhere to the meat.
Budget Buy: Use less expensive boneless pork chops, halved, in place of pork tenderloin.

2 tablespoons Dijon mustard
1 (1-pound) pork tenderloin, trimmed and cut into 8 medallions
½ cup panko (Japanese breadcrumbs)
1 tablespoon chopped fresh thyme
1 tablespoon minced fresh parsley
⅛ teaspoon salt
⅛ teaspoon freshly ground black pepper
2 tablespoons extra-virgin olive oil

1. Preheat oven to 450°.
2. Rub mustard evenly over pork medallions. Combine panko, thyme, parsley, salt, and pepper in a large bowl. Dredge pork in panko mixture. Heat a large ovenproof skillet over medium-high heat. Add oil to pan; swirl to coat. Add pork; sauté 2 minutes or until golden brown. Turn pork. Place skillet in oven; bake at 450° for 8 minutes or until pork reaches 145°. Let stand 3 minutes. Yield: 4 servings (serving size: 2 medallions).

CALORIES 210; **FAT** 9.4g (sat 1.7g, mono 5.8g, poly 1.1g); **PROTEIN** 24.5g; **CARB** 5.1g; **FIBER** 0.3g; **CHOL** 74mg; **IRON** 1.3mg; **SODIUM** 329mg; **CALC** 10mg

For the Roasted Root Vegetables:

Preheat oven to 450°. Combine 8 ounces quartered small red potatoes, 2 thinly sliced carrots, and 2 thinly sliced parsnips in a medium bowl. Add 1 tablespoon olive oil, ⅛ teaspoon salt, ⅛ teaspoon freshly ground black pepper, and 1 minced garlic clove; toss well to coat. Arrange vegetable mixture on a rack placed in a broiler pan. Bake at 450° for 28 minutes, stirring after 10 minutes. Yield: 4 servings (serving size: ¾ cup).

CALORIES 144; **FAT** 3.7g (sat 0.5g); **SODIUM** 106mg

The
SHOPPING LIST

Broccoli and Rice Casseroles
broccoli florets
onion
green bell pepper
celery
1 rotisserie chicken
1 (3½-ounce) bag boil-in-bag long-grain rice
2 ounces light processed cheese
2 ounces ⅓-less-fat cream cheese
1 ounce Parmesan cheese
2 cups 1% low-fat milk

Buttered Carrots
2 cups thinly sliced carrots
1 cup fat-free, lower-sodium chicken broth
butter
fresh parsley

The
GAME PLAN

While oven preheats:
- Cook rice and broccoli.
- Sauté veggies.
- Assemble casseroles.
While casseroles bake:
- Cook carrots.

Quick & Easy • Kid Friendly
Broccoli and Rice Casseroles
With Buttered Carrots

Time-Saver: Streamline by cooking rice and veggies in the same milk.
Shopping Tip: Look for prechopped onion, celery, and bell pepper in the produce section.
Prep Pointer: An 8-inch casserole dish will fit the whole recipe.

2 cups 1% low-fat milk
1 cup water
1 (3½-ounce) bag boil-in-bag long-grain rice
3 cups small broccoli florets
Cooking spray
⅓ cup chopped onion
⅓ cup chopped celery
⅓ cup chopped green bell pepper
¼ cup (2 ounces) ⅓-less-fat cream cheese
2 ounces light processed cheese, cubed
2 cups shredded skinless, boneless rotisserie chicken breast
¼ teaspoon salt
¼ teaspoon freshly ground black pepper
¼ cup (1 ounce) grated Parmesan cheese

1. Preheat oven to 375°.
2. Combine milk and water in a medium saucepan; bring to a boil. Add rice; cook 10 minutes. Remove rice; keep warm. Return milk mixture to a simmer. Add broccoli; cook 5 minutes. Drain; discard milk mixture.
3. Heat a Dutch oven over medium-high heat. Coat pan with cooking spray. Add onion, celery, and bell pepper; sauté 5 minutes. Add cream cheese and processed cheese, stirring until cheese melts. Remove from heat; stir in rice, broccoli, chicken, salt, and black pepper. Spoon 1 cup rice mixture into each of 4 (10-ounce) ramekins coated with cooking spray. Sprinkle each serving with 1 tablespoon Parmesan. Bake at 375° for 10 minutes or until cheese melts. Yield: 4 servings (serving size: 1 casserole).

CALORIES 327; **FAT** 9.5g (sat 5.2g, mono 2.5g, poly 0.5g); **PROTEIN** 29g; **CARB** 31.3g; **FIBER** 2.2g; **CHOL** 76mg; **IRON** 1.7mg; **SODIUM** 633mg; **CALC** 284mg

For the Buttered Carrots:
Bring 1 cup fat-free, lower-sodium chicken broth to a boil in a saucepan. Add 2 cups thinly sliced carrots. Reduce heat; simmer 6 minutes or until tender. Drain; return to pan. Stir in 1 tablespoon butter, 2 teaspoons chopped parsley, ⅛ teaspoon salt, and ⅛ teaspoon black pepper; stir until butter melts. Yield: 4 servings (serving size: ½ cup).

CALORIES 51; **FAT** 3g (sat 1.9g); **SODIUM** 148mg

OOPS! THE TURKEY HACK JOB

If you lack a surgeon's touch, carve the bird in the kitchen.
By Tim Cebula

On turkey day, you've earned the right to parade that magnificent roasted bird around the dining room. But carving is best done where there's elbow room and a stable cutting surface. You'll need a well-honed knife; have it professionally sharpened before the big day.

Now, as the pros say, "break" the bird down in the right order (this is where many cooks go wrong—trying to slice meat directly off a big, hot bird). Leg quarters come off first, and then breast meat, with the tucked-under wings serving to stabilize as you cut (for step-by-step illustrations, see page 303). Set the big pieces onto a cutting board where you can deal with them properly.

Take the breast meat off the bone in one piece, and then slice crosswise, which ensures uniformity and allows for slightly thicker slices that are juicier and less fibrous than thin portions. Cut the thigh meat into large chunks. Reserve room on the platter for legs if you have a Henry VIII in the family.

Oh, and remember—in the days leading up to Thanksgiving, you can always practice your technique on a nice roasted chicken: same configuration of bird parts, no game-day pressure.

A VERY MERRY OPEN-HOUSE MENU

Whether you go casual or elegant, we have all the tips and advice you'll need to host a warm, friendly, successful party.

In this season of giving, which many of us love, we often find that one of the hardest things to give is our time. Holiday commitments may be fun, but they come too fast and furious—they seem to crowd every moment—and leave little time for ourselves, let alone others.

One solution is not to back away from the chaos, but to throw a party!

Yes, a party: a holiday open house, a warm gesture of welcome to the wonderful people whose company we've missed far too often during a busy, busy year. Getting them to come to you has certain obvious advantages, one being that it's rather efficient. Efficient in that the advance work is not only easy, but it is also meaningful: Preparing food and drink with love is a beautiful gesture, a material way of sharing time with those who mean the most to us. And, with this open-house menu, when guests arrive, you will be free to spend real time with them, because most all the prep can be done ahead.

We designed this open-house menu for versatility: a dress-up evening or a casual day, a low-key Sunday afternoon drop-around or an elegant Saturday night, even a New Year's eve. The dishes are small, full of flavor, suitable for adults or kids, and can be dressed up or dressed down. There's a lively mix of flavors and textures, from crunchy phyllo-wrapped asparagus to a creamy caramelized onion topping for crostini. Most all are pick-up bites, both savory and sweet (including chocolate and peanut butter–dipped pretzels that are completely addictive), with a heavier "anchor" pairing of pork tenderloin in herbed biscuits alongside a colorful roasted root vegetable salad.

Oh, and along the way we talked with expert party planner Jeffrey Selden, formerly with the New York Palace Hotel and now with Marcia Selden Catering in Stamford, Connecticut; he shared some of his best tips on successful holiday open-house party planning.

INVITE EARLY

Send invitations at least four to five weeks in advance, especially if you've chosen a prime Friday or Saturday night slot, which fill up quickly this time of year. If you're going more upscale with your party, set the tone with paper invitations (you'll need to order them a few weeks before you want to send them). For a more casual gathering, e-mailed invitations from a site like evite.com are fine. Either way, be sure to ask guests to RSVP so you can plan enough food, drinks, glassware, and so on. Specify whether children are invited—and if they're not, come up with a clear but clever way to get that across, like playfully saying, "Hire a babysitter, and put on your party clothes…" Make it clear that the party will span several hours, and guests are welcome to stay the whole time or just pop by for a short visit.

OPEN-HOUSE MENU

serves 10

Whiskey Sour Punch

Warm Spiced Cran-Pom Toddies

Apple-Blue Cheese Chutney

Caramelized Onion Spread

Phyllo-Wrapped Asparagus with Prosciutto

Pork Tenderloin with Herbed Biscuits

Roasted Root Vegetable Salad

Coconut-Cardamom Macaroons

Pistachio and Pine Nut Brittle

Peanut Butter and Chocolate-Dipped Pretzels

FESTIVE-UP THE HOUSE

Your home may already be decked for the holidays, and if so, you have a great head start. For casual holiday cheer, add touches of fragrant greenery (pine or spruce) or even pretty pine cones to your mantel, coffee table, or buffet. You can also use fresh fruit as table garnishings—whole kumquats, Seckel pears, cranberries, or pomegranates. Or go more elegant with a few sparkles—silver ornaments as table decorations, or twinkly lights creating soft light in the dining room.

continued

MAKE MUSIC

Don't forget about music! It absolutely sets the tone for the party. Classic holiday tunes (Bing Crosby, Nat King Cole, and Dean Martin) are, of course, perfect, but mix in anything in a classic vein that sustains the mood. Have a playlist preset to last several hours to cover the entire party so you won't have to continually refresh. If you're set up to play music from your computer, try a free online service like Pandora that will allow you to play a variety of songs within a particular genre.

CHOOSE SUITABLE DISHES

For a Sunday afternoon open house, nice paper goods from a party-supply store are fine. Even so, nothing beats having real plates and real glasses—and if you rent them, they may be comparable in price to the paper goods. Many suppliers offer casual options like glass plates as well as china if you plan to go more elegant; you can also rent wine and cocktail glasses. Check your local party-supply stores for prices and return policies; some places only require you to rinse dishes before returning them (which certainly simplifies cleanup). If you host parties on a regular basis, it pays to keep a set (or two or three) of inexpensive wineglasses; you can find boxes of 12 for under $20.

TAKE TIME TO STUDY THE FOOD PLAN

If everyone sent an RSVP (in which case you have the most responsible and rare set of friends ever—RSVPing seems to be a dying art), you have a realistic idea of how many people to plan for. If that's not the case (and be prepared, it likely won't be), assume you'll have up to 25% more people than responded.

We designed a pick-and-choose menu for which all recipes make 10 generous servings—it's doubtful that folks will eat an entire serving of every single dish, but there should be plenty of food if you assume they will. Don't attempt to scale the recipes up in fractional increments; that will drive you crazy and invite mistakes. For example, if you think you'll have 17 people, including yourself, at the party, just double the recipes to serve 20. It's nice to send a few leftovers home with those guests who linger and help with cleanup, and it's great to snack on them in the morning.

We tend to double recipes rather than increase in half-steps. When multiplying by 1.5 or 2.5, our advice is to round down to the nearest standard measurement. For example, if you multiply the ⅛ teaspoon cardamom in our Coconut-Cardamom Macaroons (page 355) by 2.5, you come out to 0.31 teaspoons. Rounding up to ½ teaspoon would be a big mistake; the cardamom would totally overwhelm the cookies, so it's better to go down to ¼ teaspoon. You can always add a little bit more, but it's hard to take away. As you scale up recipes, keep in mind that larger amounts may increase cook times.

All our recipes can either be made completely in advance or have make-ahead components and need just a bit of assembly shortly before the party. And because no host wants to be busy cooking all day and up to the last minute, we feature dishes that can be enjoyed at room temperature—nothing has to be piping hot.

KEEP KIDS HAPPY

If you'll have kids at your party, talk frankly to your guests about the issue of food. Our recipes include options that many kids will enjoy—pork stuffed into biscuits, peanut butter and chocolate–covered pretzels, even crunchy phyllo-wrapped asparagus "cigars." If small children are picky eaters, though, you may want to design a special kids' area with a buffet designed just for them. It can be as simple as PB&J sandwiches cut into fun shapes with cookie cutters, fruit kebabs (watch the sharp sticks, though—try popsicle sticks), and veggies with ranch dip or hummus. And make sure to set aside an area where the kids can play freely—believe it or not, they tend to find grown-ups a bit boring. Think about hiring a babysitter or two to run some games or holiday movies for them. Or put together a fun holiday craft—decorating cookies, ornaments, or holiday cards.

BE PREPARED FOR GIFTS

Don't be caught off guard by what guests may bring. Though you may want to stress in the invite that potluck items aren't necessary—it nicely relieves guests of an obligation—someone may show up with a special holiday treat. Even if it's a fluorescent cheese ball in the shape of a Santa head, don't be too territorial about the food, as extra nibbles are nice to have on hand. Have a few vases set aside for the lovely gift of flowers. But—and this includes wine and spirits—you are not obligated to open gifts on the spot, unless your guest requests that you do.

WELCOME WITH REFRESHMENTS

There is nothing more festive than being offered a refreshment at the moment of arrival, like a VIP at an Oscar ball. Set up a station close to the entryway so guests can be welcomed with our Whiskey Sour Punch or Warm Spiced Cran-Pom Toddies (at right). It's a good idea to have a fun pick-up snack like the phyllo-wrapped asparagus right at that point, too. Set up a wine station elsewhere, along with plenty of nonalcoholic options for drivers and kids. If you have enough space, you can have the three sweet treats on a buffet with a coffee bar. The rest of the food can be arranged on the dining table. The idea is to spread the food out so that one area doesn't get too clogged, and people are encouraged to move about and mingle.

ENJOY!

As we said, this menu stresses advanced prep, room-temp service, and minimal last-minute fuss. You are free to actually enjoy the people you've done this work for. Here's one more stress-minimizer: Hire a presentable neighborhood teenager (they come cheap) and put her or him in charge of refreshing the food.

Warm Spiced Cran-Pom Toddies

Hands-on time: 5 min. Total time: 38 min.

For a nonalcoholic version, omit the rum or replace it with apple juice. Steep juice mixture up to a week ahead. Cool to room temperature; refrigerate. Warm over medium-low heat; add rum and lime juice shortly before serving.

2 (3-inch) cinnamon sticks
1 (64-ounce) bottle cranberry-pomegranate
   juice drink
1 (1-inch) piece fresh ginger, peeled and cut
   into thin slices
1³/4 cups gold rum
3 tablespoons fresh lime juice
Sugar cane sticks or cinnamon sticks
   (optional)

1. Combine first 3 ingredients in a large Dutch oven; bring to a simmer. Cover and cook over low heat 30 minutes. Discard cinnamon and ginger. Stir in rum and lime juice; serve warm. Garnish with sugar cane sticks or cinnamon sticks, if desired. Yield: 10 servings (serving size: about 1 cup).

CALORIES 171; FAT 0g (sat 0g, mono 0g, poly 0g);
PROTEIN 0g; CARB 19.6g; FIBER 0g; CHOL 0mg;
IRON 0mg; SODIUM 30mg; CALC 30mg

Whiskey Sour Punch

Hands-on time: 5 min. Total time: 25 min.

Make-ahead tip: Combine all ingredients except club soda up to 2 days ahead; gently stir in club soda shortly before serving.

¹/3 cup sugar
¹/3 cup water
2¹/2 cups refrigerated fresh orange juice
2 cups bourbon
¹/2 cup fresh lemon juice (about 3 large
   lemons)
3 cups chilled club soda
Fresh orange slices (optional)

1. Combine sugar and ⅓ cup water in a 1-cup glass measure; microwave at HIGH 2 minutes; stir until sugar dissolves. Cool to room temperature.
2. Combine sugar mixture, orange juice, bourbon, and lemon juice in a large pitcher; stir well. Stir in club soda just before serving. Garnish with orange slices, if desired. Yield: 10 servings (serving size: about ¾ cup).

CALORIES 160; FAT 0.1g (sat 0g, mono 0.1g, poly 0g);
PROTEIN 0.5g; CARB 14.2g; FIBER 0.2g; CHOL 0mg;
IRON 0.2mg; SODIUM 16mg; CALC 11mg

Apple–Blue Cheese Chutney

Hands-on time: 15 min. Total time: 1 hr. 10 min.

Serve with our Basic Crostini (page 354) or toasted walnut bread. Make-ahead tip: Prepare and refrigerate the chutney up to three days ahead; bring to room temperature before serving. For a prettier presentation, top crostini with chutney shortly before serving, and sprinkle cheese on top instead of stirring it into the chutney.

2 teaspoons canola oil
¹/4 cup finely chopped shallots
2¹/2 cups finely chopped peeled Braeburn
   apple (2 large)
1 cup apple cider
¹/4 cup golden raisins
2 tablespoons brown sugar
1 tablespoon cider vinegar
1¹/2 teaspoons chopped fresh thyme, divided
¹/4 teaspoon kosher salt
¹/4 teaspoon freshly ground black pepper
¹/2 cup (2 ounces) crumbled blue cheese

1. Heat a small saucepan over medium-high heat. Add oil to pan; swirl to coat. Add shallots; sauté 1 minute. Add apple and next 4 ingredients; bring to a boil. Reduce heat and simmer, uncovered, 25 minutes or until most of liquid evaporates and apples are very tender. Remove from heat; stir in ¾ teaspoon thyme, salt, and pepper. Cool to room temperature. Gently stir in cheese.

Sprinkle with remaining ¾ teaspoon thyme. Yield: 10 servings (serving size: about 3½ tablespoons).

CALORIES 83; FAT 2.6g (sat 1.1g, mono 1g, poly 0.3g);
PROTEIN 1.6g; CARB 14.3g; FIBER 0.9g; CHOL 4mg;
IRON 0.2mg; SODIUM 129mg; CALC 38mg

Caramelized Onion Spread

Hands-on time: 15 min. Total time: 1 hr. 15 min.

Serve with Basic Crostini (page 354), or try on melba toast. For a more upscale version, thinly slice the onions, and caramelize as directed. Then combine cream cheese, mayo, pepper, and salt; spread over crostini, and top with onions and chives. Make-ahead tip: Prepare and refrigerate the spread (or its components) up to two days ahead.

1 tablespoon olive oil
3 cups chopped yellow onion
4 garlic cloves, minced
¹/2 cup (4 ounces) block-style ¹/3-less-fat
   cream cheese
¹/2 cup canola mayonnaise
2 tablespoons finely chopped fresh chives
¹/2 teaspoon freshly ground black pepper
¹/4 teaspoon kosher salt

1. Heat a large skillet over medium-high heat. Add oil to pan; swirl to coat. Add onion and garlic to pan; sauté 5 minutes, stirring frequently. Reduce heat to medium-low; cook 35 minutes or until very tender and caramelized, stirring occasionally. Add cream cheese to pan; stir to combine. Remove from heat; stir in mayonnaise and remaining ingredients. Serve at room temperature or chilled. Yield: 10 servings (serving size: about 2½ tablespoons).

CALORIES 98; FAT 7.6g (sat 1.7g, mono 3.7g, poly 1.5g);
PROTEIN 1.7g; CARB 5.4g; FIBER 0.9g; CHOL 8mg;
IRON 0.2mg; SODIUM 160mg; CALC 28mg

Basic Crostini

Make-ahead tip: Bake crostini, and cool completely; store in an airtight container at room temperature for up to two days.

Preheat oven to 400°. Arrange 40 (¼-inch-thick) baguette slices on 2 baking sheets. Coat slices with cooking spray. Bake, 1 sheet at a time, at 400° for 10 minutes or until golden brown and toasted. Cool completely on a wire rack. Yield: 10 servings (serving size: 4 crostini).

CALORIES 90; **FAT** 1.7g (sat 0g); **SODIUM** 184mg

Make Ahead • Vegetarian
Roasted Root Vegetable Salad

Hands-on time: 20 min. Total time: 1 hr. 30 min.

Roast the veggies several hours ahead; toss with vinaigrette about an hour before the party. Serve at room temperature.

3 cups (¾-inch) cubed peeled butternut squash
8 small shallots, peeled and halved
4 parsnips, peeled, halved lengthwise, and cut into 1-inch pieces
4 carrots, peeled, halved lengthwise, and cut into 1-inch pieces
2 medium turnips, cut into thin wedges
5 tablespoons olive oil, divided
⅝ teaspoon kosher salt, divided
½ teaspoon freshly ground black pepper, divided
2 tablespoons white wine vinegar
2 teaspoons Dijon mustard
1½ teaspoons honey
1 garlic clove, minced
2 tablespoons chopped fresh flat-leaf parsley

1. Preheat oven to 425°.
2. Combine first 5 ingredients in a large bowl; add 2 tablespoons oil, ⅜ teaspoon salt, and ¼ teaspoon pepper. Toss well to coat; arrange in a single layer on a large jelly-roll pan. Bake at 425° for 40 minutes or until vegetables are browned and tender, stirring every 10 minutes. Remove from oven; cool to room temperature.
3. Combine remaining ¼ teaspoon salt, remaining ¼ teaspoon pepper, vinegar, mustard, honey, and garlic in a large bowl, stirring with a whisk. Gradually add remaining 3 tablespoons oil, stirring constantly with a whisk. Add vegetables; toss to coat. Sprinkle with parsley. Yield: 10 servings (serving size: ½ cup).

CALORIES 167; **FAT** 7g (sat 1g, mono 5g, poly 0.8g);
PROTEIN 2.9g; **CARB** 26.1g; **FIBER** 4.4g; **CHOL** 0mg;
IRON 1.3mg; **SODIUM** 193mg; **CALC** 60mg

Make Ahead • Kid Friendly
Phyllo-Wrapped Asparagus with Prosciutto

Hands-on time: 25 min. Total time: 45 min.

You can also chop the prosciutto and sprinkle it on the phyllo. Make-ahead tip: Arrange assembled rolls on a baking sheet, coat with cooking spray, and cover; store in the fridge for up to 4 hours. Bake an hour or two before the party.

3 ounces thinly sliced prosciutto, cut into 30 thin strips
30 asparagus spears, trimmed
10 (14 x 9–inch) sheets frozen phyllo dough, thawed
Cooking spray

1. Preheat oven to 450°.
2. Wrap 1 prosciutto strip around each asparagus spear, barber pole-style. Place 1 phyllo sheet on a cutting board or work surface (cover remaining dough to keep from drying); lightly coat phyllo with cooking spray. Cut phyllo crosswise into even thirds to form 3 (4½ x 9–inch) rectangles. Arrange 1 asparagus spear across 1 short end of each rectangle; roll up jelly-roll fashion. Arrange rolled spears on a baking sheet; lightly coat outside of rolls with cooking spray. Repeat procedure with remaining phyllo, asparagus, and cooking spray. Bake at 450° for 10 minutes or until phyllo is golden and crisp. Serve warm or at room temperature. Yield: 10 servings (serving size: 3 pieces).

CALORIES 59; **FAT** 1g (sat 0.3g, mono 0.4g, poly 0.1g);
PROTEIN 4.1g; **CARB** 8.6g; **FIBER** 1.4g; **CHOL** 5mg;
IRON 0.7mg; **SODIUM** 164mg; **CALC** 21mg

Make Ahead • Freezable • Kid Friendly
Pork Tenderloin with Herbed Biscuits

Hands-on time: 43 min. Total time: 1 hr. 7 min.

You can freeze the uncooked biscuit dough for a couple of weeks; cut out dough rounds, and freeze flat on a baking sheet. Once frozen, transfer to a zip-top freezer bag. Arrange frozen dough on a baking sheet and allow to thaw slightly as oven preheats. Bake an extra two or three minutes or until browned. You can also assemble the sandwiches about an hour or two before the party; wrap and keep warm at 150°. And just know that these meat-filled biscuits are delicious at room temperature—they don't have to be piping hot.

2 (12-ounce) pork tenderloins, trimmed
1 tablespoon olive oil
1 teaspoon coarsely ground black pepper
½ teaspoon kosher salt
11.25 ounces all-purpose flour (about 2½ cups)
1 tablespoon baking powder
⅜ teaspoon salt
¼ teaspoon baking soda
6 tablespoons unsalted chilled butter, cut into small pieces
1½ tablespoons finely chopped fresh thyme
1½ tablespoons finely chopped fresh sage
1¼ cups fat-free buttermilk
¼ cup whole-grain Dijon mustard
1 tablespoon maple syrup

1. Preheat oven to 400°.
2. Heat a large ovenproof skillet over medium-high heat. Rub pork evenly with oil; sprinkle evenly with pepper and kosher salt. Add pork to pan; cook 6 minutes, turning to brown on all sides. Place pan in oven. Bake at 400° for 17 minutes or until a thermometer inserted into thickest portion of pork registers 145°. Remove pork from pan; let stand 10 minutes.

3. Increase oven temperature to 450°.
4. Weigh or lightly spoon flour into dry measuring cups; level with a knife. Combine flour and next 3 ingredients in a large bowl, stirring with a whisk. Cut in butter with a pastry blender until mixture resembles coarse meal. Toss in thyme and sage. Add buttermilk; toss with a fork until a soft, sticky dough forms. With floured hands, gently pat dough out onto a lightly floured surface to about a ¼-inch thickness. Cut with a 2-inch biscuit cutter into 20 rounds, gently reshaping scraps as necessary. Arrange dough rounds on a baking sheet lined with parchment paper. Bake at 450° for 17 minutes or until lightly browned. Place on a wire rack.
5. Combine mustard and syrup, stirring well. Cut each pork tenderloin into 20 thin slices. Split each biscuit in half; spread about ¾ teaspoon mustard mixture onto cut side of each biscuit top. Arrange 2 pork slices on bottom half of each biscuit; top with top halves. Yield: 10 servings (serving size: 2 filled biscuits).

CALORIES 260; FAT 9.7g (sat 5g, mono 3.2g, poly 0.7g); PROTEIN 15.2g; CARB 27.2g; FIBER 1g; CHOL 52mg; IRON 2.1mg; SODIUM 473mg; CALC 124mg

Make Ahead • Kid Friendly
Coconut-Cardamom Macaroons

Hands-on time: 8 min. Total time: 33 min.

Bake cookies, and cool completely on a wire rack; store in an airtight container at room temperature for up to 1 week.

2 large egg whites
¼ cup sugar
½ teaspoon vanilla extract
⅛ teaspoon salt
⅛ teaspoon ground cardamom
1½ cups flaked sweetened coconut

1. Preheat oven to 325°.
2. Place egg whites in a medium bowl; lightly beat with a whisk. Add sugar, vanilla, salt, and cardamom; stir well with a whisk until foamy. Add coconut; toss well to combine. Loosely pack coconut mixture into a 1-tablespoon measuring spoon. Turn out onto a baking sheet lined with parchment paper. Spoon remaining coconut mixture by 1 tablespoonfuls onto prepared pan to form 20 mounds. Bake at 325° for 23 minutes or until golden all over. Cool on pan 3 minutes; cool completely on wire rack. Yield: 10 servings (serving size: 2 cookies).

CALORIES 82; FAT 3.6g (sat 3.4g, mono 0.2g, poly 0g); PROTEIN 0.1g; CARB 11.7g; FIBER 1.3g; CHOL 0mg; IRON 0.2mg; SODIUM 77mg; CALC 2mg

Make Ahead • Kid Friendly
Peanut Butter and Chocolate–Dipped Pretzels

Hands-on time: 25 min. Total time: 45 min.

Make-ahead tip: Dip the pretzels and store in the fridge on a parchment-lined tray up to five days ahead. Set out shortly before serving, but not too far ahead, as the chocolate may melt.

4 ounces semisweet chocolate, chopped
¼ cup creamy peanut butter
30 braided honey-wheat pretzel twists

1. Line a jelly-roll pan with parchment paper.
2. Place chocolate in a small microwave-safe bowl. Microwave at HIGH 1 minute or until chocolate melts, stirring every 15 seconds. Stir in peanut butter until smooth. Scrape some of chocolate mixture onto a silicone spatula; working with 1 pretzel at a time, roll 1 end of pretzel mixture to coat. Place pretzel on prepared pan. Repeat procedure with remaining pretzels and chocolate mixture. Place in freezer for 30 minutes or until set. Yield: 10 servings (serving size: 3 pretzels).

CALORIES 135; FAT 6.8g (sat 2.7g, mono 2.2g, poly 1g); PROTEIN 3.2g; CARB 16.7g; FIBER 1.4g; CHOL 0mg; IRON 0.5mg; SODIUM 183mg; CALC 3mg

Make Ahead • Kid Friendly
Pistachio and Pine Nut Brittle

Hands-on time: 20 min. Total time: 2 hr. 20 min.

Make-ahead tip: Cool the brittle completely, break into chunks, and store in an airtight container at room temperature for up to 1 week.

⅔ cup sugar
⅓ cup light-colored corn syrup
¼ cup water
½ cup unsalted dry-roasted pistachios, coarsely chopped
⅓ cup pine nuts, lightly toasted
¼ cup dried cranberries, coarsely chopped
1½ tablespoons unsalted butter, softened
¾ teaspoon baking soda
½ teaspoon vanilla extract
¼ teaspoon salt

1. Line a baking sheet with parchment paper.
2. Combine first 3 ingredients in a medium, heavy saucepan over medium-high heat, stirring just until combined; bring to a boil. Cook, without stirring, until a candy thermometer registers 335° or until syrup is dark golden brown. Remove from heat, and stir in pistachios and remaining ingredients (mixture will bubble). Quickly pour mixture onto prepared pan; spread to about ½-inch thickness. Cool completely (about 2 hours). Break brittle into bite-sized pieces. Yield: 10 servings (serving size: about 1 ounce).

CALORIES 176; FAT 7.7g (sat 1.7g, mono 2.8g, poly 2.5g); PROTEIN 2g; CARB 27.3g; FIBER 1g; CHOL 5mg; IRON 0.5mg; SODIUM 162mg; CALC 10mg

WHAT TO EAT RIGHT NOW
CHESTNUTS

Walk the streets of New York City or Paris in winter, especially at the holidays, and you're sure to be seduced by the intoxicating nutty, sweet aroma of freshly roasted chestnuts. Following the sensory delight is the anticipation of the sweet caramel flavor as you carefully peel away the tough mahogany skin. And finally comes the sheer delight of popping a toasted, still-warm, starchy nut into your mouth. Chestnuts are a true seasonal delight. At winter's first frost, they burst forth from the spiky burrs that hang on the majestic trees, but chestnuts stay fresh only a couple of months, if stored properly. These nuts are unusually versatile: divine in cakes, especially if paired with chocolate. Or try a creamy pureed chestnut soup. Stir them in with cubed bread and sausage or mushrooms for stuffing to accompany your holiday roast. Whatever you do, get them now while they're fresh.

Make Ahead • Freezable • Kid Friendly

Chestnut Ice Cream

Hands-on time: 35 min. Total time: 9 hr.

Brown sugar and roasted chestnuts combine to lend this ice cream a deliciously nutty flavor with rich caramel undertones. The chestnuts are really absorbent, so when straining the custard, be sure to press them firmly to extract as much of the liquid as possible.

3 cups 2% reduced-fat milk
1 cup half-and-half
¾ cup packed brown sugar
¼ teaspoon salt
5 large egg yolks
1½ cups coarsely chopped peeled roasted chestnuts, divided
1 teaspoon vanilla extract

1. Combine milk and half-and-half in a medium, heavy saucepan over medium-high heat; cook to 180° (do not boil). Remove from heat. Combine sugar, salt, and yolks, stirring well with a whisk. Carefully pour 1 cup hot milk mixture gradually into yolk mixture, stirring constantly with a whisk. Return mixture to pan, stirring constantly. Cook custard over medium heat until a thermometer registers 160°, stirring constantly. Combine custard and 1 cup chestnuts in a medium bowl; cover and chill 8 hours. Strain mixture through a cheesecloth-lined strainer, pressing to release liquid; discard solids. Stir in vanilla.

2. Pour custard into freezer can of an ice-cream freezer; freeze according to manufacturer's instructions. Spoon ice cream into a freezer-safe container; cover and freeze 2 hours or until firm. Top ice cream with remaining ½ cup chestnuts. Yield: 8 servings (serving size: about ¾ cup ice cream and 1 tablespoon chestnuts.)

CALORIES 242; FAT 8.5g (sat 4.4g, mono 2.9g, poly 0.8g); PROTEIN 6.2g; CARB 35.8g; FIBER 0.9g; CHOL 150mg; IRON 0.7mg; SODIUM 135mg; CALC 175mg

CONVENIENCE COOKING
PUFF PASTRY APPETIZERS

The irresistible flaky crunch of purchased puff pastry makes a delicious starting point for super-simple party snacks.

Make Ahead • Freezable • Vegetarian

Sun-Dried Tomato Palmiers

Hands-on time: 19 min. Total time: 54 min.

You can either thaw the puff pastry in the fridge overnight or leave it out at room temperature for 1 to 2 hours until it's pliable.

1 tablespoon extra-virgin olive oil
1 teaspoon fresh thyme leaves
4 oil-packed sun-dried tomatoes, drained
2 ounces pitted kalamata olives (about ½ cup)
1 garlic clove, minced
1 sheet frozen puff pastry dough, thawed

1. Place first 5 ingredients in a mini food processor; process until finely chopped.

HOW TO ROAST AND PEEL CHESTNUTS

1. Place fresh chestnuts, flat sides down, and score an X in the tough outer skin. Then soak them in water for 20 to 30 minutes and drain.

2. Arrange chestnuts in a single layer on a baking sheet and roast at 400° until toasted and skins begin to peel back (about 15 to 20 minutes); cool. Remove skins.

2. Unfold dough; roll gently to a 10 x 9–inch rectangle. Spread tomato mixture evenly over dough, leaving a ½-inch border. Roll up long sides of dough, jelly-roll fashion, until they meet in the middle. Chill 20 minutes or until firm.

3. Preheat oven to 400°.

4. Cut dough roll crosswise into 20 slices. Arrange slices in a single layer on a baking sheet lined with parchment paper. Bake at 400° for 15 minutes or until lightly browned. Yield: 10 servings (serving size: 2 palmiers).

CALORIES 168; **FAT** 12.5g (sat 1.7g, mono 4.4g, poly 5.8g); **PROTEIN** 2g; **CARB** 12.1g; **FIBER** 0.5g; **CHOL** 0mg; **IRON** 0.7mg; **SODIUM** 158mg; **CALC** 6mg

Make Ahead • Vegetarian

Caramelized Onion Tartlets

Hands-on time: 40 min. Total time: 1 hr. 5 min.

Caramelizing takes up to an hour before onions turn dark golden brown. To save time, use balsamic vinegar to add nuttiness and color.

2 teaspoons olive oil
2 small red onions, thinly sliced and separated into rings (about 8 ounces)
2 small yellow onions, thinly sliced and separated into rings (about 6 ounces)
1 tablespoon white balsamic vinegar
1 sheet frozen puff pastry dough, thawed
⅓ cup (about 1½ ounces) finely shredded Asiago cheese
¼ teaspoon kosher salt

1. Heat oil in a large skillet over medium-high heat. Add onions, and sauté 5 minutes. Reduce heat to medium, and cook 15 minutes, stirring occasionally. Add vinegar to pan, and remove from heat.

2. Preheat oven to 400°.

3. Unfold dough; place on a work surface lightly dusted with flour. Roll gently into a 10 x 9–inch rectangle. Cut dough into 20 (2¼ x 2–inch) rectangles. Score each rectangle about ⅛-inch from edge. Prick each dough piece liberally with a fork. Arrange dough pieces on a baking sheet lined with parchment paper; chill 10 minutes.

4. Sprinkle about ¾ teaspoon cheese over each tartlet; top with about 1 tablespoon onion mixture. Sprinkle salt evenly over tartlets. Bake at 400° for 15 minutes or until dough is lightly browned. Yield: 10 servings (serving size: 2 tartlets).

CALORIES 179; **FAT** 11.7g (sat 2.3g, mono 2.8g, poly 5.6g); **PROTEIN** 3.2g; **CARB** 15.3g; **FIBER** 1.1g; **CHOL** 4mg; **IRON** 0.7mg; **SODIUM** 153mg; **CALC** 42mg

Make Ahead • Kid Friendly
Vegetarian

Tomato–Baby Bell Pepper Tartlets

Hands-on time: 30 min. Total time: 55 min.

1 sheet frozen puff pastry dough, thawed
¼ cup (1 ounce) grated Parmigiano-Reggiano cheese
2 tablespoons canola mayonnaise
1 small garlic clove, minced
8 grape tomatoes, cut into ⅛-inch-thick slices
3 baby bell peppers, cut into ⅛-inch-thick rings
2 teaspoons fresh thyme leaves

1. Preheat oven to 400°.

2. Unfold dough; place on a work surface lightly dusted with flour. Roll gently into a 10 x 9–inch rectangle. Cut dough into 20 (2¼ x 2–inch) rectangles. Score each rectangle about ⅛ inch from edge. Prick each dough piece liberally with a fork. Arrange dough pieces on a baking sheet lined with parchment paper; chill 10 minutes.

3. Combine cheese, mayonnaise, and garlic, stirring well. Spread a scant ½ tea-spoon cheese mixture over each dough piece. Top each tartlet with about 2 tomato slices and 2 bell pepper rings. Bake at 400° for 15 minutes or until dough is lightly browned. Remove from oven; sprinkle evenly with thyme. Yield: 10 servings (serving size: 2 tartlets).

CALORIES 162; **FAT** 11.1g (sat 1.8g, mono 2.9g, poly 5.8g); **PROTEIN** 3.1g; **CARB** 12.4g; **FIBER** 0.7g; **CHOL** 2mg; **IRON** 0.8mg; **SODIUM** 126mg; **CALC** 39mg

TAMING PUFF PASTRY

Frozen puff pastry is a handy shortcut for appetizers, but it's important to keep it from puffing so much that toppings slide off. To prep:

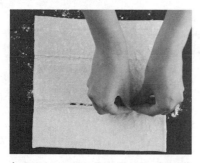

1. Pinch together dough to repair any tears.

2. Cut into shapes as directed; a fluted pastry wheel makes pretty scalloped edges.

3. Score dough close to outer edge. Prick dough inside score marks to tame puffing.

Potato-Gruyère Tartlets

Hands-on time: 27 min. Total time: 52 min.

For a varied presentation, try using a mix of yellow and purple potatoes.

6 baby Dutch or fingerling potatoes
1 sheet frozen puff pastry dough, thawed
¼ teaspoon kosher salt
⅓ cup (about 1½ ounces) finely shredded Gruyère cheese
1½ teaspoons coarsely chopped fresh rosemary

1. Place potatoes in a small saucepan; cover with water. Bring to a boil; reduce heat, and simmer 5 minutes or until almost tender. Drain and rinse with cold water until potatoes are cool enough to handle. Cut potatoes crosswise into thin slices.
2. Preheat oven to 400°.
3. Unfold dough; place on a work surface lightly dusted with flour. Roll gently into a 10 x 9–inch rectangle. Cut dough into 20 (2¼ x 2–inch rectangles). Score each rectangle about ⅛-inch from edge. Prick each dough piece liberally with a fork. Arrange dough pieces on a baking sheet lined with parchment paper; chill 10 minutes.
4. Arrange about 2 potato slices over each dough piece; sprinkle salt evenly over tartlets. Combine cheese and rosemary in a small bowl. Sprinkle about ¾ teaspoon cheese mixture over each tartlet. Bake at 400° for 15 minutes or until dough is lightly browned. Yield: 10 servings (serving size: 2 tartlets).

CALORIES 168; **FAT** 10.8g (sat 2.2g, mono 2.6g, poly 5.5g); **PROTEIN** 3.5g; **CARB** 14.2g; **FIBER** 0.6g; **CHOL** 5mg; **IRON** 0.8mg; **SODIUM** 125mg; **CALC** 46mg

TODAY'S LESSON: ROASTS

A holiday meal traditionally calls for a stately roast, and for good reason: It feeds a crowd, fills the house with savory, meaty aromas, and is mostly hands-off, freeing you to prepare side dishes or spend time with guests. Bone-in roasts take longer to cook but deliver more flavor. For a perfect "ooh-aah" centerpiece, follow the steps outlined here.

Kid Friendly

Maple-Mustard Glazed Fresh Ham

Hands-on time: 1 hr. 10 min. Total time: 11 hr. 45 min.

Fresh ham is different from the cured ham you may be used to. It's juicy, full of pork flavor, and much less salty—a wonderful special-occasion roast. Serve with Brussels sprouts and mashed sweet potatoes.

2 teaspoons garlic powder
2 teaspoons ground cumin
2 teaspoons ground coriander
2 teaspoons Hungarian sweet paprika
1¼ teaspoons kosher salt
½ teaspoon freshly ground black pepper
1 (10-pound) shank portion, bone-in fresh ham, skin removed
Cooking spray
⅓ cup maple syrup
3 tablespoons Dijon mustard
2 tablespoons unsalted butter, melted

1. Combine first 6 ingredients in a small bowl. Score outside of ham in a diamond pattern. Rub garlic powder mixture evenly over ham. Cover and chill overnight.
2. Remove ham from refrigerator; let stand at room temperature 1 hour.
3. Preheat oven to 425°.
4. Arrange ham, fat side up, on the rack of a roasting pan coated with cooking spray; place rack in pan. Place ham in oven; bake at 425° for 30 minutes. Reduce oven temperature to 350° (do not remove ham from oven); bake at 350° for 1½ hours.
5. Combine maple syrup, mustard, and butter in a small bowl. Turn ham, fat side down. Bake an additional 40 minutes, basting ham with syrup mixture every 20 minutes. Turn ham again. Baste with remaining syrup mixture; bake an additional 35 minutes or until a thermometer inserted close to the bone registers 145°. Let stand 20 minutes; remove excess fat, and slice. Yield: 16 servings (serving size: 3 ounces ham).

CALORIES 358; **FAT** 14.3g (sat 5.3g, mono 6.1g, poly 1.5g); **PROTEIN** 46.9g; **CARB** 7.3g; **FIBER** 0.2g; **CHOL** 140mg; **IRON** 2.4mg; **SODIUM** 381mg; **CALC** 26mg

> KITCHEN TIP: Have your butcher remove the skin, but leave the fat layer on the fresh ham. With a sharp knife, slice long lines about an inch apart through the fat (but not into the meat) in a crisscross pattern. This allows the rub to penetrate to the meat and helps the fat render as it roasts.

Romano and Herb Rubbed Turkey with Pan Gravy

Hands-on time: 50 min. Total time: 3 hr. 30 min.

With poultry like turkey and chicken, roasting it at a low temperature helps keep the meat moist and tender, while finishing it at a higher temperature browns the skin.

2 cups coarsely chopped onion
2 cups coarsely chopped carrot
1½ cups coarsely chopped celery
15 garlic cloves, peeled
1 bay leaf
3½ cups fat-free, lower-sodium chicken broth, divided
6 thyme sprigs, divided
1 (12-pound) fresh or frozen turkey, thawed
½ cup (2 ounces) grated fresh pecorino Romano cheese
2 tablespoons minced garlic, divided (about 6 medium cloves)
2 tablespoons chopped fresh marjoram
2 tablespoons chopped fresh sage
1 tablespoon chopped fresh thyme
2 tablespoons extra-virgin olive oil
1 teaspoon salt, divided
½ teaspoon freshly ground black pepper, divided
2 marjoram sprigs
2 sage sprigs
3 tablespoons all-purpose flour
½ cup water
2 teaspoons extra-virgin olive oil
¼ cup finely chopped shallots
¼ cup dry vermouth or dry white wine

1. Place oven rack in the lower third of oven. Preheat oven to 325°.
2. Combine first 5 ingredients, 3 cups broth, and 4 thyme sprigs in bottom of a shallow roasting pan. Remove giblets and neck from turkey; discard giblets. Add neck to onion mixture in pan. Trim excess fat. Lift wing tips up and over back; tuck under turkey. Starting at neck cavity, loosen skin from breast and drumsticks by inserting fingers, gently pushing between skin and meat. Combine cheese, 4 teaspoons garlic, chopped herbs, 2 tablespoons oil, ¾ teaspoon salt, and ¼ teaspoon pepper in a medium bowl. Rub cheese mixture under loosened skin over breast and drumsticks. Stuff body cavity with remaining 2 thyme sprigs, marjoram sprigs, and sage sprigs. Tie legs together with twine. Place a roasting rack in pan over vegetables. Arrange turkey, breast side up, on roasting rack. Bake at 325° for 2 hours, basting turkey with pan drippings every 30 minutes. Increase oven temperature to 425° (do not remove turkey from oven); bake an additional 40 minutes or until a thermometer inserted into meaty part of thigh registers 165°, basting turkey once with pan drippings. (Shield turkey breast with foil if it browns too quickly.) Remove turkey from oven; let stand 20 minutes. Discard skin.
3. Strain drippings through a colander into a bowl; discard solids. Place a zip-top plastic bag inside a 4-cup glass measure. Pour pan drippings into bag; let stand 10 minutes (fat will rise to the top). Seal bag; carefully snip off bottom corner of bag. Drain pan drippings into measuring cup, stopping before fat layer reaches opening; discard fat. Add remaining ½ cup broth to drippings.
4. Place flour in a small bowl; gradually add ½ cup water, stirring with a whisk until smooth. Heat 2 teaspoons oil in a medium saucepan over medium high heat. Add shallots and remaining 2 teaspoons garlic to pan; sauté 1½ minutes. Add vermouth; cook 2 minutes or until liquid almost evaporates. Stir in reserved drippings, flour mixture, remaining ¼ teaspoon salt, and remaining ¼ teaspoon pepper to pan; bring to a boil. Cook 2 minutes or until gravy thickens, stirring constantly with a whisk. Serve with turkey. Yield: 12 servings (serving size: about 6 ounces turkey and about 3 tablespoons gravy).

CALORIES 286; FAT 5.5g (sat 1.7g, mono 2.4g, poly 0.7g); PROTEIN 50.8g; CARB 3.3g; FIBER 0.3g; CHOL 126mg; IRON 2.6mg; SODIUM 505mg; CALC 89mg

PRIME RIB PRIMER

1. TRIM AND TEMPER
Use a sharp knife (boning or thin utility knives work well here) to remove fat from the exterior of the roast—leave about ⅛ inch of fat on to help keep the roast moist as it cooks. Let the roast stand at room temperature for 1 hour: This promotes even cooking and a desirable pink color throughout each slice.

2. SEASON
Sprinkle with salt and pepper, and then rub the meat with a flavorful mixture of herbs, spices, and condiments.

3. REST AND CARVE
Let the roast stand at room temperature at least 20 minutes before carving so the juices don't gush out when you slice (and leave you with bone-dry meat. Remove the bones by slicing along their contour, between the meat and the bone. Then slice the meat crosswise, against the grain.

Herb and Citrus Roast Leg of Lamb

Hands-on time: 20 min. Total time: 9 hr. 45 min.

Orange and lemon in the marinade make for a bright counterpoint to the earthy cumin. Stuff leftovers into pitas, and drizzle with yogurt.

3 tablespoons chopped fresh flat-leaf parsley
3 tablespoons chopped fresh shallots
2 tablespoons chopped fresh oregano
1 tablespoon grated lemon rind
1 tablespoon grated orange rind
2 tablespoons balsamic vinegar
2 tablespoons extra-virgin olive oil
2 tablespoons fresh lemon juice
2 tablespoons fresh orange juice
1 teaspoon ground cumin
2 tablespoons minced fresh garlic (about 6 medium cloves)
1 (6-pound) leg of lamb, trimmed
1 teaspoon salt
1 teaspoon freshly ground black pepper
Cooking spray

1. Combine first 11 ingredients in a small bowl, stirring well. Place lamb in a roasting pan; rub with garlic mixture. Cover with plastic wrap, and refrigerate 8 hours or overnight.
2. Remove lamb from refrigerator. Sprinkle lamb with salt and pepper. Place lamb on rack of a roasting pan coated with cooking spray; place rack in pan. Let lamb stand 1 hour at room temperature.
3. Preheat oven to 425°.
4. Roast lamb at 425° for 30 minutes; reduce oven temperature to 375° (do not remove lamb from oven); bake an additional 45 minutes or until a thermometer inserted into thickest portion of roast registers 135° or until desired degree of doneness. Let stand 20 minutes; slice. Yield: 16 servings (serving size: about 3 ounces lamb).

CALORIES 241; FAT 9.4g (sat 3g, mono 4.3g, poly 0.9g); PROTEIN 35.2g; CARB 1.8g; FIBER 0.2g; CHOL 109mg; IRON 3.3mg; SODIUM 255mg; CALC 20mg

> KITCHEN TIP: To ensure an accurate temperature reading on bone-in meats, insert the thermometer into the thickest part until you touch the bone, and then pull it back ¼ inch.

Kid Friendly

Rosemary-Dijon Crusted Standing Rib Roast

Hands-on time: 15 min. Total time: 3 hr. 5 min.

A standing rib roast is a bone-in prime rib roast. Serve with roasted potatoes and steamed green beans.

1 (5-pound) standing rib roast, trimmed
1 teaspoon salt
1 teaspoon freshly ground black pepper
5 garlic cloves
¼ cup Dijon mustard
1½ tablespoons chopped fresh thyme
1 tablespoon chopped fresh rosemary
1 tablespoon extra-virgin olive oil
Cooking spray
1½ cups fat-free, lower-sodium beef broth
⅔ cup pinot noir

1. Let beef stand 1 hour at room temperature. Sprinkle beef evenly with salt and pepper.
2. Preheat oven to 400°.
3. Place garlic in a mini chopper; pulse until finely chopped. Add Dijon, thyme, rosemary, and oil; pulse to combine. Rub Dijon mixture evenly over beef. Place roast on rack of a roasting pan coated with cooking spray; place rack in pan. Bake at 400° for 30 minutes. Reduce oven temperature to 350° (do not remove roast from oven); bake at 350° for 30 minutes. Add broth to pan. Bake an additional 30 minutes or until a thermometer registers 135° or until desired degree of doneness. Remove roast from oven; let stand 20 minutes before slicing.
4. Heat roasting pan over medium-high heat; bring broth mixture to a boil, scraping pan to loosen browned bits. Stir in wine; boil 6 minutes or until reduced to ⅔ cup (about 6 minutes). Serve with beef. Yield: 12 servings (serving size: about 3 ounces beef and about 2½ teaspoons sauce).

CALORIES 255; FAT 15.4g (sat 5.7g, mono 6.7g, poly 0.7g); PROTEIN 23g; CARB 1.9g; FIBER 0.1g; CHOL 107mg; IRON 1.6mg; SODIUM 417mg; CALC 20mg

LESS MEAT, MORE FLAVOR
EFFORTLESS HORS D'OEUVRES

By Mark Bittman

It's 5 p.m.: Do you know where your hors d'oeuvres are?

If you're anything like me, the last thing you want to be doing when your party guests start trickling in is fussing over needlessly complicated food in the kitchen. If it only takes two seconds to eat, should it take two hours to make?

Cue the smear.

Smearing (a word whose Yiddish culinary cousin, schmear, refers to the layer of cream cheese that finds its natural home on a bagel) is probably the best way I know to make hors d'oeuvres or snacks that are quick, flavorful, even elegant. All I'm talking about here is blending up a few ingredients in the food processor until they're well-combined and spreadable, and then smearing the mixture onto sliced raw vegetables, bread, crackers—really any vehicle you want—and serving.

There are three recipes here, all of them infinitely variable. The first recipe is sort of a take on a cucumber sandwich (the cucumber is the bread). What I spread (I mean smear) onto the cucumber pieces is an ode to the bagel: thick Greek yogurt instead of cream cheese, smoked salmon, and red onion whirred together in the food processor. This takes a lot less time and effort than layering each ingredient separately.

The second is a version (with some serious chef's license taken) of a French classic: radishes dipped in butter and sea salt. Since I don't always trust myself around a bowl of butter and a dish of salt, I've introduced green things to the dish, and lots of them. A small amount of butter is pulsed together with a pinch of salt, parsley, chives, mint, arugula, and iceberg lettuce. (Yes, you read that correctly.) The lettuce, which might be thought of as essentially crunchy water, mellows out the intensity of the herbs and lightens the consistency of the spread. Just smear on crisp, spicy radish halves, and that's it.

The last is baked crab toast, a variation of the classic fried Chinese shrimp toast. No deep-frying here: Just as I cut the butter with herbs and lettuce, I mix the crabmeat with either raw carrot or parsnip. You pick; it depends on whether you like the distinct earthy flavor of parsnips, or if you care that your crab toast is orange. The pureed crab and vegetable is mixed with more lump crabmeat, green onions, soy sauce, ginger—and hot sauce, if you like—and then smeared on oven-toasted baguette rounds, sprinkled with sesame seeds, and baked until golden. OK, I admit that this is smearing plus baking, but it's still a lot easier than frying.

The idea behind these recipes is ultimately a lot more useful than the recipes themselves: Hors d'oeuvres don't have to be fussy to be good. In fact, turning your favorite combinations of ingredients into a mixture that can be served simply on bread or veggies is one of the best—and certainly one of the fastest—ways to develop a lot of flavor and show it off without too many superfluous bells and whistles. Whether it's crème fraîche and caviar, goat cheese and pistachios, fresh tuna and scallions, or plain old beans and herbs that you love, sometimes all it takes is a little smear.

Quick & Easy • Make Ahead
Smoked Salmon in Cucumber Boats

Hands-on time: 16 min. Total time: 16 min.

You can make the salmon mixture up to a day in advance.

2 English cucumbers, peeled
½ cup plain fat-free Greek yogurt
½ cup chopped smoked salmon (about 4 ounces)
¼ cup chopped red onion

1. Trim ends off cucumbers. Split each cucumber in half lengthwise. Scoop out center of cucumbers, leaving a ¼- to ½-inch-thick shell. Cut into 24 (1½-inch-long) pieces. Reserve any remaining cucumber for another use.
2. Combine yogurt, salmon, and onion in a food processor; process until almost smooth, scraping sides of bowl occasionally. Spoon about 2 teaspoons salmon mixture into each cucumber piece. Yield: 8 servings (serving size: 3 pieces).

CALORIES 32; FAT 0.7g (sat 0.1g, mono 0.3g, poly 0.1g); PROTEIN 4.2g; CARB 2.1g; FIBER 0.4g; CHOL 3mg; IRON 0.2mg; SODIUM 118mg; CALC 19mg

Quick & Easy • Make Ahead
Vegetarian
Radishes with Iceberg and Herb Butter

Hands-on time: 15 min. Total time: 15 min.

You can make the herb butter a few hours ahead and store it in the fridge. Some water will seep out of the lettuce as it sits; just bring the dip to room temperature and give it a good stir to reincorporate the water before serving.

1¼ cups chopped iceberg lettuce
1¼ cups chopped arugula leaves
⅓ cup packed fresh parsley leaves
⅓ cup packed fresh mint leaves
⅓ cup chopped fresh chives
¼ cup unsalted butter, softened
¼ teaspoon salt
24 radishes, halved

1. Place first 7 ingredients in a food processor; process until combined, scraping sides of bowl occasionally. Serve with radish halves for dipping. Yield: 12 servings (serving size: 4 teaspoons butter and 4 radish halves).

CALORIES 38; FAT 3.9g (sat 2.4g, mono 1g, poly 0.2g); PROTEIN 0.3g; CARB 0.9g; FIBER 0.4g; CHOL 10mg; IRON 0.3mg; SODIUM 56mg; CALC 13mg

Quick & Easy • Kid Friendly
Crab Toast with Carrot and Scallion

Hands-on time: 25 min. Total time: 25 min.

The crab mixture is also delicious in cucumber boats—tastes like sushi.

24 (¼-inch-thick) slices whole-wheat baguette
½ cup lump crabmeat, shell pieces removed, divided
½ cup diced carrot or parsnip
2 teaspoons lower-sodium soy sauce
1½ teaspoons dark sesame oil
1 teaspoon peanut oil
¼ cup finely chopped green onions
1 teaspoon grated peeled fresh ginger
½ teaspoon Sriracha (hot chile sauce)
1 tablespoon sesame seeds, toasted

1. Preheat oven to 450°.
2. Arrange baguette slices in a single layer on a baking sheet. Bake at 450° for 4 minutes or until browned. Remove from oven, leaving bread slices on baking sheet.
3. Combine ¼ cup crabmeat, carrot, soy sauce, sesame oil, and peanut oil in a food processor; process about 1 minute or until mixture is smooth, scraping down sides as necessary. Transfer to a bowl. Stir in remaining ¼ cup crabmeat, green onions, ginger, and chile sauce.
4. Spread about 2 teaspoons crab mixture on each bread slice. Sprinkle evenly with sesame seeds. Bake at 450° for 7 minutes or until tops are golden. Let cool a few minutes before serving warm or at room temperature. Yield: 8 servings (serving size: 3 slices).

CALORIES 65; FAT 2.3g (sat 0.3g, mono 0.8g, poly 0.8g); PROTEIN 3.1g; CARB 7.9g; FIBER 0.7g; CHOL 7mg; IRON 0.7mg; SODIUM 151mg; CALC 24mg

GIFTS FROM YOUR HOLIDAY KITCHEN

Perfect for friends, neighbors, coworkers, and everyone on your shopping list, these simple treats are a beautiful and delicious way to share Christmas cheer.

ICING AND DECORATING COOKIES:

- Decorations can be as simple—just icing or a dusting of sugar—or as elaborate as you like.

- Make a batch and a half of the icing, if you need to. This will ensure that you can divide it into several small batches and tint each a different color, but you won't need to use it all.

- Ideally you want a thick icing for decorating and detail work, but a thinner coating of icing to cover the cookies. Start with the thin icing, and coat the entire cookie. Let stand until completely dry, and then do detail work with the thicker mixture.

- Make the thick icing first, and tint it to the desired shade. Then remove some to another bowl, and add a few drops of water to reach the desired consistency for a coating version of the same shade.

- You don't have to have a professional cookie-decorating kit. Place each color of icing in a small zip-top plastic bag, and snip a tiny hole in the corner to do precise decorating work. It's handy to have 4-inch skewers or wooden picks to help with detail work.

- It's always important to let the icing set and dry thoroughly before sealing the cookies in an airtight container. This prevents smearing, running, and other accidents.

Make Ahead • Freezable • Kid Friendly
Iced Sugar Cookies

Hands-on time: 45 min. Total time: 3 hr. 12 min.

Add water to icing a drop at a time for thinner spreading consistency. Decorate with dragées (sometimes called sugar pearls), gold or silver foil, and coarse or sparkling sugar. Make the cookie dough up to a month in advance. Wrap it tightly in plastic wrap; freeze until you're ready to bake the cookies. Let the dough thaw completely by placing it in the refrigerator overnight. Reroll all the dough scraps to maximize your yield.

Cookies:
9 ounces all-purpose flour (about 2 cups)
1/2 teaspoon salt
1/4 teaspoon baking powder
3/4 cup butter
2/3 cup granulated sugar
1 large egg
1 1/2 teaspoons vanilla extract
Icing:
1 1/2 cups powdered sugar
4 teaspoons egg white powder
1/8 teaspoon salt
2 tablespoons water
Additional ingredient:
Sparkling sugar (optional)

1. Preheat oven to 350°.
2. To prepare cookies, weigh or lightly spoon flour into dry measuring cups; level with a knife. Combine flour, 1/2 teaspoon salt, and baking powder, stirring with a whisk. Place butter and granulated sugar in a large bowl; beat with a mixer at high speed until well blended. Add egg; beat until light and fluffy. Beat in vanilla extract. Reduce mixer speed to low. Add flour mixture to butter mixture; beat just until combined.
3. Scrape dough into a 4-inch round; cover with plastic wrap. Chill 1 hour.
4. Roll dough to 3/8-inch thickness on a lightly floured surface. Using 3-inch cookie cutters, cut out 42 cookies, rerolling scraps as necessary. Place cookies 1 inch apart on a baking sheet lined with parchment paper. Bake at 350° for 9 minutes or until lightly browned on bottoms. Cool completely on a wire rack.
5. To prepare icing, combine powdered sugar, egg white powder, and 1/8 teaspoon salt, stirring well. Gradually add 2 tablespoons water, stirring constantly with a whisk until smooth. Decorate cookies as desired. Let cookies stand on a cooling rack until icing is completely dry (about 1 hour). Sprinkle with sparkling sugar, if desired. Yield: 40 servings (serving size: 1 cookie).

CALORIES 88; FAT 3.7g (sat 2.2g, mono 1g, poly 0.2g); PROTEIN 1.3g; CARB 12.8g; FIBER 0.2g; CHOL 14mg; IRON 0.3mg; SODIUM 66mg; CALC 5mg

Gingerbread Cookies variation
Prepare Iced Sugar Cookies, increasing flour to 11.25 ounces (about 2 1/2 cups). Stir 1 tablespoon ground ginger, 1 teaspoon ground cinnamon, 1/2 teaspoon ground cloves, and 1/4 teaspoon allspice into flour mixture. Add 1/4 cup molasses to dough when vanilla is added. Roll dough. Using a 3-inch gingerbread-shaped cutter, cut out 42 cookies. Halve icing recipe; decorate as desired. Yield: 40 servings (serving size: 1 cookie).

CALORIES 91; FAT 3.7g (sat 2.2g); SODIUM 63mg

Pecan Cookies variation
Prepare Iced Sugar Cookies, decreasing butter to 10 tablespoons. Stir 3/4 cup chopped, toasted pecans into dough. Omit icing. Dust cooled cookies with 1/3 cup powdered sugar. Yield: 40 servings (serving size: 1 cookie).

CALORIES 82; FAT 4.5g (sat 2g); SODIUM 54mg

Make Ahead • Kid Friendly

Vanilla Cupcakes with Vanilla Bean Frosting

Hands-on time: 1 hr. Total time: 2 hr. 33 min.

These cupcakes are moist, light, and delicious. Cake flour keeps them light, and butter makes them moist. Start checking for doneness a minute or two before time. Pull them from the oven when moist crumbs cling to the wooden pick so they don't overbake and become tough. Garnish tops of cupcakes with shiny dragées, sugar pearls, or sparkling sugar for a polished look.

Cupcakes:
8 ounces cake flour (about 2 cups)
½ teaspoon salt
½ teaspoon baking soda
½ teaspoon baking powder
½ cup butter, softened
1¼ cups sugar
2 large egg yolks
1 teaspoon vanilla extract
1 cup whole buttermilk
3 large egg whites
¼ teaspoon cream of tartar
Baking spray with flour
Frosting:
1 cup sugar
¼ cup water
½ vanilla bean
3 large egg whites
¼ teaspoon cream of tartar
⅛ teaspoon salt
¼ cup butter, softened

1. Preheat oven to 350°.
2. To prepare cupcakes, weigh or lightly spoon flour into dry measuring cups; level with a knife. Combine flour, ½ teaspoon salt, baking soda, and baking powder, stirring well. Place ½ cup butter and 1¼ cups sugar in a large bowl; beat with a mixer at high speed until light and fluffy. Add egg yolks, 1 at a time, beating well after each addition. Stir in vanilla extract. Reduce mixer speed to low. Add flour mixture and buttermilk alternately to butter mixture, beginning and ending with flour mixture; beat just until combined. Using clean, dry beaters, beat 3 egg whites and ¼ teaspoon cream of tartar at high speed until stiff peaks form. Fold one-third of egg white mixture into batter. Gently fold in remaining egg white mixture.
3. Line each of 24 muffin cups with a cupcake liner; coat liners with baking spray. Divide batter evenly among prepared cups. Bake at 350° for 23 minutes or until moist crumbs cling to a wooden pick inserted into centers of cupcakes. Cool in pans 10 minutes. Remove cupcakes from pans; cool completely on a wire rack.
4. To prepare frosting, combine 1 cup sugar, ¼ cup water, and vanilla bean in a saucepan; bring to a boil. Without stirring, cook 3 minutes or until a candy thermometer registers 250°; discard vanilla bean. Combine 3 egg whites, ¼ teaspoon cream of tartar, and ⅛ teaspoon salt in a large bowl; using clean, dry beaters, beat with a mixer at high speed until soft peaks form. Pour hot sugar syrup in a thin stream over egg whites, beating at high speed until stiff peaks form. Reduce mixer speed to low; continue beating until egg white mixture cools (about 12 minutes).
5. Beat ¼ cup butter until light and fluffy. Fold in 1 cup egg white mixture. Fold butter mixture into remaining egg white mixture, stirring until smooth. Top cupcakes with frosting. Yield: 24 servings (serving size: 1 cupcake).

CALORIES 174; FAT 6.6g (sat 4g, mono 1.7g, poly 0.3g); PROTEIN 2.3g; CARB 26.9g; FIBER 0.2g; CHOL 34mg; IRON 1mg; SODIUM 164mg; CALC 11mg

> # BUTTER OPTION
> Just a touch of butter folded into this dreamy meringue frosting adds rich, luxurious flavor. But, admittedly, the meringue deflates slightly. For a beautiful snow-white appearance, omit the butter.

Chocolate Cupcakes with Chocolate Frosting variation
Prepare Vanilla Cupcakes, decreasing cake flour to 7 ounces (about 1¾ cups). Stir ½ cup unsweetened cocoa into flour mixture. Increase sugar to 1½ cups. Decrease vanilla to ½ teaspoon. Melt 2 ounces unsweetened baking chocolate, and stir into batter after adding flour mixture and buttermilk. Prepare Vanilla Bean Frosting, increasing sugar to 1⅓ cups and increasing water to ⅓ cup. Omit butter. Fold ¼ cup unsweetened cocoa into meringue. Shave 1 ounce bittersweet chocolate over frosted cupcakes. Yield: 24 servings (serving size: 1 cupcake).

CALORIES 185; FAT 6.6g (sat 3.9g); SODIUM 151mg

Red Velvet Cupcakes variation
Prepare Vanilla Cupcakes, adding ¼ cup unsweetened cocoa powder to cake flour mixture. Stir 1 (1-ounce) bottle red food coloring into batter. Omit Vanilla Bean Frosting. Place 3 tablespoons butter and 1 (8-ounce) block ⅓-less-fat cream cheese in a large bowl; beat with a mixer at medium-high speed until smooth. Add 2 cups powdered sugar, ¼ teaspoon vanilla, and ⅛ teaspoon salt; beat until smooth. Add red food color paste to icing; stir. Place frosting in a zip-top plastic bag; seal. Snip a ¼-inch hole in 1 corner of bag. Pipe on top of cupcakes. Yield: 24 servings (serving size: 1 cupcake).

CALORIES 201; FAT 8.4g (sat 4.9g); SODIUM 186mg

> # STYLISH SWIRLS
> Dot the thick frosting with a few drops of red food color paste and stir gently to give it a swirled appearance. Carefully spoon into a zip-top bag and pipe out.

Make Ahead • Freezable • Kid Friendly

Buttermilk Bundt Cakes

Hands-on time: 20 min. Total time: 55 min.

Thicken the glaze with a bit more powdered sugar for a thicker, whiter coating. Make the cakes up to two weeks ahead. Wrap them tightly in plastic wrap and freeze, unglazed. Thaw in the refrigerator overnight, and glaze. Be sure to coat the cups of the mini Bundt pan well with baking spray with flour added. Cakes will stick if you use regular cooking spray. Although the mini cakes are really cute, you can bake one large cake, if you prefer. It'll just need to bake longer, about 45 minutes.

Baking spray with flour
13.5 ounces all-purpose flour (about 3 cups)
2 teaspoons baking powder
1 teaspoon baking soda
1/2 teaspoon salt
1 3/4 cups granulated sugar
12 tablespoons butter, softened
3 large eggs
1 1/2 teaspoons vanilla extract
1/2 teaspoon grated lemon rind
1 cup low-fat buttermilk
1/3 cup powdered sugar

1. Preheat oven to 350°.
2. To prepare cakes, coat 18 mini Bundt cups with baking spray.
3. Weigh or lightly spoon flour into dry measuring cups; level with a knife. Combine flour, baking powder, baking soda, and salt in a bowl, stirring well with a whisk.
4. Place granulated sugar and 12 tablespoons butter in a large bowl; beat with a mixer at medium speed until well blended. Add eggs, 1 at a time, beating well after each addition. Beat in vanilla and rind. Add flour mixture and buttermilk alternately to sugar mixture, beginning and ending with flour mixture.
5. Spoon batter evenly into prepared pans. Bake at 350° for 18 minutes or until a wooden pick inserted in center comes out with moist crumbs clinging. Cool 5 minutes in pans on a wire rack; remove from pans.

6. Dust tops of cakes with powdered sugar. Yield: 18 servings (serving size: 1 cake).

CALORIES 249; FAT 8.7g (sat 5.2g, mono 2.4g, poly 0.5g); PROTEIN 3.8g; CARB 39g; FIBER 0.6g; CHOL 51mg; IRON 1.2mg; SODIUM 261mg; CALC 53mg

Cranberry-Orange Bundt Cakes variation

Prepare Buttermilk Bundt Cakes batter, reducing vanilla to 1 teaspoon, omitting lemon rind, and decreasing buttermilk to 3/4 cup. Combine 1 cup sweetened, dried cranberries and 1/2 cup fresh orange juice in a microwave-safe dish. Microwave at HIGH 1 minute; let stand 10 minutes. Omit 1/3 cup powdered sugar. Combine 2 cups powdered sugar, 1/4 cup fresh orange juice, 1 tablespoon melted butter, and 2 teaspoons grated orange rind, stirring until smooth. Dip tops of cooled cakes in glaze; let stand until set.

CALORIES 331; FAT 9.4g (sat 5.6g); SODIUM 262mg

> ## SUGAR RUSH
> For a decorative glaze that completely covers the cakes, dip the tops of the cakes into the glaze and move them around a bit to make sure the glaze sticks and coats.

Hummingbird Bundt Cakes variation

Prepare Buttermilk Bundt Cakes, adding 1 1/2 teaspoons ground cinnamon to flour mixture. Decrease vanilla to 1 teaspoon, and omit lemon rind. Fold 1 cup chopped ripe banana, 1/2 cup chopped toasted pecans, and 1 (8-ounce) can crushed pineapple into batter. Combine 1/2 cup powdered sugar, 1 tablespoon bourbon, 1 tablespoon melted butter, and 1/4 teaspoon vanilla; stir until smooth. Drizzle over cakes.

CALORIES 291; FAT 10.9g (sat 5.4g); SODIUM 269mg

> ## DOUBLING UP
> You'll only need a touch of the bourbon glaze, but for sugar hounds, you can double the glaze and garnish with more.

LESS-THAN-A-POUND POUND CAKE

Heart-healthy canola oil helps lighten a classic dessert, while an ingenious technique deepens flavor and adds richness.

Dense, supermoist, and indulgently rich, the pound cake carries a pound each of flour, sugar, butter, and eggs. No surprise that this hefty cake weighs in at more than 700 calories and a daily dose of saturated fat per slice. Could anything replace that old-fashioned pound of butter and still maintain a tender crumb? We had to find out.

After testing a dozen cakes that came out too dry, crumbly, or spongy, we combined the butter with a flavor-infused canola oil to yield total success. Steeping a vanilla bean in this heart-healthy oil lends it an exquisitely creamier texture, resulting in the dense, rich flavor we set out to find. Nonfat buttermilk and a few eggs gave us the extra moisture we needed, while a simple yet powerful drizzle of browned butter tops the cake for maximum impact. We break tradition, dropping half the calories, 80% of the saturated fat, and a few pounds off the original.

> ## A BETTER BASE
>
> ### BUTTER/CANOLA OIL COMBO
> A combination of butter and vanilla bean–infused canola oil subs for the traditional pound (4 sticks) of butter to save 174 calories and 15.4g of saturated fat per serving.
>
> ### TWO EGGS
> Two eggs—instead of the traditional pound of 8 or 9 eggs—save 47 calories and 1g of saturated fat per serving.
>
> ### NONFAT BUTTERMILK
> To make up for the drastic reduction in fat, we add nonfat buttermilk, which provides richness and moisture to the cake.

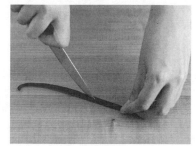

1. Lay the vanilla bean flat on the cutting board. Using a small, sharp knife with a tip, split the vanilla bean down the middle lengthwise, end to end.

2. Heating the oil with the vanilla bean speeds up the infusion process, as the heat helps release flavors from the vanilla bean. Remove the skillet from heat once it starts to simmer to avoid getting any cooked flavor from the oil. Allow the oil to come to room temperature before proceeding.

3. When the pod is cool enough to handle, hold it at one end and use the edge of the knife to scrape the seeds into the oil. Maximum flavor comes from the seeds, with more than 25,000 in the average bean. To get the most out of the bean, place your scraped pod in the container with your vanilla extract to enhance flavor.

A SIMPLE HEAT INFUSION ADDS DEPTH AND INTENSITY TO THE NEUTRAL-TASTING CANOLA OIL WITHIN MINUTES. THE USE OF HEAT HELPS TO RELEASE THE FLAVOR, AS WITH TOASTING.

Make Ahead • Freezable • Kid Friendly
Canola Oil Pound Cake with Browned Butter Glaze

Hands-on time: 25 min. Total time: 1 hr. 50 min.

Cake:
6 tablespoons canola oil
1 vanilla bean, split lengthwise
1¾ cups sugar
½ cup unsalted butter, softened
2 large eggs
12 ounces cake flour (about 3 cups)
2 teaspoons baking powder
½ teaspoon salt
1 cup nonfat buttermilk
Cooking spray with flour
Glaze:
1 tablespoon unsalted butter
¼ cup sugar
2 tablespoons 2% reduced-fat milk
½ teaspoon vanilla extract

1. Preheat oven to 350°.
2. To prepare cake, combine oil and vanilla bean in a small skillet over medium-high heat; bring to a simmer (about 3 minutes). Remove from heat. Let stand 10 minutes or until mixture cools to room temperature. Scrape seeds from bean; discard bean.
3. Combine oil mixture, 1¾ cups sugar, and ½ cup butter in a large bowl; beat with a mixer at medium speed until well blended (about 5 minutes). Add eggs, 1 at a time, beating well after each addition. Weigh or lightly spoon flour into dry measuring cups; level with a knife. Combine flour, baking powder, and salt, stirring well with a whisk. Add flour mixture and buttermilk alternately to sugar mixture, beginning and ending with flour mixture.
4. Spoon batter into a 10-inch tube pan coated with cooking spray; spread evenly. Bake at 350° for 1 hour or until a wooden pick inserted in center comes out clean. Cool in pan 10 minutes on a wire rack; remove from pan.
5. To prepare glaze, melt 1 tablespoon butter in a small skillet over medium heat; cook 2 minutes or until lightly browned. Remove from heat. Add remaining ingredients, stirring until smooth. Drizzle glaze over warm cake. Yield: 16 servings (serving size: 1 slice).

CALORIES 294; **FAT** 12.6g (sat 4.7g, mono 5.3g, poly 1.9g); **PROTEIN** 3.2g; **CARB** 42.8g; **FIBER** 0.4g; **CHOL** 44mg; **IRON** 1.7mg; **SODIUM** 149mg; **CALC** 60mg

OLD WAY	OUR WAY
707 calories per serving	294 calories per serving
39.6 grams total fat	12.6 grams total fat
23.7 grams saturated fat	4.7 grams saturated fat

A SHORT GUIDE TO TOASTING A PERSON YOU LOVE

The toast well done warms a whole room. When stumbled through, or delivered as a droning dissertation, it becomes an unfortunate bit of family lore. Here, some success tips from toast masters.

By Kate Meyers

My father gave the best toast I have ever heard. It was at my brother's wedding, in 1986. On that June day, one of the least talkative men I've ever known stood up and delivered a completely unscripted speech that was riveting, funny, and poignant. It was as if, at that unique moment in his life, my father had found a way to channel Johnny Carson, so at ease was he at the microphone. He stood, smiling and poised, entertaining an audience of more than 200. And I sat, stunned, at his perfect tribute.

Later I asked my dad, "Who was that up there? How did you do it?" He smiled and answered as if he had been toasting people in perfect fashion for his entire life: "You just have to have the right thing in your heart."

Turns out my dad was intuitively right about something that causes most of us to break out in a cold sweat: the heartfelt public tribute at a holiday dinner or special occasion. Toasting someone you love can become a great pleasure if you follow a few simple rules, gleaned here from a diverse range of experts. These rules are worth heeding because, as *Martha Stewart Weddings*' Editorial Director Darcy Miller so perfectly puts it, "There's nothing more awkward than sitting in a room where everyone is thinking, 'Oh my God, stop now!'"

Oh, and before we dive into the art of the toast, let's give a brief nod to the toastee, and her or his job. Somewhat surprisingly, Miss Manners, in her freshly updated *Guide to Excruciatingly Correct Behavior*, insists that if you are the one being toasted, it is absolutely "gauche" to raise your own glass. "All you should do," she writes, "is to sit there, hands in lap, and smile demurely while everyone else drinks to you. You are supposed to be sufficiently drunk on happiness. If you can manage a blush, that is nice, too. It is only after the toast is completed that you may join the guzzling, or not, as you see fit."

THE SAME WAY YOU GET TO CARNEGIE HALL: PRACTICE

"A good toast does not consist of walking into a room, having a bunch to drink, and then, when you're brave, standing up and going, 'OK I want to make a toast.'"
—Pat Johnson, Toastmasters International President

Everyone agrees on this one point: Preparation separates the doomed from the eloquent. "It's an interesting thing," says Johnson. "I've never seen a toast that was kind of OK. They're either absolutely disastrous or they're prepared." She suggests the very obvious idea of writing your thoughts down to help you focus and organize. Then the crucial bridge: "You really have to work to put it into your speaking voice, because we all have two voices—the written and the spoken—and the toast definitely has to be in your speaking voice."

Johnson's belief is that as you speak the toast a few times, in front of a mirror or a thoughtful (and preferably brutally honest) test listener, you begin to internalize. "When we internalize, something magical happens. We no longer have to read, and we start to speak from our hearts and say what we think and feel." Rehearsing gives you time to get comfortable with what you're saying, freeing you to connect with the audience when the time comes and make eye contact with the people or person you're honoring. This plants you firmly in the moment and brings you closer to your own emotions, hopefully allowing them to shine through your words and your anxiety.

CONSIDER THE AUDIENCE

"I always just steel myself when the best man clinks his glass. It sounds sort of like the rumbling of the guillotine into place."
—Calvin Trillin, journalist, *New Yorker* contributor, *The Nation* verse columnist

Preparation also, crucially, gives you time to think about the people you're addressing—from children to in-laws to grandparents—and to make sure what you're saying is common knowledge among those people. A toast should not spend time teaching people long, complicated things about the person being toasted; this is a celebration of things already known and loved. Inside jokes are taboo and, unless it's a stag party, off-color humor is out.

The price of not considering the audience is dreadfully high. "I suppose if you collected the most embarrassing public speeches from America every year, about half of them would be the best man's toast at the rehearsal dinner," says Trillin. "He's trying to sort of tease the groom but actually just manages to mortify the bride or somebody's mother or his own wife."

SHORT, AND TO THE SUBJECT BE TRUE

"Brevity is a virtue. … If you can hit the long ball, do it. If you can't, hit your single and get offstage."
—Dan Okrent, author, editor, and off-Broadway producer of *Old Jews Telling Jokes*

"Less is more" is the oft-repeated mantra of the seasoned toast-giver. Overstaying your welcome is another mistake you can avoid if you rehearse and time yourself. That old college high jinks story may take longer than you think, and bomb. Johnson says two to three minutes is an ideal length. "The good toasts are organized," says Trillin.

"They don't drift off somewhere. They do what people at the *New Yorker* used to call 'close the circle.' They say something, and they get around to it at the end again. And they tend to be short. I don't think anybody ever gave a very, very long toast that was appreciated."

There are exceptions: "Nothing beats a good story," says Okrent, as he recalls a long toast given by the late writer George Plimpton. "Plimpton went on for 12 minutes, but it was George Plimpton and it was brilliant and hilarious and I don't think anybody wanted it to end." Unless you're in Plimpton's league, be a good editor of your own toast. You don't need to be great, just good.

continued

10 TOAST-WORTHY SPARKLERS

When you raise a glass, make sure there's something worthy of the occasion inside. You can't go wrong with bubbly. Here are 10 great options, starting at $10 a bottle.

CAVA
Segura Viudas, Brut Cava Reserva, Spain, $10
Using the traditional Champagne method but with a blend of Spanish grapes creates a rich, mid-weight wine with plenty of complexity. Two years of bottle aging adds a layer of richness to this surprisingly affordable, creamy sparkler.

BLANC DE NOIR
Domaine Ste. Michelle, Blanc de Noirs, Brut NV, Washington, $14
Blanc de Noirs ("white from blacks") is made from the clear juice of red grapes (typically all pinot noir). While there's no pink tint to the wine, it's fruitier and more full-bodied than regular brut.

MOSCATO D'ASTI
Saracco, Moscato d'Asti, Italy, $15
The traditional Christmas wine in the Piedmont region of Italy, moscato d'Asti isn't as effervescent as its peppier cousin spumante, but its fizzy sweetness make this frothy, low-alcohol wine one of the most festive sippers around.

PROSECCO
La Marca, Prosecco, Italy, $16
Instead of Champagne-like bottle aging, this prosecco is made using the Charmat method where wine quickly undergoes a second fermentation in large tanks. This speedy step creates a refreshing, easy-drinking sparkling wine that's loaded with ripe fruit flavors.

BRUT
Piper Sonoma, Brut Select Cuvée NV, California, $16
Nonvintage (NV) brut is one of the most popular, universally food-friendly styles of sparkling wines. With ripe apple and citrus flavors, this California offshoot of French Champagne house Piper-Heidsieck has a touch of elegance usually reserved for pricier offerings.

CRÉMANT
Bailly-Lapierre, Brut Chardonnay Crémant de Bourgogne, France, $20
When French sparkling wine is made outside of Champagne, it's labeled Crémant, which means the wines use the same classic production method and the same high-quality grapes, but often at a fraction of the price. This crisp, all-chardonnay sparkler from Burgundy delivers real bang for the buck.

BLANC DE BLANCS
Schramsberg, Blanc de Blancs, California, 2007, $36
Made from 100% chardonnay, Blanc de Blancs ("white from whites") are the lightest style made in the classic Champagne method. With green apple and melon flavors, Schramsberg is a few bucks more than nonvintage Brut (which blends in pinot noir and pinot meunier), but it's a well-crafted wine and solid value if you're looking for something a bit more refined.

"GROWER CHAMPAGNE"
L. Aubry et Fils, Brut NV, France, $35
Local production is the hot new category in the world of Champagne. Often referred to as "farmer fizz," these top-notch wines are hand-crafted by small, family-owned wineries—and Aubry is one of the best. You'll pay a few bucks more per bottle, but the craftsmanship is unmistakable.

ROSÉ
Domaine Chandon, étoile Rosé NV, California, $50
Don't confuse this rich, full-bodied sparkler with a sweet blush wine because they're light years apart. With regal Moët & Chandon parentage (of Dom Perignon fame), étoile uses a small amount of pinot noir for its rosy hue. You pay for the limited production and extra bottle aging (in this case, five years). But it's worth the splurge.

VINTAGE
Gaston-Chiquet, Brut Special Club 2000, France, $65
True vintage Champagne is rare (and this is always reflected in the price), but it doesn't always translate to superior quality over its nonvintage brethren. Crisp and citrusy, yet rich with caramel complexity, Gaston-Chiquet is a tasty exception, delivering a delicious wine for the price tag.

"I think a lot of times people think the toast is supposed to be the Gettysburg Address," says Larry Meyers, hilarious father of comedians Seth *(Saturday Night Live)* and Josh *(MADtv).* "Something so profound that everyone is going to remember it. But the truth is, everybody forgets almost everything. Make it short, amusing, and, if you can, entertaining. Let the content show your affection. A lot of people forget that the toast is about the people they're toasting. They end up talking about themselves, and it tends to be sappy and long."

YOU GOTTA MEAN IT

"Any toast that evokes some kind of emotion is right on, whether it's a laugh or a tear or a lump in our throats. If you can get all that in two or three minutes, I would say it's an amazing toast."
—Pat Johnson

Everyone appreciates humor, but we're not all funny. Especially in tight clothing and high-pressure situations. It is, in fact, the long reach for humor by the person with short arms that causes the most discomfort.

"You need to be very careful," says Johnson. "Funny is not always funny." Even people who are consistently funny can't always pull that off in a toast. The overriding rule—much more important—is that you have to be genuine.

"I've found I can always get a laugh, but I can't always convince people of my sincerity," says Okrent. "So the way you do that is forget about the laugh and just go for the sincerity. For me this happened at my wife's 60th birthday party last year. My dear, dear friends know that I'm basically a clown, but I decided not to clown it and to look deeply into her eyes and tell everybody what I thought about her. She said it was the best toast ever."

MAKE IT PERSONAL

"I think the most important thing is deep familiarity with the person you're toasting. My failures as a toaster have always been for people I didn't know well enough, and I'll never do that again."
—Dan Okrent

Search for words, moments, and stories that have a deep meaning for you, and speak to your connection with the person being toasted. Okrent explains that to him, the elements of a great toast include something anecdotal and specific. "It helped that I was toasting the woman I've been married to for 34 years," he says. "That's what I mean about familiarity."

As kids, Darcy Miller and her sister had made up lyrics and performed songs at their parents' dinner parties, so for her wedding toast, Darcy's sister prepared custom-tailored lyrics to "Forever You'll Be in My Heart," and alerted the band beforehand so they could back her up. Another spot-on toast at Miller's wedding was given by her boss of almost 20 years, Martha Stewart. It was Stewart who fixed Miller up with her husband, Andy. Stewart knew, as everyone who knew Andy knew, the goofy fact that in fourth grade he learned all the prepositions in alphabetical order and to this day recites them. So Stewart's toast at their wedding included all the prepositions in alphabetical order, beginning with "above" and "beyond." "I can't tell someone what's personal to them," says Miller. "You need to think about that and you need to be yourself, let the toast reflect who you are. The best toasts come from the heart."

FORGET ABOUT THE LAUGH AND JUST GO FOR THE SINCERITY.

EVERYDAY VEGETARIAN

THE COMFORT OF CHILI

From smoky and bold to roasted and spiced, these cold-weather chilis are guaranteed to warm you from the inside out.

Make Ahead • Freezable • Vegetarian

Black Bean and Soy Chili

Hands-on time: 20 min. Total time: 40 min.

Bold, smoky-flavored soy crumble will infuse this chili with a robust flavor that belies its quick and easy preparation.

1 cup uncooked short-grain brown rice
1 tablespoon olive oil
1½ cups chopped onion
1 cup chopped red bell pepper
1 cup chopped green bell pepper
4 garlic cloves, minced
1 tablespoon chili powder
¼ teaspoon ground chipotle pepper
2 cups meatless fat-free crumbles
1 cup frozen corn kernels
⅓ cup water
2 tablespoons chopped fresh oregano
1 tablespoon cider vinegar
1 teaspoon kosher salt
¼ teaspoon freshly ground black pepper
2 (15-ounce) cans no-salt-added diced tomatoes, undrained
1 (15-ounce) can no-salt-added black beans, rinsed and drained

1. Cook rice according to package directions, omitting salt and fat.
2. Heat a large Dutch oven over medium-high heat. Add oil to pan; swirl to coat. Add onion, bell peppers, and garlic; cook 6 minutes, stirring occasionally. Add chili powder and chipotle pepper; cook 30 seconds. Add meatless crumbles and remaining

ingredients; bring to a boil. Cover, reduce heat, and simmer 25 minutes, stirring occasionally. Spoon rice into each of 6 bowls. Ladle chili over rice. Yield: 6 servings (serving size: 1⅓ cups chili and ⅓ cup rice).

CALORIES 307; FAT 3.3g (sat 0.4g, mono 1.7g, poly 0.4g); PROTEIN 13.9g; CARB 55.4g; FIBER 7.3g; CHOL 0mg; IRON 3.5mg; SODIUM 547mg; CALC 107mq

Make Ahead • Freezable • Vegetarian
White Bean and Hominy Chili

Hands-on time: 20 min. Total time: 40 min.

Vegetarian chipotle sausage packs quite a punch, adding savory depth to the entire pot.

2 (15-ounce) cans no-salt-added cannellini beans or other white beans, rinsed, drained, and divided
1 tablespoon olive oil
1 (4-ounce) meatless Mexican chipotle sausage, finely chopped
1½ cups chopped white onion
3 garlic cloves, minced
2 poblano chiles, seeded and chopped
2 teaspoons chili powder
1 teaspoon ground cumin
1½ cups water
2 tablespoons chopped fresh oregano
2 teaspoons hot pepper sauce
½ teaspoon salt
1 (15.5-ounce) can white hominy, rinsed and drained
2 tablespoons thinly sliced green onions
2 tablespoons chopped fresh cilantro
8 lime wedges

1. Mash ⅔ cup beans in a small bowl with a fork.
2. Heat a large Dutch oven over medium heat. Add oil to pan; swirl to coat. Add sausage; sauté 4 minutes. Add onion, garlic, and poblanos; sauté 6 minutes. Add chili powder and cumin; cook 30 seconds, stirring constantly. Add mashed beans, whole beans, 1½ cups water, and next 4 ingredients. Bring to a boil. Cover, reduce heat, and simmer 20 minutes or until slightly thickened. Stir in green onions and

cilantro. Serve with lime wedges. Yield: 4 servings (serving size: 1½ cups.)

CALORIES 261; FAT 6.1g (sat 0.6g, mono 3g, poly 1.6g); PROTEIN 14.4g; CARB 41.4g; FIBER 9.7g; CHOL 0mg; IRON 3.1mg; SODIUM 596mg; CALC 89mg

Kid Friendly • Vegetarian
Cincinnati 5-Way Chili

Hands-on time: 20 min. Total time: 45 min.

8 ounces uncooked whole-wheat spaghetti
1 tablespoon olive oil
2 cups chopped onion, divided
4 garlic cloves, minced
⅓ cup water
1 tablespoon chili powder
1½ teaspoons unsweetened cocoa
1 teaspoon ground cumin
¼ teaspoon ground red pepper
¼ teaspoon ground cinnamon
1 (15-ounce) can no-salt-added dark red kidney beans, rinsed and drained
1 (14.5-ounce) can fire-roasted diced tomatoes, undrained
1 tablespoon semisweet chocolate chips
½ teaspoon salt
1 cup (4 ounces) shredded reduced-fat cheddar cheese
6 tablespoons reduced-fat sour cream

1. Cook pasta according to package directions, omitting salt and fat. Drain and keep warm.
2. Heat a large Dutch oven over medium-high heat. Add oil to pan; swirl to coat. Add 1 cup onion and garlic; sauté 5 minutes. Add ⅓ cup water and next 7 ingredients; bring to a boil. Cover, reduce heat, and simmer 20 minutes or until slightly thickened. Stir in chocolate chips and salt.
3. Place ½ cup pasta into each of 6 shallow bowls. Ladle 1 cup chili into each bowl. Top each serving with about 2½ tablespoons onion, 2½ tablespoons cheese, and 1 tablespoon sour cream. Yield: 6 servings (serving size: 1 bowl).

CALORIES 311; FAT 9.4g (sat 4.2g, mono 3.7g, poly 0.9g); PROTEIN 14.8g; CARB 46.6g; FIBER 10.2g; CHOL 19mg; IRON 2.8mg; SODIUM 538mg; CALC 354mg

Make Ahead • Freezable • Vegetarian
Quinoa and Roasted Pepper Chili

Hands-on time: 25 min. Total time: 45 min.

2 red bell peppers
2 poblano chiles
4 teaspoons olive oil
3 cups chopped zucchini (about 1 large)
1½ cups chopped onion
4 garlic cloves, minced
1 tablespoon chili powder
1 teaspoon ground cumin
½ teaspoon Spanish smoked paprika
½ cup water
⅓ cup uncooked quinoa, rinsed and drained
1 (14.5-ounce) can fire-roasted diced tomatoes with chipotles, undrained
1 (15-ounce) can no-salt-added pinto beans, rinsed and drained
1 cup low-sodium vegetable juice
¼ teaspoon kosher salt

1. Preheat broiler.
2. Cut bell peppers and chiles in half lengthwise; discard seeds and membranes. Place pepper and chile halves, skin sides up, on a foil-lined baking sheet; flatten with hand. Broil 10 minutes or until blackened. Place in a paper bag; fold to close tightly. Let stand 10 minutes. Peel and coarsely chop peppers and chiles.
3. Heat a large Dutch oven over medium-high heat. Add oil to pan; swirl to coat. Add zucchini, onion, and garlic; sauté 4 minutes. Stir in chili powder, cumin, and paprika; sauté 30 seconds. Add ½ cup water, roasted peppers and chiles, and remaining ingredients; bring to a boil. Reduce heat to medium-low; cover and simmer 20 minutes or until quinoa is tender. Yield: 4 servings (serving size: 1½ cups).

CALORIES 258; FAT 6.3g (sat 0.9g, mono 3.6g, poly 1.2g); PROTEIN 9.7g; CARB 42.1g; FIBER 9.8g; CHOL 0mg; IRON 3.7mg; SODIUM 430mg; CALC 108mg

A SPANISH CHRISTMAS

The culinary treasures of Spain's Alicante province shine brightly during the holidays. Spanish food expert Colman Andrews explores the region's bounty.

The Spanish brought the domesticated turkey home in the early 16th century, and the bird soon found a place, stuffed and roasted, on the country's holiday tables—in some households reprieving the previous roasted favorite, peacock.

Not every Spaniard took to roasting the Mexican import: What Americans think of as the iconic holiday oven bird often found its way instead into the Sunday and holiday stew pot. Every region of Spain has its version of cocido (or, in some regions, *puchero*), involving one or more kinds of meat, including turkey, cooked in broth with assorted vegetables. In Spain's northern Alicante province, there's even a version made with octopus.

But turkey, stewed or roasted, was not special enough for some in Alicante. Someone decided to fancy the bird up by getting it drunk.

Last year, just before Christmas, I went searching for the province's most famous version of drunken turkey, or *pava borracha,* with Pedro Nuño de la Rosa, a well-known Alicante gastronomic critic and author. He told me this story about the origins of the inebriated fowl:

"The local aristocrats didn't like turkey very much. They had the idea that it was for common folk, maybe because it came from Mexico, and they preferred to eat quail. Then some of them traveled to France and saw farm women force-feeding geese to make foie gras, and somebody had the idea of doing the same thing with turkeys: Why not feed them expensive French cognac before slaughtering? Then they would surely be fit for an aristocrat's table! The idea, in other words, was frankly an ignorant imitation of the French."

As to what is now the iconic version of drunken turkey, it has its origins about 40 years ago at a roadside inn called El Cruce (The Cross), in Almoradí, about 25 miles southwest of Elche. There, Pedro Montesinos and his wife/chef, Pilar Berenguer, refined the classic into a dish now famous all over the province and beyond. An expedition to Almoradí before Christmas to sample El Cruce's pava borracha has become a local tradition.

Today, happily, the cognac is added to the dish, not the live turkey, though who is to say the liquor did not ease the bird's departure?

We visited El Cruce's kitchen, where Pilar was tending a big, old, flame-darkened aluminum pot of the turkey soup that is the heart of the dish, and breathed in its rich aroma. The soup cooks for as long as eight hours, Pilar told us, its flavors concentrating and melding all the while.

Then we tramped outside, through a field of artichokes—the most popular vegetable in the region—to the farm where the turkeys are raised, uncaged and grain-fed. "We use only black turkeys, because they have more flavor than the white ones," Pedro explained, "and only females, because they have more meat." Back at the restaurant, he proudly pointed to a photograph of "the first turkey we killed"—the birds are dispatched pretty much to order—back in the 1970s.

We sat down in a small private room, across the hall from a larger dining room in which an office party of about 20 men and a lone woman had already started on their pava borracha—and, judging from the volume level and the singing that broke out periodically, also on their wine. Our own meal began with appetizers of mojama, the dried, salted tuna that is a specialty of this part of Spain, sliced into transluscency and dressed with tomato coulis and capers, and with a heap of raw baby fava beans in the pod, dumped right on the table to be opened and popped into our mouths like edamame. Then Pedro brought us what a fancier place might have called "a trio of artichokes"—large pieces braised with clams, ham, and pine nuts; hearts deep-fried, light and crisp; and paper-thin slices of raw baby ones, dressed with olive oil and lemon juice.

Finally, the pava borracha—served, it turned out, not in two courses as turkey stew often is in Spain, but in three: First came the soup, a concentrated turkey broth flavored with saffron and enhanced with turkey giblets, shredded white meat, and perfect little marigold-bright egg yolks (think homemade chicken soup taken to a whole new level). Next was the meat, in the form of plump, moist turkey meatballs, surprisingly delicate in flavor, guaranteed to banish any memory of dried-out turkey burgers. Last came the vegetables—garbanzos, celery, and potatoes—with some pieces of turkey on (but falling off) the bone. Modern chefs might consider everything overcooked, but the flavors were simple and pure and they filled the mouth with delicious warmth. (Long soaked in the broth, the potatoes tasted almost more like turkey than the turkey did.)

De la Rosa and I cooled off with dishes of homemade cactus-pear sorbet, and then headed back to Alicante.

The Spanish have always celebrated Christmas enthusiastically and elaborately, not only with holiday bazaars and church services but also with public beléns, or Nativity scenes, many of them live or at least life-size, and with assorted pageants, parades, puppet shows, concerts, ornate street decorations, and certainly much festive eating and drinking. But I had come to Alicante a week or so before Christmas because this province, even more than others, takes the holiday particularly seriously.

The Alicantino city of Jijona (Xixona in the local Valencian language), to begin with, is the center of production for turrón, or nougat, the emblematic Spanish Christmastime confection—as strongly associated with the holiday here as candy canes are in America. Another Alicante town, Ibi, is the country's toy-making capital, without whose wares Papá Noel would be handing out imports. (Interestingly, the Dutch children have long believed that Sinterklaas, as they call Santa, arrives not by sleigh from the North Pole but by steamer from Alicante, perhaps because the port has long shipped oranges to northern Europe, where they were Christmas treats.)

For anyone from the American snowbelt, it's odd to contemplate Christmas palm trees, sun, and comparatively mild temperatures, but the good people of Alicante would like to remind you that their region looks a lot more like the Holy Land—where, after all, the whole thing started—than do those Christmas-card scenes of snowy streets and houses hung with holly wreaths. In any case, I was much more interested in the holiday food than the holiday weather, for Alicante is a culinary treasure.

CULINARY DIVERSITY

Curving along the Mediterranean coast in southeastern Spain, Alicante is one of the smallest Spanish provinces, but it is an unusually diverse one in geography, encompassing everything from beaches and marshlands to high plains, rugged mountains, and plenty of lush agricultural terrain. This in turn leads to an unusual diversity of dishes. Prominent Alicante chef-restaurateur Maria José San Román, whose sleekly

contemporary restaurant Monastrell updates classic local dishes with imagination and respect—and whose lively La Taberna del Gourmet is simply one of the best tapas bars in Spain—explained to me that, thanks to the province's keystone position touching other provinces with different culinary traditions, there are really four cuisines here, not just one: the seafood cooking of the capital city of Alicante itself, based on fish and shellfish of astonishing quality and variety, always impeccably fresh; the more complex, Valencian- and Catalan-inspired dishes of the Marina Alta, in the northern portion of the province; the hearty meat specialties and rich stews of inland Alicante, abutting La Mancha—Don Quixote territory; and the immense repertoire of paella-like rice dishes in the south.

Add to this variety the presence of Spain's most celebrated pastry chef, Paco Torreblanca, the so-called "father of modern Spanish confectionary," and of Quique Dacosta, arguably the most exciting and original avant-garde Spanish chef this side of Ferran Adrià (the fabled genius of the recently shuttered El Bulli), and Alicante shapes up as a prime—if not yet very well-known—destination for food-lovers.

The earliest known recipe for turrón dates from the 16th century, but nougat made like Jijona's, with egg whites, almonds, and honey, has existed around the Mediterranean since Roman times. Today, there are two main types: Alicante turrón, firm and brittle, and Jijona turrón, softer and a little chewy, with a consistency suggesting a cross between chewy caramel and fudge. "People have associated turrón with Christmas since the 1600s," says Jorge Cantó, who has a family connection to the largest turrón producer, and took me to their factory. "And to this day, about 85 percent of the annual output is sold in December. The factories are in full production for about six months every year, from the summer until the holidays. Ours turns out as much as 20 tons of turrón a week at the height of the season."

The Turrón 1880 plant is a large complex with sterile neon-lit kitchens

and a rather anonymous-looking assembly line for shaping and packaging of the turrón varieties (it could as well have been processing electronics or cosmetics). More interesting was the factory's turrón museum, a handsomely designed two-story gallery of old almond-harvesting and turrón-making equipment, vintage labels, advertising imagery, and more. (El Lobo, 1880's lower-priced brand, is represented by a lupine character who resembles Disney's Big Bad Wolf, and who, I was amused to notice, was pictured until recent years with a smoldering stogie in one paw.)

Almonds are also the basis for another popular local confection, marzipan (mazapán in Spanish), which can be formed into almost any shape. Cantó and I stopped in the middle of Jijona on a street that looked mostly residential and, stepping through a garage, past somebody's motorcycle, walked into Lopetes, a small family-run operation producing the famous sweets. Here the assembly line consisted of a dozen or so women, dressed in white, with gauze caps on their heads, sitting at long tables, talking gaily while they sculpted soft almond paste into the forms of flowers, snakes, dogs, and other living things. "Try these," said one of the women, offering us little dome-shaped marzipan buns filled with sweet potato and egg yolk—impossibly rich. "And these—carefully!" she added, holding out a tray filled with non-marzipan polvorones, delicate cookies made with almond meal, sugar, cinnamon, and lemon zest, so fragile that they disintegrate if you grasp them too firmly (*polvo* is Spanish for "powder").

HOLIDAY TRADITIONS

On our way back to Alicante, I asked Jorge what his family eats for Christmas. "At my house," he responded, "we always start with centollo, king crab legs, and then we eat whole baked fish, and usually roast turkey—but sometimes pork loin stuffed with truffles and foie gras and wrapped in puff pastry, like

continued

pork Wellington, with apple sauce on the side." Dessert? Turrón of course, he said, but also puréed frozen pineapple mixed with cava, Spain's sparkling wine.

The fruit most associated with the holidays in Spain isn't pineapple, but dates. I visited Elche, a dozen miles or so southwest of the city of Alicante, to meet an expert on the subject, "gastro-botanist" Santiago Orts. Elche is the home of the largest palm grove in Europe, designated as a UNESCO World Heritage Site in 2000, and Orts tends many hundreds of palms of his own, both strictly decorative and date-producing. "There are as many as 3,000 varieties of palm trees around the world," he told me, "but of course they're not really trees. They don't have branches, and they're made of pith, not wood. They're actually weeds." Dates are tricky business: "It takes 8 years to determine whether a palm is male or female, and even then only 4 to 10 percent of the females actually end up producing fruit."

Orts also grows exotic citrus (finger limes, pear lemons, Buddha hand citron, and such) supplying them to chefs around Spain, and to his mother, Marisol Perez, who turns them into preserves. Perez knows the whole roster of Spanish Christmas confectionary, and in the weeks before the holiday, her kitchens (she has two) are warm with the scents of baking. Among the treats she makes are rollos de anís, little doughnut-shape cookies spiked with anise-flavored spirits; the flourless cookies (just almond meal, eggs, sugar, and lemon zest) called almendrados; guirlaches, a kind of homemade nougat, sometimes based on pine nuts instead of almonds; and nueces acarameladas, walnut halves cloaked in almond-and-egg-yolk pastry and glazed with caramelized sugar. (See Perez's cookie recipe, at right.) She also makes the cookies known as mantecados, made with equal quantities of flour, sugar, almond meal, and lard. As the note accompanying one recipe for these puts it, "Mantecados are a calorie bomb, but at Christmastime we can let things slide a little."

Back in Alicante, I found myself at the annual Christmas market on the Plaza de Gabriel Miró, a few blocks from the sea. In Alicante, 10 days before Christmas—one of the dozen or so pre-holiday agglomerations of craft stalls, food stands, and religious tableaux that set up in squares around this pleasant Mediterranean port city every year. It was twilight, and the holiday lights were just coming on as I walked into the park in the middle of the square, and into another world. A tanned Madonna, babe in arms, stood quietly in a stable next to a droopy-eyed donkey and a couple of sheep munching idly on straw. Women in loose, rough-textured dresses and men in broad-striped robes, both with corded mantles on their heads, strolled past wood-and-burlap stands where sellers hawked handpainted boxes, leather bags, and exotic sweets. One of the Three Wise Men, jeweled coffer in hand, came down the path rapidly, as if he were late for a meeting. The aroma of woodsmoke and the chatter of children filled the air. There wasn't a Jolly Saint Nick or a Salvation Army bell-ringer or a snowman in sight—but somehow it felt a lot like Christmas.

Make Ahead • Kid Friendly • Freezable

Almendrados (Flourless Almond Cookies)

Hands-on time: 20 min. Total time: 1 hr.

The almond base gives these cookies a wonderfully nutty flavor.

2 cups whole blanched almonds
⅔ cup sugar
4 teaspoons grated lemon rind
Dash of salt
1 large egg
Cooking spray
1 teaspoon ground cinnamon
24 whole blanched almonds

1. Preheat oven to 350°.
2. Place 2 cups almonds in a food processor; process until finely ground. Add

sugar, rind, salt, and egg; pulse 10 times or until dough forms a ball.
3. Shape dough into 24 balls, about 1 tablespoon each. Place 1 inch apart on baking sheets coated with cooking spray. Sprinkle evenly with cinnamon. Gently press one whole almond into center of each dough ball. Bake at 350° for 16 minutes or until edges are golden brown. Cool 5 minutes on pans. Remove from pans; cool on wire racks. Yield: 24 servings (serving size: 1 cookie).

CALORIES 103; FAT 7g (sat 0.6g, mono 4.4g, poly 1.6g); PROTEIN 3.2g; CARB 8.5g; FIBER 1.5g; CHOL 8mg; IRON 0.6mg; SODIUM 13mg; CALC 32mg

Make Ahead • Kid Friendly •Freezable

Anise-Flavored "Doughnuts"

Hands-on time: 23 min. Total time: 1 hr. 53 min.

These confections, called rollos de anís in Spanish, are often washed down with small glasses of Alicante Muscat or other sweet white wine. This recipe comes from Marisol Perez of Elche.

½ cup granulated sugar
½ cup olive oil
¼ cup anisette liqueur
1 large egg
6.75 ounces all-purpose flour (about 1½ cups)
½ teaspoon baking powder
¼ teaspoon salt
Cooking spray
1 tablespoon powdered sugar

1. Combine first 3 ingredients in a large bowl; stir with a whisk until sugar dissolves. Add egg; stir with a whisk until smooth. Weigh or lightly spoon flour into dry measuring cups; level with a knife. Combine flour, baking powder, and salt in a medium bowl, stirring with a whisk. Add flour mixture to sugar mixture; stir until smooth. Cover and chill 1 hour.
2. Preheat oven to 300°.
3. Coat baking sheets with cooking spray or line with parchment paper.

Shape 1½ teaspoons dough into a 2-inch log. Connect ends of log together, forming a ring; place on prepared baking sheets. Repeat procedure with remaining dough, placing 1 inch apart. Bake at 300° for 15 minutes or until edges are golden brown. Remove cookies from pans; cool on wire racks. Sprinkle cookies evenly with powdered sugar while still warm. Yield: 24 servings (serving size: 2 cookies).

CALORIES 97; FAT 4.8g (sat 0.7g, mono 3.4g, poly 0.5g); PROTEIN 1.1g; CARB 11.5g; FIBER 0.2g; CHOL 8mg; IRON 0.4mg; SODIUM 36mg; CALC 7mg

3 MORE WAYS WITH ANISETTE LIQUEUR

1. Stir into coffee.

2. Heat, mix with powdered sugar, and drizzle over warm pound cake.

3. Add a splash to steaming liquid for shellfish like mussels or clams.

Make Ahead • Freezable
Turkey-Saffron Stock

Hands-on time: 30 min. Total time: 8 hr. 15 min.

This flavorful stock is used in the three dishes that comprise a traditional Alicante turkey feast. Freeze extra stock for up to 3 months.

15 cups water
3 pounds turkey necks, backs, or wings
8 ounces lean salt pork
1 tablespoon water
¼ teaspoon powdered saffron

1. Combine first 3 ingredients in an 8-quart stockpot. Bring to a boil over medium-high heat. Reduce heat to low, and simmer 2 hours and 45 minutes, skimming off and discarding foam as needed. Strain stock through a fine sieve into a large bowl; discard solids. Combine 1 tablespoon water and saffron in a small bowl, stirring with a whisk. Stir saffron mixture into stock.

Cool stock to room temperature; cover and refrigerate 5 hours or overnight. Skim solidified fat from surface; discard fat. Yield: 20 servings (serving size: ½ cup).

CALORIES 17; FAT 1.2g (sat 0.4g, mono 0.5g, poly 0.2g); PROTEIN 1.5g; CARB 0g; FIBER 0g; CHOL 6mg; IRON 0.1mg; SODIUM 21mg; CALC 1mg

Kid Friendly
Alicante Turkey Meatballs

Hands-on time: 25 min. Total time: 35 min.

At El Cruce in Almoradí, blood from the restaurant's fresh-slaughtered turkeys lends these meatballs richness, moisture, and complexity. We found that they have plenty of flavor and an attractive texture—not at all dry—without it. You can substitute 2 cups fat-free, lower-sodium turkey or chicken broth and ⅛ teaspoon powdered saffron for Turkey-Saffron Stock.

½ cup fresh flat-leaf parsley leaves
2 (1-ounce) slices country white bread, torn into small pieces
1 garlic clove
⅓ cup fat-free milk
1 tablespoon pine nuts, coarsely chopped
¼ teaspoon salt
4 ounces ground turkey
4 ounces ground pork
½ turkey or chicken liver, minced (about 1 tablespoon)
2 teaspoons olive oil
2 cups Turkey-Saffron Stock (at left)
2 celery stalks, cut diagonally into 1-inch pieces

1. Combine first 3 ingredients in a food processor; process until coarsely ground. Combine breadcrumb mixture and milk in a medium bowl; let stand 5 minutes. Add nuts and next 4 ingredients to milk mixture. Shape into 12 meatballs, about 1½ tablespoons each.
2. Heat a medium nonstick skillet over medium-high heat. Add oil to pan; swirl to coat. Add meatballs; cook 4 minutes, turning to brown on all sides. Remove meatballs from pan. Wipe pan clean; heat over medium heat. Add

Turkey-Saffron Stock and celery to pan; bring to a simmer. Return meatballs to pan in a single layer. Cover and simmer 10 minutes or until meatballs are done. Place 2 meatballs in each of 6 shallow bowls. Ladle about ⅓ cup broth mixture into each bowl. Yield: 6 servings.

CALORIES 173; FAT 10.4g (sat 2.9g, mono 4.6g, poly 1.6g); PROTEIN 10.7g; CARB 8.6g; FIBER 1.1g; CHOL 59mg; IRON 2.4mg; SODIUM 230mg; CALC 52mg

Alicante Turkey Soup

Hands-on time: 40 min. Total time: 5 hr. 43 min.

This is the first course in the three-part meal that constitutes a traditional Alicantino "drunken turkey" feast. El Cruce in Almoradí doesn't give out their official recipe for the meal, but this and the related recipes are a close approximation. Traditionally, this soup also includes egg yolks poached in the broth, but we skip that here for a simpler version. Have your butcher cut your turkey breast in half for you if you don't have a heavy chef's knife or cleaver.

1 (1-pound) bone-in turkey breast half, skinned
½ cup brandy
5 cups Turkey-Saffron Stock (at left)
½ teaspoon salt

1. Cut turkey breast in half crosswise. Combine turkey and brandy in a large zip-top plastic bag. Refrigerate 5 hours or overnight. Discard brandy.
2. Place Turkey-Saffron Stock in a large saucepan; bring to a boil. Stir in salt. Add turkey to pan. Cover, reduce heat, and simmer 23 minutes or until done. Remove turkey from pan; let stand 10 minutes. Remove turkey from bone; discard bones. Cut turkey into bite-sized pieces; return to pan. Ladle turkey and broth into each of 6 bowls. Yield: 6 servings.

CALORIES 112; FAT 1.9g (sat 0.7g, mono 0.7g, poly 0.3g); PROTEIN 19.8g; CARB 0g; FIBER 0g; CHOL 53mg; IRON 1mg; SODIUM 263mg; CALC 14mg

Drunken Turkey

Hands-on time: 20 min. Total time: 11 hr.

This dish, the centerpiece of an Alicante Christmas feast, gets its name from the turkey's brandy marinade. Locals like to mash the potatoes into a little broth on their plates. If your pot can't easily accommodate the turkey, cut the breast halves in half crosswise to make them easier to fit. We've added a little extra brandy to the dish as it finishes cooking because we like the complexity it lends the broth—for subtler flavor, omit the last ½ cup of brandy. Substitute 3 cups fat-free, lower-sodium turkey or chicken broth and ⅛ teaspoon powdered saffron if you haven't made the Turkey-Saffron Stock.

1 cup dried garbanzo beans (chickpeas)
1 (5½-pound) whole turkey breast, skinned
2 cups brandy, divided
1 tablespoon extra-virgin olive oil
1 (1-pound) veal shank (2 inches thick)
3 cups Turkey-Saffron Stock (page 373)
3 cups water
6 thyme sprigs, tied with kitchen string
¾ teaspoon salt
3 cups (2-inch-thick) sliced celery
1½ pounds Yukon gold potatoes, quartered

1. Sort and wash beans; place in a large Dutch oven. Cover with water to 2 inches above beans; cover and let stand overnight. Drain beans.
2. Split turkey in half lengthwise. Pierce breast liberally with a paring knife. Place breast havles, meat sides down, in a 13 x 9–inch glass or ceramic baking dish. Add 1½ cups brandy. Cover and let stand overnight. Discard marinade.
3. Heat a large Dutch oven or stockpot over medium-high heat. Add oil to pan; swirl to coat. Add veal; cook 10 minutes, turning to brown on both sides. Add drained beans, Turkey-Saffron Stock, water, and thyme; bring to a boil. Cover, reduce heat, and simmer 1 hour and 10 minutes, skimming off and discarding foam as needed. Add turkey and salt. Cover and cook 35 minutes, skimming occasionally. Add celery and potatoes. Cover and cook 40 minutes or until thermometer registers 155° when inserted into the thickest part of the breast. Remove turkey; cover with foil.

Add remaining ½ cup brandy to pan; cook, uncovered, 20 minutes or until potatoes are tender. Remove thyme; discard. Divide bean mixture evenly among 12 bowls. Slice turkey and veal across grain into thin slices. Divide turkey and veal evenly among bowls. Yield: 12 servings (serving size: about 5 ounces turkey, about 1 ounce veal, and ⅔ cup bean mixture).

CALORIES 483; FAT 12.5g (sat 3.8g, mono 4.8g, poly 1.8g); PROTEIN 62.5g; CARB 20.1g; FIBER 2.8g; CHOL 173mg; IRON 4.2mg; SODIUM 436mg; CALC 64mg

BUDGET COOKING
FEED 4 FOR LESS THAN $10

Sausage, beans, and peas offer a variety of comforting, seasonal options. Citrus and avocado add bright notes.

$2.48 per serving, $9.92 total

Shrimp, Avocado, and Grapefruit Salad

Hands-on time: 48 min. Total time: 48 min.

The segments from ruby red grapefruit add zing to this salad. Use the fruit's juice to add tang to the dressing without adding to the cost of the overall dish.

2½ tablespoons olive oil, divided
12 ounces peeled and deveined medium shrimp
½ teaspoon salt, divided
¼ teaspoon freshly ground black pepper, divided
1 red grapefruit
2 tablespoons chopped fresh tarragon
2 teaspoons brown sugar
1 teaspoon chopped shallots
6 cups chopped romaine lettuce
1 peeled avocado, cut into 12 wedges

1. Heat a large skillet over medium-high heat. Add 1½ teaspoons oil to pan; swirl to coat. Sprinkle shrimp with ¼ teaspoon salt and ⅛ teaspoon pepper. Add shrimp to pan; cook 3 minutes or until shrimp are done, stirring frequently. Remove from pan; keep warm.
2. Peel and section grapefruit over a bowl, reserving 3 tablespoons juice. Combine juice, remaining 2 tablespoons oil, remaining ¼ teaspoon salt, remaining ⅛ teaspoon pepper, tarragon, sugar, and shallots in a large bowl, stirring well with a whisk. Add lettuce; toss. Arrange 2 cups lettuce mixture on each of 4 plates. Top each serving with ½ cup shrimp and 3 avocado wedges; divide grapefruit sections evenly among servings. Yield: 4 servings.

 Sustainable Choice | *To ensure you are making an eco-friendly choice, look for the Marine Stewardship Council blue-and-white check mark to indicate the shrimp was caught (or farmed) using sustainable practices.*

CALORIES 291; FAT 17.7g (sat 2.6g, mono 11.3g, poly 2.5g); PROTEIN 19.9g; CARB 15.5g; FIBER 6g; CHOL 129mg; IRON 3.4mg; SODIUM 433mg; CALC 96mg

$1.65 per serving, $6.59 total

Make Ahead • Kid Friendly

Black-Eyed Peas and Greens

Hands-on time: 15 min. Total time: 1 hr.

Serve over hot cooked long-grain white or brown rice. Frozen black-eyed peas are economical and available year round, but in the summer months, you can use fresh shelled peas, if you prefer.

2 smoked bacon slices
1½ cups chopped onion
2 cups fat-free, lower-sodium chicken broth
2 cups water
½ teaspoon kosher salt
½ teaspoon freshly ground black pepper
1 (1-pound) bag frozen black-eyed peas, thawed
1 (12-ounce) bunch fresh turnip greens, trimmed and coarsely chopped
2 tablespoons pepper vinegar

1. Cook bacon in a Dutch oven over medium heat until crisp. Remove bacon from pan, reserving drippings in pan. Crumble bacon.

2. Add onion to drippings in pan; sauté 4 minutes. Stir in broth and next 5 ingredients; bring to a boil. Reduce heat and simmer 55 minutes or until peas are tender, stirring occasionally and skimming as necessary. Stir in vinegar. Ladle about 1⅓ cups pea mixture into each of 4 bowls; top evenly with crumbled bacon. Yield: 4 servings.

CALORIES 282; FAT 6.3g (sat 1.8g, mono 2.4g, poly 0.7g); PROTEIN 15.7g; CARB 43.2g; FIBER 11.3g; CHOL 8mg; IRON 3.9mg; SODIUM 593mg; CALC 213mg

---

$2.45 per serving, $9.80 total

Sausage Ragu over Creamy Polenta

Hands-on time: 40 min. Total time: 50 min.

Turkey sausage and bottled marinara combine for a healthy, quick, and affordable twist on this Italian classic.

3 (4-ounce) links sweet turkey Italian sausage, casings removed
1 tablespoon olive oil
1 cup finely chopped onion
4 garlic cloves, minced
1½ cups lower-sodium marinara sauce
2⅓ cups water, divided
1 cup whole milk
¾ cup instant polenta
¼ cup (1 ounce) grated fresh pecorino-Romano cheese
⅛ teaspoon freshly ground black pepper
¼ cup coarsely chopped fresh flat-leaf parsley

1. Heat a large nonstick skillet over medium-high heat. Add sausage to pan; sauté 6 minutes or until browned, stirring to crumble. Remove sausage from pan; drain. Wipe pan clean with paper towels. Return pan to medium-high heat. Add oil to pan; swirl to coat. Add onion; sauté 4 minutes, stirring occasionally. Add garlic; sauté 1 minute, stirring constantly. Stir in sausage, marinara sauce, and ⅓ cup water; bring to a boil. Reduce heat to medium-low and simmer gently 20 minutes, stirring occasionally.

2. Bring remaining 2 cups water and milk to a boil in a medium saucepan over medium heat; reduce heat to medium-low. Gradually add polenta to milk mixture; cook 3 minutes or until thick, stirring constantly with a whisk. Remove from heat; stir in cheese and pepper. Serve with sausage mixture; garnish with parsley. Yield: 4 servings (serving size: ¾ cup polenta, ½ cup sausage mixture, and 1 tablespoon parsley).

CALORIES 357; FAT 14g (sat 4.8g, mono 5.2g, poly 2.3g); PROTEIN 17.2g; CARB 50.8g; FIBER 3.7g; CHOL 65mg; IRON 1.1mg; SODIUM 712mg; CALC 137mg

---

$2.08 per serving, $8.33 total

Make Ahead • Kid Friendly

Quicker Cassoulet

Hands-on time: 31 min. Total time: 3 hr. 31 min.

This French classic normally takes days to prepare. Quick-cooking ingredients like bacon and sausage add depth and flavor to the dish, but help shave time.

1 cup dried Great Northern beans
3 cups boiling water
2 teaspoons olive oil
8 ounces boneless leg of lamb, trimmed and cut into bite-sized pieces
½ teaspoon freshly ground black pepper
¼ teaspoon kosher salt
4 ounces turkey kielbasa, chopped
1 bacon slice, chopped
1½ cups coarsely chopped onion
1 cup coarsely chopped carrot (about 2 medium)
½ cup coarsely chopped celery
6 garlic cloves, smashed
1 tablespoon no-salt-added tomato paste
2½ cups fat-free, lower-sodium chicken broth
1½ cups water
2 tablespoons brandy
1 (2-ounce) piece French bread baguette
¼ cup (1 ounce) grated fresh Parmesan cheese
3 tablespoons chopped fresh parsley

1. Preheat oven to 350°.

2. Sort and wash beans; place in a large saucepan. Cover beans with 3 cups boiling water. Cover and let stand 1 hour. Drain; set beans aside.

3. Heat a large Dutch oven over medium-high heat. Add oil to pan; swirl to coat. Sprinkle lamb evenly with pepper and salt. Add lamb to pan; sauté 5 minutes, turning to brown on all sides. Add lamb to beans.

4. Return pan to medium-high heat. Add sausage and bacon to pan; sauté 2 minutes, stirring occasionally. Add onion and next 3 ingredients to pan; sauté 3 minutes, stirring frequently. Add onion mixture to bean mixture. Add tomato paste to pan; sauté 30 seconds, stirring constantly. Stir in broth, 1½ cups water, and brandy; bring to a boil, scraping pan to loosen browned bits. Stir bean mixture into broth mixture. Cover and bake at 350° for 1 hour. Uncover; bake 1 hour.

5. Combine bread and cheese in a food processor; process until coarse crumbs measure 2 cups. Sprinkle crumbs evenly over bean mixture. Bake an additional 30 minutes or until topping is browned and beans are tender. Sprinkle with parsley. Yield: 4 servings (serving size: about 1½ cups).

CALORIES 501; FAT 17.9g (sat 6.9g, mono 7g, poly 2g); PROTEIN 32.3g; CARB 50.1g; FIBER 15.5g; CHOL 56mg; IRON 5.6mg; SODIUM 759mg; CALC 259mg

Quick & Easy • Kid Friendly

Healthy Wheat Nachos

Hands-on time: 18 min. Total time: 20 min.

Wheat crackers add texture and offer a healthy alternative to the traditional sodium- and fat-laden fried corn chips in this fresh and colorful one-dish meal that will please the whole family.

1 cup fresh corn kernels
6 ounces reduced-fat wheat crackers
1/2 cup (2 ounces) shredded extra-sharp cheddar cheese
1/3 cup (1 1/2 ounces) shredded Monterey Jack cheese
1/4 cup lower-sodium mild green salsa
3 tablespoons (1 1/2 ounces) 1/3-less-fat cream cheese, softened
1 (15-ounce) can organic black beans, rinsed and drained
1/2 teaspoon kosher salt, divided
2 cups thinly sliced romaine lettuce
1 cup chopped plum tomato
1 cup chopped peeled avocado

1. Preheat broiler to high.
2. Arrange corn in a single layer on a heavy-duty baking sheet; broil 6 minutes or until lightly browned, stirring after 4 minutes. Remove from pan.
3. Arrange crackers in a single layer on baking sheet; top evenly with cheddar and Monterey Jack cheeses. Broil 3 minutes or until cheese is bubbly and crackers are lightly toasted. Divide crackers evenly among 4 plates. Combine salsa, cream cheese, and beans in a food processor. Add 1/4 teaspoon salt to salsa mixture; pulse until mixture is chunky and well blended.
4. Arrange 1/2 cup lettuce on each plate; top each with about 6 tablespoons bean mixture, 1/4 cup corn, 1/4 cup tomato, and 1/4 cup avocado. Sprinkle evenly with remaining 1/4 teaspoon salt. Yield: 4 servings.

CALORIES 471; FAT 20.9g (sat 7.3g, mono 7.7g, poly 3.9g); PROTEIN 18g; CARB 56.8g; FIBER 12.2g; CHOL 32mg; IRON 3.5mg; SODIUM 736mg; CALC 242mg

SUPERFAST

For stress-free cooking during the holiday season, look to hearty lamb and pork, sage and rosemary, and other cozy dishes.

Quick & Easy

Currant-Glazed Lamb Chops with Pistachio Couscous

Black currant jelly would be equally tasty in this simple but luscious sauce.

1 1/2 cups fat-free, lower-sodium chicken broth, divided
4 teaspoons olive oil, divided
1/2 teaspoon salt, divided
1 cup uncooked couscous
2 teaspoons minced fresh rosemary
1/2 teaspoon garlic powder
1/4 teaspoon freshly ground black pepper
8 (3-ounce) lamb rib chops, trimmed
Cooking spray
1/3 cup red currant jelly
3 tablespoons balsamic vinegar
2 teaspoons whole-grain mustard
1/4 cup unsalted shelled dry-roasted pistachios, coarsely chopped
2 tablespoons chopped fresh mint

1. Bring 1 1/4 cups broth, 2 teaspoons oil, and 1/8 teaspoon salt to a boil in a medium saucepan. Stir in couscous; cover. Remove pan from heat.
2. Combine remaining 2 teaspoons oil, remaining 3/8 teaspoon salt, rosemary, garlic powder, and pepper in a small bowl. Rub paste evenly on both sides of chops. Heat a large skillet over medium-high heat. Coat pan with cooking spray. Add lamb to skillet; cook 6 minutes or until desired degree of doneness, turning once. Remove from pan and keep warm.
3. Add remaining 1/4 cup broth, jelly, vinegar, and mustard to pan. Bring to a boil over high heat. Reduce heat to medium; simmer 90 seconds or until slightly syrupy.
4. Fluff couscous with a fork; stir in pistachios and sprinkle with mint.

Spoon sauce over lamb. Serve with couscous. Yield: 4 servings (serving size: 2 lamb chops and about 2/3 cup couscous).

CALORIES 507; FAT 17.4g (sat 4.9g, mono 8.7g, poly 2g); PROTEIN 29.6g; CARB 56.4g; FIBER 3.5g; CHOL 70mg; IRON 2.9mg; SODIUM 595mg; CALC 42mg

Quick & Easy

Flank Steak with Romesco Sauce

Romesco also works well as a sandwich spread, with grilled chicken, or as a veggie and pita dip.

2 tablespoons sliced almonds
2 (3/4-ounce) slices whole-grain bread, torn into 2-inch pieces
4 teaspoons extra-virgin olive oil
2 teaspoons chopped fresh garlic
1/4 teaspoon Spanish smoked paprika
1 tablespoon sherry vinegar
1 (7-ounce) bottle roasted red bell peppers, drained
1/2 teaspoon salt, divided
1 (1-pound) flank steak, trimmed
1/4 teaspoon freshly ground black pepper
Cooking spray

1. Preheat broiler.
2. Arrange almonds and bread in a single layer on a baking sheet. Broil 1 minute or until lightly browned. Add almonds and bread to a food processor; process until coarsely ground. Heat oil, garlic, and paprika in a small skillet over medium heat; cook 1 minute or until garlic begins to brown. Add garlic mixture, vinegar, bell peppers, and 1/8 teaspoon salt to bread mixture; process until smooth.
3. Sprinkle steak evenly with remaining 3/8 teaspoon salt and black pepper. Place on a broiler pan coated with cooking spray; broil 5 minutes on each side or until desired degree of doneness. Let stand 5 minutes. Cut steak diagonally across grain into thin slices. Serve with sauce. Yield: 4 servings (serving size: 3 ounces steak and 1/4 cup sauce).

CALORIES 262; FAT 13g (sat 3.2g, mono 6.5g, poly 1.4g); PROTEIN 27.1g; CARB 7.8g; FIBER 1.5g; CHOL 37mg; IRON 2.5mg; SODIUM 537mg; CALC 53mg

Cider and Sage Pork

The sweet, earthy flavors of apple and sage complement the pork. Serve with steamed green beans.

1 (1-pound) pork tenderloin, trimmed
½ teaspoon salt
¼ teaspoon freshly ground black pepper
1 tablespoon olive oil, divided
¼ cup finely chopped shallots
1½ teaspoons chopped fresh sage
4 teaspoons sherry vinegar
½ cup fat-free, lower-sodium chicken broth
¼ cup apple cider
1 teaspoon Dijon mustard
¾ teaspoon cornstarch
1 tablespoon heavy whipping cream
4 fresh sage leaves

1. Cut pork crosswise into 12 (1-inch-thick) pieces. Sprinkle both sides of medallions evenly with salt and pepper. Heat 2 teaspoons oil in a large nonstick skillet over medium-high heat. Add pork to pan; cook 3 minutes on each side or until done. Remove pork from pan; keep warm.
2. Add remaining 1 teaspoon oil, shallots, and chopped sage to pan; cook 2 minutes, stirring frequently. Stir in vinegar, scraping pan to loosen browned bits. Combine broth, cider, mustard, and cornstarch in a small bowl, stirring with a whisk. Add broth mixture to pan; bring to a boil. Reduce heat to medium and cook 2 minutes or until mixture is slightly thick, stirring constantly. Remove from heat. Stir in cream. Serve sauce with pork. Garnish with sage leaves. Yield: 4 servings (serving size: 3 medallions and about 2½ tablespoons sauce).

CALORIES 190; **FAT** 7.3g (sat 2.1g, mono 3.8g, poly 0.8g); **PROTEIN** 24.5g; **CARB** 4.9g; **FIBER** 0.2g; **CHOL** 79mg; **IRON** 1.3mg; **SODIUM** 436mg; **CALC** 16mg

Chicken and Waffle Sandwiches

Breakfast meets dinner in this play on the Southern favorite.

4 lower-sodium bacon slices, halved
    crosswise
3 tablespoons canola mayonnaise
1 tablespoon low-fat buttermilk
1 teaspoon cider vinegar
¼ teaspoon sugar
¼ teaspoon garlic powder
⅛ teaspoon freshly ground black pepper
8 frozen whole-grain waffles, toasted
6 ounces thinly sliced, lower-sodium deli
    chicken breast
8 (¼-inch-thick) slices ripe tomato
4 Boston lettuce leaves

1. Cook bacon in a large nonstick skillet over medium heat until crisp. Drain on paper towels.
2. Combine mayonnaise and next 5 ingredients in a small bowl.
3. Spread mayonnaise mixture evenly over each of 4 waffles. Evenly divide chicken, bacon, tomato, and lettuce over mayonnaise. Top with remaining waffles. Yield: 4 servings.

CALORIES 355; **FAT** 19.5g (sat 2g, mono 7.6g, poly 7.4g); **PROTEIN** 16.3g; **CARB** 33.5g; **FIBER** 6.6g; **CHOL** 39mg; **IRON** 2mg; **SODIUM** 739mg; **CALC** 32mg

Sweet and Spicy Pumpkinseeds

For even more kick, add an extra ⅛ teaspoon ground red pepper.

1 cup unsalted pumpkinseed kernels
1 tablespoon canola oil
1 teaspoon sugar
½ teaspoon ground cumin
½ teaspoon chipotle chile powder
¼ teaspoon kosher salt
¼ teaspoon ground cinnamon
Dash of ground red pepper

1. Place pumpkinseed kernels in a large skillet over medium heat. Cook 4 minutes or until toasted, stirring constantly (seeds will pop slightly).
2. Combine oil and remaining ingredients in a large bowl; add seeds, tossing to coat. Arrange seeds in a single layer on a paper towel-lined baking sheet. Cool 10 minutes. Yield: 8 servings (serving size: about 2 tablespoons).

CALORIES 158; **FAT** 13g (sat 2.3g, mono 4.6g, poly 5.6g); **PROTEIN** 8.8g; **CARB** 4.3g; **FIBER** 1.2g; **CHOL** 0mg; **IRON** 4.1mg; **SODIUM** 67mg; **CALC** 14mg

Chip-Crusted Fish Fillets

The tang in the salt and vinegar chip crust mellows as it bakes in the oven, creating a crunchy spin on fish and chips.

4 (6-ounce) cod fillets (or other firm white
    fish)
2 teaspoons canola mayonnaise
⅛ teaspoon salt
1 (2-ounce) package salt and vinegar kettle-
    style potato chips, crushed
½ cup light ranch dressing

1. Preheat oven to 400°.
2. Arrange fillets on a parchment-lined baking sheet. Brush ½ teaspoon mayonnaise over top of each fillet; sprinkle evenly with salt. Gently press about 2 tablespoons crushed chips evenly on top of each fillet. Cook fish at 400° for 10 minutes or until fish flakes easily when tested with a fork. Serve with ranch dressing. Yield: 4 servings (serving size: 1 fillet and 2 tablespoons ranch dressing).

Sustainable
Choice

Look to hook-and-line-caught Atlantic or Pacific cod for the most sustainable choice.

CALORIES 291; **FAT** 11.3g (sat 1.2g, mono 5.7g, poly 2.8g); **PROTEIN** 31.7g; **CARB** 14.5g; **FIBER** 0.8g; **CHOL** 79mg; **IRON** 1.4mg; **SODIUM** 549mg; **CALC** 49mg

White Beans with Prosciutto

2 teaspoons extra-virgin olive oil
¼ cup finely chopped red onion
2 teaspoons minced fresh garlic
½ teaspoon minced fresh rosemary
2 tablespoons dry white wine
3 tablespoons fat-free, lower-sodium chicken broth
¼ teaspoon freshly ground black pepper
1 (15-ounce) can cannellini beans, rinsed and drained
2 tablespoons chopped fresh parsley
1 ounce thinly sliced prosciutto, chopped (about ¼ cup)

1. Heat a large skillet over medium heat. Add oil to pan; swirl to coat. Add onion; sauté 2 minutes. Add garlic and rosemary; sauté 30 seconds. Add wine; cook until liquid evaporates. Add broth, pepper, and beans; cook 3 minutes or until beans are thoroughly heated. Stir in parsley and prosciutto. Yield: 4 servings (serving size: about ⅓ cup).

CALORIES 94; FAT 3.1g (sat 0.6g, mono 1.7g, poly 0.3g); PROTEIN 5.9g; CARB 10.6g; FIBER 2.9g; CHOL 6mg; IRON 1.1mg; SODIUM 356mg; CALC 35mg

Spicy Escarole Sauté variation
Omit onion, rosemary, wine, parsley, and prosciutto. Increase garlic to 4 teaspoons. Heat oil in a Dutch oven over medium-high heat. Add half of a (1-pound) bag of chopped, prewashed escarole; cook 30 seconds, stirring frequently. Add remaining half of escarole; cook 30 seconds. Add ¼ cup water; cover. Cook 30 seconds or until escarole begins to wilt. Uncover and stir in ½ teaspoon crushed red pepper, 4 teaspoons, garlic, ¼ teaspoon salt, and beans. Cook 2 minutes. Stir in 1 teaspoon grated lemon rind, 2 teaspoons fresh lemon juice, and black pepper. Yield: 6 servings (serving size: about ⅔ cup).

CALORIES 62; FAT 1.7g (sat 0.3g,); SODIUM 226mg

White Bean Dip on Crostini variation
Omit onion, wine, and prosciutto. Decrease beans to 1 cup, parsley to 1 tablespoon, broth to 2 tablespoons, garlic to 1 teaspoon, and rosemary to ¼ teaspoon. Heat oil in a small saucepan over medium heat. Add garlic to pan; sauté 1 minute. Add beans; cook 1 minute or until thoroughly heated. Remove pan from heat; mash beans to desired consistency. Stir in broth, 1 teaspoon fresh lemon juice, rosemary, pepper, and ⅛ teaspoon salt. Spread bean mixture on 8 (¼-inch-thick) slices toasted baguette. Sprinkle crostini evenly with parsley. Yield: 4 servings (serving size: 2 crostini).

CALORIES 82; FAT 2.3g (sat 0.3g,); SODIUM 253mg

Lemony Salad variation
Omit wine, broth, rosemary, and prosciutto; decrease garlic to ½ teaspoon and pepper to ⅛ teaspoon. Combine 2 tablespoons fresh lemon juice, oil, garlic, ¼ teaspoon Dijon mustard, pepper, and ⅛ teaspoon sugar in a large bowl, stirring with a whisk. Add onion, parsley, and beans; toss gently to coat. Top with 2 tablespoons shaved Parmigiano-Reggiano cheese. Yield: 4 servings (serving size: ½ cup).

CALORIES 86; FAT 3g (sat 0.8g,); SODIUM 194mg

> WARM CANNELLINI BEANS ARE A WELCOME SUBSTITUTE TO A TRADITIONAL POTATO SIDE.

OOPS! YOUR COOKIES SPREAD INTO SHAPELESS BLOBS

To prevent a cookie meltdown, keep it cool.
By Hannah Klinger

Baking holiday cookies can go from a labor of love to an exercise in frustration when your gingerbread men come out more bloated than a Macy's parade float. The problem is too much heat—but not at the baking stage, at the mixing stage: Your butter is too warm.

The solution: Keep your butter cool, right until baking. Butter starts to melt at 68°, and once that happens, the water-fat emulsion breaks and there's no getting it back. Cold, emulsified butter takes in air when mixed with sugar and helps give baked goods structure—melted butter can't do that. For cookies, you want butter well below room temperature; between 50° and 65° is optimal. Cut the butter into chunks, and let it stand at room temperature to soften gradually (and nix the microwave idea entirely).

As a rule, if the butter is still cold to the touch but spreadable, you can start creaming. Butter and sugar need only be mixed (or "creamed") for about 30 seconds—much longer and the butter warms up. Once you've formed the cookie dough, chill it for 20 to 30 minutes before you bake. Lastly, don't put the cookies on a hot pan. If you're working in batches, cool the used pan for a few minutes, and then run it under cool water before reloading (don't do this while hot, though, or you'll risk warping the pan).

DINNER TONIGHT

Here is a batch of fast weeknight menus from the *Cooking Light* Test Kitchens.

READY IN 40 MINUTES

The SHOPPING LIST

Moroccan-Style Lamb and Chickpeas

2 onions
2 large carrots
1 lemon
fresh cilantro
ground cumin
ground cinnamon
ground coriander
ground red pepper
golden raisins
2 cups fat-free, lower-sodium chicken broth
tomato paste
1 (15½-ounce) can chickpeas (garbanzo beans)
extra-virgin olive oil
1 pound lean ground lamb

Couscous-Arugula Salad

2 cups arugula
¾ cup uncooked couscous
extra-virgin olive oil
1 lemon

The GAME PLAN

- Cook couscous.

While couscous stands:
- Cook lamb.

While lamb mixture simmers:
- Finish couscous salad.

Quick & Easy

Moroccan-Style Lamb and Chickpeas

With Couscous-Arugula Salad

Simple Sub: Use ground chicken or turkey if you're not a lamb fan.
Prep Pointer: Sautéing the spices briefly with the veggies allows their flavors to bloom and intensify.
Flavor Hit: A little lemon juice added at the end brightens the flavor of the dish.

1 pound lean ground lamb
2 teaspoons extra-virgin olive oil
2 cups vertically sliced onion
½ cup (¼-inch) diagonally cut carrot
¾ teaspoon ground cumin
¾ teaspoon ground cinnamon
½ teaspoon ground coriander
¼ teaspoon ground red pepper
2 cups fat-free, lower-sodium chicken broth
½ cup golden raisins
3 tablespoons tomato paste
1½ tablespoons grated lemon rind
¼ teaspoon salt
1 (15½-ounce can) chickpeas (garbanzo beans), rinsed and drained
½ cup chopped fresh cilantro
1 tablespoon fresh lemon juice

1. Heat a large nonstick skillet over medium-high heat. Add lamb to pan; cook 6 minutes, stirring to crumble. Remove lamb from pan with a slotted spoon. Discard drippings. Add oil to pan; swirl to coat. Add onion and carrot to pan; sauté 4 minutes. Add cumin, cinnamon, coriander, and pepper; sauté 30 seconds, stirring constantly. Add reserved lamb, broth, and next 5 ingredients; bring to a boil. Reduce heat and simmer 4 minutes or until mixture thickens. Remove from heat. Stir in cilantro and lemon juice. Yield: 4 servings (serving size: 1¼ cups).

CALORIES 430; **FAT** 20.3g (sat 7.3g, mono 8.8g, poly 1.6g); **PROTEIN** 27.2g; **CARB** 36.1g; **FIBER** 6.5g; **CHOL** 83mg; **IRON** 3.5mg; **SODIUM** 647mg; **CALC** 88mg

---

For the Couscous-Arugula Salad:
Bring 1 cup water to a boil in a medium saucepan. Stir in ¾ cup uncooked couscous and ¼ teaspoon salt. Remove from heat; cover and let stand 10 minutes. Fluff with a fork. Stir in 2 cups arugula, 2 tablespoons extra-virgin olive oil, 1 tablespoon lemon juice, and ½ teaspoon freshly ground black pepper. Yield: 4 servings (serving size: about ½ cup).

CALORIES 186; **FAT** 7g (sat 1g); **SODIUM** 154mg

READY IN 40 MINUTES

The SHOPPING LIST

Pork Chops with Grits and Red-Eye Gravy

2 shallots
1 (4-ounce) package sliced exotic mushroom blend
fresh thyme
extra-virgin olive oil
Madeira wine or dry sherry
sherry vinegar
quick-cooking grits
cornstarch
ground red pepper
coffee
lower-sodium tomato juice
4 (6-ounce) bone-in center-cut loin pork chops
2% reduced-fat milk
butter

Wilted Spinach

garlic
1 (9-ounce) package fresh spinach

The GAME PLAN

- Cook pork and gravy; keep warm.
- Cook grits.

While grits simmer:
- Sauté spinach.

continued

Pork Chops with Grits and Red-Eye Gravy
With Wilted Spinach

Simple Sub: Use 2 teaspoons light brown sugar in place of Madeira or dry sherry.

1 tablespoon extra-virgin olive oil
4 (6-ounce) bone-in center-cut loin pork chops, trimmed (about ½ inch thick)
½ teaspoon salt, divided
½ teaspoon freshly ground black pepper, divided
¼ cup chopped shallots
2 teaspoons chopped fresh thyme
1 (4-ounce) package sliced exotic mushroom blend
¼ cup Madeira wine or dry sherry
½ cup hot strong brewed coffee, divided
½ cup lower-sodium tomato juice
2 teaspoons sherry vinegar
⅛ teaspoon ground red pepper
2 teaspoons cornstarch
2¼ cups plus 2 tablespoons 2% reduced-fat milk, divided
½ cup uncooked quick-cooking grits
1 tablespoon butter

1. Heat a large nonstick skillet over medium-high heat. Add oil to pan; swirl to coat. Sprinkle pork with ⅜ teaspoon salt and ¼ teaspoon black pepper. Add pork to pan; cook 3 minutes on each side. Remove pork from pan; keep warm. Add shallots, thyme, and mushrooms; sauté 4 minutes. Stir in wine; cook 30 seconds, scraping pan to loosen browned bits. Stir in remaining ¼ teaspoon black pepper, ¼ cup coffee, juice, vinegar, and red pepper. Bring to a simmer; cook 3 minutes. Combine cornstarch and remaining ¼ cup coffee in a small bowl. Add cornstarch mixture to pan, stirring with a whisk; cook 2 minutes or until mixture thickens, stirring frequently.
2. Bring 2¼ cups milk and remaining ⅛ teaspoon salt to a boil in a medium saucepan. Gradually stir in grits. Cover, reduce heat, and simmer 5 minutes or until liquid is absorbed, stirring frequently with a whisk. Remove from heat; stir in remaining 2 tablespoons milk and butter. Serve immediately with gravy. Yield: 4 servings (serving size: 1 pork chop, ½ cup grits, and ¼ cup gravy).

CALORIES 465; **FAT** 15.8g (sat 6g, mono 6.4g, poly 1.4g); **PROTEIN** 45.4g; **CARB** 29.2g; **FIBER** 0.9g; **CHOL** 137mg; **IRON** 2.4mg; **SODIUM** 495mg; **CALC** 209mg

For the Wilted Spinach:

Heat 1 tablespoon olive oil and 1 teaspoon minced garlic in a large saucepan over medium-high heat 1 minute or until garlic starts to sizzle. Add 1 (9-ounce) package fresh spinach; sauté 2 minutes or until wilted. Sprinkle with ¼ teaspoon salt and ¼ teaspoon pepper. Yield: 4 servings (serving size: ⅓ cup).

CALORIES 47; **FAT** 3.6g (sat 0.5g); **SODIUM** 198mg

READY IN
40
MINUTES

The SHOPPING LIST

Chicken with Brussels Sprouts and Mustard Sauce

12 ounces Brussels sprouts
olive oil
unfiltered apple cider
fresh flat-leaf parsley
whole-grain Dijon mustard
fat-free, lower sodium chicken broth
4 (6-ounce) skinless, boneless chicken breast halves
butter

Rosemary Potatoes

12 ounces red potatoes
fresh thyme
fresh rosemary

The GAME PLAN

While oven preheats:
  ▪ Brown chicken.
  ▪ Prep potato mixture.
Roast potatoes and chicken.
While potatoes finish roasting:
  ▪ Cook Brussels sprouts.

Chicken with Brussels Sprouts and Mustard Sauce
With Rosemary Potatoes

Shopping Tip: Buy unfiltered cider, which has the pectin needed to thicken the sauce.
Kid Tweak: A teaspoon of sugar can help take the edge off bitterness in the sprouts.

2 tablespoons olive oil, divided
4 (6-ounce) skinless, boneless chicken breast halves
⅜ teaspoon salt, divided
¼ teaspoon freshly ground black pepper
¾ cup fat-free, lower-sodium chicken broth, divided
¼ cup unfiltered apple cider
2 tablespoons whole-grain Dijon mustard
2 tablespoons butter, divided
1 tablespoon chopped fresh flat-leaf parsley
12 ounces Brussels sprouts, trimmed and halved

1. Preheat oven to 450°.
2. Heat a large ovenproof skillet over high heat. Add 1 tablespoon oil; swirl to coat. Sprinkle chicken with ¼ teaspoon salt and pepper. Add chicken to pan; cook 3 minutes or until browned. Turn chicken and place pan in oven; bake at 450° for 9 minutes or until done. Remove chicken from pan; keep warm. Return pan to medium-high heat. Add ½ cup broth and cider to pan; bring to a boil, scraping pan to loosen browned bits. Reduce heat to medium-low; simmer 4 minutes or until mixture thickens; whisk in mustard, 1 tablespoon butter, and parsley.
3. Heat remaining 1 tablespoon oil and 1 tablespoon butter in a large nonstick skillet over medium-high heat. Add Brussels sprouts; sauté 2 minutes or until lightly browned. Add remaining ⅛ teaspoon salt and remaining ¼ cup broth to pan; cover and cook 4 minutes or until crisp-tender. Serve with chicken and sauce. Yield: 4 servings (serving size: 1 chicken breast half, 2 tablespoons sauce, and ⅔ cup Brussels sprouts).

CALORIES 355; **FAT** 14.9g (sat 5.2g, mono 7g, poly 1.5g); **PROTEIN** 42.8g; **CARB** 11.6g; **FIBER** 3.5g; **CHOL** 114mg; **IRON** 2.6mg; **SODIUM** 647mg; **CALC** 61mg

For the Rosemary Potatoes:

Preheat oven to 450°. Combine 1 tablespoon olive oil, 1 teaspoon chopped fresh thyme, ½ teaspoon minced fresh rosemary, ¼ teaspoon salt, ¼ teaspoon freshly ground black pepper, and 12 ounces quartered red potatoes in a bowl. Spread potatoes on a jelly-roll pan. Bake at 450° for 25 minutes or until golden brown and tender. Yield: 4 servings (serving size: about ⅓ cup).

CALORIES 90; **FAT** 3.5g (sat 0.5g); **SODIUM** 153mg

READY IN
40
MINUTES

The
SHOPPING LIST

Tofu Steaks with Shiitakes and Veggies

1 large red bell pepper
matchstick-cut carrots
garlic
1 (5-ounce) package presliced shiitake mushrooms
1 (14-ounce) package extra-firm tofu
dark sesame oil
sherry vinegar
organic vegetable broth
honey
crushed red pepper
lower-sodium soy sauce

Cashew Rice

green onions
unsalted dry-roasted cashews
long-grain rice

The
GAME PLAN

While tofu marinates:
- Cook rice.
- Sauté veggies.
- Prepare mushroom mixture.

While rice stands:
- Cook tofu.

Vegetarian
Tofu Steaks with Shiitakes and Veggies
With Cashew Rice

Technique Tip: Piercing the tofu with a fork allows it to absorb the marinade.
Simple Sub: Rice or white wine vinegar will work in place of sherry vinegar.

1 (14-ounce) package extra-firm tofu, drained
3 tablespoons dark sesame oil, divided
3 tablespoons lower-sodium soy sauce, divided
1 cup julienne-cut red bell pepper
1 cup matchstick-cut carrot
⅛ teaspoon salt
4 garlic cloves, thinly sliced
1 (5-ounce) package presliced shiitake mushrooms
½ cup organic vegetable broth
1 tablespoon honey
2 teaspoons sherry vinegar
½ teaspoon crushed red pepper
Cooking spray

1. Cut tofu in half crosswise and again in half lengthwise. Pierce entire surface of tofu liberally with a fork. Place in a shallow dish. Combine 1 tablespoon sesame oil and 1 tablespoon soy sauce in a small bowl, stirring with a whisk. Pour soy mixture over tofu; let stand 15 minutes, turning once. Set aside.
2. Heat a large nonstick skillet over medium-high heat. Add 1 tablespoon oil to pan; swirl to coat. Add bell pepper, carrot, and salt to pan; sauté 3 minutes. Remove from pan. Add remaining 1 tablespoon oil; swirl to coat. Add garlic and mushrooms to pan; sauté 4 minutes. Add remaining 2 tablespoons soy sauce, broth, and next 4 ingredients. Simmer 3 minutes or until mixture begins to thicken. Remove from heat.
3. Remove tofu from marinade; reserve marinade. Heat a grill pan over high heat. Coat pan with cooking spray. Add tofu to pan; cook 3 minutes on each side or until browned and thoroughly heated, basting occasionally with reserved marinade. Place about ⅓ cup carrot mixture on each of 4 plates. Top each serving with 1 tofu steak, and

about 2 tablespoons mushroom mixture. Yield: 4 servings.

CALORIES 268; **FAT** 16.5g (sat 2.7g, mono 5.3g, poly 7.9g); **PROTEIN** 11.4g; **CARB** 19g; **FIBER** 2.2g; **CHOL** 0mg; **IRON** 1.8mg; **SODIUM** 462mg; **CALC** 91mg

For the Cashew Rice:

Combine 1 cup water, ½ cup long-grain rice, and ¼ teaspoon salt in a small saucepan; cover. Bring to a boil; reduce heat. Simmer 12 minutes. Let stand 5 minutes. Fluff with a fork; stir in ⅓ cup thinly sliced green onions and ¼ cup chopped unsalted dry-roasted cashews. Yield: 4 servings.

CALORIES 136; **FAT** 4.1g (sat 0.8g); **SODIUM** 151mg

TIME SAVER: LOOK FOR PRECUT MATCHSTICK CARROTS IN THE SUPERMARKET.

The
SHOPPING LIST

Sautéed Flounder and Spicy Rémoulade

fresh flat-leaf parsley
lemon
canola mayonnaise
all-purpose flour
extra-virgin olive oil
orzo
capers
cornichons or dill pickles
Sriracha
whole-grain Dijon mustard
4 (6-ounce) flounder or sole fillets

Bacony Green Beans

12 ounces green beans
2 center-cut bacon slices

The
GAME PLAN

While orzo cooks:
- Prepare rémoulade.

While water comes to a boil:
- Season and dredge fish.
- Cook beans and bacon.
- Cook fish.

Sautéed Flounder and Spicy Rémoulade
With Bacony Green Beans

Time-Saver: Use thawed frozen cut green beans to shave a few minutes off prep time.
Prep Pointer: A fish spatula works best to flip these thin, delicate fillets.

3/4 cup uncooked orzo
3 tablespoons chopped fresh flat-leaf parsley, divided
1/2 teaspoon salt, divided
3/4 teaspoon freshly ground black pepper, divided
1/3 cup canola mayonnaise
1 tablespoon chopped cornichons or dill pickle
1 tablespoon fresh lemon juice
1 teaspoon chopped capers
2 teaspoons whole-grain Dijon mustard
2 teaspoons Sriracha (hot chile sauce)
2 tablespoons extra-virgin olive oil, divided
3 tablespoons all-purpose flour
4 (6-ounce) flounder or sole fillets

1. Cook orzo according to package directions, omitting salt and fat. Drain; stir in 2 tablespoons parsley, 1/4 teaspoon salt, and 1/4 teaspoon pepper.
2. Combine remaining 1 tablespoon parsley, mayonnaise, and next 5 ingredients in a small bowl.
3. Heat a large nonstick skillet over medium-high heat. Add 1 tablespoon oil; swirl to coat. Place flour in a shallow dish. Sprinkle fillets with remaining 1/4 teaspoon salt and remaining 1/2 teaspoon pepper; dredge fillets in flour. Add 2 fillets to pan; cook 1 1/2 minutes on each side or desired degree of doneness. Remove fish from pan. Repeat procedure with remaining 1 tablespoon oil and 2 fillets. Serve with rémoulade and orzo. Yield: 4 servings (serving size: 1 fillet, 4 teaspoons rémoulade, and about 1/3 cup orzo).

Sustainable Choice | *Look for flounder wild-caught in the US Pacific.*

CALORIES 495; FAT 24.1g (sat 2.8g, mono 13.3g, poly 5.3g); PROTEIN 36.8g; CARB 29.7g; FIBER 1.6g; CHOL 88mg; IRON 1.2mg; SODIUM 691mg; CALC 38mg

For the Bacony Green Beans:
Place 12 ounces (1-inch) cut green beans into a large saucepan of boiling water; cook 4 minutes or until crisp-tender; drain. Heat a medium nonstick skillet over medium-high heat. Add 2 center-cut bacon slices; cook until crisp. Remove bacon slices from pan; crumble. Add greens beans, bacon, 1/4 teaspoon freshly ground black pepper, and 1/8 teaspoon salt to drippings in pan; cook 1 minute, tossing to coat beans. Yield: 4 servings (serving size: 1/2 cup).

CALORIES 39; FAT 1.1g (sat 0.5g); SODIUM 146mg

FLAVOR HIT: PICKLES AND CAPERS GIVE THE SAUCE A GREAT BRINY TANG.

CONTRIBUTORS

Anisa Abeytia

Krista Ackerbloom

Michael Adkins

Colman Andrews

Simon Andrews

Alison Attenborough

John Autry

Quentin Bacon

Angharad Bailey

Jeremy Bearman of Rogue
   Tomate

Lisa Bell

Sabrina Bone

David Bonom

Philippa Braithwaite

Levi Brown

Brown Bird Design

Maureen Callahan

Nina Choi

Patrick Alan Coleman

Kathryn Conrad

Adam Cooke

Grant Cornett

Lori Hulston Corvin

Ruth Cousineau

Liz Crain

Daniel Croddy

Kim Cross

Helen Crowther

Claudia De Almeida

Joseph De Leo

Vanessa DiMaggio

Kathy Kitchens Downie, RD

Mary Drennan

Thom Driver

Naomi Duguid

Andrea Fazzari

Kim Ficaro

Allison Fishman

Nathan Fong

Bonnie Friedman

Sandy Gluck

Joyce Goldstein

Lesa Griffith

Paul Greenberg

Paul Grimes

Leanne Guido

Anissa Helou

Christin Holcomb

Ditte Isager

Raghavan Iyer

Bill Jamison

Cheryl Alters Jamison

Lisa Jernow

Telia Johnson

Scott Jones

Barbara Kafka

Wendy Kalen

Nicole Kaplan

Jeanne Kelley

Ana Kelly

John Kernick

Jamie Kimm

Katie Koonce

Barbara Lauterbach

Lisa Lee

Jee Levin

Karen Levin

Mindi Shapiro Levine

Irene Lilja

Jeffrey Lindenmuth

J. Kenji Lopez-Alt

Lindsey Lower

Deborah Madison

Jose Mandojana

Nicholette Manescalchi

Ivy Manning

Charles Masters

Erin McCall

Neal McLennan

Alma Meyers

Jackie Mills, MS, RD

Cynthia Mims

Pam Morris

Eunice Munn

Jackie Newgent

Marcus Nilsson

Henry Obasi

Amy O'Connor

Marisol Perez

Laraine Perri

Marge Perry

Kathy Pickens

Lori Powell

David Prince

Steve Raichlen

Kim Ricardo

Marie Rizzio

Gretchen Roberts

Anthony Rosenfeld

Susan Russo

Mark Scarbrough

Barton Seaver

Jeffrey Selden

Mary Britton Senseney/
   Wonderful Machine

Leslie Siegel

Marie Simmons

Alexander Spacher

Susan Spungen

Linda Stoneking

Susan Sugarman

Sally Swift

Karen Tedesco

Francesco Tonnelli

Rori Trovato

Jan Valdez

John Walton

Bruce Weinstein

Joanne Weir

Anna Williams

Faith Willinger

Mike Wilson

Caroline Wright

Romulo Yanes

Laura Zapalowski

Lauren Zembron

SEASONAL PRODUCE GUIDE

When you use fresh fruits, vegetables, and herbs, you don't have to do much to make them taste great. Although many fruits, vegetables, and herbs are available year-round, you'll get better flavor and prices when you buy what's in season. The Seasonal Produce Guide below helps you choose the best produce so you can create sensational meals all year long.

SPRING

Fruits
Bananas
Blood oranges
Coconuts
Grapefruit
Kiwifruit
Lemons
Limes
Mangoes
Navel oranges
Papayas
Passionfruit
Pineapples
Strawberries
Tangerines
Valencia oranges

Vegetables
Artichokes
Arugula
Asparagus
Avocados
Baby leeks
Beets
Belgian endive
Broccoli
Cauliflower
Dandelion greens
Fava beans
Green onions
Green peas
Kale
Lettuce
Mushrooms
Radishes
Red potatoes
Rhubarb
Snap beans
Snow peas
Spinach
Sugar snap peas
Sweet onions
Swiss chard

Herbs
Chives
Dill
Garlic chives
Lemongrass
Mint
Parsley
Thyme

SUMMER

Fruits
Blackberries
Blueberries
Boysenberries
Cantaloupes
Casaba melons
Cherries
Crenshaw melons
Grapes
Guava
Honeydew melons
Mangoes
Nectarines
Papayas
Peaches
Plums
Raspberries
Strawberries
Watermelons

Vegetables
Avocados
Beets
Bell peppers
Cabbage
Carrots
Celery
Chili peppers
Collards
Corn
Cucumbers
Eggplant
Green beans
Jicama
Lima beans
Okra
Pattypan squash
Peas
Radicchio
Radishes
Summer squash
Tomatoes

Herbs
Basil
Bay leaves
Borage
Chives
Cilantro
Dill
Lavender
Lemon balm
Marjoram
Mint
Oregano
Rosemary
Sage
Summer savory
Tarragon
Thyme

AUTUMN

Fruits
Apples
Cranberries
Figs
Grapes
Pears
Persimmons
Pomegranates
Quinces

Vegetables
Belgian endive
Bell peppers
Broccoli
Brussels sprouts
Cabbage
Cauliflower
Eggplant
Escarole
Fennel
Frisée
Leeks
Mushrooms
Parsnips
Pumpkins
Red potatoes
Rutabagas
Shallots
Sweet potatoes
Winter squash
Yukon gold potatoes

Herbs
Basil
Bay leaves
Parsley
Rosemary
Sage
Tarragon
Thyme

WINTER

Fruits
Apples
Blood oranges
Cranberries
Grapefruit
Kiwifruit
Kumquats
Lemons
Limes
Mandarin oranges
Navel oranges
Pears
Persimmons
Pomegranates
Pomelos
Tangelos
Tangerines
Quinces

Vegetables
Baby turnips
Beets
Belgian endive
Brussels sprouts
Celery root
Chili peppers
Dried beans
Escarole
Fennel
Frisée
Jerusalem
  artichokes
Kale
Leeks
Mushrooms
Parsnips
Potatoes
Rutabagas
Sweet potatoes
Turnips
Watercress
Winter squash

Herbs
Bay leaves
Chives
Parsley
Rosemary
Sage
Thyme

TIME-SAVING TOOLS & GADGETS

Here are some tools and gadgets our Test Kitchen crew and editors recommend for getting dinner on the table superfast. Armed with these handy equipment must-haves, you can cut down on your time in the kitchen and actually spend more time with the ones you love.

BLENDER

A blender is a necessity when making quick frozen beverages, sensational smoothies, and slushy drinks. If you make frozen beverages often, choose a blender with an ice-crushing mode.

CHEF'S KNIFE

The chef's knife is the workhorse of the *Cooking Light* Test Kitchens. It's ideal for chopping herbs, onions, garlic, fruits, and vegetables, and for cutting boneless meats, slicing and dicing, and general cutting tasks.

CITRUS PRESS

For the best flavor, fresh citrus juice can't be beat. A citrus press is a quick and easy way to get a lot of juice from your fruit. To get the most juice, bring your fruit to room temperature before pressing it.

FOOD PROCESSOR

A food processor is a handy piece of equipment that can save time. Use the shredder blade to quickly shred vegetables such as potatoes and carrots.

GARLIC PRESS

A garlic press is a real timesaver. It crushes garlic right into your pan or bowl. You don't even have to peel the clove.

GRATERS

Graters, whether handheld or box, are kitchen tools that speed up preparation time. Use the smaller holes for grating hard cheese or chocolate. For ingredients such as cheddar cheese or carrots, the largest holes work best.

GRILL PAN

A grill pan is a good alternative to a gas or charcoal grill. Meat and fish turn out juicy, with no need for added fat, and you save time by not having to heat up a traditional grill.

KITCHEN SHEARS

Keep kitchen shears on hand to mince small amounts of herbs, chop canned tomatoes, trim fat from meat and skin from poultry, and make slits in bread dough.

MICROPLANE® GRATER

When it comes to finely grating foods, nothing works better or faster than a Microplane grater. It works great on everything from hard cheese and citrus fruits to chocolate.

MEASURING CUPS AND SPOONS

While every kitchen needs these tools, we recommend at least two sets of each in a variety of sizes. With multiples, you'll save time by not having to rinse in the middle of a recipe.

PANINI PRESS

A panini press is great for making hot sandwiches quickly. You can find one at most kitchen stores.

PEELER

A peeler removes the skin from vegetables and fruits, as well as the gnarled roots of fresh ginger. Select one with a comfortable grip and an eyer to remove potato eyes and other blemishes. It also makes quick work of shaving Parmesan cheese and curling chocolate.

PEPPERMILL

Give your food a bit of pungent flavor with a quick turn of a peppermill for a sprinkle of cracked or freshly ground black pepper. It's a must-have kitchen gadget for quick cooking.

PITTER

An easy-to-use pitter is the perfect tool to easily remove olive and cherry pits.

PIZZA CUTTER

Everyone needs a pizza cutter for cutting pizza. But it also works great for cutting toast, focaccia, and even pancakes or waffles.

VEGETABLE STEAMER

Steaming vegetables helps them retain their water-soluble vitamins. It's a quick and easy process, especially when you use a collapsible metal vegetable steamer. Using this tool will assist you in getting vegetable sides on the table quickly.

NUTRITIONAL ANALYSIS

How to Use It and Why

Glance at the end of any *Cooking Light* recipe, and you'll see how committed we are to helping you make the best of today's light cooking. With chefs, registered dietitians, home economists, and a computer system that analyzes every ingredient we use, *Cooking Light* gives you authoritative dietary detail like no other magazine. We go to such lengths so you can see how our recipes fit into your healthful eating plan. If you're trying to lose weight, the calorie and fat figures will probably help most. But if you're keeping a close eye on the sodium, cholesterol, and saturated fat in your diet, we provide those numbers, too. And because many women don't get enough iron or calcium, we can help there, as well. Finally, there's a fiber analysis for those of us who don't get enough roughage.

Here's a helpful guide to put our nutritional analysis numbers into perspective. Remember, one size doesn't fit all, so take your lifestyle, age, and circumstances into consideration when determining your nutrition needs. For example, pregnant or breast-feeding women need more protein, calories, and calcium. And women older than 50 need 1,200mg of calcium daily, 200mg more than the amount recommended for younger women.

IN OUR NUTRITIONAL ANALYSIS, WE USE THESE ABBREVIATIONS

sat	saturated fat	**CHOL**	cholesterol
mono	monounsaturated fat	**CALC**	calcium
poly	polyunsaturated fat	**g**	gram
CARB	carbohydrates	**mg**	milligram

Daily Nutrition Guide

	WOMEN ages 25 to 50	WOMEN over 50	MEN ages 25 to 50	MEN over 50
CALORIES	2,000	2,000*	2,700	2,500
PROTEIN	50g	50g	63g	60g
FAT	65g*	65g*	88g*	83g*
SATURATED FAT	20g*	20g*	27g*	25g*
CARBOHYDRATES	304g	304g	410g	375g
FIBER	25g to 35g	25g to 35g	25g to 35g	25g to 35g
CHOLESTEROL	300mg*	300mg*	300mg*	300mg*
IRON	18mg	8mg	8mg	8mg
SODIUM	2,300mg*	1,500mg*	2,300mg*	1,500mg*
CALCIUM	1,000mg	1,200mg	1,000mg	1,000mg

NUTRITIONAL VALUES USED IN OUR CALCULATIONS EITHER COME FROM THE FOOD PROCESSOR, VERSION 7.5 (ESHA RESEARCH) OR ARE PROVIDED BY FOOD MANUFACTURERS.
*Or less, for optimum health.

METRIC EQUIVALENTS

The information in the following charts is provided to help cooks outside the United States successfully use the recipes in this book. All equivalents are approximate.

Cooking/Oven Temperatures

	Fahrenheit	Celsius	Gas Mark
Freeze Water	32° F	0° C	
Room Temp.	68° F	20° C	
Boil Water	212° F	100° C	
Bake	325° F	160° C	3
	350° F	180° C	4
	375° F	190° C	5
	400° F	200° C	6
	425° F	220° C	7
	450° F	230° C	8
Broil			Grill

Liquid Ingredients by Volume

¼ tsp	=					1 ml	
½ tsp	=					2 ml	
1 tsp	=					5 ml	
3 tsp	=	1 tbl	=	½ fl oz	=	15 ml	
2 tbls	=	⅛ cup	=	1 fl oz	=	30 ml	
4 tbls	=	¼ cup	=	2 fl oz	=	60 ml	
5⅓ tbls	=	⅓ cup	=	3 fl oz	=	80 ml	
8 tbls	=	½ cup	=	4 fl oz	=	120 ml	
10⅔ tbls	=	⅔ cup	=	5 fl oz	=	160 ml	
12 tbls	=	¾ cup	=	6 fl oz	=	180 ml	
16 tbls	=	1 cup	=	8 fl oz	=	240 ml	
1 pt	=	2 cups	=	16 fl oz	=	480 ml	
1 qt	=	4 cups	=	32 fl oz	=	960 ml	
				33 fl oz	=	1000 ml	= 1 l

Dry Ingredients by Weight

(To convert ounces to grams, multiply the number of ounces by 30.)

1 oz	=	1/16 lb	=	30 g
4 oz	=	¼ lb	=	120 g
8 oz	=	½ lb	=	240 g
12 oz	=	¾ lb	=	360 g
16 oz	=	1 lb	=	480 g

Length

(To convert inches to centimeters, multiply the number of inches by 2.5.)

1 in	=			2.5 cm	
6 in	=	½ ft	=	15 cm	
12 in	=	1 ft	=	30 cm	
36 in	=	3 ft	= 1 yd =	90 cm	
40 in	=			100 cm	= 1 m

Equivalents for Different Types of Ingredients

Standard Cup	Fine Powder (ex. flour)	Grain (ex. rice)	Granular (ex. sugar)	Liquid Solids (ex. butter)	Liquid (ex. milk)
1	140 g	150 g	190 g	200 g	240 ml
¾	105 g	113 g	143 g	150 g	180 ml
⅔	93 g	100 g	125 g	133 g	160 ml
½	70 g	75 g	95 g	100 g	120 ml
⅓	47 g	50 g	63 g	67 g	80 ml
¼	35 g	38 g	48 g	50 g	60 ml
⅛	18 g	19 g	24 g	25 g	30 ml

MENU INDEX

A topical guide to all the menus that appeared in *Cooking Light Annual Recipes 2011*. See page 402 for the General Recipe Index.

DINNER TONIGHT

30-Minute Dinners

BEEF

(page 159)
serves 4
Chipotle-Rubbed Flank Steak
Couscous
Spinach with Toasted Almonds

FISH & SHELLFISH

(page 45)
serves 4
Sauteed Halibut with Romesco Sauce
Nutty Rice

(page 109)
serves 4
Linguine with Clams and Fresh Herbs
Baby Romaine Salad

(page 132)
serves 4
Roasted Shrimp and Broccoli
Garlic-Basil Corn

(page 158)
serves 4
Open-Faced Blackened Catfish Sandwiches
Stewed Okra and Fresh Tomato

(page 242)
serves 4
Herbed Shrimp and White Bean Salad
Tomato Toast

LAMB

(page 107)
serves 4
Grilled Lamb Chops and Mint Chimichurri
Buttermilk Mashed Potatoes

(page 132)
serves 4
Greek Lamb Chops and Mint Yogurt Sauce
Tomato-Parsley Salad

POULTRY

(page 76)
serves 4
Chicken with Italian Sweet-Sour Fennel
Creamy Polenta
Herbed Green Beans

(page 131)
serves 4
Peach and Gorgonzola Chicken Pizza
Arugula Salad

(page 270)
serves 4
Chicken Lettuce Cups
Orzo with Spinach

SALADS

(page 243)
serves 4
Grilled Scallop Salad
Radish-Yogurt Dip and Pita Wedges

40-Minute Dinners

BEEF

(page 45)
serves 4
Beef Tagine with Butternut Squash
Scallion Couscous

(page 47)
serves 6
Cheesy Meat Loaf Minis
Salad with Balsamic Vinaigrette

(page 242)
serves 4
Peppered Flank Steak and Salsa
Two-Bean Toss

FISH & SHELLFISH

(page 77)
serves 4
Seared Scallops with Cauliflower Puree
Tarragon Carrots and Peas

(page 78)
serves 4
Arctic Char with Orange-Caper Relish
Frisée and Arugula Salad

(page 160)
serves 6
Shrimp Korma and Basmati Rice
Roasted Summer Squash with Parsley

(page 182)
serves 4
Pan-Fried Shrimp with Creole Mayonnaise
Tomato, Cucumber, and Fennel Salad

(page 271)
serves 4
Shrimp Fettuccine Alfredo
Roasted Asparagus

(page 272)
serves 4
Crab Cakes and Spicy Mustard Sauce
Tomato and Arugula Salad

(page 382)
serves 4
Sautéed Flounder and Spicy Rémoulade
Bacony Green Beans

LAMB

(page 244)
serves 4
Lamb Chops and Cilantro Relish
Fresh Lima Beans

(page 379)
serves 4
Moroccan-Style Lamb and Chickpeas
Couscous-Arugula Salad

PORK

(page 46)
serves 4
Smoky Pan-Grilled Pork Chops
Caramalized Onion Mashed Potatoes
Lemon Broccolini

(page 76)
serves 4
Caramel Pork
Radish-Squash Slaw

(page 107)
serves 4
Chipotle Pork Tacos
Radish and Fennel Salad

(page 184)
serves 4
Pork Tenderloin Medallions and Balsamic Reduction
Grilled Peaches
Wild Rice Salad

(page 296)
serves 6
Bacon, Tomato, and Arugula Pizza
Poached Pears

(page 298)
serves 6
Pepperoni, Onion, and Olive Pizza
Greens and Sherry Vinaigrette

(page 349)
serves 4
Crispy Pork Medallions
Roasted Root Vegetables

(page 379)
serves 4
Pork Chops with Grits and Red-Eye Gravy
Wilted Spinach

POULTRY

(page 108)
serves 4
Herb and Goat Cheese-Stuffed Chicken Breasts
Red Pepper Couscous

(page 133)
serves 4
Parmesan Polenta and Spicy Sausage Sauce
Sautéed Spinach and Pine Nuts

(page 160)
serves 4
Grilled Chicken Sliders and Apricot Chutney Spread
Guacamole

(page 183)
serves 4
Chicken Kebabs and Nectarine Salsa
Herbed Couscous

(page 270)
serves 4
Chicken Tostadas and Avocado Dressing
Mexican Rice

(page 297)
serves 6
Spicy Sausage and Mushroom Pizza
Lemony Arugula Salad

(page 296)
serves 6
Chicken and Herb White Pizza
Apple Iced Tea

(page 348)
serves 4
Chicken and Sausage Jambalaya
Garlic Breadsticks

(page 350)
serves 4
Broccoli and Rice Casseroles
Buttered Carrots

(page 380)
serves 4
Chicken with Brussels Sprouts and Mustard Sauce
Rosemary Potatoes

VEGETARIAN
(page 182)
serves 4
Baked Ziti and Summer Veggies
Mixed Greens Salad

(page 348)
serves 6
Baked Mac and Cheese
Spinach Salad

(page 381)
serves 4
Tofu Steaks with Shiitakes and Veggies
Cashew Rice

ENTERTAINING MENUS

Celebration of Spring Menu
(page 91)
serves 8
Beets with Walnuts, Goat Cheese, and Baby Greens
Lemon Chicken Soup with Dumplings
Quinoa Salad with Artichokes and Parsley
Brown Sugar–Glazed Capon with Bourbon Gravy
Israeli Carrots
Green Beans with Shallots and Hazelnuts
Sponge Cake with Orange Curd and Strawberries
Date and Almond Truffles

Portable 4th of July Menu
(page 178)
serves 8
Marinated Shrimp Salad
Tabbouleh Salad
Creamy Buttermilk-Herb Potato Salad
Lemony Cucumber Salad
Jalapeño-Lime Slaw
Smoky Three-Bean Bake
Fresh Cherry Cheesecake Bars

Mix & Match Taco Menu
(page 163)
serves 6
Blackberry Margaritas
Baked Black Beans with Chorizo
Flank Steak Tacos
Chimichurri Halibut Tacos
Cabbage Slaw
Grilled Pineapple-Avocado Salsa

One-Hour Dinner Party Menu
(page 117)
serves 8
Lemon-Gin Sparkling Cocktails
Pickled Onion, Blue Cheese, and Berry Salad
Beef Tenderloin with Horseradish-Chive Sauce
Truffled Roasted Potatoes
Browned Butter Asparagus
Champagne-Soaked Berries with Whipped Cream

Clambake Menu
(page 190)
Serves 8
Fresh Raspberry Lemonade
Beer-Steamed Soft-Shell Clams
Grilled Maine Lobsters
Butter Sauce
Grilled Corn on the Cob
New Potatoes with Onions and Spicy Sausage
Blueberry Crisp

A Gluten-Free Thanksgiving Menu
(page 305)
serves 8
Slow-Roasted Turkey with Cream Gravy
(Our gravy is thickened with cornstarch, which is gluten-free.)
Old-Fashioned Cranberry Sauce
Wild Rice Stuffing with Dried Cherries and Toasted Pecans
(Use a gluten-free chicken broth or water.)
Brussels Sprouts with Bacon, Garlic, and Shallots
(Use gluten-free broth.)
Truffled Pommes Anna
Ginger Pumpkin Pie with Toasted Coconut
(Forget the crust; just make the filling. Divide it and bake in individual ramekins.)

The Lactose-Free Thanksgiving Menu
(page 302)
serves 8
Roasted Rosemary Fingerling Potatoes
Old-Fashioned Cranberry Sauce
Fennel, Sausage, and Caramelized Apple Stuffing
Smoke-Roasted Turkey Breast with Pomegranate-Thyme Glaze
Brussels Sprouts with Bacon, Garlic, and Shallots
French Apple Tart
(Hold the crème fraîche.)

The Vegan Thanksgiving Menu
(page 307)
serves 8
Roasted Rosemary Fingerling Potatoes
Apple-Cranberry Sauce
Spicy Sautéed Broccoli Rabe with Garlic
Farro, Caramelized Onion, and Wild Mushroom Stuffing
French Apple Tart
(Use a vegan pastry dough—made with vegetable shortening—and leave off the crème fraîche.)

Open-House Menu
(page 351)
serves 10
Whiskey Sour Punch
Warm Spiced Cran-Pom Toddies
Apple–Blue Cheese Chutney
Caramelized Onion Spread
Phyllo-Wrapped Asparagus with Prosciutto
Pork Tenderloin with Herbed Biscuits
Roasted Root Vegetable Salad
Coconut-Cardamom Macaroons
Pistachio and Pine Nut Brittle
Peanut Butter and Chocolate-Dipped Pretzels

RECIPE TITLE INDEX

An alphabetical listing of every recipe title that appeared in the magazine in 2011. See page 402 for the General Recipe Index.

Alicante Turkey Meatballs, 373
Alicante Turkey Soup, 373
All-Purpose Spice Rub, 197
Almendrados (Flourless Almond Cookies), 372
Almost Classic Pork Fried Rice, 38
Ancho Chicken Tacos with Cilantro Slaw and Avocado Cream, 134
Anise-Flavored "Doughnuts," 372
Apple–Blue Cheese Chutney, 353
Apple-Cinnamon Bundt Cake, 328
Apple-Cranberry Sauce, 303
Apple, Goat Cheese, and Pecan Pizza, 295
Apple Iced Tea, 297
Apricot-Fig Chutney, 155
Apricot-Glazed Pork Kebabs, 254
Arctic Char and Vegetables in Parchment Hearts, 61
Arctic Char with Blistered Cherry Tomatoes, 114
Arctic Char with Duxelles and Leeks, 26
Arctic Char with Orange-Caper Relish, 78
Argentinean Pork, 249
Artichoke and Goat Cheese Strata, 60
Artichoke, Spinach, and White Bean Dip, 100
Arugula and Walnut Salad, 106
Arugula Pizza with Poached Eggs, 265
Arugula Salad, 131
Asian-Glazed Chicken Thighs, 70
Asparagus with Balsamic Tomatoes, 111
Avocado-Corn Chowder with Grilled Chicken, 196

Baby Romaine Salad, 109
Bacon and Egg Sandwiches with Caramelized Onions and Arugula, 258
Bacon and Goat Cheese Chicken, 22
Bacon-Cheddar Corn Muffins, 115
Bacon-Corn Chowder with Shrimp, 246
Bacon, Tomato, and Arugula Pizza, 296
Bacony Green Beans, 382
Baja Pork Stir-Fry, 250
Baked Black Beans with Chorizo, 164
Baked Feta with Romesco and Olive Tapenade, 324
Baked Italian-Style Cauliflower, 342
Baked Mac and Cheese, 348
Baked Mozzarella Bites, 246
Baked Pasta with Spinach, Lemon, and Cheese, 59
Baked Shrimp with Tomatoes, 35
Baked Ziti and Summer Veggies, 182
Balsamic-Glazed Green Beans and Pearl Onions, 308
Bananas Foster Parfaits, 346
Barbecue Pulled Chicken Sliders, 79
Barbecued Pork Tenderloin, 255

Basic Crostini, 354
Basil Chicken Meatballs with Ponzu Sauce, 35
Basil Plum Granita, 169
BBQ Chicken and Blue Cheese Pizza, 247
Beef and Butternut Chili, 316
Beef and Mushroom Sloppy Joes, 161
Beef-Broccoli Stir-Fry, 78
Beef Pot Roast with Turnip Greens, 56
Beef Tagine with Butternut Squash, 45
Beef Tenderloin with Cherry–Black Pepper Sauce, 292
Beef Tenderloin with Horseradish-Chive Sauce, 118
Beef Tenderloin with Mushroom–Red Wine Sauce, 27
Beer-Braised Brisket, 286
Beer-Steamed Soft-Shell Clams, 190
Beet, Blood Orange, Kumquat, and Quinoa Salad, 33
Beets with Walnuts, Goat Cheese, and Baby Greens, 91
Beet Wellingtons, 333
Bittersweet Chocolate Cookies, 275
Black Bean and Cheese Enchiladas with Ranchero Sauce, 289
Black Bean and Soy Chili, 368
Black Bean and Sweet Potato Tamales with Tomatillo Sauce, 332
Black Bean Hummus, 80
Black Beans and Yellow Rice, 157
Blackberry Margaritas, 163
Blackened Tilapia Tacos, 63
Black-Eyed Pea and Tomato Salsa, 111
Black-Eyed Peas and Greens, 374
Blue Cheese Polenta with Vegetables, 266
Blue Cheese–Stuffed Pork Chops with Pears, 291
Blueberry Crisp, 192
Blueberry-Peach Ice Pops, 208
Blueberry Thrill, 138
Bombay Shrimp Curry with Coconut Rice, 186
Bourbon-Glazed Chicken, 255
Bourbon-Glazed Peaches with Yogurt, 241
Braised Chicken with Kale, 318
Braised Turkey Roulade with Pancetta, Shallots, and Porcini Gravy, 300
Brazilian Feijoada, 57
Broccoli and Rice Casseroles, 350
Broccoli Rabe with Onions and Pine Nuts, 43
Broiled Herb-Marinated Shrimp Skewers, 52
Broiled Oysters with Garlic-Buttered Breadcrumbs, 50
Broiled Pineapple with Bourbon Caramel over Vanilla Ice Cream, 52
Broiled Tenderloin Steaks with Ginger-Hoisin Glaze, 50

Broiler Garlic Bread, 52
Brown Sugar–Glazed Capon with Bourbon Gravy, 93
Brown Sugar Soufflés with Crème Anglaise, 148
Browned Butter Asparagus, 119
Brussels Sprouts with Bacon, Garlic, and Shallots, 306
Bucatini with Green Peas and Pancetta, 96
Buffalo Chicken, 19
Buffalo Chicken Thighs, 267
Burgers with Blue Cheese Mayo and Sherry Vidalia Onions, 140
Butter Sauce, 190
Butter-Basted Turkey, 302
Buttered Carrots, 350
Buttermilk–Blue Cheese Smashed Potatoes, 267
Buttermilk Bundt Cakes, 364
Buttermilk Mashed Potatoes, 108
Butternut Squash, Caramelized Onion, and Spinach Lasagna, 331
Butternut Squash Risotto, 293

Cabbage Slaw, 164
Cabernet Short Ribs with Parmesan Polenta, 286
Caesar Salad Bagels, 205
Cajun Hot Crab Dip, 326
Cajun-Spiced Smoked Shrimp with Rémoulade, 201
Campari and Orange Sparkling Cocktail, 312
Canola Oil Pound Cake with Browned Butter Glaze, 365
Cantonese-Style Shrimp and Napa Cabbage, 344
Caramelized Onion, Gruyère, and Bacon Spread, 325
Caramelized Onion Mashed Potatoes, 46
Caramelized Onion Spread, 353
Caramelized Onion Tartlets, 357
Caramel-Pecan Dacquoise, 330
Caramel Pork, 77
Carrot Cake, 98
Cashew Rice, 381
Chai Cream Pie, 125
Champagne-Soaked Berries with Whipped Cream, 119
Cheese and Pear Pork, 252
Cheese and Squash Soufflés, 316
Cheese Ravioli with Pesto, 267
Cheesy Chicken Bagel Pizzas, 269
Cheesy Meat Loaf Minis, 47
Cherry-Almond Crisp, 147
Cherry Cheesecake Brownies, 262
Cherry–Wheat Germ Muffins, 116

Chestnut Ice Cream, 356
Chiang Mai Pork Patties, 339
Chicken and Herb White Pizza, 297
Chicken and Sausage Jambalaya, 349
Chicken and Waffle Sandwiches, 377
Chicken and White Bean Soup, 101
Chicken and Wild Rice Soup, 283
Chicken Burgers, 25
Chicken Club Soup, 283
Chicken Cutlets with Creamy Dijon Sauce, 21
Chicken Enchilada Casserole, 74
Chicken Fajitas, 20
Chicken Fried Rice, 62
Chicken Fried Rice with Leeks and Dried
    Cranberries, 39
Chicken Glace, 27
Chicken Gumbo, 282
Chicken Kebabs and Nectarine Salsa, 183
Chicken Larb, 24
Chicken Lettuce Cups, 270
Chicken Meat Loaf, 24
Chicken, Mustard Greens, and Gruyère
    Quesadillas, 100
Chicken Parmesan Burgers, 105
Chicken Puttanesca, 162
Chicken Satay, 181
Chicken Souvlaki Pitas with Tahini Sauce, 65
Chicken Tabbouleh with Tahini Drizzle, 257
Chicken Tacos, 24
Chicken Tostadas and Avocado Dressing, 271
Chicken Verde Stew with Hominy, 37
Chicken with Brussels Sprouts and Mustard
    Sauce, 380
Chicken with Cherry Tomato Sauce, 21
Chicken with Dates, Olives, and
    Cinnamon, 285
Chicken with Italian Sweet-Sour Fennel, 76
Chicken with Mushroom Sauce, 21
Chickpea Chili, 55
Chiles Rellenos Made Easy, 166
Chili-Corn Chip Pie, 282
Chilled Avocado Soup with Seared Chipotle
    Shrimp, 137
Chimichurri Halibut Tacos, 165
Chip-Crusted Fish Fillets, 377
Chipotle-Orange Thighs, 318
Chipotle Pork Tacos, 107
Chipotle-Rubbed Flank Steak, 159
Chocolate Chip Scones, 35
Chocolate–Chocolate Chip Muffins, 115
Chocolate-Granola Apple Wedges, 269
Chocolate Marshmallows, 276
Chocolate Pudding Pops, 208
Chocolate Spider Cupcakes, 275
Choucroute, 252
Ciabatta French Toast with Warm Apple Maple
    Syrup, 259
Ciabatta Stuffing with Chestnuts and
    Raisins, 304
Cider and Sage Pork, 377
Cincinnati 5-Way Chili, 369
Cinnamon-Cider Candied Apples, 274
Citrus Pudding with Whipped Cream, 34
Clam Chowder, 128

Classic Fudge-Walnut Brownies, 262
Classic Meat Loaf, 281
Classic Roast Chicken, 69
Clementine-Date Cake, 33
Clementine Sparkler, 312
Coconut-Cardamom Macaroons, 355
Coconut Chicken Fingers, 23
Coconut Cream Pie, 66
Coconut French Toast with Grilled
    Pineapple, 153
Coffee-Rubbed Texas-Style Brisket, 198
Cognac Sparkling Wine Cocktail, 312
Cold Chicken and Rice Salad, 158
Corn Bread, Chorizo, and Jalapeño
    Dressing, 305
Couscous, 159
Couscous and Pine Nuts, 114
Couscous-Arugula Salad, 379
Couscous-Stuffed Chicken, 22
Crab Cakes and Spicy Mustard Sauce, 272
Crab Toast with Carrot and Scallion, 361
Cranberry-Apple Pie, 311
Cranberry Ketchup, 313
Creamy Buttermilk-Herb Potato Salad, 179
Creamy Chicken Salad, 123
Creamy, Light Macaroni and Cheese, 260
Creamy Linguine with Shrimp and
    Veggies, 158
Creamy Polenta, 76
Crispy Buttermilk Chicken, 23
Crispy Chickpea Salad with Grilled Prawns, 40
Crispy Pork Medallions, 349
Crispy Topped Brussels Sprouts and Cauliflower
    Gratin, 52
Crusty French Boules, 334
Cucumber Gazpacho with Shrimp Relish, 111
Cumin-Spiced Chickpeas and Carrots on
    Couscous, 202
Currant-Glazed Lamb Chops with Pistachio
    Couscous, 376
Curried Chickpea Stew with Brown Rice
    Pilaf, 30
Curried Coconut Mussels, 154
Curried Potato Salad, 144
Curried Turkey, Spinach, and Cashew
    Salad, 314
Curry Chicken Wraps with Nectarine
    Chutney, 142
Curry-Spiced Noodles, 31

Date and Almond Truffles, 94
Dried Cherry-Cranberry Sauce, 303
Drunken Turkey, 374
Duxelles, 25

Easy Braised Brisket, 75
Edamame Salad with Crisp Steak Bits, 150
Endive Spears with Spicy Goat Cheese, 44
Escarole, Bean, and Sausage Soup with
    Parmesan Cheese, 80
Escarole, Sausage, and Fontina
    Quesadillas, 100

Fancy Fish Sticks, 154
Fantastic Bourbon Smoked Chicken, 200
Farfalle with Fava Beans, Morel Mushrooms,
    and Mascarpone, 97
Farro, Caramelized Onion, and Wild Mushroom
    Stuffing, 306
Fennel Salad with Lemon, 68
Fennel, Sausage, and Caramelized Apple
    Stuffing, 305
Fettuccine with Mushrooms and Hazelnuts, 43
Fettuccine with Olive Oil, Garlic, and Red
    Pepper, 106
Fig, Tomato, and Sweet Onion Salad, 143
Fingerling Potato–Leek Hash with Swiss Chard
    and Eggs, 87
Fizzy Plum Bellini, 167
Flank Steak Tacos, 163
Flank Steak with Romesco Sauce, 376
Flank Steak with Spicy Lemon Sauce, 134
Four-Herb Green Goddess Dressing, 138
Frangipane Pear Tarts, 278
French Apple Tart, 310
French Onion and Apple Soup, 62
French Toast Peanut Butter and Jelly, 266
Fresh Cherry Cheesecake Bars, 180
Fresh Lima Beans, 244
Fresh Pea and Garlic Gazpacho, 129
Fresh Raspberry Lemonade, 192
Fried Rice with Sweet Soy Sauce, 204
Frisée and Arugula Salad, 78
Frozen Orange Tortes with Cranberry
    Compote, 330
Fusilli with Caramelized Spring Onions and
    White Wine, 95

Garbanzo Beans and Greens, 42
Garganelli with Asparagus and Pecorino
    Cheese, 95
Garlic-Basil Corn, 132
Garlic Breadsticks, 349
Garlicky Leg of Lamb with Yogurt Sauce, 102
Garlicky Spinach-Sausage Gratin, 291
Gemelli Salad with Green Beans, Pistachios,
    and Lemon-Thyme Vinaigrette, 127
Ginger Pumpkin Pie with Toasted
    Coconut, 312
Ginger-Scented Corn and Asparagus
    Stir-Fry, 204
Golden Beet Salad with Wheat Berries and
    Pumpkinseed Vinaigrette, 145
Granola with Honey-Scented Yogurt and Baked
    Figs, 256
Grapefruit-Buttermilk Sherbet, 33
Greek Chicken Thighs, 318
Greek Lamb Chops and Mint Yogurt
    Sauce, 133
Greek-Style Chicken, 24
Greek Yogurt with Warm Black and Blueberry
    Sauce, 185
Green Bean Casserole with Madeira
    Mushrooms, 307
Green Beans with Shallots and Hazelnuts, 94
Green Beans with Toasted Garlic, 185
Green Chile Chili, 42

Green Chile Tamale Pie, 71
Green Curry with Bok Choy, 30
Greens and Sherry Vinaigrette, 298
Greens with Golden Raisins, 121
Grill-Braised Clams and Chorizo in Tomato-
    Saffron Broth, 139
Grilled Apricot Halves, 156
Grilled Char with Yukon Golds and Tomato–
    Red Onion Relish, 140
Grilled Chicken Caesar Salad, 344
Grilled Chicken Sliders and Apricot Chutney
    Spread, 161
Grilled Chicken Thighs with Pineapple, Corn,
    and Bell Pepper Relish, 247
Grilled Chicken with Bourbon Peach
    Butter, 194
Grilled Chicken with Cola Sauce, 255
Grilled Chicken Wraps, 157
Grilled Corn on the Cob, 191
Grilled Corn on the Cob with Roasted Jalapeño
    Butter, 145
Grilled Farmers' Market Sandwiches, 152
Grilled Flank Steak with Onions, Avocado, and
    Tomatoes, 156
Grilled Gruyère and Olive Tapenade
    Sandwiches, 265
Grilled King Salmon with Tomato-Peach
    Salsa, 186
Grilled Lamb Chops and Mint Chimichurri 108
Grilled Maine Lobsters, 191
Grilled Peaches, 184
Grilled Pineapple-Avocado Salsa, 164
Grilled Pizza with Prosciutto, Arugula, and
    Lemon, 142
Grilled Pork Salad, 254
Grilled Portobello and Poblano Tacos with Pico
    de Gallo, 290
Grilled Romaine with Creamy Herb
    Dressing, 173
Grilled Scallop Salad, 243
Grilled Steak with Onions and Scallions, 181
Grilled Stuffed Jalapeños, 174
Grilled Vegetable Gazpacho, 174
Grilled Zucchini Caprese Sandwiches, 207
Grilled Zucchini with Sea Salt, 268
Guacamole, 161
Guinness Lamb Stew, 37

Ham and Pineapple Pizza Subs, 343
Ham and Swiss Egg Sandwiches, 247
Hawaiian Chicken, 20
Healthy Wheat Nachos, 376
Herb and Citrus Roast Leg of Lamb, 360
Herb and Goat Cheese–Stuffed Chicken
    Breasts, 108
Herb-Crusted Chicken and Parsley Orzo, 43
Herb-Crusted Rack of Lamb, 103
Herb-Glazed Carrots, 27
Herbed Chicken, 19
Herbed Chicken Salad Sandwiches, 206
Herbed Couscous, 184
Herbed Green Beans, 76
Herbed Shrimp and White Bean Salad, 242
Honey-Glazed Almonds, 345

Honey-Orange Marshmallows, 276
Honey-Wheat Pizza with Pear-Prosciutto
    Salad, 279
Hungarian Goulash, 251
Iced Sugar Cookies, 362
Indian-Spiced Lentils and Lamb, 291
Indian-Spiced Pork with Raita, 250
Indian-Spiced Roasted Squash Soup, 318
Israeli Carrots, 93
Italian Beef Stew, 36
Italian-Seasoned Roast Chicken Breasts, 69
Italian-Style Beef with Polenta, 282

Jalapeño-Lime Slaw, 179

Kabocha Squash Puree, 317
Kid-tastic Pizzadillas, 245

Lamb Chops and Cilantro Relish, 244
Lemon-Almond Soufflés, 149
Lemon Broccolini, 47
Lemon Chicken Soup with Dumplings, 92
Lemon Cream Pie, 124
Lemon-Gin Sparkling Cocktails, 117
Lemon-Parmesan Broccoli, 295
Lemongrass Tofu Banh Mi, 151
Lemony Arugula Salad, 298
Lemony Chicken Saltimbocca, 43
Lemony Cucumber Salad, 179
Libanais Breakfast, 40
Limoncello Pops, 207
Linguine with Clams and Fresh Herbs, 109
Linguine with Easy Meat Sauce, 295
Linguine with Quick Lemon Ricotta, 245
Linguine with Two-Cheese Sauce, 185
Local Farmers' Market Pizza, 172
Lump Crab–Stuffed Trout, 53

Mango-Coconut Sherbet, 153
Mango-Ginger Parfaits, 195
Maple-Bourbon Pecan Pie, 310
Maple-Brined Pork, 245
Maple-Cider Brined Turkey with Bourbon-
    Cider Gravy, 302
Maple-Gingerbread Pots de Crème, 330
Maple-Mustard Chicken Thighs, 130
Maple-Mustard Glazed Fresh Ham, 358
Margarita Ice-Cream Sandwiches, 147
Marinated Lamb Chops, 103
Marinated Peppers and Mozzarella, 264
Marinated Shrimp Salad, 178
Market Salad with Goat Cheese and
    Champagne-Shallot Vinaigrette, 171
Mashed Chickpea Pitas, 294
Mashed Potato Casserole, 309
Mediterranean Barley with Chickpeas &
    Arugula, 84
Mediterranean Chicken, 22
Melon Gazpacho with Frizzled Prosciutto, 196
Mexican Chicken Casserole with Charred
    Tomato Salsa, 48
Mexican Chocolate Cream Pie, 124
Mexican Rice, 271
Mexican Stuffed Poblanos, 290

Meyer Lemon Chicken Piccata, 67
Meyer Lemon Curd Tart, 68
Microwave Smashed Potatoes, 162
Migas con Salsa Verde, 289
Mini Farfalle with Roasted Peppers, Onions,
    Feta, and Mint, 79
Minted Lemon-Lime Watermelon Agua
    Fresca, 138
Mixed Greens and Avocado Salad, 194
Mixed Greens Salad, 182
Mixed Seafood Salad, 113
Monkey Bread, 288
Moroccan Shepherd's Pie, 74
Moroccan-Style Lamb and Chickpeas, 379
Mozzarella Omelet with Sage and Red Chile
    Flakes, 258
Mushroom and Root Vegetable Potpie, 58
Mushroom, Corn, and Poblano Tacos, 345

New Potatoes with Onions and Spicy
    Sausage, 191
New Potatoes with Parsley and Saffron, 121
Nutty Rice, 46

Oatmeal-Crusted Chicken, 23
Old-Fashioned Cranberry Sauce, 303
Onion Tart, 106
Open-Faced Blackened Catfish
    Sandwiches, 159
Open-Faced Prosciutto and Plum
    Sandwiches, 184
Open-Faced Smoked Salmon Sandwiches, 321
Orange and Avocado Salsa, 325
Orecchiette with Peas, Shrimp, and Buttermilk-
    Herb Dressing, 141
Orzo Salad with Radish and Fennel, 96
Orzo Salad with Spicy Buttermilk
    Dressing, 127
Orzo with Spinach, 270
Out-N-In California Burger, 64

Paella with Poblanos, Corn, and Clams, 122
Paella with Soy Chorizo and Edamame, 85
Pan-Fried Shrimp with Creole
    Mayonnaise, 183
Pan-Fried Trout with Tomato Basil Sauté, 268
Pan-Roasted Fish with Mediterranean Tomato
    Sauce, 321
Pan-Seared Chicken with Tomato-Olive
    Relish, 344
Pan-Seared Strip Steak, 88
Pappardelle with Baby Spinach, Herbs, and
    Ricotta, 96
Parmesan-Coated Potato Wedges, 309
Parmesan Polenta and Spicy Sausage Sauce, 133
Pasta Puttanesca, 130
Pasta with Fresh Tomato Sauce and Clams, 170
Peach and Gorgonzola Chicken Pizza, 131
Peanut Butter and Chocolate–Dipped
    Pretzels, 355
Peanut Butter and Dark Chocolate Fudge, 324
Peanut Butter Caramel Corn, 274

Peanut Butter Cup Blondies, 263
Peanut-Sauced Chicken Pitas, 205
Pear and Gruyère Strata, 277
Pear Chutney Bruschetta with Pecans and Blue
    Cheese, 278
Pecan Chicken, 23
Pecan-Crusted Pork Noisettes, 251
Pepper Pork, 253
Peppered Flank Steak and Salsa, 243
Pepperoni, Onion, and Olive Pizza, 298
Phyllo-Wrapped Asparagus with
    Prosciutto, 354
Pickled Cranberries, 313
Pickled Onion, Blue Cheese, and Berry
    Salad, 118
Pickled Ramps and Asparagus, 104
Picnic-Perfect Lobster Rolls, 188
Pimiento Cheese Chicken, 22
Piña Colada Sorbet, 146
Pineapple Chicken Satay, 162
Pineapple Musubi Rolls, 322
Pistachio and Pine Nut Brittle, 355
Pistachio-Chai Muffins, 116
Pizza Supreme, 63
Plank-Grilled Salmon with Grape Relish, 153
Plum Kuchen, 167
Poached Halibut with Lemon-Herb Sauce, 34
Poached Pears, 296
Pomegranate Fizz, 313
Pork Chops with Caribbean Rub and Mango
    Salsa, 294
Pork Chops with Cherry Couscous, 181
Pork Chops with Grits and Red-Eye
    Gravy, 380
Pork Posole, 73
Pork Roulade, 253
Pork Salad Provençal, 131
Pork Satay with Peanut Sauce, 255
Pork Tenderloin Medallions and Balsamic
    Reduction, 184
Pork Tenderloin with Herbed Biscuits, 354
Pork Tenderloin with Orange Compote, 253
Pork Tenderloin with Red and Yellow Bell
    Peppers, 44
Pork Tenderloin with Tangy Grape Salad, 249
Pork with Figs and Farro, 252
Potato-Crusted Chicken Fingers, 292
Potato Gratin with Duxelles, 26
Potato-Gruyère Tartlets, 358
Prosciutto Pizza with Tangy White
    Sauce, 336
Provençal Beef Daube, 57
Pulled Pork Sandwiches with Mustard
    Sauce, 198
Pumpkin-Almond Cheesecake, 328

Quick Pastitsio, 280
Quick Shrimp Chowder, 162
Quick White Bean, Asparagus, and Mushroom
    Cassoulet, 86
Quicker Cassoulet, 375
Quince Tart with Pine Nut Caramel Glaze, 311
Quinoa and Roasted Pepper Chili, 369

Quinoa Salad with Artichokes and Parsley, 92
Quinoa-Stuffed Squash, 315

Radish and Fennel Salad, 107
Radish-Squash Slaw, 77
Radish-Yogurt Dip and Pita Wedges, 244
Radishes with Iceberg and Herb Butter, 361
Raspberry-Walnut Cranberry Sauce, 303
Real Bagels, 336
Red Flannel Hash, 71
Red Pepper Couscous, 109
Rice and Beans with Chicken and Chorizo, 326
Rice and Green Peas with Shrimp Butter, 28
Rice Noodle Salad, 203
Rich Chocolate Babka, 335
Rich Chocolate Pudding Pie, 146
Roast Beef Sandwiches with Watercress
    Slaw, 135
Roast Pork Tenderloin with Plum Barbecue
    Sauce, 168
Roast Pork with Potatoes and Butternut
    Squash, 249
Roasted Asparagus, 272
Roasted Asparagus and Tomato Penne Salad
    with Goat Cheese, 126
Roasted Asparagus with Browned Butter, 69
Roasted Banana Pudding, 202
Roasted Chile-Garlic Broccoli, 120
Roasted Eggplant Salsa, 340
Roasted Oysters with Pancetta and
    Breadcrumbs, 327
Roasted Pork Tenderloin and Maple-Glazed
    Apples, 248
Roasted Root Vegetables, 349
Roasted Root Vegetable Salad, 354
Roasted Rosemary Fingerling Potatoes, 310
Roasted Shrimp and Broccoli, 132
Roasted Summer Squash with Parsley, 160
Roasted Sweet Potato Salad with Cranberry-
    Chipotle Dressing, 285
Roasted Turkey with Rosemary-Garlic Butter
    Rub and Pan Gravy, 301
Roasted Vegetable and Ricotta Pizza, 82
Romano and Herb Rubbed Turkey with Pan
    Gravy, 359
Rosemary-Dijon Crusted Standing Rib
    Roast, 360
Rosemary–Green Peppercorn Mignonette, 327
Rosemary Potatoes, 381
Rotini with White Beans and Escarole, 264

Salad with Balsamic Vinaigrette, 47
Salmon and Bok Choy, 268
Salmon Sandwiches, 110
Salmon with Red Pepper Pesto, 293
Salsa Verde, 264
Salted Caramel Brownies, 263
Sausage and Egg Burrito, 130
Sausage Ragu over Creamy Polenta, 375
Sautéed Brussels Sprouts with Bacon, 81
Sautéed Chicken with Sage Browned Butter, 20
Sautéed Flounder and Spicy Rémoulade, 382
Sautéed Halibut with Romesco Sauce, 46
Sautéed Shrimp with Sherry and Chiles, 112

Sautéed Spinach and Pine Nuts, 134
Sautéed Tilapia Tacos with Grilled Peppers and
    Onion, 193
Savory Baked Apples, 342
Savory Bread Puddings with Ham and
    Cheddar, 260
Savory Sausage, Spinach & Onion
    Turnovers, 83
Scallion Couscous, 45
Scallops with Spinach and Paprika Syrup, 110
Seared Scallops with Cauliflower Puree, 77
Seared Scallops with Lemony Sweet Pea
    Relish, 128
Seared Scallops with Meyer Lemon Beurre
    Blanc, 68
Serrano, Manchego, and Apple Sandwiches, 279
Sesame Albacore Tuna, 114
Sesame Beef Stir-Fry, 344
Sesame-Miso Cucumber Salad, 135
Shaved Fennel Salad with Orange, Green
    Olives, and Pistachios, 284
Shaved Summer Squash Salad with Prosciutto
    Crisps, 144
Shredded Chicken Tacos with Tomatoes and
    Grilled Corn, 195
Shrimp and Arugula Salad, 163
Shrimp, Avocado, and Grapefruit Salad, 374
Shrimp Butter, 27
Shrimp Cobb Salad, 134
Shrimp Fettuccine Alfredo, 271
Shrimp Korma and Basmati Rice, 160
Shrimp Pad Thai, 64
Shrimp Sautéed with Broccolini, 28
Simmered Cabbage, Shan Style, 341
Simple Lobster Risotto, 41
Sirloin Skewers with Grilled Vegetable
    Couscous and Fiery Pepper Sauce, 177
Skillet Pork Chop Sauté with Peaches, 161
Sloppy Joe Sliders, 346
Slow-Roasted Lamb Shanks, 104
Slow-Roasted Tomato Pasta, 97
Slow-Roasted Turkey with Cream Gravy, 300
Slow-Simmered Meat Sauce, 56
Smoke-Roasted Turkey Breast with
    Pomegranate-Thyme Glaze, 299
Smoked Oysters with Olive Relish, 198
Smoked Potato Salad, 199
Smoked Salmon and Egg Sandwich, 29
Smoked Salmon in Cucumber Boats, 361
Smoky Asparagus and Mushroom Sauté, 105
Smoky Baked Beans with Chorizo, 144
Smoky Pan-Grilled Pork Chops, 46
Smoky Potato Pancakes, 42
Smoky Shrimp and Chicken Gumbo, 347
Smoky Three-Bean Bake, 180
Snapper in Tomato Broth, 44
South-of-the-Border Cranberry Sauce, 303
Southwestern White Bean Pita Pockets, 101
Soy and Cola–Braised Pork Shoulder, 287
Soy-Ginger Sesame Pork, 250
Spaghetti Bolognese, 73
Spanish Pork with Apple-Citrus Salsa, 249
Spanish Rice Salad, 120
Spanish-Style Cod in Tomato Broth, 345

Sparkling Apricot Sorbet, 156
Sparkling Meyer Lemon Cocktail, 67
Sparkling Peach Sangria, 241
Sparkling Pear Cocktail, 313
Sparkling Strawberry Pops, 207
Spice-Rubbed Flank Steak with Fresh Salsa, 176
Spiced Cinnamon Rolls with Maple Glaze, 317
Spiced Lamb Kebabs, 129
Spiced Lamb with Plum Sauce, 326
Spicy Asian Chicken and Noodle Soup, 268
Spicy Caramel Brownies, 323
Spicy Crab-Papaya Salad, 72
Spicy North African Pork Tenderloin, 248
Spicy Sausage and Mushroom Pizza, 297
Spicy Sautéed Broccoli Rabe with Garlic, 307
Spicy-Sweet Glazed Chicken, 256
Spicy Tortilla Soup with Shrimp and Avocado, 79
Spicy Tortilla Strips, 325
Spinach and Blue Cheese Chicken, 22
Spinach and Parmesan Soufflés, 149
Spinach, Endive, and Tangelo Salad, 32
Spinach, Pasta, and Pea Soup, 294
Spinach Salad, 348
Spinach with Garlic Vinaigrette, 44
Spinach with Toasted Almonds, 160
Sponge Cake with Orange Curd and Strawberries, 94
Spring Risotto, 106
Steak Baguettes with Pesto Mayo, 205
Steak with Cucumber-Radish Salad, 110
Steamed Clams with White Wine and Tomatoes, 343
Stewed Okra and Fresh Tomato, 159
Stir-Fried Chinese Egg Noodles, 266
Stir-Fried Rice Noodles with Beef and Spinach, 85
Stone Fruit Cobbler, 169
Strawberry-Avocado Salsa with Cinnamon Tortilla Chips, 135
Striped Bass with Cilantro-Onion Salad, 112
Stuffed Cuban Pork Tenderloin, 194
Stuffed Zucchini with Cheesy Breadcrumbs, 145
Summer Lemon-Vegetable Risotto, 172
Summer Pea, Watermelon, and Farro Salad, 193
Summer Squash, Bacon, and Mozzarella Quiche, 188
Summer Tomato, Feta, and Basil Galette, 143
Summer Tomato, Mozzarella, and Basil Panini with Balsamic Syrup, 247
Summer Veggie Pizza, 244
Sun-Dried Tomato Palmiers, 356
Sweet and Sour Chicken, 21
Sweet and Spicy Pumpkinseeds, 377
Sweet Onion Casserole, 129
Sweet Potato Pie with Spiced Cream Topping, 322
Sweet & Sour Plum Quencher, 167
Sweet Soy Sauce, 204
Swiss Chard with Crème Fraîche, 308

Tabbouleh Salad, 178
Tacos Al Pastor with Grilled Pineapple Salsa, 254
Tagine-Style Pork with Squash and Pearl Onions, 251
Tamarind Pork with Pineapple-Ginger Chutney, 72
Tandoori-Spiced Chicken, 19
Tangy Coffee Barbecue Sauce, 177
Tangy Cranberry Tea, 313
Tangy Ice Cream with Cashew Brittle, 323
Tarragon Carrots and Peas, 78
Tempeh and Green Bean Stir-Fry with Peanut Sauce, 86
Tempeh Greek Salad Wraps, 151
Tequila-Glazed Grilled Chicken Thighs, 141
Tequila Pork with Tomatillo Guacamole, 250
Thai Beef Cabbage Cups, 281
Thai Cashew Brittle, 274
Thai Chicken Salad with Peanut Dressing, 84
Thai Coconut Chicken, 19
Thai Curry Stew with Turkey and Zucchini, 314
Thai Sticky Rice, 337
Toasted Chickpea and Apricot Salad, 150
Toasted Parmesan Pita Crisps, 325
Tofu Steaks with Shiitakes and Veggies, 381
Tomato and Arugula Salad, 272
Tomato–Baby Bell Pepper Tartlets, 357
Tomato, Cucumber, and Fennel Salad, 183
Tomato Panzanella with Shrimp and Basil, 171
Tomato-Parsley Salad, 133
Tomato Soup with Roasted Chickpeas, 246
Tomato Toast, 242
Tortilla Meatball Soup, 280
Triple-Chocolate Cake, 329
Tropical Sherbet, 73
Truffled Pommes Anna, 308
Truffled Roasted Potatoes, 118
Tuna and White Bean Salad, 101
Tuna-Fennel Pasta Salad, 272
Tuna Melts with Avocado, 157
Turkey-Saffron Stock, 373
Turkey Sausage, Mushroom, and Potato Gratin, 342
Turkey Tenders, 60
Tuscan Lemon Muffins, 115
Tuscan-Style New York Strip with Arugula-Artichoke Salad, 175
Twice-Roasted Sweet Potatoes with Chipotle, 309
Two-Bean Toss, 243

Udon Noodle Salad with Broccolini and Spicy Tofu, 126

Vanilla Cupcakes with Vanilla Bean Frosting, 363
Vegetable and Steak Fajitas with "Killed" Jalapeños, 122
Vegetable Korma, 74
Vegetarian Country Captain, 32

Vegetarian Moussaka, 59
Vietnamese Salad, 250

Waldorf Salad with Steel-Cut Oats, 257
Walnut-Breadcrumb Pasta with a Soft Egg, 29
Warm Potato Salad with Ramps and Bacon, 105
Warm Spiced Cran-Pom Toddies, 353
Warm White Beans with Roasted Fennel, 283
Watermelon-Jalapeño Ice Pops, 146
Whiskey Sour Punch, 353
White Bean and Hominy Chili, 369
White Bean and Sage Pita Burgers, 152
White Beans with Prosciutto, 378
White Pizza with Tomato and Basil, 80
Whole Roasted Endives with Pear, Arugula, and Walnut Salad, 277
Whole-Wheat Buttermilk Pancakes with Orange Sauce, 320
Wild Rice Salad, 184
Wild Rice Stuffing with Dried Cherries and Toasted Pecans, 306
Wild Mushroom Pastitsio, 333
Wilted Spinach, 380

Yakitori, 142
Yellow Plum Salad, 168
Yogurt-Marinated Chicken with Beet Salad, 41

Zesty Green Goddess Dip, 325
Zingy Chimichurri, 177
Zucchini Angel Hair Pancake, 241

MONTH-BY-MONTH INDEX

A month-by-month listing of every food story with recipe titles that appeared in the magazine in 2011. See page 402 for the General Recipe Index.

January/February

Breakfast, Lunch & Dinner in Vancouver, 39
  Crispy Chickpea Salad with Grilled Prawns, 40
  Libanais Breakfast, 40
  Yogurt-Marinated Chicken with Beet Salad, 41
Chicken Breasts 25 Ways, 19
  Bacon and Goat Cheese Chicken, 22
  Buffalo Chicken, 19
  Chicken Burgers, 25
  Chicken Cutlets with Creamy Dijon Sauce, 21
  Chicken Fajitas, 20
  Chicken Larb, 24
  Chicken Meat Loaf, 24
  Chicken Tacos, 24
  Chicken with Cherry Tomato Sauce, 21
  Chicken with Mushroom Sauce, 21
  Coconut Chicken Fingers, 23
  Couscous-Stuffed Chicken, 22
  Crispy Buttermilk Chicken, 23
  Greek-Style Chicken, 24
  Hawaiian Chicken, 20
  Herbed Chicken, 19
  Mediterranean Chicken, 22
  Oatmeal-Crusted Chicken, 23
  Pecan Chicken, 23
  Pimiento Cheese Chicken, 22
  Sautéed Chicken with Sage Browned Butter, 20
  Spinach and Blue Cheese Chicken, 22
  Sweet and Sour Chicken, 21
  Tandoori-Spiced Chicken, 19
  Thai Coconut Chicken, 19
The Comfort of Curries, 30
  Curried Chickpea Stew with Brown Rice Pilaf, 30
  Curry-Spiced Noodles, 31
  Green Curry with Bok Choy, 30
  Vegetarian Country Captain, 32
Dinner Tonight, 45
  Beef Tagine with Butternut Squash, 45
  Caramelized Onion Mashed Potatoes, 46
  Cheesy Meat Loaf Minis, 47
  Lemon Broccolini, 47
  Nutty Rice, 46
  Sautéed Halibut with Romesco Sauce, 46
  Salad with Balsamic Vinaigrette, 47
  Scallion Couscous, 45
  Smoky Pan-Grilled Pork Chops, 46
Eggs, 29
  Smoked Salmon and Egg Sandwich, 29
  Walnut-Breadcrumb Pasta with a Soft Egg, 29
Feed 4 for Less Than $10, 42
  Garbanzo Beans and Greens, 42
  Green Chile Chili, 42
  Smoky Potato Pancakes, 42

5-Ingredient Cooking, 41
  Simple Lobster Risotto, 41
Fried Brown Rice, 38
  Almost Classic Pork Fried Rice, 38
  Chicken Fried Rice with Leeks and Dried Cranberries, 39
From Your Kitchen to Ours, 34
  Baked Shrimp with Tomatoes, 35
  Basil Chicken Meatballs with Ponzu Sauce, 35
  Chocolate Chip Scones, 35
Mexican Casserole, Two-Thirds Lighter!, 47
  Mexican Chicken Casserole with Charred Tomato Salsa, 48
OOPS! You Burn the Brown Butter, 49
  Don't cross the thin line between nutty and bitter, 49
Superfast, 43
  Endive Spears with Spicy Goat Cheese, 44
  Fettuccine with Mushrooms and Hazelnuts, 43
  Herb-Crusted Chicken and Parsley Orzo, 43
  Lemony Chicken Saltimbocca, 43
  Pork Tenderloin with Red and Yellow Bell Peppers, 44
  Snapper in Tomato Broth, 44
  Spinach with Garlic Vinaigrette, 44
3 Little Secrets for Big Flavors, 25
  Arctic Char with Duxelles and Leeks, 26
  Beef Tenderloin with Mushroom–Red Wine Sauce, 27
  Chicken Glace, 27
  Duxelles, 25
  Herb-Glazed Carrots, 27
  Potato Gratin with Duxelles, 26
  Rice and Green Peas with Shrimp Butter, 28
  Shrimp Butter, 27
  Shrimp Sautéed with Broccolini, 28
Today's Lesson: Stews, 36
  Chicken Verde Stew with Hominy, 37
  Guinness Lamb Stew, 37
  Italian Beef Stew, 36
The Winter Warmth of Citrus, 32
  Beet, Blood Orange, Kumquat, and Quinoa Salad, 33
  Citrus Pudding with Whipped Cream, 34
  Clementine-Date Cake, 33
  Grapefruit-Buttermilk Sherbet, 33
  Poached Halibut with Lemon-Herb Sauce, 34
  Spinach, Endive, and Tangelo Salad, 32

March

Comforting Casseroles, 58
  Artichoke and Goat Cheese Strata, 60
  Baked Pasta with Spinach, Lemon, and Cheese, 59

Mushroom and Root Vegetable Potpie, 58
  Vegetarian Moussaka, 59
The Completely Dreamy Coconut Cream Pie, 65
  Coconut Cream Pie, 66
The Delicious Pleasures of Slow Cooking, 55
  Beef Pot Roast with Turnip Greens, 56
  Brazilian Feijoada, 57
  Chickpea Chili, 55
  Provençal Beef Daube, 57
  Slow-Simmered Meat Sauce, 56
Dinner Tonight, 76
  Arctic Char with Orange-Caper Relish, 78
  Caramel Pork, 77
  Chicken with Italian Sweet-Sour Fennel, 76
  Creamy Polenta, 76
  Frisée and Arugula Salad, 78
  Herbed Green Beans, 76
  Radish-Squash Slaw, 77
  Seared Scallops with Cauliflower Puree, 77
  Tarragon Carrots and Peas, 78
Feed 4 for Less Than $10, 73
  Chicken Enchilada Casserole, 74
  Moroccan Shepherd's Pie, 74
  Pork Posole, 73
  Spaghetti Bolognese, 73
  Vegetable Korma, 74
5-Ingredient Cooking, 75
  Easy Braised Brisket, 75
From Your Kitchen to Ours, 60
  Arctic Char and Vegetables in Parchment Hearts, 61
  French Onion and Apple Soup, 62
  Turkey Tenders, 60
Hamburger Has a New Helper, 71
  Green Chile Tamale Pie, 71
  Red Flannel Hash, 71
A Little Ode to the Other Lemon, 67
  Fennel Salad with Lemon, 68
  Meyer Lemon Chicken Piccata, 67
  Meyer Lemon Curd Tart, 68
  Roasted Asparagus with Browned Butter, 69
  Seared Scallops with Meyer Lemon Beurre Blanc, 68
  Sparkling Meyer Lemon Cocktail, 67
OOPS! Your Bacon Is Burned and Crinkly, 81
  There's a surefire way to avoid those tangled ribbons: Bake your bacon, 81
Superfast, 78
  Barbecue Pulled Chicken Sliders, 79
  Beef-Broccoli Stir-Fry, 78
  Black Bean Hummus, 80
  Escarole, Bean, and Sausage Soup with Parmesan Cheese, 80
  Mini Farfalle with Roasted Peppers, Onions, Feta, and Mint, 79
  Sautéed Brussels Sprouts with Bacon, 81

Spicy Tortilla Soup with Shrimp and
  Avocado, 79
White Pizza with Tomato and Basil, 80
Takeout Makeovers, 62
  Blackened Tilapia Tacos, 63
  Chicken Fried Rice, 62
  Chicken Souvlaki Pitas with Tahini
    Sauce, 65
  Out-N-In California Burger, 64
  Pizza Supreme, 63
  Shrimp Pad Thai, 64
Today's Lesson: Roast Chicken, 69
  Asian-Glazed Chicken Thighs, 70
  Classic Roast Chicken, 69
  Italian-Seasoned Roast Chicken
    Breasts, 69
Tropical Fruit, 72
  Spicy Crab-Papaya Salad, 72
  Tamarind Pork with Pineapple-Ginger
    Chutney, 72
  Tropical Sherbet, 73
Your Secret Element, 50
  Broiled Herb-Marinated Shrimp
    Skewers, 52
  Broiled Oysters with Garlic-Buttered
    Breadcrumbs, 50
  Broiled Pineapple with Bourbon Caramel
    over Vanilla Ice Cream, 52
  Broiled Tenderloin Steaks with Ginger-
    Hoisin Glaze, 50
  Broiler Garlic Bread, 52
  Crispy Topped Brussels Sprouts and
    Cauliflower Gratin, 53
  Lump Crab–Stuffed Trout, 53

April

Carrot Cake, 1,000 Calories Lighter!, 98
  Carrot Cake, 98
A Celebration of Traditions, 91
  Beets with Walnuts, Goat Cheese, and
    Baby Greens, 91
  Brown Sugar–Glazed Capon with Bourbon
    Gravy, 93
  Date and Almond Truffles, 94
  Green Beans with Shallots and
    Hazelnuts, 94
  Israeli Carrots, 93
  Lemon Chicken Soup with Dumplings, 92
  Quinoa Salad with Artichokes and
    Parsley, 92
  Sponge Cake with Orange Curd and
    Strawberries, 94
Dinner Tonight, 107
  Baby Romaine Salad, 109
  Buttermilk Mashed Potatoes, 108
  Chipotle Pork Tacos, 107
  Grilled Lamb Chops and Mint
    Chimichurri, 108
  Herb and Goat Cheese–Stuffed Chicken
    Breasts, 108
  Linguine with Clams and Fresh
    Herbs, 109
  Radish and Fennel Salad, 107
  Red Pepper Couscous, 109
Feed 4 for Less Than $10, 106
  Arugula and Walnut Salad, 106
  Fettuccine with Olive Oil, Garlic, and Red
    Pepper, 106

Onion Tart, 106
Spring Risotto, 106
From Your Kitchen to Ours, 105
  Chicken Parmesan Burgers, 105
The Glorious Noodles of Spring, 95
  Bucatini with Green Peas and Pancetta, 96
  Farfalle with Fava Beans, Morel
    Mushrooms, and Mascarpone, 97
  Fusilli with Caramelized Spring Onions
    and White Wine, 95
  Garganelli with Asparagus and Pecorino
    Cheese, 95
  Orzo Salad with Radish and Fennel, 96
  Pappardelle with Baby Spinach, Herbs, and
    Ricotta, 96
Grass Versus Grain, 88
  Pan-Seared Strip Steak, 88
OOPS! Your Green Veggies Turn Brown, 109
  Baby them a bit, and your bright spring
    vegetables will stay vibrant, 109
The Perfect Dish to Pair with Chianti, 97
  Slow-Roasted Tomato Pasta, 97
Quesadillas, Done Better, 99
  Chicken, Mustard Greens, and Gruyère
    Quesadillas, 100
  Escarole, Sausage, and Fontina
    Quesadillas, 100
Start with a Can of White Beans, 100
  Artichoke, Spinach, and White Bean
    Dip, 100
  Chicken and White Bean Soup, 101
  Southwestern White Bean Pita
    Pockets, 101
  Tuna and White Bean Salad, 101
Store-Bought Shortcuts for Easy, Home-
    Cooked Meals, 82
  Mediterranean Barley with Chickpeas &
    Arugula, 84
  Roasted Vegetable and Ricotta Pizza, 82
  Savory Sausage, Spinach & Onion
    Turnovers, 83
  Stir-Fried Rice Noodles with Beef and
    Spinach, 85
  Thai Chicken Salad with Peanut
    Dressing, 84
Superfast, 110
  Asparagus with Balsamic Tomatoes, 111
  Black-Eyed Pea and Tomato Salsa, 111
  Cucumber Gazpacho with Shrimp
    Relish, 111
  Salmon Sandwiches, 110
  Scallops with Spinach and Paprika
    Syrup, 110
  Steak with Cucumber-Radish Salad, 110
Tastes of Spring, 104
  Pickled Ramps and Asparagus, 104
  Smoky Asparagus and Mushroom
    Sauté, 105
  Warm Potato Salad with Ramps and
    Bacon, 105
Today's Lesson: Roast Lamb, 102
  Garlicky Leg of Lamb with Yogurt
    Sauce, 102
  Herb-Crusted Rack of Lamb, 103
  Marinated Lamb Chops, 103
  Slow-Roasted Lamb Shanks, 104
Veggie Skillet Suppers, 85
  Fingerling Potato–Leek Hash with Swiss
    Chard and Eggs, 87

Paella with Soy Chorizo and Edamame, 85
Quick White Bean, Asparagus, and
  Mushroom Cassoulet, 86
Tempeh and Green Bean Stir-Fry with
  Peanut Sauce, 86

May

The Amazing One-Hour Dinner Party, 117
  Beef Tenderloin with Horseradish-Chive
    Sauce, 118
  Browned Butter Asparagus, 119
  Champagne-Soaked Berries with Whipped
    Cream, 119
  Lemon-Gin Sparkling Cocktails, 117
  Pickled Onion, Blue Cheese, and Berry
    Salad, 118
  Truffled Roasted Potatoes, 118
Dinner Tonight, 131
  Arugula Salad, 131
  Garlic-Basil Corn, 132
  Greek Lamb Chops and Mint Yogurt
    Sauce, 133
  Parmesan Polenta and Spicy Sausage
    Sauce, 133
  Peach and Gorgonzola Chicken Pizza, 131
  Roasted Shrimp and Broccoli, 132
  Sautéed Spinach and Pine Nuts, 134
  Tomato-Parsley Salad, 133
Feed 4 for Less Than $10, 130
  Maple-Mustard Chicken Thighs, 130
  Pasta Puttanesca, 130
  Pork Salad Provençal, 131
  Sausage and Egg Burrito, 130
Five Munchable Muffins, 115
  Bacon-Cheddar Corn Muffins, 115
  Cherry–Wheat Germ Muffins, 116
  Chocolate–Chocolate Chip Muffins, 115
  Pistachio-Chai Muffins, 116
  Tuscan Lemon Muffins, 115
5-Ingredient Cooking, 129
  Spiced Lamb Kebabs, 129
From Your Kitchen to Ours, 129
  Sweet Onion Casserole, 129
Heating Things Up with a Few Fresh
    Chiles, 121
  Paella with Poblanos, Corn, and
    Clams, 122
  Vegetable and Steak Fajitas with "Killed"
    Jalapeños, 122
Match a Dish with Chardonnay, 127
  Clam Chowder, 128
One Fish, Two Fish, Good Fish, Green
    Fish, 112
  Arctic Char with Blistered Cherry
    Tomatoes, 114
  Couscous and Pine Nuts, 114
  Mixed Seafood Salad, 113
  Sautéed Shrimp with Sherry and
    Chiles, 112
  Sesame Albacore Tuna, 114
  Striped Bass with Cilantro-Onion
    Salad, 112
OOPS! Your Salad Goes Limp, 136
  How and when you dress your greens can
    make all the difference, 136
Peas, 128
  Fresh Pea and Garlic Gazpacho, 129

Pea Shoot Salad with Radishes and Pickled
  Onion, 128
Seared Scallops with Lemony Sweet Pea
  Relish, 128
Sides for May, 119
Greens with Golden Raisins, 121
New Potatoes with Parsley and
  Saffron, 121
Roasted Chile-Garlic Broccoli, 120
Spanish Rice Salad, 120
Smarter Chicken Salad, 122
Creamy Chicken Salad, 123
Superfast, 134
Ancho Chicken Tacos with Cilantro Slaw
  and Avocado Cream, 134
Flank Steak with Spicy Lemon Sauce, 134
Roast Beef Sandwiches with Watercress
  Slaw, 135
Sesame-Miso Cucumber Salad, 135
Shrimp Cobb Salad, 134
Strawberry-Avocado Salsa with Cinnamon
  Tortilla Chips, 135
Today's Lesson: Cream Pies, 124
Chai Cream Pie, 125
Lemon Cream Pie, 124
Mexican Chocolate Cream Pie, 124
Veggie Pasta Salads, 126
Gemelli Salad with Green Beans,
  Pistachios, and Lemon-Thyme
  Vinaigrette, 127
Orzo Salad with Spicy Buttermilk
  Dressing, 127
Roasted Asparagus and Tomato Penne
  Salad with Goat Cheese, 126
Udon Noodle Salad with Broccolini and
  Spicy Tofu, 126

June

Apricots, 155
Apricot-Fig Chutney, 155
Grilled Apricot Halves, 156
Sparkling Apricot Sorbet, 156
Bean Salads with Bite, 150
Edamame Salad with Crisp Steak
  Bits, 150
Toasted Chickpea and Apricot Salad, 150
Dinner Tonight, 158
Chipotle-Rubbed Flank Steak, 159
Couscous, 159
Grilled Chicken Sliders and Apricot
  Chutney Spread, 161
Guacamole, 161
Open-Faced Blackened Catfish
  Sandwiches, 159
Roasted Summer Squash with Parsley, 160
Shrimp Korma and Basmati Rice, 160
Spinach with Toasted Almonds, 160
Stewed Okra and Fresh Tomato, 159
Feed 4 for Less Than $10, 157
Black Beans and Yellow Rice, 157
Cold Chicken and Rice Salad, 158
Creamy Linguine with Shrimp and
  Veggies, 158
Grilled Chicken Wraps, 157
Tuna Melts with Avocado, 157
5-Ingredient Cooking, 156
Grilled Flank Steak with Onions, Avocado,
  and Tomatoes, 156

Fresher, Lighter Fish Sticks, 154
Fancy Fish Sticks, 154
From Your Kitchen to Ours, 166
Chiles Rellenos Made Easy, 166
Match a Dish with Pinot Noir, 152
Plank-Grilled Salmon with Grape
  Relish, 153
OOPS! Incinerating Chicken on the Grill, 165
How to avoid a backyard poultry flame-
  out, 165
Start with a Can of Light Coconut Milk, 153
Coconut French Toast with Grilled
  Pineapple, 153
Curried Coconut Mussels, 154
Mango-Coconut Sherbet, 153
Superfast, 161
Beef and Mushroom Sloppy Joes, 161
Chicken Puttanesca, 162
Microwave Smashed Potatoes, 162
Pineapple Chicken Satay, 162
Quick Shrimp Chowder, 162
Shrimp and Arugula Salad, 163
Skillet Pork Chop Sauté with Peaches, 161
¡Taco! ¡Taco!, 163
Baked Black Beans with Chorizo, 164
Blackberry Margaritas, 163
Cabbage Slaw, 164
Chimichurri Halibut Tacos, 165
Flank Steak Tacos, 163
Grilled Pineapple-Avocado Salsa, 164
Today's Lesson: Soufflés, 148
Brown Sugar Soufflés with Crème
  Anglaise, 148
Lemon-Almond Soufflés, 149
Spinach and Parmesan Soufflés, 149
Veggie Sandwiches, 151
Grilled Farmers' Market Sandwiches, 152
Lemongrass Tofu Banh Mi, 151
Tempeh Greek Salad Wraps, 151
White Bean and Sage Pita Burgers, 152

The 25 Dishes of Summer

Hot & Cold Mains, 139
Burgers with Blue Cheese Mayo and
  Sherry Vidalia Onions, 140
Curry Chicken Wraps with Nectarine
  Chutney, 142
Grill-Braised Clams and Chorizo in
  Tomato-Saffron Broth, 139
Grilled Char with Yukon Golds and
  Tomato–Red Onion Relish, 140
Grilled Pizza with Prosciutto, Arugula, and
  Lemon, 142
Orecchiette with Peas, Shrimp, and
  Buttermilk-Herb Dressing, 141
Tequila-Glazed Grilled Chicken
  Thighs, 141
Yakitori, 142
Salads & Sides, 143
Curried Potato Salad, 144
Fig, Tomato, and Sweet Onion Salad, 143
Golden Beet Salad with Wheat Berries and
  Pumpkinseed Vinaigrette, 145
Grilled Corn on the Cob with Roasted
  Jalapeño Butter, 145
Shaved Summer Squash Salad with
  Prosciutto Crisps, 144
Smoky Baked Beans with Chorizo, 144

Stuffed Zucchini with Cheesy
  Breadcrumbs, 145
Summer Tomato, Feta, and Basil
  Galette, 143
Starters & Drinks, 137
Blueberry Thrill, 138
Chilled Avocado Soup with Seared
  Chipotle Shrimp, 137
Four-Herb Green Goddess Dressing, 138
Minted Lemon-Lime Watermelon Agua
  Fresca, 138
Sweets & Treats, 146
Cherry-Almond Crisp, 147
Margarita Ice-Cream Sandwiches, 147
Piña Colada Sorbet, 146
Rich Chocolate Pudding Pie, 146
Watermelon-Jalapeño Ice Pops, 146

July

Dinner Tonight, 182
Baked Ziti and Summer Veggies, 182
Chicken Kebabs and Nectarine Salsa, 183
Grilled Peaches, 184
Herbed Couscous, 184
Mixed Greens Salad, 182
Pan-Fried Shrimp with Creole
  Mayonnaise, 183
Pork Tenderloin Medallions and Balsamic
  Reduction, 184
Tomato, Cucumber, and Fennel Salad, 183
Wild Rice Salad, 184
Feast of the Perfect Tomatoes, 170
Pasta with Fresh Tomato Sauce and
  Clams, 170
Tomato Panzanella with Shrimp and
  Basil, 171
Feed 4 for Less Than $10, 181
Chicken Satay, 181
Grilled Steak with Onions and
  Scallions, 181
Pork Chops with Cherry Couscous, 181
From Your Kitchen to Ours, 188
Summer Squash, Bacon, and Mozzarella
  Quiche, 188
OOPS! Your Hard-Cooked Eggs Are Icky, 187
For a perfect egg every time, heat slowly
  and cool quickly, 187
Pacific Salmon, 186
Grilled King Salmon with Tomato-Peach
  Salsa, 186
Peak of the Crop, 171
Local Farmers' Market Pizza, 172
Market Salad with Goat Cheese and
  Champagne-Shallot Vinaigrette, 171
Summer Lemon-Vegetable Risotto, 172
The Perfect Dish for Rosé, 188
Picnic-Perfect Lobster Rolls, 188
Plum Wonderful, 167
Basil Plum Granita, 169
Plum Kuchen, 167
Roast Pork Tenderloin with Plum Barbecue
  Sauce, 168
Stone Fruit Cobbler, 169
Yellow Plum Salad, 168
The Portable 4th of July, 178
Creamy Buttermilk-Herb Potato
  Salad, 179
Fresh Cherry Cheesecake Bars, 180

Jalapeño-Lime Slaw, 179
Lemony Cucumber Salad, 179
Marinated Shrimp Salad, 178
Smoky Three-Bean Bake, 180
Tabbouleh Salad, 178
The Steak Lover's Guide to Lean Meat & High
    Heat, 175
    Sirloin Skewers with Grilled Vegetable
        Couscous and Fiery Pepper Sauce, 177
    Spice-Rubbed Flank Steak with Fresh
        Salsa, 176
    Tuscan-Style New York Strip with
        Arugula-Artichoke Salad, 175
Superfast, 184
    Bombay Shrimp Curry with Coconut
        Rice, 186
    Greek Yogurt with Warm Black and
        Blueberry Sauce, 185
    Green Beans with Toasted Garlic, 185
    Linguine with Two-Cheese Sauce, 185
    Open-Faced Prosciutto and Plum
        Sandwiches, 184
Today's Lesson: Grilled Vegetables, 173
    Grilled Romaine with Creamy Herb
        Dressing, 173
    Grilled Stuffed Jalapeños, 174
    Grilled Vegetable Gazpacho, 174

August

Banana Pudding: Best Dessert Ever?, 201
    Roasted Banana Pudding, 202
Chicken of the Year!, 197
    All-Purpose Spice Rub, 197
    Cajun-Spiced Smoked Shrimp with
        Rémoulade, 201
    Coffee-Rubbed Texas-Style Brisket, 198
    Fantastic Bourbon Smoked Chicken, 200
    Pulled Pork Sandwiches with Mustard
        Sauce, 198
    Smoked Oysters with Olive Relish, 198
    Smoked Potato Salad, 199
The Clambake Comes Home, 190
    Beer-Steamed Soft-Shell Clams, 190
    Blueberry Crisp, 192
    Butter Sauce, 190
    Fresh Raspberry Lemonade, 192
    Grilled Corn on the Cob, 191
    Grilled Maine Lobsters, 191
    New Potatoes with Onions and Spicy
        Sausage, 191
Cold Summer Soups, 195
    Avocado-Corn Chowder with Grilled
        Chicken, 196
    Melon Gazpacho with Frizzled
        Prosciutto, 196
Dinner Tonight, 242
    Fresh Lima Beans, 244
    Grilled Scallop Salad, 243
    Herbed Shrimp and White Bean
        Salad, 242
    Lamb Chops and Cilantro Relish, 244
    Peppered Flank Steak and Salsa, 243
    Radish-Yogurt Dip and Pita Wedges, 244
    Tomato Toast, 242
    Two-Bean Toss, 243
Feed 4 for Less Than $10, 244
    Kid-tastic Pizzadillas, 245
    Linguine with Quick Lemon Ricotta, 245

Maple-Brined Pork, 245
Summer Veggie Pizza, 244
Tomato Soup with Roasted
    Chickpeas, 246
5-Ingredient Cooking, 193
    Grilled Chicken with Bourbon Peach
        Butter, 194
    Sautéed Tilapia Tacos with Grilled Peppers
        and Onion, 193
    Shredded Chicken Tacos with Tomatoes
        and Grilled Corn, 195
    Stuffed Cuban Pork Tenderloin, 194
    Summer Pea, Watermelon, and Farro
        Salad, 193
From Your Kitchen to Ours, 241
    Zucchini Angel Hair Pancake, 241
OOPS! Your Turkey Burgers Are Parched
    Pucks, 204
    A simple stir-in makes for juicy, delicious
        patties, 204
Our First App Gets Cooking, 195
    Mango-Ginger Parfaits, 195
Peaches, 241
    Bourbon-Glazed Peaches with Yogurt, 241
    Sparkling Peach Sangria, 241
Slice, Fill, Eat, Smile, 205
    Caesar Salad Bagels, 205
    Grilled Zucchini Caprese Sandwiches, 207
    Herbed Chicken Salad Sandwiches, 206
    Peanut-Sauced Chicken Pitas, 205
    Steak Baguettes with Pesto Mayo, 205
Superfast, 246
    Bacon-Corn Chowder with Shrimp, 246
    Baked Mozzarella Bites, 246
    BBQ Chicken and Blue Cheese Pizza, 247
    Grilled Chicken Thighs with Pineapple,
        Corn, and Bell Pepper Relish, 247
    Ham and Swiss Egg Sandwiches, 247
    Summer Tomato, Mozzarella, and Basil
        Panini with Balsamic Syrup, 247
Today's Lesson: Ice Pops, 207
    Blueberry-Peach Ice Pops, 208
    Chocolate Pudding Pops, 208
    Limoncello Pops, 207
    Sparkling Strawberry Pops, 207
Veggie Stir-Fries, 202
    Cumin-Spiced Chickpeas and Carrots on
        Couscous, 202
    Fried Rice with Sweet Soy Sauce, 204
    Ginger-Scented Corn and Asparagus Stir-
        Fry, 204
    Rice Noodle Salad, 203

September

Chile Peppers, 264
    Marinated Peppers and Mozzarella, 264
    Salsa Verde, 264
Creamy, Light Mac and Cheese, 260
    Creamy, Light Macaroni and Cheese, 260
Dinner Tonight, 270
    Chicken Lettuce Cups, 270
    Chicken Tostadas and Avocado
        Dressing, 271
    Crab Cakes and Spicy Mustard Sauce, 272
    Mexican Rice, 271
    Orzo with Spinach, 270
    Roasted Asparagus, 272

Shrimp Fettuccine Alfredo, 271
Tomato and Arugula Salad, 272
Feed 4 for Less Than $10, 266
    Buffalo Chicken Thighs, 267
    Cheese Ravioli with Pesto, 267
    French Toast Peanut Butter and Jelly, 266
    Stir-Fried Chinese Egg Noodles, 266
5-Ingredient Cooking, 272
    Tuna-Fennel Pasta Salad, 272
Granola Gets Fancy, 256
    Granola with Honey-Scented Yogurt and
        Baked Figs, 256
Grill and Glaze, 255
    Bourbon-Glazed Chicken, 255
    Grilled Chicken with Cola Sauce, 255
    Spicy-Sweet Glazed Chicken, 256
Ladies and Gentlemen, Breakfast Is Now
    Served, for Dinner, 258
    Bacon and Egg Sandwiches with
        Caramelized Onions and Arugula, 258
    Ciabatta French Toast with Warm Apple
        Maple Syrup, 259
    Mozzarella Omelet with Sage and Red
        Chile Flakes, 258
    Savory Bread Puddings with Ham and
        Cheddar, 260
OOPS! Your Rice Gets Gummy, 269
    For light, fluffy grains, try a technique
        so simple you'll kick yourself for not
        thinking of it, 269
Pork Tenderloin, 25 Ways, 248
    Apricot-Glazed Pork Kebabs, 254
    Argentinean Pork, 249
    Baja Pork Stir-Fry, 250
    Barbecued Pork Tenderloin, 255
    Cheese and Pear Pork, 252
    Choucroute, 252
    Grilled Pork Salad, 254
    Hungarian Goulash, 251
    Indian-Spiced Pork with Raita, 250
    Pecan-Crusted Pork Noisettes, 251
    Pepper Pork, 253
    Pork Roulade, 253
    Pork Satay with Peanut Sauce, 255
    Pork Tenderloin with Orange
        Compote, 253
    Pork Tenderloin with Tangy Grape
        Salad, 249
    Pork with Figs and Farro, 252
    Roasted Pork Tenderloin and Maple-
        Glazed Apples, 248
    Roast Pork with Potatoes and Butternut
        Squash, 249
    Soy-Ginger Sesame Pork, 250
    Spanish Pork with Apple-Citrus Salsa, 249
    Spicy North African Pork Tenderloin, 248
    Tacos Al Pastor with Grilled Pineapple
        Salsa, 254
    Tagine-Style Pork with Squash and Pearl
        Onions, 251
    Tequila Pork with Tomatillo
        Guacamole, 250
    Vietnamese Salad, 250
Superfast, 268
    Cheesy Chicken Bagel Pizzas, 269
    Chocolate-Granola Apple Wedges, 269
    Grilled Zucchini with Sea Salt, 268
    Pan-Fried Trout with Tomato Basil
        Sauté, 268

Salmon and Bok Choy, 268
Spicy Asian Chicken and Noodle
 Soup, 268
Today's Lesson: Brownies, 262
 Cherry Cheesecake Brownies, 262
 Classic Fudge-Walnut Brownies, 262
 Peanut Butter Cup Blondies, 263
 Salted Caramel Brownies, 263
20-Minute Veggie Mains, 264
 Arugula Pizza with Poached Eggs, 265
 Blue Cheese Polenta with Vegetables, 266
 Grilled Gruyère and Olive Tapenade
  Sandwiches, 265
 Rotini with White Beans and
  Escarole, 264
Whole-Grain Salads, 256
 Chicken Tabbouleh with Tahini Drizzle, 257
 Waldorf Salad with Steel-Cut Oats, 257

October

Apples, 279
 Serrano, Manchego, and Apple
  Sandwiches, 279
Beans, Greens, and Accolades, 283
 Warm White Beans with Roasted
  Fennel, 283
Dinner Tonight, 296
 Apple Iced Tea, 297
 Bacon, Tomato, and Arugula Pizza, 296
 Chicken and Herb White Pizza, 297
 Greens and Sherry Vinaigrette, 298
 Lemony Arugula Salad, 298
 Pepperoni, Onion, and Olive Pizza, 298
 Poached Pears, 296
 Spicy Sausage and Mushroom Pizza, 297
Fall Vegetable Salads, 284
 Roasted Sweet Potato Salad with
  Cranberry-Chipotle Dressing, 285
 Shaved Fennel Salad with Orange, Green
  Olives, and Pistachios, 284
Feed 4 for Less Than $10, 291
 Blue Cheese–Stuffed Pork Chops with
  Pears, 291
 Garlicky Spinach-Sausage Gratin, 291
 Indian-Spiced Lentils and Lamb, 291
 Potato-Crusted Chicken Fingers, 292
5-Ingredient Cooking, 292
 Beef Tenderloin with Cherry–Black Pepper
  Sauce, 292
 Butternut Squash Risotto, 293
For the Love of a Perfect Pear, 277
 Frangipane Pear Tarts, 278
 Honey-Wheat Pizza with Pear-Prosciutto
  Salad, 279
 Pear and Gruyère Strata, 277
 Pear Chutney Bruschetta with Pecans and
  Blue Cheese, 278
 Whole Roasted Endives with Pear,
  Arugula, and Walnut Salad, 277
Meatless Mexican Mains, 289
 Black Bean and Cheese Enchiladas with
  Ranchero Sauce, 289
 Grilled Portobello and Poblano Tacos with
  Pico de Gallo, 290
 Mexican Stuffed Poblanos, 290
 Migas con Salsa Verde, 289
Monkey Bread Lightens Up, 287
 Monkey Bread, 288

OOPS! Your Caramel Meets a Burnt, Bitter
 End, 298
 A little water—and patience—goes a long
  way, 298
Start with a Pound of Ground Beef . . . , 280
 Chili-Corn Chip Pie, 282
 Classic Meat Loaf, 281
 Italian-Style Beef with Polenta, 282
 Quick Pastitsio, 280
 Thai Beef Cabbage Cups, 281
 Tortilla Meatball Soup, 280
Superfast, 293
 Apple, Goat Cheese, and Pecan Pizza, 295
 Lemon-Parmesan Broccoli, 295
 Linguine with Easy Meat Sauce, 295
 Mashed Chickpea Pitas, 294
 Pork Chops with Caribbean Rub and
  Mango Salsa, 294
 Salmon with Red Pepper Pesto, 293
 Spinach, Pasta, and Pea Soup, 294
3 Speedy Soups, 282
 Chicken and Wild Rice Soup, 283
 Chicken Club Soup, 283
 Chicken Gumbo, 282
Today's Lesson: Braised Meats, 285
 Beer-Braised Brisket, 286
 Cabernet Short Ribs with Parmesan
  Polenta, 286
 Chicken with Dates, Olives, and
  Cinnamon, 285
 Soy and Cola–Braised Pork Shoulder, 287
Tricks with Treats, 274
 Bittersweet Chocolate Cookies, 275
 Chocolate Marshmallows, 276
 Chocolate Spider Cupcakes, 275
 Cinnamon-Cider Candied Apples, 274
 Honey-Orange Marshmallows, 276
 Peanut Butter Caramel Corn, 274
 Thai Cashew Brittle, 274

November

Adventures in the Home Kitchens of
 Thailand, 337
 Chiang Mai Pork Patties, 339
 Roasted Eggplant Salsa, 340
 Simmered Cabbage, Shan Style, 341
 Thai Sticky Rice, 337
Beautiful Holiday Desserts, 328
 Apple-Cinnamon Bundt Cake, 328
 Caramel-Pecan Dacquoise, 330
 Frozen Orange Tortes with Cranberry
  Compote, 330
 Maple-Gingerbread Pots de Crème, 330
 Pumpkin-Almond Cheesecake, 328
 Triple-Chocolate Cake, 329
Breakfast, Lunch & Dinner in Honolulu, 319
 Open-Faced Smoked Salmon
  Sandwiches, 321
 Pan-Roasted Fish with Mediterranean
  Tomato Sauce, 321
 Pineapple Musubi Rolls, 322
 Whole-Wheat Buttermilk Pancakes with
  Orange Sauce, 320
Dinner Tonight, 348
 Baked Mac and Cheese, 348
 Broccoli and Rice Casseroles, 350
 Buttered Carrots, 350
 Chicken and Sausage Jambalaya, 349

Crispy Pork Medallions, 349
Garlic Breadsticks, 349
Roasted Root Vegetables, 349
Spinach Salad, 348
Dips: Easy, Gooey, Chewy Treats, 324
 Baked Feta with Romesco and Olive
  Tapenade, 324
 Cajun Hot Crab Dip, 326
 Caramelized Onion, Gruyère, and Bacon
  Spread, 325
 Orange and Avocado Salsa, 325
 Spicy Tortilla Strips, 325
 Toasted Parmesan Pita Crisps, 325
 Zesty Green Goddess Dip, 325
Feed 4 for Less Than $10, 342
 Baked Italian-Style Cauliflower, 342
 Ham and Pineapple Pizza Subs, 343
 Savory Baked Apples, 342
 Turkey Sausage, Mushroom, and Potato
  Gratin, 342
5-Ingredient Cooking, 326
 Rice and Beans with Chicken and
  Chorizo, 326
Fun Uses for Fresh Cranberries, 313
 Cranberry Ketchup, 313
 Pickled Cranberries, 313
 Tangy Cranberry Tea, 313
Getting Good with Gumbo, 346
 Smoky Shrimp and Chicken Gumbo, 347
Leftovers: Curry Your Turkey!, 313
 Curried Turkey, Spinach, and Cashew
  Salad, 314
 Thai Curry Stew with Turkey and
  Zucchini, 314
Legs & Thighs, 318
 Braised Chicken with Kale, 318
 Chipotle-Orange Thighs, 318
 Greek Chicken Thighs, 318
Meatless Holiday Mains, 331
 Beet Wellingtons, 333
 Black Bean and Sweet Potato Tamales with
  Tomatillo Sauce, 332
 Butternut Squash, Caramelized Onion, and
  Spinach Lasagna, 331
 Wild Mushroom Pastitsio, 333
OOPS! The Turkey Hack Job, 350
 If you lack a surgeon's touch, carve the bird
  in the kitchen, 350
Oysters, 327
 Roasted Oysters with Pancetta and
  Breadcrumbs, 327
 Rosemary–Green Peppercorn
  Mignonette, 327
Plum Good Chops, 326
 Spiced Lamb with Plum Sauce, 326
Start With . . . Sweetened Condensed
 Milk, 322
 Peanut Butter and Dark Chocolate
  Fudge, 324
 Spicy Caramel Brownies, 323
 Sweet Potato Pie with Spiced Cream
  Topping, 322
 Tangy Ice Cream with Cashew Brittle, 323
Superfast, 343
 Bananas Foster Parfaits, 346
 Cantonese-Style Shrimp and Napa
  Cabbage, 344
 Grilled Chicken Caesar Salad, 344
 Honey-Glazed Almonds, 345

Mushroom, Corn, and Poblano Tacos, 345
Pan-Seared Chicken with Tomato-Olive
  Relish, 344
Sesame Beef Stir-Fry, 344
Sloppy Joe Sliders, 346
Spanish-Style Cod in Tomato Broth, 345
Steamed Clams with White Wine and
  Tomatoes, 343
Today's Lesson: Rustic Breads, 334
Crusty French Boules, 334
Prosciutto Pizza with Tangy White
  Sauce, 336
Real Bagels, 336
Rich Chocolate Babka, 335
Winter Squash, 315
Beef and Butternut Chili, 316
Cheese and Squash Soufflés, 316
Indian-Spiced Roasted Squash Soup, 318
Kabocha Squash Puree, 317
Quinoa-Stuffed Squash, 315
Spiced Cinnamon Rolls with Maple
  Glaze, 317

The Crowd-Pleaser's Holiday Cookbook

The Cocktails, 312
Campari and Orange Sparkling Cocktail, 312
Clementine Sparkler, 312
Cognac Sparkling Wine Cocktail, 312
Pomegranate Fizz, 313
Sparkling Pear Cocktail, 313
The Pies, 310
Cranberry-Apple Pie, 311
French Apple Tart, 310
Ginger Pumpkin Pie with Toasted
  Coconut, 312
Maple-Bourbon Pecan Pie, 310
Quince Tart with Pine Nut Caramel
  Glaze, 311
The Potatoes, 308
Mashed Potato Casserole, 309
Parmesan-Coated Potato Wedges, 309
Roasted Rosemary Fingerling
  Potatoes, 310
Truffled Pommes Anna, 308
Twice-Roasted Sweet Potatoes with
  Chipotle, 309
The Stuffing, 304
Ciabatta Stuffing with Chestnuts and
  Raisins, 304
Corn Bread, Chorizo, and Jalapeño
  Dressing, 305
Farro, Caramelized Onion, and Wild
  Mushroom Stuffing, 306
Fennel, Sausage, and Caramelized Apple
  Stuffing, 305
Wild Rice Stuffing with Dried Cherries
  and Toasted Pecans, 306
The Turkey, 299
Braised Turkey Roulade with Pancetta,
  Shallots, and Porcini Gravy, 300
Butter-Basted Turkey, 302
Maple-Cider Brined Turkey with Bourbon-
  Cider Gravy, 302
Old-Fashioned Cranberry Sauce, 303
Roasted Turkey with Rosemary-Garlic
  Butter Rub and Pan Gravy, 301

Slow-Roasted Turkey with Cream
  Gravy, 300
Smoke-Roasted Turkey Breast with
  Pomegranate-Thyme Glaze, 299
The Vegetables, 306
Balsamic-Glazed Green Beans and Pearl
  Onions, 308
Brussels Sprouts with Bacon, Garlic, and
  Shallots, 306
Green Bean Casserole with Madeira
  Mushrooms, 307
Spicy Sautéed Broccoli Rabe with
  Garlic, 307
Swiss Chard with Crème Fraîche, 308

December

Chestnuts, 356
Chestnut Ice Cream, 356
Chili Creations, 368
Black Bean and Soy Chili, 368
Cincinnati 5-Way Chili, 369
Quinoa and Roasted Pepper Chili, 369
White Bean and Hominy Chili, 369
Dinner Tonight, 379
Bacony Green Beans, 382
Cashew Rice, 381
Chicken with Brussels Sprouts and
  Mustard Sauce, 380
Couscous-Arugula Salad, 379
Moroccan-Style Lamb and Chickpeas, 379
Pork Chops with Grits and Red-Eye
  Gravy, 380
Rosemary Potatoes, 381
Sautéed Flounder and Spicy
  Rémoulade, 382
Tofu Steaks with Shiitakes and
  Veggies, 381
Wilted Spinach, 380
Effortless Hors D'Oeuvres, 360
Crab Toast with Carrot and Scallion, 361
Radishes with Iceberg and Herb
  Butter, 361
Smoked Salmon in Cucumber Boats, 361
Feed 4 for Less Than $10, 374
Black-Eyed Peas and Greens, 374
Healthy Wheat Nachos, 376
Quicker Cassoulet, 375
Sausage Ragu over Creamy Polenta, 375
Shrimp, Avocado, and Grapefruit
  Salad, 374
Goodies to Gift, 362
Buttermilk Bundt Cakes, 364
Iced Sugar Cookies, 362
Vanilla Cupcakes with Vanilla Bean
  Frosting, 363
OOPS! Your Cookies Spread into Shapeless
  Blobs, 378
To prevent a cookie meltdown, keep it
  cool, 378
Pound Cake, Perfected, 364
Canola Oil Pound Cake with Browned
  Butter Glaze, 365
Puff Pastry Appetizers, 356
Caramelized Onion Tartlets, 357
Potato-Gruyère Tartlets, 358
Sun-Dried Tomato Palmiers, 356
Tomato–Baby Bell Pepper Tartlets, 357

A Short Guide to Toasting a Person You
  Love, 66
Some tips on the ritual of the toast, 366
A Spanish Christmas, 370
Alicante Turkey Meatballs, 373
Alicante Turkey Soup, 373
Almendrados (Flourless Almond
  Cookies), 372
Anise-Flavored "Doughnuts," 372
Drunken Turkey, 374
Turkey-Saffron Stock, 373
Superfast, 376
Chicken and Waffle Sandwiches, 377
Chip-Crusted Fish Fillets, 377
Cider and Sage Pork, 377
Currant-Glazed Lamb Chops with
  Pistachio Couscous, 376
Flank Steak with Romesco Sauce, 376
Sweet and Spicy Pumpkinseeds, 377
White Beans with Prosciutto, 378
Today's Lesson: Roasts, 358
Herb and Citrus Roast Leg of Lamb, 360
Maple-Mustard Glazed Fresh Ham, 358
Romano and Herb Rubbed Turkey with
  Pan Gravy, 359
Rosemary-Dijon Crusted Standing Rib
  Roast, 360
A Very Merry Open-House Menu, 351
Apple–Blue Cheese Chutney, 353
Basic Crostini, 354
Caramelized Onion Spread, 353
Coconut-Cardamom Macaroons, 355
Peanut Butter and Chocolate–Dipped
  Pretzels, 355
Phyllo-Wrapped Asparagus with
  Prosciutto, 354
Pistachio and Pine Nut Brittle, 355
Pork Tenderloin with Herbed Biscuits, 354
Roasted Root Vegetable Salad, 354
Warm Spiced Cran-Pom Toddies, 353
Whiskey Sour Punch, 353

GENERAL RECIPE INDEX

A listing by major ingredient and food category for every recipe that appeared in the magazine in 2011.

Almonds
Almendrados (Flourless Almond Cookies), 372
Crisp, Cherry-Almond, 147
Honey-Glazed Almonds, 345
Rice, Nutty, 46
Soufflés, Lemon-Almond, 149
Toasted Almonds, Spinach with, 160
Truffles, Date and Almond, 94

Appetizers. *See also* **Snacks.**
Bruschettas with Pecans and Blue Cheese, Pear Chutney, 278
Clams, Beer-Steamed Soft-Shell, 190
Crab Toast with Carrot and Scallion, 361
Crostini, Basic, 354
Dips
Artichoke, Spinach, and White Bean Dip, 100
Crab Dip, Cajun Hot, 326
Green Goddess Dip, Zesty, 325
Radish-Yogurt Dip and Pita Wedges, 244
Feta with Romesco and Olive Tapenade, Baked, 324
Oysters with Pancetta and Breadcrumbs, Roasted, 327
Pineapple Musubi Rolls, 322
Pita Crisps, Toasted Parmesan, 325
Radishes with Iceberg and Herb Butter, 361
Smoked Salmon in Cucumber Boats, 361
Spread, Caramelized Onion, 353
Tortilla Strips, Spicy, 325

Apples
Baked Apples, Savory, 342
Cake, Apple-Cinnamon Bundt, 328
Candied Apples, Cinnamon-Cider, 274
Caramelized Apple Stuffing, Fennel, Sausage, and, 305
Chocolate-Granola Apple Wedges, 269
Chutney, Apple–Blue Cheese, 353
Country Captain, Vegetarian, 32
Maple-Glazed Apples, Roasted Pork Tenderloin and, 248
Pie, Cranberry-Apple, 311
Pizza, Apple, Goat Cheese, and Pecan, 295
Salad with Steel-Cut Oats, Waldorf, 257
Salsa, Spanish Pork with Apple-Citrus, 249
Sandwiches, Serrano, Manchego, and Apple, 279
Sauce, Apple-Cranberry, 303
Syrup, Ciabatta French Toast with Warm Apple Maple, 259
Tart, French Apple, 310
Tea, Apple Iced, 297

Apricots
Chutney, Apricot-Fig, 155
Chutney Spread, Grilled Chicken Sliders and Apricot, 161
Grilled Apricot Halves, 156
Pork Kebabs, Apricot-Glazed, 254
Salad, Toasted Chickpea and Apricot, 150
Sorbet, Sparkling Apricot, 156

Artichokes
Dip, Artichoke, Spinach, and White Bean, 100
Salad, Tuscan-Style New York Strip with Arugula-Artichoke, 175
Salad with Artichokes and Parsley, Quinoa, 92
Strata, Artichoke and Goat Cheese, 60

Asparagus
Balsamic Tomatoes, Asparagus with, 111
Browned Butter Asparagus, 119
Cassoulet, Quick White Bean, Asparagus, and Mushroom, 86
Garganelli with Asparagus and Pecorino Cheese, 95
Phyllo-Wrapped Asparagus with Prosciutto, 354
Pickled Ramps and Asparagus, 104
Risotto, Spring, 106
Roasted Asparagus, 272
Roasted Asparagus with Browned Butter, 69
Salad with Goat Cheese, Roasted Asparagus and Tomato Penne, 126
Sauté, Smoky Asparagus and Mushroom, 105
Stir-Fry, Ginger-Scented Corn and Asparagus, 204

Avocados
Chowder with Grilled Chicken, Avocado-Corn, 196
Cream, Ancho Chicken Tacos with Cilantro Slaw and Avocado, 134
Dressing, Chicken Tostadas and Avocado, 271
Guacamole, 161
Guacamole, Tequila Pork with Tomatillo, 250
Melts with Avocado, Tuna, 157
Salad, Mixed Greens and Avocado, 194
Salad, Shrimp, Avocado, and Grapefruit, 374
Salsa, Grilled Pineapple-Avocado, 164
Salsa, Orange and Avocado, 325
Salsa with Cinnamon Tortilla Chips, Strawberry-Avocado, 135
Soup with Seared Chipotle Shrimp, Chilled Avocado, 137
Soup with Shrimp and Avocado, Spicy Tortilla, 79

Bacon
Brussels Sprouts with Bacon, Garlic, and Shallots, 306
Chicken, Bacon and Goat Cheese, 22
Chowder with Shrimp, Bacon-Corn, 246
Green Beans, Bacony, 382
Muffins, Bacon-Cheddar Corn, 115
Pancetta and Breadcrumbs, Roasted Oysters with, 327
Pancetta, Bucatini with Green Peas and, 96
Pancetta, Shallots, and Porcini Gravy, Braised Turkey Roulade with, 300
Pizza, Bacon, Tomato, and Arugula, 296
Potato Salad with Ramps and Bacon, Warm, 105
Quiche, Summer Squash, Bacon, and Mozzarella, 188

Sandwiches with Caramelized Onions and Arugula, Bacon and Egg, 258
Soup, Chicken Club, 283
Spread, Caramelized Onion, Gruyère, and Bacon, 325
Banana Pudding, Roasted, 202
Bananas Foster Parfaits, 346

Barbecue
Chicken and Blue Cheese Pizza, BBQ, 247
Chicken Sliders, Barbecue Pulled, 79
Pork Tenderloin, Barbecued, 255
Sauce, Roast Pork Tenderloin with Plum Barbecue, 168
Sauce, Tangy Coffee Barbecue, 177
Barley with Chickpeas & Arugula, Mediterranean, 84

Beans
Baked Beans with Chorizo, Smoky, 144
Bake, Smoky Three-Bean, 180
Black
Baked Black Beans with Chorizo, 164
Chili, Black Bean and Soy, 368
Enchiladas with Ranchero Sauce, Black Bean and Cheese, 289
Feijoada, Brazilian, 57
Hummus, Black Bean, 80
Nachos, Healthy Wheat, 376
Rice and Beans with Chicken and Chorizo, 326
Tamales with Tomatillo Sauce, Black Bean and Sweet Potato, 332
Yellow Rice, Black Beans and, 157
Cassoulet, Quicker, 375
Chickpea and Apricot Salad, Toasted, 150
Chickpea Chili, 55
Chickpea Pitas, Mashed, 294
Chickpea Salad with Grilled Prawns, Crispy, 40
Chickpeas and Carrots on Couscous, Cumin-Spiced, 202
Chickpeas & Arugula, Mediterranean Barley with, 84
Chickpea Stew with Brown Rice Pilaf, Curried, 30
Chickpeas, Tomato Soup with Roasted, 246
Chili, Green Chile, 42
Fava Beans, Morel Mushrooms, and Mascarpone, Farfalle with, 97
Garbanzo Beans and Greens, 42
Green
Bacony Green Beans, 382
Balsamic-Glazed Green Beans and Pearl Onions, 308
Casserole with Madeira Mushrooms, Green Bean, 307
Herbed Green Beans, 76
Salad with Green Beans, Pistachios, and Lemon-Thyme Vinaigrette, Gemelli, 127
Shallots and Hazelnuts, Green Beans with, 94

Stir-Fry with Peanut Sauce, Tempeh and
 Green Bean, 86
Toasted Garlic, Green Beans with, 185
Lima Beans, Fresh, 244
Moroccan-Style Lamb and Chickpeas, 379
Poblanos, Mexican Stuffed, 290
Quinoa and Roasted Pepper Chili, 369
Soup with Parmesan Cheese, Escarole, Bean,
 and Sausage, 80
Turkey, Drunken, 374
Two-Bean Toss, 243
White
 Burgers, White Bean and Sage Pita, 152
 Cassoulet, Quick White Bean, Asparagus,
  and Mushroom, 86
 Chili, White Bean and Hominy, 369
 Dip, Artichoke, Spinach, and White
  Bean, 100
 Pita Pockets, Southwestern White
  Bean, 101
 Prosciutto, White Beans with, 378
 Rotini with White Beans and
  Escarole, 264
 Salad, Herbed Shrimp and White
  Bean, 242
 Salad, Tuna and White Bean, 101
 Soup, Chicken and White Bean, 101
 Warm White Beans with Roasted
  Fennel, 283
Beef. *See also* **Beef, Ground.**
Brisket, Beer-Braised, 286
Brisket, Coffee-Rubbed Texas-Style, 198
Brisket, Easy Braised, 75
Feijoada, Brazilian, 57
Roasts
 Chili, Beef and Butternut, 316
 Pot Roast with Turnip Greens, Beef, 56
 Provençal Beef Daube, 57
 Standing Rib Roast, Rosemary-Dijon
  Crusted, 360
 Stew, Italian Beef, 36
Sandwiches with Watercress Slaw, Roast
 Beef, 135
Short Ribs with Parmesan Polenta,
 Cabernet, 286
Steaks
 Baguettes with Pesto Mayo, Steak, 205
 Crisp Steak Bits, Edamame Salad
  with, 150
 Cucumber-Radish Salad, Steak with, 110
 Fajitas with "Killed" Jalapeños, Vegetable
  and Steak, 122
 Flank Steak and Salsa, Peppered, 243
 Flank Steak, Chipotle-Rubbed, 159
 Flank Steak Tacos, 163
 Flank Steak with Fresh Salsa, Spice-
  Rubbed, 176
 Flank Steak with Onions, Avocado, and
  Tomatoes, Grilled, 156
 Flank Steak with Romesco Sauce, 376
 Flank Steak with Spicy Lemon
  Sauce, 134
 Grilled Steak with Onions and
  Scallions, 181
 New York Strip with Arugula-Artichoke
  Salad, Tuscan-Style, 175
 Sirloin Skewers with Grilled Vegetable
  Couscous and Fiery Pepper Sauce, 177
 Stir-Fried Rice Noodles with Beef and
  Spinach, 85
 Stir-Fry, Beef-Broccoli, 78
 Stir-Fry, Sesame Beef, 344

Strip Steak, Pan-Seared, 88
Tenderloin Steaks with Ginger-Hoisin
 Glaze, Broiled, 50
Tenderloin with Cherry–Black Pepper Sauce,
 Beef, 292
Tenderloin with Horseradish-Chive Sauce,
 Beef, 118
Tenderloin with Mushroom–Red Wine Sauce,
 Beef, 27
Beef, Ground
Burger, Out-N-In California, 64
Burgers with Blue Cheese Mayo and Sherry
 Vidalia Onions, 140
Cabbage Cups, Thai Beef, 281
Cabbage, Shan Style, Simmered, 341
Cauliflower, Baked Italian-Style, 342
Chili, Green Chile, 42
Hash, Red Flannel, 71
Italian-Style Beef with Polenta, 282
Meatball Soup, Tortilla, 280
Meat Loaf, Classic, 281
Meat Loaf Minis, Cheesy, 47
Pastitsio, Quick, 280
Pie, Chili-Corn Chip, 282
Pie, Green Chile Tamale, 71
Sauce, Linguine with Easy Meat, 295
Sauce, Slow-Simmered Meat, 56
Sloppy Joes, Beef and Mushroom, 161
Sloppy Joe Sliders, 346
Spaghetti Bolognese, 73
Beets
Golden Beet Salad with Wheat Berries and
 Pumpkinseed Vinaigrette, 145
Hash, Red Flannel, 71
Salad, Beet, Blood Orange, Kumquat, and
 Quinoa, 33
Salad, Yogurt-Marinated Chicken with
 Beet, 41
Walnuts, Goat Cheese, and Baby Greens,
 Beets with, 91
Wellingtons, Beet, 333
Beverages
Agua Fresca, Minted Lemon-Lime
 Watermelon, 138
Alcoholic
 Blueberry Thrill, 138
 Cocktail, Campari and Orange
  Sparkling, 312
 Cocktail, Cognac Sparkling Wine, 312
 Cocktails, Lemon-Gin Sparkling, 117
 Cocktail, Sparkling Meyer Lemon, 67
 Cocktail, Sparkling Pear, 313
 Fizz, Pomegranate, 313
 Margaritas, Blackberry, 163
 Punch, Whiskey Sour, 353
 Sangria, Sparkling Peach, 241
 Sparkler, Clementine, 312
 Toddies, Warm Spiced Cran-Pom, 353
Lemonade, Fresh Raspberry, 192
Tea, Apple Iced, 297
Tea, Tangy Cranberry, 313
Biscuits, Pork Tenderloin with Herbed, 354
Blackberries
Margaritas, Blackberry, 163
Sauce, Greek Yogurt with Warm Black and
 Blueberry, 185
Blueberries
Crisp, Blueberry, 192
Pops, Blueberry-Peach Ice, 208
Sauce, Greek Yogurt with Warm Black and
 Blueberry, 185
Thrill, Blueberry, 138

Bok Choy, Green Curry with, 30
Bok Choy, Salmon and, 268
Breads
Breadsticks, Garlic, 349
Garlic Bread, Broiler, 52
Puddings with Ham and Cheddar, Savory
 Bread, 260
Scones, Chocolate Chip, 35
Toast, Tomato, 242
Yeast
 Babka, Rich Chocolate, 335
 Bagels, Real, 336
 French Boules, Crusty, 334
 Monkey Bread, 288
 Rolls with Maple Glaze, Spiced
  Cinnamon, 317
Broccoli
Casseroles, Broccoli and Rice, 350
Lemon-Parmesan Broccoli, 295
Roasted Chile-Garlic Broccoli, 120
Roasted Shrimp and Broccoli, 132
Stir-Fry, Beef-Broccoli, 78
Broccolini
Lemon Broccolini, 47
Salad with Broccolini and Spicy Tofu, Udon
 Noodle, 126
Shrimp Sautéed with Broccolini, 28
Broccoli Rabe with Garlic, Spicy Sautéed, 307
Broccoli Rabe with Onions and Pine Nuts, 43
Brussels Sprouts
Bacon, Garlic, and Shallots, Brussels Sprouts
 with, 306
Chicken with Brussels Sprouts and Mustard
 Sauce, 380
Gratin, Crispy Topped Brussels Sprouts and
 Cauliflower, 52
Sautéed Brussels Sprouts with Bacon, 81
Budget Cooking
Arugula and Walnut Salad, 106
Baked Italian-Style Cauliflower, 342
Black Beans and Yellow Rice, 157
Black-Eyed Peas and Greens, 374
Blue Cheese–Stuffed Pork Chops with
 Pears, 291
Buffalo Chicken Thighs, 267
Buttermilk–Blue Cheese Smashed
 Potatoes, 267
Cheese Ravioli with Pesto, 267
Chicken Enchilada Casserole, 74
Chicken Satay, 181
Cold Chicken and Rice Salad, 158
Creamy Linguine with Shrimp and
 Veggies, 158
Fettuccine with Olive Oil, Garlic, and Red
 Pepper, 106
French Toast Peanut Butter and Jelly, 266
Garbanzo Beans and Greens, 42
Garlicky Spinach-Sausage Gratin, 291
Green Chile Chili, 42
Grilled Chicken Wraps, 157
Grilled Steak with Onions and Scallions, 181
Ham and Pineapple Pizza Subs, 343
Healthy Wheat Nachos, 376
Indian-Spiced Lentils and Lamb, 291
Kid-tastic Pizzadillas, 245
Linguine with Quick Lemon Ricotta, 245
Maple-Brined Pork, 245
Maple-Mustard Chicken Thighs, 130
Moroccan Shepherd's Pie, 74
Onion Tart, 106
Pasta Puttanesca, 130
Pork Chops with Cherry Couscous, 181

Budget Cooking *(continued)*

Pork Posole, 73
Pork Salad Provençal, 131
Potato-Crusted Chicken Fingers, 292
Quicker Cassoulet, 375
Sausage and Egg Burrito, 130
Sausage Ragu over Creamy Polenta, 375
Savory Baked Apples, 342
Shrimp, Avocado, and Grapefruit Salad, 374
Smoky Potato Pancakes, 42
Spaghetti Bolognese, 73
Spring Risotto, 106
Stir-Fried Chinese Egg Noodles, 266
Summer Veggie Pizza, 244
Tomato Soup with Roasted Chickpeas, 246
Tuna Melts with Avocado, 157
Turkey Sausage, Mushroom, and Potato
　Gratin, 342
Vegetable Korma, 74

Bulgur
Breakfast, Libanais, 40
Moussaka, Vegetarian, 59
Tabbouleh Salad, 178

Burrito, Sausage and Egg, 130

Butter
Bourbon Peach Butter, Grilled Chicken
　with, 194
Herb Butter, Radishes with Iceberg and, 361
Roasted Jalapeño Butter, Grilled Corn on the
　Cob with, 145
Rosemary-Garlic Butter Rub and Pan Gravy,
　Roasted Turkey with, 301
Sauce, Butter, 190
Shrimp Butter, 27

Cabbage
Cantonese-Style Shrimp and Napa
　Cabbage, 344
Cups, Thai Beef Cabbage, 281
Hash, Red Flannel, 71
Simmered Cabbage, Shan Style, 341

Cakes
Apple-Cinnamon Bundt Cake, 328
Buttermilk Bundt Cakes, 364
Carrot Cake, 98
Cheesecake, Pumpkin-Almond, 328
Chocolate Cake, Triple-, 329
Clementine-Date Cake, 33
Cupcakes, Chocolate Spider, 275
Cupcakes with Vanilla Bean Frosting,
　Vanilla, 363
Plum Kuchen, 167
Pound Cake with Browned Butter Glaze,
　Canola Oil, 365
Sponge Cake with Orange Curd and
　Strawberries, 94

Candies
Brittle, Pistachio and Pine Nut, 355
Brittle, Thai Cashew, 274
Fudge, Peanut Butter and Dark
　Chocolate, 324
Truffles, Date and Almond, 94

Caramel
Bourbon Caramel over Vanilla Ice Cream,
　Broiled Pineapple with, 52
Brownies, Salted Caramel, 263
Brownies, Spicy Caramel, 323
Corn, Peanut Butter Caramel, 274
Dacquoise, Caramel-Pecan, 330

Glaze, Quince Tart with Pine Nut
　Caramel, 311
Pork, Caramel, 77

Carrots
Buttered Carrots, 350
Cake, Carrot, 98
Crab Toast with Carrot and Scallion, 361
Cumin-Spiced Chickpeas and Carrots on
　Couscous, 202
Herb-Glazed Carrots, 27
Israeli Carrots, 93
Salad, Shrimp Cobb, 134
Tarragon Carrots and Peas, 78

Casseroles
Broccoli and Rice Casseroles, 350
Chicken Casserole with Charred Tomato
　Salsa, Mexican, 48
Chicken Enchilada Casserole, 74
Mac and Cheese, Baked, 348
Macaroni and Cheese, Creamy, Light, 260
Moussaka, Vegetarian, 59
Pasta with Spinach, Lemon, and Cheese,
　Baked, 59
Pastitsio, Quick, 280
Spinach-Sausage Gratin, Garlicky, 291
Strata, Artichoke and Goat Cheese, 60
Strata, Pear and Gruyère, 277
Turkey Sausage, Mushroom, and Potato
　Gratin, 342
Vegetable
　Brussels Sprouts and Cauliflower Gratin,
　　Crispy Topped, 52
　Green Bean Casserole with Madeira
　　Mushrooms, 307
　Mashed Potato Casserole, 309
　Onion Casserole, Sweet, 129
　Potato Gratin with Duxelles, 26

Cauliflower
Baked Italian-Style Cauliflower, 342
Gratin, Crispy Topped Brussels Sprouts and
　Cauliflower, 52
Puree, Seared Scallops with Cauliflower, 77

Cheese
Baked Mozzarella Bites, 246
Broccoli, Lemon-Parmesan, 295
Casseroles
　Mac and Cheese, Baked, 348
　Macaroni and Cheese, Creamy,
　　Light, 260
　Pastitsio, Quick, 280
　Strata, Artichoke and Goat Cheese, 60
　Strata, Pear and Gruyère, 277
Chicken Breasts, Herb and Goat Cheese-
　Stuffed, 108
Chicken, Pimiento Cheese, 22
Chiles Rellenos Made Easy, 166
Chutney, Apple-Blue Cheese, 353
Enchiladas with Ranchero Sauce, Black Bean
　and Cheese, 289
Endive Spears with Spicy Goat Cheese, 44
Garganelli with Asparagus and Pecorino
　Cheese, 95
Jalapeños, Grilled Stuffed, 174
Lemon Ricotta, Linguine with Quick, 245
Marinated Peppers and Mozzarella, 264
Mayo and Sherry Vidalia Onions, Burgers
　with Blue Cheese, 140
Meat Loaf Minis, Cheesy, 47
Muffins, Bacon-Cheddar Corn, 115
Omelet with Sage and Red Chile Flakes,
　Mozzarella, 258

Pappardelle with Baby Spinach, Herbs, and
　Ricotta, 96
Pita Crisps, Toasted Parmesan, 325
Pizza, BBQ Chicken and Blue Cheese, 247
Pizzadillas, Kid-tastic, 245
Pizza, Peach and Gorgonzola Chicken, 131
Pizza, Roasted Vegetable and Ricotta, 82
Pizzas, Cheesy Chicken Bagel, 269
Pizza with Tomato and Basil, White, 80
Polenta and Spicy Sausage Sauce,
　Parmesan, 133
Polenta, Cabernet Short Ribs with
　Parmesan, 286
Polenta with Vegetables, Blue Cheese, 266
Pork, Cheese and Pear, 252
Pork Chops with Pears, Blue Cheese-
　Stuffed, 291
Pork Tenderloin, Stuffed Cuban, 194
Potatoes, Buttermilk-Blue Cheese
　Smashed, 267
Potato Wedges, Parmesan-Coated, 309
Ravioli with Pesto, Cheese, 267
Sandwiches
　Burgers, Chicken Parmesan, 105
　Grilled Gruyère and Olive Tapenade
　　Sandwiches, 265
　Grilled Zucchini Caprese
　　Sandwiches, 207
　Ham and Swiss Egg Sandwiches, 247
　Panini with Balsamic Syrup, Summer
　　Tomato, Mozzarella, and Basil, 247
　Serrano, Manchego, and Apple
　　Sandwiches, 279
Sauce, Linguine with Two-Cheese, 185
Soufflés, Cheese and Squash, 316
Soufflés, Spinach and Parmesan, 149
Spread, Caramelized Onion, Gruyère, and
　Bacon, 325
Tartlets, Potato-Gruyère, 358
Turkey with Pan Gravy, Romano and Herb
　Rubbed, 359

Cherries
Brownies, Cherry Cheesecake, 262
Cheesecake Bars, Fresh Cherry, 180
Couscous, Pork Chops with Cherry, 181
Crisp, Cherry-Almond, 147
Muffins, Cherry-Wheat Germ, 116
Sauce, Beef Tenderloin with Cherry-Black
　Pepper, 292
Sauce, Dried Cherry-Cranberry, 303
Stuffing with Dried Cherries and Toasted
　Pecans, Wild Rice, 306

Chicken
Asian-Glazed Chicken Thighs, 70
Bacon and Goat Cheese Chicken, 22
Bourbon-Glazed Chicken, 255
Braised Chicken with Kale, 318
Brown Sugar-Glazed Capon with Bourbon
　Gravy, 93
Brussels Sprouts and Mustard Sauce, Chicken
　with, 380
Buffalo Chicken, 19
Buffalo Chicken Thighs, 267
Burgers, Chicken, 25
Buttermilk Chicken, Crispy, 23
Casserole, Chicken Enchilada, 74
Casserole with Charred Tomato Salsa,
　Mexican Chicken, 48
Cherry Tomato Sauce, Chicken with, 21
Chipotle-Orange Thighs, 318
Couscous-Stuffed Chicken, 22

Cutlets with Creamy Dijon Sauce,
Chicken, 21
Dates, Olives, and Cinnamon, Chicken
with, 285
Fajitas, Chicken, 20
Fennel, Chicken with Italian Sweet-Sour, 76
Fingers, Coconut Chicken, 23
Fingers, Potato-Crusted Chicken, 292
Fried Rice, Chicken, 62
Fried Rice with Leeks and Dried Cranberries,
Chicken, 39
Glace, Chicken, 27
Glazed Chicken, Spicy-Sweet, 256
Greek-Style Chicken, 24
Grilled Chicken, Avocado-Corn Chowder
with, 196
Grilled Chicken Thighs, Tequila-Glazed, 141
Grilled Chicken Thighs with Pineapple, Corn,
and Bell Pepper Relish, 247
Grilled Chicken with Bourbon Peach
Butter, 194
Grilled Chicken with Cola Sauce, 255
Gumbo, Chicken, 282
Gumbo, Smoky Shrimp and Chicken, 347
Hawaiian Chicken, 20
Herb-Crusted Chicken and Parsley Orzo, 43
Herbed Chicken, 19
Jambalaya, Chicken and Sausage, 349
Kebabs and Nectarine Salsa, Chicken, 183
Larb, Chicken, 24
Lettuce Cups, Chicken, 270
Maple-Mustard Chicken Thighs, 130
Meatballs with Ponzu Sauce, Basil
Chicken, 35
Meat Loaf, Chicken, 24
Mediterranean Chicken, 22
Mushroom Sauce, Chicken with, 21
Oatmeal-Crusted Chicken, 23
Pan-Seared Chicken with Tomato-Olive
Relish, 344
Pecan Chicken, 23
Piccata, Meyer Lemon Chicken, 67
Pimiento Cheese Chicken, 22
Pizza, BBQ Chicken and Blue Cheese, 247
Pizza, Chicken and Herb White, 297
Pizza, Peach and Gorgonzola Chicken, 131
Pizzas, Cheesy Chicken Bagel, 269
Puttanesca, Chicken, 162
Quesadillas, Chicken, Mustard Greens, and
Gruyère, 100
Rice and Beans with Chicken and
Chorizo, 326
Roast Chicken Breasts, Italian-Seasoned, 69
Roast Chicken, Classic, 69
Salads
Cold Chicken and Rice Salad, 158
Creamy Chicken Salad, 123
Grilled Chicken Caesar Salad, 344
Herbed Chicken Salad Sandwiches, 206
Tabbouleh with Tahini Drizzle,
Chicken, 257
Thai Chicken Salad with Peanut
Dressing, 84
Saltimbocca, Lemony Chicken, 43
Sandwiches
Burgers, Chicken Parmesan, 105
Pitas, Peanut-Sauced Chicken, 205
Pitas with Tahini Sauce, Chicken
Souvlaki, 65
Sliders and Apricot Chutney Spread,
Grilled Chicken, 161

Sliders, Barbecue Pulled Chicken, 79
Wraps, Grilled Chicken, 157
Wraps with Nectarine Chutney, Curry
Chicken, 142
Sandwiches, Chicken and Waffle, 377
Satay, Chicken, 181
Satay, Pineapple Chicken, 162
Sautéed Chicken with Sage Browned
Butter, 20
Smoked Chicken, Fantastic Bourbon, 200
Soups
Asian Chicken and Noodle Soup,
Spicy, 268
Club Soup, Chicken, 283
Lemon Chicken Soup with
Dumplings, 92
White Bean Soup, Chicken and, 101
Wild Rice Soup, Chicken and, 283
Spinach and Blue Cheese Chicken, 22
Stew with Hominy, Chicken Verde, 37
Stuffed Chicken Breasts, Herb and Goat
Cheese–, 108
Sweet and Sour Chicken, 21
Tacos, Chicken, 24
Tacos with Cilantro Slaw and Avocado Cream,
Ancho Chicken, 134
Tacos with Tomatoes and Grilled Corn,
Shredded Chicken, 195
Tandoori-Spiced Chicken, 19
Thai Coconut Chicken, 19
Tostadas and Avocado Dressing, Chicken, 271
Yakitori, 142
Yogurt-Marinated Chicken with Beet
Salad, 41
Chicken 3 Ways
Bourbon-Glazed Chicken, 255
Braised Chicken with Kale, 318
Chicken and Wild Rice Soup, 283
Chicken Club Soup, 283
Chicken Gumbo, 282
Chipotle-Orange Thighs, 318
Greek Chicken Thighs, 318
Grilled Chicken with Cola Sauce, 255
Spicy-Sweet Glazed Chicken, 256
Chili
Beef and Butternut Chili, 316
Black Bean and Soy Chili, 368
Cincinnati 5-Way Chili, 369
Green Chile Chili, 42
Pie, Chili-Corn Chip, 282
Quinoa and Roasted Pepper Chili, 369
White Bean and Hominy Chili, 369
Chimichurri, Grilled Lamb Chops and
Mint, 108
Chocolate
Apple Wedges, Chocolate-Granola, 269
Babka, Rich Chocolate, 335
Bars and Cookies
Bittersweet Chocolate Cookies, 275
Brownies, Cherry Cheesecake, 262
Brownies, Classic Fudge-Walnut, 262
Brownies, Spicy Caramel, 323
Cake, Triple-Chocolate, 329
Cupcakes, Chocolate Spider, 275
Fudge, Peanut Butter and Dark
Chocolate, 324
Marshmallows, Chocolate, 276
Muffins, Chocolate–Chocolate Chip, 115
Pie, Mexican Chocolate Cream, 124
Pie, Rich Chocolate Pudding, 146
Pops, Chocolate Pudding, 208

Pretzels, Peanut Butter and Chocolate–
Dipped, 355
Scones, Chocolate Chip, 35
Chowders
Avocado-Corn Chowder with Grilled
Chicken, 196
Bacon-Corn Chowder with Shrimp, 246
Clam Chowder, 128
Shrimp Chowder, Quick, 162
Chutneys
Apple–Blue Cheese Chutney, 353
Apricot-Fig Chutney, 155
Nectarine Chutney, Curry Chicken Wraps
with, 142
Pear Chutney Bruschetta with Pecans and
Blue Cheese, 278
Pineapple-Ginger Chutney, Tamarind Pork
with, 72
Clams
Chowder, Clam, 128
Grill-Braised Clams and Chorizo in Tomato-
Saffron Broth, 139
Linguine with Clams and Fresh Herbs, 109
Paella with Poblanos, Corn, and Clams, 122
Pasta with Fresh Tomato Sauce and
Clams, 170
Soft-Shell Clams, Beer-Steamed, 190
Steamed Clams with White Wine and
Tomatoes, 343
Coconut
Chicken Fingers, Coconut, 23
Chicken, Thai Coconut, 19
French Toast with Grilled Pineapple,
Coconut, 153
Macaroons, Coconut-Cardamom, 355
Mussels, Curried Coconut, 154
Pie, Coconut Cream, 66
Rice, Bombay Shrimp Curry with
Coconut, 186
Sherbet, Mango-Coconut, 153
Sorbet, Piña Colada, 146
Toasted Coconut, Ginger Pumpkin Pie
with, 312
Convenience Cooking
Artichoke, Spinach, and White Bean Dip, 100
Caramelized Onion Tartlets, 357
Coconut French Toast with Grilled
Pineapple, 153
Curried Coconut Mussels, 154
Mango-Coconut Sherbet, 153
Potato-Gruyère Tartlets, 358
Southwestern White Bean Pita Pockets, 101
Spicy Caramel Brownies, 323
Sun-Dried Tomato Palmiers, 356
Sweet Potato Pie with Spiced Cream
Topping, 322
Tangy Ice Cream with Cashew Brittle, 323
Tomato–Baby Bell Pepper Tartlets, 357
Tuna and White Bean Salad, 101
Cookies
Almendrados (Flourless Almond Cookies), 372
Bars and Squares
Blondies, Peanut Butter Cup, 263
Brownies, Cherry Cheesecake, 262
Brownies, Classic Fudge-Walnut, 262
Brownies, Salted Caramel, 263
Brownies, Spicy Caramel, 323
Cherry Cheesecake Bars, Fresh, 180
Bittersweet Chocolate Cookies, 275
"Doughnuts," Anise-Flavored, 372
Macaroons, Coconut-Cardamom, 355
Sugar Cookies, Iced, 362

Cooking Class
Asian-Glazed Chicken Thighs, 70
Beer-Braised Brisket, 286
Blueberry-Peach Ice Pops, 208
Brown Sugar Soufflés with Crème
  Anglaise, 148
Cabernet Short Ribs with Parmesan
  Polenta, 286
Chai Cream Pie, 125
Cherry Cheesecake Brownies, 262
Chicken Verde Stew with Hominy, 37
Chicken with Dates, Olives, and
  Cinnamon, 285
Chocolate Pudding Pops, 208
Classic Fudge-Walnut Brownies, 262
Classic Roast Chicken, 69
Crusty French Boules, 334
Garlicky Leg of Lamb with Yogurt Sauce, 102
Grilled Romaine with Creamy Herb
  Dressing, 173
Grilled Stuffed Jalapeños, 174
Grilled Vegetable Gazpacho, 174
Guinness Lamb Stew, 37
Herb and Citrus Roast Leg of Lamb, 360
Herb-Crusted Rack of Lamb, 103
Italian Beef Stew, 36
Italian-Seasoned Roast Chicken Breasts, 69
Lemon-Almond Soufflés, 149
Lemon Cream Pie, 124
Limoncello Pops, 207
Maple-Mustard Glazed Fresh Ham, 358
Marinated Lamb Chops, 103
Mexican Chocolate Cream Pie, 124
Peanut Butter Cup Blondies, 263
Prosciutto Pizza with Tangy White
  Sauce, 336
Real Bagels, 336
Rich Chocolate Babka, 335
Romano and Herb Rubbed Turkey with Pan
  Gravy, 359
Rosemary-Dijon Crusted Standing Rib
  Roast, 360
Salted Caramel Brownies, 263
Slow-Roasted Lamb Shanks, 104
Soy and Cola–Braised Pork Shoulder, 287
Sparkling Strawberry Pops, 207
Spinach and Parmesan Soufflés, 149

Corn
Chowder with Grilled Chicken, Avocado-
  Corn, 196
Chowder with Shrimp, Bacon-Corn, 246
Garlic-Basil Corn, 132
Grilled Corn on the Cob, 191
Grilled Corn, Shredded Chicken Tacos with
  Tomatoes and, 195
Muffins, Bacon-Cheddar Corn, 115
Nachos, Healthy Wheat, 376
Paella with Poblanos, Corn, and Clams, 122
Relish, Grilled Chicken Thighs with
  Pineapple, Corn, and Bell Pepper, 247
Stir-Fry, Ginger-Scented Corn and
  Asparagus, 204
Tacos, Mushroom, Corn, and Poblano, 345
Corn Bread, Chorizo, and Jalapeño,
  Dressing, 305

Couscous
Cherry Couscous, Pork Chops with, 181
Chicken, Couscous-Stuffed, 22
Chickpeas and Carrots on Couscous, Cumin-
  Spiced, 202
Couscous, 159
Herbed Couscous, 184

Pine Nuts, Couscous and, 114
Pistachio Couscous, Currant-Glazed Lamb
  Chops with, 376
Red Pepper Couscous, 109
Salad, Couscous-Arugula, 379
Scallion Couscous, 45

Crab
Cakes and Spicy Mustard Sauce, Crab, 272
Dip, Cajun Hot Crab, 326
Lump Crab–Stuffed Trout, 53
Salad, Spicy Crab-Papaya, 72
Toast with Carrot and Scallion, Crab, 361

Cranberries
Chicken Fried Rice with Leeks and Dried
  Cranberries, 39
Compote, Frozen Orange Tortes with
  Cranberry, 330
Dressing, Roasted Sweet Potato Salad with
  Cranberry-Chipotle, 285
Ketchup, Cranberry, 313
Pickled Cranberries, 313
Pie, Cranberry-Apple, 311
Sauce, Apple-Cranberry, 303
Sauce, Dried Cherry-Cranberry, 303
Sauce, Old-Fashioned Cranberry, 303
Sauce, Raspberry-Walnut Cranberry, 303
Sauce, South-of-the-Border Cranberry, 303
Tea, Tangy Cranberry, 313
Toddies, Warm Spiced Cran-Pom, 353

Cucumbers
Boats, Smoked Salmon in Cucumber, 361
Chicken Larb, 24
Gazpacho, Fresh Pea and Garlic, 129
Gazpacho with Shrimp Relish,
  Cucumber, 111
Raita, Indian-Spiced Pork with, 250
Salad, Lemony Cucumber, 179
Salad, Sesame-Miso Cucumber, 135
Salad, Steak with Cucumber-Radish, 110
Salad, Tomato, Cucumber, and Fennel, 183
Curry with Bok Choy, Green, 30

Dates
Cake, Clementine-Date, 33
Chicken with Dates, Olives, and
  Cinnamon, 285
Truffles, Date and Almond, 94
Desserts. *See also* **specific types.**
Apple Wedges, Chocolate-Granola, 269
Berries with Whipped Cream, Champagne-
  Soaked, 119
Candied Apples, Cinnamon-Cider, 274
Dacquoise, Caramel-Pecan, 330
Frozen
  Granita, Basil Plum, 169
  Ice-Cream Sandwiches, Margarita, 147
  Ice Pops, Blueberry-Peach, 208
  Ice Pops, Watermelon-Jalapeño, 146
  Pops, Chocolate Pudding, 208
  Pops, Limoncello, 207
  Pops, Sparkling Strawberry, 207
  Sherbet, Grapefruit-Buttermilk, 33
  Sherbet, Mango-Coconut, 153
  Sherbet, Tropical, 73
  Sorbet, Piña Colada, 146
  Sorbet, Sparkling Apricot, 156
  Tortes with Cranberry Compote, Frozen
    Orange, 330
Greek Yogurt with Warm Black and Blueberry
  Sauce, 185
Parfaits, Bananas Foster, 346
Peaches with Yogurt, Bourbon-Glazed, 241

Pineapple with Bourbon Caramel over Vanilla
  Ice Cream, Broiled, 52
Pots de Crème, Maple-Gingerbread, 330
Soufflés, Lemon-Almond, 149
Soufflés with Crème Anglaise, Brown
  Sugar, 148

Dinner Tonight
Apple Iced Tea, 297
Arctic Char with Orange-Caper Relish, 78
Arugula Salad, 131
Baby Romaine Salad, 109
Bacon, Tomato, and Arugula Pizza, 296
Bacony Green Beans, 382
Baked Mac and Cheese, 348
Baked Ziti and Summer Veggies, 182
Beef Tagine with Butternut Squash, 45
Broccoli and Rice Casseroles, 350
Buttered Carrots, 350
Buttermilk Mashed Potatoes, 108
Caramelized Onion Mashed Potatoes, 46
Caramel Pork, 77
Cashew Rice, 381
Cheesy Meat Loaf Minis, 47
Chicken and Herb White Pizza, 297
Chicken and Sausage Jambalaya, 349
Chicken Kebabs and Nectarine Salsa, 183
Chicken Lettuce Cups, 270
Chicken Tostadas and Avocado Dressing, 271
Chicken with Brussels Sprouts and Mustard
  Sauce, 380
Chicken with Italian Sweet-Sour Fennel, 76
Chipotle Pork Tacos, 107
Chipotle-Rubbed Flank Steak, 159
Couscous, 159
Couscous-Arugula Salad, 379
Crab Cakes and Spicy Mustard Sauce, 272
Creamy Polenta, 76
Crispy Pork Medallions, 349
Fresh Lima Beans, 244
Frisée and Arugula Salad, 78
Garlic-Basil Corn, 132
Garlic Breadsticks, 349
Greek Lamb Chops and Mint Yogurt
  Sauce, 133
Greens and Sherry Vinaigrette, 298
Grilled Chicken Sliders and Apricot Chutney
  Spread, 161
Grilled Lamb Chops and Mint
  Chimichurri, 108
Grilled Peaches, 184
Grilled Scallop Salad, 243
Guacamole, 161
Herb and Goat Cheese–Stuffed Chicken
  Breasts, 108
Herbed Couscous, 184
Herbed Green Beans, 76
Herbed Shrimp and White Bean Salad, 242
Lamb Chops and Cilantro Relish, 244
Lemon Broccolini, 47
Lemony Arugula Salad, 298
Linguine with Clams and Fresh Herbs, 109
Mexican Rice, 271
Mixed Greens Salad, 182
Moroccan-Style Lamb and Chickpeas, 379
Nutty Rice, 46
Open-Faced Blackened Catfish
  Sandwiches, 159
Orzo with Spinach, 270
Pan-Fried Shrimp with Creole
  Mayonnaise, 183
Parmesan Polenta and Spicy Sausage
  Sauce, 133

Peach and Gorgonzola Chicken Pizza, 131
Peppered Flank Steak and Salsa, 243
Pepperoni, Onion, and Olive Pizza, 298
Poached Pears, 296
Pork Chops with Grits and Red-Eye
    Gravy, 380
Pork Tenderloin Medallions and Balsamic
    Reduction, 184
Radish and Fennel Salad, 107
Radish-Squash Slaw, 77
Radish-Yogurt Dip and Pita Wedges, 244
Red Pepper Couscous, 109
Roasted Asparagus, 272
Roasted Root Vegetables, 349
Roasted Shrimp and Broccoli, 132
Roasted Summer Squash with Parsley, 160
Rosemary Potatoes, 381
Salad with Balsamic Vinaigrette, 47
Sautéed Flounder and Spicy Rémoulade, 382
Sautéed Halibut with Romesco Sauce, 46
Sautéed Spinach and Pine Nuts, 134
Scallion Couscous, 45
Seared Scallops with Cauliflower Puree, 77
Shrimp Fettuccine Alfredo, 271
Shrimp Korma and Basmati Rice, 160
Smoky Pan-Grilled Pork Chops, 46
Spicy Sausage and Mushroom Pizza, 297
Spinach Salad, 348
Spinach with Toasted Almonds, 160
Stewed Okra and Fresh Tomato, 159
Tarragon Carrots and Peas, 78
Tofu Steaks with Shiitakes and Veggies 381
Tomato and Arugula Salad, 272
Tomato, Cucumber, and Fennel Salad, 183
Tomato-Parsley Salad, 133
Tomato Toast, 242
Two-Bean Toss, 243
Wild Rice Salad, 184
Wilted Spinach, 380
"Doughnuts," Anise-Flavored, 372
Dressing, Corn Bread, Chorizo, and
    Jalapeño, 305
Dumplings, Lemon Chicken Soup with, 92

Easy Baking
Bacon-Cheddar Corn Muffins, 115
Cherry–Wheat Germ Muffins, 116
Chocolate–Chocolate Chip Muffins, 115
Pistachio-Chai Muffins, 116
Tuscan Lemon Muffins, 115
Edamame
Country Captain, Vegetarian, 32
Paella with Soy Chorizo and Edamame, 85
Risotto, Spring, 106
Salad with Crisp Steak Bits, Edamame, 150
Eggplant
Moussaka, Vegetarian, 59
Salsa, Roasted Eggplant, 340
Eggs
Breakfast, Libanais, 40
Burrito, Sausage and Egg, 130
Hash with Swiss Chard and Eggs, Fingerling
    Potato–Leek, 87
Migas con Salsa Verde, 289
Poached Eggs, Arugula Pizza with, 265
Sandwiches, Ham and Swiss Egg, 247
Sandwiches with Caramelized Onions and
    Arugula, Bacon and Egg, 258
Sandwich, Smoked Salmon and Egg, 29
Soft Egg, Walnut-Breadcrumb Pasta
    with a, 29
Enchilada Casserole, Chicken, 74

Enchiladas with Ranchero Sauce, Black Bean
    and Cheese, 289
Endive Spears with Spicy Goat Cheese, 44
Everyday Vegetarian
Artichoke and Goat Cheese Strata, 60
Arugula Pizza with Poached Eggs, 265
Baked Pasta with Spinach, Lemon, and
    Cheese, 59
Beet Wellingtons, 333
Black Bean and Cheese Enchiladas with
    Ranchero Sauce, 289
Black Bean and Soy Chili, 368
Black Bean and Sweet Potato Tamales with
    Tomatillo Sauce, 332
Blue Cheese Polenta with Vegetables, 266
Butternut Squash, Caramelized Onion, and
    Spinach Lasagna, 331
Cincinnati 5-Way Chili, 369
Cumin-Spiced Chickpeas and Carrots on
    Couscous, 202
Curried Chickpea Stew with Brown Rice
    Pilaf, 30
Curry-Spiced Noodles, 31
Fingerling Potato–Leek Hash with Swiss
    Chard and Eggs, 87
Fried Rice with Sweet Soy Sauce, 204
Gemelli Salad with Green Beans, Pistachios,
    and Lemon-Thyme Vinaigrette, 127
Ginger-Scented Corn and Asparagus
    Stir-Fry, 204
Green Curry with Bok Choy, 30
Grilled Farmers' Market Sandwiches, 152
Grilled Gruyère and Olive Tapenade
    Sandwiches, 265
Grilled Portobello and Poblano Tacos with
    Pico de Gallo, 290
Lemongrass Tofu Banh Mi, 151
Local Farmers' Market Pizza, 172
Market Salad with Goat Cheese and
    Champagne-Shallot Vinaigrette, 171
Mexican Stuffed Poblanos, 290
Migas con Salsa Verde, 289
Mushroom and Root Vegetable Potpie, 58
Orzo Salad with Spicy Buttermilk
    Dressing, 127
Paella with Soy Chorizo and Edamame, 85
Quick White Bean, Asparagus, and
    Mushroom Cassoulet, 86
Quinoa and Roasted Pepper Chili, 369
Rice Noodle Salad, 203
Roasted Asparagus and Tomato Penne Salad
    with Goat Cheese, 126
Rotini with White Beans and Escarole, 264
Summer Lemon-Vegetable Risotto, 172
Sweet Soy Sauce, 204
Tempeh and Green Bean Stir-Fry with Peanut
    Sauce, 86
Tempeh Greek Salad Wraps, 151
Udon Noodle Salad with Broccolini and Spicy
    Tofu, 126
Vegetarian Country Captain, 32
Vegetarian Moussaka, 59
White Bean and Hominy Chili, 369
White Bean and Sage Pita Burgers, 152
Wild Mushroom Pastitsio, 333

Fajitas, Chicken, 20
Fajitas with "Killed" Jalapeños, Vegetable and
    Steak, 122
Farro
Pork with Figs and Farro, 252

Salad, Summer Pea, Watermelon, and
    Farro, 193
Stuffing, Farro, Caramelized Onion, and Wild
    Mushroom, 306
Fennel
Italian Sweet-Sour Fennel, Chicken with, 76
Roasted Fennel, Warm White Beans
    with, 283
Salad with Lemon, Fennel, 68
Salad with Orange, Green Olives, and
    Pistachios, Shaved Fennel, 284
Stuffing, Fennel, Sausage, and Caramelized
    Apple, 305
Fettuccine
Mushrooms and Hazelnuts, Fettuccine
    with, 43
Olive Oil, Garlic, and Red Pepper, Fettuccine
    with, 106
Shrimp Fettuccine Alfredo, 271
Figs
Baked Figs, Granola with Honey-Scented
    Yogurt and, 256
Chutney, Apricot-Fig, 155
Pork with Figs and Farro, 252
Salad, Fig, Tomato, and Sweet Onion, 143
Fish. See also **specific types and Seafood.**
Arctic Char
    Blistered Cherry Tomatoes, Arctic Char
        with, 114
    Duxelles and Leeks, Arctic Char with, 26
    Grilled Char with Yukon Golds and
        Tomato–Red Onion Relish, 140
    Orange-Caper Relish, Arctic Char
        with, 78
    Parchment Hearts, Arctic Char and
        Vegetables in, 61
Catfish Sandwiches, Open-Faced
    Blackened, 159
Cod in Tomato Broth, Spanish-Style, 345
Fillets, Chip-Crusted Fish, 377
Flounder and Spicy Rémoulade, Sautéed, 382
Halibut with Lemon-Herb Sauce,
    Poached, 34
Halibut with Romesco Sauce, Sautéed, 46
Pan-Roasted Fish with Mediterranean Tomato
    Sauce, 321
Snapper in Tomato Broth, 44
Sticks, Fancy Fish, 154
Striped Bass with Cilantro-Onion Salad, 112
Tilapia Tacos, Blackened, 63
Tilapia Tacos with Grilled Peppers and Onion,
    Sautéed, 193
Trout, Lump Crab-Stuffed, 53
Trout with Tomato Basil Sauté,
    Pan-Fried, 268
5-Ingredient Cooking
Beef Tenderloin with Cherry–Black Pepper
    Sauce, 292
Butternut Squash Risotto, 293
Easy Braised Brisket, 75
Grilled Chicken with Bourbon Peach
    Butter, 194
Grilled Flank Steak with Onions, Avocado,
    and Tomatoes, 156
Mixed Greens and Avocado Salad, 194
Rice and Beans with Chicken and
    Chorizo, 326
Sautéed Tilapia Tacos with Grilled Peppers
    and Onion, 193
Shredded Chicken Tacos with Tomatoes and
    Grilled Corn, 195
Simple Lobster Risotto, 41

5-Ingredient Cooking *(continued)*
Spiced Lamb Kebabs, 129
Stuffed Cuban Pork Tenderloin, 194
Summer Pea, Watermelon, and Farro
Salad, 193
Tuna-Fennel Pasta Salad, 272

French Toast
Ciabatta French Toast with Warm Apple
Maple Syrup, 259
Coconut French Toast with Grilled
Pineapple, 153
Peanut Butter and Jelly, French Toast, 266
Pear and Gruyère Strata, 277
Frosting, Vanilla Cupcakes with Vanilla
Bean, 363

Fruit. *See also* **specific types.**
Berries with Whipped Cream, Champagne-
Soaked, 119
Cobbler, Stone Fruit, 169
Pudding with Whipped Cream, Citrus, 34
Salad, Pickled Onion, Blue Cheese, and
Berry, 118

Gingerbread Pots de Crème, Maple-, 330

Glazes
Browned Butter Glaze, Canola Oil Pound
Cake with, 365
Ginger-Hoisin Glaze, Broiled Tenderloin
Steaks with, 50
Maple Glaze, Spiced Cinnamon Rolls
with, 317
Pine Nut Caramel Glaze, Quince Tart
with, 311
Pomegranate-Thyme Glaze, Smoke-Roasted
Turkey Breast with, 299
Goulash, Hungarian, 251
Granola Apple Wedges, Chocolate-, 269
Granola with Honey-Scented Yogurt and Baked
Figs, 256
Grapefruit-Buttermilk Sherbet, 33
Grapefruit Salad, Shrimp, Avocado, and, 374
Grape Relish, Plank-Grilled Salmon with, 153
Grape Salad, Pork Tenderloin with Tangy, 249

Gravies
Bourbon-Cider Gravy, Maple-Cider Brined
Turkey with, 302
Bourbon Gravy, Brown Sugar–Glazed Capon
with, 93
Cream Gravy, Slow-Roasted Turkey with, 300
Pan Gravy, Roasted Turkey with Rosemary-
Garlic Butter Rub and, 301
Pan Gravy, Romano and Herb Rubbed Turkey
with, 359
Porcini Gravy, Braised Turkey Roulade with
Pancetta, Shallots, and, 300
Red-Eye Gravy, Pork Chops with Grits
and, 380

Greens
Black-Eyed Peas and Greens, 374
Golden Raisins, Greens with, 121
Mustard Greens, and Gruyère Quesadillas,
Chicken, 100
Turnip Greens, Beef Pot Roast with, 56

Grilled
Beef
Brisket, Coffee-Rubbed Texas-Style, 198
Burgers with Blue Cheese Mayo and
Sherry Vidalia Onions, 140
Flank Steak and Salsa, Peppered, 243
Flank Steak with Fresh Salsa, Spice-
Rubbed, 176

Flank Steak with Onions, Avocado, and
Tomatoes, Grilled, 156
New York Strip with Arugula-Artichoke
Salad, Tuscan-Style, 175
Steak with Onions and Scallions,
Grilled, 181
Fish and Shellfish
Char with Yukon Golds and Tomato–
Red Onion Relish, Grilled, 140
Clams and Chorizo in Tomato-Saffron
Broth, Grill-Braised, 139
Clams, Beer-Steamed Soft-Shell, 190
Halibut Tacos, Chimichurri, 165
King Salmon with Tomato-Peach Salsa,
Grilled, 186
Lobsters, Grilled Maine, 191
Oysters with Olive Relish, Smoked, 198
Prawns, Crispy Chickpea Salad with
Grilled, 40
Salmon with Grape Relish, Plank-
Grilled, 153
Scallop Salad, Grilled, 243
Shrimp with Rémoulade, Cajun-Spiced
Smoked, 201
Fruit
Apricot Halves, Grilled, 156
Pineapple-Avocado Salsa, Grilled, 164
Pizza with Prosciutto, Arugula, and Lemon,
Grilled, 142
Pork
Chops with Cherry Couscous, Pork, 181
Kebabs, Apricot-Glazed Pork, 254
Maple-Brined Pork, 245
Pulled Pork Sandwiches with Mustard
Sauce, 198
Salad, Grilled Pork, 254
Salad Provençal, Pork, 131
Salad, Vietnamese, 250
Satay with Peanut Sauce, Pork, 255
Soy-Ginger Sesame Pork, 250
Tacos Al Pastor with Grilled Pineapple
Salsa, 254
Tenderloin, Barbecued Pork, 255
Tequila Pork with Tomatillo
Guacamole, 250
Poultry
Chicken, Bourbon-Glazed, 255
Chicken, Fantastic Bourbon
Smoked, 200
Chicken Satay, 181
Chicken, Spicy-Sweet Glazed, 256
Chicken Thighs, Maple-Mustard, 130
Chicken Thighs, Tequila-Glazed
Grilled, 141
Chicken with Bourbon Peach Butter,
Grilled, 194
Chicken Wraps, Grilled, 157
Chicken Wraps with Nectarine Chutney,
Curry, 142
Cola Sauce, Grilled Chicken with, 255
Turkey Breast with Pomegranate-Thyme
Glaze, Smoke-Roasted, 299
Yakitori, 142
Vegetables
Corn on the Cob, Grilled, 191
Corn on the Cob with Roasted Jalapeño
Butter, Grilled, 145
Gazpacho, Grilled Vegetable, 174
Jalapeños, Grilled Stuffed, 174
New Potatoes with Onions and Spicy
Sausage, 191

Peppers and Onion, Sautéed Tilapia
Tacos with Grilled, 193
Portobello and Poblano Tacos with Pico
de Gallo, Grilled, 290
Potato Salad, Smoked, 199
Romaine with Creamy Herb Dressing,
Grilled, 173
Sirloin Skewers with Grilled Vegetable
Couscous and Fiery Pepper Sauce, 177
Grits and Red-Eye Gravy, Pork Chops with, 380
Guacamole, 161
Guacamole, Tequila Pork with Tomatillo, 250
Gumbo, Chicken, 282
Gumbo, Smoky Shrimp and Chicken, 347

Ham. *See also* **Bacon, Pork.**
Bread Puddings with Ham and Cheddar,
Savory, 260
Maple-Mustard Glazed Fresh Ham, 358
Prosciutto
Crisps, Shaved Summer Squash Salad
with Prosciutto, 144
Frizzled Prosciutto, Melon Gazpacho
with, 196
Pizza with Prosciutto, Arugula, and
Lemon, Grilled, 142
Pizza with Tangy White Sauce,
Prosciutto, 336
Salad, Honey-Wheat Pizza with Pear-
Prosciutto, 279
Sandwiches, Open-Faced Prosciutto and
Plum, 184
White Beans with Prosciutto, 378
Sandwiches
Egg Sandwiches, Ham and Swiss, 247
Serrano, Manchego, and Apple
Sandwiches, 279
Subs, Ham and Pineapple Pizza, 343
Hash, Red Flannel, 71
Hominy
Chili, White Bean and Hominy, 369
Pork Posole, 73
Stew with Hominy, Chicken Verde, 37
Honey
Almonds, Honey-Glazed, 345
Marshmallows, Honey-Orange, 276
Pizza with Pear-Prosciutto Salad, Honey-
Wheat, 279
Hummus, Black Bean, 80

Ice Cream, Chestnut, 356
Ice Cream with Cashew Brittle, Tangy, 323

Jambalaya, Chicken and Sausage, 349

Kale
Chicken with Kale, Braised, 318
Garbanzo Beans and Greens, 42
Kebabs
Chicken Kebabs and Nectarine Salsa, 183
Chicken Satay, 181
Lamb Kebabs, Spiced, 129
Pineapple Chicken Satay, 162
Pork Kebabs, Apricot-Glazed, 254
Pork Satay with Peanut Sauce, 255
Shrimp Skewers, Broiled Herb-Marinated, 52
Sirloin Skewers with Grilled Vegetable
Couscous and Fiery Pepper Sauce, 177
Yakitori, 142
Kumquat, and Quinoa Salad, Beet, Blood
Orange, 33

Lamb

Cassoulet, Quicker, 375

Chops
    Cilantro Relish, Lamb Chops and, 244
    Currant-Glazed Lamb Chops with Pistachio Couscous, 376
    Greek Lamb Chops and Mint Yogurt Sauce, 133
    Grilled Lamb Chops and Mint Chimichurri, 108
    Marinated Lamb Chops, 103
Indian-Spiced Lentils and Lamb, 291
Leg of Lamb
    Garlicky Leg of Lamb with Yogurt Sauce, 102
    Kebabs, Spiced Lamb, 129
    Roast Leg of Lamb, Herb and Citrus, 360
Moroccan-Style Lamb and Chickpeas, 379
Rack of Lamb, Herb-Crusted, 103
Shanks, Slow-Roasted Lamb, 104
Shepherd's Pie, Moroccan, 74
Spiced Lamb with Plum Sauce, 326
Stew, Guinness Lamb, 37
Lasagna, Butternut Squash, Caramelized Onion, and Spinach, 331

Leeks

Arctic Char with Duxelles and Leeks, 26
Chicken Fried Rice with Leeks and Dried Cranberries, 39
Hash with Swiss Chard and Eggs, Fingerling Potato–Leek, 87

Lemon

Beverages
    Agua Fresca, Minted Lemon-Lime Watermelon, 138
    Cocktails, Lemon-Gin Sparkling, 117
    Cocktail, Sparkling Meyer Lemon, 67
    Lemonade, Fresh Raspberry, 192
Broccoli, Lemon-Parmesan, 295
Broccolini, Lemon, 47
Chicken Piccata, Meyer Lemon, 67
Chicken Saltimbocca, Lemony, 43
Fennel Salad with Lemon, 68
Muffins, Tuscan Lemon, 115
Pasta with Spinach, Lemon, and Cheese, Baked, 59
Pie, Lemon Cream, 124
Pizza with Prosciutto, Arugula, and Lemon, Grilled, 142
Pops, Limoncello, 207
Relish, Seared Scallops with Lemony Sweet Pea, 128
Ricotta, Linguine with Quick Lemon, 245
Risotto, Summer Lemon-Vegetable, 172
Salad, Lemony Arugula, 298
Salad, Lemony Cucumber, 179
Sauces
    Herb Sauce, Poached Halibut with Lemon-, 34
    Meyer Lemon Beurre Blanc, Seared Scallops with, 68
    Spicy Lemon Sauce, Flank Steak with, 134
Soufflés, Lemon-Almond, 149
Soup with Dumplings, Lemon Chicken, 92
Tart, Meyer Lemon Curd, 68
Vinaigrette, Gemelli Salad with Green Beans, Pistachios, and Lemon-Thyme, 127
Lentils and Lamb, Indian-Spiced, 291

Less Meat, More Flavor

Almost Classic Pork Fried Rice, 38
Avocado-Corn Chowder with Grilled Chicken, 196
Chicken Fried Rice with Leeks and Dried Cranberries, 39
Chicken, Mustard Greens, and Gruyère Quesadillas, 100
Chicken Tabbouleh with Tahini Drizzle, 257
Crab Toast with Carrot and Scallion, 361
Curried Turkey, Spinach, and Cashew Salad, 314
Edamame Salad with Crisp Steak Bits, 150
Escarole, Sausage, and Fontina Quesadillas, 100
Melon Gazpacho with Frizzled Prosciutto, 196
Paella with Poblanos, Corn, and Clams, 122
Pasta with Fresh Tomato Sauce and Clams, 170
Radishes with Iceberg and Herb Butter, 361
Red Flannel Hash, 71
Roasted Sweet Potato Salad with Cranberry-Chipotle Dressing, 285
Smoked Salmon in Cucumber Boats, 361
Thai Curry Stew with Turkey and Zucchini, 314
Toasted Chickpea and Apricot Salad, 150
Tomato Panzanella with Shrimp and Basil, 171
Vegetable and Steak Fajitas with "Killed" Jalapeños, 122
Waldorf Salad with Steel-Cut Oats, 257

Lime

Agua Fresca, Minted Lemon-Lime Watermelon, 138
Ice-Cream Sandwiches, Margarita, 147
Salsa, Spanish Pork with Apple-Citrus, 249
Slaw, Jalapeño-Lime, 179

Linguine

Clams and Fresh Herbs, Linguine with, 109
Creamy Linguine with Shrimp and Veggies, 158
Lemon Ricotta, Linguine with Quick, 245
Meat Sauce, Linguine with Easy, 295
Two-Cheese Sauce, Linguine with, 185

Lobster

Grilled Maine Lobsters, 191
Risotto, Simple Lobster, 41
Rolls, Picnic-Perfect Lobster, 188

Macaroni

Cheese, Baked Mac and, 348
Cheese, Creamy Light Macaroni and, 260

Mangoes

Parfaits, Mango-Ginger, 195
Salsa, Pork Chops with Caribbean Rub and Mango, 294
Sherbet, Mango-Coconut, 153

Maple

Chicken Thighs, Maple-Mustard, 130
Ham, Maple-Mustard Glazed Fresh, 358
Pots de Crème, Maple-Gingerbread, 330
Marshmallows, Chocolate, 276
Marshmallows, Honey-Orange, 276

Mayonnaise

Blue Cheese Mayo and Sherry Vidalia Onions, Burgers with, 140
Creole Mayonnaise, Pan-Fried Shrimp with, 183
Pesto Mayo, Steak Baguettes with, 205

Meatballs

Chicken Meatballs with Ponzu Sauce, Basil, 35
Soup, Tortilla Meatball, 280
Turkey Meatballs, Alicante, 373

Meatless Sausage

Soy Chorizo and Edamame, Paella with, 85
Meat Loaf, Chicken, 24
Meat Loaf, Classic, 281

Melons

Gazpacho with Frizzled Prosciutto, Melon, 196
Watermelon
    Agua Fresca, Minted Lemon-Lime Watermelon, 138
    Ice Pops, Watermelon-Jalapeño, 146
    Salad, Summer Pea, Watermelon, and Farro, 193
Moussaka, Vegetarian, 59

Muffins

Cherry–Wheat Germ Muffins, 116
Chocolate–Chocolate Chip Muffins, 115
Pistachio-Chai Muffins, 116
Tuscan Lemon Muffins, 115

Mushrooms

Cassoulet, Quick White Bean, Asparagus, and Mushroom, 86
Duxelles, 25
Duxelles and Leeks, Arctic Char with, 26
Duxelles, Potato Gratin with, 26
Fettuccine with Mushrooms and Hazelnuts, 43
Gratin, Turkey Sausage, Mushroom, and Potato, 342
Madeira Mushrooms, Green Bean Casserole with, 307
Morel Mushrooms, and Mascarpone, Farfalle with Fava Beans, 97
Noodles, Curry-Spiced, 31
Noodles, Stir-Fried Chinese Egg, 266
Pastitsio, Wild Mushroom, 333
Pizza, Spicy Sausage and Mushroom, 297
Porcini Gravy, Braised Turkey Roulade with Pancetta, Shallots, and, 300
Portobello and Poblano Tacos with Pico de Gallo, Grilled, 290
Potpie, Mushroom and Root Vegetable, 58
Sauce, Beef Tenderloin with Mushroom Red Wine, 27
Sauce, Chicken with Mushroom, 21
Sauté, Smoky Asparagus and Mushroom, 105
Shiitakes and Veggies Tofu Steaks with, 381
Sloppy Joes, Beef and Mushroom, 161
Tacos, Mushroom, Corn, and Poblano, 345
Wellingtons, Beet, 333
Wild Mushroom Stuffing, Farro, Caramelized Onion, and, 306
Mussels, Curried Coconut, 154

Nectarine Chutney, Curry Chicken Wraps with, 142

Nectarine Salsa, Chicken Kebabs and, 183

Noodles

Curry-Spiced Noodles, 31
Goulash, Hungarian, 251
Pad Thai, Shrimp, 64
Rice Noodle Salad, 203
Soup, Spicy Asian Chicken and Noodle, 268
Stir-Fried Chinese Egg Noodles, 266
Stir-Fried Rice Noodles with Beef and Spinach, 85
Udon Noodle Salad with Broccolini and Spicy Tofu, 126

Oatmeal-Crusted Chicken, 23
Oats, Waldorf Salad with Steel-Cut, 257
Okra
    Gumbo, Chicken, 282
    Stewed Okra and Fresh Tomato, 159
Olives
    Chicken, Mediterranean, 22
    Chicken with Dates, Olives, and
      Cinnamon, 285
    Relish, Pan-Seared Chicken with Tomato-
      Olive, 344
    Relish, Smoked Oysters with Olive, 198
    Salad with Orange, Green Olives, and
      Pistachios, Shaved Fennel, 284
    Tapenade, Baked Feta with Romesco and
      Olive, 324
    Tapenade Sandwiches, Grilled Gruyère and
      Olive, 265
Omelet with Sage and Red Chile Flakes,
    Mozzarella, 258
Onions
    Broccoli Rabe with Onions and Pine Nuts, 43
    Caramelized Onion, and Spinach Lasagna,
      Butternut Squash, 331
    Caramelized Onion, and Wild Mushroom
      Stuffing, Farro, 306
    Caramelized Onion, Gruyère, and Bacon
      Spread, 325
    Caramelized Onion Mashed Potatoes, 46
    Caramelized Onions and Arugula, Bacon and
      Egg Sandwiches with, 258
    Caramelized Onion Spread, 353
    Caramelized Onion Tartlets, 357
    Caramelized Spring Onions and White Wine,
      Fusilli with, 95
    Chicken Glace, 27
    Flank Steak with Onions, Avocado, and
      Tomatoes, Grilled, 156
    Grilled Peppers and Onion, Sautéed Tilapia
      Tacos with, 193
    Grilled Steak with Onions and Scallions, 181
    Migas con Salsa Verde, 289
    New Potatoes with Onions and Spicy
      Sausage, 191
    Pearl Onions, Balsamic-Glazed Green Beans
      and, 308
    Pearl Onions, Tagine-Style Pork with Squash
      and, 251
    Pickled Onion, Blue Cheese, and Berry
      Salad, 118
    Pickled Onion, Pea Shoot Salad with Radishes
      and, 128
    Pizza, Pepperoni, Onion, and Olive, 298
    Pork Tenderloin with Orange Compote, 253
    Red Onion Relish, Grilled Char with Yukon
      Golds and Tomato–, 140
    Salad, Striped Bass with Cilantro-Onion, 112
    Scallion Couscous, 45
    Scallion, Crab Toast with Carrot and, 361
    Soup, French Onion and Apple, 62
    Sweet Onion Casserole, 129
    Sweet Onion Salad, Fig, Tomato, and, 143
    Tart, Onion, 106
    Turnovers, Savory Sausage, Spinach &
      Onion, 83
    Vidalia Onions, Burgers with Blue Cheese
      Mayo and Sherry, 140
Oranges
    Clementine-Date Cake, 33
    Cocktail, Campari and Orange Sparkling, 312
    Compote, Pork Tenderloin with Orange, 253

    Curd and Strawberries, Sponge Cake with
      Orange, 94
    Marshmallows, Honey-Orange, 276
    Relish, Arctic Char with Orange-Caper, 78
    Salad, Beet, Blood Orange, Kumquat, and
      Quinoa, 33
    Salad with Orange, Green Olives, and
      Pistachios, Shaved Fennel, 284
    Salsa, Orange and Avocado, 325
    Sauce, Whole-Wheat Buttermilk Pancakes
      with Orange, 320
    Sparkler, Clementine, 312
    Thighs, Chipotle-Orange, 318
    Tortes with Cranberry Compote, Frozen
      Orange, 330
Orzo
    Parsley Orzo, Herb-Crusted Chicken
      and, 43
    Salad with Radish and Fennel, Orzo, 96
    Salad with Spicy Buttermilk Dressing,
      Orzo, 127
    Spinach, Orzo with, 270
Oysters
    Broiled Oysters with Garlic-Buttered
      Breadcrumbs, 50
    Roasted Oysters with Pancetta and
      Breadcrumbs, 327
    Smoked Oysters with Olive Relish, 198

Paella with Poblanos, Corn, and Clams, 122
Paella with Soy Chorizo and Edamame, 85
Pancakes
    Potato Pancakes, Smoky, 42
    Whole-Wheat Buttermilk Pancakes with
      Orange Sauce, 320
    Zucchini Angel Hair Pancake, 241
Papaya Salad, Spicy Crab-, 72
Pasta. *See also* **specific types.**
    Angel Hair Pancake, Zucchini, 241
    Baked Pasta with Spinach, Lemon, and
      Cheese, 59
    Bucatini with Green Peas and Pancetta, 96
    Farfalle with Fava Beans, Morel Mushrooms,
      and Mascarpone, 97
    Farfalle with Roasted Peppers, Onions, Feta,
      and Mint, Mini, 79
    Fusilli with Caramelized Spring Onions and
      White Wine, 95
    Garganelli with Asparagus and Pecorino
      Cheese, 95
    Gemelli Salad with Green Beans, Pistachios,
      and Lemon-Thyme Vinaigrette, 127
    Orecchiette with Peas, Shrimp, and
      Buttermilk-Herb Dressing, 141
    Pappardelle with Baby Spinach, Herbs, and
      Ricotta, 96
    Pastitsio, Quick, 280
    Pastitsio, Wild Mushroom, 333
    Penne Salad with Goat Cheese, Roasted
      Asparagus and Tomato, 126
    Puttanesca, Pasta, 130
    Rotini with White Beans and Escarole, 264
    Salad, Tuna-Fennel Pasta, 272
    Slow-Roasted Tomato Pasta, 97
    Soup, Spinach, Pasta, and Pea, 294
    Tomato Sauce and Clams, Pasta with
      Fresh, 170
    Walnut-Breadcrumb Pasta with a Soft
      Egg, 29
    Ziti and Summer Veggies, Baked, 182
Pastitsio, Quick, 280
Pastitsio, Wild Mushroom, 333

Peaches
    Bourbon-Glazed Peaches with Yogurt, 241
    Butter, Grilled Chicken with Bourbon
      Peach, 194
    Grilled Peaches, 184
    Pizza, Peach and Gorgonzola Chicken, 131
    Pops, Blueberry-Peach Ice, 208
    Pork Chop Sauté with Peaches, Skillet, 161
    Sangria, Sparkling Peach, 241
Peanut
    Blondies, Peanut Butter Cup, 263
    Chicken Pitas, Peanut-Sauced, 205
    Corn, Peanut Butter Caramel, 274
    Dressing, Thai Chicken Salad with Peanut, 84
    French Toast Peanut Butter and Jelly, 266
    Fudge, Peanut Butter and Dark
      Chocolate, 324
    Pad Thai, Shrimp, 64
    Pretzels, Peanut Butter and Chocolate–
      Dipped, 355
    Sauce, Pork Satay with Peanut, 255
    Sauce, Tempeh and Green Bean Stir-Fry with
      Peanut, 86
Pears
    Chutney Bruschetta with Pecans and Blue
      Cheese, Pear, 278
    Cocktail, Sparkling Pear, 313
    Poached Pears, 296
    Pork, Cheese and Pear, 252
    Pork Chops with Pears, Blue Cheese–
      Stuffed, 291
    Salad, Honey-Wheat Pizza with Pear-
      Prosciutto, 279
    Salad, Whole Roasted Endives with Pear,
      Arugula, and Walnut, 277
    Strata, Pear and Gruyère, 277
    Tarts, Frangipane Pear, 278
Peas
    Black-Eyed Pea and Tomato Salsa, 111
    Black-Eyed Peas and Greens, 374
    Gazpacho, Fresh Pea and Garlic, 129
    Green Peas and Pancetta, Bucatini with, 96
    Green Peas with Shrimp, Rice and, 28
    Orecchiette with Peas, Shrimp, and
      Buttermilk-Herb Dressing, 141
    Relish, Seared Scallops with Lemony Sweet
      Pea, 128
    Salad, Summer Pea, Watermelon, and
      Farro, 193
    Salad with Radishes and Pickled Onion, Pea
      Shoot, 128
    Soup, Spinach, Pasta, and Pea, 294
    Tarragon Carrots and Peas, 78
Pecans
    Bruschetta with Pecans and Blue Cheese, Pear
      Chutney, 278
    Chicken, Pecan, 23
    Dacquoise, Caramel-Pecan, 330
    Pie, Maple-Bourbon Pecan, 310
    Pork Noisettes, Pecan-Crusted, 251
    Stuffing with Dried Cherries and Toasted
      Pecans, Wild Rice, 306
Peppers
    Chile
        Chiles Rellenos Made Easy, 166
        Chipotle-Orange Thighs, 318
        Chipotle Pork Tacos, 107
        Chipotle-Rubbed Flank Steak, 159
        Chipotle Shrimp, Chilled Avocado Soup
          with Seared, 137
        Chipotle, Twice-Roasted Sweet Potatoes
          with, 309

Green Chile Chili, 42
Green Chile Tamale Pie, 71
Hungarian Goulash, 251
Poblanos, Corn, and Clams, Paella
   with, 122
Poblanos, Mexican Stuffed, 290
Poblano Tacos with Pico de Gallo, Grilled
   Portobello and, 290
Pork Patties, Chiang Mai, 339
Salsa Verde, 264
Grilled Peppers and Onion, Sautéed Tilapia
   Tacos with, 193
Jalapeño
   Grilled Stuffed Jalapeños, 174
   Ice Pops, Watermelon-Jalapeño, 146
   "Killed" Jalapeños, Vegetable and Steak
      Fajitas with, 122
   Roasted Jalapeño Butter, Grilled Corn on
      the Cob with, 145
   Slaw, Jalapeño-Lime, 179
Marinated Peppers and Mozzarella, 264
Pizza Supreme, 63
Red
   Couscous, Red Pepper, 109
   Pesto, Salmon with Red Pepper, 293
   Pork, Pepper, 253
Red and Yellow Bell Peppers, Pork Tenderloin
   with, 44
Roasted Peppers, Onions, Feta, and Mint,
   Mini Farfalle with, 79
Sauce, Sautéed Halibut with Romesco, 46
Sauce, Sirloin Skewers with Grilled Vegetable
   Couscous and Fiery Pepper, 177
Stir-Fry, Baja Pork, 250
Tartlets, Tomato–Baby Bell Pepper, 357
Pesto, Salmon with Red Pepper, 293
Pies, Puffs, and Pastries
Chai Cream Pie, 125
Chocolate Pudding Pie, Rich, 146
Cobbler and Crisps
   Blueberry Crisp, 192
   Cherry-Almond Crisp, 147
   Stone Fruit Cobbler, 169
Coconut Cream Pie, 66
Cranberry-Apple Pie, 311
Ginger Pumpkin Pie with Toasted
   Coconut, 312
Lemon Cream Pie, 124
Main Dish
   Chili-Corn Chip Pie, 282
   Green Chile Tamale Pie, 71
   Mushroom and Root Vegetable
      Potpie, 58
   Shepherd's Pie, Moroccan, 74
Mexican Chocolate Cream Pie, 124
Pastries
   Galette, Summer Tomato, Feta, and
      Basil, 143
   Palmiers, Sun-Dried Tomato, 356
   Phyllo-Wrapped Asparagus with
      Prosciutto, 354
Pecan Pie, Maple-Bourbon, 310
Sweet Potato Pie with Spiced Cream
   Topping, 322
Tarts
   Caramelized Onion Tartlets, 357
   Frangipane Pear Tarts, 278
   French Apple Tart, 310
   Meyer Lemon Curd Tart, 68
   Onion Tart, 106
   Potato-Gruyère Tartlets, 358

Quince Tart with Pine Nut Caramel
   Glaze, 311
   Tomato–Baby Bell Pepper Tartlets, 357
Turnovers, Savory Sausage, Spinach &
   Onion, 83
Pineapple
Broiled Pineapple with Bourbon Caramel over
   Vanilla Ice Cream, 52
Chicken, Hawaiian, 20
Chutney, Tamarind Pork with Pineapple-
   Ginger, 72
Grilled Pineapple, Coconut French Toast
   with, 153
Relish, Grilled Chicken Thighs with
   Pineapple, Corn, and Bell Pepper, 247
Rolls, Pineapple Musubi, 322
Salsa, Grilled Pineapple-Avocado, 164
Salsa, Tacos Al Pastor with Grilled
   Pineapple, 254
Satay, Pineapple Chicken, 162
Sherbet, Tropical, 73
Subs, Ham and Pineapple Pizza, 343
Pistachio
Brittle, Pistachio and Pine Nut, 355
Couscous, Currant-Glazed Lamb Chops with
   Pistachio, 376
Muffins, Pistachio-Chai, 116
Pizza
Apple, Goat Cheese, and Pecan Pizza, 295
Arugula Pizza with Poached Eggs, 265
Bacon, Tomato, and Arugula Pizza, 296
BBQ Chicken and Blue Cheese Pizza, 247
Chicken and Herb White Pizza, 297
Chicken Bagel Pizzas, Cheesy, 269
Farmers' Market Pizza, Local, 172
Grilled Pizza with Prosciutto, Arugula, and
   Lemon, 142
Ham and Pineapple Pizza Subs, 343
Honey-Wheat Pizza with Pear-Prosciutto
   Salad, 279
Kid-tastic Pizzadillas, 245
Peach and Gorgonzola Chicken Pizza, 131
Pepperoni, Onion, and Olive Pizza, 298
Prosciutto Pizza with Tangy White
   Sauce, 336
Roasted Vegetable and Ricotta Pizza, 82
Sausage and Mushroom Pizza, Spicy, 297
Supreme, Pizza, 63
Veggie Pizza, Summer, 244
White Pizza with Tomato and Basil, 80
Plums
Granita, Basil Plum, 169
Kuchen, Plum, 167
Salad, Yellow Plum, 168
Sandwiches, Open-Faced Prosciutto and
   Plum, 184
Sauce, Roast Pork Tenderloin with Plum
   Barbecue, 168
Sauce, Spiced Lamb with Plum, 326
Polenta
Beef with Polenta, Italian-Style, 282
Blue Cheese Polenta with Vegetables, 266
Creamy Polenta, 76
Creamy Polenta, Sausage Ragu over, 375
Parmesan Polenta and Spicy Sausage
   Sauce, 133
Parmesan Polenta, Cabernet Short Ribs
   with, 286
Pomegranate Fizz, 313
Pomegranate-Thyme Glaze, Smoke-Roasted
   Turkey Breast with, 299

Popcorn
Peanut Butter Caramel Corn, 274
Pork. *See also* **Bacon, Ham, Sausage.**
  Chops
   Caribbean Rub and Mango Salsa, Pork
      Chops with, 294
   Cherry Couscous, Pork Chops with, 181
   Fried Rice, Almost Classic Pork, 38
   Grits and Red-Eye Gravy, Pork Chops
      with, 380
   Maple-Brined Pork, 245
   Pan-Grilled Pork Chops, Smoky, 46
   Skillet Pork Chop Sauté with
      Peaches, 161
   Stuffed Pork Chops with Pears, Blue
      Cheese–, 291
Feijoada, Brazilian, 57
Patties, Chiang Mai Pork, 339
Posole, Pork, 73
Pulled Pork Sandwiches with Mustard
   Sauce, 198
Shoulder, Soy and Cola–Braised Pork, 287
Tenderloin
   Argentinean Pork, 249
   Barbecued Pork Tenderloin, 255
   Caramel Pork, 77
   Cheese and Pear Pork, 252
   Choucroute, 252
   Cider and Sage Pork, 377
   Figs and Farro, Pork with, 252
   Grape Salad, Pork Tenderloin with
      Tangy, 249
   Herbed Biscuits, Pork Tenderloin
      with, 354
   Hungarian Goulash, 251
   Indian-Spiced Pork with Raita, 250
   Kebabs, Apricot-Glazed Pork, 254
   Medallions and Balsamic Reduction,
      Pork Tenderloin, 184
   Medallions, Crispy Pork, 349
   Noisettes, Pecan-Crusted Pork, 251
   Orange Compote, Pork Tenderloin
      with, 253
   Pepper Pork, 253
   Red and Yellow Bell Peppers, Pork
      Tenderloin with, 44
   Roasted Pork Tenderloin and Maple-
      Glazed Apples, 248
   Roast Pork Tenderloin with Plum
      Barbecue Sauce, 168
   Roast Pork with Potatoes and Butternut
      Squash, 249
   Roulade, Pork, 253
   Salad, Grilled Pork, 254
   Salad Provençal, Pork, 131
   Salad, Vietnamese, 250
   Satay with Peanut Sauce, Pork, 255
   Soy-Ginger Sesame Pork, 250
   Spanish Pork with Apple-Citrus
      Salsa, 249
   Spicy North African Pork
      Tenderloin, 248
   Stir-Fry, Baja Pork, 250
   Stuffed Cuban Pork Tenderloin, 194
   Tacos Al Pastor with Grilled Pineapple
      Salsa, 254
   Tacos, Chipotle Pork, 107
   Tagine-Style Pork with Squash and Pearl
      Onions, 251
   Tamarind Pork with Pineapple-Ginger
      Chutney, 72

Tenderloin *(continued)*

Tequila Pork with Tomatillo
Guacamole, 250
Potatoes. *See also* **Sweet Potatoes.**
Chowder, Clam, 128
Fingerling Potatoes, Roasted Rosemary, 310
Fingerling Potato–Leek Hash with Swiss
Chard and Eggs, 87
Gratin, Turkey Sausage, Mushroom, and
Potato, 342
Gratin with Duxelles, Potato, 26
Mashed
Buttermilk–Blue Cheese Smashed
Potatoes, 267
Buttermilk Mashed Potatoes, 108
Caramelized Onion Mashed Potatoes, 46
Casserole, Mashed Potato, 309
Microwave Smashed Potatoes, 162
New Potatoes with Onions and Spicy
Sausage, 191
New Potatoes with Parsley and Saffron, 121
Pancakes, Smoky Potato, 42
Pork with Potatoes and Butternut Squash,
Roast, 249
Roasted Potatoes, Truffled, 118
Rosemary Potatoes, 381
Salads
Buttermilk-Herb Potato Salad,
Creamy, 179
Curried Potato Salad, 144
Smoked Potato Salad, 199
Warm Potato Salad with Ramps and
Bacon, 105
Tartlets, Potato-Gruyère, 358
Truffled Pommes Anna, 308
Wedges, Parmesan-Coated Potato, 309
Yukon Golds and Tomato–Red Onion Relish,
Grilled Char with, 140
Pretzels, Peanut Butter and Chocolate–
Dipped, 355
Puddings
Banana Pudding, Roasted, 202
Bread Puddings with Ham and Cheddar,
Savory, 260
Chocolate Pudding Pops, 208
Citrus Pudding with Whipped Cream, 34
Pumpkin-Almond Cheesecake, 328
Pumpkin Pie with Toasted Coconut, Ginger, 312
Pumpkinseeds, Sweet and Spicy, 377

Quesadillas, Chicken, Mustard Greens, and
Gruyère, 100
Quesadillas, Escarole, Sausage, and Fontina, 100
Quiche, Summer Squash, Bacon, and
Mozzarella, 188
Quince Tart with Pine Nut Caramel Glaze, 311
Quinoa
Chili, Quinoa and Roasted Pepper, 369
Salad with Artichokes and Parsley, Quinoa, 92
Squash, Quinoa-Stuffed, 315

Radishes
Dip and Pita Wedges, Radish-Yogurt, 244
Iceberg and Herb Butter, Radishes with, 361
Salad, Radish and Fennel, 107
Salad with Radish and Fennel, Orzo, 96
Salad with Radishes and Pickled Onion, Pea
Shoot, 128
Slaw, Radish-Squash, 77
Ramps and Asparagus, Pickled, 104
Ramps and Bacon, Warm Potato Salad with, 105

Raspberry Lemonade, Fresh, 192
Raspberry-Walnut Cranberry Sauce, 303
Ravioli with Pesto, Cheese, 267
Reader Recipes
Arctic Char and Vegetables in Parchment
Hearts, 61
Baked Shrimp with Tomatoes, 35
Basil Chicken Meatballs with Ponzu
Sauce, 5
Chicken Parmesan Burgers, 105
Chiles Rellenos Made Easy, 166
Chocolate Chip Scones, 35
French Onion and Apple Soup, 62
Granola with Honey-Scented Yogurt and
Baked Figs, 256
Spiced Lamb with Plum Sauce, 326
Summer Squash, Bacon, and Mozzarella
Quiche, 188
Sweet Onion Casserole, 129
Turkey Tenders, 60
Warm White Beans with Roasted Fennel, 283
Zucchini Angel Hair Pancake, 241
Recipe Makeover
Canola Oil Pound Cake with Browned Butter
Glaze, 365
Carrot Cake, 98
Coconut Cream Pie, 66
Creamy Chicken Salad, 123
Creamy, Light Macaroni and Cheese, 260
Fancy Fish Sticks, 154
Mexican Chicken Casserole with Charred
Tomato Salsa, 48
Monkey Bread, 288
Roasted Banana Pudding, 202
Smoky Shrimp and Chicken Gumbo, 347
Relishes. *See also* **Chutneys, Pesto, Salsas,
Sauce, Toppings.**
Cilantro Relish, Lamb Chops and, 244
Grape Relish, Plank-Grilled Salmon
with, 153
Lemony Sweet Pea Relish, Seared Scallops
with, 128
Olive Relish, Smoked Oysters with, 198
Orange-Caper Relish, Arctic Char with, 78
Pico de Gallo, Grilled Portobello and Poblano
Tacos with, 290
Pineapple, Corn, and Bell Pepper Relish,
Grilled Chicken Thighs with, 247
Shrimp Relish, Cucumber Gazpacho
with, 111
Tomato-Olive Relish, Pan-Seared Chicken
with, 344
Tomato–Red Onion Relish, Grilled Char with
Yukon Golds and, 140
Rice
Basmati Rice, Shrimp Korma and, 160
Beans with Chicken and Chorizo, Rice
and, 333
Brown Rice
Apples, Savory Baked, 342
Fried Rice, Almost Classic Pork, 38
Pilaf, Curried Chickpea Stew with Brown
Rice, 30
Cashew Rice, 381
Casseroles, Broccoli and Rice, 350
Coconut Rice, Bombay Shrimp Curry
with, 186
Country Captain, Vegetarian, 32
Fried Rice, Chicken, 62
Fried Rice with Leeks and Dried Cranberries,
Chicken, 39
Fried Rice with Sweet Soy Sauce, 204

Mexican Rice, 271
Nutty Rice, 46
Risotto
Butternut Squash Risotto, 293
Lemon-Vegetable Risotto, Summer, 172
Lobster Risotto, Simple, 41
Spring Risotto, 106
Salad, Cold Chicken and Rice, 158
Salad, Spanish Rice, 120
Shrimp Butter, Rice and Green Peas with, 28
Sticky Rice, Thai, 337
Wild Rice
Salad, Wild Rice, 184
Soup, Chicken and Wild Rice, 283
Stuffing with Dried Cherries and Toasted
Pecans, Wild Rice, 306
Yellow Rice, Black Beans and, 157
Rolls with Maple Glaze, Spiced Cinnamon, 317

Salads and Salad Dressings
Arugula and Walnut Salad, 106
Arugula-Artichoke Salad, Tuscan-Style New
York Strip with, 175
Arugula Salad, 131
Arugula Salad, Lemony, 298
Balsamic Vinaigrette, Salad with, 47
Beet Salad, Yogurt-Marinated Chicken
with, 41
Beets with Walnuts, Goat Cheese, and Baby
Greens, 91
Caesar Salad Bagels, 205
Chicken
Cold Chicken and Rice Salad, 158
Creamy Chicken Salad, 123
Grilled Chicken Caesar Salad, 344
Herbed Chicken Salad Sandwiches, 206
Tabbouleh with Tahini Drizzle, Chicken,
257
Thai Chicken Salad with Peanut
Dressing, 84
Chickpea and Apricot Salad, Toasted, 150
Chickpea Salad with Grilled Prawns,
Crispy, 40
Cilantro-Onion Salad, Striped Bass with, 112
Couscous-Arugula Salad, 379
Crab-Papaya Salad, Spicy, 72
Cucumber-Radish Salad, Steak with, 110
Cucumber Salad, Lemony, 179
Edamame Salad with Crisp Steak Bits, 150
Endives with Pear, Arugula, and Walnut Salad,
Whole Roasted, 277
Fennel Salad with Lemon, 68
Fennel Salad with Orange, Green Olives, and
Pistachios, Shaved, 284
Fig, Tomato, and Sweet Onion Salad, 143
Four-Herb Green Goddess Dressing, 138
Frisée and Arugula Salad, 78
Gemelli Salad with Green Beans, Pistachios,
and Lemon-Thyme Vinaigrette, 127
Golden Beet Salad with Wheat Berries and
Pumpkinseed Vinaigrette, 145
Grape Salad, Pork Tenderloin with Tangy, 249
Green
Baby Romaine Salad, 109
Greens and Sherry Vinaigrette, 298
Mixed Greens and Avocado Salad, 194
Mixed Greens Salad, 182
Romaine with Creamy Herb Dressing,
Grilled, 173
Market Salad with Goat Cheese and
Champagne-Shallot Vinaigrette, 171
Orzo Salad with Radish and Fennel, 96

Orzo Salad with Spicy Buttermilk
   Dressing, 127
Pear-Prosciutto Salad, Honey-Wheat Pizza
   with, 279
Pea Shoot Salad with Radishes and Pickled
   Onion, 128
Pickled Onion, Blue Cheese, and Berry
   Salad, 118
Pork Salad, Grilled, 254
Pork Salad Provençal, 131
Potato
   Buttermilk-Herb Potato Salad,
      Creamy, 179
   Curried Potato Salad, 144
   Roasted Sweet Potato Salad with
      Cranberry-Chipotle Dressing, 285
   Smoked Potato Salad, 199
   Warm Potato Salad with Ramps and
      Bacon, 105
Quinoa Salad with Artichokes and Parsley, 92
Radish and Fennel Salad, 107
Rice Noodle Salad, 203
Rice Salad, Spanish, 120
Roasted Asparagus and Tomato Penne Salad
   with Goat Cheese, 126
Scallop Salad, Grilled, 243
Seafood Salad, Mixed, 113
Sesame-Miso Cucumber Salad, 135
Shrimp and Arugula Salad, 163
Shrimp and White Bean Salad, Herbed, 242
Shrimp, Avocado, and Grapefruit Salad, 374
Shrimp Salad, Marinated, 178
Slaws
   Cabbage Slaw, 164
   Cilantro Slaw and Avocado Cream,
      Ancho Chicken Tacos with, 134
   Jalapeño-Lime Slaw, 179
   Radish-Squash Slaw, 77
   Watercress Slaw, Roast Beef Sandwiches
      with, 135
Spinach, Endive, and Tangelo Salad, 32
Spinach Salad, 348
Summer Pea, Watermelon, and Farro
   Salad, 193
Summer Squash Salad with Prosciutto Crisps,
   Shaved, 144
Tabbouleh Salad, 178
Tempeh Greek Salad Wraps, 151
Tomato and Arugula Salad, 272
Tomato, Cucumber, and Fennel Salad, 183
Tomato-Parsley Salad, 133
Tuna and White Bean Salad, 101
Tuna-Fennel Pasta Salad, 272
Turkey, Spinach, and Cashew Salad,
   Curried, 314
Udon Noodle Salad with Broccolini and Spicy
   Tofu, 126
Vegetable Salad, Roasted Root, 354
Vietnamese Salad, 250
Waldorf Salad with Steel-Cut Oats, 257
Wild Rice Salad, 184
Yellow Plum Salad, 168
Salmon
Bok Choy, Salmon and, 268
Grilled King Salmon with Tomato-Peach
   Salsa, 186
Red Pepper Pesto, Salmon with, 293
Sandwiches, Salmon, 110
Smoked Salmon and Egg Sandwich, 29
Smoked Salmon in Cucumber Boats, 361
Smoked Salmon Sandwiches, Open-
   Faced, 321

Salsas. *See also* **Pesto, Relishes, Sauces.**
Apple-Citrus Salsa, Spanish Pork with, 249
Black-Eyed Pea and Tomato Salsa, 111
Charred Tomato Salsa, Mexican Chicken
   Casserole with, 48
Fresh Salsa, Spice-Rubbed Flank Steak
   with, 176
Mango Salsa, Pork Chops with Caribbean Rub
   and, 294
Nectarine Salsa, Chicken Kebabs and, 183
Orange and Avocado Salsa, 325
Pineapple Salsa, Tacos Al Pastor with
   Grilled, 254
Roasted Eggplant Salsa, 340
Strawberry-Avocado Salsa with Cinnamon
   Tortilla Chips, 135
Tomato-Peach Salsa, Grilled King Salmon
   with, 186
Verde, Migas con Salsa, 289
Verde, Salsa, 264
Sandwiches
Bacon and Egg Sandwiches with Caramelized
   Onions and Arugula, 258
Bagels, Caesar Salad, 205
Baguettes with Pesto Mayo, Steak, 205
Burger, Out-N-In California, 64
Burgers, Chicken, 25
Burgers, Chicken Parmesan, 105
Burgers, White Bean and Sage Pita, 152
Burgers with Blue Cheese Mayo and Sherry
   Vidalia Onions, 140
Chicken and Waffle Sandwiches, 377
Chicken Salad Sandwiches, Herbed, 206
French Toast Peanut Butter and Jelly, 266
Grilled Farmers' Market Sandwiches, 152
Grilled Gruyère and Olive Tapenade
   Sandwiches, 265
Grilled Zucchini Caprese Sandwiches, 207
Ham and Swiss Egg Sandwiches, 247
Melts with Avocado, Tuna, 157
Open-Faced Blackened Catfish
   Sandwiches, 159
Open-Faced Prosciutto and Plum
   Sandwiches, 184
Open-Faced Smoked Salmon
   Sandwiches, 321
Panini with Balsamic Syrup, Summer Tomato,
   Mozzarella, and Basil, 247
Pita Pockets, Southwestern White Bean, 101
Pitas, Mashed Chickpea, 294
Pitas, Peanut-Sauced Chicken, 205
Pitas with Tahini Sauce, Chicken Souvlaki, 65
Pork Tenderloin with Herbed Biscuits, 354
Pulled Pork Sandwiches with Mustard
   Sauce, 198
Roast Beef Sandwiches with Watercress
   Slaw, 135
Rolls, Picnic-Perfect Lobster, 188
Salmon Sandwiches, 110
Serrano, Manchego, and Apple
   Sandwiches, 279
Sliders and Apricot Chutney Spread, Grilled
   Chicken, 161
Sliders, Barbecue Pulled Chicken, 79
Sliders, Sloppy Joe, 346
Sloppy Joes, Beef and Mushroom, 161
Smoked Salmon and Egg Sandwich, 29
Subs, Ham and Pineapple Pizza, 343
Wraps, Grilled Chicken, 157
Wraps, Tempeh Greek Salad, 151
Wraps with Nectarine Chutney, Curry
   Chicken, 142

Sauces. *See also* **Chutneys, Gravies, Pesto,
   Relishes, Salsas, Toppings.**
Apple-Cranberry Sauce, 303
Balsamic Reduction, Pork Tenderloin
   Medallions and, 184
Beef with Polenta, Italian-Style, 282
Butter Sauce, 190
Cherry–Black Pepper Sauce, Beef Tenderloin
   with, 292
Cherry Tomato Sauce, Chicken with, 21
Chimichurri, Zingy, 177
Cola Sauce, Grilled Chicken with, 255
Cranberry Sauce, Old-Fashioned, 303
Cranberry Sauce, South-of-the-Border, 303
Dijon Sauce, Chicken Cutlets with
   Creamy, 21
Dried Cherry-Cranberry Sauce, 303
Fiery Pepper Sauce, Sirloin Skewers with
   Grilled Vegetable Couscous and, 177
Horseradish-Chive Sauce, Beef Tenderloin
   with, 118
Lemon-Herb Sauce, Poached Halibut
   with, 34
Lemon Sauce, Flank Steak with Spicy, 134
Meat Sauce, Linguine with Easy, 295
Meat Sauce, Slow-Simmered, 56
Meyer Lemon Beurre Blanc, Seared Scallops
   with, 68
Mint Yogurt Sauce, Greek Lamb Chops
   and, 133
Mushroom–Red Wine Sauce, Beef Tenderloin
   with, 27
Mushroom Sauce, Chicken with, 21
Mustard Sauce, Chicken with Brussels Sprouts
   and, 380
Mustard Sauce, Crab Cakes and Spicy, 272
Mustard Sauce, Pulled Pork Sandwiches
   with, 198
Orange Sauce, Whole-Wheat Buttermilk
   Pancakes with, 320
Peanut Sauce, Pork Satay with, 255
Peanut Sauce, Tempeh and Green Bean
   Stir-Fry with, 86
Plum Sauce, Spiced Lamb with, 326
Ponzu Sauce, Basil Chicken Meatballs
   with, 35
Ranchero Sauce, Black Bean and Cheese
   Enchiladas with, 289
Raspberry-Walnut Cranberry Sauce, 303
Rémoulade, Cajun-Spiced Smoked Shrimp
   with, 201
Rémoulade, Sautéed Flounder and Spicy, 382
Romesco Sauce, Flank Steak with, 376
Romesco Sauce, Sautéed Halibut with, 46
Rosemary–Green Peppercorn
   Mignonette, 327
Sausage Sauce, Parmesan Polenta and
   Spicy, 133
Sweet Soy Sauce, 204
Tahini Sauce, Chicken Souvlaki Pitas with, 65
Tomatillo Sauce, Black Bean and Sweet Potato
   Tamales with, 332
Tomato Sauce, Pan-Roasted Fish with
   Mediterranean, 321
Two-Cheese Sauce, Linguine with, 185
White Sauce, Prosciutto Pizza with
   Tangy, 336
Yogurt Sauce, Garlicky Leg of Lamb
   with, 102
Sausage
Apples, Savory Baked, 342
Burrito, Sausage and Egg, 130

Sausage *(continued)*

Chorizo, and Jalapeño Dressing, Corn Bread, 305
Chorizo, Baked Black Beans with, 164
Chorizo in Tomato-Saffron Broth, Grill-Braised Clams and, 139
Chorizo, Rice and Beans with Chicken and, 326
Chorizo, Smoky Baked Beans with, 144
Gratin, Garlicky Spinach-Sausage, 291
Jambalaya, Chicken and Sausage, 349
Pepperoni, Onion, and Olive Pizza, 298
Pizza, Spicy Sausage and Mushroom, 297
Pizza Supreme, 63
Quesadillas, Escarole, Sausage, and Fontina, 100
Ragu over Creamy Polenta, Sausage, 375
Sauce, Parmesan Polenta and Spicy Sausage, 133
Soup with Parmesan Cheese, Escarole, Bean, and Sausage, 80
Spicy Sausage, New Potatoes with Onions and, 191
Stuffed Squash, Quinoa-, 315
Stuffing, Fennel, Sausage, and Caramelized Apple, 305
Turnovers, Savory Sausage, Spinach & Onion, 83

Scallops
Salad, Grilled Scallop, 243
Seared Scallops with Cauliflower Puree, 77
Seared Scallops with Lemony Sweet Pea Relish, 128
Seared Scallops with Meyer Lemon Beurre Blanc, 68
Spinach and Paprika Syrup, Scallops with, 110

Seafood. *See also* **specific types and Fish.**
Prawns, Crispy Chickpea Salad with Grilled, 40
Salad, Mixed Seafood, 113

Seasonings
All-Purpose Spice Rub, 197
Caribbean Rub and Mango Salsa, Pork Chops with, 294
Chicken Glace, 27
Duxelles, 25
Rosemary-Garlic Butter Rub and Pan Gravy, Roasted Turkey with, 301
Shrimp Butter, 27

Shrimp
Baked Shrimp with Tomatoes, 35
Butter, Rice and Green Peas with Shrimp, 28
Butter, Shrimp, 27
Cajun-Spiced Smoked Shrimp with Rémoulade, 201
Cantonese-Style Shrimp and Napa Cabbage, 344
Chowder, Quick Shrimp, 162
Chowder with Shrimp, Bacon-Corn, 246
Curry with Coconut Rice, Bombay Shrimp, 186
Fettuccine Alfredo, Shrimp, 271
Gumbo, Smoky Shrimp and Chicken, 347
Korma and Basmati Rice, Shrimp, 160
Linguine with Shrimp and Veggies, Creamy, 158
Orecchiette with Peas, Shrimp, and Buttermilk-Herb Dressing, 141
Pad Thai, Shrimp, 64
Pan-Fried Shrimp with Creole Mayonnaise, 183

Panzanella with Shrimp and Basil, Tomato, 171
Relish, Cucumber Gazpacho with Shrimp, 111
Roasted Shrimp and Broccoli, 132
Salads
Arugula Salad, Shrimp and, 163
Avocado, and Grapefruit Salad, Shrimp, 374
Cobb Salad, Shrimp, 134
Herbed Shrimp and White Bean Salad, 242
Marinated Shrimp Salad, 178
Sautéed Shrimp with Sherry and Chiles, 112
Sautéed with Broccolini, Shrimp, 28
Seared Chipotle Shrimp, Chilled Avocado Soup with, 137
Skewers, Broiled Herb-Marinated Shrimp, 52
Soup with Shrimp and Avocado, Spicy Tortilla, 79
Snacks
Almonds, Honey-Glazed, 345
Apple Wedges, Chocolate-Granola, 269
Endive Spears with Spicy Goat Cheese, 44
Hummus, Black Bean, 80
Mozzarella Bites, Baked, 246
Peanut Butter Caramel Corn, 274
Pumpkinseeds, Sweet and Spicy, 377
Soufflés
Brown Sugar Soufflés with Crème Anglaise, 148
Cheese and Squash Soufflés, 316
Lemon-Almond Soufflés, 149
Spinach and Parmesan Soufflés, 149
Soups. *See also* **Chili, Chowders, Gumbo, Stews.**
Avocado Soup with Seared Chipotle Shrimp, Chilled, 137
Chicken and Noodle Soup, Spicy Asian, 268
Chicken and White Bean Soup, 101
Chicken and Wild Rice Soup, 283
Chicken Club Soup, 283
Cucumber Gazpacho with Shrimp Relish, 111
Escarole, Bean, and Sausage Soup with Parmesan Cheese, 80
French Onion and Apple Soup, 62
Gazpacho, Fresh Pea and Garlic, 129
Gazpacho, Grilled Vegetable, 174
Gazpacho with Frizzled Prosciutto, Melon, 196
Lemon Chicken Soup with Dumplings, 92
Roasted Squash Soup, Indian-Spiced, 318
Stock, Turkey-Saffron, 373
Tomato-Saffron Broth, Grill-Braised Clams and Chorizo in, 139
Tomato Soup with Roasted Chickpeas, 246
Tortilla Meatball Soup, 280
Tortilla Soup with Shrimp and Avocado, Spicy, 79
Turkey, Drunken, 374
Turkey Soup, Alicante, 373
Spaghetti
Bolognese, Spaghetti, 73
Chili, Cincinnati 5-Way, 369
Spinach
Almonds, Spinach with Toasted, 160
Chicken, Spinach and Blue Cheese, 22
Dip, Artichoke, Spinach, and White Bean, 100
Garlic Vinaigrette, Spinach with, 44
Gratin, Garlicky Spinach-Sausage, 291

Greens with Golden Raisins, 121
Orzo with Spinach, 270
Pappardelle with Baby Spinach, Herbs, and Ricotta, 96
Pasta with Spinach, Lemon, and Cheese, Baked, 59
Salads
Curried Turkey, Spinach, and Cashew Salad, 314
Endive, and Tangelo Salad, Spinach, 32
Spinach Salad, 348
Sautéed Spinach and Pine Nuts, 134
Scallops with Spinach and Paprika Syrup, 110
Soufflés, Spinach and Parmesan, 149
Soup, Spinach, Pasta, and Pea, 294
Stir-Fried Rice Noodles with Beef and Spinach, 85
Stir-Fry, Sesame Beef, 344
Turnovers, Savory Sausage, Spinach & Onion, 83
Wilted Spinach, 380
Spreads
Apricot Chutney Spread, Grilled Chicken Sliders and, 161
Caramelized Onion, Gruyère, and Bacon Spread, 325
Caramelized Onion Spread, 353
Squash
Butternut
Beef Tagine with Butternut Squash, 45
Chili, Beef and Butternut, 316
Lasagna, Butternut Squash, Caramelized Onion, and Spinach, 331
Macaroni and Cheese, Creamy, Light, 260
Pork with Potatoes and Butternut Squash, Roast, 249
Risotto, Butternut Squash, 293
Tagine-Style Pork with Squash and Pearl Onions, 251
Kabocha Squash Puree, 317
Rolls with Maple Glaze, Spiced Cinnamon, 317
Slaw, Radish-Squash, 77
Soufflés, Cheese and Squash, 316
Soup, Indian-Spiced Roasted Squash, 318
Stuffed Squash, Quinoa-, 315
Summer Squash, Bacon, and Mozzarella Quiche, 188
Summer Squash Salad with Prosciutto Crisps, Shaved, 144
Summer Squash with Parsley, Roasted, 160
Stews
Beef Stew, Italian, 36
Beef Tagine with Butternut Squash, 45
Cassoulet, Quick White Bean, Asparagus, and Mushroom, 86
Chicken Verde Stew with Hominy, 37
Chickpea Stew with Brown Rice Pilaf, Curried, 30
Curry with Coconut Rice, Bombay Shrimp, 186
Hungarian Goulash, 251
Lamb Stew, Guinness, 37
Tagine-Style Pork with Squash and Pearl Onions, 251
Thai Curry Stew with Turkey and Zucchini, 314
Strawberries
Pops, Sparkling Strawberry, 207
Salsa with Cinnamon Tortilla Chips, Strawberry-Avocado, 135

Sponge Cake with Orange Curd and
Strawberries, 94
Stuffings. *See also* **Dressing.**
Ciabatta Stuffing with Chestnuts and
Raisins, 304
Farro, Caramelized Onion, and Wild
Mushroom Stuffing, 306
Fennel, Sausage, and Caramelized Apple
Stuffing, 305
Wild Rice Stuffing with Dried Cherries and
Toasted Pecans, 306
Superfast
Ancho Chicken Tacos with Cilantro Slaw and
Avocado Cream, 134
Apple, Goat Cheese, and Pecan Pizza, 295
Asparagus with Balsamic Tomatoes, 111
Bacon-Corn Chowder with Shrimp, 246
Baked Mozzarella Bites, 246
Bananas Foster Parfaits, 346
Barbecue Pulled Chicken Sliders, 79
BBQ Chicken and Blue Cheese Pizza, 247
Beef and Mushroom Sloppy Joes, 161
Beef-Broccoli Stir-Fry, 78
Black Bean Hummus, 80
Black-Eyed Pea and Tomato Salsa, 111
Bombay Shrimp Curry with Coconut
Rice, 186
Broccoli Rabe with Onions and Pine Nuts, 43
Cantonese-Style Shrimp and Napa
Cabbage, 344
Cheesy Chicken Bagel Pizzas, 269
Chicken and Waffle Sandwiches, 377
Chicken Puttanesca, 162
Chip-Crusted Fish Fillets, 377
Chocolate-Granola Apple Wedges, 269
Cider and Sage Pork, 377
Cucumber Gazpacho with Shrimp Relish, 111
Currant-Glazed Lamb Chops with Pistachio
Couscous, 376
Endive Spears with Spicy Goat Cheese, 44
Escarole, Bean, and Sausage Soup with
Parmesan Cheese, 80
Fettuccine with Mushrooms and
Hazelnuts, 43
Flank Steak with Romesco Sauce, 376
Flank Steak with Spicy Lemon Sauce, 134
Greek Yogurt with Warm Black and Blueberry
Sauce, 185
Green Beans with Toasted Garlic, 185
Grilled Chicken Caesar Salad, 344
Grilled Chicken Thighs with Pineapple, Corn,
and Bell Pepper Relish, 247
Grilled Zucchini with Sea Salt, 268
Ham and Swiss Egg Sandwiches, 247
Herb-Crusted Chicken and Parsley Orzo, 43
Honey-Glazed Almonds, 345
Lemon-Parmesan Broccoli, 295
Lemony Chicken Saltimbocca, 43
Linguine with Easy Meat Sauce, 295
Linguine with Two-Cheese Sauce, 185
Mashed Chickpea Pitas, 294
Microwave Smashed Potatoes, 162
Mini Farfalle with Roasted Peppers, Onions,
Feta, and Mint, 79
Mushroom, Corn, and Poblano Tacos, 345
Open-Faced Prosciutto and Plum
Sandwiches, 184
Pan-Fried Trout with Tomato Basil Sauté, 268
Pan-Seared Chicken with Tomato-Olive
Relish, 344
Pineapple Chicken Satay, 162

Pork Chops with Caribbean Rub and Mango
Salsa, 294
Pork Tenderloin with Red and Yellow Bell
Peppers, 44
Quick Shrimp Chowder, 162
Roast Beef Sandwiches with Watercress
Slaw, 135
Salmon and Bok Choy, 268
Salmon Sandwiches, 110
Salmon with Red Pepper Pesto, 293
Sautéed Brussels Sprouts with Bacon, 81
Scallops with Spinach and Paprika Syrup, 110
Sesame Beef Stir-Fry, 344
Sesame-Miso Cucumber Salad, 135
Shrimp and Arugula Salad, 163
Shrimp Cobb Salad, 134
Skillet Pork Chop Sauté with Peaches, 161
Sloppy Joe Sliders, 346
Snapper in Tomato Broth, 44
Spanish-Style Cod in Tomato Broth, 345
Spicy Asian Chicken and Noodle Soup, 268
Spicy Tortilla Soup with Shrimp and
Avocado, 79
Spinach, Pasta, and Pea Soup, 294
Spinach with Garlic Vinaigrette, 44
Steak with Cucumber-Radish Salad, 110
Steamed Clams with White Wine and
Tomatoes, 343
Strawberry-Avocado Salsa with Cinnamon
Tortilla Chips, 135
Summer Tomato, Mozzarella, and Basil Panini
with Balsamic Syrup, 247
Sweet and Spicy Pumpkinseeds, 377
White Beans with Prosciutto, 378
White Pizza with Tomato and Basil, 80
Sustainable Choice
Arctic Char and Vegetables in Parchment
Hearts, 61
Arctic Char with Duxelles and Leeks, 26
Bombay Shrimp Curry with Coconut
Rice, 186
Chimichurri Halibut Tacos, 165
Chip-Crusted Fish Fillets, 377
Creamy Linguine with Shrimp and
Veggies, 158
Cucumber Gazpacho with Shrimp Relish, 111
Fancy Fish Sticks, 154
Grilled Char with Yukon Golds and Tomato–
Red Onion Relish, 140
Grilled Scallop Salad, 243
Linguine with Clams and Fresh Herbs, 109
Mixed Seafood Salad, 113
Open-Faced Blackened Catfish
Sandwiches, 159
Oysters with Pancetta and Breadcrumbs,
Roasted, 327
Pan-Fried Shrimp with Creole
Mayonnaise, 183
Pan-Fried Trout with Tomato Basil Sauté, 268
Pasta with Fresh Tomato Sauce and
Clams, 170
Poached Halibut with Lemon-Herb Sauce, 34
Quick Shrimp Chowder, 162
Roasted Shrimp and Broccoli, 132
Salmon Sandwiches, 110
Salmon with Red Pepper Pesto, 293
Sautéed Flounder and Spicy Rémoulade, 382
Shrimp, Avocado, and Grapefruit Salad, 374
Simple Lobster Risotto, 41
Smoked Oysters with Olive Relish, 198
Smoked Salmon and Egg Sandwich, 29
Snapper in Tomato Broth, 44

Spanish-Style Cod in Tomato Broth, 345
Steamed Clams with White Wine and
Tomatoes, 343
Tuna and White Bean Salad, 101
Tuna-Fennel Pasta Salad, 272
Tuna Melts with Avocado, 157
Sweet Potatoes
Pie with Spiced Cream Topping, Sweet
Potato, 322
Salad with Cranberry-Chipotle Dressing,
Roasted Sweet Potato, 285
Shepherd's Pie, Moroccan, 74
Tamales with Tomatillo Sauce, Black Bean
and Sweet Potato, 332
Twice-Roasted Sweet Potatoes with
Chipotle, 309
Swiss Chard and Eggs, Fingerling Potato–Leek
Hash with, 87
Swiss Chard with Crème Fraîche, 308
Syrups
Apple Maple Syrup, Ciabatta French Toast
with Warm, 259
Balsamic Syrup, Summer Tomato, Mozzarella,
and Basil Panini with, 247
Paprika Syrup, Scallops with Spinach and, 110

Tabbouleh Salad, 178
Tabbouleh with Tahini Drizzle, Chicken, 257
Tacos
Al Pastor with Grilled Pineapple Salsa,
Tacos, 254
Chicken Tacos, 24
Chicken Tacos with Cilantro Slaw and
Avocado Cream, Ancho, 134
Chimichurri Halibut Tacos, 165
Flank Steak Tacos, 163
Mushroom, Corn, and Poblano Tacos, 345
Pork Tacos, Chipotle, 107
Portobello and Poblano Tacos with Pico de
Gallo, Grilled, 290
Tilapia Tacos, Blackened, 63
Tilapia Tacos with Grilled Peppers and Onion,
Sautéed, 193
Tamales with Tomatillo Sauce, Black Bean and
Sweet Potato, 332
Tempeh and Green Bean Stir-Fry with Peanut
Sauce, 86
Tempeh Greek Salad Wraps, 151
Tofu
Curry with Bok Choy, Green, 30
Lemongrass Tofu Banh Mi, 151
Salad with Broccolini and Spicy Tofu, Udon
Noodle, 126
Steaks with Shiitakes and Veggies, Tofu, 381
Tomatillo Guacamole, Tequila Pork with, 250
Tomatillo Sauce, Black Bean and Sweet Potato
Tamales with, 332
Tomatoes
Balsamic Tomatoes, Asparagus with, 111
Blistered Cherry Tomatoes, Arctic Char
with, 114
Broth, Grill-Braised Clams and Chorizo in
Tomato-Saffron, 139
Broth, Snapper in Tomato, 44
Broth, Spanish-Style Cod in Tomato, 345
Chicken Tacos with Tomatoes and Grilled
Corn, Shredded, 195
Clams with White Wine and Tomatoes,
Steamed, 343
Galette, Summer Tomato, Feta, and Basil, 143
Panini with Balsamic Syrup, Summer Tomato,
Mozzarella, and Basil, 247

Tomatoes *(continued)*

Pasta, Slow-Roasted Tomato, 97
Pizza with Tomato and Basil, White, 80
Relish, Grilled Char with Yukon Golds and Tomato–Red Onion, 140
Relish, Pan-Seared Chicken with Tomato-Olive, 344
Salads
    Arugula Salad, Tomato and, 272
    Cucumber, and Fennel Salad, Tomato, 183
    Panzanella with Shrimp and Basil, Tomato, 171
    Parsley Salad, Tomato-, 133
Salsa, Grilled King Salmon with Tomato-Peach, 186
Salsa, Mexican Chicken Casserole with Charred Tomato, 48
Salsa, Spice-Rubbed Flank Steak with Fresh, 176
Sauces
    Cherry Tomato Sauce, Chicken with, 21
    Fresh Tomato Sauce and Clams, Pasta with, 170
    Mediterranean Tomato Sauce, Pan-Roasted Fish with, 321
Sauté, Pan-Fried Trout with Tomato Basil, 268
Shrimp with Tomatoes, Baked, 35
Soup with Roasted Chickpeas, Tomato, 246
Stewed Okra and Fresh Tomato, 159
Sun-Dried Tomato Palmiers, 356
Tartlets, Tomato–Baby Bell Pepper, 357
Toast, Tomato, 242
Toppings
  Savory
    Avocado Cream, Ancho Chicken Tacos with Cilantro Slaw and, 134
    Garlic Vinaigrette, Spinach with, 44
    Ketchup, Cranberry, 313
  Sweet
    Cashew Brittle, Tangy Ice Cream with, 323
    Cranberry Compote, Frozen Orange Tortes with, 330
    Spiced Cream Topping, Sweet Potato Pie with, 322
Tostadas and Avocado Dressing, Chicken, 271
Tuna
Melts with Avocado, Tuna, 157
Salad, Tuna and White Bean, 101
Salad, Tuna-Fennel Pasta, 272
Sesame Albacore Tuna, 114
Turkey
Butter-Basted Turkey, 302
Drunken Turkey, 374
Maple-Cider Brined Turkey with Bourbon-Cider Gravy, 302
Meatballs, Alicante Turkey, 373
Pizzadillas, Kid-tastic, 245
Roasted Turkey with Rosemary-Garlic Butter Rub and Pan Gravy, 301
Romano and Herb Rubbed Turkey with Pan Gravy, 359
Roulade with Pancetta, Shallots, and Porcini Gravy, Braised Turkey, 300
Salad, Curried Turkey, Spinach, and Cashew, 314
Sausage, Mushroom, and Potato Gratin, Turkey, 342
Slow-Roasted Turkey with Cream Gravy, 300

Smoke-Roasted Turkey Breast with Pomegranate-Thyme Glaze, 299
Soup, Alicante Turkey, 373
Stew with Turkey and Zucchini, Thai Curry, 314
Stock, Turkey-Saffron, 373
Tenders, Turkey, 60

Vanilla Cupcakes with Vanilla Bean Frosting, 363
Vegetables. *See also* **specific types.**
Arctic Char and Vegetables in Parchment Hearts, 61
Baked Ziti and Summer Veggies, 182
Beef Daube, Provençal, 57
Brisket, Beer-Braised, 286
Fajitas with "Killed" Jalapeños, Vegetable and Steak, 122
Gazpacho, Grilled Vegetable, 174
Korma, Vegetable, 74
Linguine with Shrimp and Veggies, Creamy, 158
Pizza, Summer Veggie, 244
Polenta with Vegetables, Blue Cheese, 266
Potpie, Mushroom and Root Vegetable, 58
Risotto, Summer Lemon-Vegetable, 172
Roasted Root Vegetables, 349
Roasted Vegetable and Ricotta Pizza, 82
Salad, Roasted Root Vegetable, 354
Salad with Goat Cheese and Champagne-Shallot Vinaigrette, Market, 171
Sandwiches, Grilled Farmers' Market, 152
Tofu Steaks with Shiitakes and Veggies 381

Waffle Sandwiches, Chicken and, 377
Walnuts
Beets with Walnuts, Goat Cheese, and Baby Greens, 91
Brownies, Classic Fudge-Walnut, 262
Pasta with a Soft Egg, Walnut-Breadcrumb, 29
Salad, Arugula and Walnut, 106
Wellingtons, Beet, 333
What to Eat Right Now
Apricot-Fig Chutney, 155
Bourbon-Glazed Peaches with Yogurt, 241
Chestnut Ice Cream, 356
Fresh Pea and Garlic Gazpacho, 129
Grilled Apricot Halves, 156
Grilled King Salmon with Tomato-Peach Salsa, 186
Marinated Peppers and Mozzarella, 264
Pea Shoot Salad with Radishes and Pickled Onion, 128
Pickled Ramps and Asparagus, 104
Roasted Oysters with Pancetta and Breadcrumbs, 327
Rosemary–Green Peppercorn Mignonette, 327
Salsa Verde, 264
Seared Scallops with Lemony Sweet Pea Relish, 128
Serrano, Manchego, and Apple Sandwiches, 279
Smoked Salmon and Egg Sandwich, 29
Smoky Asparagus and Mushroom Sauté, 105
Sparkling Apricot Sorbet, 156
Sparkling Peach Sangria, 241
Spicy Crab-Papaya Salad, 72
Tamarind Pork with Pineapple-Ginger Chutney, 72

Tropical Sherbet, 73
Walnut-Breadcrumb Pasta with a Soft Egg, 29
Warm Potato Salad with Ramps and Bacon, 105
Wheat Berries and Pumpkinseed Vinaigrette, Golden Beet Salad with, 145

Yakitori, 142
Yogurt
Dip and Pita Wedges, Radish-Yogurt, 244
Honey-Scented Yogurt and Baked Figs, Granola with, 256
Parfaits, Bananas Foster, 346
Parfaits, Mango-Ginger, 195
Pork Tenderloin, Spicy North African, 248
Raita, Indian-Spiced Pork with, 250

Zucchini
Grilled Zucchini with Sea Salt, 268
Pancake, Zucchini Angel Hair, 241
Sandwiches, Grilled Zucchini Caprese, 207
Stew with Turkey and Zucchini, Thai Curry, 314
Stuffed Zucchini with Cheesy Breadcrumbs, 145